The Ultimate Guide to
Asheville & the Western
North Carolina Mountains
Including Boone, Hendersonville, Hickory,
Lenoir, Morganton & Waynesville

Fourth Edition

Written and Illustrated by
Lee James Pantas

Foreword by
Rick Boyer

R.Brent and Company
Asheville, North Carolina
RBrent.com

The Ultimate Guide to Asheville & the Western North Carolina Mountains: Including Boone, Hendersonville, Hickory, Lenoir, Morganton & Waynesville: Fourth Edition. Copyright © 1998–2011 by Lee James Pantas.

Foreword copyright © 1998, 2000, 2006, 2011 by Rick Boyer

Published in Asheville, North Carolina
by R. Brent and Company
50 Deerwood Drive
Asheville NC 28805
828-299-0977
rbrent.com

Editor and publisher: *Robbin Brent Whittington*
Original cover design: *Gayle Graham*
Fourth edition cover design: *jb graphics, Asheville, North Carolina*
Compositor: *Rick Soldin*
Illustrations: *Lee James Pantas*

Library of Congress Data

Pantas, Lee James
    the ultimate guide to asheville & the western north carolina mountains:
including hendersonville, hickory, lenoir, morganton & waynesville—4th ed.
        p.   cm.
    ISBN-13: 978-0-9788160-7-0
    ISBN-10: 0-9788160-7-2
        (Previously published by WorldComm®, ISBN 1-56664-129-2, 1st ed.,
        ISBN 1-57090-105-8, 2nd ed.)
    1. Asheville Region (NC)—Guidebooks 2. Blue Ridge Mountains—
Guidebooks 3. Great Smoky Mountains National Park (NC and TN)—
Guidebooks 4. Hendersonville Region (NC)—Guidebooks
    I. Title
Fourth Edition   2011934577 LCCN

11 12 13 14 15   5 4 3 2 1

Printed in the United States of America.

Lee James Pantas may be contacted at 828-779-1569 or leepantas@bellsouth.net for ordering information. Visa and MasterCard accepted. This book is also available for order online at www.ashevilleguidebook.com.

Contents

Section One: Getting Acquainted   1

Section Two: The Best of
Asheville & Hendersonville   27

Contents

Section Three: Asheville, All-America City   127

Section Four: Hendersonville   223

Section Five: Western North Carolina   247

Contents

List of Maps

Contents

List of Illustrations

List of Illustrations (*continued*)

Foreword by Rick Boyer

Why I Live in the "Land of the Sky"

The Today Show, 1982:

On our fourth and final day in New York's NBC studios at Rockefeller Center promoting our new book, *Places Rated Almanac,* Jane Pauley leaned over and asked me the question:

"Okay Mr. Boyer—after doing all this research, after compiling this huge almanac based on facts, figures, and government data—what American city would you relocate to if you had a choice?"

Although I should have been expecting a question like this, I admit it took me somewhat off guard. As we filed out to the studio stage from the "green room" that morning, we were told that between eight and twelve million people would be watching. Now I had been asked to *personally choose* the one metro area in the U.S. out of 330 that had emerged as my *favorite city,* a place I would move to the next day if given the chance.

Where to start, given the fact that I had only a few seconds to come up with an answer? I knew it would not be a major city; I have always loved the countryside and knew that any population center I chose would be small to medium sized, and within an easy drive of farms and wilderness.

Although born and raised in the Middle West, I was sick and tired of the long, cold winters and hot humid summers in that region. Now, having lived in New England (Concord, Massachusetts) for a decade, I found the place charming, but the climate no better. I wanted a more southerly place. But not in the Deep South, where the heat and humidity would stifle me. The semitropical climates of Florida and Southern California, while attractive to so many people, never appealed to me; a place needs some cold weather, I reasoned, not just for variety but for hardiness. Also, places with "paradise climates" like San Diego and Honolulu, where the weather shows hardly any fluctuation from season to season, may be great for people suffering from aching joints, but I knew from experience, both researched and personal, that such monotonous climates have a long-term depressant effect on those confined to them.

The deserts and mountains of the West? Yes, they had always enthralled me. Their scenery and openness were spectacular, and their climates vigorous yet comfortable. Also, the major cities of the region, from Denver and Salt Lake to Boise and Albuquerque, were on the whole quite livable. Still, there was the inevitable drawback of isolation. How and when would I ever get to see my friends and family living like Jeremiah Johnson?

Then somewhere from the back of my mind—sifting through the endless lists and tables that my co-author and I had examined during the past four years, leapt a name. A name of a place small enough that many people outside the region had not heard of it. "I think I would move to Asheville, North Carolina," I answered.

And, less than seven months later, I did.

Basically stated, the reasons were simple: Asheville is not too far north nor too far south. It is in the eastern half of the country, but so far west in the coastal state of North Carolina that it lies directly south of Akron, Ohio. Nestled in a broad valley 2,200 feet high between the Blue Ridge and Smoky Mountains, it is shielded from the cold polar air masses that sweep down from Canada in the winter months, and likewise sheltered from most of the hot, humid air that moves inland from the Gulf and the Atlantic during the summer.

In Chicago, where I grew up, the finest season (the *only* fine season) is the fall. Too bad it only lasts two weeks. In Asheville, fall lasts at least ten weeks: the second half of September, all of October and November, and usually the first half of December. Spring begins on the Ides of March and lasts 'til June. The summers, from June until mid-September, have warm days and cool nights. For the most part, air conditioning—especially after seven in the evening—is not needed here. Nor are window screens, because there are no mosquitoes!

Although *Places Rated Almanac* is an extremely thorough publication, there was no section in it that "rated" beauty. Therefore, while I was relatively confident that I had made a good choice, *I had never actually seen the place. All my judgments had been made from printed data, not a personal visit.*

Uh oh…

So it was with some apprehension that I boarded the plane in Boston for Asheville to enjoy a paid week (courtesy of the Asheville Chamber of Commerce) in the city that I had chosen on national television as the most livable in the country, but that I had never visited. The chamber put us up in the Grove Park Inn, an historic resort hotel that was destined to triple in size within a decade after "word got out" about Asheville. My co-author and I gave out interviews and spiels in mid-April, when the dogwood blossoms speckled the mountainsides, and mountain warblers sang on every branch (it was still snowing in Boston.) A time, as Thomas Wolfe writes in *Look Homeward Angel:*

"When all the woods are a tender, smokey blur, and birds no bigger than a budding leaf dart through the singing trees… and when the mountain boy brings water to his kinsman laying fence, and as the wind snakes through the grasses hears far in the valley below the long wail of the whistle, and the faint clangor of the bell; and the blue great cup of the hills seems closer, nearer. ..."

There's a lot more we all like about Asheville: The Biltmore Estate south of town—the grandest, most exquisite chateau ever built, not on the banks of the Loire, but in the valley of the French Broad. The town's architecture, both in her city buildings and her majestic homes set on wide, sycamore-lined avenues. The native mountain people, taciturn at first, funny and kind after a time, and true to their word as a mountain oak.

And always remember this: Every January, there are always three or four days where you can play golf in a sweater. ...

—Rick Boyer, 2000

Introduction

I t is hoped that *The Ultimate Guide to Asheville & the Western North Carolina Mountains* will be just that. A complete resource for you as you visit our area, one that will allow you to make an informed decision as to what you wish to see and do during your stay. Besides being comprehensive in scope and highly factual as any good guidebook should be, *The Ultimate Guide* is unique in that it is filled with pen and ink illustrations that accompany the text. These highly detailed illustrations should also help you to make the right choices for your visit. A picture *can be* worth a thousand words!

I have tried to organize the material in the book into logical sections to help you in thinking about what to do. Section One, "Getting Acquainted," will provide you with an overview as well as vital and useful information to make your stay a successful one. Section Two, "The Best of Asheville & Hendersonville," not only represents my personal selections and favorites, but also covers topics of interest to all visitors, from accommodations and restaurants to art and crafts galleries to outdoor recreation. As a longtime resident who lives and works in this area, I am very confident in providing this vital information and very comfortable in making any recommendations, since these come from my firsthand knowledge. Sections Three and Four present the major attractions and things to see and do in "Asheville, All-America City" and "Hendersonville." Section Five presents the major attractions in all of "Western North Carolina," realizing that you may wish to stay in Asheville or Hendersonville and venture out into the surrounding mountains on day trips.

I have tried to include in this guidebook everything that would be of interest to visitors. Many of the attractions and features included are very popular and well advertised. Some however are not as well known but just as worthy. It is hoped that my experience of living and working in the Asheville and Hendersonville area has enabled me to do it right, so to speak—to write a guidebook that really is thorough and accurate, not just one that provides superficial or limited information from the perspective of a nonnative.

One of the most delightful surprises along the way, and one I hope you will discover for yourself, is the wonderful friendliness of the many people who work at the places highlighted in *The Ultimate Guide to Asheville & the Western North*

Carolina Mountains. There is such a thing as "Southern Hospitality!" The people of the mountains, those whose families have lived here for generations and those who have just arrived, are the true treasures. There are truly beautiful and inspiring places to visit in the mountains, but the folks who greet you at the door make it all the better.

—Lee James Pantas, 2011

About the Author

Lee James Pantas, originally from Greenwich, Connecticut, has lived in the Asheville area since 1989. He has a Master's degree in Ecology from the University of Vermont, and has worked as a research scientist, military officer, lecturer, parapsychologist, marketing director, painter and illustrator in Vermont, Georgia, the orient, Brazil, Colorado, Connecticut and North Carolina. He is active in youth track and field and coaches hurdles for A.C. Reynolds High School as well as the Asheville Lightning Junior Olympics Team. As coordinator of the Blue Ridge Classic, he has helped grow this annual event into the largest track and field meet in North Carolina.

Well-known throughout North Carolina for his award-winning, exquisitely detailed pen and ink drawings, Mr. Pantas has completed more than 2,000 private and corporate commissions. Distinguished clients include Former President and Mrs. George Bush, Governor and Mrs. James B. Hunt Jr., United States Ambassador and White House Chief of Staff of Protocol Joseph Verner Reed, Mr. and Mrs. Ben Holden, George Sanders, and the Estate of Guy Lombardo. He has also completed drawings for more than 200 bed and breakfasts and inns, and more than 300 churches and synagogues. He is one of the few area artists with permission from the Biltmore Company to publish and market prints of his original pen and ink drawings of Biltmore Estate.

Mr. Pantas is also known for his imaginative visionary and fantasy paintings. His work has been exhibited in New York City, San Francisco and Washington, D.C., and locally in Blue Spiral 1, Broadway Arts and Seven Sisters Gallery, among others, and is found in many private collections. He is currently at work on a ten-year project "Liza's Reef," a series of paintings of an imaginary coral reef located near an imaginary island in the South Pacific. The goal of the project is to raise funds for selected environmental organizations and orphanages in the South Pacific. The project website is www.lizasreef.com.

He lives just outside of Asheville in a mountain valley in Fairview with his wife, Elizabeth.

Correspondence should be directed to:

Lee James Pantas
Cherry Orchard Studio
18 Garren Mountain Lane   828-779-1569
Fairview, NC 28730   leepantas@bellsouth.net

Acknowledgements

I am greatly indebted to the many people who offered their time and knowledge and helped to make this book a reality. Many thanks to the management and staff at the various agencies, attractions and other listings in this book for their valuable assistance and input. I am especially grateful to Dini Pickering, Diane LeBeau, Liz Calhoun, Barbara O'Neil, Elizabeth Sims, Marinda Williams and Kathleen Morris of Biltmore Estate; Charlie C. Lytle and Reginna Swimmer of Harrah's Cherokee Casino; Jennifer F. Martin, John H. Horton and Diane Jones of the North Carolina State Preservation Office; Harry Weiss of the Preservation Society of Asheville and Buncombe County; Melody Heltman and Gabby Snyder of the Hendersonville/Flat Rock Visitors Information Center; Angie Chandler, Helen Calloway, Bill Turner, and Angie Briggs of the Asheville Area Chamber of Commerce Visitor Center; Maggie O'Conner of the Historic Resources Commission; Stephen Hill, Susan Weatherford and Ted Mitchell of the Thomas Wolfe Memorial; Maggie Schlubach and David Tomsky of the Grove Park Inn Resort; Rhonda Horton of the Woodfield Inn; Grace Pless, Sara Bissette, and all of the other dedicated volunteers of the Asheville Urban Trail; Susan Michel-Robertson of the Richmond Hill Inn; Gail Gomez of High Country Guild; Roann Bishop of the Historic Johnson Farm; Sherry Masters of the Grovewood Gallery; Cae Gibson of the Flat Rock Playhouse; Joey Moore of the Asheville Arts Alliance; Donna Garrison of the N.C. Department of Transportation; Dick Stanland of Historic Flat Rock Inc.; Weston Utter of the Western North Carolina Nature Center; Patricia R. Crisco and David W. Blynt of the Buncombe County Parks & Recreation Department; Roxanne J. Royer of Office Depot; Sondra McCrary of ARCO Blueprinters; Terry Clevenger of the Asheville Downtown Association; Lisa Smith and Gwen Chalker of the Asheville Convention and Visitors Bureau; Richard Mathews of the Albermarle Park Association; Jerry and Nancy Marstall of The Blue Book; Joan S. Baity of the Old Wilkes Jail Museum; Pam Herrington of The Cove; Mary Alice Murphy of Christmount; Laura Rathbone of Lake Junaluska Assembly; Jim Danielson of Ridgecrest; John Paul Thomas of YMCA Blue Ridge Assembly; Mike Small of UNCA; and Liz Gress of Lutheridge.

Other professionals to whom I am indebted include Lauren Abernathy, Connie Backlund, Harry Bothwell, Bill Bornstein, Irby Brinson, Katherine Caldwell,

Wayne Caldwell, Lee Creech, Carol Donnelly, Cheryl Fowler, Jessica Gosnell, Leona Haney, Tom Hardy, Larry Harmon, Carl Hill, Hosey Horton, Dr. Jack Jones, Joy Jones, Elaine McPherson, Rev. Edward Meeks, Judy and Neil Meyer, Mary Alice Nard, David Olson, Marvin Owings, David Ross, Norm Sanders, Dick Shahan, Chris Smith, David Tate and Barbara Turman.

A special thank you for their encouragement and advice to Annie Ager, Bill and Kathy Agrella, Rem and Isabel Behrer, Larry and Yolanda Bopp, Joe and Bobbi Costy, Greg and Carla Filapelli, Mike and Chris Grier, Mary Herold, Charlotte Harrell, Marge Kavanaugh, John and Agnes Laughter, Roddy Lee, Daniel Lewis, Marilyn and Dick Marino, Elizabeth McAfee, Jane McNeil, Tom and L.J. McPherson, Erich and Liz Pearson, Myra Ramsay, and Phil and Rene Thompson.

I am also grateful to Jim Curwen of the Asheville Track Club for his information about the Track Club and especially for the Kimberly Avenue run; to Mickie Booth, for her wonderful exposition on the Asheville Urban Trail; and to my assistant Kiki Cook for her encouragement and help.

I am thankful to Ralph Roberts, publisher of Alexander Books, for allowing me the opportunity to bring this book to print in the first and second editions, and to Barbara Blood, Gayle Graham, Susan Parker, Vanessa Razzano, Pat Roberts, and Vivian Terrell of Alexander Books for advice and assistance.

A special word of thanks to my mother-in-law, Hazel Nading, and to Art and Martha Nading, Vincent and Maryjean Pantas, Lynne and Bob Boie, and Louise Lea Nading.

I would also like to especially thank both Liza Schillo for her encouragement and review of the Grove Park Inn Resort & Spa, and Robbin Brent Whittington, of R. Brent & Company, for her invaluable guidance and support in bringing the third and fourth editions to life.

Finally I would like to thank my wife Elizabeth, my son Daniel, and my daughter Susanna for their patience, love, and support.

**This book is dedicated in loving memory of my parents
Leo and Alberta Pantas**

Icons, Abbreviations & Symbols Used in This Guide

NRHP	Listed in the National Register of Historic Places
NHL	National Historic Landmark
LHL	Local Historic Landmark
See	Sends you to another section of the guide for more information.

Restaurant Price Guide

$	Under $10
$$	$10-$20
$$$	$20-$30
$$$$	Over $30

The typical price for an evening meal for one person, excluding taxes, gratuity, and drinks.

Section One
Getting Acquainted

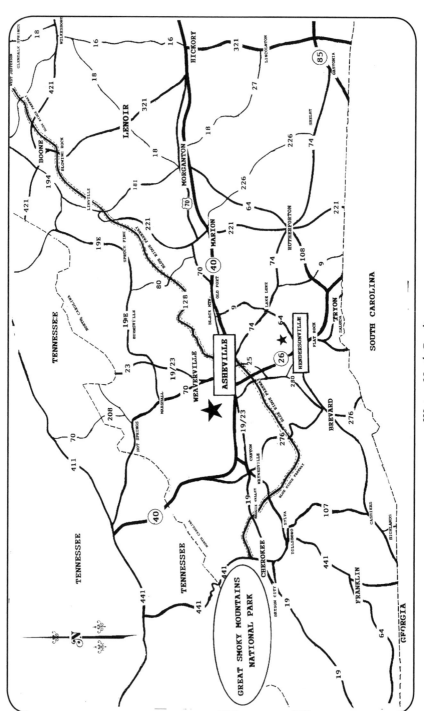

Western North Carolina

Chapter One
Getting Started

Once you arrive in Asheville, one of your first stops should be the visitor center on Montford Avenue (Exit 4C off of I-240 as it passes through downtown). There you will find friendly and informed staff eager to help, a complete array of brochures and tourist-oriented publications, and complimentary maps.

Western North Carolina Basics

Western North Carolina, the region of North Carolina that includes the Appalachian Mountains, is blessed with towering verdant mountains, lovely gentle valleys, flower-filled coves, virgin stands of untouched forest, crystal clear lakes and streams, and vibrant cities and towns. Asheville is the largest city (73,000) and receives over 5,000,000 visitors each year. It is also home to the famous Biltmore Estate, America's largest private residence and the major tourist attraction in the mountains.

Tourism is the major industry in Western North Carolina, with millions of visitors flocking each year to the mountains for outdoor recreation. The area includes the Great Smoky Mountains National Park, the Nantahala National Forest, the Pisgah National Forest and numerous State Forests. Much of Western North Carolina is wilderness and offers an abundance of recreational opportunities from mountain climbing to whitewater rafting. Other major natural attractions include the Appalachian Scenic National Trail and the Blue Ridge Parkway, both of which pass right through the mountains.

The unique character of the Western North Carolina mountains is such that Congress has even designated them a National Heritage Area and they are now officially recognized as the Blue Ridge National Heritage Area. The 24 counties in Western North Carolina have a total population of over 1,000,000. Western North Carolina covers approximately 11,000 square miles, is roughly the size of the state of Massachusetts and is generally recognized as having four distinct regions: the western, central and northern mountains, and the foothills. In the three mountain regions there are over 80 mountain peaks between 5,000 to 6,000 feet in elevation, and 43 that rise to over 6,000 feet. Major cities are Asheville,

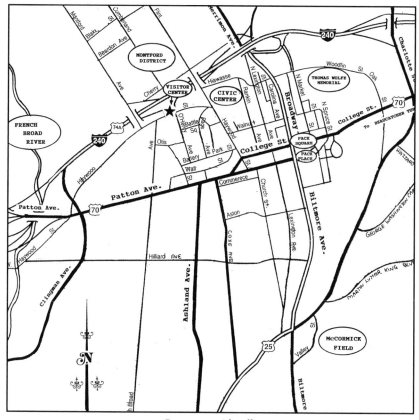

Downtown Asheville

Boone, Hendersonville and Waynesville. The foothills region, extending east from the mountains towards the North Carolina Piedmont, is characterized by rolling hills, with much lower elevations, typically between 1000 and 1500 feet. Major cities are Hickory, Lenoir and Morganton.

Major Cities in the Mountains

Western North Carolina has seven major cities with populations over 10,000, with Asheville and Hickory the two largest. Some basic facts for these seven mountain cities are presented below. Please refer to the appropriate sections in the book for more detailed information about each city. Asheville, along with nearby Hendersonville, are the two mountain cities that receive the most visitors, and because of that fact, are given more coverage in this book than the other cities and towns. This includes additional and more detailed information about the history, architecture, and local attractions of each city, and listings of more accommodations and restaurants.

Asheville

Location: Central Mountains
Elevation & Population: 2,216 feet, 73,000+
City Hall: 70 Court Plaza, PO Box 7148, Asheville NC 28802; 828-251-1122
City Website: www.ashevillenc.gov
County: Buncombe County: County Offices, 205 College Street, Asheville NC 28801; 828-250-4000; www.buncombecounty.org
Asheville Area Chamber of Commerce: 36 Montford Avenue, Asheville NC 28801; 828-258-6101; www.ashevillechamber.org
Visitor Center: 36 Montford Street, Asheville NC 28801; 800-257-1300; www.exploreasheville.com

Boone

Location: Northern Mountains, 2 hours northeast of Asheville
Elevation & Population: 3,500 feet, 15,000+
Town Offices: 567 West King Street, Boone NC 28607; 828-268-6200
City Website: www.townofboone.net
City Chamber of Commerce: Boone Area Chamber of Commerce 208 Howard Street, Boone NC 28607; 828-264-2225
County: Watauga County: County Offices, 842 West King Street, Boone NC 28607; 828-265-8000
County Chamber of Commerce: Boone Area Chamber of Commerce 208 Howard Street, Boone NC 28607; 828-264-2225
Visitor/Welcome Center: Boone Convention & Visitor Center 208 Howard Street, Boone NC 28607; 800-852-9506, 828-262-3516

Hendersonville

Location: Central Mountains, 30 minutes south of Asheville
Elevation & Population: 2,200 feet, 10,000+
City Hall: 145 5th Avenue East, Hendersonville NC 28792; 828-697-3000
City Website: www.cityofhendersonville.org
County: Henderson County: County Offices, 1 Historic Courthouse Square, Suite 2, Hendersonville NC 28792; 828-697-4809; www.hendersoncountync.org

Hendersonville Visitor Center

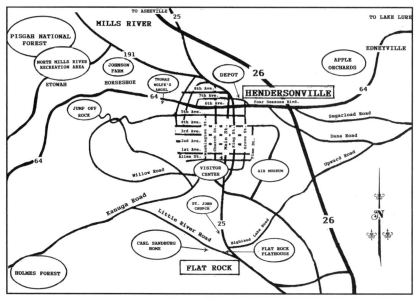

Hendersonville & Flat Rock

Hendersonville Chamber of Commerce: 330 North King Street, Hendersonville NC 28792; 828-692-1413; www.hendersonvillechamber.org

Visitor Center: 201 South Main Street, Hendersonville NC 28792; 800-828-4244; www.historichendersonville.org

Hickory

Location: Foothills, 1 hour and 15 minutes east of Asheville

Elevation & Population: 910 feet, 40,000+

Town Hall: 76 North Center Street, Hickory NC 28601; 828-323-7400

City Website: www.hickorygov.com

County: Catawba County: County Offices, 100-A South West Boulevard, Newton NC 28658; 828-465-8201

County Chamber of Commerce: 1055 Southgate Corporation Park SW, Hickory NC 28602; 828-328-6111

City Visitor/Welcome Center: Hickory Metro Convention &Visitors Bureau, 1960-A 13th Avenue Drive SE, Hickory NC 28602; 800-509-2444

County Visitor/Welcome Center: Catawba County Visitor Information Center, 1055 Southgate Corporation Park SW, Hickory NC 28602; 828-328-6111

Lenoir

Location: Foothills, 11/2 hours east of Asheville

Elevation & Population: 1,182 feet, 17,000+

Town Hall: 801 West Avenue, Lenoir NC 28645; 828-757-2200

City Website: www.cityoflenoir.com

County: Caldwell County: County Offices, 904 West Avenue NW, Lenoir NC
28645; 828-757-1300
County Chamber of Commerce: Caldwell County Chamber of Commerce,
1909 Hickory Boulevard SE, Lenoir NC 28645; 828-726-0323
County Visitor/Welcome Center: Caldwell County Chamber of Commerce
Visitor Center,1909 Hickory Boulevard SE, Lenoir NC 28645; 828-726-0323

Morganton
Location: Foothills, One hour east of Asheville
Elevation & Population: 1,182 feet, 17,000+
Town Offices: 305 East Union Street, Suite A100, Morganton NC 28655; 828-
437-8863
City Website: www.ci.morganton.nc.us
County: Burke County: Burke County Government Center, 200 Avery Avenue,
Morganton NC 28680; 828-439-4340
County Chamber of Commerce: Burke County Chamber of Commerce, 110
East Meeting Street, Morganton NC 28655; 828-437-3021
County Visitor/Welcome Center: Burke County Visitor Center, 102 East
Union Street, Morganton NC 28655; 888-462-2921

Waynesville
Location: Central Mountains, 45 minutes west of Asheville
Elevation & Population: 3,600 feet, 10,000+
Municipal Building: 16 South Main Street, Waynesville NC 28786; 828-452-
2491
City Website: www.townofwaynesville.org
County: Haywood County, Haywood City Offices, 215 North Main Street,
Waynesville NC 28786; 828-452-6625
County Chamber of Commerce: Haywood County Chamber of Commerce,
591 North Main Street, Waynesville NC 28786; 828-456-3021
County Visitor/Welcome Center: Haywood County Tourism Development
Authority Visitor Center, 20525 Great Smoky Mountain Expressway, Waynes-
ville NC 28786; 828-456-7307

Climate
The mountains surrounding Asheville and Hendersonville serve as a moderat-
ing influence from extreme conditions. Major snow storms are rare and annual
precipitation is around 50 inches and average annual snowfall is about 15 inches.
The mountains serve to keep the area cool during the summer months, and with
their higher elevations are usually 10 to 15 degrees cooler than the lowlands of
the Carolinas and Georgia. The northern mountains, including the major city of
Boone, are at higher elevations and receive more annual snowfall, with slightly
cooler year-round temperatures.

Spring in the Appalachians is a wondrous time, with mild days and nights. Wild-flowers are blooming in abundance and all chance of snow has virtually disappeared by April. Summer brings more humidity and heat, although nothing like what the lowlands experience. Late afternoon thunderstorms are common and August usually brings a few weeks when it is hot enough for air conditioning. Temperatures can reach over 90 degrees in Asheville and Hendersonville. Such extremes are rare, however, at elevations over 4,000 feet. Winter doesn't make its presence shown until after Christmas, and January and February can be very cold with temperatures dipping down below 20 degrees occasionally. Light snows and ice storms occur frequently, although the snow rarely stays on the ground for more than a few days. Big snowfalls can occur. The Blizzard of 1993 dumped three feet of snow on the ground in less than 24 hours!

Autumn Glory

One of the most beautiful seasons in the mountains is autumn, when the color-ful display of fall foliage spreads throughout the area. The peaks and valleys take on deep shades of crimson, brilliant orange, translucent yellow and earth brown every fall during September and October. Every year millions of visitors return to the mountains to admire this natural pageant of beauty, and one of the most popular touring routes is the Blue Ridge Parkway with its unbroken vistas and towering mountain peaks.

The fall foliage display usually reaches its height in October, but the intensity of color and peak for each area is also determined by elevation. The higher elevations come into color first, followed by the lower ranges. Views from the Parkway can show you various stages of this transformation, with full color above you on the higher peaks and lush green in the valleys far below. If you do plan to visit the mountains during the leaf season, make sure your book your accommodations well in advance.

Chapter Two
Asheville in Two Days

Asheville has such a wealth of attractions and things to see and do that it can be a bit overwhelming in planning your visit. Most people only have a few days, and that narrow time frame only makes choices all the more difficult. If you only have a short time for your visit, here are some recommendations of things to see and do that should be on your list. I have tried to include on this list those attractions and things to do that are unique to Asheville. They are all personal favorites of mine as well!

First and foremost, plan a visit to Biltmore Estate (*See* Section Three, Chapter 2). A national treasure, Biltmore House is the largest privately owned residence in America and is the most popular cultural attraction in the mountains. Allow at least 4 to 6 hours minimum to see the house, grounds and related buildings. Also on any list of "must-see" Asheville attractions is the historic Grove Park Inn Resort & Spa (*See* Section Three, Chapter 5), located on a mountainside overlooking Asheville. Plan to have either lunch or dinner at the hotel. The food is superb and the ambiance even better. My recommendation is the Sunset Terrace with its great views, especially if the weather is good.

For those interested in American literature, my number one choice is the Thomas Wolfe Memorial (*See* Section Three, Chapter 2), the childhood home of Asheville author Thomas Wolfe. Conveniently located downtown, it is a state-run historic site and offers a fascinating glimpse into the life of one of America's most famous authors. An alternative choice, and a must if you like arts and crafts is the famous Folk Art Center of the Southern Highland Craft Guild (*See* Section Three, Chapter 2) conveniently located inside Asheville city limits at mile marker 382 on the Blue Ridge Parkway. Here you can see and purchase authentic Appalachian crafts. Asheville is noted for its arts and crafts culture, and two commercial craft galleries also of special note are New Morning Gallery in Biltmore Village, and the Grovewood Gallery located near the Grove Park Inn Resort & Spa.

If shopping is of interest to you, my top recommendation is to visit Biltmore Village, located near the entrance to Biltmore Estate. Established by George Vanderbilt as a village for his workers while his house was being built, Biltmore Village is full of unique and special shops housed in restored turn of the century houses. It's a fascinating and charming shopping venue! (For more information *See* Section Three, Chapter 2)

Providing the weather is good, my number one choice for an experience of the vastness and beauty of the mountains is to take a drive on the Blue Ridge Parkway (*See* Section Five, Chapter 1). You can access the parkway at a number of points as it passes through Asheville. Plan to take at least a half a day and head out first north on the parkway to the Parkway Destination Center at mile-marker 384, just two miles from the Folk Art Center. Here you will get a great overview of the parkway and can further plan your outing. If you decide to go south on the parkway, plan to have lunch or dinner at the historic Pisgah Inn, located at mile marker 408. Going north plan to make Mount Mitchell at mile marker 355 your final destination for lunch or dinner.

Last but not least, the North Carolina Arboretum and the Western North Carolina Nature Center are two great choices for anyone who loves nature. The 426-acre Arboretum, located on the west side of Asheville, is an inter-institutional facility of the University of North Carolina and has wonderful varied gardens, walking trails and natural habitats. The Nature Center, located on the east side and only minutes from downtown, is one of my top recommended attractions in the Asheville area for both kids and grownups alike. *See* Section Three, Chapter 2 for more information about both of these outstanding attractions.

Chapter Three
Getting Around Asheville

Asheville is located at the junction of Interstates 26 and 40, with an I-240 connector that passes through the downtown district. Hendersonville is located to the south of Asheville off Interstate 26. The Blue Ridge Parkway also passes through the Asheville area with a number of accesses. The major airport is located in Asheville, but many people also choose to fly into the Greenville SC and Charlotte NC airports as well. Asheville is only a two hour drive from either of these cities. There is no railroad passenger service to Asheville.

Airlines

Asheville Regional Airport: 828-684-2226, www.flyavl.com. The main gateway to the area is the Asheville Regional Airport, 15 miles south of downtown Asheville on I-26. This airport is serviced daily by major carriers with connections to all major cities. The airport has an 8,000-foot runway and modern navigational aids, including a wind shear detection system.

Hendersonville Airport: 828-693-1897, 1232 Shepherd Street, Hendersonville NC 28792. Nearby Hendersonville also has a small airport that serves the Hendersonville area, has a 3,200-foot lighted runway, and provides charter service to larger airports.

Bus Travel

Asheville Transit: City bus service, located at 360 West Haywood St., Asheville NC 28801, Bus service for Asheville. 828-253-5691

Greyhound Bus Lines: Located at 2 Tunnel Rd. Asheville NC 28801, Passenger service. 828-253-5353,800-231-2222.

Young Transportation: Located at 843 Riverside Dr., Asheville NC 28804, Passenger service and charters. 828-258-0084 or 800-622-5444

Emma Bus Lines Inc.: 1 Stoner Rd., Asheville NC 28803, Charter bus service. 828-274-5719

Limousines
All American Limousine: 828-667-9935
Carolina Limousine: 828-258-2526
Special Occasions Limousine: 828-687-9918

Taxi Service
A Red Cab Co.: 828-232-1112
Beaver Lake Cab Co.: 828-252-1913
Jolly Taxi Co.: 828-253-1411
New Blue Bird Taxi: 828-258-8331
Yellow Cab Co.: 828-253-3311
Your Cab II: 828-259-9904

Chapter Four
Helpful Information For
Asheville & Hendersonville

Bookstores

Asheville:

Accent on Books: 854 Merrimon Ave., Asheville NC 28804; 828-252-6255.

B. Dalton Bookseller: 3 S. Tunnel Rd., Asheville Mall, Asheville NC 28805; 828-298-7711.

Barnes & Noble: 83 S. Tunnel Rd., Asheville Mall, Asheville NC 28805, 828-296-9330

Barnes & Noble: 33 Town Square Boulevard, Suite 100, Biltmore Park, Asheville NC 28803; 828-687-0681

Books and Breadboard: 30 All Souls Crescent, Asheville NC 28803; 828-505-8233.

Books-A-Million: 136 S. Tunnel Rd., Asheville NC 28805; 828-299-4165.

Borders: 800 Brevard Rd., Biltmore Square Mall, Asheville NC 28806; 828-665-1066.

Malaprop's Bookstore and Cafe: 55 Haywood St., Asheville NC 28801; 828-254-6734.

Hendersonville:

Waldenbooks: 1800 Four Seasons Blvd, Blue Ridge Mall, Hendersonville NC 28792; 828-692-4957.

Colleges & Schools

Colleges:

Asheville-Buncombe Technical Community College: 340 Victoria Rd., Asheville NC 28801; 828-254-1921.

Blue Ridge Community College: 180 West Campus Drive, Flat Rock NC 28731; 828-684-1700.

Mars Hill College: 100 Athletic Street, Mars Hill NC 28754; 828-689-1307.

South College: 29 Turtle Creek Drive, Asheville NC 28803; 828-277-5521.

Shaw University: 31 College Street, Asheville NC 28801; 828-252-7635.

University of North Carolina at Asheville (UNCA): One University Heights, Asheville NC 28804; 828-251-6600.

Warren Wilson College: 701 Warren Wilson Rd., Swannanoa, NC 28778; 828-298-3325.

Public Schools:

Asheville City Schools: 828-350-7000, www.ashevillecityschools.net

Buncombe County Schools: 828-255-5921, www.buncombe.k12.nc.us

Henderson County Schools: 828-697-4733, www.henderson.k12.nc.us

Emergency Numbers

Fire, Police & Ambulance: 911

Asheville Police Department Information Center: 828-259-9039

Buncombe County Sheriff's Department: (non-emergency) 828-277-3131

Hendersonville Police Department General Business: 828-697-3025

North Carolina State Highway Patrol: 828-298-4252

Hospitals

Buncombe County:

   Mission Hospital: 428 and 509 Biltmore Avenue, Asheville NC 28801; 828-213-1111.

   Care Partners Rehabilitation Hospital: 68 Sweeten Creek Road, Asheville NC 28803; 828-277-4800.

   Park Ridge Hospital: 100 Hospital Drive, Fletcher NC 28792; 828-684-8501.

   V.A. Medical Center in Asheville: Asheville; 1100 Tunnel Rd., Asheville NC 28805; 828-298-7911.

Sisters of Mercy Urgent Care Centers:

   Urgent Care South, 1812 Hendersonville Road, Asheville NC 28803; 828-274-1462.

   Urgent Care West, 1201 Patton Avenue, Asheville NC 28806; 828-252-4878.

   Urgent Care North, 155 Weaver Boulevard, Weaverville NC 28787; 828-645-5088.

   Urgent Care Airport, 77 Airport Road, Arden NC 28704; 828-651-0098.

Henderson County:

   Pardee Hospital: 715 Fleming Street, Hendersonville NC 28792; 828-696-1000.

   Park Ridge Hospital: 100 Hospital Drive, Hendersonville NC 28792; 828-684-8501.

Health and Fitness

Listed below are some of the major health and fitness centers in Asheville and Hendersonville. For a complete list of all centers and spas, visit www.asheville-guidebook.com.

Apex Fitness: 3754 Brevard Road, Hendersonville NC 28791; 828-890-4049.

Asheville Health & Fitness: 237 Sardis Road, Asheville NC 28806; 828-665-2007.

Rush Fitness: 1815 Hendersonville Highway, Asheville NC 28803; 828-274-7874 and 1070 Haywood Road, Asheville NC 28806; 828-271-4747.

Vision Sports Fitness Center: 9 Kenilworth Knoll, Asheville NC 28805; 828-252-0222

World Gym: 780 Hendersonville Road, Asheville NC 28803 828-277-8588

YMCA of Western North Carolina: Asheville YMCA, 30 Woodfin Street, Asheville NC 28801; 828-252-4726. Reuter Family YMCA, 3 Town Square Blvd, Biltmore Park, Asheville NC 28803; 828-651-9622. Woodfin YMCA, 40 N. Merrimon Avenue, Suite 101, Asheville NC 28804; 828-505-3990.

YWCA of Asheville: 185 South French Broad Avenue, Asheville NC 28801; 828-254-7206.

Libraries

Asheville/Buncombe Library System: The main library, Pack Memorial, is located next to the Civic Center downtown. 67 Haywood St., Asheville NC 28801; 828-250-4700; Hours: Monday-Wednesday: 9:30 am-8 pm; Thursday & Friday: 9:30 am-6 pm; Saturday: 9:30am-5 pm.

The Henderson County Public Library: 301 N. Washington St. Hendersonville NC 28792; 828-697-4725.Hours: Monday-Thursday: 9 am-9 pm, Friday -Saturday: 9 am-6 pm.

Movie Theaters

Asheville and Hendersonville have a large number of movie theatres, and your best resources for current movies and reviews are the weekly free publication, the *Mountain Xpress*, and the *Take Five* insert in the *Asheville Citizen Times* newspaper. Both the Hendersonville and Asheville newspapers have daily movie listings as well.

Mountain Xpress: A free weekly independent news, arts, and events newspaper for Western North Carolina. Excellent entertainment coverage, local commentary. Pick up a copy from numerous sidewalk boxes located around Asheville. P.O. Box 144, Asheville NC 28802; 828-251-1333.

Take Five: A weekly tabloid insert in the Friday edition of the Asheville Citizen-Times. It features a complete theater and events listing, articles and reviews. 14 O'Henry Ave., Asheville NC 28801; 828-252-5611, 800-800-4204.

Newspapers & Magazines

Asheville Citizen-Times: The region's largest circulation daily newspaper. 14 O'Henry Ave., Asheville NC 28801; 828-252-5611, 800-800-4204. www.citizen-times.com.

Hendersonville Times-News: Hendersonville's daily newspaper. 1717 Four Seasons Blvd, Hendersonville, NC 28792; 828-692-0505. www.blueridgenow.com.

Mountain Xpress: A free weekly independent news, arts, and events newspaper for Western North Carolina, with the focus on Asheville. Excellent entertainment coverage, local commentary. P.O. Box 144, Asheville NC 28802; 828-251-1333. www.mountainx.com.

In addition to the three major papers listed above, there are a number of other publications available that feature information on current attractions, restaurants, art gallery exhibitions and outdoor recreation activities.

Appalachian Voices: Bi-monthly newspaper published by Appalachian Voices, a nonprofit grass roots organization. Articles of general interest about the mountains, with focus on the environment. 119 Howard Street, Boone, NC 28607; 828-265-1500. www.appvoices.org.

Blue Ridge Outdoors: Monthly free publication covering all outdoor sports in the southern mountains. 434-817-2755. www.blueridgeoutdoors.com.

Bold Life: Monthly free magazine featuring Hendersonville and Asheville area dining, art, music, people and culture. PO Box 1070, Flat Rock, NC 28731; 828-692-3230. www.boldlife.com.

The Laurel of Asheville: Monthly free magazine focusing on the arts and culture of the Asheville area. 1 West Pack Square, BB&T Building, Suite 503, Asheville NC 28801; 828-670-7503. www.thelaurelofasheville.com.

Rapid River: Monthly free arts and culture magazine serving Asheville and Western North Carolina. 85 N. Main Street, Canton NC 28716; 828-646-0071. www.rapidrivermagazine.com.

Sophie: Complimentary monthly magazine for today's women, distributed throughout Western North Carolina. www.sophiemagazine.com.

Smoky Mountain News: Information from the western North Carolina region covering Haywood, Jackson, Macon and Swain county. PO Box 629, Waynesville NC 28786; 828-452-4251. www.smokymountainnews.com.

Verve: Verve Magazine provides an in-depth look at WNC women in the arts, business, fashion and design. Published six times a year. 105 South Main Street, Hendersonville NC 28792; 828-697-1414. www.vervemag.com.

Radio Stations near Asheville

WCQS/88.1 (FM -Public Radio) 828-210-4800
WKJV/1380 (AM -Gospel) 828-252-1380
WLFA/91.3 (FM-Christian)

WNCW/88.7 (FM -Public Radio) 828 -287-8000
WOXL/96.5 (FM-Light Rock Mix)
WPVM/103.5 (FM-Progressive News/Talk) 828-258-0085
WWNC/570 (AM -Country) 828-253-3835

Spas

The premier spa in Western North Carolina is the Spa at the Grove Park Inn Resort & Spa.

Ambience Day Spa and Salon: 549 Merrimon Avenue, Suite C, Asheville NC 28804; 828-252-5065

Asia Bed and Spa: 128 Hillside Street, Asheville NC 28801, 828-255-0051

Blissful Rituals Personal Spa Retreat: 57 Broadway, Asheville NC 28801; 828-545-2867

Blue Lotus Ayurveda -Ayurveda, Panchakarma Clinic & Day Spa: 822 Haywood Road, Asheville NC 28806; 828-713-4266

Center for Massage & Natural Health: 530 Upper Flat Creek Road, Weaverville NC 28787; 828-658-8198

Chestnut Hill Salon & Spa: 155 E. Chestnut Street, Asheville NC 28801; 828-236-0034

Grove Park Inn Resort & Spa: 290 Macon Avenue, Asheville NC 28804; 828-252-2711

L'eau de Vie Salon/Spa: 20 Battery Park Avenue, Suite 203, Asheville NC 28801; 828-258-9741

Namaste Yoga & Healing Center: 57 Broadway, Asheville NC 28801; 828-253-6985

Pi Salon.Spa: 16 Brook Street, Suite 150, Asheville NC 28803; 828-274-1210

Relax & Rejuvenate of Asheville, Inc.: 5 Regent Park Blvd., Suite 105, Asheville NC 28806; 828-250-9077

Revive Spa: 1000 Brevard Road, Asheville NC 28806; 828-665-4875

Sensibilities Day Spa: 59 Haywood Street, Asheville NC 28801; 828-253-3222

Two Town Square Blvd, Biltmore Park, Asheville NC 28803; 828-687-8760

Shoji Retreat: 90 Avondale Heights Road, Asheville NC 28803; 828-299-0999,

Starting Point Internal Cleansing Center & Spa: 959 Merrimon Avenue, Suite 2, Asheville NC 28804; 828-255-2898

Spa at Biltmore Village: 18 Brook Street, Suite 104, Asheville NC 28803; 828-277-2639

The Poseidon Spa: Grand Bohemian Hotel, 11 Boston Way, Asheville NC 28803; 828-398-5540

White Gate Inn & Cottage Spa: 173E Chestnut Street, Asheville NC 28801; 828-253-2553; 800-485-3045

Television Stations

WLOS TV/13 ABC: affiliate based in Asheville offering the best coverage of the mountains.

Fox Carolina/21: Coverage of the mountains, originating in Greenville SC

Chapter Five
Making the Move to the Mountains

I f you are considering a move to the mountains, the following lists should prove to be helpful in your planning. Real estate companies are listed for each city on my guidebook website city pages at www.ashevilleguidebook.com.

Real Estate Resources
Asheville Board of Realtors: 31 Montford Avenue, Asheville NC 28801; 828-255-8505, 800-392-2775.

Asheville Home Builders Association: 14 Mimidis Lane, Rte. 70, Swannanoa NC 28778; 828-299-7001.

Hendersonville Board of Realtors: 316 First Avenue E., Hendersonville NC 28792; 828-683-9642.

Homes and Land Magazine: 800-277-7800. Monthly real estate publication.

North Carolina Association of Realtors: 4511 Weybridge Lane, Greensboro NC 27407; 800-443-9956.

Western North Carolina Green Building Council: The primary resource in Western North Carolina for environmentally sustainable and health conscious building. PO Box 17026, Asheville NC 28816; 828-254-1995.

Relocation Resources
Asheville Chamber of Commerce: 36 Montford Ave., Asheville NC 28801; 828-258-6100.

Asheville Tourism and Visitor Center: 36 Montford Ave., Asheville NC 28801; 828-258-6102.

Greater Hendersonville Chamber of Commerce: 330 North King St., Hendersonville, NC 28792; 828-692-1413.

Hendersonville and Flat Rock Visitors Information Center: 201 South Main St., Hendersonville, NC 28792; 828-693-9708.

Employment Resources
Asheville Area Chamber of Commerce: 36 Montford Ave., Asheville NC 28801; 828-258-6101.

Buncombe County Human Resources Department: 205 College Street, Suite 100, Asheville NC 28801; 828-250-5206.

Mountain Area JobLink Career Center: The purpose of Mountain Area Job Training Services is to provide job seekers and employers a single place to address their employment and training needs. P.O. Box 729, Asheville NC 28802; 828-250-4761.

Senior Resources

Asheville Parks & Recreation Senior Programs: Asheville City Hall, Fourth Floor, 70 Court Plaza, Asheville NC 28801; 828-259-5800.

Buncombe County Council on Aging: 50 South French Broad Ave., Asheville NC 28801; 828-258-8027.

Buncombe County Department of Social Services: 40 Coxe Ave., Asheville NC 28801; 828-250-5500.

Council On Aging For Henderson County: 304 Chadwick Ave., Hendersonville, NC 28792; 828-692-4203.

Henderson County Department of Social Services: 246 2nd Ave. East, Hendersonville, NC 28792; 828-697-5500.

Land of Sky Regional Council Agency On Aging: 25 Heritage Dr., Asheville NC 28806; 828-2516622.

Meals On Wheels Of Asheville & Buncombe County: 146 Victoria Road, Asheville NC 28801; 828-253-5286.

Opportunity House: A multifaceted center for senior citizens in the Hendersonville area. 1411 Asheville Hwy., Hendersonville, NC 28791; 692-0575.

Senior Friendships of Hendersonville: P.O. Box 2828 Hendersonville, NC 28793.

The North Carolina Center for Creative Retirement: The University of North Carolina at Asheville, Asheville NC 28804; 828-251-6140.

Chapter Six
Environmental Issues in Western North Carolina

Paradise is not without its problems, and even though it would seem at first glance that there are really no environmental concerns in the beautiful mountains of Western North Carolina, there are a couple of issues that have just about everyone who lives here worried. Tops on the list is an air quality problem that occurs primarily in the summer. On certain days, even the most remote mountains and valleys, especially in the Great Smoky Mountains, have smog that rivals even Los Angeles and other urban centers. The primary culprits are the coal-fired power plants in the Midwest, which spew nitrous oxides and sulfur dioxides into the atmosphere, which are then carried by the prevailing west to east air currents and deposited in our area. A battle to stop this pollution is being fought on a national level, with North Carolina legislators (and those of adjoining states that are similarly affected) in the forefront of the war. Acid rain which harms higher altitude forests is another problem clearly related to this air pollution problem. Of concern also is the increasing number of mountain developments and the consequent loss of habitat.

Western North Carolina Environmental Organizations

Canary Coalition: A non-profit organization dedicated to restoring clean air in Western North Carolina and the southern Appalachian Region. PO Box 653, Sylva NC 287790; 828-631-3447; www.canarycoalition.org.

Carolina Mountain Land Conservancy: The Carolina Mountain Land Conservancy is a non-profit, voluntary organization that works directly to protect the natural diversity and beauty of Western North Carolina by preserving natural lands and scenic areas. PO Box 2822, Hendersonville NC 28793; 828-697-5777, www.carolinamountain.org.

Clean Air Community Trust: The Clean Air Community Trust is a non-profit organization chartered by the City of Asheville and Buncombe County. Their mission is the seek and secure cleaner air for the citizens of Buncombe County and surrounding communities. PO Box 2824, Asheville NC 28802; 828-258-1856, www.airtrust.org.

Cradle of Forestry: The Cradle of Forestry in America is a 6,500 acre Historic Site within the Pisgah National Forest, set aside by Congress to commemorate the beginning of forestry conservation in the United States. 828-877-3130, www.cradleofforestry.com.

ECO–Environmental & Conservation Organization: ECO is dedicated to preserving the natural heritage of Henderson County and the mountain region through **education, re**creation, service and civic action. Hendersonville. 828-692-0385, www.eco-wnc.org.

Long Branch Environmental Education Center: The Long Branch Environmental Education Center, Inc. is a small educational institute in Buncombe County's Newfound Mountains, about 18 miles northwest of Asheville, North Carolina. P.O. Box 369 Leicester, NC 28748; 828-683-3662, www.longbrancheec.org.

North Carolina Interfaith Power & Light: NC IPL works with faith communities to address the causes and consequences of global climate change, and promote practical solutions, through education, outreach, and public policy advocacy. 919-828-6501, http://www.ncipl.org

Quality Forward Asheville: Quality Forward is a volunteer based organization working to enhance the environment and quality of life for the citizens of Asheville and Buncombe County through awareness building, community activities and partnership. PO Box 22, 29 Page Avenue, Asheville NC 28801; 828-254-1766, www.qualityforward.org.

RiverLink: RiverLink is a regional nonprofit spearheading the economic and environmental revitalization of the French Broad River and its tributaries. 70 Woodfin Place, Asheville NC 28801; 828-225-0760, www.riverlink.org.

Southern Alliance for Clean Energy: SACE is a nonprofit, nonpartisan organization that promotes responsible energy choices that solve global warming problems and ensure clean, safe, and healthy communities throughout the Southeast. 828-254-6776, www.cleanenergy.org.

Southern Appalachian Biodiversity Project: SABP's goal is permanent protection for the region's public lands and sustainable management of private lands. Battery Park Ave., Asheville NC 28801; 828-258-2667, www.sabp.net.

Southern Appalachian Forest Coalition: SAFC is a nonprofit organization formed in 1994 whose objective is to protect the forests at the local level. 46 Haywood St., Asheville NC 28801; 828-252-9223, www.safc.org.

Southern Appalachian Highlands Conservancy: SAHC's mission is to conserve unique plant and animal habitats, clean water, and scenic beauty of the mountains of North Carolina and Tennessee for the benefit of present and future generations. 34 Wall St., Suite 802, Asheville NC, 28801; 828-253-0095, www.appalachian.org.

Sustainable Asheville Area Network: The Sustainable Asheville Area Network is comprised of organizations and individuals in the greater Asheville area concerned with sustainability and the environment. www.sustainableasheville.org.

Western North Carolina Alliance: The Western North Carolina Alliance is a grassroots organization that aims to promote a sense of stewardship and caring for the natural environment. 70 Woodfin Place, Asheville NC 28801; 828-258-8737, www.wnca.org.

Western North Carolina Green Building Council: WNCGBC is a nonprofit organization whose mission is to promote environmentally sustainable and health-conscious building practices through community education. PO Box 17026, Asheville NC 28801; 828-232-5080, www.wncgbc.org.

Western North Carolina Nature Center: The Western North Carolina Nature Center is the premier nature center in Western North Carolina. 75 Gashes Creek Rd., Asheville NC 28805; 828-298-5600, www.wildwnc.org.

Section Two
The Best of
Asheville & Hendersonville

Chapter One
Author's Choice Accommodations

Both Asheville and Hendersonville have a wide variety and number of accommodations, from world-class resort hotels, exotic bed & breakfasts to budget motels. In this section I have presented only the best that our area has to offer in each category. For a complete listing of all the hundreds of Asheville & Hendersonville accommodations by category, visit my guidebook website at www.ashevilleguidebook.com.

The season of the year has a lot to do with accommodation availability. Summer and the fall leaf season in October are by far the most crowded and busiest times of the year. Also, the weekend around Bele Chere Festival, the October leaf season, and Christmas and New Year's weekends are all high-volume times. Accommodations for these weekends can be hard to find if not booked in advance.

NRHP = Listed on the National Register of Historic Places

Asheville Grand Hotels, Inns & Lodges

Crown Plaza Tennis & Golf Resort: Located one mile from downtown on the west side of Asheville, this 274-room, full-service resort offers oversized rooms with Sleep Advantage Deluxe bedding and 30 vacation villas on site. Nine hole golf course, and indoor and outdoor tennis. One Resort Drive, Asheville NC 28806; 800-733-3211, 828-254-3211.

Grand Bohemian Hotel: Located in Biltmore Village opposite the entrance to Biltmore Estate, the Grand Bohemian Hotel has 104 luxurious guestrooms and suites in an atmosphere of gracious, Tudor-inspired style, reminiscent of the grand elegance of the Old World. 11 Boston Way, Asheville NC 28803; 828-274-1242.

Grove Park Inn Resort & Spa (NRHP): Superlative world-class resort hotel. Four-diamond and many other awards. 510 rooms, sports center, indoor and outdoor pools, 18-hole championship golf course. Opened in 2001, the hotel's world-famous spa is one of the finest in the world and features lush gardens, waterfalls and a wide range of treatments. 290 Macon Ave., Asheville NC 28804; 800-438-5800 or 828-252-2711.

Haywood Park Hotel (NRHP): Four-diamond hotel in the heart of downtown. 33 rooms, all suites, Jacuzzis. Continental breakfast delivered to suite daily. One Battery Park Ave., Asheville NC 28801; 800 228-2522, 828-252-2522. $$$ Luxury.

Hotel Indigo: Hotel Indigo is a 100-room boutique hotel located in the heart of downtown Asheville, one block from Grove Arcade. The hotel includes a bar and restaurant, off-street parking and spectacular views. 151 Haywood Street, Asheville NC 28801. 828-239-0239.

The Inn on Biltmore Estate: A truly world class deluxe inn with over 200 rooms located on Biltmore Estate grounds, near the Biltmore Estate Winery. Spectacular mountain vistas from porches, balconies, and guest rooms. Guest rooms ranging from deluxe to suites as well as on site dining for breakfast, lunch, and dinner. Four-star rating by both Mobil Travel Guide and AAA. One Antler Ridge Rd., Asheville NC 28801; (800) 624-1575, 828-225-1600.

Marriott Renaissance Hotel Asheville: Downtown next to Thomas Wolfe Memorial. 281 mountain-view rooms within walking distance everything downtown. Superb dining options, concierge service, 60' indoor pool, whirlpool, & fitness center. 31 Woodfin Street, Asheville NC 28801; 800-333-3333, 828-252-8211.

Princess Anne Hotel: (NRHP): Sophistication and grace describe this little gem of a historic hotel. The lovingly restored Princess Anne is characterized by its timeless, classic 1920s appeal with modern luxury and conveniences. The hotel still retains its original ambience and charm. 301 E. Chestnut St., Asheville NC 28801; 866 552-0986, 828-258-0986.

Asheville Motels

Airport Area

Clarion Inn Airport: 550 New Airport Rd., Fletcher, NC 28732; 828- 684-1213, 800-465-4329.

Comfort Inn Airport: 15 Rockwood Rd., Arden, NC 28704; 828-687-9199, 800-228-5150.

Days Inn Airport: 183 Underwood Road, Fletcher NC 28732; 828-684-2281, 800-329-7466.

Econo Lodge Airport: 196 Underwood Road, Fletcher NC 28732; 828-684-1200, 800-553-2666.

Fairfield Inn Airport: Airport Park Road, Fletcher NC 28732; 828-684-1144, 800-451-8174.

Hampton Inn & Suites: 18 Rockwood Rd., Fletcher, NC 28732; 828-687-0806, 800-426-7866.

Holiday Inn Airport: 550 New Airport Rd., Fletcher, NC 28732; 828- 684-1213, 800-465-4329.

Quality Inn & Suites -Biltmore South: 1 Skyland Drive, Arden NC 28704; 828-684-6688.

Biltmore Square Area (West of downtown)

Comfort Inn West: 15 Crowell Rd., Asheville NC 28806; 828-665-6500, 800-228-5150.

Comfort Suites Biltmore Square Mall: 890 Brevard Rd., Asheville NC 28806; 828-665-4000, 800-622-4005

Fairfield Inn & Suites: 11 Rocky Ridge Road, Asheville NC 28806; 828-665-4242.

Hampton Inn Biltmore Square: 1 Rocky Ridge Rd., Asheville NC 28806; 828-667-2022, 800-426-7866.

Hilton Asheville- Biltmore Park: 43 Town Square Boulevard, Asheville NC 28803; 828-210-8290.

Holiday Inn Express Hotel & Suites: 1 Wedgefield Dr., Asheville NC 28806; 828-665-6519, 800-465-6814.

Rodeway Inn & Suites -Biltmore Square: 9 Wedgewood Drive, Asheville NC 28806; 828-670-8800, 877-354-8800.

Biltmore Village Area (Closest to Biltmore Estate)

Baymont Inn & Suites: 204 Hendersonville Rd., Asheville NC 28803; 828-274-2022, 800-301-0200.

Biltmore Howard Johnson: 190 Hendersonville Rd., Asheville NC 28803; 828-274-2300, 800-446-4656.

Country Inn & Suites by Carlson: 845 Brevard Rd., Asheville NC 28806; 828-670-9000, 800- 456-4000.

DoubleTree Biltmore Hotel: 115 Hendersonville Rd., Asheville NC 28803; 828-274-1800.

Guesthouse International Inn -Biltmore: 234 Hendersonville Road, Asheville NC 28803; 828-274-0101.

Residence Inn by Marriott -Asheville: 701 Biltmore Ave., Asheville NC 28803; 828-281-3361, 800-331-3131.

Sleep Inn -Biltmore: 117 Hendersonville Rd., Asheville NC 28803; 828-277-1800.

Downtown Asheville

Asheville Four Points by Sheraton Downtown: 22 Woodfin Street, Asheville NC 28801; 888-854-6897, 828-2563-1851.

East of Downtown

Days Inn Biltmore East: 1435 Tunnel Road, Asheville NC 28805; 828-298-4000, 866-949-9914.

Motel 6 Asheville: 1415 Tunnel Road, Asheville NC 28805, 828-299-3040; 800-466-8356.

Quality Inn & Suites-Biltmore East: 1430 Tunnel Road, Asheville NC 28805; 828-298-5519, 877-299-5519.

North of Downtown

Days Inn North: 3 Reynolds Mtn. Rd., Asheville NC 28804; 828-645-9191; 800-329-7666.

South of Downtown (Asheville Mall -Tunnel Road Area)

Asheville Ramada: 800 Fairview Road, Asheville NC 28805; 800-836-6732, 828-298-9141.

Best Western Asheville Biltmore East: 501 Tunnel Rd., Asheville NC 28805; 828-298-5562, 888-230-1228.

Brookstone Lodge: 4 Roberts Road, Asheville NC 28803; 877-798-5888, 828-398-5888.

Country Inn & Suites by Carlson/ Tunnel Road: 199 Tunnel Road, Asheville NC 28805; 828-254-4311, 800-456-4000.

Courtyard by Marriott: Buckstone Place, Asheville NC 28805; 800-321-2211, 828-281-0041.

Days Inn Asheville Mall: 201 Tunnel Rd., Asheville NC 28805; 828-252-4000; 800-329-7466.

Econo Lodge Biltmore: 150 Tunnel Road, Asheville NC 28805, 828-254-9521; 800-553-2666.

Extended StayAmerica Asheville: 6 Kenilworth Knoll Rd., Asheville NC 28805; 828-253-3483, 800-398-7829.

Hampton Inn Tunnel Road: 204 Tunnel Rd., Asheville NC 28805; 828-255-9220; 800-426-7866.

Holiday Inn -Biltmore East at the Blue Ridge Parkway: 1450 Tunnel Rd., Asheville NC 28805; 828-298-5611.

Holiday Inn Hotel & Suites -Asheville Downtown: 2 Tunnel Road, Asheville NC 28805; 828-225-5550, 800-465-4329.

Homewood Suites by Hilton: 88 Tunnel Road, Asheville NC 28805; 800-225-5466, 828-252-5400.

Springhill Suites by Marriott -Asheville: 2 Buckstone Place, Asheville NC 28805; 828-253-4666, 888-287-9400.

Super 8 -Asheville Biltmore: 180 Tunnel Road, Asheville NC 28805; 828-505-4648.

West of Downtown

Days Inn West: 2551 Smoky Park Hwy., Candler, NC 28715; 828-667-9321, 800-329-7466.

Holiday Inn -Biltmore West: 435 Smoky Park Highway, Asheville NC 28806; 828-678-2161.

Ramada Biltmore West: 275 Smoky Park Highway, Asheville NC 28806; 828-667-4501, 800-295-5486.

Red Roof Inn: 16 Crowell Rd., Asheville NC 28806; 828-667-9803, 800-733-7663.

Rodeway Inn -Asheville: 8 Crowell Road, Asheville NC 28806; 877-577-8737.

Sleep Inn Biltmore West: 1918 Old Haywood Rd., Asheville NC 28806; 828-670-7600, 866-901-1033.

Value Place: 40 Monte Vista Road, Asheville NC 28806; 828-418-1400.

Asheville Bed & Breakfasts

A Bed of Roses (NRHP): Situated on a quiet, tree-lined street in Montford district of Asheville, A Bed of Roses was built at the end of the Victorian era by Oliver Davis Revell and meticulously renovated in 2002. Enjoy the comfort of the tastefully decorated 1897 Queen Anne house with its shaded porch and tended gardens. Many of the guest rooms have fireplaces and private baths including Jacuzzi-style tubs. 135 Cumberland Ave., Asheville NC 28801; 828-258-8700, 800-471-4182.

Abbington Green Bed & Breakfast Inn (NRHP): Richard Sharp Smith designed Colonial Revival-style home with romantic English flavor that includes antique furnishings, fine rugs, piano, library and fireplaces. Prize-winning English gardens surround the inn. Inside, the stylish guestrooms are named after parks and gardens around London. Each room has a king bed, whirlpool tub with shower, fireplace, HDTV and internet access. Five rooms plus one- and two-bedroom suites. Located in the Montford Historic District. 46 Cumberland Circle, Asheville NC 28801; 828-251-2454, 800-251-2454.

Aberdeen Inn: Six guest rooms and cottages, all with private baths, four with fireplaces. Children over 12 welcome. One of the earliest houses built in the area, the Aberdeen Inn rests comfortably on a small rise surrounded by nearly an acre of lawns, trees and gardens. Hot tub, full gourmet breakfast. 64 Linden Ave., Asheville NC 28801; 828-254-9336.

Albemarle Inn (NRHS): The Albemarle Inn is housed in a classic 1907 Southern mansion with English gardens. Period guest rooms offer clawfoot or whirlpool tubs with fragrant bath amenities, fine linens, fresh flowers and evening turndown service. Elegant canopy queen or king-size beds and a private balcony are special features of some rooms. Award winning full gourmet breakfasts are

A Bed of Roses, 135 Cumberland Avenue

Albemarle Inn, 86 Edgemont Road

served at private tables on the bright sun porch or cozy period dining room. 86 Edgemont Road, Asheville NC 28801; 828-255-0027, 800-621-7435.

Applewood Manor Inn (NRHP): A Colonial Revival-style house on almost two acres of secluded lawn and shade trees. The inn and its sizeable rooms are accented with fireplaces, private baths and balconies, antiques, art and fresh flowers. Services each day include a full delicious and plentiful 3-course breakfast, afternoon social with beverages and treats and turndown service are provide Located in the Montford Historic District. 62 Cumberland Circle, Asheville NC 28801; 828-254-2244, 800-442-2197.

Asheville Seasons Bed & Breakfast: An intimate Inn with only five guest rooms, Asheville Seasons is located in the Montford Historic District. Walk to downtown, enjoy sitting on the front porch, read a book in the parlor or just relax in your room. A delicious breakfast with fruit, a main course, juice, teas, and special blend of gourmet organic fair trade coffee is included. All of the seasonal themed rooms include private baths, king or queen beds and most have working fireplaces. 43 Watauga Street, Asheville NC 28801; 828-236-9494.

Asia Bed & Spa: East meets West at ASIA, a haven of serene privacy, with five luxurious suites. Everything you see, touch, or sense creates an experience of pampering and calm. Japanese Gardens with a fountain, exotic fabrics and finishes! Double Jacuzzis, fireplaces, king beds, robes and slippers, and a mini-bar. 128 Hillside Street, Asheville NC 28801, 828-255-0051. $$$ Luxury.

At Cumberland Falls Bed & Breakfast Inn (NRHP): Turn-of-the-century home located in Montford Historic District. Grounds are landscaped with waterfalls, koi ponds, and gardens. The inn features quilted maple woodwork and solarium. Guest rooms have wood or gas-burning fireplaces and two-person Jacuzzi tubs surrounded by marble. Gourmet breakfasts, fresh pastries, flowers, and robes in rooms, turndown service with chocolates, massage, and concierge service. 254 Cumberland Ave., Asheville NC 28801; 828-253-4085, 888-743-2557.

Beaufort House Inn (NRHP): A grand Queen Anne mansion, features wood-burning fireplaces, two-person Jacuzzis, fitness facility and mountain views. Built in 1894, this historic home has been meticulously restored as a romantic bed and breakfast inn with an air of casual luxury and elegance and has a lovely gingerbread porch, with beautifully landscaped grounds that include tea gardens. Popular afternoon tea offered on outdoor porch. 61 North Liberty St., Asheville NC 28801; 828-254-8334, 800- 261-2221.

Bent Creek Lodge: Bent Creek Lodge is a rustic mountain retreat surrounded by acres of woods and miles of trails and located less than one mile from the North Carolina Arboretum. Built in 1999, the Lodge is an ideal base for biking, hiking, canoeing, and exploring the Asheville area. Features gourmet breakfasts and intimate dinners for guests only. Amenities include a great room with stone fireplace, pool table, spacious decks, and six comfortably appointed guest rooms with private baths and air conditioning. 10 Parkway Crescent, Arden NC 28704; 828-654-9040, 877-231-6574.

Biltmore Village Inn: Located in historic Biltmore Village, this lovely B&B is the closest to Biltmore Estate. Large rooms feature Jacuzzis, fireplaces, flat screens, DVD players and wireless Internet access. Meals and conversation are enjoyed on a porch boasting mountain views and sunsets. 119 Dodge Street, Asheville NC 28803; 828-274-8707, 866-274-9779.

Carolina Bed & Breakfast (NRHP): A turn-of-the-century restoration located in the Montford district, this historic house designed in 1900 by Richard Sharp Smith has seven rooms with fireplaces, private baths, and air-conditioning. The rooms are decorated with a blend of antiques and collectibles. Porches and gardens complement the gracious interior. With its pebbledash finish, unique rooflines and abundant porches, this Smith creation blends art and nature in the true Arts and Crafts tradition. 177 Cumberland Ave., Asheville NC 28801; 828-254-3608, 888-254-3608.

1891 Cedar Crest Inn (NRHP): One of the largest and most opulent residences surviving from Asheville's 1890s boom period, is an 1891 Queen Anne mansion featuring elegant interiors created by Vanderbilt's craftsmen. Romantic guest suites, rooms and beautiful grounds. One of three accommodations in Asheville to be awarded AAA's Four Diamond rating. 674 Biltmore Ave., Asheville NC 28803; 828-252-1389, 800-252-0310.

Chestnut Street Inn (NRHP): A superbly restored Colonial Revival bed & breakfast located in the Chestnut Hill Historic District. The entire grounds are designated a "Treasure Tree" preserve. The 1905 house has been lovingly restored and has some of the most elegant interior woodwork to be found in Asheville. Eclectic furnishings with great porches and all rooms have private baths. Private suite also available. Afternoon tea and breakfast are served on antique china. 176 East Chestnut St., Asheville NC 28801; 828-285-0705, 800-894-2955.

The Corner Oak Manor Bed & Breakfast, 53 St. Dunstans Road, Asheville

Corner Oak Manor Bed & Breakfast: A 1920 English Tudor residence in a quiet neighborhood. Renovated and deco rated with oak antiques, arts and hand-crafted items. Features a full gourmet breakfast, living room fireplace with baby grand piano and an outdoor deck with Jacuzzi. 53 St. Dunstans Rd., Asheville NC 28803; 828-253-3525, 888-633-3525.

Hill House Bed & Breakfast (NRHP): Seated on an acre of beautiful gardens and century-old trees, the original tin roof still graces this 1885 Grand Victorian. Recently restored and decorated in an eclectic mix of antiques and unique pieces, the varied accommodations include AC, VCR, phone, fax, in-room coffee maker, private Jacuzzi tub and fireplaces. 120 Hillside St., Asheville NC 28801; 828-232-0345, 800-379-0002.

1900 Inn on Montford (NRHP): A 1900 Richard Sharp Smith-designed English country cottage, is furnished with period antiques from 1730 to 1910, oriental rugs and an extensive collection of antique maps. Full breakfast also served daily. Five large and comfortable guest rooms have private in-suite baths, fireplaces, and queen-sized poster beds. A large Southern porch and a massive stone fireplace grace the inn. In Montford Historic District. 296 Montford Ave., Asheville NC 28801; 828-254-9569, 800- 254-9569.

North Lodge on Oakland Bed & Breakfast (NRHP): A lovingly restored 1904 stone and cedar shingle home with private baths and TV in every room. Antiques and contemporary furnishings. Deluxe hot breakfast. No smoking. Fine hotel service at affordable rates. 84 Oakland Rd., Asheville NC 28801; 828-252-6433, 800-282-3602. $$ Moderate.

Oakland Cottage Bed & Breakfast: Circa 1905 B&B with spacious family friendly suites. Breakfast included. This 5,000 square ft "cottage" has been naturally broken into private and roomy Suites. The open common areas create

Hill House Bed & Breakfast Inn, 120 Hillside Street, Asheville

a warm and spacious feel. Conveniently located a short one and a half miles from the entrance of the Biltmore Estate and just two miles from downtown Asheville's Pack Square   74 Oakland Road, Asheville NC 28801, 828-994-2627, 866-858-0863. $$ Moderate.

The Black Walnut Bed & Breakfast Inn (NRHP): A finely preserved Shingle-style home, was built in 1899 by Richard Sharp Smith and restored into a bed & breakfast in 1992. the Inn features six rooms in the main house and two brand new, pet friendly suites in the restored carriage house. All rooms have

North Lodge Bed & Breakfast, 84 Oakland Road, Asheville

private bath, luxury bedding, and most have fireplaces. Room rates include gourmet three course breakfast and afternoon tea with wine tasting. In Montford Historic District. 288 Montford Ave., Asheville NC 28801; 828-254-3878, 800-381-3878.

The Lion & The Rose (NRHP): A Queen Anne/Georgian-style home, was built around 1898. Lovely antique-filled suites and private rooms complete with fresh flowers and linens. 24-hour guest pantry, wireless internet and TV/DVD players in each guest room. Gourmet breakfast served daily in the sunny dining room and in the afternoon, tea on the verandas or in the parlors. In Montford Historic District. 276 Montford Ave., Asheville NC 28801; 828-255-7673, 800-546-6988.

The Reynolds Mansion Bed & Breakfast (NRHP): The Reynolds Mansion Bed & Breakfast Inn (circa 1847) has graciously restored accommodations that include eight guest rooms in the main house, three guest rooms in the nearby Carriage House and two private Cottages. All guest rooms feature private baths and most offer the warming glow of a fireplace.100 Reynolds Heights, Asheville NC 28804; 828-258-1111, 888-611-1156

Sourwood Inn: Located 10 miles from downtown Asheville on one hundred acres, the Sourwood Inn has 12 guest rooms with wood-burning fireplaces, balconies, and baths. Also available is the charming Sassafras Cabin. Located near the Blue Ridge Parkway in the mountains surrounding Asheville, Sourwood Inn has two miles of walking trails and offers a unique experience of the mountains.810 Elk Mountain Scenic Hwy., Asheville NC 28804; 828-255-0690.

Sweet Biscuit Inn: 1915 Colonial Revival house with rich decorative details throughout, including 11-foot ceilings, tiger oak floors, dramatic formal staircase, and a comfortable full length porch. 3 spacious guest rooms and carriage house with private baths. Located in Kenilworth neighborhood of East Asheville. Casual comfort and unpretentious sophistication are the hallmarks of this sweet and charming B&B. Children welcomed. 77 Kenilworth Rd., Asheville NC 28803; 828-250-0170.

1889 White Gate Inn & Cottage(NRHP): One of Asheville's premier bed & breakfasts, the historic 1889 White Gate Inn & Cottage is conveniently located near downtown Asheville. Romance, elegance and tranquility perfectly describe the ambience of this New England-style inn. Sumptuous breakfasts, luxurious spa suites and award-winning gardens, complete with cascading waterfalls and koi ponds, are just part of what make this B&B special. 173 East Chestnut St., Asheville NC 28801; 828-253-2553, 800-485-3045.

1899 Wright Inn & Carriage House NRHP): One of the finest examples of Queen Anne architecture in Asheville, has eight distinctive bedrooms and a luxurious suite with fireplace. All rooms have private baths, cable TV and telephones. The three-bedroom Carriage House is ideal for groups or families. Full breakfast and afternoon tea served daily in the inn. In Montford Historic District. 235 Pearson Dr., Asheville NC 28801; 828-251-0789, 800-552-5724

Asheville Cabins, Cottages & Chalets

Asheville Cabins of Willow Winds: Twenty-five luxury cabins on delight acre property with trout pond, stream, waterfall, gardens and fountains ʌll cabins are tastefully decorated, completely equipped and furnished. Amenities include wood-burning fireplaces, hot tubs, kitchens with dishwashers, linens, towels, cooking utensils, cable television with DVD, free internet, air conditioning, washer/dryer, telephone and private decks with grills. 39 Stockwood Road Ext., Asheville NC 28803; 828-277-3948, 800-235-2474.

Asheville Swiss Chalets: Pet-friendly. Casual elegance on Beaucatcher Mountain overlooking Asheville. All chalets are smoke free & equipped with heating and air conditioning for year-round comfort. Well appointed & tastefully decorated chalets with every convenience of home with full service kitchens, internet service, cable TV, gas fireplaces and more. 5 Delano Road, Asheville NC 28805; 828-776-0509.

Cabins of Asheville: Real dovetail log cabins with modern amenities, in forest setting in Candler. 25 LIttle Stoney Fork Road, Candler NC 28715; 828-670-0084

Log Cabin Motor Court: Historic and unique log cabins from the 1930s refurbished with all the modern conveniences. Pet friendly and fully furnished. Located only 5.5 miles north of the center of downtown Asheville. All cabins are fully equipped with linens, towels, coffee maker and refrigerator. All cabins with AC, except for one. 330 Weaverville Highway, Asheville NC 28804; 828-645-6546, 800-295-3392.

Mountain Springs Cabins: Three Diamond AAA rating. Outstanding country cabins with fireplaces overlooking a rushing mountain stream. Nestled on 30 landscaped, parklike acres just off the Blue Ridge Parkway and 10 minutes west of Asheville. Breathtaking views, a really special place to stay. 27 Emma's Cove Road, Candler NC 28715; 828-665-1004.

Mountain Springs Cabins & Chalets, 151 Pisgah Hwy., Candler

Pisgah View Ranch: 19 miles southwest of Asheville at the base of Mount Pisgah. 42 cottage rooms with private baths. Famous family style country dining (three meals a day included). Nightly entertainment, swimming, tennis, hiking and horseback riding. Open May through October. 70 Pisgah View Ranch Road, Candler NC 28715; 828-667-9100, 866-252-8361.

The Pines Cottages: Over 75 years in business at the same location. 15 cottages and cabins to choose from, all with kitchens, some with fireplaces and cable TV. Children welcome. 346 Weaverville Hwy., Asheville NC 28804; 828-645-9661, 888-818-6477.

Asheville Campgrounds

Campfire Lodgings: Located on Goldview Knob just a ten minute drive outside of Asheville, Campfire Lodgings offers 100 acres of mountaintop camping at its best. Options include RV camping with large, staggered sites to tent sites with water/electric to romantic Yurts, fully furnished log cabins or Cliff House, perfect for a large group. Full hookups. 116 Appalachian Village Road, Asheville NC 28804; 828-658-8012, 800-933-8012.

French Broad River Campground: Located on the French Broad River, 13 acres with over 2,000 feet of river frontage campground sites. 1030 Old Marshall Hwy., Asheville NC 28804; 828-658-0772.

KOA Asheville-East Tanglewood: Shady RV and tent sites with full and partial hookups. Three bathhouses, 17 cabins and three furnished rental units. Amenities include two fishing lakes, boating, store, laundry, swimming, playground, mini-golf, and LP gas. Free Wi-Fi and Cable TV2708 Hwy. 70 East, Swannanoa, NC 28778; 828-686-3121, 800-562-5907.

KOA Asheville-West: Tent sites are beautifully wooded, and our "Big Rig" friendly 50- and 30-amp pull-through sites are large, level, and have cable TV and free Wi-Fi. I-40 Exit 37 & Wiggins Rd., Candler, NC 28715; 828-665-7015, (800) 562-9015.

Rutledge Lake RV Park and Cabins: Friendly professional service, and clean and well-maintained facilities. Lake fishing, boating and canoeing. 170 Rutledge Road, Fletcher NC 28732; 828 654-7873.

Hendersonville Grand Hotels, Inns & Lodges

Echo Mountain Inn: Historic inn with great views. Built in 1896 on Echo Mountain, the inn offers one or two bed-room apartments, rooms with mountain views and fireplaces, private bath, cable TV and telephones. Restaurant, swimming pool and shuffleboard. 2849 Laurel Park Hwy., Hendersonville, NC 28739; 828-693-9626, 888-324-6466.

Highland Lake Inn: Offers accommodations in the inn, cabins or cottages. Located on scenic Highland Lake and surrounded by 26 wooded acres. A full service resort destination, Highland Lake Inn offers award-winning dining, outdoor pool, walking trails, organic gardens and more. 86 Lily Pad Lane, Flat Rock, NC 28731; 828-693-6812, 800-762-1376.

Inn on Church Street: Hendersonville's premier boutique hotel, built in 1921. Located in the heart of historic downtown Hendersonville. Private bath, wireless internet, full gourmet breakfast and fresh baked cookies at check in. 201 3rd Ave. West, Hendersonville, NC 28739; 828-693-3258, 800-330-3836.

Woodfield Inn (NRHP): A historic 1852 country inn near Flat Rock Playhouse and the Carl Sandburg home. Authentic bedrooms, wine room, parlor and dining rooms all restored to their original elegance. Many of the Victorian bed-rooms offer private baths, fireplaces, and French doors leading to sweeping verandas. Park like setting on 28 acres. Tennis courts, gazebo, formal English garden, seven acres of walking trails, and entertainment facilities. Fine mountain and continental cuisine. Popular wedding setting. 2901 Greenville Hwy., P.O. Box 98, Flat Rock, NC 28731; 828-693-6016.

Hendersonville Motels

Best Western Hendersonville Inn: 105 Sugarloaf Rd., Hendersonville, NC 28792; 828-692-0521,800-528-1234.

Comfort Inn: 206 Mitchell Dr., Hendersonville, NC 28792; 828-693-8800, 800-882-3843.

Days Inn: 102 Mitchell Dr., Hendersonville, NC 28792; 828-697-5999.

Hampton Inn: 155 Sugarloaf Rd., Hendersonville, NC 28792; 828-697-2333, 800-426-7866.

Holiday Inn Express: 111 Commercial Boulevard, Flat Rock, NC 28731; 828-698-8899, 800-465-4329.

Mountain Inn & Suites: 447 Naples Road, Hendersonville NC 28792; 828-692-7772.

Mountain Lodge & Conference Center: 42 McMurray Road, Flat Rock NC 28731; 828-693-9910.

Quality Inn & Suites: 201 Sugarloaf Rd., Hendersonville, NC 28792; 828-692-7231, 800-228-5151.

Ramada Limited: 150 Sugarloaf Rd., Hendersonville, NC 28792; 828-697-0006, 800-272-6232.

Red Roof Inn: 240 Mitchell Dr., Hendersonville, NC 28792; 828-697-1223.

Hendersonville Bed & Breakfasts

Claddagh Inn (NRHP): A historic bed & breakfast, has been lovingly restored. Built between 1888 and 1906, the Claddagh Inn has 14 lovely guest rooms, all uniquely decorated. Each has a private bath, AC, telephone and TV. A full home-cooked breakfast is served every morning in the inn's large, comfortable dining room. 755 N. Main St., Hendersonville, NC 28792; 697-7778, 800-225-4700.

Elizabeth Leigh Inn (NRHP): Elegant bed and breakfast in historic 1893 residence. Four suites with king-size beds, private baths and fireplaces. Services and amenities include real estate tours, dinner reservation, massage by appointment, homemade ice cream, guest's pantry, full concierge service and wireless internet access. 908 5th Ave. West, Hendersonville NC 28792; 838-698-9707.

Melange Bed & Breakfast, 1230 5th Ave. West, Hendersonville

Flat Rock Inn Bed & Breakfast (NRHP): Victorian elegance in the country. Four theme-decorated guest rooms, each furnished to take you back to a bygone era. The inn was built in 1888 as a private residence and has been wonderfully restored. Breakfast is served family style in one of two dining rooms and is varied every day. 2810 Greenville Hwy., Flat Rock, NC 28731; 838-696-3273, 800-266-3996

Inn on Church Street: Hendersonville's premier boutique hotel, built in 1921. Located in the heart of historic downtown Hendersonville. Private bath, wireless internet, full gourmet breakfast and fresh baked cookies at check in. 201 3rd Ave. West, Hendersonville, NC 28739; 828-693-3258, 800-330-3836.

Melange: Newly restored with European flair and charm, is a unique bed & breakfast with a re-fined atmosphere and museum-quality art and sculpture, oriental rugs, Mediterranean porches, crystal chandeliers and antique furnishings. AC in all rooms, two rooms with Jacuzzis. A gourmet breakfast is served during summer in the Rose Garden and on covered porches and in winter in the formal dining room. 1230 5th Ave. West, Hendersonville, NC 28739; 828-697-5253, 800-303-5253.

Pinebrook Manor: One of the oldest historic estates in Hendersonville, this romantic five-acre property has been lovingly restored to provide the utmost in pampered hospitality for guests. 2701 Kanuga Road, Hendersonville NC 28739; 828-698-2707, 877-916-2667.

The Apple Inn: Mountain views and delicious home-cooked breakfast. Each room in this charming home is named after an apple variety. Secluded grounds with hammocks, rockers and lawn games. House built circa 1900. 1005 White Pine Dr., Hendersonville, NC 28739; 838-693-0107, 800-615-6611.

The Barker House 1891: The spacious house interior has been restored to its late Victorian elegance, with large rooms and high ceilings. The home is accented

with many antiques and interesting articles from the own[...]
interests. Originally the residence of Civil War Major Theod[...]
Greenville Highway, Hendersonville NC 28792; 828-699-32[...]

1898 Waverly Inn (NRHP): An elegant bed & breakfast established in 1898 that is famous for Southern breakfasts. Fourteen unique guest rooms and one suite, each with private bath, are named for native wildflowers. Special features include four-poster canopy beds, brass beds, claw-foot bathtubs, and pedestal sinks. 783 N. Main St., Hendersonville, NC 28792; 838-693-9193, 800-537-8195

Hendersonville Cabins, Cottages & Chalets

Lakemont Cottages: Located in Flat Rock, Lakemont Cottages features 14 individually decorated units that each sleep from two to six guests. All cottages are furnished, with separate bedrooms, air conditioning, heat, fully equipped kitchens and cable TV. Most have enclosed porches. No pets. 100 Lakemont Drive, Flat Rock, NC 28731; 828-693-5174.

Lazy Lake Cabins: Rustic comfort on a six acre hobby farm. Cabins are 750 square feet and all have a fireplace with gas logs, a carpeted loft, a Jacuzzi in the main bathroom, and a full length covered porch with porch furniture. 2322 Sugarloaf Road, Hendersonville NC 28792; 828-692-5094.

Mountain Lake Cottages: Mountain Lake Inn offers eleven large efficiency cottages available nightly, weekly or seasonally. Each cottage has a well appointed eat in kitchen including small stove, fridge, microwave, and coffee maker. All cottages offer private baths, air-conditioning, heat, ceiling fans, television with cable and free wifi. Most cottages offer a separate living room and private porch with chairs. 801 N. Lakeside Drive, Hendersonville NC 28739; 828-692-6269.

The Cottages of Flat Rock: 13 immaculate one and two bedroom cottages nestled on 2.5 acres. Each cottage has a private front porch with rocking chairs overlooking a one acre park like setting complete with gazebo and quiet stream. Laundry on grounds. 1511 Greenville Hwy., Hendersonville, NC 28792; 828-693-8805.

Villa Capri Cottages: 18 cottages situated on two landscaped acres in a residential setting. 920 Greenville Hwy., Hendersonville, NC 28792; 828-692-7660.

Hendersonville Campgrounds

Blue Ridge Travel Park: Open April-November, picnic area. Located on 10 acres in Henderson County's apple growing region. 58 lots all full hookup, with 30 AMP electrical service. 3576 Chimney Rock Road, Hendersonville NC 28792; 828-685-9207.

Lakewood RV Resort: Premier RV resort catering to adults. RV site rentals, amenities include full size pool and deck, shuffleboard, fishing pond, large fully equipped clubhouse, gym and business center. 915 Ballenger Rd., Flat Rock, NC 28731; 828-697-9523, 888-819-4200.

Park Place RV Park: Located 3 miles from downtown Hendersonville, 48 level sites, all full hook-up, 47 are pull-through. Wi-fi high speed internet now available from campsites. 501 South Allen Rd., Flat Rock, NC 28731; 828-693-3831.

Red Gates Cottages and RV Park: Located on a gently rolling meadowland with a 2 acre lake and surrounded by beautiful wooded areas. Cottages and 20 large lots with full hookups, hot showers, laundry facilities and sandy swimming beach. 314 Red Gates Lane, Hendersonville NC 28792; 828-685-8787.

Rutledge Lake RV Park and Cabins: Friendly professional service, and clean and well-maintained facilities. Lake fishing, boating and canoeing. 170 Rutledge Road, Fletcher NC 28732; 828 654-7873.

Town Mountain Travel Park: Large shady campsites with full hook-ups, a patio, and a picnic table. Cable TV is available on some sites and some sites have telephone hook-ups. Also cottage rentals. Located two miles from downtown Hendersonville. 2030 Spartanburg Highway, Hendersonville NC 28792; 828-697-6692.

Twin Ponds RV Park: Pool, clubhouse, activity room laundry facilities, mail room with keyed boxes, kitchen, tennis courts, ponds. 24 Empire Lane, Flat Rock, NC 28731; 828-693-4018.

Chapter Two
Author's Choice Dining

The choice of restaurants in the Asheville and Hendersonville area is impressive, something you would expect given the hundreds of thousands of visitors who come to the mountains each year. Restaurants of all types and quality abound, and in order to make your vacation in Asheville as enjoyable as possible, I have included a selection of the most popular and established places to eat, including my own favorites. For a complete listing of all Asheville and Hendersonville restaurants, by category, visit my guidebook website at www.ashevilleguidebook.com.

Pricing Guide

Menu changes affect the pricing of the restaurants listed; however, in an attempt to help you make choices, a basic pricing guide is provided for some idea as to what you can expect to pay for an evening meal for one person, excluding sales tax, gratuity, drinks and dessert.

$	under $10
$$	$10-20
$$$	$20-30
$$$$	over $30

Asheville Restaurants

Asian Grill: ASIAN PACIFIC-RIM ($$ South Asheville) Excellent selection of Chinese, Japanese and Thai delicacies prepared "New York Style." 1851 Hendersonville Rd., Asheville NC 28803; 828-277-1558. 11 a.m.-11 p.m. 7 days a week.

Bistro 1896: AMERICAN-CONTINENTAL ($$ Downtown) Innovative American cuisine with a decidedly chic twist, all in a great setting on historic Pack Square. Patio setting outside in the summer. 7 Pack Square, Asheville NC 28801; 828-251-1300. Lunch: Monday-Saturday 11:30 a.m.-4 p.m.; Dinner: Monday-Saturday 5-10 p.m.

Black Forest Restaurant: GERMAN-NORTHERN ITALIAN ($$ South Asheville) Authentic German and Northern Italian cuisine, steaks, and seafood. All Fireside lounge with all permits and seven distinctive dining rooms. 2155 Hendersonville Rd., Arden NC 28704; 828-687-7980. Reservations suggested, Dinner: Monday-Saturday 5-10 p.m.; Lunch: Monday-Friday 11:30 a.m.-2:30 p.m.; Sunday 11 a.m.-8:30 p.m.

Blue Ridge Dining Room at the Grove Park Inn Resort & Spa: AMERICAN ($$$ Grove Park Inn) Southern Heritage cuisine including shrimp and grits and other southern classics. Enclosed terrace dining with a wonderful sunset view. Grove Park Inn Resort & Spa, 290 Macon Ave., Asheville NC 28804; 828-252-2711. Reservations recommended. Breakfast: 6:30-11 a.m.; Sunday Brunch: 10 a.m.-2 p.m. Dinner: 3-9:30 pm.

Books & Breadboard: AMERICAN (Biltmore Village) Browse books by local authors and enjoy breakfast or lunch. Locally grown, green menu focus. 30 All Souls Crescent, Asheville NC 28805; 828-505-8233, Monday-Friday 9 a.m.-6 p.m., Saturday 9 a.m.-3 p.m.

12 Bones Smokehouse: BBQ ($ River Arts District & South Asheville) An Asheville institution, 12 Bones Smokehouse has two locations, the original down by the French Broad River and another in South Asheville. Serving baby back ribs, pulled pork, beef brisket, and more. Everything is smoked in house and all sides and desserts are made from scratch. 5 Riverside Drive, Asheville NC 28801; 828-253-4499 and 3578 Sweeten Creek Road, Arden NC 28704; 828-687-1395. Serving lunch Monday through Friday 11 a.m.-4 p.m.

Bouchon French Bistro: FRENCH ($$ Downtown) Superb restaurant offering authentic French "comfort food" (honest ingredients, in season, simply prepared, unpretentiously presented). Wonderful ambiance. 62 North Lexington Avenue, Asheville NC 28801; 828-350-1140. Dinner starting at 5 p.m. Seven days a week; Street Food, Monday-Thursday 11 a.m.-7 p.m., 11 a.m.-9 p.m. Friday-Saturday.

Chai-Pani: INDIAN ($$ Downtown) Indian street food, with signature dishes of chaat, quick snacks served by street vendors in India. 22 Battery Park Avenue, Asheville NC 28801, 828-254-4003. 7 days a week: 11:30 a.m.-4 p.m., 5-9 p.m.

Corner Kitchen: SOUTHERN ($$ S Biltmore Village): Bistro offering Southern dishes with an urban twist. 3 Boston Way, Asheville NC 28805; 828-274-2439. Breakfast and Lunch: Monday-Saturday 7:30 -11 a.m., 11:30-3 p.m.; Dinner 5:00 p.m., Sunday Brunch 9 a.m.-3 p.m.

Doc Chey's Noodle House: ASIAN NOODLE SHOP ($ Downtown): Asian cuisine with emphasis on wide variety of noodle dishes. Seating outside on Pack Square. 37 Biltmore Ave., Asheville NC 28801; 828-252-8220. Sunday-Thursday 11:30 a.m.-10 p.m.; Friday-Saturday 11:30 a.m.-11 p.m.

Early Girl Eatery: SOUTHERN ($$ Downtown) Located in the historic Wall Street section, the Early Girl Eatery offers healthy, made-from-scratch cuisine with a regional emphasis. 8 Wall Street, Asheville NC 28801;, 828-259-9292. Monday through Thursday 7:30 a.m.-3 p.m.; Dinner: Tuesday through Thursday 5 p.m.-9 p.m.; Friday and Saturday 5 p.m.-10 p.m.; Brunch: Saturday and Sunday 9 a.m.-3 p.m.

Ed Bourdreaux's Bayou Bar-B-Que: BBQ ($ Downtown) Ed Bourdeaux's Bayou offers 14 in-house sauces to and stocks 140 different beers. Live music five nights a week with no cover. Full bar available. 48 Biltmore Avenue, Asheville NC 28801; 828-296-0100. Open 7 days a week from 11:30 a.m.-11 p.m.

El Chapala Mexican Restaurant: MEXICAN ($$ North and West Asheville) Authentic Mexican cuisine—burritos, tacos, enchiladas, tamales and great margaritas. Two Asheville locations: 868 Merrimon Ave., Asheville NC 28803; 828-258-0899; and 282 Smokey Park Hwy., Asheville NC 28806; 828-665-0430. Dinner: Monday-Friday 5-10 p.m. Open Saturday and Sunday 12-10 p.m.

Fig Bistro: FRENCH ($$ Biltmore Village) Fig is a cozy bistro serving Chef William Klein's modern interpretation of classic, pure, and market-driven French cuisine. Menu changes regularly so they can offer fresh and local ingredients. 18 Brook St., Asheville NC 28803; 828-277-0889. Lunch: Monday-Saturday 11 a.m.-2 p.m., Sunday 10 a.m.-3 p.m. Dinner: Monday-Saturday 5-10 p.m., Sunday 5-10 p.m.

Frank's Roman Pizza: PIZZA ($ Tunnel Road & North Asheville) An Asheville institution since 1977. Great pizza, pastas, subs and salads. Casual and relaxed. 90 South Tunnel Rd., Asheville NC 28805; 828-298-5855 and 85 Weaverville Hwy., Asheville NC 28804;, 828-645-2910. Monday-Sunday 11 a.m.-9 p.m.

Fiore's Ristorante Toscana: ITALIAN ($$$ Downtown): Tuscan-inspired Italian cuisine served in a great Old World atmosphere. Like a trip to Italy. 122 College Street, Asheville NC 28801; 828-281-0710, Lunch: Monday-Friday 11 a.m.-3:30 p.m.; Dinner: Monday-Thursday 4:30-9:30 p.m., Friday—Saturday 4:30-10:00 p.m.

Grovewood Cafe: AMERICAN-SOUTHERN($$$ Behind Grove Park Inn) Features regional and classic cuisine with a Southern flare. Located in a cozy cottage setting within walking distance to the Grove Park Inn Resort & Spa. 111 Grovewood Rd., Asheville NC 28804; 828-258-8956. Open Monday-Sunday Lunch: 11 a.m.-2:30 p.m. Dinner: 5-8:30 p.m.

Heiwa Shokudo: JAPANESE ($$ Downtown) A little jewel of a Japanese restaurant offering authentic Japanese cuisine. Tempura, teriyaki, sukiyaki, vegetarian dishes and more. 87 North Lexington Ave., Asheville NC 28801; 828-254-7761. Lunch: Monday-Friday 11:30 a.m. -2:30 p.m.; Dinner: Monday-Saturday 5:30-9:30 p.m.

Horizons: AMERICAN-CONTINENTAL ($$$$ Grove Park Inn) One of the few area restaurants to be awarded the prestigious DiRoNA Award given by members of the Distinguished Restaurants of North America. Known for its innovative, classic cuisine and extensive wine list. Grove Park Inn Resort & Spa, 290 Macon Ave., Asheville NC 28804; 828-252-2711; reservations required, jacket and tie. Dinner: 6:30-9:30 p.m.

Iannucci's Pizzeria and Italian Restaurant: ITALIAN-PIZZA ($$ South Asheville) Iannucci's is a family-owned and operated authentic Italian pizzeria and restaurant. Iannucci's has been serving the south Asheville area for 25 years. 1981 Hendersonville Road, Asheville NC 28803; 828-684-5050. Monday thru Friday 11:30 a.m.-9 p.m.

Jerusalem Garden Cafe: MEDITERRANEAN-MIDDLE EASTERN ($$ Downtown) Moroccan and Mediterranean cuisine at its best. And belly dancing with live music every Thursday, Friday and Saturday night. 78 Patton Avenue, Asheville NC 28801; 828-254-0255. Lunch, dinner and Sunday Brunch. Monday-Thursday 11 a.m.-9 p.m., Friday 11 a.m.-10 p.m., Saturday 10 a.m.-10 p.m., Sunday 9 a.m.-9 p.m.

J&S Cafeteria: CAFETERIA ($$ Outskirts of Asheville) Since 1984, outstanding quality cafeterias. Pleasant decor, friendly service and expansive selection. 3 locations in the Asheville area: River Ridge Mall, 800 Fairview Rd., Asheville NC 28803,828-298-1209; 30 Airport Park Road, Fletcher NC 28732; 828-684-3418 and Westridge Market Place, 900 Smokey Park Hwy. Enka NC 28792; 828-665-1969. Open seven days a week. Call for hours.

Mamacita's: MEXICAN ($ Downtown) Mamacita's serves up fresh, made from scratch Mexican cuisine in a casual downtown location. Specializes in hand-crafted burritos, huge fresh salads, quesadillas, Baja-style fish tacos and a number of vegetarian options. 77 Biltmore Avenue, Asheville NC 28801; 828-255-8090. Open 7 days a week, 11 a.m.-10 p.m.

Marco's Pizzeria: PIZZA ($ North and South Asheville) One of the best pizzerias around since 1933! Wide range of pies. Two locations: 640 Merrimon Ave., Asheville NC 28804; 828-285-0709 and 1854 Hendersonville Road, Asheville NC 28803; 828-277-0004. Open 7 days a week, 11 30 a.m.- 9:30 p.m. (9 p.m. on Sundays)

Mela Indian Restaurant: INDIAN ($$ Downtown) Authentic North and South Indian dishes. 70 N. Lexington Avenue, Asheville NC 28801; 828-225-8880. Open 7 days a week, Lunch buffet: 11:30 a.m. -2:30 p.m., Dinner: 5:30-9:30 p.m. or later.

Mellow Mushroom: PIZZA ($ Downtown) Located in an old gas station and featuring an 1960's ambiance, Mellow Mushroom serves up pizzas and calzones made with spring water dough and baked on stone. . 50 Broadway, Asheville NC 28801, 828-236-9800. Monday-Thursday 11 a.m.-11:30 p.m.; Friday-Saturday 11 a.m.-12:30 a.m.; Sunday noon-10:30 p.m.

New French Bar Courtyard Cafe: FRENCH-CONTINENTAL ($$ Downtown) Casual dining, live entertainment and a wide range of tapas-style entrees, hearty sandwiches and hand-crafted deserts. 12 Biltmore Avenue, Asheville NC 28801; 828-225-6445. Tuesday-Friday 3 p.m-2 a.m., Saturday 11 a.m-2 p.m., Sunday 10:30 a.m.-4 p.m., Dinner until 10 p.m.

Red Stag Grill: CONTINENTAL ($$ Biltmore Village) Old-world ambience in Grand Bohemian Hotel, traditional favorites , chops and game. Grand Bohemian Hotel, 11 Boston Way, Asheville NC 28803; 828-717-8756. Open 7 days a week. Breakfast 6:30-10:30 a.m., Lunch 11 a.m.-2:30 p.m., Dinner 5-10 p.m.

Rezaz Restaurant: MEDITERRANEAN ($$ Biltmore Village) Eclectic Mediterranean cuisine in sleek, contemporary setting. Located in historic building, modern minimalist setting. 28 Hendersonville Rd., Asheville NC 28803;

828-277-1510. Lunch: Monday-Saturday: 11:30 a.m.-2 p.m. Dinner: Monday-Friday 5:30-9 p.m., Saturday 5-10 p.m.

Salsa's: CUBAN-CARIBBEAN ($$ Downtown) Wonderful blend of Cuban-Caribbean and Mexican cuisine. Innovative and distinctive food that includes such dishes as trout tacos and Mandingo burritos. 6 Patton Ave., Asheville NC 28801; 828-252-9805. Monday-Thursday 5-9:30 p.m.; Friday-Saturday 5-10 p.m.

Stoney Knob Cafe: ECLECTIC-CONTINENTAL ($$ North Asheville): Unique restaurant offering cuisine from near and far, with an eclectic menu including American contemporary, Greek, Asian and European dishes with fantastic hors d'oeuvres and southern comfort foods. 337 Merrimon Avenue, Asheville NC 28787; 828-645-3309. Monday through Friday 11 a.m. to 9 p.m.; Saturday 11 a.m. to 9:30 p.m.; Sunday brunch 9:30 a.m.-3 p.m.

Sunset Terrace at the Grove Park Inn Resort & Spa: AMERICAN ($$$ Grove Park Inn) One of the most beautiful places for dining anywhere in Asheville is the Sunset Terrace at the historic Grove Park Inn. Here you can enjoy the outdoors (weather permitting), have an elegant dinner and experience a magnificent view of the lights of Asheville as darkness falls. Grove Park Inn Resort & Spa, 290 Macon Ave., Asheville NC 28804; 828-252-2711. Dinner: 6-9 p.m.

Table: AMERICAN ($$ Downtown) American cuisine with focus toward seasonal, organic and local ingredients, and an obsession with freshness. 48 College Street, Asheville NC 28801; 828-254-8980, Lunch: 11:00 a.m.-2:30 p.m. Dinner: 5:30 -10:00 p.m. Monday-Saturday and Sunday brunch: 10:30 a.m.-2:30 p.m. Closed Tuesdays.

Tupelo Honey Café: SOUTHERN ($$) Elegant southern cuisine with an uptown twist. The Tupelo Honey Cafe has an upscale, yet casual environment with touches of an authentic Charleston/New Orleans style. Two locations: 2 College St., Asheville NC 28801, 828-255-4863 and 1829 Hendersonville Road, Asheville NC 28704; 828-505-7676. Breakfast & Lunch: Tuesday-Sunday 9 a.m.-3 p.m.; Dinner" Tuesday-Thursday 5:30-10 p.m., Friday-Saturday 5:30-11:00 p.m.

The Laughing Seed: VEGETARIAN ($$ Downtown) Great vegetarian restaurant. Casual atmosphere and sumptuous vegetarian delicacies! 40 Wall St., Asheville NC 28801; 828-252-3445. Monday-Saturday 11:30 a.m.-9 p.m.; Sunday 10 a.m.-8 p.m.

The Lobster Trap: SEAFOOD ($$$ Downtown) A local favorite offering fresh seafood and an oyster bar. Famous for flying in fresh seafood from Maine, the Lobster Trap also live music and in-house micro brewery beer. 35 Patton Ave., Asheville NC 28801; 828-250-0505. Dinner: seven nights a week, from 5 p.m.

Urban Burrito: CAL-MEX ($ North and East Asheville) Wide selection of California-style burritos, as well as great salsas. Voted best burritos of WNC. Two locations: 640 Merrimon Ave., #303, Asheville NC 28804; 828-251-1921 and 129 Bleachery Boulevard, Asheville NC 28805; 828-298-9802. Monday-Saturday 11 a.m.-10 p.m.; Sunday 12-10 p.m.

Vincenzo's Ristorante & Bistro: ITALIAN-CONTINENTAL ($$ Downtown) Chic and trendy restaurant, yet warm and friendly. Offering the finest in Northern Italian and continental cuisine. 10 North Market St., Asheville NC 28801; 828-254-4698. Reservations suggested. Dinner: Monday-Thursday 5:30-10 p.m., Friday-Saturday 5:30-11 p.m., Sunday 5:30-9 p.m.

Zambra: SPANISH-MEDITERRANEAN TAPAS ($$ Downtown) Spanish, Portuguese and Moroccan cuisine served in an exotic European setting. Like taking a trip to Spain for dinner. Tapas bar and restaurant. Not to be missed. 85 Walnut St., Asheville NC; 828-232-1060. Dinner: Monday-Thursday 5:30-9 p.m.; Friday-Saturday 5:00-until.; Sun 5:30-9 p.m. Lounge service menu starts an hour earlier.

Asheville Coffeehouses

Lots of coffeehouses in Asheville, these are the best!

Chelsea's and The Village Tea Room: ENGLISH TEAROOM (Biltmore Village) Step back in time and enjoy lunch or a traditional English tea. A charming restaurant offering outdoor dining in season. 6 Boston Way, Biltmore Village, 288-5: 274-0701. Monday through Saturday 11:30 a.m. to 3 p.m.; Afternoon Tea 3:30 p.m. to 4:45 p.m.; Sunday brunch 10:30 a.m.-3 p.m.; Shop open daily 10 a.m.-5 p.m.

Dobra Tea: COFFEEHOUSE (Downtown) An absolutely unique coffeehouse. Cheaper than taking a trip to China, Nepal, India and Japan. Traditional and authentic teas from around the world. A tearoom, light-fare restaurant and loose-leaf teashop (100+ varieties) all rolled into one. 78 North Lexington Avenue, Asheville NC 28801; 828-575-2424. Open 7 days a week, 11 a.m.-11 p.m.

Dripolator Coffee Bar: COFFEEHOUSE (Downtown) Wide selection of Fair-Trade and organic coffees and espresso, and open for lunch. Pioneer Building at 102 Broadway, Asheville NC 28801; 828-398-0209. Monday -Thursday 7 a.m.-8 p.m., Friday 7 a.m.-11 p.m., Saturday 8 a.m.-11 p.m., Sunday 8 a.m.-8 p.m.

French Broad Chocolate Lounge: CHOCOLATE LOUNGE (Downtown) A sacred space for chocophiles. Hand-craft artisan chocolate truffles, salted honey caramels, beautiful pastries and classic cakes, featuring superb local and organic ingredients. Not to be missed! 10 South Lexington Avenue, Asheville NC 28801; 828-252-4181. Monday -Thursday 11 a.m.-11 p.m.; Friday—Saturday 11 a.m.-12 midnight; Sunday 1 p.m.-8 p.m.

Green Sage Coffeehouse & Cafe: COFFEEHOUSE (Downtown) A great coffeehouse & cafe offering fair-trade organic coffee, natural and organic food, and operated sustainably as a model ecologically-driven business. The Green Sage is one of Asheville's premier coffeehouses, conveniently located downtown. 5 Broadway Street, Asheville NC 28801; 828-252-4450. Coffeehouse: Monday

through Wednesday 7:30 a.m.-9 p.m.; Thursday 7:30 a.m.-10 p.m.; Friday 7:30
a.m.-11 p.m.; Saturday 8 a.m.-11 p.m.; Sunday 8 a.m.-9 p.m.

Malaprop's Bookstore and Café: BOOKSTORE & COFFEEHOUSE (Downtown) A booklover's favorite, locally as well as nationally! Great books, great
food, great coffee. Live music performances and author events throughout the
year. Offering a wide variety of coffees and teas as well as soups, sandwiches
and light lunches. Live music Friday and Saturday evenings. 55 Haywood St.,
Asheville NC 28801; 828-254-6734. Monday through Thursday 8 a.m.-9 p.m.;
Friday and Saturday 8 a.m.-10 p.m.; Sunday 8 a.m.-7 p.m.

Hendersonville Restaurants

Binion's Roadhouse: COUNTRY-WESTERN ($$ Four Seasons Boulevard)
Country style and casual, wild west atmosphere. 1565 Four Seasons Boulevard,
Hendersonville NC 28792; 828-693-0492. Sunday-Thursday 11 a.m.-10 p.m.;
Friday-Saturday 11 a.m.-11 p.m.

Black Rose Public House: IRISH-AMERICAN ($$ Downtown) Menu features
a wide array of great selections, always made from the highest quality ingredi-
ents and always made from scratch. 222 N Main Street, Hendersonville NC
28792; 828-698-2622.

Champa Sushi & Thai Cuisine: PAN-ASIAN ($$ Downtown) Full ABC bar,
elegant decor, Pan-Asian menu with focus on Thai cuisine. 437 North Main
Street, Hendersonville NC 28792; 828-696-9800. Lunch: Monday-Friday 11
a.m.-3 p.m., Saturday-Sunday 12 -3 p.m.; Dinner: Monday-Friday 4:30-10
p.m., Saturday-Sunday 3-10 p.m.

Cypress Cellar: CAJUN ($$ Downtown) Authentic South Louisiana cuisine.
Gumbo, jambalaya and red beans & rice. Beer, wine, liquor permits. 321-C
North Main St., Hendersonville, 28793; 828-698-1005. Tuesday-Thursday 11
a.m.-9 p.m.; Friday-Saturday 11 a.m.-10 p.m.

Flight Wood Grill & Wine Bar: AMERICAN ($$$ Downtown) Fine dining in
the retro-modern decor of the historic 1920's Stillwell bank building. Several
dining options, from main floor or balcony level. Extensive wine list and over
40 wines by the glass. 401 N Main Street, Hendersonville NC 28792; 828-694-
1030. Dinner only, Monday-Saturday.

Hannah Flanagan's Pub & Eatery: IRISH ($$ Downtown): A little bit of
Ireland in the mountains. Full menu that ranges from sandwiches to Irish
stew and shepherd's pie. Children's menu. Featuring authentic fish and chips
every Friday. 300 N. Main Street, Hendersonville NC 28792; 828-696-1665.
Monday-Wednesday 11 a.m.-1 a.m.; Thursday-Saturday 11 a.m.-2 a.m.; Sunday
11 a.m.-midnight.

Haus Heidelburg German Restaurant: GERMAN ($$ South of Downtown)
German cuisine prepared only with the freshest ingredients. 630 Greenville
Highway, Hendersonville NC 28792; 828-693-8227. Open for lunch and
dinner seven day a week.

Inn On Church Street: AMERICAN-REGIONAL ($$ Downtown) Regional cuisine in the elegant casual setting of the historic Inn on Church Street. Emphasis is on using local, organic produce. 201 West 3rd Avenue, Hendersonville NC 28792; 828-693-3258. Lunch: Daily 11:30 a.m.-2 p.m.; Sunday Brunch: 11 a.m.-2 p.m.; Dinner: Thursday-Saturday 5 p.m. until.

Kelsey's: AMERICAN ($$ South of downtown) In operation since 1985 Kelsey's offer casual fine dining in a setting that includes outdoor gardens, waterfall and mountain views. Homemade soups, fresh salads as well as their signature corn pudding. 840 Spartanburg Highway, Hendersonville NC 28730; 828-693-6688. Monday-Thursday 11 a.m. -9:30 p.m., Friday-Saturday 11 a.m.-10 p.m., Sunday 11 a.m.-8 p.m.

Mike's on Main Street: SANDWICHES -ICE CREAM ($ Downtown): An old-fashioned ice cream parlor that serves soup, sandwiches and breakfast. Like stepping back into the 1920s! 303 N. Main St., Hendersonville NC 28792; 828-698-1616. Monday-Saturday 7:30 a.m.-5 p.m.; Sunday noon-5 p.m.

Poplar Lodge Restaurant: AMERICAN ($$ Laurel Park) Poplar Lodge offers exceptional dining in a casual rustic setting. 2550 Hebron Rd. Hendersonville NC 28792; 828-693-8400. Dinner: Tuesday-Sunday 5-9:30 p.m.; Friday and Saturday 5-10:30 p.m.

Seasons at Highland Lake Inn: AMERICAN ($$$ Highland Lake) World-class, award winning cuisine in a casual, elegant country setting at the Highland Lake Inn. Local, organic produce (much of it grown in the Inn's 2 acre gardens). Lavish family-friendly Sunday buffets year-round. 180 Highland Lake Drive, Hendersonville NC 28731; 828-696-9094. Breakfast, lunch, dinner, Sunday Brunch Buffet; please call for hours.

Sinbad Restaurant: MEDITERRANEAN ($$$ Downtown): Featuring Mediterranean specialties and contemporary American cuisine. Elegantly decorated dining rooms overlooking beautifully landscaped gardens. 202 S. Washington Street, Hendersonville NC 28792; 828-696-2039. Tuesday-Saturday, Lunch: 11:30 a.m -2 p.m., Dinner: 5:00 p.m. until.

Square 1 Bistro: AMERICAN ($$ Downtown): Emphasis on using local organic produce and meats. Fine dining in a casual elegant atmosphere. 111 S Main Street, Hendersonville NC 28792; 828-698-5598. Lunch 11 a.m.-4 p.m. 7 days a week; Dinner 4-9 p.m. Sunday-Thursday, 4-10 p.m. Friday-Saturday; Sunday Brunch 11 a.m.- 4p.m.

Three Chopt: SANDWICH SHOP ($ Downtown): An excellent sandwich shop located downtown. Luncheon only. 103 Third Ave., Hendersonville NC 28792; 828-692-0228. Open Monday-Saturday 11 a.m.-2:30 p.m.

Umi: JAPANESE ($$ Downtown): Authentic Japanese entrees, fresh sushi and a wide range of organic and special sakes. 633 North Main Street, Hendersonville NC 28792; 828-698-8048. Open 7 days a week, Monday-Friday Lunch 11 a.m.-3 p.m., Dinner 4:30-9 p.m., Saturday 12-10 p.m.

Hendersonville Coffeehouses

Black Bear Coffee Co.: COFFEHOUSE (Downtown) 318 N. Main St., Hendersonville,28792; 828-692-6333. Monday-Friday 8 a.m.-6 p.m.; Saturday 9 a.m.-6 p.m.; Sunday 11 a.m.-5 p.m.

Picasso's: COFFEHOUSE (Downtown) Patisseries, coffee bar and cafe that offers a variety of made-from-scratch pastries, gourmet coffees. Cafe walls are covered with European art. 240 North Main Street, Hendersonville NC 28792; 828-694-0907. Monday-Saturday 8 a.m.-5 p.m.

Chapter Three
Festivals & Events

Western North Carolina has a wide range of festivals throughout the year, from small town gatherings to one of the largest street festivals in the South. Most of these occur annually, during the same month each year. However, in planning your visit, be sure to check the festival website to verify exact dates. It is beyond the scope of this book to present each and every festival in the mountains, only the major and more established ones will be presented, month by month. The two major street festivals in the mountains are Bele Chere in Asheville and the North Carolina Apple Festival in Hendersonville. For a complete listing of all major mountain festivals and events, visit my guidebook website at www.ashevilleguidebook.com.

January:
(ASHEVILLE) All That Jazz and Big Band Dance Weekends at Grove Park Inn Resort & Spa: The inn hosts a fabulous lineup of entertainers and events, all jazz-related. 800-438-5800. www.groveparkinn.com

March:
(ASHEVILLE) Heritage Classic DanceSport Championships at the Grove Park Inn Resort & Spa: One of the nation's premier dancesport events. 800-438-5800. www.groveparkinn.com

April:
(ASHEVILLE) Festival of Flowers at Biltmore Estate: A celebration that highlights the spring blooming of flowers at Biltmore Estate. Guided tours through the gardens alive with color from more than 50,000 tulips, azaleas, flowering shrubs and much more. Live music and other special events. Ongoing April through May. 800-543-2961, 828-225-1333. www.biltmore.com

May:
(ASHEVILLE) Asheville Herb Festival: The largest herb festival in the Southeast. More than 50 herb vendors marketing herbs, herb plants and herb

products. Held at the Western North Carolina Farmers Market. 828-253-1691. www.ashevilleherbfestival.com

(ASHEVILLE) Mountain Sports Festival: Focus is on outdoor sports, including mountain biking, rock climbing, triathlon, road and trail races. 828-251-4029. www.mountainsportsfestival.com

(BLACK MOUNTAIN) Lake Eden Arts Festival (LEAF): Located at a mountain retreat, Camp Rockmont, LEAF is held twice a year in the spring and fall features music from dozens of national and regionally known musicians as well as crafts, storytelling, drumming, dancing and a healing arts tent. 828-686-8742. www.theleaf.com

(HOT SPRINGS) French Broad River Festival: Music, whitewater rafting and activities centered around the French Broad River. www.frenchbroadriverfestival.com

June:

(BAKERSVILLE) North Carolina Rhododendron Festival: Street fair, car show, ducky derby, beauty pageant, 10K run and street dance are highlights of this local mountain city festival. 828-688-5901. www.bakersville.com

(BREVARD) Brevard Music Festival: Held at the Brevard Music Center over a seven week period each summer during June, July and August, this world-class music festival features over 70 different concerts, from symphony orchestra to Broadway musicals. 828-862-2100. www.brevardmusic.org

(TRYON) Blue Ridge Barbecue Festival: Two days of BBQ competitions from over 50 top BBQ-cooking teams. Music, games, foothills craft fair, and of course, BBQ. 828-859-7427. www.blueridgebbqfestival.com

July:

(ASHEVILLE) Bele Chere: A community celebration in downtown Asheville with annual attendance of over 300,000. One of the greatest street festivals in America. Not to be missed! 828-259-5800. www.belecherefestival.com

(ASHEVILLE) Shindig on the Green: Held every Saturday night during July, August and September at Martin Luther King Jr. Park in downtown Asheville. Bluegrass music, dancing, clogging. This festival has been around for over 43 years! 828-2586101. www.folkheritage.org

(LINVILLE) Grandfather Mountain Highland Games: Scottish athletes and musicians share their heritage from bagpipes and Celtic music to border collies and sheep herding at the largest gathering of Scottish clans in North America. 828-733-1333. www.gmgh.org

(WAYNESVILLE) Folkmoot USA: North Carolina's official international festival, Folkmoot USA is a world-class folk festival with international dancers and musicians performing their countries' traditional folk dances. Over 350 performers at numerous venues. 828-452-2997. www.folkmootusa.org

August:

(ASHEVILLE) Mountain Dance and Folk Festival: The oldest festival in America. For more than 70 years, a celebration of traditional mountain music and dance. Held at various venues in Asheville. 828-258-6101. www.folkheritage.org

(ASHEVILLE) Goombay: Since 1982, a street festival in the historic black business district in downtown Asheville. A celebration of African-Caribbean culture. 828-252-4614. www.ymicc.org

(ASHEVILLE) Village Art & Craft Fair: A long-standing, premier outdoor art and craft fair that hosts over 100 exhibitors representing all media. Held on the beautiful tree covered grounds of the Cathedral of All Souls in historic Biltmore Village for over 39 years. 828-274-2831

(BLACK MOUNTAIN) Sourwood Festival: Art & crafts, dancing, music, food and games. 828-669-2300. www.blackmountain.org

(BURNSVILLE) Mt. Mitchell Crafts Fair: The oldest and largest crafts fair in the Blue Ridge with more than 200 artists. Live entertainment and kid's activities. 828-682-7413. www.yanceychamber.com

September:

(ASHEVILLE) North Carolina Mountain State Fair: Great state fair held at the Western North Carolina Agricultural Center. Rides, farm animals and great food. For the whole family. 828-687-1414. www.mountainfair.org

(ASHEVILLE) Brewgrass Festival: One of the most popular beer and bluegrass festivals in the southeast. American breweries and national and regional bluegrass musicians. www.brewgrassfestival.com

(HENDERSONVILLE) North Carolina Apple Festival: Another not-to-be-missed festival. A celebration of apples and the fall season. 828-697-4557. www.ncapplefestival.org

October:

(ASHEVILLE) Craft Fair of the Southern Highland Craft Guild: Held at the Civic Center. World-class traditional mountain arts & crafts show. Hosted by the prestigious Southern Highland Craft Guild; 828-298-7928. www.southernhighlandguild.org

(ASHEVILLE) Thomas Wolfe Festival: A festival centered on the life and times of the Asheville-born author Thomas Wolfe. Walking tours, concerts, plays, Wolfe workshops, road race and other events centered on Wolfe's life. 828-253-8304. www.thomaswolfememorial.com

(BANNER ELK) Woolly Worm Festival: The stripes on the winner of the woolly worm race will be inspected by the town elders. Brown signals a mild winter, black predicts severe weather. Nonstop music, food, crafts, and children's rides. 800-972-2183. www.woolyworm.com

(BLACK MOUNTAIN) Lake Eden Arts Festival (LEAF): Located at a mountain retreat, Camp Rockmont, LEAF is held twice a year in the spring and fall features music from dozens of national and regionally known musicians as well as crafts, storytelling, drumming, dancing and a healing arts tent.828-686-8742. www.theleaf.com

November:

(ASHEVILLE) Christmas at Biltmore House: Biltmore House is especially memorable during the Christmas season. During Candlelight Christmas Evenings, Biltmore's doors open to a world of crackling fires, festive music performances, glittering trees and the warm glow of hundreds of candles illuminating the richly decorated rooms. Ongoing during December. 800-543-2961, 828-225-1333. www.biltmore.com

December:

(ASHEVILLE) Christmas at Biltmore House: Biltmore House is especially memorable during the Christmas season. During Candlelight Christmas Evenings, Biltmore's doors open to a world of crackling fires, festive music performances, glittering trees and the warm glow of hundreds of candles illuminating the richly decorated rooms. Ongoing during December. 800-543-2961, 828-225-1333. www.biltmore.com

(ASHEVILLE) Biltmore Village Dickens Festival: Ongoing Christmas festivities in picturesque Biltmore Village during the month of December. 828-274-8788. www.biltmorevillage.com

(ASHEVILLE) Victorian Christmas Celebration at the Smith-McDowell House: A celebration of Christmas the old-fashioned way. The Museum's time-line of authentically decorated period rooms showcases the evolution of Christmas celebrations and includes hand-crafted decorations and live trees. 828-253-9231. www.wnchistory.org

Chapter Four
Bele Chere

O ne of the largest and most outstanding street festivals in America, Bele Chere attracts more than 300,000 people each year and is usually held on the last weekend in July. Bele Chere, which roughly translates as "beautiful living," always begins with a parade on Friday at noon with the festival continuing through Sunday until 6 p.m. The festival includes local restaurants in two food courts, children's activities, music at numerous venues, a 5K road race, an arts & crafts section and hundreds of vendors offering everything from homemade toys to BBQ.

If you are planning to attend this great festival, please keep in mind that accommodations in Asheville fill up every year, so make your reservations early in the year. For more information about Bele Chere contact their office at 828-259-5800 or visit their website at www.belecherefestival.com.

Chapter Five
Author's Favorites

No guidebook would be complete without a list of the author's personal favorite places and attractions. I have included my favorites hoping that it will help you in making your decisions about what to see and do while visiting our mountains.

Man-Made Awesome Majesty
Biltmore Estate: An absolute stunner. Not to be missed. Breathtaking gardens and grounds. (*See* Section Three, Chapter 3)

Grove Park Inn Resort & Spa: Monumental building. Great ambience. Wonderful special events and facilities. (*See* Section Three, Chapter 4)

Historical Treasures
Thomas Wolfe Memorial: A fascinating time capsule. Superb restoration. (*See* Section Three, Chapter 2)

Smith-McDowell House: A historic gem. Wonderful at Christmas in its Victorian finery. (*See* Section Three, Chapter 2)

Thomas Wolfe Angel Statue: In Oakdale Cemetery in Hendersonville. Possible to take a close-up look. (*See* Section Four, Chapter 3)

Architectural Masterpieces
Asheville City Building: An Art Deco masterpiece. (*See* Section Three, Chapter 4)

Basilica of St. Lawrence: Wonderful stained glass and interior. Amazing rose gardens in season. Make time to take the self-guided art and architecture tour. (*See* Section Three, Chapter 4)

Cathedral of All Souls: Inside and out, this elegant church is truly inspirational. One of the most beautiful buildings in Asheville. (*See* Section Three, Chapter 4)

Your Kids Will Thank You!
Western North Carolina Nature Center: Animals from otters to cougars. A must! (*See* Section Three, Chapter 2)

Pack Place Education, Arts & Science Center: Fascinating stuff for all ages. (*See* Section Three, Chapter 2)

Pisgah National Forest: A perfect day trip in the summer. Take a picnic lunch. Visit Looking Glass Falls, Sliding Rock's natural waterslide, and the National Forest Fish Hatchery to let the kids feed the huge trout. Finish up at the Forest Discovery Center at the Cradle of Forestry. (*See* Section Two, Chapter 8 -Waterfalls & Trout)

Sweet Treats

The Chocolate Fetish: 36 Haywood Street, Asheville NC 28801. Handmade truffles rated "America's best" by the Los Angeles Times. They're right!

French Broad Chocolate Lounge: 10 South Lexington Avenue, Asheville NC 28801. A sacred space for chocophiles. Hand-craft artisan chocolate truffles, salted honey caramels, beautiful pastries and classic cakes, featuring superb local and organic ingredients.

Festivals

Bele Chere in Asheville: One of the best street festivals in America! (*See* Section Two, Chapter 4)

Apple Festival in Hendersonville: Small-town friendliness and wonderful mountain culture. (*See* Section Two, Chapter 3)

Unbelievable Views/Natural Wonders

Chimney Rock Park: This place will take your breath away. Take a good pair of walking shoes and go on a clear day. (*See* Section Five, Chapter 1)

Blue Ridge Parkway: Head out in any direction. Be sure to take a picnic lunch. (*See* Section Five, Chapter 1)

Looking Glass Falls: Pisgah National Forest. One of the most accessible and spectacular waterfalls around. (*See* Section Five, Chapter 1)

Gardener's Delights

Formal Flower Gardens at Biltmore Estate: World-class. Especially wonderful in April-May during the Festival of Flowers. Will leave you dazzled. (*See* Section Three, Chapter 3)

North Carolina Arboretum: Extraordinary gardens and educational center. Inspirational. (*See* Section Three, Chapter 2)

Chapter Six
Great Things To Do With Kids

A trip to Western North Carolina doesn't have to be a bore for the kids. Here is a listing of things to do that will bring smiles to the faces of kids and kids-at-heart alike.

Asheville

Asheville's Fun Depot: Kid centered activities, commercial venue but well done. (*See* Section Three, Chapter 2)

Biltmore Estate: Educational, awe-inspiring and fascinating (for older kids). (*See* Section Three, Chapter 3)

Folk Art Center: Art and craft exhibits, craft demonstrations. (*See* Section Three, Chapter 2)

Lake Julian District Park: Swimming, fishing, boating and picnic area. (*See* Section Three, Chapter 9)

McCormick Field: Asheville Tourists baseball games. (*See* Section Three, Chapter 2)

North Carolina Arboretum: Wonderful gardens and botanical exhibits. (*See* Section Three, Chapter 2)

Outdoor Activities: The lineup of choices can be found in Section Two, Chapter 15.

Pack Place Education, Arts & Science Center: Art, science, exhibits (*See* Section Three, Chapter 2)

Western North Carolina Nature Center: Animals of all types, Appalachian nature exhibits, and much more. (*See* Section Three, Chapter 2)

Zebulon B. Vance Birthplace: Pioneer history exhibits and demonstrations. (*See* Section Five, Chapter 2)

Hendersonville

Carl Sandburg Home: Historical exhibits, goat farm, hiking trails. (*See* Section Four, Chapter 2)

Historic Johnson Farm: Farm animals, exhibits, farm history. (*See* Section Four, Chapter 2)

Holmes Educational Forest: Trails, nature center, exhibits, picnic areas. (*See* Section Four, Chapter 2)

Western North Carolina

Blue Ridge Parkway: (Enter from Asheville area) Picnics, hiking. (*See* Section Five, Chapter 1)

Cherokee Indian Reservation: (Cherokee) Plan to spend a day. History and fun for kids. (*See* Section Five, Chapter 2)

Chimney Rock Park: (Lake Lure) Spectacular hiking trails, nature center. (*See* Section Five, Chapter 1)

Cradle of Forestry: (Brevard) Educational and inspiring. (*See* Section Five, Chapter 2)

Foothills Equestrian Nature Center (FENCE): (Tryon) A great nature center plus horse stuff! (*See* Section Five, Chapter 2)

Ghost Town In The Sky: (Maggie Valley) The wild west in Western North Carolina. (*See* Section Five, Chapter 2)

Grandfather Mountain: (Linville) World class mountain park and nature center (*See* Section Five, Chapter 1)

Great Smoky Mountains Railroad: (Bryson City, Dillsboro) Your kids will love this one! (*See* Section Five, Chapter 2)

Lake Lure: (Lake Lure) Swimming, fishing, wonderful boat tours of lake. (*See* Section Five, Chapter 1)

Joyce Kilmer Memorial Forest: (Robbinsville area) A chance for your children to old growth, huge trees! (*See* Section One, Chapter 2)

Linville Caverns: (Linville) Underground, guided adventure for kids and adults (*See* Section Five, Chapter 1)

Outdoor Activities: The lineup of choices can be found in Section Two, Chapter 15.

Pisgah National Forest: (Brevard) Plan a day trip and include stops at Looking Glass Falls, Sliding Rock, State Fish Hatchery and Cradle of Forestry. (*See* Section Two, Chapter 8, "Waterfalls & Trout!")

Tweetsie Railroad: (Blowing Rock) A child centered railroad adventure (*See* Section Five, Chapter 2)

Waterfalls: (Brevard area) Great natural attractions. Looking Glass Falls is closest to Asheville. (*See* Section Five, Chapter 1)

Whitewater Rafting: Numerous places to do so. (*See* Section Two, Chapter 15)

Chapter Seven
Planning a Gourmet Picnic

A wonderful way to highlight a day trip into the surrounding mountains, no matter what your itinerary or destination, is to bring along a picnic lunch. This is particularly true if your exploring takes you for a ride on the Blue Ridge Parkway or deep into one of the national forests. Restaurants are few and far between there, and besides, what could be better than eating a picnic lunch beside a wilderness waterfall or on a rocky overlook perched high above the green valleys below? If this idea appeals to you, then you are in luck, because not only does Western North Carolina have an unlimited supply of really great picnic spots, but there are some stores in Asheville within minutes of each other where you can purchase the ingredients for an unforgettable picnic lunch. They are located on Biltmore Avenue just as you leave Pack Square heading south.

Laurey's Catering (yum!) & Gourmet to Go: Catering and gourmet takeout, as well as easy going breakfast. 67 Biltmore Ave., Asheville NC 28801; 828-252-1500.

Asheville Wine Market: Right next door. Extremely good selection of fine wines and quality beers. 65 Biltmore Ave., Asheville NC 28801; 828-253-0060.

French Broad Food Co-op: Just down the street is an outstanding organic grocery, run by a local cooperative. Fresh vegetables, fruit, cheese, crackers and more. 90 Biltmore Ave., Asheville NC 28801; 828-255-7650.

Chapter Eight
Great Itineraries & Tours

For visitors new to an area, planning some day trips or itineraries can be a challenge, especially in an area as rich in interesting things to do as Asheville, Hendersonville and Flat Rock. Considering the size and scope of the whole Western North Carolina mountains, the task can seem overwhelming. In an attempt to make your visit easier, I have presented below a number of tours and itineraries, both local and farther afield, from which you can choose.

Another great option for you is to find these daytrips and many more on DayZipping, (www.dayzipping.com) a reliable and comprehensive online resource for planning and taking daytrips throughout the world.

Guided Tours of Asheville
Ghost & Haunt Tours
Tour Description: A leisurely, narrated walking tour taking approximately 90 minutes and covering less than a mile.

Days of Operation: Mar 1 -Oct 31, 9:00 PM, departure nightly, rain or shine. Nov 1- Feb 27 tour starts at 7:00 PM.

Length of Tour: 90 minutes

Cost: Adults: $189, Children: $10

Ticket Locations: Haywood Park Hotel, located on the corner of Haywood Street and Battery Park in downtown Asheville.

Boarding and Departure: Same

Telephone: 828-355-5855

Notes:. Reservations required

Gray Line Trolley Tours

Tour Description: Live narrated tours on replica antique "Red" Trolleys. Tours encompass all major points of interest, including the Montford Historic District, Grove Park Historic District, Grove Park Inn Resort & Spa, downtown Asheville, the River Arts District and Biltmore Village.

Days of Operation: Tours operate daily, seven days a week, March through December except Easter, Thanksgiving, Christmas, Christmas Eve, New Year's Day and during the Bele Chere Festival.

Length of Tour: Tour lasts approximately 1-5 to 1.75 hours. There is an additional 15 minute stop at the Asheville Visitor Center.

Cost: Adults: $20, Children; (5-11) $10, children under 5 are carried free. AAA members get 10% discount. Special pricing available for groups of 10 or more.

Ticket Locations: Tickets available at the Asheville Visitor Center. You may also board the trolley at any one of the 8 stops and purchase your ticket on-board during the tour.

Boarding and Departure: You can board the trolley at any of their convenient trolley stops. See website for departure times. Main departure at Asheville Visitor Center, 36 Montford Avenue, Asheville NC 28801.

Telephone: 828-251-8687, 866-592-8687

Notes: Unlimited hop-on & hop-off privileges. 2nd day free.

LaZoom Comedy Tours

Tour Description: Rolling comedy tour bus

Days of Operation: April -October, Tuesday through Saturday, 6:00 pm

Length of Tour: 90 minutes

Cost: Adults: $22, Children (5-12): $12, Senior: $18

Ticket Locations: Reserve seating on-line, by phone or arrive 15 minutes prior to departure and get on bus if seating remains available.

Boarding and Departure: Tours depart from the French Broad Food Co-op at 90 Biltmore Avenue, in downtown Asheville.

Telephone: 828-225-6932

Segway Tours

Tour Description: Guided Segway tours of downtown Asheville, including the Grove Arcade, Urban Trail and historic architecture.

Days of Operation: 9am, 1pm and 5pm daily.

Length of Tour: Required 20-45 minutes of training followed by 2 to 2.5 hour tour.

Cost: $55

Ticket Locations: Asheville Visitor Center, 36 Montford Avenue, Asheville NC 28801.

Boarding and Departure: Asheville Visitor Center, 36 Montford Avenue, Asheville NC 28801.

Telephone: 828-776-8687

Notes: Riders must weigh between 100 and 260 lbs.

Self-Guided Tours & Itineraries
Urban Trail
One of the best ways to experience downtown Asheville is by walking the Urban Trail. This self-guided tour takes a few hours and follows thematic markers (*See* Section Three, Chapter 5).

Historic Asheville
If you are interested in history and especially architecture, then there are a number of self-guided tours by car that you might be interested in doing. These tours visit four of Asheville's eleven Historic Districts and highlight all of the interesting and really important buildings and sites. The four are Montford, Chestnut Hill, Grove Park and Biltmore Village. (*See* Section Three, Chapter 4)

Historic Hendersonville
A self-guided walking tour by car of historic Main Street in downtown Hendersonville. (*See* Section Four, Chapter 3)

Biltmore Estate
A visit to Biltmore Estate is one of the high points of any visit to Asheville and is highly recommended. You will want to allow a minimum of half a day to see the grounds and estate as well as allowing time to eat at one of the Estate's three fine restaurants. Afterwards, be sure to take some time to visit the historic Biltmore Village just outside the estate entrance. (*See* Section Three, Chapter 3)

High Country Adventure
For this tour, allow a whole day or more. Start off by packing a gourmet picnic (*See* Section Two, Chapter 7) and heading east on the Blue Ridge Parkway. Your first stop will be the Folk Art Center (*See* Section Three, Chapter 2) just east of Asheville at milepost 382; then continue north to Craggy Gardens at milepost 364. Here you will find nature trails, native rhododendron and magnificent views. Continue on to Mount Mitchell State Park at milepost 355 (*See* Section Five, Chapter 1) and hike the short distance to the tower on the summit. Mount Mitchell will be a great place to picnic. After lunch continue up the parkway to Grandfather Mountain at milepost 305. (*See* Section Five, Chapter 1) After visiting Grandfather, if you have time, there are a couple of excellent options. You can visit Linville Caverns (*See* Section Five, Chapter 1) or take in Tweetsie Railroad. (*See* Section Five, Chapter 2) Return to Asheville by Highway 19 East through Burnsville.

The Land of the Cherokee
Allow one full day for this outing that will take you two hours west to Cherokee Indian Reservation. (*See* Section Five, Chapter 2) Take I-40 west from Asheville and get off at Exit 27. Follow 19/23 & 74 to Cherokee. At Cherokee you will want to also visit the Oconaluftee Indian Village and the Cherokee Indian Museum. During the

View of Craggy Gardens off the Blue Ridge Parkway at milepost 364

afternoon you may wish to drive south on U.S. 441 about 14 miles to Dillsboro and take a ride on the Great Smoky Mountains Railway. (*See* Section Five, Chapter 2)

Waterfalls & Trout!

This day trip is a great one for kids. Be sure and bring a picnic lunch. You will be visiting the Pisgah District of the Pisgah National Forest and seeing some spectacular waterfalls. Take the Blue Ridge Parkway south and stop at the Pisgah Inn for some wonderful views of the mountains. Just beyond, get on 276 south and follow this into the forest. Stop at the Cradle of Forestry and visit the Forest Discovery Center. (*See* Section Five, Chapter 2) Continue on and turn right on Forest Road 445 to the Fish Hatchery. The kids will really love this. They can hand-feed monster trout! After the fish hatchery, continue on to Sliding Rock, where they can put on their bathing suits and slide down a wonderful natural waterslide. After Sliding Rock, the nearby Looking Glass Falls is the perfect place for a picnic lunch. If you have time, you may wish to see other waterfalls in the area (*See* Section Five, Chapter 1) or return to Asheville by way of Highway 280.

Last of the Mohicans

This day trip is also a great one for kids. It will take you from an historic site in Asheville to the exact spot where the famous trail scene in "The Last of the Mohicans" was filmed. Begin your tour in Asheville by taking Charlotte Street to #265, The Manor. This impressive historic building (*See* Section Three, Chapter 4) was where the headquarters scene in the movie "Last of the Mohicans" was filmed. Cast members of an earlier movie, "The Swan," including Grace Kelly, also stayed here while filming. After visiting the Manor, return by way of Charlotte Street and get on I-240 east. Get off at exit 9 (Bat Cave, Lake Lure) and take

Scenic Byway 74A through beautiful Fairview to Hickory Nut Gap. While passing through Hickory Nut Gap, you will see the historic Sherrill's Inn. (*See* Section Three, Chapter 4) Continue on 74A through Bat Cave (so named for the numerous bat caves in the area) and down into Chimney Rock. This will be your major destination (*See* Section Five, Chapter 1) and at Chimney Rock you will be able to hike the wonderful trails with their unbelievable views.

After Chimney Rock, which will take you two-three hours, return to your car and journey on 74A to Lake Lure. At the beginning of the lake is a public beach where the kids can swim. Finish out the day with a wonderful boat tour of Lake Lure. (*See* Section Five, Chapter 1) Lake Lure is one of the most beautiful man-made lakes in the world and this boat ride is a real treat. The boats are operated by Lake Lure Tours and are located at the Lake Lure Marina on Highway 64/74A.

Return to Asheville by taking 74A west from Lake Lure through Chimney Rock and then turning left on Highway 64 towards Hendersonville. This will take you through some lovely apple growing sections (See Section Four, Chapter 7) and to I-26, which you will take north to Asheville.

Famous Authors

If the lives of famous writers interest you, this is the day trip for you. Begin by visiting the Thomas Wolfe Memorial (*See* Section Three, Chapter 2) in the morning. After touring the historic boyhood home of Thomas Wolfe, travel to nearby Riverside Cemetery in the Montford Historic District, where Wolfe and author O. Henry (William Sidney Porter) are buried. (*See* Section Three, Chapter 4) From the Wolfe memorial get on I-240 heading west and get off at the next exit, Montford. Take Montford Avenue north into the Montford area and turn left onto Cullowee Street. Turn right onto Pearson Drive and then left onto Birch Street to the cemetery. After visiting the grave sites (refer to cemetery map in Riverside Cemetery section), drive to the famous Grove Park Inn Resort (*See* Section Three, Chapter 4) for lunch by retracing your steps to I-240 and going east to the Charlotte Street exit. Take Charlotte Street to Macon Avenue and then to the hotel. Many famous authors, including F. Scott Fitzgerald and his wife, Zelda, have stayed at this historic resort. After lunch, travel to Hendersonville via I-240 west and I-26 south. Take exit 18 off I-26 onto 64 west. Follow 64 west to just beyond Hendersonville. Look for Oakdale Cemetery on your left and the State Historic Highway Marker indicat-

Chimney Rock Park

Connemara, former home of poet Carl Sandburg, located in Flat Rock

ing the Thomas Wolfe Angel. (*See* Section Four, Chapter 4) You may park your car and get out and visit this lovely statue which Wolfe immortalized in his famous novel *Look Homeward Angel.* After viewing the statue, return to Hendersonville by way of 64 east. Turn right on Main Street (Highway 25 south) and follow this through Hendersonville to Flat Rock, a few miles south. In Flat Rock, you will pass by the famous Flat Rock Playhouse (*See* Section Four, Chapter 2), where the dramatic works of legendary authors are performed every summer. Turn right onto Little River Road just beyond the playhouse and visit the home of poet Carl Sandburg, "Connemara." After touring the home and seeing the grounds, return to Asheville by Highway 25 north through Hendersonville and then on I-26.

Chapter Nine
Historic Churches

The greater Asheville and Hendersonville area has over 350 religious institutions with the Baptist Church (150+ churches) and Methodist Church (60+ churches) being the two largest denominations. Of special interest to visitors and residents alike are the beautiful historic churches. Some of the more noteworthy and historic are presented below. For a complete listing of all of the historic churches, visit my guidebook website at www.ashevilleguidebook.com.

Basilica of St. Lawrence

To the north of the Grove Arcade area in downtown Asheville is the remarkable Basilica of Saint Lawrence, Deacon and Martyr, built in 1909. A Spanish Baroque Revival Roman Catholic Church built of red brick with polychrome glazed terra-cotta inserts and limestone trim, it was designed by world-famous architect/engineer Raphael Guastavino. The church employs his "cohesive construction" techniques in its large oval tile dome and Catalan-style vaulting in its two towers. The massive stone foundations and the solid brick superstructure give silent testimony to the architect's desire to build an edifice that would endure for generations. There are no beams of wood or steel in the entire structure; all walls, floors, ceilings and pillars are of tile or other masonry materials. The dome is entirely self supporting, has a clear span of 58 x 82 feet and is reputed to be the largest unsupported dome in North America. The Crucifixion tableaux of the Basilica altar feature a rare example of seventeenth century Spanish woodcarving. The windows are of German origin, and the Basilica has two chapels. Attached by an arcade is the 1929 Neo-Tuscan Renaissance brick rectory designed by Father Michael of Belmont Abbey. Self-guided tour brochures are available at the church, and guided tours are given after Sunday masses.

Denomination: Catholic
Address: 97 Haywood Street, Asheville NC 28801
Telephone: 828-252-6042
Directions: From Pack Square take Patton Avenue west to Pritchard Park. Turn right onto Haywood Street.

Cathedral of All Souls

Originally known as All Souls Church, this edifice was designated an Episcopal Cathedral in January 1995. The largest structure in Biltmore Village, it is an exquisite, lovely building of fine Romanesque style. Designed by Richard Morris Hunt, this complex building combines pebbledash wall surfaces, brick and wood trim, and expansive tiles roofs. In spite of the complexity, however, the church is a simple cruciform with a tall tower rising in the center which contains most of the interior space. The Parish House features the same materials but is considerably different in design. The interior is relatively simple but no less elegant and features wonderful stained glass windows created for the Vanderbilts by Maitland Armstrong and his daughter Helen. They illuminate a variety of scenes from the Old and New Testaments. George Vanderbilt was one of the organizers of the congregation in 1896. He financed the construction of the church and parish house and selected the furnishings. The church was consecrated on November 8, 1896.

Denomination: Episcopal
Address: 9 Swan Street, Biltmore Village, Asheville NC 28803
Telephone: 828-274-2681
Directions: From Pack Square, take Biltmore Avenue south to Biltmore Village. The Cathedral of All Souls will be on your left as you pass through the village.

First Baptist Church

Built in 1927, the First Baptist Church of Asheville was designed by noted architect Douglas Ellington from his sketches of a cathedral in Florence, Italy. Two major additions have been made to the building. The Children's Wing was added in 1968, and the Sherman Family Center in 1980. This wonderfully elegant building is an unusual combination of an Early Italian Renaissance form and color scheme arranged in a beaux arts plan with Art Deco detailing. Of particular interest is the Art Deco copper lantern atop the dome and the subtle gradation of color in the roofing tiles. The walls are an effective combination of orange bricks, terra-cotta moldings and pink marble.

Denomination: Baptist
Address: 5 Oak Street, Asheville NC 28801
Telephone: 828-252-4781
Directions: From Pack Square go east on Broadway and turn right onto Woodfin Street to Oak Street. The First Baptist Church will be on your left.

St. James Episcopal Church

St. James Episcopal Church, located on Main Street in downtown Hendersonville, is one of the area's most picturesque churches. Consecrated in 1861, the first rector was Rev. N. Collin Hughes. From 1970 to 1980, Henderson County experienced an unprecedented population growth. New economic developments, the discovery of Hendersonville as an outstanding retirement area, and growth in tourism marked this period. Consequently, St. James Church flourished and became the largest parish in the Episcopal Diocese of Western North Carolina during that time.

Denomination: Episcopal
Address: 766 North Main Street, Hendersonville NC 28792
Telephone: 828-693-7458
Directions: North side of downtown on Main Street.

St. John in the Wilderness Church

A unique spot of southern history in a setting of idyllic beauty, St. John in the Wilderness Episcopal Church in Flat Rock is a gable roof brick church that has at its southeast corner a three-story square tower with pyramidal roof. In 1833, Charles and Susan Baring built the church as a private chapel, and at the formation of the Episcopal Diocese of Western North Carolina in 1836, the Baring family gave up their rights to the church as a private chapel, turning the deed over to the bishop of the newly-formed diocese. Among the family plots in the graveyard are the graves of Christopher Memminger, first secretary of the Confederate treasury; Rev. John Grimke Drayton, developer of the world famous Magnolia Gardens; members of families of three signers of the Declaration of Independence; and Edward P. King, the World War II general who led the infamous Bataan death march.

Denomination: Episcopal
Address: 1895 Greenville Highway, Flat Rock NC
Telephone: 828-693-7458
Hours: The church and graveyard are open daily 9 a.m.-4 p.m. for visitation.
Directions: From downtown Hendersonville take Highway 25 south towards Flat Rock. St. John in the Wilderness Church will be on your right.

St. Mary's Church in Grove Park

Described in the year of her founding in 1914 as a "Wayside Shrine in the Mountains of Western North Carolina," beautiful little St. Mary's Church has attracted countless visitors over the years. Designed by Richard Sharp Smith and built in 1914, the church is English Gothic in style and cruciform in plan. Constructed out of red brick with steeply pitched gable roofs, the building is like those dotting the hilly landscape of Counties Durham, Northumberland and Cumbria in northern England. The English cottage-style Rectory, also designed by Smith, was built and set in beautiful landscaped grounds. The landscape architect was Frederick Law Olmsted, architect for Biltmore Estate and designer of New York's Central Park. International attention was brought to St. Mary's by the writer Gail Godwin when she immortalized the church in her novel *"Father Melancholy's Daughter"*.

Denomination: Episcopal
Address: 337 Charlotte Street, Asheville NC 28801
Telephone: 828-254-5836
Directions: From Pack Square, go south on College Street and turn left onto Charlotte Street east to 337 on your right.

Chapter Ten
Art Galleries

Asheville

For a complete listing of all current exhibitions and ongoing art-related events, pick up copies of the following free weekly publications.

Mountain Xpress: A free weekly independent news, arts, and events newspaper for Western North Carolina. Excellent entertainment coverage, local commentary. P.O. Box 144, Asheville NC 28802; 828-251-1333.

Take Five: A weekly tabloid insert in the *Asheville Citizen-Times* on Fridays. It features a complete theater and events listing, articles and reviews. 14 O. Henry Ave., Asheville NC 28801; 828-252-5611, 800-800-4204.

Asheville Area Arts Council: Located in Asheville, the Asheville Area Arts Council is a nonprofit umbrella service organization that represents the interests of more than 100 cultural and arts related groups. 346 Depot Street, the ARTERY, Asheville NC 28801; 828-258-0710.Website: ashevillearts.com

River Arts District: While most of the galleries exist in the downtown Asheville area, the River Arts District, located on the French Broad River, is the newest artist hotspot. This former industrial and warehouse district now is home to a growing number of artists and crafts persons, many of whom open their studios to the public. The River Arts District is defined clearly by small "River District" signs along the roads and streets and is easy to find. To get to the River Arts District from Pack Square, go west on Patton Avenue and turn left on Clingman Avenue. Clingman Avenue takes you directly to the River Arts District. Website: www.riverartsdistrict.com

Art Galleries

Aesthetic Gallery: Textiles, photography, painting, sculpture, ceramics and jewelry from local, national and international artists and crafters. 6 College Street, Asheville NC 28801; 828-236-2889

American Folk: Contemporary Southern folk art, North Carolina wood-fired pottery, custom picture frames and a generous helping of whimsy, exuberance and inspiration. 64 Biltmore Avenue, Asheville NC 28801; 828-281-2134.

Asheville Art Museum: Ongoing exhibits of local and nationally known artists. The museum's permanent collection features 100 years worth of images, including those of America's acclaimed impressionists, regionalists and abstract artists. 2 South Pack Sq., Asheville NC 28801; 828-253-3227.

Asheville Gallery of Art: Top quality original paintings by local artists. Cooperative artist-run gallery. 16 College St., Asheville NC 28801; 828-251-5796.

Atelier 24 Lexington: Local art from more than 40 artists in a 5,000 sq. ft. exhibition space. 24 North Lexington Avenue, Asheville NC 28801; 828-505-3663.

Bella Vista Art Gallery: A Biltmore Village gallery represented both emerging and mid-career artists, from many media, whose works challenge and interest art collectors now and for many years to come. 14 Lodge Street, Asheville NC 28803, 828-768-0248.

Black Mountain College Museum + Arts Center: The Black Mountain College Museum + Arts Center is an exhibition space and resource center dedicated to exploring the history and legacy of the world's most acclaimed experimental educational community. 56 Broadway, Asheville NC 28801; 828-350-8484.

Black Bird Frame & Art: Original art by local, regional artists in a variety of media.365 Merrimon Ave., Asheville NC 28801; 828-252-6036.

Blue Spiral 1: Features changing shows of sculptures and paintings. Oils, pastels, mixed media and watercolor. More than 11,000 square feet of gallery space. World-class gallery. 38 Biltmore Ave., Asheville NC 28801; 828-251-0202.

Cherry Orchard Studio: Pen & ink drawings of Asheville & Western North Carolina. 828-779-1569. www.cherryorchardstudio.com

Echo Gallery at Biltmore Park: Echo Gallery is a joint venture between Biltmore Farms and eight Asheville artists. Paintings, ceramics, textile art and photography.

Europa Art Gallery: Europa features artists from, France, Italy, Germany, Czech republic as well as artists from the USA and South Africa. 29 Page Avenue, Asheville NC 28801; 828-258-5600.

Flood Gallery Fine Arts Center: The Flood Gallery Fine Art Center is a non-profit arts organization dedicated to promoting the arts in Asheville through the exhibition of established and emerging artists from all over the world. 109 Roberts Street, Asheville NC 28801; 828-254-2166.

Gallery Minerva: Fine art featuring landscapes, still life, sculpture and photography. Local and international artists. 8 Biltmore Avenue., Asheville NC 28801; 828-255-8850.

Grand Bohemian Gallery: Located in the Grand Bohemian Hotel in Biltmore Village and other luxury Kessler Collection Hotels throughout the country. Contemporary painting, art glass, ceramics, jewelry and sculpture. 11 Boston Way, Asheville NC 28803; 828-274-1242.

Lee James Pantas: Asheville artist noted for his fantasy coral reef paintings. Studio and gallery visits by appointment. 18 Garren Mountain Lane, Fairview NC 28730; 828-779-1569. www.leepantas.com

16 Patton: Regional artists who work with oils and pastels. Also wood furniture and wood crafts. 16 Patton Ave., Asheville NC 28801; 828-236-2889.

Pura Vida: Local and regional artwork in a warm and friendly gift store. Featuring paintings, ceramics, jewelry, candles and art-apparel. 39 Biltmore Avenue, Asheville NC 28801; 828-439-3568

Studio B: One of Asheville's premier framing store and art galleries. Museum, conservation and shadowbox framing by Patti Bell (over 40 years of framing experience). Also original art by regional, national and international artists. 171 Weaverville Highway, Asheville NC 28804; 828-225-5200

The Bender Gallery: One of Asheville's premier studio art glass galleries and its largest on two sun filled levels. 57 Haywood Street, Asheville NC 28801; 828-933-5530.

The Complete Naturalist Wildlife Art Gallery: Biltmore Village gallery representing local as well as internationally-known nature artists that include Carl Brenders, Robert Bateman, Bev Doolittle, Charles Frace, Charley Harper, Terry Isaac, Roger Tory Peterson, and John James Audubon. 2 Brook Street, Asheville NC 28802; 828-274-5730.

The Haen Gallery: The Haen Gallery is committed to providing access to stunning and unique artwork for discerning collectors and the local community in general. 52 Biltmore Avenue, Asheville NC 28801; 828-254-8577.

The Satellite Gallery: Specializing in artwork that represents the next wave of artists that are rising from the underground of contemporary street and pop culture. 55 Broadway, Asheville NC 28801; 828-505-2225

University of North Carolina at Asheville Gallery: The University has two galleries located in Owen Hall, Second Floor Gallery and University Gallery, that have monthly exhibitions. UNCA, Owen Hall, One University Heights, Asheville NC 28804; 828-251-6559.

Hendersonville

For a complete listing of all current exhibitions and ongoing art-related events, pick up a free local entertainment guide at the Hendersonville/Flat Rock Visitors Information Center. The *Hendersonville Times-News* also has current listings in the "Preview Page" of the Friday edition

Arts Council of Henderson County: The Arts Council of Henderson County is a community organization that advocates for the arts and provides opportunities to enrich the lives of Henderson County's children and adults through the arts by offering exhibits and art education programs. 538-A North Main Street, Hendersonville NC 28972; 828-693-8504. Website: www.acofhc.org

Art League of Henderson County: The purpose of the Art League of Henderson County is the promotion, development, and enjoyment of the visual arts. The Art League has more than 200 members. PO Box 514, Hendersonville NC 28793. Website: www.artleague.net

Art Galleries

Arts Council of Henderson County Gallery: Ongoing exhibits of national and regional artists. 538A North Main Street, Hendersonville NC 28792; 828-693-8504.

Art League of Henderson County Gallery: Monthly ongoing exhibits of original work by local guest artists. Located at Opportunity House, 1411 Asheville Hwy., Hendersonville NC 28791; 828-692-0575.

Framing Arts: Regional artists and prints. Authorized Winn-Devon art group dealer. Distinctive custom framing. 119 Third Ave. West, Hendersonville NC 28792; 828-696-3818.

Gallery Studio B: Gallery representing Soviet Era artists from the 1940's to the present. Concentration in both the Russian Impressionism and Soviet Socialist Realism styles. 2760 Greenville Highway, Hendersonville NC 28792; 828-551-8773.

Oliver's Southern Folk Art: Gallery represents over 100 authentic and self-taught southern folk artists and potters. 1034D Greenville Highway, Hendersonville NC 28792; 828-698-7877.

The Conn-Artists Studios & Art Gallery: Original art, one-of-kind cards, pottery, a bit of funky jewelry and offer commissions by represented local and regional artists. Art instruction. 611 Greenville Highway, Hendersonville NC 28792; 828-329-2819.

The Portrait Source: Top quality, nationally recognized and award winning portrait artists, 318 N. Main Street; 828-692-7056.

Chapter Eleven
Craft Galleries

Asheville

Resources:
For a complete listing of all current exhibitions and ongoing art-related events, pick up copies of the following free weekly publications.

Mountain Xpress: A free weekly independent news, arts, and events newspaper for Western North Carolina. Excellent entertainment coverage, local commentary. P.O. Box 144, Asheville NC 28802; 828-251-1333.

Take Five: A weekly tabloid insert in the *Asheville Citizen-Times* on Fridays. It features a complete theater and events listing, articles and reviews. 14 O. Henry Ave., Asheville NC 28801; 828-252-5611, 800-800-4204.

Odyssey Center for Ceramic Arts: Studio school located in the River Arts District whose mission is to promote understanding, appreciation and development in the ceramic arts. Classes, workshops and gallery. 238 Clingman Avenue, Asheville NC 28801; 828-285-0210. Website: www.highwaterclays.com

Craft Galleries
Allanstand Craft Shop at the Folk Art Center: One of Appalachia's oldest and best-known craft shops. Sells the work of more than 200 members of the Southern Highland Craft Guild. Milepost 382, Blue Ridge Parkway in Asheville, 298-7928.

American Folk: Contemporary Southern folk art, North Carolina wood-fired pottery, custom picture frames and a generous helping of whimsy, exuberance and inspiration. 64 Biltmore Avenue, Asheville NC 28801; 828-281-2134.

Appalachian Crafts: Traditional hand-made Appalachian crafts, including pottery, heirloom quality quilts, hand blown glass and wood carvings. Two locations: 10 North Spruce St., Asheville NC 28801 and in the Renaissance Asheville Hotel, 1 Thomas Wolfe Plaza, Asheville NC 28801; 828-253-8499.

Ariel Gallery: A cooperative gallery featuring local artists working within a range of fine crafts, offering original works in pottery, sculpture, glass, furniture, jewelry, fiber wearables, decorative fiber and mixed media. 19 Biltmore Avenue, Asheville NC 28801; 828-236-2660.

Bellagio: Biltmore Village gallery that features exquisitely handcrafted jewelry and clothing. One of top craft galleries in the Asheville area. 5 Biltmore Plaza, Asheville NC 28803; 828-277-8100.

Blue: Biltmore Village gallery offering jewelry designs in four colors of gold, plus sterling. Also works by local artists in raku, pottery, photography and glass. 1 Swan Street, Asheville NC 28803; 828-277-2583.

Gallery of the Mountains: Extensive selection of fine mountain crafts by regional and national artisans. Hand-dyed and hand-painted silk vests, hand-woven coats, wraps and scarves, pottery, woodwork and jewelry. Located in the Grove Park Inn Resort & Spa. 290 Macon Ave., Asheville NC 28804; 800-692-2204.

Grovewood Gallery: A spacious shop displaying the work of some of the Southeast's finest craftspeople. Highest quality innovative work on display. A must-see gallery located in the Homespun Shops next to the Grove Park Inn Resort & Spa. 111 Grovewood Road, Asheville NC 28804; 828-253-7651.

Guild Crafts: Features the work of regional artists who are members of the Southern Highland Handicraft Guild. 930 Tunnel Rd., Asheville NC 28805; 828-298-7903.

Jewels That Dance: Exquisite handcrafted jewelry from gold, silver, diamonds and other precious gems and metals. 63 Haywood St., Asheville NC 28801; 828-254-5088.

Kress Emporium: Original crafts and art by local artists and crafters as well as home furnishings and decorative accessories. 19 Patton Ave., Asheville NC 28801; 828-281-2252.

Mountain Made: Regional crafts, including jewelry, pottery, glass, wood, and metal. Local books and music. Owned by nonprofit Mountain BizWorks, located in the Grove Arcade Public Market. 1 Page Ave., Suite 123, Grove Arcade Asheville NC 28801, 828-350-0307.

New Morning Gallery: Located in Biltmore Village, New Morning Gallery is one of Asheville's premier craft galleries. Functional and sculptural pottery, fine art glass, furniture, jewelry and other handmade objects. 7 Boston Way, Biltmore Gallery, Asheville NC 28803; 828-274-2831.

Odyssey Gallery: Located in the River District, the Odyssey Gallery features pottery and works of art in clay and ceramics by Odyssey Center for Ceramic Arts instructors and artist. 238 Clingman Avenue, Asheville NC 28801; 828-285-0210.

Stuart Nye Jewelry: Hand wrought jewelry since 1933. Originator of the Dogwood Jewelry. 940 Tunnel Road, Asheville NC 28805, 828-298-7988.

Woolworth Walk: Over 150 artists and crafts persons selling and making jewelry, fine art, decorative art and crafts in a nearly 20,000 square foot air-conditioned display and studio space. 25 Haywood Street, Asheville NC 28801; 828-254-9234.

Hendersonville
Resources:
For a complete listing of all current exhibitions and ongoing art-related events, pick up a free local entertainment guide at the Hendersonville/Flat Rock Visitors Information Center. *The Hendersonville Times-News* also has current listings in the "Preview Page" of the Friday edition.

Arts Council of Henderson County: The Arts Council of Henderson County is a community organization that advocates for the arts and provides opportunities to enrich the lives of Henderson County's children and adults through the arts by offering exhibits and art education programs. 538-A North Main Street, Hendersonville NC 28972, 828-693-8504. Website: www.acofhc.org.

Art League of Henderson County: The purpose of the Art League of Henderson County is the promotion, development, and enjoyment of the visual arts. The Art League has more than 200 members. PO Box 514, Hendersonville NC 28793. Website: www.artleague.net.

Craft Galleries
Carolina Mountain Artists: Arts and crafts by regional artists. Fine art and traditional crafts 444 N. Main Street, Hendersonville NC 28792; 828-696-0707.

Hand in Hand Gallery: High-quality arts and crafts by over 150 regional artists working in all media. Decorative porcelain pottery by David Voorhees and silver and gold jewelry by Molly Sharp. 2720 Greenville Hwy., Flat Rock NC 28731; 828- 697-7719.

Narnia Studios: Established in 1982, Narnia Studios features affordable original art by Hendersonville artists, including local pottery and art glass. Narnia is the creator of "Chalk It Up1" one of the country's oldest chalk art contests. 315 N. Main St., Hendersonville NC 28972; 828-697-6393.

Red Step Art Works: Work by local and regional artists, including fiber art, jewelry, oil painting, pottery, sculpture and furniture, and featuring the jewelry and pottery of owners Kelli Redmond and Andrew Stephenson. 142 3rd Avenue West, Hendersonville NC 28792; 828-697-1447.

Silver Fox Gallery: Contemporary American art, craft & furniture. 508 N. Main St., Hendersonville, 28801; 828-698-0601.

Chapter Twelve
Shopping

Asheville has a great range of shopping opportunities, from charming historic shopping districts to major malls. Downtown Asheville is a mix of art and craft galleries, specialty shops, bookstores and antique shops. Especially noteworthy is the historic Wall Street district, with its fascinating collection of shops, the recently restored Grove Arcade Public Market, and Biltmore Village, a historic district of specialty and gift shops.

Asheville Malls and Shopping Districts

Asheville Mall: Asheville's major mall located on Tunnel Road. Take Exit 7 off I-240. 3 South Tunnel Road, Asheville NC 28805, 828-298-5080.

Biltmore Square Mall: Located on the west side of Asheville off I-26. Take Exit 2 off I-26. 800 Brevard Road, Asheville NC 28806, 828-667-2308.

Biltmore Village: Built in the late 1890's as a classic planned community at the entrance to George Vanderbilt's Biltmore Estate in Asheville, North Carolina,

Grove Arcade Public Market: Built by E.W. Grove, creator of the Grove Park Inn Resort & Spa, the Grove Arcade opened in 1929 and thrived until World War II as one of the country's leading public markets. Restored and reopened to the public in 2002, the Grove Arcade is not only one of Asheville's architectural jewels, it is also home to a large number of unique shops and restaurants. The Arcade is located downtown just to the west of Haywood Street.

Lexington Avenue District: The Lexington Avenue district is located in downtown Asheville, just north of Pack Square and is home to some of the city's most interesting and diverse stores. The lineup ranges from neo-hippy to contemporary chic and features shops known for funk, punk and creative gifts, as well as coffee shops and sidewalk cafes.

River Arts District: Located in a former industrial area of Asheville along the French Broad River, the River Arts District today is now one of the arts and crafts centers of Asheville.

Hendersonville Malls and Shopping Districts

Blue Ridge Mall: Located on the east side of Hendersonville on Highway 64.

Main Street: Downtown Hendersonville is the primary shopping district in Hendersonville. Specialty shops, gift stores, card stores, galleries, craft outlets, antiques and much more. This pleasant street is unique not only for its rich collection of stores but also the beautiful flowers, benches, and shady trees.

Flea Markets

Smiley's Flea Market: Friday-Sunday, 7 a.m.-5 p.m. Located halfway between Asheville and Henderson. One of the largest outdoor flea markets in North Carolina. Every weekend. 5360 Hendersonville Road, Fletcher NC 28732; 828-684-3532.

Auctions

Bagwell & Associates: Full-service auctions for businesses, estates and individuals and specialty auctions of entire collections. 29 Fanning Bridge Road, Fletcher NC 28732; 828-651-9699.

Brunk Auctions: Asheville's version of Sotheby's. Elegant and respected, and includes world-class antiques that go up for sale. 117 Tunnel Rd., Asheville NC 28805; 828-254-6846.

Tommy Tuten and Johnny Penland Auctions: Everything goes, even if it's for only $1. Coffee and hot dogs sold, and be sure to bring a chair. 6 p.m. every Friday, 155 Craven St., Asheville NC 28806; 828-255-0455.

Asheville Antique Stores

Asheville is a shopping mecca for antique lovers from all over the world. Here they can stroll through antique shops conveniently grouped in two different parts of town (Lexington Avenue District and Biltmore Village) or visit often larger antique "malls" sprinkled throughout the city.

Antique Market Gallery: Offering a large selection of functional antique items for the home including seating, beds and paintings. 52 Broadway, Asheville NC 28801; 828-259-9977.

Antique Tobacco Barn: The Antique Tobacco Barn is a 25-year-old, 77,000-square-foot antique store located in a historic tobacco barn that has the largest selection of antiques in North Carolina. Over 75 dealers offering antique furniture, collectibles, and fine art. 75 Swannanoa River Rd., Asheville NC 28805; 866-676-5146.

Archive Antiques: General antiques and collectibles. 57 Broadway, Asheville NC 28801, 828-254-4568.

Chatsworth Art & Antiques: Antiques, oils, etchings, European collectibles and more. 54 N. Lexington Ave., Asheville NC 28801; 828-252-6004.

Fireside Antiques & Interiors: Twenty-five years experience importing English antiques. A premier source of antiques in Western North Carolina. Extensive selection of Oriental and European porcelain as well as reproduction gift items.30 All Souls Crescent, Asheville NC 28803; 828-274-5977.

King-Thomasson Antiques: Specializes in English County Furniture. 65 Biltmore Ave., Asheville NC 28801; 828-252-1565.

L.O.F.T. Lost Objects Found Treasures: Unique furniture, handmade paper journals, ironwork, art, baskets, French soaps, scented candles, pottery and garden stuff... 53 B roadway Street, Asheville NC 28801; 828-259-9303.

Oddfellows Antique Warehouse: Over 16,000 sq. ft of hand-picked European Antiques from England, France and much of Western Europe. They also have select dealers at our shop featuring antiques from the states and abroad giving an overall European flair to their warehouse. 124 Swannanoa River Road, Asheville NC 28805; 828-350-7800.

Stuf Antiques: General antiques and collectibles. 52 Broadway, Asheville NC 28801; 828-254-4054,

Sweeten Creek Antiques & Collectibles: 31,000 Sq. Ft of antiques and collectibles of all types. 1156 Sweeten Creek Road, Asheville NC 28803; 828-277-6100.

Village Antiques: Since 1989, a destination shop for designers and collectors of fine antique furniture and art. Regularly imports from France, and their shop in offers over 25,000 square feet of antiques, fine art, and decorative arts, both European and American, as well as specialized collections of Southern Furniture, pottery, and folk art, and African art. 755 Biltmore Ave., Asheville NC 28803; 828-252-5090.

Hendersonville Antique Stores

Jane Asher Antiques & Fine Traditions: 344 N. Main Street, Hendersonville NC 28792; 828-698-0018.

JRD's Classics & Collectibles: 520-4 South Allen Road, Flat Rock NC 28739, 576 Upward Road, Suite 5, Flat Rock NC 28731; 828-698-0075.

Mehri & Company: 501 N. Main St., Hendersonville NC 28792; 828-693-0887.

Nana's Antiques: 122 West Allen Street, Hendersonville NC 28792; 828-697-8979.

Nancy Roth Antiques: 127 4th Avenue West, Hendersonville NC 28792; 828-697-7555.

Piggy's & Harry's: 102 Duncan Hill Rd., Hendersonville NC 28792; 828-692-1995.

Scotties Jewelry & Fine Art: 314 N. Main St., Hendersonville NC 28792; 828-692-1350.

Village Green Antique Mall: 424 N. Main Street, Hendersonville NC 28792; 828-692-9057.

Chapter Thirteen
Nightlife

Asheville has a vibrant downtown, and the combination of great historic architecture, fine restaurants, coffeehouses, specialty stores, art galleries and nightclubs, pubs and cafes all add to the mix that has made the city an exciting nighttime destination. Downtown Asheville is especially interesting and eclectic after dark, with street musicians and the popular long-running drum circle. The number one music venue in Asheville is The Orange Peel.

Listed below is a selection of the more established venues and places to check out. The best way to get a handle on what is happening in Asheville is to pick up a copy of one of these two publications.

Mountain Xpress: A free weekly independent news, arts, and events newspaper for Western North Carolina. Excellent entertainment coverage, local commentary. P.O. Box 144, Asheville NC 28802; 828-251-1333.

Take Five: A weekly tabloid insert in the *Asheville Citizen-Times* on Fridays. It features a current performers and events, articles and reviews. 14 O. Henry Ave., Asheville NC 28801; 828-252-5611

Asheville Microbreweries

Over the past ten years, a number of microbreweries have sprung up in the Asheville area, enough so that Asheville is gaining a reputation as a beer-lover's city! Four local breweries are turning out a wide selection of local ales and lagers and while most have focused on darker pale ales and bitters, some are now producing lighter varieties. The breweries are Highland Brewing Company (www.highlandbrewing.com), Asheville Pizza and Brewing Company (www.ashevillepizza.com), French Broad River Brewing, and Jack of the Wood (www.jackofthewood.com). Local Asheville watering holes for these great beers and ales are Barley's Taproom (www.barleys-taproom.com.asheville), 42 Biltmore Ave., 255-0504; Asheville Pizza and Brewing Company, 675 Merrimon Ave., 254-1281; Jack of the Wood, 95 Patton Ave., 252-5445; and The Bier Garden, 46 Haywood St., 285-0002. These establishments are covered in greater detail in this chapter.

Asheville

Asheville Pizza & Brewing: One screen, second-run Hollywood and independent films at discount prices. Pizza and micro-brews available in theater or adjoining restaurant. Live entertainment and tons of dance floor. 675 Merrimon Ave., Asheville NC 28804; 828-254-1281.

Barley's Taproom & Pizzeria: One of Asheville's most popular watering holes. Great selection of beer, including micro-brews, and wonderful pizzas. Entertainment Tuesday, Thursday, Saturday and Sunday with a blend of jazz, bluegrass and more. Billiard tables and dart boards available upstairs. 42 Biltmore Ave., Asheville NC 28801; 828-255-0504.

Jack of The Wood: In addition to making their own unique beers and ales, Jack of the Wood offers a distinctively British-style pub atmosphere. They also feature fresh-baked breads and desserts to go along with the local performers. 95 Patton Ave., Asheville NC 28801; 828-252-5445.

Malaprop's Bookstore and Café: Cafe located downtown in the Asheville's best privately owned bookstore. Live music (no cover charge) most Friday and Saturdays. 55 Haywood Street, Asheville NC 28801; 828-254-6734.

Orange Peel Social Aid & Pleasure Club: Asheville's premier entertainment venue. Always a great lineup of big-name talent, huge concert hall with room enough for almost 1,000. Most shows start early, are standing only and non-smoking. Beer and wine. 101 Biltmore Ave., Asheville NC 28801; 828-225-5851.

Stella Blue: Live music that ranges from blues and jazz to reggae, techno and hip-hop. 31 Patton Avenue, Asheville NC 28801; 828-236-2424.

Tressa's Downtown Jazz and Blues: Live jazz and blues every night in a unique setting. Old New Orleans elegance, great service and world-class jazz and blues performers. 28 Broadway, Asheville NC 28801; 828-254-7072.

The Garage at Biltmore: Live music venue sharing the same building with French Broad Brewery and Monte Vecchia Music and Arts Studio. 101 Fairfield Road, Suite B, Asheville NC 28803; 828-505-2663.

The Grey Eagle: The Grey Eagle has become one of Asheville's premier music halls. Situated in Asheville's vibrant French Broad River district, the Grey Eagle is known for presenting local and nationally known artists, making it a cornerstone of the Asheville music scene. 185 Clingman Ave., Asheville NC 28801; 828-232-5800.

The Rocket Club: Open seven days a week, The Rocket Club offers live music and a vast array of drinks in a small, intimate setting. 401 Haywood Street, Asheville NC 28806; 828-505-2494.

Westville Pub: Something happening seven evenings a week, including open mike nights. Non-smoking pub serving a light menu. 777 Haywood Rd., Asheville NC 28806; 821-225-9782.

Hendersonville

Eleanor's Sports Tavern & Grill: 12 drafts and full service bar, 10 H.D.TVs, 430 N. Main Street, Hendersonville NC 28792; 828-692-3100.

Hannah Flanagan's Pub & Eatery: More than 30 beers on tap, pub food and Irish dishes. Live music. 300 N. Main St., Hendersonville NC 28792; 828-696-1665.

Margaritagrille: Sports tavern and grill. 430 North Main Street, Hendersonville NC 28792; 828-692-3100.

Chapter Fourteen
Theatre & Dance

Theatre is alive and well in Western North Carolina, especially in the Asheville, Hendersonville and Flat Rock area. Big-city ensembles regularly return each year. There is a strong local theatre, which ranges from innovative and cutting-edge performances by the Montford Park Players to the full-scale productions at the Diana Wortham Theatre (*See* Section Three, Chapter 2, Pack Place Education, Arts & Science Center). You can even find Shakespeare in the summer from the Montford Park Players. Asheville also has an established theater in the Asheville Community Theatre (ACT), which regularly schedules award-winning shows. (*See* Section Three, Chapter 2). Located in Flat Rock, the Flat Rock Playhouse has been rated one of the top ten summer theaters in the nation. Home to the Vagabond Players, this theater is a major attraction. (*See* Section Four, Chapter 2).

Theatre
For a complete listing of all current performances, pick up copies of the following free weekly publications.

Mountain Xpress: A free weekly independent news, arts, and events newspaper for Western North Carolina. Excellent entertainment coverage, local commentary. P.O. Box 144, Asheville NC 28802; 828-251-1333.

Take Five: A weekly tabloid insert in the *Asheville Citizen-Times* on Fridays. It features a complete theater and events listing, articles and reviews. 14 O. Henry Ave., Asheville NC 28801; 828-252-5611, 800-800-4204.

Asheville Area Theatres
(For a complete listing of all theatres in Western North Carolina, visit my guidebook website at www.ashevilleguidebook.com)

Asheville Community Theatre: Asheville's primary community theatre. 35 Walnut Street, Asheville NC 28801; 828-254-1320.

Blue Ridge Performing Arts Center: Featuring a grand marble lobby, a cozy 100 seat theatre and a 20 seat digital screening room, the center is a venue for all types of musical entertainment, comedy, live theatre, host to various writers, speakers, community events, parties and children's events. 538 North Main Street, Hendersonville NC 28702; 828-693-0087

Flat Rock Playhouse, home of the Vagabond Players

Brevard Little Theatre: Official community theater of Transylvania County. American Legion Hall, 55 East Jordan Street, Brevard NC 28712; 828-884-2587

Diana Wortham Theatre: 500 seat theatre & performance venue located in Pack Place downtown Asheville. 2 South Pack Square, Asheville NC 28801; 828-257-4530.

Flat Rock Playhouse: State Theatre of North Carolina. Located in nearby Flat Rock (25 miles south of Asheville). 2661 Greenville Highway, Flat Rock NC 28731; 828-693-0731.

Hendersonville Little Theatre: Since 1996, staging five shows annually. Located at the Barn, State Street between Kanuga and Willow, PO Box 66, Hendersonville NC 28793; 828-692-1082.

Southern Appalachian Repertory Theatre: 44 College Street, Mars Hill NC 28754;, 828-689-1239

The Magnetic Field: The Magnetic Field is a River Arts District's cafe, bar and performance house. 372 Depot Street, Asheville NC 28801; 828-674-2036

Performance Organizations & Concert Series

Asheville Lyric Opera: Opera at its best in Asheville. 2 South Pack Square, Asheville NC 28801; 828-236-0670.

Asheville Symphony Orchestra: Asheville's major symphony orchestra. PO Box 2852, Asheville NC 28802; 828-254-7046.

Hendersonville Symphony: Hendersonville's symphony orchestra, performances at the Blue Ridge Conference Hall. PO Box 1811, Hendersonville NC 28793; 828-697-5884.

Bravo Concerts: World-class opera, symphony and dance performances at Thomas Wolfe Auditorium, Asheville. PO Box 685, Asheville NC 28802, 828-225-5887.

North Carolina Stage Company: Professional theatre in an intimate off-Broadway style in downtown Asheville. 15 Stage Lane, Asheville NC 28801; 828-239-0263.

Poetry Alive: Performance poetry like nothing else! 70 Woodfin Place, Suite WW4C, Asheville NC 28801, 800-476-8172.

Western North Carolina Jazz Society: Performances at Diana Wortham Theatre by acclaimed local and nationally recognized jazz artists. 828-257-4530.

W.C. Reid Center for the Creative Arts: The W.C. Reid Center, sponsored and supported by the City of Asheville, is the home to a variety of creative cultural art programs for all ages focusing on visual, performing and computer arts. 133 Livingston Street, Asheville NC 28801; 828-350-2048.

Dance

For a complete listing of all current performances and ongoing dance-related events, pick up copies of the following free weekly publications.

Mountain Xpress: A free weekly independent news, arts, and events newspaper for Western North Carolina. Excellent entertainment coverage, local commentary. P.O. Box 144, Asheville NC 28802; 828-251-1333.

Take Five: A weekly tabloid insert in the *Asheville Citizen-Times* on Fridays. It features a complete theater and events listing, articles and reviews. 14 O. Henry Ave., Asheville NC 28801; 828-252-5611, 800-800-4204.

Suppliers

A Dancer's Place: Complete inventory of dance wear, shoes and accessories all types of dance. 14 Patton Ave., Asheville NC 28801; 828-253-1434.

Dance Etc: Dancewear and dancer's supplies. 615 Greenville Hwy., Hendersonville, NC 28792; 828-696-2806.

Dance Theaters and Venues

Asheville Contemporary Dance Theatre: The Asheville Contemporary Dance Theatre is a non-profit professional dance company created in 1979 that performs up to 80 times a year in Asheville and throughout the world. Repertory consists of both full-length modern dance ballets and children's shows. 20 Commerce Street, Asheville NC 28801; 828-254-2621. www.acdt.org

Dance Troupes, Schools & Organizations

Asheville Academy of Ballet & Contemporary Dance: 4 Lynwood Rd., Asheville NC 28804; 828-258-1028 (ballet, contemporary)

Asheville Center of Performing Arts: The Asheville Center of Performing Arts was founded in 1996 and offers classes in ballet, tap, jazz, modern, acrobatics and preschool. They are also home to the Asheville City Ballet, Asheville Jazzworks and Asheville Tap Company. 193 Charlotte Street, Asheville NC 28801; 828-258-3377. www.theperformancecenter.org

Asheville Contemporary Dance Theatre: ACDT is a non-profit professional dance company created in 1979 that performs up to 80 times a year in Asheville and throughout the world. Repertory consists of both full-length modern dance ballets and children's shows. 20 Commerce Street, Asheville NC 28801; 828-254-2621. www.acdt.org

Ballet Conservatory of Asheville: Instruction in all forms of dance for children through pre-professional. Performances locally. 6 East Chestnut Street, Asheville NC 28801; 828-255-5777. www.balletconservatoryofasheville.com

Blue Ridge Ballroom: Ballroom classes. New Bridge Shopping Center, Asheville NC 28804; 828-253-9108

Center Stage Dance Studio: Center Stage Dance Studio offers instruction in tap, jazz, ballet, pre-ballet, lyrical, modern, hip-hop, acro and creative movement. Rosscraggon Business Park, 7 Long Shoals Rd., Asheville NC 28803;828-654-7010.

DC Dance Studio: A private ballroom specializing in social and sequenced ballroom dance instruction for both singles and couples.16 Dancing Creek Lane, Fletcher NC 28732, 828-654-0798.

Miss Kellie's Dance Studio: Creative movement, preschool, jazz, tap, ballet. Royal Pines Plaza, Arden, NC 28803; 828-684-7999.

Merles Dance Place: Tap, jazz ballet, tumbling for children and adults. 126 West Blue Ridge Rd., Flat Rock, NC 28731; 828-692-4907.

Southside Dance Studio: Ages 3 through adult, professional training in ballet, tap, jazz, hip-hop and ballroom dancing. 3445 Hendersonville Road, Fletcher NC 28732; 828-684-2118.

Terpsicorps Theatre of Dance: Professional contemporary ballet company, showcasing local talent as well as acclaimed dancers from nationally recognized dance companies in two summer concerts a year at Pack Place. 2 South Pack Square, Asheville NC 28801; 828-252-6342.

Chapter Fifteen
Outdoor Recreation in Western North Carolina

Western North Carolina abounds with numerous outdoor recreational opportunities, many of them rare in other areas but plentiful here. Whitewater rafting, llama trekking, mountain biking and mountain climbing are prime examples.

Both Asheville and Hendersonville have excellent city parks (*See* Section Three, Chapter 9 Asheville Parks; and Section Four, Chapter 7 Hendersonville Area Parks) that provide various outdoor sporting venues. The Buncombe County Parks and Recreation Department also manages a number of parks that are used for various outdoor and sporting activities. Their offices are at 205 College Street, Asheville NC 28801; 828-255-5526.

Outdoor Stores & Outfitters

Asheville:
Black Dome: 140 Tunnel Road, Asheville NC 28805; 828-251-2001.
Diamond Brand Outdoors: 2623 Hendersonville Road, Arden NC 28704; 828-684-6262.
Frugal Backbacker Outdoor Outlet: 2621 Hendersonville Road, Arden NC 28704; 828-209-1530.
REI: 31 Schenck Parkway, Asheville NC 28803, 828-687-0918.
Ski Country Sports: 1000 Merrimon Avenue, Asheville NC 28804; 828-254-0901.

Banner Elk:
High Mountain Expeditions: 3149 Tynecastle Highway, Banner Elk NC 28604; 828-262-9036.

Blowing Rock:
Footsloggers of Blowing Rock: 921 Main Street, Blowing Rock NC 28605; 828-295-4453.

Boone:
Footsloggers of Boone: 139 South Depot Street, Boone NC 28607; 828-262-5111.

Bryson City:
Nantahala Outdoor Center: 13077 Highway 19W, Bryson City NC; 888-905-7238.

Cashiers:
Highland Hiker: 47 Highway 107 South, Cashiers NC 28717; 828-743-1732.

Cullowhee:
Adventure Depot: 200 Yellow Mountain Road, Cullowhee NC 28723; 800-903-4401.

Fontana Dam:
Fontana Village Adventure Center: Highway 28 North, Fontana Dam NC 28733; 800-849-2258.

Hot Springs:
Bluff Mountain Outfitters: 152 Bridge Street, Hot Springs NC 28743; 828-622-7162.

Murphy:
Appalachian Outfitters: 104A Tennessee Street, Murphy NC 28906; 828-837-4165.

Pisgah Forest:
Looking Glass Outfitters: 90 New Hendersonville Highway, Pisgah Forest NC 28768; 866-351-2176
Backcountry Outdoors: 49 Pisgah Highway, Suite 6, Pisgah Forest NC 28768; 828-884-4262.

Robbinsville:
Cherohala Outfitters: 260 Snowbird Road, Robbinsville NC 28711; 828-479-4464.

Valle Crucis:
Mast General Store: Highway 194, Valle Crucis NC 28691; 828-963-6511.

West Jefferson:
Mountain Outfitters: 102 South Jefferson Avenue, West Jefferson NC 29694; 336-246-9133.

Airplane and Helicopter Tour Services
Shadowhawk Aviation: Based one hour from Asheville in Greenville South Carolina, Shadowhawk Aviation provides specialized helicopter tours over South Carolina and Western North Carolina; 864-640-4327.
Smoky Mountain Aero: Based at the Andrews/Murphy airport offering scenic flights year-round. 5840 Airport Road, Andrews NC 28901, 828-321-5114; 888-284-5114.
Western North Carolina Air Tours, LLC: Based in Shiflet Field in Marion NC, Western North Air Tours will arrange for 1-3 passenger flights to take off from either the Asheville, Brevard, Hendersonville, Hickory, Marion, Morganton, Rutherfordton or Spruce Pine airports; 828-403-9955

Bird Watching
The mountains of Western North Carolina are a bird watcher's paradise and since they cover regions of unspoiled territory, farmlands and woodlands, seeing birds is no problem. Still finding the best bird watching sites can be a bit tricky. The best resource to solve this dilemma is the NC Wildlife Resources Commission North Carolina Birding Trail. The trail is divided into three sections, including

⌐ ountains. From their website you may order trail guides which will help you in planning your outings. The trail physically links great bird watching sites and birders with communities, businesses and other local historical and educational attractions. Efforts to develop the North Carolina Birding Trail began in October 2003. As of summer 2009, the Trail is now complete across the entire state—coastal plain, piedmont, and mountain regions.

In Asheville, the North Carolina Arboretum (a site on the North Carolina Birding Trail) offers great bird watching, as does the Blue Ridge Parkway which runs through Asheville. The Western North Carolina Nature Center, located in Asheville, is also a place of interest if you are a bird watcher. In north Asheville, off of Merrimon Avenue, is the Beaver Lake Bird Sanctuary, known locally as a great bird watching site also. From downtown follow Merrimon Avenue north about two miles, and begin watching for the Beaver Lake Bird Sanctuary on your left. After you pass the North Asheville Public Library, look for stone pillars at a pair of driveways leading to the Sanctuary parking lot.

In Hendersonville, one of the best sites for bird watching is Jackson Park located at 801 Glover Street, arguably one of the finest migration spots in North Carolina, with a wide range of habitats being represented in the park's 317 acres. In late September it is possible to see over 70 bird species as they pass through the park on their way south.

Directions: From I-26 Eastbound from Asheville and take U.S. 64 West exit (Exit # 18B) towards downtown Hendersonville. Continue through the traffic light at end of exit ramp onto 4 Seasons Boulevard (U.S. 64) for 1.6 miles (passing 4 more traffic lights). After a wetland area on the left, turn left at the 5th traffic light (Harris Street). Go 0.2 mile to stop sign at end of street. Turn left onto E. 4th Avenue, enter park and follow road to Administration Building (red-brick house on left) and parking.

Resources

Elisha Mitchell Audubon Society (Asheville Chapter): PO Box 18711, Asheville NC 28814; see website for local phone numbers (http://main.nc.us/emas/index.html)

North Carolina Birding Trail: North Carolina Wildlife Resources Commission, 1722 Mail Service Center, Raleigh NC 27699; 919-604-5183.

Mountains Region NC Birding Trail: List of 105 great birding sites in Western North Carolina. 919-604-5183.

Boating

Western North Carolina is an area blessed with many lakes, the vast majority of them man-made, with most having public boating access. The larger lakes generally are in the far western part of the state, with Lake Lure, southeast of Asheville, and Lake James, east of Asheville, exceptions. If whitewater rafting of interest to you, see Whitewater Rafting in this chapter for more on that popular mountain activity.

Boat Rides & Tours

Bryson City:

Paddlefish Kayaking, Inc: Calm water lake kayaking on Lake Fontana, PO Box 2696, Bryson City NC 28713; 828-488-8797.

Bryson City:

Smoky Mountain Jet Boats: 12-passenger jet boat rides on Lake Fontana. 22 Needmore Road, Bryson City NC 28713;, 828-488-0522.

Fontana Dam:

Fontana Village Marina: Pontoon boat trips on Fontana Lake. Highway 28 North, Fontana Dam NC 28733, 828-498-2211; 800-849-2258.

Lake Lure:

Lake Lure Tours: Covered pontoon boat trips on Lake Lure. 2930 Memorial Highway, Lake Lure NC 28746; 828-625-1373.

Boating Associations, Clubs & Resources

Asheville Rowing Club: Non-profit athletic and social organization dedicated to promoting health, fitness and fun through the sport of rowing. Has boathouse on Lake Julian. Asheville Rowing Club, PO Box 861, Asheville NC 28802. www.ashevillerowing.org

Asheville Youth Rowing Association: Non-profit organization dedicated to promoting the sport of rowing among teenagers between the ages of 13 and 18. www.ashevilleyouthrowing.com

North Carolina Boating Law Basics: North Carolina Wildlife Resources Commission, 1717 Mail Services Center, Raleigh NC 27699. www.ncwildlife.org

North Carolina Online Boating Safety Course and Exam: North Carolina Wildlife Resources Commission, 1751 Varsity Drive, Raleigh NC 27606; 919-707-0031. www.ncwildlife.org

Western Carolina Paddlers: Asheville based canoe, kayak and rafting club. http://boatingbeta.com

Outfitters, Marinas & Boat Dealers

Asheville:

Boats Etc: 60 Dogwood Road, Asheville NC 28806; 828-670-9595.

Diamond Brand Outdoors: 2623 Hendersonville Road, Arden NC 28704; 828-684-6262.

Bryson City (Fontana Lake):

Alarka Boat Dock: 7230 Grassy Branch Road, Bryson City NC 28713; 828-488-3841.

Fontana Village Marina: Highway 28 North, Fontana Dam NC 28733, 828-498-2211, 800-849-2258.

Hayesville (Lake Chatuge):
Chatuge Cove Marina: 2397 Highway 175, Hayesville NC 28904.

Hendersonville:
Todd's RV and Marine: 2918 North Rugby Road, Hendersonville NC 28791; 828-651-0007.
Driftwood Marine LLC: 3769 Chimney Road Road, Hendersonville NC 28792; 828-685-1313.

Lake Lure (Lake Lure):
Lake Lure Town Marina: 2975 Memorial Highway, Lake Lure NC 28746; 828-625-2889.

Murphy (Lake Hiwassee):
Mountain View Marina: 200 Dean Aldrich Drive, Murphy NC 28906; 828-644-5451.

Nebo (Lake James):
Bear Creek Marina: 608 Marina Drive, Nebo NC 28761; 828-655-1400.
Mountain Harbour Marina: 9066 Highway 126, Nebo NC 28761; 828-584-0666.

Robbinsville (Lake Santeetlah):
Santeetlah Marina: 1 Marina Drive, Robbinsville NC 28711; 828-479-8180.

West Jefferson:
Mountain Outfitters: 102 South Jefferson Avenue, West Jefferson NC 29694; 336-246-9133.

Camping

Given the vast amount of wilderness area in the Western North Carolina mountains, one would expect to find a staggering array of campgrounds and camping facilities. Indeed this is exactly the case and it is beyond the scope of this guidebook to present all of the camping options available. Instead, this chapter presents some general resources and information about the most popular camping regions: the Blue Ridge Parkway, Pisgah National Forest, the Great Smoky Mountains National Park, the Appalachian Trail and three campgrounds close to Asheville: The Davidson River Campground, the North Mills River Recreation Area and the Lake Powhatan Recreational Area. It is highly recommended that you visit one of the outdoor stores or outfitters listed before heading out into the mountains. There you will not only get knowledgeable advice but can also pick up maps and specific guides to the area you plan to visit.

If you are looking for RV campgrounds, check out the Asheville Campgrounds or Hendersonville Campgrounds sections also in this chapter. Maps of the Pisgah National Forest and other wilderness areas can be ordered from the Cradle of Forestry in America Interpretive Association Forest Place Store. Their address is The Forest Place Store, 66 South Broad St., Brevard, NC 28712. 800-660-0671.

Popular Asheville Area Campgrounds

Davidson River Campground

About: Located at the entrance to Pisgah National Forest in the Brevard area. The Davidson River is a premier trout stream. Located nearby is the Cradle of Forestry.
Address: 1 Davidson River Circle, Pisgah Forest NC 28768
Telephone: 828-862-5960, 877-457-4023
Reservations: 877-444-6777, or online at www.recreation.gov
Open: Year round
Fees: Yes, Federal Interagency Pass, Senior and Access discounts accepted.
Sites: 160 spacious shaded sites, singles and doubles. Sites with river access.
Facilities: Hot showers within walking distance of each site.
Directions: From I-26, take Exit 40 (US 280 to Brevard), right on US 276. Enter Pisgah National Forest, one mile on 276, turn left into Davidson River Campground.

North Mills River Recreation Area

About: The North Mills River runs through this recreation area and camping facility. Each campsite is only a short stroll from the river. Swimming, fishing and river tubing. Located between Asheville and Hendersonville.
Address: 5289 N. Mills River Road, Mills River NC 28742
Telephone: 828-890-3284, 877-457-4023
Reservations: 877-444-6777, or online at www.recreation.gov
Open: Year round with limited service November thru March.
Fees: Yes, Federal Interagency Pass, Senior and Access discounts accepted.
Sites: 32 primitive sites, including 9 double sites. No hooks up available.
Facilities: Restrooms close to sites.
Directions: From Exit 40 on Interstate 26, travel west on US 280 past the airport six miles to traffic light at North Mills River Road. Turn right and travel five miles to the North Mills River Recreation Area.

Lake Powhatan Recreational Area

About: Located just minutes from Asheville, Lake Powhatan offers peace, quiet and solitude on the border of Bent Creek. Camping, swimming, fishing, hiking trails. Beach and fishing pier.
Address: 375 Wesley Branch Road, Asheville NC 28806
Telephone: 828-670-5627, 877-457-4023
Reservations: 877-444-6777, or online at www.recreation.gov

Open: April through October

Fees: Yes, Federal Interagency Pass, Senior and Access discounts accepted.

Sites: 98 sites, singles and doubles. Limited hook-ups available.

Facilities: Modern facilities with hot showers.

Directions: From I-26, take Exit 33 onto US 191. Travel south on US 191 approximately 2 miles to traffic light, turn right to the Lake Powhatan entrance.

Popular Camping Regions In The Mountains

Blue Ridge Parkway Campgrounds

There are six campgrounds open to the public on the Parkway in North Carolina from May 1 through October or into early November, depending on weather conditions. Facilities are limited in winter. Fees are charged and length of stay may be limited. Camping is permitted only in designated campgrounds. Drinking water and comfort stations are provided; shower and laundry facilities are not. Sites in each campground are designated for trailers but none is equipped for utility connections. Campgrounds have sanitary dumping stations. Each campsite has a table and fireplace. Limited supplies may be purchased at most Parkway gasoline stations and camp stores. For further information, call the Blue Ridge Parkway headquarters at 828-298-0398. (*See* also Section 5, Chapter 1)

Milepost 241.1: Doughton Park

Milepost 297.1: Julian Price Memorial Park

Milepost 316.4: Linville Falls

Milepost 339.5: Crabtree Meadows

Milepost 408.6: Mount Pisgah

Milepost 418.8: Graveyard Fields

Pisgah National Forest Campgrounds

The Pisgah National Forest is a land of mile-high peaks, cascading waterfalls and heavily forested slopes. It is an ideal place, as are all of the national forests, for outdoor recreation. Located on two sides of Asheville, the forest is more than 490,000 acres and spreads over 12 Western North Carolina counties. The forest is more or less divided in half by the Blue Ridge Parkway, and the Appalachian Trail runs along its border with Tennessee. The Mountains-to-the-Sea Trail crosses through the forest. Pisgah National Forest contains three wilderness areas: Middle Prong, Linville Gorge and the Shining Rock section, and is divided into four districts: Pisgah District, French Broad District, Grandfather District and Tocane District. The Pisgah District of the forest borders the Asheville/Hendersonville area. This magnificent forest is easily accessible from many points and offers wonderful camping facilities. Keep in mind that there are some rules governing camping in national forests. You can pitch your tent just about anywhere providing you are 100 feet or more from all water sources, at least 1,000 feet from the road and there are no signs prohibiting camping. Pets must be under control and on a leash when you are near people or a campground. For more information about camping in the forest, call 828-257-4200. (*See* also Section 5, Chapter 1)

Great Smoky Mountains National Park Campgrounds

The Great Smoky Mountains, which lie along the common border of Tennessee and North Carolina, form a majestic climax to the Appalachian Highlands. With outlines softened by a forest mantle, the mountains stretch away to remote horizons in sweeping troughs that recede to evenness in the distance. Shrouding the peaks is a smoke-like mist that rises from the dense plant growth. The mountains get their name from this deep blue mist. The park's boundary wraps around 800 square miles of mountain wilderness, most of it virtually unspoiled. Many peaks rise above 6,000 feet. A great variety of trees, shrubs, herbs and other plants are nourished by the fertile land and heavy rainfall and rushing streams. The Great Smoky Park contains more than 700 miles of rivers and streams, over 200,000 acres of virgin forests, and over 850 miles of trails. It is the most visited national park with over 9,000,000 visitors a year. (*See* also Section 5, Chapter 1)

Appalachian Trail

The Appalachian Trail is a 2,167 mile footpath from Maine to Georgia which follows the ridge tops of the fourteen states through which it passes. Each day, as many as two hundred backpackers are in the process of hiking the full length of the trail. More than 250 backcountry shelters are located along the Appalachian Trail at varying intervals, as a service to all Appalachian Trail hikers. A typical shelter, sometimes called a "lean-to," has a shingled or metal roof, a wooden floor and three walls and is open to the elements on one side. Most are near a creek or spring, and many have a privy nearby. Hikers occupy them on a first-come, first-served basis until the shelter is full. They are intended for individual hikers, not big groups. (*See* also Section 5, Chapter 1)

Cycling & Mountain Biking

Biking is a very popular recreation in the mountains, with road cycling the main attraction followed closely by off-road and mountain biking. Scenic vistas winding country and mountain roads and a wide variety of terrain make for some of the best bicycle touring in the world. Because of this fact, Asheville was one of the stops in the Tour Dupont, which used the Grove Park Inn Resort as race headquarters, and notable biking professionals regularly visit the mountains to ride. And as far as mountain and off-road biking goes, Western North Carolina is second to none in that category. Some of the

world's greatest mountain biking trails can be found in Western North Carolina and thousands of enthusiasts flock here every year for just that reason.

Local bookstores and bicycle shops carry specialty guidebooks on biking in Western North Carolina that offer maps and trails advice, beyond the scope of what is presented here. One of the best for visitors who wish to find some road biking routes is *Road Bike Asheville*. This informative guide describes sixteen road-biking routes in and around Asheville that the Blue Ridge Bicycle Club of Asheville sees as tops. The bicycle shops listed below can give you personal advice as to mountain biking trails in the mountains as well as additional road routes.

Near Asheville, excellent off-road riding can be found in the nearby Pisgah District of the Pisgah National Forest. This section of the forest has more than 400 miles of trails. Check in at the Ranger Station Visitor Center, 1½ miles west of NC 280 on U.S. 276 and pick up a copy of their trail map. The Bent Creek section of the forest near Asheville is an especially popular riding area, as is the nearby North Mills River Recreation Area and the Dupont State Forest near Hendersonville. An excellent online resource for mountain biking, including area maps and trail information can be found on the Mountain Biking in Western North Carolina website.

In addition to the many opportunities for road and mountain biking, Asheville also has its own racing oval located at 220 Amboy Road in the Asheville Parks and Recreation Carrier Park. Formerly the old Asheville Motor Speedway, this park is open to the public for multiple outdoor activities, including track racing. Cyclocross racing also has caught on in Western North Carolina as well. This discipline involves short off-road races in a circuit-race format with a one to two mile course, short, steep hills and a variety of surfaces from pavement to mud and sand.

Asheville Area Bicycle Clubs, Organizations & Training Centers

Asheville Bicycle Racing Club: Non-profit Asheville based organization established for the purpose of promoting amateur bicycle racing in Western North Carolina. www.abrc.net

Asheville Triathlon Club: Non-profit multisport club based in Asheville. www.ashevilletri.com

Asheville Women's Cycling Club: All-female cycling club. Road racing, mountain biking, cyclo-cross, track racing, triathlons and adventure racing. Also professional all-female racing team. www.ashevillewomenscycling.com

Blue Ridge Bicycle Club of Asheville: Premier Western North Carolina bicycle club includes both mountain and road cyclists. Blue Ridge Bicycle Club, PO Box 309, Asheville NC 28802. www.ashevillewomenscycling.com

Velosports Performance Center: Cycle training and performance center. Indoor facility. 200 Racquet Club Road, Asheville NC 28803, 828-274-3361. www.ashevillevelosports.com

Pisgah Area SORBA: Pisgah chapter of the Southeastern Off-Road Bike Association. PO Box 61, Skyland NC 28776. 770-654-3291. www.pisgahareasorba.org

Western North Carolina Unicyclists: http://wncunicycle.webs.com

Other Bicycle Clubs, Organizations & Training Centers

Blue Ridge B.I.T.S.: Local Hendersonville road and mountain biking club. http://sports.groups.yahoo.com/group/BlueRidgeBITS/

Bushy Mountain Cyclists Club: Club based in North Wilkesboro, North Carolina. PO Box 1281, North Wilkesboro NC 28659 http://www.bmcc.us

Great Smoky Mountains Triathlon Club: Non-profit multisport club based in Hayesville.828-389-6982. http://thebeastoftheeast.net/index1.htm

IMBA International Mountain Bicycling Association: IMBA works to keep trails open for mountain bikers by encouraging responsible riding and supporting volunteer trail work. 207 Canyon, Suite 301, Boulder CO 80302. 303-545-9011. http://www.imba.com/nmbp

Southern Appalachian Bicycling Association: PO Box 461, Hayesville NC 28804. http://sabacycling.com/

USA Cycling: National cycling organization based in Colorado Springs, Colorado. 719-434-4200. http://www.usacycling.org/mtb/

Bicycle Shops in the Asheville-Hendersonville Area

Bike Ways: 607 Greenville Highway, Hendersonville NC 29792; 828-692-0613

Biowheels: 81 Coxe Avenue, Asheville NC 28801; 828-236-2455.

Carolina Fatz Cycling Center: 1240 Brevard Road, Suite #3, Asheville NC 28806; 828-665-7744

Hearn's Cycling & Fitness: 34 Broadway, Asheville NC 28801; 828-253-4800.

Liberty Bicycles: 1378 Hendersonville Hwy., Asheville NC 28803, 828-274-2453.

Suspension Experts: (Bike repair, parts) 89 Thompson Street, Unit K, Asheville NC 28803; 828-255-0205

The Bicycle Company: 779 N. Church Street, Hendersonville NC 28792; 828-696-1500.

Pro Bikes: 610-B Haywood Road, Asheville NC 28806; 828-253-2800.

Ski Country Sports: 1000 Merrimon Avenue, Asheville NC 28804; 828-254-0901.

Youngblood Bicycles: 233 Merrimon Avenue, Asheville NC 28801; 828-251-4686.

Bicycle Shops in Western North Carolina

Boone: Boone Bike and Touring: 899 Blowing Rock Road, Boone NC 28807; 828-262-5750.

Franklin: Smoky Mountain Bicycles: 179 Highlands Road, Franklin NC 28734; 828-369-2881.

Pisgah Forest: Sycamore Cycles: 112 New Hendersonville Highway, Pisgah Forest, NC 28768; 828-877-5790.

Saluda: Keiths Triathlon Shop: 171 East Main Street, Saluda NC 28773; 828-749-1816.

Sylva: Motion Makers Bicycle Shop: 552 West Main Street, Sylva NC 28779; 828-586-6925.

Disc Golf & Ultimate Frisbee

Disc Golf and Ultimate Frisbee are two sports that are growing in popularity throughout Western North Carolina. There are a number of PDGA disc golf courses in the greater Asheville area, as well as others scattered throughout the mountains. If ultimate Frisbee is your game, your best resource is the Asheville-based Asheville Ultimate Club. They can be reached at 828-777-6115 for more information. The annual Mountain Sports Festival features competitions in both disc golf and ultimate Frisbee. The disc golf courses in the Asheville area are listed below. For a complete listing of all disc golf courses in Western North Carolina, visit my guidebook website at www.ashevilleguidebook.com.

Crookston Disc Golf Course: 9 holes, 4312 feet, occupies half of a 60- acre park with some open holes and several curving into the woods along a large creek.; 85 Howard Gap Road, Fletcher NC 28732; 828-687-0751.

Richmond Hill Park Disc Golf Course: 18 holes, 4935 feet, hilly, wooded course.; 280 Richmond Hill Drive, Asheville NC 28806; 828-251-1122.

Buncombe County Sports Park: 6 holes; 58 Apac Circle, Candler NC 28715; 828-250-4260.

Golf in the Mountains

Golf is a major attraction in the mountains and the mild climate offers nearly four seasons on courses that range from wide river valleys and rolling terrains to fairways that pitch and roll to challenge even the most experienced golfer. The golf courses that allow public play in the greater Asheville area are listed below. For a complete listing of all golf courses in Western North Carolina, visit my guidebook website at www.ashevilleguidebook.com.

Asheville's standout courses are the prestigious Grove Park Inn Resort & Spa and the beautiful Reems Creek Golf Club course in Weaverville. Access to the Grove Park Inn Resort & Spa course is generally limited to guests of the hotel while the Reems Creek Golf Club course is open to the public. Asheville has a number of driving ranges. These include Jake's Driving Range, Highway 25 North, Naples NC 28760 (just south of Asheville), 828-684-8086, and the Practice Tee & Golf Shop at 161 Azalea Rd. East, Asheville NC 28805. 828-298-0123.

Asheville/Hendersonville Area Golf Courses That Allow Public Play

Asheville Municipal Golf Course: 226 Fairway Dr., Asheville NC 28805, 828-298-1867; Public; 18-holes.

Black Mountain Golf Club: 18 Ross Drive, Black Mountain NC 28711; 828-669-2710; Semi-Private; 18-holes; travel time from Asheville: 30 minutes east.

Broadmoor Golf Links: 101 French Broad Lane, Fletcher NC 28732; 866-578-5847; Public; 18-holes.

Migration of the Monarch Butterflies

A marvelous natural phenomenon that can be seen in the fall is the migration of the Monarch butterflies through the Western North Carolina mountain valleys as they make their way south on their long pilgrimage to Mexico, where they spend the winter in the Sierra Madre mountains.

Monarchs that emerge in late summer and autumn in the Western North Carolina mountains are different than their cousins born earlier in the summer, as the shorter, cooler days of fall postpone the development of their reproductive organs. This, plus changes in light and temperature (perhaps along with other factors not yet understood) cues these butterflies to take to the skies, migrating hundreds and even thousands of miles across the continent to warmer wintering grounds. They are strong, fast fliers, reaching speeds of ten to thirty miles per hour. Along the way, they get nourishment from plants, fattening themselves for the coming winter. This migration usually takes place from August to October, reaching a peak usually the third week in September. An excellent viewing site is the Cherry Cove Overlook on the Blue Ridge Parkway seven miles south of Pisgah Inn.

Connestee Falls Golf Course: 33 Connestee Trail, Brevard NC 28712; 828-885-2005; Semi-Private; 18-holes; travel time from Asheville: 1 hour west.

Crooked Creek Golf Course: Crooked Creek Rd., Hendersonville NC 28739; 828-692-2011; Public; 18-holes; travel time from Asheville: 45 minutes south.

Crowne Plaza Golf Course: One Resort Drive, Asheville NC 28806; 828-253-5874; Resort/public; 18-holes.

Cummings Cove Golf & Country Club: 20 Cummings Cove Parkway, Hendersonville NC 28739; 828-891-9412; Semi-private; 18-holes; travel time from Asheville: 45 minutes south.

Glen Cannon Country Club: 337 Glen Cannon Road, Brevard NC 28712; 828-883-8175; Semi-private; 18 holes; travel time from Asheville: 1 hour west.

Grove Park Inn Resort & Spa: 290 Macon Ave., Asheville NC 28804; 800-438-5800; Resort; 18-holes.

High Vista Country Club: 88 Country Club Road, Mills River NC 28759; 828-891-1986; Semi-private;18-holes.

Orchard Trace Golf Club: 942 Sugarloaf Rd., Hendersonville NC 28792; 828-685-1006; Public; 18-holes; travel time from Asheville: 1 hour south.

Reems Creek Golf Club: 36 Pink Fox Cove Rd., Weaverville NC 28787; 828-645-4393; Semi-Private; 18-holes.

Southern Tee Golf Course: 111 Howard Gap Road, Fletcher NC 28732; 828-687-7273; Semi-Private; 18-holes.

Course Road: Waynesville NC 28786; 828-456-5777; Public; 18-holes; travel time from Asheville: 1 hour west.

Hiking & Backpacking

The mountains and valleys around Asheville and Hendersonville are a hiker's paradise. Hundreds of thousands of visitors come to this region every year just to hike and to experience the countless trails that range from short day hikes to the world famous Appalachian Trail.

The choice of possible hikes is to vast to be covered here. I strongly suggest that you first visit one of the outfitters mentioned at the start of this chapter. They will be able to help you make some good choices based on your preferences and skill level. These stores also have maps and books for sale about hiking in the mountains. There are also a number of hiking clubs in the mountains. For a complete list of these visit my guidebook website at www.ashevilleguidebook. com. The local office of the U.S. Forest Service is another valuable resource and can also answer questions you might have regarding hiking trails in the Pisgah and other national forests. Contact them at the U.S. Forest Service, P.O. Box 7148, Asheville NC 28802; 828-257-4200.

Because of the vast territory involved for possible hiking, some considerations should be made concerning planning and safety. For the most part, the Western North Carolina mountains are wilderness or semi-wilderness areas. That means there are a lot more trees and woods than people. Getting lost is a possibility if proper planning and cautions are not taken. In order to prevent any problems, you should always take the following precautions before venturing out into the woods on any hike that takes you away from civilization.

1. **Always check in at a ranger station or park headquarters** for the latest trail information before you leave. Trail conditions often change due to weather conditions, and knowing about any changes in advance can prevent much aggravation later. In addition, rangers know the trails and can best advise you regarding which trails to take, length of hikes and so on.
2. **Always leave word with someone about where you're going,** when you plan to leave and when you plan to return. In the worst case, this will insure that you will be searched for should you not return at the designated time.
3. **Always take a trail map on your hike,** unless it is a short self-guided nature trail or similar trail. Know how to read the map. Check with a local forest ranger if you have any questions about the map and the trail you intend to hike.
4. **If at all possible, never hike alone.** An injury alone in the woods can be life-threatening without someone else to assist or go for help.
5. **Lock valuables in the trunk of your car** or take them with you.
6. **Be prepared! Do your homework before you even start out.** Talk to professional outfitters to insure that you have the right hiking shoes, equipment,

food, first aid supplies and maps. Take plenty of food and water, and cold weather gear in the fall or spring.

7. **Never leave the trail.** Even experienced hikers can get lost by taking off-the-trail shortcuts.

8. **Do not drink the water in streams or springs.** Bacterial diseases can be contracted by drinking untreated "wild waters."

Hiking Trails Accessible From the Blue Ridge Parkway

Listed below are the hiking trails in North Carolina that can be accessed from the Blue Ridge Parkway. Keep in mind that Asheville is located around milepost 380 and getting to milepost 260, for example, 100 miles on the parkway, will take a good three hours driving time.

Milepost	Trail	Mileage*	Difficulty
217.5	Cumberland Knob Trail (ideal lazy-day walk)	0.5	Easy
217.5	Gully Creek Trail (rewarding loop that meanders by stream)	2.0	Strenuous
218.6	Fox Hunters Paradise Trail (view)	0.2	Easy
230.1	Little Glade Millpond (easy loop stroll around pond)	0.4	Easy
238.5	Cedar Ridge Trail (great for day hike; vistas and forests)	4.2	Moderate
238.5	Bluff Mountain Trail (parallels Parkway to milepost 244.7)	7.5	Moderate
241.0	Fodder Stack Trail (great variety of plants)	1.0	Moderate
241.0	Bluff Ridge Trail (primitive trail with steep slopes)	2.8	Moderate
243.7	Grassy Gap Fire Road (wide enough for side-by-side hiking)	6.5	Moderate
243.7	Basin Creek Trail (access from back-country campground)	3.3	Moderate
244.7	Flat Rock Ridge Trail (forest path with vistas)	5.0	Moderate
260.3	Jumpingoff Rocks Trail (forest path to vista)	1.0	Easy
264.4	The Lump Trail (to hilltop view)	0.3	Easy
271.9	Cascades Trail (self-guiding loop to view of falls)	0.5	Moderate
272.5	Tompkins Knob Trail (to Jesse Brown Cabin)	0.6	Easy
294.0	Rich Mountain Carriage, Horse & Hiking Trail	4.3	Moderate
294.0	Flat Top Mountain Carriage, Horse & Hiking Trail	3.0	Moderate
294.0	Watkins Carriage, Horse & Hiking Trail	3.3	Easy/Moderate
294.0	Black Bottom Carriage, Horse & Hiking Trail	0.5	Easy
294.0	Bass Lake Carriage, Horse & Hiking Trail	1.7	Easy
294.0	Deer Park Carriage, Horse & Hiking Trail	0.8	Moderate
294.0	Maze Carriage, Horse & Hiking Trail	2.3	Moderate
294.0	Duncan Carriage, Horse & Hiking Trail	2.5	Moderate
294.0	Rock Creek Bridge Carriage, Horse & Hiking Trail	1.0	Easy
294.1	Figure 8 Trail (short self-guiding loop around nature trail)	0.7	Easy
294.6	Trout Lake Hiking & Horse Trail (loop)	1.0	Easy
295.9	Green Knob Trail (to Green Knob)	2.3	Moderate/Strenuous
296.5	Boone Fork Trail (stream, forest and meadows)	5.5	Moderate/Strenuous
297.0	Price Lake Loop Trail (loop around Price Lake)	2.7	Moderate

* Mileage indicates length of trail one-way unless otherwise noted

Milepost	Trail	Mileage*	Difficulty
304.4	Linn Cove Viaduct Access Trail	0.16	Easy
305.2	Beacon Heights Trail (10 minutes to view)	0.2	Moderate
305.5	Tanawha Trail (diverse features, parallels Parkway to Price Park)	13.5	Moderate/Strenuous
308.2	Flat Rock Trail (self-guiding loop)	0.6	Easy
315.5	Camp Creek Trail (leg stretcher through laurel and rhododendron)	0.1	Easy
316.4	Linville Falls Trail (view of upper falls)	0.8	Moderate
316.4	Linville Gorge Trail (view of lower falls)	0.5	Strenuous
316.4	Duggers Creek Trail (loop to view of Duggers Falls)	0.25	Easy
316.5	Linville River Bridge Trail (leg stretcher to view of unusual bridge)	0.1	Easy
320.8	Chestoa View Trail (30-minute loop to vista)	0.6	Easy
339.5	Crabtree Falls Loop Trail (loop to view of falls)	2.5	Strenuous
344.1	Woods Mountain Trail (USES)	2.0	Moderate
350.4	Lost Cove Ridge Trail (USFS)	0.6	Moderate
351.9	Deep Gap Trail (USFS)	0.2	Easy
355.0	Bald Knob Ridge Trail (USFS)	0.1	Easy
359.8	Big Butt Trail (USFS) (trail continues on USFS lands)	0.2	Strenuous
361.2	Glassmine Falls (view of falls)	0.05	Moderate
364.2	Craggy Pinnacle Trail (to panoramic view)	0.7	Moderate
364.6	Craggy Gardens Trail (first portion is self-guiding nature trail)	0.8	Moderate
374.4	Rattlesnake Lodge Trail (woodland walk)	0.5	Moderate
382.0	Mountain-to-Sea Trail/MTS Trail (Folk Art Center to Mt. Mitchell; spring wildflowers & views, parallels Parkway; many accesses to trail segments)		Moderate/Strenuous
393.7	Shut-in Trail/MTS Trail (Bent Creek-Walnut Cove)	3.1	Strenuous
396.4	Shut-in Trail/MTS Trail (Walnut Cove-Sleepy Gap)	1.7	Moderate
397.3	Grassy Knob Trail (steep trail to USFS area)	0.9	Strenuous
397.3	Shut-in Trail/MTS Trail (Sleepy Gap-Chestnut Cove)	0.7	Moderate
398.3	Shut-in Trail/MTS Trail (Chestnut Cove-Bent Creek Gap)	2.8	Strenuous
400.3	Shut-in Trail/MTS Trail (Bent Creek Gap-Beaver Dam Gap)	1.9	Moderate
401.7	Shut-in Trail/MTS Trail (Beaver Dam Gap-Stoney Bald)	0.9	Moderate
402.6	Shut-in Trail/MTS Trail (Stoney Bald-Big Ridge)	1.2	Strenuous
403.6	Shut-in Trail/MTS Trail (Big Ridge-Mills River Valley)	1.1	Moderate/Strenuous
404.5	Shut-in Trail/MTS Trail (Elk Pasture Gap-Mt. Pisgah)	1.7	Strenuous
407.6	Mt. Pisgah Trail (summit view)	1.3	Moderate/Strenuous
407.6	Buck Springs Trail (Pisgah Lodge to view)	1.06	Easy/Moderate
408.5	Frying-Pan Mountain Trail	1.06	Moderate/Strenuous
417.0	East Fork Trail (USFS, access to Shining Rock Trail System)	0.1	Easy/Moderate
418.8	Graveyard Fields Loop Trail (loop by a stream)	2.3	Moderate
419.4	John Rock Trail (leg stretcher to view)	0.1	Easy

* Mileage indicates length of trail one-way unless otherwise noted

Milepost	Trail	Mileage*	Difficulty
422.4	Devil's Courthouse Trail (panoramic summit view)	0.4	Moderate/Strenuous
427.6	Bear Pen Gap Trail (access to Mountains-to-Sea Trail)	0.2	Easy
431.0	Richland Balsam Trail (self-guiding loop through spruce-fir forest	1.5	Moderate
433.8	Roy Taylor Overlook Trail (paved trail to overlook)	0.1	Easy
451.2	Waterrock Knob Trail (summit view; .6 mile one way)	1.2	Moderate/Strenuous

* Mileage indicates length of trail one-way unless otherwise noted

Horseback Riding

Horseback riding and horse shows are very popular activities in the mountains. Many local horse stables provide not only traditional riding instruction and facilities but also can serve as outfitters for trail rides into the hills and mountains. Asheville area stables and riding facilities are presented below. For a complete listing of most of the horse facilities in the mountains, visit my guidebook website at www.ashevilleguidebook.com.

Of interest to horse lovers is the Western North Carolina Agricultural Center in Asheville which regularly schedules championship horse shows and related events. Another major equestrian facility fairly close to Asheville and Hendersonville is the Foothills Equestrian Nature Center (FENCE), located in Tryon, which is about an hour's drive south. They have world-class equestrian facilities, steeplechase and cross-country courses and regularly host horse shows of all types and classes. Asheville has a number of tack stores including Balsam Quarter Tack at 521 Long Shoals Rd., Arden NC 28704, 828-684-8445, and Jackson's Western Store at 641 Patton Avenue, Asheville NC 28806, 828-254-1812.

Asheville/Hendersonville Area Riding Stables

Big Pine Ranch: 2-4 hour and all-day trail rides, overnight pack trips, lessons. Open 7-days a week; 2279 South Fork Road, Marshall NC 28753; 828-649-3176; travel time from Asheville: travel time from Asheville: 45 minutes north.

Biltmore Estate Equestrian Center: Lessons, boarding, clinics and 80 miles of estate trails, the same paths used by the Vanderbilts and guests at the turn of the century; Biltmore Estate, Asheville NC 28803; 828-225-1454.

Cane Creek Farm: 65-acre equestrian center offering boarding and training programs for both horse and rider; 912 Cane Creek Road, Fletcher NC 28732; 828-681-5975; travel time from downtown Asheville: 30 minutes.

Horseback riding is a popular pastime in WNC.

Clear Creek Guest Ranch: Guided trail rides for non ranch guests depending on availability; 100 Clear Creek Drive, Burnsville NC 28714; 828-675-4510; travel time from Asheville: 45 minutes north.

Encore Stables: Dressage and Hunter/Jumper instruction, full board with daily turnout and pasture board; 338 Young Drive Extension, Candler NC 28715; 828-665-0790; travel time from Asheville: 30 minutes west.

Foothills Equestrian Nature Center (FENCE): 380-acre non-profit nature and outdoor recreation center. FENCE's riding trails are normally open only to members of the Foothills Equestrian Trails Association; 3381 Hunting Country Road, Tryon NC 28782; 828-859-9021; travel time from Asheville: 1 hour south.

Laurel Park Riding Stables: Trail rides on 36 acres of forest, lighted riding arena and boarding; 1790 Davis Mountain Road, Hendersonville NC 28739; 828-692-0709: travel time from Asheville: 45 minutes south.

Pisgah Forest Riding Stables: 1-3 hour mountaintop or waterfall trail rides in Pisgah National Forest; 476 Pisgah Circle, Brevard NC 28712; 828-883-8258; travel time from Asheville: 1 hour west.

Pisgah View Ranch: Dude ranch and resort. Twice daily 1-3 hour trail rides; 70 Pisgah View Ranch Road, Candler NC 28715; 828-667-9100; travel time from Asheville: 30 minutes west.

Randal Glen Stables: Horses outfitted with Australian saddles, trails at 3100 feet above sea level and higher; 96 Randall Cove Road, Leicester NC 28748; 828-683-5758; travel time From downtown Asheville: 45 minutes.

Sandy Bottom Trail Rides: Trail rides for all ages accompanied by friendly, experienced guides; 1459 Caney Fork Road, Marshall NC 28753; 828-649-3464; travel time from Asheville: 1 hour north.

Wolf Laurel Stables at The Preserve at Wolf Laurel: Established equestrian facility, offering trail rides in the mountains around Wolf Laurel; 5860 Bald Mountain Road, Burnsville NC 28714; 828-682-1200; travel time from Asheville: 1 hour north.

Hot Air Balloon Rides

Are you interested in seeing the beautiful mountains and meadows of Western North Carolina from a unique perspective? Then a hot air balloon ride is for you! Flight times vary but a typical outing is from 45 minutes to an hour in the air and leave daily from April until January, weather permitting, at sunrise. The entire process from start to finish, including flight time, takes about 2½ hours. The balloon floats in the direction of the wind and can rise from 500 to 2000 feet in the air. Flights offered by the Asheville Hot Air Balloon Company (in business since 1981 and the only hot air balloon outfit in WNC) are typically above the countryside west of Asheville and include parts of the Pisgah National Forest.

Asheville Hot Air Balloons: 901 Smoky Park Highway, Candler NC 28715; 828-667-9943.

Llama Trekking

An unusual and popular way to experience the mountain trails is by llama trek. A couple of local companies offer guide service, camping gear, food and gentle llamas to carry the equipment. These friendly relatives of the camel are sure-footed and capable of carrying loads of up to 90 pounds. They are also kind to the trails and do much less damage than horses.

Hawksdene House Llama Treks: Short treks for guests of the Hawkedene House, April thru October; 381 Phillips Creek Road, Andrews NC 28901; 828-321-6027; Travel time from Asheville: 2 hours west.

English Mountain Llama Treks: Llama treks from day (picnic) hikes to two day hiking trips or longer. English Mountain has special use permit for both Pisgah and Nantahala National Forest; 767 Little Creek Road, Hot Springs NC 28743; 828-622-9686. Travel time from Asheville: 45 minutes northwest.

Miniature Golf

Throughout Western North Carolina there are a number of cities and towns that have miniature or "putt-putt" golf courses. This is family fun that even non-golfers enjoy! The Asheville area courses are presented below. For a complete listing of all miniature golf courses in the mountains, visit my guidebook website at www.ashevilleguidebook.com.

Asheville's Fun Depot: 18-hole indoor mini golf course with waterfall, bridges and pond; 7 Roberts Road #B, Asheville NC 28801; 828-277-2386.

Boyd Park: Hendersonville city park that has a free miniature golf course; Located between N. Main and Church Streets at 8th Street, Hendersonville NC 28792; 828-697-3084 (City of Hendersonville Parks Department); Travel time from Asheville: 45 minutes -1 hour south.

Outdoor Family Fun Center: 18-hole Harris designed mini golf course with waterfalls, ponds and spillways; 485 Brookside Camp Road, Hendersonville NC 28792; 828-698-1234; Travel time from Asheville: 45 minutes -1 hour south.

Shadowbrook Golf & Games: Two championship miniature golf courses with natural landscaping and water features; 701 Highway 9, Black Mountain NC 28711; 828-669-5499: Travel time from Asheville: 30 minutes east.

Tropical Gardens Mini Golf: Miniature golf course; 3956 Patton Avenue, Asheville NC 28806; 828-252-2207.

Rock & Mountain Climbing

The mountains of Western North Carolina offer a fabulous wealth of climbing opportunities if you are interested in rock, ice or mountain climbing. Rock cliffs, outcroppings, and slopes are to be found in endless abundance, and every year, thousands of professional and amateur climbers alike visit our area to test their skills. There are three outdoor stores in Asheville that can offer you professional and competent advice on local climbs: Black Dome, Diamond Brand Outdoors and REI. See the section at the start of this chapter for addresses of these stores.

Climbing Centers

Climbmax Climbing Center: A climbing center located in downtown Asheville offering instruction, guide services, apparel sales, and two on-site climbing walls -one 40-foot outdoor wall and an indoor climbing gym with a 20-foot wall geared to all skill levels, with staff on duty at all times to insure safety. 43 Wall Street, Asheville NC 28801, 828-252-9996.

Guide Services

Appalachian Mountain Institute: Guided rock and ice climbing near Asheville and Brevard North Carolina. AMGA certified guides. 77 Rhododendron Drive, Brevard NC 28712; 828-553-6323.

Climbmax Mountain Guides: Outdoor guided climbs range from local one-day climbs to multi-day Alpine-class climbs. AMGA certified guides. 43 Wall Street, Asheville NC 288801; 828-252-9996.

Fox Mountain Guides and Climbing School: Trips near Asheville, Boone, Chimney Rock and Charlotte. AMGA Certified guides. 951 Crab Creek Road, Hendersonville NC 28739; 888-284-8433.

Granite Arches Climbing Guides: Rock, ice and mountain climbing in the American Southeast and South America. AMGA Certified guides. 423-413-1432.

Rock Dimensions: Guided rock climbing, rappelling and caving. Courses range from beginner to advanced. 131-B S. Depot St. Boone, North Carolina 28607; 828-265-3544.

Rock Hounding & Gem Hunting

The mountains of Western North Carolina are one of the richest areas in the United States for gemstones and minerals. Two of the more popular gemstone areas in the mountains are centered around Franklin in the west and Spruce Pine in the east. There are close to 40 different minerals that rock hounds look for in the mountains. Corundum, beryl, moonstone, garnet, olivine, quartz, opal, amethyst, emerald, jasper, ruby, sapphire, spinel, turquoise, chrysoprase and zircon are among the most sought after. Gold also can still be found in some of the foothills streams.

Gemstone mines are very popular attrations open to the public, where you may sift through buckets of dirt to discover any treasure. Most mines sell "gem dirt" in a bucket or bag (few allow digging) and you may have to pay an admission fee for the day. You are provided with a screen for washing and there is a flume—a trough of running water—with a bench along its length. The dirt goes in the screen, the screen goes in the water and the mud is washed away. Depending on the mine, the buckets provided are either native ore or enriched with ore from other countries. A list of those mines that use only native ore is presented in this chapter.

For serious rock hounds, the best resource available in planning your visit to the mountains is MAGMA (Mountain Area Gem and Mineral Association,www. wncrocks.com, 828-683-1048). There are privately owned mines in the mountains where you may collect for modest daily fees, but you need to plan in advance. Two of these are Crabtree Emerald Mine in Spruce Pine and Little Pine Garnet Mine in Madison County.

A great place to see gems in Asheville is the Colburn Earth Science Museum at Pack Place. Also fairly close to Asheville is the Museum of North Carolina Minerals at Milepost 331 on the Blue Ridge Parkway. In the Hendersonville area is the newly opened Mineral & Lapidary Museum of Henderson County. The Franklin Gem and Mineral Museum in Franklin also has interesting exhibits of regional minerals and gemstones.

Resources

Henderson County Gem & Mineral Society: PO Box 6391, Hendersonville NC 28793. http://hcgms.org

M.A.G.M.A -Mountain Area Gem and Mineral Association: PO Box 542, Leicester NC 28748; 828-683-1048. http://www.wncrocks.com/magma/ magma.html

North Carolina Geological Survey: Division of Land Resources, 1612 Mail Center, Raleigh NC 27699; 919-733-2423. http://www.geology.enr.state. nc.us/

Southern Appalachian Mineral Society: PO B ox 15461, Asheville NC 28813; 828-285-9470. http://www.main.nc.us/sams

U.S. Geological Survey (USGS): 12201 Sunrise Valley Drive, Reston VA 20192; 888-275-8747. www.usgs.gov

Museums & Mineral Centers

(See also SECTION FIVE, Chapter Two for more information on most of the centers listed below.)

Colburn Earth Science Museum: 2 South Pack Square, Asheville NC 28801; 828-254-7162

Emerald Village: 331 McKinney Mine Road, Spruce Pine NC 28777; 828-765-6463

Franklin Gem and Mineral Museum: 25 Phillips St., Franklin, NC 28734; 828-369-7831

Hiddenite Center: 316 Church Street, Hiddenite, NC 28636; 828-632-6966

Linville Caverns: Highway 19929 US Highway221 North, Marion NC 28752; 800-419-0540

Mineral & Lapidary Museum of Henderson County: 400 N. Main Street, Hendersonville NC 28792; 828-698-1977

Museum of North Carolina Minerals: Blue Ridge Parkway, Milepost 331, Spruce Pine; 828-765-2761

North Carolina Mining Museum: 331 McKinney Mine Road, Spruce Pine NC 28777; 828-765-6463

Ruby City Gems Museum: 130 East Main Street, Franklin NC 28734; 828-524-3967

Gem Mines

For a complete listing of all gem mines in the mountains, visit my guidebook website at www.ashevilleguidebook.com. The mines presented below are a selection of established facilities that do not "enhance" their ore with imported gemstones but use only native ore.

Cherokee Ruby and Sapphire Mine: Only native gemstone ore from the Cowee Valley; 41 Cherokee Mine Road, Franklin NC 28734; 828-349-2941; Travel time From Asheville: 2 hours west.

Emerald Hollow Mine: Native gem ore, including emeralds, from their own mine;484 Emerald Hollow Mine Drive, Hiddenite NC 28636; 866-600-4367;

The World's Largest Blue Star Sapphire

Located just a short drive west of Asheville in Canton is the Old Pressley Sapphire Mine. In 1986 and 1987, two blue sapphires were found there that were truly spectacular. Craig Peden and Steve Meyers, prospecting in the area of the mine, found one that was 1035 carats and was named the "Southern Star." At the time it was the world's largest. Around the same time, Bruce Camanitti found an even larger one. When it was cut in 1988, it was named the "Star of the Carolinas" and was an astounding 1445 carats! It is listed in the Guiness Book of World Records, and was cut by the master gem cutter, John Robinson.

Travel time from Asheville: 1-1½ hours east.

Emerald Village: Native gem ore from their mine and other area mines; 331 McKinney Mine Road, Spruce Pine NC 28777; 828-765-6463, 828-765-0000; Travel time from Asheville: 1-1½ hours east.

Gem Mountain Gemstone Mine: Covered flumes. Gem ore brought in daily from mines; Highway 226, Spruce Pine NC 28777; 888-817-5829; travel time from Asheville: 1-1½ hours east.

Mason's Ruby & Sapphire Mine: Native gem ore where you dig your dirt from their own mine; 6961 Upper Burningtown Road, Franklin NC 28734; 828-369-9742; Travel time from Asheville: 2 hours west.

Old Pressley Sapphire Mine: World's largest blue star sapphires were found at this mine. Only native gemstone ore; 240 Old Pressley Mine Road, Canton NC 28716; 828-648-6320; Travel time from Asheville: 45 minutes west.

Mason Mountain Mine & Cowee Gift Shop: Native gem ore where you dig your dirt from their own mine. Also enriched buckets with imported ore; 5315 Bryson City Road, Franklin NC 28734; 828-524-4570; Travel time from Asheville: 2 hours west.

Rose Creek Mine: Native gem ore where you dig your own dirt from their own mine; 115 Terrace Ridge Drive, Franklin NC 28734; 828-349-3774; Travel time from Asheville: 2 hours west.

Sheffield Mine: Native ruby and sapphire gem ore from their own mine; 385 Sheffield Farms Road, Franklin NC 28734; 828-369-8383; Travel time from Asheville: 2 hours west.

Spruce Pine Gemstone Mine: Native gem ore from local gem mines; 15090 Highway 226 South, Spruce Pine NC 28777; 828-765-7981; Travel time from Asheville: 1-1½ hours east.

Running

Asheville Track Club: Since its founding in 1972, the Asheville Track Club has been instrumental in promoting running as a sport and providing a means for interested individuals to participate and improve as runners. Their website (http://ashevilletrackclub.org) has the most comprehensive race calendar for Western North Carolina. One of the more important annual races on the calendar is their Bele Chere 5K, held in August in downtown Asheville during the festival.

Asheville Lightning Junior Olympics Team: For youths aged 6 to 18, Asheville also has one of the country's premier summer youth track and field teams, the Asheville Lightning. For more information visit their website at www.ashevillelightning.org.

Blue Ridge Classic: For track and field enthusiasts, an outstanding high school track and field meet, the Blue Ridge Classic, is held at A.C. Reynolds High School in Asheville every spring. This popular Saturday meet features thousands of elite high school athletes from all over the southeast, a Friday evening 5K open to the public, and great food in a beautiful mountain setting. More information on meet website at www.blueridgeclassic.org.

Running Stores in the Asheville-Hendersonville Area

Foot RX Running: 63 Turtle Creek Drive, Asheville NC 28803; 828-277-5151.

Jus' Running: 523 Merrimon Avenue, Asheville NC 28804; 828-252-7867.

Shuffleboard

Toms Park: Located on West Allen Street in Hendersonville, it is the site of state and national shuffleboard tournaments. 27 shuffleboard courts. For more information, call the Hendersonville Shuffleboard Club at 828-697-3016.

Skateboarding

Western North Carolina has a number of cities and towns that have public skate parks. The more popular ones are the City of Asheville Food Lion Skate Park, Zero Gravity Skate Park, the huge indoor facility in Brevard, and the City of Hendersonville Skate Park.

Asheville Food Lion Skate Park: 17,000 square feet, unique concrete park with three distinctive areas in the beginner bowl, intermediate street course and an advanced vertical bowl. Safe challenging skate park facility for all ages.; 50 North Cherry Street, Asheville NC 28801; 828-225-7184.

Black Mountain Skate Park: Skate park maintained by the Black Mountain Recreation Department.; 101 Carver Avenue, Carver Community Center, Black 28711; 828-669-2052; Travel time from Asheville: 30 minutes east.

BP Skate Park: Indoor facility. Quarter and mini ramps, bank with 2 huba ledges and hand rail, camel humps and vert walls.; 171A Muse Business Park, Waynesville NC 28786; 828-452-0011; Ttravel time from Asheville: 1 hour west.

Hendersonville Skate Park: 20,000 square feet, skate park in Patton Park.; Asheville Highway and Clairmont Drive, Hendersonville NC 28792;828-551-3270; Travel time from Asheville: 45 minutes south.

Zero Gravity Skate Park: 12,000 square feet indoor skating facility, largest in Western North Carolina Spine mini-ramp, fun boxes, mini three-quarter bowl, bank ramps, launch boxes, a pyramid, ledges and roll-ins.; 1800 Old Hendersonville Road, Brevard NC 28712; 828-862-6700; Travel time from Asheville: 1 hour west.

Skiing & Snowboarding

The slopes of the Western North Carolina mountains provide a wide variety of trails, from easy beginner to expert. The views are breathtaking and the facilities modern. Many of the resorts feature their own snow making equipment. Most people don't associate the south with skiing, but the Western North Carolina mountains, with their higher elevations and colder winters, do have excellent skiing and snowboarding. Wolf Ridge Ski Slopes, the closest to Asheville is a 30-minute drive north on Highway 19/23.

Skiing & Snowboarding Facilities

Appalachian Ski Mountain: Ten slopes, two quad chairlifts, one double chairlift, outdoor ice skating. Excellent ski school and a large number of family-oriented programs; 940 Ski Mountain Road, Blowing Rock NC 28605; 828-295-7828, 800-322-2373; travel time from Asheville: 2 hours east

Beech Mountain Resort: Beech Mountain is the highest ski area in eastern North America at 5,506 feet. One high-speed quad lift, six doubles, one J-bar and one rope tow. Skiing, snowboarding and tubing; 1007 Beech Mountain Parkway, Beech Mountain NC 28604; 828-387-2011; travel time from Asheville: 2 hours east.

Cataloochee Ski Area: Fourteen slopes and trails. Full-service rental shop and PSIA ski school. Cataloochee is the oldest ski resort in North Carolina; 1080 Ski Lodge Road, Maggie Valley NC 28751; 828-926-0285, 800-768-0285; travel time from Asheville: 2 hours east.

Hawksnest Tubing Park: Biggest snow tubing operation on the east coast. Four different areas to snow tube with over 20 lanes. Two moving carpet lifts.

Located between Boone and Banner Elk; 2058 Skyland Drive, Seven Devils NC 28604; 828-963-8681, 800-822-4295; travel time from Asheville: 1½-2 hours west.

Sapphire Valley Ski Area: Two runs, one each for for beginner and intermediate skiing and snowboarding; 4350 Highway 64 West, Sapphire NC 28774; 828-743-7663; travel time from Asheville 1½-2 hours west.

Scaly Mountain Outdoor Center: Four slopes, snow tubing only. Also summer tubing on artificial turf slopes; 7420 Dillard Road, Scaly Mountain NC 28775; 828-526-3737; travel time from Asheville: 2-2½ hours west.

Sugar Mountain Resort: A full-service alpine snow ski and snowboard area. Features a 1,200-foot vertical drop, 18 slopes and trails, eight lifts, and a longest run of 1½ miles. Tubing, ice skating and snowshoeing also; 1009 Sugar Mountain Drive, Banner Elk NC 28604; 828-898-4521, 800-784-2768; travel time from Asheville: 1½ hours east.

Wolf Ridge Ski Slopes: 4 lifts/ and 4 magic carpet lifts: 2 full service Ski Lodges: 23 ski runs. 25 minutes north of Asheville NC and only 5 miles off the new I-26 Wolf Laurel Exit # 3 Interchange. 578 Valley View Circle, Mars Hill NC 28754; 800-817-4111; travel time from Asheville: 30 minutes north.

Spelunking & Caving

Spelunking is the official name used for the recreational activity of exploring caves but it is more commonly referred to as "caving". Like skydiving and rock climbing, caving is about as adventurous as it gets, and while going out on your own is possible, the best advice is to hook up with a professional cave guide company and let them plan your outing and guide you. The Linville Caverns, located south of Boone, are open to the public and are a good place to experience caving in a safe and controlled environment without the need of hiring a guide.

Linville Caverns: Hwy. 221 North (P.O. Box 567), Marion NC 28752; 800-419-0540, 828-756-4171; Travel time from Asheville: 1 hour east.

Caving Guides

High Mountain Expeditions: 3149 Tynecastle Highway, Banner Elk 28604; 800-262-9036, 828-264-7368; Travel time from Asheville: 2 hours east.

River and Earth Adventures, Inc: 1655 Highway 105, Boone NC 28607; 800-411-7238, 828-963-5491; Travel time from Asheville: 2-2½ hours west.

Rock Dimensions: 131-B South Depot Street, Boone NC 28607; 828-265-3544; Travel time from Asheville: 2 hours east.

Swimming

In Asheville, the Buncombe County Parks, Greenways and Recreation Services offers five outdoor pools located in different areas of Buncombe County. The pools are open in June, July and the early part of August. The water is heated in every pool and there is a small admission fee per person. The City of Asheville

Parks, Recreation and Cultural Arts Department has three outdoor public swimming pools, with Recreation Park on Gashes Creek Road the nearest to downtown of any county or city pool. The city pools are open June through Mid-August and also charge a small fee for swimming.

If lake swimming is what you want, nearby Lake Lure has a public beach and is your best bet. While there, plan to check out the famous Chimney Rock attraction and also consider an evening boat ride on the lake. Tours leave from the town dock area.

An absolutely unique mountain water experience, especially on a hot summer day, is the extremely popular Sliding Rock located on the Davidson River in Pisgah National Forest, about an hour's drive west from Asheville in the Brevard area, Sliding Rock is a natural 60-foot long waterslide ending in a 7-foot deep pool that has been developed by the US Forest Service into a recreation area. From the intersection of US 276 and US 64 in Pisgah Forest, NC (near Brevard), go about eight miles north into the National Forest on US 276 toward the Blue Ridge Parkway. You will pass Looking Glass Falls on the right after five miles. Look for signs directing you to the Sliding Rock recreation area parking lot on the left.

Selected City of Asheville and Buncombe County Pools

Cane Creek Pool: 590 Lower Brush Creek Rd., Fletcher NC 28732; 828-628-4494

Erwin Community Pool: 55 Lees Creek Rd., Asheville NC 28806; 828-251-4992

North Buncombe Park Pool: 82 Clarks Chapel Rd., Weaverville NC 28787; 828-645-1080

Owen Pool: 117 Stone Dr., Swannanoa NC 28778; 828-686-1629

Recreation Park: (Closest to downtown) 65 Gashes Creek Road, Asheville NC 28805; 828-298-0880

Tennis

For tennis players, many mountain cities and towns have city parks that have tennis courts available for public play. In Asheville, the Asheville Parks and Recreation Department lists a total of 32 public tennis courts on their website. Information about these courts, as well as the annual city Open Tennis Tournament for Junior and Adult divisions held each July, can be obtained by calling the Asheville Parks and Recreation Department, 828-259-5800. Asheville area courts are presented below. For a complete listing of tennis facilities open to the public, visit my guidebook website at www.ashevilleguidebook.com.

Aston Park Tennis Center: City of Asheville Parks and Recreation public facility. Aston Park Tennis Center is one of the finest public clay court facilities in the United States. There are 12 lighted clay courts designed and constructed of the HarTru Fast Dry clay court material. Open April to December. Reservations & fees to play; 336 Hilliard Avenue, Asheville NC 28801; 828-251-4074.

Jackson Park: Eight tennis courts in the best Hendersonville park; 801 Glover Street, Hendersonville NC 28792; 828-697-4884.

Weaver Park: Very easy to find North Asheville park located on Merrimon Avenue. Park and tennis courts will be on the right. No reservations needed—first come, first served basis; Merrimon Avenue, Asheville NC 28801; 828-258-2453.

Whitewater Rafting, Canoeing & Kayaking

The rivers of Western North Carolina and the Tennessee border offer Class I through Class IV rapids for whitewater rafting. Major rafting rivers are the French Broad, Nolichucky, Nantahala, Ocoee, Chattooga and Green River. These six rivers mountains are considered the best whitewater in the Southeast. Of the many whitewater rafting companies in the mountains, none has a better reputation than the Nantahala Outdoor Center. Their center, located on the Nantahala River near Bryson City, is a sure bet if you are looking for a first class, professional whitewater experience.

The closest whitewater rafting companies to Asheville are USA Raft, Blue Heron Whitewater and French Broad Rafting Expeditions, all located on the French Broad River, 30 minutes north in Marshall. If you want to get on a river, and whitewater is not a must, check out the Asheville Outdoor Center located right in Asheville. They offer gentle tubing, rafting, kayaking and canoeing on the French Broad River.

There are few better ways to experience the excitement of the mountains than a whitewater rafting trip, and Western North Carolina has it all, from peaceful gentle streams to big tumbling rivers that roar through the deepest gorges. The most popular whitewater stream for professional and amateur alike is the Nantahala River in the Bryson City area. A class II and III stream, the Nantahala begins in the mountains of Macon County and flows northward through the beautiful Nantahala Gorge and on into Graham County where it joins the Little Tennessee River. The eight-mile run on the Nantahala takes about three hours. Be advised, though, on summer weekends the river can get very crowded.

Located north of Asheville in Woodfin on the French Broad River, the Ledges Whitewater Park is the closest whitewater section of the river for canoeing and kayaking without guided service. This is recommended for experienced canoeists and kayakers only. The Ledges play spots, of which there are several, begin to warm up at levels over 1,000 cfs, and rise to 3,500 cfs. The park is complete with movable holding "gates" that kayakers can paddle through to practice for slalom competition and to improve their dexterity and water skills. To get there from Asheville, take I-240 to 19-23 North (Exit 4) and continue six miles to the New Stock Road exit. Turn left off the exit ramp and drive 0.7 miles to left on Aiken Road, then first right onto Goldview Road. Follow Goldview Road to the river. Turn right onto NC 251. The Ledges Whitewater Park and Picnic Area will be on your right almost immediately. If you wish, you can continue north on NC 251 2.0 miles to the Alexander Bridge for put-in.

Stream Classifications

Class I: Easy. Moving water with a few riffles, small waves and few obstructions. Requires basic paddling know-ledge.

Class II: Moderate. Easy rapids with up to three-foot waves and few obstructions. Requires intermediate skill level.

Class III: Difficult. High rapids and narrow channels. Requires intermediate skill level.

Class IV: Very difficult. Long difficult rapids, constricted channels and turbulent water. Requires experienced skill level.

Class V: Exceedingly difficult. Extremely difficult, long and often violent rapids. Requires high skill level.

Class VI: Utmost difficulty. Very dangerous and for experts only.

Western Mountains (From Murphy to Waynesville)

Adventurous Fast Rivers Rafting: Nantahala River; 14690 Highway 19 West, Bryson City NC 28713; 800-438-7238, 828-488-2386; Travel time from Asheville: 1½ -2 hours west to Nantahala River location.

Appalachian Rivers Raft Company: Nantahala River; US Highway 19, Topton NC 28781; 800-330-1999; Travel time from Asheville: 1½ -2 hours west to Nantahala River location.

Blue Ridge Outing Co: Nantahala and Tuckaseegee Rivers; 11044 Highway 19 West, Bryson City NC 28713; 800-468-7238, 828-488-6345; Travel time from Asheville: 1½ -2 hours west to Nantahala River location.

Carolina Outfitters: Nantahala River; 12121 Highway 19 West, Bryson City NC 28713; 800-572-3510; Travel time from Asheville: 1½ -2 hours west.

Dillsboro River Company: Tuckaseegee River; 18 Macktown Road, Sylva NC 28799; 866-586-3797; Travel time from Asheville: 1 hour west.

Endless River Adventures: Nantahala, Cheoah and Ocoee Rivers; 14157 US Highway 19/74 West, Bryson City NC 28713; 800-224-7238, 828-488-6199; Travel time from Asheville: 1½ -2 hours west to Nantahala River location.

Great Smokey Mountain Fish Camp & Safaris: Little Tennessee (Tubing & Canoe Rentals only); 1136 Bennett Road, Franklin NC 28734; 828-369-5295; Travel time from Asheville: 2 hours west to Franklin.

Headwater Outfitters: Canoeing, kayaking and tubing on the French Broad River. No whitewater rafting; 25 Parkway Road, Rosman NC 28772; 828-877-3106; Travel time from Asheville: 1½ hours west.

Nantahala Outdoor Center: Nantahala, Ocoee, Chattooga, Cheoah, Pigeon, French Broad and Nolichucky Rivers; 13077 Highway 19 West, Bryson City NC 28713; 828-488-2176, 888-905-7238; Travel time from Asheville: 1½ -2 hours west to Nantahala River location.

Paddle Inn Rafting Company: Nantahala River; 14611 US Highway 19 West, Bryson City NC 28713; 800-711-7238; Travel time from Asheville: 1½ -2 hours west.

Rolling Thunder River Company: Nantahala River; 10160 Highway 19 West, Bryson City NC 28713; 800-408-7238; Travel time from Asheville: 1½ -2 hours west.

Tuckaseegee Outfitters: Tuckaseegee River; 4909 Highway 74, Whittier NC 28789; 888-593-5050; Travel time from Asheville: 1½ -2 hours west.

USA Raft: Nantahala River; Bryson City NC 28713; 866-872-7238; Travel time from Asheville: 1½ -2 hours west

Wildwater Ltd. Rafting: Pigeon, Nantahala, Chattooga, Ocoee and Cheoah Rivers; 10345 Highway 19, Bryson City NC 28713; 866-319-8870, 828-488-2384; Travel time from Asheville: 1½ -2 hours west to Nantahala River location.

Central Mountains (From Waynesville through Asheville to Burnsville)

Asheville Outdoor Center: Canoeing, Kayaking, Rafting and Tubing the French Broad River. No whitewater rafting; 521 Amboy Road, Asheville NC 28806; 800-849-1970, 828-232-1970; Travel time from Asheville: In Asheville.

Big Creek Expeditions: Pigeon River; 3541 Hartford Road, Hartford TN 37753; 877-642-7238, 423-487-0178; Travel time From Asheville: 1 hour northwest.

Blue Heron Whitewater: French Broad River; 35 Little Pine Road, Marshall NC 28753; 888-426-7238; Travel time from Asheville: 30-45 minutes north.

Cherokee Adventures Inc: Rivers: Nolichucky, Watauga and Holston Rivers; 2000 Jonesborough Road, Erwin TN 37650; 800-445-7238, 423-743-7733; Ttravel time from Asheville: 1 hour northwest to Nolichucky River location.

French Broad Rafting Expeditions: French Broad River; 9800 US Highway 25-70, Marshall NC 28753; 800-570-7238: Travel time from Asheville: 30-45 minutes north.

Green River Adventures: Green River; 1734 Holbert Cove Road, Saluda NC 28773; 800-335-1530, 828-749-2800; Travel time from Asheville: 45 minutes south.

Huck Finn Rafting Adventures: French Broad River; 158 Bridge Street, Hot Springs NC 28743; 877-520-4658; Travel time from Asheville: 45 minutes northwest.

Loafers Glory Rafting: Toe and French Broad Rivers; 2637 Highway 226 North, Bakersville NC 28705; 828-208-9202, 866-933-5628; Travel time from Asheville: 1 hour west to Bakersville location.

Outdoor Rafting Adventures: Pigeon River; 3635 Trail Hollow Road, Hartford TN 37753; 866-333-7238, 423-487-2085; travel time from Asheville: 1 hour northwest.

Rapid Descent River Co: Pigeon River; 3195 Hartford Road, Hartford TN 37753; 800-455-8808; Travel time from Asheville: 1 hour northwest.

Rafting in the Smokies: Pigeon River; 3595 Hartford Road, Hartford TN 37753; 800-776-7238; Travel time from Asheville: 1 hour northwest.

Rip Roaring Adventures: Pigeon River; 3375 Hartford Road, Hartford TN 37753; 800-449-7238; Travel time from Asheville: 1 hour northwest.

USA Raft: French Broad River; 13490 US Highway 25-70, Marshall NC 28753; 866-872-7238; Travel time from Asheville: 30- 45 minutes north to the French Broad River location.

Wahoo Adventures: Watauga and Nolichucky Rivers; 1201 Rock Creek Road, Erwin TN 37650; 800-444-7238, 828-262-5774; Travel time from Asheville:.45 minutes -1 hour northwest to Nolichucky River location.

White Water Rafting: Pigeon River; 453 Brookside Village Way, Gatlinburg TN 37738; 800-771-7238, 865-430-3838; Travel time from Asheville: 1½ -2 hours northwest.

Northern Mountains (From Burnsville to Sparta)

High Mountain Expeditions: Watauga and Nolichucky Rivers, Wilson's Creek; 3149 Tynecastle Highway, Banner Elk NC 28604; 800-262-9036; Travel time from Asheville: 1½ -2 hours east to Banner Elk location.

River and Earth Adventures, Inc : Watauga and Nolichucky Rivers; 1655 Highway 105, Boone NC 28607; 800-411-7238, 828-963-5491; Travel time from Asheville: 2-2½ hours east.

Riverside Canoe: South Fork of the New River (Tubing and canoeing only), 2966 Garvey Bridge Road, Crumpler NC 28617; 336-982-9439; Travel Time From Asheville: 3 hours east.

Zip Line Riding

Are you on the adventurous side, and interested in seeing the beautiful forests of Western North Carolina from a different perspective? Then a forest canopy zip line ride may be for you. This unique experience takes limited energy to participate in, and is not designed to scare but rather offers a gentle, self-controlled gliding experience. In 2009, Nantahala Gorge Canopy Tours became the first zip line facility in the mountains, and offers rides during the summer season. Their rides take you through multiple ecosystems in the Nantahala Gorge area.

Nantahala Gorge Canopy Tours: Nantahala Rafting Center, 10345 Highway 19 South, Bryson City NC 28713; 877-398-6222.

Navitat Canopy Adventures: 242 Poverty Branch Road, Barnardsville NC 28709; 828-626-3700.

The Beanstalk Journey at Catawba Meadows: 229 Catawba Meadows Drive, Morganton NC 28655; 828-430-3440

Section Three
Asheville, All-America City

Chapter One
About Asheville

L ocated at the hub of the Great Smoky and Blue Ridge mountains, 2,216 feet above sea level on the Asheville Plateau, Asheville is the largest city in Western North Carolina and the tenth largest municipality in the state, covering an area of 40.99 square miles. Asheville's population is estimated at over 70,000 and the city is located at the confluence of the French Broad and Swannanoa rivers in a river-formed valley that runs 18 miles north and south. Chartered in 1797 and named after Samuel Ashe, a former governor of North Carolina, Asheville attracts millions of visitors and tourists each year who come for the timeless natural beauty, the crisp highland air, the magnificent mountains and vibrant cosmopolitan hospitality the city offers. Every year publications of every type list Asheville and the Western North Carolina mountains as one of the best places in the world to live.

Surrounded by thousands of acres of majestic mountains, plateaus, rolling valleys and mystical coves, Asheville is a city not easily forgotten once visited. With its winding hilly streets graced by architectural gems from the past, Asheville has been called the "Paris of the South." Every section of this enchanting city is blessed with unique and irreplaceable buildings that few cities in America can match. From the awesomely majestic Biltmore House to the Art Deco masterpiece S&W Building to the stately rock-hewn beauty of the Grove Park Inn, Asheville is overflowing with architectural treasures. More than 170 historic buildings have been preserved, some of which were designed by world-famous architects Richard S. Smith, Douglas Ellington, Richard M. Hunt and Rafael Guastavino. Couple this with all of the cultural, business and entertainment possibilities and you have an extraordinary city to experience.

A major tourist destination with more than 5,000,000 visitors annually, Asheville is also known for its varied and rich arts and crafts communities. Hundreds of galleries, craft shops, and artisans studios are to be found here. Asheville has become an important center for traditional Appalachian as well as contemporary crafts. The variety and quality of the craft galleries and the many craft exhibits and shows attest to this fact. Located only minutes from national forests and green valleys, outdoor recreation opportunities also abound. White-water rafting, golf, hiking, fishing, horseback riding, llama trekking, rock climbing, camping and ballooning are just a few of the choices.

As you would expect, Asheville is rich in museums, nature centers, historic sites and other attractions for the visitor. During your stay, you may wish to attend a performance of the Civic Ballet, the Asheville Symphony Orchestra or one of the many local theatre companies. A wonderful way to spend a summer evening is to take in a game at historic McCormick Field, where Babe Ruth once played baseball. Throughout the year, Asheville celebrates with many festivals, from the renowned fairs of the Southern Highland Handicraft Guild to the world famous street festival, Bele Chere. Asheville is also a major medical center. Modern hospitals and numerous specialized medical facilities, as well as a large resident population of doctors and medical professionals combine to make Asheville the regional center for health care.

The largest city in Western North Carolina, Asheville is the regional center for manufacturing, transportation, banking and professional services and shopping. Asheville boasts a vibrant downtown, where nightclubs, cafes, galleries, theatres, coffeehouses, pubs and superb restaurants all add to the mix that now creates one of the most exciting and cosmopolitan downtown districts in the South. Voted an All-America City in 1997 by the National Civic League, Asheville was one of only ten U.S. cities to receive this prestigious award. An abundance of local micro-breweries notably the Highland Brewery, French Broad Brewery and others, have also earned Asheville the title of "Beer City USA". Asheville is home to numerous venues, including many restaurants and most bars, where local handcrafted beers can be sampled. In September, the wildly popular Brewgrass Festival, a celebration of Asheville's many microbreweries and bluegrass music takes place.

Asheville has a number of unincorporated communities and distinct areas that are constellated in and around the city. These include Arden, Biltmore Forest, Candler, Enka, Fairview and Leicester. Of these, Biltmore Forest is the most historic. An incorporated town located right in the heart of Asheville, this residential community is immediately adjacent to the world famous Biltmore Estate and is known for its many elegant homes.

History

Surrounded by towering mountains, Asheville was a small crossroads town when it was founded by pioneer town planner John Burton in 1792. Known as Morristown during the early years, the city was also called Buncombe Courthouse until 1797, when it was incorporated and named Asheville in honor of North Carolina governor Samuel Ashe.

Buncombe County attained county status in 1792 and was named for Revolutionary War hero Col. Edward Buncombe. Growth was slow until 1880, when the first railroad system was constructed. This first steam train changed Asheville forever, bringing in the outside world. This small mountain settlement went from a population of 2,616 to 10,328 in just ten years. A trickle of summer visitors that had journeyed to Asheville for half a century turned into a torrent. By 1886, an estimated 30,000 "summer people" visited the city annually. In 1885, the building of the first Battery Park Hotel was noted as the beginning of a great period of expansion for Asheville. Near the turn of the century, George Vanderbilt also began construction of the now world famous Biltmore House.

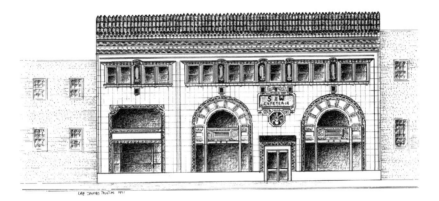

The S&W Cafeteria, 56 Patton Avenue, Asheville

The greatest boom period in Asheville's history came during the 1920s with the construction of many new buildings throughout downtown, including the Grove Arcade, City Hall, Buncombe County Courthouse, Flat Iron Building and others. Many Art Deco buildings were also constructed in this period such as the S&W Cafeteria building.

Today, Asheville is experiencing another period of tremendous growth and revitalization. The downtown district, with its wealth of historic buildings, is one of the most vibrant city centers in the South. Major, ecologically sound riverfront development is also occurring along the French Broad River, with parks, greenways and cultural centers emerging. Asheville continues to attract people from around the world as an exciting vacation destination, and as a wonderful and beautiful place to live.

Downtown Neighborhoods

As a visitor to Asheville, it will be helpful to know that the downtown district is divided into a number of diverse neighborhoods, each with its own unique history and ambience. One of the very best ways to experience these neighborhoods is to walk the Asheville Urban Trail. This short self-guided walking tour visits all four of the neighborhoods discussed below, with stations and thematic markers along the way. For more information about this extraordinary way to trace the footsteps of Asheville's historic past, see Section Three, Chapter 5, The Asheville Urban Trail.

For those interested in historic architecture, see Section Three, Chapter 4, Historic Asheville. Each of Asheville's official historic districts are presented and the most important and historic buildings are highlighted. For some districts, self-guided tours are presented.

1. **Battery Hill Neighborhood:** This neighborhood is crowned by the magnificent Basilica of St. Lawrence, D.M., the former Battery Park Hotel and the historic Grove Arcade. This area contains some of Asheville's best shopping and dining. Be sure to take a stroll down quaint Wall Street and visit some of its interesting and unusual stores. Farther down on Haywood Street is the Asheville Civic Center and the main library.
2. **Lexington Park Neighborhood:** This is Asheville's antique shop district. If you are at all interested in antiques, a visit to this district is a must. There you will also find trendy boutiques, neo-hippie stores, coffeehouses and nightclubs.
3. **Pack Square Neighborhood:** The heart of Asheville is Pack Square, a wonderful space surrounded by stunning architecture, from Art Deco to contemporary. This is a district which overflows with nightlife from the many art galleries, pubs, coffeehouses, theatres and restaurants. Asheville's Pack Place and YMI Center for African-American Culture are also found here.
4. **Thomas Wolfe Plaza Neighborhood:** Crowned by the historic home of author Thomas Wolfe, the Thomas Wolfe Plaza area is home to the Asheville Community Theatre, historic churches, craft shops and art galleries.

In addition to the districts already mentioned, there are some others of special interest to visitors. You will want to be sure and visit Biltmore Village, located just outside the entrance to the Biltmore Estate. There you will find unique and enchanting gift shops, art and craft galleries, and specialty stores, including Chelsea's Village Cafe and Tea Room, where lunch begins at 11:30 a.m. and their quintessentially English afternoon tea begins at 3:30 p.m.

Four other districts that have distinctive and historically important architecture in abundance are Montford, Chestnut Hill, Albermarle Park and the Grove Park areas. All of these neighborhoods, including Biltmore Village, are presented in depth in Section Three, Chapter 4 Historic Asheville.

Quick Facts
City Hall: 70 Court Plaza, PO Box 7148, Asheville NC 28802; 828-251-1122
Website: www.ashevillenc.gov
Elevation & Population: 2,216 feet, 73,000+
Visitor Center: 36 Montford Street, Asheville NC 28801; 800-257-1300; www.exploreasheville.com
Directions To Visitor Center: From I-240, take exit 4C to Montford Avenue.
Asheville Area Chamber of Commerce: 36 Montford Avenue, Asheville NC 28801; 828-258-6101; www.ashevillechamber.org
County: Buncombe County: County Offices, 205 College Street, Asheville NC 28801; 828-250-4000; www.buncombecounty.org

Biltmore Village Shops, Asheville

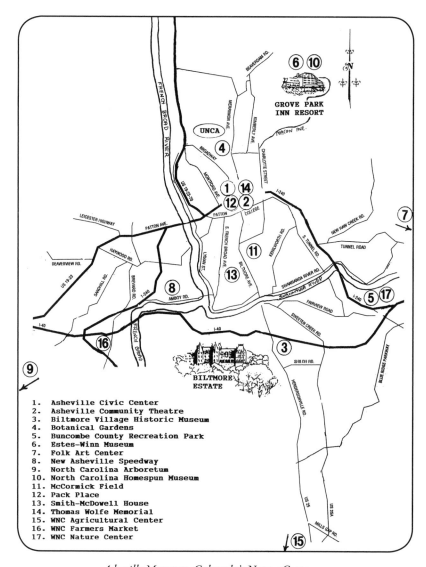

1. Asheville Civic Center
2. Asheville Community Theatre
3. Biltmore Village Historic Museum
4. Botanical Gardens
5. Buncombe County Recreation Park
6. Estes-Winn Museum
7. Folk Art Center
8. New Asheville Speedway
9. North Carolina Arboretum
10. North Carolina Homespun Museum
11. McCormick Field
12. Pack Place
13. Smith-McDowell House
14. Thomas Wolfe Memorial
15. WNC Agricultural Center
16. WNC Farmers Market
17. WNC Nature Center

Asheville Museums, Cultural & Nature Centers

Chapter Two
Asheville Cultural Attractions

This chapter is devoted to the major cultural attractions and centers that Asheville has to offer. Those included here are very important to the life of Asheville as a city and each attracts thousands of visitors each year. The range of attractions is wide, from world-class crafts to baseball games at a park where Babe Ruth once swung a bat.

Asheville Art Museum

Located in the heart of downtown Asheville on Pack Square in the Pack Place Education, Art & Science Center, the Asheville Art Museum is set within the elegance of a restored 1926 structure of Italian Renaissance design. The museum's permanent collection features America's impressionists, as well as regionalist and contemporary abstract artists. In the spacious galleries above, traveling exhibitions spotlight a broad range of artistic talent in a full spectrum of media and highlight nationally renowned collections of sculpture, paintings, and traditional and contemporary crafts.

The Asheville Art Museum annually presents an exciting, inviting and active schedule of exhibitions and public programs based on its permanent collection of 20th and 21st century American art. Any visit will also include experiences with works of significance to Western North Carolina's cultural heritage including Studio Craft, Black Mountain College and Cherokee artists. Special exhibitions feature renowned regional and national artists and explore issues of enduring interest. The Museum also offers a wide array of innovative, inspiring and entertaining educational programs for people of all ages.

Location: Downtown Asheville
Address: 2 South Pack Square, Asheville NC 28801
Telephone: 828-253-3227
Hours: All Year: 10 a.m.-5 p.m. Tuesday-Saturday, June-October Only: 1:00-5 p.m. Sunday
Fees: $6.00 adults, $5.00 students & seniors, children under 4 free.
Allow: 1-3 hours
Website: www.ashevilleart.org

The Asheville Civic Center, 87 Haywood St., Asheville

Directions: From I-240 take exit 5A Merrimon Avenue and follow signs for Highway 25 south for three blocks. Pack Place is located on Pack Square, directly in front of the Vance Monument.

Asheville Civic Center

Located on Haywood Street, the Asheville Civic Center is the major entertainment facility for Western North Carolina. It includes an Exhibition Hall on the bottom level, an Arena Floor immediately above, and a third level complex which includes a glass-enclosed concourse. The Civic Center is home to the Thomas Wolfe Auditorium, the venue for many dramas, music performances, pageants, conventions, and festivals. Equipped with excellent acoustic and lighting systems, it is also the performance space for the Asheville Symphony Orchestra. The building itself contains historic elements from the previous Art Deco auditorium. The lobby of the current structure features Art Deco terrazzo floors and gilded plaster molding and anthemia-ornamented columns.

Location: Asheville NC
Address: 87 Haywood St., Asheville NC 28801
Telephone: 828-259-5736
Website: www.ashevillenc.gov/departments/civic_center
Hours: Business office open Monday-Friday 8:30 a.m.-5 p.m.; ticket office open Monday-Friday 10 a.m.-5:30 p.m., Saturday 10 a.m.-1 p.m.
Directions: Walking from Pack Square in downtown Asheville, take Patton Avenue to Pritchard Park. Turn right onto Haywood Street.

Asheville Community Theatre (ACT)

For more than 50 years, the Asheville Community Theatre has presented productions that have ranged from classics to contemporary comedies. The theater's Heston Auditorium (named after Charlton Heston and his wife, actress Lydia Clark, who served as artistic co-directors in 1947) is designed to provide an intimate theatre setting; the back row is only 55 feet from the stage edge. Air-conditioned and equipped with a Bose sound enhancement system, ACT is also

Asheville Community Theatre (ACT), 35 Walnut Street, Asheville

home to youth acting classes, special student matinees and the Autumn Players outreach program produced by senior citizens.

Location: Downtown Asheville
Address: 35 Walnut St., Asheville NC 28801
Telephone: Box Office: 828-254-1320, Business Office: 828-254-2939
Hours: Business hours Monday-Friday 10 a.m.-4 p.m.
Website: www.ashevilletheatre.org
Directions: From I-240 heading east, take exit 5A Merrimon Avenue. Go straight up the hill through the light onto Market Street. Make first left, in front of Magnolia's Grill and Bar. I-240 heading west, left off exit ramp. Left at light onto Woodfin Street. Right on Market Street. First left on Walnut Street.

Asheville's Fun Depot

The Asheville Fun Depot is one of Asheville's most popular family-oriented attractions, designed with kids in mind. Facilities include a state-of-the-art arcade gallery, 18-hole indoor mini-golf, an outdoor go-kart track, multi-level laser tag, a soft play area, a climbing wall, batting cages and the Depot Diner.

Location: Southeast Asheville just off Interstate 1-40 at exit 5
Address: 7 Roberts Road, Asheville NC 28803
Telephone: 828-277-2386, 866-303-4386
Hours: 10:00 a.m.-10:00 p.m. Monday-Friday; 9:00 a.m.-10:00 p.m. Saturday; 1:00-8:00 p.m. Sunday
Fees: Call for prices
Website: www.ashevillesfundepot.com
Directions: Take exit 51 off of Interstate 1-40, turn left at bottom of the ramp onto Sweeten Creek Road. Turn left onto Roberts Road.

Asheville Urban Trail

One of the most creative projects that has accompanied the revitalization of downtown Asheville has been the development of the Asheville Urban Trail, a walking route through downtown that is centered around Pack Square, the birthplace of Asheville. The trail is highlighted by interpretive displays which commemorate people, places and events of historic, cultural and architectural significance. In walking the trail, a good starting point is the Pack Place Education, Arts & Science Center located on Pack Square across from the Vance Monument. Here you can pick up a free map for the self-guided tour, which should take only an hour or so, depending on your walking pace. And of course, along the way there are plenty of opportunities for refreshment in Asheville's many cafes and coffeehouses.

Location: Downtown Asheville
Address: Pick up maps and rent cassettes at main desk of Pack Place, located on Pack Square
Telephone: 828-258-0710 (Asheville Area Arts Council)
Hours: None, walk anytime
Fees: Audiocassettes available for self-guided tours for a small fee.

Basilica of St. Lawrence

To the north of the Grove Arcade area in downtown Asheville is the Basilica of Saint Lawrence, Deacon and Martyr, built in 1909. A Spanish Baroque Revival Roman Catholic Church built of red brick with polychrome glazed terra-cotta inserts and limestone trim, it was designed by world-famous architect/engineer Raphael Guastavino. The church employs his "cohesive construction" techniques in its large oval tile dome and Catalan-style vaulting in its two towers. The massive stone foundations and the solid brick superstructure give silent testimony to the architect's desire to build an edifice that would endure for generations. There are no beams of wood or steel in the entire structure; all walls, floors, ceilings and pillars are of tile or other masonry materials. The dome is entirely self supporting, has a clear span of 58 x 82 feet, and is reputed to be the largest unsupported dome in North America. The Crucifixion tableaux of the Basilica altar feature a rare example of seventeenth century Spanish woodcarving. The windows are of German origin, and the Basilica has two chapels. Attached by an arcade is the 1929 Neo-Tuscan Renaissance brick rectory (now housing church offices) designed by Father Michael of Belmont Abbey. Self-guided tour brochures are available at the church, and guided tours are given after Sunday masses.

Location: Asheville NC
Address: 97 Haywood Street, Asheville NC 28801
Telephone: 828-252-6042
Hours: Open daily to the public. The Basilica is an active church, and note that masses may be in session.
Website: www.saintlawrencebasilica.org

Directions: From Pack Square go east on Broadway Street and turn left onto College Street. Proceed to Pritchard Park and turn right onto Haywood Street. The Basilica will be on your right.

Biltmore Estate

See Section Three, Chapter 3 (next chapter)

Biltmore Village

When George W. Vanderbilt began building Biltmore Estate near Asheville in the late 1880s, he planned a picturesque manorial village to be built just outside the entrance to Biltmore Estate. Constructed in the early 1900s, the Village was primarily the work of Richard Hunt, Frederick Law Olmsted and Richard Smith. Today, Biltmore Village is a charming community of shops, restaurants and galleries offering world class shopping in an historic setting.

Be sure to take time to park your car and take a walking tour of the many shops housed in the original historic buildings. Buildings of special historical interest are the Cathedral Of All Souls, the Administration Building at 1 Biltmore Plaza, the Depot, The Samuel Harrison Reed House at 119 Dodge Street and the cottages throughout the main section of the village. Buildings were added to the Village until about 1910, and shortly after Vanderbilt's death, the Village was sold. It was declared a National Historic District and a Local Historic District in 1989. (See Section Three, Chapter 4, Historic Asheville for an in-depth look at the history and architecture of the Biltmore Village Historical District). Biltmore Village is also noted for its Christmas festival that surrounds the enacting of Charles Dickens' "A Christmas Carol." This enchanting festival includes concerts, lighting displays and arts and crafts exhibits.

Website: www.biltmorevillage.com

Directions: I-40 Exit 50 North on Highway 25/Biltmore Avenue. Right immediately after All Souls Cathedral. From downtown Asheville, take Biltmore Avenue south from Pack Square through the hospital district

Black Mountain College Museum + Arts Center

The Black Mountain College Museum + Arts Center is an exhibition space and resource center dedicated to exploring the history and legacy of one of the world's most acclaimed experimental educational communities. The Center offers changing exhibitions, a video archive, research materials, and a selection of books and other materials for sale. The Center was founded in 1993 by Mary Holden to honor and pay tribute to the spirit and history of Black Mountain College and to acknowledge the College's role as a forerunner in progressive, interdisciplinary education with a focus on the arts.

Location: Downtown Asheville

Address: 56 Broadway, Asheville NC 28801

Telephone: 828-350-8484
Hours: Wednesday thru Saturday, 12 p.m.-4 p.m.
Fees: None
Allow: 1-2 hours
Website: www.blackmountaincollege.org
Directions: From I-240 take exit 5A Merrimon Avenue and go west on Broadway towards the center of town.

Blue Ridge Parkway Destination Center

A joint project of the National Park Service and the Blue Ridge National Heritage Area, the Blue Ridge Parkway Destination Center is a regional exhibit and education center focusing on the Blue Ridge Parkway. The center, housed in a LEED-certified "green" environmentally friendly building, features exhibits on the natural and cultural diversity and recreational opportunities found on the 469 mile length of the parkway. A key feature is the I-Wall, an oversized interactive, interpretive map of the parkway. The design, planning and construction of the 12,800 square foot center cost $9.8 million and was completed in 2007. There is also a gift shop and a 70-seat theatre showing a short movie about the parkway throughout the day.

Location: Milepost 384 on the Blue Ridge Parkway, two miles south of the Folk Art Center.
Address: 195 Hemphill Knob Road, Asheville NC 28803
Telephone: 828-298-5330
Hours: 9 a.m. 5 p.m. seven days a week except Christmas and New Year's Day.
Fees: None
Allow: Two hours
Website: www.blueridgeparkway.org
Directions: Located on the Blue Ridge Parkway just east of Asheville at Milepost 384. Access the highway at Highway 74A (I-240, Exit 9) and head east.

Botanical Gardens at Asheville

The Botanical Gardens at Asheville are located on a ten-acre site next to the campus of the University of North Carolina at Asheville. The Gardens were organized in 1960 by the Asheville Garden Club and were designed by Doan Ogden, a nationally known landscape architect. They were created to preserve and display the native plants and flowers of the Southern Appalachian Mountains and are noted for their landscaping and as well as the great variety of plant life. The gardens are open year round and are intertwined with peaceful walking trails through varied habitats. There is a Botany Center, library and gift shop on the premises.

Location: North Asheville
Address: 151 W.T. Weaver Blvd., Asheville NC 28804
Telephone: 828-252-5190

Botanical Gardens at Asheville, 151 W.T. Weaver Boulevard, Asheville

Hours: Open year round, dawn to dusk
Fees: None
Allow: About two hours
Website: www.ashevillebotanicalgardens.org
Directions: From I-240 take Exit 5A Merrimon Avenue. Go north to W.T. Weaver Boulevard and turn left.

Colburn Earth Science Museum

Located in the heart of downtown Asheville, the Colburn Earth Science Museum is part of the Pack Place Education, Art & Science Center. Here you can explore the beauty of crystals, the magnificence of gemstones and the fantastic shapes and colors of minerals from around the world. The museum highlights the treasures that make North Carolina a geologic destination for gem hunters and rock hounds, and regularly schedules exhibitions covering the full range of gem and mineral related subjects.

Exhibits include the Hall of Minerals, which features many items from the Colburn Earth Science Museum's primary collection of more than 4,500 specimens from around the world; the Grove Stone Room, whose displays explore the geology of North Carolina and the entire Earth; the History of Mining in North Carolina, which chronicles mining activity in North Carolina, including the activities of prehistoric Native Americans, Spanish explorers and 20th-century Western North Carolinians. The museum's gem collection includes over 1,000 cut gemstones from around the world.

Location: Asheville NC
Address: 2 South Pack Square, Asheville NC 28801
Telephone: 828-254-7162
Hours: All Year: 10 a.m.-5 p.m. Tuesday-Saturday, 1:00-5 p.m. Sunday
Fees: $4 adults, $3 students, children 4-17 and adults 60 or older.
Allow: 1-2 hours
Website: www.colburnmuseum.org
Directions: From I-240 take exit 5A Merrimon Avenue and follow signs for
    Highway 25 south for three blocks. Pack Place is located on Pack Square,
    directly in front of the Vance Monument.

Diana Wortham Theatre

Located in the heart of downtown Asheville, the Diana Wortham Theatre is part of the Pack Place Education, Art & Science Center. The theatre features state-of-the-art acoustics and lighting, exquisitely detailed woodwork, plus a full-sized stage and orchestra pit. Excellent sight lines and accessibility for the handicapped make this a gem of a performance space for audiences, performers and technicians alike. The 500-seat theater is a dramatic and sophisticated setting that attracts a diverse range of local, regional, and national companies, and touring shows.

Location: Asheville NC
Address: 2 South Pack Square, Asheville NC 28801
Telephone: 828-257-4530
Hours: All Year: 10 a.m.-5 p.m. Tuesday-Saturday, June-October Only: 1:00-5 p.m.
    Sunday
Website: www.dwtheatre.com
Directions: From I-240 take exit 5A Merrimon Avenue and follow signs for
    Highway 25 south for three blocks. Pack Place is located on Pack Square,
    directly in front of the Vance Monument.

Estes-Winn Memorial Automobile Museum

Located in the Homespun Shops area next to the Grove Park Inn Resort is the Estes-Winn Memorial Automobile Museum. More than twenty restored cars, including a 1926 Cadillac, a 1927 La Salle convertible and a 1922 La France fire engine now fill this building. Greeting you at the door is a 1913 Model T much like the ones Henry Ford and Thomas Edison traveled to Asheville in during their stays at the Grove Park Inn.

Location: Asheville NC
Address: 111 Grovewood Rd., Asheville NC 28804
Telephone: 828-253-7651
Hours: Saturday 10 a.m.- 5 p.m.; Sunday 11 a.m.-5 p.m.; closed January thru March.
Fees: None
Allow: One hour
Website: www.grovewood.com/about-us/estes-winn-antique-car-museum

Estes-Winn Memorial Automobile Museum, 111 Grovewood Road, Asheville

Directions: From I-240 take Exit 5B. North on Charlotte Street. Right on Macon Avenue to Grove Park Inn. Museum is in Homespun Shops area behind the inn, opposite the Vanderbilt wing garage.

Folk Art Center of the Southern Highland Craft Guild

Opened in 1980 on the 50th anniversary of the Southern Highland Craft Guild (SHCG), the Folk Art Center is home to Allanstand Craft Shop, one of Appalachia's oldest and best-known craft shops. Allanstand sells the work of more than 200 members of the SHCG. Both the finest in traditional mountain crafts of the region as well as the very best in contemporary American crafts are available for the discriminating visitor.

The center's upper level contains the museum space of the SHCG as well as the offices and the center's comprehensive craft library. The changing exhibition schedule showcases the works of SHCG members in addition to specially selected traveling exhibitions reflecting the traditions of the Southern Highlands. If crafts are of interest to you, a visit to the Folk Art Center is a must. Set in a forested glen just off the Blue Ridge Parkway, this special Asheville attraction is for young and old alike.

Location: Milepost 382 just east of Asheville on the Blue Ridge Parkway
Address: P.O. Box 9545, Asheville NC 28815
Telephone: 828-298-7928
Hours: Open daily 9 a.m.-5 p.m. except Thanksgiving, Christmas, and New Year's Day
Fees: None

The Folk Art Center, off the Blue Ridge Parkway at milepost 382

Allow: Two hours

Website: www.southernhighlandguild.org

Directions: Located on the Blue Ridge Parkway just east of Asheville at milepost 382.

Grove Arcade Public Market

The Grove Arcade was the dream of E.W. Grove, a self-made millionaire who moved to Asheville in the early 1900s, where he conceived of the Arcade as "the most elegant building in America," and as a new type of retail center. When the Arcade opened in 1929, it quickly became home to a collection of local shops and services. For 13 years, the Arcade was the major commercial and civic center in Western North Carolina. The Federal Government took over the building in 1942, following America's entry into World War II, evicting all retail and office tenants. Following the war's end, the Arcade continued under Federal ownership. In 1997 the City of Asheville acquired title to the Grove Arcade under the National Monument Act, and the revitalized Grove Arcade now features over 50 specialty stores, restaurants, offices and apartments and is open to the public daily. The Arcade is located just west of Haywood Street and the Civic Center, an easy 10-minute walk from Pack Square.

Website: www.grovearcade.com

Directions: From Pack Square proceed east on Patton Avenue, turn left onto Haywood Street and then left onto Battery Park. The Arcade will be ahead on your right.

McCormick Field & the Asheville Tourists

Opened in 1924, McCormick Field is one of the oldest operating minor-league baseball parks in North America. A 1992 remodeling replaced the field's rickety wooden grandstand with one of steel and brick and expanded the concession area. Despite the facelift, the field retained its signature short right field, a scant 300 feet down the line from home plate. As a result of remodeling, though, the wall is now an imposing 35 feet high. The entire outfield wall is surrounded by tall, verdant trees, and during the summer the smell of honeysuckle is heavy throughout the park. Scenes from the movie "Bull Durham" were filmed at the park. McCormick Field is home to the Asheville Tourists, a Class A farm team of the Colorado Rockies. Ty Cobb, Jackie Robinson and the immortal Babe Ruth all played at McCormick Field.

Historic McCormick Field, opened in 1924 and remodeled in 1992, can be seen in the film "Bull Durham."

Location: Asheville NC
Address: 30 Buchanan Pl., Asheville NC 28802
Telephone: 828-258-0428
Hours: Most games are played at night, starting at 7:05 p.m., Sunday games begin at 5:05 p.m.
Fees: Box seats start at around $10
Directions: Take I-240 to Exit 5B Charlotte Street. Go south on Charlotte Street to McCormick Place.

North Carolina Arboretum

Established in 1986 as an inter-institutional facility of the University of North Carolina, the Arboretum is located within the 6,300-acre Bent Creek Experimental Forest and is surrounded by the 480,000-acre Pisgah National Forest. The 426-acre site is nestled in one of the most beautiful natural settings in the Southeast. The Arboretum has wonderful varied gardens, walking trails and natural habitats.

The Arboretum focuses on education, economic development, research, conservation, and garden demonstration with respect to landscape architecture and plant sciences. It is becoming the major state-supported attraction in Western North Carolina. A wide variety of classes and workshops are taught by the garden's staff and other plant experts. Educational programs target all ages and range from bonsai demonstrations to nature walks.

North Carolina Arboretum, 100 Frederick Law Olmsted Way, Asheville

Location: Asheville NC
Address: 100 Frederick Law Olmsted Way, Asheville NC 28806
Telephone: 828-665-2492
Hours: Daily from 7 a.m.-9 p.m. (daylight savings time) and 8 a.m.-9 p.m. (Eastern Standard Time)
Fees: None
Allow: Three hours
Website: www.ncarboretum.org
Directions: From the Blue Ridge Parkway: N.C. 191 exit (Milepost 393.6). On the exit ramp, the entrance is on the left. From I-40: Exit 40 (Farmers Market). 191 south, follow signs.

North Carolina Homespun Museum

The North Carolina Homespun Museum is located next to the Grove Park Inn Resort & Spa and presents a historical overview of Biltmore Industries and its internationally renowned wool cloth. Inside the museum, photographs depict important events from Biltmore Industries history, including its founding in 1901 by Eleanor Vance and Charlotte Yale. The museum showcases memorabilia such as letters, photographs, and tailored suits made from homespun fabric.

Location: Asheville NC
Address: 111 Grovewood Rd., Asheville NC 28804
Telephone: 828-253-7651
Hours: Monday-Saturday 10 a.m.- 5 p.m.; Sunday 11 a.m.-5 p.m.; closed January thru March.

Fees: None
Allow: One hour
Website: www.grovewood.com/about-us/nc-homespun-museum
Directions: From I-240 take Exit 5B. North on Charlotte Street. Right on Macon Avenue to Grove Park Inn. Museum is in Homespun Shops area behind the inn, opposite the Vanderbilt wing garage.

Pack Place Education, Arts & Science Center

Located in the heart of downtown Asheville on Pack Square, the Pack Place Education, Arts & Science Center is a marvelous combination of science, arts, culture and entertainment all under one roof. This 92,000 square-foot complex boasts museums, performance spaces, courtyards, exhibition and lobby galleries, as well as a permanent exhibit "Here is the Square" which traces the story of Asheville from its earliest days. Attractions within Pack Place include the Asheville Art Museum, the Colburn Earth Science Museum, the Diana Wortham Theatre, the Health Adventure and the YMI Cultural Center.

Location: Asheville NC
Address: 2 South Pack Square, Asheville NC 28801
Telephone: 828-257-4500
Hours: 10 a.m.-5 p.m. Tuesday-Saturday; 1:00-5 p.m. Sunday. Closed Mondays
Fees: Different fees depending on attraction
Allow: Two to four hours to see all exhibits
Website: www.packplace.org
Directions: From I-240 take exit 5A Merrimon Avenue and follow signs for Highway 25 south for three blocks. Pack Place is located on Pack Square, directly in front of the Vance Monument.

Pack Place at Pack Square is many museums in one complex.

Smith-McDowell House, 283 Victoria Road, Asheville

Smith-McDowell House

Delve into mountain history and enjoy the Victorian splendor of Asheville's oldest brick residence by visiting the Smith-McDowell House. This elegant structure, circa 1840, is now open to the public as a local history museum. The house was built by James McConnell Smith as a private residence. A later owner, Charles Van Bergen, commissioned the famous Olmsted Brothers firm to landscape the property. In 1974, Asheville-Buncombe Technical College purchased the structure, and leased it to the Western North Carolina Historical Association. Five years later, after restoration, it was opened as a museum.

One of Asheville's architectural jewels, the Smith-McDowell House presents a wonderful opportunity to experience the past in a truly elegant restoration. It is especially delightful at Christmas time when all of the Victorian decorations are up. For an in-depth look at Smith-McDowell House's architecture and history, see Section Three, Chapter 4 Historic Asheville.

Location: Asheville NC
Address: 283 Victoria Rd., Asheville NC 28801
Telephone: 828-253-9231
Hours: Wednesday through Saturday:10:00 a.m. to 4:00 p.m., Sunday: 12:00 to 4:00 p.m.
Fees: $7 adults, $3 children
Allow: Two hours
Website: www.wnchistory.org

Directions: From Pack Square take Biltmore Avenue south toward hospitals. Just before Memorial Mission Hospital, make a right onto Victoria Road.

Southern Appalachian Radio Museum

The Southern Appalachian Radio Museum has a wide range of radio memorabilia including exhibits of Atwater Kent, Philco, Silvertone, Edison phonographs, Crosley, Hammarlund, Harvey Wells, test instruments, spark gap transmitters, keys and ancient QSL cards. This is a museum where you can touch the radios and do things, and they also have an amateur radio station, W4AFM, on premises where you can take a turn at the mike!

Location: Campus of Asheville-Buncombe Technical Community College, Asheville NC
Address: Room 315 Elm Building, AB-Tech College, Asheville NC 28801
Telephone: 828-298-1847
Hours: Friday 1-3 p.m. or call for a tour at other times
Fees: None
Allow: 1 hour
Website: www.saradiomuseum.org
Directions: From Pack Square proceed south on Biltmore Avenue. As you pass the hospitals turn right onto Victoria Road for about .9 mile. When you see a pedestrian overpass, turn right (up the hill) at the electronic message board. Park in any of the spaces marked with white strips in several lots; and enter the nearby Elm Building. Take the elevator to the 3rd floor, room 315.

The Health Adventure

The Health Adventure, located in the Pack Place Education, Art & Science Center, is a health and science museum for children and today's families dedicated to improving health awareness, promoting wellness lifestyles, and increasing science literacy through programs and exhibits. Founded in 1968, The Health Adventure is one of the first health education centers in the country to let you explore the wonders of the body and mind with dozens of exhibits full of amazing health and science information and fascinating photography.

Location: Asheville NC
Address: 2 South Pack Square, Asheville NC 28801
Telephone: 828-254-6373
Hours: 10 a.m.-5 p.m. Monday-Saturday; 1:00-5 p.m. Sunday.
Fees: $8.50 Adults, $7.50 Students (12 and up), $6 Children (2-11)
Allow: One hour
Website: www.thehealthadventure.org
Directions: From I-240 take exit 5A Merrimon Avenue and follow signs for Highway 25 south for three blocks. Pack Place is located on Pack Square, directly in front of the Vance Monument.

Thomas Wolfe Memorial

Thomas Wolfe left an indelible mark on American letters. His mother's boardinghouse in Asheville, now the Thomas Wolfe Memorial, has become one of literature's most famous landmarks. In his epic autobiographical novel, *Look Homeward Angel,* Wolfe immortalized the rambling Victorian structure, originally called "Old Kentucky Home," as "Dixieland." A classic of American literature, *Look Homeward Angel* has never gone out of print since its publication in 1929, keeping interest in Wolfe alive and attracting visitors to the setting of this great novel.

The Memorial is administered by the North Carolina Department of Cultural Resources and is open to the visiting public. For an in-depth look at the architecture and history of the Thomas Wolfe House, see Section Three, Chapter 4 Historic Asheville.

Location: Asheville NC
Address: 52 North Market St., Asheville NC 28801
Telephone: 828-253-8304
Hours: Tuesday-Saturday 9 a.m.-5 p.m., Sunday 1-5 p.m., closed Monday
Fees: $1.00 Adults, 50¢ Students
Allow: Two hours
Website: www.wolfememorial.com
Directions: I-240 heading east: Take Exit 5A straight up hill through light onto North Market Street. I-240 heading west: turn left off exit, then left onto Woodfin Street and right onto North Market Street.

Thomas Wolfe Memorial, 52 North Market Street, Asheville

Western North Carolina Agricultural Center

One of the country's premier agricultural centers, the WNC Agricultural Center schedules over 50 events yearly, including 35 horse shows. The Center has a 65,000 square-foot fully enclosed show arena, with a 3,000-person seating capacity. There is also a 120' x 240' show ring, outdoor covered rings, and two outside, well-lighted warm-up rings. The Agricultural Center is host yearly to horse and livestock events, trade shows, RV and car shows, festivals, cat and dog shows, and many other events. This world-class multiuse facility is open year round. It is also home to the annual North Carolina Mountain State Fair.

Location: Fifteen minutes south of Asheville
Address: 1301 Fanning Bridge Rd., Fletcher, NC 28732
Telephone: 828-687-1414
Website: www.wncagcenter.org
Directions: I-26 Exit 9. Follow airport signs off ramp. Continue past airport to make left onto Fanning Bridge Road.

Western North Carolina Farmers Market

The Western North Carolina Farmers Market first opened for business in September 1977. This model project, involving input from local, state and national leaders, is one of the most modern and best planned markets in the United States. Hundreds of thousands of visitors come to the market each year not only to shop, but to take in the wonderful country atmosphere. Fruits and vegetables can be purchased by the piece, pound, bushel or truckload. Former Commissioner of Agriculture James A. Graham stated it this way: "Think of shopping at a 36-acre roadside stand featuring farm-fresh fruits and vegetables, flowers and ornamental plants, mountain crafts and scores of gift items."

Retail vendors offer a year-round selection of farm fresh produce, canned goods, honey and handcrafted items. Five truck sheds provide space for farmers and dealers to display and sell their produce. Restaurants and a retail garden center are also located on Market grounds.

Location: Asheville NC
Address: 570 Brevard Rd., Asheville NC 28806
Telephone: 828-253-1691
Hours: Open year-round, 7 days a week. (April-October) 8 a.m. to 6 p.m. (November-March) 8 a.m. to 5 p.m.
Website: www.ncagr.gov/markets/facilities/markets/asheville
Directions: I-40 Exit 47. South on Highway 191/Brevard Road. The market is on the left a short distance from Interstate.

At the Western North Carolina Farmers Market, 570 Brevard Road, Asheville

Western North Carolina Nature Center

Owned and maintained by Buncombe County, the Western North Carolina Nature Center is open year-round with indoor and outdoor exhibits. This outstanding 42-acre center features indigenous wildlife and plant life of the Appalachian region. A great outing for kids and adults alike, the center has animals both large and small, from cougars and wolves to the tiniest insects. Special programs, demonstrations and "hands-on" activities are available for anyone who wishes to learn about the rich natural heritage of the Southern Appalachian mountains. Nowhere else in WNC will you find such diverse wildlife, gardens, trails, indoor exhibits, habitats and farm animals in one setting.

Location: Asheville NC
Address: 75 Gashes Creek Rd., Asheville NC 28805
Telephone: 828-298-5600
Hours: Open 7 days a week, 10 a.m. -5 p.m.
Fees: $8 Adults, $7 Seniors, $4 Youth (3-14)
Allow: 2-4 hours
Website: www.wildwnc.org
Directions: I-240 Exit 8 (74A West). East off ramp. Right onto Swannanoa River Road. Right onto Gashes Creek Road.

Cougars can be seen at WNC Nature Center

YMI Cultural Center

The YMI Cultural Center, located in the Pack Place Education, Arts & Science Center, is an enduring asset for the city of Asheville. Housed in a local landmark building that is listed on the National Register of Historic Places, the YMICC runs programs in cultural arts, community education and economic development. Commissioned by George Vanderbilt in 1892, this beautiful pebbledash and brick building of Tudor design was built by and to serve several hundred African-American craftsmen who helped construct the Biltmore Estate. Today, the newly refurbished center continues its tradition of community service. Its galleries feature exhibits, programs, classes and performance that present African-American art, culture and history at their best. The YMI Cultural Center is located behind Pack Place at Eagle and Market Streets.

Location: Asheville NC
Address: 39 South Market Street, Asheville NC 28801
Telephone: 828-252-4614
Hours: 10 a.m.-5 p.m. Tuesday-Friday; 1:00-5 p.m. Saturday by appointment
Fees: $5 Adults, $3 Students (12 and up), $3 Children (2-11)
Allow: Two hours
Website: www.ymicc.org
Directions: From I-240 take exit 5A Merrimon Avenue and follow signs for Highway 25 south for three blocks. Pack Place is located on Pack Square, directly in front of the Vance Monument.

Vintage Mercury

The Red Wolf: A Nature Center Project

The Red Wolf, one of the lesser-known wolf species native to North America, once roamed throughout much of the Southeastern United States but have been eliminated from almost all of their natural range. The Nature Center located in Asheville is part of a breeding program to raise red wolves for eventual release into the wild.

Red Wolves average between 55 and 80 pounds, somewhat smaller than the better known gray wolf, but larger than the coyote which it resembles. Although many red wolves have a reddish cast to their fur, some do not. The usual coloration is a blend of cinnamon-brown, black and grayish-brown.

Western North Carolina Nature Center, 75 Gashes Creek Road, Asheville

Not as much is known about the red wolf as it's more well-known cousin, and it is believed that they do not form large packs like gray wolves. Most of their food consists of smaller animals such as raccoons, rabbits, rodents and birds. Like other wolf species, the red wolf has been persecuted by man because of our hatred, fear and misconception of these large predators. Over the years, the red wolves were shot, trapped and poisoned as their habitat was cleared for use by man. Today, thanks to the efforts of organizations such as the Western North Carolina Nature Center, the red wolf is returning to the wild habitats of its ancestors.

Chapter Three
Biltmore Estate

T his chapter is devoted exclusively to Biltmore Estate. A national treasure, Biltmore Estate's importance to Asheville cannot be understated, and as one of the major attractions in Western North Carolina it warrants a chapter unto itself. A visit to Biltmore Estate, in the opinion of the author, is a must for anyone coming to Asheville.

Although it is not formally part of the present Biltmore Estate, Biltmore Village (*See* Section Three, Chapter Two) was also originally conceived of by George Vanderbilt. The architecture of the original village buildings, especially the Cathedral of All Souls, clearly reflects the spirit of Vanderbilt's vision.

Biltmore Estate
Your Visit

A visit to Biltmore is an event, so you'll want to give yourself at least 4-6 hours to explore the house, grounds, and winery. You'll find numerous shops throughout the estate, all with an uncommon selection of special gifts, accessories, and mementos of your visit. Don't forget to allow time to browse through them all. Like the estate itself, Biltmore's restaurants offer a delicious blend of American and European flavors. Dining choices range from the distinctly American fare of the Stable Café to the seasonal buffets of the Deerpark Restaurant.

Every trip to Biltmore, no matter the time of year, is a new and exciting experience, whether you come for the breathtaking Festival of Flowers in the spring or the celebrated Candlelight Christmas Evenings. The beauty of Biltmore Estate is ever-changing, with new wonders and delights appearing every season. In the springtime, the gardens explode with brilliant color, calling for the celebration of the spring Festival of Flowers. Summertime brings lush greenery to the hillsides, deep shade in the cool, wooded groves, and Summer Evening Concerts performed on the South Terrace. December brings the splendor of an elaborate 19th century Christmas to every corner of the decorated mansion. Finally, winter is a time when guests can enjoy the special presentations regarding many of the preservation projects taking place in the house.

George Vanderbilt's dream first began to take shape in 1887, when he visited Asheville on holiday. Enchanted by the remote majesty of the Blue Ridge Mountains, he decided to make Asheville the site of his country estate. Commissioning architect Richard Morris Hunt, he set out to create a mansion modeled after the châteaux of France's Loire Valley. They began to collect the finest building materials from all over the United States. It took an army of stonecutters and artisans six years to construct Biltmore House, which is today the largest private home in America, situated on more than eight thousand acres.

George Vanderbilt filled his 250-room mansion with treasures he had collected during his world travels. Works by Albrecht Dürer, John Singer Sargent, and Pierre Auguste Renoir cover the walls. Exquisite furniture and Oriental rugs fill each room. Minton china graces elaborate table settings. Guests of Mr. Vanderbilt had their choice of 32 guest rooms, and could pass the time in the Billiard Room, Winter Garden, Tapestry Gallery, or countless other sitting rooms, and be entertained in the Gymnasium, Bowling Alley, or indoor swimming pool. Ever mindful of his guest's comfort, Mr. Vanderbilt equipped his house with a centralized heating system, mechanical refrigeration, electric lights and appliances, and indoor bathrooms—all unheard of luxuries at the turn of the century.

Today, Biltmore House visitors can see the house virtually as it was in George Vanderbilt's day because its sculptures, paintings, furnishings, and household items have been carefully preserved.

Biltmore Estate Information

Location: South Asheville, adjacent to Biltmore Village
Address: Corporate Offices: Biltmore Estate, One North Pack Square, Asheville NC 28801
Telephone: General Information: 800-543-2961, 828-274-6333
Corporate Offices: 818-255-1776
Individual Ticket Sales: 800-411-3812
Group Ticket Sales: 828-274-6230
Inn on Biltmore Estate: 800-858-4130, 828-225-1600
Website: www.biltmore.com
Hours: Biltmore Estate is closed Thanksgiving and Christmas but open on New Year's Day. Biltmore Estate also has a number of special events including Summer Evenings Concerts and Candlelight Christmas Evenings (early November through Christmas, taking place after normal hours.) Reservations are required.
Estate Entrance Hours (Subject to change without notice): 8:30 a.m.- 7 p.m. Admissions gate closes at 4 p.m. Biltmore House front door closes at 4:30 p.m.
Admission Gate and Welcome Center: 8:30 a.m. -4 p.m.
Biltmore House Hours: January-December daily 9 a.m.-4:30 p.m.
Fees: Prices vary seasonally and depending on method of purchase (*Online or at gate*). 2011 prices are quoted. Adults $69.00, Youth 10-16 $34.50 Children nine and under free when accompanied by paying adult.

Admission Tickets Includes: Self-guided visit of Biltmore House, all-day access to gardens and Antler Hill Village, complimentary wine tasting and guided tour at the Winery, dining and shopping opportunities and free parking.

Outdoor Activities: Stop by the Outdoor Center in Antler Hill Village to check the many outdoor activities available at Biltmore Estate. These include Carriage Rides, Horseback Riding, River Float Trips, Biking, Hiking, Segway Tours, Sporting Clays, Fly-fishing School and Land Rover Driving School. Estate outdoor activities are available by reservation to estate daytime guests, Biltmore Twelve-Month Passholders, and Inn on Biltmore Estate guests. Call 800-411-3812 for more information

Allow: Four to six hours minimum.

Directions: From I-40: Exit 50 or 50B. North on Highway 25. Left at fork. Entrance gate on left. From downtown Asheville: Biltmore Avenue south from Pack Square through hospital district. Left on Lodge Street.

Antler Hill Village and Winery

Antler Hill Village is a casual place extending the Biltmore experience, from the fun and relaxing Winery to exhibits at The Biltmore Legacy to delectable pub fare and ale at Cedric's Tavern. You can also enjoy live entertainment on the Village Green, explore farm life in the early 1900s at the Farm, and get ready to explore the 8,000-acre backyard at the Outdoor Adventure Center. The village's name comes from Antler Hill, the "fine high ridge" where the Inn on Biltmore Estate is located. From the Civil War into the 1930s, the ridge was the site of Antler Hall, a residence and social center for many estate families. Main features at Antler Hill Village include:

Winery: Guests enter the Winery from Antler Hill Village where they walk underground through the old dairy's original tunnel, designed to immediately engage all of the senses into the winemaking process. As part of the tours offered at the Winery, guests can enjoy wines in the Tasting Rooms. On display also at the Winery is Edith Vanderbilt's 1913 Stevens-Duryea Model C-Six. This rare piece is the only car George Vanderbilt purchased that remains in the estate's collection.

The Biltmore Legacy: Discover the many sides of Edith Vanderbilt, George Vanderbilt's wife, or learn how the Cecils preserve Biltmore's legend of gracious hospitality. This facility includes exhibits filled with slices of estate life, including archival letters, photos, and drawings illustrating how the Vanderbilts lived. A small theater features a film narrated by Dini Cecil Pickering that shares the family story of the Vanderbilts.

Village Green and Bandstand: The centerpiece of Antler Hill Village, the Village Green has a gently sloping area perfect for people watching, listening to live music each afternoon, or relaxing with a snack or picnic.

Outdoor Adventure Center: Outdoor activities available at Biltmore Estate include Carriage Rides, Horseback Riding, River Float Trips, Biking, Hiking, Segway Tours, Sporting Clays, Fly-fishing School and Land Rover Driving School. Tickets are available at the Outdoor Adventure Center, as well as outdoor gear and clothing.

Antler Hill Farm: The Farm offers a glimpse into the agricultural past of Biltmore Estate. Traditional farming demonstrations take place there, including authentic blacksmithing by local crafters. The Farmyard houses sheep, goats, chickens, cows and horses that children can see up close and personal. The Kitchen Gardens showcase fragrant herbs and vegetables used in Biltmore's restaurants.

Cedric's Tavern: Named after George Vanderbilt's beloved St. Bernard, Cedric, this warm, relaxing pub reflects the less formal side of Biltmore dining and entertaining. Specialties include shepherd's pie and fish and chips.

Tours & Seminars

Audio Guide to Biltmore House: Storytelling audio guide that leads you room-by-room sharing stories of occupants.

Biltmore House Architect's Tour: Guided 60-minute tour that offers a closer look at the design and construction of Biltmore House by going into areas not on regular house visit. The tour provides stunning photo opportunities from rooftop and balconies.

Biltmore House Butler's Tour: See how Biltmore House functioned, past and present, and learn about the work of the domestic servants during this 60-minute guided tour, which takes you into unrestored rooms and mechanical areas not open to the public on the regular house visit.

Vanderbilt Family & Friends Tour: This new guided tour spurs your imagination about staying at Biltmore with the Vanderbilts as your hosts. Tour bedrooms not on the regular house visit that are outfitted with clothing and accessories from the 1900s as your hear stories from your host about customs of the time and the fascinating people who visited Biltmore.

Premium Biltmore House Tour: Tour the house for two hours with a guide assigned to you exclusively. Includes areas seen in the Butler's Tour, Architect's Tour, and House Tours.

Legacy of the Land Tour: Take a motorcoach tour of the estate and learn about the history of the land, structures, and former residents. Visit areas not usually open to guests.

Winery Behind The Scenes Guided Walking Tour: Guests are guided on a walking tour of the Winery production areas. See and learn the difference between making red wine and white wine, as well as the bottling process. The tour ends in the Champagne finishing room where guests learn how true French style sparkling wines are made.

Farm Guided Walking Tour: Take a tour of what everyday life was like on the estate at the turn of the century. Meet friendly farmyard animals, a blacksmith, a woodworker, and try your hand at churning butter. Stroll through the stunning Kitchen Garden.

Farm Wagon Rides: Tours departs from the Farm's Kitchen Garden entrance in Antler Hill Village.

Red Wine & Chocolate Seminar at Winery: Discover why chocolate and red wine is a match made in heaven. Please register at the Winery Portal area in Antler Hill Village.

Biltmore Estate Lodging

Inn on Biltmore Estate: Superb is the one word to describe the Inn on Biltmore Estate. Opened in 2001, it is the newest addition to George Vanderbilt's turn-of-the-century retreat. The 213-room luxury accommodation provides guests with an opportunity to enjoy Vanderbilt-style hospitality firsthand. Located on the east side of the estate above the Winery, it affords spectacular views of Biltmore House. At 165,000 sq. ft., the Inn offers banquet meeting rooms, two executive boardrooms, 213 exquisitely appointed guest rooms and suites, a 150-seat dining room, library, lobby bar, exterior swimming pool and fitness center. Amenities offered to guests include walking and hiking trails, carriage rides, horseback riding, mountain hiking and river float trips. The design of this world-class facility is in keeping with gracious resorts of the turn-of-the-century, and elements and accents from the magnificent Biltmore House are everywhere. Many design materials and elements reflect other estate structures. Fieldstone stucco and a slate roof similar to that found on the house have been incorporated. The large lobby fireplace, the inn library and Indiana fieldstone reception desk all further reinforce the perception that one is truly in a creation inspired by the vision of George Vanderbilt. Landscaping reflects the style of landscape architect Frederick Law Olmstead and his overall plan for Biltmore Estate.

Address: One Antler Ridge Rd., Asheville NC 28801
Telephone: 800-858-4130, 828-225-1600.

Biltmore Estate Dining

Restaurants:

Arbor Grill: (Antler Hill Village) Savor al fresco dining beside the wintery. Delicious food, wine and the natural beauty of Biltmore come together at the Arbor Grill to give you an ultimate Biltmore experience. Live musicians entertain Friday through Sunday. Open year round for lunch and dinner, 12:00-8:00 p.m., weather permitting.

Bistro: (Antler Hill Village) Open daily for lunch and dinner. The menu includes soups, salads, wood-fired pizza, homemade pasta, desserts, a children's menu, and entrées featuring estate-raised beef, lamb, and veal. Located at the Winery, the Bistro opens year-round from 12 -8 pm. 828-274-6341

Cedric's Tavern: (Antler Hill Village) Offering satisfying pub fare alongside robustly flavored American and global cuisine presented with Biltmore flair. Open daily for lunch, dinner, and late night entertainment.

Deerpark Restaurant: Originally part of the estate's farm operation, Deerpark is open late March-December 11 a.m.-3 p.m. Deerpark offers delicious southern specialties served buffet-style in an outdoor atmosphere. To make arrangements for group dining, call 828-274-6260.

Stable Cafe: (Stable courtyard next to Biltmore House) Formerly the Biltmore Estate carriage house and stables, the Stable Café is open from 11 a.m. to 5 p.m. The menu includes rotisserie chicken, Biltmore beef, fresh salads, burgers, desserts, and a full selection of drinks including wine and beer. Open year-round from 11 a.m.-4 p.m. 828-274-6370.

The Dining Room: (Inn on Biltmore Estate) The Dining Room at the Inn on Biltmore Estate with breakfast, lunch and dinner available to inn guests. The restaurant features estate-raised products and a regional cuisine paired with Biltmore Estate wines.

Light Bites:

Bake Shop: (Stable courtyard next to Biltmore House) Serves espresso, gourmet coffees, herbal teas, and freshly baked goods daily 9 a.m.-5 p.m.

Conservatory Cafe: (Conservatory) Good news for garden lovers—you really can spend the whole day wandering the gardens and greenhouses, and when you're ready for refreshment, the Conservatory Café is right there in the open air with Biltmore wines, frozen daiquiris, light snacks and deli sandwiches.

Courtyard Market: (Stable courtyard next to Biltmore House) Specializing in Sicilian-style thin crust pizza, great hot dogs, snacks, beer, wine, and cold beverages.

Creamery: (Antler Hill Village) Ice cream, gourmet coffee, cupcakes, deserts and drinks.

Ice Cream Parlor: (Stable courtyard next to Biltmore House) Located in the stable courtyard next to the house, the Ice Cream Parlor serves specialty ice cream, yogurt treats, beverages, and picnics for two. Open year-round 11 am.-5 p.m. seasonally.

Smokehouse: (The Farm in Antler Hill Village) Carolina barbeque, quick sandwiches and light snacks at the Farm.

Wine Bar: (Winery in Antler Hill Village) Biltmore wines accompanied with light far.

Biltmore Estate Shopping

A Christmas Past: (Stable area near Biltmore House) Offers an assortment of Christmas ornaments and music.

A Gardener's Place: (Conservatory lower level) Features estate-grown plants, gardening accessories, books and gifts.

Bookbinder's: (Stable area near Biltmore House) Filled with books relating to the Vanderbilt family and the Gilded Age.

Carriage House: (Stable area near Biltmore House) Carries gifts, decorative accessories, and Biltmore Estate wines.

Confectionery: (Stable area near Biltmore House) Offers a delectable array of sweets.

Cottage Door: (The Inn on Biltmore Estate) Unique children's items, gourmet snacks, chocolates and amenities such as newspapers, magazine and toiletries.

Gate House: (Just outside main entrance to Biltmore Estate). Features Biltmore Estate reproductions, decorative accessories, and a full selection of fine estate wines. The only estate shop accessible without ticket purchase.

Marble Lion: (The Inn on Biltmore Estate) Sophisticated apparel and luxury items.

Mercantile: (The Barn at the Farm at Antler Hill Village) Appalachian crafts, dry goods and old-fashioned candy.

Outdoor Adventure Center: (Village Green in Antler Hill Village) Explore the many different outdoor activities offered at Biltmore Estate, plus purchase clothing and sundries.

Toymaker's: (Stable area near Biltmore House) Features old-fashioned toys and games.

Traditions: (Village Green in Antler Hill Village) Offers a graceful mix of products inspired by envisioning how Edith Vanderbilt would entertain her guests today—carrying forward her renowned hospitality and sense of style. Decorative home accents including tabletop accessories and home décor that blend perfectly in today's homes, plus pottery and jewelry crafted by local artisans.

Wine Shop: (Winery in Antler Hill Village) offering fine wines, gourmet foods, kitchen accessories, and other gifts.

The Gardens

George Vanderbilt commissioned Frederick Law Olmsted, designer of New York's Central Park, to create the stunning backdrop for his château. The resulting gardens and grounds are as spectacular as the house itself. A feast for the eyes, the ten acres of gardens also feature a remarkable array of flowers—many blooming through most of the year. From the orderly, manicured grounds framing the house to the lush forestland covering the mountains, the estate was carefully planned and designed by Olmsted's judicious hand. Today the grounds are still exquisitely maintained, and you are invited to explore them at your leisure.

Equestrian Center

Bring your own horse and explore more than 80 miles of estate trails—the same paths used by the Vanderbilts and their guests at the turn of the century. Enjoy wide, well-marked trails through pristine forests, green pastures, and along the banks of the French Broad River. Choose from five different 10–30 mile loops. Several trails include optional jumps and are suitable for carriages. Horseback riding is also offered for visitors who do not bring their own horses. For more information call the Estate Equestrian Center at 828-225-1454.

Lodge Gate

The entrance to Biltmore Estate is through the Lodge Gate opposite Biltmore Village. Both its bricks and roof tiles were made on the Estate. Beyond the Lodge Gate, the approach road winds for three miles through a deliberately controlled landscape. The road runs along the ravines instead of the ridges, creating a deep natural forest with pools, springs

The Lodge Gate at Biltmore Estate

and streams. Around the last turn, the visitor passes through the iron gates and pillars that are topped by early 19th century stone sphinxes, and then into the expansive court of Biltmore House.

Statue of Diana

Statue of Diana

Located inside a small temple at the top of the hill, beyond the Rampe Douce at Biltmore Estate, is a statue which represents Diana. Diana was the daughter of Zeus and Leto, twin sister of Apollo and one of the twelve Olympians. As protector of wild animals, deer were especially sacred to her, which is particularly appropriate for Biltmore, with its large native deer population. Diana is usually portrayed with a bow and arrow and quiver, as she is here. The dog next to her in the statue could represent fidelity or chastity.

The Entrance Lions

Guarding the main entrance at Biltmore House are two massive carved stone lions

that survey visitors with magnificently serene countenances. Carved of Rosso di Verona marble that is from near San Ambrogio Valpolicello in Italy, these lions are believed to date to the late nineteenth century and were not put in place until late 1899 or early 1900.

One of the Entrance Lions

Biltmore House

George Vanderbilt commissioned two of America's most renowned designers to help plan his estate. His friend Richard Morris Hunt, the first American to receive an architectural degree from the Ecole des Beaux Arts in Paris, was the architect of Biltmore House, and Frederick Law Olmsted was chosen to lay out the gardens and parks surrounding the house.

For his house, Mr. Vanderbilt chose the period of the great 16th century châteaux, known as the Francis I style. In 1895, when the house was formally opened, it was named Biltmore from Bildt, the name of the Dutch town from which the family's ancestors came (van der Bildt), and "more," an old English word for rolling, upland country. Biltmore House became a favorite home for Mr. Vanderbilt and his wife, Edith Stuyvesant Dresser and their only child, Cornelia. Upon Cornelia's marriage to John Francis Amherst Cecil, it became the Cecils' residence.

To build Biltmore House, beginning in the summer of 1890, a thousand workers were steadily engaged for six years. A three-mile railway spur from the present Biltmore Station had to be built to carry materials to the site. Hundreds of workmen from the local area and artisans from all over the country and Europe came to carve and fit limestone that came from Indiana. So massive are some of these limestone blocks that one in the retaining wall weighs over three tons. So great was the project that a brick manufacturing facility was established on the estate grounds to satisfy the need for building materials. One of the greatest private houses in America, Biltmore House, once seen, will never be forgotten.

Biltmore House

The Building of a Legend

The following section was provided courtesy of The Biltmore Company for use in this chapter:

Biltmore House took six years and 1,000 men to build it; it opened its doors on Christmas Eve in 1895. With its 390-foot facade, the House has more than 11 million bricks, 250 rooms, 65 fireplaces, 43 bathrooms, 34 bedrooms, and three kitchens, all of which are contained in more than four acres of floor space. The massive stone spiral staircase rises four floors and has 102 steps. Through its center hangs an iron chandelier suspended from a single point containing 72 electric light bulbs.

At its completion, Biltmore House was one of the most innovative and technologically advanced homes in the world. Imagine having hot and cold running water, elevators, indoor heating, a fire alarm system, refrigeration, electric light bulbs and 10 Bell telephones—all of which were unheard of luxuries at the turn of the century.

Imagine what it must have been like to call this your home. Dozens of servants to meet your every need. A vast collection of art and furniture comprising more than 70,000 items, including approximately 23,000 books, furniture from 13 countries, over 1,600 art prints, and many paintings.

If you were lucky enough to be one of Vanderbilt's guests, your choice of inside activities included bowling, billiards, an exercise room, swimming, and games of all sorts. Outdoors, guests could ride horseback, swim, play croquet, hunt, camp, fish, and hike, The Vanderbilts could entertain as many as 64 guests at their dinner table in the massive Banquet Hall. The room spans 72 feet by 42 feet and is 70 feet high. Meals served in the Banquet Hall were usually seven courses and required as many as 15 utensils per person. Enough fresh fish to feed 50 people was often shipped daily from New York, and the same amount of lobster was often shipped twice a week to feed the ever-changing guest list.

You'll experience a different kind of awe when you walk the Estate's grounds. Originally more than 125,000 acres of land, the Estate includes wooded parks, six pleasure gardens, a conservatory, and 30 miles of paved roadway. You will be overwhelmed every spring with the sight of tens of thousands of tulips in the Walled Garden. Or stroll among the carpets of mums that decorate the grounds each fall. The rest of the year the grounds will amaze you with their colors, shapes, aromas, and natural beauty.

The Tea House

The Tea House in the southwest corner of the South Terrace was an addition landscape-architect Frederick Law Olmsted advocated throughout the construction of Biltmore House. He viewed it as a much-needed focal point and an ideal spot from which to contemplate the mountains.

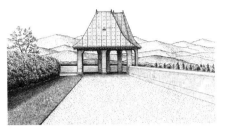

The Tea House

Italian Garden at Biltmore House

The Italian Garden

Designed by Olmsted, the Italian Garden is located to the east of the lower terrace adjacent to Biltmore House. Its three formal pools are part of a design concept that dates back to the 16th century. These gardens have an architectural purity in which the plantings are secondary to the design. Nature is completely controlled and the gardens serve as an extension of the house. The outline of the three pools, grass areas and the paths are all part of a symmetrical design. The nearest pool contains the sacred lotus of Egypt. In the second are aquatic plants and in the third, water lilies.

The Conservatory at Biltmore House

The Conservatory

The Conservatory was used to provide citrus fruit, flowers, and plants for Biltmore House during Vanderbilt's time. It is located at the far end of the four-acre Walled Garden, the lower half of which contains the Rose Garden featuring 159 of 161 All-American Rose selections as well as more than 2,300 other roses of the finest varieties. The Conservatory, restored in 1999, serves the same function today as it did in Vanderbilt's time: providing cut flowers and ornamental plants for the house and growing bedding plants for the estate's gardens.

The Winery Clock Tower

One of the highlights at Biltmore Estate's Winery is Richard Morris Hunt's European winery clock tower. Since the winery was previously a dairy, the central clock tower with its "candle-snuffer" roof originally had only three working faces; the side toward the pasture featured a painted-on clock, as the grazing cows did not need to know the time.

The Clock Tower at the Winery

The Winery

The Winery, opened in 1985, followed George Vanderbilt's original concept of a self-supporting European estate. The 96,500 square-foot facility is located in buildings designed by Richard Morris Hunt as part of the dairy operation on Biltmore Estate. The winery complex with its half-timbered woodwork, pebbledash plaster and

The Winery on Biltmore Estate

decorative brickwork is reminiscent of a rural landscape of the 19th century. Today the buildings house state-of-the-art wine making equipment, cellars for wine storage, an elaborately stenciled tasting room, and the spacious Wine Shop.

Deerpark Restaurant

Deerpark Restaurant is part of a series of handsome outbuildings designed by architect Richard Morris Hunt in the 1890s for George Vanderbilt's farm operations at Biltmore Estate. Originally a dairy barn, Deerpark has been renovated into a unique open-air restaurant in a beautiful pastoral setting. The historic architectural detailing includes pebbledash plaster, half-timbered woodwork, and decorative brickwork. The name Deerpark is taken from a nearby area of the estate which George Vanderbilt set aside as a deer preserve.

Deerpark Restaurant on Biltmore Estate

Vignette:
George Washington Vanderbilt, III

William Henry Vanderbilt's youngest son, George, was born in the Vanderbilt farmhouse in New Dorp, Staten Island, New York on November 18, 1862, the youngest of eight children. Little interested in his father's business affairs, Vanderbilt was influenced instead by the collection of art and antiques in his father's home.

A quite shy person, he began collecting books and art objects at a young age. After his mother died, George inherited the family home at 640 Fifth Avenue in New York City and all the art objects within it, including the large collection of paintings his father had assembled. He showed no interest in the social world of the Vanderbilt family, instead preferring the adventure of travel and the world of books.

After visiting Asheville in the 1880s, which was then a fashionable resort, he decided to create a home for himself away from the noise and pace of New York City. During the five years of the construction of Biltmore House, he was a bachelor. However, on a trip to Europe in 1896 he met Edith Stuyvesant Dresser and on June 1, 1898, they were married in a civil ceremony in Paris, followed the next day by a religious ceremony at the American Church. Their only child, Cornelia, was born on August 22, 1900.

While George Vanderbilt is well known for his creation of Biltmore Estate, he also accomplished a number of important good works in his lifetime. He established the first school of scientific forestry management practices in the United States and he also brought modern farming techniques to the relatively rural area surrounding his estate. Together, the Vanderbilts started Biltmore Estate Industries in 1901. In this apprenticeship program, young people were instructed in skills to produce furniture, baskets, needlework and woven fabric for resale.

George Vanderbilt died in 1914 and was buried in the family vault on Staten Island. In the memorial service held at All Souls Church in Biltmore Village, the following remarks were made:

"Courteous in manner, dignified in deportment, kind in heart and pure in morals, he was beloved by his friends, honored by his acquaintances and respected by everyone."

Chapter Four
Historic Asheville

One encounters Asheville today as a modern city that is rapidly growing and expanding out into the surrounding Buncombe County. Asheville today does not look at all like the Asheville from before the turn of the century. Regrettably, much of the best of that time has vanished, including the elegant Queen Anne style Battery Park Hotel and the very hilltop on which it stood and dominated the city landscape. Only scattered buildings remain from that period.

Much of the city landscape remains, however, from the early days of the century through to the present day, especially downtown Asheville, which retains a strong presence from the early third of the twentieth century. Asheville's slow recovery from the Great Depression did not allow it to demolish wholesale these early buildings as did so many American cities, and because of that, they have been preserved intact to this day. Within the central downtown district for example, one can find excellent examples of Neo-Gothic, Neo-Georgian, Commercial Classical, Art Deco, Romanesque Revival and other style structures that make up the most extensive collection of early twentieth century architecture in the state. They remain an open-air museum, reminders of the optimism and unbounded investment that characterized Asheville in its boom period. Asheville is the only city of its magnitude in which such an urban landscape survives almost intact.

Asheville, through the efforts of local preservation and historic resources organizations, as well as the North Carolina Department of Cultural Resources, has been divided into a number of historic districts. These districts form the basis for this chapter and also the framework for a series of mini-tours, should you wish to experience some of the wonderful and diverse architectural heritage of Asheville during your visit.

Historic Designations
Historic District

Historic District refers to a district of Asheville that has been so designated by the United States Department of the Interior. These districts serve as frameworks for further discussion of the historic buildings and sites of Asheville and in some cases as self-guided mini-tours. Some of these Historic Districts include whole neighborhoods while others are only a small cluster of buildings.

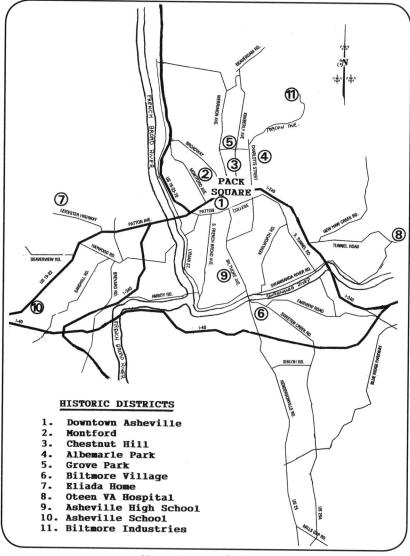

HISTORIC DISTRICTS

1. Downtown Asheville
2. Montford
3. Chestnut Hill
4. Albemarle Park
5. Grove Park
6. Biltmore Village
7. Eliada Home
8. Oteen VA Hospital
9. Asheville High School
10. Asheville School
11. Biltmore Industries

Historic Districts of Asheville

Local Historic Landmarks (LHL)

These are designated by the Asheville City Council or the Buncombe County Board of Commissioners.

National Historic Landmarks (NHL)

National Historic Landmark are structures, buildings or sites which are of significance to all Americans. This designation is by the Secretary of the Interior and the listings are registered with the United States Department of the Interior National Park Service.

National Register of Historic Places (NRHP)

The National Register is the official list of the nation's cultural resources worthy of preservation. The National Register includes all historic areas in the National Park System, National Historic Landmarks, and properties significant to the nation, state or community which have been nominated by the states, federal agencies and others and have been approved by the National Park Service.

Downtown Asheville Historic District

Downtown Asheville itself has four distinct neighborhoods, each with their own distinctive qualities and ambience: **Battery Park,** the area that includes Haywood Street, Wall Street, and Battery Park Avenue; **Lexington Park,** spanning Lexington Avenue and Broadway; Pack Square, encompassing **Pack Square,** South Pack Square, Biltmore Avenue, and Patton Avenue; and **Thomas Wolfe Plaza,** centered on Market Street and Spruce Street.

One of the very best ways to experience these neighborhoods and most of the downtown Asheville historic buildings presented below is to walk the Asheville Urban Trail. This self-guided walking tour visits all four of the neighborhoods discussed here, with stations and thematic markers along the way. For more information about this extraordinary way to trace the footsteps of Asheville's historic past, see Section Three, Chapter 5, The Asheville Urban Trail.

Pack Square (NRHP)

Pack Square, and the nearby South Pack Square, Biltmore Avenue, and Patton Avenue, is the heart of Asheville. Located at the intersection of Biltmore Avenue, Broadway, and College Street, it was once known as Public Square and was renamed in 1901 for city benefactor George Willis Pack when he moved the courthouse off the square and, in agreement with county commissioners, the square was designated a public park. This spacious square is surrounded by wonderful examples of Classical, Gothic, Art Deco, and Contemporary architecture.

Today, Pack Square and its surrounding streets are a vibrant and historic city center that not only boasts elegant architecture but superb museums, shops, music halls, art galleries and world class restaurants. A visit to Pack Square will show you immediately why Asheville has been called "Paris of the South."

Pack Square, the heart of downtown Asheville

Vance Monument (NRHP)   Pack Square
Located in the square's center is a 75-foot tall granite obelisk, the Vance Monument, erected in 1896 and named in honor of Zebulon B. Vance, an Asheville attorney who was twice governor of North Carolina and was also a U.S. Senator. Two-thirds of the $3,000 cost was paid by philanthropist George W. Pack, and the architect R.S. Smith donated his services. The granite obelisk was cut from the Pacolet quarries in Henderson County.

Pack Memorial Library Building (NRHP, LHL)   2 South Pack Square
Located on the southern side of Pack Square is the Pack Memorial Library Building. Today this noble Second Renaissance Revival structure is home to the Asheville Art Museum, part of the Pack Place Education, Arts & Science Center. Built in 1925-26 and designed by New York Library architect Edward L. Tilton, the four-story building presents symmetrically arranged elevations faced with white Georgia marble and ornamented with a low-relief classical cornice.

Jackson Building (NRHP)   22 South Pack Square
To the left of the Library Building is the wonderfully elegant Jackson Building. Built in 1923-24 by real estate developer L.B. Jackson and it was the first skyscraper in Western North Carolina. The architect was Ronald Greene and the building he designed rises 13 stories on a small 27 x 60 foot lot. Neo-Gothic in style, the building originally had a searchlight on top that illuminated the surrounding mountains.

Asheville City Hall (NRHP, LHL)   70 Court Plaza

To the east of Pack Square is the Art Deco masterpiece designed by Douglas D. Ellington, and built in 1926-28. One of the crown jewels of Asheville it is set on a marble base and topped with a pink and green tiled octagonal ziggurat roof. A wonderful unity of appearance is achieved through the luxurious use of color and form. The main entrance is through a loggia of pink marble with multicolored groin vaults. One of the most striking and beautiful buildings in all of North Carolina, City Hall is a show stopper in a city graced by many unusual and beautiful buildings.

Asheville City Hall

Buncombe County Courthouse (NRHP)   60 Court Plaza

To the left of the City Hall is the Buncombe County Courthouse. Designed by Milburn and Heister of Washington, DC, and built in 1927-28, this steel frame seventeen-story courthouse has a brick and limestone classical surface. It has an opulent lobby ornamented with polychrome classical plaster work and marble balustrades. Polished granite columns at the entrance are echoed by similar columns above at the jail section. The large superior court room has a coffered plaster ceiling and elegant woodwork.

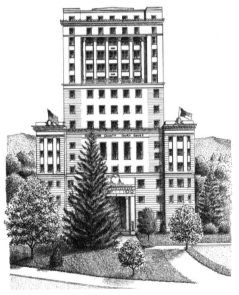

Buncombe County Courthouse

Young Men's Institute Building (NRHP, LHL)   Market and Eagle St.

Located behind the Pack Place Education, Arts, & Science Center on the corner of South Market and Eagle streets is the Young Men's Institute (YMI) Building, built by George Vanderbilt in 1892 to serve as a recreational and cultural center for black men and boys. It was sold to the Young Men's Institute in 1906 and became a center for social activity in the black community and contained professional offices and a black public library. Designed by R.S. Smith in a simplified English Cottage style with a pebbledash and brick surface, today it houses the YMI Cultural Center, part of Pack Place Education, Arts & Science Center.

Eagle and Market Streets District (NRHP)

This district was the heart of the black community in Asheville in the early days and today contains many fine buildings of historic importance, including the YMI Building mentioned earlier. Of interest are the Campbell Building at 38 South Market Street, originally an office building, and the former Black Masonic Temple Building at 44 South Market Street.

Mount Zion Missionary Baptist Church (NRHP)   47 Eagle St.

Also in this historic area is the large and handsome Mount Zion Missionary Baptist Church. A three-tower red brick Late Victorian Gothic structure built in 1919, it has a tin-shingled roof that has ornamental sheet-metal finials. The large number of Art Glass windows that grace the church are another unusual feature. It was home to one of Asheville's largest black congregations, organized in 1880 by the noted Reverend Rumley.

Kress Building (NRHP, LHL)   21 Patton Ave.

Just down from Pack Square on Patton Avenue, you will encounter one of Asheville's finest commercial buildings, the Kress building. Housing today an antique and crafts emporium, this four-story building was built in 1926-27. Distinctive features are the cream colored glazed terra-cotta with orange and blue rosette borders that face the front three bays of the building. In addition the side elevations above the first level are tan brick with terra-cotta inserts. This classical design preceded the many Art Deco Kress stores built around the country in the late 1930s and is unique in that sense.

Drhumor Building (NRHP)   48 Patton Ave.

Farther west is the splendid Romanesque Revival Drhumor Building. Built in 1895, this structure is an imposing four stories of brick trimmed with rock-faced limestone and graced by a marvelous first floor frieze by sculptor Fred Miles. One of the bearded visages is supposedly of local merchant E.C. Deake, who watched Miles sculpt. Miles was also the sculptor who did the figures atop the Basilica of St. Lawrence. A complementary limestone frontispiece was added to the north side of the building in the 1920s and the original corner entrance was filled in.

Detail from Drhumor Building

The building was designed by A.L. Melton for Will J. Cocke and his relatives, Mrs. Marie Johnson and Miss Mattie. The name Drhumor comes from teh Johnson family's ancestral home in Ireland.

S&W Cafeteria Building (NRHP, LHL)   56 Patton Ave.

A little farther down Patton Avenue is another of the crown jewels of Asheville, and one of the finest examples of Art Deco architecture in North Carolina, the S&W Cafeteria Building. It was built in 1929 for the cafeteria chain which occupied the building until 1973. The building was designed by Douglas D. Ellington, and is two stories with a polychrome cream, green, blue, black and gilt glazed terra cotta facade that employs geometrically-stylized Indian and classical motifs. The interior is divided into dining rooms and lobbies with Art Deco decorations of superb quality. The building today is used for catering of meetings, receptions and banquets. (*See* illustration Section Three, Chapter 1)

Public Service Building (NRHP, LHL)   89-93 Patton Ave.

Farther west is the Public Service Building built in 1929. This imposing eight-story Neo-Spanish Romanesque steel frame office building is one of North Carolina's most attractive 1920s skyscrapers. Built of red brick and glazed terra cotta, its first two and upper floors are lavishly ornamented with polychrome terra cotta including such whimsical details as Leda-and-the-Swan spring blocks on the second-floor windows.

Flatiron Building (NRHP, LHL)

10-20 Battery Park Ave.

The Flatiron Building is an eight-story tan brick building that has classical detailing and a "flatiron" plan. Built in 1925-26, and designed by Albert C. Wirth, this elegant and unique building is faced with limestone ashlar and is perched at the entrance to the historic Wall Street district. A large metal sculpture of a household iron sits outside on the Wall Street side of the building.

The Flatiron Building

Wall Street (NRHP)

This charming one-block street of small shops was named Wall Street after the retaining wall built behind the structures that face Pritchard Park. In 1926 Tench Coxe and Ed Ray remodeled and repainted the rear entrances to these building to create a boutique district, which they called "Greenwich Village." That name never caught on, and the district was simply called Wall Street. Today it is a one of Asheville's most interesting shopping districts, with many top-quality gift and specialty shops. When there, notice the unusual gingko trees planted along the street.

Grove Arcade (NRHP, LHL)   10-20 Battery Park Ave.

Located just north of Wall Street, the grand Grove Arcade building occupies a full city block. This imposing building was begun in 1926 by E.W. Grove to be a commercial mall topped with an office skyscraper. Completed after Grove's death minus the skyscraper, the building is surfaced with cream glazed terra-cotta in a Neo-Tudor Gothic style. It is one of several major buildings for which the millionaire was responsible, with the most noteworthy among them being the Grove Park Inn. The arcade was designed by Charles N. Parker. Among the most interesting details are a pair of winged Griffin statues guarding the Battle Square entrance of the building. After years of service as offices for the federal government, the Grove Arcade is now home to commercial shops and venues.

Griffin from Grove Arcade

Battery Park Hotel (NRHP, LHL)

1 Battle Square

The hotel is a huge 14-story T-plan Neo-Georgian hotel erected by E.W. Grove in 1923-24. This extraordinary building was designed by hotel architect W.L. Stoddart of New York and replaced a previous Queen Anne style hotel of the same name. It is surfaced in brick with limestone and terra-cotta trim. The hotel building today houses apartments and is located just north of the Grove Arcade.

United States Post Office and Courthouse (NRHP)   100 Otis St.

Located just west of the Grove Arcade is the former post office and courthouse building, one of the state's finest Depression-era Federal buildings. This Art-Deco influenced building was designed by the Federal Architect's Office under James A. Wetmore. The building has a majestically massed central entrance in which the Art Deco influence can be seen.

First Church of Christ Scientist (NRHP)

64 North French Broad Ave.

First Church of Christ Scientist

The First Church of Christ Scientist is of a refined Jeffersonian, Neo-Classical Revival style, constructed of orange brick. Built between 1909 and 1912, it was designed by S.S. Beaman of Chicago.

Basilica of Saint Lawrence, D.M. (NRHP)

97 Haywood St.

To the north of the Grove Arcade area is the Basilica of Saint Lawrence, Deacon and Martyr, built in 1909. A Spanish Baroque Revival Roman Catholic Church built of red brick with polychrome glazed terra-cotta inserts and limestone trim, it was designed by world-famous architect/engineer Raphael Guastavino. The church employs his "cohesive construction" techniques in its large oval tile dome and Catalan-style vaulting in its two towers. The massive stone foundations and the solid brick superstructure give silent testimony to the architect's desire to build an edifice that would endure for generations. There are no beams of wood or steel in the entire structure; all walls, floors, ceilings and pillars are of tile or other masonry materials. The dome is entirely self supporting, has a clear span of 58 x 82 feet and is reputed to be the largest unsupported dome in North America. The Crucifixion tableaux of the Basilica altar features a rare example of seventeenth century Spanish woodcarving. The windows are of German origin, and the Basilica has two chapels. Attached by an arcade is the 1929 Neo-Tuscan Renaissance brick rectory designed by Father Michael of Belmont Abbey.

Basilica of Saint Lawrence, D.M.

Loughran Building (NRHP, LHL)   43 Haywood St.
The Loughran Building was in 1923 and is a six-story steel-frame commercial building that has a restrained white glazed terra cotta classical facade. It was designed by Smith and Carrier for Frank Loughran and its first occupant was Denton's Department Store.

Central United Methodist Church (NRHP)   27 Church St.
Located on Church Street, south of Patton Avenue, this Gothic limestone-faced church was designed by R.H. Hunt of Chattanaooga, Tennessee. The church is noted for its fine stained and Art Glass windows and was built between 1902 and 1905.

First Presbyterian Church (NRHP)   40 Church St.
This Gothic Revival church is home to one of Asheville's oldest congregations and is one of the oldest church buildings in the city. Located on the corner of Church and Aston streets, the brick nave and steeple were constructed in 1884-85 and have deep, corbelled cornices, hoodmolded windows and blind arcading at the eaves. The north chapel and the south building were added in 1968.

Trinity Episcopal Church (NRHP)   Church and Aston St.
Located on the opposite corner of Church and Aston Streets, Trinity Episcopal Church is the third of three churches in this Church Street neighborhood. Built in 1921, it is a Tudor Gothic Revival style brick with granite trim building and was designed by Bertram Goodhue of Cram, Goodhue and Ferguson, well-known church architects. This lovely building has a simple gable roofed sanctuary with transepts and a short gable-roofed blunt tower.

Ravenscroft School Building (NRHP, LHL)   29 Ravenscroft Dr.
Built in the 1840s, this two-and-a-half story brick Greek Revival house is probably the oldest structure in the downtown area and one of the oldest in Asheville. It housed the Ravenscroft Episcopal Boys' Classical and Theological School after 1856 until the Civil War. Thereafter it was used as a training school for the ministry. In 1886 it was used again as a boys' school. After the turn of the century, it was a rooming house, and today it is used for professional offices. Details of the house in Academic Greek Revival are of a type not common to Western North Carolina.

Ravenscroft School Building

Mears House (NRHP) 137 Biltmore Ave.

Located on Biltmore Avenue, the Mears House is a wonderful example of Queen Anne style architecture. Built around 1885, this brick residence has a slate-shingled mansard roof, gables and dormers. This is the most distinguished of the remaining late nineteenth century residences near downtown.

Scottish Rite Cathedral and Masonic Temple Building (NRHP) 80 Broadway

Built in 1913, this imposing four-story building is constructed of pressed brick and trimmed in limestone and grey brick. A two-story limestone portico with a pair of Ionic columns graces the Broadway entrance. The building was designed by Smith and Carrier.

Lexington Avenue (NRHP)

This once thriving market district was where farmers and others once came to water their horses and buy and sell local produce. Because natural springs kept it wet, Lexington Avenue was first called Water Street. Double doorways accommodating farmers' wagons are still evident on renovated buildings. Lexington Avenue is Asheville's premier antique district and also home to Asheville's oldest store, T.S. Morrison (circa 1891). Many antique shops, specialty stores, galleries and nightclubs are found today in this interesting neighborhood.

Lexington Avenue is home to T.S. Morrison, Asheville's oldest store.

First Baptist Church of Asheville

First Baptist Church of Asheville (NRHP)   5 Oak St.

Built in 1927, the First Baptist Church of Asheville was designed by noted architect Douglas Ellington from his sketches of a cathedral in Florence, Italy. Three major additions have been made to the building. The Children's Wing was added in 1968, and the Sherman Family Center in 1980. This wonderfully elegant building is an unusual combination of an Early Italian Renaissance form and color scheme arranged in a beaux arts plan with Art Deco detailing. Of particular interest is the Art Deco copper lantern atop the dome and the subtle gradation of color in the roofing tiles. The walls are an effective combination of orange bricks, terra-cotta moldings and pink marble. This striking building is at the corner of Oak and Woodfin Streets.

First Christian Church (NRHP)   20 Oak St.

Right across the street is the First Christian Church, built between 1925 and 1926 in a traditional Late Gothic Style, and constructed of rock-faced grey granite masonry with smooth granite trim. Designed by the home office, it has an unusual feature in that the placement of the tower is at the intersection of the nave and transept.

Montford Historic District

The Montford Historic District is Asheville's oldest and largest with over 600 buildings reflecting a variety of late 19th and early 20th century styles. Montford is a culturally diverse and thriving community, and was the creation of Asheville's boomtimes, having its origins as an upper middle class suburb in 1889. Asheville's most famous son, writer Thomas Wolfe, describes Montford Avenue in *Look Homeward Angel* as "the most fashionable street in town."

Montford's Riverside Cemetery is well worth a visit for scenic beauty alone; but is also notable as the final resting place for two of America's most important writers: O. Henry (William Sidney Porter) and Thomas Wolfe.

Located just across I-240 from downtown Asheville, a drive through Montford reveals a collection of architecture from the Queen Anne to Georgian Revival styles, with many variations in between. Quite a few of these majestic old homes have been converted to bed & breakfasts, making Montford one of Asheville's premier destinations for those seeking a pleasant stay in a historic setting. The best way to see Montford is by car and the historic sites in this section will be presented as a self guided tour. Plan at least an hour, perhaps more if you wish to get out and visit Riverside Cemetery on foot, for the tour.

From I-240, take Exit 4C Haywood Street/Montford Avenue. Begin at the top of Montford Avenue just on the north side of I-240. Montford Avenue turns off of Haywood Street just west of the Asheville Visitor Center. Continue down Montford to 276, The Lion and The Rose Bed & Breakfast on your left.

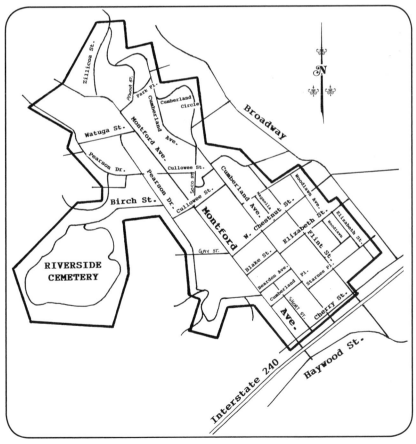

Montford Historic District

The Lion & The Rose Bed & Breakfast (NRHP)   276 Montford Ave.

This beautifully landscaped bed & breakfast is housed in a charming three-story Queen Anne/Georgian Revival style pebbledash building and is officially known as the Craig-Toms House. Interesting features are the double Doric posts on stone pedestals and the elaborate center gable. Built in 1898, this house has been faithfully restored to its original elegance, with all its rooms furnished with antiques, oriental rugs and period appointments. High embossed ceilings, golden oak, classic leaded and stained glass windows create a feeling of the Victorian era.

Right next door is The Black Walnut Bed & Breakfast Inn.

The Black Walnut Bed & Breakfast Inn (NRHP)   288 Montford Ave.

This large handsome residence, designed by Richard Sharp Smith was constructed around 1900. Known historically as the Otis Green House, after Otis Green who owned the residence for many years, it embodies the eclecticism characteristic of Smith's work, combining flourishes of the Shingle style, Queen Anne and Colonial Revival styles of architecture. Beautifully landscaped also, this striking building is faithfully restored and decorated throughout with antiques and fine traditional furniture.

The third of three bed & breakfasts located on this side of the street is The Inn on Montford, next door to The Black Walnut.

The Inn on Montford (NRHP)   296 Montford Ave.

Originally known as the Dr. Charles S. Jordan House, this "Old English" style house at 296 Montford Avenue was designed by Richard Sharp Smith. The house is typical of architect Smith's interpretation of the "Old English" style. Two major gables with splayed eaves are presented to the street at attic level, and a combination of shingles and pebbledash are employed. Construction of the house dates back to around 1900. This lovely bed & breakfast has period landscaping with rows of neatly trimmed boxwoods and other plantings. Queen-sized poster beds, English and American antiques and fine paintings all add to the atmosphere of an "English Cottage." After viewing these three inns, turn left on Watauga Street and proceed to Pearson Drive. Turn left on Pearson. On your left will be the romantic Wright Inn.

The Wright Inn and Carriage House (NRHP)   235 Pearson Dr.

The Wright Inn is one of the finest examples of Queen Anne architecture in the Montford District and in all of Western North Carolina. With stylized Doric porch posts on paneled pedestals, multiple gables and slate roof, this wonderfully restored building is a delight to behold. Elegantly appointed inside with antiques and family heirlooms, the 1899-1900 Victorian masterpiece was designed by George Barber.

Right across the street is the Colby House, another bed & breakfast.

The Colby House (NRHP)   230 Pearson Dr.

This bed & breakfast was built in 1924, and is a Dutch Colonial Revival-style dwelling with Gambrel roof. Interesting features include the elliptical leaded fanlight at the entrance door and the exterior of North Carolina blue granite with beaded mortar joints. Originally called the Dr. Charles Hartwell Cocke House, the Colby House today welcomes guests to a relaxing refined environment.

Continue down Pearson Drive and turn right onto Birch Street to the historic Riverside Cemetery.

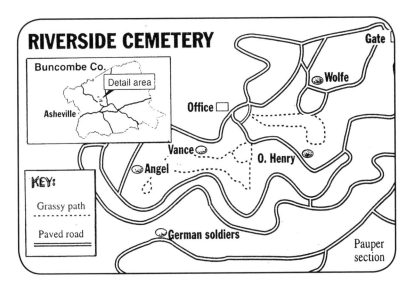

Riverside Cemetery (NRHP)   53 Birch St.

Historic Riverside Cemetery at the end of Birch Street and is operated under the direction of the City of Asheville Parks, Recreation and Public Facilities Department. It is the burial site of Thomas Wolfe, O. Henry (William Sidney Porter), Zebulon Vance (N.C. Governor and U.S. Senator), three Civil War Confederate Generals, Thomas L. Clingman and Robert R. Reynolds (U.S. Senators), and many of Asheville's founding families. Group tours are welcomed at this 87-acre cemetery. A walk through Riverside Cemetery is a walk through a rich source of area history. More than 13,000 people lie in marked graves, many with grave sites marked with angels and lambs crafted of Italian Carrera marble. The cemetery is open around the clock, but office hours are Monday-Friday, 8 a.m.-4:30 p.m. The office phone number is 258-8480. Website: www.ci.asheville.nc.us/parksrec/riversid.htm

Leaving the cemetery, return by way of Birch Street back to Pearson Drive and turn right. Continue down Pearson to West Chestnut Street and turn left. On West Chestnut you will cross Montford Avenue and continue on to Cumberland Avenue. Turn left at Cumberland and look for another lovely Victorian bed & breakfast, A Bed of Roses, immediately on your right.

Thomas Wolfe's gravestone at Riverside Cemetery in historic Montford

A Bed of Roses (NRHP)   135 Cumberland Ave.

This splendidly restored house dates back to around 1897 and is a playful variant of the Queen Anne style, with the dominant feature being the large second store polygonal corner projection with a broad ogee roof. The front porch also has stylized Doric type posts on stone pedestals. It was built by O.D. Revell and is officially named after the first long-term occupant Marvin B. Wilkinson who purchased it in 1904. Today, the house welcomes guests to its rooms furnished with antiques, handmade quilts and fresh flowers. (*See* illustration Section Two, Chapter 1)

Continuing on down Cumberland Avenue you will see the Maria T. Brown House on your right at 177, restored as the Carolina Bed & Breakfast.

The Carolina Bed & Breakfast (NRHP)   177 Cumberland Ave.

This 2½-story stucco dwelling was designed by Richard Sharp Smith and built before 1901. The porch has unusual brackets, shed dormers and a high hipped roof. The pebbledash stucco is typical of that period of architecture. The Carolina Bed & Breakfast has been graciously restored and features warm heart-pine floors, spacious rooms and seven working fireplaces.

Farther down Cumberland on your left is The Arbor Rose Inn at 254 Cumberland Avenue.

Cumberland Falls Bed & Breakfast (NRHP)   254 Cumberland Ave.

This early 20th century house is a 2½-story vernacular shingle dwelling which features shingles over weatherboards, bay windows and porch. Charming rooms with antique furnishings, ornamental fireplaces and ceiling fans await the visitors to this graciously restored dwelling.

At this point you will want to take the right fork onto Cumberland Circle. Ahead on the left will be the Wythe Peyton House at 46 Cumberland Circle, known today as Abbington Green Bed & Breakfast Inn.

Abbington Green Bed & Breakfast Inn (NRHP)   46 & 48 Cumberland Cir.
This stunning Colonial Revival home was built in 1908 for businessman David Latourette Jackson and was officially named the Wythe Peyton House for another prominent resident who lived here during the 1950s. It was designed by Richard Sharp Smith and has been lovingly restored to all of its former glory. It features shingles over weatherboards, Doric porch posts, molded trim and a central gable. Inside, each of the eight stylishly appointed guest rooms is named after parks and gardens in London.

Continuing on Cumberland Circle you will see the red Applewood Manor Inn on your left.

Applewood Manor Inn (NRHP)   62 Cumberland Cir.
Built before 1917, this shingle-sided Colonial Revival building features a pedimented entrance supported on Doric columns and flanking porches. Located on an acre and a half this finely restored bed & breakfast is a touch of country in the city!

Continue on Cumberland Circle until it rejoins Cumberland Avenue and turn right. Take Cumberland Avenue until you reach Panola Street. Turn left and go to Montford Avenue. Turn right on Montford and then right again on Zillicoa Street. Directly ahead on your left is the Homewood School Building and just beyond it is the magnificent Rumbough House.

Applewood Manor Inn

Homewood (NRHP)   19 Zillicoa St.

Constructed in 1934 and designed by Dr. Robert S. Carroll, founder of Highland Hospital, Homewood was for many years the home to Dr. Carroll and his second wife Grace Potter Carroll. The castle-like Homewood was constructed of uncoursed stone masonry, with an asymmetrical facade and entrance deeply recessed beneath a basket arch. A crenellated polygonal tower at the building's southeast corner and additional crenellation atop a projecting bay at the north end give the former residence the romantic image of a fortified castle.

Rumbough House (NRHP)   49 Zillicoa St.

Built in 1892 by James H. Rumbough, this elegant building, featuring a combination of Queen Anne, Colonial Revival and Neoclassical elements, is generally considered to be the most impressive residence in the Montford area. It features weatherboarding, wide porches and pairs of tapered and molded porch posts on stone pedestals. It is also known for its elaborately finished rooms. The house was owned by James Edwin Rumbough (1861-1941) who became the first and only mayor of the autonomous village of Montford when it was incorporated in 1893. Among his various other distinctions he is credited with being the first person to drive an automobile across the Appalachian Mountains, a feat that he accomplished in 1911. The house was purchased in 1952 by Duke University to become the administration building for the former Highland Hospital. It now houses the Carolina Center for Metabolic Medicine.

Turn around here and return on Zillicoa Street to Montford Avenue and turn left. Continue down Montford for 3 blocks to Blake Street and turn left on Blake to the stop sign. Turn right onto Cumberland Avenue and you'll find The Redwood House immediately on your right.

Redwood House (NRHP)   90 Cumberland Ave.

This early 20th century house is officially known as Redwood House and is a fine example of Colonial Revival architecture. It features shingles over stucco, Doric porch posts and a high pitched roof.

Turn left in front of Redwood House onto Elizabeth Street and continue to Flint Street. Turn right on Flint. Just ahead on your right you'll see the Flint Street Inns.

Flint Street Inns (NRHP)   100 & 116 Flint St.

The Flint Street Inns are two, side by side, distinguished old family homes that date back to the turn of the century. The structure at 100 Flint Street is a half-timbered stucco gable end dwelling. 116 Flint Street is thought to be one of Richard Sharp Smith's designs and features shingle over weatherboard, bracketed eaves, Montford brackets and a large dormer. Rooms in the Inns are furnished in turn-of-the-century style.

Your tour of Historic Montford is now over. Continue straight ahead up Flint Street to Haywood Street and downtown Asheville.

Vignette:
Richard Sharp Smith

Few persons have left their mark upon the face of a city as British-born Richard Sharp Smith has upon Asheville. Employed in his younger years by the prestigious architectural firm of Hunt and Hunt, he was sent to Asheville to supervise the construction of Biltmore House, which had been designed by Richard Morris Hunt. Smith stayed in Asheville, married here and raised two sons and two daughters. He became an American citizen and opened a private practice. During his life, he designed scores of private homes and dozens of commercial buildings in downtown Asheville. His distinctive architectural style has a British accent and Smith is remembered today as one of the most prominent of the many architects who helped shape Asheville.

Chestnut Hill Historic District

The Chestnut Hill Historic District is centered around Chestnut Hill, the apex of a knoll running west from Patton Mountain just 500 yards north of the center of Asheville. The neighborhood surrounding the hill was once an extension of the nineteenth-century residential streets that began a block off the city's Public Square. This district is a relatively compact late-nineteenth and early-twentieth-century residential neighborhood whose architectural styles and landscaping form a well-defined place. Tree-lined streets, brick-paved sidewalks and granite curbing are all unique features.

Practically all of the more than 200 buildings in the district were originally dwellings. Architecturally they range from the local in-town vernacular of the period to sophisticated versions of the nationally popular Queen Anne, Colonial Revival and Shingle styles.

The district dates from Asheville's post-railroad (post-1880) boom period and its finer homes reflect the relative sophistication of the city's more substantial citizens of that time. Besides a continuous growth in permanent residents, Asheville experienced an annual influx of thousands of summer and winter tourists and a number of Chestnut Hill "cottages" were built as high quality rental properties.

In this section, some of the more important houses will be presented as a self-guided driving tour. This is a very convenient way to see the Chestnut Hill district. Allow about an hour for the tour, and slightly more if you wish to park occasionally to get out and examine some of the buildings closer. As a note, Chestnut Hill District and the following two districts, Albermarle Park and Grove Park are very close together. It is possible to see all three of these important neighborhoods in a few hours.

Begin your tour by taking Merrimon Avenue north to Hillside Street. Turn right onto Hillside and go to second right North Liberty Street. Turn right onto North Liberty. A short distance on the left you'll see a classic Victorian House.

North Liberty Victorian House   76 North Liberty St.

A wonderful example of Victorian architecture, the elegant house is intricate in its detail and styling. It is a multi-gabled structure with flaring eaves and standing-seam tin roof, and has a square tower with a mansard-like shingled cap dominating the house adjacent to two projecting bays. The house's elaborate porch features turned posts, a scroll-bracketed cornice above a ladder frieze and a Chinese-Chippendale-like balustrade. Currently the building is undergoing restoration.

Continuing on North Liberty you will come upon the historic Beaufort House Bed & Breakfast on your left.

Beaufort House   61 North Liberty St.

This Victorian bed & breakfast is a grand 2½-story pink Queen Anne style house built in 1895 by former State Attorney general and prominent Asheville resident Theodore Davidson. This elegant building features a roof line that sweeps down upon an ample veranda accented at its southern end by a fanciful pergola. Elaborate interior woodwork includes paneled wainscoting and a closed-stringer stairway with intricately carved newel post and balusters. The building has been wonderfully restored as Beaufort House Bed & Breakfast and is furnished with antiques and period furniture.

From this unique house continue down North Liberty and turn left on East Chestnut Street. Located just one block down are two wonderfully restored bed & breakfasts. Chestnut Street is noted for its many fine examples of Colonial Revival, Queen Anne-influenced and bracketed Victorian homes.

White Gate Inn & Cottage   173 East Chestnut St.

Known officially as the Kent House, it was built circa 1889 and is a tall 2½-story Shingle style house. The building features tall exterior chimneys centered on minor gables. Mr. Kent who owned the house reportedly ran the Asheville Ice Company. Today it houses the White Gate Inn that is beautifully furnished with period antiques, fine furniture and collectibles.

Directly across the street is the newly restored Chestnut Street Inn.

Chestnut Street Inn   176 East Chestnut St.

Officially known as the William R. Whitson house, this Grand Colonial Revival House was built circa 1905. The house is constructed out of pressed brick and is two and a half stories with hip-on-hip roof with central Palladian dormer. The house, constructed for Whitson by J. M. Westall, has some of the finest woodwork in Asheville, including a graceful closed stringer stairway, beautiful arts & crafts wainscoting, and elaborate mirrored mantles. Today, Chestnut Street Inn

Chestnut Street Inn

welcomes visitors to its gracious and exquisite interior impeccably furnished with antiques and period decorations.

Just down the street on the right is the Annie West House.

Annie West House   189 East Chestnut St.

Built around 1900, this picturesque half-timbered cottage was designed by Richard Sharp Smith. Standing 1½ stories, it features a "veranda" across facade beneath a large central gable and smaller flanking dormers. This detail links it stylistically to early Biltmore Village architecture. Continue down East Chestnut to the Jeter Pritchard House.

Jeter Pritchard House   223 East Chestnut St.

This imposing two-story frame house was built by architect and builder James A. Tennent, who sold it to Senator Jeter Conly Pritchard in 1904. Construction dates back to around 1895. The building is a boxy weatherboard form under a multi-gabled roof. The interior of the house features exceptional woodworking.

Continue down East Chestnut to Charlotte Street and turn left. Take a right onto Baird Street and take your second left onto Albemarle Place to find The Carl Von Ruck House on your left.

Carl Von Ruck House (NRHP, LHL)   52 Albemarle Pl.

This rambling three-story house was built in three distinct stages by Dr. Carl Von Ruck, famed tuberculosis specialist who founded the Winyah Sanitorium on Sunset Mountain. In 1904 he bought twenty acres, including two houses that were on the property. One of the houses is incorporated into the north end of the present structure. In 1912 he built a separate house for his resident MDs just to the south and in 1915 he built between these two buildings, connecting them with a grand two-story music room with twin elliptic conservatories to either side. The music room features Viennese-crafted mahogany woodwork and houses Dr. Ruck's sixty-seven rank Aeolian Organ, with 4800 handmade wooden pipes rising two stories behind a curved mahogany screen.

At this point, turn around and return down Albemarle Place to Baird Street. At Baird turn left and look on the left for the Edward I. Holmes House.

Edward I. Holmes House   60 Baird St.
Built around 1883, this wonderfully restored house is an elaborated frame two-story double-pile plan design. There is a hip roof with internal brick chimneys and gabled projecting bays on each elevation. Other unique features are chamfered posts on opaque shoulder brackets and an elaborate scrollwork balustrade. No other 20th-century building in Asheville, especially of the finer structures, is as little altered as this house.

Edward I. Holmes House

Turn right onto Furman Avenue across from the Holmes House and continue down to East Chestnut Street. Turn right onto East Chestnut and just before you reach Charlotte Street you will see the white Thomas Patton House on your left. The main entrance is off Charlotte Street but virtually impossible to see from that direction because of the trees and landscaping. Turn left onto Charlotte Street and continue south to downtown Asheville.

Thomas Patton House   95 Charlotte St.
Built in 1869, the Thomas Patton House is a two-story frame house formally organized around central and traverse hallways. It has very interesting external features in chevron-latticed bargeboards. Tradition maintains that the house was

built by black carpenters working from the plans of Thomas Patton. Patton was the grandson of James Patton, mayor of Asheville and active public servant.

Albemarle Park Historic District

Albemarle Park, located off Charlotte Street, is a planned residential community that is composed of 45 residences reflecting diverse and very attractive architectural styles that were built on a 32.42-acre tract of land acquired by William Green Raoul in 1886. Raoul, who served as president of both Georgian and Mexican railroads, was the visionary who conceived of Albemarle Park and who purchased the land from a local farmer named Deaver. It was his third son, Thomas Wadley Raoul, however who was to be the foreman of the project and the one who made the vision a reality. For almost twenty-five years he devoted his energies to overseeing the construction and management of The Manor and cottages.

The main building, The Manor, was built in 1898 by Thomas. He conceived the idea of a twenty-five room English style country inn to be used as a boarding house. He later modified his plan to include several individually designed cottages to complement the main house. From these beginnings the Albemarle Park neighborhood began to take shape, with Raoul insisting upon only the finest materials and workmanship to be used in the construction.

This neighborhood has very narrow curving streets that preserve much of the wooded landscape of the area. It is situated on the western slope of Sunset Mountain and is crowned by The Manor that graces a knoll that slopes down to Charlotte Street. This district is evocative of Asheville's dramatic turn-of-the century resort town boom era, and its rich craftsmanship and informal quaintness is related to Biltmore Village.

The original site plan was designed by Samuel Parsons Jr., the landscape architect of New York's Central Park. The design catered to wealthy lowlanders from Georgia and North and South Carolina who saw the mountains as a summer refuge. The crown jewel of this marvelous complex is The Manor, one of the last intact grand hotels from the late 19th century resort era. It was used for the filming of one of the scenes for the recent movie "The Last of the Mohicans." This historic building also hosted the film crews for the movie, "The Swan," and Grace Kelly, who starred in the film was a guest at the inn. Her former rooms are now known as the Princess Suite. Alec Guiness, Agnes Morehead and Louis Jordan also stayed at The Manor during that time.

The Manor was converted to a retirement hotel in 1961 by Charles Lavin. By 1976 The Manor had changed owners again and at this time it became a residential hotel, and in 1984, after severe winter damage, it was closed. The Preservation Society bought The Manor in 1989 when it was threatened with demolition, and in 1991, it was sold and restored in an historically sensitive way as an apartment complex. Without the efforts of this important local organization, this historical treasure would have been lost forever.

Each building in the neighborhood was intended to have a distinctive architectural style. A walk through the neighborhood reveals cottages that show Italian, French and Swiss influences as well as Georgian Revival, Appalachian and Adirondack styles of architecture. The primary architect of Albemarle Park was Bradford Lee Gilbert, who also designed the Virginia Beach Hotel (1888) in Virginia Beach, Virginia, and the Berkeley Arms Hotel (1883) in Berkeley, New Jersey.

To reach Albemarle Park take Charlotte Street north till you come to the original Gatehouse on your right at 265. Turn right onto Cherokee Road. The Manor will be on your left. Park your car if you wish in the small parking lot on Cherokee Road.

The Manor (NRHP, LHL)   265 Charlotte St.

Constructed in 1889, The Manor is a rambling group of interconnecting wings which combine elements of Shingle, Tudoresque and Dutch Colonial Revival architecture. The main portion of The Manor was built soon after the property, originally part of the Deaver Farm, was purchased in 1886 by the elder Raoul. This main portion of the inn is a twenty-five room five-part structure of rough field rock above which is a stucco and timber level.

A second wing, built in 1903, angles out from the main body of the inn towards the road. The main level of this wing is Tudoresque and has cross timbering beneath the windows that is painted a deep red color.

A third wing projects in the opposite direction and is composed of rough stone below green shingles. This wing was added in 1913-1914.

The interior of The Manor is wonderfully executed craftsmanship that is believed to have been done by Italian workmen from Biltmore Estate. An immense brick fireplace, a long, curved glass-enclosed sun corridor and Tiffany-type stained glass windows are among the notable features.

Just below The Manor are the Gatehouse and the Clubhouse.

The Manor

The Gatehouse (NRHP)

Also referred to as the Lodge, this building was the first structure built in Albemarle Park, erected by James A. Tennent in 1898. It was designed by Gilbert in the Tudoresque Shingle style with pebbledash stucco at the first floor and granite foundation. The Lodge arched over the entrance drive leading from Charlotte Street into The Park. During the early years of the development, the offices of the Albemarle Park Company were on the ground floor of the two-story shingle and stone turret. Today the Gatehouse is used for commercial office space.

The Club House (NRHP)

Built around 1903, it originally contained the tennis courts, bowling alleys, pool and billiard rooms and a reading lounge. It is an L-shaped building of stone and timber that has a long gallery on the second floor. Three small hexagonal offices now dot the area between the old tennis court and the Gatehouse, and though modern, are in character with the round and polygonal forms found on several of the earlier buildings. The Club House today is used for commercial office space.

After viewing these main buildings, you may wish to venture on foot to see some of the lovely cottages throughout Albemarle Park. Dogwood Cottage, Foxhall and Rose Bank are all within walking distance.

Dogwood Cottage Inn (NRHP)   40 Canterbury Rd.

This large 1½-story rustic shingle cottage is now operated as a bed & breakfast, the Dogwood Cottage Inn. Main features are a continuous shed dormer across the main facade, casement windows and a bracketed hood over the entrance. It was built as a home for William Green and Mary Raoul in 1910 and sits on a commanding mountainside site offering views of the mountains to the west. The rustic style of the Dogwood Cottage relates to the traditional architecture of the Appalachians.

Dogwood Cottage Inn

Foxhall and Fox Den (NRHP)　　　　　60 Terrace Rd.

Foxhall is the larger of the two and was built in 1914 by E.A. Fordtran, who was the owner of the New Orleans Times/Picayune newspaper. It is a 2½-story building, originally stucco and shingle, which has been refaced with brick veneer and siding. The building has graceful roof lines and fenestration and is beautifully landscaped. Fox Den is a two-story gambrel roofed garage apartment of stucco and timber that adjoins Foxhall.

Rose Bank (NRHP)　　　　　106 Orchard Rd.

Rose Bank is a two-story shingle cottage with a projecting Dutch gambrel wing and double porches, designed in the Dutch Colonial Revival Style. Built around 1905, Rose Bank has distinctive windows that have diamond-paned upper sashes playfully arranged. Windows of various sizes and shapes are tied together with simple trim.

Grove Park Historic District

The Grove Park Historic District is located in an area that adjoins the Grove Park Country Club golf course and extends on either side of Charlotte Street. This district also includes part of Kimberly Avenue that runs along side the golf course in a northerly direction.

The Grove Park neighborhood was designed and developed by St. Louis entrepreneur Edwin Wiley Grove with the help of Chauncey Beadle, landscape designer and later superintendent of Biltmore Estate and is a superb example of early twentieth century planned residential development. Grove wanted his development, like every other real estate venture he engaged in, to be exciting and innovative. Some of his ventures, such as the Grove Arcade and the Battery Park Hotel, were on the cutting edge of design and planning and his Grove Park Inn stands today as a monument to Grove's vision and genius.

The early phases of Grove Park were laid out by Chauncey Beadle and have curvilinear streets, large tree canopies, stone retaining walls and a grand entry park. There are many architectural styles represented and these include Shingle, Neo-Classical, American Foursquare, Colonial Revival, Tudor Revival, Georgian Revival, Bungalow, Italian Renaissance, Queen Anne and Chateauesque. Many nationally known and historically important architects worked within the Grove Park neighborhood. These included Richard Sharp Smith, Ronald Greene, Henry I. Gaines and James Gamble Rogers. Local Asheville developers E.A. Jackson and W.H. Westall also contributed to Grove Park's growth, buying and developing many lots in the 1920s.

Especially notable in this lovely neighborhood are the large number of deciduous and evergreen trees. Stonework in retaining walls and stairs are found throughout and many of the houses are on terraced grounds.

Like the Montford and Chestnut Hill historic districts, Grove Park is easily seen by car, and a self-guided tour is presented below.

To reach Grove Park take Charlotte Street north to 324 Charlotte Street where you will see Mr. Grove's Real Estate Office on the left.

E.W. Grove's Office (NRHP)   324 Charlotte St.

This building is a small one-story rubble rock structure with rough-faced ashlar covering. It features a tile-on-gable roof. It was constructed around 1909 and is said to have been used by Grove when he was building the Grove Park Inn and developing the Grove Park neighborhood. The building was designed by Richard Sharp Smith and is the only structure of its type in the area. Grove left the building and the adjacent park to the City of Asheville. Note also the handsome stone gates to the right, entrances into the park.

Continue on Charlotte Street to 337 where you will see the beautiful St. Mary's Parish Church just ahead on your right.

St. Mary's Parish, Grove Park (NRHP)   337 Charlotte St.

Described in the year of her founding in 1914 as a "Wayside Shrine in the Mountains of Western North Carolina," beautiful little St. Mary's Church has attracted countless visitors over the years. Designed by Richard Sharp Smith and built in 1914, the church is English Gothic in style and cruciform in plan. Constructed out of red brick with steeply pitched gable roofs, the building is like those dotting the hilly landscape of County Durham, Northumberland and Cumbria in northern England. The English cottage-style Rectory, also designed by Smith, was built and set in beautiful landscaped grounds. The landscape architect was the famous Frederick Law Olmsted, architect for Biltmore Estate and designer

St. Mary's Parish at Grove Park

of New York's Central Park. International attention was brought to St. Mary's by the writer Gail Godwin when she immortalized the church in her novel Father Melancholy's Daughter.

From St. Mary's Parish, return down Charlotte Street and turn left onto Sunset Parkway. Continue on Sunset to the end where you will turn left onto Glendale Road. Look for 50 on your right, the Edgar Fordtran House. It is up on a hill at the intersection of Ridgewood Street, behind ivy covered stone walls.

Edgar Fordtran House (NRHP)   50 Glendale Rd.
This Tudor Revival style house was built in 1936 for Edgar Fordtran for $30,000. It is constructed of cut ashlar stone with stucco infill as part of the half-timbering in the front gable. This lovely building features outstanding chimneys and a decorative wrought iron front door. The landscaping is especially noteworthy and includes a winding drive, stone retaining wall and large wrought iron gates. This residence was the ASID Designer House for 1994.

Continue on Glendale Road to the stop sign and turn left onto Macon Avenue. Look for the Ralph Worthington House on your left.

Edgar Fordtran House

Ralph Worthington House (NRHP)   41 Macon Ave.
This handsome house was built in 1920 by Ralph Worthington and is a wonderful example of the quality of the houses that abound in the Grove Park District. The ASID Designer House for 1992, it is an excellent blend of Colonial Revival and Spanish Revival styles of architecture. It was operated as a boarding house from 1942 to 1959 but is now a private residence.

Continue on Macon to Charlotte Street and at the stop sign take a right onto Charlotte Street. Turn left onto Evelyn Place just beyond the park. Immediately on your left, just past the intersection of Gertrude Place, is the J.R. Oates House.

Ralph Worthington House

J.R. Oates House (NRHP)
90 Gertrude Pl.

Built in 1913 for J.R. Oates, a local banker, the house was designed by the architectural firm of Smith and Carrier. It is an excellent example of the Prairie style of architecture. A striking two-story house with smooth stucco and a cross gable roof with wide overhanging eaves. According to the portfolio of Richard Sharp Smith, the building was designated as "fireproof." It is noteworthy also for the superb craftsmanship of the interior as well as the exterior spaces, including the beautifully landscaped grounds.

Directly across the street on Evelyn Place is the Reuben Robertson House.

Reuben Robertson House (NRHP)   1 Evelyn Pl.

This elegant house was built for Reuben Robertson in 1922 and was designed by New York architect James Gamble Rogers. This is an excellent example of the Colonial Revival style of architecture.

Continue on Evelyn Place to 107, The William Bryan Jennings House, which will be on your right.

Reuben Robertson House

Residence on Kimberly Avenue

William Jennings Bryan House (NRHP)   107 Evelyn Pl.

William Jennings Bryan, famous orator, statesman, politician and presidential candidate spent many summers in this house. Built in 1917, it was designed also by Richard Sharp Smith, and is a refined example of a Colonial Revival style house. Exceptional details include paired columns and pilasters on front stoop and dentil molding beneath the roof lines.

After viewing the Jennings House, turn right onto Kimberly Avenue and continue on up Kimberly.

Kimberly Avenue

Kimberly Avenue is one of the finer residential streets in all of Asheville, bordered on one side by the Grove Park Inn golf course and one the other by grand houses from the 1920s. The Avenue is a favorite for local walkers and joggers and the views of the Grove Park Inn and nearby mountains from the tree-lined street are outstanding.

This concludes your tour of the historic Grove Park District. To return to downtown Asheville, retrace your path down Kimberly Avenue and Edwin Place to Charlotte Street. While you are in the vicinity, you may wish to visit the Grove Park Inn and The Biltmore Industries Buildings which are close by. Both of these are presented later in this chapter.

Biltmore Village Historic District

Biltmore Village was built by George W. Vanderbilt on the south bank of the Swannanoa River at the edge of his vast estate. Much has changed over the years by the flood tide of urban sprawl, Biltmore Village nonetheless has some remaining buildings from that early period. Many of these form a small neighborhood which

evokes the village's original ambience. The landscaping, the quaintness of the cottages, the presence of
other remaining buildings and the
street pattern all form an important
historic district.

The symmetrical, fan-shaped
street plan is the least changed
element of the original design. At
the north end, Brook and Lodge
streets join at an obtuse angle at the
railway station and plaza. All Souls
Crescent swings south from these
streets to form the boundaries of
the village, and within the village
itself a network of streets forms the
fan pattern.

Vanderbilt planned Biltmore
Village as a picturesque manorial
village, to complement his estate
and grounds and as a practical solu-
tion to solving the housing problem
of estate workers and servants. This
model village, English in flavor with

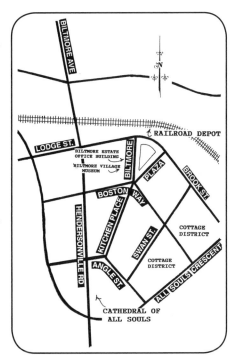

Biltmore Village

its Tudor buildings, was primarily the work of three men: Richard Morris Hunt
(1827-1895), the nationally prominent architect who designed Biltmore House
itself, the village church of All Souls, the railway station and the estate office;
Frederick Law Olmsted (1822-1903), the renowned landscape architect who
designed the grounds of the estate and the village plan; and Richard Sharp Smith
(1852-1924), an architect employed by Hunt who designed the cottages, school,
post office, infirmary and other village buildings.

The site along the Swannanoa River, a small crossroads known as Asheville
Junction or Best (for William J. Best, an owner of the Western North Carolina
Railroad) was chosen for Biltmore Village, planning for which began in 1889.
Vanderbilt bought the village, relocated the residents and constructed an entirely
new town. Construction was largely complete by 1910. Shortly after Vanderbilt's
death, the village was sold and over the years, many changes were made, not all
compatible with the original concept and design of Vanderbilt and his architects.
Recently however, through the efforts of the Historic Resources Commission
of Asheville and Buncombe County, the Preservation Society and the Biltmore
Village Merchants Association, much restoration has been accomplished and an
enlightened program of adaptive use instituted. At the heart of Biltmore Village's
recent revival has been the conversion of former cottages into commercial spaces
that include gift shops, restaurants, art and craft galleries and clothing stores.

The Village is a Local as well as a National Historic District which will insure its preservation and continued restoration.

Biltmore Village is an ideal setting for a walking self-guided tour and the historic buildings highlighted in this section will be presented in that fashion. I suggest also that you visit the Biltmore Village Historic Museum at 7 Biltmore Plaza, one building to the left of the Biltmore Estate Office Building on the plaza. (*See* Section Three, Chapter 2)

Begin your walking tour by parking near the plaza, across from the old railroad depot, which will be your first stop.

Biltmore Village Railway Depot Building (NRHP)   1 Biltmore Plaza

This Southern Railway passenger depot was designed by Richard Morris Hunt and is a symmetrical one-story structure with half-timbered pebbledash walls. It is significant as one of the four structures that were designed by Hunt for the Village and it serves as one of the major functional and architectural landmarks of the community. It was built in 1896.

Walk across the Plaza and you will see the Biltmore Estate Office on your right.

Biltmore Estate Office Building (NRHP)   10 Biltmore Plaza

Another of the four structures designed by Hunt it is a combination of the design motifs and materials utilized in other structures in the village. It is a 1½-story building that features pebbledash walls, half-timbering, brick trim, chamfered and bracketed porch posts and stylized classical ornament. This building served as the office for the operations of Biltmore Estate and was constructed also in 1896. It is still in use today by the Biltmore Company for offices.

After viewing the Biltmore Estate Office Building, you will see the Biltmore Village Historic Museum, also on the plaza. If they are open, stop in for a visit. After leaving the museum, continue on your way from the plaza area and walk south on Kitchen Place towards The Cathedral of All Souls directly ahead.

The Cathedral of All Souls (NRHP)   9 Swan St.

Originally known as All Souls Church, it was designated an Episcopal Cathedral in January 1995. The largest structure in Biltmore Village, it is an exquisite, lovely building of fine Romanesque style. Designed by Richard Morris Hunt, this complex building combines pebbledash wall surfaces, brick and wood trim, and expansive tiles roofs. In spite of the complexity however, the church is a simple cruciform with a tall tower rising in the center which contains most of the interior space. The Parish House features the same materials but is considerably different in design.

The interior is relatively simple but no less elegant and features wonderful stained glass windows created for the Vanderbilts by Maitland Armstrong and his daughter Helen. They illuminate a variety of scenes from the Old and New Testaments.

The Cathedral of All Souls

George Vanderbilt was one of the organizers of the congregation in 1896, financed the construction of the church and parish house and selected the furnishings. The church was consecrated on November 8, 1896.

From this lovely building, you may now begin to explore the Cottage District which is found on Swan Street, All Souls Crescent, and Boston Way. There are fourteen cottages in this district, which will be on your left and behind you as you face the front of the church and the Parish House.

Biltmore Village Cottage District (NRHP)

The English Tudor cottages on the east side of Biltmore Village were designed by architect Richard Sharp Smith. All are one-and-one-half to two-story pebbledash cottages with recessed porches, multiple gables and steeply pitched roofs. No two cottages are alike although they are closely similar and in some cases mirror images. They are located at 1 and 3 Swan Street, 2, 4, 6, 7, 10 and 11 All Souls Crescent and 5 and 6 Boston Way. Besides being architecturally interesting, these cottages now house specialty shops and restaurants.

This concludes the walking tour of Biltmore Village. Another structure of historical importance, The Reed House, is in the district and can be visited by car. From the plaza area take Lodge Street to Hendersonville Road (Highway 25) and turn left. Go south on Hendersonville Road to Irwin Street and turn left. Turn left at the end onto Dodge Street and look for 119, The Samuel Harrison Reed House.

Biltmore Cottage District

Samuel Harrison Reed House (NRHP) 119 Dodge St.

Built in 1892, this house is one of the most important Queen Anne style residences in Asheville. The frame structure features a prominent corner turret with an ogee dome and a wraparound porch. It is historically significant for its associations with Mr. Reed, who sold to George Vanderbilt and his land agents the property on which Biltmore Village was constructed.

Eliada Home Historic District

The Eliada Home is a youth home complex located in the Leicester neighborhood of Asheville. This historic district includes the early administrative, residential and agricultural buildings of the home as well as associated sites that include a residence, a tabernacle site, a log guest cabin and cemetery. Eliada Home is in a parklike setting with concrete walks and shade trees, and is situated on a hilltop.

Eliada Home was founded by Lucius B. Compton as a refuge for unwed mothers in 1903. The first facility was "Faith Cottage" on Atkinson Street in Asheville. The children's home was established in 1906, with buildings on the property dating back to 1907, and is still in operation today.

To reach Eliada Home, take Patton Avenue west from Asheville and turn right onto Leicester Highway. Turn right again onto Compton Drive. Eliada Home is at the end of Compton Drive. www.eliada.org

Main Building (NRHP)   2 Compton Dr.

The main building is a two-and-a half story, five-course American-bond brick structure that originally served as a dormitory and was used also for administration, food processing (canning) and as an outlet store for excess clothing and as a chapel. The exterior style is Colonial Revival and Foursquare-inspired, and was designed by architect Thomas E. Davis.

Located behind the Main Building and accessible down a short gravel drive is the most impressive of the structures at Eliada Home, the Dairy Barn.

Dairy Barn (NRHP)

This magnificent barn was built between 1930 and 1931 and is a two-level, six course American-bond brick building with room for forty dairy cows on the fire-proof first level and machinery and tools on the second level. The barn was used for milk production and the motto "Eliada Dairy, Pure Bred Guernseys" was originally painted on the west side of the roof. This has been replaced with the motto "Eliada Home Outlet Barn," indicating its use as a retail outlet since the late 1970s.

Oteen Veterans Administration Hospital Historic District

Located in the Oteen district of Asheville on US Highway 70 just beyond the intersection of Highway 70 and Riceville Road, the Oteen Veterans Administration Hospital District is a striking collection of massive yellow stucco Georgian Revival and white frame Colonial Revival buildings. As Riceville Road leaves Highway 70 at the foot of the hospital's lawn it runs north through the district and divides employees' dormitories and other residential structures to its west from the facility's main campus.

The structures included in the Historic District were built between 1924 and 1940 to replace a large collection of frame buildings which had served as U.S. Army General Hospital No. 19 in the late teens and early twenties. The work accomplished at the Oteen location turned out to be one of the nation's best and most beautiful permanent military hospitals. The focus of care at the hospital was tubercular and respiratory treatment. Today the hospital still functions as a major care center, although some of the outlying buildings have been converted to apartment use. For more information about the current medical programs at the VA Hospital, see Section Three, Chapter 8 Asheville VA Medical Center.

Asheville High School Historic District (NRHP)

To reach the Asheville High School Historic District, take Patton Avenue west from Pritchard Park. Turn left onto Asheland Avenue until you reach McDowell Street. Continue on McDowell until you reach the high school at 419.

Asheville High School is an Italian Renaissance and Art Deco pink granite building that was a state-of-the-art facility when it opened February 5, 1929. It cost $1,362,601 when it was built by general contractor Palmer-Spivey Construction Co. of Charlotte, using the plans of architect Douglas D. Ellington. The main school building is visible from McDowell Street and is a large Art Deco/Italian Renaissance style structure that features a tile roof. The landscaping in front is extraordinary and the formal stairs, drives and walkways of Ellington's plan serve as a graceful setting for the magnificent building. The whole school complex is

Asheville High School

contained within this district. Originally named Asheville High School, it was renamed Lee H. Edwards High School but was changed back to Asheville High School in 1969 when the city schools were integrated.

Asheville School Historic District (NRHP)

To reach the Asheville School Historic District, take Patton Avenue west from Pritchard Park. Continue on Patton Avenue (19-23 South); 3.4 miles after you cross over the French Broad River, look for Asheville School Road on your left just beyond Goodwill Industries.

The Asheville School and its attendant buildings compose the Asheville School Historic District. This lovely parklike campus is approximately 276 acres, with a winding entrance road lined with native evergreens. These were planted by Chauncey Beadle, landscape gardener for Biltmore Estate, who donated his design services to the school. Asheville School is still in operation today, many years after its founding in 1900, and still provides excellent secondary education as a private boarding school. It was founded by Newton Anderson and Charles Mitchell. Over the years, they commissioned many prominent architects to design the campus buildings, including John Milton Dyer, Thomas Hibben, and Anthony Lord. The result was a collection of wonderful and architecturally impressive buildings. www.asheville-school.org

Following the entrance road you will pass in front of the three main administration buildings and then around to the larger structures, Anderson Hall, Mitchell Hall and Lawrence Hall, all on your right.

Anderson Hall (NRHP)   Asheville School Rd.

This building was built as the main academic building in 1900 and is the oldest one on the campus. It was designed by John Milton Dyer of Cleveland and is Tudor Revival in style. Constructed primarily of brick with limestone lintels and sills on the first and second floor windows, it is three stories tall.

Mitchell Hall, Asheville School Historic District

Mitchell Hall (NRHP)   Asheville School Rd.

Built in 1903, this building was also designed by Dyer and is a long, linear plan with porches on the front and rear of the building. Walls on the lower floors are brick, with half-timbering on the uppermost floors. The exterior and interior design of this superb building is Art Deco with Tudor Revival detailing.

Lawrence Hall (NRHP)   Asheville School Rd.

Lawrence Hall is the third of the main campus buildings and was constructed in 1907. It is likely that Dyer also designed this building. The building was originally used as a dormitory, which it remains today along with administrative use. Three stories high, it is Tudor Revival in style.

Biltmore Industries Historic District (NRHP)

Directions: Take Charlotte Street to Macon Avenue. Turn right on Macon and go to Grove Park Inn Resort, 290 Macon Avenue. Turn left into the inn's parking area and bear right to go down the hill and left at the stop sign to Grovewood Road and Grovewood Shops area.

The Biltmore Industries complex of buildings is situated on an eleven and one-half acre tract adjacent to the Grove Park Inn Resort. The seven buildings of the grouping, which vary in size and form, lie in a row along the top of a ridge. These cottages were constructed in 1917 under the supervision of Fred Seely, designer and owner of the Grove Park Inn. The purpose was to provide workshops for the production of high-quality crafts and fine hand-woven cloth that would be pleasing to the workers, and to provide a special to visitors at the Grove Park by offering the opportunity to observe the manufacturing process and to purchase completed items.

*Biltmore Industries buildings include Estes-Winn Automobile Museum.
The buildings are adjacent to the Grove Park Inn Resort & Spa.*

Today the Biltmore Industries Buildings house the Grovewood Gallery, the Estes-Winn Automobile Museum, the North Carolina Homespun Museum and the Grovewood Cafe.

Other Historic Asheville Sites & Buildings

This section of Historic Asheville is devoted to those sites and buildings of architectural or historic importance that have not been covered in the previous section.

Albemarle Inn Bed & Breakfast (NRHP, LHL)   86 Edgemont Rd.

Officially known as the Dr. Carl V. Reynolds House, this large frame Neo-Classical Greek Revival building is today the Albemarle Inn Bed & Breakfast. It is distinguished by a gable roof and a two-story portico with twin pairs of Corinthian columns and half-round pilasters. The interior features oak paneling and an exquisite carved oak stairway with a unique circular landing and balcony. Dr. Carl Reynolds built this house in 1909 and occupied it until 1920. Thereafter it was leased to the Grove Park School and then to the Plonk sisters, who operated an arts school there until it became the Albemarle Inn in 1941. Hungarian composer Bela Bartok stayed at the Inn during 1943 and while there completed his Third Piano Concerto, also known as the Asheville Concerto or Concerto of Birds. (*See also Section Two, Chapter 1*)

Directions: From Pack Square, take College Street east to Charlotte Street. Turn left and go 0.9 miles. Turn right onto Edgemont Road.

Albemarle Inn Bed & Breakfast

Beaucatcher Tunnel (NRHP) College St.

This two-lane tunnel was originally built in 1930 to replace a winding road that went over Beaucatcher Mountain. The tunnel was blasted out of solid granite and has served Asheville for these many years. In 1997 it was refurbished and modernized and new granite stonework installed over the entrances.

Directions: From Pack Square take College Street east to the nearby tunnel entrance.

Biltmore Estate (NRHP, NHL) Entrance opposite Biltmore Village

This magnificent estate built by George Vanderbilt is a national treasure. Biltmore House, the largest privately owned house in America, is visited by hundreds of thousands of visitors each year. For architectural and historical information see Section Three, Chapter 3 Biltmore Estate.

Biltmore Forest

Biltmore Forest is an area of fine residential homes that adjoins part of Biltmore Estate. Driving through this lovely parklike neighborhood you will see many architecturally interesting and historic buildings. Notice also the street lamps, antique ornamental fixtures still in use throughout that combine lighting and signage functions. The high quality copper and bronze swan-neck lamp posts are thought to have been manufactured in California and bought by a Judge Adams before 1928. Of special interest are the Biltmore Forest Municipal Buildings (circa 1927) at Vanderbilt Place, the Silver Shop Building (circa 1930) at 365 Vanderbilt Road and the Biltmore Forest Country Club (circa 1922) at Country Club Road.

Residence in Biltmore Forest

Although Biltmore Forest is not a Historic District, many of the buildings are individually listed in the National Register of Historic Places.

Directions: Biltmore Forest can be entered at many places along Hendersonville Road going south from Biltmore Village. An easy-to-find entrance is Vanderbilt Road that enters the Forest just to the right of the Quality Inn Biltmore.

Cedar Crest (NRHP, LHL)   674 Biltmore Ave.

Officially known as the William E. Breese, Sr. House, this is one of the largest and most opulent residences surviving from Asheville's 1890s boom period. A wonderful Queen Anne-style dwelling, it was constructed by contractor Charles B. Leonard in 1891. It features a prominent turret, expansive side and rear porches and interior woodwork of extraordinary beauty. It was opened as a tourist home with the present name "Cedar Crest" in the 1930s. Today, it is a Victorian bed & breakfast. (*See* also Section Two, Chapter 1)

Directions: From Pack Square take Biltmore Avenue south.

Church of the Redeemer (NRHP)   1201 Riverside Dr.

This small, coursed-ashlar church was reportedly built in 1886 by a Dr. Willis, an immigrant from England. It features a cruciform plan, patterned slate roof and round arched windows with beautiful stained glass. An Episcopal Church, it still is in operation and visitors are welcome.

Directions: From Pack Square take Broadway north to Riverside Drive. Turn right onto Riverside Drive.

Grove Park Inn Resort & Spa (NRHP, NHL) 290 Macon St.

The Grove Park Inn Resort & Spa is one of the largest resort and conference centers in the Carolinas. Built in 1913 by Edwin Wiley Grove of native granite boulders, the main block of the inn is four double bays wide and four stories deep with a deep hip roof pierced by two rows of eyelid dormers, thus making six floors in all. The granite for the inn was quarried locally from nearby Sunset Mountain.

A magnificent building, it has many noteworthy architectural features including more than 600 handmade solid copper lighting fixtures still in use, the main lobby with the huge fireplaces at each end and the striking red clay tile roof. Recently wings were added to each side of the hotel, thus providing over 500 rooms. (*See* Section Three, Chapter 6 for more about the history of the Grove Park Inn Resort & Spa)

Directions: Take exit 5B onto Charlotte Street off I-240. Go one-half mile north on Charlotte Street to Macon Avenue. Turn right. The Inn is one-half mile up Macon Avenue.

Grove Park Inn Country Club Building (NRHP) Country Club Rd.

Formerly the Asheville Country Club, this rambling stucco-on-masonry structure was designed in a chateauesque style by English architect H.T. Linderberg in 1925. Distinctive features include a diminutive round tower with tall conical cap and weathervane adjacent to the archway drive and a grand Flemish bond chimney on the west side of the north-south section of the building. The Country Club building is owned today by the Grove Park Inn Resort and houses the Golf Pro Shop, swimming pool facilities and is also used to host meetings and weddings.

Directions: Take exit 5B onto Charlotte Street off I-240. Go one-half mile north on Charlotte Street to Macon Avenue. Turn right. Inn is one-half mile up Macon. Enter into main driveway and in front of the hotel bear right. Go down hill to stop sign and turn left and then left again at stop sign onto access road. Country Club building in on your left.

Longchamps Apartments (NRHP) 185 Macon Ave.

This imposing six-story structure was designed by Ronald Greene and built around 1925. Chateauesque and Tudor elements are combined in the unusual facade. The body of the building is a combination of half-timbers, rectilinear and half-round towers and brick and slate. A controversial building because of the unusual combination of elements, the building is nevertheless pleasing and has a majestic presence.

Directions: From I-240 take the Charlotte Street exit 5B. Take Charlotte Street north and turn right onto Macon Avenue.

The Old Reynolds Mansion (NRHP)   100 Reynolds Heights.

Officially known as the Reynolds-Reynolds House, this two-story American bond brick structure is supposed to have been built around 1846. During the 1920s the house was completely remodeled at which time a third floor within a mansard roof with dormers as well as other rooms were added giving the house a Second-Empire look. Today the house is known as The Old Reynolds Mansion and is operated as a bed breakfast.

Directions: From Pack Square, take Broadway to the juncture of Merrimon Avenue. Follow Merrimon Avenue north past Beaver Lake and turn right just past next stop light onto Beaver Drive. Turn left up gravel lane.

Sherrill's Inn (NRHP)   Highway 74A, Fairview

This large weatherboarded house was operated as an inn that served travelers passing through Hickory Nut Gap during the 19th century. Bedford Sherrill began operating the inn in 1834. It is a two-story saddlebag-plan structure that probably dates back to around 1801. Also located on the property is a very old smokehouse and tradition maintains that this building served as a frontier "fort" in the 1790s. More than likely this small rectangular building is the area's oldest structure. The inn, which is a private residence today, is visible on the right as you drive up the winding Hickory Nut Gap Road from Fairview going towards the Lake Lure area. As a note, if you happen to be in Asheville or Hendersonville in the fall during apple harvest the owners of the house sell excellent homemade cider and fresh apples grown in the property's orchards.

Directions: From Asheville take I-240 east to exit 9 (Bat Cave, Lake Lure and Highway 74A east). Take Highway 74A east through Fairview to the very end of the valley. As you climb up the winding road to Hickory Nut Gap, look for the State Historic Sign and Sherrill's Inn on your right up on a hill.

St. Luke's Episcopal Church (NRHP)   219 Chunns Cove Rd.

St. Luke's is a tiny historic country frame church located in the Chunns Cove section of Asheville. The building was consecrated on July 9th, 1898 and features triangular arched windows with simple geometric stained glass. The building is noteworthy for its simple, honest beauty.

Directions: From I-240 take Exit 6 Chunns Cove Road. Look for the church on your right.

St. Matthias Church (NRHP)   One Dundee St.

Saint Matthias began as Trinity Chapel in 1867 on land donated by Captain Thomas Patton. It has the distinction of being Asheville's first black congregation. In addition, a strong Sunday School and Day School flourished on the site and offered the only formal education at that time for the children of the black community. However, they soon outgrew the smaller structure and the present building was begun in 1894. It was completed two years later under

St. Matthias Church

the supervision of James Vester Miller, whose crew then went to begin work on Biltmore House. At this time it was renamed Saint Matthias to honor the 13th apostle and the first missionary to Africa. A handsome Gothic-brick structure, the building features elaborate interior woodwork.

Directions: Located in downtown Asheville. Take exit 5B off I-240 onto Charlotte Street heading south. Take a left on Carver Street, then a quick right on Grail Street, and then turn right onto Dundee Street.

Smith-McDowell House (NRHP, LHL) 283 Victoria Rd.

The Smith-McDowell House is one of Asheville's major historic structures. Built around 1848, the house is an impressive two-story double-pile plan Flemish-bond brick house with a graceful two-tier porch. It is one of the oldest buildings surviving in Asheville and definitely the oldest brick structure in Buncombe County. The house was constructed for James M. Smith, one of the wealthiest and most influential men in antebellum Asheville. It is open today as a museum. See Section Three, Chapter 2, Smith-McDowell House for more information about the museum and the programs offered.

Directions: From Pack Square take Biltmore Avenue south. Just past St. Joseph Hospital and just before Memorial Mission Hospital turn right onto Victoria Road.

The Smith-McDowell House as it appeared in 1848

Thomas Wolfe House, "Dixieland"

Thomas Wolfe House (NHL, NRHP, LHL)   48 Spruce St.

This historic two-story Queen Anne style house was the childhood home of North Carolina's most famous writer, Thomas Wolfe. The building was built around 1883 and features a decoratively-shingled slate roof, colored glass windows and bracketed cornice. In 1906 it was purchased by Wolfe's mother, Julia, who operated it as a boarding house that she called Dixieland. Wolfe immortalized it in his novel *Look Homeward Angel*. Almost destroyed by fire in 1998, the house was authentically restored in 2004. It is operated today as the Thomas Wolfe Memorial and is open to the public. For more information about this important house, see Section Three, Chapter 2, Thomas Wolfe Memorial.

Directions: From Pack Square take Broadway north and turn right onto Woodfin Street. Take first right onto Market Street. Memorial parking lot is ahead on the left (Spruce Street, the official address for the house no longer exists as a operational city street.)

Chapter Five
The Grove Park Inn Resort & Spa

The Grove Park Inn was the dream of Edwin Wiley Grove and his son-in-law, Fred Loring Seely, who envisioned the building of a resort hotel in the beautiful and restful mountains of the Southern Appalachians. Mr. Grove, who was the owner of a pharmaceutical company in St. Louis, Missouri, had come to Asheville for health reasons and liked the area so much he bought land here, including acreage on the western slope of Sunset Mountain. It was on this land that he eventually built a unique resort, the Grove Park Inn, patterned after the Old Faithful Inn in Yellowstone National Park, but built of native stone instead of logs.

Over the years, this grand hotel has had many distinguished guests. President Franklin D. Roosevelt and his wife, Eleanor, President Woodrow Wilson, F. Scott Fitzgerald, William Jennings Bryan and Will Rogers all journeyed to E.W. Grove's luxurious mountainside inn. The attraction of the inn was compelling and guests came in great numbers from all over the world. Other noteworthy visitors were John D. Rockefeller, General Pershing, Chief Justice Taft and Thomas Edison.

The hotel was designed by Mr. Seely and was constructed of granite boulders which were brought from nearby Sunset Mountain or from land owned by Mr. Grove. Hundreds of North Carolina laborers helped in the construction was well as Italian stone masons. Each rock was used only if it fit perfectly where it was needed, and the great fireplaces, which are thirty-six feet wide required one hundred and twenty tons of boulders to build. The hotel was completed in just over a year and was opened on July 1, 1913.

Originally a guard house protected the main entrance to the hotel grounds. The roads leading up the hill along Macon Avenue were also originally paved in smooth brick and converged on a circular parking area in front of the east porch, now the main entrance. Seven hundred pieces of furniture and over six hundred lighting fixtures were handmade by Roycrofters of East Aurora, New York, and the bedroom furniture was made by the White Furniture Company of Mebane, North Carolina. The rugs were woven in Aubusson, France, and lasted until 1955, when Charles and Elaine Sammons of Dallas came to the resort and refurnished the entire property. In the early years, entertainment at the hotel included bowling,

Grove Park Inn Resort & Spa on Sunset Mountain

swimming and billiards, and in the Great Hall there were concerts, organ recit-als and movies, after which each guest received an apple wrapped in gray paper for depositing the core. Another hotel practice which amazed visitors was the presenting of change at the cashier's window in washed and polished silver and crisp new paper money.

The rocking chairs on the porches and terraces were very popular as guests would sit for hours enjoying the mountain views and refreshing air. Walking paths on the grounds were also provided for the guests. During the years of the Second World War, the U.S. State Department leased the property for an internment center for Axis diplomats. Later, the Navy Department took over the hotel as a rest and rehabilitation center for soldiers returning from the war, and the Philippine Gov-ernment in exile functioned from the Presidential Cottage on the hotel grounds. For a decade after the war, the hotel was operated as such by the owner, Ike Hall.

The complete restoration and modernization, begun in 1955, included private baths in every room, electric and water lines replaced, American fabrics and rugs installed and furniture cleaned, restored and reupholstered. A beautiful swimming pool was added, tennis courts were resurfaced and a putting green constructed. In later years, wings were added to the original stone hotel body to provide needed guest accommodations.

In 1917, the Biltmore Industries, a cottage craft industry started by Mrs. George Vanderbilt, was sold to Mr. Seely who installed it in the Old English type shops at the edge of the Grove Park Inn grounds. Visitors to the Grove Park Inn could watch the spinning and carding of wool and the looming of cloth. These cottages still operate in much the same spirit and are home to the Grovewood Gallery, the Estes-Winn Memorial Automobile Museum and the North Carolina Homespun Museum.

In the early 1980s the famous resort hotel was converted from a seasonal enterprise into a year-round resort and convention center. Refurbishing of all the guest rooms, public areas, dining rooms and meeting rooms was undertaken, and the electric and plumbing system fully modernized. New wings included complete meeting and conference facilities.

Today, the Grove Park Inn Resort & Spa is the epitome of a world-class resort. This great hotel has it all—superb facilities, a rich history, overwhelmingly beautiful mountain setting, a Four Diamond Restaurant, and championship golf course. Recent renovations and additions to the resort include an updated Sports Center with indoor pool, the restoration of the historic main Inn's roof, new outdoor tennis courts and an extraordinary 40,000 sq. ft. spa complex that is one of the finest in the world (*See* review of the spa below).

> ## Vignette: Stone Poems
>
> One of the many surprises that await guests of the Grove Park Inn are the two magnificent fireplaces that grace both ends of the great entrance hall. Made out of massive boulders and large enough for a bunch of kids to camp out in, these transcendently massive stone structures also have a delicate literary side, and if you look closely, you will find written here and there on some of the stones poems and quotations. The one below is from the north fireplace:
>
> "This old world we're living in
> is mighty hard to beat
> We get a thorn with every rose
> but ain't the roses sweet?

Location: Asheville NC
Address: 290 Macon Ave., Asheville NC 28804
Telephone: 800-438-5800, 828-252-2711
Website: www.groveparkinn.com
Directions: From I-40 or I-26, take I-240 into Asheville. Take exit 5B, Charlotte Street. Proceed north on Charlotte Street for ½ miles, then turn right on Macon Avenue. After ½ mile, take Grove Park Inn entrance on left.

The Spa at The Grove Park Inn Resort

Completed in 2001, the 40,000 square foot spa is one of the finest in the world and features stone and timber construction, cascading waterfalls, waterscaped gardens and harmonious landscaping. Built into the face of Sunset Mountain and largely underground, the spa reflects the strong mountain arts and crafts traditions with a palette of soft greens, rust and ochre. Arts and crafts decorations abound, including torchieres that illuminate the main spa pool. The pool area, with its ocean themes, is absolutely spectacular. In addition to a relaxation pool and a lap pool, the area also boasts plunge pools and whirlpools. Saunas, steam rooms, inhalation rooms, treatment rooms and outdoor sun decks are only steps away. There are a wide range of services and treatments offered and these can be reviewed at the spa's website (www.groveparkinn.com). The following personal account of her own experience by writer Liza Schillo will give you an insider's view of just how wonderful the Spa at the Grove Park Inn Resort really is.

In order to get to The Spa at the Grove Park Inn, you must walk through the resort's grand lobby, which is breathtaking enough—all stone, vast ceiling and a fireplace at each end large enough to fit a handful of people. But stepping out onto the Sunset Terrace overlooking Asheville, and descending the stone steps winding through the garden and around a lit waterfall, pennies scattered over every rock the water touches, a feeling quite overwhelming wells inside me. The anticipation and excitement of spending an entire day of pampering, inside one of the world's best spas! The feeling augments the closer I get to the entrance, where I can catch the fragrant scent of herbs, and that warm, spicy smell that saunas give when they are warm.

Upon stepping inside I was amazed at the interior design. The theme I was told is "Rock, Water, Fire, and Light," and this is apparent as the lighting resembles torches in increments along the walls, which are all of rock. The ambience is one of an ancient library, or a revered museum. I am immediately greeted with the fine manners of one of their receptionists, who takes my name and hands me a black notebook in which is an itinerary and a question sheet. He courteously explains to me what I will be doing, and I take a seat. Not a minute later another spa employee comes out to give me and the other waiting ladies a tour before our treatments! We are lead through the back and I learn that only paying customers over the age of 18 are allowed here, to ensure maximum comfort and quiet to The Spa's clients. I also learned that no matter what treatment you are undergoing, you are permitted to remain at the spa, using the full facilities, for the entirety of the day, coming and going as you please! The spa divides into men and women's halves, and we are all taken to a very classy locker room where we change into robes and flip flops. The robes I was pleased to learn may be found in the spa store, as well as most of the products used during massages. A hall leading to the ladies' fireside lounge stems from it a shower room (with large showers, all of tile in a teal color, the "water" portion of their decorating theme I'd assume), bathroom and vanity room. Let me speak some on the vanity room: it was built for two Marilyn Monroes. The Hollywood lights that run above the wrap-around mirror highlight every amenity you could possibly need during your stay at The Spa. Mouthwash, hair gel, razors, deodorant, you name it and it is there at your fingertips!

Tiny windows throughout the interior allow peeks at things to come, some looking over the huge pool room that I will come to momentarily. In the lounge fancy snacks and cucumber water are provided, as well as a spot by the fireplace, but if you'd rather, the ladies' sundeck, complete with a hammock, is right outside. I was soon led to my massage, but I do not want to ruin this surprise for you! Let me just say that after I came out, my skin was literally glowing and my head was huge from so much attention given just to me for a solid 80 minutes! I can't remember the last time my body felt so good, so cool and relaxed, yet strengthened. It is a feeling that can only be created when you allow yourself enough time to drop everything you are currently worrying with and simply focus on the now, on how your body feels and what can ease that stress that so many of us today are under too often. You can be assured that every masseuse at the Grove Park Inn Spa is an absolute expert. I myself have applied for various positions at the resort with an above-average resume, and I know from experience that there is quite an extensive and selective application process. They know exactly what they are looking for, and at the Grove Park, they get it. My masseuse was one of the younger ones; he told me that a lot of the staff is around 50 years of age. He also described to me some of the other massage rooms, and all are different; mine was The Dome Room: waterproof, containing a bathtub and a water massager, as well as other special treats.

After my treatment, I am taken to another lounge and provided with a neck warmer until I am guided through another tour. This one leads me to the pool that I've seen so many pictures of. However there is much more to it than just the simple lap pool. There are of course more king-size showers, and an unlimited stock of towels. Then the women rejoin the men in this cavernous space containing several pools and whirlpools. There is a sauna, what I caught a waft of outside. To get to the sauna however you enter a room I'd never heard of, an Inhalation Room. This room remains at room temperature but inside is burning essential oils to breathe in! There is a double whirlpool next to it titled the Contrast Pools. One pool of 103 degrees and an adjoining one of 65. After minutes in the hot one, you are to plunge into the icy one! This is good for circulation and detoxification of the bloodstream, especially good after massages or strenuous workouts. Needless to say I did not spend much time here but my body certainly tingled with a refreshing cleanliness afterwards. I decide to try the large pools next. There is one in the back of the "cave," where the lights are dimmer. This pool is unique because in the ceiling there are tiny, twinkling fiber optic cable stars, just beautiful. A waterfall cuts through between this pool and the front one, which is a mineral salts pool. This was my favorite, at 86 degrees (several degrees above the latter), I could open my eyes without the burning of strong chlorine! Both pools are no deeper than 4 feet, and have speakers underwater so that their soft, soothing music may still be heard while you are swimming. Massage waterfall whirlpools bank this pool on either side, and I test them out. These are like hot tubs but with two streams of water that are just strong enough to sit beneath for a good, hard massage on the shoulders. For the remainder of the day I rotate between these varying pools of water, and spend a good deal of time on their large patio with comfy lounge chairs and another large fireplace. Here I order lunch, and it is brought to me on a silver platter! The spa café is not just hot dogs; I enjoyed the vegetarian BLT—their menu is clearly health conscious, though if you're not counting calories I recommend their fruit creams, made with real fruit! Though menu items may seem a little pricey, believe me you get more than what you pay for. That is probably the most remarkable thing I found during my visit. I noticed two outdoor gazebos while on the patio, and learned that these are available if you wish to upgrade a massage to the outdoors, with a view of our Blue Ridge Mountains. I shared the patio with a good number of people, though I was astounded at how vacant and spacious it seemed for such a renowned spa. Upon questioning I found that there is usually a constant 30 to 40 people at The Spa during busy summer months, yet even in the winter they stay pretty full. This is because they have found that now spouses and other acquaintances of people arriving at the Grove Park for business have discovered The Spa! These otherwise stay-at-homes now tag along for treatment while their significant other is in meetings (a good idea, I think). Though 30 to 40 people may sound like a lot, spread throughout The Spa it is a tiny number for the size of the building, which I greatly appreciated. For most of the day I had the pools to myself! It is good to make reservations several weeks in advance, especially on weekends and summer days.

After inspection of the spa's store in the front (in which I was very happy to find that my robe is carried there!), I exit the building sometime around dusk, sorry to be returning to what I'd left behind that morning. But as I stare into the wishing well of the waterfall as I climb the steps, I feel no need to toss a penny in, because tonight, I can't wish for anything else.

Chapter Six
Asheville Parks

Surrounded on all sides by majestic mountains, with a major river, the French Broad, flowing through its center, Asheville is blessed with nearby outdoor recreation opportunities and natural attractions for visitors. Excellent golf courses, parks, lakes and the river itself are within a few minutes' drive from downtown.

Asheville parks are full of activity in the summer.

Asheville Parks

Woven throughout the Asheville community are 11 neighborhood recreation centers, two pools, over 35 parks and play areas, 20 tennis courts, and a stadium complex supervised and maintained by the Asheville Parks and Recreation Department (828-259-5800)

Recommended Parks

The following listing of Asheville Parks were recommended to the author by the Asheville Parks and Recreation Department for first-time Asheville visitors. They are easy to find, and offer outstanding facilities.

French Broad River Park: One of the most popular parks in Asheville, it is located on Amboy Road along the French Broad River. Also one of Asheville's most beautiful parks, this 14-acre park meanders alongside the tranquil French Broad River. The property features a vast area of open green space with gracious old trees, a wildflower garden, a paved half-mile walking path, a large gazebo, picnic tables and grills, a fishing/observation deck, and a small playground. The natural beauty of this park makes it a popular spot for warm weather weddings

219

The French Broad River runs through 117 miles of Western North Carolina.

and romantic picnics in the meadow. The newest addition of the property is the Dog Park, which features a large fenced-in area made just for exercising and socializing your pooch! Off-street parking and restrooms are also available.

Martin Luther King Jr. Park: (Martin Luther King Jr. Dr., 828-259-5800) Ball field, concession stand, fitness course, soccer field, picnic tables, playground, restrooms, open shelters.

Montford Park: (Montford Ave., 828-253-3714) Outdoor basketball court, playground, restrooms, open shelters, tennis.

Murphy-Oakley Park: (Fairview Rd., 828-274-7088) Ball field, outdoor basketball court, concession stand, picnic tables and grills, playground, restrooms.

Weaver Park: (Murdock/Merrimon Ave., 828-258-2453) Ball field, outdoor basketball court, concession stand, soccer field, picnic tables and grills, playground, restrooms, open shelters, summer playground.

West Asheville Park: (Vermont Ave., 828-258-2235) Ball field, concession stand, picnic tables, restrooms, open shelters, summer playground, tennis.

Lake Julian District Park

Lake Julian is an ideal family recreational facility and an excellent spot for the fishing enthusiast. Located near Skyland, N.C., the park offers opportunities for picnicking, canoeing, sailing and outdoor games. The park is open year-round for all county residents and visitors to enjoy. Lake Julian was named in honor of Julian Byrd Stepp.

Lake Julian, off Long Shoals Road in South Asheville

Location: South Asheville
Address: Entrance is off Long Shoals Rd. (Hwy 146)
Telephone: 828-684-0376
Hours: Open year-round except Thanksgiving, Christmas, and New Year's Day. October-March: 8 a.m.-6 p.m.; April: 8 a.m.-8 p.m.; May-September: 8 a.m.-9 p.m.
Fees: Fees for fishing boat and canoe rentals, and picnic area rentals
Directions: Take Hendersonville Highway south from Biltmore Village. Turn left onto Long Shoals Road in south Asheville. The entrance to the park is a few miles on the left opposite Overlook Road.

Jewel of the Appalachians

Visitors to the mountains are often surprised by how often during the summer months they encounter the ruby-throated hummingbird. This tiny creature belongs to a family that numbers more than 300 tropical species, but the ruby-throated is the only one found in the mountains. It is a great migratory flier and strong enough to make the 500-mile flight across the Gulf of Mexico each spring and fall. During the summers it can be found in the mountains sipping nectar from flowers garden variety and wildflower alike. They are very good flyers and posses incredible stamina and endurance. In fact, they can hover in mid-air and even go backwards when necessary.

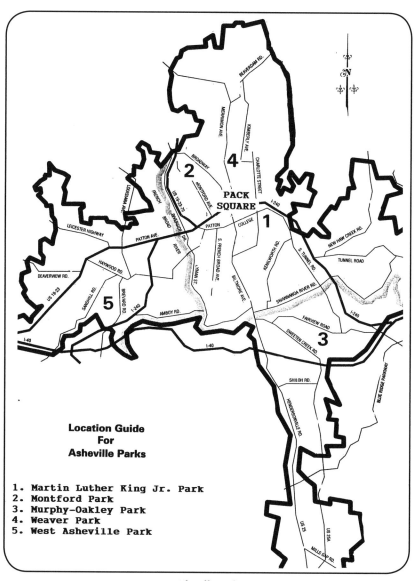

Asheville Parks

Section Four
Hendersonville

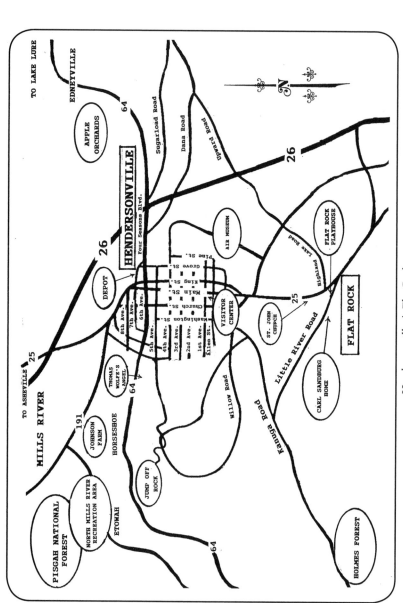

Hendersonville & Flat Rock

Chapter One
Hendersonville

Located amidst the majestic mountains of the Southern Appalachians, Hendersonville (population approximately 10,000) has come to be known as the "City of Four Seasons" and as an ideal retirement community. Since before the turn of the century, Hendersonville has attracted visitors and families seeking a gentle climate, lovely mountain scenery, and great recreational resources. It is located in Henderson County, which has a population of over 90,000.

Situated 2,200 feet above sea level, on a mountain plateau between the Blue Ridge and the Great Smoky Mountains, Hendersonville is blessed with a moderate and mild climate, yet the area still experiences the four seasons. With a mean summer temperature of around 70 degrees and 40 degrees in the winter, the climate is conducive to year-round outdoor recreation.

Tourism is a major industry in Hendersonville, with agriculture and industry also strong economic forces. Noted for its scenic beauty and tranquility, Hendersonville has industrial development restrictions that encourage small industries that will not disturb the peaceful quality of Henderson County life. Retirement development is also a major economic force in Hendersonville as retirees continue to flock to the area.

Blessed with an abundance of cultural opportunities, Hendersonville offers something for all ages. A symphony orchestra, theatres, libraries, and festivals throughout the year enrich the life of Hendersonville residents. Henderson County is also rich in parks, picnic areas, hiking trails and other outdoor attractions.

Over the years, Hendersonville has preserved its traditional downtown Main Street area from the decline which has happened in so many other cities. Main Street has been transformed into a beautiful tree-lined avenue complete with flower-filled brick planters. A stroll down this lovely thoroughfare will surround you with sounds of classical music, sights of exquisite seasonal plantings in a hometown setting of boutiques, numerous antique and clothing shops and an old fashioned pharmacy, plus benches on which to sit and people-watch. Few hometowns have remained as beautiful, vital, and alive as historic downtown Hendersonville. The streets bring history to life and bring the best of yesteryear into the excitement of today.

Hendersonville was an uninhabited Cherokee hunting ground before Revolutionary War solder William Mills discovered it in the late 1780s. He received one

Downtown Hendersonville

of the first land grants west of the Blue Ridge and established the first community. By right of discovery, Mills christened some of Henderson County's picturesque regions: Mills River and Mills Gap are names that are still in use today.

The county was named for Chief Justice of the State Supreme Court Judge Leonard Henderson and has four incorporated areas: the city of Hendersonville, the village of Flat Rock, the town of Fletcher, and the town of Laurel Park. Agriculture was the sole industry for early Hendersonville citizens. Tourism came later as visitors from the lowlands in South Carolina and Georgia discovered the scenic beauty and cooler climate. Industrial development became important after World War II, with the founding of the Chamber of Commerce program. Henderson County has long been known for its superior apples, and apple production still continues to be a major industry. Hendersonville celebrates this fact every summer with its famous "Apple Festival."

Hendersonville has two small towns, Laurel Park and Mills River, both primarily residential, and a number of unincorporated communities that are constelled in and around the city. The unincorporated communities, all rural with some light industry and businesses, include Edneyville, Etowah, Horse Shoe, Mountain Home and Tuxedo.

City Hall: 145 5th Avenue East, Hendersonville NC 28792; 828-697-3000

Website: www.cityofhendersonville.org

Elevation & Population: 2,200 feet, 10,000+

Visitor Center: 201 South Main Street, Hendersonville NC 28792; 800-828-4244; www.historichendersonville.org

Directions To Visitor Center: Take exit 18B off I-26. Travel south on Highway 64 for about 2½ miles. Turn left onto Main Street and continue eight blocks to 201 South Main Street.

Hendersonville Chamber of Commerce: 330 North King Street, Hendersonville NC 28792; 828-692-1413; www.hendersonvillechamber.org

County: Henderson County: County Offices, 1 Historic Courthouse Square, Suite 2, Hendersonville NC 28792; 828-697-4809; www.hendersoncountync.org

Chapter Two
Hendersonville
Cultural Attractions

Carl Sandburg Home

A very popular attraction, Pulitzer Prize-winning writer Carl Sandburg's farm, "Connemara," is open to the public for visitation. The farm includes 264 acres of rolling hills, forests, lakes, pastures, goat barn, and buildings. Located in Flat Rock, three miles south of Hendersonville, the grounds are open for self-guided tours. Guided tours of the home are also scheduled daily. The barn

Carl Sandburg Home

and the many delightful goats are a hit with the kids!

Location:	Flat Rock, NC
Address:	1928 Little River Rd., Flat Rock, NC 28731
	Telephone: 828-693-4178
Hours:	Open-year round, 9 a.m. to 5 p.m. Closed Christmas Day.
Fees:	Guided house tour $5 adults, $3 seniors, children under 15 free
Allow:	Two hours
Website:	www.nps.gov/carl
Directions:	Connemara is located 3 miles south of Hendersonville in Flat Rock. Take Highway 25 south from Hendersonville and turn right just beyond the Flat Rock Playhouse onto Little River Road.

Fifth Avenue Mask Museum

The Fifth Avenue Mask Museum houses a masks and related artifacts collected by retired art teacher Ellen Hobbs. The collection includes over 500 masks as well as dolls in native costume from Africa, Asia and North and South America.

Location:	Hendersonville, NC
Address:	317 Fifth Avenue, Hendersonville NC 28792
Telephone:	828-693-7108
Hours:	By appointment only
Fees:	None
Allow:	1 hour
Directions:	From Asheville take I-26 South. Take exit 49B onto US Highway 64 toward Hendersonville. Turn left at North Grove Street, take the 1st left onto 5th Avenue East.

Flat Rock Playhouse

The State Theatre of North Carolina, Flat Rock Playhouse, is one of the top ten summer theatres in the nation. Broadway-mountain style is the best way to describe this professional equity theatre found in a lovely forested setting in Flat Rock. Actors at the Playhouse come from across the nation and have acting credits including Broadway, feature films, national tours, television, off-Broadway and regional theatres. Sets are designed by the resident scenic designer and in the scenic studio adjacent to the theatre by Playhouse carpenters.

Flat Rock Playhouse (The Vagabond School of the Drama, Inc.) was established in 1952. In 1961, the playhouse was given special status with the honorary title of The State Theatre of North Carolina by the N.C. State Legislation in recognition of its high production standards. As the State Theatre, the Playhouse strives to offer a variety of fare each year with an emphasis on diversity.

Flat Rock Playhouse, home of the Vagabond Players

Location:	Flat Rock, NC
Address:	2661 Greenville Hwy., Flat Rock, NC 28731
Telephone:	Box Office: 828-693-0731, Business Office: 828-693-0403
Allow:	Performances last from two to three hours.
Website:	www.flatrockplayhouse.org
Directions:	From downtown Hendersonville take Highway 25 south to Flat Rock. The Playhouse is on the right at the intersection of Highway 25 and Little River Road.

Hands On! A Child's Gallery

Hands On! A Child's Gallery offers an affordable, educational and fun way to spend the day with your children, grandchildren, and students ages 1 – 10. This is a safe gathering place where kids can be kids while learning is nurtured. Field trips, special events, and birthday parties are welcome.

Location:	Hendersonville, NC
Distance:	40 minutes from Asheville
Address:	318 N. Main Street, Hendersonville NC 28792
Telephone:	828-697-8333
Admission:	$5 per person (1-100)
Hours:	Saturday 10 a.m.-5 p.m.
Website:	www.handsonwnc.org
Directions:	From Asheville take I-26 South. Get off at exit 49B onto US 64. Turn left onto Main Street.

Henderson County Curb Market

The Curb Market, in continuous operation in Hendersonville since 1924, offers home-grown fresh vegetables and fruits, baked goods, home-made jams and jellies as well as gifts and handicrafts of all kinds. It was started on Main Street in 1924 with eight sellers using umbrellas and has grown to the present number of 137 selling spaces, with many sellers being third and fourth generation. The sellers are required to be residents of Henderson County and to make or grow all items sold.

Henderson County Curb Market

Location:	Hendersonville, NC
Address:	221 N. Church St., Hendersonville NC 28739
Telephone:	828-692-8012
Website:	www.curbmarket.com
Hours:	Tuesday, Thursday and Saturday, 8 a.m.-2 p.m.

Fees: None
Directions: From Asheville take I-26 South. Get off at exit 49B onto US 64. Turn left onto Main Street. Heading south on Main Street in Hendersonville, take any right turn to take you to Church Street. It parallels Main Street. The market is behind the historic old Courthouse.

Henderson County Heritage Center

The Henderson County Heritage Museum opened on April 11th, 2008, and uses displays and multimedia technology to tell the story of the people of Henderson County, from the Cherokee and pioneers who carved homes out of the wilderness to today's residents and events. The displays include rare artifacts, artwork, photographs, maps, video tours, oral histories, re-enactments, music, stories and legends. The museum is housed in the Historic Courthouse with rooms portraying periods in Henderson County's history: Wilderness to 1860, 1860-1920, 1920 to the Present, and the "Window on Main Street".

Location: Hendersonville, in the Historic Henderson County Courthouse building.
Distance: 30 minutes from Asheville
Address: One Historic Courthouse Square, Suite 4, Hendersonville NC 28792.
Telephone: 828-694-1619
Hours: Hours: 10 a.m.-5 p.m. Wednesday thru Saturday, 1-5 p.m. Sunday
Fees: None
Allow: 1 hour
Website: www.hendersoncountymuseum.org
Directions: From Asheville take I-26 South. Get off at exit 49B onto US 64. Turn left onto Main Street and proceed down Main Street. The Historic Courthouse building will be on your right.

Henderson County History Center

Located on Main Street in downtown Hendersonville, the Henderson County Historical Center consists of four separate entities under one roof: 1) Henderson County Historical Museum, 2) Henderson County Archives, 3) Henderson County Genealogical and Historical Society, and 4) Mineral and Lapidary Museum of Henderson County. The Henderson County Historical Center has grown over the years under the direction of Dr. Jack Jones, noted local historian, into one of the area's most prestigious attractions.

Location: Hendersonville, NC
Distance: 30 minutes from Asheville
Address: 400 North Main Street, Hendersonville NC 28792
Telephone: 828-693-1531, County Archives: 828-693-1531; County Historical Museum: 828-693-1531; Mineral and Lapidary Museum: 828-693-1531

Hours:	Monday -Friday 10 a.m.-4 p.m.
Fees:	None
Allow:	1-2 hours
Website:	www.hcghs.com
Directions:	From Asheville take I-26 South. Get off at exit 49B onto US 64. Turn left onto Main Street and proceed down Main Street.

Hendersonville Antique Toy Museum

The Hendersonville Antique Toy Museum showcases toys from the 1880's to 1960, and the collection includes dollhouses, dolls, windup toys and trains from the USA, England and Germany. The museum has forty dollhouses or miniature rooms on display ranging from 1900 to 1950. The dollhouses are furnished with furniture and accessories that are the same age as the house. The dolls in the museum are from 1860 to 1960, and are made of wood, wax, paper mache, china, composition and cloth. The trains on display in the museum range in age from 1887 to 1942 and include Lionel, American Flyer, Ives Hornby, Bing, and Karl Bub.

Location:	Hendersonville, NC
Distance:	40 minutes from Asheville
Address:	154 White Street, Hendersonville NC 28793
Telephone:	828-702-1922
Admission:	$2 Adults, $1 Children (6 to 12)
Hours:	Saturday & Sunday 1-4 p.m.
Allow:	1 hour
Website:	www.hendersonvilleantiquetoymuseum.com
Directions:	From Asheville take I-26 South. Get off at exit 49B onto US 64. Turn left at N. Church Street and then slight right at S. Main Street. Take the 1st right onto White Street.

Hendersonville Railroad Depot

The Hendersonville Railroad Depot was the second station to be built by Southern Railway in the city and was built between 1902 and 1904. A frame structure with characteristics of the Craftsman style of architecture, it originally was 87 feet long and consisted of two waiting rooms, an agent's office and had indoor plumbing. In 1906, 15 more feet were added to each end of the station to provide a ladie's waiting room and more baggage space. A few years later, an open pavilion area was added to the north end, and in 1916 another 50 feet were added to the roofed-over, open pavilion area.

Recently the depot has been restored to its original color, and a Southern Railway caboose is located at the south end. The depot currently houses an operating model railroad, maintained by the Apple Valley Model Railroad Club, in the former baggage room.

Location:	Hendersonville NC
Distance:	30 minutes from Asheville

Address:	650 Maple Street, Hendersonville NC 28792.
Telephone:	Apple Valley Model Railroad Club, 828-698-5465
Hours:	Saturday 10 a.m.-2 p.m.
Fees:	None
Allow:	1 hour
Directions:	From Asheville take I-26 South. Get off at exit 49B onto US 64. Turn right at North Grove Street, take the 1st right onto 7 Avenue East and then the 1st right onto Maple Street.

Historic Johnson Farm

The Johnson Farm originally was the home of a wealthy tobacco farmer, Oliver Moss. Construction began in 1876 and was completed by 1880. It is handmade entirely of bricks fired on site from French Broad River mud. Over the years various outbuildings were added, including a tool shed and blacksmith shop, barn, boarding house and cottage. In 1913 Sallie Leverett Johnson inherited the farm and a new era began. The farm was now operated as a farm and summer boarding home for tourists. Historic Johnson Farm is a non-profit education center and farm museum for area school children and the community. It features an 1880's home, a barn loft museum, 10 historic buildings, animals, nature trails, and 15 acres of fields, forest and streams. It is owned and administered by the Henderson County Board of Education and operates today as a community museum and heritage center, with guided tours available for visitors.

Location:	Hendersonville, NC
Address:	3346 Haywood Road, (Route 191), Hendersonville, NC 28791
Telephone:	828-891-6585
Hours:	September-May: Tuesday-Friday. Tours for public at 10:30 a.m. and 1:30 p.m.; June-August Tuesday-Thursday

Historic Johnson Farm, just northwest of Hendersonville

Fees:	Tours: $5 adults, $3 students, preschoolers free.
Allow:	Two hours
Website:	www.co.henderson.k12.nc.us/teachers/johnsonfarm-web
Directions:	From Hendersonville take Haywood Road (Rt. 191) north four miles. From Asheville take Highway 280 West past the airport and turn left onto Highway 191 in Mills River

Mineral & Lapidary Museum of Henderson County

Founded by Larry Hauser, the Mineral & Lapidary Museum of Henderson County, is a small institution with exhibits that include fossils, Cherokee Indian artifacts, and gems and minerals found in North Carolina. The purpose of the museum is to support the education of the children of Henderson and neighboring counties in the Earth Science areas of Mineralogy, Geology, Paleontology and the associated Lapidary Arts. The museum has ongoing exhibits of regional minerals and gemstones of interest to the general public, a workshop where gem-cutting and polishing demonstrations are held, and a gift shop.

Location:	Hendersonville NC
Address:	400 N. Main Street, Hendersonville NC 28792
Telephone:	828-698-1977
Website:	www.mineralmuseum.org
Hours:	Monday-Friday 1:00-5:00, Saturday 10:00 -5:00
Fees:	Free
Allow:	One hour
Directions:	From Asheville take I-26 South. Get off at exit 49B onto US 64. Turn left onto Main Street and proceed down Main Street.

Mountain Farm & Home Museum

The Mountain Farm & Home Museum has displays of agricultural and domestic equipment, buildings, implements, utensils, methods and literature typical of rural life in 19th century Western North Carolina. Noteworthy also is the museum's outstanding collection of over 40 unique restored tractors.

Location:	Hendersonville NC
Address:	10 Brookside Camp Road, Hendersonville NC 28792
Telephone:	828-697-8846
Hours:	Monday-Friday 9 a.m.-3 p.m., by special appointment at other times
Fees:	None
Allow:	1-2 hours
Website:	http://mfhmuseum.homestead.com
Directions:	From Asheville take I-26 South, take exit 44 for US/25 toward Fletcher/Mountain Home. Turn right off exit onto Highway 25 south towards Naples. After approximately 3 miles turn left onto Brookside Camp Road.

Thomas Wolfe Angel

The marble angel statue immortalized by Thomas Wolfe in his novel Look Homeward Angel now stands at Oakdale Cemetery in Hendersonville. The completed statue was imported from Carrara, Italy by Wolfe's father, and was bought by members of the Johnson family after the death of Mrs. Johnson in 1905. The gravesite belongs to Reverend and Mrs. H.F. Johnson and their son. In 1975, when the statue was accidentally knocked from its stand, the Henderson County Commissioners had the graves enclosed with a six-foot tall iron picket fence set on a stone wall. This still allows visitors to view the statue and reduces the possibility of damage to the monument.

Location:	Hendersonville NC
Distance:	40 minutes from Asheville
Address:	Oakdale Cemetery, Highway 64 West, Hendersonville NC 28972
Directions:	From downtown Hendersonville, take Highway 64 west. Look for Oakdale Cemetery on your left. The Angel Statue is visible from the road, and the location is indicated by a State Highway Marker.

Western North Carolina Air Museum

The Western North Carolina Air Museum, founded in 1989, is dedicated to preserving and promoting the flying heritage of the Western North Carolina Mountains region. They have over 15 vintage aircraft on display. In addition to the historic aircraft, the Western North Carolina Air Museum has exhibits of flight manuals and engines from historic aircraft as well as more modern reciprocating and jet engines, photographs of historic airplanes and pilots, and models of historic airplanes.

Impromptu rides sometimes happen at the N.C. Air Museum

Location:	Hendersonville NC
Address:	1340 Gilbert St., Hendersonville, NC 28792
Telephone:	828-698-2482
Hours:	April-October: Saturday 10 a.m.- 5 p.m., Sunday & Wednesday 12-5 p.m.; November-March: 12-5 p.m.
Fees:	None
Allow:	1-2 hours
Website:	www.wncairmuseum.com
Directions:	From I-26 south take exit 22 Upward Road. Take right onto Spartanburg Highway (US 176) and then another right onto Shepherd Street. Museum is on Gilbert Street.

Chapter Three
Historic Hendersonville

Hendersonville, while in existence as early as 1841, did not reach its peak of development until the late 19th and early 20th centuries. The boom started in 1879 when the railroad arrived and commercial development expanded greatly, both in the downtown Main Street area and in the district around the railroad depot. The influx of tourists at that time greatly increased and this in turn spurred the building of resort hotels and boarding houses, as well as fine residential homes for those tourists who decided to stay in Hendersonville. This building and development continued into the early 20th century but stopped abruptly in 1929 with the advent of the Great Depression.

During the early years of development, two individuals, W.F. Edwards and Erle G. Stilwell had major influence on the shape and character of Hendersonville. Edwards was a builder, and was responsible for the construction of many important commercial and residential buildings, including the early Town Hall and Opera House which stood on Main from 1893 to the 1920s, the Neo-Classical People's Bank at 225-231 North Main Street and the historic Henderson County Courthouse. Stilwell was an architect who had considerable influence on the shape of municipal, religious and commercial architecture in Hendersonville by bringing a new level of sophistication and competence to the local architecture. Among his important works were the Hendersonville High School, City Hall and the Citizens National Bank.

The face of domestic architecture was changed significantly with the arrival of the railroad. The industrial growth that the railroads brought also resulted in fine homes being built in the Queen Anne, Eastlake, Colonial Revival and Neo-Classical styles to house the wealthy industrialists. Today, in modern Hendersonville, many of these remaining significant residential properties in downtown have survived and continue to grace the city with their historic presence.

In this chapter, a selection of important historic buildings and structures will be presented, both as part of the two major downtown historic districts; Main Street and the 7th Avenue Depot area, and as separate structures not part of any designated historic district.

As in the chapter on Historic Asheville, certain abbreviations will be used to signify buildings of historical importance. NRHP indicates the structure is listed in the National Register of Historic Places, NHL indicates a National Historic Landmark property and LHL means the building is a Local Historic Landmark. Discussion of these designations is given in depth in the Historic Asheville chapter. (*See* Section Three, Chapter 4)

The Hendersonville Historic Preservation Society is instrumental in the preservation and restoration of historic properties. They are a valuable resource for anyone interested in historic Hendersonville. The Preservation Society may be reached by calling the Henderson County Genealogical & Historical Society offices at 828-693-1531, also an excellent historical resource. They are located at 400 North Main Street, Hendersonville, NC 28792.

Historic Districts of Hendersonville
Main Street Historic District

This district will be presented in the form of a self-guided walking tour. The best place to start is to park at the Hendersonville and Flat Rock Area Visitors Information Center located at 201 South Main Street. From there your tour will take you up and back on Main Street. Allow about an hour for the stroll.

Leaving the Visitors Center proceed north up Main Street. One block up on your left will be the Historic Henderson County Courthouse.

Historic Henderson County Courthouse (NRHP)   113 North Main Street

Built in 1905, the historic Henderson County Courthouse overlooks Main Street. Graced with a gold dome and a statue of Lady Justice, this imposing building was constructed by W.F. Edwards, father of A.V. Edwards, who served as

The Historic Henderson County Courthouse

Hendersonville's mayor for 36 years. Neo-Classical Revival in style, this building replaced an earlier two-story stuccoed brick structure. The architect was Richard Sharp Smith and is Smith's only structure in Hendersonville. The most notable feature of the courthouse is the gold domed three-stage cupola, which consists of a columned drum and domical roof, crowned by a statue of Lady Justice. This Lady Justice is thought to be the only one in the United States that does not wear a blindfold.

Although its main function was as a courthouse, the graceful building served other purposes over the years. The main courtroom was used in the early 1900s for various purposes, including speeches by governors, and as a gathering place for church congregations. Although it no longer is Henderson County's courthouse, it remains a dignified and majestic reminder of the past. The sophistication and grandeur reflect the past aspirations of a small county seat at a time when the economy was booming and whose population was beginning to soar.

Farther up Main Street in the next block you will see the People's National Bank Building on your left.

People's National Bank Building (NRHP) 227-231 North Main Street
This building, dating back to around 1910, is a two story Neo-Classical structure of cream colored brick and was built by W.F. Edwards. It has a recessed central entrance beneath entablature supported by Ionic columns, and storefronts to either side. The bank building was the earliest use of Neo-Classical style and reinforced concrete construction for a commercial building in Hendersonville.

Continuing on up North Main Street to the end, look for the Maxwell Store Building on your left, which is now home to Mast General Store.

People's National Bank Building

Maxwell Store Building (NRHP)   529 North Main Street

This building once housed a fancy grocery business run by Maxwell Brown, a longtime proprietor. It was built around 1910 and is a two-story pressed brick structure. Highlights are round and segmentally arched windows with fanlights.

Turn around at this point and continue south on North Main. Turn left at 5th Avenue and look for the Hendersonville City Hall on your left.

Hendersonville City Hall Building (NRHP)   145 5th Avenue East

Built between 1926 and 1928, this Neo-Classical Revival building was designed by Erle Stilwell. A flight of stairs leads up to the main entrance which is under a tetrastyle portico, on which is inscribed '"Erected by the People, Dedicated to the Perpetuation of Civic Progress, Liberty and the Security of Public Honor." This building reflects the prosperity of Hendersonville during the 1920s and the architectural refinement that Stilwell brought to the city.

After viewing the City Hall, return to Main Street, and turn left. Proceed south on Main. The Ripley-Shepherd Building will be three blocks down on your left.

Ripley-Shepherd Building (NRHP)   218 North Main Street

This building is believed to be the second-oldest building on Main Street, one of several buildings built by Colonel Valentine Ripley and once known as the "Ripley Brick Store House." It is said to have served as a district commissary under a Major Noe during the Civil War. Later it was also a post office for Hendersonville. Later still it was the home of Shepherd and Hart's furniture store and undertaking business. Notable features are the high hip roof and bracketed eaves.

7th Avenue Depot Historic District

This district is located two blocks northeast of Main Street and separated from Main Street by new commercial development. The district still shows a cohesive grouping of commercial, residential and transportation-related structures typical of the early development of Hendersonville, especially the period after the arrival of the railroad.

Seventh Avenue East developed as a commercial district during the late 19th and early 20th centuries and was centered around the first depot built in 1879. The majority of buildings are one and two story brick commercial and warehouse structures located along 7th Avenue. Only minor alterations to the commercial buildings have occurred and these are mainly at the storefront level. Very little construction took place after the Great Depression. This district, with its frame depot, approximately 28 brick commercial buildings and the Station Hotel is one of the best surviving examples of a railroad district in western North Carolina. The buildings in the district are primarily commercial in function and provided services that were associated with a shipping point for locally grown cash crops.

Directions: Take North Main Street north to 6th Avenue. Turn right and go 2 blocks. Turn left onto North Grove Street. Proceed on North Grove across Four Seasons Boulevard. Take a right onto East 7th Avenue. The Depot is just ahead on your right.

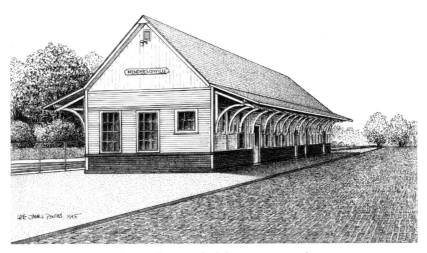

Hendersonville Depot, built between 1902 and 1904

Hendersonville Depot (NRHP)   SE Corner of 7th Avenue and Maple Street

This depot was the second station to be built by Southern Railway in the city and was built between 1902 and 1904. A frame structure with characteristics of the Craftsman style of architecture, it originally was 87 feet long and consisted of two waiting rooms, an agent's office and had indoor plumbing. In 1906, 15 more feet were added to each end of the station to provide a ladies waiting room and more baggage space. A few years later, an open pavilion area was added to the north end, and in 1916 another 50 feet were added to the roofed over, open pavilion area.

The railroad line was opened from Spartanburg, S.C. to Hendersonville in 1879, a year before Asheville was to receive a line from the east. The railroad brought large numbers of visitors to Hendersonville and allowed the county's produce to reach a wider market in other cities. The last passenger service ended in 1968. Since then the depot has been restored to its original color, and a Southern Railway caboose located at the south end. Restoration is ongoing, and the depot currently houses an operating model railroad in the baggage room. Visitors are invited to visit this historic station. The Depot is open for visitors year-round, Saturday 10 a.m.-2 p.m. Free.

Just north of the Depot, on the same side of the railroad tracks is the Station Hotel Building.

Station Hotel (NRHP)   729 Maple Street

Built between 1912-1922, the Station Hotel is a two story brick building that features a low tripped roof and a two tiered, full facade frame porch. This relatively plain hotel was built near the tracks to serve the visitors who came to Hendersonville by the railroad. The building is still operated today as a hotel, although without its former polish and poise.

Other Historic Sites & Buildings

This section of Historic Hendersonville is devoted to those sites and buildings of architectural or historic importance that have not been covered in the previous section.

Aloah Hotel Building (NRHP)   201 3rd Avenue West

The Aloah Hotel, called the Hendersonville Inn since the 1930s, is a large three-story brick building built in the early years of the 20th century. The building has a modest Classical Revival porch and entrance and is remarkably unaltered on its exterior and very well preserved on the interior. One of the few hotels in Hendersonville still operated as such, it was also known as the Carson House and then the Hendersonville Inn. Its plain sturdy brick design and great wraparound porch reflect comfort and integrity, and is a good example of the type of hotel built to handle the influx of visitors and tourists to Hendersonville in the early years. This sector of town was originally filled with other hotels catering to the tourist boom.

Directions: From Main Street take 3rd Avenue heading west. The Aloah Hotel, known today as the Hendersonville Inn, is on your right just beyond Church Street.

The Cedars (NRHP)   227 7th Avenue

The Cedars is a large 3½-story brick veneer hotel built in a Neo-Classical Revival style. It derives its name from the large ancient cedars on the lot in which it stands. The building is highlighted by a monumental Ionic portico that has a deck with railing. The Cedars is the largest and one of the most important of the historic tourist accommodations in Hendersonville. It was built in 1914 for Jennie Bailey, wife of a local Southern Railroad executive. Mrs. Bailey and, later, her daughter operated the hotel until 1976. Today it is privately owned and used for weddings, receptions, parties and club meetings.

The Cedars

Directions: Take 7th Avenue west off of Main Street.

Chewning House (NRHP) 755 North Main Street

Located on the same shady street as the Waverly Inn, Chewning House is also one of Hendersonville's treasures. Built sometime between 1888 and 1906 by W.A. Smith, the inn's original name was "The Smith-Green House." The house underwent a complete transformation between 1912 and 1922 when it was enlarged from a two-story building to the present three-story structure. It is a prime example of the simpler domestic architectural styles of the 1920s. Chewning House, like the Waverly next door, still serves its original purpose and today is known as the Claddagh Inn.

Directions: Located on Main Street in downtown Hendersonville.

Clarke-Hobbs-Davidson House (NRHP) 229 5th Avenue West

Built about 1907, the Clarke-Hobbs-Davidson House is one of the most imposing historic residences remaining near downtown Hendersonville. Purchased by the Masons in 1958, it is a 2½-story brick Queen Anne-Colonial Revival style house that has had a rear brick wing added, nearly doubling the size of the building. The house was probably built by Charles S. Clarke and his wife Louise, and in 1907 it was sold to Alfred J. Hobbs, and thereafter to Charles A. Hobbs and his wife Harriet. In 1911 it was again sold to a Mrs. Davidson who left the property to her brother Edgar Sutton and his wife Eleanor. Since that time it has had a number of other owners, including the Masons, who now operate it as a Masonic Lodge. It is a rare example of a large brick house in Hendersonville at the time of the tourism boom during the early part of the 20th century.

Directions: From Main Street, take 5th Avenue heading west. The Clarke-Hobbs-Davidson House will be on your right.

Connemara (NRHP, NHL) Little River Road, Flat Rock

Designated a National Historic site because of its association with Carl Sandburg, who lived there from 1945 until his death in 1967. It was built in 1838-1839 by Christopher Gustavus Memminger, later secretary of the treasury of the Confederacy, on land purchased from Charles Baring. Memminger named the house Rock Hill and after his death, the new owner Captain Ellison Adder Smyth, a textile executive, changed the name to Connemara. The farm today includes 264 acres of rolling hills, forests, lakes, goat barn and buildings. The grounds and farm are open for self-guided tours, and guided tours (admission charged) of the home are scheduled daily. (*See* Section Four, Chapter 2 Carl Sandburg Home)

Directions: Take Highway 225 (Greenville Highway) south from Hendersonville. Turn right on Little River Road in Flat Rock

The Henderson County Courthouse, dedicated in 1995

Henderson County Courthouse   200 North Grove Street

Dedicated on April 29, 1995, the Henderson County Courthouse occupies approximately 99,100 square feet on a 13-acre site. Designed by Grier-Fripp Architects of Charlotte, NC, and built by M.B. Kahn Construction Company of Greenville, SC, this imposing structure replaced the historic old courthouse on Main Street.

The ceilings in the lobby and court waiting areas are painted to resemble the sky with clouds. The clock over the main steps is over five feet in diameter, and the grounds are planted with Japanese Yoshino cherry trees, Japanese Zelkova, and Sugar Maples.

Directions: Located in downtown Hendersonville on North Grove Street. North Grove Street parallels North Main Street and is two blocks to the east.

King-Waldrop House (NRHP)   103 South Washington Street

The King-Waldrop House was built around 1881 and shows features of both the Queen Anne and the Italianate building styles. Its main feature is a square three-stage cupola with a concave pyramidal roof. The general condition of the house is excellent and both the inside, with its dark woodwork and Victorian detailing, and the outside are little altered. The house is an excellent example of the large spacious residences built for the wealthy in Hendersonville in the 1880s. It is one of the few surviving 19th century dwellings in downtown Hendersonville. It was built for Laura V. King, the daughter of Colonel Valentine Ripley, one of Hendersonville's earliest businessmen and entrepreneurs. In 1897, Laura King and Dr. J.G. Waldrop traded houses, and the residence was then titled "Maple Grove" by Dr. Waldrop, who occupied the home with his wife, Nancy, and their eight children.

Directions: Take First Avenue west from Main Street and turn left onto Washington Street. The King-Waldrop House is on your right at 103.

Mary Mills Coxe House (NRHP)   1210 Greenville Highway

The Mary Mills Coxe House is located south of Hendersonville on the Greenville Highway, formerly known as Flat Rock Road. Built around 1911 as a single family residence, it is notable as one of only a handful of pebbledash houses remaining in Henderson County. A Colonial-Revival style dwelling, it is two-and-a-half stories and has as distinctive features a large porch formed by fifteen columns and a roof of pressed metal shingles. The house was built by Mary Mills Coxe, widow of Colonel Franklin Coxe, one of the more influential and wealthy men in Henderson and Buncombe counties. The building is significant historically since it is a very well-preserved pebbledash house that is a rare, unchanged structure that has not been modernized stylistically. The pebbledash stucco walls reflect the influence of noted Asheville architect Richard Sharp Smith.

Directions: Take Main Street heading south. This street turns into Greenville Highway. The Mary Mills Coxe House is on your left heading toward Flat Rock.

Reese House (NRHP) 202 South Washington Street

The Reese House, built in 1885 by Harriet Louise and William Reese is one of the best preserved Queen Anne style houses in Hendersonville. Wonderfully restored, the house boasts rich, red heart of pine floors, seven fireplaces and hand-carved gingerbread mouldings. On the front lawn is a buckeye tree that was one of the original plantings.

Directions: Just down the street to the south of the King-Waldrop House on South Washington Street.

St. James Episcopal Church 766 North Main Street

St. James Episcopal Church, located on Main Street in downtown Hendersonville, is one of the area's most picturesque churches. Consecrated in 1861, the first rector was Rev. N. Collin Hughes. From 1970 to 1980, Henderson County experienced an unprecedented population growth. New economic developments, discovery of Hendersonville as an outstanding retirement area, and growth in tourism marked this period. Consequently, St. James Church flourished and became the largest parish in the Episcopal Diocese of Western North Carolina during that time.

Directions: Located on North Main Street.

St. James Episcopal Church

St. John in the Wilderness Church (NRHP)
1895 Greenville Highway, Flat Rock

A unique spot of southern history in a setting of idyllic beauty, St. John in the Wilderness Episcopal Church in Flat Rock is a gable roof brick church that has at its southeast corner a three-story square tower with pyramidal roof.

In 1833, Charles and Susan Baring built the church as a private chapel, and at the formation of the Episcopal Diocese of Western North Carolina in 1836, the Baring family gave up their rights to the church as a private chapel, turning the deed to the bishop of the newly-formed diocese. The church and graveyard are open daily 9 a.m.-4 p.m. for visitation.

Thomas Wolf's Angel in Oakdale Cemetery

Directions: Take Highway 225 (Greenville Highway) south from Hendersonville.

Thomas Wolfe's Angel Oakdale Cemetery   Highway 64 West

The marble angel statue immortalized by Thomas Wolfe in his novel Look Homeward Angel now stands at Oakdale Cemetery in Hendersonville. The statue was imported from Carrara, Italy by Wolfe's father, and was bought by members of the Johnson family after the death of Mrs. Johnson in 1905. The gravesite belongs to Reverend and Mrs. H.F. Johnson and their son. In 1975, when the statue was accidentally knocked from its stand, the Henderson County Commissioners had the graves enclosed with a six-foot tall iron picket fence set on a stone wall. This still allows visitors to view the statue and reduces the possibility of damage to the monument.

Directions: From downtown Hendersonville, take Highway 64 west. Look for Oakdale Cemetery on your left. The Angel Statue is visible from the road, and the location is indicated by a State Highway Marker.

The Waverly Inn (NRHP)   783 North Main Street

Built just after 1898, the Waverly Inn is a three-story Queen Anne style inn. The third story was added in 1910 after a fire did extensive roof damage. With the exception of minor changes, the Waverly has undergone relatively little change and is in remarkably pristine condition. The interior boasts a magnificent Eastlake style stair and twenty-one guest rooms, with seventeen bathrooms. Today the Waverly is still operated as an inn.

Directions: Located on North Main Street in downtown Hendersonville.

Chapter Four
Hendersonville Parks

Natural beauty abounds in the Hendersonville and Flat Rock areas, from enchanting apple orchards to lush green valleys and rugged mountains. Visitors to the area are only minutes away from a wide variety of natural attractions and opportunities for outdoor recreation. Chimney Rock Park, Lake Lure, and area waterfalls are covered separately in Section Five, Chapter 1.

Hendersonville City Parks

Hendersonville maintains seven city parks, listed below, that are easily accessible. The most popular is the 20-acre Patton Park located on Patton Avenue. Hendersonville City Parks, Public Works Department, 415 8th Avenue East, Hendersonville, NC 28792. 828-697-3084.

Patton Park: Hwy. 25 north to Patton Avenue
Boyd Park: 840 Church Street
Edwards Park: North Main Street and Locust Street
Green Meadows Park: Ash Street and Park View Drive
King Memorial Park: 7th Avenue and Robinson Terrace
Toms Park: Allen Street and Lily Pond Road, shuffleboard
Lennox Park: Park Drive off Whitted Street

Henderson County Parks

Maintained by the Henderson County Parks and Recreation Department, there are seven parks total over 259 acres of playing fields, recreation facilities, woodland and playgrounds. The major park is Jackson Park on Glover Street. Henderson County Parks & Recreation Department, 801 Glover St., Hendersonville, NC 28792. 828-697-4884.

Jackson Park: 801 Glover Street, Hendersonville NC 28792. 828-697-4888.
Established in 1974, is located conveniently near downtown Hendersonville, and covers 212 acres in Henderson County. The parks' facilities include 4 picnic shelters, 9 baseball fields, cross country courses for local middle and high schools,

soccer fields, 8 tennis courts, a BMX track, playgrounds, and many walking trails, providing a central location for many community sports and activities. The park is home to several species of birds, wildlife, and plants, making the park a great place to observe nature. Jackson Park is noted for its great bird watching also.

Black Bears:
Spirit of the Mountains

If any animal personifies the spirit of the Western North Carolina mountains, it is the black bear. They inhabited these mountains long before the Cherokees arrived and it is estimated that the entire population numbers around 4,000 for the Southern Appalachians, with the heart of bear country located in the Great Smoky Mountains National Park. With over 500,000 acres, it is the largest protected bear habitat east of the Mississippi. Over 1,000 bears are estimated to live in the park, one of the highest densities anywhere.

Although only one human death has ever been recorded in the Great Smokies, bears are to be respected. Each year there are an average of seven bear incidents reported that involve human injury, and over 150 incidents each year of property damage—coolers destroyed, backpacks ripped open, cars scratched and tents torn down. Most of these incidents involved violation of a primary rule—don't feed the bears!

The black bear has long been held as a symbol of power by the Cherokee Indians, both on the land and in the psyche. And to visitors, the bear is the one animal that is hoped to be seen, perhaps for similar reasons. More than any other animal, it is an embodiment of the wilderness and represents the mystery and power of the mountains.

Section Five
Western North Carolina

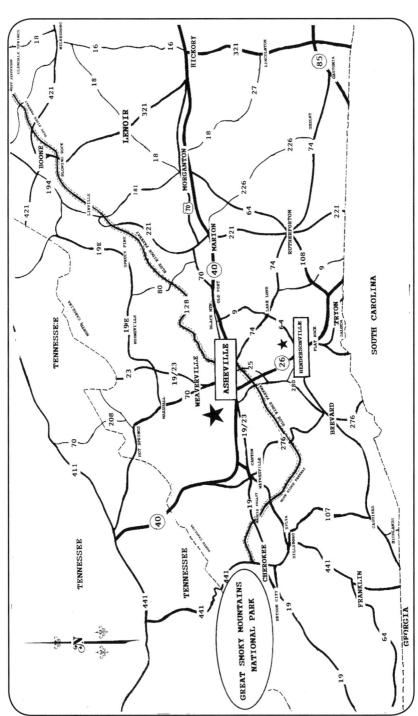

Western North Carolina

Chapter One
Natural Attractions

Waterfalls in Western North Carolina

In Transylvania County within an hour's drive of Asheville are a number of truly spectacular waterfalls. These Brevard area waterfalls are a national treasure and worth a visit at any time of the year. In fact Transylvania County is known as "The Land of Waterfalls. " There are hundreds to choose from, many of which are easy to get to, and some even visible from the highway. The most popular and easily accessible is Looking Glass Falls in the Pisgah National Forest. It is suggested that if you wish to visit the waterfalls, you first check into the Brevard Chamber of Commerce Visitor Center in Brevard and pick up a copy of their "Land of the Waterfalls" guide and map. A great day trip can be planned to visit these falls. Be sure to take a picnic lunch. Besides these Brevard area waterfalls, there are others worth mentioning and these are listed below.

Looking Glass Falls in the Brevard Area

Location: Pisgah National Forest

Distance: 1 hour from Asheville

Address: Highway 276, Pisgah National Forest

Telephone: Pisgah District Office: 828-877-3350, 828-257-4203

Website: www.cs.unca.edu/nfsnc/recreation/wncwaterfalls/lookingglassfalls

Fees: None

Cautionary Note: While all of the falls are beautiful, they can be treacherous. Death or injury may be only seconds away if one misjudges the force of moving water or height of the cascades. Rocks are slippery when wet. Do not attempt to climb the rocks beside the falls or venture near the top. Viewing the falls is safe, family fun only if you stay on the designated trails and viewing areas.

Directions: From Asheville, take NC 280 South. NC 280 begins as Airport Rd. after you leave Hendersonville Hwy. (US 25). Take a right into Pisgah National Forest at Highway 276 in Pisgah Forest just before you reach Brevard. Follow 276 for 6 miles.

Other Notable Waterfalls

Brevard Area west of Asheville:

Bird Rock Falls: Take Highway 64 West from Brevard 8.5 miles and turn right on NC 215. Continue approximately 9 miles. Falls are on the left just below the confluence of Shoal Creek and the North Fork of the French Broad River in the Balsam Grove Community.

Bridal View Falls: Bridal Veil Falls is unique because you can drive your car right underneath it! The water falls 120 feet from above, right over the highway. From Brevard take Highway 64 West, and look for the sign 2.5 miles west of Highlands in the Cullasaja Gorge.

Cullasaja Falls: The lower portion of Cullasaja Falls is a cascade of water which flows about 250 feet down. It is located on the Cullasaja River, 9 miles west of Highlands off Highway 64 in the Cullasaja Gorge. Cullasja Falls is only visible from your car, there is no adequate pull-off spot from the road.

Rainbow Falls: Follow Highway 64 West from Brevard 18 miles to Whitewater Rd. (NC 281) and turn left 2.5 miles. A trail begins at a turn in the road and continues downstream past Drift Falls a half-mile to the 200 foot high Rainbow Falls.

Silver Run Falls: Silver Run Falls has a drop of 30 feet into a quiet pool below, and are located off NC 197, 4.1 miles south of Cashiers. Park in the pull-off on the left.

Toxaway Falls: Take Highway 64 West from Brevard 15.5 miles. The highway crosses the top of the falls 123 feet just below Toxaway Dam. The area was named Toxaway (Red Bird) by the Cherokee Indians. Easily visible from the road.

Whitewater Falls: A spectacular plunge of 411 feet makes this the tallest waterfall east of the Mississippi. A park with parking and restrooms provides easy access. Take US 64 West from Brevard, go 18 miles to Whitewater Rd. (NC 281), turn left 8 miles to park entrance on left. Falls can be viewed from the end of a paved road 100 yards from the parking area.

Chimney Rock Area south of Asheville:

Hickory Nut Falls: Located in Chimney Rock Park, this waterfall is 404 feet high, making it one of the tallest in the eastern United States. The park has an short hiking trail, which leads to the base of this magnificent falls. To see this waterfall, you must purchase a ticket to enter Chimney Rock Park. While you are there visit the famous Chimney Rock attraction. (*See* Section Five, Chapter 1)

Franklin Area west of Asheville:

Dry Falls: Dry Falls is located on Highway 64 between Franklin and Highlands, and you can find the falls with a short, easy walk. Once there you can walk right behind them without getting wet! A well-marked path and hand rail to guide you behind and around the 75-foot curtain of rushing water.

Blue Ridge Parkway north of Asheville:

Linville Falls: Linville Falls is located on the Blue Ridge Parkway at mile post 316.3. Two main hiking trails lead to great views of the falls which drop into the spectacular Linville Gorge. It is probably the most photographed in the state, and is considered one of the most beautiful. Both begin at the Linville Falls Visitor Center, which is operated by the National Park Service (open only in the late spring to fall). The trails range in difficulty from moderate to strenuous. Access is from the Blue Ridge Parkway (closed in winter) or by taking a slightly faster route using I-40 east to Marion, getting off at the US Hwy 221 exit in Marion and heading north. Take 221 all the way to the Blue Ridge Parkway, go north on the Parkway about a mile to Linville Falls.

Morganton Area east of Asheville

Upper Creek Falls: A steep, 0.8-mile trail leads to this popular cascading waterfall. Upper Creek Falls is located in the Jonas Ridge Area of Burke County, and is only accessible by hiking in. The Falls are located 13.5 miles from Morganton. Take NC 181 North from Morganton. The parking area is on the right about 6 miles north of the Pisgah National Forest boundary.

Natural Attractions North of Asheville
Appalachian National Scenic Trail

The Appalachian Trail is a 2,167-mile footpath from Maine to Georgia which follows the ridge tops of the fourteen states through which it passes. Each day, as many as two hundred backpackers are in the process of hiking the full length of the trail. On average, it takes about four to five months to hike the entire length. More than 250 backcountry shelters are located along the Appalachian Trail at varying intervals, as a service to all Appalachian Trail hikers. A typical shelter, sometimes called a "lean-to," has a shingled or metal roof, a wooden floor and three walls, and is open to the elements on one side. Most are near a creek or spring, and many have a privy nearby. Hikers occupy them on a first-come, first-served basis until the shelter is full. They are intended for individual hikers, not big groups.

The Appalachian Trail Conservancy website has more complete information for hikers who intend to camp on the trail. The Trail, which passes though North Carolina, was conceived by Benton MacKaye in the 1920s. With the support of local hiking clubs and interested individuals, MacKaye's dream eventually became a reality. By 1937 the trail was completed by opening a two-mile stretch in a densely wooded area between Spaulding and Sugarloaf Mountains in Maine. It may be entered at many points as it passes through North Carolina for over 300 miles.

Swallowtail butterfly

Location:	The trail passes to the north of Asheville
Address:	Appalachian Trail Conference Southern Regional Offices: 160-A Zillicoa St., Asheville NC 28801
Telephone:	Appalachian Trail Conservancy 828-254-3708
Website:	www.appalachiantrail.org
Distance:	From Asheville, approximately 30 miles (a 45-minute drive)
Resources:	Appalachian National Scenic Trail, (National Park Service) Appalachian National Scenic Trail, PO Box 50, Harpers Ferry WV 25425; 304-535-6278
Directions:	Closest access is at Sams Gap, on the North Carolina/Tennessee line. Take US 19/23 north to the state line. Look for the parking on the west side. Just before the parking lot at the crest of the ridge is a trail sign. The parking lot is just before 19/23 becomes a four-lane road. After parking, walk back along 19/23 about 100 meters to access the trail.

Max Patch

Max Patch is one of Western North Carolina's best kept secrets, and it is located about 40 miles north of Asheville in the Hot Springs area. It is 300 acres of a grassy bald that is 4,629 feet at its highest point, and from which, on clear days, one can see Mount Mitchell to the east and the Great Smokies far off in the west! Some balds are naturally occurring areas in the mountains where trees do not grow and only flowers and grasses have taken hold. In Max's case, evidently it was cleared by sheep and cattle in the 1800s and has remained as such, with a little mowing help from the U.S. Forest Service. Max Patch is a premier example of a southern mountain bald, and if you have a half-day free, it is well worth the trip. Great panoramic views and a hundreds of places to picnic or camp await those making the trip.

The area is closed to motor vehicles however, although there is road access and parking near the summit, which requires about a 1/4 mile uphill walk. Visitors are encouraged to travel the area by foot and enjoy the fresh mountain air and clear views of open country. Many visitors come to Max Patch to camp, fly kites and walk the Appalachian Trail.

Location:	Madison County, NC
Distance:	1 hour from Asheville
Directions:	From Asheville take Leicester Hwy. North 30 miles to NC 209. Follow 209 about 7 miles to Meadow Fork Rd. (State Rd. 1175). Follow this road south 5.3 miles to State Rd. 1181. Follow 1181 for 2 miles (will turn into gravel). At the top of the mountain, the road intersects with State Rd. 1182. Turn right and drive about 3 miles to the Max Patch parking area, which will be on your right. From the parking area, it is a short 1.4 miles to the top.

Natural Attractions South of Asheville
Apple Orchards in Henderson County

Henderson County, North Carolina, is the seventh largest apple producing county in the United States and is one of the leading producer of apples in the Southeast, producing over 85% of the apples grown in North Carolina. Its main city, Hendersonville, is home to the famous North Carolina Apple Festival, held every summer. Apple orchards in the county range in size from small family backyard plantings to some with over 600 acres. The most popular varieties are Rome, Red Delicious, Golden Delicious, Gala, Fugi, and Jonagold. An average of one million mature apple trees are growing on nine thousand acres producing approximately 5 million bushels of apples per year. A drive in the country out Route 64 heading east through Edneyville towards Chimney Rock will take you past some very scenic apple orchards as well as past roadside stands that sell fresh apples and cider. There are also a number of orchards where you may pick you own apples. The Blue Ridge Farm Direct Market Association website, www.ncapples.com, has more information about specific apple orchards and roadside stands, as well as maps to these locations.

Location: South of Asheville in Henderson County
Telephone: Blue Ridge Farm Direct Market Association (Hendersonville NC Apple Growers) 828-697-4891
Website: www.ncapples.com
Directions: From Asheville take I-26 south towards Hendersonville. Take Exit 49 and proceed east on NC Highway 64 towards Edneyville. The apple orchards begin a few miles down Highway 64.

Chimney Rock State Park

Chimney Rock Park is a natural scenic attraction nestled in the foothills of the Blue Ridge Mountains just above Lake Lure. Southeast of Asheville and only a short drive from Hendersonville, this 1000-acre park provides breathtaking views from its many trails and from the top of the 315-foot monolithic "Chimney Rock." Towering 315 feet over the village of Chimney Rock, the park which was privately owned, in 2007 became Chimney Rock State Park, one of the newest North Carolina state parks. With an elevation range from about 1,100 feet to 2,800 feet, the park is expanding to include some 5,000 acres.

Chimney Rock Park

The park features three hiking trails that lead to the 404-foot Hickory Nut Falls, one of the highest waterfalls in the eastern United States. At 2,280 feet above sea level, Chimney Rock is a 535-million-year-old remnant of igneous rock. You can climb a trail to its top, or take the 26-story elevator carved out of solid rock if you wish. The movie "Last of the Mohicans" was filmed at Chimney Rock, and you may recognize part of the Cliff Trail from scenes in the film. Picnic tables and grills are located along the roadway to the Chimney Rock, and a less strenuous trail leads to the base of Hickory Nut Falls. There is also a nature center on the access road where you may learn about the flora, fauna and geology of the park.

Location: Southeast of Asheville
Address: Box 39, Chimney Rock, NC 28740
Distance: From Asheville, approximately 25 miles
Telephone: 828-625-9611, 800-277-9611
Website: www.chimneyrockpark.com
Hours: Open year-round except Thanksgiving, Christmas and New Year's Day; 8:30 a.m.-4:30 p.m.
Fees: $14 Adults, $6 Children 6-15, Children under 6 free
Allow: 2-3 hours
Directions: From Asheville, take I-240 East to Exit 9 (Bat Cave, Blue Ridge Parkway) and continue on Hwy. 74A through Fairview and Hickory Nut Gap to Chimney Rock. From Hendersonville, take Hwy. 64 East. Turn right on Hwy. 74 to Chimney Rock.

Holmes Educational State Forest

North Carolina has six Educational State Forests that have been developed as living environmental education centers. These forests are designed to promote a better understanding of the value of forests in our lives. Holmes Forest, located in the Blue Ridge Mountains, offers a rich mixture of mountain hardwoods, rhododendron, flame azaleas and a variety of wildflowers. These features are accessible to the visiting public by a series of well-marked trails accented by exhibits and displays depicting the ecology of the managed forest. Picnic sites with tables and grills are provided, and ranger-conducted programs are available to groups visiting the 235-acre forest.

Location: Just west of Hendersonville
Address: 1299 Crab Creek Road, Hendersonville, NC 28739
Telephone: 828-692-0100
Website: www.ncesf.org/HESF/home
Hours: Mid-March to the day Friday before Thanksgiving. Closed Mondays. 9 a.m.-5 p.m. Tuesday through Friday, 11 a.m.-8 p.m. DST/11 a.m.-5 p.m. ST Saturday and Sunday.
Fees: None
Allow: Two hours
Directions: From Hendersonville take Kanuga Road west 8 miles. Forest is on the left.

Jump Off Rock

Legend has it that more than 300 years ago a young Indian maiden leapt from this rock to her death when she learned that her lover, a Cherokee chief, had been killed in battle. Indian lore to this day maintains that on some moonlit nights the ghost of the heartbroken maiden can be seen on the rock. Views from the rock are breathtaking of the valleys below during daylight hours and are also especially noteworthy at sunset. The rock itself is surrounded by landscaped grounds.

Location: South of Asheville in the Laurel Park section of Hendersonville.
Fees: None
Directions: From Asheville take I-26 south towards Hendersonville. Get off at Exit 49 and take NC Highway 64 west towards Hendersonville. After it passes North Main Street, it becomes 7th Avenue West. Continue on this road a short distance and turn left on Buncombe Street. Proceed down Buncombe Street two blocks and turn right onto 5th Avenue West. Continue on 5th Avenue West as it turns into Laurel Park Highway. Follow Laurel Park Highway to the very end and Jump Off Rock.

Lake Lure

Located southeast of Hendersonville just below Chimney Rock is sparkling Lake Lure, selected by National Geographic as one of the ten most spectacular and beautiful man-made lakes in the world. Over 1,500 acres of crystal clear water and 27 miles of inviting shoreline await the visitor to this majestic body of water. A marina and sandy beaches are open to the public and boat tours of the lake, offered by Lake Lure Tours, are a popular attraction. The boat tour dock is located at Lake Lure Marina, off of highway 64/74A.

Location: Southeast of Asheville
Distance: From Asheville, approximately 30 miles, a 45-minute drive
Address: Lake Lure Boat Tours, 2830 Memorial Highway, Lake Lure, NC 28746 (located at Lake Lure Marina)
Telephone: Lake Lure Tours: 828-625-1373, 877-386-4255
Website: www.lakelure.com
Hours: Lake Lure Tours: March-November. Daily cruises on the hour from 10 a.m.-5 p.m
Fees: Lake Lure Tours: $14 adults, $6 children 6-15, 5 and under free; Swimming at beach, no fee.
Allow: Cruises take one hour
Directions: From Hendersonville, take Hwy. 64 West. Turn right on Hwy. 74. Go through Chimney Rock to Lake Lure. From Asheville, take I-240 East to Exit 9 (Bat Cave, Blue Ridge Parkway) and continue on Hwy. 74A through Hickory Nut Gap and Chimney Rock. Lake Lure is one mile past Chimney Rock.

North Mills River Recreation Area

The North Mills River Recreation Area and Campground is part of the Pisgah District of the Pisgah National Forest and is a great place to take kids on a picnic. Bring inner tubes and rubber rafts. A gentle yet bold stream provides the perfect place for summer fun. The section of the stream where the kids tube even has a natural beach area. There are over 39 picnic units with grills along the river for cookouts, and large ball playing fields and walking trails along the river. For campers there are 32 excellent primitive campsites which can accommodate tents and some sites that can accommodate RVs up to 22 feet in length. No hookups available.

Location:	20 minutes west of Hendersonville
Address:	5289 North Mills River Rd. Mills River NC 28742
Telephone:	828-890-3284, 877-457-4023, Reservations: 877-444-6777
Hours:	Open year round with limited service November thru March
Fees:	Yes, Federal Interagency Pass, Senior and Access discount accepted.
Directions:	From downtown Hendersonville take Highway 191 north towards the community of Mills River. Go approximately 13 miles. Turn left onto North Mills Road to the recreation area.

Pearson's Falls

This botanical preserve, owned and maintained by the Tryon Garden Club, is comprised of 268 acres of native forest, granite, spring-fed streams and a moderate ¼ mile trail to a 90 ft. waterfall. There are over 200 species of rare wildflowers, as well as plants. Mosses, lichens and trees are in the glen which is classified as a deciduous climax forest.

Location:	Between Tryon and Saluda NC
Distance:	1 hour from Asheville
Address:	2720 Pearson Falls Road, Saluda NC 28773
Telephone:	828-749-3031
Website:	www.pearsonsfalls.org
Hours:	March-October: Monday-Saturday 10 a.m.-5:15 p.m., Sunday 12-5:15 p.m.; November-February: Monday-Saturday 10 a.m.-4:15 p.m., Sunday 12-4:15 p.m.
Fees:	Adults: $5.00, Youth: (6-12) $1.00, Under Six: Free
Directions:	From Asheville take I-26 south towards Hendersonville. Take exit 59 toward Saluda and turn right at State Rd 1142 . Take 3rd left onto Thompson Road for 2 miles and turn left at US-176E. Turn right at Old Melrose Road/Pearson Falls Road.

Natural Attractions East of Asheville
Blue Ridge Parkway

The Blue Ridge Parkway is ranked "America's most scenic drive" by leading travel writers. Following mountain crests from the Shenandoah National Park in Virginia to the Great Smoky Mountains National Park in North Carolina and Tennessee, the Parkway is the gateway to a wondrous mountain empire. The Parkway's 469 toll-free miles of awesome natural beauty, combined with the pioneer history of gristmills, weathered cabins and split-rail fences, create one of the most popular areas in the national park system. This extraordinary region encompasses a world of mountain forest, wildlife and wildflowers thousands of feet above a patchwork of villages, fields and farms.

Passing right through Asheville, the Parkway is easily accessible to visitors. Located at Milepost 384 just southeast of Asheville is the newly constructed Blue Ridge Parkway Destination Center. A unique feature about the Parkway is that there are no tolls. Speed limits are set at a leisurely 45 miles per hour, and stops are frequent with more than 250 overlooks on the parkway that offer magnificent uninterrupted views. More that 600 million visitors have traveled the Parkway over the years since it opened in the 1930s.

A free Parkway trip planning information packet is available by writing to the Blue Ridge Parkway Association, P.O. Box 2136, Asheville NC 28802. This packet contains maps, the official Park Service Trip map, guides, and other useful information. Much of this information is also available at the parkway website (www.blueridgeparkway.org). A complete list of hiking trails that can be accessed from the Blue Ridge Parkway is presented in Section Two, Chapter 16.

A nonprofit organization, Friends of the Blue Ridge Parkway, continues to work towards the preservation of the environmental heritage of the Parkway. This grass-roots organization welcomes memberships in its work to preserve and protect the Parkway. Information about Friends of the Blue Ridge Parkway can be obtained by calling 828-687-8722, (800) 228-7275 or by writing them at 3536 Brambleton Avenue S.W., Building B, Roanoke, VA 24108. Another organization dedicated to preserving the Blue Ridge Parkway is the Blue Ridge Parkway Foundation. They fund specific programs and projects that further the parkway's preservations, protection, and enhancement. For further information, call 336-721-0260 or write 717 South Marshall Street, Suite 105B, Winston-Salem, NC 27101.

Camping is allowed along the parkway May-October at designated sites, many requiring a small fee that covers the use of a fireplace and table. Winter camping is allowed, weather permitting. Facilities are limited and you will need to check in advance. Copies of campground regulations are available at Parkway Visitor Centers, and are posted at all campgrounds. Campgrounds near Asheville are at Linville Falls (Milepost 316.3; 50 tent, 20 RV sites), Crabtree Meadows (Milepost 339.5; 71 tent, 22 RV sites) and Mount Pisgah (Milepost 408.6; 70 tent, 70 RV sites).

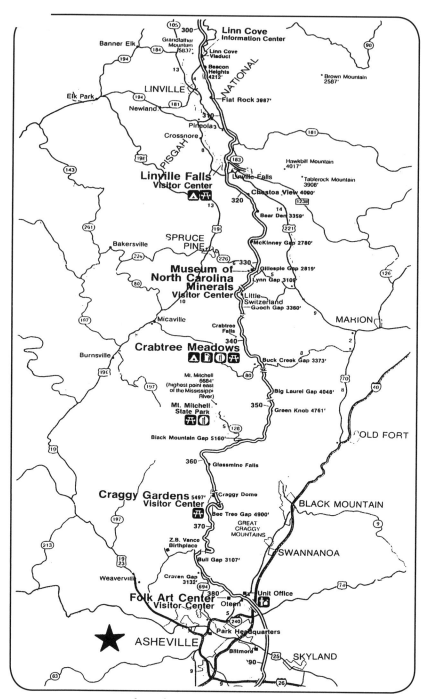

Blue Ridge Parkway North of Asheville

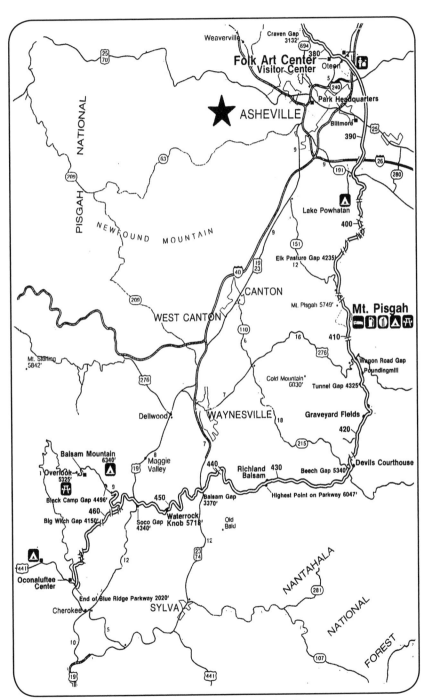

Blue Ridge Parkway South of Asheville

Location: The Parkway begins at Fort Royal, Virginia, and ends in Cherokee, North Carolina. It goes right through the east side of Asheville, running north to south overall.

Address: 199 Hemphill Knob Road, Asheville NC 28803

Telephone: Parkway Information: 828-298-0398, 828-259-0701, 828-271-4779
Emergency Parkway Telephone: 800-727-5928
Parkway Headquarters: 828-271-4779
Visitor Information: 828-271-4779

Website: www.blueridgeheritage.com

Fees: None

Directions: From Asheville, take I-240 East and get off at Exit 9 (Bat Cave, Blue Ridge Parkway). Take Hwy. 74A East to parkway entrance roads. It is also accessible off of Tunnel Rd. (US 70) near the V.A. Hospital in East Asheville and Brevard Rd. (Hwy. 191) in South Asheville past the Biltmore Square Mall.

Tips: The Parkway is closed intermittently during the winter due to ice and snow. Peak traffic is during the summer months and especially the autumn leaf season. With a 45-mph speed limit on a winding two-lane road, be prepared for a leisurely trip.

Parkway Attractions Near Asheville Heading North:

Milepost 384, Blue Ridge Parkway Destination Center: The Blue Ridge Parkway Destination Center is the major exhibit and education center on the parkway. (*See* Section Three, Chapter 2)

Milepost 382, Folk Art Center: Located just east of Asheville, the Folk Art Center offers a look at traditional and contemporary crafts of the Appalachian region through interpretive programs, a museum and library. (*See* Section Three, Chapter 2

Milepost 364, Craggy Gardens: Craggy Gardens is an area of exposed rocks and high peaks that provides breathtaking views. Large expanses of native rhododendron cover its slopes and summits. In mid-June, pink and purple blooms of these Catawba rhododendrons are at their peak. This popular stop has restrooms, nature exhibits, and is open May-October. Well-marked trails lead through the rhododendron thickets to Craggy Dome's awe-inspiring views.

Milepost 355, Mount Mitchell: Mount Mitchell State Park offers tent camping, trails, nature study, picnic area, natural history museum and restaurant. At 6,684 feet

Craggy Gardens

above sea level, it is the highest peak in the eastern United States. 675-4611. (*See* other listing on Mount Mitchell in this chapter for complete information)

Milepost 331, Museum of North Carolina Minerals: Displays of over 300 varieties of minerals found in North Carolina. Open 9-5 daily. (*See* Section Five, Chapter 2)

Milepost 317, Linville Caverns: North Carolina's only caverns open year-round. Smooth paths takes visitors deep into the innermost recesses of this beautiful underground fairyland. Located on route 221, between Linville and Marion, NC. (*See* main Linville Caverns listing later in this chapter for complete information)

Milepost 316, Linville Gorge: Located off NC 105 in the Pisgah National Forest. Excellent hiking trails that lead to superb views of Linville Falls. Linville Gorge is one of the most spectacular sites in North Carolina. (*See* main Linville Gorge listing later in this chapter for complete information)

Milepost 305, Grandfather Mountain: One of North Carolina's top scenic attractions. Extraordinary views, wildlife habitats, famous Mile High Swinging Bridge, trails, picnic areas, nature museum, restaurant and theatre. (*See* main Grandfather Mountain listing in this chapter for complete information)

Milepost 304, Linn Cove Viaduct: Linn Cove Viaduct is a spectacular bridge that offers outstanding views and is noteworthy for its elegant and unique construction. Opened in 1987, this engineering marvel represents the final link in the construction of the Blue Ridge Parkway. The Viaduct is the most complicated concrete bridge ever built, snaking around boulder-strewn Linn Cove in a sweeping "S" curve.

Linn Cove Viaduct

The old Pisgah Inn

Milepost 294, Moses H. Cone Memorial Park: This great mountain park has hiking and horseback riding trails, and Flat Top Manor houses the Parkway Craft Center. No fees, and the Craft Center is open from Mid-March to November, 9:00 a.m. to 5:00 p.m. Ranger-guided activities are also available throughout the summer.

Parkway Attractions Near Asheville Heading South:

Milepost 408, Pisgah Inn at Mount Pisgah: Mount Pisgah was part of the original 145,000 acre parcel bought in the 1800's by George Vanderbilt to build his estate. The area is now the Pisgah National Forest. Located on the parkway is the historic Pisgah Inn, a great place to stop for a meal. A moderately strenuous hiking trail leads from the inn to the Mount Pisgah Overlook.

Milepost 412, Cradle of Forestry: Four miles south of the parkway on US 276 is the Cradle of Forestry, a National Historic Site located in the Pisgah National Forest. The Cradle of Forestry was the birthplace of American forestry. Visitors will find forestry exhibits, guided tours, restored historic buildings, craft exhibits and more. 1002 Pisgah Hwy. (*See* Section Five, Chapter 2)

Milepost 419, Graveyard Fields: An unusual flat area that takes its name from the mounds dotting the site, which are remains of fallen trees, victims of a 1925 Thanksgiving Eve fire.

Milepost 469, Mountain Farm Museum: Located at the southern end of the Parkway on US Hwy. 441, the Mountain Farm Museum is a National Park Service reconstruction of early pioneer farm buildings that show a past lifestyle. 497-1900. Located nearby also is Oconoluftee Visitors Center, which has restrooms, exhibits and park information.

Brown Mountain Lights

To the east of Asheville, near Morganton in Burke County, lies Brown Mountain. Rising to an elevation of only 2,600 feet, this foothills mountain has been at the center of a mystery since the earliest days of recorded history. For hundreds of years, lights have been seen on the mountain to the astonishment of all that have seen them. Cherokee Indians were familiar with the lights as far back as the year 1200, and their legends claim the lights are the spirits of Indian maidens searching for their fallen husbands and sweethearts. Early scientists, including German engineer Gerard Will de Brahm, Dr. W.J. Humphries of the Weather Bureau, and members of the U.S. Geological Survey, studied the lights and offered various explanations, none of which has stood the test of time. In fact, there has been no satisfactory explanation to date, making the lights one of North Carolina's most enduring mysteries as well as one of its most famous legends. Possible explanations that have been rejected by the scientific community include nitrous vapor emissions, locomotive or automobile reflections, "Andes Light" manifestations, marsh gas spontaneous combustion, moonshine still reflections, electrical phenomenon such as St. Elmo's Fire, mirages, UFOs, radioactive uranium ore emissions, and atmospheric reflections from nearby Hickory, Lenoir, or other area towns.

The lights are visible from several locations, the most popular being Brown Mountain Overlook, located 20 miles north of Morganton on NC Hwy.181 one mile south of the Barkhouse Picnic area; Wiseman's View Overlook, located five miles south of the village of Linville Falls on Kistler Memorial Hwy. (Old NC 105/SR 1238); and Lost Cove Cliffs Overlook, located on the Blue Ridge Parkway at Milepost 310, two miles north of the NC 181 junction.

Brown Mountain's lights have been seen as far away as Blowing Rock and the old Yonahlosse Trail over Grandfather Mountain twelve miles away. The lights are an irregular and somewhat rare occurrence and are not always visible. Your best chance of seeing them is on a night with clear weather conditions, good visibility, and little to no moonlight. Witnesses have reported seeing them at all hours of the night between sundown and sunrise. The lights vary widely in appearance, at times seeming like large balls of fire from a Roman candle, sometimes rising to various heights and fading, at other times expanding as they rise to finally burst without a sound.

It is best to keep your expectations low since there is absolutely no certainty that the lights will be visible. In this case, the journey is just as important as the destination. The adventure of looking, not finding, should be your focus. In any event, you will be participating in a North Carolina mystery that has baffled plenty of smart people over the years!

Location: Near Morganton, North Carolina (see viewing locations above)
Distance: 1½-2 hours from Asheville
Telephone: 828-433-6793 (Morganton Visitor Information Center)

Directions: To Lost Cove Cliffs Overlook on Blue Ridge Parkway: From Asheville, take I-40 East to Morganton and NC 181 North. The Blue Ridge Parkway is a more scenic though slower alternative (allow three hours). Follow the parkway north from the Tunnel Rd. (US 70) entrance to Milepost 310.

Grandfather Mountain and Grandfather Mountain State Park

Grandfather Mountain is one of the most environmentally significant mountains in the world. It is set apart by the United Nations as an International Biosphere Reserve and in 2009, 2,456 acres along the crest of Grandfather Mountain were purchased by the State of North Carolina to create North Carolina's newest state park, Grandfather Mountain State Park This purchase was made possible through support by The Conservation Fund and The Nature Conservancy. Grandfather Mountain is famous for its swinging bridge, the highest in America. Crossing this bridge suspends visitors more than a mile above sea level. Hiking and picnicking are favorite activities at Grandfather, and the mountain boasts wildlife habitats with bears, deer, panthers, otters and eagles. There is also a Nature Museum and gift shop.

Location: Linville, N.C.
Distance: 2 hours from Asheville
Address: 2050 Blowing Rock Highway, Linville, NC 28846
Telephone: 800-468-7325, 828-733-4337
Website: www.grandfather.com
Hours: 8 a.m. to dusk year-round except Thanksgiving and Christmas.
Fees: $15 adults, $7 children 4-12, under 4 free
Directions: Take Linville exit, Milepost 305 off of Blue Ridge Parkway onto US 221 or take I-40 from Asheville. Get off in Marion and take Hwy. 221 North 35 miles to Linville. Look for Grandfather Mountain signs.

Lake James State Park

Tucked away in rolling hills at the base of Linville Gorge is Lake James, a 6,510-acre lake with more than 150 miles of shoreline. This impressive waterway is the centerpiece of Lake James State Park. The park offers a variety of activities, including swimming, boating and fishing. The park has a well-maintained campground for public use, with twenty backpack campsites, each with fire pit, picnic table and tent space. Water and a washhouse with showers are also nearby. Campsites are available March though November for a modest fee on a first-come basis.

Location: Nebo, NC.
Distance: About an hour's drive
Address: 2785 NC Highway 126, Nebo, NC 28761
Telephone: 828-652-5047

Website: www.ncparks.gov/Visit/parks/laja/main
Hours: 8 a.m.-9 p.m. in summer, check website for hours in other seasons.
Directions: Traveling east on I-40: From I-40, take the Nebo/Lake James exit (Exit 90) and head north. After a half-mile, turn right onto Harmony Grove Rd., and follow it for 2 miles to a stoplight. Proceed straight across the intersection and past Nebo Elementary School to a stop sign. Turn right onto NC 126, and follow the signs to the park entrance 2.3 miles on the left.

Linville Caverns

At the head of beautiful Linville Valley, Linville Caverns lie deep under Humpback Mountain. The caverns entrance is in a beautiful glade and they are open year-round. In the winter many of the skiers from various popular ski slopes in the Banner Elk, Boone and Blowing Rock areas add a visit to Linville Caverns, "Inside the Mountain" as a delightful contrast to their skiing on the slopes above. The wondrous splendors deep inside Humpback Mountain were unknown to the white man until they were explored by H.E. Colton, an eastern Carolinian, and his local guide, Dave Franklin, more than one hundred years ago. The mysterious appearance of fish swimming out of the mountains led the explorers to probe deep into the mountain, following the underground stream through passageways and rooms whose ceilings, when lit by torches," looked like the arch of some grand cathedral." Linville Caverns have lighted smooth paths that take visitors deep into the innermost recesses. Courteous and experienced guides accompany each party through the caverns, pointing out the most interesting features and answering all questions.

Location: Marion, NC
Distance: 1 hour from Asheville
Address: 19929 Us Highway 221 North, Marion NC 28752
Telephone: 800-419-0540, 828-756-4171
Website: www.linvillecaverns.com
Hours: Open year-round, closed Thanksgiving and Christmas. June 1-Labor Day: 9 a.m.-6 p.m.; April, May, September, October: 9 a.m.-5 p.m.; November-March: weekends only 9 a.m.-4:30 p.m.
Fees: $7 adults, $5 children 5-12, under 5 free, seniors (62+) $5.50
Directions: Take Linville Falls exit on Blue Ridge Parkway and turn left on US 221. Caverns are 4 miles south of Linville on US 221 north of Marion. A faster route is I-40 from Asheville. Exit in Marion and take Hwy. 221 North.

Linville Gorge

Linville Gorge is a rugged wilderness area in Pisgah National Forest. Excellent hiking trails lead to superb views of Linville Falls. Linville Gorge, carved by the Linville River forming Jonas Ridge on the east and Wiseman's View on the western rim, is one of the most spectacular sites in North Carolina. The Linville Gorge area was originally donated to the Parkway by John D. Rockefeller. Linville Falls is perhaps the best-known waterfall in the entire Appalachian Mountains, and certainly it is one of the most scenic. The waterfall marks the beginning of the gorge, one of the deepest canyons in the east, with walls rising to almost 2,000 feet in places. Peregrine falcons and numerous other rare animals and plants are found in the gorge. One species of plant, the mountain golden heather (Hudsonia montana) is found nowhere else in the world.

Location:	Linville, NC
Distance:	Two hours from Asheville
Address:	Linville Falls Visitor Center, spur road off of Blue Ridge Parkway at Milepost 316.4.
Telephone:	Grandfather District Ranger Station: 828-652-2144
	Linville Falls Visitor Center: 828-765-1045
	U.S. Forest Service: 828-768-6062
Website:	http://ncnatural.com/Resources/Adventure/Gorge/Linville-Gorge
Hours:	The Linville Falls Visitor Center is open 9 a.m.-5:30 p.m.
Fees:	None, but permit must be obtained at Information Cabin along top of Gorge in order to enter Gorge area. This cabin is open 8 a.m.-4:30 p.m.
Directions:	Turn off of the Blue Ridge Parkway at Milepost 316.3, and follow the paved road 1.4 miles to Linville Falls Visitor Center. Faster route is I-40 East from Asheville. Get off in Marion and take Hwy. 221 North for 26 miles to Linville Falls Community. At intersection of Hwy. 183, take right and go east ¼ mile to entrance.

Mount Jefferson State Natural Area

Mount Jefferson in the Mount Jefferson State Natural Area is a National Natural Landmark. Two short trails give hikers spectacular views of the New River and the surrounding mountains. One of the more interesting features of the area is Luther's Rock Overlook. No bicycles or camping are allowed. There are picnic areas, and canoeing can be done at the nearby New River State Park. Mount Jefferson has a self-guided nature trail for hikers who wish to take their time and learn about the natural history of the area. By special request, park naturalists lead guided walks explaining the area's natural history and legends. The Park Service also offers a program history that advertises upcoming hikes and events.

Location:	Ashe County, NC
Distance:	2½-3 hours from Asheville
Address:	State Road 1152, Jefferson, NC 28604
Telephone:	336- 246-9653 (park office)
Website:	http://ncnatural.com/Resources/Adventure/Gorge/Linville-Gorge
Hours:	June-August 9 a.m.-8 p.m.; call for hours other times of the year.

Fees: None
Directions: From Asheville, take I-40 East to Hickory. Use 321 North through Blowing Rock and West Jefferson to US 221 North. Mount Jefferson State Natural Area is located a half-mile south of Jefferson. From NC 163, take SR 1149 to the park entrance on SR 1152.

Mount Mitchell State Park

Mount Mitchell State Park is in the Black Mountain range, which reaches higher than the Blue Ridge or Smoky Mountains. At 6,684 feet, its dominant mountain, Mount Mitchell, is the highest peak in the eastern United States. A cool climate, unique flora and fauna and easy access from the Blue Ridge Parkway make this a very popular vacation spot. Mount Mitchell State Park offers tent camping, six trails of varying difficulty, nature study, picnic areas, Natural History Museum and restaurant. The Park is 1,727 acres in size, and the summit of Mount Mitchell is famous for its spectacular views. On a clear day it is possible to see for more than 70 miles. The Natural History Museum located on the way to the Stone Observation Tower at the summit has dioramas, exhibits and recordings that present some of the unusual higher elevation plants and wildlife.

These high elevations give Mount Mitchell a cooler climate than the surrounding lowlands, a climate more typical of the boreal forests that dominate Canada and Alaska. Flora and fauna associated with the mountain's ecosystem are atypical of the southern Appalachians. Rare and uncommon plant and animal species live in the spruce-fir forest that covers the summit. This spruce-fir forest is among the rarest of forest environments in North Carolina, and one of the most endangered. The Park was created in 1916 by individuals concerned with the destruction of virgin forests by logging, and the mountain was named for Dr. Elisha Mitchell, the first person to take measurements of the Black Mountains, which include Mt. Mitchell. Dr. Mitchell is buried on the summit of Mount Mitchell at the base of the observation tower.

Location: Northeast of Asheville.
Distance: 1½ hours from Asheville
Address: Milepost 355 on the Blue Ridge Parkway
Telephone: 828-675-4611, Park Office
Website: http://ncnatural.com/Resources/Adventure/Gorge/Linville-Gorge
Hours: June- August: 8 a.m.-9 p.m.; call for hours in other times of the year.
Fees: None; campsites $8 per night
Directions: Take the Blue Ridge Parkway north from Asheville. The entrance to the park is at Milepost 355.

New River State Park

One of the oldest rivers in the world, the New River is designated as a National Wild and Scenic River and an American Heritage River. At the New River State Park, it is possible to canoe the more than 26 miles of the river's South Fork, embarking for your journey from any of three access points. A trip down the gentle New River promises excellent canoeing and picnicking as well as inspiring mountain scenery. The park itself encompasses 1,580 acres and is located in Ashe and Alleghany counties.

The park has a number of hiking trails, picnic areas including a 12-table covered picnic shelter with fireplace and grill, and a community building which includes a large meeting room, kitchen facilities, and restrooms. The community building is available for rent per day and is often used for family reunions and other groups' meetings. Canoe camping is very popular on the New River and the three access areas provide over 30 canoe-in or walk-in primitive campgrounds with tables and grills. Pit toilets and drinking water are located nearby. Campers must first register with the park staff or at registration boxes. Campsites require a small fee.

Easy paddling and beautiful scenery make canoeing the New River a spectacular and rewarding trip. Gentle waters with some rapids make it fun for both beginning and advanced paddlers. Canoes may be launched at the three access sites as well as from several bridges and roadways that cross the river.

Location: Jefferson, NC
Distance: 2½-3 hours from Asheville
Address: 1477 Wagoner Access Rd., Jefferson, NC 28640-
Telephone: Park Office: 336- 982-2587
Website: www.ncparks.gov/Visit/parks/neri/main
Hours: November-February 8 a.m.-6 p.m.; March & October 8 a.m.-7 p.m.; April, May, & September 8 a.m.-8 p.m.; June-August 8 a.m.-9 p.m.; Closed Christmas. Gates remain locked after hours.
Fees: Small fees for camping only
Directions: From Asheville, take I-40 East to Hickory. From there, take US 321 North through Blowing Rock and West Jefferson to US 221 to Jefferson. Wagoner Access Rd. off NC 88 can reach the Wagoner Rd. Access Area, which is eight miles southeast of Jefferson, 1.2 miles east of the intersection of NC 16 and NC 88. The US 221 Access Area, at river mile 15, is located eight miles northeast of Jefferson.

Rendezvous Mountain Educational State Forest

North Carolina has six Educational State Forests that have been developed as living environmental education centers. These forests are designed to promote a better understanding of the value of forests in our lives. Rendezvous Mountain Educational State Forest, located near Purlear, offers a rich mixture of mountain hardwoods, rhododendron, flame azaleas and a variety of wildflowers. These features are accessible to the visiting public by a series of well-marked trails accented by exhibits and displays depicting the ecology of the managed forest. The Talking Tree Trail features" talking trees," each with a recorded message about itself, its site, and the forest history. Also, actual forestry practices are explained on the

Forest Demonstration Trail. Close to the start of the trail, a natural amphitheater is available for special sessions or groups.

Location:	2½ hours west of Asheville
Address:	1956 Rendezvous Mountain Road, Purlear NC 28651
Telephone:	336-667-5072
Website:	www.ncesf.org/RMESF/rmesf_about.htm
Hours:	Third season in March to the day after Thanksgiving. Call office for hours.
Fees:	None
Allow:	Two hours
Directions:	From Asheville take 1-40 East towards Statesville. Take Exit 123 to Highway 321 North to Boone. In Boone take US 421 East. Take the exit toward Blue Ridge Parkway, turn left at Parkway and stay right on Parkway. Take the 1st right onto Phillips Gap Road and then turn left at State Road 1300/Summit Road. Turn right and the Forest will be on the right.

South Mountains State Park

Nestled deep in the woods, rugged South Mountains State Park is a phenomenal place to enjoy nature. The 132,747-acre park includes elevations that range from 1000 feet in the rolling piedmont to majestic mountain ranges towering over 3,000 feet. Other highlights are the beautiful High Shoals Falls that drops 80 feet, and more than 40 miles of trails including a 17-mile mountain bike loop. From equestrian camping to trout fishing, mountain biking to picnicking, a number of activities are available at the park.

Location:	Connelly Springs, NC. .
Distance:	1 hour and 30 minutes east of Asheville
Address:	3001 South Mountain State Park, Connelly Springs NC 28612
Telephone:	828-433-4772
Website:	www.ncparks.gov/Visit/parks/somo/main
Hours:	May-August: 8 a.m.-9 p.m., call for hours other times of the year.
Directions:	Traveling east on I-40: From I-40, turn south on NC 18, travel 11.1 miles and make a right turn onto SR 1913 (Sugarloaf Road). Take SR 1913 to Old NC 18 4.3 miles and turn left. Travel 2.7 miles and make a right turn onto SR 1901 (Ward's Gap Road). The park is 1.4 miles off SR 1901 on SR 1904 (South Mountains Park Avenue). Travel one mile from the beginning of South Mountain Park Avenue to the South Mountains State Park gate.

Stone Mountain State Park

Stone Mountain is not immediately visible upon entering the park that bears its name, but this magnificent 600-foot granite dome is well worth the wait. The 132,747-acre park offers 17 miles of designated trout waters and more than 16 miles of hiking trails. Designated as a National Natural Landmark in 1975, Stone Mountain is bounded on the north by the Blue Ridge Parkway and on the west by the Thurmond Chatham Game Lands.

Location: Roaring Gap, NC

Distance: 3 hours

Address: 3042 Frank Parkway, Roaring Gap, NC 28668

Telephone: 336-957-8185

Website: www.ncparks.gov/Visit/parks/stmo/main

Hours: June-August: 8 a.m.-9 p.m., call for hours other times of the year.

Directions: Stone Mountain State Park is located in Wilkes and Alleghany counties, seven miles southwest of Roaring Gap. From I-77, turn west onto US 21. Veer left onto Traphill Rd. (SR 1002), and follow it to the John P. Frank Parkway. Turn right and follow the parkway to the park. From the west, take NC 18 North and turn right onto Traphill Rd. (SR 1002). Follow the road to the John P. Frank Parkway and turn left, following the parkway to the park.

The Blowing Rock

The Blowing Rock, located near Boone, is an immense cliff rising about 1,000 feet above the Johns River Gorge below. The rock is named Blowing Rock because the cliff walls of the gorge form a flume through which the northwest wind sweeps with such force that it returns light objects cast over the cliff. This phenomena prompted the Ripley's "Believe It or Not" cartoon about "the only place in the world where snow falls upside down."

The Blowing Rock

Location: Blowing Rock, NC

Distance: 2 hours from Asheville

Address: Hwy. 321 South, Blowing Rock, NC 28605

Telephone: 828-295-7111

Website: www.theblowingrock.com

Hours: March, April, May and November: 9 a.m.-6 p.m.; June-October: 8 a.m. to 8 p.m.; Closed December-February

Fees: $6 adults, $5 seniors, $1 ages 6-11, under 5 free

Directions: From Blue Ridge Parkway take Boone exit to 321 South to Blowing Rock. A faster route from Asheville is to take I-40 East to Marion and take Hwy. 221 North to Blowing Rock

Tuttle Educational State Forest

North Carolina has six Educational State Forests that have been developed as living environmental education centers. These forests are designed to promote a better understanding of the value of forests in our lives. Tuttle Educational State Forest, located near Lenoir, offers a rich mixture of mountain hardwoods and pines, rhododendron, flame azaleas and a variety of wildflowers. These features are accessible to the visiting public by a series of well-marked trails accented by exhibits and displays depicting the ecology of the managed forest. Tuttle boasts a wide variety of pines and hardwoods plus rolling terrain and clear streams. These features are accessible by a series of well-marked trails accented by exhibits and displays which explain the ecology of the managed forest.

Location:	1½ hours east of Asheville
Address:	3420 Playmore Beach Road, Lenoir NC 28655
Telephone:	828-757-5608
Website:	http://www.ncesf.org/TESF/home.htm
Hours:	Mid-March to Mid-November. Closed Mondays, Call office for hours.
Fees:	None
Allow:	Two hours
Directions:	From Asheville take Exit 103 Burkmont Avenue to Highway 18-64 north towards Lenoir. Turn left onto SR 1311. The forest will be on your right.

W. Scott Kerr Dam & Reservoir

W. Scott Kerr Dam and Reservoir are named in honor of William Kerr Scott, 1896-1958, former Governor of North Carolina and U.S. Senator. The project was included in the general plan for the improvement of the Yadkin-Pee Dee River for the purpose of reducing flood damage such as was caused by the devastating floods of 1899, 1916, and 1940.

User Fees are required in some park areas for day use activities and boat launching. The remaining parks, access areas, fringe shorelines and all water areas are open to the public without charge for public and recreational use. Public use facilities have been provided by the Corps of Engineers in the recreational areas, including seven boat launching ramps, four swimming areas, paved access roads, picnic areas and campsites with potable water and sanitary facilities. Flush type toilets, laundry trays, and shower facilities are available in Bandit's Roost and Warrior Creek Parks. Public service facilities consisting of a marina, snack bar, and fueling and bait supplies are available at the Skyline Marina. Anyone visiting the reservoir for the first time should check in at the Visitor Assistance Center on Reservoir Road.

Location:	Wilkesboro
Distance:	2½ hours from Asheville

Address: Visitor Assistance Center, 499 Reservoir Road, Wilkesboro NC
            28697
Telephone: 336-921-3390
Directions: (To the Visitor Assistance Center) From Asheville take I-40 East
            and get off at Exit 100 toward Jamestown Road. Turn left at James-
            town Road and go 2 miles to right at Carbon City Road. In one
            mile turn left at the US64 Bypass and go 2.7 miles to NC18. Follow
            NC18 over 30 miles to the Wilkesboro area, and turn left at Boomer
            Road. Turn right onto Highway 268, go 3 miles, turn right onto
            Reservoir Road at the W. Kerr Scott Dam and Reservoir sign, go
            1/4 mile, then turn left beside Shady Grove Baptist Church

Natural Attractions West of Asheville
Bent Creek Experimental Forest
Bent Creek Experimental Forest (SRS-4101), located just outside Asheville, is one of the oldest research areas maintained by the USDA Forest Service. Since 1925, scientists at Bent Creek have been developing and practicing sound forestry practices. The fruits of their research on fire, insects, wildlife, water, diseases, and recreational uses are being applied today in forests all around the world and in particular the Southern Appalachians. Open to visitors, Bent Creek is popular with area hikers and runners.

Location: Just west of Asheville
Distance: 30 minutes west of Asheville
Address: 1577 Brevard Rd., Asheville NC 28806
Telephone: 828-667-5261
Website: www.srs.fs.usda.gov/bentcreek
Hours: 8 a.m.-4:30 p.m. Monday-Friday
Fees: None
Directions: I-26 Exit 2 (Biltmore Square Mall exit). Follow Hwy. 191 South
            1½-2 miles. Turn right onto Bent Creek Ranch Rd. and follow signs
            to Lake Powatan and the Experimental Forest.

Cades Cove
Cades Cove is a broad, verdant 6,800-acre valley near Townsend, Tennessee in the Great Smoky Mountains National Park. It is surrounded by mountains and is one of the most popular destinations in the park. It offers some of the best opportunities for wildlife viewing in the park. Large numbers of white-tailed deer are frequently seen, and sightings of black bear, coyote, ground hog, turkey, raccoon, skunk, and other animals are also possible.

For hundreds of years Cherokee Indians hunted in Cades Cove, but archeologists have found no evidence of major settlements. The first Europeans settled in the cove sometime between 1818 and 1821. By 1830 the population of the area had already swelled to 271. Cades Cove offers the widest variety of historic buildings of any area in the national park. Scattered along the loop road are three churches, a working grist mill, barns, log houses, and many other faithfully restored eighteenth and nineteenth century structures. An inexpensive self-guiding tour booklet available at the entrance to the road provides in-depth information about the buildings and the people who built and used them.

An 11-mile, one-way loop road circles the cove, offering motorists the opportunity to sightsee at a leisurely pace. Allow at least two to four hours to tour Cades Cove, longer if you walk some of the area's trails. Traffic is heavy during the tourist season in summer and fall and on weekends year-round. While driving the loop road, please be courteous to other visitors and use pulloffs when stopping to enjoy the scenery or view wildlife. A visitor center (open daily), restrooms, and the Cable Mill historic area are located half-way around the loop road.

Numerous trails originate in the cove, including the five-mile roundtrip trail to Abrams Falls and the short Cades Cove Nature Trail. Longer hikes to Thunderhead Mountain and Rocky Top (made famous by the popular song) also begin in the cove. Several designated backcountry campsites (camping by permit only) are located along trails. A campground with 159 sites is open year round in Cades Cove. Tents and RVs up to 35 feet can be accommodated in the campground.

Only bicycle and foot traffic are allowed on the loop road until 10:00 a.m. every Saturday and Wednesday morning from early May until late September. Otherwise the road is open to motor vehicles from sunrise until sunset daily, weather permitting.

Location:	Great Smoky Mountains National Park, West of Asheville near Townsend TN
Distance:	3-4 hours from Asheville
Address:	The Cades Cove Visitor Center is near the western entrance of the park in Tennessee
Telephone:	General Information 423-436-1200, Cades Cove Campground: 828-448-4103
Website:	http://www.nps.gov/grsm/planyourvisit/cadescove.htm
Directions:	From Asheville take I-40 west towards Tennessee. After you reach Tennessee take Exit 443 onto Foothills Parkway towards Gatlinburg and Great Smoky Mountains National Park. Go 6.3 miles and turn left at TN 73/US321 heading west to Gatlinburg. In Gatlinburg take 441 toward the National Park and turn at the Sugarlands Visitor Center. From here you will take Little River Road to Laurel Creek Rd which runs straight into Cades Cove.

Chatuge Lake

Chatuge Lake was created in 1942 when the Tennessee Valley Authority constructed a dam across the Hiwassee River. The lake has over 133 miles of shoreline, is over 7,200 acres in size and is in both North Carolina and Georgia. Chatuge Dam is 144 feet high and stretches 2,850 feet across the Hiwassee River. Chatuge was originally built to store water to help prevent flooding downstream. A single hydropower generating unit was added in 1954. The Weir, just north of the dam, offers picnic tables and a launch for canoes and tubes for a trip on the Hiawassee River to a takeout area near Fires Creek Wildlife Management Area. Call the Tennessee Valley Authority for information regarding water conditions and release schedules at 828-837-7395.

There are three public boat ramps accessible from North Carolina: Jackrabbitt Mountain Campground off Highway 175, Ledford Chapel Wildlife Access Ramp on Highway 64, and Gibson Cove Campground, on Myers Chapel Road. Contact the Clay Country Chamber of Commerce office at 828-389-3704 for more information. Clay County operates two campgrounds on the lake with spaces available for tents and campers. Call 828-389-3532 evenings. Both have: public swimming areas with a sandy beach, BBQ grills and picnic tables. Other amenities include a boat launch, playground, ball park, pavilions and showers.

Location:　Near Hayesville NC
Distance:　From Asheville allow 2-2½ hours
Resources:　Clay County Chamber of Commerce 388 Business Highway 64, Hayesville NC 28904; 828-389-3704 and Tennessee Valley Authority/Lake Hiwassee, 221 Old Ranger Road, Murphy NC 28906; 828-837-7395
Directions:　From Asheville take I-40 West towards Knoxville. Take Exit 27 to merge into US Highway 74/19 West towards to Waynesville/Murphy. In approximately 25 miles take Exit 81 to merge onto US 23/441 towards Franklin/Dillsboro. Continue on Murphy Highway/US 64 and after approximately 28 miles take sharp left onto Highway 175. This will take you to the lake in the Hayesville area.

Cherohala Skyway

The Cherohala Skyway was completed and dedicated in 1996 and cost over $100,000,000 to construct. Spectacular to say the least, the road has been designated a National Scenic Byway. The Skyway crosses through the Cherokee National Forest in Tennessee and the Nantahala National Forest in North Carolina. The Skyway connects Tellico Plains, Tennessee, with Robbinsville, North Carolina, and is about 50 miles long. It is a wide, paved 2-laned road maintained by the Tennessee Department of Transportation and the North Carolina Department of Transportation, and the elevations range from 900 feet above sea level at the Tellico River in Tennessee to over 5400 feet above sea level at the Tennessee-North Carolina state line at Haw Knob (mile marker 11).

The name "Cherohala" comes from the names of the two National Forests: "Cher" from the Cherokee and "ahala" from the Nantahala. The Cherohala Skyway is located in southeast Tennessee and southwest North Carolina. Keep in mind that the skyway can be desolate at night and dangerous driving in the winter months. Also, keep in mind that there are no gas stations also for the entire 50 miles.

Location:	West of Asheville
Address:	Graham County Visitor Center: 12 North Main Street, Robbinsville NC 28711
Distance:	From Asheville, approximately 2½ hours driving time.
Telephone:	828-479-3790
Website:	www.cherohala.org
Directions:	From Asheville take 1-40 West. Take Exit 27 to merge onto US Highway 74 West towards Waynesville/Murphy/US19. Turn right at Highway19West/74 and continue to follow US 19/74. Turn right at US 129/Tallulah Rd. Continue to follow US 129 into Robbinsville. Turn left at Massey Branch Road/NC 1116/NC 143. Turn right at NC 1127/NC143/Snowbird Road. Turn right at NC 143/Santeetlah road and continue to follow 143 to the Skyway.

Dupont State Forest

The Dupont State Forest is located between Hendersonville and Brevard and its 10,400 acres of forest feature four major waterfalls on the Little River and several on the Grassy Creek. Originally 7,600 acres and established in 1996 through a donation from the Dupont Corporation, the forest was expanded in 2000 by two property additions, including the spectacular 2,200-acre tract in the center of the forest. It lies in the upland plateau of the Little River valley with elevation between 2,300 and 3,600 feet. Key waterfalls, all of which are easily accessed by short trails, include Triple Falls (a series of three waterfalls), High Falls, Hooker Falls (an 11-foot drop into Cascade Lake), Bridal Veil Falls (the most unique falls in the State Forest, with a long, shallow veil-like whitewater incline along the lower section), Wintergreen Falls (20-foot cascade on Grassy Creek) and Grassy Creek Falls. Cedar Rock Mountain in the forest has hundreds of acres of exposed granite, making it a very popular destination for cyclists and hikers, and Stone Mountain is the forest's high point at 3,600 feet. It offers a 180-degree view during the summer and a full 360 degrees during the winter months.

Location:	Between Hendersonville and Brevard
Distance:	Approximately 45 minutes to 1 hour from Asheville
Telephone:	828-251-6509
Website:	www.dupontforest.com
Address:	Division of Forest Resources, 14 Gaston Mountain Rd., Asheville NC 28806
Fees:	None
Directions:	From Asheville, take I-26 West to Exit 9, and then take Hwy. 280 to Pisgah Forest. Turn left on US 64 in Pisgah Forest and travel 3.7 miles to the Texaco station in Penrose. Turn right on Crab Creek Rd. and continue 4.3 miles and turn right onto Dupont Rd. As the road climbs the hill, turn left at Sky Valley Rd. and continue about a mile past the farmhouse to the parking lot on the right.

...ɒroad River

The third oldest river in the world, trailing only the Nile in Africa and the New in West Virginia, the French Broad River flows north through 117 miles of Western North Carolina from its headwaters in Rosman to Tennessee. In Tennessee it joins the Holston to form the Tennessee River and eventually reaches the Mississippi. It is a great recreational resource offering splendid scenery, perfect picnic spots, Class I through IV whitewater, and good fishing. It flows right though Asheville on its journey north. One of the river's Cherokee names was Tahkeeostee, "racing waters." Others, frequently used for only a part of the river, were Poelico, Ariqua, and Zillicoah. By 1776 the present name French Broad River was in use. The name French Broad comes from the fact that this river used to flow into French Indian territory in Tennessee during colonial days.

On its way through Asheville, the river is accessible at a number of places. These access sites are maintained by the Buncombe County Department of Parks, Recreation & Greenways and are listed below. The City of Asheville Parks, Recreation & Cultural Arts Department also maintains a number of river parks on the French Broad River in the Asheville area. One of these, the Jean Webb Park is located on Riverside Drive which parallels the river. This small park is convenient from downtown and a good spot for a picnic lunch. The major river park in the Asheville area is the French Broad River Park, also maintained by the city of Asheville. One of Asheville's most beautiful parks, it features a vast area of open green space with old trees, a wildflower garden, a paved trail, a gazebo, picnic tables and grills, an observation deck, and a small playground. Riverlink, an important non-profit river preservation organization, was instrumental in helping to develop this park, the Jean Webb Park and others. Riverlink's website (www.riverlink.org) has an extensive "River Guide" which has maps and directions to all of the access points on the river.

If you are interested in whitewater rafting, the French Broad River north of Asheville is home to a number of whitewater rafting companies. In Asheville, the Asheville Outdoor Center is conveniently located minutes from downtown. They offer gentle tubing, rafting, kayaking and canoeing trips, including ones that go through lands owned by Biltmore Estate.

Location: West of downtown Asheville

Resources: Riverlink: PO Box 15488, Asheville NC 28813; 828-252-8474; www.riverlink.org; Buncombe County Department Parks, Recreation & Greenways: 828-250-4260; City of Asheville Parks, Recreation & Cultural Arts Department: 828-251-1122

Directions: The French Broad River is accessible from many points in Asheville. To reach the Riverlink French Broad River Park, take Meadow Road west from Biltmore Village. This road eventually begins to parallel the river. Turn left at Amboy Road to access the park.

Buncombe County River Access Sites & River Parks

Bent Creek: 1592 Brevard Rd., Asheville NC 28806; From Asheville take 26 East & take Exit 2–go left at light on to Bre-vard Road & travel 2.4 mile–see the park on the left.

Jean Webb Park: 30 Riverside Drive, Asheville NC 28801;From downtown Asheville head west on Patton Avenue and turn left at South French Broad Avenue. Turn right at Hilliard Avenue, turn left at Clingman Avenue and then turn right on Lyman Street. Turn right at Riverside Drive and park will be on your left.

French Broad River Park: 508 Riverview Drive, Asheville NC 28806;From downtown Asheville head west on Patton Avenue and turn left at South French Broad Avenue. Turn right at Hilliard Avenue, turn left at Clingman Avenue and then turn left on Lyman Street. Turn right on Amboy Road and the immediate right on Riverview Drive

Corcoran Paige: 9 Pinners Rd., Arden NC 28704; From Asheville take 26 East & take Exit #6–turn left on to Long Shoals Road & travel 1.8 miles–turn right on to Hendersonville Road & travel 1.4 miles–turn right on to Glen Bridge Road & travel 1.0 mile–turn left on to Pinner Road–see park on right.

Glen Bridge: 77 Pinners Rd., Arden NC 28704; From Asheville take 26 East & take Exit #6–turn left on to Long Shoals Road & travel 1.8 miles–turn right on to Hendersonville Road & travel 1.4 miles–turn right on to Glen Bridge Road & tra-vel 1.0 mile–turn left on to Pinner Road & travel .5 mile–see park on right.

Hominy Creek: 194 Hominy Creek Rd., Asheville NC 28806; From Asheville take I-240 West. Take exit #1B. At the end of the ramp, turn right. After about .1 mile, turn left onto Shelburne then left onto Hominy Creek Road & travel .7 mile–see park on left.

Ledges Whitewater: 1080 Old Marshall Hwy, Alexander NC 28701;From Asheville take 19/23 North & immediately take the Hill Street Exit–go left & travel .1 mile–turn right on to Riverside Drive & travel 8.1 miles–see park on left.

Walnut Island: 3042 Old Marshall Hwy, Alexander NC 28701;From Asheville take 19/23 North & immediately take the Hill Street Exit–go left and travel .1 mile–turn right on to Riverside Drive & travel 13.3 miles–see park on left.

Fontana Lake

Fontana Lake, located in Swain and Graham counties, is surrounded on the north side by the Great Smoky Mountains National Forest, and by national forest on the remainder of the shoreline. At 10,230 acres, Fontana Lake is the largest in the Western North Carolina mountains and offers visitors an abundance of recreational opportunities. There are over 39 miles of hiking trails along its shores, and the Appalachian Trail actually passes over the top of Fontana Dam. The hot showers available at the trail shelter maintained by TVA have led grateful hikers to dub it the Fontana Hilton. There are over 238 miles of shoreline, and most of it is protected from development, since 90% is owned by the National Park and U.S. Forest Service.

Fontana Dam, which forms the lake, is the highest dam east of the Rockies is a Tennessee Valley Authority project. It towers an amazing 480 feet in height and stretches 2,365 feet across the Little Tennessee River. The dam itself is a major tourist attraction, with thousands of visitors each year. The construction of the dam began in 1942 to provide electric power for the war effort and was completed in 1944. The lake is fed by Chambers Creek, Eagle Creek, Forney Creek, Hazel Creek, Lands Creek, Nolands Creek and Pilkeys Creek, and reaches depths of over 440 feet. The Fontana Dam Visitor Center is open to the public from 9 a.m. to 7 p.m. daily from May through November.

Tsali Recreational Area, located on the southeastern shore of Fontana Lake, has a well-deserved reputation as a great spot for hiking, mountain biking, bird watching and horseback riding. Fontana Village Resort in Fontana Dam is a good place to begin when you arrive in the Fontana Lake area. From there the dam is a short drive, and the village offers restaurants and resources for more lake information.

Location:	Swain and Graham Counties, NC
Distance:	From Asheville allow 2-2½ hours
Resources:	Tennessee Valley Authority/Lake Hiwassee, 221 Old Ranger Road, Murphy NC 28906;
Telephone:	828-837-7395
Directions:	(To Fontana Village) take I-40 west. Take the exit for Hwy 74 (Great Smoky Mountain Expressway). Stay on Hwy 74 (four lane) you will pass Clyde, Sylva, and 8 miles past Bryson City (last chance for groceries, restaurants) turn right on Hwy 28. Continue on Hwy 28 for 25 miles.

Joyce Kilmer Memorial Forest

The 526,798-acre Nantahaha National Forest located to the west of Asheville is home to the Joyce Kilmer Memorial Forest, one of the nation's most impressive preserves of old-growth forest. Here you may view magnificent examples of over 100 species of trees, including hemlocks and tulip-poplars over 20 feet in circumference and 100 feet high. Some of these trees are over 450 years old. Explored in 1540 by Spanish Conquistador Hernando DeSoto and established in 1920 under the 1911 Weeks Act, this 3,800-acre forest was set aside in 1936 as a memorial to Joyce Kilmer, the soldier/poet who wrote the famous poem "Trees."

The only way to see the impressive memorial forest is on foot. The figure-eight Joyce Kilmer National Recreation Trail covers 2 miles and has two loops: t h e 1.25-mile lower loop passes the Joyce Kilmer Memorial plaque, and the upper 0.75-mile loop swings through Poplar Cove—a grove of the forest's largest trees. The trailhead parking area has a flush toilet and picnic tables. No camping or overnight parking is allowed.

Location:	West of Asheville
Distance:	2-3 hours from Asheville

Address: Cheoah District Ranger Office, 1133 Massey Branch Rd., Robbinsville, NC 28771
Telephone: Nantahala National Forest Cheoah District Ranger 828-479-6431
Hours: Daily 8 a.m.-4:30 p.m. (Ranger Office hours)
Fees: None
Directions: Take I-40W to Exit 27. Exit right onto U.S. 19/74 toward Waynesville. Go about 47 miles, and bear right on NC 28N. Go 5 miles, and turn left on NC 143 to Robbinsville. From Robbinsville take NC 143W. After about 12 miles, turn right on Joyce Kilmer Road (SR1134). Go 2 miles and turn left to memorial forest.

Gorges State Park

Located near Sapphire, Gorges State Park contains spectacular waterfalls, sheer rock walls, rugged river gorges, and one of the greatest concentrations of rare and unusual plant species in the Eastern United States. An elevation that rises over 2,000 feet in only three to five miles and an annual rainfall in excess of 80 inches creates a unique temperate rain forest. Gorges' 7,484 acres were designated a state park in April of 1999 to protect these nationally significant natural resources, and it is the newest state park in North Carolina. Park highlights are Horsepasture River (a National Wild and Scenic River), Toxaway River, Bearwallow Creek, Thompson River, Bearcamp Creek, Windy Falls, Lower Bearwallow Falls, Toxaway Creek Falls, Chestnut Mountain, Grindstone Mountain, Misery Mountain, many major trout streams, and numerous wildflowers including rare species.

Location: Sapphire, North Carolina
Distance: Approximately 2 hours from Asheville
Address: NC Highway 281 South, Sapphire, NC 28774
Telephone: 828-966-9099
Website: www.ncparks.gov/Visit/parks/gorg/main
Hours: June-August 8 a.m.-9 p.m.; call for hours during other times of the year.
Fees: None
Directions: From Asheville, take the I-26 Airport Rd. Exit (US 280 South) past the airport to Brevard where it will turn into US 64. Continue on Hwy. 64 to Sapphire. Gorges State Park is located in Transylvania County and overlaps the North Carolina/South Carolina state lines. It is approximately 45 miles west of Asheville.

Great Smoky Mountains National Park

The Great Smoky Mountains National Park, which lies along the common border of Tennessee and North Carolina, forms a majestic climax to the Appalachian Highlands. With outlines softened by a forest mantle, the mountains stretch away to remote horizons in sweeping troughs that recede to evenness in the distance. Shrouding the peaks is a smokelike mist that rises from the dense plant growth. The mountains get their name from this deep blue mist.

The park's boundary wraps around 800 square miles of mountain wilderness, most of it virtually unspoiled. Many peaks rise above 6,000 feet. A great variety of trees, shrubs, herbs and other plants are nourished by the fertile land and heavy rainfall and rushing streams. The Great Smoky Park contains more than 700 miles of rivers and streams, over 200,000 acres of virgin forests, and over 850 miles of trails. It is the most visited national park with over 9,000,000 visitors a year.

When you get to the border of the park coming from the Asheville direction you will want to check in at the Oconaluftee Visitor Center in Cherokee. Although there are many opportunities to drive through the park, the most rewarding experiences are found along the trails. More than 650 miles of horse and foot trails wind along the crystal clear streams and waterfalls, past forest giants that have been living for hundreds of years, through the wild beauty of flower-filled coves and into high mountain meadows. One of the most popular attractions in the park is Cades Cove, a lush beautiful valley complete with historic buildings (*See* Cades Cove, earlier in this same section).

The park offers guided nature walks as well as self-guided tours. Copies of maps and schedules are available at Visitors Centers and at all ranger stations. Not to be missed during your visit is the Mountain Farm Museum, located at the Oconaluftee Visitor Center. It is part of an effort to preserve some of the cultural heritage of the Smokies and is a collection of buildings that were moved from their original locations to form an open-air museum. Highly recommended auto tours include the Roaring Fork Auto Tour, the Newfound Gap Road Auto Tour, the Cades Cove Auto Tour and the Cataloochee Auto Tour. Self-guided tour books are available and will enrich your stops at the many historical sites and natural wonders along the way.

The famed Appalachian Trail (*See* Appalachian Trail, earlier in this same section), which stretches from Maine to Georgia, enters the park near the eastern boundary. Straddling the boundary line of two states, it zigzags a course for 71 miles along the crest of some of the highest peaks and ultimately leaves the park again at Fontana Dam. If you wish to hike the full distance in the park, you can cover the 71 miles in 6 to 8 days. Trailside shelters and campsites are spaced about a day's journey apart. Many other horse and foot trails are scattered throughout the park. There are short, self-guiding trails that are perfect for beginners. Just pick up a leaflet at the start of each trail. A backcountry-use permit, required for all overnight hiking parties, can be obtained free at ranger stations or visitors centers (except Cades Cove Visitors Center).

There are ten developed campgrounds in the park; fees are charged at each. Reservations are recommended at Cades Cove, Elkmont and Smokemont from May 15 to October 31; they can be made by calling 800-365-2267. Sites may be reserved up to three months in advance. All other campgrounds are first-come, first-served. Cosby and Look Rock campgrounds rarely fill up. Campgrounds have tent sites, limited trailer space, water, fireplaces, tables and restrooms. There are no showers or hookups for trailers. No more than six people may occupy a campsite. Two tents or one RV and one tent are allowed per site. The camping limit is seven days between May 15 and October 31, and 14 days between November 1 and May 14. Some campgrounds close in winter. Sewage disposal stations are located at Smokemont, Cades Cove, Deep Creek and Cosby campgrounds, and across from the Sugarlands Visitor Center. They are not available for use in the winter.

Saddle horses are available from April 1 to October 31 at Cades Cove, Smokemont, Deep Creek (near Greenbrier on U.S. 321), and near park headquarters. Bicycles are permitted on park roads but prohibited on all trails except Gatlinburg, Oconaluftee River, and lower Deep Creek. Bicycles may be rented from the Cades Cove Store, near the Cades Cove Campground.

One of the most biologically diverse regions in all of North America, the Park has been designated an International Biosphere Reserve under the UNESCO "Man in the Biosphere" program. Within its boundaries there are over 1500 species of flowering plants; 100 different types of trees; 600 mosses, lichens and liverworts; 50 species of mammals including black bears, whitetail deer, raccoons, foxes, bobcats, opossum, coyotes, and possibly cougars; more than 80 types of snakes and amphibians; and 70 kinds of fish from small colorful darters to brook, brown and rainbow trout. And over 200 kinds of birds have been observed within the park borders. Bring along your bird book and binoculars; the Great Smokies are a bird watcher's paradise.

The Great Smoky Mountains National Park was formally dedicated on February 6, 1930 by both Tennessee and North Carolina governors. Its mission continues today; to preserve and protect the wild beauty and natural charm of the Great Smoky Mountains for all time. LeConte Lodge (accessible by trail only) provides the only lodging in the park. Call (423) 429-5704 for more information on this secluded retreat.

Location: West of Asheville

Distance: 2-3 hours from Asheville

Address: Headquarters: Great Smoky Mountains National Park, 107 Park Headquarters Rd., Gatlinburg, TN 37738. There are three visitor centers that provide maps and information: Sugarlands (Tennessee side), Cades Cove (Near the western entrance of the park), and Oconaluftee (in North Carolina). Oconaluftee is the nearest entrance to Asheville. Oconaluftee Visitor Center: 150 Hwy. 441 N., Cherokee, NC 28719.

Telephone: General Information: 423-436-1200
Communications Center: 423-436-1230
Back Country Information: 423-436-1297
Oconaluftee Visitor Center: 423-497-1900, 423-497-1904
Park Headquarters: 423-436-1294
Campground Reservations: 800-365-2267
National Park Service: (Washington DC) 202-208-6843
Friends of the Smokies: 828-452-0720

Website: www.nps.gov/grsm

Hours: Visitor Centers open daily except Christmas. Winter: 9 a.m.-5 p.m., Summer: 8 a.m.-7 p.m. Hours vary depending on time of year.

Fees: None to enter park. Fees are charged at developed campgrounds and for certain special programs.

Camping: There are ten developed campgrounds in the park including Cades Cove in Tennessee and Smokemont in North Carolina, which are open year-round. The other developed campgrounds are generally open from late March or April to early November. Fees range from $10-$15 per night. Backcountry camping, on the other hand, is free but requires a permit. Most campsites use self-registration at visitor centers or ranger stations, but shelters and rationed sites require reservations. Reservations can be made 30 days in advance by calling 423-436-1231 or 800-365-2267 between 8 a.m. and 6 p.m. any day of the week.

Lodging: LeConte Lodge, which is accessible only by foot or horseback, sits atop 6,593-foot tall Mt. LeConte. This is the Park's third highest peak. Reservations are required and can be made by calling 423-429-5704. The lodge is open mid-March to mid-November. A variety of lodging facilities are available in the outlying communities.

Directions: From Asheville, take I-40 West to Exit 27. Follow Hwy. 19 South to Cherokee. In Cherokee, take 441 North and follow signs to the park entrance.

Of Note: The most visited National Park in America. Hosts the International Biosphere Reserve and the World Heritage Site. Elevations in the park range from 800-6643 feet and topography affects local weather. Temperatures are 10-20 degrees cooler on the mountaintops. Annual precipitation averages 65 inches in lowlands to 88 inches in high country. Spring often brings unpredictable weather, particularly in higher elevations. Summer is hot and humid, but more pleasant in higher elevations. Fall has warm days and cool nights and is the driest period. Frosts occur starting in late September and continue into April. Winter is generally moderate, but extreme conditions become more likely as elevation increases.

Tips: In summer time the park is heavily visited. Expect long lines during this season. Late spring is a great time to visit because of the wildflowers, pleasant weather, and absence of crowds. The Great Smoky Mountains are vast. Plan your trip carefully. Write or call ahead for information to help in planning. During the summer and fall, the park provides regularly scheduled ranger-led interpretive walks and talks, slide presentations, and campfire programs at campgrounds and visitor centers.

Hiwassee Lake

Lake Hiwassee was formed in 1940 with the construction of the Tennessee Valley Authority dam, which currently has the highest dam overspill in the world at 307 feet. The dam was created for flood control and hydroelectric power generation, with the resulting 6090 acre Lake Hiwassee, which has almost 180 miles of shoreline, measures 22 miles long, and is more than 200 feet deep in places. Hiwassee Dam stretches 1,376 feet across the Hiwassee River.

Lake Hiwassee is surrounded by the Nantahala National Forest and offers extraordinary scenery, boating and lake activities. Easy access for boaters and kayakers can be found at the Hanging Dog Recreation Area, which also offers a campground, picnic area and hiking trails as well as a boat launching ramp. To get to the Hanging Dog Recreation Area from Murphy, go 4.4 miles northwest on Peachtree Road which turns into Joe Brown Highway. Entrance to the lake is on the left.

Location:	Near Murphy, NC
Distance:	From Asheville allow 2-2½ hours
Telephone:	828-837-7395
Resources:	Tennessee Valley Authority/Lake Hiwassee, 221 Old Ranger Road, Murphy NC 28906;
Directions:	From Asheville take I-40 West towards Knoxville. Take Exit 27 to merge into US Highway 74/19 West towards to Murphy.

Nantahala National Forest

This 526,798-acre National Forest located to the west of Asheville offers family camping, boating, fishing, horse trails and miles of hiking trails. Nantahala is home to the Joyce Kilmer Memorial Forest, one of the nation's most impressive preserves of old-growth forest. Here you may view magnificent examples of over 100 species of trees, some over 20 feet in circumference and 100 feet high. Explored in 1540 by Spanish Conquistador Hernando DeSoto and established in 1920 under the 1911 Weeks Act, this 3,800-acre forest was set aside in 1936 as a memorial to Joyce Kilmer, the soldier/poet who wrote the famous poem Trees. Scenic drives, excellent fishing and rafting the whitewaters of the Nantahala River are among the forest's

"Trees" by Joyce Kilmer
(1886-1918)

I think I shall never see
A poem lovely as a tree.
A tree whose hungry mouth is pressed
Against the earth's sweet flowing breast;
A tree that looks at God all day
And lifts her leafy arms to pray;
A tree that may in summer wear
A nest of robins in her hair;
Upon whose bosom snow has lain;
Who intimately lives with rain.
Poems are made by fools like me,
But only God can make a tree.

biggest attractions. Nantahala is also renowned for waterfalls and its beautiful chain of pristine lakes. Black bears, bobcats, white-tailed deer and other animals indigenous to the Appalachians abound in the Forest.

Location: West of Asheville
Distance: 2-3 hours from Asheville
Address: Cheoah District Ranger Office, Massey Branch Rd., Rt. 1 (PO Box 16A), Robbinsville, NC 28771
Highlands Ranger District: 2010 Flat Mountain Rd., Highlands, NC 28741; 828-526-3765
Telephone: Nantahala National Forest Cheoah District Ranger 828-479-6431
Highlands Ranger District 828-526-3765
Website: www.cs.unca.edu/nfsnc
Hours: Ranger Office: April-November Daily 8 a.m.-4:30 p.m.; December-March 8 a.m.-4:30 p.m. Monday-Friday
Fees: None to enter park
Camping: Tsali campground, Cheoah, Horse Cove, and Cable Cove campgrounds.
Directions: From Asheville take I-40 West. Take Exit 27 to 74 West, then to NC 19. Follow NC 19 to Nantahala.

Pisgah National Forest

Pisgah National Forest is a land of mile-high peaks, cascading waterfalls and heavily forested slopes. It is an ideal place, as are all of the national forests, for outdoor recreation. The forest gets its name from Mount Pisgah, a prominent peak in the area. In the 1700s a Scotch-Irish minister saw the peak and named it for the Biblical mountain from which Moses saw the promised land after 40 years of wandering in the wilderness. Located on two sides of Asheville, the forest has more than 490,000 acres and spreads over 12 western North Carolina counties. The forest is more or less divided in half by the Blue Ridge Parkway, and the Appalachian Trail runs along its border with Tennessee. The Mountains-to-the-Sea Trail crosses through the forest. Pisgah National Forest contains three wilderness areas. Middle Prong, Linville Gorge and the Shining Rock section and is divided into four districts: Pisgah District, French Broad District, Grandfather District and Tocane District.

A short drive from downtown Asheville, the Pisgah District of the National Forest has a number of outstanding features and points of interest. This district is the most popular of all four, and receives over five million visitors a year. Over 156,000 acres in size, it encompasses parts of Buncombe, Haywood, Henderson, and Transylvania counties. There are over 275 miles of trails for hiking, horseback riding, and mountain biking. Two of the three wilderness areas, Shining Rock and Middle Prong, are in this district. There is a Ranger Station and Visitor Center located on US 276 a few miles into the forest from Hwy. 280 in Brevard. I recommend you visit the center before continuing on into the forest.

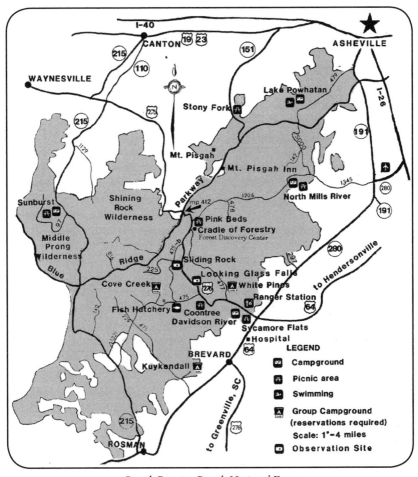

Pisgah District, Pisgah National Forest

Location: The Pisgah District of the Pisgah National Forest is located to the west of Asheville

Distance: 45 minutes-1 hour from Asheville

Address: Pisgah District Office, 1001 Pisgah Hwy., Pisgah Forest, NC 28768

Telephone: Pisgah District Office: 828-877-3350, 828-257-4203
Appalachian Ranger District, French Broad Station: 828-622-3202
Appalachian Ranger District, Toecane Ranger Station: 828-682-6146
Grandfather Ranger District: 828-652-2144

Website: www.cs.unca.edu/nfsnc

Hours: Pisgah District Ranger Station Visitor Center: Monday-Friday 8 a.m.-5 p.m.; holidays and Saturday 9 a.m.-5 p.m.; Sundays noon-5 p.m.

Fees: None to enter park

Camping: Davidson River, Lake Powhatan, North Mills River, Sunburst

The Pisgah View Ranch in Candler, showing Mount Pisgah in the distance

Directions: From Asheville: Take Airport Rd. (Hwy. 280) off of Hendersonville Hwy. in Arden. Continue on 280 past Asheville airport to Wal-Mart Shopping Plaza just before Brevard. Turn right onto US 276 into Pisgah Forest. The R anger Visitor Center will be located on the right a few miles in. From Hendersonville: Take US 64 West from downtown to the intersection of Hwy. 280 and Hwy. 276 at the Wal-Mart Shopping Plaza. Continue straight through light to US 276 and into the Forest. Look for the Ranger Visitor Center on your right.

Tips: Obtain maps and information at Visitor Center. You may order maps through the mail by calling 828-884-4734.

Major Points of Interest:

Andy Cove Nature Trail: A self-guided trail located behind Pisgah Ranger Station (0.7 miles), that goes through several forest habitats. The trail takes about 30 minutes to walk.

Forest Heritage National Scenic Byway: A 79-mile highway loop (US 276, US 64 NC 215 & FS 475) provides numerous opportunities to view the outstanding scenery of the forest, in an area rich in forest history.

The Forest Discovery Center at The Cradle of Forestry in America: This National Historic Site commemorates the birthplace of American forestry and forest education. The Forest Discovery Center features two interpretive exhibits and a gift shop, guided tours on two trails featuring eight historic buildings, restored stationary logging locomotive and living history interpretation by local crafters. www.cradleofforestry.com. Open 9 a.m.-5 p.m. April-October. 828-877-3130. (*See* Section Five, Chapter 2 "Cradle of Forestry")

Lake Powhatan: A family recreation area in Asheville's backyard, Lake Powhatan is located off NC 191 at the end of Bent Creek Rd. The park provides picnic tables with grills and water sources, fishing, swimming beach and hiking trails.

Looking Glass Falls: A beautiful 30-foot wide waterfall that drops more than 60 feet down to a rock cliff. A trail with steps leads to an overlook and to the bottom of the falls. Located along Hwy. 276. Parking is provided.

North Mills River Recreation Area: This popular area offers picnic tables with grills along the beautiful North Mills River. A popular activity here is tubing on the river, as well as trout fishing. 13 miles north of Hendersonville. (*See* Section Four, Chapter 7)

Pisgah Forest State Fish Hatchery and Pisgah Center for Wildlife Education: Different species and size of trout can be observed in the raceways and fish food is available to feed the fish. For group programs and information call 828-877-4423. www.ncwildlife.org. Located off Hwy. 276 on Davidson River Rd. (FS Rd. 475).

Sliding Rock Recreation Area: This very popular observation and water play area is a natural waterslide located on Hwy. 276. Visitors can slide down a 60-foot rock into a 7-foot deep pool; restrooms, changing areas, large parking lot, observation deck, site attendant on duty Memorial Day through mid-August. Small fee.

Santeetlah Lake

Santeetlah Lake, located in Graham County, has 76 miles of mostly natural forested shoreline, is over 3,000 acres in size and is surrounded by the Cheoah District of the Nantahala National Forest. Almost 80% of the shoreline is public land which is managed by the North Carolina Forest Service. Boating, kayaking and canoeing are popular activities and Cheoah Point on the east side of the Santeetlah Lake offers swimming at a lakeside beach, picnic areas, over 26 campsites and hiking trails. Cheoah Point is the only campground with facilities on Santeetlah Lake. Since most of the surrounding land is public access, there are many primitive campsites scattered along the shoreline. These free sites however have no facilities, no toilets or grills.

Nearby Forest Service Campgrounds are Horse Cove, located on Big Santeetlah Creek with 17 camp sites, toilets, and no showers (Modest fee per day/open winter with no fees/first come first served), and the group camp at Rattler Ford which has four sites (up to 50 people each site), showers, and toilets (Fee per site by reservation). For more information contact the Cheoah District Office at 828-479-6431.

The lake was created in 1928 by the damming of the Cheoah River to create hydroelectric power as it flows northward to join the Little Tennessee River. During the last decades of the twentieth century non-public lands were developed as scenic residences and vacation homes, most notably in the area now incorporated as the town of Lake Santeetlah. Cheoah Dam was also one site of the film "The Fugitive" starring Harrison Ford.

Location: Along US Highway 129 in Graham County, NC.
Distance: From Asheville 2-2½ hours

Website: www.grahamcountytravel.com/activities_santeetlah

Resources: Graham County NC Travel and Tourism Authority, 12 Main Street, Robbinsville NC,28711; 828-479-3790

Directions: From Asheville take I-40 West towards Knoxville. Take Exit 27 to merge into US Highway 74/19 West towards Waynesville/Murphy. Approximately 20 miles past Bryson City take right onto Highway 129 to Robbinsville. Santeetlah Lake is six miles north of Robbinsville on Highway 129.

Chapter Two
Cultural Attractions

Asheville

For information about the attractions listed below, *see* Section Three, Chapter 2, Asheville Cultural Attractions.

Asheville Art Museum
Asheville Community Theatre (ACT)
Asheville's Fun Depot
Asheville Urban Trail
Basilica of St. Lawrence
Biltmore Estate (*See* Section Three, Chapter 3 Biltmore Estate)
Biltmore Village
Black Mountain College Museum + Art Center
Blue Ridge Parkway Destination Center
Botanical Gardens at Asheville
Colburn Earth Science Museum
Diana Wortham Theatre
Estes-Winn Memorial Automobile Museum
Folk Art Center of the Southern Highland Craft Guild
Grove Arcade Public Market
Grove Park Inn Resort & Spa (*See* Section Three, Chapter 5 Grove Park Inn Resort & Spa)
McCormick Field & the Asheville Tourists
North Carolina Arboretum
North Carolina Homespun Museum
Pack Place Education, Arts & Science Center
Smith-McDowell House
Southern Appalachian Radio Museum
The Health Adventure
Thomas Wolfe Memorial
Western North Carolina Agricultural Center

Western North Carolina Farmers Market
Western North Carolina Nature Center
YMI Cultural Center

Cultural Attractions North of Asheville
Dry Ridge Historical Museum

The Dry Ridge Historical Museum, housed in the Weaverville Public Library, documents the life of the area's first settlers dating back to 1787, especially residents of the Reems Creek and Flat Creek Townships. The museum displays a collection of artifacts that include furniture, tools, clothing, letters, ledgers, books, photographs, and portraits.

Location:	Weaverville, NC
Distance:	30 minutes from downtown Asheville
Address:	Weaverville Public Library, Lower Level, 41 N. Main St. Weaverville, NC 28787
Telephone:	828-250-6482
Hours:	March-November: Saturdays only from 10 a.m.-4 p.m.
Fees:	None

Allow:	1 hour minimum
Directions:	From I-240, take the Weaverville Exit 4A onto 19/23 North. Go seven miles and take the New Stock Rd. Exit. Turn right off the ramp and left onto US 25/70 North. Make a left onto Main Street.

Penland Gallery & School of Crafts

The Penland Gallery, located at the Penland School of Crafts, features work by artists affiliated with the school. The Penland School of Crafts is a national center for craft education dedicated to helping people live creative lives. The school offers one-, two-, and eight-week workshops in books & paper, clay, drawing, glass, iron, metals, photography, printmaking and letterpress, textiles, and wood. Tours of the Penland School are available on Tuesday at 10:30 a.m. and Thursday at 1:30 p.m. Reservations are required.

Location:	Penland, NC
Distance:	1 hour from Asheville
Address:	67 Dora's Trail, Penland NC 28765
Telephone:	Gallery: 828-765-6211, School: 828-765-2359
Website:	www.penland.org
Admission:	Free
Hours:	Early March through mid-December Tues-Sat: 10 a.m.-5 p.m.; Sun: 12-5 p.m.;(Closed Mon)
Directions:	From Asheville take 19/23 North and get off at exit 9 towards Burnsville/Spruce Pine. Continue on US 19 for approximately 16 miles. Turn left at NC 1160 Rabbit Hop Road then take first right onto NC 1162 Penland Road. Turn left at Bailey's Peak Road.

Rural Life Museum

This small museum is housed in the Montague building on the campus of Mars Hill College and is dedicated to preserving mountain farm and craft culture. It focuses on Pre-Industrial Appalachia as well as the Industrial period that followed, with depictions of hearth and home, exhibits of farm and craft implements, and historic photographic murals. An exhibit honoring the Hooked-Rug Industry, which existed in Madison County and other parts of Western North Carolina, is one of the museum's most fascinating displays.

Location:	Mars Hill College, Mars Hill, NC
Distance:	30 minutes from Asheville
Address:	NC 213, Montague Building, Mars Hill College, Mars Hill, NC 28754
Telephone:	828-689-1424
Hours:	Monday-Friday 2-4 p.m. and by appointment
Fees:	None
Allow:	1 hour

Directions: From I-240, take Weaverville Exit 4A (19/23N) to the Mars Hill Exit. Follow Hwy. 213 to the first light. Just ahead will be the college campus. The museum is housed in the native stone Montague building just inside the gate on the right.

Rush Wray Museum of Yancey County History

Located within the historic McElroy House, this museum focuses on Yancey County's local history and Appalachian mountain heritage. One of their permanent exhibits is "Our people, our heritage, our pride," which features the settlement of Yancey County and Burnsville, NC. The Revolving Exhibit Room hosts changing exhibits including "The Pisgah Village," "Cane River Archeological Site," "The Civil War and the Home Guard," and "The McElroy House."

Location: Burnsville, NC
Distance: 45 minutes to 1 hour from Asheville
Address: 11 Academy Street, Burnsville, NC 28714
Telephone: 828-682-3671
Hours: April 10-October 10, Saturdays 1-7 p.m. Call for weekday hours.
Fees: None
Allow: 1 hour
Directions: From Asheville, take 19/23 North to Mars Hill/Burnsville Exit. Follow 19E to Burnsville. The museum is located behind the visitor center.

Zebulon B. Vance Birthplace

The birthplace of the dynamic "War Governor of the South," Zebulon B. Vance, is located in Weaverville, just a few miles north of Asheville. Administered by the N.C. Department of Cultural Resources, the Vance birthplace is one of North Carolina's Historic Sites and is open to the public year-round. The homestead, a large two-story structure of hewn yellow pine logs, has been reconstructed around the original chimney with its two enormous fireplaces. The furnishings and household items on display today are representative of the period from 1790 to 1840 and include a few pieces original to the home. Clustered about the grounds of the house are six log outbuildings, loom house, slave house, and tool house. Nearby the Visitor Center/Museum houses exhibits portraying the life of Governor Vance.

Each spring and again in the fall, visitors to the Vance home have the opportunity to experience Pioneer Living Days; the grounds come alive with history as costumed staff members and volunteers demonstrate the skills and cherished occupations of settlers in the early days.

Location: Weaverville, NC
Distance: 30 minutes from Asheville
Address: 911 Reems Creek Rd., Weaverville, NC 28787
Telephone: 828-645-6706
Website: www.nchistoricsites.org/vance/vance

Zebulon B. Vance Birthplace

Hours: Tuesday-Saturday 9 a.m.-5 p.m.
Fees: None; donations accepted.
Allow: 1-2 hours
Directions: From Asheville take the I-240 Weaverville Exit 4A off of I-240 (US 19/23N) to New Stock Rd. Turn right off the ramp, left onto US 25/70 North, and follow to Reems Creek Rd. where you will turn right.

Cultural Attractions South of Asheville
Hendersonville

For information about the attractions listed below, *See* Section Four, Chapter 2 Hendersonville Cultural Attractions

Carl Sandburg Home
Flat Rock Playhouse
Fifth Avenue Mask Museum
Flat Rock Playhouse
Henderson County Curb Market
Henderson County Heritage Center
Henderson County History Center
Hendersonville Antique Toy Museum
Hendersonville Railroad Dept
Historic Johnson Farm
Holmes Educational State Forest

Mountain Farm & Home Museum
Thomas Wolfe Angel
Western North Carolina Air Museum

Bennett Classics Antique Auto Museum

Located in Forest City, the Bennett Classics Antique Auto Museum has a collection of over 50 antique and completely restored automobiles. They also have a show room with resorted cars for sale, and well as displays of automotive memorabilia.

Location:	Forest City, NC
Distance:	1 hour from Asheville
Address:	241 Vance Street, Forest City NC 28043
Telephone:	828-247-1767
Website:	www.bennettclassics.com
Hours:	Monday–Saturday 10 a.m.-5 p.m.
Fees:	None
Allow:	1-2 hours
Directions:	From Asheville take I-26 south past Hendersonville to exit for US 74 towards Columbus/Rutherforton, Shelby. Highway. Take exit 181 off of MC 74 and travel north. Turn right on Church Street, and then left on Main Street. Go two stop lights and turn right onto Vance Street.

Foothills Equestrian Nature Center (FENCE)

The Foothills Equestrian Nature Center, also known as FENCE, provides the South Carolina Upstate and Western North Carolina with a nature preserve of 380 acres, open to the public year-round. FENCE has an award-winning equestrian facility that hosts local, regional and national events, offers birding activities and programs, and is a learning center for children. FENCE also hosts youth cross-country meets. The are over five miles of trails for walking, riding and carriage use, a wildlife pond, quiet meadows and sweeping panoramas. FENCE also hosts steeplechases, horse trails, dressage shows, pleasure driving and cross-country races. Stabling is available for over 180 horses, and there are lighted show rings, and cross-country and steeplechase courses.

Location:	Tryon, NC
Distance:	1 hour from Asheville
Address:	3381 Hunting Country Rd. Tryon, NC 28782
Telephone:	828-859-9021
Website:	www.fence.org
Hour:	Dawn to dusk daily; Office Hours: 9 a.m.-4 p.m.
Fees:	None for hiking and nature trails. Equestrian fees charged for Bed and Barn Program (Bring your own horse, rental stalls and apartment are available. Call the Equestrian Director)

Directions: Take I-26 East from Asheville or Hendersonville. Take S.C. Exit 1. Turn right towards Landrum. Go 1½ miles and take a right onto Bomar Rd. Go one short block and turn right onto Prince Rd. After 1.7 miles, turn left onto Hunting Country Rd., just before the I-26 overpass. Go slightly over ½ mile to FENCE's entrance on the right.

Green River Plantation

The Green River Plantation, located in Rutherfordton, is a 42-room antebellum mansion built circa 1804-1807 on 356 acres. It is open to the public for tours by reservation only. The Plantation also hosts: weddings, receptions, rehearsal dinners, parties, picnics & other special events. The Green River Plantation is listed in the National Register of Historic Places. If you are interested in seeing a classic example of a southern plantation home, then a visit to Green River will be worth the trip.

Location: Rutherfordton, NC
Distance: 1 hour, 30 minutes from Asheville
Address: 6333 Coxe Road, Rutherfordton NC 28138
Telephone: 828-286-1461.
Website: www.green-river.net/Green_River_Plantation/Home
Fees: Tours by reservation only: $15 adult, $12 senior, $6 children (12 and under)
Allow: Tours last approximately one hour.
Directions: From Asheville take 1-26 south past Hendersonville and take the exit for US74 towards Columbus and Rutherfordton. Take exit 173 off of 74 and turn right at Union Road. Turn left at Coxe Road.

KidSenses Children's InterACTIVE Museum

KidSenses Chidren's InterACTIVE Museum is located in Rutherfordton, and has exhibits and special workshops to stimulate the imagination and educate the minds of young children. Discovery Garden, Virtual Reality Ride and Lights! Camera! Action! are a few of the many themed interactive exhibits.

Location: Rutherfordton, NC
Address: 172 North Main Street, Rutherfordton NC 28139
Distance: 1 hour from Asheville
Telephone: 828-286-2120
Website: www.kidsenses.com
Hours: Tuesday–Thursday, Saturday 9 a.m.-5 p.m., Friday 9 a.m.-8 p.m.
Fees: $5
Directions: From Asheville Take I-40 east to NC 221 and get off at exit 85. Go right toward Rutherfordton.

Polk County Historical Museum

Located in a historic railroad depot, the Polk County Historical Museum contains a large collection that includes artifacts from the Cherokee Indians, early

e Revolutionary War, the Civil War, and World War II. Museum items include tools and clothing of the settlers, various railroad treasures, photos and paintings of historic sites in Polk County, and memorabilia from local residents. They also have a large collection of early maps, records, and pictures including important items in American history.

Location:	Tryon, NC
Distance:	45 minutes from Asheville
Address:	1 Depot St., Tryon, NC 28782
Telephone:	800-440-7848
Hours:	Tuesday-Thursday 10 a.m.-noon and by appointment
Fees:	None
Allow:	1 hour
Directions:	From Asheville, take I-26 East to Exit 36 for Columbia/Tryon. Go right, towards Tryon, and proceed through town on Trade Street to the 4th light. Turn right and then another right onto Depot Street.

Rutherford County Farm Museum

The Rutherford County Farm Museum has exhibits of antique farm equipment and items dating back to the earliest days of the nineteenth century. Two large murals, depicting the cycle of growing cotton and the early textile mills of the county, are outstanding features of the museum.

Location:	Forest City, NC
Distance:	45 minutes from Asheville
Address:	240 Depot Street, Forest City, NC 28043
Telephone:	828-248-1248
Hours:	Wed-Sat: 10-4
Fees:	$2 adults, children free
Allow:	1 hour
Directions:	From Asheville take I-26 South to Exit 35. Take Hwy. 74 East to Columbus/Rutherfordton. Take exit 182 to US221 to Forest City. In Forest City turn left at South Broadway, then turn left at Florence Street and continue to Depot Street.

Tryon Arts & Crafts Heritage Gallery

The Tryon Arts & Crafts Heritage Gallery, run by Tryon Arts & Crafts, has permanent exhibitions of over 200 artifacts native to Western North Carolina, and specifically the Tryon Area, some dating back as far as 1775. On display are animals, dolls and tiny pieces of furniture from the original Tryon Toy-Makers and Wood Carvers, including a small version of Morris, made by Eleanor Vance, an original founder of the Tryon Toy-Makers.

Cherokee artifacts include a large collection of pottery and several collections of arrowheads, tomahawks, dolls and baskets. The Pisgah Forest pottery collection includes a pitcher featuring a fine cameo or pate sure embellishment. Other exhibits include original forged work and kitchen tools, quilts, furniture, musical instruments and paintings by local artists.

The mission of Tryon Arts & Crafts is to preserve, enhance and promote native mountain arts & crafts by providing education, instruction and opportunity to express, develop and showcase creative talent. The organization has its home in the former Tryon Middle School, a building of over 10,000 square feet. Classes and instruction in arts and crafts are offered at the center on a regular basis, and there is a gift shop on the premises as well.

Location:	Tryon, NC
Distance:	45 minutes from Asheville
Address:	373 Harmon Field Road, Tryon NC 28782
Telephone:	828-859-8323
Website:	www.tryonartsandcrafts.org/gallery/index.php
Hours:	Open daily at 9 a.m.
Fees:	None
Allow:	1-2 hours
Directions:	From Asheville, take Interstate 26 South to Exit 67 (Columbus, North Carolina). Turn right onto Hwy 108 & West Will Street and continue straight to 373 Harmon Field Road.

Tryon Fine Arts Center

The Tryon Fine Arts Center has a 315-seat auditorium, a Mural Room for gatherings, an Exhibition Gallery, work rooms, an outdoor garden and is home to the Tryon Little Theater, with more than 900 members It also houses Tryon Crafts, whose classes include weaving, silver making, enameling on copper, rug hooking, crewel and needlepoint, macramé, wood carving, knitting, stained glass and lampshades. The center is home to the Carolina Camera Club, and the Tryon Painters & Sculptors, whose members, both professional and amateur, regularly exhibit in the gallery and other public areas. The center has a retail shop which is open to the public.

Location:	Tryon, NC
Distance:	45 minutes from Asheville
Address:	34 Melrose Avenue, Tryon NC 28782
Telephone:	828-859-8322
Website:	www.tryonarts.org
Hours:	Weekdays 10 a.m.-4 p.m.
Fees:	None
Allow:	1-2 hours
Directions:	From Asheville, take Interstate 26 South to Exit 67 (Columbus, North Carolina). Turn right onto Hwy 108. Head towards Tryon approximately 6.5 miles. Hwy 108 joins Hwy 176 at traffic light (Texaco at corner). Count this as first traffic light and continue on Hwy 176 east until you reach fourth traffic light. (Big wooden horse

across and right of intersection.) At fourth traffic light turn right onto Pacolet Street, up over railroad tracks, then make second left onto Chestnut Street (before the Bank of America Building). Drive to top of hill and turn right onto Melrose Avenue.

Cultural Attractions East of Asheville
Alleghany County Courthouse
Built in 1933-34 following the destruction by fire of the first courthouse, this two-story brick County Courthouse with white columns is an example of Classical Revival architecture of the period. The architect was Harry Barton. Alleghany County is nestled in the Blue Ridge Mountains of Northwestern North Carolina. Alleghany County was formed out of Ashe County by an act of the 1858-1859 session of the North Carolina legislature. The Courthouse is listed on the National Register of Historic Places and continues to the present day as a functioning courthouse.

Location: Sparta, NC
Distance: 3 hours from Asheville
Address: 100 North Main Street, Sparta, NC 28675
Telephone: 336-372-4179
Admission: Free
Directions: From Asheville, take I-40 East to Marion and take Hwy. 221 North to through Boone to Sparta.

Appalachian Heritage Museum
The Appalachian Heritage Museum is a living history museum in the same complex as Mystery Hill in Blowing Rock NC. It is housed in the historic Dougherty House, which was the home of the Dougherty Brothers, D.D. and B.B., founders of Appalachian State University. The purpose of the museum is to show visitors how middle class mountain families lived at the turn of the century.

Location: Mystery Hill complex between Boone and Blowing Rock, NC
Distance: 2 hours, longer if using the Blue Ridge Parkway
Address: 129 Mystery Hill Lane, Blowing Rock, NC 28605
Telephone: 828-264-2792
Hours: June-August 8 a.m.-8 p.m.; September-May 9 a.m.-5 p.m.
Fees: Rates vary. Call for current rate schedule. Senior, military, group, and AAA discounts are available.
Allow: 1 hour
Directions: From Asheville, take I-40 East to Marion. Take Hwy. 221 North to Blowing Rock. Then, take 321 North four miles to the Mystery Hill complex. Alternately, take the Blue Ridge Parkway north to exit at mile marker 291 and take Hwy. 321 North for 1½ miles.

Ashe County Arts Council Gallery

Located in the Ashe Arts Center, The Ashe County Arts Council Gallery consists of changing exhibits of local artists and performances of music, poetry, literature and more. The spectrum of work shown ranges from traditional to contemporary, from quilts to pottery to abstract fine art.

Location:	West Jefferson, NC
Address:	303 School Avenue, West Jefferson 28694
Telephone:	336-847-2787
Website:	www.ashecountyarts.org/gallery
Hours:	Monday-Saturday 9 a.m.-4 p.m.
Fees:	None
Allow:	1-2 hours
Directions:	From Asheville take I-40 west to exit 72 and merge onto US70 toward Old Fort. After 11 miles turn left at US 221 and follow US 221 through Boone to West Jefferson.

Avery County Historical Museum

The Avery County Historical Museum is housed in the historic (circa 1912) Avery County Jail and has displays of early Avery County life. The jail house is one of the last intact old jails in North Carolina. The museum was formed in 1976 to collect, preserve and display vital information, photographs and artifacts about people, events and places that make up the history of Avery County and this area.

Location:	Newland, NC
Distance:	2 hours from Asheville
Address:	1829 Schultz Circle, Newland, NC 28657
Telephone:	828-733-7311
Website:	http://www.averymuseum.com/avery_county_museum%20guide.htm
Admission:	Free
Hours:	10 am-4 pm Friday, 11 am-3 pm Saturday
Directions:	From Asheville, take I-40 East to Morganton and take Hwy. 181 North to Pineola, just past the Blue Ridge Parkway. Turn left on Hwy. 221 and then right onto 194 North to Newland.

Banner House Museum

The Banner House Museum presents a glimpse of 19th century life in Banner Elk and the High Country in the home of Samuel Henry Banner, one of Banner Elk's original settlers. The restored household dates back to the 1870-80s and is an authentic window into that period of history.

Location:	Banner Elk, NC
Distance:	2 hours from Asheville
Address:	7990 Hickory Nut Gap Road, Banner Elk NC 28604

Telephone: 828-898-3634
Website: www.bannerhousemuseum.org
Hours: June 20th-October 17th, Tuesday-Saturday: 11 a.m.-4 p.m. Private
tours available
Fees: $5 adults, $1 children (6-12)
Directions: From Asheville take i-40 West. Get off at exit 72 and merge onto
US70 towards Old Fort. Turn left at NC 226/US221 and take 221
north. In Linville take 105 north and turn left at NC184.Tynecastle
Highway to Banner Elk. Turn right on Hickory Nut Gap Road.
After you cross the bridge, you will see the museum on your left.

Ben Long Frescoes

Western North Carolina is home to four churches that are graced by Ben
Long's frescoes. Fresco painting is an ancient art form based on the immediate
application of pigment to wet plaster, and Western North Carolina artist Ben
Long is considered one of the few American masters of the art. The marvelous
luminous beauty of his frescoes in these churches attract over 80,000 visitors annually from around the world. The closest of Long's frescoes to Asheville is located
in the Black Mountain area, in Montreat College's Chapel of the Prodigal Son.
Farther east, the Holy Trinity Church in Glendale Springs features his fresco of
the Lord's Supper and other assorted artworks. St. Mary's Church in nearby West
Jefferson is home to frescoes of the Mystery of Faith, Mary Great with Child, and
John the Baptist. The fourth church, St. Paul's Episcopal Church in Wilkesboro
is home to Long's fresco depicting the story of St. Paul.

Locations: Montreat, Glendale Springs, West Jefferson and Wilkesboro NC
Distance: Glendale Springs, West Jefferson and Wilkesboro (2- 3 hours from
Asheville); Montreat (30 minutes from Asheville)
Address: Montreat – Lookout Road, Montreat NC 28757
Address: Glendale Springs – Holy Trinity Church, 195 J.W. Luke Rd., Glen-
dale Springs, NC 28629
Telephone: 336-982-3076
Address: West Jefferson – St. Mary's Church, 400 Beaver Creek School Rd.,
West Jefferson, NC 28694
Telephone: 336-246-3552
Address: Wilkesboro – St. Paul's Episcopal Church, 200 West Cowles Street,
Wilkesboro NC 28697
Hours: Please call and ask about hours for viewing.
Fees: None
Allow: ½ to 1 hour each church
Directions to Montreat: From Asheville take I-240 East to I-40. Take I-40 to Exit 64
(Black Mountain/Montreat).Turn left onto NC-9/Broadway. Stay
in the left-hand lane. Drive over the railroad tracks and through the
traffic light. At the second traffic light, continue through. At the
third traffic light, continue through; the street changes to Montreat

Road. At the stone Montreat Gate, the road changes to Assembly Drive. Turn right on Lookout Road to Chapel on the right.

Directions to Wilkesboro, Glendale Springs, and West Jefferson: From Asheville, take I-40 East to Hickory. Take Exit 131 to NC 16 North to Wilkesboro to St. Paul's Church. To see the other two churches, take 421 North towards Watauga. Turn left onto NC 16 North again to Glendale Springs and Holy Trinity Church. From Glendale Springs take NC 16 North to NC 221. Turn left onto NC 221 to West Jefferson and St. Mary's Church.

Bunker Hill Covered Bridge

Designated as a National Civil Engineering Landmark in 2001, the Bunker Hill Covered Bridge is the only remaining example in wood of the Improved Lattice Truss patented by General Herman Haupt. It joins the Cape Hatteras Lighthouse, the Blue Ridge Parkway, and Dorton Arena in representing North Carolina on this prestigious list.

One of only two original remaining covered bridges in North Carolina, the other being Mt. Pisgah in Randolph County. The bridge was built in 1895 by Andy L. Ramsour. In 1894 Catawba County Commissioners had called on nearby owners of Bunker Hill Farm to build and maintain a bridge that would cross Lyle's Creek on the old Island Ford Road, a former Native American trail. The landowners hired Ramsour, keeper of the Horseford covered bridge that spanned the Catawba River north of Hickory. He likely found Haupt's design in a popular book on bridge building. Originally constructed as an open span, the Bunker Hill Covered Bridge, whose roof is ninety-one feet long, was covered in 1900. In 1921 its wooden shingles were replaced with a tin roof.

Location:	Claremont, NC
Distance:	1 hour and 30 minutes from Asheville
Address:	Highway 70, Claremont NC 28610
Telephone:	828-322-4731
Website:	www.catawbahistory.org/bunker_hill_covered_bridge.php
Hours:	Open 24/7 365 days a year
Fees:	None
Allow:	½ hour
Directions:	From Asheville take I-40 East towards Statesville. Take Exit 135 toward Claremont. Turn right at North Oxford Street and then then left at West Main Street/US Highway 70. Follow Highway 70 two miles east of town.

Burke Arts Council Jailhouse Gallery

The Jailhouse Gallery is a public gallery dedicated to promoting the art and crafts of Burke County artists and craftsmen as well as out of state artists, and is run by the Burke Arts Council. The Council was founded in 1975 and is a non-profit, tax-exempt corporation funded by individual membership and corporate donors. It hosts three galleries which provide space for both local and out of state artists.

Location:	Morganton, NC
Address:	115 Meeting Street, Morganton NC 28655
Telephone:	828-433-7282
Website:	www.burkearts.org
Hours:	9 a.m.-5 p.m. Tuesday- Friday
Fees:	None
Allow:	1-2 hours
Directions:	Take I-40 East from Asheville, take the US-64 exit- Exit 103- toward Morganton & Rutherfordton, turn left onto US-64, turn right onto West Union Street/US-64 /US-70, Continue to follow US-64 E/ S-70, end at 115 E Meeting St.

Caldwell Heritage Museum

The Caldwell Heritage Museum was opened in 1991 and is dedicated to preserving and presenting the history of Caldwell County, North Carolina, through about two dozen permanent exhibits and rotating special exhibits. The museum is housed in the last remaining building of Davenport College, a prestigious institution of higher learning for women that was supported by the Methodist Church from 1855 to 1933.

Over 35,000 square feet of vertical, horizontal, and floor space have been utilized in the Caldwell Heritage Museum to show Caldwell Country's history and culture from pre-colonial, pioneer, Revolutionary, and Civil War eras to the present day. Specialized collections and exhibits also include antique furniture and farm implements; Native American artifacts; World War I and II memorabilia; the Caldwell County Music Preservation collection; an antique phonograph, radio, and TV exhibit; and Plains and Western Indian exhibits.

Location:	Lenoir, NC
Distance:	1 hour from Asheville
Address:	112 Vaiden St. SE (PO Box 2165), Lenoir, NC 28645
Telephone:	828-758-4004
Website:	www.caldwellheritagemuseum.org
Hours:	Tuesday through Friday from 10:00am until 4:30pm, and on Saturdays from 10:00am until 3:00pm.
Fees:	None, donations accepted
Allow:	1-2 hours
Directions:	From Asheville, take I-40 East to Rte. 321 in Hickory. Follow 321 North to Lenoir. In Lenoir, you will come to a major intersection (Burger King and Eckerd's Drugstore). Take a left and after 100 yards, bear again to your left. The road turns into Harper Avenue. Stay on Harper and bear to the right in front of the Fire Department and Post Office. Turn right after the Police Department and

then left onto Willow. Left again at the stop sign will take you onto Harper. Make a right at the first light and then left at the stop light at the top of the hill. The first street on your right will be Vaiden Street. The museum is on Vaiden at the top of the hill.

Catawba County Museum of History

The Catawba County Museum of History offers testimony to the hardy settlers of the Catawba River Valley and their resourceful descendants who carved a world-renowned furniture and textile empire out of the backwoods. The story is artfully displayed in the unique setting of the former Catawba County Courthouse, an imposing National Register Renaissance Revival structure built in 1924, on the square in downtown Newton.

Museum collections include agricultural tools and implements forged from hand-dug iron ore, as well as handcrafted household cupboards, wagon benches, beds, tables, chests, cradles, plantation desks, a firkin, and miniature furniture samples shown by "drummers" or early salesmen. There are treasured military uniforms, including a British Red Coat from the Revolutionary War era (one of the few such coats in existence) and a major repository of Civil War objects.

Two full-scale, original antebellum parlors have been reconstructed and preserved in the museum: the Shuford-Jarett from 1830, featuring deft molding-plane embellishments and pegged muntins, and the Munday Parlor from 1840, with trompe l'oeil dentils, marbleized wooden baseboards, and a dazzling hand-painted central medallion. Visitors can also walk through Dr. Hambrick's 1920's medical office, containing his ice-cold stainless steel examination table and an extensive variety of instruments from the period. Also on permanent exhibit at the museum is a 1930's racecar which roared around the county fairgrounds, complemented with a photograph gallery of the first race at the Hickory Motor Speedway, in 1951.

Location:	Newton, NC
Distance:	1 hour and 15 minutes from Asheville
Address:	30 North College Street, Newton NC 28658
Telephone:	828-465-0383
Website:	http://www.catawbahistory.org/catawba_county_museum_of_his tory.php
Hours:	Wednesday-Saturday 9 a.m.-4 p.m., Sunday 1:30-4:30 p.m.
Fees:	None
Allow:	1-2 hours
Directions:	From Asheville take I-40 East towards Statesville. Take Exit 130 toward Old US 70. Turn left at West 1st Street, take the 2nd right onto 1st Avenue South. Continue onto North Main Avenue, and turn left at East 1st Street. Take the 1st right onto North College Avenue in Newton.

Catawba Science Center

The Catawba Science Center has permanent exhibit areas that explore the physical, natural and earth sciences, and interactive traveling exhibits that rotate throughout the years. CSC also has some outstanding freshwater and saltwater aquarium exhibits, featuring North Carolina's only marine touch pool with live sharks and stingrays.

One of the main highlights of the Science Center is the Millholland Planetarium, a state of the art theater, featuring 30-ft full dome illuminated by digital technology-MEDIAGLOBE 3-D, created by Konica Minolta of Japan-and a powerful surround sound system. In addition to traditional planetarium shows, the Millholland Planetarium also has an AVI Skylase full-dome laser system, enabling visitors to experience dynamic laser light shows accompanied by modern pop, alternative, holiday and classic rock presentations.

CSC also offers many and varied educational programs to the general public on an on-going basis, and also maintains two science-oriented gift shops as well as a climbing wall in the courtyard. One of the more popular features of the center is the Naturalist Center where exhibits of live reptiles, amphibians, insects and arachnids are presented.

Location: Hickory, NC
Distance: 1 hour and 15 minutes from Asheville
Address: 243 3rd Avenue, Hickory NC 28603
Telephone: 828-322-8169
Website: www.catawbascience.org
Hours: Tuesday-Friday 10 a.m.-5 p.m., Saturday 10 a.m.-4 p.m., Sunday 1-4 p.m.
Fees: Adults $6, Seniors $4, Youth (2-18) $4, Children under 3-Free; Planetarium-$3
Allow: 1-2 hours
Directions: From Asheville take I-40 East towards Statesville. Take Exit 123A-123B for US 321 toward Hickory. Continue on US 321 North. Turn right at 2nd Avenue NW, turn left at 3rd Street NE and take the 1st left onto 3rd Avenue.

Catherine Smith Gallery

The Catherine Smith Gallery is a program of Appalachian State University and is located within Farthing Auditorium at the University. The gallery is a non-profit institution, in the service of society and its development and open to the public. The gallery is committed to researching, exhibiting and interpreting, for the purpose of study, education, and enjoyment of objects, activities and documents which are part of the focus of visual arts. The mission of the gallery is to become a center for the presentation of the visual arts in Northwestern North Carolina by establishing a regionally significant exhibition and research program in support of the educational mission of Appalachian State University.

Location:	Boone, NC
Address:	Farthling Auditorium, 733 Rivers Street, ASU, Boone NC 28607
Telephone:	828-262-7338
Website:	www.art.appstate.edu/cjs
Hours:	Monday through Friday from 10 a.m. to 5 p.m.
Fees:	None
Allow:	1-2 hours
Directions:	From Asheville take I-40 east. At exit 72 merge onto US-70 E toward Old Fort. Turn left onto US-221 N. Continue on US-221 N to Linville. Turn left onto NC-105 N. Follow NC-105 N to Boone. To go Directly to Farthing Auditorium: Turn left onto US-321 N. Turn left onto Rivers Street. Holmes Convocation Center and Appalachian welcome sign will be on the left. Farthing Auditorium is on the left at the 3rd stoplight. Parking for evening events is on the right at the 3rd stoplight in the Raley Parking Lot.

Chapel of Rest

The Chapel of Rest Preservation Society was created in 1984 to preserve the historical integrity of the Chapel of Rest and to maintain the building and grounds. The Chapel, built in1887, is in the heart of Happy Valley and situated on a knoll, is reminiscent of a more simple life when locals lined the pews in their Sunday best clothing. Travelers who stop in for a rest along the Scenic Byway will find the chapel as peaceful today as those did who visited many years ago.

Location:	Lenoir, NC (nine miles north of Lenoir, adjacent to the Patterson School)
Distance:	1 hour and 30 minutes east of Asheville
Address:	NC Highway 268, Lenoir NC 28645
Telephone:	828-758-8619, 828-758-0906
Website:	www.chapelofrest.org
Admission:	Free
Hours:	Open daily during daylight hours
Directions:	From Asheville, take I-40 East to Exit 100 towards Jamestown Road. Turn left at Jamestown Road and after 2 miles right at Carbon City Road. Go 1 mile and turn left at US-64 Bypass West. After 2.7 miles turn left at NC Highway 18 and continue for 14.5 miles. Turn right at Harper Avenue NW and then a quick left at US 321 North. Turn right at NC Highway 268 to the Chapel.

Crossnore Fine Arts Gallery

The Crossnore Fine Arts Gallery is located at the Crossnore School in Crossnore, which has been providing residential child care for disadvantaged children since 1913. A significant portion of the proceeds from the sale of artwork in the gallery goes towards helping children through Crossnore's social outreach programs. Artwork displayed ranges from traditional to contemporary in all mediums.

Location: Crossnore, NC
Distance: 1 hour from Asheville
Address: 205 Johnson Lane, Crossnore NC 28816
Telephone: 828-733-3144
Website: http://crossnoregallery.org
Hours: 9 a.m.-5 p.m. April-Dec (Mon- Sat); Dec- Mar (Thur- Sat)
Fees: None
Allow: 1 hour
Directions: From I-40, Exit 105 Morganton on Highway 181, travel north
             about 30 miles to Pineola to the intersection of Highway 181 and
             US Highway 221. At Pineola, turn left on 221 S. for 1.5 miles, turn
             right onto Crossnore Drive .6 miles, turn right onto Johnson Lane
             at The Blair Fraley Sales Store. Gallery is third building on the left.

Davidson's Fort

Davidson's Fort is located on eighteen acres inside the Old Fort city limits,
and is a replica of the original historic fort that existed in the area during colonial
days. It is a living history site dedicated to telling the true story of the families of
Western North Carolina during the 18th Century and the American Revolution.
Facilities include a welcome center/museum area as well as the replicated fort.
The fort interprets living conditions and daily life during the late 18th and 19th
centuries, and also includes a replica Cherokee village where other reenactments
and interpretations are performed.

Location: Old Fort, NC
Distance: 30 minutes east of Asheville
Address: Lackey Town Road, Old Fort NC 28762
Telephone: 828-668-4831
Website: http://davidsonsfort.com
Admission: Free, donations accepted
Hours: April 1st until end of November. Saturdays from 8:00 a.m. to 5 p.m.,
             or by appointment
Allow: 1-3 hours
Directions: From Asheville take I-40 west to exit 72 and follow Hwy 70. At the
             stop light turn right, cross the RR and make a left at water street and
             the Mountain Gateway Museum. Take the next left, then the next
             right and follow the road to the fort on your left. From the East on
             I-40—Take exit 73, turn right at the bottom of the ramp turn right
             on Water St make your next left, then right and follow the road to
             the fort on your left.

Emerald Village

Emerald Village features the North Carolina Mining Museum, a historic tour,
gem-cutting shops with resident goldsmith, gem mining with stone identification,
and gem cutters at work. In this famous historic mining area, over 45 different

rocks, minerals and gems have been found including aquamarine, beryl, emerald, garnet and smoky quartz. The North Carolina Mining Museum is located underground in a real mine. Authentic mining equipment and displays bring to life the early days of North Carolina mining.

Location:	Little Switzerland, NC
Distance:	1-2 hours from Asheville
Address:	331 McKinney Mine Rd., Little Switzerland, NC 28749.
Telephone:	828-765-6463, 828-765-0000
Website:	www.emeraldvillage.com
Hours:	9 a.m.-5 p.m., seven days a week, May through October. Museum is open April-November
Fees:	Museum and Displays free. Underground Mine Tour: $6 adults, $5 students (1-12), $5.50 seniors.
Allow:	2 hours
Directions:	From Asheville, take I-40 East to Marion. Take NC 221 North to NC 226. Left on NC 226 and go 9 miles to the Blue Ridge Parkway. Go south on parkway and get off at next exit, Little Switzerland, Milepost 334. Take right under parkway onto Chestnut Grove Rd. Turn left onto McKinney Mine Rd.

Fort Defiance

The home of Revolutionary War hero, General William Lenoir, is open to the public. Original clothing and furnishings of this1792 house are on display. General Lenoir was a member of the Council of State, served in both houses of the Legislature and was President of the NC Senate. The history of this house is the history of the opening of the Western North Carolina frontier. Furnishings include more than 300 original pieces, from teacups to bedsteads.

Location:	Lenoir, NC
Distance:	1½-2 hours from Asheville
Address:	Highway 268, Lenoir, NC 28645
Telephone:	828-758-1671
Website:	www.fortdefiancenc.org
Hours:	April-October, Thursday-Saturday 10 a.m.-5 p.m., Sunday 1-5 p.m.; November-March: Weekends.
Allow:	1 hour
Directions:	Take I-40 East from Asheville to Rte. 321 in Hickory. North on Rte. 321 to Patterson. Take 268 East 5½ miles.

From This Day Forward

Held in the Old Colony amphitheater, From This Day Forward is a seasonal outdoor drama produced by the Old Colony Players that portrays the compelling story of the Waldensian struggle for religious freedom in the 17th century and their eventual migration to Valdese in 1893.

Location: Valdese, NC
Distance: 1 hour from Asheville
Address: 410 Church Street, Valdese, NC 28690
Telephone: 828-874-0176
Website: www.oldcolonyplayers.com/ftdf.html
Hours: 16 evening performances held on Friday, Saturday, & Sunday at 8:15 p.m. in July and August.
Fees: $12 adults,$10 seniors and students
Allow: 2½ hours
Directions: From Asheville, take I-40 East to Exit 111. Take Carolina Street and turn left onto Main Street. Turn right on Church Street. You will see signs at every intersection.

Granite Falls History & Transportation Museum

The Granite Falls History & Transportation Museum, located in the restored former home of Andrew Baird, showcases local history for Granite Falls, with a special emphasis on history as it relates to transportation in the Granite Falls area. The museum opened to the public in 2006. Exhibits include photographs, furniture and memorabilia dating back over 100 years.

Location: Granite Falls, NC
Distance: 1 hour from Asheville
Address: 107 Falls Avenue, Granite Falls NC 28630
Telephone: 828-396-3131
Website: www.granitefallsnc.com/transportationmuseum.html
Hours: Saturday 10 a.m.-4 p.m., Sunday 2-4 p.m.
Fees: None
Directions: From Asheville take I-40 west to exit 123B for US 321 toward Hickory & Lenoir. Take the Falls Avenue exit.

Happy Valley

From Patterson east to the Wilkesboro Reservoir, this rural route follows NC 268 along the upper Yadkin River from the mountains to the gently rolling foothills of the Piedmont. Historically a farming region, today travelers can see acres of horticultural nurseries and turf farms alongside more traditional crops. This road twists and turns through a river valley dotted with historic homes and old barns. Around Happy Valley, visitors can stop at the Chapel of Rest, a restored Episcopal Church that served The Patterson School in the early 1900s; and Fort Defiance, the 18th century home of Revolutionary War hero William Lenoir. Driving towards Wilkesboro, history buffs will find Whippoorwill Academy and Village where a replica log-cabin village has been reconstructed, or they can find Kerr Scott Dam and Reservoir, a 3,754-acre recreational area for camping, fishing, swimming, boating, hiking, or camping. Frontiersman Daniel Boone also lived here in the mid-18th century with his wife and six children before settling in Kentucky.

As you drive along this scenic 28-mile stretch of road, listen as valley residents describe the area's musical traditions, stories, legends, and traditional farming practices. They're captured in the world-famous ballad, Hang Down Your Head, Tom Dooley, and brought to life by Charles Frazier's award-winning book, Cold Mountain.

Location:	Just north of Lenoir-NC Highway 268 between Patterson NC and the Wilkesboro Reservoir
Distance:	1 hour and 45 minutes from Asheville to start of Happy Valley in Patterson
Website:	www.happyvalleync.org
Directions:	From Asheville take I-40 East to Exit 100 towards Jamestown Road. Turn left at Jamestown Road for 2 miles and then right at Carbon City Road. Go 1 mile and turn left at US-64 Bypass W. Go 2.7 miles and turn left at NC 18N/US 64. Continue 14.5 miles and turn right at Harper Avenue and then quick left at US 321. Continue for 5.8 miles and turn right at NC 268. Follow 268 North to Happy Valley.

Harper House/Hickory History Center

Considered by the North Carolina Department of Archives and History to possess "the finest Queen Anne interior styling in the entire state," the Harper House and the accompanying Craftsman style Bonniwell-Lyerly House, another of Hickory's finest structures, serve a broad spectrum of visitors and local residents as the Harper House & Hickory History Center. Through a momentous preservation project, with the Catawba County Historical Association having raised $2,000,000 for restorations, the Harper House today welcomes visitors as a house museum, interpreting both Hickory history, through the numerous significant families who lived in the house, and Victorian life in the South, circa 1887, the date of the house's construction.

On the same lot, the Lyerly House, rescued and moved for preservation on June 24, 2004, is devoted to the further interpretation of Hickory's rich past, serving as the Betty Allen Education Center and Margaret Huggins Gallery, as well as a conference facility. Current exhibits include quilts from the CCHA's extensive collection, historical photographs of Hickory, and "Panoramic Catawba," the CCHA's collection of Benjamin Porter panoramic photographs of significant Catawba County sites, events, and groups. The Harper House/Hickory History Center is maintained by the Catawba County Historical Association.

Location:	Hickory, NC
Distance:	1 hour and 15 minutes from Asheville
Address:	310 North Center Street, Hickory NC 28601
Telephone:	828-324-7294
Website:	www.catawbahistory.org/harper_house_hickory_history_center.php
Hours:	Thursday-Saturday 9 a.m.-4 p.m., Sunday 1:30-4:30 p.m. Open Tuesday & Wednesday by appointment for groups of ten or more.

Fees: Tours of the Harper House itself are $5, exhibits in the Bonniwell-
             Lyerly House are free.
Allow: 1-2 hours
Directions: From Asheville take I-40 East towards Statesville. Take Exit 123A-
             123B for US 321 toward Hickory. Continue on US 321 North.
             Turn right at 2nd Avenue NW and turn left at North Center Street.

Hickory Furniture Mart

The Hickory Furniture Mart is a unique mix of nearly 100 furniture outlet
stores, shops and galleries. Within this four-story complex, you'll find home furnishings, accessories, lighting, art, fine rugs, fabrics and more, all with discounts
up to 80% off retail. Over 500,000 visitors travel to the Mart every year to visit
these renowned discounted furniture destination. The mart also offers valuable
amenities and an exceptional array of furniture-related services including guest,
shipping, decorating, design, and upholstery services, a gourmet cafe, coffee bar
and group tours. This extraordinary shopping complex has over a million square
feet of furniture.

Location: Hickory, NC
Distance: 1 hour and 15 minutes from Asheville
Address: 2220 Hwy 70 SE, Hickory, NC 28602
Telephone: 828-322-3510,888-640-0025
Website: www.hickoryfurniture.com
Hours: Monday-Saturday 9 a.m.-6 p.m.
Directions: Take I-40 East to Hickory, leaving the highway at Exit 126. Turn
             right at the off-ramp, then right onto Hwy 70 West. Hickory Fur-
             niture Mart is on the left.

Hickory Motor Speedway

The Hickory Motor Speedway has been in operation for over 50 years and is
the oldest professional sporting venue in Catawba County. Hickory Motor Speedway also stands as the oldest continually operated motor speedway in the country
and is known as the "Birthplace of the NASCAR Stars" and "The World's Most
Famous Short-Track" (the oval is .363 miles in length).The Speedway has three
fully equipped concession stands, a souvenir stand, six large restrooms areas, and
three enclosed air-conditioned hospitality suites. There is also a game room and
kid's fenced-in area with a climbing gym and swings. RV parking is also available.

Location: Newton, NC
Distance: 1 hour and 30 minutes from Asheville
Address: 3130 Highway 70 SE, Newton NC 28658
Telephone: 828-464-3655
Website: www.hickorymotorspeedway.com
Hours: Call for hours

Wildflowers on the Roadsides

As you drive along some of the major roads and interstates in North Carolina in the spring, summer and fall, you can't help but notice the spectacular plantings of wildflowers. In 1985, the North Carolina Department of Transportation (NCDOT) began planting wildflower beds as an integral part of the highway beautification. The program has been a great success and visitors and residents alike are treated to wonderful colorful displays as they travel throughout the state. If you are planning a trip to North Carolina, I suggest you write to the North Carolina Department of Transportation offices for a copy of their wildflower identification booklet. This guide will allow you to identify and learn about each type of wildflower planting you encounter on your travels. The cost is $6. Checks should be made payable to the NC Wildflower Program. Their address is Roadside Environmental Unit, PO Box 25201, Raleigh, NC 27611.

Fees:	Adults $10, Teens/Seniors $7.00, Ages 7-12 $4.00, 6 & Under Free
Directions:	From Asheville take I-40 East towards Statesville. Take Exit 126 for US 70 toward Newton. Turn right at McDonald Parkway and turn left at Conover Boulevard to Speedway.

Hickory Museum of Art

The Hickory Museum of Art is located in a 3-story brick building on the SALT block in the right wing of the Arts and Science Center of Catawba Valley. The museum has permanent and rotating exhibits and feature their Permanent Collection of American Art and works borrowed from private collectors and other institutions. The museum operates the HMA Galleria, a shop that sells unique gifts and collectibles. The shop is open during regular museum hours. The Museum also offers many learning opportunities and regularly holds classes for youth, high school students and adults.

Location:	Hickory, NC
Distance:	1 hour and 15 minutes from Asheville
Address:	243 Third Avenue NE, Hickory NC 28601
Telephone:	828-327-8576
Website:	http://www.hickorymuseumofart.org/home.php
Hours:	Tuesday-Thursday 10 a.m.-4 p.m., Sunday 1-4 p.m.
Fees:	None
Allow:	1-2 hours
Directions:	From Asheville take I-40 East towards Statesville. Take Exit 123A-123B for Hickory. Take US 321 North and turn right at 2nd Avenue NW, turn left at 3rd Street NE, and take the 1st left onto Third Avenue NE.

Hickory Ridge Homestead

Hickory Ridge Homestead is an eighteenth-century living history museum that highlights the daily lives of the early settlers of the Appalachian Mountains. Early furniture, period clothing, utensils, farm implements, and many other early artifacts, as well as displays and exhibits, contribute to the experience of Hickory Ridge. This is a great place to take the kids.

Location:	Located at Horn in the West, Boone, NC
Distance:	2 hours from Asheville
Address:	591 Horn in the West Rd., Boone, NC 28607
Telephone:	828-264-2120
Website:	www.horninthewest.com/museum
Hours:	May-June Saturday 9 a.m.-8 p.m., Sunday noon-8 p.m.; July-Oct 9 a.m.-8 p.m. daily; Nov-April by appointment
Fees:	Donations accepted
Allow:	1 hour minimum
Directions:	From Asheville, take I-40 East to Marion. In Marion, take NC 221 North to Boone. Located just past the intersection of NC 321.

Hiddenite Center

Housed in the historic Lucas Mansion, the Hiddenite Center is a step back in time. This folk and cultural arts center features an exhibition of native gems and minerals, one of which is the 294-pound Carolina crystal, as well as a superb doll collection dating from the 1800s. The changing exhibitions of the gallery and the period house furnishings all contribute to the unique experience of the Hiddenite Center and allow the visitors to this lovely turn-of-the-century Victorian mansion not only to learn about the past, but to experience it. Educational activities and arts programming are held on a regular basis.

Location:	Hiddenite, NC
Distance:	1 hour from Asheville
Address:	316 Church Street, Hiddenite, NC 28636
Telephone:	828-632-6966
Website:	www.hiddenitecenter.com
Hours:	Monday-Friday 9 a.m.-4:30 p.m.
Fees:	Gallery areas free, fees for House Museum tours.
Allow:	1-2 hours
Directions:	From Asheville, take I-40 East to Exit 149 in Statesville. Go north on NC 90 to Hiddenite. The center is located three blocks north of NC 90.

Historic Carson House

Built in 1793 by Colonel John Carson, the Carson House today is a privately owned history museum that is open to the public. This plantation home is filled with furnishings typical of the upper-class of that period. Exhibits and artifacts

describe not only the influential Carson famil,y but the culture and history of the region and state.

Location: Marion, NC
Distance: 45 minutes from Asheville
Address: 1805 Highway 70 West, Marion NC 28752
Telephone: 828-724-4948
Website: www.historiccarsonhouse.com
Hours: April through November, Wednesday-Saturday 10 a.m.-4 p.m., Sunday 2-5 p.m.
Fees: None
Allow: 1 hour
Directions: From Asheville, take I-40 East to Old Fort. Take NC 70 North through Pleasant Gardens to the House. It is located on the right just beyond the intersection of NC 80.

Historic Murray's Mill

Maintained by the Catawba County Historical Association, the Historic Murray's Mill is a complex of historic building preserved intact. Included are the 1913 mill (the centerpiece of the complex), the 1890's Murray & Minges General Store, the 1880's Wheathouse, used as an exhibit gallery, the 1913 John Murray House, furnished to the period, and numerous outbuildings. Run by three generations of the Murray Family, who abandoned operations in 1967, the picturesque structures and surrounding land form the last milling complex in the county, meticulously preserved and interpreted by the Catawba County Historical Association.

Location: Hickory, NC
Distance: 1 hour and 30 minutes from Asheville
Address: 1489 Murray's Hill Road, Catawba NC 28609
Telephone: 828-241-4299
Website: www.catawbahistory.org/historic_murrays_mill.php
Hours: Closed January-March. In season, Saturday 9 a.m.-4 p.m., Sunday 1:30-4:30 p.m.
Fees: $3.00
Allow: 1-2 hours
Directions: From Asheville take I-40 East towards Statesville. Take Exit 138 at Wike Road, and take the first right onto Oxford School Road (NC 10). Turn right at 2nd Avenue SW and then left at Murray's Hill Road.

Historic Newton, NC Depot

The Historic Newton, NC Depot is open to visitors on Saturdays, and features displays and exhibits of local railroad history. The building, built in 1924, served both the Southern Railway and the Carolina & North-Western lines which traversed Catawba County. Railroad service into the area started in 1860 when rails of the Western North Carolina Railroad reached the county. In 1881, tracks of the Chester & Lenoir Narrow Gauge railroad also reached Newton and joined the rails of the WNCRR.

The renovated depot, which was built an all-brick structure by the Elliott Building Company, opened to the public in September, 2006, and houses a railroad museum, model railroad club, and a banquet room. The banquet room of the depot can seat up to 80 people at one time and is available for rent for family, church, business or civic events. Currently, the Depot Authority is exploring the feasibility of creating the North Carolina Narrow Gauge Museum, with displays of North Carolina railroad equipment that is smaller than the typical standard gauge railroad. Preliminary plans call for a covered car-barn with three storage tracks on land adjacent to the depot.

Location:	Newton NC
Distance:	1 hour and 15 minutes from Asheville
Address:	1123 North Main Avenue, Newton NC 28658
Telephone:	828-695-4317
Website:	Historic Newton NC Depot
Hours:	Saturday 1-3 p.m., other times by appointment only.
Fees:	None
Allow:	1-2 hours
Directions:	From Asheville take I-40 East towards Statesville. Take Exit 130 toward Old US 70. Turn left at West 1st Street, take the 2nd right onto 1st Avenue South. Continue onto Highway 16 Business/Main Street to depot.

History Museum of Burke County

The History Museum of Burke County seeks to promote the collection, preservation, educational interpretation and display of those artifacts, documents, and events most representative of Burke County–its prehistory and history, its cultural and economic development, its people and institutions. The museum is housed in the Old City Hall, and has 22 rooms, each with its own theme, devoted to various aspects of local history.

Location:	Morganton, NC
Distance:	1 hour from Asheville
Address:	201 West Meeting Street, Morganton NC 28655
Telephone:	828-437-1777
Website:	www.thehistorymuseumofburke.org
Hours:	Tuesday-Friday: 10 a.m.-4 p.m.; Saturday 10 a.m.-2 p.m.
Fees:	None
Allow:	1 hour
Directions:	From Asheville take I-40 west to exit 103 toward Morganton. Turn left at Burkemont Avenue (US Highway 64) and then right at West Union Street. Continue on West Meeting Street.

Horn in the West

One of North Carolina's best know outdoor dramas, Horn in the West, is a re-creation of North Carolina's early pioneers, including Daniel Boone, and their struggle for independence from Britain. The production takes place in pre-Revolutionary days and lasts two hours. Horn in the West first premiered in 1952.

Location:	Boone, NC
Distance:	2 hours from Asheville
Address:	591 Horn in the West Rd., Boone, NC 28607
Telephone:	828-264-2120
Website:	www.horninthewest.com
Hours:	Season is mid-June to mid-August. Performances begin at 8:30 p.m. No show on Mondays.
Fees:	$18 adults, $9 children 12 and under, $16 seniors
Allow:	Performances last about two hours
Directions:	From Asheville, take I-40 East to Marion. In Marion take NC 221 to Boone. Just past intersection of NC 321 look for the Horn in the West sign.

Hudson Depot Railroad Museum

The Hudson Depot Railroad Museum is housed in a former train depot built around the turn of the 20th century and chronicles the history of the town of Hudson and the local railroad industry through photographs and artifacts. The depot was in operation until the 1970's. A highlight of the museum is its collection of several restored cabooses including a restored 1912 wood-sided Rear Cupola Caboose furnished with railroad artifacts, and a Delaware & Hudson.

Location:	Hudson, NC
Distance:	1½ hours east of Asheville
Address:	550 Central Street, Hudson NC 28638
Telephone:	828-728-8272
Website:	http://www.explorecaldwell.com/historic
Hours:	Open by appointment and during special events
Fees:	Free
Allow:	1 hour
Directions:	From Asheville, take I-40 East to Exit 113 toward Rutherford College Road/NC 1001, turn right at Cajah Mountain Road/NC 1130 and then right at Elm Avenue in Hudson. Take the 1st left onto Central Avenue.

J. Summie Propst House Museum

The J. Summie Propst house, built between 1881 and 1883, is the only remaining example of the Second Empire Style of architecture in Hickory. J. Summie Propst (1853-1940) was the son of Absalom Propst and was born in the Propst Crossroads section of Catawba County. A carpenter and cabinetmaker by trade, he built this house soon after his marriage to Nancy Jane Abernathy. Still in their twenties, they represented the new generation. Amenable to change, they accepted the new styles of architecture printed in the latest pattern books and erected an asymmetrical, spacious, modest house. This house remained in the family until it was vacated for a short period prior to its acquisition by the Hickory Landmarks Society in 1968.

The Society moved the house to the present site in the Shuford Memorial Gardens, from its original location on Tenth Avenue (now Main Avenue SW). An early twentieth-century kitchen wing was not moved to the new site. Since its relocation to Shuford Park, the house has been rehabilitated and is used as a museum. Trained docents serve as guides at the museum.

Location:	Hickory, NC
Distance:	1 hour and 15 minutes from Asheville
Address:	332 Sixth Street NW, Hickory NC 28601
Telephone:	828-322-4731
Website:	www.hickorylandmarks.org/j_summie_propst_house_museum. htm
Hours:	March 15- December 15; Thursday and Sunday, 1:30-4:30 p.m.
Fees:	None
Allow:	1-2 hours
Directions:	From Asheville take I-40 East towards Statesville. Take Exit 123A-123B for US 321 toward Hickory. Continue on US 321 North. Turn right at 2nd Avenue NW and turn right at 2nd Avenue NW, then turn left at 6th Street NW.

Maple Grove Historical Museum

Built in 1883 and listed on the National Register of Historic Places, this restored Italianate style house features authentic Victorian furnishings and was the home of Adolphus Lafayette Shuford and his family, and is one of the oldest remaining houses in Hickory. It is a simple but handsome representation of the Italianate style. A.L. Shuford was a prominent early citizen of Hickory. He was one of the six founding commissioners when the first attempt to incorporate the village of Hickory Tavern was made in 1863. He was also the first agent in Hickory of the Western North Carolina Railroad, and he played an important role in the founding of Claremont College. Shuford is credited with having imported the first Jersey cattle to Catawba County.

Maple Grove is a two-story frame house with weather-board siding, a pedimented-gable roof, gable-end brick chimneys, a three-bay facade, and a two-story rear ell. One of the most distinctive features of the house is its two-tier front porch with paired chamfered posts, bracketed cornices, and decorative sawn-work balustrades. The main body of the house has a center-hall plan with simple detailing. One of the most striking interior features is the closed-string stairs with its heavy chamfered and molded newel and unusual sawn work balustrade reminiscent of the front porch balustrades. In 1973, it was listed on the National Register of Historic Places.

Location:	Hickory NC
Distance:	1 hour and 15 minutes from Asheville
Address:	542 2nd Street NE, Hickory NC 28601
Telephone:	828-322-4731
Website:	www.hickorylandmarks.org/maple_grove_historical_museum.HTM
Hours:	Monday-Friday 9 a.m.-5 p.m.
Fees:	Hone
Allow:	1 hour
Directions:	From Asheville take I-40 East towards Statesville. Take Exit 123A-123B for US 321 toward Hickory. Continue on US 321 North. Turn right at 2nd Avenue NW and turn left at 2nd Street NE.

Mariam & Robert Hayes Performing Arts Center

The Blowing Rock Community Arts Center Foundation, Inc. was formed in December 2000 by community members to promote the advancement of cultural arts and humanities in Blowing Rock and the North Carolina High Country through a regional Arts Center, The Mariam & Robert Hayes Performing Arts Center. Home to the Blowing Rock Stage Company, the Arts Center benefits residents and visitors by providing a permanent home for a multitude of arts groups and a facility in which to host live theatre, dance groups, a variety of musical performances, visual arts displays, classic films, and children's theatre workshops.

Location:	Blowing Rock, NC
Distance:	2 hours from Asheville
Address:	152 Jamie Fort Road, Blowing Rock NC 28605
Telephone:	828-295-9627
Website:	www.brcac.org/blog
Directions:	From Blue Ridge Parkway take Boone exit to 321 South to Blowing Rock. A faster route from Asheville is to take I-40 East to Marion and take Hwy. 221 North to Blowing Rock.

McDowell Arts Council Association Gallery

Located in the McDowell Arts Council Association building, this art gallery features local and regional artists and craft persons working in a variety of media. It is known locally for their annual Holiday Show showcasing the work of McDowell County artisans exhibiting pottery, woodworking, basketry, jewelry, textile arts and other fine crafts.

Location:	Marion, NC
Distance:	1 hour from Asheville
Address:	50 South Main Street, Marion NC 28752
Telephone:	828-652-8610
Website:	http://mcdowellarts.net/taxonomy/term/1
Hours:	Monday-Saturday, 10 a.m.-6 p.m.

Fees:	None
Allow:	1 hour
Directions:	From Asheville take I-40 east towards Statesville. Take exit 81 toward Marion, turn left at Sugar Hill road. Continue for 2 miles onto West Henderson Street and turn left onto South Main Street.

Mast General Store

The century-old Mast General Store is one of the best remaining examples of old country stores in America. It has featured traditional clothing and quality goods since 1883. There are four other Mast General Stores: Asheville, Boone, Hendersonville, and Waynesville. However, the store in Valle Crucis is the original and as such, is a landmark.

Location:	Valle Crucis, NC
Distance:	2 hours from Asheville
Address:	Hwy. 194, Valle Crucis, NC 28691
Telephone:	828-963-6511
Website:	www.mastgeneralstore.com
Hours:	7 a.m.-6:30 p.m. Monday through Saturday; 12-6 p.m. Sunday.
Directions:	From Asheville take I-40 East to Marion. Take Hwy. 221 North to Hwy. 105. Take 105 North and turn left on Hwy. 194 into Valle Crucis.

20 Miles of Furniture

Thousands of people visit Lenoir and Hickory each year with one thing on their minds-furniture! With 20 miles of furniture stores located along or near a stretch of U.S. Highway 321 between Lenoir and Hickory, North Carolina, the area is a required destination for any serious shopper looking for discount furniture. Nearly all manufacturers including Bernhardt, Broyhill, Fairfield Chair, Hammary, Kincaid and Thomasville can be found here along with an abundance of smaller, perhaps lesser known companies that also produce top-quality furnishings. Highway 321 passes through the towns of Granite Falls, Sawmills and Hudson.

Location:	Highway 321 Between Hickory and Lenoir, NC
Distance:	1 hour and 15 minutes from Asheville
Telephone:	800-737-0782
Website:	www.20milesoffurniture.com
Directions:	From Asheville take I-40 East towards Statesville. Take Exit 123A-123B for Hickory. Take US 321 North towards Lenoir.

Morganton 1916 Railroad Depot

The Morganton 1916 Railroad Depot was built in 1886, and restored to its 1916 appearance in 2004. The Depot is open to the public on Saturdays and features exhibits of original station master and railroad equipment memorabilia and photos from the 19th and 20th centuries. The Depot is maintained by the History Museum of Burke County.

Location:	Morganton, NC
Distance:	1 hours from Asheville
Address:	624 South Green Street, Morganton NC 28655
Telephone:	828-437-1777
Website:	www.thehistorymuseumofburke.org/depot
Hours:	Saturdays 2-4 p.m., other times by appointment
Allow:	30 minutes-1 hour
Directions:	From Asheville take I-40 East to Morganton. Get off at exit 103 onto US 64 towards Morganton. Within one mile turn left at Burkemont Avenue, turn right at West Flemming Drive and then slight left at South Sterling Street. Continue onto South Green Street.

Mountain Gateway Museum

The Mountain Gateway Museum offers visitors an opportunity to learn about North Carolina's mountain region. Exhibits, programs, and living history demonstrations depict area history from the earliest original inhabitants through the settlement period and into the twentieth century. The museum site includes a picnic area, amphitheater, two pioneer-era log cabins and the museum itself, all located on the banks of historic Mill Creek, a Catawba River tributary.

Location:	Old Fort, NC
Distance:	45 minutes from Asheville
Address:	102 Water St., Old Fort, NC 28762
Telephone:	828-668-9259
Website:	http://www.facebook.com/pages/Mountain-Gateway-Museum-and-Heritage-Center/52168779289
Hours:	Monday: 12-5 p.m., Tuesday-Saturday: 9 a.m-5 p.m., Sunday: 2-5 p.m.
Fees:	None
Allow:	1 hour
Directions:	From Asheville take I-40 East to Old Fort and get off at Exit 73 onto Catawba Avenue. Go left 2 blocks to Water Street.

Museum of Ashe County History

The Museum of Ashe County History is located in the historic 1904 Ashe County Courthouse building and has exhibits pertaining to the history of Ashe County and its people. The major permanent exhibit presents the story of the "Virginia Creeper" Railroad.

Location:	Jefferson, NC
Distance:	3 hours from Asheville
Address:	301 East Main Street, Jefferson NC

ne:	336-846-1904
Website:	www.ashehistory.org
Hours:	April–October: 10 a.m.-4 p.m. Tuesday–Friday
Fees:	None
Allow:	1-2 hours
Directions:	From Asheville take I-40 west to exit 72 and merge onto US70 toward Old Fort. After 11 miles turn left at US 221 and follow US 221 through Boone to Jefferson.

Museum of North Carolina Minerals

The Museum of North Carolina Minerals opened in 1956 as a joint project of the National Park Service and the North Carolina Department of Conservation and Development and displays more than 300 varieties of minerals found in North Carolina. Renovated in 2002, the museum also has numerous interpretative exhibits and a gift shop.

Location:	Milepost 331 Blue Ridge Parkway, Spruce Pine area
Distance:	1-1½ hours
Address:	Blue Ridge Parkway, Milepost 331
Telephone:	828-765-2761
Website:	www.blueridgeheritage.com/attractions-destinations/museum-of-north-carolina-minerals
Hours:	9 a.m.-5 p.m. Monday-Sunday, early May through October
Fees:	None
Allow:	1-2 hours
Directions:	Take Blue Ridge Parkway north out of Asheville to Milepost 331

Mystery Hill

Mystery Hill is a hands-on entertainment center for kids and grown-ups alike that has been around for over 50 years. The self-guided tour includes the famous Mystery House where you stand at a 45-degree angle and experience unusual gravitational effects. Other venues include the Hall of Mystery with over 40 puzzles and science-based experiments, the Bubble-Rama with bubble experiments including human-sized bubbles the kids can enter, the Native American Artifacts Museum with over 50,000 relics on display, and the Appalachian Heritage Museum.

Location:	Between Boone and Blowing Rock, NC
Distance:	2 hours from Asheville
Address:	129 Mystery Hill Lane, Blowing Rock, NC 28605
Telephone:	828-264-2792
Website:	www.mysteryhill-nc.com
Hours:	June-August 8 a.m.-8 p.m.; September-May 9 a.m.-5 p.m.
Fees:	Rates vary. Call for current prices. Senior, military, group, and AAA discounts are available.
Allow:	1-2 hours

Directions: From Asheville, take I-40 East to Marion, take Hwy. 221 North to Blowing Rock, and then take 321 North four miles to Mystery Hill. From the Blue Ridge Parkway north out of Asheville, get off at mile marker 291. Take Hwy. 321 North 1½ miles.

Native American Artifacts Museum

The Native American Artifacts Museum is part of the Mystery Hill complex and houses over 50,000 pieces of authentic Native American artifacts. Almost every time period of American Indian history is represented in the collection that took over 70 years to collect. From arrowheads and effigy pipes to bowls, celts and awls, this is one of the largest collections of its kind in North Carolina.

Location: Blowing Rock, NC
Distance: 2 hours from Asheville
Address: 129 Mystery Hill Lane, Blowing Rock, NC 28605
Telephone: 828-264-2792
Website: www.mysteryhill-nc.com
Hours: June-August 8 a.m.-8 p.m.; September-May 9 a.m.-5 p.m.
Fees: Rates vary. Call for current prices. Senior, military, group, and AAA discounts are available
Allow: 1 hour
Directions: From Asheville, take I-40 East to Marion, take Hwy. 221 North to Blowing Rock, and then take 321 North four miles to Mystery Hill. From the Blue Ridge Parkway north out of Asheville, get off at mile marker 291. Take Hwy. 321 North 1½ miles.

North Carolina Mining Museum

The large North Carolina Mining Museum is part of Emerald Village and is located adjacent to and inside the historic Bon Ami Mine and features a general mining history exhibit, information on the minerals extracted and their uses, authentic mining equipment, and fascinating information on the Bon Ami Mine and Bon Ami Company.

Location: Little Switzerland, NC
Distance: 1-2 hours from Asheville
Address: 331 McKinney Mine Rd., Little Switzerland, NC 28749.
Telephone: 828-765-6463, 828-765-0000
Website: www.emeraldvillage.com
Hours: 9 a.m.-5 p.m., seven days a week, May through October. Museum is open April-November
Fees: None
Allow: 1 hour
Directions: From Asheville, take I-40 East to Marion. Take NC 221 North to NC 226. Left on NC 226 and go 9 miles to the Blue Ridge Parkway. Go south on parkway and get off at next exit, Little Switzerland,

Milepost 334. Take right under parkway onto Chestnut Grove Rd. Turn left onto McKinney Mine Rd.

North Carolina School for the Deaf Museum

The North Carolina School for the Deaf Historical Museum is located in Morganton, and is a museum run by the Historic Rusmisell Museum Society. The museum contains yearbooks, scrapbooks, histories, photographs and other artifacts documenting the school and its community since its founding in 1894.

Location:	Morganton, NC
Distance:	1 hour from Asheville
Address:	517 West Fleming Drive, Morganton NC 28655
Telephone:	828-433-2971
Website:	www.ncsdmuseum.net
Hours:	Call for hours
Fees:	None
Allow:	1 hour
Directions:	From Asheville take I-40 west to exit 103. Take Highway 64 toward Morganton and turn left at Burkemont Avenue. Turn right onto West Fleming Drive to the museum.

Old Burke County Courthouse & Heritage Museum

The Old Burke County Courthouse & Heritage Museum features a restored 19th-century courthouse with displays and exhibits about the building, the early court system, and local history. Exhibits include a restored turn-of-the-century lawyer's office, including information on the North Carolina Supreme Court justices who held summer sessions of the Supreme Court in the Old Courthouse from 1847 to 1862. The museum also has changing exhibits on selected aspects of early Burke County life and culture as well as a 20-minute slide presentation on Burke County heritage.

Location:	Morganton, NC
Distance:	1 hour from Asheville
Address:	102 East Union St. Morganton, NC 28655
Telephone:	828-437-4104
Website:	www.historicburke.org/museum
Hours:	Monday-Friday 9 a.m.-4 p.m., Saturday 10 a.m.-1 p.m.
Fees:	None
Allow:	1 hour
Directions:	From Asheville, take I-40 East to Exit 105. Turn left off the exit and continue straight into Morganton to Courthouse Square.

Old Depot & Caboose Museum

The Old Depot Gallery & Caboose Museum are located in Black Mountain, and are operated by the Old Depot Association. The Gallery, located in the historic restored railroad depot, sells only original and juried crafts of local Western North Carolina Artists. Separate from the depot building is the Caboose Museum housed in an authentic railroad caboose. The little museum display features a photographic history of the depot, train memorabilia, and period music.

Location:	Black Mountain, NC
Distance:	20 minutes from Asheville
Address:	207 Sutton Avenue, Black Mountain 28711
Telephone:	828-669-5483
Website:	www.olddepot.org/galleryindex.html
Hours:	Tuesday-Saturday, 10 a.m.–5 p.m.
Fees:	None
Allow:	1 hour
Directions:	From Asheville take I-40 west to exit 64. Turn left at exit ramp onto Highway 9 toward Black Mountain. Turn left at Sutton Avenue.

Old Fort Railroad Museum

The Old Fort Railroad Museum presents the impact of the railroads in the mountains of North Carolina. Train exhibits, original tools and signal lights, furniture and signs are housed in the historic 1890s vintage Old Fort Depot. There is also an original caboose on display.

Location:	Old Fort, NC
Distance:	45 minutes from Asheville
Address:	25 West Main Street, Old Fort, NC 28762
Telephone:	828-668-7223
Website:	www.mcdowellnc.org/links/144
Admission:	None
Hours:	Monday-Saturday 9 a.m.-5 p.m.
Directions:	Take I-40 East to Old Fort exit 72. Take US70 West towards Old Fort and Main Street.

Old Wilkes Jail Museum

Built in 1859, the Old Wilkes Jail was in continuous use as a jail until 1915. The first jail had four cells and included a residence for the jailer and his family. It is now restored as a history museum. One famous inmate, Tom Dula (of the famous ballad "Hang Down Your Head Tom Dooley") was incarcerated here until a change of venue was obtained by his defense attorney, former NC Governor Zebulon Vance. The building was restored to its original state using as many of the original building materials as possible. Access to the cells are through the original iron and wood doors. The old Wilkes County jail is one of the best preserved examples of nineteenth century penal architecture in North Carolina.

Location:	Wilkesboro, NC
Distance:	2 hours from Asheville

Address:	203 North Bridge Street, Wilkesboro, NC 28697
Telephone:	336-667-3712
Website:	www.wilkesboro.com/oldwilkesinc/jail/jail.htm
Hours:	9 a.m.-4 p.m., Monday-Friday; weekends by appointment
Fees:	None
Allow:	45 minutes
Directions:	From Asheville take I-40 East to Hickory. Exit at Hickory and take Hwy. 16 North to downtown Wilkesboro. Turn right at the light and go through town past the courthouse. Take first left onto to Broad Street to behind the courthouse. Turn left onto North Street and then right onto North Bridge Street.

Orchard at Atlapass

The Orchard at Altapass is a unique Blue Ridge experience. This is a great place to take the kids and enjoy an afternoon of Appalachian culture, music, and fun. In addition to the splendid apple orchards, activities include hayrides, storytelling, clogging, performances by local mountain musicians, cider and apple butter making, picnic lunches and craft exhibits.

Located on land right next to the Blue Ridge Parkway, the Orchard has always been an important economic base for the local folks. In the 1930s, the Orchard was split in two by the building of the parkway. Because of that proximity, it is the only private business with direct access to the parkway. Nearby railroad lines bring up to thirty trains a day to the area and train whistles are part of the Orchard experience. The trees grown at Altapass are heritage varieties including the much-prized Virginia Beauty, King Luscious, and Stayman Winesap apples.

Location:	Milepost 328.3 at Orchard Rd. near Spruce Pine, NC
Distance:	2 hours by way of the Blue Ridge Parkway
Address:	102 Orchard Road, Spruce Pine NC
Telephone:	888-765-9531, 828-765-9531
Website:	www.altapassorchard.com
Hours:	May 1 to November 1, Monday, Wednesday-Saturday: 10 a.m.-6 p.m. Sunday: 12-6 p.m., Closed Tuesday
Fees:	Orchard: Free; Various fees for other activities
Allow:	2-3 hours
Directions:	Take the Blue Ridge Parkway! Hard to find, even with directions by any other route. Get off 3 miles north of the Spruce Pine exit at Milepost 328.3 onto Orchard Rd. Look for little brown Orchard at Altapass signs.

Presbyterian Historical Society Museum

The Presbyterian Historical Society Museum is located at the Montreat Conference Center in Black Mountain, and is maintained by the Presbyterian

Historical Society. The museum contains collections of items related to the history of the Presbyterian Church, USA and its missions.

Location: Montreat, NC
Distance: 30 minutes from Asheville
Address: 318 Georgia Terrace, Montreat, NC 28757
Telephone: 828-669-7061
Hours: Monday-Friday 8:30 a.m.-4:30 p.m. Closed all major holidays.
Fees: $5 fee for any research done by the Society. Otherwise free.
Allow: ½-1 hour
Directions: From Asheville, take I-40 East to Exit 64. Take Rte. 9 North through Black Mountain and the Montreat Gate. Continue on Assembly Dr. one mile and turn left onto Georgia Terrace.

Quaker Meadows Plantation

Quaker Meadows Plantation is the restored 1812 Catawba Valley Plantation House of Captain Charles McDowell, Jr. It was the site of the 1780 gathering of the Overmountain Men, patriots that marched to Kings Mountain and helped defeat the British in the Revolutionary War. This authentically furnished house museum interprets antebellum culture in Burke Country from that era.

Location: Morganton, NC
Distance: 1 hour from Asheville
Address: 119 St. Mary Church Rd., Morganton, NC 28655
Telephone: 828-437-4104
Hours: Sunday 2-5 p.m. or by appointment
Fees: Small admission fee for adults
Allow: 1 hour
Directions: From Asheville, take I-40 East to Exit 100. Turn left onto Hwy. 181 and go two blocks to St. Mary's Church Rd. Turn right and the plantation will be on the left.

Rutherford County Farm Museum

The Rutherford County Farm Museum has exhibits of antique farm equipment and items dating back to the earliest days of the nineteenth century. Two large murals, depicting the cycle of growing cotton and the early textile mills of the county, are outstanding features of the museum.

Location: Forest City NC
Distance: 45 minutes from Asheville
Address: 240 Depot Street, Forest City, NC 28043
Telephone: 828-248-1248
Hours: Wednesday-Saturday: 10 a.m.-4 p.m.
Fees: $2 adults, children free
Allow: 1 hour

Directions: From Asheville take I-26 South to Exit 35. Take Hwy. 74 East to Columbus/Rutherfordton. Take exit 182 to US221 to Forest City. In Forest City turn left at South Broadway, then turn left at Florence Street and continue to Depot Street.

Rutherford Hospital Museum

The Rutherford Hospital Museum opened in October of 2005 and was created because the Hospital played an important role in Rutherford County history. The design of the museum features vignettes that showcase several areas of hospital life. It is a treasure trove of artifacts including many pieces of medical equipment and furniture from earlier years at the hospital. Other items were used privately by physicians in Rutherford County who were once associated with the hospital.

Among the prized pieces of the collection are a massive roll-top desk used by Dr. Henry Norris, one of the three founders of Rutherford Hospital located in the Founders' Corners. He used the roll-top desk in the 1906 hospital and later in the 1911 building.

Location: Rutherfordton, NC
Distance: 1 hour from Asheville
Address: 288 South Ridgecrest Avenue, Rutherfordton NC 28139
Telephone: 828-286-5000
Hours: Monday-Friday 6 a.m.-5 p.m.
Fees: Free
Allow: 1 hour
Directions: From Asheville Take I-40 east to Exit 85 (NC 221). Go north toward Rutherfordton on NC 221. In Rutherfordton turn left onto Maple Street to hospital on South Ridgecrest Avenue.

Senator Sam J. Ervin Jr. Library

The Senator Sam J. Erwin Jr. Library is located on the campus of Western Piedmont Community College in the Phifer Learning Resources Center, and is a replica of the late Senator Ervin's home library, as it existed at 515 Lenoir Street in Morganton. A 7,500-item collection of Ervin's books and professional and family memorabilia is housed in the library. Senator Ervin is best known for serving as the Chairman of the Senate Watergate Committee in the 1970s.

Location: Morganton, NC
Distance: 1 hour from Asheville
Address: Western Piedmont Community College, 1001 Burkemont Ave., Morganton, NC 28655
Telephone: 828-438-6195
Website: www.samervinlibrary.org
Hours: Monday-Friday 8 a.m.-5 p.m.
Fees: None

Allow: 1 hour
Directions: Driving east on I-40 from Asheville, take Exit #103 and turn left onto Burkemont Avenue. Cross the bridge over I-40. Western Piedmont Community College is on the right, 1 block up.

Sparta Teapot Museum of Craft & Design

The Sparta Teapot Museum of Craft & Design has ongoing exhibits of traditional and contemporary arts and crafts, with the focus on regional artists.

Location: Sparta, NC
Distance: 3 hours from Asheville
Address: 18 South Main Street, Sparta NC 28675
Telephone: 336-372-6879, 336-372-7238
Website: http://spartateapotmuseum.com
Hours: Thursday-Saturday, 10 a.m.-5 p.m.
Fees: None
Directions: From Asheville take I-40 east to exit 152B north to I-77 towards Elkin. After approximately 30 miles turn left at US21 towards Sparta.

Swannanoa Valley Museum

The Swannanoa Valley Museum resides in what was formerly the Black Mountain Fire Department and was founded in 1989 by the Swannanoa Valley Historical and Preservation Association. Exhibits focus on Swannanoa Valley history and culture and include Native American exhibits, artifacts and early tools, plants indigenous to the region and photographic displays.

Location: Black Mountain, NC
Distance: 20 minutes from Asheville
Address: 223 West State Street, Black Mountain, NC 28711
Telephone: 828-669-9566
Website: www.swannanoavalleymuseum.org
Hours: April April-October: Tuesday-Friday 10 a.m.-5 p.m.; Saturday 12-4 p.m., Sunday 2-5 p.m.
Fees: None
Allow: 1 hour
Directions: From Asheville, take I-40 East to Black Mountain. Get off at Exit 64 and turn left onto Hwy. 9. Proceed to State Street and turn left. The museum is two blocks on the left.

Town of Catawba Historical Museum

Catawba is one of the oldest towns between Salisbury and Asheville, having been selected as an early railroad station. Trains ran to the town before the War Between the States, beginning about 1859. The museum opened to the public in 2003 to present the history of the region, including the impact of the railroad.

The museum is housed in the oldest brick building in Catawba, the Dr. Q. M. Little House built around 1873. This Federal-style building, which contains five rooms of unique local history, and a room dedicated to the National Little Family Archives, features a two-tier porch, exterior stairway, six front doors and vintage handmade brick construction. The museum is maintained by the Town of Catawba Historical Society. Nearby is the Catawba Historic District, where visitor may enjoy a walking tour that features brick-detailed commercial buildings, homes and churches dating from the 1860's.

Location:	Catawba, NC
Distance:	1 hour and 30 minutes from Asheville
Address:	101 First Street S.W.
Telephone:	828-241-4077
Website:	www.townofcatawbanc.org
Hours:	Call for hours
Fees:	None
Allow:	1 hour
Directions:	From Asheville take 1-40 East to Exit 138.Take NC10, Oxford School Road south to Catawba.

Trail of Faith

The Trail of Faith is a walk-through outdoor trail showing the terrible religious persecution of the Waldensians in Northern Italy and their eventual settling in Valdese. There are over nine life-sized exhibits are on the trail with more being added yearly. Summer evening dramas reenact the historic struggles of Waldensians (*See* "From This Day Forward," earlier in this section).

Location:	Valdese, NC
Distance:	1 hour from Asheville
Address:	401 Church Street, Valdese, NC 28690
Telephone:	800-635-4778, 828-874-1893
Website:	www.waldensiantrailoffaith.org
Hours:	Saturday-Sunday 2-5 p.m.
Fees:	Small admission fee
Allow:	1-2 hours for the trail
Directions:	From Asheville, take I-40 East to Exit 111. Take Carolina Street and turn left at traffic light and travel Main Street to Church Street. Turn right onto Church Street. The Trail of Faith is located on top of the hill to the right.

Turchin Center for the Visual Arts

The Turchin Center for the Visual Arts presents exhibition, education, and collection programs that support Appalachian State University's role as a key regional educational, cultural, and economic resource. The center has exhibits that focus on a blend of new and historically important artworks, and features the work of regional, national and international artists.

Location:	Boone, NC
Distance:	2 hours from Asheville
Address:	423 West King Street, Appalachian State University, Boone, NC 28608
Telephone:	828-262-3017
Website:	www.turchincenter.org
Admission:	Free
Directions:	From Asheville, take I-40 East to Marion and take Hwy. 221 North to Blowing Rock. Then take US 321 North to Boone. In Boone turn left on US 421 and then left onto West King Street.

Tweetsie Railroad

Tweetsie Railroad is an exciting Western theme park. An authentic early American, full-size coal-fired steam locomotive takes you on a 3-mile trip over a scenic route with an enacted Indian raid. There is a complete old-time western town that features live entertainment at the Palace Variety Show. A petting zoo, gift shops, and rides for the kids make for great family entertainment.

Location:	Highway 321 between Boone and Blowing Rock, NC
Distance:	2 hours from Asheville
Address:	300 Tweetsie Lane, Blowing Rock, NC 28605
Telephone:	800-526-5740
Website:	www.tweetsie-railroad.com
Hours:	May 22-August 23: Open seven days a week, 9 a.m.-6 p.m.; May 1-May 17, August 28-November 1: Open Friday, Saturday & Sunday, 9 a.m.-6 p.m.
Fees:	$30 adults; $22 children
Directions:	Exit at Milepost 291, Boone Exit, off Blue Ridge Parkway. Tweetsie Railroad is located on US 321 between Boone and Blowing Rock. Faster route: Take I-40 from Asheville and take Hwy. 221 North at Marion. Proceed to Linville and take Hwy. 105 North into Boone. In Boone take 321 South 5 miles.

Waldensian Heritage Museum

The Waldensian Heritage Museum is dedicated to preserving the rich heritage and culture of the Waldensian settlers. It features several rooms and thousands of items that date back to the earliest immigrants, including: clothing, tools, books, pictures, and household items.

Location:	Valdese, NC
Distance:	1 hour from Asheville
Address:	208 Rodoret Street South, Valdese, NC 28690

Telephone: 828-874-1111
Website: www.waldensianpresbyterian.org/13-museum
Fees: None
Allow: 1 hour
Directions: From Asheville, take I-40 East to Valdese, Exit 111. Turn right at
             Millstone Avenue towards Valdese. In approximately one mile take
             the 1st right onto Carolina Street. Then left at Massel Avenue and
             take the 2nd right onto Rodoret Street.

Whippoorwill Academy and Village

The Whippoorwill Academy and Village was created by Mrs. Edith Ferguson
Carter by moving historical buildings to the family farm many years ago. The
complex today features historical museums, including: Tom Dooley Museum,
Daniel Boone Replica Cabin, Smokehouse Art Gallery, Matt's Store, Indian Tee-
pee, Jail, School House, Chapel, Tavern, Blacksmith shop and Weaving room.

Location: Ferguson, NC
Distance: 2 hours from Asheville
Address: 11929 Hwy 268 West, Ferguson NC 28624
Telephone: 336-973-3237
Website: http://www.ncagr.gov/ncproducts/ShowSite.asp?ID=100673
Hours: April- December: Saturday- Sunday 3-5 p.m. and during the
             week by appointment
Fees: None
Allow: 1 hour
Directions: From Asheville take I-40 east. Take exit 103 and follow US 64 north
             to US 321 in Lenoir. Take US 321 north and turn right onto NC
             268 to Whippoorwill Academy and Village.

Wilkes Art Gallery

The Wilkes Art Gallery is a 10,000 square foot facility which includes over
3,500 square feet of exhibition space, an education center with a complete ceramics studio, painting and drawing studios, two multi-purpose classrooms, and a
Gallery Gift Shop. The art gallery that has changing monthly exhibitions of local,
regional, student, and nationally known artists.

Location: North Wilkesboro, NC
Distance: 2 hours from Asheville
Address: 913 C Street, North Wilkesboro, NC 28659
Telephone: 336-667-2841
Website: http://www.wilkesartgallery.org/
Hours: Tuesday 10 a.m.-8 p.m.; Wednesday-Friday 10 a.m.-5 p.m.; Saturday
             10 a.m.-2 p.m.
Fees: None
Allow: 1-2 hours

Directions: From Asheville, take I-40 East to Exit 131 just beyond Hickory. Take NC 16 North to Wilkesboro. At the juncture of East Main Street, turn right and then left Wilkesboro Boulevard towards North Wilkesboro. At NC 421 turn right and then right at 10th Street. Take the 1st left onto C Street.

Wilkes Heritage Museum & Blue Ridge Music Hall of Fame

The Wilkes Heritage Museum, located in the restored historic Wilkes County Courthouse, opened in November of 2005 and celebrates the unique heritage of Wilkes County. Through a collection of artifacts and images, stories of all facets of life in Wilkes County are told. Self-guided tours feature exhibits that include early settlement, medicine, military history, moonshine, and early stock-car racing. The Blue Ridge Music Hall of Fame is also located at the museum and showcases the rich musical heritage of the greater Blue Ridge Mountains area from northern Georgia to northern Virginia. The Hall of Fame educates, defines and interprets the history of music in the Blue Ridge area and musicians in all genres from the region with exhibits and an annual celebration of inductees.

Location: Wilkesboro, NC
Distance: 2 hours from Asheville
Address: 100 East Main Street, Wilkesboro NC 28697
Telephone: 336-667-3171
Website: www.wilkesheritagemuseum.com
Hours: Tuesday-Saturday 10 a.m.-4 p.m.
Fees: $5 adults, $4 students & seniors, children 4 & under are free.
Allow: 1-2 hours
Directions: From Asheville, take I-40 East to Exit 131 just beyond Hickory. Take NC 16 North to Wilkesboro.

Cultural Attractions West of Asheville
Allison-Deaver House

The Allison-Deaver house is one of Western North Carolina's finest surviving examples of early 19th-century architecture. Located in Transylvania County in Brevard, NC, the superbly restored house and farmstead are open to the public. The main house, a two story, wood timber structure with a full two-tiered porch, sits on a steep hill overlooking an old Indian trail which later became a main road for settlers into the Davidson River region of what was Old Buncombe County. The house, built by Benjamin Allison in 1815, was added onto by William Deaver in 1840.

Location: Brevard, NC
Distance: 45 minutes from Asheville
Address: 200 Highway 280, Brevard, NC 28712
Telephone: 828-884-5137, Transylvania Historical Society

Website: www.preservingourpast.org/allison_deaver_house.html
Hours: April-October: Friday-Saturday 10 a.m.-4 p.m., Sunday 1-5 p.m.
Fees: Donations accepted
Allow: 1 hour
Directions: From Asheville, take I-26 East or US 25 South to Airport Rd. Follow
            Airport Rd. south towards Brevard. The Allison-Deaver House is on
            a hill just before you reach the intersection of NC 64. From Hender-
            sonville, take Hwy. 64 West to the intersection of NC 280. Turn right.
            The Allison-Deaver House will be a short distance on your left.

Andrews Art Museum

The Andrews Art Museum is housed on the mezzanine floor of the Cultural
Arts Center in Andrews and is run by the Valleytown Cultural Arts and Historical
Society. The museum hosts regularly scheduled exhibitions of local and regional
artists in the museum's gallery spaces. The historic building that is home to the
Andrews Art Museum was originally the First Baptist Church of Andrews.

Location: Andrews, NC
Distance: 2 hours from Asheville
Address: Corner of Chestnut and Third Streets, Andrews NC 28901
Telephone: 828-361-8602
Website: www.andrewsvalleyarts.com/the-museum.asp
Hours: Saturdays and Sundays, call for hours
Fees: None
Allow: 1-2 hours
Directions: From Asheville take I-40 West to Exit 27.Proceed on US 74 West,
            by-passing the towns of Waynesville, Cherokee, Sylva and Bryson
            City. The four lane then becomes two lane US 19/74 West as you
            approach the Nantahala Gorge. You will travel about 15 miles be-
            fore entering Cherokee County at Topton. In Andrews turn left at
            the first red light. Make a right onto Main Street followed by a left
            onto Chestnut Street to the second building on the left.

Brevard Music Center

In operation for more than 60 years, the Brevard Music Center is known for
its premiere festivals, pleasant setting and the highest standards in music education. With more than fifty concert events scheduled each year, the Music Center
provides not only wonderful entertainment but a unique training environment
for over 400 gifted students from across the nation.

Location: Brevard, NC
Distance: 45 minutes from Asheville
Address: 1000 Probart Street, Brevard, NC 28712
Telephone: 828-884-2011
Website: www.brevardmusic.org/index.php

Hours:	Box Office: Monday-Wednesday noon-4:30 p.m. Other days ... show intermission. Performances June 26-August 10.
Fees:	Vary with performances
Allow:	Performances average two hours.
Directions:	From Asheville, take NC 280 South to Brevard. From downtown Brevard follow Probart Street to the Brevard Music Center. Street signs mark the way.

Canton Area Historical Museum

The Canton Area Historical Museum is a history heritage museum focusing on the culture and history of Canton and Haywood County. The museum has extensive photo archives, exhibits, as well as coverage of Champion Paper Mill and the area's early logging railroads.

Location:	Canton, NC
Distance:	30 minutes from Asheville
Address:	58 Park St., Canton, NC 28716
Telephone:	828-646-3412
Hours:	Monday-Friday 10 a.m.-noon, 1-4 p.m.; weekends by appointment only
Fees:	None
Allow:	1 hour
Directions:	From Asheville, take I-40 West to East Canton, Exit 37. Take 19/23 South to Park Street in Canton.

Cherokee County Historical Museum

Housed in the old Carnegie Library in downtown Murphy, the Cherokee County Historical Museum has a collection of more than two thousand artifacts from the time of the infamous Trail of Tears. Many of the artifacts were collected in Cherokee County, excavated from Indian mounds, or purchased from area citizens over the past seventy years. For the most part, the museum reflects the lifestyle of the Cherokee Indians, although some exhibits also focus on the early white settlers as well as the 16th century Spanish explorers who passed through the area in search of gold and other precious metals. The museum also has an exhibit of over 700 antique dolls, the oldest dating back to around 1865.

The museum serves as an interpretive center for the Trail of Tears National Historic Trail. Murphy was once the site of Fort Butler, one of the main holding areas for Cherokees who were being removed from North Carolina in the 1830's. Other sites in and around Murphy play a prominent role in Cherokee history, mythology, and culture.

The museum houses a replica of the log cabin dwellings used by the Cherokee residents of the area at the time of their removal. This type of dwelling was also typical of that used by pioneer settlers, many of whom moved into the vacated Cherokee cabins.

Location:	Murphy, NC
Distance:	2 hours from Asheville
Address:	87 Peachtree St., Murphy, NC 28906
Telephone:	828-837-6792
Hours:	Monday-Friday 9 a.m.-5 p.m.; Closed national holidays.
Fees:	$3 adults, $1 children
Allow:	1-2 hours
Directions:	From Asheville, take I-40 West. Take Exit 27 to 74 West. Follow 74 West to NC 19. Follow 19 into Murphy. The Museum is right behind the courthouse in the center of town.

Cherokee Indian Reservation

The 56,000-acre Cherokee Indian Reservation is home to more than 10,000 members of Eastern Band of the Cherokee Indians. Each year, thousands of visitors from across the country come to discover this enchanted land and to share the natural mountain beauty the Cherokee have treasured for centuries.

A visit to Cherokee is like stepping into the past. You'll find a nation still linked to ancient customs and traditions that enable them to live in harmony with nature as their ancestors did. The Reservation, known as the Qualla Boundary, has a number of outstanding attractions. Among them is the Museum of the Cherokee Indian, Qualla Arts & Crafts Mutual, "Unto These Hills" Outdoor Drama, Oconaluftee Indian Village, and Harrah's Cherokee Casino & Hotel. There are 28 campgrounds on the Reservation, and many motels and cabins. Be sure to visit the Cherokee Welcome Center at 489 Tsali Boulevard in downtown Cherokee. Be prepared, however, to be turned off by the somewhat glitzy atmosphere on Main Street, which overflows with tourist stores selling "Indian" souvenirs made in China, and street performers wearing non-Cherokee Plains Indian costumes.

Location:	Cherokee, NC
Distance:	1-1½ hours from Asheville
Address:	Cherokee Welcome Center, 498 Tsali Boulevard, Cherokee, NC 28719
Telephone:	800-438-1601
Website:	www.cherokee-nc.com/index.php
Allow:	Plan to spend the whole day
Directions:	From Asheville take I-40 west to exit 27 (Great Smoky Mountains Expressway). Continue west on U.S. 74 past Waynesville, Sylva, and Dillsboro to exit 74, Cherokee. U.S. Highway 441 will take you into Cherokee.

Clay County Historical & Arts Council Museum

The Clay County Historical & Arts Council Museum is housed in the Old County Jail which was constructed in 1912 and used as a jail until 1972. The Museum displays items pertinent to the history of the area through changing exhibits. Displays include school house artifacts, a collection of farm equipment, Indian artifacts from a local excavation and a replica of the office of Dr. Paul Killian, along with many of his medical implements. Ongoing exhibitions are also regularly scheduled for local and regional artists and crafters.

Location: Hayesville, NC
Distance: 1½ hours from Asheville
Address: 212 Davis Loop, Hayesville NC 38904
Telephone: 828-389-6814
Website: www.clayhistoryarts.org
Hours: May through Labor Day: Tues-Sat 10 a.m.-4 p.m.; September-October, Fri-Sat 10 a.m.-4 p.m.
Fees: None
Allow: 1-2 hours
Directions: From Asheville take I-40 west to exit 27. Take 19/23 Hwy. 74 West to the Dillsboro area. Take exit 81 for US441 toward Franklin. In Franklin area take Highway 64 to Hayesville and in Hayesville turn left at Davis Loop.

Cradle of Forestry

The Cradle of Forestry, a National Historic Site, is located in Pisgah National Forest. It is the site where scientific forestry was first practiced in America over 85 years ago. In 1889, George Vanderbilt began buying land southwest of Asheville to build a country estate. His plans included a palatial home surrounded by a large game preserve. To manage the forest property, Vanderbilt hired Gifford Pinchot, father of American forestry. Pinchot's management proved profitable through the sale of wood products, so Vanderbilt purchased an additional 100,000 acres in the mountains surrounding Mt. Pisgah. Pisgah Forest, as it became known, was the first large tract of managed forest land in America. It later became the nucleus of the Pisgah National Forest.

In 1895, a German forester, Dr. Carl Schenck, succeeded Pinchot as manager of Pisgah Forest. Schenck intensified forest operations and three years later launched the first forestry school in America, the Biltmore Forest School. The school lasted until 1914. In 1968, Congress passed the Cradle of Forestry in America Act, establishing 6,400 acres of the Pisgah National Forest to preserve and make available to the public the birthplace of forestry and forestry education in America.

Public facilities at the Cradle of Forestry provide visitors with exciting programs and displays on the rich history of American forestry. The Forest Discovery Center, two paved interpretative trails, and living history exhibits are major attractions at the historic site. A 1900 portable steam powered sawmill and a restored 1915 Climax locomotive are also on exhibit.

Location: Pisgah District of the Pisgah National Forest
Distance: 1 hour from Asheville
Address: Cradle of Forestry, Pisgah National Forest, 1001 Pisgah Hwy., Pisgah Forest, NC 28768

Telephone: 828-877-3130
Website: www.cradleofforestry.com
Hours: Open April to October, 9 a.m.-5 p.m.
Fees: $5 adults, youth ages 15 and younger free
Allow: 3 hours
Directions: From Asheville: Take Airport Rd. (NC 280) off of Hendersonville Hwy. in Arden. Continue on 280 past Asheville Airport to Wal-Mart Shopping Plaza just before Brevard. Turn right onto US 276 into Pisgah Forest to Cradle of Forestry. From Hendersonville: Take US 64 West from Hendersonville to intersection of Hwy. 280 and US 276 at the Wal-Mart Shopping Plaza. Continue straight through light to US 276 into Pisgah Forest and Cradle of Forestry.

Fine and Performing Arts Center at Western Carolina University

The $30 million Fine and Performing Arts Center at Western Carolina University is an exciting cultural arts and art education destination and combines state-of-the-art educational opportunities for students and instructors with a fresh and inspiring venue for world-class performers and artists. Major features include an elegant 1,000 seat concert hall, fine arts academic wing, and a Fine Art Museum with nearly 10,000 feet of exhibit space and a growing permanent collection.

Location: Cullowhee NC
Distance: 45 minutes from Asheville
Address: Centennial Drive, Western Carolina University, Cullowhee NC 28723
Telephone: 828-227-2479
Website: www.wcu.edu/fapac/index
Hours: Fine Art Museum: Tuesday–Friday 10 a.m.-4 p.m., Saturday 1-4 p.m.
Fees: Museum: None, Performances & Theatre: vary with performances
Allow: 1-2 hours
Directions: From Asheville follow I-40 West to exit 27 (Highway 74 West). Follow Highway 74 West to exit 85 in Sylva. At third light turn left onto Highway 107 South. Follow Highway 107 South to campus.

Franklin Gem & Mineral Museum

Housed in the historic old jail (circa 1850) of Macon County, the Franklin Gem and Mineral Museum has many fascinating exhibits concerning North Carolina gems and minerals. The "Jail House Museum" now imprisons thousands of specimens on display in eight rooms. The museum displays not only specimens of local minerals and Cowee Valley gem stones but gems, minerals and artifacts from around the world, among these a 2¼ pound ruby.

Location: Franklin, NC
Distance: 1½ to 2 hours from Asheville
Address: 25 Phillips St., Franklin, NC 28734

Telephone: 828-369-7831
Website: http://fgmm.org
Hours: May 1-Oct. 31 Mon-Fri: 10 a.m.-4 p.m.; Sat: 11 a.m.-3 p.m.,
6-9 p.m.; Nov 1-April 30: Sat only 11 a.m.-3 p.m.
Fees: None
Allow: ½-1 hour
Directions: From Asheville, take I-40 West to Exit 27. Take Hwy. 74 West to
Hwy. 441 South (Exit 81). Follow 441 South to Franklin.

Ghost Town In The Sky

Ghost Town In The Sky is a family-fun theme park that features staged gunfights, theme park rides, live music and shows, crafts and food located on a mountaintop in Maggie Valley. An unusual aspect of this park is that it is located atop a mountain which can only be accessed by visitors via a 3370' long chair lift or an inclined railway. The highest elevation in the park is 4650 feet above sea level.

The park is divided into several "towns," which are located at different elevations of the mountain, each of which has a slightly different theme. Among these are the "Indian Village," "Mountain Town," and "Mining Town." The heart of the park is the re-created old Western town complete with two saloons, a schoolhouse, bank, jail, and church, and various other businesses typical of the day. Each hour, a gunfight is staged right in the street, with visitors lining up on the board sidewalks to watch the action. In the "Silver Dollar Saloon" there are hourly shows featuring Old West can-can dancers, while the Red Dog Saloon features live country and bluegrass music performances throughout the day.

Location: Maggie Valley, NC
Address: 16 Fie Top Road, Maggie Valley NC 28751
Telephone: 828-926-1140
Fees: Prices begin at around $20 per adult.
Allow: 3 hours
Note: In 2009-2010 Ghost Town In The Sky was closed because of mud slides in the area. Call to see if they have reopened before visiting the park.
Directions: From Asheville take I-40 west. Take exit 27 towards Waynesville and then take exitn103 onto US-19 toward Maggie Valley. After approximately 8 miles, turn right onto Fie Top Road.

Graham County Museum of Prehistoric Relics

The Graham County Museum of Prehistoric Relics is housed in The Hike Inn, and is a collection of thousands of prehistoric artifacts from North, South and Central America. They also have a rock bed in front of the museum from which kids can take home samples.

Location: The Hike Inn in Fontana Dam, NC

Distance: 2 hours from Asheville
Address: 3204 Fontana Road, Fontana Dam NC 28733
Telephone: 828-479-3667
Hours: 9 a.m.-6 p.m. (Please call ahead from Dec 1 though Feb 15)
Fees: None
Allow: 1 hour
Directions: From Asheville take I-40 west. Take the exit for Hwy 74 (Great
             Smoky Mountain Expressway). Stay on Hwy 74 (four lane) you will
             pass Clyde, Sylva, and 8 miles past Bryson City (last chance for gro-
             ceries, restaurants) turn right on Hwy 28 to #3204, The Hike Inn.

Great Smoky Mountains Railroad

The Great Smoky Mountains Railroad gives passengers a chance to recapture the thrills and romance of early trains with its excursions through the mountain countryside. Steam and diesel locomotives pull authentic passenger cars on half-day excursions through the mountains and valleys of Western North Carolina. With 53 miles of track, 2 tunnels and 25 bridges, the Great Smoky Mountains Railroad offers a variety of excursions that explore the amazing landscape of the mountains.

There are open cars, coaches and club cars to choose from, as well as a popular weekly dinner train. Excursions leave from a number of sites: Dillsboro, Bryson City and Andrews. The trains run on passenger schedules for half-day round trips. Passengers ride in comfortable, reconditioned coaches, crown coaches, club cars, cabooses and even open cars. The club cars and dining cars have historic pasts and have been lovingly restored, as have the cabooses. A full excursion schedule is offered, including summer season "Raft and Rail" trips that combine a train ride and whitewater rafting experience into one package, Gourmet Dinner Trains, and many other special events.

Location: Departures from Dillsboro, Bryson City and Andrews, NC
Distance: 1-3 hours depending upon departure point
Address: Great Smoky Mountains Railroad, 1 Front St., Dillsboro, NC
             28752
Telephone: 800-872-4681, 828-586-8811
Website: www.gsmr.com
Hours: March-December, times vary.
Fees: Adult $34-$53, Children 2-12 $19-$31, depending on season and
             excursion.
Allow: 3½ to 4½ hours round trip.
Directions: From Asheville to Dillsboro (closest departure point), take I-40
             West to Exit 27. Take 19/23 Hwy. 74 West to Exit 81 (Dillsboro).
             Go to first red light and turn left on Haywood Street. Proceed to
             post office and turn right onto Depot Street.

Harrah's Cherokee Casino

Located on a site that was known as the "Magic Waters" in Cherokee is the visually stunning complex of Harrah's Cherokee Casino. Superbly designed to blend in with the breathtaking natural surroundings beside a sparkling trout stream, the huge 175,000 square-foot casino building is barely visible from Hwy. 19. The approach drive features landscaping highlighting native plants and trees and nearing the casino, one is greeted by massive stone columns and a waterfall. The overall effect upon first seeing the building in its natural setting is that of a remote mountain lodge nestled deep in some immense wilderness.

The casino cost $85 million to build and is situated on 37 acres, tucked tightly between two mountains that reflect the bluish haze that gives the Great Smoky Mountains their name, featuring virgin forest and a stunning panoramic backdrop. Harrah's Cherokee Casino is owned by the Eastern Band of Cherokee Indians and was designed by one of the nation's leading casino and destination resort design firms, the Minneapolis-based Cunningham Group. Harrah's Cherokee Casino is an architectural triumph. Inside, the mountain lodge theme is continued, with colorful Native American art and artifacts, the use of natural materials indigenous to the area and a truly spectacular display of neon lightning in the ceiling that comes to life, complete with rolling bursts of thunder whenever a jackpot is won at one of the 1,800 video gaming machines.

Location:	Cherokee, NC
Distance:	1½ to 2 hours from Asheville
Address:	Intersection of Hwy. 19 and Business Rte. 441, Cherokee NC 28719
Telephone:	800-427-7247, 828-497-7777
Website:	www.harrahscherokee.com/casinos/harrahs-cherokee/hotel-casino/property-home.shtml
Hours:	Casino: 24 hours a day, seven days a week, all year.; Hotel: Harrah's Casino Hotel, 777 Casino Drive, Cherokee NC 28719; 828-497-7777, 800-427-7247
Fees:	None to enter casino, parking is free. Fees for childcare facilities.
Directions:	From Asheville take I-40 West to Exit 27. Follow US-74 West through Waynesville. Take Hwy. 441 North to Cherokee. Take right at first light. Harrah's is at the next intersection.

Highlands Biological Station

Founded in 1927, the Highlands Biological Station acquired its first laboratory for scientific research in 1931. Since that time, scientists based at the Station have made significant contributions in a number of fields, particularly in the study of salamander biology, plant ecology, mycology, and aquatic ecology. The mission of the Station is to foster education and research focused on the rich natural heritage of the Highlands Plateau, while preserving and celebrating the integrity of the "biological crown of the southern Appalachian Mountains." The Highlands

Biological Station offers courses and tours, and also has an onsite botanical garden open to the public.

Location:	Highlands, NC
Distance:	1½ hours from Asheville
Address:	265 North Sixth Street, Highlands, NC 28741
Telephone:	828-526-2602
Website:	www.wcu.edu/hbs/Home.htm
Fees:	None
Hours:	Botanical Gardens are open year-round, sunrise to sunset.
Allow:	1-2 hours
Directions:	From Asheville, take NC 280 West to Brevard (280 begins as Airport Rd., accessible from US 25 or I-26). NC 280 joins NC 64 just before reaching Brevard. Follow 64 West to Highlands. In Highlands, turn left at the first light onto Main Street. Proceed to left onto Sixth Street and make a right turn into the Station driveway.

Highlands Museum & Historical Village

The Highlands Museum & Historical Village is composed of a number of restored buildings which make up the Historical Village. These include the House-Trapier-Wright Home, the Highlands Historical Museum, and Bug Hill Cottage. The House-Trapier-Wright Home is the oldest existing house in Highlands and was built in 1877. The museum house exhibits consist of artifacts, photographs and memorabilia relating to the history of the Highlands area.

Location:	Highlands, NC
Distance:	1 hour from Asheville
Address:	524 N. 4th Street, Highlands NC 28741
Telephone:	828-787-1050
Website:	www.highlandshistory.com
Hours:	May 23-October 31, Friday & Saturday, 10 a.m.-4 p.m., or by appointment
Fees:	None
Allow:	1-2 hours
Directions:	From Asheville, take NC 280 West to Brevard (280 begins as Airport Rd., accessible from US 25 or I-26). NC 280 joins NC 64 just before reaching Brevard. Follow 64 West to Highlands. In Highlands, turn left at the first light onto Main Street.

Highlands Nature Center

Live animal exhibits, garden tours, and children's programs are all facets of this excellent nature center. Their emphasis is on Southern Appalachian biodiversity and geology. They also have exhibitions of Native American artifacts and culture, and exhibits of native wildflowers that are currently in bloom in their Botanical Garden.

Location:	Highlands, NC
Distance:	1-1½ hours from Asheville
Address:	930 Horse Cove Road, Highlands, NC 28741
Telephone:	828-526-2623
Website:	www.wcu.edu/hbs/Naturecenter.htm
Hours:	March-October: Monday-Saturday 1-5 p.m.
Fees:	None
Allow:	1-2 hours
Directions:	From Asheville, take NC 280 West to Brevard (280 begins as Airport Rd., accessible from US 25 or I-26). NC 280 joins NC 64 just before reaching Brevard. Follow 64 West to Highlands. In Highlands, turn left at the first light onto Main Street. Proceed through the next light (Main Street turns into Horse Cove Rd.) and look for the Nature Center on your left.

John C. Campbell Folk School

Established in 1925, the John C. Campbell Folk School is one of America's premier folk art schools. Listed on the National Register of Historic Places, the school offers a wide range of instruction in traditional and contemporary art, crafts, music, dance, nature studies, gardening and cooking. The Folk School's Craft Shop represents more than 300 juried craftspeople and features an impressive collection of traditional and contemporary Appalachian craft, including jewelry, pottery, wood, fiber, ironwork, basketry and other disciplines. The school's fascinating 82-year background is captured in their History Center, where you'll find interesting examples of 20th-century Appalachia on display, including visual art, fine and folk craft, music, historic film footage, photographs and written panels.

Location:	Brasstown, NC
Distance:	2 hours from Asheville
Address:	One Folk School Rd., Brasstown, NC 28902
Telephone:	800-365-5724, 828-837-2775
Website:	www.folkschool.org
Hours:	Craft Shop and History Center: Monday-Saturday 8 a.m.-5 p.m.; Sunday 1-5 p.m.
Admission:	Free
Directions:	I-40 West to Exit 27, US 19/23/74. Take 23/74 to Waynesville/Sylva. At Exit 81 take US 23/441 South to Franklin. In Franklin, the US 441 bypass merges with US 64 West. Follow 64 West from Franklin towards Hayesville. Eight miles west of Hayesville, turn left on Settawig Rd. Follow the signs to the Folk School.

Junaluska Memorial & Museum

The Junaluska Memorial & Museum, located at the burial site of Cherokee Warrior Junaluska in the Great Smoky Mountains near the Nantahala River, is dedicated to preserving Cherokee history and culture. Displays include: arrowheads, spear points and other artifacts found here in the Cheoah Valley, artwork and crafts by Snowbird Indian community members, and information about this valley, its people and its place in American history as the starting point of the Trail of Tears.

Location:	Robbinsville, NC
Distance:	2 hours from Asheville
Address:	1 Junaluska Drive, Robbinsville NC 28771
Telephone:	828-479-4727
Website:	www.junaluska.com
Hours:	Monday-Saturday, 8:00 a.m.-4:00 p.m.
Fees:	None
Allow:	1-2 hours
Directions:	From Asheville, take I-40 West to Exit 27. Take Highway 74 South through Sylva and Nantahala. Turn right on NC 129 to Robbinsville. Turn left at East Main Street in Robbinsville and take the 1st left onto South Main Street. Junaluska Drive will be on the left.

Macon County Historical Society & Museum

Housed in the historic Pendergrass Building (circa 1904), the Macon County Museum collection including clothing, antiques, photographs, textiles, documents, and other artifacts pertaining to the history and culture of Macon County and other areas of Western North Carolina. They also have extensive genealogy files and archives relating to local history.

Location:	Franklin, NC
Distance:	1½-2 hours from Asheville
Address:	36 West Main St., Franklin, NC 28734
Telephone:	828-524-9758
Website:	www.maconnchistorical.org/museum
Hours:	November-April: Monday-Friday 10 a.m.-4 p.m.; Saturday 1-4 p.m.; May-October: Monday-Friday 10 a.m.-5 p.m.; Saturday 1-5 p.m.
Fees:	None
Allow:	1 hour
Directions:	From Asheville, take I-40 West to Exit 27. Take Hwy. 74 West to Hwy. 441 South (Exit 81). Follow 441 South to Franklin.

Mountain Farm Museum

The Mountain Farm Museum is located in the Great Smoky Mountains National Park and is a collection of historic log buildings gathered from throughout the Smoky Mountains and preserved on a single site. Buildings include a house, barns, springhouse, and smokehouse.

Location:	Great Smoky Mountains National Park
Distance:	2-3 hours from Asheville

Address:	Great Smoky Mountains National Park. Oconaluftee Visitor Center (Closest to Mountain Farm Museum), 150 Hwy. 441 N., Cherokee, NC 28719.
Telephone:	General Information: 423-436-1200 Oconaluftee Visitor Center: 423-497-1900
Website:	www.nps.gov/grsm/planyourvisit/mfm.htm
Fees:	None to enter park.
Allow:	2-4 hours
Directions:	From Asheville, take I-40 West to Exit 27. Follow Hwy. 19 South to Cherokee. In Cherokee, take 441 North and follow signs to the park entrance.

Mountain Heritage Center

This museum highlights Southern Appalachian history through exhibitions, publications, educational programs and demonstrations and promotes the rich mountain traditions. The "Migration of the Scotch Irish People" is the center's permanent exhibit. The center also produces temporary exhibits highlighting blacksmithing, mountain trout, the southern handicraft movement, the enduring popularity of handwoven coverlets and other subjects. The Center maintains three major galleries. Gallery A houses the Center's only permanent exhibit, while Galleries B and C house traveling or temporary exhibits.

Location:	Campus of Western Carolina University in Cullowhee, NC
Distance:	1 hours from Asheville
Address:	H.F. Robinson Building, Western Carolina University, Cullowhee, NC 28723
Telephone:	828-227-7129
Website:	www.wcu.edu/2389.asp
Hours:	8 a.m.-5 p.m. Monday through Friday; 10 a.m.-5 p.m. Saturdays June through October only.
Fees:	None
Allow:	1 to 2 hours
Directions:	From Asheville, take I-40 West to Exit 27 and follow Hwy. 19/23, Hwy. 74 to Exit 85 for Western Carolina University.

Museum of American Cut and Engraved Glass

The Museum of American Cut and Engraved Glass, in Highlands, is considered one of the finest collections of its kind in the world. The museum exhibits cut and engraved glass primarily from the American Brilliant Period, 1876-1916. The museum seeks to educate people about glass from this period and increase awareness of and appreciation for this American art form. Housed in a rustic log cabin, the collection's brilliance is a direct contradiction to its humble setting.

Location:	Highlands, NC
Distance:	1½ hours from Asheville

Address:	472 Chestnut Street, Highlands NC 28741
Telephone:	828-526-3415, 828-521-3427
Hours:	May–October: Tuesday, Thursday & Saturday 1-4 p.m., November-April: Saturday 1-4 p.m.
Fees:	None
Directions:	From Asheville take NC 280 South to Brevard. Continue on through Brevard on NC 64 to Highlands.

Museum of North Carolina Handicrafts

Located in the historic 1875 Shelton House, the Museum of North Carolina Handicrafts features a unique collection of the works of some of the state's most renowned artisans. Special collections of pottery are exhibited in nearly every room of the Shelton House including examples from Seagrove and rare pieces from Jugtown Potteries and Pisgah Potteries. There is also an extensive collection of Native American artifacts as well. Other rooms house collections of coverlets, quilts, china painting, jewelry, period furniture and musical instruments.

Location:	Waynesville, NC
Distance:	1 hour from Asheville
Address:	307 Shelton St., Waynesville, NC 28786
Telephone:	828-452-1551
Hours:	May-October: 10 a.m.-4 p.m. Tuesday–Saturday. Call for winter hours.
Fees:	$5 adults, $4 seniors, $1 children, under 5 years free
Allow:	1 hour
Directions:	From Asheville take I-40 West to Exit 27 and follow NC 19/23 South to Waynesville onto Hwy. 276. This road turns into Main Street. Past the 1st Baptist Church bear left 2 blocks to intersection of 276 and Shelton Street. Museum is on corner.

Museum of the Cherokee Indian

The mission of the Museum of the Cherokee Indian is "to perpetuate the history, culture, and stories of the Cherokee people". To accomplish this mission, the museum maintains a permanent exhibit, extensive artifact collection, archives, education programs, artist series and a gift shop. The Museum of the Cherokee Indian opened in 1948 and moved to its present facility in 1976. Its exhibit was totally renovated in 1998, when a new 12,000-square-foot exhibit was installed. The museum has helped to revitalize the stamped pottery tradition by creating and working with the Cherokee Potters Guild as well as traditional dance by sponsoring the Warriors of AniKituhwa, who wear traditional 18th century Cherokee dress; feather capes; and language. There are a number of permanent exhibits in the museum, including some that combine state-of-the-art computer-generated imagery, special effects and audio with an extensive artifact collection.

Location:	Cherokee, NC
Distance:	1-1½ hours from Asheville
Address:	589 Tsali Boulevard, Cherokee, NC 28719
Telephone:	828-497-3481
Website:	www.cherokeemuseum.org
Hours:	Daily 9 a.m.-5 p.m. year round except for Thanksgiving Day, Christmas Day and New Year's Day.
Allow:	2-3 hours
Fees:	Adults $9, Children(6-13) $6
Directions:	From Asheville take Interstate 40 west to exit 27 (Hwy. 74), and travel west on Hwy. 74 to Exit 74 (the Cherokee/Great Smoky Mountains National Park exit). Bear right on Exit 74 and proceed approximately five miles on Hwy. 441 N to the fourth traffic light. Turn right and proceed about a half mile to the next traffic light. Turn left onto Hwy. 441 N/Tsali Boulevard. Proceed .6 mile to the next traffic light (intersection of Hwy. 441/Tsali Boulevard and Drama Road). Turn left and the museum will be on your left at 589 Tsali Boulevard.

Oconaluftee Indian Village

The Oconaluftee Indian Village, located on the Cherokee Indian Reservation, is an authentic replica of an 18th-century Cherokee village and offers guided and self-guided tours to explore the village with dwellings, residents, and artisans right out of the 1750's. Visitors can experience traditional medicine and interact with villagers as they hull canoes, make pottery and masks, weave baskets and beadwork, and participate in their daily activities. The Village also hosts live reenactments, interactive demonstrations, "Hands-On Cherokee" arts and crafts classes, villager outfit rentals for children, and evening storytelling performances.

Location:	Cherokee, NC
Distance:	1-1½ hours from Asheville
Address:	Drama Road, Cherokee, NC 28719
Telephone:	828-554-4557
Hours:	Daily 9 a.m.-5 p.m. , May 1 to October 24
Allow:	2-3 hours
Fees:	Adults $15, Children (6-13) $6
Directions:	From Asheville take Interstate 40 west to exit 27 (Hwy. 74), and travel west on Hwy. 74 to Exit 74 (the Cherokee/Great Smoky Mountains National Park exit). Bear right on Exit 74 and proceed approximately five miles on Hwy. 441 N to the fourth traffic light. Turn right and proceed about a half mile to the next traffic light. Turn left onto Hwy. 441 N/Tsali Boulevard. Proceed .6 mile to the next traffic light (intersection of Hwy. 441/Tsali Boulevard and Drama Road). Turn onto Drama Road.

Perry's Water Garden

Located in Franklin and established in 1980, Perry's Water Gardens is a wholesale-retail aquatic plant nursery by Perry D. Slocum and is known for shipping high quality mature plants. Perry's Water Garden also has the country's largest collection of aquatic gardens and is a major tourist attraction. Perry Slocum created over 147 ponds on 13 acres featuring exotic sunken gardens highlighted with old fashioned antique rose beds and other above-ground flowers. Naturalized grass and dirt paths meander throughout. In addition to the multitude of iris, water lilies, and lotus, the gardens are home to thousands of brightly colored koi and goldfish. If you love flowers and gardens, this center is a must!

Location:	Franklin, NC
Distance:	2 hours from Asheville
Address:	Gibson Aquatic Farm Rd., Franklin, NC 28734
Telephone:	828-524-3264
Website:	www.perryswatergarden.net
Hours:	April 1 through Labor Day. Monday–Saturday 9 a.m.-5 p.m., Closed Sunday
Fees:	None
Allow:	2 hours
Directions:	From Asheville, take I-40 West to Exit 27. Take Hwy. 74 West to Hwy. 441 South (Exit 81). Follow 441 for 14 miles and turn right on Sanders Town Rd., then right on Bryson City Rd. for 2 miles. Turn right on Cowee Creek for 1 mile, then left on Leatherman Gap Rd. ¼ mile. Turn right onto Gibson Aquatic Farm Rd.

Pisgah Center for Wildlife Education

Located in the Pisgah National Forest at the site of the Bobby N. Setzer Fish Hatchery, the Pisgah Center for Wildlife Education features a reception and orientation area that includes aquarium exhibits, the NC Wild Store gift shop, and wildlife exhibits. Run by the NC Wildlife Resources Commission, this facility is a wonderful place to become acquainted with the diverse wildlife and habitats of the Blue Ridge and Appalachian mountains.

Besides the fascinating dish hatchery, with thousands of trout both large and small, informative exhibits strung along an interpretive trail are another of the Center's popular aspects. The outdoor exhibits on the trail include stations that focus on wildlife conservation, the geology of the Blue Ridge Mountains, unique NC habitats, preservation of streams and wetlands, responsibility and safety in the woods, the science of wildlife management, NC Wild Education Sites, the ecology of wetlands, and ways to get involved in wildlife conservation.

Location:	Pisgah District of the Pisgah National Forest
Distance:	1 hour from Asheville
Address:	1401 Fish Hatchery Road, Pisgah Forest, NC 28768

Telephone: 828-877-4423
Website: www.ncwildlife.org/Education_Workshops/Pisgah_Center.htm
Hours: Open Monday–Saturday 8 a.m.-4:45 p.m. Closed on Sunday. Closed on Easter weekend and other state holidays except for Good Friday, Memorial Day, Independence Day and Labor Day.
Fees: None
Allow: 2-3 hours
Directions: From Asheville: Take I-26 East or US 25 South to Airport Rd. (NC 280). Follow 280 past the airport to the Wal-Mart Shopping Plaza just before Brevard. Turn right onto US 276 into Pisgah Forest. Turn left onto Forest Service Rd. 475. From Hendersonville: Take US 64 West to the intersection of Hwy. 280 and US 276 at the Wal-Mart. Take US 276 into Pisgah Forest. Turn left onto Forest Service Rd. 475.

Qualla Arts & Crafts Mutual

The Qualla Arts & Crafts Mutual located in Cherokee is considered to be one of the premier such organizations in any Indian community in America. The store offers a wide range of traditional and contemporary Cherokee arts and crafts. Groups are welcome to experience Qualla "Hands-On" and learn a specific art from one of Qualla's artists.

Location: Cherokee, NC
Distance: 1-1½ hours from Asheville
Address: 645 Tsali Boulevard, Cherokee, NC 28719
Telephone: 828-497-3103
Hours: Monday–Saturday: 8 a.m.-7 p.m., Sunday: 9 a.m.-5 p.m. year round except for Thanksgiving Day, Christmas Day and New Year's Day. Winter hours (September-May) 8 a.m.-5 p.m.
Fees: None
Allow: 2-3 hours
Directions: From Asheville take Interstate 40 west to exit 27 (Hwy. 74), and travel west on Hwy. 74 to Exit 74 (the Cherokee/Great Smoky Mountains National Park exit). Bear right on Exit 74 and proceed approximately five miles on Hwy. 441 N to the fourth traffic light. Turn right and proceed about a half mile to the next traffic light. Turn left onto Hwy. 441 N/Tsali Boulevard. Proceed .6 mile to the next traffic light (intersection of Hwy. 441/Tsali Boulevard and Drama Road). Turn left and the museum will be at 645 Tsali Boulevard.

Red Barn Mountain Museum

The Red Barn Mountain Museum presents the history of rural mountain life in the Haywood County area from mountain men to the 1920's through exhibits and interpretation of artifacts, photographs, and memorabilia from the local region and from local families. On display are horse-drawn farming equipment, quilts, area photographs, tools, Civil War artifacts and mountain lore.

Location:	Waynesville NC
Distance:	1 hour from Asheville
Address:	1856 Dellwood Rd., Waynesville, NC 28786
Telephone:	828-926-1901
Hours:	10 a.m.-5 p.m. Monday-Saturday. Call to confirm hours as they can vary seasonally.
Admission:	None
Allow:	1 hour
Directions:	From Asheville take I-40 West and take exit 27 to US74W towards Waynesville. Take exit 102 and merge onto Russ Avenue. Turn right at Dellwood Road.

Ruby City Gems Museum

The Ruby City Gems Museum has on display thousands of gem and mineral specimens, including fluorescent (glow-in-the-dark) pieces, fossils dating to millions of years old, petrified wood from all over the world, an expansive Native American collection of pipes, tools, and other daily artifacts, and one of the largest, private pre-Columbian collections in the world.

Location:	Franklin NC
Distance:	2 hours from Asheville
Address:	131 East Main Street, Franklin NC 28734
Telephone:	828-524-3967
Website:	www.rubycity.com
Hours:	Monday-Friday 9 a.m.-5 p.m., Saturday 9 a.m.-5 p.m.
Fees:	None
Allow:	1 hour
Directions:	From Asheville, take I-40 West to Exit 27. Take Hwy. 74 West towards Waynesville/Franklin. After approximately 16 miles take exit 81 to US23/US441. Continue straight onto East Main Street in Franklin.

Scottish Tartans Museum

Located in Franklin, NC, the Scottish Tartans Museum focuses on the history of Scottish Tartans—how they were woven and used in dress over the centuries since 325 A.D. Cultural programs of weaving, music, and dance are also provided at the Center throughout the year by Friends of the Museum and volunteers. Ongoing educational programs and exhibits interpret Scottish history and culture, including migrations of the Scots, concentrating on the Scots who settled in Western North Carolina. The museum is over 2,200 square feet and contains the official registry of all publicly known tartans and is the only American extension of the Scottish Tartans Society. Visitors are invited to view their family tartan on computer and trace their Scottish heritage in the tartan research library. The Center also has a gift shop offering a large selection of Scottish and Celtic treasures.

Location:	Franklin, NC
Distance:	1½-2 hours from Asheville
Address:	86 East Main St., Franklin, NC 28734
Telephone:	828-524-7472
Website:	www.scottishtartans.org
Hours:	Monday-Saturday 10 a.m.-5 p.m., Closed Sunday and major holidays.
Fees:	$2 Adults, $1 Children
Allow:	1-2 hours
Directions:	From Asheville, take I-40 West to Exit 27. Hwy. 74 West to Hwy. 441 South (Exit 81). Take the first Franklin exit at the Days Inn, and go straight into town to Main Street.

SEJ Heritage Center at Lake Junaluska

The mission of the SEJ Heritage Center at Lake Junaluska is to preserve and keep alive the stories of the remarkable persons and events that make up the unique history of United Methodists in the Southeast. The museum features exhibits depicting the history of the United Methodist Church and its antecedents with special emphasis on the Southeastern Jurisdiction. The archives contain records of SEJAC, journals and newspapers of the SEJ Annual Conferences, some local church histories and clergy biographical information and books on a variety of subjects related to Methodism and its people in the Southeastern Jurisdiction. A special portion of the archives is dedicated to the correspondence and other personal papers of Harry Denman.

Location:	Lake Junaluska, NC
Distance:	1 hour from Asheville
Address:	Harrell Center, 710 North Lakeshore Drive, Lake Junaluska, NC 28745
Telephone:	828-452-2881
Website:	www.sejumc.org/archives-history
Hours:	Monday-Friday 9 a.m.-4:30 p.m., Saturdays 9:30 a.m.-1:30 p.m., other times by appointment
Fees:	None
Allow:	1-2 hours
Directions:	From Asheville, take I-40 West to Exit 27. Take Hwy. 19/23 South to Lakeshore Drive.

Shook Museum

The Shook Museum is housed in the historic Shook-Smathers house in Clyde NC. The original "Shook" portion of the house dates back to between 1810 and 1820. It is the oldest frame structure still standing in Haywood County.

Outstanding in its architectural detail, the Shook-Smathers house offers a fascinating glimpse into life in North Carolina years ago. The museum docents give regularly scheduled tours.

Location:	Clyde, NC
Address:	178 Morgan Street, Clyde NC 28721
Distance:	45 minutes from Asheville
Telephone:	828-620-2300
Website:	www.shookmuseum.org
Hours:	Saturday 10 a.m.-2 p.m. Tours at other times by appointment only
Fees:	$5 adults, $3 students.
Allow:	2 hours
Directions:	From Asheville take I-40 west and take exit 27 and US 74 towards Waynesville/Murphy. Take exit 106 to merge onto Great Smoky Mountain Expressway/US 19 toward Clyde. Turn left at Morgan Street in Clyde.

Smoky Mountain Trains

Smoky Mountain Trains is an outstanding train museum with a collection of 7,000 Lionel engines, cars and accessories, impressive operating layout, children's activity center, and gift & toy shop. The extensive collection dates back to 1918 and features such classics as the 1934 Blue Comet Passenger set and the more recent Joshua Lionel Cowen Challenger Steam Locomotives.

Location:	Bryson City, NC
Distance:	1 hour from Asheville
Address:	100 Greenlee Street, Bryson City NC 28713
Telephone:	828-488-5200, 800-872-4681
Website:	www.smokymountaintrains.com
Hours:	9 a.m.-5 p.m. 7 days a week.
Fees:	$9 adults, $5 children
Directions:	From Asheville take I-40 west. Take exit # 27 US 74 West toward Waynesville and Sylva. Take US 74 West to Bryson City. Take the second Bryson City exit # 67, turn right at the bottom of the exit ramp, turn right onto Main Street and then turn left onto Everett Street. Turn right onto Frye Street and you will see Smoky Mountain Trains straight ahead.

Stecoah Valley Cultural Arts Center

The Stecoah Valley Cultural Arts Center has its roots in the Stecoah Union School in Robbinsville, which first opened its doors in 1916. The historic school property is now the heart of the center, and consists of the restored original main school building, and adjacent gymnasium building and grounds. The Center now offers over 20 programs each year to approximately 10,000 people, and brings music to the mountains through the summer performing arts series An

Appalachian Evening, as well as the annual Mountain Music Championship, Folkmoot USA, Harvest Festival and other events. Additionally, the new Stecoah Artisans Gallery & Guild provides sales promotion and support for over 100 local and regional artists.

Location:	Robbinsville, NC
Distance:	1½-2 hours from Asheville
Address:	121 Schoolhouse Road, Robbinsville NC 28711
Telephone:	828-479-3364, Gallery 828-479-3098
Website:	www.stecoahvalleycenter.com
Hours:	Gallery: Monday-Friday 10 a.m.-5 p.m.
Fees:	None
Allow:	1-2 hours
Directions:	From Asheville take I-40 west. Take the exit for Hwy 74 (Great Smoky Mountain Expressway). Stay on Hwy 74 (four lane) you will pass Clyde, Sylva, and 8 miles past Bryson City (last chance for groceries, restaurants) turn right on Hwy 28. Turn left on Stecoah Road in Robbinsville and then sharp left at Schoolhouse Road.

The Bascom

The Bascom, a nonprofit center for the visual arts in Highlands, has a six-acre, "green," architect-designed pastoral campus where it serves people through high-quality rotating exhibitions, classes and educational presentations. The campus features historic buildings, a covered bridge, a nature trail, a 27,500 square foot main building for two-dimensional adult and children's art, a separate reconstructed Studio Barn for three-dimensional art, a café, a shop, a terrace for venue rentals, and much more. The Bascom complex and landscape, evocative of the former horse stable and agrarian landscape that once thrived there, inspires audiences of all ages and backgrounds. Individuals come together, participate in studio art classes and public programs, share cultural experiences, and enjoy the synergy of art and nature.

Location:	Highlands, NC
Distance:	1½ hours from Asheville
Address:	323 Franklin Road, Highlands, NC 28741
Telephone:	828-526-4849
Website:	http://thebascom.org
Hours:	Tuesday through Saturday, 10 a.m.–5 p.m.
Fees:	None
Allow:	1-2 hours
Directions:	From Asheville, take NC 280 West to Brevard (280 begins as Airport Rd., accessible from US 25 or I-26). NC 280 joins NC 64 just before reaching Brevard. Follow 64 West to Highlands. In Highlands, turn right onto Main Street and continue to Franklin Street.

Transylvania Heritage Museum

The Transylvania Heritage Museum presents the historical heritage of Transylvania County and its families through exhibits, educational programs, collections of artifacts, and heritage-related cultural activities. Temporary and permanent exhibits include displays of heirlooms, artifacts, genealogical exhibits, vintage photographs, and other memorabilia reflective of the history and heritage of the county.

Location:	Brevard, NC
Distance:	45 minutes from Asheville
Address:	40 West Jordan Street, Brevard NC 28712
Telephone:	828-884-2347
Website:	www.transylvaniaheritage.org
Hours:	Wednesday-Saturday 10 a.m.-5 p.m.
Fees:	None
Allow:	1 hour
Directions:	From Asheville take I-26 south and get off at exit 40. Take left onto NC280 past the Asheville Airport to Brevard. In Brevard continue past Main Street and turn right onto West Jordan Street.

Unto These Hills

One of America's most popular outdoor dramas, "Unto These Hills", is presented at the Cherokee Indian Reservation, and is the tragic and triumphant story of the Cherokee Indians. Set against the backdrop of the Great Smoky Mountains, the drama is performed under the stars on three stages in the beautiful Mountainside Theatre. Since opening in 1950, "Unto These Hills" has been seen by over five million people (*See* Section Five, Chapter 2 "Cherokee Indian Reservation").

Location:	Cherokee, NC
Distance:	2 hours from Asheville
Address:	Mountainside Theatre, Drama Road, Cherokee, NC 28719
Telephone:	866-554-4557, 800-438-1601
Hours:	Shows nightly except Sunday (June-August).
Fees:	$18 adults, $8 children (12 and under)
Allow:	Drama takes about 2 hours. Pre-show entertainment begins 40 minutes before show times.
Directions:	From Asheville, take I-40 West to Exit 27. Take Hwy. 19/23, Hwy. 74 West to Cherokee. In Cherokee turn right at Hospital Road which turns into Drama Road.

Wheels Through Time Museum

The Wheels Through Time Museum is a vintage motorcycle and automobile museum in Maggie Valley that houses a collection of over 250 rare antique motorcycles and automobiles, accompanied by an outstanding collection of memorabilia.

Location:	Maggie Valley, NC
Distance:	1½ hours from Asheville
Address:	62 Vintage Lane, Maggie Valley, NC 28751
Telephone:	828-926-6626
Website:	www.wheelsthroughtime.com
Hours:	9 a.m.-5 p.m.
Fees:	$12 adults, $10 seniors, $6 children
Directions:	From Asheville take I-40 West to exit 27 onto US-74 W toward Clyde/Waynesville (1.3 Miles). Merge onto Great Smoky Mountain ExpresswayUS-19/ 74. Exit on to U.S. 19 South to Maggie Valley (6.7 Miles). Wheels Through Time is located on the right, three miles past junction of 276 N.

World Methodist Museum

Located at beautiful Lake Junaluska, the World Methodist Museum includes the largest collection in America of artifacts and memorabilia of John Wesley and the Wesley family. The collection includes displays of antique Wedgwood pottery and oil portraits of John Wesley and other Methodist church founders.

Location:	Lake Junaluska, NC
Distance:	1 hour from Asheville
Address:	575 Lakeshore Drive, Lake Junaluska, NC 28745
Telephone:	456-9432
Hours:	Monday-Friday 9 a.m.-5 p.m.
Fees:	None
Allow:	1-2 hours
Directions:	From Asheville, take I-40 West to Exit 27. Take Hwy. 19/23 South to Lakeshore Dr., which circles the lake.

Zachary-Tolbert House Museum

Built by Mordecai Zachary in 1842, the Greek Revival Zachary-Tolbert House remains in its original state along with the world's largest collection of plain style furniture made by one craftsman where the craftsman's identity is known.

Location:	Cashiers, NC
Distance:	1½ hours from Asheville
Address:	1940 Hwy. 107 Cashiers, NC 28771
Telephone:	828-743-7710
Website:	www.cashiershistoricalsociety.org/zacharytolberthouse.htm
Hours:	11 a.m.-3 p.m. Friday & Saturday, Grounds: open daily
Fees:	None
Directions:	From Asheville take NC 280 South to Brevard. Continue on through Brevard on NC 64 to Cashiers.

Chapter Three
Retreat & Conference Centers

Western North Carolina, due in part to its overwhelming natural beauty, is home to a number of religious retreat and conference centers. These are included in this book since you may be interested in visiting one or more during your stay. As would be expected, all are in breathtaking settings and immaculately maintained. The administration at each center has indicated that they welcome all visitors.

Billy Graham Training Center at The Cove

Located in a lovely mountain cove just east of Asheville, the Billy Graham Training Center holds year-round seminars and retreats for those seeking in-depth Bible studies, and a deeper experience of God's love. The Cove features two inns: Shepherd's Inn and Pilgrim's Inn. The facilities and grounds at the Cove are especially beautiful in design and landscaping.

Telephone: 828-298-2092, 800-950-2092

Directions: From Asheville take I-40 East. Get off at Exit 55 Porters Cove Rd. Center entrance is on immediate right.

Bonclarken

Located in historic Flat Rock in the Blue Ridge Mountains of Western North Carolina, Bonclarken is nestled among acres of tall white pines, hemlocks, spruce and rhododendron.

Chatlos Chapel at The Cove

Bonclarken is owned by the Associate Reformed Presbyterian Church and is available for use year-round by any groups desiring to rent the facilities and agreeing to live within the rules and regulations governing its use. Rich in history and tradition, Bonclarken has served the Associate Reformed Presbyterian Church and others since 1922. The

Bonclarken, a haven for birds and others

beautiful hotel on the grounds was built in 1886 as a private home. Dr. Arthur Rose Guerard, a Charlestonian, came to Flat Rock to build a home for his German bride. He used only the finest materials in the parquet floors and the wainscoting, and the mantels were carved in Germany of rosewood, ebony and cherry. Bonclarken today offers a variety of facilities to individuals and groups. Complete dining, meeting, recreational and camping facilities round out the total service offering.

Telephone: 828-692-2223
Directions: From Main Street in Hendersonville go south on Hwy. 25 four miles to Pine Dr. Look for Bonclarken sign on left.

Christmount

Christmount, an agency of the Christian Church (Disciples of Christ), is located one mile south of Black Mountain. The Christmount conference center occupies one square mile of mountain land, cooled by numerous springs and creeks, at an elevation of just under 3,000 feet. Christmount is open year-round with a variety of accommodations including the Gaines M. Cook Guest House, the Guest House East, Davis

Prayer garden at Christmount

Hall, Holly Park, and camp cabins. Most camps and conferences are related to the Christian Church (Disciples of Christ).

Telephone: 828-669-8977
Directions: Exit from I-40 in Black Mountain onto Hwy. 9 (Exit 54). Go south one mile to gate on left.

Kanuga Lake

Kanuga

Kanuga is a year-round conference facility, closely affiliated with the Episcopal Church. Kanuga maintains the following programs: Kanuga-sponsored conferences, two summer camps for young people, parish family weekends, guest accommodations, Mountain Trail Outdoor School, retreats, national and regional programs sponsored by the Episcopal Church, and a special camp session for homeless, abused, and disadvantaged children.

Located near Hendersonville, Kanuga's extensive conference center and camp facilities are situated on 1,400 acres of woodland, crisscrossed by streams, ridges and valleys. There is a 30-acre lake, ponds, and complete outdoor recreational facilities and accommodations that range from rustic cottages to the spacious and modern Kanuga Inn.

Telephone: 828-692-9136
Directions: From I-26, take Exit 18 onto US 64 West into Hendersonville. Turn left on Hwy. 25 South (Church Street) and drive 9 blocks. Turn right onto Kanuga Street, go 4 miles to Kanuga triangular sign. Turn right, drive 1½ miles to Kanuga Entrance Park. Turn right and go ½ mile.

Lake Junaluska

Lake Junaluska Assembly

Nestled in the mountains of Western North Carolina west of Asheville, Lake Junaluska Assembly is the conference and retreat center for the Southeastern Jurisdiction of the United Methodist Church, and home of the SEJ Administrative Council. The Assembly provides a wide variety of accommodations and conference facilities which will comfortably support groups ranging in size from 5 to 2,000. The Assembly welcomes individuals, families, church groups, educational organizations and many other groups. The 200-acre Lake Junaluska is surrounded by 1,200 acres of beautiful rolling hills and valleys. Located on the lake is the Cokesbury Gift Shop, which carries gifts, books and crafts.

Telephone: 828-452-2881, 800-222-4930
Directions: From Asheville, take I-40 West to Exit 27 to 19/23. Lake Junaluska is a few miles on the right.

Lifeway Ridgecrest Conference Center

Lifeway Ridgecrest Conference Center began in 1907 as a summer retreat for Southern Baptists. Today Ridgecrest thrives as a year-round conference center, attracting over 60,000 guests a year. While the Sunday School Board of the Southern Baptist Convention owns and operates the conference center, Ridgecrest attracts Christian groups from diverse backgrounds, as well as nonprofit organizations, school groups, and government groups. Ridgecrest offers over 52,000 square feet of conference space, eighty-one conference rooms, and three auditoriums of various sizes. Outstanding dining and recreational facilities are also available to guests.

Telephone: 828-669-8022, 800-588-7222
Directions: From Asheville, take I-40 East and get off at Exit 66. At top of ramp, turn left. At the first junction, turn right onto Old US 70 and continue a short distance to Ridgecrest

Lutheridge Conference Center & Camp

Lutheridge is a 160-acre conference center and camp atop scenic Crescent Hill just south of Asheville.
The Center offers an intimate setting that boasts a mix of comfortable adult lodging and rustic cabins for youth, modern conveniences, and beautiful year-round scenery. Lutheridge is owned and operated by the North Carolina, South Carolina, Southeastern and Florida-Bahamas synods of the Evangelical Lutheran Church in America (ELCA).

Entrance gate at Lutheridge

Telephone: 828-684-2361
Directions: Take Exit 9 Airport Rd. off I-26 South. Proceed to Rt. 25, Hendersonville Rd. Lutheridge is located south on Hendersonville Rd.

Montreat Conference Center

Montreat Conference Center, a conference center of the Presbyterian Church (U.S.A.) is located 15 miles east of Asheville, just outside Black Mountain. Montreat is a special place to meet and enjoy the refreshing sights and sounds of the Blue Ridge Mountains. With 29 meeting facilities, Montreat offers a comfortable environment for conferences, retreats seminars or other special gatherings. Year-round facilities include a number of options

Left Bank Building on Lake Susan at Montreat Conference Center

available for housing, dining, classrooms, and recreation. Montreat's beautiful setting makes it the perfect place for all types of outdoor recreation. Hiking on marked trails in the surrounding mountains, swimming in the outdoor Olympic-size pool, and boating and canoeing on Lake Susan are among the many options. Montreat also has superb guest accommodations including Assembly Inn, and the Winnsborough.

Telephone: 828-669-2911, 800-572-2257

Directions: Take I-40 West from Asheville. Get off at Exit 64, Black Mountain. Go north on Route 9 through Black Mountain, two miles to the Montreat Gate.

YMCA Blue Ridge Assembly

Located in Black Mountain, 15 miles east of Asheville, is the YMCA Blue Ridge Assembly. Founded in 1906 as a YMCA student conference center, the Assembly has hosted over half a million people in its rich history. Blue Ridge serves a diverse mix of not-for-profit religious, social, educational and family groups. Nestled on over 1,200 acres of woodlands, YMCA Blue Ridge Assembly provides restful surroundings for groups large and small and a variety of comfortable accommodations that range from hotel-style to cottages. Blue Ridge also offers a diverse range of meeting facilities, and numerous recreational options. In the summer, Blue Ridge is known for its plentiful and delicious food served family style.

Telephone: 828-669-8422

Directions: From Asheville take I-40 East. Get off at Exit 64 and go south on Hwy. 9. Proceed less than ½ mile and bear right on Blue Ridge Rd. Turn left at the small Blue Ridge Assembly sign.

Robert E. Lee Hall at YMCA Blue Ridge Assembly

Valle Crucis Conference Center

Secluded in an area of spectacular beauty near Boone, the Valle Crucis Conference Center overlooks a peaceful, rural valley in the Blue Ridge Mountains. An outreach of the Episcopal Diocese of Western North Carolina, the Conference Center is located on 448 acres of lush wooded mountain and open valley land, with bold rushing streams and waterfalls. Groups come to Valle Crucis for spiritual and personal renewal, including family reunions, and the Center offers a ministry of hospitality to a diverse range of church and non-profit groups from around the Southeast. The Center is also right up the road from the original Mast General Store. Grandfather Mountain is close by, and Blowing Rock and Boone are nearby for shopping, etc.

Telephone: 828-963-4453; e-mail: vccc@highsouth.com; web site: www.high-south.com/vallecrucis

Directions: From Asheville take take I-40 East to US-70 exit (Old Fort exit). Exit onto US-70 East toward Old Fort and Marion. Drive approximately eleven (11) miles to intersection with US-221 in Marion. Turn left onto US-221 North. Drive approximately 35 miles to the intersection with NC-105 in Linville. Turn left onto NC-105 North. Drive approximately twelve (12) miles to the traffic light at Broadstone Road (State Road 1112, just before the Watauga River Bridge). Turn left onto Broadstone Road. Drive approximately three (3) miles to the intersection with NC-194 (in front of Valle Crucis Elementary School). Turn left onto NC-194 South. Drive approximately 1.3 miles, past the Valle Crucis Conference Center.

Chapter Four
Western North Carolina Cities & Towns

Andrews

Andrews is a beautiful small town located within the heart of the Western North Carolina Mountains that is largely untouched by large city influences. In today's hectic, modern world, Andrews remains a place that enjoy a more leisurely pace of life. The city has a thriving downtown with restaurants, retail shops, bed and breakfast inns, and artists' galleries and is a great jumping off point for outdoor adventures in the surrounding mountains.

The highest elevation near Andrews in Cherokee County is 5,149 feet, near Tusquitee Bald in the Fires Creek area, and the 466 square mile county encompasses 300,000 acres, with over 90,000 of those owned by the US Forest Service. Andrews is also home to the Andrews Art Museum run by the Valleytown Cultural Arts and Historical Society. The museum has rotating exhibits of local and regional artists. A unique activity in Andrews is the annual Western North Carolina Wagon Train, where wagon train enthusiasts annually make the trek from Andrews to Walhalla, South Carolina in covered wagons and on horseback.

Location: Western Mountains, 2 hours west of Asheville
Town Hall: 1101 Main Street, Andrews NC 28901; 828-321-3113
Website: www.andrewsnc.com
County: Cherokee County: County Offices, 75 Peachtree Street, Murphy NC 28906; 828-837-5527
Elevation & Population: 2,350 feet, 1,600+
Visitor/Welcome Center: Cherokee County Welcome Center, 805 West Highway 64, Murphy NC 28906, 828-837-2242
City Chamber of Commerce: Andrews Chamber of Commerce, 345 Locust Street, Andrews NC 28901, 877-558-0005
County Chamber of Commerce: Cherokee County Chamber of Commerce, 805 West Highway 64, Murphy NC 28906, 828-837-2242

Newspaper: Andrews Journal, PO Box 250, Chestnut Street, Andrews NC 28901; 828-321-4271

Movie Theatres: Andrews Twin Cinema, 125 Main Street, Andrews NC 28901, 828-321-3333

High School: Andrews High School, 50 High School Drive, Andrews NC 28901; 828-321-5415

Area Major Festivals: Andrews Valley Music Festival (June)

Area Natural Attractions: Chatuge Lake, Joyce Kilmer Memorial Forest, Lake Santeetlah, Nantahala Lake, Nantahala National Forest, Nantahala River

Area Cultural Attractions: Andrews Art Museum, Cherokee County Historical Museum, Great Smoky Mountains Railroad

Recommended Restaurants: (For a complete list of all restaurants visit www.ashevilleguidebook.com)

> **Chestnuts Cafe:** (County-American) 493 Main Street, Andrews NC 28901; 828-321-4566
>
> **Elsie's Steak and Seafood:** (American, Seafood) 358 W. Main Street, Andrews NC 28901; 828-321-4915

Recommended Places To Stay: (For a complete list of all accommodations visit www.ashevilleguidebook.com)

> **Andrews Southern Charm Bed & Breakfast:** (B&B) 11 Railroad Street, Andrews NC 28901; 828-321-2348
>
> **Country Hearth Inn:** (County Inn) 138 Country Hearth Lane, Andrews NC 28901; 888-777-7901
>
> **Cozad-Cover House:** (B&B) 1194 Main Street, Andrews NC 28901; 828-321-1017
>
> **Hawkesdene House Mountain Retreat:** (County Lodge) 381 Phillips Creek Road, Andrews NC 28901; 800-447-9549

Bakersville

Bakersville, founded in the mid 1800's and incorporated in 1870, is the home of the famous North Carolina Rhododendron Festival held every spring during the height of the blooming season. The county seat of Mitchell County, Bakersville still retains the charm of a small mountain community, and is a convenient jumping-off point to explore the surrounding mountains. Every spring the Bakersville Creek Walk Arts Festival is held along the banks of Cane Creek, with over 50 artists and crafters displaying their work. Bakersville also has two farmer's markets open every Saturday morning-the Bakersville Farmers Market and the Community Market held at the Creek Walk pavilion.

Location: Central Mountains, 1 hour northeast of Asheville
Town Hall: 26 South Mitchell Avenue, Bakersville NC 28705; 828-688-2113
Website: www.bakersville.com
County: Mitchell County: County Administration Building, 26 Crimson Laurel Circle, Bakersville NC 28705; 828-688-2139

Elevation & Population: 2,460 feet, 350+

County Visitor Center: Mitchell County Visitor Center; Located in the Museum of NC Minerals, Milepost 331, Blue Ridge Parkway; Spruce Pine NC 28777; 800-227-3912

County Chamber of Commerce: Mitchell County Chamber of Commerce: 11 Crystal Street, Spruce Pine NC 28777; 828-765-9033

Newspaper: Mitchell News-Journal 291 Locust Avenue, Spruce Pine 28777; 828-765-2071

Movie Theatres: None

High School: Mitchell High School, 416 Ledger School Road, Bakersville NC 28705; 828-688-2101

Area Major Festivals: North Carolina Rhododendron Festival (June)

Area Natural Attractions: Mount Mitchell State Park

Area Cultural Attractions: Penland Gallery & School of Crafts

Recommended Restaurants: (For a complete list of all restaurants visit www. ashevilleguidebook.com)

> **Dot's Coffee Shoppe Cafe:** (County-American) 24 Mitchell Avenue, Bakersville NC 28705; 828-688-3789

> **Helen's Restaurant:** (County-American) 99 N 226 Hwy, Bakersville NC 28705; 828-688-9999

> **White Wolf Restaurant:** (County-American) 5253 Hwy 226, Bakersville NC 28705; 828-688-4770

Recommended Places To Stay: (For a complete list of all accommodations visit www.ashevilleguidebook.com)

> **Bakersville Bed & Breakfast:** (B&B) 79 N. Mitchell Avenue, Bakersville NC 28705; 877-688-6012

> **Doanie Mama's Big House and Guest House:** (County Lodge) 309 N. Mitchell Avenue, Bakersville NC 28705; 828- 688-3456

Banner Elk

Banner's Elk, as the village was once called, was settled around 1850, and is located in the northeast section of the mountains in Avery County, Banner Elk is a quaint mountain community that offers tourist activities including skiing and snowboarding at the world famous Sugar Mountain Resort. Golf, hiking & backpacking, horseback riding and whitewater rafting are also available. Surrounded by high peaks and rugged ridges, Banner Elk has strong historic and cultural ties with the neighboring mountainous regions of Tennessee and Virginia as well as Western North Carolina. Lees-McRae College has been located in the area for over 100 years and the College Drama Department presents theatrical productions during the summer months. Banner Elk is also host every October to the famous Woolly Worm Festival.

Location: Northern Mountains, 2 hours east of Asheville

Town Offices: 200 Park Avenue, Banner Elk NC 28604; 828-898-5398

Website: www.townofbannerelk.org

County: Avery County: County Administrative Building, 175 Linville Street, Newland NC 28657; 828-733-8202

Elevation & Population: 3,739 feet, 950+

City Chamber of Commerce: Banner Elk Chamber of Commerce: 100 West Main Street, Banner Elk NC 28604; 828-898-8395

County Chamber of Commerce: Avery County Chamber of Commerce: 4501 Tynecastle Highway, Unit #2, Banner Elk NC 28604; 800-972-2183

Newspaper: The Mountain Times PO Box 1815, Boone NC 28607; 828-264-6397

High School: Avery County High School, 401 High School Road, Newland NC 28657; 828-733-0151

Colleges and Universities: Lees-McRae College, 191 Main Street, Banner Elk NC 28604; 828-898-5241

Area Major Festivals: Woolly Worm Festival (October)

Area Natural Attractions: Blue Ridge Parkway, Grandfather Mountain, Linville Caverns, Linville Gorge,

Area Cultural Attractions: Avery County Historical Museum, Banner House Museum, Crossnore Fine Arts Gallery, Horn in the West, Mast General Store, Mystery Hill, Orchard at Altapass, Tweetsie Railroad

Recommended Restaurants: (For a complete list of all restaurants visit www. ashevilleguidebook.com)

> **Hearthstone Tavern & Grille:** (Casual-American) 3990 Highway 105, Banner Elk NC 28604; 828-898-3461
>
> **Jackalope's View:** (Casual-Continental) 2489 Beech Mountain Parkway, Banner Elk NC 28604; 888-827-6155
>
> **Louisana Purchase Food and Spirits:** (Cajun) 537 Shawneehaw Avenue, Banner Elk NC 28694; 828-963-5087
>
> **Sorrentos Bistro:** (Italian) 147 Azalea Circle, Banner Elk NC 28604; 828-898-5214
>
> **The Mast Farm Inn:** (American) 2543 Broadstone Road, Banner Elk NC 28604; 828-963-5857

Recommended Places To Stay: (For a complete list of all accommodations visit www.ashevilleguidebook.com)

> **Archers Mountain Inn:** (Hotel) 2489 Beech Mountain Parkway, Banner Elk NC 28604; 888-827-6155
>
> **Banner Elk Inn B&B and Cottages:** (B&B) 407 E. Main Street, Banner Elk NC 28604; 888-487-8263
>
> **Little Main Street Inn & Suites:** (Village Inn) 607 Main Street East, Banner Elk NC 28604; 800-851-4397
>
> **The Mast Farm Inn:** (B&B) 2543 Broadstone Road, Banner Elk NC 28604; 888-963-5857
>
> **1902 Turnpike House Bed & Breakfast:** (B&B) 317 Old Turnpike Road, Banner Elk NC 28604; 888-802-4487

Beech Mountain

The town of Beech Mountain, originally begun as a private resort development in the mid 1960's and incorporated in 1981, is today known for its world-famous ski resort, Beech Mountain Resort, as well as its cool summer weather where temperatures rarely get above 72 degrees. Located in the northeast section of the Western North Carolina mountains, upscale Beech Mountain is the highest in elevation of all towns in the northeastern United States at 5,506 feet above sea level. Offering a nice selection of stores and restaurants, as well as a large choice of outdoor sports, Beech Mountain is a year-round destination. When October rolls around, Beech Mountain magically transforms into the Land of Oz in their annual Autumn at Oz Festival, complete with all your favorite people and places from Frank Baum's silver screen classic.

Location: Northern Mountains, 2 hours east of Asheville
Town Offices: 403 Beech Mountain Parkway, Beech Mountain NC 28604; 828-387-4862
Website: www.townofbeechmountain.com
County: Avery County: County Administrative Building, 175 Linville Street, Newland NC 28657; 828-733-8202
Elevation & Population: 5,506 feet, 300+
City Chamber of Commerce: Beech Mountain Chamber of Commerce 403-A Beech Mountain Parkway, Beech Mountain NC 28604; 800-468-5506
County Chamber of Commerce: Avery County Chamber of Commerce: 4501 Tynecastle Highway, Unit #2, Banner Elk NC 28604; 800-972-2183
Newspaper: The Mountain Times PO Box 1815, Boone NC 28607; 828-264-6397
High School: Avery County High School, 401 High School Road, Newland NC 28657; 828-733-0151
Area Major Festivals: Autumn at Oz Festival (October), Annual Roasting of the Hog & Fireworks Display (July)
Area Natural Attractions: Blue Ridge Parkway, Grandfather Mountain, Linville Caverns, Linville Gorge,
Area Cultural Attractions: Avery County Historical Museum Banner House Museum, Crossnore Fine Arts Gallery, Horn in the West, Mast General Store, Mystery Hill, Orchard at Altapass, Tweetsie Railroad
Recommended Restaurants: (For a complete list of all restaurants visit www.ashevilleguidebook.com)
    Alpen Restaurant & Bar: (American) 700 Beech Mountain Parkway, Beech Mountain NC 28604; 828-387-2011
    Jackalope's View: (Casual-Continental) 2489 Beech Mountain Parkway, Beech Mountain NC 28604; 888-827-6155
Recommended Places To Stay: (For a complete list of all accommodations visit www.ashevilleguidebook.com)

Archers Mountain Inn: (Hotel) 2489 Beech Mountain Parkway, Beech Mountain NC 28604; 888-827-6155

Beech Alpen Inn: (Country Inn) 700 Beech Mountain Parkway, Beech Mountain NC 28604; 866-284-2770

Black Mountain

Located just fifteen miles east of Asheville on Interstate 40 is the charming mountain city of Black Mountain, known as "The Front Porch of Western North Carolina". One of the hallmarks of Black Mountain is the magnificent view of the nearby Black Mountains, including Mount Mitchell, the highest peak east of the Mississippi River and the famous Seven Sisters range. Known for its arts & crafts and antiques, Black Mountain has many top quality galleries, antique and specialty shops, bookstores, and furniture stores. The epicenter of this eclectic mix of stores is the historic Cherry Street district. The community also offers a diverse program of outdoor recreation with golf at the Black Mountain Golf Club, public tennis, ball-fields, croquet, and walking paths, including a spectacular one at Lake Tomahawk.

In the Swannanoa Valley, where Black Mountain is located, there are several religious conference centers including Montreat Conference Center, Lifeway Ridgecrest Conference Center, and the YMCA Blue Ridge Assembly. Famous residents include Evangelist Billy Graham, former NBA star Brad Dougherty, and Minnesota Vikings quarterback Brad Johnson. In the late summer, Black Mountain also is host to the famous Sourwood Festival and the bi-annual Lake Eden Arts Festival, also known as LEAF.

The Swannanoa Valley, home to the unincorporated community of Swannanoa, has been a coveted spot for hundreds of years. The Cherokee Indians guarded the mountainous ridges while would-be settlers from what is now Old Fort looked westward towards the game-filled forests. The Cherokee boundary was moved farther west in the late 1780s and settlers rapidly rushed through the Swannanoa Gap into the coves to establish homesteads along the many creeks and rivers. By 1850, there was a turnpike up the mountains from the east, but one so steep that wheels on the wagons had to be larger on one side to make the journey up and then switched to the other side to make the journey down. In 1879, the railroad arrived and changed things forever. Black Mountain has been known as a tourist destination and a wonderful place to vacation and live ever since.

Montreat is a small residential community adjacent to Black Mountain, located in a secluded mountain cove at the foot of Greybeard Mountain. Montreat is home to the Montreat Conference Center which currently hosts religious conferences throughout the year, and Montreat College, a four-year Christian liberal arts college affiliated with the Presbyterian Church (USA).

Location: Central Mountains, 15 minutes east of Asheville
Town Offices: 160 Midland Avenue, Black Mountain NC 28711; 828-419-9300
Website: www.townofblackmountain.org

County: Buncombe County: County Offices, 205 College Street, Asheville NC 28801; 828-250-4000

Elevation & Population: 2405 feet, 7500+

Visitor/Welcome Center: Black Mountain-Swannanoa Visitor Center 201 East State St., Black Mountain, NC 28711; 800-669-2301

City Chamber of Commerce: Black Mountain-Swannanoa Chamber of Commerce 201 East State St., Black Mountain, NC 28711; 800-669-2301

County Chamber of Commerce: Buncombe County Chamber of Commerce 205 College Street, Asheville NC 28801; 828-250-4100

Newspaper: Black Mountain News 14 O Henry Avenue, Asheville NC 28801; 828-669-8727

High School: Owen High School, 99 Lake Eden Road, Black Mountain NC 28711; 828-686-3852

Colleges and Universities: Montreat College, 310 Gaither Circle, Montreat NC 28757; 800-622-6968

Area Major Festivals: Lake Eden Arts Festival (LEAF) (May & October) Sourwood Festival (August).

Area Natural Attractions: Mount Mitchell State Park, Pisgah National Forest

Area Cultural Attractions: Lifeway Ridgecrest Conference Center, Montreat Conference Center, Old Depot Gallery & Caboose Museum, Swannanoa Valley Museum, YMCA Blue Ridge Assembly

Recommended Restaurants: (For a complete list of all restaurants visit www.ashevilleguidebook.com)

> **Que Sera Restaurant:** (American) 400 East State Street, Black Mountain NC 28711; 828-664-9472
>
> **Red Rocker Inn:** (American) 136 N. Dougherty Street, Black Mountain NC 28711; 888-669-5991
>
> **The Madison Inn:** (American) 15 Dixon Drive, Black Mountain NC 28711; 828-669-4785
>
> **Black Mountain Bistro:** (American) 203 E. State Street, Black Mountain NC 28711; 828-669-5041
>
> **Morning Glory Cafe:** (Cafe-Breakfast & Lunch) 6 East Market Street, Village of Cheshire, Black Mountain NC 28711; 828-669-6212.
>
> **Veranda Cafe:** (Cafe) 119 Cherry Street, Black Mountain NC 28711; 828-669-8864

Recommended Places To Stay: (For a complete list of all accommodations visit www.ashevilleguidebook.com)

> **Arbor House of Black Mountain:** (B&B) 207 Rhododendron Avenue, Black Mountain NC 28711; 866-669-9303
>
> **Bella Luna Inn:** (B&B) 99 Terry Estate Drive, Black Mountain NC 28711; 800-249-6979
>
> **Raspberry Hill Bed & Breakfast:** (B&B) 77 Stroud Valley Road, Black Mountain NC 28711; 828-669-7031

Red Rocker Inn: (Hotel-Village Inn) 126 N. Dougherty Street, Black Mountain NC 28711; 888-6690-5991

The Madison Inn: (B&B) 15 Dixon Drive, Black Mountain NC 28711; 828-669-4785

Tree Haven Bed &Breakfast: (B&B) 1120 Montreat Road, Black Mountain NC 28711; 888-448-3841

Blowing Rock

The quaint upscale resort village of Blowing Rock sits aside the Eastern Continental Divide in the Northern Mountains of Western North Carolina and is centrally located to most of the major area attractions. There is a professional summer stock theatre (the Blowing Rock Stage Company), wonderful festivals, Art in the Park and the Blue Ridge Wine and Food Festival, and abundant outdoor recreational opportunities, including skiing at Appalachian Ski Mountain. Its rich history stretches back to the 1500s, when the famous explorer Desoto supposedly looked for gold in the area. The town is named after its main attraction, The Blowing Rock, cliff walls that form a flume through which the north-west wind sweeps with such force that it returns light objects cast over the cliff. Another of Blowing Rock's main attractions is the Moses H. Cone Memorial Park. The park, once a 3,500 acre estate, was donated by Moses H. Cone and now includes 26 miles of horse and carriage trails, which are also used for hiking and cross-country skiing, and a deer park.

Location: Northern Mountains, 2 hours west of Asheville
Town Offices: 1036 Main Street, Blowing Rock NC 28605; 828-95-5200
Website: www.townofblowingrock.com
County: Watauga County: County Offices, 814 West King Street, Suite 205, Boone NC 28607; 828-265-8000
Elevation & Population: 4,000 feet, 1,500+
Visitor/Welcome Center: Blowing Rock Visitor Center, 7738 Valley Boulevard, Blowing Rock, NC 28605; 877-750-4636
City Chamber of Commerce: Blowing Rock Chamber of Commerce, 7738 Valley Boulevard, Blowing Rock NC 28605; 828-295-7851
Newspaper: The Blowing Rocket, 452-1 Sunset Drive, Blowing Rock NC 28605; 828-295-7522
High School: Watauga High School, 400 High School Drive, Boone NC 28607; 828-264-2407
Hospitals: Blowing Rock Hospital, 418 Chestnut Drive, Blowing Rock NC 28605; 828-295-3136
Area Major Festivals: Art in the Park (Monthly: May-October) Blue Ridge Wine and Food Festival (April)
Area Natural Attractions: Blue Ridge Parkway, Grandfather Mountain, Linville Caverns, Linville Gorge, Moses H Cone Memorial Park, Pisgah National Forest, The Blowing Rock

Area Cultural Attractions: Appalachian Heritage Museum, Appalachian Ski Mountain, Mariam & Robert Hayes Performing Arts Center, Mystery Hill, Orchard at Altapass, Tweetsie Railroad

Recommended Restaurants: (For a complete list of all restaurants visit www. ashevilleguidebook.com)

> **Best Cellar:** (American) The Inn at Ragged Garden, 203 Sunset Drive, Blowing Rock NC 28605; 828-295-3466
>
> **Bistro Roca:** (American Bistro) 143 Wonderland Trail, Blowing Rock NC 28605; 828-295-4008
>
> **Blowing Rock Grille and Bert's Bar:** (American) 349 Sunset Drive, Blowing Rock NC 28605; 828-295-9474
>
> **Canyons:** (American-Eclectic) 8960 Valley Boulevard, Blowing Rock NC 28605; 828-295-7661
>
> **Crippens Restaurant:** (Fine Dining) 239 Sunset Drive, Blowing Rock NC 28605; 877-295-3487
>
> **Speckled Trout Cafe & Oyster Bar:** (American) 922 Main Street, Blowing Rock NC 28605; 828-295-9819
>
> **Storie Street Grille:** (American Bistro-Mediterranean) 1167 Main Street, Blowing Rock NC 28605; 828-295-7075
>
> **Twigs Restaurant:** (Continental) 7956 Valley Boulevard, Blowing Rock NC 28605; 828-295-5050

Recommended Places To Stay: (For a complete list of all accommodations visit www.ashevilleguidebook.com)

> **Azalea Garden Inn:** (Village Inn) 793 North Main Street, Blowing Rock NC 28605; 828-295-3272
>
> **Blowing Rock Victorian Inn:** (B&B) 242 Ransom Street, Blowing Rock NC 28605; 828-295-0034
>
> **Chetola Resort at Blowing Rock:** (Resort Inn) 185 Chetola Lake Drive, Blowing Rock NC 28605; 800-243-8652
>
> **Gideon Ridge Inn:** (County Inn) 202 Gideon Ridge Road, Blowing Rock NC 28605; 828-295-3644
>
> **Maple Lodge Bed & Breakfast:** (B&B) 152 Sunset Drive, Blowing Rock NC 28605; 866-795-3331
>
> **Meadowbrook Inn:** (Hotel) 711 Main Street, Blowing Rock NC 28605; 828-295-4300
>
> **Ridgeway Inn:** (Village Inn) 131 Yonahlossee Road, Blowing Rock NC 28605; 828-295-7321
>
> **Yonahlossee Resort:** (Resort) Shulls Mill Road, Blowing Rock NC 28605; 800-962-1986
>
> **Westglow Resort & Spa:** (Resort) 2845 US Highway 221 South, Blowing Rock NC 28605; 800-562-0807

Boone

Located just off the Blue Ridge Parkway in the northeast section of the mountains, Boone, incorporated in 1872, is a destination in very much the same way Asheville is. Consistently ranked as one of the "Best Small Towns in America," Boone is a bustling town and the center of tourism and commerce for Watauga County and the region. With a population of over 15,000, the city is home to Appalachian State University, which adds a distinctive college atmosphere to the already vibrant, outdoors oriented mountain city. Boone is located in the "Heart of the High Country" and has a wide array of stores, restaurants, galleries and things to do. It is even known as the "Firefly Capital of America!" Named for Daniel Boone, the frontiersman who lived in the area from 1760 to 1769, this tourist-oriented mountain city has much to offer the visitor.

Boone also has the highest elevation of any town of its size east of the Mississippi River and because of that, on average, the city receives over 40" of snowfall a year, far more than most other cities in North Carolina. In 2005, Boone was recognized by travel journalists as the ultimate outdoor adventure destination in the Southeast. Along with Durango, Colorado, Bend, Oregon and North Vancouver, British Columbia, Boone was selected as one of four multi-sport vacation destinations in North America, featured in an article in the May 2005 issue of Adventure Sports Magazine. In the winter, one of the major draws to Boone is the many ski and snowboarding resorts in the area. These include Appalachian Ski Mountain, Sugar Mountain Resort, Beech Mountain Resort and Hawksnest Tubing Park.

Boone also has one of North Carolina's most progressive public school systems. All eight K-8 schools are ranked as Schools of Excellence, a claim to fame no other public school district in the state can match.

Location: Northern Mountains, 2 hours east of Asheville
Town Offices: 567 West King Street, Boone NC 28607; 828-268-6200
Website: www.townofboone.net
County: Watauga County: County Offices, 842 West King Street, Boone NC 28607; 828-265-8000
Elevation & Population: 3,500 feet, 15,000+
Visitor/Welcome Center: Boone Convention & Visitor Center, 208 Howard Street, Boone NC 28607; 800-852-9506, 828-262-3516
City Chamber of Commerce: Boone Area Chamber of Commerce, 208 Howard Street, Boone NC 28607; 828-264-2225
County Chamber of Commerce: Boone Area Chamber of Commerce 208 Howard Street, Boone NC 28607; 828-264-2225
Newspaper: The Watauga Democrat 474 Industrial Park Drive, Boone NC 28607; 828-264-3612 and The Mountain Times PO Box 1815, Boone NC 28607; 828-264-6397
Movie Theatres: Regal Boone Cinema 7 210 New Market Street Centre, Boone NC 28607; 828-262-3330

High School: Watauga High School, 400 High School Drive, Boone NC 28607; 828-264-2407

Colleges and Universities: Appalachian State University, ASU Box 32003, Boone NC 28608; 828-262-2000

Hospitals: Watauga Medical Center, 336 Deerfield Road, Boone NC 28607; 828-262-4100

Area Major Festivals: Daniel Boone Days (Sept), High Country Bluegrass Festival (June), MusicFest 'n Sugar Grove (July)

Area Natural Attractions: Blue Ridge Parkway, Grandfather Mountain, Pisgah National Forest

Area Cultural Attractions: Hickory Ridge Homestead, Horn in the West, Mast General Store, Turchin Center for Visual Arts, Tweetsie Railroad

Recommended Restaurants: (For a complete list of all restaurants visit www.ashevilleguidebook.com)

   Cafe Portofino: (Eclectic-Thai, Eurasian, Italian) 970 Rivers Street, Boone NC 28607; 828-264-7772

   Capone's Pizza & Bar: (Pizza) 454 B West King Street, Boone NC 28607; 828-265-1886

   Casa Rustica: (Italian-American) 1348 Highway 105 South, Boone NC 28607; 828-262-5128

   Char: (American) 179 Howard Street, Boone NC 28607; 828-266-2179

   Daniel Boone Inn: (American Family Style) 130 Hardin Street, Boone NC 28607; 828-264-8657

   Dos Amigos: (Mexican) 187 New Market Center, Boone NC 28607; 828-265-1674

   Makoto: (Japanese) 2124 Blowing Rock Road, Boone NC 28607; 828-264-7770

   Pepper's Restaurant: (American) 240 Shadowline Drive #4, Boone NC 28607; 828-262-1250

   Red Onion Café: (Cafe-Eclectic) 227 Hardin Street, Boone NC 28607; 828-264-5470

   The Gamekeeper Restaurant: (Southern-Gourmet) 3005 Shulls Mill Road, Boone NC 28607; 828-963-7400

Recommended Places To Stay: (For a complete list of all accommodations visit www.ashevilleguidebook.com)

   Broyhill Inn & Appalachian Conference Center: (Hotel) 775 Bodenheimer Drive, Boone NC 28607; 800-951-6048

   Country Inn & Suite: (Motel) 818 East King Street, Boone NC 28607; 828-264-4234

   Crestwood Resort: (Resort, Spa) 3236 Shulls Mill Road, Boone NC 28607; 877-836-5046

   Fairfield Inn & Suites by Marriott: (Motel) 2060 Blowing Rock Road, Boone NC 28607; 828-268-0677

   Hampton Inn: (Motel) 1075 Highway 105; Boone NC 28607; 828-264-8845

Highland Hills Motel & Cabins: (Cabins) 2748 Highway 105 South, Boone NC 28607; 800-948-5276

Lovill House Inn: (B&B) 404 Old Bristol Road, Boone NC 28607; 800-849-9466

Parkway Cabins: (Cabins) 749 Turkey Knob, Boone NC 28607; 866-679-3002

Whispering Hills Resort: (Resort) 136 Virgil Day Road, Boone NC 28607; 828-963-0018

Brevard

Located in the heart of Transylvania County, Brevard is a wonderful small town that is not only a great place to live but also a renowned tourist destination. In downtown Brevard you'll find all of the familiar touchstones of a classic American small town-an old-fashioned soda shop, a 1930s-era movie theater, even a locally-owned hardware store. And surrounding the city are hundreds of thousands of acres of pristine wilderness, protected forever in the Dupont State Forest, Gorges State Park, and Pisgah National Forests. Brevard is also right at the center of one of the most famous waterfall regions in America. In fact Transylvania County is known as "The Land of Waterfalls." Over 250 are located within a short drive of downtown.

Brevard is also home to a colony of white squirrels that even have their own festival, the White Squirrel Festival, and to the Brevard Music Festival, one of the best music festivals in America. Brevard College, a small, private, United Methodist liberal arts college, is the educational centerpiece of Brevard, and its lovely campus is located just east of downtown.

Location: Central Mountains, 45 minutes west of Asheville

Municipal Building: 151 West Main Street, Brevard NC 28712; 828-885-5601

Website: www.cityofbrevard.com

County: Transylvania County: County Offices, 21 East Main Street, Brevard NC 28712; 828-884-3100

Elevation & Population: 2,200 feet, 7,000+

Visitor/Welcome Center: Transylvania County Tourism Development Authority, 175 East Main Street, Brevard NC 28712; 800-648-4523

Resource Website: Heart of Brevard 175 East Main Street, Suite 200, Brevard NC 28712; 828-884-3278

City Chamber of Commerce: Brevard Transylvania Chamber of Commerce, 175 East Main Street, Brevard NC 28712; 828-883-3700

Newspaper: The Transylvania Times 37 North Broad Street, Brevard NC 28712; 828-883-8156

Movie Theatres: Falls Co-Ed Cinema, 79 W. Main Street, Brevard NC 28712; 828-883-2200

High School: Brevard High School, 747 Country Club Road, Brevard NC 28712; 828-884-4103

Colleges and Universities: Brevard College, One Brevard College Drive, Brevard NC 28712; 828-883-8292

Hospitals: Transylvania County Hospital, 260 Hospital Drive, I 28712; 828-884-9111

Area Major Festivals: Brevard Music Festival (June-August), White Squirrel Festival (May), Mountain Song Festival (September)

Area Natural Attractions: Dupont State Forest, Gorges State Park, Pisgah National Forest, Waterfalls in Western North Carolina,

Area Cultural Attractions: Allison-Deaver House, Brevard Little Theatre, Brevard Music Center, Cradle of Forestry, Pisgah Center for Wildlife Education, Transylvania Heritage Museum

Recommended Restaurants: (For a complete list of all restaurants visit www.ashevilleguidebook.com)

    Dugan's Pub: (Irish) 29 West French Broad Street, Suite 101, Brevard NC 28712; 828-862-6527

    Hobnob: (European-American) 226 West Main Street, Brevard NC 28712; 828-966-4662

    Marco Trattoria: (Italian) 230 West Main Street, Brevard NC 28712; 828-883-4841

    Sora Japanese Restaurant: (Japanese) 300 Forest Gate Center, Pisgah Forest NC 28768; 828-883-9808

    The Falls Landing Restaurant: (Seafood) 18 East Main Street, Brevard NC 28712; 828-884-2835

    The Quarry: (American) 14 South Gaston Street, Brevard NC 28712; 828-877-2244

    The Square Root: (American) 5 Times Arcade Alley, Brevard NC 28712; 828-884-6171

Recommended Places To Stay: (For a complete list of all accommodations visit www.ashevilleguidebook.com)

    Ash Grove Resort Cabins & Camping: (Cabins)749 East Fork Road, Brevard NC 28712; 828-885-7216

    Morningside Farm Bed & Breakfast: (B&B) 246 Morningside Drive, Brevard NC 28712; 828-577-2413

    Red House Inn: (B&B) 266 West Probart Street; Brevard NC 28712; 828-884-9349

    The Inn at Brevard: (Village Inn) 315 East Main Street, Brevard NC 28712; 828-884-2105

    The Inn on Main Street: (Village Inn) 243 West Main Street, Brevard NC 28712; 888-884-4770

Bryson City

Unique among mountain communities, Bryson City, the county seat of Swain County, is located right next to the Great Smoky Mountains National Park. Over 40 percent of this great national park is located in Swain County, and the park sets the tone for this lovely mountain city, with outdoor recreation as one of the major highlights. There are a large number of accommodations for such a small city, largely because of the number of visitors who wish to visit the park.

Bryson City, because of its central location in the mountains, is also a great jumping off point to many of Western North Carolina's natural and cultural attractions as well, including the popular Great Smoky Mountains Railroad, which has departures from downtown, and the nearby Cherokee Indian Reservation. The train depot at Bryson City is also the venue for "Music in the Mountains," live performances that take place every Saturday evening from June through October. Motorcycle and sports car enthusiasts also make Bryson City their base camp for riding the "Tail of the Dragon" at nearby Deal's Gap, a section of Highway 129 that has 318 curves in only 11 miles. A number of great mountain rivers flow through Swain County, the most popular of which are the Nantahala and the Tuckaseegee. Both offer great whitewater rafting and other recreational opportunities. A famous and long established outdoor center is also located near Bryson City on the Nantahala, the Nantahala Outdoor Center, offers everything from great dining on the river to world-class whitewater rafting.

Location: Western Mountains, 45 minutes west of Asheville

Town Offices: 45 Everett Street, Bryson City NC 28713; 828-488-3335

County: Swain County: County Administration Building, 101 Mitchell Street, Bryson City NC 28713; 828-488-9273

Elevation & Population: 2,000 feet, 1,400+

Visitor/Welcome Center: Bryson City-Swain County Chamber of Commerce & Visitor Center 210 Main Street, Bryson City NC 28713; 800-867-9246

City & County Chamber of Commerce: Bryson City-Swain County Chamber of Commerce & Visitor Center 210 Main Street, Bryson City NC 28713; 800-867-9246

Newspaper: Smoky Mountain Times 114 Everett Street, Bryson City, NC 28713; 828-488-2189

Movie Theatres: Cherokee Phoenix Theatre, 61 Sequoyah Trail, Cherokee NC 28719; 828-487-7384

High School: Swain County High School, 1415 Fontana Road, Bryson City NC 28713; 828-488-2152

Colleges and Universities: Southwestern Community College, 60 Almond School Road, Bryson City NC 28713; 828-488-6413

Hospitals: Swain County Hospital, 45 Plateau Street, Bryson City NC 28713; 828-488-2155

Area Major Festivals: Music in the Mountains 800-867-9246 (Saturday evenings June-October), Smoky Mountains Bluegrass Festival (May)

Area Natural Attractions: Blue Ridge Parkway, Fontana Lake, Great Smoky Mountains National Park, Whitewater Rafting

Area Cultural Attractions: Cherokee Indian Reservation, Great Smoky Mountains Railroad, Harrah's Cherokee Casino & Hotel, Mountain Farm Museum, Museum of the Cherokee Indian, Oconaluftee Indian Village, Qualla Arts &

Crafts Mutual, Smoky Mountains Train Museum, Smoky Mountain Community Theatre, Smoky Mountain Trains, Unto These Hills

Recommended Restaurants: (For a complete list of all restaurants visit www.ashevilleguidebook.com)

> **Hemlock Inn:** (American-Family Style) Galbraith Creek Road, Bryson City NC 28713; 828-488-2885
>
> **Mountain Perks Espresso Bar & Cafe:** (Cafe) 9 Depot Street, Bryson City NC 28713; 828-488-9561
>
> **Pasqualino's Italian Restaurant:** (Italian) 25 Everett Street, Bryson City NC 28713; 828-488-9555
>
> **Relia's Garden Restaurant:** (American) Nantahala Outdoor Center, US19/74 West, Bryson City NC 28713; 800-232-7238
>
> **The Filling Station Deli & Sub Shop:** (Deli) 145 Everett Street, Bryson City NC 28713; 828-488-1919
>
> **Thirteen Moons:** (Fine Dining) Nantahala Village, 9400 Highway 19 West, Bryson City NC 28713; 828-488-2826

Recommended Places To Stay: (For a complete list of all accommodations visit www.ashevilleguidebook.com)

> **Charleston Inn:** (B&B) 208 Arlington Avenue, Bryson City NC 28713; 888-285-1555
>
> **Falling Waters Adventure Resort:** (Resort) 10345 US Highway 74 West, Bryson City NC 28713; 800-451-9972
>
> **Folkestone Inn:** (B&B) 101 Folkestone Road, Bryson City NC 28713; 888-812-3385
>
> **Hemlock Inn:** (B&B) 911 Galbraith Creek Road, Bryson City NC 28713; 828-488-2885
>
> **Lloyd's on the River Country Inn:** (Country Inn) 5370 Ela Road, Bryson City NC 28713; 888-611-6872
>
> **Nantahala Adventure Resort:** (Resort) 13077 Highway 19 West, Bryson City NC 28713; 888-905-7238
>
> **The Fryemont Inn:** (County Inn) 245 Fryemont Street, Bryson City NC 28713; 800-845-4879
>
> **The Historic Calhoun House Hotel:** (Hotel) 135 Everett Street, Bryson City NC 28713; 828-488-1234

Burnsville

Located about halfway between Asheville and Boone, Burnsville is nestled among nineteen of the highest mountains in the east. Nearby Mount Mitchell, at 6,684 feet, is the highest peak east of the Mississippi River, and it is accompanied by 18 other peaks over 6,300 feet. The county seat of Yancey County, Burnsville was established in 1833, and has as many artisans and crafts persons per capita as any town in the United States, with nearly 400 full-time and 200 part-time residing in Yancey County. Burnsville is also home to the Yancey County Farmers'

Market, one of the oldest and largest tailgate markets in western North Carolina, held on Saturday mornings behind the Burnsville Town Center.

The major festival is the Mount Mitchell Craft Fair, held every August on the beautiful town square of Burnsville. This great arts and crafts festival is one of the longest running in the mountains and has been held for over 50 years. Burnsville is also home to the historic Nu Wray Inn, also located on the town square.

Location: Central Mountains, 45 minutes north of Asheville
Town Offices: 2 Town Square, Burnsville NC 28714; 828-682-2420
Website: www.townofburnsville.org
County: Yancey County: County Offices, Yancey County Courthouse, 110 Town Square, Burnsville NC 28714; 828-682-3971
Elevation & Population: 2,815 feet, 7,000+
Visitor Center: Yancey County/Burnsville Chamber of Commerce 106 West Main Street, Burnsville NC 28714; 828-682-7413
City & County Chamber of Commerce: Yancey County/Burnsville Chamber of Commerce 106 West Main Street, Burnsville NC 28714; 800-948-1632
Newspaper: Yancey Common Times Journal (Weekly), 22 North Main Street, Burnsville NC 28714; 828-682-2120
Movie Theatres: Yancey Theatre, 119 West Main Street, Burnsville NC 28714; 828-678-3322
High School: Mountain Heritage High School, 333 Mountain Heritage High School Road, Burnsville NC 28714; 828-682-6103
Colleges and Universities: Mayland Community College, Yancey Campus, 107 Wheeler Hills Road, Burnsville NC 28714; 828-682-7315
Area Major Festivals: Mount Mitchell Craft Fair (August), Music in the Mountains Festival (October)
Area Natural Attractions: Blue Ridge Parkway, Mount Mitchell State Park
Area Cultural Attractions: Parkway Playhouse, Rush Wray Museum
Recommended Restaurants: (For a complete list of all restaurants visit www.ashevilleguidebook.com)
　Garden Deli: (Deli) 107 Town Square, Burnsville NC 28714; 828-682-3946
　In The Garden: (American) 117 West Main Street, Burnsville NC 28714; 828-682-1680
　Nu Wray Inn: (American) 105 Town Square, Burnsville NC 28714; 800-368-9729
Recommended Places To Stay: (For a complete list of all accommodations visit www.ashevilleguidebook.com)
　Celo Inn: (Country Inn) 45 Seven Mile Ridge Road, Burnsville NC 28714; 828-675-5132
　Clear Creek Ranch: (Dude Ranch) 100 Clear Creek Drive, Burnsville NC 28714; 800-651-4510
　Nu Wray Inn: (Village Inn) 105 Town Square, Burnsville NC 28714; 800-368-9729

Terrell House Bed & Breakfast: (B&B) 109 Robertson Street, Burnsville NC 28714; 888-682-4505

The Buck House Bed & Breakfast: (B&B) 5860 Bald Mountain Road, Burnsville NC 28714; 888-689-5001

Canton

Canton is a small town nestled among five hills along the banks of the Pigeon River in the mountains of Western North Carolina, near major highways and within easy driving distance of the regional airport in Asheville. Canton's beautiful residential communities lie along tree-lined streets in this quaint town. Canton is also the home of Blue Ridge Papers, Haywood County's largest industry. The mill produces paper and allied products and has made great strides in reducing the amount of air and water pollution spewed with devastating effects into the environment, especially the Pigeon River, by the former owner, the Champion Paper Company. Blue Ridge Papers today is a partner with the community in not only providing jobs for local residents, but also in reducing the environmental impact of the company's manufacturing operation.

Canton has a recreation program as part of its services to its citizens and guests. The Recreation Park has a large, modern swimming pool, playground, picnic tables, lighted tennis courts, and ball fields adjacent to the park. The community was named for Canton, OH, the source of the steel used in construction of the bridge over the Pigeon River.

One of the largest mountains in Haywood County, the now famous Cold Mountain lies in the Bethel Community near Canton. Popularized by the novel which was turned into a major motion picture, Cold Mountain was written by Charles Frazier, who was born in Haywood County and spent weekends and summers in the area. While here, he explored the mountains and decided to immortalize Cold Mountain in his memorable novel. Another of Canton's claims to fame are the Star of the Carolinas (1445 carats), and the Southern Star (1035 carats), two of the world's largest star sapphires, both found in Canton's Old Pressley Sapphire Mine, now open to the public.

Location: Central Mountains, 20 minutes west of Asheville

Town Hall: 58 Park Street, Canton NC 28716; 828-646-3412

Website: www.cantonnc.com

County: Haywood County: County Offices, 215 North Main Street, Waynesville NC 28786; 828-452-6625

Elevation & Population: 2,589 feet, 2,500+

Visitor/Welcome Center: Haywood County Tourism Development Authority Visitor Center, (Exit 31 off I-40) 761 Champion Drive, Canton NC 28716; 828-235-9238

County Chamber of Commerce: Greater Haywood County Chamber of Commerce: 591 North Main Street, Waynesville NC 28786; 828-456-3021

Newspaper: The Mountaineer, 220 North Main Street, Waynesville NC 28786; 828-452-0661

Movie Theatres: Colonial Theatre 58 Park Street, Canton NC 28716; 828-235-2760

High School: Pisgah High School, 1 Black Bear Drive, Canton NC 28716; 828-646-3440

Area Major Festivals: Christmas Parade (December), Folkmoot USA (July)

Area Natural Attractions: Blue Ridge Parkway, Old Pressley Sapphire Mine, Pisgah National Forest

Area Cultural Attractions: Canton Area Historical Museum, Shook Museum

Recommended Restaurants: (For a complete list of all restaurants visit www.ashevilleguidebook.com)

    Sagebrush Steakhouse: (American) 1941 Champion Drive, Canton NC 28716; 828-646-3750

Recommended Places To Stay: (For a complete list of all accommodations visit www.ashevilleguidebook.com)

    Springdale Country Club: (Country Club) 200 Golfwatch Road, Canton NC 28716; 800-553-3027

Cashiers

Nestled in the southwestern section of the mountains, Cashiers is a beautiful, upscale little resort town that has welcomed visitors for over 150 years. Nineteen easily accessible pristine waterfalls in the immediate area are one of the main attractions as well as the numerous restaurants and gift, antique and craft shops that line the streets coming into town.

Cashiers has long had a reputation as a mountain retreat, and as early as 1850, people from nearby South Carolina flocked to this region during the summer to escape the hot and humid lowland weather. Eventually, investment in second and vacation homes started and this transformed the Cashiers area into the affluent resort destination it is today. No one knows for sure the origin of the name Cashiers but one good guess is that it was a crossroads where miners (this part of the mountain is known for its mines and gemstones) cashed out after success in the field.

Near Cashiers itself are a number of beautiful mountain lakes, including Lake Toxaway, Lake Glenville, and Sapphire Lake, and the surrounding communities of Lake Toxaway, Glenville and Sapphire. The Sapphire Valley Ski Area is also located in Sapphire and has two runs open to the public during the ski season.

Location: Western Mountains, 1½ hours west of Asheville

County: Jackson County: County Offices, 401 Grindstaff Cove Road, Suite A-207, Sylva NC 28779; 828-631-2207

Elevation & Population: 3,486 feet, 1,500 full-time, 10,000 part-time residents

Visitor/Welcome Center: Cashiers Area Chamber of Commerce Visitor Center, 202 Highway 64 West, Cashiers NC 28717; 828-743-5191

City Chamber of Commerce: Cashiers Area Chamber of Commerce, 202 Highway 64 West, Cashiers NC 28717; 828-743-5191

County Chamber of Commerce: Jackson County Chamber of Commerce, 773 West Main Street, Sylva NC 28779; 800-962-1911

Newspaper: Crossroads Chronicle, PO Box 1040, Cashiers NC 28717; 828-743-5101

High School: Blue Ridge School, 95 Bobcat Drive, Cashiers NC 28717; 828-743-2646

Colleges and Universities: Southwestern Community College, 217 Frank Allen Road, Cashiers NC 28717; 800-447-4091

Area Major Festivals: Cashiers Mountain Music Festival (July), Highlands-Cashiers Chamber Music Festival (July-August), Leaf Festival of Cashiers Valley (October)

Area Natural Attractions: Pisgah National Forest, Waterfalls in Western North Carolina

Area Cultural Attractions: Mountain Heritage Center, Zachery-Tolbert House Museum

Recommended Restaurants: (For a complete list of all restaurants visit www.ashevilleguidebook.com)

> **Brown Trout Mountain Grille:** (American) 502 Blue Ridge Road, Lake Toxaway NC 28747; 828-877-3474
>
> **Carolina Smokehouse:** (BBQ) 281 US Highway 64 West, Cashiers NC 28717; 828-743-3200
>
> **Sapphire Mountain Brewing Company:** (Pizza-Cafe) Sapphire National Golf Club, 50 Spicers Avenue, Sapphire NC 28774; 888-813-7622
>
> **The Gamekeeper's Tavern:** (American) 3646 US Highway 64 East, Sapphire NC 28774; 828-743-4263
>
> **The Orchard:** (American with Southern flavor) 905 Highway 107 South, Cashiers NC 28717; 828-743-7614
>
> **Zeke & Earl's:** (Cafe) 95 Highway 107 South, Cashiers NC 28717; 828-743-5055

Recommended Places To Stay: (For a complete list of all accommodations visit www.ashevilleguidebook.com)

> **Earthshine Mountain Lodge:** (Resort) 1600 Golden Road, Lake Toxaway NC 28747; 828-862-4207
>
> **High Hampton Inn & Country Club:** (Resort) 1525 Highway 107 South, Cashiers NC 28717; 800-334-2551
>
> **Innisfree Inn By-The-Lake:** (Country Inn) 8 Innisfree Drive, Cashiers NC 28736; 828-743-2946
>
> **Laurelwood Mountain Inn:** (Village Inn) 58 Highway 107 North, Cashiers NC 28717; 800-346-6846
>
> **The Cabins at Seven Foxes:** (Cabins) Seven Foxes Lane, Lake Toxaway NC 28747: 828-877-6333

The Greystone Inn: (Resort) Greystone Lane, Lake Toxaway NC 28747; 800-824-5766
The Inn at Millstone: (County Inn) 119 Lodge Lane, Cashiers NC 28717; 828-743-6513

Catawba

Catawba is a small town in the heart of the beautiful Catawba Valley in the foothills, and is one of only two municipalities in Catawba County that borders the Catawba River. The name "Catawba" recalls the tribe of Native Americans which once inhabited the area. Catawba is one of the oldest towns between Salisbury and Asheville as a result of having been selected to be the site of an early railroad station. Trains ran to the town before the Civil War, as early as 1859, and continue to do so today.

The Town of Catawba Historical Association maintains a museum in the oldest brick building in town, the former residence of Dr. Q.M. Little, circa 1873, to showcase local history. The museum is located at 101 First Street SW downtown and contains five rooms. Visitors to the museum should call 828-241-4077 for scheduling and information. Catawba has an annual Catawba Festival and Parade held each November, which features vendors offering everything from crafts and toys to festival food.

Location: Foothills, 1 hour and 15 minutes east of Asheville
Town Hall: 102 First Street NW, Catawba NC 28609; 828-241-2215
Website: www.townofcatawbanc.org
County: Catawba County: County Offices, 100-A South West Boulevard, Newton NC 28658; 828-465-8201
Elevation & Population: 886 feet, 700+
County Visitor/Welcome Center: Catawba County Visitor Information Center, 1055 Southgate Corporation Park SW, Hickory NC 28602; 828-328-6111
County Chamber of Commerce: Catawba County Chamber of Commerce, 1055 Southgate Corporation Park SW, Hickory NC 28602; 828-328-6111
Newspapers: The Claremont Courier, 3283 White Oak Court, Claremont NC 28610; 828-320-8450 and the Hickory Daily Record, 1100 Park Place, Hickory NC 28603; 828-322-4510
High Schools: Bandys High School, 5040 East Bandys Road, Catawba NC 28609; 828-241-3171
Area Major Festivals: Catawba Festival and Parade (November), Catawba Valley Pottery Festival (March)
Area Natural Attractions: Pisgah National Forest, South Mountains State Park
Area Cultural Attractions: Bunker Hill Covered Bridge, Catawba County Museum of History, Catawba Science Center, Town of Catawba Historical Association Museum, Harper House/Hickory History Center, Hickory Furniture Mart, Hickory Motor Speedway, Hickory Museum of Art, Hiddenite Center, Historic Murray's Mill

Recommended Restaurants: (For a complete list of all restau
ashevilleguidebook.com)
   Old Company Store: (Deli) 101 North Main Street, Cataᴠ
   828-241-4200
Recommended Places To Stay: (For a complete list of all accommodations visit
www.ashevilleguidebook.com)
   There are no accommodations in Catawba

Cherokee
   Located in the heart of the 56,000-acre Cherokee Indian Reservation, the village of Cherokee is a major destination. Offering a wide range of accommodations, restaurants and things to do, Cherokee is host to a great number of visitors each year. Cherokee is home to more than 10,000 Eastern Band of the Cherokee members. Each year, thousands of visitors from across the country come to discover this enchanted land and to share the natural mountain beauty the Cherokee people have treasured for centuries.
   A visit to Cherokee is like stepping into the past. You'll find a nation still linked to ancient customs and traditions that enable them to live in harmony with nature as their ancestors did. The Reservation, known as the Qualla Boundary, has a number of outstanding attractions. The main attraction in the area is Harrah's Cherokee Casino, but other more historical and cultural attractions are also very popular, especially the 12,000 square-foot. Museum of the Cherokee Indian, Oconaluftee Indian Village, Qualla Arts & Crafts Mutual and Unto These Hills outdoor drama.
   Surrounded by the vast forests of the Cherokee Indian Reservation and adjacent to the Great Smoky Mountains National Park, a visit to Cherokee affords countless outdoor recreational opportunities, and one of the most accessible is the popular Oconaluftee Islands Park, a beautiful multi-faceted family-oriented park in the middle of the Oconaluftee River right in town.

Location: Western Mountains, 1½ hours west of Asheville
Website: www.cherokee-nc.com
County: Jackson County: County Offices, 401 Grindstaff Cove Road, Suite A-207, Sylva NC 28779; 828-631-2207
Elevation & Population: 3,000 feet, 13,000+
Visitor/Welcome Center: Cherokee Welcome Center, 498 Tsali Boulevard, Cherokee NC 28719; 800-438-1601
City Chamber of Commerce: Cherokee Chamber of Commerce, 1148 Tsali Boulevard, Cherokee NC 28719; 828-497-6700
County Chamber of Commerce: Jackson County Chamber of Commerce, 773 West Main Street, Sylva NC 28779; 828-586-2155
Newspaper: The Cherokee One Feather, 828-487-1751
Movie Theatres: Cherokee Phoenix Theatres, 61 Sequoyah Trail, Cherokee NC 28719; 828-497-7384

High School: Cherokee Central School, 200 Ravensford Drive, Cherokee NC 28719; 828-554-5030

Colleges and Universities: Southwestern Community College, Acquoni Road, Cherokee NC 28719; 828-497-7233

Hospitals: Cherokee Indian Hospital, 188 Hospital Road, Cherokee NC 28719; 828-497-9163

Area Major Festivals: North Carolina State Bluegrass Festival (June) Festival of Native Peoples (July) Cherokee Indian Fair (October)

Area Natural Attractions: Blue Ridge Parkway, Great Smoky Mountains National Park

Area Cultural Attractions: Cherokee Indian Reservation, Harrah's Cherokee Casino & Hotel, Mountain Farm Museum, Museum of the Cherokee Indian, Oconaluftee Indian Village, Qualla Arts & Crafts Mutual, Unto These Hills

Recommended Restaurants: (For a complete list of all restaurants visit www.ashevilleguidebook.com)

> **Brushy Mountain Smokehouse and Creamery:** (BBQ) 667 Casino Trail, Cherokee NC 28719; 8280497-7675
>
> **Granny's Kitchen:** (County) 1098 Painttown Road, Cherokee NC 28719; 828-497-5010

Recommended Places To Stay: (For a complete list of all accommodations visit www.ashevilleguidebook.com)

> **Best Western Great Smokies Inn:** (Motel) 1636 Acquoni Road, Cherokee NC 28719; 828-497-2020
>
> **Cherokee Campground & Craig's Cabins:** (Cabins) US 19N/US 441 Bus, Cherokee NC 28719; 828-497-9838
>
> **Cherokee KOA:** (Campground) 92 KOA Kampground Road, Cherokee NC 28719; 828-497-9711
>
> **Fairfield Inn & Suites Cherokee:** (Motel) 568 Painttown Road, Cherokee NC 28719; 828-497-0400
>
> **Hampton Inn:** (Motel) 185 Tsalagi Road, Cherokee NC 28719; 828-497-3115
>
> **Harrah's Cherokee Casino & Hotel:** (Hotel) 777 Casino Drive, Cherokee NC 28719; 800-427-7247
>
> **Inn of the Seven Clans:** (Motel) 196 Painttown Road, Cherokee NC 28719; 828-497-4231

Chimney Rock

Located just south of Asheville, the Village of Chimney Rock, incorporated in 1921, sits at the base of the famous Chimney Rock and along the Rocky Broad River. Primarily catering to tourists who are visiting the Rock and nearby Lake Lure, the Village is a convenient stopping spot for lunch or some souvenir shopping. A number of restaurants are also located right on the bold Rocky Broad River, which flows right through the Village on its way to nearby Lake Lure. Most buildings downtown, just outside Chimney Rock Park, date to the 1920s. The

Village became a resort town around Chimney Rock Park, which began to be developed in 1902.

Towering over the Village, Chimney Rock Park, which was privately owned, recently became Chimney Rock State Park, one of the newest North Carolina state parks. With an elevation range from about 1,100 feet to 2,800 feet, the park ultimately will include over 5,000 acres. The nearby 404-foot Hickory Nut Falls is among the most dramatic waterfalls in Western North Carolina, and movie fans should be aware that parts of "The Last of the Mohicans" were filmed at the park.

Location: Central Mountains, 45 minutes south of Asheville
Website: www.chimneyrock.org
County: Rutherford County: County Offices, 289 North Main Street, Rutherfordton NC 28139; 828-287-6060
Elevation & Population: 1,000 Feet, 200+
Visitor/Welcome Center: Hickory Nut Gorge Visitor Center, 2926 Memorial Highway, Lake Lure NC 28746; 877-625-2725
City Chamber of Commerce: Hickory Nut Gorge Chamber of Commerce, PO Box 32, Chimney Rock NC 28720; 877-625-2725
County Chamber of Commerce: Rutherford County Chamber of Commerce, 162 North Main Street, Rutherfordton NC 28139; 828-287-3090
County Tourism Development: Lake Lure & the Blue Ridge Foothills, 1990 US Highway 221 South, Forest City NC 28043; 828-245-1492
Newspaper: The Digital Courier, PO Box 1149, Forest City NC 28043; 828-245-6431
Area Major Festivals: Lure of the Dragons (May)
Area Natural Attractions: Apple Orchards in Henderson County, Chimney Rock Park, Lake Lure
Recommended Restaurants: (For a complete list of all restaurants visit www.ashevilleguidebook.com)
  Duncan's Bar-B-Que: (BBQ) 461 Main Street, Chimney Rock N 28720; 828-625-1579
  Old Rock Cafe: (Cafe) 431 Main Street, Chimney Rock NC 28720; 828-625-2329
Recommended Places To Stay: (For a complete list of all accommodations visit www.ashevilleguidebook.com)
  Chimney Rock Inn: (Village Inn) 126 Main Street, Chimney Rock NC 28720; 828-625-1429
  Evening Shade River Lodge & Cabins: (Lodge) 745 Main Street, Chimney Rock NC 28720; 828-625-4774
  Fibber MaGee's "Riverfront Inn: (B&B) 339 Main Street, Chimney Rock NC 28720; 866-480-0466
  The Esmeralda Inn: (Village Inn) 910 Main Street, Chimney Rock NC 28720; 888-897-2999

Claremont

Claremont is a small town located in the foothills of Western North Carolina in Catawba County, and has roots that date back to the early 1800's when the area around present day Claremont was first referred to as "Charlotte Crossing." Later, the name was changed again to "Setzer's Depot" but ultimately the name was changed in 1892 to Claremont, after an early settler, Clare Sigmon. The town has seen strong economic growth over the years and is blessed with large and small businesses that provide a good tax base. These include high quality furniture industries and two fiber optical and coaxial cable manufacturing plants within the city limits. The Norfolk-Southern Railroad also passes through the city limits.

An attraction in the Claremont area is the Bunker Hill Covered Bridge located on Highway 70, a few miles east of town. The bridge spans Lyles Creek as part of a road that originally followed a Native American trail and is one of only two covered bridges left in the state. Claremont also has a lovely downtown park, Claremont Park, located on East Main Street, next to Claremont Elementary School. This park is 21 acres, and has tennis courts, horseshoe pits, sheltered picnic areas, a pavilion and an amphitheater, and a paved quarter mile walking trail.

Location: Foothills, 1 hour and 15 minutes east of Asheville
City Hall: 3288 East Main Street, Claremont NC 28610; 828-459-7009
Website: www.cityofclaremont.org
County: Catawba County: County Offices, 100-A South West Boulevard, Newton NC 28658; 828-465-8201
Elevation & Population: 981 feet, 1,050+
County Visitor/Welcome Center: Catawba County Visitor Information Center, 1055 Southgate Corporation Park SW, Hickory NC 28602; 828-328-6111
County Chamber of Commerce: Catawba County Chamber of Commerce, 1055 Southgate Corporation Park SW, Hickory NC 28602; 828-328-6111
Newspapers: The Claremont Courier, 3283 White Oak Court, Claremont NC 28610; 828-320-8450 and the Hickory Daily Record, 1100 Park Place, Hickory NC 28603; 828-322-4510
High Schools: Bunker Hill High School, 4675 Oxford School Road, Claremont NC 28610; 828-241-3355
Area Major Festivals: Catawba Valley Pottery Festival (March)
Area Natural Attractions: Pisgah National Forest, South Mountains State Park
Area Cultural Attractions: Bunker Hill Covered Bridge, Catawba County Museum of History, Catawba Science Center, Harper House/Hickory History Center, Hickory Furniture Mart, Hickory Motor Speedway, Hickory Museum of Art, Hiddenite Center, Historic Murray's Mill
Recommended Restaurants: (For a complete list of all restaurants visit www.ashevilleguidebook.com)
    Claremont Cafe: (Cafe) 4485 South Depot Street, Claremont NC 28610; 828-459-2190

Hannah's Bar-B-Que: (BBQ) 2942 North Oxford Street, Claremont NC 28610; 828-459-9889

Recommended Places To Stay: (For a complete list of all accommodations visit www.ashevilleguidebook.com)

Super 8: (Motel-only accommodation in Claremont) 3054 North Oxford Street, Claremont NC 28610; 828-459-7777

Clyde

Clyde is a small town located just west of Asheville and has the distinction of being "away from it all" but without the isolation usually associated with mountain living. Long associated with neighboring Canton, Clyde is also home to Haywood Community College and the Haywood Regional Medical Center. Recently two industrial parks have been developed just north of Clyde. Clyde Township was formed in 1877 from Pigeon, Beaverdam and Waynesville. At first it was called Lower Pigeon, with the name later changed to Clyde.

Clyde is surrounded by mountains and valleys which afford numerous outdoor recreational opportunities to the visitors and residents. Clyde is also the home of the Shook Museum, housed in one of the oldest buildings still standing in Haywood county. Build circa 1795 by Jacob Shook for his son Peter, this historic house is known and associated with the founding of Methodism in Haywood County.

Location: Central Mountains, 30 minutes west of Asheville

Town Hall: 8437 Carolina Boulevard, Clyde NC 28721; 828-627-2566

Website: www.townofclyde.com

County: Haywood County: County Offices, 215 North Main Street, Waynesville NC 28786; 828-452-6625

Elevation & Population: 2,543 feet, 1,300+

County Visitor/Welcome Center: Visitor/Welcome Center: Haywood County Tourism Development Authority Visitor Center, (Exit 31 off I-40) 761 Champion Drive, Canton NC 28716; 828-235-9238

County Chamber of Commerce: Haywood County Chamber of Commerce: 591 North Main Street, Waynesville NC 28786; 828-456-3021

Newspaper: The Mountaineer, 220 North Main Street, Waynesville NC 28786; 828-452-0661

High School: Pisgah High School, 1 Black Bear Drive, Canton NC 28716; 828-646-3440

Colleges and Universities: Haywood Community College, 185 Freelander Drive, Clyde NC 28721; 828-627-2821

Hospitals: Haywood Regional Medical Center, 262 Leroy George Drive, Clyde NC 28721; 800-834-1729

Area Major Festivals: Folkmoot USA (July)

Area Natural Attractions: Blue Ridge Parkway, Pisgah National Forest

Recommended Restaurants: (For a complete list of all restaurants visit www.ashevilleguidebook.com)

Sherrill's Pioneer Restaurant: (County-American) 8363 Carolina Boulevard, Clyde NC 28721; 828-626-9880

Recommended Places To Stay: (For a complete list of all accommodations visit www.ashevilleguidebook.com)

No accommodations currently available in Clyde. *See* Canton and Waynesville

Columbus

Columbus is the Polk County seat where the government offices and the historic 1857 Polk County Courthouse are located. The beautiful courthouse building is one of the oldest still in use in North Carolina and has been fully restored to its original grandeur. Of historical interest is the ancient slave block that still remains on the courthouse lawn as a daily reminder of that terrible period of American history.

Dr. Columbus Mills, for whom the town was named, has been called the "Father of Polk County." It was largely through his efforts as a state senator that Polk County was established by sectioning off parts of Rutherford and Henderson Counties, deliberately carved from 100 acres of wilderness on what was then known as Foster Race path in the shadow of Foster's Mountain, known today as Chocolate Drop.

Columbus has all the charm of a small mountain city, and has two major festivals, the Fabulous 4th in July and the Columbus Day Farm Festival in October. It is also home to the Howard Monument, a landmark in the County for over 100 years, and the famous Doughboy statue. Originally laid out with a church at each corner of the main streets, only two of these are in their original locations today, the Columbus Baptist Church and the Columbus Presbyterian Church.

Location: Foothills, 45 minutes south of Asheville

Town Hall: 95 Walker Street, Columbus NC 28722; 828-894-8236

Website: http://columbusnc.com

County: Polk County: County Offices, 40 Courthouse Street, Columbus NC 28722; 828-894-3301

Elevation & Population: 1,131 feet, 1,000+

Visitor/Welcome Center: Polk County Travel & Tourism 20 East Mills Street, Columbus NC 28722; 800-440-7848

County Chamber of Commerce: Carolina Foothills Chamber of Commerce 2753 Lynn Road, Suite A, Tryon NC 28782; 828-859-6236

Newspaper: Tryon Daily Bulletin 16 North Trade Street, Tryon NC 28782; 828-859-9151 and Polk County News Journal PO Box 576, Columbus NC 28722; 864-457-3337

High School: Polk County High School, 1681 East NC Highway 108, Columbus NC 28722; 828-894-2525

Hospitals: St. Luke's Hospital, 101 Hospital Drive, Columbus NC 28722; 828-894-3311

Area Major Festivals: Fabulous 4th (July), Columbus Day Farm Festival (October)

Area Natural Attractions: Pisgah National Forest
Area Cultural Attractions: Foothills Equestrian Nature Center (FENCE), Polk
   County Courthouse, Polk County Historical Museum, Tryon Fine Arts Center
Recommended Restaurants: (For a complete list of all restaurants visit www.
   ashevilleguidebook.com)
   Giardini: (Italian) 2411 Highway 108 East, Columbus NC 28722; 828-894-0341
   Larkin's Carolina Grill: (Grill) 115 West Mills Street, Columbus NC
   28722; 828-894-8800
Recommended Places To Stay: (For a complete list of all accommodations visit
   www.ashevilleguidebook.com)
   Butterfly Creek: (B&B) 780 Smith Dairy Road, Columbus NC 28722;
   828-894-6393
   Green River Vineyard Bed & Breakfast: (B&B) 3043 John Watson Road,
   Green Creek NC 28139; 828-863-4705

Connelly Springs

Connelly Springs is located in eastern Burke County between Hickory and
Morganton, and was originally named Happy Home. The first settler in the area
was William Lewis Connelly and in the 1880's the town's name was changed to
Connelly Springs after the discovery of mineral springs by Mrs. Elmira Connelly.
The town, because of the popularity of the springs for natural healing, soon
became a resort destination with a number of large hotels constructed for visitors.
These former hotels included The Connelly Mineral Springs Hotel, The Sides
Boarding House, The Connelly Springs Inn and The Haliburton Hotel.

Connelly Springs was incorporated in 1920, and later again in 1989, and
eventually became a bedroom community with residents employed in the textile
and furniture manufacturing facilities in neighboring towns. Recently Connelly
Springs has seen considerable growth: a new town hall was opened in
2002 and numerous community projects undertaken as well as a revitalization of
the business sector along NC Highway 70. Connelly Springs is also home to the
Raintree Cellars winery, and adjacent to the community is the beautiful South
Mountains State Park.

Location: Foothills, one hour and fifteen minutes east of Asheville
Town Hall: 1030 US Highway 70, Connelly Springs NC 28612; 828-879-2321
County: Burke County: Burke County Government Center, 200 Avery Avenue,
   Morganton NC 28680; 828-439-4340
Elevation & Population: 1236 feet, 1,900+
County Visitor/Welcome Center: 102 East Union Street, Morganton NC
   28655; 888-462-2921
County Chamber of Commerce: Burke County Chamber of Commerce, 110
   East Meeting Street, Morganton NC 28655; 828-437-3021
Newspaper: The News Herald, 301 Collett Street, Morganton NC 28655; 828-
   437-2161

High Schools: East Burke High School, 3695 East Burke Boulevard, Connelly Springs NC 28612; 828-397-5541 and Jimmy C. Draughn High School, 709 Lovelady Road NE, Valdese NC 28690, 828-879-4200

Area Major Festivals: Connelly Springs Fall Festival (October)

Area Natural Attractions: Brown Mountain Lights, Lake James State Park, South Mountains State Park

Area Cultural Attractions: History Museum of Burke County, North Carolina School For The Deaf Museum, Old Burke County Courthouse Heritage Museum, Quaker Meadows Plantation, Senator Sam J. Erwin Jr. Museum

Recommended Restaurants: (For a complete list of all restaurants visit www. ashevilleguidebook.com)

    Granny's Country Kitchen: (Country) 3448 Miller Bridge Road, Icard NC 28666; 828-325-0005

Recommended Places To Stay: (For a complete list of all accommodations visit www.ashevilleguidebook.com)

No accommodations currently available in Connelly Springs. *See* Morganton.

Conover

Conover is located in the foothills of Western North Carolina, in Catawba County, and is a small town that offers historic charm, access to excellent recreational opportunities, entertainment and shopping, especially if you are in the market for furniture. Historically, Conover was home to a number of important furniture manufacturers, including the former Conover Furniture Company. The origin of the name Conover is uncertain but it is known the city was chartered in 1876 and incorporated in 1877. Conover was also home at one time to Concordia College, an institution of higher education that trained Lutheran ministers. The college closed in 1935 after the college buildings were destroyed by fire. Today the city has several large industrial parks which make Conover one of the main employment bases in Catawba County, and daytime residency, because of this, is over 20,000.

Conover has eight neighborhood parks;the most centrally located is the Downtown Park located on 2nd Avenue NE just across from both the city hall and the police department. This great little park is the geographical and cultural heart of Conover, and is home to a large gazebo that has become the unofficial symbol of the town. Along with the gazebo, the park also contains walking trails, benches, picnic tables and play equipment for children. Another of the town's outstanding parks is Hunsucker Park. This 1.13 acre park has playground equipment, including a slide, merry-go-round and other recreational equipment.

Location: Foothills, 1 hour and 15 minutes east of Asheville

City Hall: 101 First Street East, Conover NC 28613; 828-464-1191

Website: www.conovernc.gov

County: Catawba County: County Offices, 100-A South West Boulevard, Newton NC 28658; 828-465-8201

Elevation & Population: 1,060 feet, 7,500+

County Visitor/Welcome Center: Catawba County Visitor Information Center, 1055 Southgate Corporation Park SW, Hickory NC 28602; 828-328-6111

County Chamber of Commerce: Catawba County Chamber of Commerce, 1055 Southgate Corporation Park SW, Hickory NC 28602; 828-328-6111

Newspapers: The Claremont Courier, 3283 White Oak Court, Claremont NC 28610; 828-320-8450 and the Hickory Daily Record, 1100 Park Place, Hickory NC 28603; 828-322-4510

High Schools: Newton-Conover High School 338 West 15th Street, Newton NC 28658; 828-465-0920 and Newton-Conover Science High School, 605 North Ashe Avenue, Newton NC 28658; 828-464-3191

Area Major Festivals: Catawba Valley Pottery Festival (March)

Area Natural Attractions: Pisgah National Forest, South Mountains State Park

Area Cultural Attractions: Bunker Hill Covered Bridge, Catawba County Museum of History, Catawba Science Center, Harper House/Hickory History Center, Hickory Furniture Mart, Hickory Motor Speedway, Hickory Museum of Art, Hiddenite Center, Historic Murray's Mill

Recommended Restaurants: (For a complete list of all restaurants visit www. ashevilleguidebook.com)

> **Alexander's Restaurant:** (Continental-Fine Dining) Rock Barn Golf & Spa, 3791 Clubhouse Drive, Conover NC 28613; 828-459-1125
>
> **Dos Amigos:** (Mexican) 1222 Conover Boulevard W, Conover NC 28613; 828-466-1920
>
> **Drum's Restaurant:** (American) 310 1st Avenue S, Conover NC 28613; 828-464-1450

Recommended Places To Stay: (For a complete list of all accommodations visit www.ashevilleguidebook.com)

> **La Quinta Inn & Suites:** (Motel) 1607 Fairgrove Church Road, Conover NC 28613; 800-753-3757
>
> **Lake Hickory RV Resort:** (RV Campground) 6641 Monford Drive, Conover NC 28613; 828-256-4303
>
> **Rock Barn Golf & Spa:** (Resort) 3791 Clubhouse Drive, Conover NC 28613; 828-459-1125

Cullowhee

The community of Cullowhee is home to Western Carolina University, a member of the University of North Carolina system, and is located in a scenic valley in Jackson County about 45 minutes west of Asheville. A college town with the median resident age of 20.7 (the university has over 10,000 students), Cullowhee is also a stopping point for the millions of visitors who are drawn to this mid-mountain region for its spectacular landscapes and vast array of outdoor recreational opportunities, including world-class mountain biking, backpacking and whitewater rafting. The beautiful Tuckasegee River flows though the Cullowhee area and passes right by the Western North Carolina campus.

Cullowhee is also home to the Jackson County Recreational Complex, a public-use park located on Cullowhee Mountain Road that includes a 24,000 square-foot facility complete with full size gym, state of the art fitness room and multipurpose meeting rooms. The park has softball and soccer fields, a basketball court, picnic shelters, playgrounds and 10,000 feet of running trails.

Location: Western Mountains, 1 hour west of Asheville

County Visitor/Welcome Center Website: www.mountainlovers.com

County: Jackson County: County Offices, 401 Grindstaff Cove Road, Suite A-20: , Sylva NC 28: : 9; 828-631-220:

Elevation & Population: 2,400 ft, 4,000+

County Chamber of Commerce: Jackson County Chamber of Commerce : : 3 West Main Street, Sylva NC 28: : 9; 828-586-2155

Newspaper: The Sylva Herald 539 West Main Street, Sylva NC 28: : 9; 800-849-3193

High School: Smoky Mountain High, 100 Smoky Mountain Drive, Sylva NC 28: : 9; 828-586-21: :

Colleges and Universities: Western Carolina University, University Way, Cullowhee NC 28: 23; 828-22: -: 211

Area Major Festivals: Mountain Heritage Day (September), Mountain Artisans Arts & Crafts Shows (July and November)

Area Natural Attractions: Pisgah National Forest, Waterfalls in Western North Carolina, Great Smoky Mountains National Park

Area Cultural Attractions: Cherokee Indian Reservation, Fine and Performing Arts Center at WCU, Great Smoky Mountains Railroad, Mountain Heritage Center, Western Carolina University

Recommended Restaurants: (For a complete list of all restaurants visit www.ashevilleguidebook.com)

    Cullowhee Cafe: (Cafe) 3050 Old Cullowhee Road, Cullowhee NC 28: 23; 828-293-3334

    Rolling Stone Burrito: (Mexican) 56: Centennial Drive, Cullowhee NC 28: 23; 828-293-: 200

Recommended Places To Stay: (For a complete list of all accommodations visit www.ashevilleguidebook.com)

    Bear Lake Reserve: (Resort-Rentals) 412 Lake Forest Drive, Tuckasegee NC 28: 83; 866-389-232:

    The River Lodge Bed & Breakfast: (B&B) 619 Roy Tritt Road, Cullowhee NC 28: 23; 8: : -384-4400

    The University Inn: (Motel) 563 North County Club Drive, Cullowhee NC 28: 23; 8: : -293-5442

Dillsboro

Founded by Williams Dills in 1884 just after the coming of the Western North Carolina Railroad, Dillsboro was incorporated in 1889. An early destination stop not only because of its scenic mountain location and railroad, this quaint mountain village had many popular restaurants and tourist hotels, one of which, the historic Jarrett House, is still serving meals. Today Dillsboro is well-known as one of the best places to board the Great Smoky Mountains Railroad, a very popular tourist excursion train.

Dillsboro is also going to be the future home to the Southern Appalachian Women's Museum located in the Monteith Community Park. This local history museum will be open to the public in the near future, and will honor and recognize generations of Appalachian women for their work both in and out of the home. Plans include permanent displays of historical artifacts, traveling exhibits and educational shows, and a restored landscape plan that will showcase local heritage and heirloom gardening.

Location: Western Mountains, 1 hour west of Asheville

Website: http://visitdillsboro.org/index.html

County: Jackson County: County Offices, 401 Grindstaff Cove Road, Suite A-207, Sylva NC 28779; 828-631-2207

Elevation & Population: 1,800 ft, 200+

County Chamber of Commerce: Jackson County Chamber of Commerce 773 West Main Street, Sylva NC 28779; 828-586-2155

Newspaper: The Sylva Herald 539 West Main Street, Sylva NC 28779; 800-849-3193

High School: Smoky Mountain High, 100 Smoky Mountain Drive, Sylva NC 28779; 828-586-2177

Area Major Festivals: Dillsboro Arts & Music Festival (June), Dillsboro Lights & Luminaries (December)

Area Natural Attractions: Pisgah National Forest, Waterfalls in Western North Carolina, Great Smoky Mountains National Park

Area Cultural Attractions: Appalachian Women's Museum, Cherokee Indian Reservation, Fine and Performing Arts Center at WCU, Great Smoky Mountains Railroad, Mountain Heritage Center

Recommended Restaurants: (For a complete list of all restaurants visit www.ashevilleguidebook.com)

Dillsboro Smokehouse: (BBQ) 403 Haywood Road, Dillsboro NC 28725; 828-586-9556

Jarrett House: (American Family-Style) 100 Haywood Road, Dillsboro NC 28725; 828-586-0265

Recommended Places To Stay: (For a complete list of all accommodations visit www.ashevilleguidebook.com)

Dillsboro Inn: (Village Inn) 146 North River Road, Dillsboro NC 28725; 866-586-3898

Jarrett House: (B&B) 100 Haywood Road, Dillsboro NC 28725; 828-586-0265

Drexel

Drexel was named after Anthony Joseph Drexel, a Philadelphia financier and philanthropist who served on the board of directors of the Norfolk Southern Railroad, which ran through the middle of this small community. On February 5, 1913, the North Carolina General Assembly granted a charter to incorporate the Town of Drexel. Drexel's corporate limits were determined by using the railroad depot as a central point and establishing the town limits one-half mile in all direction, thus the town was round. In the early 1900's the Drexel Knitting Mills Company and Drexel Furniture Factory were established and the city prospered. These important textile and furniture industries were at the heart of Drexel's existence for the rest of the 20th century and now into the 21st. Both companies made significant contributions to the Town of Drexel and are an important part of its heritage.

Location: Foothills, one hour and fifteen minutes east of Asheville
Town Offices: 202 Church Street, Drexel NC 28619; 828-437-7421
Website: www.ci.drexel.nc.us
County: Burke County: Burke County Government Center, 200 Avery Avenue, Morganton NC 28680; 828-439-4340
Elevation & Population: 1,194 feet, 1,900+
County Visitor/Welcome Center: Burke County Visitor Center, 102 East Union Street, Morganton NC 28655; 888-462-2921
County Chamber of Commerce: Burke County Chamber of Commerce, 110 East Meeting Street, Morganton NC 28655; 828-437-3021
Newspaper: The News Herald, 301 Collett Street, Morganton NC 28655; 828-437-2161
High School: Jimmy C Draughn High School, 709 Lovelady Road NE, Valdese NC 28690, 828-879-4200
Area Major Festivals: Waldensian Festival (August)
Area Natural Attractions: Brown Mountain Lights, Lake James State Park
Area Cultural Attractions: History Museum of Burke County, North Carolina School For The Deaf Museum, Old Burke County Courthouse Heritage Museum, Quaker Meadows Plantation, Senator Sam J. Erwin Jr. Museum
Recommended Restaurants: (For a complete list of all restaurants visit www.ashevilleguidebook.com)
   Papa Johns: (Pizza) 114 North Main Street, Drexel NC 28619; 828-433-7272
Recommended Places To Stay: (For a complete list of all accommodations visit www.ashevilleguidebook.com)
No accommodations currently available in Drexel. *See* Morganton

Flat Rock

Flat Rock began about a century and a half ago with large summer estates being built in the English manner by the affluent Charlestonians, Europeans and prominent plantation owners of the South's low country. The first great estate was built in 1827 by Charles Baring of Baring Brothers Banking firm of London, consisting of 3,000 acres, which he named Mountain Lodge. Baring also built a private chapel on his estate which is now St. John in the Wilderness Episcopal Church. The second large estate was built by Judge Mitchell King of Charleston, South Carolina, and was named Argyle. He later donated the land on which Hendersonville was built and directed the laying out of Main Street.

Many other coastal families soon followed, until the settlement grew to about fifty estates. They came to Flat Rock to escape the sweltering heat, yellow fever and malaria, which were running rampant. Summers in Flat Rock became a round of southern gaiety in antebellum days. South Carolina's low country gentry called Flat Rock "The Little Charleston of the Mountains." Most of these old estate homes still stand, surrounded by wide lawns, gardens, towering trees and virtually all graced by white pillar porches. A few of these gracious homes remain in the possession of the families of the original owners, although many of these grand estates are now centerpieces of planned residential communities.

Flat Rock is built around a tremendous outcropping of granite which is said to have been the site of Cherokee gatherings, most of which has been blasted away and used for highway material. The main "rock" can be found on the grounds of the Flat Rock Playhouse. Besides the Flat Rock Playhouse, the other main attraction in Flat Rock is Connemara, the Carl Sandburg Home, now a State Historic Site open to the public.

Location: Central Mountains. 45 minutes south of Asheville
Town Offices: 2685 Greenville Highway, Flat Rock NC 28731; 828-697-8100
County: Henderson County: County Offices, 1 Historic Courthouse Square, Hendersonville NC 28792; 828-697-4809
Elevation & Population: 2,205 feet, 2,500+
Visitor/Welcome Center: Hendersonville/ Flat Rock Visitors Information Center 201 South Main Street, Hendersonville NC 28792; 800-828-4244
County Chamber of Commerce: Henderson County Chamber of Commerce 204 Kanuga Road, Hendersonville NC 28739; 828-692-1413
Newspaper: Hendersonville Times-News 1717 Four Seasons Blvd, Hendersonville, NC 28792; 828-692-0505.
Movie Theatres: Flat Rock Cinema First-run foreign, independent and classic films. 2700 Greenville Highway, Flat Rock NC 28731; 828-697-2463
High School: East Henderson High School, 110 Upward Road, East Flat Rock NC 28726; 828-697-4768
Colleges and Universities: Blue Ridge Community College, 180 West Campus Drive, Flat Rock NC 28731; 828-694-1700
Area Major Festivals: North Carolina Apple Festival (September)
Area Natural Attractions: Apple Orchards in Henderson County, Dupont State Forest, Holmes Educational State Forest, Pisgah National Forest
Area Cultural Attractions: Carl Sandburg Home, Flat Rock Playhouse

Recommended Restaurants: (For a complete list of all restaurants visit www. ashevilleguidebook.com)

> **Hubba Hubba Smokehouse:** (BBQ) 2724 Greenville Highway, Flat Rock NC 28731; 828-694-3551

> **Season's Restaurant:** (American) Highland Lake Inn, 116 Water Lily Drive, Flat Rock NC 28731; 800-762-1376

> **Woodfield Inn:** (American) 2905 Greenville Highway, Flat Rock NC 28731; 828-693-6016

Recommended Places To Stay: (For a complete list of all accommodations visit www.ashevilleguidebook.com)

> **Flat Rock Inn:** (B&B) 2810 Greenville Highway, Flat Rock NC 28731; 800-266-3996

> **Highland Lake Inn:** (Resort) 116 Water Lily Drive, Flat Rock NC 28731; 800-762-1376

> **Woodfield Inn:** (County Inn) 2905 Greenville Highway, Flat Rock NC 28731; 828-693-6016

Fletcher

The Town of Fletcher, which was incorporated in 1989, is located in Henderson County, North Carolina. The town contains 6.1 square miles of land area and measures six miles in an east-west direction and less than four miles from north to south. Fletcher was incorporated in 1989 by way of an activist movement spearheaded by local politician Sara Waechter, who then became the first interim mayor of Fletcher.

Fletcher consists of primarily level and at times hilly terrain, which is dominated by Cane Creek and the French Broad River and their tributaries. Several major roadways provide easy access to Fletcher. US Highway 25 runs north-south through the center of the Town and is the main thoroughfare for residents. Interstate 26 is located to the west and travels through North Carolina to Tennessee and South Carolina. Fletcher is also home to a number of great parks, including the extensive Fletcher Community Park, which has youth and adult baseball and softball fields, multiple soccer fields, a playground, disc golf course, arboretum gardens and walking trails.

Location: Central Mountains, approximately 13 miles south of downtown Asheville

Town Offices: 4005 Hendersonville Road, Fletcher NC 28732; 828-687-3985

County: Henderson County: County Offices, 1 Historic Courthouse Square, Hendersonville NC 28792; 828-697-4809

Elevation & Population: 2,123 feet, 4,200+

County Chamber of Commerce: Henderson County Chamber of Commerce 204 Kanuga Road, Hendersonville NC 28739; 828-692-1413

Newspaper: Hendersonville Times-News 1717 Four Seasons Blvd, Hendersonville, NC 28792; 828-692-0505 or Asheville Citizen-Times,14 O'Henry Ave., Asheville NC 28801; 828-252-5611, 800-800-4204.

High School: North Henderson High School, 35 Fruitland Road, Hendersonville NC 28792; 828-697-4500 and West Henderson High School, 3600 Haywood Road, Hendersonville NC 28791; 828-891-6571

Hospitals: Park Ridge Hospital: 100 Hospital Drive, Fletcher NC 28792, 828-684-8501

Area Major Festivals: Bele Chere (Asheville-July), North Carolina Mountain State Fair (Asheville-September)

Area Natural Attractions: North Mills River Recreation Area, Pisgah National Forest, French Broad River

Area Cultural Attractions: Historic Johnson Farm

Recommended Restaurants: (For a complete list of all restaurants visit www.ashevilleguidebook.com)

> **Blue Sky Cafe:** (American) 3987 Hendersonville Road, Fletcher NC 28732; 828-684-1247

Recommended Places To Stay: (For a complete list of all accommodations visit www.ashevilleguidebook.com)

> **Chateau on the Mountain:** (B&B) 22 Vineyard Hill Drive, Fletcher NC 28732; 828-651-9810

> **Hampton Inn & Suites I-26:** (Motel) 18 Rockwood Road, Fletcher NC 28732; 828-687-0806

Forest City

Located on the far eastern edge of the mountains, Forest City began as a crossroads on the Shelby-Rutherfordton and Spartanburg-Lincolnton Roads and was incorporated in 1877 as Burnt Chimney, with the name changed to Forest City in 1887 after a prominent citizen, Forest Davis. This small city in the foothills, once a bustling mill town, still has much to offer visitors, including a large selection of stores and restaurants. In 1914, the Forest City Betterment Club embarked on a project to beautify the town's Main Street and today the original landscaped medians and fountain still exist. In 1927, the town was selected as one of the ten most beautiful and best planned towns in the United States by the US Department of Agriculture.

Forest City is famous for the great display of Christmas lights that brighten the city every holiday season; over half a million lights sparkle in the downtown area alone at Christmastime. Forest City is also home to the Bennett Classics Antique Auto Museum, the Rutherford County Farm Museum, and McNair Field, the home of the semi-professional baseball team the Forest City Owls.

Location: Foothills, 1 hour southeast of Asheville

Town Hall: 128 North Powell Street, Forest City NC 28403; 828-248-5202

County: Rutherford County: County Offices, 229 North Main Street, Rutherfordton NC 28139; 828-287-6045

Elevation & Population: 860 feet, 7500+

County Visitor/Welcome Center: Rutherford County Tourism 1990 US Highway 221 South, Forest City NC 28043; 800-849-5998

County Chamber of Commerce: Rutherford County Chamber of Commerce 162 North Main Street, Rutherfordton NC 28139; 828-287-3090

Newspaper: The Daily Courier 601 Oak Street, Forest City NC 28043; 828-245-6431

Movie Theatres: Retro Cinema 4 2270 US 221 South, Forest City NC 28043; 828-248-1670

High School: Chase High School, 1603 Chase High Road, Forest City NC 28043; 828-245-7668

Area Major Festivals: Christmas Festivities & Lights (December)

Area Natural Attractions: Chimney Rock Park, Lake Lure

Area Cultural Attractions: Bennett Classics Antique Auto Museum, KidSenses Children's InterACTIVE Museum, McNair Field/Forest City Owls, Rutherford County Farm Museum, Rutherford County Museum

Recommended Restaurants: (For a complete list of all restaurants visit www. ashevilleguidebook.com)

> **Big Dave's Family Seafood:** (Seafood) 123 Commercial Drive, Forest City NC 28043; 828-245-9844
>
> **City Table Barbeque:** (BBQ) 110 Powell Street, Forest City NC 28043; 828-247-8730
>
> **Hickory Log Barbecue:** (BBQ) 1163 West Main Street, Forest City NC 28043; 828-245-6241
>
> **Ol Blue's House of BBQ:** (BBQ) 1237 Piney Ridge Road, Forest City NC 28043; 828-245-2274
>
> **Rollins Cafeteria:** (Cafeteria) 2270 US Highway 74A Bypass, Forest City NC 28043; 828-245-9999
>
> **Scott's on Broadway:** (American) 753 South Broadway, Forest City NC 28043; 828-245-9811
>
> **Sisk Restaurant:** (American) 1168 West Main Street; Forest City NC 28043; 828-245-4222

Recommended Places To Stay: (For a complete list of all accommodations visit www.ashevilleguidebook.com)

> **Jameson Inn:** (Motel) 164 Jameson Inn Drive, Forest City NC 28043; 828-287-8788
>
> **Ramada Worldwide:** (Motel) 2600 Highway 74A Bypass, Forest City NC 28043; 828-248-1711

Franklin

Known as the "Gem of the Smokies," Franklin is the county seat of Macon County and is next to the Little Tennessee River. Settled in the early 1800's, much of the land around Franklin is still wilderness, making the town an excellent stopping-off point if your destination is the outdoors. In fact, nearly half of Macon County lies within the Nantahala National Forest which is comprised of over a half-million acres of unspoiled natural beauty. Franklin is also situated between two popular scenic gorges, the Cullasaja and the Nantahala. In its rush downhill, the Cullasaja River takes some spectacular spills, creating lower Cullasaja Falls with a drop of 250 feet. Dry Falls is a favorite with visitors, who can actually walk behind the roaring 75 foot wall of water.

The Franklin area is also famous for its many gem mines, with rubies, sapphires and garnets the major gemstones found. The area is so important as a gem hunting region that it has earned the name "Gem Capital of the World." In September, the Macon County Fair, the state's only true agricultural fair, is held here and in October, Scottish Heritage Week brings to life traditional concerts, lectures and highland games. Franklin is also home to the regional Macon County Airport, one of the few airports in the mountains.

Location: Western Mountains, 2 hours west of Asheville

Town Hall: 188 West Main Street, Franklin NC 28744, 828-524-2516

Website: www.franklinnc.com

County: Macon County: County Offices, 5 West Main Street, Franklin NC 28734; 828-349-2025

Elevation & Population: 1,900 feet, 3,000+

Visitor/Welcome Center: Franklin Chamber of Commerce 425 Porter Street, Franklin NC 28734; 866-372-5546

City Chamber of Commerce: Franklin Chamber of Commerce, 425 Porter Street, Franklin NC 28734; 866-372-5546

Newspaper: The Franklin Press 40 Depot Street, Franklin NC 28744; 828-524-2010

Movie Theatres: Ruby Cinemas, 2097 Georgia Road, Franklin NC 28734; 828-524-2076

High School: Franklin High School, 100 Panther Drive, Franklin NC 28734; 828-524-6467

Colleges and Universities: Southwestern Community College, 44 Siler Farm Road, Franklin NC 28734; 800-447-4091

Hospitals: Angel Medical Center, 120 Riverview Street, Franklin NC 28734; 828-524-8411

Area Major Festivals: Macon County Fair (September), Macon County Gemboree (July), Pumpkinfest (October), Window Wonderland (December)

Area Natural Attractions: Appalachian Scenic National Trail, Fontana Lake, Great Smoky Mountains National Park, Joyce Kilmer Memorial Forest, Nantahala National Forest, Waterfalls in Western North Carolina

Area Cultural Attractions: Franklin Gem & Mineral Museum, Macon County Historical Society & Museum, Perry's Water Gardens, Ruby City Gems Museum, Scottish Tartans Museum, Smoky Mountain Center for the Performing Arts

Recommended Restaurants: (For a complete list of all restaurants visit www.ashevilleguidebook.com)

    Cajun Connection: (Cajun Seafood) 549 Highlands Road, Franklin NC 28734; 828-369-6288

> **Frog & Owl Mountain Bistro:** (International) 46 East Main Street, Franklin NC 28734; 828-349-4112
>
> **Jer's Kitchen:** (Cafe) 1231 Georgia Road, Whistle Stop Mall, Franklin NC 28734; 828-524-1960
>
> **Lucio's Italian Restaurant:** (Italian) 313 Highlands Road, Franklin NC 28734; 828-369-6670
>
> **Stamey's Cafe:** (BBQ) 1111 East Main Street, Franklin NC 28734; 828-524-8198
>
> **The Hidden Gem Cafe:** (Cafe-American) 24 Lotla Street, Franklin NC 28734; 828-369-0575
>
> **Yati's International Bistro:** (International) 2726 Georgia Road, Franklin NC 28734; 828-349-9284

Recommended Places To Stay: (For a complete list of all accommodations visit www.ashevilleguidebook.com)

> **Buttonwood Inn Bed & Breakfast:** (B&B) 50 Admiral Drive, Franklin NC 28734; 888-368-8985
>
> **Carolina Motel:** (Motel) 2601 Georgia Road, Franklin NC 28734; 828-524-3380
>
> **Hampton Inn:** (Motel) 244 Cunningham Road, Franklin NC 28734; 800-426-7866
>
> **Microtel Inns & Suites:** (Motel) 81 Allman Drive, Franklin NC 28734; 888-403-1700
>
> **Oak Grove Cabins:** (Cabins) 9835 Bryson City Road, Franklin NC 28734; 828-369-0166
>
> **Oak Hill Country Inn Bed & Breakfast:** (B&B) 1689 Old Murphy Road, Franklin NC 28734; 800-587-6374
>
> **Wayah Creek Cottages & Gardens:** (Cabins, Cottages) 26 Wayah Way, Franklin NC 28734; 800-559-8280

Glen Alpine

With roots that date back to the mid 1800's, Glen Alpine began with the arrival of the Southern Railroad. Originally called Turkey Tail by railroad workers, Glen Alpine also was named Sigmundsburg, after Edmund Sigmund, a mill founder, and then later Glen Alpine Station. In the early 1870's the town was home to one of the then largest wooden structures in North Carolina, the Glen Alpine Springs Hotel, which was said to have had as many as 100 guests at a time. After the hotel closed in 1890's, the town's name was finally changed to just Glen Alpine. Glen Alpine today is primarily a residential community, and is also home to the Lake James Cellars winery.

Location: Foothills, 1 hour east of Asheville
Town Hall: 103 Pitts Street, Glen Alpine NC 28628; 828-584-2622
Website: www.townofglenalpinenc.org

County: Burke County: Burke County Government Center, 200 Avery Avenue, Morganton NC 28680; 828-439-4340
Elevation & Population: 1,201 feet, 1,100+
County Visitor/Welcome Center: Burke County Visitor Center, 102 East Union Street, Morganton NC 28655; 888-462-2921
County Chamber of Commerce: Burke County Chamber of Commerce, 110 East Meeting Street, Morganton NC 28655; 828-437-3021
Newspaper: The News Herald, 301 Collett Street, Morganton NC 28655; 828-437-2161
High School: Freedom High School, 511 Independence Boulevard, Morganton NC 28655; 828-433-1310
Area Major Festivals: Glen Alpine Fall Festival (October), Glen Alpine Christmas Parade (December), Glen Alpine 4th of July Parade (July)
Area Natural Attractions: Brown Mountain Lights, Lake James State Park
Area Cultural Attractions: History Museum of Burke County, North Carolina School For The Deaf Museum, Old Burke County Courthouse Heritage Museum, Quaker Meadows Plantation, Senator Sam J. Erwin Jr. Museum
Recommended Restaurants: (For a complete list of all restaurants visit www.ashevilleguidebook.com)
    Doogies Pizza & Subs: (Pizza) 500 West Main Street, Glen Alpine, NC 28628; 828-584-1111
    Glen Alpine Depot: (Country-American) 102 Linville Street, Glen Alpine NC 28628; 828-584-0202
Recommended Places To Stay: (For a complete list of all accommodations visit www.ashevilleguidebook.com)
    The Inn at Glen Alpine: (B&B) 105 Davis Street, Glen Alpine NC 28628; 828-584-9264

Granite Falls

Granite Falls, established in 1899, is located in southern Caldwell County just north of Hickory on U. S. Highway 321. Its history dates back before the Revolutionary War and its roots can be traced to land grants as early as 1754. Granite Falls was incorporated on May 1, 1899 and was named after the Falls on Gunpowder Creek, where a solid formation of granite spans the creek.

Home to the nationally recognized Bank of Granite, the Town of Granite Falls' economy has been centered on manufacturing, with tourism and the retirement industry also diversifying the economic base. Granite Falls is also home to one of the world's largest collection of soda pop memorabilia housed in the Antique Vending Company showroom. Recreational opportunities for visitors include the nearby Pisgah National Forest and the town's Lakeside Park on scenic Lake Rhodhiss. The Granite Falls History & Transportation Museum is also located in Granite Falls and is housed in the historic home of Andrew Baird, one of the town's original founders.

Rhodhiss is a small, quaint community near Granite Falls with a unique claim to fame. The town is known for a sign that proudly proclaims that the flags planted on the moon by the United States were woven in Rhodhiss. Located in both Caldwell and Burke counties, Rhodhiss is situated alongside the Catawba River just below Duke Energy's Rhodhiss Dam.

Location: Foothills, 1½ hours east of Asheville
Town Hall: 30 Park Square, Granite Falls NC 28630; 828-396-3131
Website: www.granitefallsnc.com
County: Caldwell County: County Offices, 904 West Avenue NW, Lenoir NC 28645; 828-757-1300
Elevation & Population: 1,191 feet, 4,600+
County Visitor/Welcome Center: Caldwell County Chamber of Commerce Visitor Center,1909 Hickory Boulevard SE, Lenoir NC 28645; 828-726-0323
County Chamber of Commerce: Caldwell County Chamber of Commerce, 1909 Hickory Boulevard SE, Lenoir NC 28645; 828-726-0323
Newspaper: News-Topic, 123 Pennton Avenue, Lenoir NC 28645; 828-758-7381
Movie Theatres: Carmike Westgate Twin, 1966 Morgantontown Boulevard SW, Lenoir NC 28645; 828-758-9902
High School: South Caldwell High School, 7035 Spartan Drive, Hudson NC 28638; 828-396-2188
Area Major Festivals: Granite Falls Art in the Park (June), Christmas Parade (December)
Area Natural Attractions: Pisgah National Forest, Tuttle Educational State Forest, Wilson Creek
Area Cultural Attractions: Caldwell Heritage Museum, Chapel of Rest, Fort Defiance, Granite Falls History &Transportation Museum, Happy Valley, 20 Miles of Furniture
Recommended Restaurants: (For a complete list of all restaurants visit www. ashevilleguidebook.com)
　　Huffy's: (Cafe) 23-3 Falls Avenue, Granite Falls NC 28630; 828-396-6111
　　Wise Guys Pizza: (Pizza) 30 Falls Avenue, Granite Falls NC 28630; 828-313-1013
Recommended Places To Stay: (For a complete list of all accommodations visit www.ashevilleguidebook.com)
　　Thistle House Bed & Breakfast: (B&B) 25 Hillside Avenue, Granite Falls NC 28630; 828-313-3989

Hayesville

Hayesville, incorporated in 1913, is the county seat of Clay County and is located at the far western edge of the North Carolina Mountains. The focal point of the town is the historic county seat courthouse, built in 1888, where many of the county's festivities are held. Hayesville is also home to the Clay County Historical & Arts Council Museum and the Peacock Playhouse where performances by the local theatrical group, The Licklog Players, can be seen. The museum is housed in the Old County Jail, which was constructed in 1912 and used until 1972. Another doorway to history is The People's Store (68 Church Street), a general store in operation since 1946 and now open as a small museum. Hours by appointment only by calling 828-557-0759.

Nearby Chatuge Lake, a TVA lake, has over 130 miles of shoreline, much of which can never be developed, and provides wonderful recreational opportunities for residents and visitors alike. This beautiful lake sets the tone for Hayesville. Few mountain cities can boast of such a great natural resource right in their own backyard.

Location: Western Mountains, 2 hours west of Asheville
County: Clay County: County Offices, 33 Main Street, Hayesville NC 28904; 828-389-0089
Elevation & Population: 2,200 feet, 300
County Visitor/Welcome Center: Clay County Chamber of Commerce, 388 Highway Business 64, Hayesville NC 28904; 828-389-3704
County Chamber of Commerce: Clay County Chamber of Commerce, 388 Highway Business 64, Hayesville NC 28904; 828-389-3704
Newspaper: Clay County Progress 43 Main Street, Hayesville NC 28904; 828-389-8431 and Smoky Mountain Sentinel 116 Sanderson Street, Hayesville NC 28904; 828-389-8338
Movie Theatres: Fieldstone Cinemas Six 1159 Jack Dayton, Young Harris GA 30582; 706-898-6843
High School: Hayesville High School, 250 Yellow Jacket Drive, Hayesville NC 28904; 828-389-6532
Area Major Festivals: Hayesville Festival on the Square (July)
Area Natural Attractions: Chatuge Lake, Joyce Kilmer Memorial Forest, Nantahala National Forest
Area Cultural Attractions: Clay County Historical & Arts Council Museum, John C. Campbell Folk School, Peacock Playhouse, The People's Store
Recommended Restaurants: (For a complete list of all restaurants visit www.ashevilleguidebook.com)
   Angelos Downtown Pizza: (Pizza-Italian) 45 Main Street, Hayesville NC 28904; 828-389-2500
   Cottage Salad Station Market & Deli: (Deli) 955 Highway 69, Hayesville NC 28904; 828-389-8473
   Hayesville Family Restaurant: (Country-American) 495 Highway 64 Business, Hayesville NC 28904; 828-389-4888
Recommended Places To Stay: (For a complete list of all accommodations visit www.ashevilleguidebook.com)
   Chatuge Mountain Inn: (Country Inn) 4238 Highway 64 East, Hayesville NC 28904; 828-389-9340

Deerfield Inn: (Country Inn) 40 Chatuge Lane, Highway 64 East, Hayesville NC 28904; 828-389-8272

LaForte's Country Cottages: (Cottages) 23 LaForte Lane, Hayesville NC 28904; 828-361-3367

Hickory

Located in the foothills of Western North Carolina, Hickory is the second largest city in the mountains and a great destination for furniture shopping as well as for culture activities and outdoor recreation. Hickory and surrounding Catawba County uniquely enjoy a world-wide reputation as one of the premier destinations for shoppers looking for fine furniture and home furnishings. Over fifty percent of America's furniture is produced within a 200-mile radius of Hickory, and virtually every major furniture manufacturer has a presence here. There are a number of malls featuring furniture stores and manufacturer's outlets in the greater Hickory area. These include the Catawba Furniture Mall and the prestigious Hickory Furniture Mart, both located on Highway 70. The Hickory Furniture Mart is the largest of its kind in the country and houses over 100 factory outlets, stores and galleries, representing over 1000 manufacturers. The mall also is home to the Catawba Valley Furniture Museum, which includes in its collections some of the area's first pieces of furniture ever produced. It is estimated that this mall receives over 500,000 visitors every year. Hickory is also one end of the "20 Miles of Furniture," a stretch of US Highway 321 between Lenoir and Hickory where numerous furniture outlets and stores also offer deep discounts. Think of this as a 20-mile-long furniture mall!

Hickory started in the 1850's when Henry Robinson built a tavern of logs under a huge Hickory tree. The city of "Hickory Tavern" was established shortly afterwards in 1863, and in 1873, the name was changed to Hickory. Hickory was known in the years after World War II for the "Miracle of Hickory." In 1944 the area around Hickory became the center of one of the worst outbreaks of polio ever recorded. Since local facilities were inadequate to treat the victims, the citizens of Hickory and the March of Dimes decided to build a hospital to care for the children of the region. From the time the decision was made until equipment, doctors, and patients were in a new facility, took less than 54 hours.

The cultural hub of Hickory is the famous SALT Block (an acronym that stands for Science, Art and Literature Together), where on one block downtown clustered together are the Catawba Science Center, the Hickory Museum of Art, the Hickory Public Library, the Western Piedmont Symphony, the United Arts Council of Catawba County and the Hickory Choral Society. A unique concentration of science and art, the SALT block is a major tourist destination in Hickory, with over 200,000 visitors a year. The block's anchor is the iconic former Claremont High School, built in 1925 and transformed 60 years later into the 74, 923 square-foot Arts and Science Center of Catawba Valley that houses many of the SALT Block organizations and institutions.

Hickory is also home to the Hickory Community Theatre and other important cultural institutions. These include the Harper House/Hickory History Center, located in the historic and stunningly beautiful Harper House, one of the finest examples of Queen Anne architecture and interior design to be found in North Carolina, and two historical houses that also are local cultural history museums, the Maple Grove Historical Museum and the J. Summie Propst House Museum.

Hickory has a Class A minor league baseball team, the Hickory Crawdads, that play at L.P. Frans Stadium, located at 2500 Clement Boulevard NW, and also the Hickory Motor Speedway, a racing facility that has presented competitions for over 50 years and is hailed as the birthplace of NASCAR stars Dale Earnhardt, Junior Johnson, Ned and Dale Jarrett and Harry Gant.

Recreational opportunities abound in the area, with more than 10 public golf courses in the Hickory metro area, and numerous parks and recreational facilities. One of the most convenient is the city park, Glenn C. Hilton, Jr. Memorial Park, located at 2000 6th Street NW, which features five picnic shelters, gazebo, lighted and paved walking trails, disc golf course, and fitness and nature trails. Other popular parks in Hickory include Bakers Mountain Park, at 6680 Bakers Mountain Road, the Ivey Arboretum in Carolina Park located at 1441 9th Avenue NE, and St. Stephens Park at 2247 36th Avenue NE. Bakers Mountain Park is located at the highest point in Catawba County (1780 feet) and features 189 acres of mature Chestnut Oak forest with nearly six miles of trails. The Ivey Arboretum in Carolina Park contains a collection of over 400 labeled species of native and rare trees and shrubs within a three-acre park and St. Stephens Park, a 9.1 acre park that features walking trails, a playground, educationally-themed landscaping and a dog park.

Hickory has been named an "All-America City" three times, the last time in 2007. This prestigious award is given annually to only ten cities in the United States. The Hickory Metro area has also been named the 10th best place to live and raise a family in America by Readers Digest. Higher educational institutions include Lenoir-Rhyne University and Catawba Valley Community College. Hickory, as one would expect for a city of 40,000 residents, has a strong lineup of festivals and cultural events. One of the major festivals is the famous Catawba Valley Pottery Festival held every March in the Hickory Metro Convention Center. Another popular annual event is the Hickory Alive program, featuring free concerts held every Friday evening in June and July in downtown Hickory.

Getting to Hickory is easy since the city is conveniently located on Interstate highway I-40. Hickory also has a small regional airport as well, the Hickory Regional Airport, for non-commercial aircraft.

Location: Foothills, 1 hour and 15 minutes east of Asheville
Town Hall: 76 North Center Street, Hickory NC 28601; 828-323-7400
Website: www.hickorygov.com
County: Catawba County: County Offices, 100-A South West Boulevard, Newton NC 28658; 828-465-8201

Elevation & Population: 910 feet, 40,000+

City Visitor/Welcome Center: Hickory Metro Convention & Visitors Bureau, 1960-A 13th Avenue Drive SE, Hickory NC 28602; 800-509-2444

County Visitor/Welcome Center: Catawba County Visitor Information Center, 1055 Southgate Corporation Park SW, Hickory NC 28602; 828-328-6111

County Chamber of Commerce: 1055 Southgate Corporation Park SW, Hickory NC 28602; 828-328-6111

Newspaper: Hickory Daily Record, 1100 Park Place, Hickory NC 28603; 828-322-4510

Movie Theatres: Carmike 14, 2000 SE Catawba Valley Boulevard, Hickory NC 28603; 828-304-0004 and Carolina Theater, 221 1st Avenue NW, Hickory NC 28601; 828-322-7210

High Schools: St. Stephens High School, 3205 34th Street Drive NE, Hickory NC 28601; 828-256-9841 and Challenger High School, 2550 Highway 70 SE, Hickory NC 28602; 828-485-2980

Colleges and Universities: Lenoir-Rhyne University, 625 7th Avenue NE, Hickory NC 28601; 828-328-1741 and Catawba Valley Community College, 2550 US Highway 70 SE, Hickory NC 28602; 828-327-7000

Hospitals: Frye Regional Medical Center, 420 North Center Street, Hickory NC 28601; 828-315-5000 and Catawba Valley Medical Center, 810 Fairgrove Church Road SE, Hickory NC 28602; 828-326-3000

Parks: Bakers Mountain Park, Glenn C. Hilton, Jr. Memorial Park, Ivey Arboretum in Carolina Park, St. Stephens Park

Area Major Festivals: Catawba Valley Pottery Festival (March), Hickory Alive (Friday evenings June & July), Hickory American Legion Fair (September), Oktoberfest (October)

Area Natural Attractions: Pisgah National Forest, South Mountains State Park

Area Cultural Attractions: Bunker Hill Covered Bridge, Catawba County Museum of History, Catawba Science Center, Harper House/Hickory History Center, Hickory Community Theatre, Hickory Crawdads, Hickory Furniture Mart, Hickory Motor Speedway, Hickory Museum of Art, Hiddenite Center, Historic Murray's Mill, J. Summie Propst House Museum, Maple Grove Historical Museum

Recommended Restaurants: (For a complete list of all 100+ Hickory restaurants visit www.ashevilleguidebook.com)

> **Applebee's:** (American) 2180 US Highway 70 SE; Hickory NC 28602; 828-324-9011
>
> **Atlanta Bread Company:** (American) 1756 Catawba Valley Boulevard, Hickory NC 28602; 828-325-8008
>
> **Beef 'O' Brady's:** (American) 1423 29th Avenue Drive NE; Hickory NC 28601; 828-256-2333
>
> **1859 Cafe:** (Continental-American Fine Dining) 443 2nd Avenue SW, Hickory NC 28602; 828-322-1859

Cafe Gouda: (Cafe) Belle Hollow, 2960 North Center Street, Hickory NC 28601; 828-267-1300

Carrabba's Italian Grill: (Italian) 1954 13th Avenue Drive SE, Hickory NC 28602; 828-322-9032

Chili's: (American) 2181 US Highway 70E, Hickory NC 28602; 828-328-8447

Cracker Barrel: (American) 1250 11th Street Court SE, Hickory NC 28602; 828-261-0508

Flat Rock Grill: (American) 1340 Highway 321 NW, Hickory NC 28601; 828-324-7339

Golden Corral: (American-Western) 1053 Lenoir-Rhyne Boulevard SE, Hickory NC 28602; 828-324-2122

Hannah's BBQ: (BBQ) 3198 Highway 127 South, Hickory NC 28602; 828-294-4227

International House of Pancakes: (American-Breakfast) 2415 US Highway 70 SE, Hickory NC 28602; 828-261-0150

J&S Cafeteria: (Cafeteria) 1940 13th Avenue Drive SE, Hickory NC 28602; 828-326-8926

Kobe Japanese House of Steak & Seafood: (Japanese) 1103 13th Avenue Drive SE, Hickory NC 28602; 828-328-5688

Longhorn Steakhouse: (American-Western) 1332 Highway 70 SE; Hickory NC 28602; 828-322-2944

Old German Schnitzel Haus: (German) 403 Highway 70 SW; Hickory NC 28602; 828-325-0800

Olive Garden Italian Restaurant: (Italian) 2261 Highway 70; Hickory NC 28602; 828-345-1015

Outback Steakhouse: (Australian) 1435 13th Avenue Drive SE, Hickory NC 28602; 828-328-6283

Red Lobster: (Seafood) 1846 US Highway 70 SE, Hickory NC 28602; 828-327-6113

Ruby Tuesday's: (American) 1821 US Highway 70 SE; Hickory NC 28602; 828-267-2981

Sagebrush Steakhouse: (American-Western) 2410 Highway 70 SE, Hickory NC 28602; 828-267-7243

Texas Roadhouse: (American-Western) 1020 Lenoir-Rhyne Boulevard SE, Hickory NC 28602; 828-325-9815

Tripp's Restaurant: (American) 1187 Lenoir-Rhyne Boulevard SE, Hickory NC 28602; 828-324-4400

Wild Wok Hickory Asian Bistro: (Asian) 2403 Catawba Valley Boulevard SE, Hickory NC 28602; 828-328-1688 and 303 N. Center Street, Hickory NC 28602; 828-322-1115

Youssef 242: (Continental Fine Dining) 242 11th Avenue NE, Hickory NC 28601; 828-324-2005

Recommended Places To Stay: (For a complete list of all accommodations visit www.ashevilleguidebook.com)

> **Comfort Suites:** (Motel) 1125 13th Avenue Drive SE, Hickory NC 28602; 828-323-1211
>
> **Courtyard by Marriott:** (Motel) 1946 13th Avenue Drive SE, Hickory NC 28602; 828-267-2100
>
> **Crowne Plaza Hotel:** (Hotel) 1385 Lenoir-Rhyne Boulevard SE; Hickory NC 28602; 828-323-1000
>
> **Fairfield Inn:** (Motel) 1950 13th Avenue Drive SE, Hickory NC 28602; 828-431-3000
>
> **Hampton Inn:** (Motel) 1520 13th Avenue Drive SE, Hickory NC 28602; 828-323-1150
>
> **Holiday Inn Express:** (Motel) 2250 US Highway 70 SE, Hickory NC 28602; 828-328-2081
>
> **Indian Springs Campground:** (RV Campground) 4361 Whitener Drive, Hickory NC 28602; 828-397-5700
>
> **Jameson Inn:** (Motel) 1120 13th Avenue Drive SE, Hickory NC 28602; 828-304-0410
>
> **Quality Inn & Suites:** (Motel) 1725 13th Avenue Drive NW, Hickory NC 28601; 828-431-2100
>
> **Red Roof Inn:** (Motel) 1184 Lenoir-Rhyne Boulevard SE, Hickory NC 28602; 828-323-1500
>
> **The Inn at Hickory:** (B&B) 464 Seventh Street SW, Hickory NC 28601; 828-324-0548
>
> **The Pecan Tree Inn of Hickory:** (B&B) 2303 Ewing Drive, Hickory NC 28602; 704-462-0822

Highlands

Highlands, incorporated in 1883, is located in the heart of the beautiful Nantahala National Forest. An affluent and quaint resort town with a large annual influx of families that own second homes, Highlands has an abundance of fine restaurants, shops, accommodations and upscale stores. Outdoor recreational opportunities abound, including hiking, fishing, boating, horseback riding and rock climbing. Highlands is also home to the Highlands Playhouse, which for over 50 years has provided summer stock theatre. Other great local resources in this cultural rich mountain town are the Highlands Nature Center, the Highlands Biological Station, The Bascom Center for the Visual Arts, the Martin-Lipscomb Performing Arts Center (Home to the Highlands Cashiers Players) and the Hudson Library located at 554 Main Street.

The Scaly Mountain Outdoor Center in nearby Scaly Mountain offers snow tubing in the winter and summer tubing on artificial turf slopes. Also, only two miles from Highlands is the Dry Falls waterfall in the Nantahala National Forest, easily accessible and worth the trip.

Location: Western Mountains, 1½ hour west of Asheville
Town Hall: 210 South 4th Street, Highlands NC 28741; 828-526-2118
Website: www.highlandsnc.org
County: Macon County: County Offices, 5 West Main Street, Franklin NC 28734; 828-349-2025
Elevation & Population: 4,118 feet,1,000+
Visitor/Welcome Center: Highlands Chamber of Commerce Visitor Center 269 Main Street, Highlands NC 28741; 866-526-5841
City Chamber of Commerce: Highlands Chamber of Commerce 269 Main Street, Highlands NC 28741; 828-526-5841
Newspaper: The Highlander 134 North 5th Street, Highlands NC 28741; 828-526-4114
High School: Highlands School, 545 Pierson Drive, Highlands NC 28741; 828-526-2147
Hospitals: Highlands-Cashiers Hospital, 190 Hospital Drive, Highlands NC 28741; 828-526-1200
Area Major Festivals: Highlands-Cashiers Chamber Music Festival (July-August)
Area Natural Attractions: Joyce Kilmer Memorial Forest, Nantahala National Forest, Waterfalls in Western North Carolina
Area Cultural Attractions: Highlands Biological Station, Highlands Museum & Historical Village, Highlands Nature Center, Macon County Historical Society & Museum, Museum of American Cut and Engraved Glass, The Bascom
Recommended Restaurants: (For a complete list of all restaurants visit www.ashevilleguidebook.com)

> **Buck's Coffee Cafe:** (Cafe) 384 Main Street, Highlands NC 28741; 828-526-0020
>
> **Cafe 460 in Main Street Pharmacy:** (Breakfast-Lunch, Cafe) 460 Main Street, Highlands NC 28741; 828-526-8926
>
> **Cyprus Restaurant:** (International) 490 Dillard Road, Highlands NC 28741; 828-526-4429
>
> **Nick's Fine Foods:** (American) 108 Main Street, Highlands NC 28741; 828-526-2706
>
> **Madison's Restaurant and Wine Garden:** (American-Fine Dining) Old Edwards Inn and Spa, 445 Main Street,
> **Highlands NC 28741; 828-526-5477**
>
> **Oak Street Cafe:** (Fine Dining-American) 332 Main Street, Highlands NC 28741; 828-787-2200
>
> **On The Verandah:** (American/International-Fine Dining) 1536 Franklin Road, Highlands NC 28741; 828-526-2338
>
> **Ristorante Paoletti:** (Italian) 440 Main Street, Highlands NC 28741; 828-526-4906
>
> **Wild Thyme Gourmet:** (Cafe) 490 Carolina Way, Highlands NC 28741; 828-526-4035

Wolfgang's Restaurant and Wine Bistro: (Eclectic Contemporary American-Fine Dining) 474 Main Street, Highlands NC 28741; 828-526-3807

Recommended Places To Stay: (For a complete list of all accommodations visit www.ashevilleguidebook.com)

Colonial Pines Inn Bed & Breakfast: (B&B) 541 Hickory Street, Highlands NC 28741; 866-526-2060

Hampton Inn: (Motel) 96 Log Cabin Lane, Highlands NC 28741; 800-426-0352

Highlands Inn: (Village Inn) 420 Main Street, Highlands NC 28741; 800-964-6955

Highlands Suite Hotel: (Hotel) 200 Main Street, Highlands NC 28741; 877-553-3761

Inn at Half Mile Farm: (Country Inn) 214 Half Mile Drive, Highlands NC 28741; 800-946-6822

Main Street Inn: (Village Inn) Main Street Inn, 270 Main Street, Highlands NC 28741; 800-213-9142

Mitchell's Lodge & Cottages: (Country Lodge) 264 Dillard Road, Highlands NC 28741; 800-522-9874

Old Edwards Inn and Spa: (Hotel and Spa) 445 Main Street, Highlands NC 28741; 866-526-8008

4 1/2 Street Inn: (B&B) 55 4½ Street, Highlands NC 28741; 888-799-4464

Hildebran

Hildebran, incorporated in 1910, was originally known as Switch but was later changed to Hildebran after J. A. Hildebran, a local lumber dealer. Today, the town has nearly 1,800 residents. Each Christmas, this small community stages an annual Christmas parade and is working to build its business and industrial base. Hildebran is home also to the Hildebran Farmer's Market, held every Thursday May through October in the Town Hall parking lot.

Location: Foothills, 1½ hours east of Asheville

Town Hall: 202 South Center Street, Hildebran NC 28637; 828-397-5801

County: Burke County: Burke County Government Center, 200 Avery Avenue, Morganton NC 28680; 828-439-4340

Elevation & Population: 1,188 feet, 1,800+

County Visitor/Welcome Center: Burke County Visitor Center, 102 East Union Street, Morganton NC 28655; 888-462-2921

County Chamber of Commerce: Burke County Chamber of Commerce, 110 East Meeting Street, Morganton NC 28655; 828-437-3021

Newspaper: The News Herald, 301 Collett Street, Morganton NC 28655; 828-437-2161

High School: East Burke High School, 3695 East Burke Boulevard, Connelly Springs NC 28612; 828-397-5541

Area Major Festivals: Hildebran Heritage Festival (October), Hildebran Christmas Parade (December), Hildebran Festival of Lights (December)

Area Natural Attractions: Brown Mountain Lights, Lake James State Park

Area Cultural Attractions: History Museum of Burke County, North Carolina School For The Deaf Museum, Old Burke County Courthouse & Heritage Museum, Quaker Meadows Plantation, Senator Sam J. Erwin Jr. Museum

Recommended Restaurants: (For a complete list of all restaurants visit www.ashevilleguidebook.com)

Chubby's: (Cafe) 511 US Highway 70, HIldebran NC 28637; 828-397-3911

Recommended Places To Stay: (For a complete list of all accommodations visit www.ashevilleguidebook.com)

No accommodations currently available in Hildebran. *See* Morganton.

Hot Springs

Hot Springs, located on the French Broad River about 40 minutes north of Asheville, was started when hot mineral springs were discovered in 1792. It is reported that people were visiting the springs by 1778 for the waters' reported healing properties. In 1828 a major road, the Buncombe Turnpike, was constructed through the current town making the area more accessible and Hot Springs became a famous resort town that catered to folks looking for relaxation in the mountains as well as healing in the mineral springs. Today Hot Springs still welcomes visitors who wish to explore and play in the surrounding mountains, and the naturally occurring hot springs are still an attraction. The major center, if you are interested in trying the hot springs, is the Hot Springs Resort & Spa located on Bridge Street.

The Appalachian Trail runs along downtown's Bridge Street and climbs the mountains on either side of the river and Whitewater Rafting and kayaking are popular on the French Broad River itself. There are numerous other hiking, mountain biking, backpacking, and sightseeing opportunities in the nearby Pisgah National Forest.

Location: Central Mountains, 1 hour northwest of Asheville

City Hall: 186 Bridge Street, Hot Springs NC 28743; 828-622-7591

Website: www.townofhotsprings.org

County: Madison County: County Offices, 2 North Main Street, Marshall NC 28753; 828-649-2854

Elevation & Population: 1,330 feet, 700+

City Visitor/Welcome Center: Hot Springs Visitors Center Highway 25-70, Hot Springs NC 28743; 828-622-7611

County Visitor/Welcome Center: Madison County Visitors Center 635-4 Carl Eller Road, Mars Hill NC 28754; 877-262-3476, 828 680-9031

County Chamber of Commerce: Madison County Chamber of Commerce 635-4 Carl Eller Road, Mars Hill NC 28754; 828-689-9351

Newspaper: News-Record & Sentinel 58 Back Street, Marshall NC 28753; 828-649-1075

High School: Madison High School, 5740 US Highway 25/70, Marshall NC 28753; 828-649-2876

Area Major Festivals: French Broad River Festival (May), Bluff Mountain Music Festival (June), Civil War Warm Springs Skirmish (June)

Area Natural Attractions: Appalachian Scenic National Trail, French Broad River, Pisgah National Forest, Max Patch

Area Cultural Attractions: Rural Life Museum, Zebulon B. Vance Birthplace

Recommended Restaurants: (For a complete list of all restaurants visit www. ashevilleguidebook.com)

> **Martha's at Mountain Magnolia Inn:** (American-Fine Dining) 204 Lawson Street, Hot Springs NC 28743; 800-622-9553
>
> **Sweet Imaginations Cafe:** (Cafe) 170 Bridge Street, Hot Springs NC 28753; 828-622-7522
>
> **The Iron Horse Restaurant and Tavern:** (American) 24 South Andrew Avenue, Hot Springs NC 28743; 866-402-9377

Recommended Places To Stay: (For a complete list of all accommodations visit www.ashevilleguidebook.com)

> **Duckett House Inn & Farm:** (B&B) 433 Lance Avenue, Hot Springs NC 28743; 828-622-7621
>
> **Mountain Magnolia Inn and Retreat:** (Country Inn) 204 Lawson Street, Hot Springs NC 28743; 800-622-9553
>
> **Iron Horse Station:** (Village Inn) 24 South Andrew Avenue, Hot Springs NC 28743; 866-402-9377
>
> **Treehouse Cabins:** (Cabins) High Mountain Road, Hot Springs NC 28743; 828-622-7296

Hudson

The Town of Hudson, incorporated in 1905, is located in Caldwell County approximately 15 miles north of Interstate 40 and was named after the Hudson brothers, Monroe and Johnnie, who were among the first lumber men in the area and became leaders of what was then known as Hudsonville. Hudson started as a sawmill camp and as the city grew textile and furniture industries played prominent roles in the economy. Hudson today has a vibrant economy based on small business and tourism, and there are approximately 150 businesses currently established. Hudson is home to many of the county's industrial leaders, including Kincaid Furniture, Shurtape Technologies, Shurford Mills and Sealed Air Corporation.

The town has two parks: Redwood Park, which features a beautiful playground with children's slides and activities, a swimming pool and several ball fields; and the Hickman Windmill Park which features the Hudson Railroad Depot Museum as well as a 100-year-old windmill. Hudson is also home to South Caldwell High

School and Caldwell Community College, which has a campus in Hudson with an enrollment of 4,000 students.

Caldwell County, known as the Furniture Capital of the South, is home to the "20 Miles of Furniture" where numerous outlets and stores offer deep discounts. Located along or near a stretch of U.S. Highway 321 between Lenoir and Hickory, the area, which passes though Hudson, is a required destination for any serious shopper looking for furniture. Hudson's downtown features a mix of mom-and-pop businesses and is a short drive to the Hudson Uptown Building, known locally as the HUB. This former renovated school building has become a favorite for community gatherings and Hudson's acclaimed annual dinner theatres.

Cajah's Mountain, founded in 1983, is one of Caldwell County's most popular residential communities. The town is located near Hudson and has seen recent expansion in residential growth along with commercial and industrial development.

Location: Foothills, 1½ hours east of Asheville
Town Hall: 550 Central Street, Hudson N C 28638; 828-728-8272
Website: www.ci.hudson.nc.us
County: Caldwell County: County Offices, 904 West Avenue NW, Lenoir NC 28645; 828-757-1300
Elevation & Population: 1,263 feet, 3,000+
County Visitor/Welcome Center: Caldwell County Chamber of Commerce Visitor Center,1909 Hickory Boulevard SE, Lenoir NC 28645; 828-726-0323
County Chamber of Commerce: Caldwell County Chamber of Commerce, 1909 Hickory Boulevard SE, Lenoir NC 28645; 828-726-0323
Newspaper: News-Topic, 123 Pennton Avenue, Lenoir NC 28645; 828-758-7381
Movie Theatres: Carmike Westgate Twin, 1966 Morganton Boulevard SW, Lenoir NC 28645; 828-758-9902
High School: South Caldwell High School, 7035 Spartan Drive, Hudson NC 28638; 828-396-2188
Colleges and Universities: Caldwell Community College, 2855 Hickory Boulevard, Hudson NC 28638; 828-726-2200
Area Major Festivals: Butterfly Festival, (May), Foothills Pottery Festival (October), 4th of July Kiddie Kar Parade (July)
Area Natural Attractions: Pisgah National Forest, Tuttle Educational State Forest, Wilson Creek
Area Cultural Attractions: Caldwell Heritage Museum, Chapel of Rest, Fort Defiance, Granite Falls History &Transportation Museum, Happy Valley, 20 Miles of Furniture
Recommended Restaurants: (For a complete list of all restaurants visit www. ashevilleguidebook.com)
   Vintage Cafe & Bakery: (Cafe) 540 Central Street, Hudson NC 28638; 828-728-3043
   Yellow Submarine Sandwich Shop: (Sandwiches) 564 Central Street, Hudson NC 28638; 828-726-1988

Recommended Places To Stay: (For a complete list of all accommodations visit www.ashevilleguidebook.com)

No accommodations currently available in Hudson. *See* Lenoir and Granite Falls.

Jefferson

Jefferson, the county seat of Ashe County, was established in 1800 and was one of the first towns in the United States to be named after President Thomas Jefferson, who at the time was Vice-President. Originally called Jeffersonton, the name was later changed to Jefferson. The ancient New River, one of the oldest rivers in the world, flows through the town. The Museum of Ashe County History is located in the historic 1904 Ashe County Courthouse building and has exhibits pertaining to the history of Ashe County and its people. The largest hospital in Ashe County is located also in Jefferson, Ashe Memorial Hospita,l as well as the Ashe campus of Wilkes Community College.

Nearby Lansing is home to the famous Ola Belle Reed Homecoming Festival, a celebration of mountain music. Lansing's classic small town setting is enhanced by the surrounding hills and Phoenix Mountain (elevation 4,170 feet) in the background as well as the homes dotting the narrow, tree lined streets.

Location: Northern Mountains, 2½ hours east of Asheville

Lansing Town Hall: 173 B Street, Lansing NC 28643; 336-384-3938

County: Ashe County: County Offices, 150 Government Circle, Suite 2500, Jefferson NC 28640; 336-846-5501

Elevation & Population: 3,000 feet, 1400+

County Chamber of Commerce: Ashe County Chamber of Commerce 01 North Jefferson Street, Suite C, West Jefferson NC 28694: 336-846-9550

Newspaper: Jefferson Post, 203 South Second Street, West Jefferson NC 28694; 336-846-7164

High School: Ashe County High School, 184 Campus Drive, West Jefferson NC 28694; 336-846-2400

Colleges and Universities: Wilkes Community College, 363 Campus Drive, Jefferson NC 28640; 336-846-3900

Hospitals: Ashe Memorial Hospital, 200 Hospital Avenue, Jefferson NC 28640; 336-846-7101

Area Major Festivals: Ola Belle Reed Homecoming Festival (August)

Area Natural Attractions: Blue Ridge Parkway; Mount Jefferson State Natural Area, New River State Park

Area Cultural Attractions: Ashe County Arts Council Gallery, Ben Long Frescoes, Museum of Ashe County History

Recommended Restaurants: (For a complete list of all restaurants visit www.ashevilleguidebook.com)

Blue Ridge Cafe and Bakery: (Cafe) 246 J. W. Luke Road, Glendale Springs NC 28629; 336-982-4811

Los Arcoiris: (Mexican) 327 E. Main Street, Jefferson NC 28640; 336-846-1639

Shatley Springs Inn: (Family Style-American) 407 Shatley Springs Road, Crumpler NC 28617; 336-982-4466

Sweet Aromas Bakery and Cafe: (Cafe) 406 Court Street, Jefferson NC 28640; 336-846-2914

Recommended Places To Stay: (For a complete list of all accommodations visit www.ashevilleguidebook.com)

Best Western Eldreth Inn: (Motel) 829 East Main Street, Jefferson NC 28640; 336-246-4499

Highlander Motel: (Motel) 891 Highway 16 South, Jefferson NC 28640; 336-246-2383

Jefferson Landing: (Resort) Highway 16/88, Jefferson NC 28640; 800-292-6274

Rocking Chair Inn: (B&B) 1115 Highway 16 South, Jefferson NC 28640; 336-246-9833

Lake Lure

Located on the beautiful northern end of 720-acre man-made Lake Lure, the town of Lake Lure offers an eclectic and tourist-oriented selection of shops, restaurants and accommodations. The town also has a boating facility, the Lake Lure Marina where boats can be rented, a public beach for swimming and a lovely lakeside park at the Morse Park peninsula that is open to residents and visitors. The lake was created in 1927 by the creation of a hydroelectric dam on the Rocky Broad River and is considered one of the most beautiful man-made lakes in America by National Geographic. Covered, pontoon boat tours of Lake Lure are offered at the Marina and are a wonderful way to see this extraordinary lake. In recent years, the Lake Lure area has served as the filming location for several major motion pictures including Last of the Mohicans with Daniel Day-Lewis; My Fellow Americans, a 1996 comedy starring Jack Lemmon and James Garner; and Dirty Dancing starring Patrick Swayze. Lake Lure, for a town of its small size, is fortunate to have an outstanding library, the Mountain Branch Library, located at 150 Bill's Creek Road.

Location: Central Mountains, 45 minutes south of Asheville

Town Hall: 2948 Memorial Highway, Lake Lure NC 28746; 828-625-9983

Website: www.townoflakelure.com

County: Rutherford County: County Tourism Development Authority Offices, 1990 Highway 221 South, Forest City NC 28043; 828-245-1492

Elevation & Population: 1,000 Feet, 1,000+

Visitor/Welcome Centers: (Two) Hickory Nut Gorge Visitor Center, 2926 Memorial Highway, Lake Lure NC 28746; 877-625-2725 and Rutherford Tourism Development Authority Center, 1990 Highway 221 South, Forest City NC 28043; 828-245-1492

City Chamber of Commerce: Hickory Nut Gorge Chamber of Commerce, PO Box 32, Chimney Rock NC 28720; 877-625-2725

County Chamber of Commerce: Rutherford County Chamber of Commerce, 162 North Main Street, Rutherfordton NC 28139; 828-287-3090

County Tourism Development: Lake Lure & the Blue Ridge Foothills, 1990 US Highway 221 South, Forest City NC 28043; 828-245-1492

Newspaper: The Mountain Breeze, 828-625-9330

High School: R.S. Central High School, 641 US Highway 221 North, Rutherfordton NC 28139; 828-287-3304

Area Major Festivals: Lure of the Dragons (May)

Area Natural Attractions: Apple Orchards in Henderson County, Chimney Rock Park, Lake Lure, Pisgah National Forest

Recommended Restaurants: (For a complete list of all restaurants visit www.ashevilleguidebook.com)

> **Beachside Grill:** (Grill) 2793 Memorial Highway, Lake Lure NC 28746; 828-625-0937
>
> **La Strada at Lake Lure:** (Italian) 2693 Memorial Highway, Lake Lure NC 28746; 828-625-1118
>
> **Lake Lure Dinner Cruise:** (Gourmet on the water dining) Departures from Rumbling Bald Resort, 112 Mountains
>
> **Boulevard, Lake Lure NC 28746; 828-694-3015**
>
> **Larkin's On The Lake:** (American) 1020 Memorial Highway, Lake Lure NC 28746; 828-625-4075
>
> **The Veranda Restaurant:** (American) 1927 Lake Lure Inn & Spa, 2771 Memorial Highway, Lake Lure NC 28746; 828-625-2525

Recommended Places To Stay: (For a complete list of all accommodations visit www.ashevilleguidebook.com)

> **Gaestehaus Salzburg Bed & Breakfast:** (B&B) 1491 Memorial Highway, Lake Lure NC 28746; 877-694-4029
>
> **1927 Lake Lure Inn & Spa:** (Resort) 2771 Memorial Highway, Lake Lure NC 28746; 828-625-2525
>
> **Lodge on Lake Lure:** (B&B) 361 Charlotte Drive, Lake Lure NC 28746; 800-733-2785
>
> **Rumbling Bald Resort on Lake Lure:** (Resort) 112 Mountains Boulevard, Lake Lure NC 28746; 800-419-3854
>
> **Wyndham Resort at Fairfield Mountains:** (Resort) 747 Buffalo Creek Road, Lake Lure NC 28746; 800-829-3149

Lenoir

Lenoir, the county seat of Caldwell County, is a foothills city rich in history, diverse recreational and cultural opportunities, local attractions and a rich quality of life. The largest city in Caldwell County, Lenoir is also home to the Caldwell County Historical Society Heritage Museum and Tuttle Educational State Forest. The first settlement in Lenoir was known as Tucker's Barn, named for the family who settled in the area around the 1760s. The settlement became a large meeting place for many gatherings and became so popular a fiddle tune was composed and written titled "Tucker's Barn." Doc Watson eventually recorded this tune in 1964 on an album titled, The Watson Family Tradition.

Caldwell County, known as the Furniture Capital of the South, is home to the "20 Miles of Furniture" where numerous outlets and stores offer deep discounts. Located along or near a stretch of U.S. Highway 321 between Lenoir and Hickory, the area is a required destination for any serious shopper looking for furniture. The County also contains more than 50,000 acres of recreational land, much of it part of the Pisgah National Forest. Two of the outstanding local attractions in the county near Lenoir are the Wilson Creek Gorge area and the beautiful T.H. Broyhill Park, on Lakewood Street, which has a half-mile nature loop circling a man-made lake. A joint project of the Broyhill Family Foundation and the city of Lenoir, Oriental gardens on the park set the tone of elegance and serenity where walkers and joggers can enjoy a lovely nature sanctuary.

Stretching from Lenoir towards Wilkesboro along Highway 268 is historic "Happy Valley." Located on the banks of the Yadkin River, Happy Valley was so named by the early settlers who described the valley as "a place of beauty, peace and tranquility" and the name aptly remains. A number of attractions are in the valley, including Fort Defiance, the Chapel of Rest and Whippoorwill Academy and Village.

The Village of Cedar Rock is the smallest and the youngest of Caldwell County's municipalities. Built around Cedar Rock Country Club, the town is nestled at the foot of the Brushy Mountains. Gamewell, incorporated in 1981, is situated midway between Lenoir and Morganton along NC Highway 18 and is primarily residential.

Location: Foothills, 1½ hours east of Asheville
Town Hall: 801 West Avenue, Lenoir NC 28645; 828-757-2200
Website: www.cityoflenoir.com
County: Caldwell County: County Offices, 904 West Avenue NW, Lenoir NC 28645; 828-757-1300
Elevation & Population: 1,182 feet, 17,000+
County Visitor/Welcome Center: Caldwell County Chamber of Commerce Visitor Center, 1909 Hickory Boulevard SE, Lenoir NC 28645; 828-726-0323
County Chamber of Commerce: Caldwell County Chamber of Commerce, 1909 Hickory Boulevard SE, Lenoir NC 28645; 828-726-0323
Newspaper: News-Topic, 123 Pennton Avenue, Lenoir NC 28645; 828-758-7381
Movie Theatres: Carmike Westgate Twin, 1966 Morgantontown Boulevard SW, Lenoir NC 28645; 828-758-9902
High School: West Caldwell High School, 300 West Caldwell Drive, Lenoir NC 28645; 828-758-5583 and Hibriten High School, 1350 Panther Trail, Lenoir NC 28645; 828-758-7376
Hospitals: Caldwell Memorial Hospital, 321 Mulberry Street SW, Lenoir NC 28645; 828-757-5100

Area Major Festivals: Blackberry Festival (July), Historic Happy Valley Heritage Old-time Fiddler's Convention (September)

Area Natural Attractions: Pisgah National Forest, Tuttle Educational State Forest, Wilson Creek

Area Cultural Attractions: Caldwell Heritage Museum, Chapel of Rest, Fort Defiance, Granite Falls History &Transportation Museum, Happy Valley, 20 Miles of Furniture

Recommended Restaurants: (For a complete list of all restaurants visit www.ashevilleguidebook.com)

    Giovanni's: (Italian) 925 Wilkesboro Boulevard NE, Lenoir, NC 28645. 828-754-1000

    Hannah's Bar-B-Q: (BBQ) 137 Blowing Rock Boulevard, Lenoir NC 28645; 828-754-7032

    Meedo's: (Italian) 211 Arrowood Street SE, Lenoir NC 28645; 828-758-1180

    Our Place: (American) 813 West Avenue NW, Lenoir NC 28645; 828-754-3645

    The Wine Cellar and Bistro: (International-Fine Dining) 128 Main Street NW, Lenoir NC 28645; 828-754-2828

    Uptown Cafe & Bakery: (Cafe, Bakery) 104 Main Street SW, Lenoir NC 28645; 828-757-3381

Recommended Places To Stay: (For a complete list of all accommodations visit www.ashevilleguidebook.com)

    Comfort Inn: (Motel) 970 Blowing Rock Boulevard NE, Lenoir NC 28645; 828-754-2090

    Days inn: (Motel) 206 Blowing Rock Boulevard, Lenoir NC 28645; 828-754-0731

    Irish Rose Bed & Breakfast: (B&B) 1344 Harper Avenue NW, Lenoir NC 28645; 828-758-2323

    Jameson Inn: (Motel) 350 Wilkesboro Boulevard, Lenoir NC 28645; 828-758-1200

Little Switzerland

Little Switzerland is an unincorporated community in Mitchell County, and was formed in 1909 on eleven hundred acres surveyed from the top of Grassy Mountain by the "Switzerland Company." It began as a private resort on the Blue Ridge Parkway and continues today as a primarily summer vacation destination.

The elevations in the Little Switzerland area range from 3200 feet in the village to 4000 feet at the top of Grassy Mountain, offer incredible views of Mt. Mitchell to the west, Table Rock, Hawksbill and Grandfather Mountain to the east, and the valleys of the South Toe, Turkey Cove and the bustling Catawba. Little Switzerland was named because of its sweeping panoramas of deep valleys and distant ranges resembling those of the foothills of the Swiss Alps.

Location: Northern Mountains, 2 hours east of Asheville

County: Mitchell County: 26 Crimson Laurel Circle, Bakersville NC 28705; 828-688-3295

Elevation & Population: 3,500 feet, 200+

County Visitor/Welcome Center Website: Mitchell County Visitor Center In Museum of North Carolina Minerals, Milepost 331, Blue Ridge Parkway, Spruce Pine NC 28777; 800-227-3912

County Chamber of Commerce: Mitchell County Chamber of Commerce 11 Crystal Street, Spruce Pine NC 28777; 828-765-9033

Newspaper: Mitchell News-Journal 291 Locust Avenue, Spruce Pine 28777; 828-765-2071

High School: Mitchell High School, 416 Ledger School Road, Bakersville NC 28705; 8280688-2101

Area Natural Attractions: Blue Ridge Parkway, Pisgah National Forest

Area Cultural Attractions: Emerald Village, Museum of North Carolina Minerals, North Carolina Mining Museum, Orchard at Altapass

Recommended Restaurants: (For a complete list of all restaurants visit www.ashevilleguidebook.com)

Cavern Tavern at the Skyline Village Inn: (American) Skyline Village Inn, 12255 Highway 226A, Little Switzerland NC 28749; 828-994-0027

Switzerland Cafe: (American) 9440 Highway 226A, Little Switzerland NC 28749; 828-765-5289

Recommended Places To Stay: (For a complete list of all accommodations visit www.ashevilleguidebook.com)

Alpine Inn: (Country Inn) 8576 Highway 226A, Little Switzerland NC 28749; 877-765-5380

Big Lynn Lodge: (Country Lodge) Highway 226A, Little Switzerland NC 28749; 800-654-5232

Skyline Village Inn & Cavern Tavern: (Village Inn) 12255 Highway 226A, Little Switzerland NC 28749; 828-994-0027

Switzerland Inn: (Country Inn) 86 High Ridge Road, Little Switzerland NC 28749; 800-654-4026

Long View

Long View is a small city located primarily in Catawba County in the foothills of Western North Carolina and adjacent to the much larger city of Hickory. Long View was incorporated in 1907, and part of it also extends into nearby Burke County. Long View is primarily a residential community and is continuous with Hickory, where most Long View residents work. It has an outstanding Recreation Center for public use which is located on 2nd Avenue, with nearby facilities that include a playground for children, walking track, tennis courts and a ball field. Long View also is home to a number of businesses of note, including the industrial service Maple Springs Laundry, and furniture companies Drexel Heritage and Century Furniture. The Hickory Regional Airport is located in the Long View area and the city is also close to the home field of the Hickory Crawdads, a Class A minor league baseball team.

Location: Foothills, 1 hour and 15 minutes east of Asheville
City Government Center: 2404 1st Avenue SW, Long View, NC 28602; 828-322-3921
County: Catawba County: County Offices, 100-A South West Boulevard, Newton NC 28658; 828-465-8201
Elevation & Population: 1,155 feet, 4,700+
County Visitor/Welcome Center: Catawba County Visitor Information Center, 1055 Southgate Corporation Park SW, Hickory NC 28602; 828-328-6111
County Chamber of Commerce: Catawba County Chamber of Commerce, 1055 Southgate Corporation Park SW, Hickory NC 28602; 828-328-6111
Newspapers: The Claremont Courier, 3283 White Oak Court, Claremont NC 28610; 828-320-8450 and the Hickory Daily Record, 1100 Park Place, Hickory NC 28603; 828-322-4510
High Schools: Hickory High School, 1234 3rd Street NE, Hickory NC 28601; 828-322-5860 and East Burke High School, 3695 East Burke Boulevard, Connelly Springs NC 28612; 828-397-5541
Area Major Festivals: Catawba Valley Pottery Festival (March)
Area Natural Attractions: Pisgah National Forest, South Mountains State Park
Area Cultural Attractions: Bunker Hill Covered Bridge, Catawba County Museum of History, Catawba Science Center, Harper House/Hickory History Center, Hickory Furniture Mart, Hickory Motor Speedway, Hickory Museum of Art, Hiddenite Center, Historic Murray's Mill
Recommended Restaurants: (For a complete list of all restaurants visit www.ashevilleguidebook.com)
No restaurants currently available in Long View. *See* Hickory
Recommended Places To Stay: (For a complete list of all accommodations visit www.ashevilleguidebook.com)
No accommodations currently available in Long View. *See* Hickory

Maggie Valley

Maggie Valley is a well-known tourist-oriented village that occupies a lush green valley in Haywood County and gets its name from Maggie Mae Setzer. Her father, John "Jack" Sidney Setzer, founded the area's first post office and named it after Maggie, one of his daughters. The main street through town is lined with craft, antique and gift shops, campgrounds, motels and restaurants. Some of the more popular outdoor activities in Maggie Valley are whitewater rafting, horseback riding, and skiing and snowboarding in the winter. Maggie Valley, with its central location in the mountains, has a lot to offer visitors. The Great Smoky Mountains National Park and the Blue Ridge Parkway are both nearby and the surrounding Pisgah National Forest also offers many choices for exploring the surrounding mountains. The oldest ski resort in North Carolina, the Cataloochee Ski Area, is also located in Maggie Valley.

Maggie Valley is home to Eaglenest Entertainment, a music venue featuring regional and national performers, and the famous Ghost Town In The Sky, a western-themed adventure park high in the mountains above Maggie Valley. For automotive buffs, the Wheels Thru Time Museum is an obligatory stop on your itinerary. Maggie Valley hosts a number of festivals, the best known are the Great Smoky Mountain Trout Festival and the Maggie Valley Summer Arts & Craft Show.

Location: Western Mountains, 45 minutes west of Asheville
Town Hall: 3987 Soco Road, Maggie Valley NC 28751; 828-926-0866
Website: www.townofmaggievalley.com
County: Haywood County: County Offices, 215 North Main Street, Waynesville NC 28786; 828-452-6625
Elevation & Population: 3,020 feet, 600+
Visitor/Welcome Center: Maggie Valley Visitors Bureau & Visitor Center, 2511 Soco Road, Maggie Valley NC 28751; 800-624-4431
City Chamber of Commerce: Maggie Valley Visitors Bureau, 2511 Soco Road, Maggie Valley NC 28751; 800-624-4431
County Chamber of Commerce: Greater Haywood County Chamber of Commerce: 591 North Main Street, Waynesville NC 28786; 828-456-3021
Newspaper: The Mountaineer, 220 North Main Street, Waynesville NC 28786; 828-452-0661
High School: Tuscola High School, 564 Tuscola School Road, Waynesville NC 28786; 828-456-2408
Area Major Festivals: Great Smoky Mountain Trout Festival (May), Maggie Valley Summer Arts & Craft Show (July)
Area Natural Attractions: Blue Ridge Parkway, Great Smoky Mountains National Park, Pisgah National Forest
Area Cultural Attractions: Cherokee Indian Reservation, Ghost Town In The Sky, HART-Haywood Arts Regional Theatre, Harrah's Cherokee Casino & Hotel, Wheels Thru Time Museum
Recommended Restaurants: (For a complete list of all restaurants visit www.ashevilleguidebook.com)
    Garlic Knots Pizzeria: (Pizza) 3914 Soco Road, Maggie Valley NC 28751; 828-926-8383
    Grizzly Grill: (Grill) 2550 Soco Road, Maggie Valley NC 28751; 828-926-7440
    Guayabitos: (Mexican) 3422 Soco Road, Maggie Valley NC 28751; 828-926-7777
    Hurley's Creekside Dining and Rhum Bar: (American-Dinner only) 4352 Soco Road, Maggie Valley NC 28751; 828-926-1566
    J. Arthur's Restaurant: (American-Fine Dining) 2843 Soco Road, Maggie Valley NC 28751; 828-926-1817
    Joey's Pancake House: (Breakfast) 4309 Soco Road, Maggie Valley NC 28751; 828-926-0212

Maggie Valley Restaurant: (American) 2804 Soco Road, Maggie Valley NC 28751; 828-926-0425

Renaissance at the Maggie Valley Club: (American-Fine Dining) Maggie Valley Club, 1819 Country Club Drive, Maggie Valley NC 28751; 828-926-1616

Rendezvous Restaurant & Lounge: (American) Maggie Valley Inn, 70 Soco Road, Maggie Valley NC 28751; 828-926-0201

Snappy's Italian Restaurant: (Italian) 2769 Soco Road, Maggie Valley NC 28751; 828-926-6126

Recommended Places To Stay: (For a complete list of all accommodations visit www.ashevilleguidebook.com)

Best Western-Mountainbrook Inn: (Motel) 3811 Soco Road, Maggie Valley NC 28751; 800-213-1914

Brooksong B&B: (B&B) 252 Living Waters Lane, Maggie Valley NC 28751; 866-926-5409

Cataloochee Ranch: (Resort-Guest Ranch) 119 Ranch Road, Maggie Valley NC 28751; 828-926-1401

Comfort Inn: (Motel) 3282 Soco Road, Maggie Valley NC 28751; 866-926-9106

Jonathan Creek Inn and Creekside Villas: (Motel, Villas) 4324 Soco Road, Maggie Valley NC 28751; 800-577-7812

Maggie Valley Club: (Golf Resort) 1819 Country Club Drive, Maggie Valley NC 28715; 800-438-3861

Maggie Valley Creekside Lodge: (Country Lodge) 2716 Soco Road, Maggie Valley NC 28751; 800-621-1260

Maggie Valley Inn & Conference Center: (Hotel) 70 Soco Road, Maggie Valley NC 28751; 866-926-0201

Ramada Limited: (Motel) 4048 Soco Road, Maggie Valley NC 28751; 800-305-6703

Riverlet Creekside Motel: (Motel) 4102 Soco Road, Maggie Valley NC 28751; 800-691-9952

Timberwolf Creek Bed & Breakfast: (B&B) 391 Johnson Branch Road, Maggie Valley NC 28751; 888-525-4218

Maiden

Maiden, incorporated in 1883, is a small town located primarily in Catawba County in the foothills of Western North Carolina. Part of the township extends also into adjacent Lincoln County. Local historians agree that Maiden was named after Maiden Creek, and in the early days the township was the site of a cotton mill and also became a trading center for the region. Maiden is noted for its enthusiastic support of the local Maiden High School Blue Devils football team, and is known as "The Biggest Little Football Town in the World." While that may not be completely true, it is a true reflection of the great vitality and home-town spirit of the residents of Maiden.

Over the years the city has enjoyed a large industrial base, and continues to do so today. A number of textile and furniture manufacturing companies, typical of the greater Hickory area, call Maiden home. Maiden has a number of parks and recreational facilities. These include the superb Recreation Center located on East Klutz Street that is open to the general public, and the Maiden Municipal Park. The Recreation Center facilities include a gym, banquet room, classrooms, softball complex, playgrounds, picnic shelters and a walking trail. Maiden has an annual Christmas Parade held the Saturday after Thanksgiving and a spring festival, Springfest, held every May.

Location: Foothills, 1 hour and 15 minutes east of Asheville
Town Hall: 113 West Main Street, Maiden NC 28650; 828-428-5010
Website: www.maidennc.com
County: Catawba County: County Offices, 100-A South West Boulevard, Newton NC 28658; 828-465-8201
Elevation & Population: 899 feet, 3,300+
County Visitor/Welcome Center: Catawba County Visitor Information Center, 1055 Southgate Corporation Park SW, Hickory NC 28602; 828-328-6111
County Chamber of Commerce: Catawba County Chamber of Commerce, 1055 Southgate Corporation Park SW, Hickory NC 28602; 828-328-6111
Newspapers: The Claremont Courier, 3283 White Oak Court, Claremont NC 28610; 828-320-8450 and the Hickory Daily Record, 1100 Park Place, Hickory NC 28603; 828-322-4510
High Schools: Maiden High School, 600 West Main Street, Maiden NC 28650; 828-428-8197
Area Major Festivals: Christmas Parade (November), Catawba Valley Pottery Festival (March), Springfest (May)
Area Natural Attractions: Pisgah National Forest, South Mountains State Park
Area Cultural Attractions: Bunker Hill Covered Bridge, Catawba County Museum of History, Catawba Science Center, Harper House/Hickory History Center, Hickory Furniture Mart, Hickory Motor Speedway, Hickory Museum of Art, Hiddenite Center, Historic Murray's Mill
Recommended Restaurants: (For a complete list of all restaurants visit www.ashevilleguidebook.com)
  Brookwood Cafe & Catering: (American) 202 Providence Mill Road, Maiden NC 28650; 828-428-8944
  Papa's Pizza To Go: (Pizza) 201 Island Ford Road, Maiden NC 28650; 828-428-0504
  Scottie's BBQ: (BBQ) 102 South Main Avenue, Maiden NC 28650; 828-428-2297
Recommended Places To Stay: (For a complete list of all accommodations visit www.ashevilleguidebook.com)
  No accommodations currently available in Maiden. *See* Hickory

Marion

Marion is the county seat of McDowell County and has as its motto "where Main Street meets the mountains". The motto is reinforced by Mount Ida, the dominant feature of the landscape in downtown. Marion is a thriving small city located on the eastern edge of the mountains along the Catawba River Basin and is home to many small industries including those that manufacture medical supplies, lumber and paper products, electronics and transportation equipment, tools, apparel, textiles and furniture.

Marion was planned and built on land selected by the first McDowell County Commissioners on March 14, 1844 at the Historic Carson House on Buck Creek. It was not until 1845, however, that the official name of Marion was sanctioned as the county seat by the state legislature. The name of Marion came from Francis Marion, the American Revolutionary War hero, known as the "Swamp Fox" and the man upon whom the movie "The Patriot" was based.

The city is home to a number of historic buildings open to the public, including the Historic Carson House, the Joseph McDowell House built in 1787, and the Marion Depot, the oldest surviving depot on the Western Rail Line. Nearby Lake James State Park is only minutes away and is a popular recreational attraction for both residents and visitors alike. Between 1804 & 1827, McDowell County contributed to North Carolina's gold legacy as the nation's leader in gold production. There are still opportunities for visitors to pan for gold in the Marion area.

Location: Foothills, 45 minutes east of Asheville

Town Hall: 194 North Main Street, Marion NC 28752; 828-652-3551

Website: www.marionnc.org

County: McDowell County: County Offices, 21 South Main Street, Marion NC 28752; 828-652-7121

Elevation & Population: 1,395 feet, 8000+

County Tourism Development: McDowell Tourism Development, Historic Depot, 25 Highway 70 West, Old Fort NC 28762; 888-233-6111

County Visitor/Welcome Center: McDowell County Visitor Center, 1170 West Tate Street, Marion NC 28752; 828-652-4240

County Chamber of Commerce: McDowell Chamber of Commerce, 1170 West Tate Street, Marion NC 28752; 828-652-4240

Newspaper: The McDowell News, 136 Logan Street, Marion NC 28752; 828-652-3313

Movie Theatres: McDowell Twin Cinemas, 520 North Main Street, Marion NC 28752; 828-652-8368

High School: McDowell High School, 334 South Main Street, Marion NC 28752; 828-652-7920

Colleges and Universities: McDowell Technical Community College, 54 College Drive, Marion NC 28752; 828-652-6021

Hospitals: McDowell Hospital, 100 Rankin Drive, Marion NC 28752; 828-659-5000

Area Major Festivals: Mountain Glory Festival (October), North Carolina Gold Festival (May)

Area Natural Attractions: Lake James State Park, Linville Caverns

Area Cultural Attractions: Historic Carson House, Joseph McDowell House, McDowell Arts Council Association Gallery, Mountain Gateway Museum & Heritage Center

Recommended Restaurants: (For a complete list of all restaurants visit www.ashevilleguidebook.com)

  Bruce's Fabulous Foods: (Cafe) 63 South Main Street, Marion NC 28752; 828-659-8023

  Countryside Barbeque: (BBQ) 2070 Rutherford Road, Marion NC 28752; 828-652-4885

  Eddie's Pizza & Pasta: (Pizza-Italian) 1284 Rutherford Road, Marion NC 28752; 828-652-4777

  Jalapeno's Fresh Mexican Grill: (Mexican) 1582 Rutherford Road, Marion NC 28752; 828-652-5154

  Little Siena Restaurant: (Italian) 2050 US 70 West, Marion NC 28752; 828-724-9451

  Moondoggy's Classic Diner: (1950's Style Diner) 909 North Main Street, Marion NC 28752; 828-655-1557

  Open Flame Buffet & Grill: (Grill) 4231 US 221 S, Marion NC 28752; 828-738-7027

Recommended Places To Stay: (For a complete list of all accommodations visit www.ashevilleguidebook.com)

  Comfort Inn: (Motel) 178 Highway 70 West, Marion NC 28752; 877-424-6423

  Days Inn: (Motel) 4248 US 221 South, Marion NC 28752; 828-659-2567

  Hampton Inn: (Motel) 3560 US 221 South, Marion NC 28752; 800-426-7866

  Robardajen Woods Bed and Breakfast: (B&B) 5640 Robardajen Woods, Nebo NC 28761; 828-584-3191

  The Cottages at Spring Farm House: (Cottages-Eco Retreat) 219 Haynes Road, Marion NC 28752; 877-738-9798

Mars Hill

Mars Hill is a small college town perched on a hill a few miles north of Asheville. Dominated by the Mars Hill College campus, this quaint village is surrounded by picturesque rolling mountains and valleys. The college, a Christian liberal arts school, is the oldest educational institution in North Carolina and attracts students from all across America. Wolf Ridge Ski Slopes, the closest ski resort to Asheville, is also found on the outskirts of Mars Hill. Mars Hill is also known for its rich music and crafts heritage. Renowned musicologist Bascom Lamar Lunsford, founder of the Mountain Dance and Folk Festival, grew up here and brought international recognition to the region's traditional mountain music.

Every autumn the Heritage Festival celebrates mountain crafts, arts, and music, and highlights the town's role as the historic center of the clogging dance tradition.

Location: Central Mountains, 30 minutes northwest of Asheville
Town Hall: 280 North Main Street, Mars Hill NC 28754; 828-689-2301
Website: www.townofmarshill.org
County: Madison County: County Offices, 2 North Main Street, Marshall NC 28753; 828-649-2854
Elevation & Population: 2,325 feet, 2,000+
County Visitor/Welcome Center: Madison County Visitors Center 635-4 Carl Eller Road, Mars Hill NC 28754; 877-262-3476, 828 680-9031
County Chamber of Commerce: Madison County Chamber of Commerce 635-4 Carl Eller Road, Mars Hill NC 28754; 828-689-9351
Newspaper: News-Record & Sentinel 58 Back Street, Marshall NC 28753; 828-649-1075
High School: Madison High School, 5740 US Highway 25/70, Marshall NC 28753; 828-649-2876
Colleges and Universities: Mars Hill College, 100 Athletic Street, Mars Hill NC 28754; 866-642-4968
Area Major Festivals: Bascom Lamar Lunsford Music Festival (October), Madison County Heritage Festival (October)
Area Natural Attractions: Appalachian Scenic National Trail, French Broad River, Pisgah National Forest, Max Patch
Area Cultural Attractions: Southern Appalachian Repertory Theatre, Rural Life Museum
Recommended Restaurants: (For a complete list of all restaurants visit www.ashevilleguidebook.com)
    El Dorado Latin Grill: (Latin Cuisine) 14 South Main Street, Mars Hill NC 28754; 828-689-9704
    Main Street Deli & Grill: (Deli, Grill) 40 North Main Street, Mars Hill NC 28754; 828-689-9849
    Papa Nicks Original Pizza: (Pizza) 15 College Street, Mars Hill NC 28754; 828-689-8566
Recommended Places To Stay: (For a complete list of all accommodations visit www.ashevilleguidebook.com)
    Bed & Breakfast at Ponder Cove: (Dog-Friendly B&B) 1067 Ponder Creek Road, Mars Hill NC 28754; 828-689-7304
    Comfort Inn: (Motel) 167 J. F. Robinson Lane, Mars Hill NC 28754; 828-689-9000
    The Inn at Mars Hill: (B&B) 139 South Main Street, Mars Hill NC 28754; 828-680-1020

Marshall

Located right on the beautiful French Broad River, Marshall, the county seat of Madison County, is one of the most picturesque villages in all of Western North Carolina. The village has a rich history, with the Buncombe County Turnpike passing through it in colonial days, as the location of notorious Civil War events, and as the hub of Madison County commerce for many years. A fun place to visit, Marshall, like other true mountain towns, retains much of its past and is like stepping back into time. There is a good selection of stores and restaurants, and an historic 1906 Neo-Classical Revival courthouse. Marshall's location along the river is a great jumping-off place to further adventures, including whitewater rafting on the river.

Location: Central Mountains, 45 minutes northwest of Asheville
Town Hall: 180 South Main Street, Marshall NC 28753; 828-649-3031
Website: www.townofmarshall.org
County: Madison County: County Offices, 2 North Main Street, Marshall NC 28753; 828-649-2854
Elevation & Population: 1,920 feet, 900+
County Visitor/Welcome Center: Madison County Visitors Center 635-4 Carl Eller Road, Mars Hill NC 28754; 877-262-3476, 828 680-9031
County Chamber of Commerce: Madison County Chamber of Commerce 635-4 Carl Eller Road, Mars Hill NC 28754; 828-689-9351
Newspaper: News-Record & Sentinel 58 Back Street, Marshall NC 28753; 828-649-1075
High School: Madison High School, 5740 US Highway 25/70, Marshall NC 28753; 828-649-2876
Area Major Festivals: Hot Doggett 100 Cycling Tour (July), Madison County Fair (August)
Area Natural Attractions: Appalachian Scenic National Trail, French Broad River, Pisgah National Forest, Max Patch
Recommended Restaurants: (For a complete list of all restaurants visit www.ashevilleguidebook.com)
    Bacchus Bistro: (Italian) 18 North Main Street, Marshall NC 28753; 828-649-0000
    Longnecks Bar and Restaurant: (Grill) 5145 US 25/70 Bypass, Marshall NC 28753; 828-649-0400
Recommended Places To Stay: (For a complete list of all accommodations visit www.ashevilleguidebook.com)
    Bend of Ivy Lodge: (Country Lodge) 3717 Bend of Ivy Road, Marshall NC 28753; 888-658-0505
    Marshall House Bed & Breakfast Inn: (B&B) 100 Hill Street, Marshall NC 28753; 828-649-9205
    River Dance: (B&B) 179 Deer Leap, Marshall NC 28753; 847-809-3098

Morganton

Morganton, the county seat, is the largest city in Burke County and encompasses an area of over nineteen square miles. It was named after Revolutionary War General Daniel Morgan. The community is located on Interstate 40 and is bisected by US 70 and 64 and North Carolina Highways 181, 18, and 126.

Morganton offers big city services wrapped in small town charm while embracing technology, new development and progressive thinking. The heart of Morganton is its vibrant downtown filled with restaurants, galleries, clothiers and antique shops. One of the must-see art galleries downtown is the Burke Arts Council Jailhouse Gallery, located at 115 Meeting Street. The City of Morganton's 1,058-seat CoMMA Municipal Auditorium at 401 South College Street also showcases a wide variety of ever changing entertainment ranging from Broadway performances to the best in Celtic music and dance. One of the artistic highlights of the Auditorium is the Ben Long Fresco of the Nine Muses on the ceiling of the atrium.

Major festivals include The Red, White and Bluegrass Festival that brings the best in bluegrass to Morganton's Catawba Meadows Park every July 1-4. Residents also enjoy great music and the family-friendly atmosphere of Morganton's TGIF Free Friday night concerts during the summer. Each September the annual two-day Historic Morganton Festival attracts upwards of 40,000 people. Craft and food booths line the downtown streets and well known musical entertainers offer free concerts. Another unique event in Morganton is the Festival of Lights in November, when the city kicks off the Christmas season.

The city is also home to the Morganton Farmer's Market, located at 300 Beach Street, open Saturday mornings from May to October, and a number of outstanding local cultural attractions. These include the History Museum of Burke County, the North Carolina School For The Deaf Museum, the Old Burke County Courthouse Heritage Museum, Quaker Meadows Plantation, the Morganton 1916 Railroad Depot and the Senator Sam J. Erwin Jr. Museum.

Near Morganton lies Brown Mountain, home to a mysterious phenomena referred to as the Brown Mountain Lights. Rising to an elevation of only 2,600 feet, Brown Mountain has been at the center of a mystery since the earliest days of recorded history. For hundreds of years, unexplained lights have been seen on the mountain to the astonishment of all that have seen them.

Morganton has a superb greenway system. The Catawba River Greenway Park offers year-round biking, jogging and strolling, canoeing and picnicking, and features children's playgrounds, fishing piers, a 1200-foot multilevel observation deck and a 170-foot bridge that crosses Silver Creek.

Location: Foothills, 1 hour east of Asheville
Town Offices: 305 East Union Street, Suite A100, Morganton NC 28655; 828-437-8863
Website: www.ci.morganton.nc.us

County: Burke County: Burke County Government Center, 200 Avery Avenue, Morganton NC 28680; 828-439-4340
Elevation & Population: 1,182 feet, 17,000+
County Visitor/Welcome Center: Burke County Visitor Center, 102 East Union Street, Morganton NC 28655; 888-462-2921
County Chamber of Commerce: Burke County Chamber of Commerce, 110 East Meeting Street, Morganton NC 28655; 828-437-3021
Newspaper: The News Herald, 301 Collett Street, Morganton NC 28655; 828-437-2161
Movie Theatres: Marquee Cinemas Mimosa 7, 103 South Green Street, Morganton NC 28655; 828-437-8084
High School: Freedom High School, 511 Independence Boulevard, Morganton NC 28655; 828-433-1310 and Robert L. Patton High School, 701 Enola Road, Morganton NC 28655; 828-433-3000
Colleges and Universities: Western Piedmont Community College, 1001 Burkemont Avenue, Morganton NC 28655; 828-438-6000
Hospitals: Grace Hospital, 2201 South Sterling Street, Morganton NC 28655; 828-580-5000
Area Major Festivals: Red, White and Bluegrass Festival (July), Historic Morganton Festival (September), Festival of Lights (November)
Area Natural Attractions: Brown Mountain Lights, Lake James State Park
Area Cultural Attractions: Burke Arts Council Jailhouse Gallery, History Museum of Burke County, North Carolina School For The Deaf Museum, Old Burke County Courthouse Heritage Museum, Quaker Meadows Plantation, Morganton 1916 Railroad Depot, Senator Sam J. Erwin Jr. Museum
Recommended Restaurants: (For a complete list of all restaurants visit www.ashevilleguidebook.com)

    Abele's: (Southern) 2156 South Sterling Street, Morganton NC 28655; 828-433-5400

    Butch's BBQ & Breakfast: (BBQ) 1234 Burkemont Avenue, Morganton NC 28655; 828-432-5040

    Churchill's Restaurant & Pub: (Continental-Fine Dining) 108 East Meeting Street, Morganton NC 28655; 828-433-9909

    Friday Friends: (American) 315 Sanford Drive, Morganton NC 28655; 828-430-3024

    Grind Cafe: (Coffeehouse-Cafe)141 West Union Street, Morganton NC 28655; 828-430-4343

    Judge's Riverside Restaurant: (American) 128 Greenlee Ford Road, Morganton NC 28680; 828-433-5798

    Limbertwig Cafe: (Cafe) 120 North Sterling Street, Morganton NC 28655; 828-438-4634

    Pat's Snack Bar: (American) 124 Sterling Street, Morganton NC 28655; 828-437-5744

Timberwoods Family Restaurant: (American) 1301 Bethel Road, Morganton NC 28655; 828-433-1767

Yianni's Restaurant: (Mediterranean) 112 West Union Street, Morganton NC 28655; 828-430-8700

Recommended Places To Stay: (For a complete list of all accommodations visit www.ashevilleguidebook.com)

Fairway Oaks Bed & Breakfast: (B&B) 4640 Plantation Drive, Morganton NC 28655; 828-584-7677

Comfort Inn and Suites: (Motel) 1273 Burkemont Avenue, Morganton NC 28655; 828-430-4000

Days Inn and Suites: (Motel) 1100 Burkemont Avenue, Morganton NC 28655; 828-430-8778

Hampton Inn: (Motel) 115 Bush Drive, Morganton NC 28655; 828-434-2000

Quality Inn: (Motel) 2400 South Sterling Street, Morganton NC 28655; 828-437-0171

The Bed & Breakfast at Historic Bridgewater Hall: (B&B) 3140 Bridgewater Road, Morganton NC 28655; 828-584-3622

Murphy

Murphy, founded in 1835, is the county seat of Cherokee County and is the westernmost county seat in North Carolina. It is closer to the capitals of six other states (Georgia, Alabama, Tennessee, South Carolina, Kentucky, and West Virginia) than to Raleigh, the capital of North Carolina, and occupies a serene corner of the mountains highlighted by hundreds of creeks, waterfalls and deep lush forests. This delightful mountain city offers to visitors a quaint downtown for shopping, the historic Murphy County Courthouse, a public library and an historical museum, the Cherokee County Historical Museum. Originally named Huntington, the town later became Murphy, named after Archibald D. Murphy, state senator and advocate of education in Western North Carolina. In 1851 Murphy became the county seat.

Murphy is also home to an historic movie theater, the Henn Theater, built in 1934 and still showing movies. This little single screen, 174-seat theater combines modern cinema technology with a classic setting. Another historic highlight of the village is the L&N Depot (circa 1887), a remnant of the Southern and Louisville & Nashville railroad, which ran through Murphy prior to 1974. The Murphy Pyramid (circa 1930) is also of interest, and is a wooden pyramid erected by Hitchcock Coit in honor of her grandfather, ARS Hunter, who was the first white settler in the area.

Cherokee County has several unique communities sprinkled throughout its mountains and valleys, the best known is the nearby crafts-oriented community of Brasstown which is home to the famous John C. Campbell Folk School.

Location: Western Mountains, 2½ hours west of Asheville

City Offices: 5 Wofford Street, Murphy NC 28906, 828-837-2510
Website: townofmurphync.com
County: Cherokee County,75 Peach Street, Murphy NC 28906; 828-837-5527
Elevation & Population: 1,604 feet, 1,600+
County Visitor/Welcome Center: Cherokee County Welcome Center, 805
  West Highway 64, Murphy NC 28906; 828-837-2242
County Chamber of Commerce: Cherokee County Chamber of Commerce,
  805 West Highway 64, Murphy NC 28906; 828-837-2242
Newspaper: Cherokee Scout, 89 Sycamore Street, Murphy NC 28906; 828-837-
  5122
Movie Theatres: Henn Theater, 110 Tennessee Street, Murphy NC 28906; 828-
  837-2618
High School: Murphy High School, 234 High School Circle, Murphy NC
  28906; 828-837-2426 and Hiwassee Dam High School, 267 Blue Eagle Circle,
  Murphy NC 28906; 828-644-5916
Colleges and Universities: Tri-County Community College, 21 Campus Circle,
  Murphy NC 28906; 828-837-6810
Hospitals: Murphy Medical Center: 3990 East Highway 64 Alternate, Murphy
  NC 28906; 828-837-8161
Area Major Festivals: Spring Festival (June), Heritage Walk & Festival (July),
  Hometown Christmas Celebration Parade and Christmas Festival (December)
Area Natural Attractions: Chatuge Lake, Joyce Kilmer Memorial Forest, Lake
  Santeetlah, Nantahala National Forest, Nantahala River
Area Cultural Attractions: Cherokee County Historical Museum, Great Smoky
  Mountains Railroad, John C. Campbell Folk School, L&N Depot, Murphy
  Pyramid
Recommended Restaurants: (For a complete list of all restaurants visit www.
  ashevilleguidebook.com)
  Brother's Restaurant: (American) 5722 Highway 64 West, Murphy NC
    28906; 828-835-9100
  Chevelles: (Grill) 66 Hiwassee Street, Murphy NC 28906; 828-935-7001
  Doyle's Cedar Hill Restaurant: (International-Fine Dining) 925 Andrews
    Road, Murphy NC 28906; 828-837-3400
  Herb's Pit Bar-B-Que: (BBQ) 15896 Highway 64 West , Murphy NC
    28906; 828-494-5397
  Murphy's Chophouse: (American-Fine Dining) 130 Valley River Avenue,
    Murphy NC 28906; 828-835-3287
  Shoebooties Cafe: (Cafe) 25 Peachtree Street, Murphy NC 28906; 828-
    837-4589
  The Daily Grind & Wine: (Cafe-Coffeehouse) 46 Andrews Road, Murphy
    NC 28906; 828-837-3400
Recommended Places To Stay: (For a complete list of all accommodations visit
  www.ashevilleguidebook.com)

Angels Landing Inn Bed & Breakfast: (B&B) 94 Campbell Street, Murphy NC 28906; 828-835-8877

Bella Luna: (B&B) 215 Peachtree Street, Murphy NC 28906; 828-837-1515

Cobb Creek Cabins: (Cabins) 106 Cobb Circle, Murphy NC 28906; 828-837-0270

Hampton Inn: (Motel) 1550 Andrews Road, Murphy NC 28906; 828-837-1628

Huntington Hall Bed & Breakfast: (B&B) 272 Valley River Avenue, Murphy NC 28906; 828-837-9567

Morgan Creek Manor: (B&B) 181 Alf Branch Drive, Murphy NC 28906; 828-837-3202

PeaceValley Campground: (Campground) 117 Happy Valley Road, Murphy NC 28905; 828-837-6223

Newland

Newland, incorporated in 1913, is the county seat of Avery County and has the distinction of being the highest county seat east of the Mississippi. A recently remodeled classical courthouse overlooks a quaint town square, bordered by shops and churches and a memorial to Avery County veterans. Newland is also home to the Avery County Historical Museum. Historically, Newland's original name was "Old Fields of Toe" because it is located in a broad flat valley and is at the headwaters of the Toe River. It was also a mustering place for Civil War troops. Newland today is also known for the many Christmas tree farms which thrive in the surrounding mountains.

The nearby little community of Linville, located at the foot of Grandfather Mountain, takes its name from the Linville River. Linville was originally developed as a summer resort where families from the North Carolina Piedmont could escape the heat and mosquitoes that characterize summers in the south. Nestled at the confluence of Highways 221 and 183, Linville Falls is a convenient stopping point for travelers from all directions. Linville Falls is named after a beautiful two-tiered waterfall located nearby in Linville Gorge.

Location: Northern Mountains, 2 hours east of Asheville

Town Offices: 301 Cranberry Street, Newland NC 28657; 828-733-2023

Website: www.newlandgov.com

County: Avery County: County Administrative Building, 175 Linville Street, Newland NC 28657; 828-733-8202

Elevation & Population: 3,621 feet, 700+

County Chamber of Commerce: Avery County Chamber of Commerce: 4501 Tynecastle Highway, Unit #2, Banner Elk NC 28604; 800-972-2183

Newspaper: The Mountain Times PO Box 1815, Boone NC 28607; 828-264-6397

High School: Avery County High School, 401 High School Road, Newland NC 28657; 828-733-0151

Colleges and Universities: Mayland Community College, Avery Campus, 785 Cranberry Street, Newland NC 28657; 828-733-5883

Area Major Festivals: Avery County Christmas Parade (December)

Area Natural Attractions: Blue Ridge Parkway, Grandfather Mountain, Linville Caverns, Linville Gorge,

Area Cultural Attractions: Avery County Historical Museum Banner House Museum, Beech Mountain Resort, Crossnore Fine Arts Gallery, Horn in the West, Mast General Store, Mystery Hill, Orchard at Altapass, Tweetsie Railroad

Recommended Restaurants: (For a complete list of all restaurants visit www. ashevilleguidebook.com)

Fabio's Restaurant: (Italian) 106 Pineola Street, Newland NC 28646; 828-733-1314

Spears BBQ & Grill: (American) Linville Falls Lodge, 800 Claude Franklin Road, Linville Falls NC 28647; 800-634-4421

The Italian Restaurant: (Italian) 2855 Linville Falls Highway, Pineola NC 28662: 828-733-1401

Recommended Places To Stay: (For a complete list of all accommodations visit www.ashevilleguidebook.com)

Dogwood Bed and Breakfast: (B&B) 7242 Dogwood Knob Road, Newland NC 28757; 828-733-0102

Linville Falls Lodge & Cottages: (Country Lodge) 800 Claude Franklin Road, Linville Falls NC 28647; 800-634-4421

The Eseeola Lodge at Linville Golf Club: (Country Lodge) 175 Linville Avenue, Linville, NC 28646; 800-742-6717

Newton

Newton is located in Catawba County in the foothills of Western North Carolina and is the county seat. Selected as the seat in 1843, Newton was incorporated in 1855. Today it is the second largest city in the county after Hickory. The city has experienced a steady rate of growth since 1970, expanding from 7,600 residents to the current population of over 13,600. Newton has a number of qualities that have contributed to this growth-challenging places to work, a low cost of living, diverse cultures, a strong array of recreational opportunities and a vibrant arts community. The city has earned a number of awards over the years, including seven Public Power Awards of Excellence in 2009.

Newton is home to the Catawba County Museum of History, located in the historic Catawba County Courthouse, an imposing National Register Renaissance Revival structure built in 1924. Other attractions in the area include the historic Newton Depot, the Newton-Conover Auditorium, the Green Room Community Theatre and the Hickory Motor Speedway. The City Parks & Recreation Department also maintain five parks that include numerous ball fields, tennis courts, walking & jogging trails, picnic tables & shelters, a swimming pool and two recreational centers complete with gymnasiums and a fitness center. One of the more popular is the 27-acre Southside Park located on Highway 3212 Business South.

Location: Foothills, 1 hour and 15 minutes east of Asheville
Town Hall: 401 North Main Avenue, Newton NC 28658; 828-695-4300
Website: www.newtonnc.gov
County: Catawba County: County Offices, 100-A South West Boulevard, Newton NC 28658; 828-465-8201
Elevation & Population: 1,001 feet, 13,000+
County Visitor/Welcome Center: Catawba County Visitor Information Center, 1055 Southgate Corporation Park SW, Hickory NC 28602; 828-328-6111
County Chamber of Commerce: Catawba County Chamber of Commerce, 1055 Southgate Corporation Park SW, Hickory NC 28602; 828-328-6111
Newspapers: The Claremont Courier, 3283 White Oak Court, Claremont NC 28610; 828-320-8450;
Hickory Daily Record: 1100 Park Place, Hickory NC 28603; 828-322-4510 and The Observer News Enterprise, 309 North College Avenue, Newton NC 28656; 828-464-0221
Movie Theatres: State Cinema, 117 North College Street, Newton NC 28658; 828-464-2171
High Schools: Fred T. Foard High School, 3407 Plateau Road, Newton NC 28658; 704-462-1496; Newton-Conover High School 338 West 15th Street, Newton NC 28658; 828-465-0920 and Newton-Conover Science High School, 605 North Ashe Avenue, Newton NC 28658; 828-464-3191
Area Major Festivals: MayFest (May), Soldiers Reunion (August), Newton Art-FEST (October), Catawba Valley Pottery Festival (March), Newton Light Up The Town Celebration (November)
Area Natural Attractions: Pisgah National Forest, South Mountains State Park
Area Cultural Attractions: Bunker Hill Covered Bridge, Catawba County Museum of History, Catawba Science Center, Green Room Community Theatre, Harper House/Hickory History Center, Hickory Furniture Mart, Hickory Motor Speedway, Hickory Museum of Art, Hiddenite Center, Historic Murray's Mill, Historic Newton Depot
Recommended Restaurants: (For a complete list of all restaurants visit www.ashevilleguidebook.com)
   Drum's Restaurant-Balls Creek: (American) 2852 Buffalo Shoals Road, Newton NC 28658; 828-464-3635
   Italy Grill: (Italian) 2725 Northwest Boulevard, Newton NC 28658; 828-466-1446
   The Artist's Cafe: (Cafe) 100 North Main Avenue, Newton NC 28658; 828-465-7497
   Tosaka Authentic Japanese Cuisine: (Japanese) 2725 Northwest Boulevard, Newton NC 28658; 828-465-9977
Recommended Places To Stay: (For a complete list of all accommodations visit www.ashevilleguidebook.com)
   The Peacock Inn: (B&B) 1670 Southwest Boulevard, Newton NC 28658; 828-464-5780

The Trott House Inn Bed & Breakfast: (B&B) 802 North Main Avenue, Newton NC 28658; 877-435-7994

North Wilkesboro

North Wilkesboro, located in Wilkes County, was founded in 1891 when the Norfolk and Southern Railroad build a line into Wilkes County that ended on the northern bank of the Yadkin River opposite Wilkesboro, the county seat. The town of North Wilkesboro quickly developed around the railroad tracks and became home to many furniture, textile and leather factories. Lowe's Foods, one of the southeast's largest supermarket chains, and Lowe's Home Improvement Warehouse both started in North Wilkesboro, the former in 1954 and the latter in 1946. North Wilkesboro is also home to the Wilkes Regional Medical Center, the major medical facility in Wilkes County and the historic Kleeberg Liberty Theatre, still in operation, on Main Street.

Due to the town's proximity to the nearby Blue Ridge Mountains, North Wilkesboro for many years was nicknamed the "Key to the Blue Ridge". Nearby Stone Mountain State Park and W. Kerr Scott Dam and Reservoir make North Wilkesboro a perfect spot to visit while enjoying these great outdoor attractions. North Wilkesboro recently opened the Yadkin River Greenway. The Greenway contains biking, jogging, and walking trails which follow the Yadkin River and Reddies River for several miles between the towns of North Wilkesboro and Wilkesboro. One of the most popular spots on the Greenway is a 156-foot-long bridge which spans the Reddies River at its mouth, where it joins the Yadkin River.

The major festival for the city is the Brushy Mountain Apple Festival, which is held annually to celebrate the local apple harvest. It is one of the largest single-day arts and crafts festivals in the South. Stretching from the North Wilkesboro and Wilkesboro area towards Lenoir along Highway 268 is the historic "Happy Valley." Located on the banks of the Yadkin River, Happy Valley was so named by the early settlers who described the valley as "a place of beauty, peace and tranquility" and the name aptly remains. A number of attractions are in the valley, including Fort Defiance, the Chapel of Rest and Whippoorwill Academy and Village.

Location: Foothills, 2½ hours east of Asheville
Town Hall: 832 Main Street, North Wilkesboro NC 28659; 336-667-7129
Website: www.north-wilkesboro.com
County: Wilkes County: County Offices, 110 North Street, Wilkesboro NC 28697; 336-651-7346
Elevation & Population: 1,016 feet, 4,200+
County Chamber of Commerce: Wilkes County Chamber of Commerce, 717 Main Street, North Wilkesboro NC 28659; 336-838-8662
County Tourism Development: Wilkes County Tourism, 203 West Main Street, Wilkesboro NC 28697; 336-838-3951
Newspaper: The Record, 911 Main Street, North Wilkesboro NC 28659; 336-667-0134

Movie Theatres: Kleeberg Liberty Theatre, 816 Main Street, North Wilkesboro NC 28659; 336-838-4561

High School: North Wilkes High School, 2986 Traphill Road, Hays NC 28635; 336-957-8601

Hospitals: Wilkes Regional Medical Center, 1370 West D Street, North Wilkesboro NC 28659; 336-651-8100

Area Major Festivals: MerleFest (April), Carolina In The Fall Festival (September), Brushy Mountain Apple Festival (October)

Area Natural Attractions: Rendezvous Mountain Educational State Forest, Stone Mountain State Park, W. Kerr Scott Dam and Reservoir, Yadkin River Greenway

Area Cultural Attractions: Ben Long Frescoes in St. Paul's Episcopal Church, Happy Valley, Old Wilkes Jail Museum, Whippoorwill Academy and Village, Wilkes Art Gallery, Wilkes Heritage Museum

Recommended Restaurants: (For a complete list of all restaurants visit www.ashevilleguidebook.com)

> **Big Bob's Getaway:** (American) 713 Cherry Street, North Wilkesboro NC 28659; 336-838-1977
>
> **Branciforte's Brick Oven:** (Italian) 810 Main Street, North Wilkesboro NC 28659; 336-838-1110
>
> **Brushy Mountain Smokehouse and Creamery:** (American) 201 Wilkesboro Boulevard, North Wilkesboro NC 28659; 336-667-9464
>
> **Key City Grille:** (Eclectic American-Fine Dining) 211 10th Street, North Wilkesboro NC 28659; 336-667-7878
>
> **Sixth and Main:** (American) 6th and Main, North Wilkesboro NC 28659; 336-903-1166
>
> **Woodhaven Family Restaurant:** (American) 1301 West D Street, North Wilkesboro NC 28659; 336-667-6201

Recommended Places To Stay: (For a complete list of all accommodations visit www.ashevilleguidebook.com)

> **Best Western:** (Motel) 1713 NC Highway 67, Jonesville NC 28642; 336-835-6000
>
> **Comfort Inn:** (Motel) 1633 Winston Road, Jonesville NC 28642; 336-835-9400
>
> **Days Inn:** (Motel) 1540 NC Highway 67, Jonesville NC 28642; 336-526-6777
>
> **Fairfield Inn & Suites:** (Motel) 628 CC Camp Road/268 Bypass, Elkin NC 28621; 336-353-2008
>
> **Hampton Inn:** (Motel) 1632 NC Highway 67, Jonesville NC 28642; 336-835-1994

Old Fort

In existence as a village since 1869 and originally a fort built by the colonial militia before the Declaration of Independence, Old Fort was a settlement that served for many years as the western outpost of the early United States. In the center of town at 25 West Main Street is a hand-chiseled rose granite arrowhead, 14 feet tall, erected in 1930 to honor the peace finally achieved between the pioneer settlers and the Native Americans. At the unveiling, over 6,000 people attended including chiefs from both the Catawba and Cherokee tribes. These two tribes had never smoked a pipe of peace together until that day.

Old Fort is also known for its weekly Mountain Music Concerts, which draw a large audience and many musicians from the surrounding areas to Old Fort's downtown each Friday evening at 7:00. The performances are held in the Rockett Building on Main Street. Other historic and cultural highlights include the Appalachian Artisan Society Gallery, which showcases the work of over 60 local craft persons and artists, Davidson's Fort, a replica of the original, Revolutionary War-era fort built in 1776, the Mountain Gateway Museum & Heritage Center and the Old Fort Railroad Museum.

Of interest, located just outside of Old Fort is the locally famous man-made Andrews Geyser. The geyser's water comes from a lake located on a mountain high above it, and comes with enough pressure to produce a stream of water 80 feet high.

Location: Foothills, 30 minutes east of Asheville
Town Hall: 38 South Catawba Street, Old Fort NC 28762; 828-668-4244
Website: www.oldfort.org
County: McDowell County: County Offices, 21 South Main Street, Marion NC 28752; 828-652-7121
Elevation & Population: 1,447 feet, 900+
County Visitor/Welcome Center: McDowell Tourism Development, Historic Depot, 25 Highway 70 West, Old Fort NC 28762; 888-233-6111
City Chamber of Commerce: Old Fort Chamber of Commerce, 25 West Main Street, Old Fort NC 28762; 828-668-7223
County Chamber of Commerce: McDowell Chamber of Commerce, 1170 West Tate Street, Marion NC 28752; 828-652-4240
Newspaper: The McDowell News, 136 Logan Street, Marion NC 28752; 828-652-3313
High School: McDowell High School, 334 South Main Street, Marion NC 28752; 828-652-4535
Area Major Festivals: Pioneer Day (April), Oktoberfest (October),
Area Natural Attractions: Andrews Geyser, Pisgah National Forest
Area Cultural Attractions: Davidson's Fort, Historic Carson House, Mountain Gateway Museum & Heritage Center, Old Fort Arrowhead Monument, Old Fort Railroad Museum, The Appalachian Artisan Society Gallery
Recommended Restaurants: (For a complete list of all restaurants visit www.ashevilleguidebook.com)
> **Catawba Vale Cafe:** (Cafe) 32 East Main Street, Old Fort NC 28762; 828-668-9899
> **Whistle Stop Pizza & Subs:** (Cafe) 27 West Main Street, Old Fort NC 28762; 828-668-7676

Recommended Places To Stay: (For a complete list of all accommodations visit www.ashevilleguidebook.com)

    Rivers Ridge Lodge: (Country Lodge) 506 Sunrise Bluff Drive, Old Fort NC 28762; 828-243-5762

    The Inn on Mill Creek: (B&B) 3895 Mill Creek Road, Old Fort NC 28762; 828-668-1115

Robbinsville

Located at the far western end of the state, Robbinsville, the Graham County seat, was incorporated in 1893. Robbinsville is a delightful small town that is a welcome stop for visitors seeking recreation in the vast wilderness areas that surround it. The village is located in a region of Western North Carolina that contains hundreds of thousands of acres of wilderness and one that is home to some of the highest and most remote mountains east of the Mississippi. Two-thirds of Graham County is National Forest. The county is the home of Joyce Kilmer Memorial Forest and the Nantahala National Forest, and borders the Great Smoky Mountains National Park. Robbinsville, as county seat, is home to the Graham County Courthouse, an elegant building constructed of locally quarried quartzite.

Robbinsville is close to a number of mountain highways that are famous for their scenic beauty and challenging drives-the Cherohala Skyway and the Tail of the Dragon, considered by many to be one of the world's best motorcycling and sports car roads. This extraordinary stretch of highway has 318 curves in just 11 miles. Just a short distance from Robbinsville also is the beautiful Lake Santeetlah, a pristine mountain lake that has 76 miles of mostly natural forested shoreline and is over 3,000 acres in size. Nearby 10,230 acre Fontana Lake with its world-famous dam is also a major tourist destination. Fontana Lake is the largest lake in Western North Carolina and offers visitors an abundance of recreational opportunities.

Location: Western Mountains, 2½ hours west of Asheville

County: Graham County: County Offices, 12 North Main Street, Robbinsville NC 28771; 828-479-7961

Elevation & Population: 2,044 feet, 2000+

County Visitor/Welcome Center: Graham County Travel and Tourism Authority, 12 North Main Street, Robbinsville NC 28771; 800-470-3790

Newspaper: The Graham Star, 774 Tallulah Road, Robbinsville NC 28771; 828-479-3383

High School: Robbinsville High School, 301 Sweetwater Road, Robbinsville NC 28771; 828-479-3330

Colleges and Universities: Tri-County Community College, Graham County Center, 145 Moose Branch Road, Robbinsville NC 28771; 828-479-9256

Area Major Festivals: Graham County 4th of July Celebration & Fireworks (July)

Area Natural Attractions: Appalachian Scenic National Trail, Cherohala Skyway, Fontana Lake, Great Smoky Mountains National Park, Joyce Kilmer

Memorial Forest, Lake Santeetlah, Nantahala National Forest, Slickrock Creek Wilderness Area, Tail of the Dragon

Area Cultural Attractions: Stecoah Valley Cultural Arts Center

Recommended Restaurants: (For a complete list of all restaurants visit www. ashevilleguidebook.com)

    Mountainview Bistro: (American-Fine Dining) Fontana Village Resort, Fontana Dam NC 28733; 800-849-2258

    Phillips Smokey Mountain Restaurant: (American) 248 North Main Street, Robbinsville NC 28771; 828-479-8811

    Snowbird Mountain Lodge: (American-Fine Dining) 4633 Santeetlah Road, Robbinsville NC 28771; 800-941-9290

    Wildwood Grill: (Grill) Fontana Village Resort, 50 Fontana Road, Fontana Dam NC 28733; 800-849-2258

Recommended Places To Stay: (For a complete list of all accommodations visit www.ashevilleguidebook.com)

    Blue Boar Inn: (Country Inn) 1283 Blue Boar Road, Robbinsville NC 28771; 828-479-8126

    Blue Waters Mountain Lodge: (Country Lodge) 292 Pine Ridge Road, Robbinsville NC 28771; 888-828-3978

    The Lodge at Fontana: (Resort) Fontana Village Resort, 50 Fontana Road, Fontana Dam NC 28733; 800-849-2258

    Snowbird Mountain Lodge: (Country Lodge) 4633 Santeetlah Road, Robbinsville NC 28771; 800-941-9290

Rutherford College

The village of Rutherford College began in 1853, when a small private academy known as Owl Hollow School was located in the eastern part of Burke County. The school received funding from local resident John T. Rutherford which allowed it to expand. Prior to the Civil War, the school taught military tactics and philosophy but it was forced to close its doors when the Civil War began. It later reopened in 1871 as a four-year college. The town of Rutherford College, originally named Excelsior, was founded 1871 and today is a bedroom community with approximately 1,300 residents. It incorporated in 1977.

The town is bordered by Lake Rhodhiss on the north, and by Mineral Springs Mountain on the south, and is home to the Rutherford College Summer Festival, held on the first Saturday in August. The main street, Malcolm Boulevard, runs for approximately three miles, with numerous homes, Methodist and Baptist churches, banks, pharmacies, doctor's clinics, a car dealership, convenience stores, and a post office.

Location: Foothills, 1 hour and 15 minutes east of Asheville

Town Offices: 980 Malcolm Boulevard, Rutherford College NC 28761; 828-874-0333

Website: http://rutherfordcollegenc.us/index.html

County: Burke County: Burke County Government Center, 200 Avery Avenue, Morganton NC 28680; 828-439-4340

Elevation & Population: 1178 feet, 1,300+

County Visitor/Welcome Center: Burke County Visitor Center, 102 East Union Street, Morganton NC 28655; 888-462-2921

County Chamber of Commerce: Burke County Chamber of Commerce, 110 East Meeting Street, Morganton NC 28655; 828-437-3021

Newspaper: The News Herald, 301 Collett Street, Morganton NC 28655; 828-437-2161

High School: East Burke High School, 3695 East Burke Boulevard, Connelly Springs NC 28612; 828-397-5541 and Jimmy C. Draughn High School, 709 Lovelady Road NE, Valdese NC 28690; 828-879-4200

Area Major Festivals: Rutherford College Summer Festival (August)

Area Natural Attractions: Brown Mountain Lights, Lake James State Park, South Mountains State Park

Area Cultural Attractions: History Museum of Burke County, North Carolina School For The Deaf Museum, Old Burke County Courthouse Heritage Museum, Quaker Meadows Plantation, Senator Sam J. Erwin Jr. Museum

Recommended Restaurants: (For a complete list of all restaurants visit www.ashevilleguidebook.com)

Dos Arcos: (Mexican) 1311 Malcolm Boulevard, Rutherford College NC 28761; 828-260-4243

Recommended Places To Stay: (For a complete list of all accommodations visit www.ashevilleguidebook.com)

No accommodations currently available in Rutherford College. *See* Morganton and Valdese

Rutherfordton

Rutherfordton, the county seat of Rutherford County, was established in 1787, and is one of the oldest towns in Western North Carolina. Both the county and the town were named after General Griffith Rutherford, a popular Western North Carolina politician and general during the Revolutionary War. During that war the corps of Patriots known as the Over Mountain Men marched through present-day Rutherfordton on their way to the Battle of King's Mountain. The Patriots defeated British troops under the command of Maj. Patrick Ferguson on October 7, 1780.

Rutherfordton has managed to retain many of its historic buildings, and the downtown district is listed on the National Register of Historic Places. Rutherfordton is home to the only remaining cluster of antebellum houses and public structures in the southern foothills of North Carolina. These include 1849 St. John's Church and 1932 "Holly Hill" on North Main Street, the 1830's Bechtler family residence on Sixth Street, the Gothic-Revival Rucker-Eaves home (circa 1858-1870) on North Washington Street and the Byrnum House on Sixth and North Washington Streets. The village center is home to the Rutherford County Courthouse and an eclectic selection of stores and restaurants. Rutherforton is also home to an innovative hands-on children's museum, the KidSenses Children's InterACTIVE Museum and the Rutherford Hospital Museum.

Location: Foothills, 1 hour southeast of Asheville
Town Hall: 129 North Main Street, Rutherfordton NC 28139; 828-287-3520
Website: www.rutherfordton.net
County: Rutherford County: County Offices, 229 North Main Street, Rutherfordton NC 28139; 828-287-6045
Elevation & Population: 1075 feet, 4100+
County Visitor/Welcome Center: Rutherford County Tourism 1990 US Highway 221 South, Forest City NC 28043; 800-849-5998
County Chamber of Commerce: Rutherford County Chamber of Commerce 162 North Main Street, Rutherfordton NC 28139; 828-287-3090
Newspaper: The Daily Courier 601 Oak Street, Forest City NC 28043; 828-245-6431
Movie Theatres: Retro Cinema 4 2270 US 221 South, Forest City NC 28043; 828-248-1670
High School: Chase High School, 1603 Chase High Road, Forest City NC 28043; 828-245-7668
Hospitals: Rutherford Hospital, 288 South Ridgecrest Avenue, Rutherforton NC 28139; 828-286-5000
Area Major Festivals: Mayfest Festival (May), Hilltop Fall Festival (October)
Area Natural Attractions: Chimney Rock Park, Lake Lure
Area Cultural Attractions: Bennett Classics Antique Auto Museum, KidSenses Children's InterACTIVE Museum, Rutherford County Farm Museum, Rutherford County Museum, Rutherford Hospital Museum
Recommended Restaurants: (For a complete list of all restaurants visit www.ashevilleguidebook.com)
  Courtside Steaks: (American) 161 Park Lane Drive, Rutherfordton NC 28139; 828-286-3855
  Gregory's on Main Street: (American) 211 North Main Street, Rutherfordton NC 28139; 828-287-2171
  Legal Grounds Restaurant, Bar & Coffee House: (American) 109 West 2nd Street, Rutherfordton NC 28139; 828-286-9955
  Mi Pueblito Mexican Restaurant: (Mexican) 139 South Washington Street, Rutherfordton NC 28139; 828-286-2860
  The Water Oak Restaurant: (Southern Mediterranean Fine Dining) 205 Fashion Circle, Rutherfordton NC 28139; 828-287-2932
Recommended Places To Stay: (For a complete list of all accommodations visit www.ashevilleguidebook.com)
  Carrier Houses Bed & Breakfast: (B&B) 255 North Main Street, Rutherfordton NC 28139; 800-835-7071
  The Firehouse Inn: (Village Inn) 125 West First Street, Rutherfordton NC 28139; 828-286-9030

Saluda

Saluda, situated in the foothills to the south of Asheville, is a town of old-fashioned charm and beauty, with sixteen of its buildings listed on the National Register. Many years ago, before the railroad and the town existed, this area was known as Pace's Gap, a crossroad for traders and herders. The Pace's Gap community included separated homesteads and a Drovers Inn. The roads were used by traders who carried goods and by people who herded livestock through Pace's Gap from the western towns and villages.

Nestled peacefully in the mountains, Saluda became a railroad stop on the way to Asheville from the lowlands and, to this day, the steep climb up the mountains is called the "Saluda Grade." The historic railroad district allows visitors a chance to catch a glimpse of local railroad history. Main Street is also a National Historic District and offers restaurants, galleries and a variety of small shops. Saluda's main festival is Coon Dog Days held each July.

A noteworthy local attraction is nearby Pearson's Falls, located off Highway 176 between Tryon and Saluda. This botanical preserve is comprised of 268 acres of native forest, spring-fed streams and a 1/4 mile trail to a 90 ft. waterfall. There are over 200 species of fern, flowering plants, algae and mosses in the wildflower preserve.

Location: Central Mountains, 45 minutes south of Asheville
Town Offices: PO Box 248, Saluda NC 28773; 828-749-2581
Website: www.cityofsaludanc.com
County: Polk County: County Offices, 40 Courthouse Street, Columbus NC 28722; 828-894-3301
Elevation & Population: 2,060 feet, 575+
County Visitor/Welcome Center: Polk County Travel & Tourism 20 East Mills Street, Columbus NC 28722; 800-440-7848
County Chamber of Commerce: Carolina Foothills Chamber of Commerce 2753 Lynn Road, Suite A, Tryon NC 28782; 828-859-6236
Newspapers: Tryon Daily Bulletin 16 North Trade Street, Tryon NC 28782; 828-859-9151 and Polk County News Journal PO Box 576, Columbus NC 28722; 864-457-3337
High School: Polk County High School, 1681 East NC Highway 108, Columbus NC 28722; 828-894-2525
Area Major Festivals: Coon Dog Days (July) Saluda Arts Festival (May)
Area Natural Attractions: Pearson's Falls, Pisgah National Forest
Area Cultural Attractions: Foothills Equestrian Nature Center (FENCE), Polk County Courthouse, Polk County Historical Museum, Tryon Fine Arts Center
Recommended Restaurants: (For a complete list of all restaurants visit www.ashevilleguidebook.com)
> **Green River Bar-B-Que:** (BBQ) 131 Main Street, Saluda NC 28773; 828-749-28773
> **Saluda Grade Cafe:** (Cafe) 40 Main Street, Saluda NC 28773; 828-749-5854

The Purple Onion: (Mediterranean) 16 Main Street, Saluda NC 28773; 828-749-1179
Recommended Places To Stay: (For a complete list of all accommodations visit www.ashevilleguidebook.com)
    The Orchard Inn: (Country Inn) 7305 Highway 176, Saluda NC 28773; 800-581-3800
    The Oaks Bed & Breakfast: (B&B) 339 Greenville Street, Saluda NC 28773; 800-893-6091

Sawmills

Sawmills lies between Hudson to the north and Granite Falls to the southeast in Caldwell County and is positioned on both Lake Rhodhiss and US 321. The name Sawmills was chosen in 1988 because of the many sawmills that supplied wood for local furniture plants. The town has the county's second highest population and is among the largest in land area. The town operates two parks, Veteran's Park on Lake Rhodhiss, which features a paved walking trail and fishing pier, and Baird Drive Park, that features a picnic area, walking track, playground, and athletic fields. Caldwell County, known as the Furniture Capital of the South, is home to the "20 Miles of Furniture" where numerous outlets and stores offer deep discounts. Located along or near a stretch of U.S. Highway 321 between Lenoir and Hickory, the area, which passes through Sawmills, is a required destination for any serious shopper looking for furniture.

Location: Foothills, 1½ hours east of Asheville
Town Hall: 4076 US Highway 321-A, Sawmills NC 28630; 828-396-7903
Website: www.townofsawmills.com
County: Caldwell County: County Offices, 904 West Avenue NW, Lenoir NC 28645; 828-757-1300
Elevation & Population: 1,247 feet, 4,900+
County Visitor/Welcome Center: Caldwell County Chamber of Commerce Visitor Center,1909 Hickory Boulevard SE, Lenoir NC 28645; 828-726-0323
County Chamber of Commerce: Caldwell County Chamber of Commerce, 1909 Hickory Boulevard SE, Lenoir NC 28645; 828-726-0323
Newspaper: News-Topic,123 Pennton Avenue, Lenoir NC 28645; 828-758-7381
Area Major Festivals: Christmas Parade (December)
Area Natural Attractions: Pisgah National Forest, Tuttle Educational State Forest, Wilson Creek
Area Cultural Attractions: Caldwell Heritage Museum, Chapel of Rest, Fort Defiance, Granite Falls History &Transportation Museum, Happy Valley, 20 Miles of Furniture
Recommended Restaurants: (For a complete list of all restaurants visit www.ashevilleguidebook.com)
    No restaurants currently available in Sawmills. *See* Lenoir and Granite Falls

Recommended Places To Stay: (For a complete list of all accommodations visit www.ashevilleguidebook.com)

No accommodations currently available in Sawmills. *See* Lenoir and Granite Falls.

Sparta

Located at the center of Alleghany County and its county seat, Sparta is a classic southern small mountain town, with the historic Allegheny County Courthouse as the primary building. There is an older business district with overtones of years gone by and two shopping centers, a satellite campus of Wilkes Community College and Alleghany Memorial Hospital. Sparta is also home to the Sparta Teapot Museum of Craft & Design which has ongoing exhibits of traditional and contemporary arts and crafts in addition to teapots.

The town also features one of the most complete public parks for a community of its size, Crouse Park. The park features a basketball and volleyball court, horseshoes, walking course and exercise and play equipment for all ages from toddlers through adults. Near to Sparta are two state parks-Stone Mountain State Park and the New River State Park, home to the famous New River, the second oldest river in the world.

Nearby Lansing has a history of mining and dairy farming, both of which have been replaced by Christmas tree farming. Frazier firs from Lansing are shipped nationwide each Christmas. Lansing has a number of festivals each year, including the famous Ola Belle Reed Homecoming Festival which is held every August and highlights folk and bluegrass music.

Location: Northern Mountains, 3 hours northeast of Asheville
Town Office: 304 South Main Street, Sparta NC 28675
County: Alleghany County: County Offices, 348 South Main Street, Sparta NC 28675; 336-372-4179
Elevation & Population: 2,939 feet, 1,800+
Visitor/Welcome Center: Alleghany Chamber of Commerce Visitor Center, 58 South Main Street, Sparta NC 28675; 800-372-5473
County Chamber of Commerce: Alleghany Chamber of Commerce 58 South Main Street, Sparta NC 28675; 800-372-5473
Newspaper: The Alleghany News, 20 South Main Street, Sparta NC 28675; 336-372-8999
High School: Alleghany High School, 404 Trojan Avenue, Sparta NC 28675; 336-372-4554
Colleges and Universities: Wilkes Community College, Alleghany Campus, 115 Atwood Street, Sparta NC 28675; 336-372-5061
Hospitals: Alleghany Memorial Hospital, 233 Doctors Street, Sparta NC 28675; 336-372-5511
Area Major Festivals: Alleghany County Fiddler's Convention (July)

Area Natural Attractions: Blue Ridge Parkway, New River State Park, Stone Mountain State Park

Area Cultural Attractions: Allegheny County Courthouse, Sparta Teapot Museum of Craft & Design

Recommended Restaurants: (For a complete list of all restaurants visit www. ashevilleguidebook.com)

> **Brown's Family Restaurant:** (American) 115 Jones Street, Sparta NC 28675; 336-372-3400
>
> **Mustard Seed Cafe:** (Cafe) 38 South Main Street, Sparta NC 28675; 336-372-7444
>
> **Ship's Wheel:** (American) 577 North Main Street, Sparta NC 28675; 336-372-4900

Recommended Places To Stay: (For a complete list of all accommodations visit www.ashevilleguidebook.com)

> **Alleghany Inn:** (Motel) 341 North Main Street, Sparta NC 28675; 888-372-2501
>
> **Harmony Hill Bed & Breakfast:** (B&B) 1740 Halsey Knob Road, Sparta NC 28675; 336-372-6868

Spindale

Located midway between Forest City and Rutherfordton, Spindale features a diverse selection of specialty shops, long-established businesses, restaurants and service professionals. It is also home to Isothermal Community College, the cultural and learning center for the entire region. Concerts at The Foundation for Performing Arts and Conference Center, the college's new convention and performance facility, are among the highlights of every cultural season. Spindale also offers a stretch of the Thermal Belt Walking Trail, following an old railroad right of way, a well established Farmer's Market, and on Main Street, Spindale House, the town Community Center. Spindale has gained fame in recent years as the home of Public Radio Station WNCW FM 88.7, which is licensed to Isothermal Community College. The station has a worldwide listener base and features programming of an eclectic blend of music styles.

Location: Foothills, 1 hour southeast of Asheville

Town Hall: 103 Revely Street, Spindale, NC 28160; 828-286-3466

Website: www.spindalenc.net

County: Rutherford County: County Offices, 229 North Main Street, Rutherfordton NC 28139; 828-287-6045

Elevation & Population: 960 feet, 4,000+

Visitor/Welcome Center: Rutherford County Tourism 1990 US Highway 221 South, Forest City NC 28043; 800-849-5998

County Chamber of Commerce: Rutherford County Chamber of Commerce 162 North Main Street, Rutherfordton NC 28139; 828-287-3090

Newspaper: The Daily Courier 601 Oak Street, Forest City NC 28043; 828-245-6431

High School: Chase High School, 1603 Chase High Road, Forest City NC 28043; 828-245-7668

Colleges and Universities: Isothermal Community College, 286 ICC Loop Road, Spindale NC 28160; 828-286-3636

Area Major Festivals: Spring Foothills Antique & Artisan Show (April)

Area Natural Attractions: Chimney Rock Park, Lake Lure

Area Cultural Attractions: Bennett Classics Antique Auto Museum, KidSenses Children's InterACTIVE Museum, Rutherford County Farm Museum, Rutherford County Museum

Recommended Restaurants: (For a complete list of all restaurants visit www.ashevilleguidebook.com)

> **Barley's Taproom & Pizzeria:** (Pizza) 115 West Main Street, Spindale NC 28160; 828-0288-8388
>
> **M2 Restaurant:** (American) 125 West Main Street, Spindale NC 28160; 828-288-4641
>
> **Soda Fountain at Spindale Drug Store:** (Cafe) 101 West Main Street, Spindale NC 28160; 828-286-3746

Recommended Places To Stay: (For a complete list of all accommodations visit www.ashevilleguidebook.com)

> **Super 8 Motel:** (Motel-only accommodation) 210 Reservation Drive, Spindale NC 28160; 828-286-3681

Spruce Pine

Located in Mitchell County on the banks of the Toe River and just off the Blue Ridge Parkway at mile marker 331, Spruce Pine is a vibrant mountain town with a past rich in gem mining history and lore. In the early 1900s, Spruce Pine was a booming mining town and the Clinchfield Railroad operated to bring materials and supplies to and from the growing community. Chartered in 1913, Spruce Pine was built around the Carolina, Clinchfield and Ohio Railroad Depot. The railroad is still going strong, and train enthusiasts continue today to come from far and wide to Spruce Pine to enjoy watching the frequent passage of CSX trains through the downtown area. Over 30 trains a day pass by, often blowing their horns in greeting.

Historically, the White House Christmas tree has come from the Spruce Pine region and with so many Christmas tree farms in the area, the town has appropriately become known as the "Christmas Tree Capital of the World," a title it shares along with "The Mineral City." Located in a region of the mountains that is known for gem mines, Spruce Pine is famous for the world-class rubies and emeralds that have been found in local mines. The surrounding mountains have a more concentrated wealth of feldspar than any other area on earth, supplying 60% of the United States production of the mineral. Additionally, almost 100%

of the United States and the world supply of ultra-pure quartz, which is used in the production of semi-conductors, comes from the Spruce Pine region.

Spruce Pine has the distinction of having two Main Streets, Upper Street (Oak Avenue) and Lower Street (Locust Street), with nicknames given because of respective altitudes. Spruce Pine also has two municipal parks, Riverside Park on Tappan Street with a wonderful walking path and access to the Toe River, and Brad Ragan Park on Laurel Creek Court.

Location: Northern Mountains, 2 hours northeast of Asheville
Town Hall: 138 Highland Avenue, Spruce Pine NC 28777; 828-765-3000
Website: www.townofsprucepine.com
County: Mitchell County: County Administration Building, 26 Crimson Laurel Circle, Bakersville NC 28705; 828-688-2139
Elevation & Population: 2,517 feet, 2,000+
County Visitor Center: Located in the Museum of NC Minerals, Milepost 331, Blue Ridge Parkway; Spruce Pine NC 28777; 800-227-3912
County Chamber of Commerce: Mitchell County Chamber of Commerce: 11 Crystal Street, Spruce Pine NC 28777; 828-765-9033
Newspaper: Mitchell News-Journal 291 Locust Avenue, Spruce Pine 28777; 828-765-2071
High School: Mitchell High School, 416 Ledger School Road, Bakersville NC 28705; 828-688-2101
Colleges and Universities: Mayland Community College, 200 Mayland Drive, Spruce Pine NC 28777; 828-765-7351
Hospitals: Blue Ridge Regional Hospital, 125 Hospital Drive, Spruce Pine NC 28777; 877-777-8230
Area Major Festivals: Fire on the Mountain Blacksmith Festival (April), Toe River Storytelling Festival (July), Mineral City Heritage Festival (October)
Area Natural Attractions: Blue Ridge Parkway, Grandfather Mountain State Park, Pisgah National Forest
Area Cultural Attractions: Emerald Village, Museum of North Carolina Minerals, North Carolina Mining Museum, Orchard at Altapass
Recommended Restaurants: (For a complete list of all restaurants visit www.ashevilleguidebook.com)
  DT's Blue Ridge Java: Coffee Shop & Cafe: (Cafe) 169 Locust Street, Spruce Pine NC 28777; 828-766-8008
  Knife and Fork Restaurant: (American) 61 Locust Street, Spruce Pine NC 28777; 828-765-1511
  Skyline Cavern Tavern: (American) Skyline Village Inn, 12255 Highway 226A, (Milepost 334 Blue Ridge Parkway),
  Spruce Pine NC 28777; 828-994-0027
Recommended Places To Stay: (For a complete list of all accommodations visit www.ashevilleguidebook.com)

Pinebridge Inn: (Hotel &Conference Center) 207 Pinebridge Avenue, Spruce Pine NC 28777; 800-356-5059

Richmond Inn: (B&B) 51 Pine Street, Spruce Pine NC 28777; 877-765-6993

Skyline Village Inn: (County Inn) 12255 Highway 226A, (Milepost 334 Blue Ridge Parkway) Spruce Pine NC 28777; 828-994-0027

Sugar Mountain

Sugar Mountain is a small resort village nestled in the middle of the High Country located at the eastern end of Avery County and is a year-round vacation destination offering golf, hiking, tennis, skiing and other outdoor activities. The major attraction is the Sugar Mountain Resort located in nearby Banner Elk, a full-service alpine snow ski and snowboard area that features a 1,200-foot vertical drop and 18 slopes and trails with eight lifts. With an average annual snowfall of 78" and state-of-the-art snowmaking equipment, Sugar Mountain offers winter sports enthusiasts a fabulous white playground. Besides Sugar Mountain for skiing, the popular Hawksnest Tubing Park is located in nearby Seven Devils.

Location: Northern Mountains, 2 hours east of Asheville

Town Hall: 251 Dick Trundy Lane, Sugar Mountain NC 28604; 828-898-9292

Website: www.townofsprucepine.com

County: Avery County: County Administrative Building, 175 Linville Street, Newland NC 28657; 828-733-8202

Elevation & Population: 4,432 feet, 250+

County Chamber of Commerce: Avery County Chamber of Commerce: 4501 Tynecastle Highway, Unit #2, Banner Elk NC 28604; 800-972-2183

Newspaper: The Mountain Times PO Box 1815, Boone NC 28607; 828-264-6397

High School: Avery County High School, 401 High School Road, Newland NC 28657; 828-733-0151

Area Major Festivals: Sugar Mountain Oktoberfest (October), Sugarfest (December)

Area Natural Attractions: Blue Ridge Parkway, Grandfather Mountain, Linville Caverns, Linville Gorge,

Area Cultural Attractions: Avery County Historical Museum, Banner House Museum, Crossnore Fine Arts Gallery, Horn in the West, Mast General Store, Mystery Hill, Orchard at Altapass, Tweetsie Railroad

Recommended Restaurants: (For a complete list of all restaurants visit www.ashevilleguidebook.com)

Bella's: (Italian) 3585 Tynecastle Highway, Sugar Mountain NC 28604; 828-898-9022

Recommended Places To Stay: (For a complete list of all accommodations visit www.ashevilleguidebook.com)

Sugar Ski & Country Club: (Resort) 100 Sugar Drive, Banner Elk NC 28604; 800-634-1320

Sylva

Sylva is a quaint town in Western North Carolina that is surrounded by beautiful mountains and conveniently located near many of the major natural and cultural attractions in Western North Carolina. The town has a delightful downtown area with many restaurants and shops, and is also home to the historic Jackson County Courthouse and Southwestern Community College. Recreational opportunities abound and nearby outdoor mountain attractions include the Cataloochee Ski Area, the Blue Ridge Parkway and three great forests and parks: the Great Smoky Mountains National Park, the Nantahala National Forest and the Pisgah National Forest. Sylva also has a state of the art children's playground, and a wonderful park, Pinnacle Park, that boasts hiking trails, waterfalls and a view of the town from 5,000 feet.

Of interest also is the famous Judaculla Rock, a large stone covered with cryptic markings that predates the Cherokee Indians and which are thought to be over 2,000 years old. The rock is the largest and best-known example of rock art in North Carolina and is open to the public. To get there, take Route 23 from downtown 1.3 miles to NC 107, then turn left onto 107. Drive 8 miles south on 107 and take a left onto Caney Fork Road, County Road 1737. Go 2.5 miles, then turn left onto a gravel road and drive 0.45 mile. The rock is on the right, with parking on the left.

Location: Western Mountains, 1 hour west of Asheville
Town Hall: 83 Allen Street, Sylva NC 28779; 828-586-2719
City Websites: http://sylvanc.govoffice3.com
County Visitor/Welcome Center Website: www.mountainlovers.com
County: Jackson County: County Offices, 401 Grindstaff Cove Road, Suite A-207, Sylva NC 28779; 828-631-2207
Elevation & Population: 2,036 ft, 2,600+
County Chamber of Commerce: Jackson County Chamber of Commerce 773 West Main Street, Sylva NC 28779; 800-962-1911
Newspapers: The Sylva Herald 539 West Main Street, Sylva NC 28779; 800-849-3193 and The Smoky Mountains News 633 West Main Street, Sylva, NC 28779; 828-631-4829
Movie Theatres: Quin Theaters East Sylva Shopping Center, Sylva NC 28779; 828-586-5918
High School: Smoky Mountain High, 100 Smoky Mountain Drive, Sylva NC 28779; 828-586-2177
Colleges and Universities: Southwestern Community College, 447 College Drive, Sylva NC, 28779; 828-586-4091 and Western Carolina University, University Way, Cullowhee NC 28723; 828-227-7211
Hospitals: Harris Regional Hospital, 68 Hospital Road, Sylva NC 28779; 828-586-7000
Area Major Festivals: Greening Up The Mountains (April), Mountain Artisans Arts & Crafts Shows (July and November), Concerts on the Creek (Summer), Mountain Heritage Day (September)

Area Natural Attractions: Judaculla Rock, Pisgah National Forest, Waterfalls in Western North Carolina, Great Smoky Mountains National Park

Area Cultural Attractions: Cherokee Indian Reservation, Fine and Performing Arts Center at WCU, Great Smoky Mountains Railroad, Mountain Heritage Center, Western Carolina University

Recommended Restaurants: (For a complete list of all restaurants visit www. ashevilleguidebook.com)

> **Annie's Naturally Bakery:** (Cafe-Lunch Only) 506 West Main Street, Sylva NC 28779; 828-586-9096
>
> **Guadalupe Cafe:** (Tapas, Caribbean) 606 West Main Street, Sylva NC 28779; 828-586-9877
>
> **Lulu's On Main:** (American Gourmet) 612 West Main Street, Sylva NC 28779; 828-586-8989
>
> **Mill & Main:** (American) 462 West Main Street, Sylva NC 28779; 828-586-6799
>
> **Nick & Nate's Pizzeria:** (Pizza) Asheville Highway, #38 The Overlook Village, Sylva NC 28799; 828-586-3000
>
> **Soul Infusion Tea House & Bistro:** (Bistro, Tea House) 628 East Main Street, Sylva NC 287790; 828-586-1717
>
> **Sapphire Mountain Brewing Company:** (Pizza) 553 W. Main Street Sylva, NC 28779; 828-587-0220

Recommended Places To Stay: (For a complete list of all accommodations visit www.ashevilleguidebook.com)

> **Balsam Mountain Inn:** (Country Inn) 68 Seven Springs Drive, Balsam NC 28707; 800-224-9498
>
> **Mountain Brook Cottages:** (Cottages) 208 Mountain Brook Road, Sylva NC 28779; 800-258-4052
>
> **The Freeze House Bed & Breakfast:** (B&B) 71 Sylvan Heights, Sylva NC 28779; 828-586-8161
>
> **The Sylva Inn:** (Motel) 2897 US 74, Sylva NC 28779; 828-586-3315

Tryon

The small mountain town of Tryon, located southeast of Asheville, is well-known for the equestrian events held at the Foothills Equestrian Nature Center almost every weekend from April through October. Incorporated in the late 1800s when the Spartanburg and Asheville Railroad came to the area, it is the largest town in its region. Many of the historic buildings on Trade Street were in place by 1900, including a general store, a pharmacy and a post office. Tryon quickly grew as a resort town, drawing tourists to the area to enjoy the mountain views and good climate. Over the years, Tryon has been home to many artists and writers including the stage actor William Gillette, most famous for his portrayal of Sherlock Holmes, and F. Scott Fitzgerald. This mix of locals, artists and retirees continues today, creating a vibrant, active community. The village also has a number of art and craft galleries, and a nice selection of restaurants and accommodations, and over the years Tryon has earned the reputation as one of the friendliest towns in the south. The premier event in Tryon is the running of the annual Block House Steeplechase, presented by the Tryon Riding & Hunt Club.

Nearby Pearson's Falls is located off Hwy. 176 between Tryon and Saluda. This botanical preserve is comprised of 268 acres of native forest, spring-fed streams and a moderate ¼ mile trail to a 90 ft. waterfall. There are over 200 species of fern, flowering plants, algae and mosses in the wildflower preserve.

Location: Central Mountains, 45 minutes south of Asheville

Town Hall: North Trade Street, Tryon NC 28782; 828-859-6655

Website: www.tryon-nc.com

County: Polk County: County Offices, 40 Courthouse Street, Columbus NC 28722; 828-894-3301

Elevation & Population: 1,100 feet, 1,750+

County Visitor/Welcome Center: Polk County Travel & Tourism 20 East Mills Street, Columbus NC 28722; 800-440-7848

County Chamber of Commerce: Carolina Foothills Chamber of Commerce 2753 Lynn Road, Suite A, Tryon NC 28782; 828-859-6236

Newspaper: Tryon Daily Bulletin 16 North Trade Street, Tryon NC 28782; 828-859-9151 and Polk County News Journal PO Box 576, Columbus NC 28722; 864-457-3337

Movie Theatres: Tryon Theatre, 45 South Trade Street, Tryon NC 28782; 828-859-6811

High School: Polk County High School, 1681 East NC Highway 108, Columbus NC 28722; 828-894-2525

Area Major Festivals: Block House Steeplechase (April)

Area Natural Attractions: Pearson's Falls, Pisgah National Forest

Area Cultural Attractions: Foothills Equestrian Nature Center (FENCE), Polk County Courthouse, Polk County Historical Museum, Tryon Fine Arts Center

Recommended Restaurants: (For a complete list of all restaurants visit www.ashevilleguidebook.com)

    Carter's Restaurant & Wine Cellar at the 1906 Pine Crest Inn: (Fine Dining) Pine Crest Inn, 85 Pine Crest Lane,

    Tryon NC 28782; 800-633-3001

    Kyoto Japanese Steak House & Seafood: (Japanese) 112 North Trade Street, Tryon NC 28722; 828-859-9043

    10 North Trade Cafe Bakery: (Cafe-Breakfast & Lunch) 10 North Trade Street, Tryon NC 28782; 828-859-3010

    The Mimosa Inn Restaurant: (Fine Dining) 65 Mimosa Inn Drive, Tryon NC 28792; 828-859-7688

Recommended Places To Stay: (For a complete list of all accommodations visit www.ashevilleguidebook.com)

    Butterfly Creek: (B&B) 780 Smith Dairy Road, Tryon NC 28782; 828-894-6393

Stone Hedge Inn: (Country Inn) 222 Stone Hedge Lane, Tryon NC 28782; 800-859-1974

The Mimosa Inn: (Village Inn) 65 Mimosa Inn Drive, Tryon NC 28792; 828-859-7688

1906 Pine Crest Inn: (Country Inn) 85 Pine Crest Lane, Tryon NC 28782; 800-633-3001

Tryon Old South Bed & Breakfast: (B&B) 27 Markham Road, Tryon NC 28792; 800-288-7966

Valdese

Valdese, a town located about eight miles east of Morganton, ranks second in size for Burke County with a population of 4,600. The community has a heritage that dates back to the Middle Ages in Europe and was settled about 113 years ago by the Waldensians, a sect from the Cottian Alps located in northern Italy and southern France that found their way to Burke County where they could freely practice their religion. For centuries in Italy they had been persecuted for their religious beliefs. Sites to visit in Valdese include the Trail of Faith, the outdoor drama "From This Day Forward" and the Waldensian Heritage Museum.

Valdese today is a tourist destination, a city rich in history, and remains a town still linked by its roots to Italy. The Old Rock School, built in 1923 by the original settlers of Valdese, was renovated in the 1970's and remains the focal point of the town. The facility now houses art galleries and a 473-seat auditorium where bluegrass music, "Bluegrass at The Rock" is performed on a regular basis throughout the year. Valdese also has a Farmer's Market, held across from the town hall, on Wednesdays and Fridays during the summer season and also a great recreational park at McGalliard Falls Parks, complete with a restored grist mill. Not to be missed while downtown is the Village Park Mural, a stunning outdoor painting on Main Street.

Location: Foothills,1 hour and 15 minutes east of Asheville

Town Offices: 121 Faet Street, Valdese NC 28690; 828-879-2120

Website: www.ci.valdese.nc.us

County: Burke County: Burke County Government Center, 200 Avery Avenue, Morganton NC 28680; 828-439-4340

Elevation & Population: 1,203 feet, 4,600+

Visitor/Welcome Center: Valdese Visitor Center, 400 West Main Street, Valdese NC 28690; 828-879-2129

County Chamber of Commerce: Burke County Chamber of Commerce, 110 East Meeting Street, Morganton NC 28655; 828-437-3021

Newspaper: The News Herald, 301 Collett Street, Morganton NC 28655; 828-437-2161

High School: Jimmy C Draughn High School, 709 Lovelady Road NE, Valdese NC 28690; 828-879-4200

Hospitals: Valdese Hospital, 720 Malcolm Boulevard, Valdese NC 28690; 828-874-2251

Area Major Festivals: July 4th Fireworks (July), Waldensian Festival (August)
Area Natural Attractions: McGalliard Falls Parks, South Mountains State Park
Area Cultural Attractions: From This Day Forward, Trail of Faith, Waldensian Heritage Museum
Recommended Restaurants: (For a complete list of all restaurants visit www. ashevilleguidebook.com)
> **Dew Drop Inn:** (American) 508 East Main Street, Valdese NC 28690; 828-879-1600
> **Giovanni's Pizza:** (Pizza) East Main Street, Valdese NC 28690; 828-874-3601
> **Myra's Little Italy:** (Italian) 155 Bobo Avenue NW, Valdese NC 28690; 828-874-7086

Recommended Places To Stay: (For a complete list of all accommodations visit www.ashevilleguidebook.com)
> No accommodations currently available in Long View. *See* Morganton

Valle Crucis

Located high in the mountains near Boone, Valle Crucis is an historic community that has been around for 200 years. It is home to the famous Mast General Store, the Holy Cross Episcopal Church and the Valle Crucis Conference Center, as well as many shops, galleries and studios featuring handmade crafts and art, rustic furniture and pottery. The town is North Carolina's first rural historic district and the entire community is listed on the National Register of Historic Places.

Valle Crucis' name means "Vale of the Cross", a reference to a valley in the area where three streams converge to form a shape similar to an archbishop's cross. Valle Crucis began in the 1840's when an Episcopalian missionary, William West Skiles, came to the area. He founded the first Episcopal Church in the region as well as the Valle Crucis Mission School. Skiles also founded the first monastic order within the Episcopal Church in the United States, the Brotherhood of the Holy Cross.

During recent years, Valle Crucis has transformed from a little-known rural community to a popular destination for tourists and new residents. The valley's serene scenic beauty and protected location in the mountains proximate to the Pisgah National Forest have been factors in this recent development. The major attraction in town is the original Mast General Store, which offers visitors a true glimpse into bygone days.

Location: Northern Mountains, 2 hours east of Asheville
Website: www.vallecrucis.com
County: Watauga County: County Offices, 842 West King Street, Boone NC 28607; 828-265-8000
Elevation & Population: 2,800 feet; 800+
Visitor/Welcome Center: Boone Convention & Visitor Center 208 Howard Street, Boone NC 28607; 800-852-9506, 828-262-3516
City Chamber of Commerce: Boone Area Chamber of Commerce 208 Howard Street, Boone NC 28607; 828-264-2225

County Chamber of Commerce: Boone Area Chamber of Commerce 208 Howard Street, Boone NC 28607; 828-264-2225

Newspaper: The Watauga Democrat 474 Industrial Park Drive, Boone NC 28607; 828-264-3612 and The Mountain Times PO Box 1815, Boone NC 28607; 828-264-6397

High School: Watauga High School, 300 Go Pioneers Drive, Boone NC 28607; 828-264-2407

Area Major Festivals: Valle Crucis Creekside Bluegrass Festival (June), Valley Country Fair (October)

Area Natural Attractions: Blue Ridge Parkway, Grandfather Mountain, Pisgah National Forest

Area Cultural Attractions: Hickory Ridge Homestead, Horn in the West, Mast General Store, Turchin Center for Visual Arts, Tweetsie Railroad

Recommended Restaurants: (For a complete list of all restaurants visit www. ashevilleguidebook.com)

     The Ham Shoppe: (Cafe) 124 Broadstone Road, Valle Crucis NC 28691; 828-963-6310

Recommended Places To Stay: (For a complete list of all accommodations visit www.ashevilleguidebook.com)

     The Baird House: (B&B) 1451 Watauga River Road, Valle Crucis NC 28691; 800-297-1342

Waynesville

Incorporated in 1871, Waynesville is Haywood County's oldest city, and the fifth largest city in Western North Carolina after Asheville, Hickory, Morganton and Hendersonville. It was founded in 1810 by Colonel Robert Love, who donated land for the courthouse, jail and public square, and who named the town after his former commander in the Revolutionary War, General "Mad" Anthony Wayne. Rich in history dating back almost 200 years and known for its southern hospitality and magnificent views of the surrounding mountains, Waynesville is a tourist destination in its own right and has a wealth of unique shops, arts and crafts galleries, restaurants and accommodations.

The Waynesville area began to see major development after the arrival of the railroad in the late 1800's, with agriculture, lumber and tourism becoming the major industries. The last passenger train to Waynesville was in 1949, but the railroad line is still active and today Norfolk Southern Railway freight trains still pass though the city on their way to Sylva in the west.

Waynesville has a number of distinct neighborhoods: Downtown, Frog Level, Hazelwood, Laurel Ridge, West Waynesville and Russ Avenue. The downtown area, once the primary retail business center of the town, is now home to town government and administration buildings, cafes, restaurants, shops, art galleries and professional offices. It is known for its lofty shade trees, brick sidewalks, benches, water fountains, and outdoor sculptures. Frog Level is an historic railroad district that was so named because of frequent flooding of nearby Richland Creek and as the early home of Waynesville's railroad depots. Today, Frog Level has experienced the same type of revitalization as the downtown Main Street area.

Hazelwood was primarily a working class town before annexation by Waynesville, and is similar to West Waynesville, the industrial part of city. The town is dominated by the Waynesville Commons shopping center which is anchored by a Wal-Mart Super Store. Russ Avenue is a newer business district of Waynesville and features restaurants, retail stores, auto dealerships, banks and grocery stores.

Waynesville has two outstanding recreational facilities: the Waynesville Recreation Center located at 550 Vance Street, and the Old Armory Recreation Center at 44 Boundary Street. These facilities serve the entire region and together offer an eight-lane pool, water playground, gymnasium, weight room and indoor and outdoor tracks. The Parks and Recreation Department also maintains an 18-hole disc golf course, five neighborhood parks, two dog parks, tennis courts, softball fields, a soccer field and a Greenway near Richland Creek.

Waynesville is also host every year to the world-famous FOLKMOOT USA, North Carolina's official international music and dance festival, as well as the Haywood Arts Regional Theatre, Museum of North Carolina Handicrafts, and the Red Barn Mountain Museum. Nearby outdoor mountain attractions include the Cataloochee Ski Area, the Blue Ridge Parkway and three great forests and parks: the Great Smoky Mountains National Park, the Nantahala National Forest and the Pisgah National Forest. Close by also is the famous Cherokee Indian Reservation as well as the Lake Junaluska Conference and Retreat Center. Lake Junaluska is notable as the site of the headquarters of the World Methodist Council, a consultative body linking almost all churches in the Methodist tradition.

Location: Central Mountains, 45 minutes west of Asheville
Municipal Building: 16 South Main Street, Waynesville NC 28786; 828-452-2491
Website: www.townofwaynesville.org
County: Haywood County, Haywood City Offices, 215 North Main Street, Waynesville NC 28786; 828-452-6625
Elevation & Population: 3,600 feet, 10,000+
County Visitor/Welcome Center: Haywood County Tourism Development Authority Visitor Center, 20525 Great Smoky Mountain Expressway, Waynesville NC 28786; 828-456-7307
County Chamber of Commerce: Haywood County Chamber of Commerce, 591 North Main Street, Waynesville NC 28786; 828-456-3021
Newspaper: The Mountaineer, 220 North Main Street, Waynesville NC 28786; 828-452-0661
Movie Theatres: Smoky Mountain Cinemas, 235 Waynesville Plaza, Russ Avenue, Waynesville NC 28786; 828-452-9091
High School: Tuscola High School, 564 Tuscola School Road, Waynesville NC 28786; 828-456-2408
Area Major Festivals: FOLKMOOT USA (July-August), Smoky Mountain Folk Festival (September), Church Street Art & Craft Show (October)

Area Natural Attractions: Blue Ridge Parkway, Great Smoky Mountains National Park, Nantahala National Forest, Pisgah National Forest

Area Cultural Attractions: Cataloochee Ski Area, Cherokee Indian Reservation, Ghost Town In The Sky, HART-Haywood Arts Regional Theatre, Museum of North Carolina Handicrafts, Red Barn Mountain Museum, Wheels Thru Time Museum, World Methodist Museum, SEJ Heritage Center at Lake Junaluska

Recommended Restaurants: (For a complete list of all restaurants visit www.ashevilleguidebook.com)

Bogart's Restaurant: (American) 303 South Main Street, Waynesville NC 28786; 828-452-1313

Bocelli's Italian Eatery: (Italian) 319 North Haywood Street, Waynesville NC 28786; 828-456-4900

Cafe 50: (Cafe) 50 North Main Street, Waynesville NC 28786; 828-246-9130

Chef's Table: (American-Fine Dining) 30 Church Street, Waynesville NC 28786; 828-452-6210

Clyde's Restaurant: (Country) 2107 South Main Street, Waynesville NC 28786; 828-456-9135

Cork & Cleaver: (American-Fine Dining) Waynesville Inn, 176 Country Club Road, Waynesville NC 28786; 800-627-6250

Maggie's Galley Oyster Bar: (Seafood) 49 Howell Mill Road, Waynesville NC 28786; 828-456-8945

The Sweet Onion Restaurant: (American) 39 Miller Street, Waynesville NC 28786; 828-456-5559

Recommended Places To Stay: (For a complete list of all accommodations visit www.ashevilleguidebook.com)

Andon Reid Inn Bed & Breakfast: (B&B) 92 Daisy Avenue, Waynesville NC 28786; 800-293-6190

Balsam Mountain Inn: (Country Inn) 68 Seven Springs Drive, Balsam NC 28707; 800-224-9498

Bed and Breakfast at Prospect Hill: (B&B) 274 South Main Street, Waynesville NC 28786; 800-219-6147

Best Western Smoky Mountain Inn: (Motel) 130 Shiloh Trail, Waynesville NC 28786; 828-456-4402

Oak Hill on Love Lane Bed & Breakfast: (B&B) 224 Love Lane, Waynesville NC 28786; 888-608-7037

The Old Stone Inn Mountain Lodge: (Country Lodge) 109 Dolan Road, Waynesville NC 28786; 800-432-8499

The Swag Country Inn: (Country Inn) 2300 Swag Road, Waynesville NC 28785; 800-789-7672

The Waynesville Inn Golf Resort & Spa: (Resort) 176 Country Club Road, Waynesville NC 28786; 800-627-6250

The Yellow House on Plott Creek Road: (B&B) 89 Oakview Drive, Waynesville NC 28786; 800-563-1236

Weaverville

Located just 12 miles north of Asheville, Weaverville is a small vibrant community that was incorporated in 1874. It was the birthplace of Zebulon T. Vance, Civil War governor of North Carolina in 1862-65 and 1877-79, who was born in the nearby Reems Creek Valley. His birthplace, the Zebulon B. Vance Birthplace, is a state historical site and worth a visit if you are interested in North Carolina history and historical sites.

Weaverville in the 1800's was home to a number of grand hotels, all now gone. These included the Dula Springs Hotel and Blackberry Lodge, where Low Country visitors came to escape the heat of South Carolina summers. These destination hotels, as well as Weaverville's natural charm and mountain beauty, helped solidify the town's reputation as a resort destination. This continues to this day, although Weaverville as a destination is greatly overshadowed by nearby Asheville.

The town has a lovely park, Lake Louise Park, and a number of excellent restaurants and places to stay, including some world-class bed and breakfasts. The Reems Creek Valley, to the east of the town center, is considered one of the most scenic valleys in the greater Asheville area. Weaverville also has the distinction of being named a "Tree City USA" every year since 1990. Weaverville is home to many residents who work in nearby Asheville but also is hosts a number of manufacturing businesses, including a branch of Arvato Digital Services, the world's second-largest replicator of CD's and DVD's.

Location: Central Mountains, 15 minutes north of Asheville
Town Hall: 30 South Main Street, Weaverville NC 28787; 828-645-7116
Website: www.weavervillenc.org
County: Buncombe County: County Offices, 205 College Street, Asheville NC 28801; 828-250-4000
Elevation & Population: 2,176 feet, 2,600+
County Chamber of Commerce: Buncombe County Chamber of Commerce 205 College Street, Asheville NC 28801; 828-250-4100
Newspaper: The Weaverville Tribune, 113 North Main Street, Weaverville NC 28787; 828-645-8911
High School: North Buncombe High School, 890 Clark's Chapel Road, Weaverville NC 28787; 828-645-4221
Area Major Festivals: Candlelight Tours at Vance Birthplace (December), Weaverville Art Safari (April & November),
Area Natural Attractions: Blue Ridge Parkway, Mount Mitchell State Park, Pisgah National Forest
Area Cultural Attractions: Biltmore Estate, Dry Ridge Historical Museum, Pack Place Education, Arts & Science Center, Thomas Wolfe Memorial, Zebulon B. Vance Birthplace
Recommended Restaurants: (For a complete list of all restaurants visit www.ashevilleguidebook.com)

Stoney Knob Cafe: (Continental-American Fine Dining) 337 Merrimon Avenue, Weaverville NC 28787; 828-645-3309

Sunnyside Cafe: (American- Fine Dining) 18 North Main Street, Weaverville NC 28787; 828-658-3338

Weaverville Milling Company Restaurant: (American) 1 Old Mill Lane, Weaverville NC 28787; 828-645-4700

Recommended Places To Stay: (For a complete list of all accommodations visit www.ashevilleguidebook.com)

Dry Ridge Inn: (B&B) 26 Brown Street, Weaverville NC 28787; 800-839-3899

Inn on Main Street: (B&B) 88 South Main Street, Weaverville NC 28787; 877-873-6074

Ox-ford Farm: (B&B) 75 Ox Creek Road, Weaverville NC 28787; 828-658-2500

West Jefferson

West Jefferson is located in the eastern part of the North Carolina mountains in Ashe County, and is in an area known for the famous New River, spectacular views and Christmas tree farming. The town has a thriving business district and is noted for the murals that create an art and history focused walking tour. The murals are the works of local artists in North Carolina that depict the area's history.

As with many small towns, West Jefferson has a number of distinctive and unique festivals, one of which is Christmas in July, featuring the very best in traditional mountain music and handmade crafts. The Ashe County Farmer's Market, open seasonally, is also located in West Jefferson on the Backstreet in downtown and is considered one of the premier farmer's markets in the mountains. St. Mary's Church on Beaver Creek Road also features the Ben Long Frescoes of the Mystery of Faith, Mary Great with Child, and John the Baptist.

Overlooking West Jefferson is the Mount Jefferson State Natural Area, which occupies the summit of Mount Jefferson. Hiking trails, picnic tables and pavilions are some of the amenities offered there. The Ashe County Arts Council Gallery is located in the Ashe Arts Center at 303 School Avenue, and has regularly changing exhibits of local artists and performances of music, poetry and literature.

Location: Northern Mountains, 2½ hours east of Asheville

Town Hall: 01 South Jefferson Avenue, West Jefferson NC 28694; 336-246-3551

Website: www.townofwj.com

County: Ashe County: County Offices, 150 Government Circle, Suite 2500, Jefferson NC 28640; 336-846-5501

Elevation & Population: 3,200 feet, 1100+

County Chamber of Commerce: Ashe County Chamber of Commerce 01 North Jefferson Street, Suite C, West Jefferson NC 28694; 336-846-9550

Newspaper: Jefferson Post, 203 South Second Street, West Jefferson NC 28694; 336-846-7164

Movie Theatres: Parkway Theatre, 10 East Main Street, West Jefferson NC 28694; 336-846-3281
High School: Ashe County High School, 184 Campus Drive, West Jefferson NC 28694; 336-846-2400
Area Major Festivals: Christmas in July (July), Ola Belle Reed Homecoming Festival (August)
Area Natural Attractions: Blue Ridge Parkway; Mount Jefferson State Natural Area, New River State Park
Area Cultural Attractions: Ashe County Arts Council Gallery, Ben Long Frescoes, Museum of Ashe County History
Recommended Restaurants: (For a complete list of all restaurants visit www.ashevilleguidebook.com)
   Frasers Restaurant & Pub: (American) 108 South Jefferson Avenue, West Jefferson NC 28694; 336-246-5222
   Mathew's 102 North: (American-Fine Dining) 102 North Jefferson Avenue, West Jefferson NC 28694; 336-846-5504
   Mountain Aire Seafood & Steaks: (American-Seafood) 9930 Highway 16 South, West Jefferson NC 28694; 336-982-3060
Recommended Places To Stay: (For a complete list of all accommodations visit www.ashevilleguidebook.com)
   Buffalo Tavern Bed & Breakfast: (B&B) 958 West Buffalo Road, West Jefferson NC 28694; 877-615-9678

Wilkesboro

Wilkesboro, founded in 1800 and incorporated in 1847, is the county seal of Wilkes County, and is located along the south bank of the Yadkin River, directly opposite the slightly larger town of North Wilkesboro. Wilkesboro is probably best known as the home to the celebrated MerleFest, an internationally acclaimed acoustic and bluegrass music festival held every April. Nearby outdoor attractions, including nearby Stone Mountain State Park and W. Kerr Scott Dam and Reservoir, the many downtown shops and galleries, and the multifaceted cultural life in this charming foothills town ensure a great visit. Wilkesboro's largest industry is the Tyson Foods poultry processing plant; it is one of the largest poultry plants east of the Mississippi River. The town also contains several textile and furniture factories; one of the largest is the Key City Furniture factory.

Noteworthy also is the fact that Daniel Boone, the famous explorer and pioneer, lived for several years where Wilkesboro and North Wilkesboro are located before moving west to Kentucky. Wilkesboro is also the place the Tom Dula saga took place. The incident was immortalized in song and legend, most notably in the murder ballad Hang Down Your Head, Tom Dooley recorded in 1958 by the Kingston Trio. Each summer the Wilkes Playmakers also present a popular play based on the legend. Visitors to Wilkesboro interested in local history may take a self-guided walking tour which includes stops at thirteen historic buildings.

One of the many artistic highlights of Wilkesboro are the beautiful Ben Long Frescoes in St. Paul's Episcopal Church, located at 200 Cowles Street. These classically-executed frescoes of St. Paul the Apostle are open for viewing by the public. Wilkesboro is also home to Wilkes Community College, a public coeducational two-year college which has an enrolment of over 3,500 students. Located on the campus is The Walker Center, one of the major cultural arts and performance venues in the area. Also in Wilkesboro is the Wilkes Heritage Museum, located in the historic Old Courthouse.

Stretching from the North Wilkesboro and Wilkesboro area towards Lenoir along Highway 268 is the historic "Happy Valley". Located on the banks of the Yadkin River, Happy Valley was so named by the early settlers who described the valley as "a place of beauty, peace and tranquility" and the name aptly remains. A number of attractions are in the valley, including Fort Defiance, the Chapel of Rest and Whippoorwill Academy and Village.

Location: Foothills, 2½ hours east of Asheville
Town Hall: 203 West Main Street, Wilkesboro NC 28697; 336-838-3951
Website: www.wilkesboronorthcarolina.com
County: Wilkes County: County Offices, 110 North Street, Wilkesboro NC 28697; 336-651-7346
Elevation & Population: 1,042 feet, 3,200+
County Chamber of Commerce: Wilkes County Chamber of Commerce, 717 Main Street, North Wilkesboro NC 28659; 336-838-8662
County Tourism Development: Wilkes County Tourism, 203 West Main Street, Wilkesboro NC 28697; 336-838-3951
Newspaper: The Record, 911 Main Street, North Wilkesboro NC 28659; 336-667-0134
High School: Wilkes Central High School, 1179 Moravian Falls Road, Wilkesboro NC 28697; 336-667-5277
Colleges and Universities: Wilkes Community College, 1328 South Collegiate Drive, Wilkesboro NC 28697; 336-838-6100
Area Major Festivals: MerleFest (April), Carolina In The Fall Festival (September), Brushy Mountain Apple Festival (October)
Area Natural Attractions: Happy Valley, Rendezvous Mountain Educational State Forest, Stone Mountain State Park, W. Kerr Scott Dam and Reservoir, Yadkin River Greenway
Area Cultural Attractions: Ben Long Frescoes in St. Paul's Episcopal Church, Chapel of Rest, Old Wilkes Jail Museum, The Walker Center, Whippoorwill Academy and Village, Wilkes Art Gallery, Wilkes Heritage Museum,
Recommended Restaurants: (For a complete list of all restaurants visit www.ashevilleguidebook.com)
    See also North Wilkesboro restaurants
    Amalfi's Italian Restaurant & Pizzeria: (Italian) 1919 Highway 421, Wilkesboro NC 28697; 336-838-3188

The 50s Cafe: (American) 109 West Main Street, Wilkesboro NC 28697; 336-838-5050

Recommended Places To Stay: (For a complete list of all accommodations visit www.ashevilleguidebook.com)

See also North Wilkesboro accommodations

Graystone Manor Bed & Breakfast: (B&B) 406 Woodland Boulevard, Wilkesboro NC 28697; 336-667-7282

Hampton Inn: (Motel) 1300 Collegiate Drive, Wilkesboro NC 28697; 336-838-5000

Leatherwood Mountains: (Resort) 512 Meadow Road, Ferguson NC 28624; 800-462-6867

Wilderness Lodge: (Country Lodge) 185 Edmiston Lane, Boomer NC 28606; 336-921-2277

Woodfin

Located north of and adjacent to Asheville, Woodfin was named in honor of Nicholas Washington Woodfin, a former lawyer and statesman of North Carolina. Woodfin is the only municipality bearing the name Woodfin in the United States. Woodfin was incorporated in 1971, and has roots back to the mid-19th century.

The history of Woodfin is closely tied to manufacturing. Much of the remaining early housing stock is characteristic of early 20th century mill villages. Many neighborhoods within the community are easily recognized for the mill village style and bear names such as "Martel Village" and "Company Bottom." The decline of American industry in the 1970's and 80's brought a decline in the fortunes of Woodfin as well. The loss of many manufacturing jobs led to a decline in population and property values. During the 1990's and into the present, however, Woodfin has grown rapidly from an influx of new residential growth in the region, including the development of luxury private mountain communities, most notably Reynolds Mountain, and from its proximity to neighboring Asheville.

The Town of Woodfin has a number of superb parks: Woodfin River Park, located at 1050 Riverside Drive; Roy Pope Memorial Park, located at 90 Elk Mountain Road; and South Woodfin Park, located at the intersection of Lookout Road and Midwood Drive. Woodfin River Park offers an ideal spot for a picnic by the meandering French Broad Rive which flows through the city.

Location: Central Mountains, immediately north of Asheville
City Offices: 90 Elk Mountain Road, Woodfin NC 28804; 828-253-4887
Website: www.woodfin-nc.gov
County: Buncombe County: County Offices, 205 College Street, Asheville NC 28801; 828-250-4000
Elevation & Population: 2,113 feet, 6,000+
County Chamber of Commerce: Buncombe County Chamber of Commerce 205 College Street, Asheville NC 28801; 828-250-4100

Newspaper: Asheville Citizen-Times,14 O'Henry Avenue, Asheville NC 28801; 828-252-5611, 800-800-4204.

High School: Asheville High School, 419 McDowell Street, Asheville NC 28803; 828-350-2500

Area Major Festivals: French Broad River Festival (May), Bele Chere (July), Craft Fair of the Southern Highland Craft Guild (October)

Area Natural Attractions: French Broad River, Blue Ridge Parkway

Area Cultural Attractions: Biltmore Estate, Dry Ridge Historical Museum, Thomas Wolfe Memorial, Zebulon B. Vance Birthplace

Recommended Restaurants: (For a complete list of all restaurants visit www.ashevilleguidebook.com)

    See Asheville restaurants

Recommended Places To Stay: (For a complete list of all accommodations visit www.ashevilleguidebook.com)

    See Asheville accommodations

Chapter Five
Western North Carolina Wineries

Many visitors to Western North Carolina are surprised at the number of vineyards and wineries that are found here. Out of the more than ninety wineries in the state of North Carolina as a whole, over twenty are found in the mountains. Commonly planted varieties include Cabernet Sauvignon, Cabernet Franc, Merlot, Syrah, Chambourcin, Chardonnay, Viognier, Sauvignon Blanc, Riesling, Seyval Blanc and Vidal Blanc.

The largest winery in the mountains is the world famous Biltmore Estate, in operation since May of 1985, when the Biltmore Estate Wine Company opened its 6.5 million dollar state of the art winery to the public. Small quantities of wine produced from experimental vineyards were first sold to Biltmore visitors in 1977. Current production averages 100,000 gallons of over a dozen varietal wines, utilizing grapes from the estate's 75 acres of vinifera grapes, other North Carolina vineyards and juice from California. For visitors to Western North Carolina who are interested in wines and wine making, a visit to this world-class winery is a must-see on any travel itinerary.

Western Mountains
Calaboose Cellars: 565 Aquone Road, Andrews NC 28901; 828-321-2006; www.calaboosecellars.com

Valley River Vineyards: 4689 Martins Creek Road, Murphy NC 28906; 828-321-5333; www.valleyrivervineyards.com

Central Mountains
Biltmore Estate Winery: Biltmore Estate, Asheville NC 28803; 800-543-2961; www.biltmore.com

Ritler Ridge Vineyards: 5 Piney Mountain Church Road, Candler NC 28715; 828-280-0690

Rockhouse Vineyards: 1525 Turner Road, Tryon NC 28782; 828-863-2784; www.rockhousevineyards.com

Northern Mountains

Banner Elk Winery and Blueberry Villa: 60 Deer Run Lane, Banner Elk NC 28604; 828-898-9090; www.bannerelkwinery.com

Chateau Laurinda: 690 Reeves Ridge Rd., Sparta, NC 28675; 800-650-3236; http://chateaulaurindavineyards.com

New River Winery: 163 Piney Creek Road, Lansing NC 28643; 336-384-1213; http://newriverwinery.com

Thistle Meadow Winery: 102 Thistle Meadow, Laurel Springs NC 28644; 800-233-1505; www.thistlemeadowwinery.com

Foothills

Brushy Mountain Winery: 125 West Main Street, Elkin NC 28621; 336-835-1313; www.brushymountainwine.com

Carolina Mist Winery: 126 Mulberry Street, Lenoir NC 28645; 828-754-4660; www.carolinamistwinery.com

Cerminaro Vineyard: 4399 Wilkesboro Blvd, Boomer, NC 28606; 828-754-9306; www.cerminarovineyard.com

Elkin Creek Vineyard: 318 Elkin Creek Mill Road, Elkin NC 28621; 336-526-5119; www.elkincreekvineyard.com

Green Creek Winery: 413 Gilbert Road, Columbus NC 28722; 828-863-2182; www.greencreekwinery.com

Green River Vineyard: 3043 John Watson Road, Green Creek NC 28139; 828-863-4705; http://www.greenriverbb.com

Lake James Cellars: 204 East Main Street, Glen Alpine NC 28628; 828-584-4551; www.lakejamescellars.com

McRitchier Winery & Ciderworks: 315 Thurmond PO Road, Thurmond NC 28683; 336-874-3003; www.mcritchiewine.com

Raffaldini Vineyards: 450 Groce Road, Ronda NC 28670: 336-835-9463; www.raffaldini.com

Raintree Cellars: 3813 Sain Avenue, Connelly Springs NC 28612; 828-397-5643; www.raintreecellars.com

Rendezvous Ridge: 172 Benny Parsons Road, Purlear NC 28665; 336-973-7375; www.rendezvousridge.com

South Creek Vineyards and Winery: 2240 South Creek Road, Nebo NC 28761; 828-652-5729; www.southcreekwinery.com

Waldensian Heritage Winery: 4940 Villar Lane NE, Valdese, NC 28690; 828-879-3202; www.visitvaldese.com

Index

B

backpacking, 110
Baird House, 454
Bakers Mountain Park, 405
Bakersville, 364
Bakersville Bed & Breakfast, 365
Balsam Mountain Inn, 450, 456
Banner Elk, 365
Banner Elk Inn B&B and Cottages, 366
Banner House Museum, 299
Barker House 1891, 42
Barley's Taproom & Pizzeria, 90
Barnes & Noble, 13
Bascom, 351
Bascom Lamar Lunsford Music Festival, 426
Basilica of Saint Lawrence, D.M, 177
Basilica of St. Lawrence, 73, 138
Bat Cave, 71
Battery Hill Neighborhood, 132
Battery Park Hotel, 176
B. Dalton Bookseller, 13
Beaufort House, 188
Beaufort House Inn, 35
Bed & Breakfast at Historic Bridgewater Hall, 430
Bed & Breakfast at Ponder Cove, 426
bed & breakfasts, 33
Beech Alpen Inn, 368
Beech Mountain, 367
Beech Mountain Resort, 120
Beer City USA, 130
Bele Chere, 56, 59
Bellagio, 82
Bella Luna, 432
Bella Vista Art Gallery, 78
Bender Gallery, 79
Bend of Ivy Lodge, 427
Ben Long Frescoes, 300
Bennett Classics Antique Auto Museum, 294
Bent Creek
 Bent Creek Experimental Forest, 272

Bent Creek Lodge, 35
bicycle clubs, 106
bicycle shops, 107
Big Band Dance Weekends, 55
Big Creek Expeditions, 125
Big Lynn Lodge, 419
biking, 105
Billy Graham Training Center at The Cove, 355
Biltmore Estate, 63, 69, 155, 164
Biltmore Estate Office Building, 200
Biltmore Forest, 130, 207
 Biltmore Forest School, 335
Biltmore House, 163
Biltmore Industries Historic District, 205
Biltmore Square Mall, 85
Biltmore Village, 69, 139, 198
 Biltmore Village Historic District, 69
Biltmore Village Cottage District, 201
Biltmore Village Dickens Festival, 58
Biltmore Village Historic District, 198
Biltmore Village Inn, 35
Biltmore Village Railway Depot Building, 200
Binion's Roadhouse, 51
Bird Rock Falls, 250
bird watching, 99, 281
Bistro 1896, 45
Black Bear Coffee Co, 53
black bears, 246, 281, 284
Blackberry Festival, 418
Black Bird Frame & Art, 78
Black Dome, 97
Black Forest Restaurant, 45
Black Mountain, 356, 359, 368
Black Mountain College Museum + Arts Center, 139
Black Mountains, 267
Black Mountain-Swannanoa Visitor Center, 369
Black Rose Public House, 51
blacksmithing, 343

Library and Archives Canada Cataloguing in Publication

Title: The world on either side / Diane Terrana.

Names: Terrana, Diane, 1951– author.

Identifiers: Canadiana (print) 20190069708 | Canadiana (ebook) 20190069716 |
ISBN 9781459822177 (softcover) | ISBN 9781459822184 (PDF) |
ISBN 9781459822191 (EPUB)

Classification: LCC PS8639.E772 W67 2019 | DDC jC813/.6—dc23

Library of Congress Control Number: 2019934059
Simultaneously published in Canada and the United States in 2019

Summary: In this work of fiction for teens, Valentine and her
mother travel to Thailand after the death of her boyfriend.

*Orca Book Publishers is committed to reducing the consumption of nonrenewable resources in the
making of our books. We make every effort to use materials that support a sustainable future.*

Orca Book Publishers gratefully acknowledges the support for its publishing
programs provided by the following agencies: the Government of Canada,
the Canada Council for the Arts and the Province of British Columbia
through the BC Arts Council and the Book Publishing Tax Credit.

Edited by Sara Cassidy
Cover design by Rachel Page
Cover image by Maria Nguyen
Author photo by Helen Tansey

Excerpt from "The Dead Woman" by Pablo Neruda,
from *The Captain's Verses*, copyright © 1972 by Pablo Neruda and Donald D. Walsh.
Reprinted by permission of New Directions Publishing Corp.
Back-cover excerpt from "Renascence," by Edna St. Vincent Millay. Public domain.

ORCA BOOK PUBLISHERS
orcabook.com

Printed and bound in Canada.

22 21 20 19 • 4 3 2 1

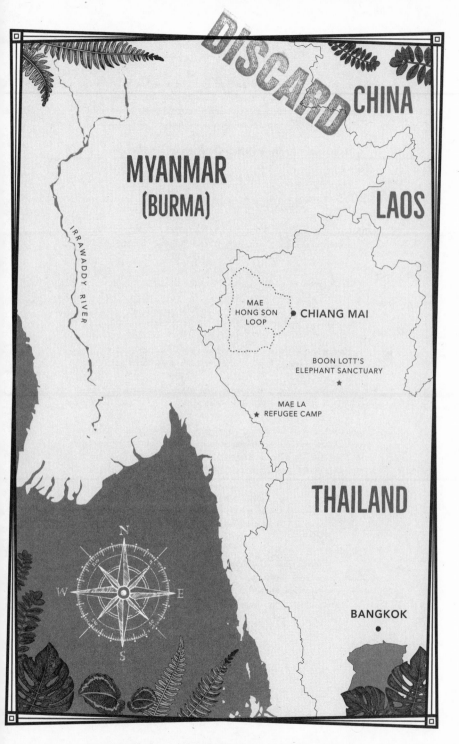

CHINA

MYANMAR
(BURMA)

LAOS

IRRAWADDY RIVER

MAE
HONG SON
LOOP

● CHIANG MAI

BOON LOTT'S
ELEPHANT SANCTUARY
★

MAE LA
★ REFUGEE CAMP

THAILAND

N
W   E
S

BANGKOK
●

THE WORLD ON EITHER SIDE

DIANE TERRANA

ORCA BOOK PUBLISHERS

Cuba	**peso** *PEH-soh*
Ecuador	**sucre** *SOO-kray*
Guatemala	**quetzal** *kayt-SAHL*
Honduras	**lempira** *lem-PEER-ah*
México	**peso** *PEH-soh*
Nicaragua	**córdoba** *KOHR-doh-bah*
Panamá	**balboa** *bahl-BOH-ah*
Paraguay	**guaraní** *gwahr-ah-NEE*
Perú	**sol** *sohl*
República Dominicana	**peso** *PEH-soh*
El Salvador	**colón** *koh-LOHN*
Spain (España)	**peseta** *peh-SEH-tah*
Uruguay	**peso** *PEH-soh*
Venezuela	**bolívar** *boh-LEE-bahr*

Note: 1. When writing numbers, Spanish uses a comma where English uses a decimal point, and vice versa. One thousand pasetas in Spanish is 1.000 pesetas. 2. Pesos from different countries have different values depending on the current rate of exchange in that country.

EXCHANGING MONEY

| Where can I find an ATM machine? | **¿Dónde hay un cajero automático?** *DOHN-day AH-ee oon kah-HEHR-oh ow-toh-MAH-tee-koh* |

Where is the currency exchange (bank)?	**¿Dónde hay un banco para cambiar moneda extranjera?** *DOHN-day AH-ee oon BAHN-koh pah-rah kahm-bee-AHR moh-NAY-dah ehs-trahn-HEHR-ah*
I wish to change ____.	**Quiero cambiar ____.** *kee-YEHR-oh kahm-bee-YAHR*
money	**dinero** *dee-NEHR-oh*
dollars (pounds)	**dólares (libras)** *DOH-lahr-ays (LEE-brahs)*
travelers checks	**cheques de viajero** *CHEH-kays day bee-ah-HAIR-oh*
Can I cash a personal check?	**¿Puedo cambiar un cheque personal?** *PWEH-doh kahm-bee-YAHR oon CHEH-kay pehr-sohn-AHL*
At what time do they open (close)?	**¿A qué hora abren (cierran)?** *ah kay ohra AH-brehn (SYEHR-ahn)*
Where is the cashier's window?	**¿Dónde está la caja, por favor?** *DOHN-day eh-STAH lah KAH-hah pohr fah-BOHR*

The current exchange rates are posted in those banks that exchange money and are also published daily in the newspapers. Since the rates fluctuate from day to day, it may be useful to convert the common amounts here for your quick reference.

PESETA	YOUR OWN CURRENCY	OTHER	YOUR OWN CURRENCY
10	_____	1	_____
100	_____	10	_____
500	_____	20	_____
1000	_____	50	_____
5000	_____	100	_____
10.000	_____		

What's the current exchange rate for dollars (pounds)?	**¿A cómo está el cambio hoy del dólar (de la libra)?** *ah KOH-moh ehs-TAH ehl KAHM-bee-oh oy del DOH-lahr (day lah LEE-brah)*
What commission do you charge?	**¿Cuál es el interés que ustedes cobran?** *kwahl ehs ehl een-tehr-AYS kay oos-TEHD-ays KOH-brahn*
I'd like to cash this check.	**Quisiera cobrar este cheque.** *kee-SYEHR-ah koh-BRAHR EHS-teh CHEH-kay*
Where do I sign?	**¿Dónde debo firmar?** *DOHN-day DEH-boh feer-MAHR*
I'd like the money ____.	**Quisiera el dinero ____.** *kee-SYEHR-ah ehl dee-NEHR -oh*
▦ in (large) bills	**en billetes (grandes)** *ehn bee-YEH-tehs (GRAHN-days)*

▓ in small change   **en suelto** *ehn SWEHL-toh*

Give me two twenty-peso bills.   **Déme dos billetes de a veinte pesos.** *DEH-may dohs bee-YEH-tays day ah BAYN-tay PAY-sohs*

▓ fifty-peso bills   **cincuenta** *seen-KWEHN-tah*

▓ one hundred-peseta bills   **cien** *see-YEHN*

Do you accept credit cards?   **¿Acepta usted tarjetas de crédito?** *a-SEHP-tah oo-STEHD tahr-HAY-tahs day KREHD-ee-toh*

BUSINESS AND BANKING TERMS

ATM	**el cajero automático** *ehl kah-HEHR-oh ow-toh-MAH-tee-koh*
account	**la cuenta** *lah KWEHN-tah*
amount	**la cantidad** *lah kahn-tee-DAHD*
bad check	**un cheque sin fondos** *oon CHEH-kay seen FOHN-dohs*
banker	**el banquero** *ehl bahn-KEH-roh*
bill	**el billete** *ehl bee-YEH-tay*
borrow (to)	**pedir prestado** *peh-DEER prehs-TAH-doh*
cashier	**el (la) cajero(a)** *ehl (lah) kah-HEHR-oh(ah)*
capital	**el capital** *ehl kah-pee-TAHL*
cashier's office	**la caja** *lah KAH-hah*
check	**el cheque** *ehl CHEH-kay*

```
           COLES BOOK STORES
          CALGARY INT'L AIRPORT
             (403)291-3540
          GST-FED #: 897152666

AVID     000303  0113 004  00002 81790
            03/06/25              11:14
         AVIDREADER       10%


LANG & DICTIONAR 0764112570  127
  1 @                         9.95
  10% DISC                   -1.00
TOTAL DISCOUNT        -1.00
  AVIDREADER: 43992726
    07.0% GST - FED           0.63
         TOTAL SALE           9.58
              CASH           10.00
            CHANGE            0.42

     SHOP ONLINE AT INDIGO.CA
```

checkbook	**el libreto de cheques** *ehl lee-BREH-toh day CHEH-kays*
endorse (to)	**endosar** *ehn-doh-SAHR*
income	**el ingreso** *ehl een-GREHS-oh*
interest rate	**el tipo de interés** *ehl TEE-poh day een-tehr-AYS*
investment	**la inversión** *lah een-behr-SYOHN*
to lend	**prestar** *prehs-TAHR*
loss	**la pérdida** *lah PEHR-dee-dah*
make change (to)	**dar (el) cambio** *dahr (ehl) KAHM-bee-oh*
money	**el dinero** *ehl dee-NEHR-oh*
mortgage	**la hipoteca** *lah eep-oh-TEH-kah*
open an account (to)	**abrir una cuenta** *ah-BREER oo-nah KWEHN-tah*
premium	**el premio** *ehl PRAY-mee-oh*
profit	**la ganancia** *la gah-NAHN-see-ah*
safe	**la caja fuerte** *lah KAH-ha FWEHR-tay*
savings account	**la cuenta de ahorros** *lah KWEHN-tah day ah-OHR-ohs*
savings book	**la libreta de ahorros** *la lee-BREH-tah day ah-OHR-ohs*
secretary	**el (la) secretario(a)** *ehl (lah) sehk-reh-TAHR-ee-oh(ah)*

| signature | **la firma** *lah FEER-mah* |
| window | **la ventanilla** *lah ben-tah-NEE-yah* |

TIPPING

In many areas, service charges are often included in the price of the service rendered. These usually come to about 10 to 15% and should be indicated on the bill.

Usually a customer will leave some small change in addition to any charge that has been included if the service has been satisfactory. At times, a set amount should be given.

Tips will vary from country to country and from time to time due to inflation and other factors. It is therefore advisable to ask some knowledgeable person (hotel manager, tour director, etc.) once you get to the country, or to check the current rate of exchange.

Travel Tips Touring on a budget? Then it pays to do your homework. Look for hotels or bed-and-breakfast establishments that include a morning meal in the price of a room. Often the breakfast is hearty enough to allow a light lunch. Carry nutrition bars from home in your tote bag for snacking when only expensive airport or restaurant food is available. Use public transportation whenever possible. Rail and air passes are sold for Europe and other regions but often can only be purchased in the U.S. before departure. If you must rent a car and have booked one from home, double-check local prices. Sometimes better deals can be arranged on the spot. When you first arrive in a country, check with a visitors' bureau. Agents there will explain discount cards or money-saving packets offered by local governments or merchants. The discount plans often cover transportation, food, lodging, museums, concerts, and other entertainment.

AT THE HOTEL

If you are unfamiliar with the city to which you are going, you'll probably find it best to make a hotel reservation in advance from home. It is possible that you would do better on prices for a room in some Mexican hotels, however, if you bargain for your room once you get there.

You can buy a *Guía de Hoteles* at a Spanish National Tourist Office, which gives official government listings of hotels in Spain by category. Ratings run from 5-star deluxe to plain 1-star. Every hotel has a plaque outside with an "H" (for hotel) on it and the star rating it has been allocated. "HS" on the plaque stands for Hostal; "HR" signifies Hotel-residencia, which means the hotel serves breakfast only. "P" stands for Pensión.

The following is a listing of the types of hotels you will encounter in Spain.

Hoteles	hotels
Hostales	small hotels or inns with no restaurant
Pensiones	guesthouses providing full board only
Paradores	first-class hotels run by the state located in places of historical interest and attractive surroundings. Many are converted castles, palaces, or monasteries
Refugios	retreats or rustic lodges, which are located in scenic mountain areas and are popular with hunters, hikers, and fishermen
Albergues Nacionales de Carretera	state-run roadside inns (period of stay is restricted). They also provide gas station and car repair services

| **Albergues juveniles** | youth hostels provide cheap accommodations for young people who are members of the international Youth Hostels Association; maximum length of stay at any one hostel is 3 nights |

Note: Paradores are extremely popular with tourists. There are more than 80 located throughout Spain, but because they have relatively few rooms and prices are modest (for value received), they are often booked far in advance. Arrangements to stay at a parador can be made by writing directly or by contacting their U.S. representative, Marketing Ahead, 515 Madison Avenue, New York, NY 10022. Brochures on paradores, albergues, and refugios are available free from the Spanish National Tourist Office.

Hotels include a service charge in the bill. It is customary, though, to tip the porter carrying your luggage, maids, room service, and the doorman who summons your cab. A helpful concierge might receive a tip for doing special favors, such as securing theater tickets or making phone calls and reservations.

GETTING TO YOUR HOTEL

I'd like to go to the ____ Hotel.	**Quisiera ir al Hotel ____.** *kee-SYEH-rah eer ahl oh-TEL*
Is it near (far)?	**¿Está cerca (lejos) de aquí?** *ehs-TAH SEHR-kah (LAY-hohs) day ah-KEE*
Where can I get a taxi?	**¿Dónde puedo tomar un taxi?** *DOHN-day PWEH-doh toh-MAHR oon TAHK-see*
What buses go into town?	**¿Qué autobuses van al centro?** *kay ow-toh-BOOS-ehs bahn ahl SEHN-troh*

| Where is the bus stop? | **¿Dónde está la parada?** *DOHN-day ehs-TAH lah pah-RAH-dah* |
| How much is the fare? | **¿Cuánto cuesta el billete?** *KWAHN-toh KWEHS-tah ehl bee-YEH-tay* |

CHECKING IN

Most first-class or deluxe hotels will have personnel who speak English. If you are checking in to a smaller hotel, you might find these phrases useful in getting what you want. In Spain, all visitors are required to fill out a registration form *(una ficha de identidad)* requiring certain information.

Apellido _____
(Surname)

Nombre _____
(First name)

Fecha de Nacimiento _____
(Date of birth)

Nacionalidad _____
(Nationality)

Lugar de Nacimiento _____
(Place of birth)

Dirección _____
(Address)

No. de Pasaporte _____
(Passport number)

Exp. en _____
(Issued at)

Firma del Viajero _____
(Signature)

I'd like a single (double) room for tonight.	**Quisiera una habitación con una sola cama (con dos camas) para esta noche.** *kee-SYEHR-ah OO-nah ah-bee-tah-SYOHN kohn OO-nah SOH-lah KAH-mah (kohn dohs KAH-mahs) pah-rah EHS-tah NOH-chay*
How much is the room ____?	**¿Cuánto cuesta el cuarto ____?** *KWAHN-toh KWEHS-tah ehl KWAHR-toh*

- with a shower **con ducha** *kohn DOO-chah*
- with a private bath **con baño privado** *kohn BAHN-yoh pree-BAH-doh*
- with a balcony **con balcón** *kohn bahl-KOHN*
- facing the ocean **con vista al mar** *kohn bees-tah ahl mahr*
- facing the street **que dé a la calle** *kay day ah lah KAH-yeh*

facing the court-yard	**que dé al patio** *kay day ahl PAH-tee-oh*
in the back	**al fondo** *ahl FOHN-doh*
Does it have ___?	**¿Tiene ___?** *tee-YEH-neh*
air-conditioning	**aire acondicionado** *AH-ee-ray ah-kohn-dee-syohn-AH-doh*
television	**televisión** *teh-lay-bee-SYOHN*
a hair dryer	**un secador de pelo** *oon seh-kah-DOHR day PEH-loh*
a mini-bar	**un minibar** *oon mee-nee-BAHR*
Is there ___ at the hotel?	**¿Hay ___ en el hotel?** *AH-ee ehn ehl oh-TEL*
a fitness center	**un gimnasio** *oon heem-NAH-see-yoh*
a restaurant	**un restaurante** *oon rest-ow-RAHN-teh*
a swimming pool	**una piscina** *oo-nah pee-SEE-nah*
a gift shop	**una tienda de regalos** *oo-nah TYEHN-dah day reh-GAH-lohs*
valet parking	**personal de estacionamiento** *pehr-sohn-AHL day es-tah-syohn-ah-MYEHN-toh*
a laundry	**una lavandería** *oo-nah lah-bahn-dehr-EE-ah*
dry cleaning service	**servicio de limpiado en seco** *sehr-BEE-syoh day leem-PYAH-doh en SEH-koh*
I (don't) have a reservation.	**(No) tengo reserva.** *(noh) ten-goh reh-SEHR-bah*
Could you call another hotel to see if they have something?	**¿Podría llamar a otro hotel para ver si tienen algo?** *poh-DREE-ah yah-MAHR ah OH-troh O-TEL pah-rah behr see tee-YEN-ehn AHL-goh*

May I see the room?	**¿Podría ver la habitación?** *poh-DREE-ah behr lah ah-bee-tah-SYOHN*
I (don't) like it.	**(No) me gusta.** *(noh) may GOOS-tah*
Do you have something ____?	**¿Hay algo ____?** *AH-ee ahl-goh*
▦ better	**mejor** *may-HOHR*
▦ larger	**más grande** *mahs GRAHN-day*
▦ smaller	**más pequeño** *mahs peh-KAYN-yo*
▦ cheaper	**más barato** *mahs bah-RAH-toh*
▦ quieter	**donde no se oigan ruidos** *DOHN-day noh say OY-gahn RWEE-dohs*
What floor is it on?	**¿En qué piso está?** *ehn kay PEE-soh ehs-TAH*
Is there an elevator?	**¿Hay ascensor?** *AH-ee ah-sen-SOHR*
Is everything included?	**¿Está todo incluído?** *eh-STAH toh-doh een-kloo-EE-doh*
How much is the room with ____?	**¿Cuánto cobra usted por la habitación ____?** *KWAHN-toh KOH-brah oos-TEHD pohr lah ah-bee-tah-SYOHN*
▦ the American plan (2 meals a day)	**con media pensión** *kohn MEH-dee-yah pen-SYOHN*
▦ bed and breakfast	**con desayuno** *kohn dehs-ah-YOO-noh*
▦ no meals	**sin la comida** *seen lah koh-MEE-dah*
The room is very nice. I'll take it.	**La habitación es muy bonita. Me quedo con ella.** *lah ah-bee-tah-SYOHN ehs mwee boh-NEE-tah may KAY-doh kohn EH-ya*

We'll be staying ____.	**Nos quedamos ____.** *nohs kay-DAH-mohs*
▓ one night	**una noche** *oo-nah NOH-chay*
▓ a few nights	**unas noches** *oo-nahs NOH-chays*
▓ one week	**una semana** *oo-nah seh-MAH-nah*
How much do you charge for children?	**¿Cuanto cobra por los niños?** *kwahn-toh KOH-brah pohr lohs NEEN-yohs*
Could you put another bed in the room?	**¿Podría poner otra cama en la habitación?** *poh-DREE-ah poh-NEHR oh-trah KAH-mah ehn lah ah-bee-tah-SYOHN*
Is there a charge? How much?	**¿Hay que pagar más? ¿Cuánto?** *AH-ee kay pah-GAHR mahs? KWAHN-toh*
Do you have a crib for the baby?	**¿Tiene una cuna para el nene (la nena)?** *TYEHN-eh oo-nah COO-nah pah-rah el NEH-neh (lah NEH-nah)*
Do you know someone who baby-sits? (a sitter)	**¿Conoce a alguien que pueda cuidar a los niños? (un síter)** *coh-NOH-say AHL-ghee-ehn kay PWEH-day kwee-DAHR ah lohs NEE-nyohs (oon SEE-tehr)*
Does the room have T.V.?	**¿Hay televisión en la habitación?** *AH-ee tel-eh-bee-SYOHN en lah ah-bee-tah-SYOHN*
Do you receive satellite programs (cable, CNN, programs in English)?	**¿Recibe programas de satélite (cable, CNN, en inglés)?** *reh-SEE-beh pro-GRAH-mahs deh sah-TEL-ee-tay (KAH-blay seh ehn-eh ehn-eh ehn een-GLEHS)*

Are there porno programs?	**¿Hay espectáculos pornográficos?** *AH-ee es-pec-TAH-koo-lohs por-no-GRAHF-ee-kohs*
On what channels? At what time?	**¿En qué canales? ¿A qué hora?** *En kay kah-NAH-lehs Ah kay OR-ah*
Can they be blocked?	**¿Hay bloqueo de canales?** *AH-ee bloh-KAY-oh deh kah-NAH-lehs*
Is there a sports (cartoon, news, movie) channel?	**¿Hay un canal de deportes (dibujos animados, noticias, películas)?** *AH-ee oon kah-NAHL deh deh-POR-tehs (dee-BOO-hohs ah-nee-MAH-dos no-TEE-see-yahs pel-EE-koo-lahs)*
Can we rent (video games)?	**¿Podemos alquilar películas (juegos de video)?** *po-DAY-mohs ahl-kee-LAHR pel-EE-koo-lahs (WAY-gohs deh BEE-deh-oh)*
Is there automatic checkout?	**¿Hay horario de salida automático?** *AH-ee or-AH-ree-oh day sah-LEE-dah ow-toh-MAH-tee-coh*

OTHER ACCOMMODATIONS

I'm looking for ____.	**Busco ____.** *BOOS-koh*
a boardinghouse	**una pensión (una casa de huéspedes)** *oo-nah pen-SYOHN (oo-nah kah-sah day WES-pehd-ays)*
a private house	**una casa particular** *oo-na kah-sah pahr-teek-oo-LAHR*
I want to rent an apartment.	**Quiero alquilar un apartamento.** *kee-YEHR-oh ahl-kee-LAHR oon ah-pahr-tah-MEHN-toh*

CHECKING IN • 41

I need a living room, bedroom, and kitchen	**Necesito una sala, un dormitorio, y una cocina.** *neh-seh-SEE-toh oon-nah SAH-lah oon dohr-mee-TOHR-ee-oh ee oo-nah koh-SEE-nah*
Do you have a furnished room?	**¿Tiene un cuarto amueblado?** *tee-YEN-ay oon KWAHR-toh ah-mway-BLAH-doh*
How much is the rent?	**¿Cuánto es el alquiler?** *KWAHN-toh ehs ehl ahl-kee-LEHR*
I'll be staying here for ____.	**Me quedaré aquí ____.** *may kay-dahr-AY ah-KEY*
▧ two weeks	**dos semanas** *dohs seh-MAH-nahs*
▧ one month	**un mes** *oon mehs*
▧ the whole summer	**todo el verano** *toh-doh ehl behr-AH-noh*
I want a place that's ____.	**Quiero un sitio ____.** *kee-yehr-oh oon SEE-tee-yo*
▧ centrally located	**en el centro de la ciudad** *ehn ehl SEHN-troh day lah syoo-DAHD*
▧ near public transportation	**cerca del transporte público** *SEHR-kah del trahns-POHR-tay POOB-lee-koh*
▧ in a quiet, safe neighborhood	**en un barrio tranquilo y seguro** *en oon BAH-ree-oh trahn-KEE-loh ee seh-GOOR-oh*
Is there a youth hostel around here?	**¿Hay un albergue juvenil por aquí?** *AH-ee oon ahl-BEHR-gay hoo-ben-EEL pohr ah-KEE*

TRAVELERS WITH SPECIAL NEEDS

The following organizations provide advice and referrals to travelers with disabilities:

Moss Rehab Hospital—(215) 456-9600

American Foundation for the Blind—(800) 232-5463

Society for the Advancement of Travel for the Handicapped (SATH)—(212) 447-7284

Mobility International—(541) 343-1284

Information Center for Individuals with Disabilities—(800) 462-5015

Do you have facilities for the disabled?	**¿Tienen facilidades para los incapacitados?** *tee-EH-nen fah-see-lee-DAH-dehs PAH-rah lohs een-kah-pah-see-TAH-dohs*
Is there a reduced rate?	**¿Hay un precio rebajado?** *AH-ee oon PRAY-see-oh ray-bah-HAH-doh*
Do you have a toilet equipped for the handicapped?	**¿Tienen baños equipados para gente incapacitada?** *tee-YEN-en BAHN-yohs eh-kee-PAH-dos par-rah HEN-teh een-kah-pah-see-TAH-dah*
Can you provide a wheelchair?	**¿Podría facilitar una silla de ruedas?** *po-DREE-ah fah-see-lee-TAHR oo-nah SEE-yah day RWAY-dahs*
Is there room in the elevator for a wheelchair?	**¿Tiene espacio el ascensor para una silla de ruedas?** *tee-YEN-eh es-PAH-see-oh el ah-sen-SOHR pah-rah oo-nah SEE-yah day RWAY-dahs*
I cannot climb stairs/walk by myself.	**No puedo subir las escaleras/ caminar por mí mismo.** *noh PWAY-doh soo-BEER lahs es-cah-LEHR-ahs/ kah-mee-NAHR por mee MEES-moh*

Is there an ambulance (ambulette, taxi, private car) service available?	**¿Hay un servicio de ambulancia (transporte médico especializado, taxi, coche privado) disponible?** *AH-ee oon sehr-BEE-see-yoh day ahm-boo-LAHN-syah (trahns-POHR-teh MEH-dee-koh ehs-peh-see-ah-lee-SAH-doh TAHK-see COH-chay pree-BAH-doh) dees-pohn-EE-blay*
Is there a doctor in the hotel?	**¿Hay un médico en el hotel?** *AH-ee oon MED-ee-ko en ehl oh-TEL*
How can we get a doctor in an emergency?	**¿Cómo podemos conseguir un médico en caso de emergencia?** *KOH-moh poh-day-mohs kohn-say-GEER oon MED-ee-koh en KAH-soh day ehm-ehr-HEN-syah.*
Are there doctors (nurses) who will come to the hotel?	**¿Hay médicos (enfermeras) que vengan al hotel?** *AH-ee MED-ee-kohs (en-fehr-MEHR-ahs) kay BEHN-gahn ahl oh-TEL*
Do you have oxygen available?	**¿Hay oxígeno disponible?** *AH-ee ohks-EE-hen-oh dees-poh-NEE-blay*
Is there a kneeling bus?	**¿Hay un autobús con sistema de arrodillaje?** *AH-ee oon ow-toh-BOOS cohn sees-TAY-may deh ah-roh-dee-YAH-hay*
Do you allow seeing-eye dogs?	**¿Se permiten perros de guía?** *say pehr-MEE-ten PEH-rohs day GHEE-ah*
I have asthma/heart problems.	**Padezco de asma/de problemas del corazón.** *pah-DES-coh deh AHS-mah/dey pro-BLAY-mahs dehl cohr-ah-SOHN*
I'm diabetic.	**Soy diabético(a).** *soy dee-ah-BET-ee-koh(ah)*

I'm (not) allergic to pencillin (cortisone).	**(No) soy alérgico a la penicilina (cortisona).** *(noh) soy ah-LEHR-hee-koh ah lah pen-ee-see-LEE-nah (cohr-tee-SOHN-ah)*
My father (mother) is elderly (blind, deaf).	**Mi padre (madre) es un anciano (una anciana) (ciego(a), sordo(a)).** *mee PAH-dray (MAH-dray) es oon ahn-SYAH-no (ahn-SYAH-nah) (see-AY-goh(ah) SOHR-doh(ah))*
We need a crutch (crutches, a walker, a cane).	**Necesitamos una muleta (muletas, un caminante, un bastón).** *neh-ses-ee-TAH-mohs oo-nah moo-LET-ah (moo-LET-ahs, oon cah-mee-NAHN-tay, oon bah-STOHN)*
Are there access ramps for wheelchairs?	**¿Hay rampas de acceso para sillas de ruedas?** *AH-ee RAHM-pahs day ahk-SES-oh pah-rah SEE-yahs day RWAY-das*
In case of emergency, are there agencies (overnight drugstores, emergency rooms) we can contact?	**En caso de emergencia, ¿hay agencias (farmacias de guardia, salas de emergencia) que podemos notificar?** *en KAH-soh day em-her-HEN-syah, AH-ee ah-HEN-syahs (far-MAH-syahs day GWAR-dee-yah, SAH-lahs day em-her-HEN-syah) kay poh-DAY-mohs noh-tee-fee-KAHR*
I cannot eat sugar (salt, dairy products, meat, pork, shell-fish, peanuts).	**No puedo comer azúcar (sal, productos lácteos, carne, puerco (or cerdo), mariscos, cacahuetes).** *no PWEH-doh koh-MEHR ah-SOO-kar (SAHL pro-DOOK-tohs LAHK-tay-ohs KAHR-nay PWER-coh (SEHR-doh) mah-REES-kohs kah-kah-WAH-tays)*

I want it without caffeine (alcohol, meat).	**Lo quiero descafeinado (sin alcohol, sin carne).** *lo kee-YEHR-oh des-cah-fey-NAH-doh (seen ahl-koh-OHL seen KAHR-nay)*
I'm a vegetarian.	**Soy vegetariano(a).** *soy beh-heh-tahr-ee-AH-noh(ah)*
Do you have food low in cholesterol (fat, calories)?	**¿Tiene comida baja en colesterol (grasa, calorías)?** *TYEH-nay koh-MEE-dah BAH-hah en koh-les-tair-OHL (GRAH-sah kah-lohr-EE-ahs)*
Do you have saccharine (an artificial sweetener)?	**¿Tiene sacarina (un endulzador artificial)?** *TYEHN-eh sah-kah-REE-nah (oon en-dool-sah-DOHR ahr-tee-fees-YAHL)*

ORDERING BREAKFAST

Larger hotels will offer breakfast. The Spanish breakfast is a simple one—**café con leche** (hot coffee mixed half and half with steaming milk), with a sweet roll or **churro** (fried pastry). Mexican breakfasts tend to be a little more elaborate, usually **café con leche** and perhaps a tortilla topped with fried eggs, tomatoes and spices or toasted **bollitos** (small boat-shaped yeast rolls). At hotels that cater to American and British tourists, you will also be able to order an English breakfast (juice, eggs, bacon, and toast). Larger hotels will have a dining room where you can eat breakfast, but the usual procedure is to have breakfast sent up to your room or to go out to a café or chocolatería (the hot chocolate in Spain is marvelous) or, in Mexico, to a street vendor who fries up your breakfast at her curbside stand.

I'll eat breakfast downstairs.	**Voy a desayunar abajo.** *boy ah dehs-ah-yoo-NAHR ah-BAH-ho*

We'll have breakfast in the room.	**Queremos desayunar en nuestra habitación.** *keh-RAY-mohs dehs-ah-yoo-NAHR ehn NWEHS-trah ah-bee-tah-SYOHN*
We'd like ____.	**Quisiéramos ____.** *kee-SYEHR-ah-mohs*
Please send up ____.	**Haga el favor de mandarnos.** *AH-gah ehl fah-BOHR day mahn-DAHR-nohs*
▧ one (two) coffee(s)	**una taza (dos tazas) de café** *oo-nah TAH-sah (dohs TAH-sahs) day kah-FAY*
▧ butter	**mantequilla** *mahn-teh-KEE-yah*
▧ cold cuts	**fiambres** *fee-AHM-brehs*
▧ cereal	**cereal** *sehr-eh-AHL*
▧ grapefruit	**toronja (pomelo)** *tohr-OHN-ha (poh-MEH-loh)*
▧ white bread	**pan blanco** *pahn BLAHN-koh*
▧ black bread	**pan moreno (pan negro)** *pahn morh-EH-noh (pan NEH-groh)*
▧ rye bread	**pan de centeno** *pahn day sehn-TEH-noh*
▧ margarine	**margarina** *mahr-gahr-EE-nah*
▧ tea	**una taza de té** *oo-nah TAH-sah day teh*
▧ hot chocolate	**una taza de chocolate** *oo-nah TAH-sah day cho-koh-LAH-tay*
▧ a sweet roll	**un pan dulce** *oon pahn DOOL-say*
▧ fruit (juice)	**un jugo (de fruta)** *oon HOO-goh day FROO-tah*
▧ bacon and eggs	**huevos con tocino** *WEH-bohs kohn toh-SEE-noh*

scrambled (fried, boiled) eggs	**huevos revueltos (fritos, pasados por agua)** *WEH-bohs ray-BWEHL-tohs (FREE-tohs pah-SAH-dohs pohr AH-gwah)*
toast	**pan tostado** *pahn tohs-TAH-doh*
jam (marmalade)	**mermelada** *mehr-may-LAH-dah*

Please don't make it too spicy. **No lo haga muy picante.** *noh loh AH-gah mwee pee-KAHN-tay*

NOTE: See the food section (pages 122–161) for more phrases dealing with ordering meals.

HOTEL SERVICES

Where is ____? **¿Dónde esta ____?** *dohn-day ehs-TAH*

the dining room	**el comedor** *ehl koh-meh-DOHR*
the bathroom	**el baño** *ehl BAHN-yo*
the elevator (lift)	**el ascensor** *ehl ah-sen-SOHR*
the phone	**el teléfono** *ehl tel-EF-oh-no*

What is my room number? **¿Cuál es el número de mi cuarto?** *kwahl ehs ehl NOO-mehr-oh day mee KWAR-toh*

May I please have my key? **Mi llave, por favor.** *mee YAH-bay pohr fah-BOHR*

I've lost my key. **He perdido mi llave.** *eh pehr-DEE-doh mee YAH-bay*

I need ____. **Necesito ____.** *neh-seh-SEE-toh*

| a bellhop | **un botones** *oon boh-TOH-nays* |
| a chambermaid | **una camarera** *oo-nah kah-mah-REHR-ah* |

Please send ____ to my room.	**Haga el favor de mandar ____ a mi habitación.** *AH-gah ehl fah-BOHR day mahn-DAHR ah mee ah-bee-tah-SYOHN*
a towel	**una toalla** *oo-nah toh-AH-yah*
a bar of soap	**una pastilla de jabón** *oo-nah pahs-TEE-yah day hah-BOHN*
some hangers	**unas perchas** *oo-nahs PEHR-chahs*
a pillow	**una almohada** *oo-nah ahl-moh-AH-dah*
a blanket	**una manta** *oo-nah MAHN-tah*
some ice cubes	**cubitos de hielo** *koo-BEE-tohs day YEH-loh*
some ice water	**agua helada** *ah-guah eh-LAH-dah*
a bottle of mineral water	**una botella de agua mineral** *oo-nah boh-TEH yah day AH-guah mee-nehr-AHL*
an ashtray	**un cenicero** *oon sen-ee-SEHR-oh*
toilet paper	**papel higiénico** *pah-PEHL ee-HYEHN-ee-koh*
an electric adapter	**un adaptador eléctrico** *oon ah-dahp-tah-DOHR eh-LEK-tree-koh*

AT THE DOOR

Who is it?	**¿Quién es?** *kee-EHN ehs*
Just a minute.	**Un momento.** *oon moh-MEN-toh*
Come in.	**Adelante.** *ah-del-AHN-tay*
Put it on the table.	**Póngalo en la mesa.** *POHN-gah-loh ehn lah MAY-sah*
Please wake me tomorrow at ____.	**¿Puede despertarme mañana a ____?** *PWEH-day dehs-pehr-TAHR-may mahn-YAH-nah ah*

COMPLAINTS

There is no ____.	**No hay ____.** *noh AH-ee*
▓ running water	**agua corriente** *AH-gwah kohr-YEN-tay*
▓ hot water	**agua caliente** *AH-gwah kahl-YEN-tay*
▓ electricity	**electricidad** *eh-lek-tree-see-DAHD*
The ____ doesn't work.	**No funciona ____.** *noh foon-SYOHN-ah*
▓ air-conditioning	**el aire acondicionado** *ehl AH-ee-ray ah-kohn-dees-yohn-AH-doh*
▓ fan	**el ventilador** *ehl ben-tee-lah-DOHR*
▓ faucet	**el grifo** *ehl GREE-foh*
▓ lamp	**la lámpara** *lah LAHM-pah-rah*
▓ light	**la luz** *lah loos*
▓ radio	**la radio** *lah RAH-dee-oh*
▓ electric socket	**el enchufe** *ehl ehn-CHOO-fay*
▓ light switch	**el interruptor** *ehl een-tehr-oop-TOHR*
▓ television	**el televisor** *ehl tel-eh-bee-SOHR*
Can you fix it ____?	**¿Puede arreglarlo ____?** *PWEH-day ah-ray-GLAHR-loh*
▓ now	**ahora** *ah-OH-rah*
▓ as soon as possible	**lo más pronto posible** *loh mahs PROHN-toh poh-SEE-blay*

AT THE DESK

Are there any ____ for me?	**¿Hay ____ para mí?** *AH-ee pah-rah MEE*
▓ letters	**cartas** *KAHR-tahs*
▓ messages	**recados** *ray-KAH-dohs*
▓ packages	**paquetes** *pah-KEH-tays*

▦ postcards	**postales** *pohs-TAH-lays*
Did anyone call for me?	**¿Preguntó alguien por mí?** *preh-goon-TOH AHL-ghee-ehn pohr MEE*
I'd like to leave this in your safe.	**Quisiera dejar esto en su caja fuerte.** *kee-SYEHR-ah day-HAHR EHS-toh ehn soo KAH-ha FWEHR-tay*
Will you make this call for me?	**¿Podría usted hacerme esta llamada?** *poh-DREE-ah oos-TEHD ah-SEHR-may EHS-tah yah-MAH-dah*

CHECKING OUT

I'd like the bill, please.	**Quisiera la cuenta, por favor.** *kee-SYEHR-ah lah KWEHN-tah pohr fah-BOHR*
I'll be checking out today (tomorrow).	**Pienso marcharme hoy (mañana).** *PYEHN-soh mahr-CHAR-may oy (mahn-YA-nah)*
Please send someone up for our baggage.	**Haga el favor de mandar a alguien para recoger nuestro equipaje.** *AH-gah ehl fah-BOHR day mahn-DAHR ah AHL-ghy-ehn pah-rah ray-koh-HEHR NWEHS-troh AY-kee-PAH-hay*

GETTING AROUND TOWN

In most cities, you will find that getting around town to sightsee is an easy affair. You'll get more of the flavor of a city if you use public transportation, but oftentimes a taxi will be the quicker way to go somewhere, and usually they are not too expensive. For information on train or plane travel, see pages 76–81.

THE BUS

Public transportation in most large cities is cheap, efficient, and frequent. In Spain, bus stops are clearly marked by number, and each number's stops are clearly delineated. Be sure to signal when you want the bus to stop, as the driver doesn't stop automatically at every stop on the route. Free bus maps often are available at the hotels (if not, ask the concierge about getting one). Most bus routes run from 6 A.M. to midnight, though some have 24-hour service. There are no free transfers, but the fare is cheap—about 40 pesetas.

In Mexico City, an unusually large urban area, there are bus routes that crisscross the entire town. Bus routes are at times confusing, so it is best to obtain specific instructions from your hotel concierge. Buses are more expensive than the subway (underground), but since both are so cheap in comparison to other cities' systems, the difference is negligible.

Where is the bus stop (terminal)?	**¿Dónde esta la parada (la terminal) de autobús?** *DOHN-day ehs-TAH lah pah-RAH-dah (lah tehr-mee-NAHL) day AH-oo-toh-BOOS*
Which bus do I take to get to ____?	**¿Qué autobús hay que tomar para ir a ____?** *kay AH-oo-toh-BOOS AH-ee kay toh-MAHR PAH-rah eer ah*

Do I need exact change?	**¿Necesito tener cambio exacto?** *neh-seh-SEE-toh ten-EHR KAHM-bee-oh ehk-SAHK-toh*
In which direction do I have to go?	**¿Qué rumbo tengo que tomar?** *kay ROOM-boh TEN-goh kay toh-MAHR*
How often do the buses run?	**¿Con qué frecuencia salen los autobuses?** *kohn kay freh-KWEHN-see-ah SAH-lehn lohs AH-oo-toh-BOOS-ehs*
Do you go to ____?	**¿Va usted a ____?** *bah oos-TEHD ah*
Is it far from here?	**¿Está lejos de aquí?** *eh-STAH LAY-hos day ah-KEE*
How many stops are there?	**¿Cuántas paradas hay?** *KWAHN-tahs pah-RAH-dahs AH-ee*
Do I have to change?	**¿Tengo que cambiar?** *TEN-goh kay kahm-bee-AHR*
How much is the fare?	**¿Cuánto es el billete?** *KWAHN-toh ehs ehl bee-YEH-tay*
Where do I have to get off?	**¿Dónde tengo que bajarme?** *DOHN-day ten-goh kay bah-HAHR-may*
Please tell me where to get off.	**Dígame, por favor, dónde debo bajarme.** *DEE-gah-may pohr fa-BOHR DOHN-day deh-boh bah-HAHR-may*

THE SUBWAY (UNDERGROUND)

The subways (metros) in Madrid and Barcelona are clean, cheap, safe, and comfortable. And graffiti-free. There are nine lines in Madrid with interchange points.

The subway (metro) in Mexico City is a very busy one and often too crowded for most tourists, although the system itself is clean and efficient. Best to avoid it during peak hours. There are also subways in several Latin American cities; such as the Santiago and Buenos Aires Metro, which are modern and well run.

Is there a subway (underground) in this city?	**¿Hay un metro en esta ciudad?** *AH-ee oon MEHT-roh ehn EHS-tah syoo-DAHD*
Where is the closest subway (underground) station?	**¿Dónde está la estación más cercana?** *DOHN-day eh-STAH lah ehs-tah-SYOHN mahs sehr-KAH-nah*
How much is the fare?	**¿Cuánto es la tarifa?** *KWAHN-toh ehs lah tah-REE-fah*
Where can I buy a token (a ticket)?	**¿Dónde puedo comprar una ficha (un billete)?** *DOHN-day PWEH-doh kohm-PRAHR oo-nah FEE-chah (oon bee-YEH-teh)*
Which is the line that goes to _____?	**¿Cuál es la línea que va a _____?** *kwahl ehs lah LEEN-eh-ah kay bah ah*
Does this train go to _____?	**¿Va este tren a _____?** *bah ehs-teh trehn ah*
Do you have a map showing the stops?	**¿Tiene un mapa que indique las paradas?** *TYEH-nay oon MAH-pah kay een-DEE-kay lahs pahr-AH-dahs*
How many more stops?	**¿Cuántas paradas más?** *KWAHN-tahs pah-RAH-dahs mahs?*
What's the next station?	**¿Cuál es la próxima estación?** *kwahl ehs lah PROHK-see-mah ehs-tah-SYOHN*

Where should I get off?	**¿Dónde debo bajarme?** *DOHN-day deh-boh bah-HAHR-may*
Do I have to change?	**¿Tengo que hacer trasbordo?** *ten-goh kay ah-SEHR trahs-BOHRD-oh*
Please tell me when we get there.	**Haga el favor de avisarme cuando lleguemos.** *AH-gah ehl fah-BOHR day ah-bee-SAHR-may kwahn-doh yeh-GAY-mohs*

TAXIS

Taxis are plentiful, metered, and, generally speaking, cheap. There are legitimate surcharges for baggage, night fares, holiday fares, and extras on certain other occasions. These are legitimate "extras," as the printed surcharge chart in each cab verifies. It is customary on entering a taxi to greet the driver with "Good morning," "Good day," or "Good evening." It is a politeness that is appreciated—and expected.

Is there a taxi stand near here?	**¿Hay una parada de taxis por aquí?** *AH-ee oo-nah pah-RAH-dah day TAHK-sees pohr ah-KEE*
Please get me a taxi.	**¿Puede usted conseguirme un taxi, por favor?** *PWEH-day oos-TEHD kohn-say-GHEER-may oon TAHK-see pohr fah-BOHR*
Where can I get a taxi?	**¿Dónde puedo tomar un taxi?** *DOHN-day PWEH-doh toh-MAHR oon TAHK-see*
Taxi! Are you free (available)?	**¡Taxi! ¿Está libre?** *TAHK-see ehs-TAH LEE-bray*
Take me (I want to go) ____.	**Lléveme (Quiero ir) ____.** *YEHV-eh-may (kee-EHR-oh eer)*

■ to the airport   **al aeropuerto** *ahl ah-ehr-oh-PWEHR-toh*

■ to this address   **a esta dirección** *ah ehs-tah dee-rehk-SYOHN*

■ to the hotel   **al hotel** *ahl o-TEL*

■ to the station   **a la estación** *ah lah ehs-tah-SYOHN*

■ to ____ street   **a la calle ____** *ah lah KAH-yeh*

Do you know where it is?   **¿Sabe dónde está?** *sah-bay DOHN-day ehs-TAH*

How much is it to ____?   **¿Cuánto cuesta hasta ____?** *KWAHN-toh KWEHS-tah AHS-tah*

Faster! I'm in a hurry.   **¡Más rápido, tengo prisa!** *mahs RAH-pee-doh ten-goh PREE-sah*

Please drive slower.   **Por favor, conduzca más despacio.** *pohr fah-BOHR kohn-DOOS-kah mahs dehs-PAH-see-oh*

Stop here ____.	**Pare aquí ____.** *PAH-ray ah-KEE*
▓ at the corner	**en la esquina** *ehn lah ehs-KEE-nah*
▓ at the next block	**en la otra calle** *ehn lah OH-trah KAH-yeh*

Wait for me. I'll be right back.	**Espéreme. Vuelvo pronto.** *ehs-PEHR-eh-may BWEHL-boh PROHN-toh*

I think you are going the wrong way.	**Creo que me está llevando por una dirección equivocada.** *KRAY-oh kay may ehs-TAH yeh-BAHN-doh pohr oo-nah dee-rek-SYOHN eh-kee-boh-KAH-dah*

How much do I owe you?	**¿Cuánto le debo?** *KWAHN-toh lay DEHB-oh*

This is for you.	**Esto es para usted.** *ehs-toh ehs PAH-rah oos-TEHD*

SIGHTSEEING AND TOURS

You'll want to visit a variety of sights—cathedrals, plazas, shopping areas, parks, and museums—and we give you here some phrases to help you locate the English-language tours, when available.

Where is the Tourist Information Office?	**¿Dónde está la oficina de turismo?** *DOHN-day ehs-TAH lah of-fee-SEEN-ah day toor-EES-moh*

I need a(n) (English-speaking) guide.	**Necesito un guía (de habla inglesa).** *neh-seh-SEE-toh oon GHEE-ah (day AH-blah een-GLAY-sah)*

How much does he charge ____?	**¿Cuánto cobra ____?** *KWAHN-toh KOH-brah*

■ per hour   **por hora**   *pohr OHR-ah*

■ per day   **por día**   *pohr DEE-ah*

There are two (four, six) of us.
Somos dos (cuatro, seis).   *soh-mohs dohs (KWAHT-roh sayss)*

Where can I buy a guidebook (map)?
¿Dónde puedo comprar una guía (un mapa)?   *DOHN-day PWEH-doh kohm-PRAHR oo-nah GHEE-ah (oon MAH-pah)*

What are the main attractions?
¿Cuáles son los puntos principales de interés?   *KWAHL-ehs sohn lohs poon-tohs preen-see-PAHL-ays day een-tehr-AYS*

What are the things of interest here?
¿Qué cosas interesantes hay aquí?   *kay KOH-sahs een-tehr-ehs-AHN-tays AH-ee ah-KEE*

Are there trips through the city?
¿Hay excursiones por la ciudad?   *AH-ee ehs-koor-SYOHN-ehs pohr lah see-oo-DAHD*

BOOKING A TOUR

When does the tour begin?
¿Cuando empieza la excursión?   *KWAHN-doh ehm-PYEH-sah lah ehs-koor-SOYHN*

How long is the tour?
¿Cuánto tiempo dura?   *KWAHN-toh TYEHM-poh DOOR-ah*

Where do they leave from?
¿De dónde salen?   *day DOHN-day SAHL-ehn*

We want to see ____.
Queremos ver ____.   *kehr-EHM-ohs behr*

■ the botanical garden
el jardín botánico   *ehl har-DEEN boh-TAHN-ee-koh*

▨ the bullring	**la plaza de toros**	*lah plah-sah day TOHR-ohs*
▨ the business center	**el centro comercial**	*ehl SEN-troh koh-mehr-SYAHL*
▨ the castle	**el castillo**	*ehl kahs-TEE-yoh*
▨ the cathedral	**la catedral**	*lah kah-tay-DRAHL*
▨ the church	**la iglesia**	*lah eeg-LEHS-ee-ah*
▨ the concert hall	**la sala de conciertos**	*lah SAH-lah day kohn-see-EHR-tohs*
▨ the downtown area	**el centro de la ciudad**	*ehl SEN-troh day lah see-oo-DAHD*
▨ the fountains	**las fuentes**	*lahs FWEHN-tays*
▨ the library	**la biblioteca**	*lah beeb-lee-oh-TAY-kah*
▨ the main park	**el parque central**	*ehl pahr-kay sen-TRAHL*
▨ the main square	**la plaza mayor**	*lah plah-sah my-YOR*
▨ the market	**el mercado**	*ehl mehr-KAH-doh*
▨ the mosque	**la mezquita**	*lah mehs-KEE-tah*
▨ the museum (of fine arts)	**el museo (de bellas artes)**	*ehl moo-SAY-oh (day bel-yahs AHR-tays)*
▨ a nightclub	**un club nocturno**	*oon kloob nohk-TOOR-noh*
▨ the old part of town	**la ciudad vieja**	*lah see-oo-DAHD BYEH-ha*
▨ the opera	**la ópera**	*lah OH-pehr-ah*
▨ the palace	**el palacio**	*ehl pah-LAH-see-oh*
▨ the stadium	**el estadio**	*ehl ehs-TAHD-ee-oh*
▨ the synagogue	**la sinagoga**	*lah seen-ah-GOH-gah*
▨ the university	**la universidad**	*lah oon-ee-behr-see-DAHD*
▨ the zoo	**el parque zoológico**	*ehl PAHR-kay soh-oh-LOH-hee-koh*

ADMISSIONS

Is it all right to go in now?	**¿Se puede entrar ahora?** *say PWEH-day ehn-TRAHR ah-OHR-ah*
Is it open (closed)?	**¿Está abierto (cerrado)?** *ehs-TAH ah-bee-YEHR-toh (sehr-AH-doh)*
At what time does it open (close)?	**¿A qué hora se abre (cierra)?** *ah kay OHR-ah say AH-bray (see-YEHR-ah)*
What's the admission price?	**¿Cuánto es la entrada?** *KWAHN-toh ehs lah ehn-TRAH-dah*
How much do children pay?	**¿Cuánto pagan los niños?** *KWAHN-toh pah-GAHN lohs NEEN-yohs*
Can they go in free? Until what age?	**¿Pueden entrar gratis? ¿Hasta qué edad?** *PWEH-dehn ehn-TRAHR GRAH-tees ah-stah kay eh-DAHD*
Is it all right to take pictures?	**¿Se puede sacar fotos?** *say PWEH-deh sah-KAHR FOH-tohs*
How much extra does it cost to take pictures?	**¿Hay que pagar para poder sacar fotos?** *AH-ee kay pah-GAHR pah-rah poh-DEHR sah-KAHR FOH-tohs*
I do (not) use a flash attachment.	**(No) uso flash (luz instantánea).** *(noh) oo-soh flahsh (loos een-stahn-TAHN-ay-ah)*

Prohibido Tomar Fotografías	(no picture-taking allowed)

A SIGHTSEEING ITINERARY—SPAIN

Spain is one of the great tourist destinations in the world today, and deservedly so. Many visitors from northern Europe view the country primarily as a place where they can escape the rigors of the cold by relaxing on the beaches of the Costa del Sol while soaking up the hot sun and swimming in the warm, clear-blue waters of the southern Mediterranean.

Spain does offer this, but also much more. Spain is a land of startling contrasts, offering the traveler large modern cities with urban amenities: department stores, museums, theaters, restaurants, high-fashion boutiques, and nightlife. In addition, the country is full of charming tiny villages with ancient churches, palaces, and looming castles that recall other eras.

Here are some of the highlights:

MADRID

The capital and largest city (3.7 million inhabitants), Madrid offers a vast variety of things to see and do.

- *The Prado Museum*   Houses one of the most magnificent art collections in the world, particularly strong in Spanish, Flemish, and Italian art.

- *La Puerta del Sol*   Considered the center of the city. It is a major transportation hub.

- *La Plaza Mayor*   A beautiful seventeenth-century square lined with shops and a couple of outdoor cafés. One of the entrances to the plaza is the Arco de Cuchilleros, which leads into Old Madrid, one of the most intriguing tourist areas of the city. Crowds throng the narrow streets with their many bars or *tascas* to sample *tapas* (snacks), drink wine, and listen to music.

- *Retiro Park*   A former palace grounds, this popular park near the Prado has tree-shaded paths, fountains, rose gardens, an enormous artificial lake for boating, two nightclubs, and over a dozen outdoor cafés.

■ *Calle Serrano*   Madrid's best shopping street—blocks and blocks of chic shops and small restaurants.

■ *Museum of Lázaro Galdiano*   A superb art collection displayed in the home of the collector, a writer and scholar.

■ *Museum of Decorative Arts*   Five floors of an old mansion filled with ceramics, tiles, silver, crystal.

■ *Botanical Gardens (El Jardín Botánico)*   Has a huge number of species of trees and plants from throughout the world.

■ *La Calle de Alcalá* and *La Gran Vía (Avenida de San José)*   Wide boulevards which are two of Madrid's main thoroughfares.

■ *El Palacio Real* (Royal Palace)   Used nowadays for important state functions. You can visit the luxurious throne room and see the collections of tapestries, porcelain, crystal, clocks, and fine art. The Royal Armory and Carriage Museum are also well worth a visit.

■ *El Rastro* (flea market)   Located on Ribera de Curtidores Street, this fascinating open-air market is a place where on Sunday morning one can buy anything from antiques, junk, old clothes, toys and trinkets to furniture and art work. The rest of the week you can visit antique shops in the area. Bargaining is expected here.

■ *Teatro de la Zarzuela*   Located behind the Spanish Parliament building (Las Cortes), this theater offers operas, ballets, and authentic Spanish zarzuelas (light operas).

■ *Museum of the Americas*   Has a collection of dolls, toys, masks, and other Indian items brought back from pre-Columbian America.

■ *Archeological Museum*   Features a reconstruction of the thirty-thousand-year-old prehistoric Altamira cave, paintings of Altamira, more than 2,000 archeological objects, and the rare statues called *Dama de Elche* and *Dama de Baza*.

■ *Casa de Campo*   The largest park in Madrid, with a zoo, a wooded area, a lake, and an amusement park which can be

reached by cable car from Paseo del Pintor Rosales. The car passes over the Manzanlares River and affords a spectacular view of the city.

▨ *Museo del Pueblo Español* This unusual museum contains dress and household items from the different regions of Spain.

▨ *Plaza de España* A spacious plaza with two skyscrapers. (El Edificio España—the tallest building in Spain—and the Torre de Madrid.) Note the small park with statues of Miguel de Cervantes, Don Quixote, and Sancho Panza.

▨ *Temple of Debod* An Egyptian temple of the fourth century, transported from Aswan to rescue it from the flooded dam area.

▨ *Centro de Arte Reina Sofía* Madrid's museum of modern art. Filled with the works of Dalí, Gris, Miró and Picasso, including the famous *Guérnica*.

▨ *Thyssen-Bornemisza Museum* Madrid's newest art museum. It contains an extensive collection of works of the great masters including El Greco, Velázquez, Rembrandt, Goya, Manet, Monet, Dalí, Trintoretto, Caravaggio, and many others.

PLACES NEAR MADRID

▨ *El Escorial* An enormous monastery, mausoleum, and palace constructed by King Felipe II.

▨ *El Valle de los Caídos* (Valley of the Fallen) General Francisco Franco's tomb and monument dedicated to the memory of those who fell in the Spanish Civil War.

EASY DAY TRIPS FROM MADRID

▨ *Segovia* Known for its first-century Roman aqueduct and its fairytalelike *Alcázar* on a hilltop overlooking the medieval town.

▨ *Avila* A medieval city of churches, with the oldest, best-preserved city walls in Spain, possibly in all of Europe.

▨ *Aranjuez* With its eighteenth-century Royal Palace and fabulous gardens.

■ *Toledo*   A jewel of a city, still medieval in feeling, famous for its many El Greco paintings and for its mix of Moorish, Jewish, and Christian legacies. Don't miss the cathedral; El Greco's house and museum; Church of Santo Tomé with one of El Greco's masterpieces; and the Museum of Santa Cruz.

BARCELONA

Spain's principal seaport and industrial heart has a population of approximately two million people. Among its many attractions are:

■ *The Ramblas*   A wide, tree-lined boulevard that goes from the center of the city to the waterfront, where one can stroll past flower stalls, caged birds, newspaper and magazine stands, and book shops.

■ *The Pueblo Español*   Located on top of Montjuic (reachable by cable railway), is a model village, featuring buildings from the various regions of the country. In the village the visitors can see pottery making, glass blowing, and other arts and crafts.

■ *The Plaza de Cataluña*   A beautiful and spacious plaza located in the center of the city.

■ *The Catedral*   A Gothic monument located in the *barrio gótico* (the Gothic quarter), the old part of the city; this is the site of sardana dancing on weekends.

■ *The Picasso Museum*   Contains one of the world's largest collections of the famous modern Spanish artist, installed in a thirteenth-century palace.

■ *Museum of Catalonian Art*   A rare collection of eleventh- and twelfth-century Romanesque art, as well as works by El Greco, Tintoretto, and others.

■ *Museum of Federico Marés*   An unusual and rare sculpture collection located in a palace near the Cathedral.

■ *The Church of the Sagrada Familia* (Holy Family)   The spectacular unfinished work of the architect Antonio Gaudí.

■ *Parque Güell*   The whimsical park designed by Gaudí.

SEVILLA

One of the most picturesque and romantic of all Spanish cities. In Sevilla, you can see:

- *Museo Provincial de Bellas Artes* A collection of Spanish paintings, lodged in an old convent.
- *La Catedral* The largest cathedral in all of Spain.
- *La Giralda* The bell tower of the cathedral which was constructed originally as the minaret of a mosque. City views from the top are extraordinary.
- *El Alcázar* A Christian and Moorish fortress with beautiful gardens.
- *Barrio Santa Cruz* Onetime Jewish quarter of narrow, winding streets.
- *La Calle de las Sierpes* (Snake Street) The principal business thoroughfare of the city, lined with sidewalk cafés, restaurants, and shops.
- *Itálica* Remains of a Roman city just outside Sevilla.

GRANADA

When in Granada, don't miss the following:

- *The Alhambra* Exquisitely beautiful Moorish palace, one of the major sights of Spain.
- *El Albaicín* The gypsy quarter whose inhabitants dwell in furnished caves with electricity.
- *El Generalife* Summer palace of the Moorish kings, famous for its beautiful gardens.

CORDOBA

One can visit the imposing Mezquita (the Great Mosque), with its beautiful marble columns and intricate mosaics and its superimposed Christian church inside. Also visit *Judería*, the old Jewish quarter of Cordova with a tiny synagogue, the only one left in town.

MARBELLA AND TORREMOLINOS

Fashionable resort areas on the Costa del Sol, with its Mediterranean beaches, luxurious hotels, and fine restaurants.

IN THE NEW WORLD: MEXICO

In this large country, don't miss these, all in Mexico City and its vicinity:

- ■ *Chapultepec Castle and Park*   A magnificent park containing a zoo, museums, lakes, and concert halls. One of the largest parks in the world.

- ■ *The Palacio de Bellas Artes* (Palace of Fine Arts)   Contains the famous murals of Rivera, Siqueiros, and Orozco.

- ■ *La Ciudad Universitaria* (University City)   An architectural and artistic wonder, the site of the past Olympic Games. The library building is completely covered with brilliantly colored mosaic tiles depicting the history of Mexico.

- ■ *La Torre Latinoamericana*   The tallest building in Mexico. The magnificent view from the top lets you see the entire city.

- ■ *El Zócalo*   The main square of the city. Here one finds the National Palace with its magnificent Diego Rivera murals.

- ■ *The Plaza de Garibaldi*   The center for the mariachis, strolling musicians who rent themselves out for tips.

- ■ *Floating Gardens of Xochimilco*   The Venice of the Americas. Boats can be rented to travel through the miles of flower-lined canals.

- ■ *Teotihuacán*   Famous Toltec ruins, which include the Pyramids of the Sun and of the Moon and the Temple of Quetzalcoatl.

BEACHES AND RESORTS

With over 6,000 miles of beaches along Mexico's coastlines, on four different seas, no other country in the world offers vacationers such a variety of beaches and resorts.

All of Mexico's beaches are open to the public, with free access for all. You may sunbathe, swim, and use the watersport facilities of any beach you'd like, including those of the beachfront hotels.

Though peak time for vacationers generally runs from October through May, Mexico's coastal sun is in season all year round.

THE CARIBBEAN AND GULF COAST

Many regard the Caribbean beaches of the Yucatan's east coast as the most beautiful in all of Mexico. The fine, powdery white sand, derived from limestone, is unique to the area.

The Caribbean coast is ideal beach vacation territory. The weather is warm and temperate, and waters are excellent for snorkeling, diving, boating, and waterskiing.

- *Cancún* Cancun is actually an island—a thin stretch of sand connected to the mainland by two bridges. The beaches are exquisite everywhere. There are boating, fishing, and diving charters available from its pier. The numerous beachfront hotels also offer watersports. In addition, there are many tennis courts, a Robert Trent Jones golf course, and a host of restaurants, shops, and discos.

  No Cancun vacation is complete without a visit to the Mayan ruins that dot the Yucatan—including two of the most famous sites in Mexico: Chichén-Itza and Uxmal.

  South of Cancun, along the coast to Tulum, is the village of Xel-Ha. Xel-Ha boasts a beautiful swimming beach, and the best snorkeling on the mainland.

- *Cozumel* First to be discovered by the international jet set, Cozumel has still managed to be virtually unspoiled. Most of the land is still in its natural state.

  Cozumel's main attraction is Palancar Reef—the world's second largest coral reef—which surrounds the island. Scuba enthusiasts rate Cozumel as one of the world's best diving areas, and there are many diving shops and schools

on the island. Chancnab Lagoon, on the southern end of the island, is the best spot for snorkeling. The island's beaches are lovely, but take care to swim at beaches that are free of sharp underwater coral.

Cozumel offers a full range of resort hotels, restaurants, and night spots. It is 12 miles off the Yucatan coast and easily accessible by air or hydrofoil from Cancun.

■ *Veracruz* The coastal city is Mexico's principal port. The water is calm, warm, and shallow for a long wade into the Gulf, and you can rent beach chairs and umbrellas from seaside vendors.

Mocambo Beach, five miles south of the city, is the most beautiful in Veracruz. Villa del Mar and Hornos Costa are nearer town and are both good swimming beaches. Fishing charters can be arranged at any number of piers in the city.

While in Veracruz, visit the Plaza de Armas, the old center of town surrounded by a high wall, and the fort of San Juan de Ulloa, both dating back to the sixteenth century.

You may want to plan your trip to coincide with the Carnival of Veracruz in March—Mexico's own Mardi Gras celebration.

THE PACIFIC COAST

This is a stretch of coastline with 2,000 miles of spectacular and varied beaches.

■ *Mazatlán* The original lure of Mazatlan was deep-sea sport fishing, with marlin and sailfish the prize catches. But beach lovers now predominate, and there are plenty of beaches to accommodate all of them.

North Beach, which extends some six miles beyond the city's oceanfront boulevard, is the largest. Farther north is the Playa Sabalo, probably the most beautiful of all Mazatlan beaches. Las Gaviotas is the beach nearest town, whereas the island beach of Venados offers exceptionally calm and clear waters.

For a break from sunbathing, Mazatlan offers plenty of golf, tennis, sailing, and surfing. Horseback riding is popular at Playa Sabalo.

■ *Puerto Vallarta* This once sleepy fishing village is now one of the most popular resorts in the world. Puerto Vallarta boasts luxurious hotels, colorful restaurants and nightclubs, and nearly every popular resort pastime imaginable.

The town's main beach, the Playa del Sol, is the center of action. There are also several quieter alternatives nearby, such as Chino Beach, Playa de Oro, and Playa Las Estacas. From any of these beaches you can enjoy the spectacular Puerto Vallarta scenery.

■ *Manzanillo* The docks of this port city provide Mexico with a vital link to Asia, while its thick jungle, tropical fruit plantations, and deserted beaches make a lush setting for vacationers. Land and water sports, golf, tennis, hunting and deep-sea fishing are available at the beachfront hotels.

The Playa Azul is a curving, seven-mile-long beach that extends from Manzanillo city. Most of the beachfront hotels in the area are built along this spectacular beach, and the smaller but equally lovely Playa Las Brisas.

Nearby is the famous Mexican resort, Las Hadas. The brainchild of a South American millionaire, Las Hadas is most notable for its unusual architecture, with domed roofs that give the development a North African feeling.

■ *Ixtapa/Zihuantanejo* Luxurious Ixtapa was carved from the jungle by the Mexican government for development into a tourist resort. It is sparkling clean and elegant, featuring first-class hotels, a Robert Trent Jones 18-hole golf course, inviting shops, gourmet restaurants, and an exciting nightlife. Visitors enjoy waterskiing, diving, snorkeling, windsurfing, and sailing. Excursions to nearby beaches such as Playa Quieta, Playa Linda, and Ixtapa Island are also available.

Just a few miles north of Ixtapa is the picturesque fishing village of Zihuantanejo. Here is a place where you can still see fisherman mending nets on the beaches. The village has several small but very attractive hotels, including the world-class Villa del Sol, and the popular Las Gatas Beach, where you can swim with the sea turtles and enjoy a lunch of freshly caught fish.

■ *Acapulco* Known as the "Pearl of the Pacific" and the "Riviera de las Americas," Acapulco is Mexico's most famous beach resort. There are over 20 beaches on and around Acapulco Bay: Playa Condesa, Caleta-Caletilla (the "morning beach"), Hornos (the "afternoon beach"), are some of the most popular. La Roqueta, located on an uninhabited island across Boca Chica Channel, offers the calmest waters for swimming.

A must-see for anyone visiting Acapulco are the world-renowned cliff divers. From the top of La Quebrada they dive 136 feet to the shallow inlet below, timing their dives so that they enter the water at the exact time the wave pours into the inlet.

BAJA

Jutting a thousand miles out of San Diego, the Baja Peninsula offers vacationers a coastline of rugged desert mountain ranges and sunny beaches.

■ *Los Cabos* Twenty miles of secluded beaches with an average of 360 sunny days per year, located at the very tip of the Baja peninsula.

At the western end of the Los Cabos area is the town of Cabo San Lucas, whose surrounding waters may have the finest marlin fishing in the world.

■ *La Paz* The capital of the Baja, La Paz is an easygoing resort town famous for its pearl divers. The fishing is excellent, along with every other watersport, from jet skiing to scuba.

ELSEWHERE IN MEXICO

■ *Taxco* Famous for the silver shops and silver factories that line its streets, Taxco is known as the most picturesque city in Mexico.

■ *Guadalajara* Mexico's second largest city has over 3 million inhabitants and is the home of the largest U.S. retirement community. Close to it is Lake Chapala, the country's largest lake.

■ *Cuernavaca*   Called the "city of eternal springtime,"
Cuernavaca is famous for its flowers and its year-round
pleasant climate. Here too there is a large community of
Americans who have retirement homes.

OTHER LATIN AMERICAN COUNTRIES

PUERTO RICO

A tourist's delight, just $3^{1}/_{2}$ hours from New York. When
there, visit San Juan's University at Río Piedras, a large
modern university with over 50,000 students. Also see Old
San Juan, the original city built by the Spaniards in the
sixteenth century. One main attraction is El Morro, a fortress
constructed to ward off attacks by English pirates. Also in
Puerto Rico, visit El Yunque, a luxurious rain forest with
exotic vegetation, waterfalls, and tropical birds.

DOMINICAN REPUBLIC

Santo Domingo is the capital and largest city (half a million
inhabitants) of this pleasant and friendly Caribbean island.
The old cathedral is visited by tourists who come to see the
tomb of Christopher Columbus. When here, also see:

■ *The Alcázar*   The restored palace of Diego Columbus. It is
richly furnished with paintings, furniture, and tapestries of
the sixteenth century.

■ *Los Tres Ojos* (the three eyes)   Located on the outskirts of
the capital, this is a marvelous natural phenomenon of
three underground springs.

■ *Puerto Plata*   Noted for its white, sandy beaches on the
northern coast of the island.

ARGENTINA

Arguably the most cosmopolitan city of South America,
Buenos Aires offers varied and interesting architecture dating
from the eighteenth century (the Cathedral, the Town Hall or
Cabildo, and the churches of La Merced, Santa Catalina, and
San Francisco) as well as nineteenth century buildings in the

French Second Empire style. When one becomes tired of visiting the city's numerous museums, it is always a pleasure to sit in Palermo Park or to listen to opera at the Teatro Colón. Other important places include:

- ◼ *Iguazú Falls* Higher than Niagara and twice as wide, this is the world's mightiest waterfall where three countries, Argentina, Brazil, and Paraguay, meet.

- ◼ *San Carlos de Bariloche* A Latin Alpine town, 2,600 feet above sea level. Latin America's favorite mountain and lake resort (fishing, hunting, skiing).

- ◼ *Ushuaia* Southernmost town in the world. Fishing, rock climbing, cross-country skiing, snowmobiling, scuba diving, whale and dolphin watching.

BOLIVA

- ◼ *La Paz* The highest capital city in the world (two and one half miles above sea level). Many open-air Indian markets, wonderful eighteenth-century architecture.

- ◼ *Lake Titicaca* With a surface of 3,500 square miles, it is the highest navigable lake in the world (13,000 feet above sea level). There are hydrofoil excursions to the Inca islands of the Sun and Moon.

- ◼ *Potosí* Once the largest city in the Americas. Renowned for its silver mines, which engendered the still-used expression, "It's worth a Potosí!" Visit La Casa de la Moneda, a museum taking up an entire city block, containing colonial paintings and equipment used for producing silver ingots and coins.

CHILE

Plagued by earthquakes, Chile's main attractions are natural. The north includes the awesome Atacama Desert, rich in mineral deposits that color the land in various hues. The south is green, cool, hospitable, and offers magnificent lakes and mountains.

- ◼ *Santiago* Chile's capital and largest city with over four million people. Not far from Santiago are the slopes of Portillo, scene of the World Alpine Ski Championships.

■ *Valparaíso* Chile's second largest city and chief seaport. Built on hills, with its cable cars and cobblestone streets, it resembles San Francisco.

■ *Viña del Mar* Not far from Valparaiso, the "Pearl of the Pacific" has famous beaches, while the casino and racetrack draw thousands of tourists daily.

■ *Torres del Paine National Park* An area of almost a half million acres in Chile's cold deep south, it shelters lakes, lagoons, waterfalls and glaciers, sculpted by the wind and snow during 12 million years. View wildlife such as guanacos, condors, Darwin rheas, ducks, geese, and more than 100 different species of birds.

COLOMBIA

■ *Bogotá* Capital city of over six million people. Plenty of museums and art galleries, numerous churches from the Colonial period. Don't miss the Baroque Cathedral, as well as the famous Salt Cathedral, located in the depths of the salt mine 31 miles north of the city. El Museo del Oro (The Gold Museum) is Bogota's most famous museum. It contains over 8,000 gold pieces (rings, bracelets, crowns, and so on) and a fabulous collection of emeralds, including the four largest emeralds in the world. (Colombia is the world's number one source of emeralds.)

■ *Cartagena* One hour by air from Bogota lies the Caribbean city of Cartagena. Surrounded by fortress-like walls (originally built to protect the inhabitants from pirates), the city looks as it did centuries ago. Its beautiful beaches make it a prime tourist destination.

ECUADOR

■ *Quito* Although it is located on the equator, Quito's climate is springtime the year round because of its altitude. From Quito, you can take one-day trips to Indian settlements in the Amazon jungle.

■ *Galapagos Islands* Located 600 miles off the coast, the islands are the site where Darwin made scientific observations leading to his theory of evolution. The

Galapagos are home for a mixture of creatures found nowhere else on earth. A visit always becomes an unforgettable experience. However, for ecological reasons many restrictions apply. Make sure to contact the Equadorian consulate before you travel.

PERU

- *Lima*   Founded by the conquistadores as a Spanish colonial city, Lima is now a huge metropolis of over seven million people, with stylish and sophisticated suburbs as well as old neighborhoods that still reflect its colonial past.

- *Cuzco*   The imperial city of the Incas, once the largest and most important city in the New World, is today a city whose present population is almost totally native American, living today much as it did hundreds of years ago.

- *Machu Picchu*   The incredible lost city of the Incas, a beautiful jewel in a beautiful setting, suspended in the mist like a ghost from the past.

URUGUAY

- *Montevideo*   A pleasant city with great views of Montevideo Bay. Don't miss the Rambla, a riverfront drive, which runs along the waterfront for 12 miles, linking all the beaches along the city's coast.

- *Punta del Este*   World famous international beach resort, the site of movies, festivals, and international conferences.

VENEZUELA

- *Caracas*   A modern metropolis of over three million people. At 3,000 feet above sea level, Caracas has one of the world's best climates. Take a cable car ride down to the Caribbean beaches below. Macuto Beach is one of the most popular ones.

- *Colonia Tovar*   Forty miles from Caracas is a "Black Forest" village founded by Bavarian immigrants—a mountain resort popular for its German food and culture.

▪ *Margarita Island*   A Caribbean resort and major tourist destination because of its lovely beaches and picturesque towns. A duty-free port, it has many shops catering to the thousands of visitors who arrive from Caracas by plane or hydrofoil.

COSTA RICA

A small democratic country, rich in natural beauty, offering an incredible variety of landscapes and comfortable climates. It is a country for nature lovers, who will marvel at the diverse and abundant flora and fauna, the abrupt and active volcanoes, and the sunny and exotic beaches of the Pacific Ocean and the Caribbean Sea. You may start with its beautiful capital city, San Jose, visit its popular beaches, and then move on to other unforgettable places.

▪ *Lake Coter Region*   Visit the Ecoadventure Lodge and the impressive Cloud Forest.

▪ *Arenal Lake*   Hiking, horseback riding, water skiing, windsurfing, fishing, hot springs of Tabacon, and the Arenal Volcano.

▪ *Tortuguero National Park*   Costa Rica's rich tropical rain forest where you can see over 800 species of birds (more than all of the U.S. and Canada combined), including brilliantly colored parrots, toucans and macaws, monkeys, iguanas, and many other species.

▪ *Monteverde Cloud Forest Reserve*   Mountain trail walking tours.

BELIZE

There are few places on earth that can match the diversity found in Belize. Its lowland rain forests, mangrove swamps, and coral reefs offer an astonishing variety of flora and fauna. A place for physically active tourists.

GUATEMALA

■ *Lake Atitlan* Its lake shore villages offer scenery and entertainment. Several handicraft markets sell belts, ponchos, blankets, and other sought-after items.

■ *Tikal* Nestled in the jungle, the capital of the Mayan Empire with its many pyramids, temples and palaces, is one of the major archaeological sites of the Americas.

■ *Chichicastenango* One of the largest native American open-air markets in the world.

PANAMA

■ *Panama City* A cosmopolitan urban metropolis of over one half million people located on the Pacific Ocean. Plenty of nightlife with many discos, nightclubs, and plush gambling casinos.

   Because of low import duties you can purchase many goods (cameras, laptops, camcorders, watches, jewelry, perfumes, etc.) at bargain prices.

■ *Panama Canal Tour* Still an awesome feat of engineering, the Canal should be seen because of its visual, technological, and political significance.

■ *San Blas Islands* An archipelago off Panama's Caribbean coast. Day trips to visit the villages of the San Blas's Native Americans.

PLANNING A TRIP

During your stay you may want to plan some excursions into the country or to other cities. In most countries you can move about by airplane, train, bus, boat, and car (see Driving a Car). For air travel within a country, look for signs to the domestic terminal (sometimes separate from the international terminal).

AIR SERVICES

Within Spain, two domestic airlines—Iberia and Avianco—fly to more than 36 cities. Unfortunately, to reach city A from B, you often have to go via Madrid and transfer. Barajas is ten miles from Madrid, but most airports are located within a few miles of a given city. A special ticket called "Visit Spain" gives unlimited air travel within Spain on Iberia for 45 days (you must fly Iberia to and from Spain; check for current price).

Flights within Mexico are easily arranged, particularly to other major tourist cities, such as Acapulco or the Yucatán. For trips among other Central and South American cities, consult your travel agent.

When is there a flight to ____?	**¿Cuándo hay un vuelo a ____?** *KWAHN-doh AH-ee oon BWEHL-oh ah*	
I would like a ____ ticket.	**Quisiera un billete ____.** *kee-see-YEHR-ah oon bee-YEH-tay*	
▪ round trip	**de ida y vuelta** *day EE-dah ee BWEHL-tah*	
▪ one way	**de ida** *day EE-dah*	
▪ tourist class	**en clase turista** *ehn KLAH-say toor-EES-tah*	
▪ first class	**en primera clase** *ehn pree-MEHR-ah KLAH-say*	

I would like a seat ____.	**Quisiera un asiento ____.** *kee-see-YEHR-ah oon ah-SYEHN-toh*
▪ in the smoking section	**en la sección de fumadores** *ehn lah sehk-SYOHN day foo-mah-DOHR-ehs*
▪ in the nonsmoking section	**en la sección de no fumadores** *ehn lah sehk-SYOHN day noh foo-mah-DOHR-ehs*
▪ next to the window	**de ventanilla** *day behn-tah-NEE-yah*
▪ on the aisle	**de pasillo** *day pah-SEE-yoh*
What is the fare?	**¿Cuál es la tarifa?** *kwahl ehs lah tah-REE-fah*
Can I use the ticket for frequent flyer miles?	**¿Puedo usar el billete para recibir bonos de vuelo (kilometraje)?** *PWAY-doh oo-SAHR ehl bee-YET-eh pah-rah reh-see-BEER BO-nohs day BWEH-loh (kee-loh-meh-TRAH-heh)*
Are meals served?	**¿Se sirven comidas?** *say seer-behn koh-MEE-dahs*
When does the plane leave (arrive)?	**¿A qué hora sale (llega) el avión?** *ah kay oh-ra SAH-lay (YEH-gah) ehl ah-BYOHN*
When must I be at the airport?	**¿Cuándo debo estar en el aeropuerto?** *KWAHN-doh deh-boh ehs-TAHR en ehl ah-ehr-oh-PWEHR-toh*
What is my flight number?	**¿Cuál es el número del vuelo?** *kwahl ehs ehl NOO-mehr-oh dehl BWEH-loh*
What gate do we leave from?	**¿De qué puerta se sale?** *day kay PWEHR-tah say sah-lay*

I want to confirm (cancel) my reservation for flight ____.	**Quiero confirmar (cancelar) mi reservación para el vuelo ____.** *kee-YEHR-oh kohn-feer-MAHR (kahn-say-LAHR) mee reh-sehr-bah-SYOHN pah-rah ehl BWEH-loh*
I'd like to check my bags.	**Quisiera facturar mis maletas.** *kee-SYEHR-ah fahk-too-RAHR mees mah-LEH-tahs*
I have only carry-on baggage.	**Tengo solo equipaje de mano.** *TEN-goh so-loh ay-kee-PAH-hay day MAH-noh*
Can you pass my film (camera) through by hand?	**¿Podría inspeccionar el film (la cámara) a mano?** *poh-DREE-ah een-spek-syohn-AHR ehl feelm (lah KAH-mahr-ah) ah MAHN-oh*

Note: Some high-speed film can be damaged by airport security x-rays. It is best to pack film in your suitcase, protected in a lead-insulated bag. If you have film in your camera or carry-on baggage, avoid problems and ask the guard to pass it through by hand. If the guard refuses, bow to his wishes.

TRAIN SERVICE

RENFE offers a kilometric ticket that can save you up to 20% of your fare; round-trip fares on some routes save 25%. A *Tarjeta Dorada* (Gold Card) can save you up to 50% on rail trips—available only to those 65 years or older.

The Eurailpass is good in Spain, as well as 15 other countries. Tickets for unlimited train travel are available for 15 or 21 days or 1, 2 or 3 months. Note that the tickets should be purchased in your country of origin before you travel to Spain.

The following is a brief description of the varieties of Spanish trains.

AVE	Spain's new bullet train connecting Madrid and Seville in three hours.
Talgo	A luxury diesel express with reclining seats and air conditioning. It operates between Madrid and major cities—Barcelona, Bilbao, Cadiz, Malaga, Seville, Valencia, Zaragoza.
Electrotren	A luxury train, but it is slower than Talgo, makes more stops, and covers more of the country. It is cheaper than Talgo.
TER	A luxury diesel express train, slower than Talgo and makes more stops.
TAF	A second-class diesel train.
Expreso	A long-distance night train, with only a few major stops.
Rápido	A fast train (slower than the Expreso).
Omnibuses or ferrobuses	Local trains.

A first (second) class ticket to ____ please.	**Un billete de primera (segunda) clase a ____ por favor.** *oon bee-YEH-teh day pree-MEHR-ah (say-GOON-dah) KLAH-say ah pohr fah-BOHR*
Give me a half price ticket	**Deme un medio billete** *DEH-meh oon MEH-dee-oh bee-YEH-teh*
Give me a round trip ticket	**Deme un billete de ida y vuelta** *DEH-meh oon bee-YEH-teh day EE-dah ee BWEHL-tah*
Give me a one way ticket	**Deme un billete de ida** *DEH-meh oon bee-YEH-teh day EE-dah*
I'd like a (no) smoking compartment.	**Quisiera un departamento para (no) fumadores.** *kee-SYEHR-ah oon day-pahr-tah-MEHN-toh pah-rah (noh) foo-mah-DOHR-ays*

When does the train arrive (leave)?	**¿Cuándo llega (sale) el tren?** *kwahn-doh YEH-gah (SAH-lay) ehl trehn*
From (at) what platform does it leave (arrive)?	**¿De (A) qué andén sale (ilega)?** *day (ah) kay ahn-DEHN SAH-lay (YEH-gah)*
Does this train stop at ___?	**¿Para este tren en ___?** *PAH-rah ehs-tay trehn ehn*
Is the train late?	**¿Tiene retraso el tren?** *tee-YEH-nay ray-TRAH-soh ehl trehn*
How long does it stop?	**¿Cuánto tiempo para?** *kwahn-toh tee-EHM-poh PAH-rah*
Is there time to get a bite?	**¿Hay tiempo para tomar un bocado?** *ahy tee-EHM-poh PAH-rah toh-MAHR oon boh-KAH-doh*
Do we have to stand in line?	**¿Tenemos que hacer cola?** *tehn-EH-mohs kay ah-SEHR KOH-lah*
Are there discounts for students (seniors, groups, the handicapped)?	**¿Hay descuentos para estudiantes (ancianos, grupos, los invalidos)?** *AH-ee des-KWEHN-tohs pah-rah ehs-too-dee-YAHN-tehs (ahn-see-YAH-nohs GROO-pohs lohs een-BAH-lee-dohs)*
How can I obtain a refund?	**¿Cómo puedo obtener un reembolso?** *KOH-moh PWAY-doh ob-ten-EHR oon ray-ehm-BOHL-so*
Are there special (weekly, monthly, group, tourist) passes?	**¿Hay pases especiales (para una semana, para un mes, para turistas)?** *AH-ee PAH-sehs ehs-pehs-YAHL-ehs (pah-rah oo-nah seh-MAH-nah oon mehs pah-rah toor-EES-tahs)*

ON THE TRAIN

Is there a dining car (sleeping car)?	**¿Hay coche-comedor (cochecama)?** *ahy KOH-chay koh-may-DOHR (KOH-chay KAH-mah)*
Is it ____?	**¿Es ____?** *ehs*

■ a through train   **un tren directo** *oon trehn dee-REHK-toh*

■ a local   **un tren local (ómnibus, ordinario)** *oon trehn loh-KAHL (OHM-nee-boos ohr-dee-NAH-ree-oh)*

■ an express   **un expreso (rápido)** *oon eks-PREHS-oh (RAH-pee-doh)*

Do I have to change trains?	**¿Tengo que trasbordar?** *TEHN-goh kay trahs-bohr-DAHR*
Is this seat taken?	**¿Está ocupado este asiento?** *ehs-TAH oh-koo-PAH-doh EHS-tay ah-SYEHN-toh*
Where are we now?	**¿Dónde estamos ahora?** *DOHN-day ehs-TAH-mohs ah-OHR-ah*
Will we arrive on time (late)?	**¿Llegaremos a tiempo (tarde)?** *yeh-gahr-EH-mohs ah tee-EHM-poh (tahr-day)*
Can I check my bag through to ____?	**¿Puedo facturar mi maleta hasta ____?** *PWEH-doh fahk-toor-AHR mee mah-LEH-tah AHS-tah*
Excuse me, but you are in my seat.	**Perdón, creo que está ocupando mi asiento.** *pehr-DOHN KRAY-oh key ehs-TAH oh-koo-PAHN-doh mee ah-SYEHN-toh*

SHIPBOARD TRAVEL

If you want to visit any surrounding islands, then you'll want to arrange to take a boat there.

Where is the dock?	**¿Dónde está el muelle?** *DOHN-day ehs-TAH ehl MWEH-yeh*
When does the next boat leave for ____?	**¿Cuándo sale el próximo barco para ____?** *KWAHN-doh SAH-lay ehl PROHKS-ee-moh BAHR-koh PAH-rah*
How long does the crossing take?	**¿Cuánto dura la travesía?** *KWAHN-toh DOO-rah lah trah-beh-SEE-ah*
Do we stop at any other ports?	**¿Hacemos escala en algunos puertos?** *ah-SAY-mohs ehs-KAH-lah ehn ahl-GOO-nohs PWEHR-tohs*
How long will we remain in the port?	**¿Cuánto tiempo permaneceremos en el puerto?** *KWAHN-toh tee-EHM-poh pehr-mah-neh-sehr-EH-mohs ehn ehl PWEHR-toh*

When do we land?	**¿Cuándo desembarcamos?** *KWAHN-doh dehs-ehm-bahr-KAH-mohs*
At what time do we have to be back on board?	**¿A qué hora debemos volver a bordo?** *ah kay OHR-ah deh-BAY-mohs bohl-BEHR ah BOHR-doh*
I'd like a ____ ticket.	**Quisiera un pasaje ____.** *kee-SYEHR-ah oon pah-SAH-hay*
▨ first class	**de primera clase** *day pree-MEHR-ah KLAH-say*
▨ tourist class	**de clase turista** *day KLAH-say toor-EES-tah*
▨ cabin	**para un camarote** *PAH-rah oon kah-mah-ROH-tay*
I don't feel well.	**No me siento bien.** *noh may SYEHN-toh byehn*
Can you give me something for sea sickness?	**¿Puede usted darme algo contra el mareo?** *PWEH-day oos-TEHD DAHR-may AHL-goh KOHN-trah ehl mah-RAY-oh*

Travel Tips Luggage is sometimes lost or arrives long after you do. To avoid problems, some people travel light and carry on everything. At the very least, take one complete change of clothing, basic grooming items, and any regular medication aboard with you. Because airlines will not replace valuable jewelry when paying for lost luggage, it should be carried on your person. Safer yet, select one set of basic, simple jewelry that can be worn everywhere—even in the shower—and wear it during your whole trip. Remember, carry-on bags must be small enough to fit in overhead bins or to slide under your seat.

DRIVING A CAR

Driving is an easy way to travel in Spain. Roads are generally good, though there are just a few superhighways **(autopistas).** More common are national and country roads, which are usually two- or three-lane asphalt roads. Roads are well marked with international highway symbols. Mileage is designated in kilometers. A mile is five eighths of a kilometer; see chart on page 90. Gas prices are the same at stations all over the country. In smaller towns, gas stations are few and far between, so it is wise to "gas up" when you can. Note that seat belts are mandatory. If stopped by the police, you will be fined for not wearing a belt.

The western United States and the western Latin American countries (except Colombia) are connected by the Panamerican Highway **(Carretera panamericana).** It is possible to go south from Alaska to Canada to Washington State and all the way to Panama, get your car on a ferry, disembark in Ecuador, and continue south until you reach the southern Chilean city of Puerto Montt. From Santiago, in Chile, you can start a journey to the east, cross into Argentina through the Andes Mountains **(Cordillera de los Andes)** and from Argentina you can reach Uruguay, Paraguay, Brazil, and Bolivia. Quite a trip!

However, geography and finances are factors that make it impossible to draw a general picture. Driving conditions in Latin America, including availability of good hotels and motels, gas stations, and so on change from country to country, so it is best to check with the tourist information office of the country you plan to visit before you start your trip.

CAR RENTALS

In Spain rentals can be arranged before departure through a travel agent or upon arrival at a rental office in the major airports and in or near the railroad station in a larger city or town. You'll find Hertz, Avis, Atesa (Budget), Europcar, and Godfrey Davis, among other car rental agencies. The usual

rate is by the day or week, with a charge per kilometer. Requirements: you must be 18 years old or older and hold a valid U.S. or international driver's license. A credit card is the preferred method of payment.

In Latin America the satisfaction derived from car rental depends on the country. Contact the tourist information offices and talk to your travel agent.

Where can I rent ____?	**¿Dónde puedo alquilar ____?** *dohn-day PWEH-doh ahl-kee-LAHR*
▨ a car	**un coche** *oon KOH-chay*
▨ a four-wheel-drive vehicle	**un vehículo con tracción en las cuatro ruedas** *oon-beh-EE-koo-loh kohn trahk-SYOHN en lahs KWAH-troh roo-WAY-dahs*
▨ a minivan	**un mínivan** *oon MEE-nee-bahn*
I want a ____.	**Quiero ____.** *kee-EH-roh*
▨ small car	**un coche pequeño** *oon KOH-chay peh-KAYN-yoh*
▨ large car	**un coche grande** *oon KOH-chay GRAHN-day*
▨ sports car	**un coche deportivo** *oon KOH-chay day-pohr-TEE-boh*
I prefer automatic transmission (power steering, power windows, power mirrors).	**Prefiero el cambio automático (dirección asistida, ventanillas eléctricas, espejos eléctricos).** *preh-fee-EHR-oh ehl KAHM-bee-oh AH-oo-toh-MAH-tee-koh dee-rehk-SYOHN ah-sees-TEE-dah ben-tah-NEE-yahs eh-LEK-tree-kahs ehs-PEH-hohs eh-LEK-tree-kohs*
How much does it cost ____?	**¿Cuánto cuesta ____?** *KWAHN-toh KWEHS-tah*
▨ per day	**por día** *pohr DEE-ah*
▨ per week	**por semana** *pohr seh-MAHN-ah*

■ per kilometer	**por kilómetro** *pohr kee-LOH-meht-roh*
■ with unlimited mileage	**con kilometraje ilimitado** *kohn kee-loh-may-TRAH-hay ee-lee-mee-TAH-doh*
How much is the insurance?	**¿Cuánto es el seguro?** *KWAHN-toh ehs ehl seh-GOOR-oh*
Is the gas included?	**¿Está incluída la gasolina?** *ehs-TAH een-kloo-EE-dah lah gahs-oh LEEN-ah*
Do you accept credit cards?	**¿Acepta usted tarjetas de crédito?** *ah-sehp-tah oos-TEHD tahr-HAY-tahs day KREH-dee-toh*
Here's my driver's license.	**Aquí tiene mi licencia de conducir.** *ah-KEE tee-EH-nay mee lee-SEN-see-ah day kohn-doo-SEER*
Do I have to leave a deposit?	**¿Tengo que dejar un depósito?** *ten-goh kay day-hahr oon day-POHS-ee-toh*
I want to rent the car here and leave it in ____.	**Quiero alquilar el coche aquí y dejarlo en ____.** *kee-YEHR-oh ahl-kee-LAHR ehl KOH-chay ah-KEE ee day-HAHR-loh ehn*
What kind of gasoline does it take?	**¿Qué tipo de gasolina necesita?** *kay TEE-poh day gah-so-LEE-nah neh-seh-SEE-tah*

PARKING

In a town or city, park only in designated places, usually marked by a sign with a big "E" or "P" (for parking). If you park in a no-parking zone, you run the very real risk of having your car towed away.

Is this a legal parking place?	**¿Es ésto un lugar para estacionar?** *ehs EHS-toh oon loo-GAHR pah-rah ehs-tah-syohn-AHR*
What is the parking fee?	**¿Cuánto cuesta estacionar aquí?** *KWAHN-toh KWEHS-tah ehs-tah-syohn-AHR ah-KEE*
Where can I find a place to park?	**¿Dónde puedo encontrar un sitio de estacionamiento?** *DOHN-day PWEH-doh ehn-kohn-TRAHR oon SEE-tee-oh day ehs-tah-syohn-ah-mee-YEHN-toh*

ON THE ROAD

In Spain turnpikes are called **autopistas** and are marked as "A" roads on the map. **Autopistas de peaje** are toll roads.

National highways are called **carreteras nacionales** and are marked with a red "N" on the map. Regional highways are reasonably good and are numbered with the prefix "C." Speed limits are:

autopistas	120 km/h (74 1/2 m.p.h.)
double-lane highways	100 km/h (62 m.p.h.)
other roads	90 km/h (56 m.p.h.)
populated areas	60 km/h (37 m.p.h.)

And pay attention to speed limits. They are enforced. Radar control is commonplace, and if you exceed the limit, you may receive a ticket by mail after you have returned home. Driving in a city can be confusing. Many streets are one-way and are very narrow, twisting, and crowded.

Latin American roads cover the full range, from excellent to terrible, often within the same country, so it is not possible to present a coherent picture. Speed limits vary, as does their enforcement.

Excuse me, can you tell me ____?	**Por favor, ¿puede usted decirme ____?** *pohr fah-BOHR pweh-day oos-TEHD day-SEER-may*
Which way is it to ____?	**¿Por dónde se va a ____?** *pohr DOHN-day say bah ah*
I think we're lost.	**Creo que estamos perdidos.** *KRAY-oh kay ehs-TAH-mohs pehr-DEE-dohs*
Is this the way to ____?	**¿Es éste el camino a ____?** *ehs EHS-tay ehl kah-MEE-noh ah*
Is it a good road?	**¿Es buena la carretera?** *ehs BWAY-nah la kahr-ray-TEHR-ah*
Where does this highway go to?	**¿Adónde va esta carretera?** *ah-DOHN-day bah ehs-tah kah-ray-TEHR-ah*

Is this the shortest way?	**¿Es éste el camino más corto?** *ehs EHS-tay ehl kah-MEE-noh mahs KOHR-toh*
Are there any detours?	**¿Hay desviaciones?** *AH-ee des-bee-ah-SYOHN-ays*
Do I go straight?	**¿Sigo derecho?** *see-goh deh-RAY-choh*
Do I turn to the right (to the left)?	**¿Doblo a la derecha (a la izquierda)?** *DOH-bloh ah lah deh-RAY-chah (ah lah ees-kee-YEHR-dah)*
How far is it from here to the next town?	**¿Cuánta distancia hay de aquí al primer pueblo?** *KWAHN-tah dees-TAHN-see-ah ah-ee day ah-KEE ahl pree-MEHR PWEH-bloh*
How far away is ____?	**¿A qué distancia está ____?** *ah kay dees-TAHN-see-ah ehs-tah*
Do you have a road map?	**¿Tiene usted un mapa de carreteras?** *tee-yehn-ay oos-TEHD oon MAH-pah day kahr-ray-TEHR-ahs*
Can you show it to me on the map?	**¿Puede indicármelo en el mapa?** *PWEH-day een-dee-KAHR-may-loh ehn ehl MAH-pah*

AT THE SERVICE STATION

Gasoline (petrol) is sold by the liter, and for the traveler accustomed to gallons, it may seem confusing, especially if you want to calculate your mileage per gallon (kilometer per liter). Here are some tips on making those conversions.

LIQUID MEASURES (Approximate)			
LITERS	GALLONS	LITERS	GALLONS
1	0.26	50	13.0
5	1.3	60	15.6
10	2.6	70	18.2
20	5.2	80	20.8
30	7.8	90	23.4
40	10.4	100	26.0

DISTANCE MEASURES (Approximate)			
KILOMETERS	MILES	KILOMETERS	MILES
1	0.62	30	18.6
5	3.1	35	21.7
10	6.2	40	24.8
15	9.3	45	27.9
20	12.4	50	31.1
25	15.5	100	62.1

Where is there a gas (petrol) station? **¿Dónde hay una estación de gasolina?** *DOHN-day AH-ee oo-nah ehs-tah-SYOHN day gahs-oh-LEE-nah*

Fill it up with ____. **Llénelo con ____.** *YAY-nay-loh kohn*
- diesel   **diesel** *dee-EH-sel*
- regular (90 octane)   **normal** *nohr-MAHL*
- super (96 octane)   **super** *SOO-pehr*
- extra (98 octane)   **extra** *EHS-trah*

Give me ____ liters. **Déme ____ litros.** *DAY-may LEE-trohs*

Please check _____.   **¿Quiere inspeccionar ___?** *kee-YEHR-ay eens-pehk-syohn-ahr*

▧ the battery   **la batería** *lah bah-tehr-EE-ah*

TIRE PRESSURE			
LB/SQ. IN.	KG/SQ. CM.	LB/SQ. IN.	KG/SQ. CM.
18	1.3	30	2.1
20	1.4	31	2.2
21	1.5	33	2.3
23	1.6	34	2.4
24	1.7	36	2.5
26	1.8	37	2.6
27	1.9	38	2.7
28	2.0	40	2.8

▧ the caburetor   **el carburador** *ehl kahr-boor-ah-DOHR*

▧ the oil   **el aceite** *ehl ah-SAY-tay*

▧ the spark plugs   **las bujías** *lahs boo-HEE-ahs*

▧ the tires   **las llantas, los neumáticos** *lahs YAHN-tahs lohs new-MAH-tee-kohs*

▧ the tire pressure   **la presión de las llantas** *lah preh-SYOHN day lahs YAHN-tahs*

▧ the antifreeze   **el agua del radiador** *ehl AH-gwah dehl rah-dee-ah-DOHR*

Change the oil.   **Cambie el aceite.** *KAHM-bee-ay ehl ah-SAY-tay*

Charge the battery.   **Cargue la batería.** *KAHR-gay lah bah-tehr-EE-ah*

Change the tire.   **Cambie esta llanta.** *KAHM-bee-ay ehs-tah YAHN-tah*

Wash the car.	**Lave el coche.** *LAH-bay ehl KOH-chay*

ACCIDENTS AND REPAIRS

My car has broken down.	**Mi coche se ha averiado.** *mee KOH-chay say ah ah-behr-ee-AH-doh*
It overheats.	**Se calienta demasiado.** *say kahl-YEN-tah day-mahs-ee-AH-doh*
It doesn't start.	**No arranca.** *noh ah-RAHN-kah*
I have a flat tire.	**Se me ha pinchado una rueda.** *say may ah peen-CHAH-doh oon-ah RWEH-dah*
The radiator is leaking.	**El radiador tiene un agujero.** *ehl rah-de-ah-dohr tee-YEHN-ay oon ah-goo-HEHR-oh*
The battery is dead.	**Tengo la batería descargada.** *ten-goh lah bah-tehr-EE-ah des-kahr-GAH-dah*
The keys are locked inside the car.	**Las puertas están cerradas con las llaves adentro.** *lahs PWEHR-tahs ehs-TAHN sehr-AH-dahs kohn lahs YAH-bays ah-DEN troh*
Is there a garage (repair shop) near here?	**¿Hay un garage (taller) por aquí?** *AH-ee oon gah-RAH-hay (tah-YEHR) pohr ah-KEE*
I need a mechanic (tow truck).	**Necesito on mecánico (remolcador).** *neh-seh-SEE-toh oon meh-KAHN-ee-koh (ray-mohl-kah-DOHR)*

Can you ____?	¿Puede usted ____? *PWEH-day oos-TEHD*
▪ give me a push	**empujarme** *ehm-poo-HAHR-may*
▪ help me	**ayudarme** *ah-yoo-DAHR may*

| I don't have any tools. | No tengo herramientas. *oh ten-goh ehr-ah-MYEHN-tahs* |

Can you lend me ____?	¿Puede usted prestarme ____? *PWEH-day oos-TEHD prehs-TAHR-may*
▪ a flashlight	**una linterna** *oo-nah leen-TEHR-nah*
▪ a hammer	**un martillo** *oon mahr-TEE-yoh*
▪ a jack	**un gato** *oon GAH-toh*
▪ a monkey wench	**una llave inglesa** *oo-nah YAH-beh een-GLAY-sah*
▪ pliers	**alicates** *ah-lee-KAH-tays*
▪ a screwdriver	**un destornillador** *oon des-tohrn-EE-yah-DOHR*

I need ____.	Necesito ____. *neh-seh-see-toh*
▪ a bolt	**un perno** *oon PEHR-noh*
▪ a bulb	**una bombilla** *oo-nah bohm-BEE-yah*
▪ a filter	**un filtro** *oon FEEL-troh*
▪ a nut	**una tuerca** *oo-nah TWEHR-kah*

| Can you fix the car? | ¿Puede usted arreglar el coche? *PWEH-day oos-TEHD ah-ray-GLAHR ehl KOH-chay* |

| Can you repair it temporarily? | ¿Puede repararlo temporalmente? *PWEH-day ray-pahr-AHR-loh tem-pohr-AHL-men-tay* |

Do you have the part?	**¿Tiene la pieza?** *tee-EHN-ay lah pee-ay-sah*
I think there's something wrong with ____.	**Creo que pasa algo con ____.** *KRAY-oh kay PAH-sah AHL-goh kohn*

■ the directional signal — **el indicador de dirección** *ehl een-dee-kah-DOHR day dee-rek-SYOHN*

■ the door handle — **el tirador de puerta** *ehl teer-ah-DOHR day PWEHR-tah*

■ the electrical system — **el sistema eléctrico** *ehl sees-TAY-mah eh-LEK-tree-koh*

■ the fan — **el ventilador** *ehl ben-tee-lah-DOHR*

■ the fan belt — **la correa de ventilador** *lah koh-ray-ah day ben-tee-lah-DOHR*

■ the fuel pump — **la bomba de gasolina** *lah BOHM-bah day gahs-oh-LEE-nah*

■ the gearshift — **el cambio de velocidad** *ehl KAHM-bee-oh day beh-loh-see-DAHD*

■ the headlight — **el faro delantero** *ehl fah-ROH deh-lahn-TEHR-oh*

■ the horn — **la bocina** *lah boh-SEEN-ah*

■ the ignition — **el encendido** *ehl ehn-sehn-DEE-doh*

■ the radio — **la radio** *lah RAH-dee-oh*

■ the starter — **el arranque** *ehl ah-RAHN-kay*

■ the steering wheel — **el volante** *ehl boh-LAHN-tay*

■ the taillight — **el faro trasero** *ehl fah-ROH trah-SEHR-oh*

■ the transmission — **la transmisión** *lah trahns-mee-SYOHN*

■ the water pump — **la bomba de agua** *lah BOHM-bah day AH-gwah*

■ the windshield (windscreen) wiper — **el limpiaparabrisas** *ehl LEEM-pee-ah-pah-rah-BREE-sahs*

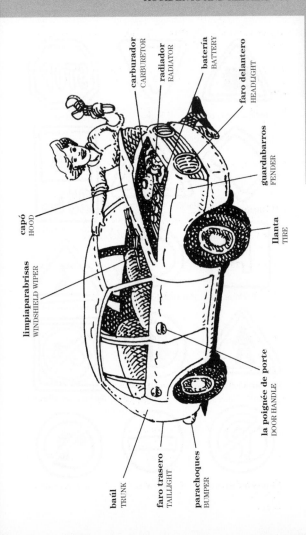

carburador
CARBURETOR

radiador
RADIATOR

batería
BATTERY

faro delantero
HEADLIGHT

guardabarros
FENDER

llanta
TIRE

la poignée de porte
DOOR HANDLE

capó
HOOD

limpiaparabrisas
WINDSHIELD WIPER

baúl
TRUNK

faro trasero
TAILLIGHT

parachoques
BUMPER

Guarded railroad crossing

Yield

Stop

Right of way

Dangerous intersection ahead

Gasoline (petrol) ahead

Parking

No vehicles allowed

Dangerous curve

Pedestrian crossing

Oncoming traffic has right of way

No bicycles allowed

No parking allowed

No entry

No left turn

No U-turn

No passing

Border crossing

Traffic signal ahead

Speed limit (kilometers)

Traffic circle (roundabout) ahead

Minimum speed limit (kilometers)

All traffic turns left

End of no passing zone

One-way street

Detour

Danger ahead

Entrance to expressway

Expressway ends

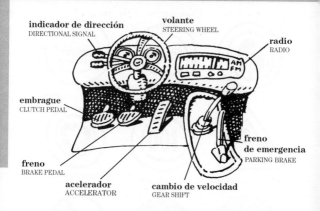

indicador de dirección
DIRECTIONAL SIGNAL

volante
STEERING WHEEL

radio
RADIO

embrague
CLUTCH PEDAL

**freno
de emergencia**
PARKING BRAKE

freno
BRAKE PEDAL

acelerador
ACCELERATOR

cambio de velocidad
GEAR SHIFT

Can you look at (check out) ____?	**¿Quiere mirar (revisar) ____?** *kee-YEHR-ay meer-AHR (reh-bee-SAHR)*
▦ the brakes	**los frenos** *lohs FRAY-nohs*
▦ the bumper	**el parachoques** *ehl pah-rah-CHOH-kays*
▦ the exhaust system	**el escape** *ehl ehs-KAH-pay*
▦ the fender	**el guardabarros** *ehl gwahr-dah-BAH-rohs*
▦ the gas tank	**el tanque** *ehl TAHN-kay*
▦ the hood	**el capó** *ehl kah-POH*
▦ the trunk (boot)	**el baúl** *ehl bah-OOL*
What's the matter?	**¿Qué pasa?** *kay PAH-sah*
Would it be possible to fix it today?	**¿Sería posible arreglarlo hoy?** *sehr-EE-ah poh-SEE-blay ah-ray-GLAHR-loh oy*

How long will it take?	**¿Cuánto tiempo tardará?** *KWAHN-toh tee-EHM-poh tahr-dahr-AH*
Thank you very much. How much do I owe you?	**Muchas gracias. ¿Cuánto le debo?** *moo-chas GRAH-see-yahs KWAHN-toh lay DEH-boh*

ENTERTAINMENT AND DIVERSIONS

MOVIES, THEATER, CONCERTS, OPERA, BALLET

To find out what's doing in Madrid, consult the daily newspaper *ABC*, under the heading **"Espectáculos";** *En Madrid*, a monthly English-Spanish leaflet available at the Madrid Tourist Office; or *Guía del Ocio* (Leisure Guide), a weekly listing of entertainment, hours, and admission fees.

The latest movies are at theaters along the Gran Vía in Madrid. The movies are dubbed into Spanish. Admission is usually 250 pesetas or less. Ushers should be tipped 5 pesetas.

There are 23 theaters in Madrid. **Teatro Zarzuela** is the most fun for tourists who are not well-versed in Spanish. Zarzuela consists of nineteenth-century light operas or operettas, with lots of music, dance, and pretty costumes. Classical Spanish theater can be seen at **Teatro Español** and **María Guerrero Theater.** Theater prices range from 200 to 1200 pesetas. Everything runs late in Spain. Matinees are at 7 or 7:30 P.M., evening performances are at 10:30 P.M.

Symphonic concerts can be heard at the beautiful ninteenth century **Teatro Real,** the Madrid Cultural Center auditorium, **Fundación Juan March,** or Sundays in the Plaza del Maestro Villa in Retiro Park. Pop, rock, and jazz music can be heard in many discos, certain movie theaters, college auditoriums, and at various bars and pubs. Check the above-mentioned listings to determine where and when.

Theater and concert schedules and procedures vary throughout the rest of the Spanish-speaking world, so we advise you to check with your hotel concierge or the tourist office in the town in which you are staying in order to find out what is going on and where to get tickets.

Let's go to the ____.	**Vamos al ____.** *BAH-mohs ahl*
▧ movies (cinema)	**cine** *SEE-nay*
▧ theater	**teatro** *tay-AH-troh*
What are they showing today?	**¿Qué ponen hoy?** *kay POH-nehn oy*
Is it a ____?	**¿Es ____?** *ehs*
▧ mystery	**un misterio** *oon mee-STEHR-ee-oh*
▧ comedy	**una comedia** *oo-nah koh-MEH-dee-ah*
▧ drama	**un drama** *oon DRAH-mah*
▧ musical	**una obra musical** *oo-nah OH-brah moo-see-KAHL*
▧ romance	**una obra romántica** *oo-nah OH-brah roh-MAHN-tee-kah*
▧ Western	**una película del Oeste** *oo-nah pehl-EE-koo-lah del OWEST-ay*
▧ war film	**una película de guerra** *oo-nah pehl-EE-koo-lah day GHEHR-ah*

■ science fiction
film

una película de ciencia ficción
oo-nah pehl-EE-koo-lah day see-EHN-see-ah feek-SYOHN

■ cartoon

una película de dibujos animados
oo-nah pehl-EE-koo-lah day dee-BOO-hohs ah-nee-MAH-dohs

Is it in English?

¿Es hablada en inglés? *ehs ah-BLAH-dah ehn een-GLAYSS*

Has it been dubbed?

¿Ha sido doblada? *ah SEE-doh doh-BLAH-dah*

Where is the box
office?

¿Dónde está la taquilla? *DOHN-day ehs-TAH lah tah-KEE-yah*

What time does the
(first) show begin?

¿A qué hora empieza la (primera) función? *ah kay OHR-ah ehm-PYEH-sah lah (pree-MEHR-ah) foon-SYOHN*

What time does the
(last) show end?

¿A qué hora termina la (última) función? *ah kay OHR-ah tehr-MEEN-ah lah (OOL-tee-mah) foon-SYOHN*

I want a seat near
the middle (front,
rear).

Quisiera un asiento en el centro (al frente, atrás). *kee-SYEHR-ah oon ah-SYEHN-toh ehn ehl SEHN-troh (ahl FREHN-tay ah-TRAHS)*

Can I check my
coat?

¿Puedo dejar mi abrigo? *PWEH-doh day-HAHR mee ah-BREE-goh*

BUYING TICKETS

I need two ____
tickets for tonight.

Necesito dos entradas ____ para esta noche. *neh-seh-SEE-toh dohs ehn-TRAH-dahs pah-rah ehs-tah NOH-chay*

■ orchestra

de platea *day plah-TAY-ah*

■ balcony

de galería *day gahl-ehr-EE-ah*

■ mezzanine | **de anfiteatro** *day ahn-fee-tay-AH-troh*

We would like to attend ___. | **Quisiéramos asistir a ___.** *kee-SYEHR-ah-mohs ah-sees-TEER ah*
■ a ballet | **un ballet** *oon bah-LEH*
■ a concert | **un concierto** *oon kohn-SYEHR-toh*
■ an opera | **una ópera** *oo-nah OH-pehr-ah*

What are they playing (singing)? | **¿Qué están interpretando?** *kay ehs-TAHN een-tehr-pray-TAHN-doh*

Who is the conductor? | **¿Quién es el director?** *kee-YEHN ehs ehl dee-rehk-TOHR*

I prefer ___. | **Prefiero ___.** *preh-fee-YEHR-oh*
■ classical music | **la música clásica** *lah MOO-see-kah KLAH-see-kah*
■ popular music | **la música popular** *lah MOO-see-kah poh-poo-LAHR*
■ folk dance | **el ballet folklórico** *ehl bah-LEH fohl-KLOHR-ee-koh*
■ ballet | **el ballet** *ehl bah-LEH*

Are there any seats for tonight's performance? | **¿Hay localidades para la representación de esta noche?** *AH-ee loh-kahl-ee-DAHD-ays pah-rah lah rep-reh-sen-tah-SYOHN day ehs-tah NOH-chay*

When does the season begin (end)? | **¿Cuándo empieza (termina la temporada?** *KWAHN-doh ehm-PYEH-sah (tehr-MEEN-ah) lah tem-pohr-AH-dah*

Should I get the tickets in advance? | **¿Debo sacar las entradas de antemano?** *deh-boh sah-KAHR lahs ehn-TRAH-dahs day ahn-tay-MAH-noh*

Do I have to dress formally?	**¿Tengo que ir de etiqueta?** *TEN-goh kay eer day eh-tee-KEH-tah*
How much are the front row seats?	**¿Cuánto vaten los asientos delanteros?** *KWAHN-toh bah-lehn lohs ahs-YEHN-tohs day-lahn-TEHR-ohs*
What are the least expensive seats?	**¿Cuáles son los asientos más baratos?** *KWAHL-ays sohn lohs ahs-YEHN-tohs mahs bah-RAH-tohs*
May I buy a program?	**¿Puedo comprar un programa?** *PWEH-doh kohm-PRAHR oon pro-GRAHM-ah*
What opera (ballet) are they performing?	**¿Qué ópera (ballet) ponen?** *kay OH-pehr-ah (bah-LEH) POH-nen*
Who's singing (tenor, soprano, baritone, contralto)?	**¿Quién canta (tenor, soprano, barítono, contralto)?** *kee-YEHN KAHN-tah (ten-OHR soh-PRAH-noh bah-REE-toh-noh kohn-TRAHL-toh)*

NIGHTCLUBS, DANCING

There are **discotecas** and nightclubs and big Las Vegas-type shows at some of the larger, new hotels. There are even a few satirical reviews in cafe settings. Madrid is now as wide-open after dark as any European capital, more so than some. You will find **flamenco** performed in small clubs, such as Café de Chintas, off the Gran Vía.

Hours at discos are approximately 7 P.M. to 3 A.M. Nightclub shows are at 11 P.M. or midnight or 1 A.M. **Tablao flamenco** places are open from 10 P.M. to 3 A.M., with shows at 12 and 1:30 or so. It is customary, but not required, to dine at the nightclub or flamenco place before the show, in which case you would arrive about 10 or 11 P.M., then stay for the midnight show.

Let's go to a nightclub	**Vamos a un cabaret.** *BAH-mohs ah oon kah-bah-REH*
Is a reservation necessary?	**¿Hace falta una reserva?** *ah-say FAHL-tah oo-nah reh-SEHR-bah*
Is it customary to dine there as well?	**¿Se puede comer allá también?** *say PWEH-day koh-MEHR ah-YAH tahm-BYEHN*
Is there a good discotheque here?	**¿Hay aquí una buena discoteca?** *AH-ee ah-KEE oo-nah BWEH-nah dees-koh-TAY-kah*
Is there dancing at the hotel?	**¿Hay un baile en el hotel?** *AH-ee oon BAH-ee-lay ehn ehl oh-TEL*
We'd like a table near the dance floor.	**Quisiéramos una mesa cerca de la pista.** *kee-SYEHR-ah-mohs oo-nah MAY-sah SEHR-kah day lah PEES-tah*
Is there a minimum (cover charge)?	**¿Hay un minimo?** *AH-ee oon MEE-nee-moh*
Where is the check-room?	**¿Dónde está el guardarropa?** *DOHN-day eh-STAH ehl gwahr-dah-ROH-pah*
At what time does the floor show go on?	**¿A qué hora empieza el espectáculo?** *ah kay OH-rah ehm-pee-EH-sah ehl ehs-peh-TAH-kool-oh*

QUIET RELAXATION

Tourists don't often take the time to relax, but you'll have a more enjoyable trip if you occasionally break from the sightseeing and have a quiet game. Also, games are an excellent way to occupy the children's spare time.

Where can I get a deck of cards?	**¿Dónde puedo conseguir una baraja?** *DOHN-day PWEH-doh kohn-seh-GHEER oo-nah bah-RAH-ha*
Do you want to play ____?	**¿Quiere usted jugar ____?** *kee-YEHR-ay oos-TEHD hoo-GAHR*
■ bridge	**al bridge** *ahl breech*
■ blackjack	**al veintiuno** *ahl bayn-ee-OO-noh*
■ poker	**al póker** *ahl POH-kehr*

BOARD GAMES

Do you want to play ____?	**¿Quiere jugar ____?** *kee-YEHR-ay hoo-GAHR*
■ checkers (draughts)	**a las damas** *ah lahs DAH-mahs*
■ chess	**al ajedrez** *ahl ah-hay-DREHS*
■ dominoes	**al dominó** *ahl dohm-ee-NOH*
We need a board (dice) (the pieces).	**Necesitamos un tablero (los dados) (las piezas).** *neh-ses-ee-TAH-mohs oon tah-BLEHR-oh (lohs DAH-dohs) (lahs pee-AY-sahs)*

SPECTATOR SPORTS

THE BULLFIGHT

The bullfight season in Spain runs from March to October. Sunday is the day, 5 or 7 P.M. the time. In Madrid there are two **plaza de toros**—the larger is Plaza de Toros Monumental de las Ventas, the smaller is Plaza de Toros de Vista Alegre. Ticket prices vary depending on sun or shade locations. You can purchase tickets through your hotel concierge, at the **plaza de toros,** or at the official city box office at 3 Calle de la Victoria.

If you have not seen a bullfight before, you may wish to reconsider, especially if you have children along. A growing number of people, including many Spaniards, view the **corrida** as too cruel and refuse to support it.

el matador	kills the bull with his **espada** (sword)
el banderillero	thrusts three sets of long darts (**banderillas**) into the bull's neck to enfuriate him
el picador	bullfighter mounted on a horse who weakens the bull with his lance (**pica**)
la cuadrilla	a team of helpers for the torero, who confuse and tire the bull with their capes (**capas**)
el monosabio	assistant who does various jobs in the **redondel** (bullring)
Is there a bullfight this afternoon? (every Sunday)?	**¿Hay una corrida de toros esta tarde (todos los domingos)?** *AH-ee oo-nah koh-REE-dah day TOH-rohs ehs-tah TAHR-day (toh-dohs lohs doh-MEEN-gohs)*
Take me to the bullring.	**Lléveme a la Plaza de Toros.** *YEH-bay-may ah lah PLAH-sah day TOHR-ohs*
I'd like a seat in the shade (in the sun).	**Quisiera un sitio a la sombra (al sol).** *kees-YEH-rah oon SEE-tee-oh ah lah SOHM-brah (ahl sohl)*
When does the parade of the bullfighters begin?	**¿Cuándo empieza el desfile de la cuadrilla?** *KWAHN-doh ehm-PYEH-sah ehl dehs-FEEL-ay day lah kwahd-REE-yah*
When does the first bull appear?	**¿Cuándo sale el primer toro?** *KWAHN-doh sah-lay ehl pree-MEHR TOH-roh*
Bravo!	**¡Ole!** *oh-LAY*

SOCCER

Soccer—called **fútbol**—is the most popular sport in Spain and Latin America. In season, between September to June, you're sure to find a game somewhere any Sunday at 5 P.M. Madrid has two teams: *Atlético de Madrid* plays in the Vicente Calderón Stadium and *Real Madrid* plays in Santiago Bernabeu Stadium. Tickets are available through your hotel concierge or at the stadium.

I'd like to watch a soccer match.	**Quisiera ver un partido de fútbol.** *kee-SYEHR-ah behr oon pahr-TEE-doh day FOOT-bohl*
Where's the stadium?	**¿Dónde está el estadio?** *DOHN-day ehs-TAH ehl ehs-TAH-dee-oh*
When does the first half begin?	**¿Cuándo empieza el primer tiempo?** *KWAHN-doh ehm-pee-EH-sah ehl pree-MEHR tee-EM-poh*
What teams are going to play?	**¿Qué equipos van a jugar?** *kay eh-KEE-pohs bahn ah hoo-GAHR*
What is the score?	**¿Cuál es la anotación?** *kwahl ehs lah ah-noh-tah-SYOHN*

JAI ALAI

Pelota *(jai alai)* is a very fast Basque game played in a court called a **frontón.** There are two teams of two players each. The players each have a **cesta** (curved basket) to throw and catch the ball with. During the match, spectators may place bets on the teams. Hours are 5:30 P.M. daily, in Spain.

Are you a jai alai fan?	**¿Es usted aficionado a la pelota?** *ehs oos-TEHD ah-fee-syohn-AH-doh ah lah pel-OH-tah*
I'd like to see a jai alai match.	**Me gustaría ver un partido de pelota.** *may goos-tahr-EE-ah behr oon par-TEE-doh day pel-OH-tah*

Where can I get tickets?	**¿Dónde puedo conseguir billetes?** *DOHN-day pweh-doh kohn-seh-GEER bee-YEH-tays*
Where is the jai alai court?	**¿Dónde está el frontón?** *DOHN-day ehs-TAH ehl frohn-TOHN*
Who are the players?	**¿Quiénes son los jugadores?** *kee-YEHN-ehs sohn lohs hoo-gah-DOHR-ays*
Where do I place my bet?	**¿Dónde hago la apuesta?** *DOHN-day ah-goh lah ah-PWEH-stah*
■ at that window	**en esa ventanilla** *ehn EH-sah ben-tah-NEE-yah*

HORSE RACING

There is no horse racing in Spain in the summer. In season, it is available at El Hipódromo de la Zarzuela on La Carretera de la Coruña.

Is there a racetrack here?	**¿Hay un hipódromo aquí?** *AH-ee oon ee-POH-droh-moh ah-KEE*
I want to see the races.	**Quiero ver las carreras de caballos.** *kee-EHR-oh behr lahs kahr-EHR-ahs day kah-BAH-yohs*

ACTIVE SPORTS

I like to ____.	**Me gusta ____.** *may GOOS-tah*
■ play baseball	**jugar béisbol** *hoo-GAHR BAYS-bohl*
■ play basketball	**jugar básquetbol** *hoo-GAHR BAHS-ket-bohl*
■ ride a bicycle	**andar en bicicleta** *ahn-DAHR en bee-see-KLEH-tah*

▨ go boating	**navegar**	*nah-bay-GAHR*
▨ go canoeing	**remar en canoa**	*ray-MAHR en kah-no-ah*
▨ fish	**pescar**	*pehs-KAHR*
▨ play football	**jugar fútbol americano**	*hoo-GAHR FOOT-bohl ah-mehr-ee-KAH-no*
▨ play golf	**jugar golf**	*hoo-GAHR gohlf*
▨ play hockey	**jugar hockey**	*hoo-GAHR HOH-kee*
▨ go horseback riding	**andar a caballo**	*ahn-DAHR ah kah-BAH-yo*
▨ hunt	**cazar**	*kah-SAHR*
▨ ice skate	**patinar sobre hielo**	*pah-tee-NAHR soh-breh YEH-loh*
▨ play jai alai	**jugar al jai alai**	*hoo-GAHR al HAH-ee ah-LAH-ee*
▨ jog	**hacer footing**	*ah-SEHR FOO-teen*
▨ go mountain climbing	**el alpinismo**	*ehl ahl-pee-NEES-moh*
▨ parasail	**volar en parapente**	*bo-LAHR en pahr-ah-PEN-teh*
▨ play ping-pong	**jugar pimpón**	*hoo-GAHR peem-POHN*
▨ roller skate	**patinar**	*pah-tee-NAHR*
▨ go sailing	**navegar a vela**	*nah-beh-GAHR ah BEH-lah*
▨ scuba dive	**bucear con escafandra**	*boo-say-AHR kohn es-kah-FAHN-drah*
▨ skate	**patinar**	*pah-tee-NAHR*
▨ ski	**esquiar**	*es-kee-AHR*
▨ play soccer	**jugar fútbol**	*hoo-GAHR FOOT-bohl*
▨ go surfing	**ir surfing**	*eer SOOR-feen*
▨ swim	**nadar**	*nah-DAHR*
▨ play tennis	**jugar tenis**	*hoo-GAHR TEN-ees*

■ do track and field	**hacer atletismo**	*ah-SEHR aht-let-EES-moh*
■ play volleyball	**jugar voleibol**	*hoo-GAHR bol-eh-BOHL*
■ waterski	**el esquí acuático**	*ehl es-KEE ah-KWAH-tee-koh*

PLAYING FIELDS

Shall we go to the ____?	**¿Vamos ____?**	*BAH-mohs*
■ beach	**a la playa**	*ah lah-PLAH-yah*
■ court	**al patio**	*ahl PAH-tee-yoh*
■ field	**a la cancha**	*ah lah KAHN-chah*
■ golf course	**al campo de golf**	*ahl KAHM-poh day gohlf*
■ gymnasium	**al gimnasio**	*ahl heem-NAH-see-yoh*
■ jai alai court	**a la cancha de jai alai**	*ah lah KAHN-chah day HA-ee ah-LAH-ee*
■ mountain	**a la montaña**	*ah lah mohn-TAHN-yah*
■ ocean	**al océano**	*ahl oh-SAY-ah-no*
■ park	**al parque**	*ahl PAHR-keh*
■ path	**al camino**	*ahl kah-MEE-no*
■ pool	**a la piscina**	*ah lah pee-SEE-nah*
■ rink	**a la pista de patinaje**	*ah lah PEES-tah day pah-tee-NAH-hay*
■ sea	**al mar**	*ahl MAHR*
■ stadium	**al estadio**	*ahl es-TAH-dee-yo*
■ track	**a la pista**	*ah lah PEES-tah*

SPORTS EQUIPMENT

I need a ____.   **Necesito ____.** *Neh-seh-SEE-toh*

- ball
  una pelota *oo-nah pel-OH-tah*
- bat
  un bate *oon BAH-tay*
- bicycle
  una bicicleta *oo-nah bee-see-KLAY-tah*
- boat
  un bote *oon BOTT-tay*
- canoe
  una canoa *oo-nah kah-NO-ah*
- diving suit
  un traje de buceo *oon trah-hay day boo-SAY-oh*
- fishing rod
  una caña de pescar *oo-nah KAHN-yah day pes-KAHR*
- flippers
  aletas *ah-LET-ahs*
- golf clubs
  palos de golf *pah-lohs day GOHLF*
- hockey stick
  un palo de hockey *oon pah-loh day HOH-kee*
- ice skates
  patines de hielo *pah-teen-ays day YEHL-oh*
- in-line skates
  patines en línea *pah-teen-ays ehn LEE-nay-ah*
- jogging shoes
  zapatillas de footing *sah-pah-TEE-yahs day FOO-teen*
- jogging suit
  un traje de footing *oon TRAH-hay day FOO-teen*
- kneepads
  rodilleras *roh-dee-YEHR-ahs*
- mitts
  mitones *mee-TOH-nays*
- net
  una red *oo-nah red*
- roller skates
  patines *pah-TEEN-ays*
- skateboard
  tabla de patinar *tah-blah day pah-tee-NAHR*
- ski bindings
  fijaciones de esquís *fee-hah-SYOH-nays day es-KEES*
- ski boots
  botas de esquí *boh-TAHS day es-KEE*

■ ski poles **bastones de esquí** *bahs-TOH-nays day es-KEE*

■ skis **esquís** *es-KEES*

■ surfboard **acuaplano** *ah-kwah-PLAH-no*

■ swimsuit **traje de baño** *trah-hay day BAHN-yoh*

■ waterskis **esquí acuático** *es-KEE ah-KWAH-tee-koh*

■ weights **pesas** *PEH-sahs*

Where is a safe place to run? **¿Dónde hay un sitio seguro para correr?** *DOHN-day AH-ee oon SEE-tee-oh seh-GOOR-oh pah-rah kohr-EHR*

Where is there a health club (spa)? **¿Dónde hay un gimnasio (balneario)?** *DOHN-day AH-ee oon heem-NAH-see-oh (bahl-nay-AHR-ee-oh)*

Where can I rent a (mountain, racing, touring) bike, in-line skates, a skateboard? **¿Dónde puedo alquilar una bicicleta (de montaña, de carrera, de turismo), patines en línea, una tabla de patinar?** *DOHN-day PWEH-doh ahl-kee-LAHR oo-nah bee-see-KLAY-tah (day mohn-TAH-nyah day kahr-REH-rah day toor-EES-moh) pah-TEE-nehs en LEE-neh-ah oo-nah TAH-blah day pah-tee-NAHR*

TENNIS

Do you play tennis? **¿Sabe usted jugar al tenis?** *SAH-bay oos-TEHD hoo-GAHR ahl TEN-ees*

I (don't) play very well. **(No) juego muy bien.** *(noh) hoo-AY-goh mwee bee-EHN*

Do you play singles (doubles)?	**¿Juega usted solo (en pareja)?** *HWAY-gah oos-TEHD SOH-loh (ehn pahr-AY-hah)*
Do you know where there is a court?	**¿Sabe usted dónde hay una cancha?** *SAH-bay oos-TEHD DOHN-day AH-ee oo-nah KAHN-chah*
Is it a private club? I'm not a member.	**¿Es un club privado? No soy socio.** *ehs oon kloob pree-BAH-do noh soy SOH-see-oh*
Can I rent a racquet?	**¿Se puede alquilar una raqueta?** *say PWEH-day ahl-kee-LAHR oo-nah rah-KAY-tah*
How much do they charge per hour (per day)?	**¿Cuánto cobran por hora (por día)?** *KWAHN-toh KOH-brahn pohr OH-rah (pohr DEE-ah)?*
Do you sell balls for a hard (soft) surface?	**¿Vende pelotas para una superficie dura (blanda)?** *BEN-day peh-LOH-tahs pah-rah oo-nah soo-pehr-FEE-syeh DOO-rah (BLAHN-dah)*
I serve (You serve) first.	**Yo saco (Usted saca) primero.** *yoh SAH-koh (oos-TEHD SAH-kah) pree-MEHR-oh*
You play very well.	**Usted juega muy bien.** *oos-TEHD hoo-EH-gah mwee bee-EHN*
You've won.	**Usted ha ganado.** *oos-TEHD oh gah-NAH-doh*

AT THE BEACH/POOL

Let's go to the beach (to the pool).	**Vamos a la playa (piscina).** *BAH-mohs ah lah PLAH-ee-ah (pee-SEEN-ah)*
Which bus will take us to the beach?	**¿Qué autobús nos lleva a la playa?** *kay AH-oo-toh-BOOS nohs yeh-bah oh lah PLAH-ee-ah*
Is there an indoor pool (outdoor) in the hotel?	**¿Hay una piscina cubierta (al aire libre) en el hotel?** *AH-ee oo-nah pee-SEE-nah ehn ehl oh-TEL*
I (don't) know how to swim well.	**(No) sé nadar bien.** *(noh) say nah-DAHR bee-EHN*
Is it safe to swim here?	**¿Se puede nadar aquí sin peligro?** *say PWEH-day nah-DAHR ah-KEE seen peh-LEE-groh*
Is it dangerous for children?	**¿Hay peligro para los niños?** *AH-ee pel-EE-groh pah-rah lohs NEEN-yohs*
Is there a lifeguard?	**¿Hay salvavidas?** *AH-ee sahl-bah-BEE-dahs*
Help! I'm drowning!	**¡Auxilio! ¡Socorro! ¡Me ahogo!** *owk-SEEL-yo so-COHR-oh may ah-OH-go*
Where can I get ____?	**¿Dónde puedo conseguir ____?** *DOHN-day PWEH-doh kohn-seh-GHEER*
■ an air mattress	**un colchón flotante** *oon kohl-CHOHN floh-tahn-tay*
■ a bathing suit	**un traje de baño** *oon trah-hay day BAHN-yoh*

▦ a beach ball	**una pelota de playa** *oo-nah pel-OH-tah day PLAH-ee-ah*
▦ a beach chair	**un sillón de playa** *oon see-YOHN day PLAH-ee-ah*
▦ a beach towel	**una toalla de playa** *oo-nah toh-AH-yah day PLAH-ee-yah*
▦ a beach umbrella	**una sombrilla playera** *oo-nah sohm-BREE-yah plah-YEHR-ah*
▦ diving equipment	**equipo de buceo** *eh-KEE-poh day boo-SAY-oh*
▦ sunglasses	**gafas de sol** *GAH-fahs day sohl*
▦ suntan lotion	**loción para broncear** *loh-SYOHN pah-rah brohn-SAY-ahr*

ON THE SLOPES

The main ski areas in Spain are the Pyrenees, the Guadarrama mountains, the Sierra Nevada, and the Cantabrian mountains. **Pistas** (ski runs) are marked with colored arrows according to their difficulty.

Green	very easy slopes
Blue	easy slopes
Red	difficult slopes for experienced skiers
Black	very difficult slopes for professionals

In South America, skiing choices are very limited. Most skiers head for the Andes, for resorts in Argentina and Chile.

| Which ski area do you recommend? | **¿Qué sitio de esquiar recomienda usted?** *kay SEE-tee-oh day ehs-kee-AHR ray-koh-MYEHN-dah oos-TEHD* |

I am a novice (intermediate, expert) skier.	**Soy principiante (intermedio, experto).** *soy preen-seep-YAHN-tay (een-tehr-MEHD-ee-oh ehs-PEHR-toh)*
Is there enough snow at this time of year?	**¿Hay bastante nieve durante esta temporada?** *AH-ee bahs-TAHN-tay nee-EHB-ay door-ahn-tay ehs-tah temp-ohr-AH-dah*
How would I get to that place?	**¿Por dónde se va a ese sitio?** *pohr DOHN-day say bah ah eh-say SEE-tee-oh*
Can I rent ____ there?	**¿Puedo alquilar ____?** *PWEH-doh ahl-kee-lahr*
■ equipment	**equipo** *eh-KEEP-oh*
■ poles	**palos** *PAH-lohs*
■ skis	**esquís** *ehs-KEES*
■ ski boots	**botas de esquiar** *BOH-tahs day ehs-kee-AHR*

Do they have ski lifts?	**¿Tienen funicular?** *TYEHN-eh foo-nee-koo-LAHR*
How much does the lift cost?	**¿Cuánto cobran?** *KWAHN-toh KOH-brahn*
Do they give lessons?	**¿Dan lecciones?** *dahn lek-SYOHN-ays*
Where can I stay?	**¿Dónde puedo alojarme?** *DOHN-day PWEH-doh ah-loh-HAHR-may*

ON THE LINKS

Is there a golf course?	**¿Hay un campo de golf?** *AH-ee oon KAHM-poh day gohlf*
Can one rent clubs?	**¿Se puede alquilar los palos?** *say PWEH-day ahl-kee-LAHR lohs PAH-lohs*

CAMPING

There are over 700 campgrounds in Spain. About 500 are located along the coast. Many of them have excellent facilities such as swimming pools, sport areas, restaurants, and supermarkets. The Spanish National Tourist Office furnishes a list of approved campsites.

Campsites (**campamentos**) are classified as follows.

de lujo	luxury
primera clase	first class
segunda clase	second class
tercera clase	third class

In parts of Latin America, a tourist must have a permit to camp, and camping only in designated sites is recommended.

Is there a camping area near here?	**¿Hay un camping cerca de aquí?** *AH-ee oon KAHM-peeng sehr-kah day ah-KEE*
Do we pick our own site?	**¿Escogemos nuestro propio sitio?** *ehs-koh-HAY-mohs NWEHS-troh PROH-pee-oh SEE-tee-oh*
We only have a tent.	**Tenemos solo una tienda.** *ten-AY-mohs SOH-loh oo-nah TYEHN-dah*
Can we camp for one night only?	**¿Se puede acampar por una noche sola?** *say PWEH-day ah-kahm-pahr pohr oo-nah noh-chay SOH-lah*
Can we park our trailer (our caravan)?	**¿Podemos estacionar nuestro coche-vivienda (nuestra caravana)?** *poh-DAY-mos eh-stah-syohn-AHR nwehs-troh KOH-chay bee-bee-EHN-dah (NWEHS-trah kahr-ah-BAHN-ah)*
Is (are) there ____?	**¿Hay ____?** *AH-ee*
■ camp guards	**guardias de campamento** *GWAHR-dee-yahs day kahm-pah-MEN-toh*
■ a children's playground	**un parque infantil** *oon PAHR-kay een-fahn-TEEL*
■ cooking facilites	**instalaciones para cocinar** *een-stah-lah-SYOHN-ays pah-rah koh-see-NAHR*
■ drinking water	**agua potable** *AH-gwah poh-TAH-blay*
■ electricity	**electricidad** *eh-lek-tree-see-DAHD*
■ fireplaces	**hogueras** *oh-GEHR-ahs*
■ flush toilets	**servicios** *sehr-BEE-see-ohs*

■ a grocery store	**una tienda de comestibles** *oo-nah tee-EHN-dah day koh-mes-TEE-blays*
■ picnic tables	**mesas de camping** *may-sahs day KAHM-peeng*
■ showers	**duchas** *DOO-chahs*
How much do they charge per person (per car)?	**¿Cuánto cobran por persona (por coche)?** *KWAHN-toh KOH-brahn pohr pehr-SOHN-ah (pohr koh-chay)*
We intend staying ____ days (weeks).	**Pensamos quedamos ____ días (semanas).** *pen-SAH-mohs kay-DAHR-nohs DEE-ahs (seh-MAHN-ahs)*

IN THE COUNTRYSIDE

Are there tours to the countryside?	**¿Hay excursiones al campo?** *AH-ee ehs-koor-SYOHN-ays ahl KAHM-poh*
What a beautiful landscape!	**¡Qué paisaje tan bonito!** *kay pah-ee-SAH-hay tahn boh-NEE-toh*
Look at ____.	**Mire ____.** *MEER-ay*
■ the barn	**el granero** *ehl grah-NEHR-oh*
■ the birds	**los pájaros** *lohs PAH-hahr-ohs*
■ the bridge	**el puente** *ehl PWEHN-tay*
■ the cottages	**las casitas** *lahs kah-SEE-tahs*
■ the farm	**la granja** *lah GRAHN-hah*
■ the fields	**los campos** *lohs KAHM-pohs*
■ the flowers	**las flores** *lahs FLOHR-ays*
■ the forest	**el bosque** *ehl BOHS-kay*
■ the hill	**la colina** *lah koh-LEE-nah*
■ the lake	**el lago** *ehl LAH-goh*

■ the mountains	**las montañas** *lahs mohn-TAHN-yahs*
■ the ocean	**el mar** *ehl mahr*
■ the plants	**las plantas** *lahs PLAHN-tahs*
■ the pond	**el estanque** *ehl ehs-TAHN-kay*
■ the river	**el río** *ehl REE-oh*
■ the stream	**el arroyo** *ehl ah-ROY-yoh*
■ the trees	**los árboles** *lohs AHR-boh-lays*
■ the valley	**el valle** *ehl BAH-yeh*
■ the village	**el pueblo** *ehl PWEHB-loh*
■ the waterfall	**la catarata** *lah kah-tahr-AH-tah*

Where does this path lead to?

¿Adónde lleva el sendero? *ah-DOHN-day YEH-bah ehl sen-DEHR-oh*

These gardens are beautiful.

Estos jardines son lindos. *EHS-tohs hahr-DEEN-ays sohn LEEN-dohs*

How long does it take to get to ____?

¿Cuánto tiempo toma para llegar a ____? *KWAHN-toh TYEHM-poh TOH-mah pah-rah yehg-AHR ah*

I am lost.

Estoy perdido(a). *es-TOY pehr-DEE-doh(dah)*

Can you show me the road to ____?

¿Puede usted mostrarme el camino a ____? *PWEH-day oos-TED mohs-TRAHR-may ehl kah-MEE-no ah*

FOOD AND DRINK

The Spanish-speaking world is a vast one, so any information on its food is, of necessity, very general. There are many similarities between the foods and eating habits of Spain and those of Latin America, since Latin American culture was largely shaped by Spanish invaders. Likewise, foods were brought back from the New World and rapidly incorporated into the cooking in Spain. But Latin American cooking is also greatly influenced by the preferences of its ancient peoples—the Incas, Aztecs, and Mayans. To sort all this out most clearly for you, we have divided the information in this chapter into two portions when appropriate: one for references to Spain, and the other for information on Latin America. Of the latter, most tips pertain to Mexico, with only minor variations for the remainder of Latin America.

IN SPAIN

Spanish restaurants are officially ranked from 5-fork (luxury) to 1-fork (4th class). The ratings—which you will see designated by forks on a sign outside each establishment—are based on the number of dishes served in specific categories, not on the quality of the establishment.

Dining hours in Spain, except for breakfast, are late: the midday meal, **comida,** is served from 1:30 to 4 P.M., dinner, **cena,** from 8:30 P.M. to midnight. Outside Madrid, the hours are a little earlier. Restaurants post their menus outside their doors, so you may study the menu and make your decision before entering.

Madrid, as Spain's capital, has restaurants specializing in the cuisine of all its regions. You will find restaurants with Basque, Catalan, Galician, Asturian, Andalusian, and other specialties. Madrid, as the center of Castile, naturally has a wide number of Castilian restaurants, where roast pork and roast lamb are the premier specialties.

Some pointers about dining out in Spain: Spaniards customarily do their drinking and have their aperitifs in a bar or **tasca,** usually standing and socializing, before going into a restaurant to sit down and dine. Drinking at the table usually

■ a soup spoon	**una cuchara de sopa**	*oo-nah koo-CHAH-rah day SOH-pah*
■ a glass	**un vaso**	*oon BAH-soh*
■ a cup	**una taza**	*oo-nah TAH-sah*
■ a saucer	**un platillo**	*oon plah-TEE-yoh*
■ a plate	**un plato**	*oon PLAH-toh*
■ a napkin	**una servilleta**	*oo-nah sehr-bee-YEH-tah*

APPETIZERS (STARTERS)

Tapas (bar snacks) are very popular in Spain. For a listing of typical tapas, see page 149, given with information on food specialties. The following are items you are likely to see on a restaurant menu.

alcachofas	artichokes
almejas	clams
anguilas ahumadas	smoked eels
calamares	squid
caracoles	snails
champiñones	mushrooms
chorizo	spicy sausage, usually pork
cigalás	crayfish
gambas (Spain only)	shrimp
huevos	eggs
jamón serrano (Spain only)	cured ham

melón	melon
moluscos	mussels
ostras (ostiones)	oysters
quisquillas (Spain only)	small shrimp
sardinas	sardines

And in Latin America, there would be some of the following:

camarones	shrimp
guacamole	puréed avocado spread
tostadas	tortilla chips with various pepper and cheese toppings

SOUPS

Soups are wonderful, whether you are enjoying them in Spain or Latin America.

gazpacho	a highly variable purée of fresh, uncooked vegetables, including cucumbers, peppers, onions, and tomatoes; served cold
potaje madrileño	a thick soup of puréed chick peas, cod, and spinach
sopa de ajo	garlic soup
sopa de cebolla	onion soup
sopa de fideos	noodle soup
sopa de mariscos	seafood soup

sopa de gambas	shrimp soup
sopa de albóndigas	soup with meatballs
sopa de pescado	fish soup
sopa de verduras	soup made from puréed greens and vegetables

In Latin America, particularly Mexico, you are also likely to find:

cazuela	a spicy soup-stew, simmered for a long time in an earthenware pot; can be fish, vegetables, or meat
pozole	a hearty pork and hominy stew
sopa de aguacate	creamed avocado soup
sopa de huitlacoche	black corn soup made from the fungus that grows on corn cobs

ENTREES (MEAT AND FISH DISHES)

The main course of a meal in Spain is likely to be meat if you are inland and seafood if you are along the coast. First the meat.

carne de	*KAHR-nay day*	meat of
■ **buey**	*bway*	beef
■ **cabrito**	*kah-BREE-toh*	goat (kid)
■ **carnero**	*kahr-NEHR-oh*	mutton
■ **cerdo**	*SEHR-doh*	pork
■ **cordero**	*kohr-DEHR-oh*	lamb
■ **ternera**	*tehr-NEHR-ah*	veal
■ **vaca, res**	*BAH-kah rehs*	beef

Some common cuts of meat, plus other terms you'll find on a menu.

albóndigas	*ahl-BOHN-dee-gahs*	meatballs
bistec	*bees-TEHK*	beef steak
carne picada	*kahr-nay pee-KAH-dah*	ground (minced) meat
chuletas	*choo-LEH-tahs*	chops
churrasco	*choo-RAHS-koh*	charcoal-grilled steak
cocido	*koh-SEE-doh*	stew
costilla	*kohs-TEE-yah*	cutlet
corazón	*koh-rah-SOHN*	heart
criadillas	*kree-ah-DEE-yahs*	sweetbreads
filete	*fee-LEH-tay*	filet
hígado	*EE-gah-doh*	liver
jamón	*ha-MOHN*	ham
lechón	*leh-CHOHN*	suckling pig
lengua	*LEN-gwah*	tongue
morcilla	*mohr-SEE-yah*	blood sausage
rabo de buey	*RAH-boh day BWAY*	oxtails
riñones	*reen-YOH-nays*	kidneys
salchichas	*sahl-CHEE-chahs*	sausages

sesos	*SAY-sohs*	brains
solomillo	*soh-loh-MEE-yoh*	pork tenderloin steak
tocino	*toh-SEE-noh*	bacon
tripas	*TREE-pahs*	tripe

You won't always recognize the types of fish available, since the waters around Spain or the Latin American countries are generally warmer, with more tropical varieties. Here is a general guide, with our advice that you sample what's offered and discover new types that you like.

almejas	*ahl-MAY-has*	clams
anchoas	*ahn-CHOH-ahs*	anchovies
anguilas	*ahn-GHEE-lahs*	eels
arenque, ahumado	*ah-REHN-kay ah-oo-MAH-doh*	smoked herring
atún	*ah-TOON*	tuna
bacalao	*bah kah-LAH-oh*	codfish
besugo	*beh-SOO-goh*	sea bream
boquerones	*boh-keh-ROH-nehs*	whitebait
caballa	*kah-BAH-yah*	mackerel
calamares	*kahl-ah-MAHR-ayss*	squid
camarones	*kah-mah-ROH-nayss*	shrimp
cangrejos	*kahn-GRAY-hohs*	crabs

caracoles	*kahr-ah-KOH-layss*	snails
cigalas	*see-GAH-lahs*	large crayfish
congrio	*KOHN-gree-oh*	conger eel
gambas	*GAHM-bahs*	large shrimp
lampreas	*lahm-PRAY-ahs*	lamprey
langosta	*lahn-GOH-stah*	spiny lobster
langostino	*lahn-gohs-TEE-noh*	small crayfish
lenguado	*len-GWAH-doh*	flounder, sole
mejillones	*meh-hee-YOH-nayss*	mussels
mújol	*MOO-hohl*	mullet
merluza	*mehr-LOOS-ah*	bass, hake
pescadilla	*pehs-kah-DEE-yah*	whiting
pulpo	*POOL-poh*	octopus
quesquillas	*kehs-KEE-yahs*	shrimp
rape	*RAH-pay*	monkfish, anglerfish
salmón	*sahl-MOHN*	salmon
sardinas	*sahr-DEE-nahs*	sardines
trucha	*TROO-chah*	trout

And some terms for fowl and game:

capón	*kah-POHN*	capon

codorniz	*koh-dohr-NEES*	quail
conejo	*kohn-AY-hoh*	rabbit
faisán	*fah-ee-SAHN*	pheasant
ganso	*GAHN-soh*	goose
pato	*PAH-toh*	duck
pavo	*PAH-boh*	turkey
perdiz	*pehr-DEES*	partridge
pichón	*pee-CHOHN*	squab
pollo	*POH-yoh*	chicken
venado	*beh-NAH-doh*	venison

Is the meat ____?	**¿Es carne ____?** *ehs KAHR-nay*
baked	**al horno** *ahl OHR-noh*
boiled	**guisada** *ghee-SAH-dah*
braised (stewed)	**estofada** *ehs-toh-FAH-dah*
broiled	**a la parrilla** *ah lah pahr-EE-yah*
roasted	**asada** *ah-SAH-dah*
poached	**escalfada** *ehs KAHL-fah-dah*

I like the meat ____.	**Me gustaría la carne ____.** *may goos-tah-REE-ah lah KAHR-nay*
well done	**bien hecha** *bee-EHN EH-chah*
medium	**término medio** *TEHR-mee-noh MED-yoh*
rare	**poco hecha** *POH-koh EH-chah*
tender	**tierna** *tee-EHR-nah*

RICE DISHES

Rice forms the foundation of several dishes in Spain, especially **paella.** This specialty varies with the region, but always features saffron-flavored rice. You are likely to see it on a menu in any of these forms.

a la campesina	with ham, chicken, sausage, and small game birds
a la catalana	with sausages, pork, squid, chilies, and peas, or with chicken, snails, beans, and artichokes
alicantina	with rabbit, mussels, and shrimp
bruta	with pork, chicken, and whitefish
de mariscos	with crayfish, anglerfish, and other seafood
valenciana	with chicken, seafood, peas, and tomatoes—the most well-known version

TORTILLA-BASED DISHES

In Mexico particularly, the **tortilla** forms the basis for many dishes; this flat cornmeal cake is roughly the equivalent of bread there, and it is served along with some dishes as well as a main dish, rolled and stuffed, layered with other ingredients and sauced, and fried until crisp. Here are some of the items you'll see on menus featuring tortilla dishes.

chalupas	tortillas that have been curled at the edges and filled with cheese or a ground pork filling, served with a green chili sauce
chilaquiles	layers of tortillas, alternated with beans, meat, chicken, and cheese, then baked

enchiladas	soft corn tortillas rolled around meat and topped with sauce and melted cheese
flautas	sort of a tortilla sandwich that is then rolled and deep-fried
quesadillas	tortillas that are stuffed with cheese and deep-fried
tacos	crisp toasted tortillas stuffed with a variety of fillings (chopped beef, refried beans, turkey, chicken) topped with shredded lettuce, cheese, and sauce

SALADS

In Spain, salads are often part of the appetizer and consist of a zesty mixture of seafood or vegetables. In Latin America, the salad is frequently served along with the main course. (Tourists should be wary of ordering salads of raw vegetables or greens, since these items may have been washed in water that has not been treated for bacteria.) Here are some useful terms for ordering salads.

aceitunas	*ah-say-TOO-nahs*	olives
lechuga	*leh-CHOO-gah*	lettuce
pepino	*pep-EE-noh*	cucumber
tomate	*toh-MAH-tay*	tomato

EGG DISHES

In Spain, eggs are not usually eaten as a breakfast food, and when served usually are in an omelet (**tortilla**) with other ingredients such as ham, potatoes, peppers, shrimp, or mushrooms. Eggs are also served baked with a tomato sauce, or boiled with fish, or scrambled with vegetables.

eggs	**huevos**	*WEH-bohs*
omelet	**tortilla**	*tohr-TEE-yah*

In Latin America, if you want an omelet you can ask for a **tortilla** but in Mexico you are more likely to get a cornmeal cake. When in Mexico, ask for a **tortilla de huevo.** As for other egg preparations, you will be better off with an English (American) breakfast.

fried eggs	**huevos fritos**	*WEH-bohs FREE-tohs*
hard-boiled eggs	**huevos duros**	*WEH-bohs DOOR-ohs*
scrambled eggs	**huevos revueltos**	*WEH-bohs ray-BWEHL-tohs*
soft-boiled eggs	**huevos pasados por agua**	*WEH-bohs pah-SAH-dohs pohr AH-gwah*

On a menu, you are likely to see:

huevos con chorizo eggs with a spicy sausage

huevos rancheros fried eggs on a tortilla, served with spicy ranchero sauce (chopped green peppers, tomatoes and onions) and guacomole or sliced avocado.

VEGETABLES

alcachofas	*ahl-kah-CHOH-fahs*	artichokes
apio	*AH-pee-oh*	celery
berenjena	*behr-ehn-HAY-nah*	eggplant (aubergine)
calabacín	*kah-lah-bah-SEEN*	zucchini

cebollas	*seh-BOH-yahs*	onions
col	*kohl*	cabbage
coliflor	*kohl-ee-FLOHR*	cauliflower
espinacas	*eh-spee-NAH-kahs*	spinach
espárragos	*ehs-PAHR-ah-gohs*	asparagus
champiñones	*chahm-peen-YOH-nays*	mushrooms
garbanzos	*gahr-BAHN-sohs*	chickpeas
guisantes	*ghee-SAHN-tays*	peas
judías	*hoo-DEE-ahs*	green beans
papas, patatas	*PAH-pahs pah-TAH-tahs*	potatoes
■ **papas fritas**	*PAH-pahs FREE-tahs*	french fries
pimiento	*pee-MYEHN-toh*	pepper
puerros	*PWEHR-ohs*	leeks
maíz	*mah-EES*	corn
tomate	*toh-MAH-tay*	tomato
zanahorias	*sah-nah-OHR-ee-ahs*	carrots

In parts of Latin America you are likely also to see the following on a menu:

chile	*CHEE-lay*	chili peppers, of any variety (see pages 141–142)

frijoles	*free-HOH-lays*	beans, usually kidney or pinto
huitlacoche	*WEET-lah-koh-chay*	corn fungus
nopalito	*noh-pah-LEE-toh*	prickly pear cactus
yuca	*YOO-kah*	root vegetable, from yucca plant

SEASONINGS AND CONDIMENTS

Seasonings in Spain tend to be lively but not fiery hot. Personal preferences sometimes intercede, however, and you might want something additional for your meal. Here's how to ask for what you want.

butter	**la mantequilla** *lah mahn-teh-KEE-yah*
horseradish	**el rábano picante** *ehl RAH-bah-noh pee-KAHN-tay*
lemon	**el limón** *ehl lee-MOHN*
margarine	**la margarina** *lah mahr-gahr-EE-nah*
mayonnaise	**la mayonesa** *lah mah-ee-oh-NAY-sah*
mustard	**la mostaza** *lah mohs-TAH-sah*
oil	**el aceite** *ehl ah-SAY-tay*
pepper (black)	**la pimienta** *lah pee-mee-EHN-tah*
pepper (red) (Spain only)	**el pimiento** *ehl pee-mee-EHN-toh*
pepper (red) (Latin America)	**ají** *ah-HEE*

salt	**la sal** *lah sahl*
sugar	**el azúcar** *ehl ah-SOO-kahr*
saccharine	**la sacarina** *lah sah-kah-REE-nah*
vinegar	**el vinagre** *ehl bee-NAH-gray*
Worchestershire sauce	**la salsa inglesa** *lah SAHL-sah een-GLAY-sah*

In Latin America, foods tend to be more heavily spiced, especially in Mexico. Here are some terms you might encounter on menus, describing the dish in terms of its major flavoring.

achiote	*ah-chee-OH-tay*	annatto
albahaca	*ahl-bah-AH-kah*	basil
azafrán	*ah-sah-FRAHN*	saffron
cilantro	*see-LAHN-troh*	coriander
orégano	*oh-REH-ga-noh*	oregano
romero	*roh-MEHR-oh*	rosemary

Descriptions of the different types of chilies could fill an entire book. Here we will mention a few of the major ones likely to be seen on menus.

ancho	mild to hot, with mild most common
chipotle	medium hot to hot, with a smokey flavor
jalapeño	hot, with a meaty flavor
pasilla	mild to medium hot, with a rich sweet flavor

pequín	hot
pimiento	sweet bell pepper
poblano	mild to hot, with a rich flavor
serrano	hot to very hot, with a bright flavor

And in sauces, you'll find:

salsa cruda	an uncooked tomato sauce, often served as a dip or table seasoning
salsa de tomatillo	delicate sauce made from Mexican green tomatoes (a husk tomato unlike the regular red tomato)
salsa de perejil	parsley sauce
ají de queso	cheese sauce
adobo	sauce made with ancho and pasilla chilies, sesame seeds, nuts, and spices
mole	a sauce of varying ingredients, made from chilies, sesame seeds, cocoa, and spices
pipián	sauce made from pumpkin seeds, chilies, coriander, and bread crumbs
verde	sauce of green chilies and green tomatoes

Oftentime, the Mexicans drink **atole,** a cornmeal drink that resembles a milk shake, with spicy foods. It is commonly served in a large pitcher for all at the table to drink.

DESSERTS—SWEETS

Desserts are not extensive in Spanish-speaking countries, but here are a few items that you may be offered.

arroz con leche	*ah-ROHS kohn LEH-chay*	rice pudding
crema catalana or **flan**	*krem-ah kah-tah-LAN-nah* or *flahn*	caramel custard
galletas	*gah-YEH-tahs*	cookies (biscuits)
helado	*ay-LAH-doh*	ice cream
■ **de chocolate**	*day cho-koh-LAH-tay*	chocolate
■ **de pistacho**	*day pees-TAH-choh*	pistachio
■ **de vainilla**	*day bah-ee-NEE-yah*	vanilla
■ **de nueces**	*day NWEH-says*	walnut
■ **de fresa**	*day FRAY-sah*	strawberry
mazapán	*mah-sah-PAHN*	marzipan
merengue	*meh-REHN-gay*	meringue
natilla	*nah-TEE-yah*	cream pudding
pastel	*pahs-TEHL*	pastry
tarta	*TAHR-tah*	tart, usually fruit

FRUITS AND NUTS

What kind of fruit do you have?	**¿Qué frutas tiene?**	*kay FROO-tahs tee-YEHN-ay*
albaricoque	*ahl-bahr-ee-KOH-kay*	apricot
banana, plátano	*bah-NAH-nah PLAH-ta-noh*	banana, plantain (green banana)

cereza	*sehr-AY-sah*	cherry
ciruela	*seer-WEH-lah*	plum
coco	*KOH-koh*	coconut
dátil	*DAH-teel*	date
frambuesa	*frahm-BWEH-sah*	raspberry
fresa	*FRAY-sah*	strawberry
guayaba	*gwah-ee-AH-bah*	guava
higo	*EE-goh*	fig
jicama	*hee-KAH-mah*	jicama
lima	*LEE-mah*	lime
limón	*lee-MOHN*	lemon
mandarina	*mahn-dahr-EE-nah*	tangerine
mango	*MAHN-goh*	mango
manzana	*mahn-SAH-nah*	apple
melocotón	*mel-oh-koh-TOHN*	peach
melón	*meh-LOHN*	melon
naranja	*nah-RAHN-hah*	orange
pera	*PEH-rah*	pear
piña	*PEEN-yah*	pineapple
pomelo	*poh-MEH-loh*	grapefruit

sandía	*sahn-DEE-ah*	watermelon
tuna	*TOO-nah*	prickly pear
uva	*OO-bah*	grape

For some common varities of nuts:

almendras	*ahl-MEN-drahs*	almonds
castañas	*kahs-TAHN-yahs*	chestnuts
avellanas	*ah-bay-YAHN-ahs*	hazelnuts (filberts)
nueces	*NWEH-sayss*	walnuts

SPECIAL CIRCUMSTANCES

Many travelers have special dietary requirements, so here are a few phrases that might help you get what you need or avoid what does you wrong.

I am on a diet.	**Estoy en dieta.** *es-TOY en DYEH-tah*
I am a vegetarian.	**Soy vegetariano(a).** *soy beh-heh-tahr-ee-YAH-no(nah)*
I want a dish ____.	**Quiero un plato ____.** *KYEHR-oh oon PLAH-toh*
◾ high in fiber	**con mucha fibra** *kohn MOO-chah FEE-brah*
◾ low in cholesterol	**con poco colesterol** *kohn POH-koh koh-les-tehr-OHL*
◾ low in fat	**con poca grasa** *kohn POH-kah GRAH-sah*
◾ low in sodium	**con poco contenido de sodio** *kohn POH-koh kohn-ten-EE-doh day SO-dee-oh*

◼ nondairy	**sin productos lácteos** *seen pro-DOOK-tohs LAHK-tay-ohs*
◼ salt-free	**sin sal** *seen sahl*
◼ sugar-free	**sin azúcar** *seen ah-SOO-kahr*
◼ without artificial coloring	**sin colorantes artificiales** *seen koh-lohr-AHN-tays ahr-tee-fee-SYAHL-ays*
◼ without preservatives	**sin preservativos** *seen pray-sehr-bah-TEE-bohs*
◼ without garlic	**sin ajo** *seen AH-ho*

I don't want anything fried (salted).	**No quiero nada frito (salado).** *noh kee-YEHR-oh nah-dah FREE-toh (sah LAH-doh)*
Do you have anything that is not spicy?	**¿Tiene algo que no sea picante?** *tee-YEHN-ay AHL-goh kay noh SAY-ah pee-KAHN-tay*
Do you have any dishes without meat?	**¿Tiene platos sin carne?** *tee-YEHN-ay PLAH-tohs seen KAHR-nay*

BEVERAGES

See pages 150–151 for information on Spanish wines and liquors. As for other beverages, we give you the following phrases to help you ask for exactly what you wish.

Waiter, please bring me ____.	**Camarero, tráiganos por favor ____.** *kah-mah-REHR-oh, TRAH-ee-gah-nohs pohr fah-BOHR*
coffee	**café** *kah-FAY*
◼ black coffee	**café solo** *kah-FAY SOH-loh*
◼ with cream	**café con crema** *kah-FAY kohn KRAY-mah*
◼ with milk	**un cortado** *oon kohr-TAH-doh*

■ espresso	**un exprés (un expreso)** *oon ehs-PRESS (oon ehs-PRESS-oh)*
■ half coffee/half milk (drunk in morning)	**café con leche** *kah-FAY kohn LEH-chay*
■ iced coffee	**café helado** *kah FAY eh-LAH-doh*
tea	**té** *tay*
■ with milk	**con leche** *kohn LEH-chay*
■ with lemon	**con limón** *kohn lee-MOHN*
■ with sugar	**con azúcar** *kohn ah-SOO-kahr*
■ iced tea	**té helado** *tay eh-LAH-doh*
chocolate (hot)	**chocolate** *choh-koh-LAH-tay*
water	**agua** *AH-gwah*
■ cold	**agua fría** *AH-gwah FREE-ah*
■ ice	**agua helada** *AH-gwah ay-LAH-dah*
■ mineral, with gas (without gas)	**agua mineral, con gas (sin gas)** *AH-gwah mee-nehr-AHL kohn gahs (seen gahs)*
cider	**una sidra** *oo-nah SEE-drah*
juice	**un jugo** *oon HOO-goh*
lemonade	**una limonada** *oo-nah lee-moh-NAH-dah*
milk	**leche** *LEH-chay*
■ malted milk	**una leche malteada** *oo-nah LEH-chay mahl-tay-AH-dah*
■ milk shake	**un batido de leche** *oon bah-TEE-doh day LEH-chay*
orangeade	**una naranjada** *oo-nah nahr-ahn-HAH-dah*

punch	**un ponche** *oon POHN-chay*
soda	**una gaseosa** *oo-nah gah-say-OH-sah*
tonic water	**un agua tónica** *oon AH-gwah TOH-nee-kah*

You might also wish to try an old Spanish favorite, **horchata de churas,** an ice-cold drink made from ground earth almonds. It is a thin, milk-like substance that is mildly sweet and very refreshing on a hot day. Usually it is scooped up from large vats that are kept chilled, and served in a tall glass.

The check, please.	**La cuenta, par favor.** *lah KWEHN-tah pohr fah-BOHR*
Separate checks.	**Cuentas saparadas.** *KWEHN-tahs sep-ahr-AH-dahs*
Is the service (tip) included?	**¿Está incluida la propina?** *ehs-TAH een-kloo-EE-dah lah proh-PEE-nah*
I haven't ordered this.	**No he pedido ésto.** *noh ay ped-EE-doh EHS-toh*
I don't think the bill is right.	**Me parece que hay un error en la cuenta.** *may pah-RAY-say kay AH-ee oon ehr-OHR ehn lah KWEHN-tah*
This is for you.	**Esto es para usted.** *EHS-toh ehs pah-rah oos-TEHD*
We're in a hurry.	**Tenemos prisa.** *ten-EH-mohs PREE-sah*

DRINKS AND SNACKS

In Spain, bars and cocktail lounges sometimes also call themselves pubs. **Cervecerías** are tascas or pubs that specialize in German beer in the barrel, as well as wine. Some pubs are more like piano bars, others are like classical-music coffee houses.

Spanish beer, a German-style brew, is both national (San Miguel and Aguila brands) and local (such as Alhambra in Granada, Vitoria in Malaga, Cruz Campo in Seville) in nature. Regular, light, and dark **(negra)** are the types, usually served ice cold.

Sidra, or cider, is available still or sparkling. The most famous sparkling sidra is produced in the north in Asturias and is called **sidra champaña.**

TAPAS (BAR SNACKS)

One of the delights of Spain is its **tapas,** light snacks that are varied samplings of Spanish cuisine. These hors d'oeuvres might include some of the following items.

aceitunas	olives
alcachofas a la vinagreta	artichokes with vinaigrette dressing
almejas en salsa de ajo	clams in a garlic sauce
anguilas	fried baby eels
calamares a la romana	batter-fried squid strips
caracoles en salsa	snails in a tomato sauce
chorizo al diablo	sausage, especially spicy

entremeses variados	platter of assorted snacks
gambas a la plancha	grilled shrimp
huevos rellenos	stuffed hard-boiled eggs
palitos de queso	cheese straws
pan con jamón	toast slices with ham
pinchitos	kebabs
salchichón	salami

SPANISH WINES

Wine is as much the "drink of the country" in Spain as in France and Italy. Premier table wines are the Bordeaux and Burgundy types produced in the Rioja area along the Ebro River in the north. Sherry, Spain's most famous white wine, is produced in the south. There are five sherry types: fino, manzanilla, amontillado, oloroso, and cream. Fino and manzanilla are the driest and are favorite aperitifs. The others are served with dessert or as after-dinner drinks.

Spanish brandy and numerous liqueurs are produced in Spain and are inexpensive.

WINE	REGION	DESCRIPTION	ORDER WITH
Chacoli	Basque	A light, refreshing petillant white	Seafood, poultry
Espumoso	Catalonia	Superb, champagne-like white	Celebrations, desserts
Málaga	Malaga	Heavy, sweet muscatel	Desserts, after-dinner
Panades	Catalonia	Fine, robust reds, some with great character —also some pleasant whites	Meats, game Seafood, poultry
Priorato	Tarragona	Astringent whites, table reds	Seafood Meats
Ribeiro	Galicia	Light, refreshing, crackling whites	Seafood, cheese
Rioja	Old Castile, Navarra	Long-lived, deep rich reds of great character —also Riesling-type whites	Meats, game, spicy foods Seafood, cheese
Sherry	Andalucia	*fino* (very dry) *manzanilla* (dry) *amontillado* (slightly sweet) *oloroso* (sweet and nutty) *cream* (sweet, syrupy nectar)	aperitif aperitif Dessert, cheese Dessert or after-dinner After-dinner

I would like ____.	**Quisiera ____.** *kee-SYEHR-ah*
■ a glass of wine	**un vaso de vino** *oon BAH-soh day BEE-noh*
■ a bottle of wine	**una botella de vino** *oo-nah boh-TEH-yah day BEE-noh*

Is it ____?	**¿Es ____?** *ehs*
■ red	**tinto** *TEEN-toh*
■ white	**blanco** *BLAHN-koh*
■ rosé	**rosado** *oh-SAH-doh*
light	**ligero** *lee-GEH-roh*
sparkling	**espumoso** *ehs-poo-MOH-soh*
dry	**seco** *SAY-koh*
sweet	**dulce** *DOOL-say*

Sangría is a refreshing fruit punch made from red wine, brandy, fruit, sugar, and soda water. It is usually enjoyed on picnics and in the afternoon, but not at dinner.

LATIN AMERICAN DRINKS

From the Caribbean come a variety of colorful drinks, most of which use rum combined with tropical fruits such as pineapple, coconut, passion fruit, and papaya. Many of these drinks are also available in other Latin American countries, including Mexico. First we list a few of these, then give you descriptions of some of the less familiar Mexican drinks that are particular to that country.

In Mexico **tequila** is a very popular drink, drunk neat (straight) with salt and lime and often also jalapeño peppers. It is distilled from the juice of the agave (maguey) plant (a cactus-like succulent) and comes in both clear and amber; the amber has been aged and has a more mellow flavor.

cuba libre	rum, lime juice, and Coca Cola

margarita	tequila, lime juice, and salt
piña colada	coconut cream, pineapple juice, and rum
ponche	fruit juice and rum or tequila
pulque	the fermented juice of the agave (maguey) plant, often with flavorings added such as herbs, pineapple, celery; available in special pulque bars
tequila sunrise	orange juice, grenadine, tequila

SOUTH AMERICAN WINES

Wine grapes only grow well in moderate climates, so the countries with any wines at all are Argentina, Chile, Uruguay, and parts of Brazil. Chile's wine is one of the world's best, and prices are still rather modest. Ask for it wherever you are. Argentina produces the most wine (quite a bit, as compared with North America), and most of it is quite good. Elsewhere, you will be able to enjoy European wines and California wines in the larger hotels and restaurants that cater to tourists.

FOOD SPECIALTIES OF SPAIN

There are no hard-and-fast rules for Spanish cooking. Seasonings and ingredients will vary from region to region, depending on what's available and what the background is of the people. In Basque country, the helpings are large and the food is heavy with seafood: fried cod, fried eels, squid, and sea bream. Along the Cantabrian coast are excellent cheeses and exquisite sardines. **Sopa montañesa** (a regional soup) is famous, as are **caracoles a la santona** (snails) and **tortilla a la montañesa,** the regional omelet. In Asturias, have a good plate of **fabada,** the beans and blood sausage stew. Tripe is also good. In Galicia, the **pote gallego** (hot pot) is

tasty, as is **merluza a la gallega** (hake). Santiago clams, spider crabs, and rock barnacle (**centollas** and **percebes**), are succulent.

Along the eastern coast, in Catalonia, you'll sample **escudella i carn d'olla,** a vegetable and meat stew, or **butifarra con judías,** pork sausage with beans. **Habas estofadas** is stewed broad beans. Toward Valencia is the land of **paella,** the famous saffron-tinted rice that is mixed with a variety of seafood and meats. If you travel to the Balearic Islands, sample **sopas mallorqinas** (soups), sausages, sardine omelet, or Ibiza-style lobster.

Castilian cuisine is famous for a chickpea and blood sausage stew (**cocido a la madrileña).** In Segovia and Sepulveda you should eat the lamb and suckling pig. **Chorizo** and smoked ham (**jamón serrano**) are world famous. In Toledo, enjoy the **huevos a caballo,** stewed partridge, and marzipan.

Andalusian food is famous for **gazpacho,** a cold, spicy soup of raw tomatoes, peppers, cucumber, and other ingredients depending on the cook. Also here try the mixed fried fishes.

Some other specialties include the following.

bacalao a la vizcaína	salt cod stewed with olive oil, peppers, tomatoes and onions
calmares en su tinta	baby squid cooked in its own ink
callos a la andaluza	tripe stew, with sausages, vegetables and seasonings
camarones en salsa verde	shrimps in a green sauce
capón relleno a la catalana	roasted capon stuffed with meat and nuts
carnero verde	stewed lamb with herbs and pignolis

cocido madrileño	mixed meat stew with chickpeas and vegetables
criadillas fritas	fried prairie oysters
empanadas	deep-fried pies filled with meat and vegetables
fabada asturiana	spicy mixture of white beans, pork, and sausages
gallina en pepitoria	chicken (fish with nuts, rice, garlic, and herbs)
huevos a la flamenca	baked eggs with green vegetables, pimento, tomato, chorizo and ham (a popular first course or light supper)
langosta a la barcelonesa	spiny lobster sauteed with chicken and tomatoes, garnished with almonds
lenguado a la andaluza	stuffed flounder or sole with a vegetable sauce
liebre estofada	hare and green beans, cooked in a tart liquid
marmitako	Basque tuna stew
pato a la sevillana	duck with olives
pescado a la sal	a white fish, packed in salt and roasted
pisto manchego	vegetable stew of tomatoes, peppers, onions, eggplant, and zucchini
rabo de toro	oxtail stewed in wine sauce
riñones al jerez	kidneys in sherry wine
sesos en caldereta	calves brains, simmered in wine

zarzuela	fish stew; varies greatly depending on region but usually similar to a bouillabaisse

SOME MEXICAN SPECIALTIES

The Mexican restaurants that proliferate throughout the U.S. are not truly representative of Mexican cooking. What is most familiar to non-Mexicans are the tortilla-based dishes described on page 136 and other dishes such as tamales (corn meal mixture stuffed with meat and steamed in a corn husk) but Mexicans view these as snacks. True Mexican cooking is as varied as the country itself, with much seafood along the coasts and other unusual dishes inland. Almost all Mexican cooking, however, is united in its use of chiles—those marvelously varied flavoring agents that range from very sweet to fiery hot. Also serving to unify Mexican cuisine are corn, beans, and rice, plus the herbs coriander and cumin and the spices cinnamon and cloves. As mentioned earlier, tortillas are the bread of this culture. Most often they are made from cornmeal, but in some parts of the country they are made from wheat flour instead.

In the vicinity of Mexico City, the food is fairly sophisticated, with a variety of ingredients appearing in dishes made with chicken, seafood, and various types of meat. Perhaps most famous is the **mole poblano,** in which turkey is served with a dark brown sauce that contains a variety of spices, ground poblano chiles, and a hint of chocolate.

Along the Mexican coast around Acapulco, as well as along the Gulf Coast, the dishes are mostly made with fresh ingredients, including seafood and fruit. In the Yucatán, the dishes reflect very strongly the ancient Mayan culture, and include **pollo pibil,** a chicken dish that is colored with annato, rolled in banana leaves, and steamed in a pit.

Wherever you are, ask for the local specialties. You are apt to sample one of the following.

amarillito	chicken or pork stew with green tomatoes, pumpkin, and chilies

carne asada	marinated pieces of beef that have been grilled
ceviche acapulqueño	raw fish or shellfish marinated in lime juice
chile relleno	stuffed chile (usually with cheese), that is coated with a light batter and fried
cochinita pibil	a suckling pig stuffed with fruits, chilies, and spices, then wrapped and baked in a pit
coloradito	chicken stew made with ancho chilies, tomatoes, and red peppers
frijoles refritos	kidney or pinto beans that have been cooked then mashed and reheated, often with chilies
guajolote relleno	turkey stuffed with fruit, nuts, and chilies and braised in wine
gorditas	bits of meat and cheese, fried and served with guacamole
guacamole	a purée of avocado, onion, garlic, and chilies, used as a condiment and a sauce for a variety of dishes
huachinango a la veracruzana	red snapper marinated in lime juice and baked with tomatoes, olives, capers, and chilies
jaibas en chilpachole	crabs cooked in a tomato sauce, flavored with the Mexican spice epazote
mancha manteles	a stew of chicken or pork, with a mixture of vegetables and in a sauce of nuts, green tomatoes, and chilies

muk-bil pollo	chicken pie with a cornmeal topping
papazul	rolled tortillas in a pumpkin sauce
panuchos	chicken dish baked with black beans and eggs
puchero	a stew made from a variety of meats, vegetables, fruits; served as a soup, then a main course
sopa de lima	a chicken soup laced with lime

SOUTH AND CENTRAL AMERICAN FOODS

This is a large area to cover, and any attempt to describe all the dishes is likely to be a bit foolish. Nevertheless, whereas Spain and Mexico have established readily identifiable cuisines, most countries in South and Central America also have some special dishes.

Peru and Ecuador, and parts of Bolivia and Chile, have a heritage of Incan culture and so the food is a combination of Indian and Spanish. Here are some specialties of this region.

anticuchos	skewered chunks of marinated beef heart, served with a hot sauce
caldillo de congrio	conger eel in a stew
humitas	cornmeal bits flavored with onion, peppers, and spices
llapingachos	potato-cheese croquettes
papas a la huancaína	potatoes in a spicy cheese sauce

pupusas **(El Salvador)**	cornmeal tortillas, stuffed with mashed kidney beans and crumbled fried bacon, cheese or pork

Argentina, Uruguay, and Paraguay are countries that favor beef, so some of their notable dishes include **carbonada,** a stew of meat with vegetables served in a pumpkin shell. **Carne con cuero** is roasted beef (done in the skin), and **matambre** is a large steak stuffed with spinach, eggs, and carrots, then braised. The **parrillada** is a type of English mixed grill, but just about every part of the animal is served (sweetbreads, kidney, liver). It usually comes with *chimichurri*, a piquant sauce made with garlic, parsley and olive oil. **Yerba mate** is a tea drunk in this region made by steeping leaves from a holly bush.

Colombia and Venezuela are noted for their **arepas,** which are cornmeal buns filled with meat, chicken or cheese. **Buñuelos** are balls of fried cornmeal, dusted with powdered sugar. **Empanadas** are also popular here, and these pies are usually stuffed with meat, onions, and raisins. **Hallacas** is a seasoned mixture of meat stuffed into cornmeal dough and wrapped in banana leaves—sort of a tamale. For fish, the Colombians have **vindo de pescado,** a fish stew that is cooked on an outdoor grill.

Bolivia is well known for its roast suckling pig, as well as **picante de pollo,** a fried chicken that is rather spicy. **Lomo montado** is a steak topped with a fried egg.

The Central American countries reflect the tastes and dishes of the Spanish, but incorporate many tropical fruits in their food. Look for **gallo en sidra** (chicken in cider), tripe and vegetable stews, and a whole range of meat stews-soups.

FOODS OF THE CARIBBEAN

There are some Spanish influences in Caribbean cooking, but you'll also find that West Africans have contributed to this food as have the French. If we concentrate on those islands where Spanish is spoken, the following items are likely to be found on menus.

asopao	a chicken and rice soup-stew with ham, peas, and peppers
chicharrones	deep-fried pork cracklings
frituras de bacalao (bacalaítos)	fish cakes that are fried in hot oil
mondongo	thick stew of beef tripe, potatoes, tomatoes, pumpkin, chickpeas and tropical vegetables
moros y cristianos	black beans and rice
pasteles	a mixture of plantain and seasonings, steamed in a banana leaf
picadillo	mixture of chopped pork and beef with peppers, olives, raisins, and tomatoes
plátanos fritos	sliced, fried green bananas (plantains)
relleno de papa	potato dough stuffed with a mixture of meat, olives, and tomatoes
ropa vieja	literally "old clothes," this is shredded beef cooked with tomatoes and peppers
sancocho	a hearty Dominican stew with beef, pork, chicken, potatoes, tomatoes, and tropical vegetables (plantains, yams, pumpkin, yucca, yautía)
sandwich cubano	a half-loaf of crisp Italian or French bread filled with fresh pork, ham, cheese, and pickle, served oven-warmed

tostones   fried green plantain slices

yuca con mojo   stewed yucca root (cassava), in a
                        garlic sauce

Travel Tips Save receipts on foreign
purchases for declaring at customs on re-entry to the
U.S. Some countries return a sales or value-added tax
to foreign visitors. Take receipts to a special office at
the store or to a tax rebate window at the airport of
departure. Americans who buy costly objects abroad
may be surprised to get a bill from their state tax
collector. Most states with a sales tax levy "use" tariff
on all items bought outside the home state, including
those purchased abroad. Most tax agencies in these
states will send a form for declaring and paying the
assessment.

MEETING PEOPLE

Here are some greetings, introductions, and invitations, plus some phrases you might need if dating. Remember to shake hands when meeting people; a Spanish person may feel offended if you do not.

The Spanish, like ourselves, don't ask questions that are too personal at the beginning of an acquaintance. *Never* tell how much money you make, nor ask how much money the other person makes, unless you are lifelong friends.

Spanish people often invite recent acquaintances to their homes. In such cases, remember that modesty and diplomacy are your best assets.

SMALL TALK

My name is ____.	**Me llamo ____.** *may YAH-mo*
Do you live here?	**¿Vive usted aquí?** *BEE-bay oos-TEHD ah-KEE*
Where are you from?	**¿De dónde es usted?** *day DOHN-day ehs oos-TEHD*
I am ____.	**Soy ____.** *soy*
■ from the United States	**de Estados Unidos** *day ehs-TAH-dohs oo-NEE-dohs*
■ from Canada	**del Canadá** *del cah-nah-DAH*
■ from England	**de Inglaterra** *day een-glah-TEHR-ah*
■ from Australia	**de Australia** *day ow-STRAHL-yah*
I like Spain (South America) very much.	**Me gusta mucho España (Sud América).** *may GOOS-tah MOO-choh ehs-PAHN-yah (sood ah-MEHR-ee-kah)*

How long will you be staying?	**¿Cuánto tiempo va a quedarse?** *KWAHN-toh tee-EHM-poh bah ah kay-DAHR-say*
I'll stay for a few days (a week).	**Me quedaré unos días (una semana).** *may kay-dahr-AY oo-nohs DEE-ahs (oo-nah sehm-AHN-ah)*
What hotel are you at?	**¿En qué hotel está?** *ehn kay oh-TEL ehs-TAH*
I think it's ____.	**Creo que es ____.** *KREH-oh kay ehs*

- (very) beautiful **(muy) bonito(a)** *(mwee) bohn-EE-toh(ah)*
- interesting **interesante** *een-tehr-ehs-AHN-tay*
- magnificent **magnífico(a)** *mahg-NEEF-ee-koh(kah)*
- wonderful **maravilloso(a)** *mahr-ah-bee-YOH-soh(sah)*
- boring **aburrido(a)** *ah-boo-REE-doh(ah)*
- ugly **feo(a)** *FEH-oh(ah)*
- too expensive **demasiado caro(a)** *day-mah-SYAH-doh KAR-oh(ah)*
- inexpensive **barato(a)** *bah-RAH-toh(ah)*

INTRODUCTIONS

May I introduce my ____?	**Le presento a mi ____.** *lay pray-SENT-oh ah mee*

- brother (sister) **hermano(a)** *ehr-MAH-noh(nah)*
- father (dad) [mother (mom)] **padre (papá) [madre (mamá)]** *PAH-dray (pah-PAH) MAH-dray (mah-MAH)*
- friend **amigo(a)** *ah-MEE-goh(gah)*
- husband (wife) **marido (esposa)** *mahr-EE-doh (ehs-POH-sah)*

■ sweetheart	**novio(a)**	*NOH-bee-oh(ah)*
■ son (daughter)	**hijo(a)**	*EE-hoh(hah)*

How do you do? (Glad to meet you.) — **Mucho gusto (en conocerle).** *MOO-choh GOOS-toh (ehn koh-noh-SEHR-lay)*

How do you do? (The pleasure is mine.) — **El gusto es mío.** *ehl GOOS-toh ehs MEE-oh*

I am a _____. — **Soy _____.** *soy*

■ teacher	**maestro(a)**	*mah-EHS-troh(trah)*
■ doctor	**médico**	*MED-ee-koh*
■ lawyer	**abogado**	*ah-boh-GAH-doh*
■ businessperson	**persona de negocios**	*pehr-SOHN-ah day neh-GOH-see-ohs*
■ student	**estudiante**	*ehs-too-DYAHN-tay*
■ accountant	**contador**	*kohn-tah-DOHR*
■ dentist	**dentista**	*den-TEES-tah*
■ jeweler	**joyero**	*hoy-EHR-oh*
■ merchant	**comerciante**	*koh-mehr-SYAHN-teh*
■ nurse	**enfermera**	*en-fehr-MEHR-ah*
■ manager	**gerente**	*hehr-EN-teh*
■ salesman	**vendedor**	*ben-deh-DOHR*
■ I'm retired	**estoy jubilado(a)**	*es-toy hoo-bee-LAH-doh(ah)*

Would you like a picture (snapshot)? — **¿Quiere una foto?** *kee-YEHR-ay oo-nah FOH-toh*

Stand here (there). — **Párese aquí (allá).** *PAH-ray-say ah-KEE (ah-YAH)*

Don't move. — **No se mueva.** *noh say MWEH-bah*

Smile. That's it.	**Sonría. ¡Asi es!**	*sohn-REE-ah ah-SEE ehs*
Will you take a picture of me (us)?	**¿(Nos)Me quiere sacar una foto?**	*(nos)may kee-YEHR-ay sah-KAHR oo-nah FOH-toh*

DATING AND SOCIALIZING

May I have this dance?	**¿Quiere usted bailar?**	*kee-YEHR-ay oos-TEHD bah-ee-LAHR*
Yes, of course.	**Sí, con mucho gusto.**	*see kohn MOO-choh GOOS-toh*
Would you like a cigarette (drink)?	**¿Quiere fumar (tomar algo)?**	*kee-YEHR-ay fo-MAHR (toh-MAHR AHL-goh)*
Do you have a light (a match)?	**¿Tiene fuego (un fósforo)?**	*tee-YEH-nay FWAY-goh (oon FOHS-fohr-oh)*
Do you mind if I smoke?	**¿Le molesta que fume?**	*lay moh-LEHS-tah kay FOO-may*
May I take you home?	**¿Me permite llevarle a casa?**	*may pehr-MEE-tay yeh-BAHR-lay ah KAH-sah*
May I call you?	**¿Puedo llamarle?**	*PWEH-doh yah-MAHR-lay*
Are you doing anything tomorrow?	**¿Está libre mañana?**	*eh-STAH LEE-bray mahn-YAH-nah*
Are you free this evening?	**¿Está usted libre esta tarde?**	*eh-STAH oos-TEHD LEE-bray ehs-tah TAHR-day*

Would you like us to go together to ____?	**¿Quiere acompañarme a ____?** *kee-YEHR-ay ah-kohm-pahn-YAHR-may ah*
I'll wait for you in front of the hotel.	**Le espero delante del hotel.** *lay ehs-PEHR-oh del-AHN-tay del oh-TEL*
I'll pick you up at your house (hotel).	**Le recogeré en su casa (hotel).** *lay ray-koh-hehr-AY ehn soo KAH-sah (oh-TEL)*
What is your telephone number?	**¿Cuál es su número de teléfono?** *kwahl ehs soo NOO-mehr-oh day tel-EH-foh-noh*
Here's my telephone number (address).	**Aquí tiene mi número de teléfono (mi dirección).** *ah-KEE tee-EH-nay mee NOO-mehr-oh day tel-EH-foh-noh (mee dee-rehk-SYOHN)*
Will you write to me?	**¿Me escribirá?** *may ehs-kree-beer-AH*
I'm single (married).	**Soy soltero(a) casado(a).** *soy sohl-TEHR-oh(ah) kah-SAH-doh(ah)*
Is your husband (wife) here?	**¿Está aquí so esposo (esposa)?** *eh-STAH ah-KEE soo ehs-POH-soh (ehs-POH-sah)*
I'm here with my family.	**Estoy aquí con mi familia.** *ehs-TOY ah-KEE kohn mee fah-MEEL-yah*
Do you have any children?	**¿Tiene usted hijos?** *tee-EH-nay oos-TEHD EE-hohs*
How many?	**¿Cuántos?** *KWAHN-tohs*

SAYING GOOD-BYE

Nice to have met you.	**Ha sido un verdadero gusto.** *ah SEED-oh oon behr-dah-DEHR-oh GOOS-toh*
The pleasure was mine.	**El gusto ha sido mío.** *ehl GOOS-toh ah SEE-doh MEE-oh*
Regards to ____.	**Saludos a ____ de mi parte.** *sah-LOO-dohs ah day mee PAHR-tay*
Thanks for a wonderful evening.	**Gracias por su invitación. Ha sido una noche extraordinaria.** *GRAH-see-ahs pohr soo een-bee-tah-SYOHN. Ah see-doh oo-nah NOH-chay ehs-trah-ohr-dee-NAHR-ee-ah*
I must go home now.	**Tengo que marchame ahora.** *TEN-goh kay mahr-CHAR-may ah-OH-rah*
You must come to visit us.	**Debe venir a visitarnos.** *DEH-bay ben-EER ah bee-see-TAHR-nohs*

SHOPPING

Madrid is a city where you can still have clothes, suits, shoes, boots, and other things custom-made. Prices are not cheap, but for fine workmanship, the price is still considerably lower than in many other countries. Ready-to-wear shoes are also a good value—in style, workmanship, and price.

Handicrafts, such as pottery, leather work, weaving, and embroideries, are still found in many regions of Spain. Official government handicraft stores, called **Artespania**, are located in cities throughout Spain. There are three in Madrid alone. There are regional specialties, such as pottery, in Talavera (near Toledo) and Manises (near Valencia); damascene ware and steel knives and swords in Toledo; weaving and rug-making in Granada; fans, dolls, combs, and mantillas in Seville; leatherwork in Cordoba and Majorca and Menorca; olive wood products, pottery, embroideries, glassware, and artificial pearls in Majorca; and trendy, boutique sports clothes and jewelry in Ibiza.

Antiques are also widely available in Spain, ranging from **santos** (small wooden sculptures of saints) and rare books to painted cabinets, portable desks, and glass paintings. Many fine antique shops in Madrid are located along Calle de Prado, Carrera de San Jerónimo, and in El Rastro. There is a stamp-and-coin market held every Sunday morning from 10 A.M. to 2 P.M. on the Plaza Mayor in Madrid.

Modern art is also a good buy, especially in Madrid and Barcelona, where you will find works by internationally known Spanish artists such as Miró, Tapies, Sempere, and others. Kreister II, Galería Vijande, and Galería Egam are among the many reputable galleries in Madrid. In Barcelona there are many galleries along Rambla de Cataluña.

Madrid has three major department stores with branches in many other cities. They are Galerías Preciados, with three Madrid locations; El Corte Inglés, with four Madrid locations; and Celso García, with two Madrid stores.

Prices are fixed in department stores and most shops. In flea markets, antique shops, and some art galleries and custom workshops, you can attempt to "negotiate" prices if you wish.

In Mexico, because of recent devaluations, your money will bring you great values for crafts and handmade goods. In particular, Mexico has to offer some fine embroidery, silver items, and paper goods. You'll also find small, detailed figurines made from straw, wood carvings, pottery, and leather goods. Since it is such a large country, with so many different specialties, we can only suggest that you look about where you are, go to local markets, and see what you like. In the markets you will have to bargain for what you want; in shops, the prices are often fixed or there is only a small margin for bargaining.

The remainder of Latin America is too vast an area to be able to offer tips on specialty items. We suggest you read some tourist guides before leaving on your trip. In Latin American countries, shops are generally open from about 9 A.M. to 1 P.M., then open again about 3 P.M. and remain open until early evening, about 7. On Sunday, most shops are closed, but some markets are open and bustling.

GOING SHOPPING

Where can I find _____?	**¿Dónde se puede encontrar _____?** *DOHN-day say pweh-day ehn-kohn-TRAHR*
■ a bakery	**una panadería** *oo-nah pah-nah-dehr-EE-ah*
■ a bookstore	**una librería** *oo-nah leeb-rehr-EE-ah*
■ a butcher shop	**una carnicería** *oo-nah kahr-nee-sehr-EE-ah*
■ a camera shop	**una tienda de fotografía** *oo-nah tee-EHN-dah day foh-toh-grah-FEE-ah*
■ a candy store	**una confitería** *oo-nah kohn-fee-tehr-EE-ah*
■ a clothing store	**una tienda de ropa** *oo-nah tee-YEHN-dah day ROH-pah*

■ a delicatessen **una tienda de ultramarinos** *oo-nah tee-YEHN-dah day ool-trah-mah-REE-nohs*

■ a department store **un almacén** *oon ahl-mah-SEHN*

■ a pharmacy (chemist) **una farmacia** *oo-nah fahr-MAH-see-ah*

■ a florist **una florería** *oo-nah flohr-ehr-EE-ah*

■ a gift (souvenir) shop **una tienda de regalos (recuerdos)** *oo-nah tee-YEHN-dah day ray-GAHL-ohs (ray-kwehr-dohs)*

■ a grocery store **una tienda de comestibles** *oo-nah tee-YEHN-dah day koh-mehs-TEE-blays*

■ a hardware store (ironmonger) **una ferretería** *oo-nah feh-reh-teh-REE-ah*

■ a jewelry store **una joyería** *oo-nah hoy-ehr-EE-ah*

■ a liquor store **una licorería** *oo-nah lee-kohr-ehr-EE-ah*

■ a newsstand **un puesto de periódicos** *oon PWEHS-toh day peh-ree-OH-dee-kohs*

■ a record store **una tienda de discos** *oo-nah tee-yehn-dah day DEES-kohs*

■ a shoe store **una zapatería** *oo-nah sah-pah-tehr-EE-ah*

■ a supermarket **un supermercado** *oon SOO-pehr-mehr-KAH-doh*

■ a tobacco shop **un estanco** *oon ehs-TAHN-koh*

■ a toy store **una juguetería** *oo-nah hoo-get-ehr-EE-ah*

BEING HELPED

Young man. Can you wait on me? **Joven. ¿Puede usted atenderme?** *HOH-ben PWEH-day oos-TEHD ah-ten-DEHR-may*

Miss. Can you help me?	**Señorita. ¿Me podría ayudar?** *sehn-yohr-EE-tah may poh-DREE-ah ah-yoo-DAHR*
Do you take credit cards?	**¿Acepta tarjetas de crédito?** *ah-SEP-tah tahr-HAY-tahs day KRED-ee-toh*
Can I pay with a traveler's check?	**¿Puedo pagar con un cheque de viajero?** *PWEH-doh pah-GAHR kohn oon CHEH-kay day bee-ah-HEHR-oh*

BOOKS

Is there a store that carries English-language books?	**¿Hay una tienda que lleve libros en inglés?** *AH-ee oo-nah TYEHN-dah kay YEH-bay LEE-brohs ehn een-GLAYS*
What is the best (biggest) bookstore here?	**¿Cuál es la mejor librería (la librería más grande) de aquí?** *kwahl ehs lah meh-HOHR lee-brehr-EE-ah (lah lee-brehr-EE-ah mahs grahn-day) day ah-KEE*
I'm looking for a copy of ____.	**Busco un ejemplar de ____.** *boos-koh oon eh-hem-PLAHR day*
I don't know the title (author).	**No sé el título (autor).** *noh say ehl TEE-too-loh (AH-oo-TOHR)*
I'm just looking.	**Estoy sólo mirando.** *ehs-TOY SOH-loh meer-AHN-doh*
Do you have books (novels) in English?	**¿Tiene usted libros (novelas) en inglés?** *tee-EHN-eh oos-TEHD LEE-brohs (noh-BEL-ahs) ehn een-GLAYSS*

Do you have paper-back copies?	**¿Tiene usted ejemplares en rústica?** *tee-EHN-ay oos-TEHD eh-hem-PLAHR-ays ehn ROOS-tee-kah*
I want a ____.	**Quiero ____.** *kee-EHR-oh*
■ guidebook	**una guía** *oon-ah GHEE-ah*
■ map of this city	**un plano de esta ciudad** *oon PLAH-noh day ehs-tah see-oo-DAHD*
■ pocket dictionary	**un diccionario de bolsillo** *oon deek-syohn-AHR-ee-oh day bohl-SEE-yoh*
■ Spanish-English dictionary	**un diccionario español-inglés** *oon deek-syohn-AHR-ee-oh ehs-pahn-YOHL-een-GLAYSS*
Where can I find ____?	**¿Dónde están ____?** *DOHN-day ehs-TAHN*
■ detective stories	**las novelas policíacas** *lahs noh-BEH-lahs poh-lee-SEE-ah-kahs*
■ history books	**los libros de historia** *lohs LEE-brohs day ee-STOHR-ee-ah*
■ short story books	**los libros de cuentos** *lohs LEE-brohs day KWEHN-tohs*
■ cookbooks	**los libros de cocina** *lohs LEE-brohs day koh-SEE-nah*
I'll take these books.	**Me quedo con estos libros.** *may kay-doh kohn EHS-tohs LEE-brohs*
Will you wrap them, please?	**¿Quiere envolverlos, por favor?** *kee-YEHR-ay ehn-bohl-BEHR-lohs pohr fah-BOHR*

CLOTHING

Would you please show me ____?	**¿Quiere enseñarme ____, por favor?** *kee-YEHR-ay ehn-sehn-YAHR-may pohr fah-BOHR*
■ a bathing suit	**un traje de baño** *oon TRAH-hay day BAHN-yo*
■ a belt	**un cinturón** *oon seen-toor-OHN*
■ a blouse	**una blusa** *oon-ah BLOO-sah*
■ boots	**botas** *BOH-tahs*
■ a bra	**un sostén** *oon soh-STEHN*
■ a dress	**un vestido** *oon bes-tee-doh*
■ an evening gown	**un traje de noche** *oon TRAH-hay day NOH-chay*
■ leather (suede) gloves	**guantes de cuero (de gamuza)** *GWAHN-tays day KWEHR-oh (day gah-MOOS-ah)*
■ handkerchiefs	**pañuelos** *pahn-yoo-EH-lohs*
■ a hat	**un sombrero** *oon sohm-BREHR-oh*
■ a jacket	**una chaqueta** *oon-nah chah-KAY-tah*
■ a pair of jeans	**un par de vaqueros, un par de jeans** *oon pahr day bah-KEHR-ohs oon pahr day jeens*
■ a jogging suit	**un traje de footing** *oon trah-hay day FOO-teen*
■ an overcoat	**un abrigo** *oon ah-BREE-goh*
■ pajamas	**piyamas** *pee-YAH-mahs*
■ panties	**bragas** *BRAH-gahs*
■ pants	**pantalones** *pahn-tah-LOHN-ays*
■ pantyhose	**pantimedias** *pahn-tee-MEHD-ee-ahs*
■ a raincoat	**un impermeable** *oon eem-pehr-may-AH-blay*

■ a robe	**una bata** *oon-nah BAH-tah*
■ sandals	**sandalias** *sahn-DAHL-ee-ahs*
■ a scarf	**una bufanda** *oo-nah boo-FAHN-dah*
■ a shirt	**una camisa** *oo-nah kah-MEES-ah*
■ (a pair of) shoes	**(un par de) zapatos** *(oon pahr day) sah-PAH-tohs*
■ shorts (briefs)	**calzoncillos** *kahl-sohn-SEE-yohs*
■ stockings	**medias** *MED-ee-ahs*
■ a t-shirt	**una camiseta** *oo-nah kah-mee-SEH-tah*
Do you have something ___?	**¿Tiene algo ___?** *tee-EH-nay AHL-goh*
■ else	**más** *mahs*
■ larger	**más grande** *mahs grahn-day*
■ less expensive	**menos caro** *may-nohs KAHR-oh*
■ longer	**más largo** *mahs LAHR-goh*
■ of better quality	**de más alta calidad** *day mahs AHL-tah kahl-ee-DAHD*
■ shorter	**más corto** *mahs KOHR-toh*
■ smaller	**más pequeño** *mahs peh-KAYN-yoh*

COLORS AND FABRICS

I (don't) like the color.	**(No) me gusta este color.** *(noh) may GOOS-tah ehs-tay koh-LOHR*
Do you have it in ___?	**¿Tiene algo en ___?** *tee-EHN-ay ahl-goh ehn*
■ black	**negro** *NEH-groh*
■ blue	**azul** *ah-SOOL*
■ brown	**marrón, pardo** *mah-ROHN PAHR-doh*
■ gray	**gris** *grees*
■ green	**verde** *BEHR-day*

- orange **anaranjado** *ah-nah-rahn-HAH-do*
- pink **rosado** *roh-SAH-doh*
- red **rojo** *ROH-hoh*
- white **blanco** *BLAHN-koh*
- yellow **amarillo** *ah-mah-REE-yoh*

I want something in ____. **Quiero algo en ____.** *kee-YEHR-oh AHL-goh ehn*

- chiffon **gasa** *GAH-sah*
- corduroy **pana** *PAH-nah*
- cotton **algodón** *ahl-goh-DOHN*
- denim **dril de algodón, tela tejana** *dreel day ahl-goh-DOHN TEH-la tay-HAH-nah*
- felt **fieltro** *fee-EHL-troh*
- flannel **franela** *frah-NEHL-ah*
- gabardine **gabardina** *gah-bahr-DEEN-ah*
- lace **encaje** *ehn-KAH-hay*
- leather **cuero** *KWEHR-oh*

■ linen	**hilo**	*EE-loh*
■ nylon	**nilón**	*nee-LOHN*
■ satin	**raso**	*RAH-soh*
■ silk	**seda**	*SAY-dah*
■ suede	**gamuza**	*gah-MOO-sah*
■ taffeta	**tafetán**	*tah-fay-TAHN*
■ terrycloth	**tela de toalla**	*TEHL-ah day toh-AH-yah*
■ velvet	**terciopelo**	*tehr-see-oh-PEHL-oh*
■ wool	**lana**	*LAH-nah*
■ worsted	**estambre**	*ehs-TAHM-bray*
■ synthetic (polyester)	**sintético**	*seen-TET-ee-koh*

I prefer ____.	**Prefiero ____.**	*preh-FYEHR-oh*
■ permanent press	**algo inarrugable**	*AHL-goh een-ah-roo-GAH-blay*
■ wash and wear	**algo que no se necesita planchar**	*AHL-goh kay noh seh neh-seh-SEE-tah plahn-CHAHR*

Show me something ____.	**Muéstreme algo ____.**	*MWEHS-ray-may AHL-goh*
■ in a solid color	**de color liso**	*day koh-LOHR LEE-soh*
■ with stripes	**de rayas**	*day RAH-ee-ahs*
■ with polka dots	**de lunares**	*day loo-NAHR-ays*
■ in plaid	**de cuadros**	*day KWAH-drohs*

Please take my measurements,	**¿Quiere tomarme la medida?**	*kee-YEHR-ay toh-MAHR-may lah meh-DEE-dah*
I take size (My size is) ____.	**Llevo el tamaño (Mi talla es)**	*YEH-boh ehl tah-MAHN-yoh (mee TAH-yah ehs)*

- small **pequeño(a)** *peh-KAYN-yoh(yah)*
- medium **mediano(a)** *meh-dee-AH-noh(yah)*
- large **grande** *GRAHN-day*

Can I try it on?
¿Puedo probármelo? *PWEHD-oh proh-BAHR-may-loh*

Can you alter it?
¿Puede arreglarlo? *PWEH-day ah-ray-GLAHR-loh*

Can I return the article?
¿Puedo devolver el artículo? *PWEH-doh day-bohl-BEHR ehl ahr-TEE-koo-loh*

Do you have something handmade?
¿Tiene algo hecho a mano? *tee-YEH-nay AHL-goh AY-choh ah MAH-noh*

CLOTHING MEASUREMENTS

MEN							
SHOES							
American	7	8	9	10	11	12	
British	6	7	8	9	10	11	
Continental	39	41	43	44	45	46	
SUITS, COATS							
American	34	36	38	40	42	44	46	48
British	44	46	48	50	54	56	58	60
Continental	44	46	48	50	52	56	58	60
SHIRTS							
American	14	$14\frac{1}{2}$	15	$15\frac{1}{2}$	16	$16\frac{1}{2}$	17	$17\frac{1}{2}$
British	14	$14\frac{1}{2}$	15	$15\frac{1}{2}$	16	$16\frac{1}{2}$	17	$17\frac{1}{2}$
Continental	36	37	38	39	40	41	42	43

WOMEN						
SHOES						
American	4	5	6	7	8	9
British	3	4	5	6	7	8
Continental	35	36	37	38	39	40
DRESSES, SUITS						
American	8	10	12	14	16	18
British	10	12	14	16	18	20
Continental	36	38	40	42	44	46
BLOUSES, SWEATERS						
American	32	34	36	38	40	42
British	34	36	38	40	42	44
Continental	40	42	44	46	48	50

The zipper doesn't work.	**No funciona la cremallera.** *noh foon-SYOHN-ah lah kray-mah-YEH-rah*
It doesn't fit me.	**No me queda bien.** *noh may KAY-dah BYEHN*
It fits very well.	**Me queda muy bien.** *may KAY-dah mwee BYEHN*
I'll take it.	**Me lo llevo.** *may loh YEH-boh*
Will you wrap it?	**¿Quiere envolverlo?** *kee-YEHR-ay ehn-bohl-BEHR-loh*
I'd like to see the pair of shoes (boots) in the window.	**Quisiera ver el par de zapatos (botas) de la vitrina.** *kee-see-YEH-rah behr ehl pahr day sah-PAH-tohs (BOH-tahs) day lah bee-TREE-nah*

They're too narrow (wide).	**Son demasiado estrechos (anchos).** *sohn day-mahs-ee-AH-doh ehs-TRAY-chohs (AHN-chohs)*
I'll take them.	**Me los llevo.** *may lohs YEH-boh*
I also need shoe-laces.	**También necesito cordones de zapato.** *tahm-BYEHN neh-say-SEE-toh kohr-DOHN-ays day sah-PAH-toh*
That's all I want for now.	**Eso es todo por ahora.** *eh-soh ehs TOH-doh pohr ah-OHR-ah*

ELECTRICAL APPLIANCES

Electric current in the U.S. is 110V AC, whereas in Spain it is 220V AC. Unless your electric shaver or alarm clock is able to handle both currents, you will need to purchase an adapter. When making a purchase, please be aware that *some* Spanish products are engineered to work with either system while others will require an adapter. When making a purchase, be careful to check the warranty to ensure that the product is covered internationally.

I want to buy ____.	**Quiero comprar ____.** *kee-YEHR-oh kohm-PRAHR*
■ a battery	**una pila** *OO-nah PEE-lah*
■ an electric shaver	**una máquina de afeitar eléctrica** *oo-nah MAH-kee-nah day ah-fay-TAHR eh-LEK-tree-kah*
■ a hair dryer	**un secador de pelo** *oon say-kah-DOHR day PEH-loh*
■ a (portable) radio	**una radio (portátil)** *oo-nah RAH-dee-oh (pohr-TAH-teel)*
■ an alarm clock	**un despertador** *oon dehs-pehr-tah-DOHR*

■ a blender   **una licuadora**   *oo-nah lee-kwah-DOHR-ah*

■ a toaster   **una tostadora**   *oo-nah tohs-tah-DOHR-ah*

■ an electric adapter   **un adaptador eléctrico**   *oon ah-dahp-tah-DOHR eh-LEK-tree-coh*

FOODS AND HOUSEHOLD ITEMS

Always keep in mind the restrictions you will face at customs when you return to your own country. Fresh foods often are not permitted.

When you go to a food market or shop, bring your own bag along with you to tote home your groceries. A collapsible net bag is very useful.

I'd like ____.   **Quisiera ____.**   *kee-SYEHR-ah*

■ a bar of soap   **una pastilla de jabón**   *oo-nah pahs-TEE-yah day hah-BOHN*

■ a bottle of juice   **una botella de jugo**   *oo-nah boh-TEH-yah day HOO-goh*

■ a box of cereal   **una caja de cereal**   *oo-nah KAH-hah day sehr-ay-AHL*

■ a can (tin) of tomato sauce   **una lata de salsa de tomate**   *oo-nah LAH-tah day SAHL-sah day toh-MAH-tay*

■ a dozen eggs   **una docena de huevos**   *oo-nah doh-SAY-nah day WAY-bohs*

■ a jar of coffee   **un pomo de café**   *oon POH-moh day kah-FAY*

■ a kilo of potatoes (2.2 lbs)   **un kilo de papas (patatas)**   *oon KEE-loh day PAH-pahs (pah-TAH-tahs)*

■ a half-kilo of cherries — **medio kilo de cerezas** *MED-ee-oh KEE-loh day sehr-AY-sahs*

■ a liter of milk — **un litro de leche** *oon LEE-troh day LEH-chay*

■ a package of candies — **un paquete de dulces** *oon pah-KEH-tay day dool-sayss*

■ 100 grams of cheese — **cien gramos de queso** *see-EHN GRAH-mohs day KAY-soh*

■ a roll of toilet paper — **un rollo de papel higiénico** *oon ROH- yoh day pah-pel ee-hee-EHN-ee-koh*

What is this (that)? — **¿Qué es esto (eso)?** *kay ehs EHS-toh (EHS-oh)*

Is it fresh? — **¿Está fresco?** *ehs-TAH FRES-koh*

I'd like a kilo (about 2 pounds) of oranges.* — **Quisiera un kilo de naranjas.** *kee-SYEHR-ah oon KEE-loh day nah-RAHN-hahs*

■ a half-kilo of butter — **medio kilo de mantequilla** *MED-ee-oh KEE-loh day mahn-tay-KEE-yah*

■ 200 grams (about ¹/₂ pound) of cookies (cakes) — **doscientos gramos de galletas (pasteles)** *dohs-SYEHN-tohs GRAH-mohs day gah-YEH-tahs (pahs-TEH-lehs)*

■ 100 grams (about ¹/₄ pound) of ham — **cien gramos de jamón** *SYEHN GRAH-mohs day hah-MOHN*

* Note: Common measurements for purchasing foods are a kilo, or fractions thereof, and 100, 200, and 500 grams. See also the pages on numbers, 14–17.

METRIC WEIGHTS AND MEASURES

Solid Measures
(approximate measurements only)

OUNCES	GRAMS (GRAMOS)	GRAMS	OUNCES
$\frac{1}{4}$	7	10	$\frac{1}{3}$
$\frac{1}{2}$	14	100	$3\frac{1}{2}$
$\frac{3}{4}$	21	300	$10\frac{1}{2}$
1	28	500	18

POUNDS	KILOGRAMS (KILOS)	KILOGRAMS	POUNDS
1	$\frac{1}{2}$	1	$2\frac{1}{4}$
5	$2\frac{1}{4}$	3	$6\frac{1}{2}$
10	$4\frac{1}{2}$	5	11
20	9	10	22
50	23	50	110
100	45	100	220

METRIC WEIGHTS AND MEASURES

Liquid Measures
(approximate measurements only)

OUNCES	MILLILITERS (MILILITROS)	MILLILITERS	OUNCES
1	30	10	$\frac{1}{3}$
6	175	50	$1\frac{1}{2}$
12	350	100	$3\frac{1}{2}$
16	475	150	5

GALLONS	LITERS (LITROS)	LITERS	GALLONS
1	$3\frac{3}{4}$	1	$\frac{1}{4}$ (1 quart)
5	19	5	$1\frac{1}{3}$
10	38	10	$2\frac{1}{2}$

JEWELRY

I'd like to see ____.	**Quisiera ver ____.**	*kee-SYEHR-ah behr*
■ a bracelet	**un brazalete**	*oon brah-sah-LAY-tay*
■ a brooch	**un broche**	*oon BROH-chay*
■ a chain	**una cadena**	*oon-nah kah-DAY-nah*
■ a charm	**un dije**	*oon DEE-hay*
■ some earrings	**unos aretes** (in Spain, **pendientes**)	*oo-nohs ah-REH-tays (pen-DYEHN-tays)*
■ a necklace	**un collar**	*oon koh-YAHR*
■ a pin	**un alfiler**	*oon ahl-fee-LEHR*
■ a ring	**un anillo (una sortija)**	*oon ahn-EE-yoh (oo-nah sohr-TEE-hah)*
■ a rosary	**un rosario**	*oon roh-SAHR-ee-oh*
■ a (wrist) watch	**un reloj (de pulsera)**	*oon ray-LOH (day pool-SEHR-ah)*
Is this ____?	**¿Es esto ____?**	*ehs EHS-toh*
■ gold	**oro**	*OH-roh*
■ platinum	**platino**	*plah-TEE-noh*
■ silver	**plata**	*PLAH-tah*
■ stainless steel	**acero inoxidable**	*ah-SEHR-oh een-ohks-ee-DAH-blay*
Is it solid or gold-plated?	**¿Es macizo o dorado?**	*ehs mah-SEE-soh oh dohr-AH-doh*
How many carats is it?	**¿De cuántos quilates es?**	*day KWAHN-tohs kee-LAH-tays ehs*
What is that stone?	**¿Qué es esa piedra?**	*kay ehs EHS-ah pee-YEHD-drah*

I want _____.	**Quiero _____.** *kee-YEHR-oh*
◼ an amethyst	**una amatista** *oo-nah ah-mah-TEES-tah*
◼ an aquamarine	**una aguamarina** *oo-nah ah-gwah-mah-REE-nah*
◼ a diamond	**un diamante** *oon dee-ah-MAHN-tay*
◼ an emerald	**una esmeralda** *oon-nah ehs-mehr-AHL-dah*
◼ ivory	**marfil** *mahr-FEEL*
◼ jade	**jade** *HAH-day*
◼ onyx	**ónix** *OH-neeks*
◼ pearls	**perlas** *PEHR-lahs*
◼ a ruby	**un rubí** *oon roo-BEE*
◼ a sapphire	**un zafiro** *oon sah-FEER-oh*
◼ a topaz	**un topacio** *oon toh-PAH-see-oh*
◼ turquoise	**turquesa** *toor-KAY-sah*
How much is it?	**¿Cuánto vale?** *KWAHN-toh BAH-lay*

NEWSPAPERS AND MAGAZINES

Do you carry English newspapers (magazines)?	**¿Tiene usted periódicos (revistas) en inglés?** *tee-YEHN-ay oos-TEHD peh-ree-OH-dee-kohs (ray-BEES-tahs) en een-GLAYSS*
I'd like to buy some postcards.	**Quisiera comprar postales.** *kee-SYEHR-ah kohm-PRAHR pohs-TAHL-ays*
Do you have stamps?	**¿Tiene sellos?** *tee-YEHN-ay SEH-yohs*
How much is that?	**¿Cuánto es?** *KWAHN-toh ehs*

PHOTOGRAPHY AND VIDEO EQUIPMENT

Please see the note under Electrical Appliances on page 179. In addition, Europe uses broadcasting and recording systems that are often incompatible with those of the U.S. Unless expressly warranted, Spanish TVs, VCRs, VCR tapes, computers, and telephone answering systems will not operate properly in the U.S.

For phrases dealing with camera repairs, see page 205.

Where is there a camera shop?	**¿Dónde hay una tienda de artículos fotográficos?** *DOHN-day AH-ee oo-nah tee-YEHN-dah day ahr-TEEK-oo-lohs foh-toh-GRAHF-ee-kohs*
Do you develop film here?	**¿Aquí revelan películas?** *ah-KEE ray-BEHL-ahn pel-EE-koo-lahs*
How much does it cost to develop a roll?	**¿Cuánto cuesta revelar un carrete?** *KWAHN-toh KWEHS-tah ray-behl-AHR oon kahr-REH-tay*
I want ____.	**Quiero ____.** *kee-YEHR-oh*
■ one print of each	**una copia de cada uno** *oo-nah KOH-pee-ah day kah-dah oo-noh*
■ an enlargement	**una ampliación** *oo-nah ahm-plee-ah-SYOHN*
■ with a glossy (matte) finish	**con acabado brillante (mate)** *kohn ah-kah-bah-doh bree-YAHN-tay (MAH-tay)*
I want a roll of color (black and white) film.	**Quiero un rollo de películas en colores (en blanco y negro).** *kee-YEHR-oh oon roh-yoh day pehl-EE-koo-lahs ehn koh-lohr-ays (ehn BLAHN-koh ee NEH-groh)*

When can I pick up the pictures?	**¿Cuándo puedo recoger las fotos?** *KWAHN-doh PWEH-doh ray-koh-HEHR lahs FOH-tohs*
Do you sell cameras?	**¿Vende usted cámaras?** *ben-day oos-TEHD KAH-mah-rahs*
I want an inexpensive camera.	**Quiero una cámara barata.** *kee-YEHR-oh oo-nah KAH-mah-rah bah-RAH-tah*

- a disposable camera — **una cámara desechable** *oo-nah KAH-mah-rah des-eh-CHAH-blay*
- a digital camera — **una cámara digital** *oo-nah KAH-mah-rah dee-hee-TAHL*
- a point-and-shoot camera — **una cámara automática** *oo-nah KAH-mah-rah ow-toh-MAH-tee-kah*
- an SLR camera — **una cámara réflex** *oo-nah KAH-mah-rah RAY-fleks*
- a flash — **un flash** *oon flahsh*
- a roll of slide film — **un rollo para diapositivas** *oon ro-yoh pah-rah dee-ah-poh-see-TEE-bahs*
- a slide projector — **una proyectora de diapositivas** *oo-nah pro-yek-TOHR-ah de dee-ah-poh-see-TEE-bahs*
- a tripod — **un trípode** *oon TREE-poh-day*
- a zoom lens — **un lente zoom** *oon len-tay soom*

Do you have ____?	**¿Tiéne usted ____?** *tee-YEHN-ay oos-TEHD*

- a camcorder — **una filmadora** *oo-nah feel-mah-DOHR-ah*
- a digital camcorder — **una filmadora digital** *oo-nah feel-mah-DOHR-ah dee-hee-TAHL*
- digital videofilm — **película digital de vídeo** *pel-EE-koo-lah dee-hee-TAHL day VEE-day-oh*

■ DVD movies   **películas en DVD** *pel-EE-koo-lahs en day-bay-day*

■ a DVD player   **un tocadiscos DVD** *oon toh-kah-DEES-kohs day-bay-day*

■ a DVD recorder   **una grabadora DVD** *oo-nah grah-bah-DOHR-ah day-bay-day*

■ a VCR   **una videograbadora** *oo-nah bee-day-oh-grah-bah-DOHR-ah*

■ VCR tape   **cinta de vídeo** *oo-nah seen-tah day BEE-day-oh*

Do you have VCR or DVD movies with English subtitles?   **¿Tiene películas de vídeo o DVD con subtítulos en inglés?** *TYEHN-ay pel-EE-koo-lahs day BEE-day-oh o day-bay-day kohn soob-TEE-too-lohs en een-GLAYS*

Will the warranty be honored in the US?   **¿Sera válida la garantía en los Estados Unidos?** *sehr-AH BAH-lee-dah lah gahr-ahn-TEE-ah en lohs es-TAH-dohs oo-NEE-dohs*

Who should I contact if this malfunctions?   **¿A quién debo contactar si ésto deja de funcionar?** *ah KYEHN deh-boh kohn-tahk-TAHR see ES-toh DEH-hah day foon-syohn-AHR*

AUDIO EQUIPMENT

Is there a record shop around here?   **¿Hay una tienda de discos por aquí?** *AH-ee oo-nah tee-yehn-dah day DEES-kohs pohr ah-KEE*

Do you sell ____?   **¿Vende usted ____?** *BEN-day oos-TEHD*

■ analog cassettes   **casetes analógicos** *kah-SEH-tehs ah-nah-LO-hee-kohs*

- cassette players **caseteros** *kah-seh-TEHR-ohs*
- cassette recorders **grabadoras** *grah-bah-DORH-ahs*
- CD players **tocadiscos** *toh-kah-DEES-kohs*
- CD recorders **grabadiscos** *grah-bah-DEES-kohs*
- CDs **discos** *DEES-kohs*
- digital cassettes **casetes digitales** *kah-SEH-tehs dee-hee-TAH-lays*
- headphones **audífonos** *ow-DEE-foh-nohs*
- metal cassettes **casetes metálicos** *kah-SEH-tays meh-TAHL-ee-kohs*
- minidisk players **tocadoras de minidiscos** *toh-kah-DOHR-ahs day mee-nee-DEES-kohs*
- minidisk recorders **grabadoras de minidiscos** *grah-bah-DOHR-ahs day mee-nee-DEES-kohs*
- minidisks **minidiscos** *mee-nee-DEES-kohs*
- recordable CDs **discos grabables** *DEES-kohs grah-BAH-blays*
- wireless headphones **audífonos inalámbricos** *ow-DEE-foh-nohs een-ah-LAHM-bree-kohs*

Do you have an album of ____? **¿Tiene un álbum de ____?** *tee-EHN-ay oon AHL-boom day*

Where is the ____ section? **¿Dónde está la sección de ____?** *DOHN-day ehs-TAH lah sek-SYOHN day*

- classical music **la música clásica** *lah MOO-see-kah KLAHS-ee-kah*
- folk music **la música folklórica** *lah MOO-see-kah fohl-KLOHR-ee-kah*
- latest hits **los últimos éxitos** *lahs OOL-tee-mohs EHK-see-tohs*
- rock 'n roll **el rocanrol** *ehl rohk-ahn-ROHL*
- opera **la ópera** *lah OH-pehr-ah*

■ popular music   **la música popular**   *lah MOO-see-kah poh-poo-LAHR*

■ Spanish music   **la música española**   *lah MOO-see-kah ehs-pahn-YOH-lah*

■ Latin music   **la música latina**   *lah MOO-see-kah lah-TEEN-ah*

SOUVENIRS, HANDICRAFTS

I'd like ____.   **Quisiera ____.**   *kee-SYEHR-ah*

■ a pretty gift   **un regalo bonito**   *oon ray-GAH-loh boh-NEE-toh*

■ a small gift   **un regalito**   *oon ray-gah-LEE-toh*

■ a souvenir   **un recuerdo**   *oon ray-KWEHR-doh*

It's for ____.   **Es para ____.**   *ehs pah-rah*

I don't want to spend more than ____ dollars.   **No quiero gastar más de ____ dólares.**   *noh kee-YEHR-oh gahs-TAHR mahs day ____ DOH-lahr-ays*

Could you suggest something?   **¿Podría usted sugerir algo?**   *poh-DREE-ah oos-TEHD soo-hehr-EER AHL-goh*

Would you show me your selection of ____?   **¿Quiere enseñarme su surtido de ____?**   *kee-YEHR-ay ehn-sen-YAHR-may soo soor-TEE-doh day*

■ blown glass   **vidrio soplado**   *BEE-dree-oh soh-PLAH-doh*

■ carved objects   **objetos de madera tallada**   *ohb-HET-ohs day mah-DEHR-ah tah-YAH-dah*

■ cut crystal   **vidrio tallado**   *BEE-dree-oh tah-YAH-doh*

■ dolls   **muñecas**   *moon-YEH-kahs*

- earthenware (pottery) — **loza** *LOH-sah*
- fans — **abanicos** *ah-bah-NEE-kohs*
- jewelry — **joyas** *HOY-ahs*
- lace — **encaje** *ehn-KAH-hay*
- leather goods — **objetos de cuero** *ohb-HET-ohs day KWEHR-oh*
- liqueurs — **licores** *lee-KOHR-ays*
- musical instruments — **instrumentos musicales** *een-stroo-MEN-tohs moo-see-KAHL-ays*
- perfumes — **perfumes** *pehr-FOO-mays*
- pictures — **dibujos** *dee-BOO-hohs*
- posters — **carteles** *kahr-TEHL-ays*
- religious articles — **artículos religiosos** *ahr-TEE-koo-lohs ray-lee-hee-OH-sohs*

LITTLE TREASURES

Is this an antique?	**¿Es una antigüedad?** *ehs oo-nah ahn-tee-gway-DAHD*
How old is it?	**¿Cuántos años tiene?** *KWAHN-tohs anh-yohs tee-YEHN-ay*
Is it a reproduction?	**¿Es una reproducción?** *ehs oo-nah ray-proh-dook-SYOHN*
Is the artist well known?	**¿Es conocido el artista?** *ehs kohn-oh-SEE-doh ehl ahr-TEES-tah*
Where has he (she) exhibited?	**¿Dónde está exhibiendo?** *DOHN-day ehs-TAH eks-ee-BYEHN-doh*
Is this handmade?	**¿Está hecho a mano?** *eh-STAH AY-choh ah MAH-noh*

What is the name of this type of work?	**¿Cómo se llama este tipo de trabajo?** *KOH-moh say YAH-mah EHS-tay TEE-poh day trah-BAH-ho*
Is this a specialty of this region? This town?	**¿Es una especialidad de esta región? De este pueblo?** *ehs oo-nah ehs-pehs-yah-lee-DAHD day ehs-tah ray-HYOHN day ehs-tay PWEHB-loh*
What are the local specialties of ____?	**¿Cuáles son las especialidades locales de ____?** *KWAHL-ays sohn lahs ehs-pehs-yah-lee-DAHD-ays loh-KAHL-ays day*
Is this washable?	**¿Es lavable?** *ehs lah-bah-blay*
Will it shrink?	**¿Se encoge?** *say ehn-KOH-hay*
Should it be washed by hand?	**¿Debe lavarse a mano?** *DEH-bay lah-BAHR-say ah MAH-noh*
Should it be washed in cold water?	**¿Debe lavarse en agua fría?** *DEH-bay lah-BAHR-say ehn AH-gwah FREE-ah*
Can it go in the dryer?	**¿Se puede meter en la secadora?** *say PWEHD-ay meh-TEHR ehn lah seh-kah-DOHR-ah*
Can this go in the dishwasher?	**¿Se puede meter esto en el lava-platos?** *say PWEH-day meh-TEHR ehs-toh ehn ehl lah-bah-PLAH-tohs*
Is it ovenproof?	**¿Está a prueba de horno?** *ehs-TAH ah PRWEH-bah day OR-noh*
Is this safe to use for cooking?	**¿Se puede usar sin peligro para cocinar?** *say PWEH-day oo-SAHR SEEN pe-LEE-groh pah-rah koh-see-NAHR*

What is the lead content?	**¿Qué contenido de plomo tiene?** *kay kohn-ten-EE-doh day PLOH-moh tee-YEHN-ay*
Did you make this yourself?	**¿Lo ha hecho usted?** *loh ah AY-choh oss-TEHD*

BARGAINING

In Latin American open markets you will be expected to bargain for everything you want to purchase. The key to successful bargaining is to end up with a price that is fair for both you and the merchant. Begin by asking the price, then make your own offer about half to two-thirds of the asking price. Usually the merchant will make another offer and you can listen and consider the object, perhaps finding a little problem with it—a tear, a scrape, some unevenness. A little discussion back and forth, and you'll soon have it at a fair price. If you do not understand numbers, then the seller will write the number down for you. At the conclusion, smile and thank the merchant, expressing your happiness with the result.

Please, madam, how much is this?	**Por favor, señora, ¿cuánto vale ésto?** *pohr fah-BOHR sehn-YOHR-ah KWAHN-toh BAH-lay EHS-toh*
Oh, no, that is more than I can spend.	**Ay, no, eso es más de lo que puedo gastar.** *AH-ee noh EHS-oh ehs MAHS day loh kay PWEH-doh gahs-TAHR*
How about ___?	**¿Y si le doy ____?** *EE see lay doy*
No, that is too high. Would you take ____?	**No, eso es demasiado. ¿Aceptaría ____?** *noh EHS-oh ehs day-mahs-ee-AH-doh ah-sep-tahr-ER-ah*

But there seems to be a scratch (tear) here.	**Me parece que hay un arañazo (un roto) aquí.** *may pahr-ay-say kay AH-ee oon ah-rahn-YAH-soh ah-KEE*
Yes, that's fine. I'll take it.	**Así está bien. Me lo llevo.** *ah-SEE ehs-TAH byehn may loh YEH-boh*
Thank you. Have a nice day.	**Gracias. Que lo pase bien.** *GRAH-see-ahs kay loh PAH-say byehn*

STATIONERY ITEMS

I want to buy ____.	**Quiero comprar ____.** *kee-YEHR-oh kohm-PRAHR*
■ a ball-point pen	**un bolígrafo** *oon boh-LEE-grah-foh*
■ a deck of cards	**una baraja** *oo-nah bahr-AH-hah*
■ envelopes	**sobres** *SOH-brays*
■ an eraser	**una goma de borrar** *oo-nah GOH-mah day bohr-AHR*
■ glue	**cola de pegar** *koh-lah day peh-GAHR*
■ a notebook	**un cuaderno** *oon kwah-DEHR-noh*
■ pencils	**lápices** *LAH-pee-sayss*
■ a pencil sharpener	**un sacapuntas** *oon sah-kah-POON-tahs*
■ printing paper	**papel para impresora** *pah-PEL PAH-rah eem-preh-SOH-rah*
■ a ruler	**una regla** *oo-nah REHG-lah*
■ Scotch tape	**cinta adhesiva** *SEEN-tah ahd-ehs-EE-bah*
■ some string	**cuerda** *KWEHR-dah*
■ typing paper	**papel de máquina** *pah-PEL day MAH-kee-nah*

- wrapping paper   **papel de envolver** *pah-PEL day ehn-bohl-BEHR*

- a writing pad   **un bloc de papel** *oon blohk day pah-PEL*

TOBACCO

Attitudes toward smoking and smokers are much more liberal in Spain and Latin America than in the United States. However, many governments are conducting health campaigns in schools and workplaces, and there are places where smoking is forbidden or frowned upon. Therefore, it always pays to be polite and ask, "May I smoke?" (**¿Puedo fumar?**) (*PWEH-doh foo-MAHR*).

In Latin America you can buy cigarettes and other related items at a **tabaquería** (*tah-bah-kehr-EE-ah*).

In Spain, you would go to an **estanco** (*ehs-TAHN-koh*).

A pack (carton) of cigarettes, please.	**Un paquete (cartón) de cigarrillos, por favor.** *oon pah-KAY-tay (kahr-TOHN) day see-gahr-EE-yohs pohr fah-BOHR*
■ filtered	**con filtro** *kohn FEEL-troh*
■ unfiltered	**sin filtro** *seen FEEL-troh*
■ menthol	**de mentol** *day mehn-TOHL*
■ king-size	**extra largos** *EHS-trah LAHR-gohs*
Are these cigarettes (very) strong (mild)?	**¿Son (muy) fuertes (suaves) estos cigarrillos?** *sohn (mwee) FWEHR-tays (SWAH-bays) ehs-tohs see-gahr-EE-yohs*
Do you have American cigarettes?	**¿Tiene usted cigarrillos norteamericanos?** *tee-YEHN-ay oos-TEHD see-gahr-EE-yohs nohr-tay-ah-mehr-ee-KAH-nohs*

What brands?	**¿De qué marcas?** *day kay MAHR-kahs*
Please give me a pack, of matches also.*	**Déme una caja de fósforos también.** *DAY-may oo-nah KAH-hah day FOHS-for-ohs tahm-bee-EHN*
Do you sell ____?	**¿Vende usted ____?** *BEHN-day oo-STEHD*
■ a cigarette holder	**una boquilla** *oo-nah boh-KEE-yah*
■ cigars	**cigarros** *see-GAHR-rohs*
■ flints	**piedras de encendedor** *pee-EH-drahs day ehn-sen-day-DOHR*
■ lighter fluid	**líquido de encendedor** *LEE-kee-doh day ehn-see-day-DOHR*
■ lighters	**encendedores** *ehn-sen-day-DOHR-ays*
■ pipes	**pipas** *PEE-pahs*
■ pipe tobacco	**tabaco de pipa** *tah-BAH-koh day PEE-pah*

*Matches are often not free; you must pay for them.

TOILETRIES

In Spain, a drugstore (chemist) doesn't carry toiletries. There you will have to go to a **perfumería.** In Latin America, however, you'll find cosmetics and other toiletries at drugstores and pharmacies as well.

Do you have ____?	**¿Tiene usted ____?** *tee-YEHN-ay oo-STEHD*
■ bobby pins	**horquillas** *ohr-KEE-yahs*
■ a brush	**un cepillo** *oon sep-EE-yoh*
■ cleansing cream	**crema limpiadora** *KRAY-mah leem-pee-ah-DOHR-ah*

■ a comb	**un peine** *oon PAY-nay*
■ deodorant	**un desodorante** *oon dehs-oh-dohr-AHN-tay*
■ (disposable) diapers	**pañales (desechables)** *pahn-YAH-lays (dehs-ay-CHAH-blays)*
■ emery boards	**limas de cartón** *LEE-mahs day kahr-TOHN*
■ eyeliner	**un lápiz de ojos** *oon LAH-pees day OH-hohs*
■ hairspray	**laca** *LAH-kah*
■ lipstick	**lápiz de labios** *LAH-pees day LAH-bee-ohs*
■ makeup	**maquillaje** *mah-kee-YAH-hay*
■ mascara	**rimel** *ree-MEHL*
■ a mirror	**un espejo** *oon ehs-PAY-ho*
■ mouthwash	**un lavado bucal** *oon lah-bah-doh boo-kahl*
■ nail clippers	**un cortauñas** *oon kohr-tah-oon-yahs*
■ a nail file	**una lima de uñas** *oo-nah lee-mah day OON-yahs*
■ nail polish	**esmalte de uñas** *ehs-MAHL-tay day OON-yahs*
■ nail polish remover	**un quita-esmalte** *oon kee-tah ehs-MAHL-tay*
■ a razor	**una navaja** *oo-nah nah-BAH-hah*
■ razor blades	**hojas de afeitar** *OH-hahs day ah-fay-TAHR*
■ sanitary napkins	**servilletas higiénicas** *sehr-bee-YEH-tahs ee-HYEHN-ee-kahs*
■ (cuticle) scissors	**tijeras (de cutículas)** *tee-HAIR-ahs (day koo-TEE-kool-ahs)*
■ shampoo	**champú** *chahm-POO*

- shaving lotion   **loción de afeitar**   *loh-SYOHN day ah-fay-TAHR*

- soap   **jabón**   *hah-BOHN*

- a sponge   **una esponja**   *oo-nah ehs-POHN-hah*

- tampons   **tapones**   *tah-POHN-ays*

- tissues   **pañuelos de papel**   *pahn-yoo-EH-lohs day pah-PEL*

- toilet paper   **papel higiénico**   *pah-PEL ee-hy-EHN-ee-koh*

- a toothbrush   **un cepillo de dientes**   *oon sep-EE-yoh day dee-YEHN-tays*

- toothpaste   **pasta de dientes**   *pah-stah day dee-YEHN-tays*

- tweezers   **pinzas**   *PEEN-sahs*

PERSONAL CARE AND SERVICES

If your hotel doesn't offer these services, ask the attendant at the desk to recommend someone nearby.

AT THE BARBER

Where is there a good barber shop?	**¿Dónde hay una buena barbería?** *DOHN-day AH-ee oo-nah BWEH-nah bahr-behr-EE-ah*
Do I have to wait long?	**¿Tengo que esperar mucho?** *ten-goh kay ehs-pehr-AHR MOO-choh*
Am I next?	**¿Me toca a mí?** *may TOH-kay ah mee*
I want a shave.	**Quiero que me afeiten.** *kee-YEHR-oh kay may ah-FAY-tehn*
I want a haircut (razorcut).	**Quiero un corte de pelo (a navaja)** *kee-YEHR-oh oon KOHR-tay day PEH-loh (ah nah-BAH-hah)*
Short in back, long in front.	**Corto por detrás, largo por delante.** *KOHR-toh pohr day-TRAHS lahr-goh pohr day-LAHN-tay*
Leave it long.	**Déjelo largo.** *DAY-hay-loh LAHR-goh*
I want it (very) short.	**Lo quiero (muy) corto.** *loh kee-YEHR-oh (mwee) KOHR-toh*
You can cut a little ____.	**Puede cortar on poquito ____.** *PWEH-day kohr-TAHR oon poh-KEE toh*

■ in back   **por detrás** *pohr day-TRAHS*

■ in front   **por delante** *pohr day-LAHN-tay*

■ off the top   **de arriba** *day ah-REE-bah*

■ on the sides   **a los lados** *ah lohs LAH-dohs*

Cut a little bit more here.   **Córteme on poco más aquí.** *KOHR-tay-may oon POH-koh mahs ah-KEE*

That's enough.   **Eso es bastante.** *EH-soh ehs bah-STAHN-tay*

I (don't) want ____.   **(No) quiero ____.** *(noh) kee-YEHR-oh*

■ shampoo   **champú** *chahm-POO*

■ tonic   **tónico** *TOHN-ee-koh*

Use the scissors only.   **Use sólo las tijeras.** *oo-say soh-loh lahs tee-HAIR-ahs*

Trim my ____.   **Recórteme ____.** *ray-KOHR-tay-may*

■ beard   **la barba** *lah bahr-bah*

■ moustache   **el bigote** *ehl bee-GOH-tay*

■ sideburns   **las patillas** *lahs pah-TEE-yahs*

I'd like to look at myself in the mirror.   **Quisiera mirarme al espejo.** *kee-SYEHR-ah meer-AHR-may ahl ehs-PAY-hoh*

How much do I owe you?   **¿Cuánto le debo?** *KWAHN-toh lay DEH-boh*

Is tipping included?   **¿Está incluída la propina?** *eh-STAH een-kloo-EE-dah lah proh-PEE-nah*

AT THE BEAUTY PARLOR

Is there a beauty parlor (hairdresser) near the hotel?	**¿Hay un salón de belleza (una peluquería) cerca del hotel?** *AH-ee oon sah-LOHN day beh-YEH-sah (oo-nah pel-oo-kehr-EE-ah) SEHR-kah del oh-TEL*
I'd like an appointment for this afternoon (tomorrow).	**Quisiera hacer una cita para esta tarde (mañana).** *kee-SYEHR-ah ah-SEHR oo-nah SEE-tah pah-rah EHS-tah TAHR-day (mahn-YA-nah)*
Can you give me ____?	**¿Puede darme ____?** *PWEH-day DAHR-may*
■ a color rinse	**un enjuague de color** *oon ehn-hoo-AH-gay day koh-LOHR*
■ a facial massage	**un masaje facial** *oon mah-SAH-hay fah-see-AHL*
■ a haircut	**un corte de pelo** *oon KOHR-tay day PEH-loh*

■ a manicure	**una manicura**	*oon-nah mah-nee-KOOR-ah*
■ a pedicure	**una pedicura**	*oo-nah ped-ee-KOOR-ah*
■ a permanent	**una permanente**	*oon-nah pehr-mah-NEN-tay*
■ a shampoo	**un champú**	*oon-chahm-POO*
■ a tint	**un tinte**	*oon TEEN-tay*
■ a touch-up	**un retoque**	*oon ray-TOH-kay*
■ a wash and set	**un lavado y peinado**	*oon lah-bah-doh ee pay-NAH-doh*
■ just a trim	**sólo las puntas**	*soh-loh lahs POON-tahs*

I'd like to see a color chart. **Quisiera ver un muestrario.** *kee-SYEHR-ah behr oon mwehs-TRAHR-ee-oh*

I want a ____ color. **Quiero un color ____.** *kee YEHR-oh oon koh-LOHR*

■ auburn	**rojizo**	*roh-HEE-soh*
■ (light) blond	**un rubio (claro)**	*oon ROO-bee-oh (KLAHR-oh)*
■ brunette	**castaño**	*kas-TAHN-yo*
■ a darker color	**un color más oscuro**	*oon koh-LOHR mahs oh-SKOOR-oh*
■ a lighter color	**un color más claro**	*oon koh-LOHR mahs KLAH-roh*
■ the same color	**el mismo color**	*ehl MEES-moh koh-LOHR*

Don't apply any hair-spray. **No me ponga laca.** *noh may POHN-gah LAH-kah*

Not too much hair-spray. **Sólo un poco de laca.** *SOH-loh oon POH-koh day LAH-kah*

I want my hair ____.	**Quiero el pelo ____.** *kee-YEHR-oh ehl peh-loh*
with bangs	**con flequillo** *kohn fleh-KEE-yoh*
in a bun	**con un moño** *kohn oon MOHN-yoh*
in curls	**con bucles** *kohn boo-KLAYS*
with waves	**con ondas** *kohn OHN-dahs*
I'd like to look at myself in the mirror.	**Quiero mirarme al espejo.** *kee-YEHR-oh meer-AHR-may ahl ehs-PAY-hoh*
How much do I owe you?	**¿Cuánto le debo?** *KWAHN-toh lay DEH-boh*
Is tipping included?	**¿Está incluída la propina?** *es-TAH een-kloo-EE-dah lah proh-PEE-nah*

LAUNDRY AND DRY CLEANING

Where is the nearest laundry (dry cleaners)?	**¿Dónde está la lavandería (la tintorería) más cercana?** *DOHN-day ehs-TAH lah lah-bahn-deh-REE-ah (lah teen-TOHR-ehr-EE-ah) mahs sehr-KAH-nah*
I have a lot of (dirty) clothes to be ____.	**Tengo mucha ropa (sucia) que ____.** *TEN-goh MOO-chah ROH-pah (SOO-see-ah) kay*
(dry) cleaned	**limpiar (en seco)** *leem-pee-AHR (ehn SEH-koh)*
washed	**lavar** *lah-BAHR*
mended	**arreglar** *ah-ray-GLAHR*
ironed	**planchar** *plahn-CHAHR*
Here's the list.	**Aquí tiene la lista.** *ah-KEE tee-EH-neh lah LEES-tah*

◼ 3 shirts (men's)	**tres camisas (de hombre)** *trays kah-mee-sahs (day OHM-bray)*
◼ 12 handkerchiefs	**doce pañuelos** *doh-say pahn-yoo-AY-lohs*
◼ 6 pairs of socks	**seis pares de calcetines** *sayss pah-rays day kahl-say-TEEN-ays*
◼ 1 blouse (nylon)	**una blusa (de nilón)** *oo-nah BLOO-sah (day nee-LOHN)*
◼ 4 shorts (underwear)	**cuatro calzoncillos** *KWAH-troh kahl-sohn-SEEL-yohs*
◼ 2 pyjamas	**dos pijamas** *dohs pee-HAHM-ahs*
◼ 2 suits	**dos trajes** *dohs TRAH-hays*
◼ 3 ties	**tres corbatas** *trays kohr-BAH-tahs*
◼ 2 dresses (cotton)	**dos vestidos (de algodón)** *dohs behs-tee-dohs (day ahl-go-DOHN)*
◼ 2 skirts	**dos faldas** *dohs FAHL-dahs*
◼ 1 sweater (wool)	**un suéter (de lana)** *oon soo-EH-tehr (day LAH-nah)*

I need them for ____.	**Las necesito para ____.** *lahs neh-seh-SEE-toh PAH-rah*
◼ tonight	**esta noche** *EHS-tah NOH-chay*
◼ tomorrow	**mañana** *mahn-YAH-nah*
◼ next week	**la semana próxima** *lah seh-MAH-nah PROHK-see-mah*
◼ the day after tomorrow	**pasado mañana** *pah-SAH-doh mahn-YAH-nah*
When will you bring it back?	**¿Cuándo la traerá?** *KWAHN-doh lah trah-ehr-AH*
When will it be ready?	**¿Cuándo estará lista?** *KWAHN-doh ehs-tah-RAH LEES-tah*
There's a button missing.	**Falta on botón.** *FAHL-tah oon boh-TOHN*

Can you sew it on?	**¿Puede usted coserlo?** *PWEH-deh oos-TEHD koh-SEHR-loh*
This isn't my laundry.	**Esta no es mi ropa.** *EHS-tah noh ehs mee ROH-pah*

SHOE REPAIRS

A shoemaker, **el zapatero** *(ehl sah-pah-TEHR-oh)* will repair shoes.

Can you fix these (boots)?	**¿Puede arreglar estos zapatos (estas botas)?** *PWEH-day ah-ray-GLAHR ehs-tohs sah-PAH-tohs (ehs-tahs BOH-tahs)*
Put on (half) soles and rubber heels.	**Póngales (medias) suelas y tacones de goma.** *POHN-gah-lays (MED-ee-ahs) SWAY-lahs ee tah-KOHN-ays day GOH-mah*
I'd like to have my shoes shined too.	**Quiero que me limpien los zapatos también.** *kee-YEHR-oh kay may LEEM-pee-ehn lohs sah-PAH-tohs tahm-BYEHN*
When will they be ready?	**¿Para cuándo los tendrá?** *pah-rah KWAHN-doh los ten-DRAH*
I need them by Saturday (without fail).	**Los necesito para el sábado (sin falta).** *lohs nes-ehs-see-toh pah-rah ehl SAH-bah-doh (seen FAHL-tah)*

WATCH REPAIRS

A watchmaker, **un relojero** *(oon reh-loh-HER-oh)*, in his shop, **la relojería** *(lah ray-loh-hehr-EE-ah)* will repair watches and clocks.

Can you fix this watch (alarm clock) (for me)?	**¿(Me) puede arreglar este reloj (despertador)?** *(may) PWEH-day ah-ray-GLAHR EHS-tay ray-LOH (dehs-pehr-tah-dohr)*
Can you clean it?	**¿Puede usted limpiarlo?** *PWEH-day oos-TEHD leem-pee-AHR-loh*
I dropped it.	**Se me cayó.** *say may kah-YOH*
It's running slow (fast).	**Se atrasa (se adelanta).** *say ah-TRAH-sah (say ah-deh-LAHN-tah)*
It's stopped.	**Está parado.** *ehs-TAH pah-RAH-doh*
I need ____.	**Necesito ____.** *neh-say-SEE-toh*
▪ a crystal, glass	**un cristal** *oon kree-STAHL*
▪ an hour hand	**un horario** *oon ohr-AH-ee-oh*
▪ a minute hand	**un minutero** *oon mee-noo-TEHR-oh*
▪ a stem	**un tornillo** *oon tohr-NEE-yoh*
▪ a second hand	**un segundario** *oon say-goon-DAH-ree-oh*
▪ a battery	**una pila** *oo-nah PEE-lah*
When will it be ready?	**¿Cuándo estará listo?** *KWAHN-doh ehs-tah-RAH LEES-toh*
May I have a receipt?	**¿Me puede dar un recibo?** *may PWEH-day dahr oon ray-SEE-boh*

CAMERA REPAIRS

| Can you fix this camera? | **¿Puede usted arreglar esta cámara?** *PWEH-deh oos-TEHD ah-ray-GLAHR ehs-tah KAH-mah-rah* |
| The film doesn't advance. | **El carrete no se mueve.** *ehl kah-REH-tay noh say MWEH-bay* |

I think I need new batteries.

Creo que necesito una nueva pila.
KRAY-oh kay neh-seh-SEE-toh oo-nah NWEH-bah PEE-lah

How much will the repair cost?

¿Cuánto costará el arreglo?
KWAHN-toh kohs-tah-RAH ehl ah-REG-loh

When can I come and get it?

¿Cuándo puedo venir a buscarla?
KWAHN-doh PWEH-doh ben-EER ah boos-KAHR-lah

I need it as soon as possible.

La necesito lo más pronto posible.
lah neh-say-SEE-toh loh mahs PROHN-toh poh-SEE-blay

MEDICAL CARE

THE PHARMACY (CHEMIST)

La farmacia *(fahr-MAH-see-ah)* in Spain can be recognized by its sign with a green cross. If it is closed, look for a list on the door indicating the nearest stores that are open. Note that in Spain a pharmacy mainly sells drugs; for toiletries, you must go to a **perfumería**.

Where is the nearest (all-night) pharmacy (chemist)?	**¿Dónde está la farmacia (de guardia) más cercana?** *DOHN-day ehs-TAH lah fahr-MAH-see-ah (day GWAHR-dee-ah) mahs sehr-KAH-nah*
At what time does the pharmacy open (close)?	**¿A qué hora se abre (se cierra) la farmacia?** *ah kay OH-rah say AH-bray (say SYEHR-ah) lah fahr-MAH-see-ah*
I need something for _____.	**Necesito algo para _____.** *neh-seh-SEE-toh AHL-goh pah-rah*
▪ a cold	**on catarro** *oon kah-TAH-roh*
▪ constipation	**el estreñimiento (constipación estomacal)** *ehl ehs-trayn-yee-MYEHN-toh*
▪ a cough	**la tos** *lah tohs*
▪ diarrhea	**la diarrea** *lah dee-ahr-RAY-ah*
▪ a fever	**la fiebre** *lah fee-YEHB-ray*
▪ flatulence	**flatulencia** *flah-too-LEN-see-ah*
▪ hay fever	**la fiebre del heno** *lah fee-YEHB-ray del AY-noh*
▪ a headache	**un dolor de cabeza** *oon doh-LOHR day kah-BAY-sah*
▪ insomnia	**el insomnio** *ehl een-SOHM-nee-oh*
▪ nausea	**náuseas** *NAH-oo-say-ahs*

■ sunburn	**la quemadura del sol** *lah kay-mah-DOOR-ah del SOHL*
■ a toothache	**un dolor de muelas** *oon doh-LOHR day MWEH-lahs*
■ an upset stomach	**la indigestión** *la een-dee-hes-TYOHN*
I do not have a prescription.	**No tengo la receta.** *noh TEN-goh lah reh-SAY-tah*
May I have it right away?	**¿Me la puede dar en seguida?** *May lah PWEH-day DAHR ehn seh-GHEE-dah*
It's an emergency!	**¡Es urgente!** *ehs oor-HEN-tay*
How long will it take?	**¿Cuánto tiempo tardará?** *KWAHN-toh tee-YEHM-poh tahr-dahr-AH*
When can I come for it?	**¿Cuándo puedo venir a recogerla?** *KWAHN-doh PWEH-doh ben-EER ah ray-koh-HAIR-lah*
I would like ____.	**Quisiera ____.** *kee-see-YEHR-ah*
■ adhesive tape	**esparadrapo** *ehs-pah-rah-DRAH-poh*
■ alcohol	**alcohol** *ahl-koh-OHL*
■ an antacid	**un antiácido** *oon ahn-tee-AH-see-doh*
■ an antihistamine	**un antihistamínico** *oon ahn-tee-ees-tah-MEEN-ee-koh*
■ an antiseptic	**un antiséptico** *oon ahn-tee-SEP-tee-koh*
■ aspirins	**aspirinas** *ahs-peer-EE-nahs*
■ Band-Aids	**curitas** *koor-EE-tahs*
■ contraceptives	**contraceptivos** *kohn-trah-sep-TEE-bohs*
■ corn plasters	**callicidas** *kah-yee-SEE-dahs*
■ cotton	**algodón** *ahl-goh-DOHN*

■ cough drops	**pastillas para la tos** *PAHS-TEE-yahs pah-rah lah TOHS*
■ cough syrup	**jarabe para la tos** *hah-RAH-bay PAH-rah lah TOHS*
■ ear drops	**gotas para los oídos** *GOH-tahs PAH-rah lohs oh-EE-dohs*
■ eye drops	**gotas para los ojos** *GOH-tahs PAH-rah lohs OH-hohs*
■ iodine	**yodo** *YOH-doh*
■ a (mild) laxative	**un laxante (ligero)** *oon lahk-SAHN-tay (lee-HEHR-oh)*
■ milk of magnesia	**una leche de magnesia** *oo-nah leh-chay day mahg-NAY-see-ah*
■ prophylactics	**profilácticos** *pro-fee-LAHK-tee-kohs*
■ sanitary napkins	**servilletas higiénicas** *sehr-bee-YEH-tahs ee-HYEHN-ee-kahs*
■ suppositories	**supositorios** *soo-pohs-ee-TOHR-ee-ohs*
■ talcum powder	**polvos de talco** *POHL-bohs day TAHL-koh*
■ tampons	**tapones** *tah-POHN-ays*
■ a thermometer	**un termómetro** *oon tehr-MOH-met-roh*
■ tranquilizers	**un tranquilizante** *oon trahn-kee-lee-SAHN-tay*
■ vitamins	**vitaminas** *bee-tah-MEE-nahs*

WITH THE DOCTOR

I don't feel well.	**No me siento bien.** *noh may SYEHN-toh BYEHN*
I need a doctor (right now).	**Necesito un médico (ahora mismo).** *neh-seh-SEE-toh oon MEH-dee-koh (ah-OHR-ah MEES-moh)*

Do you know a doctor (chiropractor) who speaks English?	**¿Conoce un médico (quiropráctico) que hable inglés?** *koh-NOH-say oon MEH-dee-koh (kee-rho-PRAHK-tee-koh) kay ah-blay een-GLAYSS*
Where is his office (surgery)?	**¿Dónde está su consultorio?** *DOHN-day ehs-TAH soo kohn-sool-TOHR-ee-oh*
Will the doctor come to the hotel?	**¿Vendrá el medico al hotel?** *ben-DRAH ehl MED-ee-koh ahl oh-TEL*
I feel dizzy.	**Estoy mareado.** *ehs-TOY mahr-ay-AH-doh*
I feel weak.	**Me siento débil.** *may SYEHN-toh DAY-beel*
My temperature is normal (37°C).	**Tengo la temperatura normal (treinta y siete grados).** *TEN-goh lah tem-pehr-ah-TOOR-ah nohr-MAHL (TRAYN-tah ee see-EH-tay GRAH-dohs)*
I (think I) have ____.	**(Creo que) tengo ____.** *KRAY-oh kay TEN-goh*
■ an abscess	**un absceso** *oon ahb-SEHS-oh*
■ a broken bone	**un hueso roto** *oon WAY-soh ROH-toh*
■ a bruise	**una contusión** *oo-nah kohn-too-SYOHN*
■ a burn	**una quemadura** *oo-nah kay-mah-DOOR-ah*
■ something in my eye	**algo en el ojo** *AHL-goh ehn ehl OH-hoh*
■ the chills	**escalofríos** *ehs-kah-loh-FREE-ohs*
■ a chest (head) cold	**un catarro (resfriado)** *oon kah-TAHR-oh (res-free-AH-doh)*

constipation	**estreñimiento**	*ehs-trayn-yee-mee-YENT-oh*
stomach cramps	**calambres**	*kahl-AHM-brays*
a cut	**una cortadura**	*oo-nah kohr-tah-DOOR-ah*
diarrhea	**diarrea**	*dee-ah-RAY-ah*
a fever	**fiebre**	*fee-YEHB-bray*
a fracture	**una fractura**	*oo-nah frahk-TOOR-ah*
a backache	**un dolor de espalda**	*oon doh-LOHR day es-PAHL-dah*
an earache	**un dolor de oído**	*oon doh-LOHR day oh-EE-doh*
a headache	**un dolor de cabeza**	*oon doh-LOHR day kah-BAY-sah*
an infection	**una infección**	*oo-nah een-fek-SYOHN*
a lump	**un bulto**	*oon BOOL-toh*
a sore throat	**un dolor de garganta**	*oon doh-LOHR day gahr-GAHN-tah*
a stomachache	**un dolor de estómago**	*oon doh-lohr day ehs-TOH-mah-goh*

It hurts me here.	**Me duele aquí.** *may DWEH-lay ah-KEE*
My whole body hurts.	**Me duele todo el cuerpo.** *may DWEH-lay toh-doh ehl KWEHR-poh*
Can you check my blood pressure (pulse, temperature)?	**¿Puede verificar mi presión (pulso, temperatura)?** *PWEH-day behr-ee-fee-KAHR mee preh-SYOHN (POOL-soh tem-pehr-ah-TOOR-ah)*

PARTS OF THE BODY

ankle	**el tobillo** *ehl toh-BEE-yoh*
appendix	**el apéndice** *ehl ah-PEN-dee-say*
arm	**el brazo** *ehl BRAH-soh*
back	**la espalda** *lah ehs-PAHL-dah*
breast	**el pecho** *ehl PAY-choh*
cheek	**la mejilla** *lah meh-HEE-yah*
ear	**el oído** *ehl oh-EE-doh*
elbow	**el codo** *ehl KOH-doh*
eye	**el ojo** *ehl OH-hoh*
face	**la cara** *lah KAH-rah*
finger	**el dedo** *ehl DAY-doh*
foot	**el pie** *ehl pee-AY*
glands	**las glándulas** *lahs GLAHN-doo-lahs*

hand	**la mano** *lah MAHN-oh*
head	**la cabeza** *lah kah-BAY-sah*
heart	**el corazón** *ehl kohr-ah-SOHN*
hip	**la cadera** *lah kah-DEHR-ah*
knee	**la rodilla** *lah roh-DEE-yah*
leg	**la pierna** *lah pee-YEHR-nah*
lip	**el labio** *ehl LAH-bee-oh*
liver	**el hígado** *ehl EE-gah-doh*
mouth	**la boca** *lah BOH-kah*
neck	**el cuello** *ehl KWEH-yoh*
nose	**la nariz** *lah nah-REES*
shoulder	**el hombro** *ehl OHM-broh*
skin	**la piel** *lah pee-YEHL*
thumb	**el pulgar** *ehl pool-GAHR*
throat	**la garganta** *lah gahr-GAHN-tah*
toe	**el dedo del pie** *ehl DAY-doh del pee-YEH*
tooth	**el diente** *ehl dee-YEHN-tay*
wrist	**la muñeca** *lah moon-YEH-kah*

TELLING THE DOCTOR

I've had this pain since yesterday.	**Tengo este dolor desde ayer.** *TEN-goh EHS-tay doh-LOHR des-day ah-YEHR*
There's a (no) history of asthma (diabetes) in my family.	**(No) hay incidencia de asma (diabetes) en mi familia.** *(noh) AH-ee een-see-DEN-see-ah day AHS-mah (dee-ah-BEH-tays) ehn mee fah-MEEL-yah*
I'm (not) allergic to antibiotics (penicillin).	**(No) soy alérgico(a) a los antibióticos (penicilina).** *(noh) soy ah-LEHR-hee-koh(kah) ah lohs ahn-tee-bee-OH-tee-kohs (pen-ee-see-LEE-nah).*
I have a pain in my chest.	**Tengo dolor en el pecho.** *TEN-goh doh-LOHR ehn ehl PAY-choh*
I have heart trouble.	**Tengo problemas cardíacos** *TEN-goh pro-BLAY-mahs kahr-DEE-ah-kohs*
I had a heart attack ____ year(s) ago.	**Tuve on ataque al corazón hace ____ año(s).** *TOO-bay oon ah-TAH-kay ahl kohr-ah-SOHN ah-say ahn-yoh(s)*
I'm taking this medicine (insulin).	**Tomo esta medicina (insulina).** *TOH-moh EHS-tah med-ee-SEE-nah (een-soo-LEE-nah)*
I'm pregnant.	**Estoy embarazada.** *EHS-toy ehm-bahr-ah-SAH-dah*
I feel better (worse).	**Me siento mejor (peor).** *may see-YEN-toh may-HOHR (pay-OHR)*
Is it serious (contagious)?	**¿Es grave (contagioso)?** *ehs GRAH-bay (kohn-tah-hee-OH-soh)*

Do I have to go to the hospital?	**¿Tengo que ir al hospital?** *TEN-goh kay eer ahl ohs-pee-TAHL*
When can I continue my trip?	**¿Cuándo puedo continuar mi viaje?** *KWAHN-doh PWEH-doh kon-teen-oo-AHR mee bee-AH-hay*

DOCTOR'S INSTRUCTIONS AND REQUIREMENTS

Abra la boca.	Open your mouth.
Saque la lengua.	Stick out your tongue.
Tosa.	Cough.
Respire fuerte.	Breathe deeply.
Quítese la ropa	Take off your clothing.
Acuéstese.	Lie down.
Levántese.	Stand up.
Vístase.	Get dressed.

FOLLOWING UP

Do I need ____?	**¿Necesito ____?**
■ an MRI	**una imagen por resonancia magnética** *oo-nah ee-MAH-hen pohr reh-soh-NAHN-see-ah mahg-NET-ee-kah*
■ a sonogram	**un sonograma** *oon soh-noh-GRAH-mah*
■ an angiogram	**un angiograma** *oon ahn-hee-oh-GRAH-mah*
■ an ECG	**un electrocardiograma** *oon eh-lek-tro-KAHR-dee-oh-GRAH-mah*

■ a CAT scan

una tomografía computarizada
oo-nah toh-moh-grah-FEE-ah kohn-poo-tahr-ee-SAH-dah

■ x-rays

rayos equis *RAH-ee-ohs EH-kees*

■ a blood (urine, stool) test

un examen de sangre (orina, excremento) *oon ek-SAH-men day SAHN-gray (oh-REE-nah eks-cray-MEN-toh)*

Are you giving me a prescription?

¿Va a darme una receta? *bah ah DAHR-may oo-nah ray-SAY-tah*

How often must I take this medicine (these pills)?

¿Cuántas veces al día tengo que tomar esta medicina (estas píldoras)? *KWAHN-tahs BEH-says ahl DEE-ah TEN-goh kay toh-MAHR EHS-tah med-ee-SEE-nah (EHS-tahs PEEL-dohr-ahs)*

(How long) do I have to stay in bed?

¿(Cuánto tiempo) tengo que quedarme en cama? *(KWAHN-toh tee-YEHM-poh) TEN-goh kay kay-DAHR-may ehn KAH-mah*

Thank you (for everything), doctor.

Muchas gracias (por todo), doctor. *MOO-chahs GRAH-see-ahs (pohr TOH-doh) dohk-TOHR*

How much do I owe you for your services?

¿Cuánto le debo? *KWAHN-toh lay DEHB-oh*

Will you accept my medical insurance?

¿Acepta mi seguro médico? *ah-SEP-tah mee seh-GOOR-oh MED-ee-koh*

IN THE HOSPITAL (ACCIDENTS)

Help!	**¡Socorro!** *soh-KOH-roh*
Get a doctor, quick!	**¡Busque un médico, rápido!** *BOO-skay oon MED-ee-koh RAH-pee-doh*
Call an ambulance!	**¡Llame una ambulancia!** *YAH-may oo-nah ahm-boo-LAHN-see-ah*
Take me to the hospital!	**¡Lléveme al hospital!** *YEV-eh-may ahl ohs-pee-TAHL*
I've fallen.	**Me he caído.** *may ay kah-EE-doh*
I was knocked down (run over).	**Fui atropellado(a).** *fwee ah-troh-peh-YAH-doh*
I think I've had a heart attack.	**Creo que he tenido un ataque al corazón.** *KRAY-oh kay ay ten-EE-doh oon ah-TAH-kay ahl kohr-ah-SOHN*
I need my nitroglycerine.	**Necesito mi nitroglicerina** *neh-seh-SEE-toh mee nee-troh-glee-sehr-EE-nah*
I burned myself.	**Me quemé.** *may kay-MAY*
I cut myself.	**Me corté.** *may kohr-TAY*
I'm bleeding.	**Estoy sangrando.** *ehs-toy sahn-GRAHN-doh*
I think the bone is broken (dislocated).	**Creo que el hueso está roto (dislocado)** *KRAY-oh kay ehl WAY-soh ehs-TAH ROH-toh (dees-loh-KAH-doh)*
My leg is swollen.	**La pierna está hinchada.** *lah pee-EHR-nah ehs-TAH een-CHAH-dah*

I have sprained (twisted) my wrist (ankle).	**Me he torcido la muñeca (el tobillo).** *may ay tohr-SEE-doh lah moon-YEH-kah (ehl toh-BEE-yoh)*
I can't move my elbow (knee).	**No puedo mover el codo (la rodilla).** *noh pweh-doh moh-BEHR ehl KOH-doh (lah roh-DEE-yah)*
I don't have medical insurance.	**(No) Tengo seguro médico.** *noh ten-goh seh-GOO-roh MED-ee-koh*

AT THE DENTIST

Can you recommend a dentist?	**¿Puede recomendar un dentista?** *PWEH-day reh-koh-men-DAHR oon den-TEES-tah*
I have a toothache that's driving me crazy.	**Tengo un dolor de muela que me vuelve loco.** *ten-goh oon doh-LOHR day MWEH-lah kay may BWEHL-bay loh-koh*
I've lost a filling.	**Se me ha caído un empaste.** *say may ah kah-EE-doh oon ehm-PAHS-tay*
I've broken a tooth.	**Me rompí un diente.** *may rohm-PEE oon dee-EHN-tay*
My gums hurt.	**Me duelen las encías.** *may DWEH-len lahs ehn-SEE-ahs*
Is there an infection?	**¿Hay una infección?** *AH-ee oo-nah een-fehk-SYOHN*
Will you have to extract the tooth?	**¿Tendrá que sacar la muela (el diente)?** *ten-DRAH kay sah-kahr lah MWEH-lah (ehl dee-EHN-tay)*

Can you fill it ___?	**¿Podría empastarlo ___?** *poh-DREE-ah ehm-pahs-TAHR-loh*
■ with amalgam	**con platino** *kohn plah-TEE-noh*
■ with gold	**con oro** *kohn OHR-oh*
■ with silver	**con plata** *kohn PLAH-tah*
■ for now	**por ahora** *pohr ah-OHR-ah*
Can you fix ___?	**¿Puede usted reparar ___?** *PWEH-day oo-STEHD ray-pah-RAHR*
■ this bridge	**este puente** *EHS-tay PWEHN-tay*
■ this crown	**esta corona** *EHS-tah kohr-OH-nah*
■ these dentures	**estos dientes postizos** *EHS-tohs dee-EHN-tays pohs-TEE-sohs*
When should I come back?	**¿Cuándo debo volver?** *KWAHN-doh DEH-boh bohl-BEHR*
How much do I owe you for your services?	**¿Cuánto le debo?** *KWAHN-toh lay DEH-boh*

WITH THE OPTICIAN

Can you repair these glasses (for me)?	**¿Puede usted arreglar(me) estas gafas? (estos lentes)** *PWEH-day oos-TEHD ah-ray-GLAHR (may) EHS-tahs GAH-fahs (EHS-tohs LEN-tehs)*
I've broken a lens (the frame).	**Se me ha roto un cristal (la armadura).** *say may oh ROH-toh oon krees-TAHL (lah ahr-mah-DOOR-ah)*
Can you put in a new lens?	**¿Puede usted ponerme un cristal nuevo?** *PWEH-day oos-TEHD poh-NEHR-may oos krees-TAHL NWEH-boh*

I have transition lenses (bifocals)

Tengo lentes polarizados (bifocales). *TEN-go LEN-tehs poh-lahr-ee-SAH-dohs (bee-foh-KAH-lehs)*

Do you have (prescription) sunglasses?

¿Tiene lentes (de receta) de sol? *TYEH-neh LEN-tehs (day ray-SAY-tah) day sohl*

I (do not) have a prescription.

(No) tengo receta. *noh TEN-goh ray-SAY-tah*

I'm nearsighted (farsighted)

Soy miope (présbita) *soy mee-OH-peh (PREHS-bee-tah)*

Can you tighten the screws?

¿Puede usted apretar los tornillitos? *PWEH-day oos-TEHD ah-pray-tahr lohs tohr-NEE-yee-tohs*

I need the glasses as soon as possible.

Necesito las gafas urgentemente. *neh-seh-SEE-toh lahs GAH-fahs oor-hen-tay-MEN-tay*

I don't have any others.

No tengo otras. *noh TEN-goh OH-trahs*

I've lost a contact lens.

Se me ha perdido un lente de contacto. *say may ah pehr-DEE-doh oon LEN-tay day kohn-TAHK-toh*

Can you replace it quickly?

¿Puede reemplazarlo rápidamente? *PWEH-day ray-ehm-plah-SAHR-loh rah-pee-dah-MEN-tay*

COMMUNICATIONS

POST OFFICE

In Spain, postcards and stamps can be purchased at **estancos** (tobacconists) and kiosks (these can be distinguished by their red and yellow signs) in addition to the official post office **(Correos y Telégrafos).**

The post office is open from 9:00 to 1:30 and from 4:00 to 7:00 Monday to Saturday.

Hours may differ somewhat in Latin America, and postcards are seldom sold at post offices.

I want to mail a letter.	**Quiero echar una carta al correo.** *kee-YEHR-oh ay-CHAHR oo-nah KAHR-tah ahl kohr-AY-oh*
Where's the post office?	**¿Dónde está correos?** *DOHN-day ehs-TAH kohr-AY-ohs*
Where's a letterbox?	**¿Dónde hay un buzón?** *DOHN-day AH-ee oon boo-SOHN*
What is the postage on ___ to the United States (Canada, England, Australia)?	**¿Cuánto es el franqueo de ___ a los Estados Unidos (al Canadá, a Inglaterra, a Australia)?** *KWAHN-toh ehs ehl frahn-KAY-oh day ah lohs ehs-TAH-dohs oo-NEE-dohs (ahl kahn-ah-DAH ah eeng-lah-TEHR-ah ah ow-STRAHL-yah)*
▪ a letter	**una carta** *oo-nah KAHR-tah*
▪ an insured letter	**una carta asegurada** *oo-nah KAHR-tah ah-say-goor-AH-dah*
▪ a registered letter	**una carta certificada** *oo-nah KAHR-tah sehr-teef-ee-KAH-dah*
▪ a special delivery letter	**una carta urgente** *oo-nah KAHR-tah oor-HEN-tay*

■ a package	**un paquete postal** *oon pah-kay-tay pohs-TAHL*
■ a postcard	**una postal** *oo-nah pohs-TAHL*
When will it arrive?	**¿Cuándo llegará?** *KWAHN-doh yeh-gahr-AH*
Which is the ____ window?	**¿Cuál es la ventanilla de ____?** *kwahl ehs lah ben-tah-NEE-yah day*
■ general delivery	**la lista de correos** *lah LEES-tah day kohr-AY-ohs*
■ money order	**los giros postales** *lohs HEER-ohs pohs-TAHL-ays*
■ stamp	**los sellos** *lohs SEH-yohs*
Are there any letters for me? My name is ____.	**¿Hay cartas para mí? Me llamo ____.** *AH-ee KAHR-tahs pah-rah mee may YAH-moh*
I'd like ____.	**Quisiera ____.** *kee-see-YEHR-ah*
■ 10 envelopes	**diez sobres** *dee-EHS SOH-brays*
■ 6 postcards	**seis postales** *sayss pohs-TAHL-ays*
■ 5 (air mail) stamps	**cinco sellos (aéreos)** *SEEN-koh SEH-yohs (ah-EHR-ay-ohs)*
Do I fill out a customs receipt?	**¿Hay un recibo de adana?** *AH-ee oon ray-SEE-boh day ah-DWAHN-ah*

TELEPHONES

In Spain telephones use coins of 5, 25, and 50 pesetas.

You can use a telephone card **(tarjeta telefónica)** for local and long distance calls. Cards may be purchased at post offices and tobacco shops.

To call another country, dial 07, wait for a dial tone and then dial the country code followed by the area code and the number.

Public telephones can be found in many stores and cafes; there are also many telephone booths (**cabinas telefónicas**) or you can call at the telephone exchange (**la central telefónica**).

Many telephone booths are for local calls only. To call another city or country, you must find a booth with a green stripe across the top marked **"interurbano."**

If you have difficulty operating the telephone or feel you will not be able to understand the person who answers the call, ask the clerk at your hotel to place the call for you.

Where is ____?	**¿Donde hay ____?** *DOHN-day AH-ee*
■ a public telephone	**un teléfono público** *oon tel-EHF-oh-noh POO-blee-koh*
■ a telephone booth	**una cabina telefónica** *oo-nah kah-BEE-nah tel-eh-FOHN-ee-kah*
■ a telephone directory	**una guía telefónica** *oo-nah GHEE-ah tel-eh-FOHN-ee-kah*

May I use your phone?	**¿Me permite usar su teléfono?** *may pehr-MEE-tay oo-sahr soo tel-EHF-oh-noh*
I want to make a ____ call.	**Quiero hacer una llamada ____.** *kee-YEHR-oh ah-SEHR oo-nah yah-MAH-dah*
▨ local	**local** *loh-kahl*
▨ long distance	**a larga distancia** *ah LAHR-gah dees-TAHN-see-ah*
▨ person to person	**personal** *pehr-SOHN-ahl*
▨ collect	**a cobro revertido** *ah KOH-broh ray-behr-TEE-doh*
Can I call direct?	**¿Puedo marcar directamente?** *PWEH-doh mahr-KAHR dee-rehk-tah-MEN-tay*
Do I need tokens for the phone? (a phone card)	**¿Necesito fichas para el teléfono? (una tarjeta telefónica)** *neh-seh-SEE-toh FEE-chahs pah-rah ehl tel-EHF-oh-no (oo-nah tahr-HEH-ta tel-eh-FOHN-ee-kah)*
How do I get the operator?	**¿Cómo puedo conseguir la central?** *KOH-moh PWEH-doh kon-seh-GHEER lah sehn-TRAHL*
Operator, can you get me number ____?	**Señorita, quiere comunicarme con ____?** *sehn-yohr-EE-tah, kee-YEHR-ay koh-moo-nee-KAHR-may kohn*
My number is ____.	**Mi número es ____.** *mee NOO-mehr-oh ehs*
May I speak to ____?	**¿Puedo hablar con ____?** *PWEH-doh ah-BLAHR kohn*
▨ Speaking.	**Con él habla.** *kon ehl AH-blah*

■ Hello.	**Diga.** *DEE-gah*
■ Who is this?	**¿Con quién hablo?** *kohn kee-YENN AH-bloh*
■ I can't hear.	**No oigo.** *noh OY-goh*
■ Speak louder, please.	**Hable más alto, por favor.** *AH-blay mahs AHL-toh pohr fah-BOHR*
■ Don't hang up. Hold the wire.	**No cuelgue.** *noh KWEHL-gay* **No se retire.** *noh seh reh-TEE-reh*
This is ____.	**Habla ____.** *AH-blah*
Operator, there's no answer (they don't answer).	**Señorita, no contestan.** *sen-yohr-EE-tah noh kohn-TEST-ahn*
The line is busy.	**La línea está ocupada.** *lah LEE-nay-ah ehs-TAH oh koo-PAH-dah*
You gave me (that was) a wrong number	**Me ha dado (fue) un número equivocado.** *may ah DAH-doh (fway) oon NOO-mehr-oh ay-kee-boh-KAH-doh*
I was cut off.	**Me han cortado.** *may ahn kohr-TAH-doh*
Please dial it again.	**Llame otra vez, por favor.** *YAH-may OH-trah bes pohr fah-BOHR*
I want to leave a message.	**Quiero dejar un recado.** *kee-YEHR-oh day-HAHR oon ray-KAH-doh*
How much do I have to pay?	**¿Cuánto tengo que pagar?** *KWAHN-toh TEN-goh kay pah-GAHR?*
Will you help me place a long-distance call?	**¿Podría ayudarme a hacer una llamada a larga distancia?** *poh-DREE-ah ah-yo-DAHR-may ah ah-SEHR oo-nah yah-MAH-dah ah LAHR-gah dees-TAHN-see-ah*

Where can I rent a cellular phone (cellphone)?	**¿Dónde puedo alquilar un teléfono celular?** *DOHN-day PWEH-doh ahl-kee-LAHR oon tel-EH-foh-noh seh-loo-LAHR*
Does it have voice mail (pager service)?	**¿Tiene mensajes electrónicos (servicios de bíper)?** *TYEHN-eh men-SAH-hehs eh-lek-TROH-nee-cohs (sehr-BEE-see-ohs day BEE-pehr)*
How much does it cost per day (per week, per month)?	**¿Cuánto cuesta por día (semana, mes)?** *KWAHN-tow KWES-tah pohr DEE-ah (sem-AH-nah MEHS)*

BUSINESS SERVICES AND ELECTRONIC COMMUNICATION

Deluxe hotels and other major cities usually can arrange secretarial services in English, French, and German for business guests.

FAX

Do you have a fax machine?	**¿Tiene usted una máquina de fax?** *TYEHN-eh oos-TED oo-nah MAH-kee-nah day-FAHKS*
What is your fax number?	**¿Cuál es su número de fax?** *KWAHL ehs soo NOO-mehr-oh day FAHKS*
I want to send a fax.	**Quiero mandar un fax.** *KYEHR-oh mahn-DAHR oon FAHKS*
Can I send a fax from here?	**¿Puedo enviar un fax desde aquí?** *PWEH-do en-bee-YAHR oon FAHKS DES-day ah-KEE*

Fax it to me.	**Mándemelo por fax.**	*MAHN-day-may-loh pohr FAHKS*
I didn't get your fax.	**No recibí su fax.**	*No reh-see-BEE soo fahks*
Did you receive my fax?	**¿Recibió usted mi fax?**	*reh-see-BYOH oos-TED mee fahks*
Your fax is illegible.	**Su fax está ilegible.**	*soo fahks ehs-TAH ee-leh-HEE-blay*
Please send it again.	**Por favor, mándelo de nuevo.**	*Por fah-BOHR MAHN-day-lo day NWEH-boh*

COMPUTERS

Note that a computer in Latin America is a **computadora,** whereas in Spain it is an **ordenador.**

To get information on Spain on the internet:

1. Go to the location box in your net browser
2. Type **http://www.altavista.digital.com** or **www.hotbot.com**
3. Click **Enter**
4. You will see a search screen. Click **Any Language**
5. Select **Spanish**
6. You can search for any subject.

Do you have ____?	**¿Tiene usted ____?**	*TYEHN-eh oos-TED*
■ a Macintosh computer	**una computadora (un ordenador) Macintosh**	*oo-nah kohm-poo-tah-DOHR-ah (oon or-day-nah-DOHR) mah-keen-TOHS*
■ a PC	**una computadora (un ordenador) PC**	*oo-nah kohm-poo-tah-DOHR-ah (oon or-day-nah-DOHR) pay-say*

Are there computers (laptops) available?	**¿Hay computadoras (computadoras portátiles) disponibles?** *AH-ee kohm-poo-tah-DOHR-ahs (kohm-poo-tah-DOHR-ahs por-TAH-tee-lehs) dees-poh-NEE-blehs*
Does it have a (color) printer, scanner, floppy disk, modem, CD-ROM drive, antivirus software?	**¿Tiene una impresora (de color), un escáner, un diskette, un modulador, una disquetera de CD-ROM, datos de aplicación antivirus?** *TYEHN-eh oo-nah eem-preh-SOHR-ah (day ko-LOHR) oon es-KAHN-ehr oon dees-KET oon moh-doo-lah-DOHR oo-nah dees-ket-eh-rah day say-day-ROHM DAH-tos day ah-plee-kah-SYOHN AHN-tee-BEE-roos*
Is is possible to access the internet from here?	**¿Es posible tener acceso al internet desde aquí?** *es poh-SEE-blay ten-EHR ahk-SES-oh ahl EEN-tehr-net DES-day ah-KEE*
What do I do if the line is busy?	**¿Qué hago si la línea está ocupada?** *kay AH-go see lah LEE-nay-ah ehs-TAH oh-koo-PAH-da*
Who is the provider?	**¿Quién es el proveedor?** *kee-YEHN ehs ehl pro-beh-eh-DOHR*
What operating system are you using?	**Qué sistema operativo está ¿usando?** *kay sees-TAY-mah boh-pehr-ah-TEE-boh ehs-TAH oo-SAHN-doh*
What word processing program are you using?	**¿Qué programa de procesamiento de texto está usando?** *kay pro-GRAH-mah day pro-sehs-ah-MYEN-toh day TEKS-toh es-TAH oo-SAHN-doh*

What spreadsheet program are you using?	**¿Qué programa de hoja de cálculo está usando?** *kay pro-GRAH-mah day OH-hah day KAHL-koo-loh es-TAH oo-SAHN-doh*
What peripherals do you have?	**¿Qué sistemas periféricos posee?** *kay sees-TAY-mahs pehr-ee-FEHR-ee-kohs poh-SAY-ay*
Are our systems compatible?	**¿Son compatibles nuestros sistemas?** *sohn kohm-pah-TEE-blays NWEHS-trohs sees-TAY-mahs*
What is your email address?	**¿Cuál es su dirección de correo electrónico?** *KWAHL es soo dee-rek-SYOHN day kohr-AY-oh eh-lek-TROHN-ee-koh*
The computer doesn't work.	**La computadora no funciona.** *Lah kohm-poo-tah-DOHR-ah no foon-SYOHN-ah*
Where can I have it repaired?	**¿Dónde me la pueden reparar?** *DOHN-day may lah PWEH-den reh-pah-RAHR*

COMPUTER MINI-DICTIONARY

access	**el acceso** *ehl ahk-SES-oh*
backup disk	**la copia de seguridad** *lah KOH-pee-yah day seh-goor-ee-DAHD*
byte	**byte** *BAH-eet*
cable	**el cable** *ehl KAH-blay*
CD-ROM disk	**el disco CD-ROM** *ehl DEES-koh seh deh ROHM*
chip	**el chip** *ehl CHEEP*

(to) click	**hacer clic** *ah-SEHR kleek*
clipboard	**el fichero temporal** *ehl fee-CHEH-roh tehm-poh-RAHL*
CPU	**la Unidad de Proceso Central** *lah oon-ee-DAHD day pro-SES-oh sen-TRAHL*
computer programmer	**el programador (de computación)** *ehl pro-grah-mah-DOHR (day kohn-poo-tah-SYOHN)*
(to) copy	**reproducir (or duplicar)** *ray-pro-doo-SEER (doo-plee-KAHR)*
cursor	**el cursor** *ehl koor-SOHR*
(to) cut	**cortar** *kohr-TAHR*
database	**el banco de datos** *ehl BAHN-koh day DAH-tohs*
disk	**el diskette** *ehl dees-KET*
disk drive	**la disquetera** *lah dees-kay-TEHR-ah*
diskette	**el diskette flexible** *ehl dees-KET flek-SEE-blay*
document	**el documento** *ehl do-koo-MEN-toh*
DOS	**el sistema operativo de disco** *ehl sees-TAY-mah oh-pehr-ah-TEE-boh day DEES-koh*
(to) download	**bajar la carga** *bah-HAHR lah KAHR-gah*
email	**el correo electrónico** *ehl kohr-AY-oh eh-lek-TROHN-ee-koh*

file	**el fichero** *ehl fee-CHEHR-oh*
font	**el tipo de letra** *ehl TEE-poh day LET-rah*
graphics	**los gráficos** *lohs GRAH-fee-kohs*
hardware	**los elementos mecánicos** *lohs eh-leh-MEHN-tohs meh-KAH-nee-kohs*
icon	**el símbolo** *ehl SEEM-boh-loh*
inkjet printer	**la impresora de inkjet** *lah eem-preh-SOHR-ah day EENK-jet*
internet	**el internet** *ehl EEN-tehr-net*
joystick	**la palanca de juego** *lah pah-LAHN-kah day WAY-goh*
key	**la tecla** *lah TEK-lah* (or **la llave**) *(lah YAH-bay)*
keyboard	**el teclado** *ehl tek-LAH-do*
(to) keyboard	**teclar** *tek-LAHR*
laptop	**la computadora portátil** *lah kohm-poo-tah-DOHR-ah por-TAH-teel*
laser printer	**la impresora láser** *lah eem-pray-SOHR-ah LAH-sehr*
memory	**la memoria** *lah mem-OHR-ee-yah*
modem	**el módem** *ehl MOH-dem* (or **el modulador** *el moh-doo-lah-DOHR* or **el demodulador** *ehl day-moh-doo-lah-DOHR*)

motherboard	**la placa madre** *la PLAH-kah MAH-dray*
mouse	**el ratón** *ehl rah-TOHN*
network	**la red** *lah red*
on-line service	**el servicio de en-línea** *ehl sehr-BEE-syoh day en-lee-nay-ah*
(to) paste	**pegar** *peh-GAHR*
program	**el programa** *ehl pro-GRAH-mah*
(to) save	**guardar** *gwahr-DAHR*
scanner	**el escáner** *ehl es-KAHN-ehr*
screen	**la pantalla** *lah pahn-TAH-yah*
search engine	**el motor de búsqueda** *ehl mo-TOHR day BOOS-kay-dah*
site	**el sitio** *ehl SEE-tyoh*
software	**datos de aplicación** *DAH-tohs day ah-plee-kah-SYOHN*
speed	**la velocidad** *lah behl-oh-see-DAHD*
spell checker	**el corrector ortográfico** *ehl kohr-ehk-TOHR or-toh-GRAH-fee-koh*
symbol	**el símbolo** *ehl-SEEM-boh-loh*
thesaurus	**el tesauro (diccionario de sinónimos)** *ehl teh-SAU-roh (deek-see-oh-NAHR-ee-oh deh see-NOH-nee-mohs)*
website	**el website** *ehl WEB-sah-eet*

| zip disk | **el diskette zip** *el dees-KET zip* |
| zip drive | **la disquetera zip** *lah dees-kay-TEHR-ah zip* |

PHOTOCOPYING

Where can I get photocopying done?	**¿Dónde puedo hacer una fotocopia?** *DOHN-day PWEH-doh ah-SEHR oo-nah foh-toh-KOH-pee-ah*
Do you have a photocopy machine?	**¿Tiene una fotocopiadora?** *TYEHN-eh oo-nah foh-toh-koh-pee-ah-DOHR-ah*
Does it make color copies?	**¿Hace copias en color?** *AH-say KOH-pee-ahs ehn koh-LOHR*
Does it enlarge (reduce)?	**¿Puede aumentar (reducir) el documento?** *PWEH-day ow-men-TAHR (reh-doo-SEER) ehl doh-koo-MEN-toh?*

TELEGRAMS

Where's the telegraph office?	**¿Dónde está Correos y Telégrafos?** *DOHN-day ehs-TAH kohr-AY-ohs ee tel-AY-grah fohs*
How late is it open?	**¿Hasta cuándo está abierto?** *AH-stah KWAHN-doh ehs-TAH ah bee-YEHR-toh*
I'd like to send a telegram (night letter) to ____.	**Quisiera mandar un telegrama (un cable nocturno) a ____.** *kee-see-YEHR-ah mahn-DAHR oon teh-lay-GRAH-mah (oon KAH-blay nohk-TOOR-noh) ah*

May I please have a form?	**¿Puede darme un formulario, por favor?** *PWEH-deh DAHR-may oon fohr-moo-LAHR-ee-oh pohr fah-BOHR*
How much it is per word?	**¿Cuánto cuesta por palabra?** *KWAHN-toh KWEHS-tah pohr pah-LAH-brah*
I need to send a telex.	**Tengo que enviar un télex.** *TEN-goh kay ehm-bee-AHR oon TEL-eks*
I want to send it collect.	**Quiero mandarlo con cobro revertido.** *kee-YEHR-oh mahn-DAHR-loh kohn KOH-broh reh-behr-TEE-doh*
When will it arrive?	**¿Cuándo llegará?** *KWAHN-doh yeh-gahr-AH*

Travel Tips   Even if you are fluent in the language of the country you are visiting, you may crave news from home in English. Large hotels often subscribe to the television service, Cable News Network (CNN). *The International Herald Tribune*, which is assembled jointly by *The New York Times* and *The Washington Post*, is distributed in more than 150 countries.

GENERAL INFORMATION

TELLING TIME

What time is it?	**¿Qué hora es?**	*kay OH-rah ehs*

When telling time in Spanish, *It is* is expressed by **Es la** for 1:00 and **Son las** for all other numbers.

It's 1:00.	**Es la una.**	*ehs lah oo-nah*
It's 2:00.	**Son las dos.**	*sohn lahs dohs*
It's 3:00, etc.	**Son las tres, etc.**	*sohn lahs trehs*

The number of minutes after the hour is expressed by adding **y** (and) followed by the number of minutes.

It's 4:10.	**Son las cuatro y diez.**	*sohn lahs KWAH-troh ee dyehs*
It's 5:20.	**Son las cinco y veinte.**	*sohn lahs SEEN-koh ee BAYN-tay.*

A quarter after and half past are expressed by placing **y cuarto** and **y media** after the hour.

It's 6:15.	**Son las seis y cuarto.**	*sohn lahs sayss ee KWAHR-toh*
It's 7:30.	**Son las siete y media.**	*sohn lahs SYEH-tay ee MEH-dyah*

After passing the half-hour point on the clock, time is expressed in Spanish by *subtracting* the number of minutes from the next hour.

It's 7:35.	**Son las ocho menos veinticinco.** *sohn lahs OH-choh MEH-nohs bayn-tee-SEEN-koh*
It's 8:50.	**Son las nueve menos diez.** *sohn lahs NWEH-bay meh-nohs dyehs*
At what time?	**¿A qué hora?** *ah kay OH-rah*
At 1:00.	**A la una.** *ah lah OO-nah*
At 2:00 (3:00, etc.)	**A las dos (tres, etc.)** *ah lahs dohs (trehs)*
A.M.	**de la mañana (in the morning)** *day lah man-YAH-nah*
P.M.	**de la tarde (in the afternoon)** *day lah TAHR -day* **de la noche (at night)** *day lah NOH-chay*
It's noon.	**Es mediodía.** *ehs meh-dee-ohd-EE-oh*
It's midnight.	**Es medianoche.** *ehs MEH-dee-ah-NOH-chay*
It's early (late).	**Es temprano (tarde).** *ehs temp-RAH-noh (TAHR-day)*

Official time is based on the 24-hour clock. You will find train schedules and other such times expressed in terms of a point within a 24-hour sequence.

The train leaves at 15:30.	**El tren sale a las quince y media.** *ehl trehn SAH-lay ah lahs KEEN-say ee MEH-dee-ah*
The time is now 21:15.	**Son las veintiuna y cuarto.** *sohn lahs bayn-tee-OO-nah ee KWAHR-toh*

DAYS OF THE WEEK

What day is today?	**¿Qué día es hoy?** *kay DEE-ah ehs oy*

The days are *not* capitalized in Spanish.

Today is ____.	**Hoy es ____.** *oy ehs*
■ Monday	**lunes** *LOO-nehs*
■ Tuesday	**martes** *MAHR-tays*
■ Wednesday	**miércoles** *MYEHR-kohl-ays*
■ Thursday	**jueves** *HWEB-ays*
■ Friday	**viernes** *bee-EHR-nays*
■ Saturday	**sábado** *SAH-bah-doh*
■ Sunday	**domingo** *doh-MEEN-goh*
yesterday	**ayer** *ah-YEHR*

the day before yesterday	**anteayer** *ant-ay-ah-YEHR*
tomorrow	**mañana** *mahn-YAH-nah*
the day after tomorrow	**pasado mañana** *pah-SAH-doh mahn-YAH-nah*
last week	**la semana pasada** *ah seh-MAH-nah pah-SAH-dah*
next week	**la semana próxima** *lah seh-MAH-nah PROHK-see-mah*
tonight	**esta noche** *EHS-tah NOH-chay*
last night	**anoche** *ahn-OH-chay*

MONTHS OF THE YEAR

The months are *not* capitalized in Spanish.

January	**enero** *ay-NEHR-oh*
February	**febrero** *fay-BREH-roh*
March	**marzo** *MAHR-soh*
April	**abril** *ah-BREEL*
May	**mayo** *MAH-yoh*
June	**junio** *HOO-nee-oh*
July	**julio** *HOO-lee-oh*
August	**agosto** *ah-GOHS-toh*

September	**septiembre**	*sep-tee-EHMB-ray*
October	**octubre**	*ohk-TOO-bray*
November	**noviembre**	*noh-bee-EHMB-ray*
December	**diciembre**	*dee-SYEHM-bray*
What's today's date?	**¿Cuál es la fecha de hoy?**	*kwahl ehs lah FAY-chah day oy*

The first of the month is *el primero* (an ordinal number). All other dates are expressed with *cardinal* numbers.

Today is August ____.	**Hoy es ____ de agosto.**	*oy ehs ____ day ah-GOHS-tah*
■ first	**el primero**	*ehl pree-MEHR-oh*
■ second	**el dos**	*ehl dos*
■ fourth	**el cuatro**	*ehl KWAH-troh*
■ 25th	**el veinticinco**	*ehl bayn-tee-SEENK-oh*
this month	**este mes**	*EHS-tay mehs*
last month	**el mes pasado**	*ehl mehs pah-SAH-doh*
next month	**el mes próximo**	*ehl mehs PROHK-see-moh*
last year	**el año pasado**	*ehl AHN-yoh pah-SAH-doh*
next year	**el año que viene**	*ehl AHN-yoh kay bee-EN-ay*
May 1, 1876	**El primero de mayo de mil ochocientos setenta y seis.**	*ehl pree-MEHR-oh day MAH-ee-oh day meel oh-choh-SYEHN-tohs say-TEN-tah ee SAYSS*

July 4, 1984   **El cuatro de julio de mil novecientos ochenta y cuatro.** *ehl KWAH-troh day HOOL-ee-oh day meel noh-bay-SYEHN-tohs oh-CHEN-tah ee KWAH-troh*

THE FOUR SEASONS

spring   **la primavera** *lah pree-mah-BEHR-ah*

summer   **el verano** *ehl behr-AH-noh*

fall   **el otoño** *ehl oh-TOHN-yoh*

winter   **el invierno** *ehl eem-BYEHR-noh*

THE WEATHER

How is the weather today?   **¿Qué tiempo hace hoy?** *kay TYEHM-poh ah-say oy*

It's nice (bad) weather.   **Hace buen (mal) tiempo.** *ah-say bwehn (mahl) TYEHM-poh*

It's raining.   **Llueve.** *YWEHB-ay*

It's snowing.   **Nieva.** *NYEHB-ah*

It's ____.   **Hace ____.** *AH-say*

■ hot   **calor** *kah-LOHR*

■ cold   **frío** *FREE-oh*

■ cool   **fresco** *FREHS-koh*

■ windy   **viento** *BYEHN-toh*

■ sunny   **sol** *sohl*

RELIGIOUS SERVICES

In addition to viewing the churches and cathedrals, you may wish to attend services.

Is there a ____ near here?	**¿Hay una ____ cerca de aquí?** *AH-ee oo-nah SEHR-kah day ah-KEE*
■ Catholic church	**iglesia católica** *ee-GLAY-see-ah kah-TOHL-ee-kah*
■ Protestant church	**iglesia protestante** *ee-GLAY-see-ah pro-test-AHN-tay*
■ Synagogue	**sinagoga** *see-nah-GOH-gah*
■ Mosque	**mezquita** *mehs-KEE-tah*
When is the service (mass)?	**¿A qué hora es la misa?** *ah kay OH-rah ehs lah MEE-sah*
I want to speak to a ____.	**Quiero hablar con ____.** *kee-EHR-oh ah-BLAHR kohn*
■ priest	**un cura** *oon KOO-rah*
■ minister	**un ministro** *oon mee-NEES-troh*
■ rabbi	**un rabino** *oon rah-BEEN-oh*

COUNTRIES AND NATIONALITIES

COUNTRY		NATIONALITY
Argentina	**la Argentina**	argentino
Bolivia	**Bolivia**	boliviano
Brazil	**el Brasil**	brasileño
Canada	**el Canadá**	canadiense
Chile	**Chile**	chileno
China	**China**	chino

COUNTRY		NATIONALITY
Colombia	**Colombia**	colombiano
Costa Rica	**Costa Rica**	costarricense
Cuba	**Cuba**	cubano
Denmark	**Dinamarca**	danés
Dominican Republic	**la República Dominicana**	dominicano
Ecuador	**el Ecuador**	ecuatoriano
Egypt	**Egipto**	egipcio
England	**Inglaterra**	inglés
Europe	**Europa**	europeo
Finland	**Finlandia**	finlandés
France	**Francia**	francés
Germany	**Alemania**	alemán
Great Britain	**Gran Bretaña**	inglés
Greece	**Grecia**	griego
Guatemala	**Guatemala**	guatemalteco
Holland	**Holanda**	holandés
Iceland	**Islandia**	islandés
Ireland	**Irlanda**	irlandés
Israel	**Israel**	israelí
Italy	**Italia**	italiano
Japan	**el Japón**	japonés
Mexico	**México or Méjico**	mexicano
Nicaragua	**Nicaragua**	nicaragüense
Norway	**Noruega**	noruego
Panama	**Panamá**	panameño
Paraguay	**el Paraguay**	paraguayo
Peru	**el Perú**	peruano
Poland	**Polonia**	polaco
Portugal	**Portugal**	portugués

COUNTRY		NATIONALITY
Puerto Rico	**Puerto Rico**	puertorriqueño
Russia	**Rusia**	ruso
El Salvador	**El Salvador**	salvadoreño
Spain	**España**	español
Sweden	**Suecia**	sueco
Switzerland	**Suiza**	suizo
Turkey	**Turquía**	turco
United States	**los Estados Unidos**	estadounidense (norteamericano)
Uruguay	**Uruguay**	uruguayo
Venezuela	**Venezuela**	venezolano

IMPORTANT SIGNS

Abajo	Down
Abierto	Open
Alto	Stop
Arriba	Up
Ascensor	Elevator
Caballeros	Men's room
Caja	Cashier
Caliente or "C"	Hot
Carretera particular	Private road
Cerrado	Closed

Completo	Filled up
Cuidado	Watch out, caution
Damas	Ladies room
Empuje	Push
Entrada	Entrance
Frío or **"F"**	Cold
Libre	Vacant
No obstruya la entrada	Don't block entrance
No pisar el césped	Keep off the grass
No tocar	Hands off, don't touch
Ocupado	Busy, occupied
¡Pase!	Walk, cross
Peligro	Danger
Prohibido	Forbidden, No ____
■ ____ **el paso**	No entrance, Keep out
■ ____ **escupir**	No spitting
■ ____ **fumar**	No smoking
■ ____ **estacionarse**	No parking
■ ____ **bañarse**	No bathing
Reservado	Reserved
Sala de espera	Waiting room
Salida	Exit

Se alquila	For rent	
Señoras	Ladies room	
Servicios	Toilets	
Se vende	For sale	
Tire	Pull	
¡Veneno!	Poison!	
Venta	Sale	

COMMON ABBREVIATIONS

apdo.	**apartado de correos**	post office box
Av., Avda.	**avenida**	avenue
C., Cía	**compañía**	company
c.	**calle**	street
D.	**don**	title of respect used before a masculine first name: don Pedro
Da., Dª	**doña**	title of respect used before a feminine first name: doña María
EE.UU	**los Estados Unidos**	United States (U.S.)
F.C.	**ferrocarril**	railroad
Hnos.	**hermanos**	brothers

N°, num.	**número**	number
1°	**primero**	first
pta.	**peseta**	peseta (Spanish monetary unit)
RENFE	**Red Nacional de Ferrocarriles**	Spanish National Railroad System
2°	**segundo**	second
S., Sta.	**San, Santa**	Saint
S.A.	**Sociedad Anónima**	Inc.
Sr.	**Señor**	Mr.
Sra.	**Señora**	Mrs.
Sres., Srs.	**Señores**	Gentlemen
Srta.	**Señorita**	Miss
Ud., Vd.	**Usted**	You (polite sing.)
Uds., Vds.	**Ustedes**	You (polite & familiar plural)

CENTIMETERS/INCHES

It is usually unnecessary to make exact conversions from your customary inches to the metric system, but to give you an approximate idea of how they compare, we give you the following guide.

Centímetros

Pulgadas

1 **centímetro** (centimeter)	=	0.39 inches (**pulgadas**)
1 **metro**	=	39.37 inches 3.28 feet (**pies**) 1.09 yards (**yardas**)
1 inch	=	2.54 centimeters
1 foot	=	30.5 centimeters 0. 3 meters
1 yard	=	91.4 centimeters 0.91 meters

To convert **centímetros** into inches, multiply by .39.
To convert inches into **centímetros,** multiply by 2.54.

METERS/FEET

How tall are you in meters? See for yourself.

FEET	METERS	FEET	METERS
5	1.52	5.7	1.70
5.1	1.54	5.8	1.73
5.2	1.57	5.9	1.75
5.3	1.59	5.10	1.78
5.4	1.62	5.11	1.80
5.5	1.64	6	1.83
5.6	1.68	5.1	1.85

WHEN YOU WEIGH YOURSELF

1 ___ (kilogram)	=	2.2 ___ (pounds)
1 pound	=	.45 kilograms

KILOS	POUNDS	KILOS	POUNDS
40	88	75	165
45	99	80	176
50	110	85	187
55	121	90	198
60	132	95	209
65	143	100	220
70	154	105	231

LIQUID MEASUREMENTS

1 **litro** (liter)	=	1.06 ___ (quarts)
4 liters	=	1. 06 ___ (gallons)

For a quick approximate conversion, multiply the number of gallons by 4 to get liters. Divide the number of liters by 4 to get gallons.

Note: You'll find other conversion charts on pages 89–91, 177, 178, 182, and 247.

MINI-DICTIONARY FOR THE BUSINESS TRAVELER

amount (value)	**el importe**	*ehl eem-POHR-tay*
appraise (to)	**valuar**	*bahl-WAHR*

authorize (to)	**autorizar**	*ow-tohr-ee-SAHR*
authorized edition	**la edición autorizada**	*lah eh-dee-SYOHN ow-tohr-ee-SAH-dah*
bill (noun)	**la cuenta**	*lah KWEHN-tah*
■ bill of exchange	**la letra de cambio**	*lah LEH-trah day KAHM-bee-oh*
■ bill of lading	**el conocimiento de embarque**	*ehl koh-noh-see-MYEHN-toh day ehm-BAHR-kay*
■ bill of sale	**la escritura de venta**	*lah ehs-kree-TOOR-ah day BEN-tah*
business operation	**la operación comercial**	*lah oh-pehr-ah-SYOHN koh-mehr-SYAHL*
cash (money)	**el dinero contante**	*ehl-dee-NEHR-oh kohn-TAHN-tay*
■ to buy for cash	**pagar al contado**	*pa-GAHR ahl kon-TAH-doh*
■ to sell for cash	**vender al contado**	*ben-DEHR ahl kon-TAH-doh*
■ to cash a check	**cobrar un cheque**	*koh-BRAHR oon CHEH-kay*
certified check	**el cheque certificado**	*ehl CHEH-kay sehr-tee-fee-KAH-doh*
chamber of commerce	**la cámara de comercio**	*lah KAH-mah-rah day koh-MEHR-see-oh*
compensation for damage	**la indemnización de danos y perjuicios**	*lah een-dehm-nee-sah-SYOHN day DAHN-yohs ee pehr-WEE-see-ohs*
competition	**la competición**	*la kohm-peh-tee-SYOHN*

■ competitive price   **el precio competidor** *ehl PREH-see-oh kohm-peh-tee-DOHR*

contract   **el contrato** *ehl kohn-TRAH-toh*

■ contractual obligations   **las obligaciones contractuales** *lahs oh-blee-gah-SYOHN-ays kohn-trahk TWAHL-ays*

controlling interest   **el interés predominante** *ehl een-tehr-AYS pray-doh-mee-NAHN-tay*

down payment   **el pago inicial** *ehl PAH-goh ee-nees-YAHL*

due   **vencido** *ben-SEE-doh*

enterprise   **la empresa** *lah ehm-PRAY-sah*

expedite (to) delivery (of goods)   **facilitar la entrega (de mercancía)** *fah-see-lee-TAHR lah ehn-TRAY-gah (day mehr-kahn-SEE-ah)*

■ expedite delivery (of letters)   **facilitar el reparto (de cartas)** *fah-seel-ee-TAHR ehl ray-PAHR-toh (day KAHR-tahs)*

expenses   **los gastos** *lohs GAHS-tohs*

goods   **las mercancías** *lahs mehr-kahn-SEE-ahs*

infringement of patent rights   **violación de derechos de patente** *bee-oh-lah-SYOHN day deh-RAY-chohs day pah-TEN-tay*

insurance against all risks   **seguros contra todo riesgo** *seh-GOOR-ohs kohn-trah TOH-doh ree-EHS-goh*

international law   **la ley internacional** *lah lay een-tehr-nah-syohn-AHL*

lawful possession	**la posesión legal**	*lah poh-seh-SYOHN lay-GAHL*
lawsuit	**el pleito**	*ehl PLAY-toh*
lawyer	**el abogado**	*ehl ah-boh-GAH-doh*
letter of credit	**la carta de crédito**	*lah KAHR-tah day KREH-dee-toh*
mail-order business	**el negocio de ventas par correo**	*ehl neh-GOH-see-oh day BEN-tahs pohr kohr-AY-oh*
market-value	**el valor comercial**	*ehl bah-LOHR koh-mehrs-YAHL*
manager	**el gerente**	*ehl hehr-EN-tay*
owner	**el dueno**	*ehl DWAYN-yoh*
partner	**el socio**	*ehl SOH-see-oh*
payment	**el pago**	*ehl PAH-goh*
■ partial payment	**el pago parcial**	*ehl PAH-goh pahr-SYAHL*
past due	**vencido**	*ben-SEE-doh*
post office box	**el apartado**	*ehl ah-pahr-TAH-doh*
property	**la propiedad**	*lah proh-pee-eh-DAHD*
purchasing agent	**el comprador**	*ehl kohm prah-DOHR*
put (to) on the American market	**poner en el mercado norteamericano**	*poh-NEHR ehn ehl mehr-KAH-doh nohr-tay-ah-mehr-ee-KAH-noh*

sale	**la venta**	*lah BEN-tah*
sell (to)	**vender**	*ben-DEHR*
send (to)	**mandar**	*mahn-DAHR*
■ to send back	**devolver**	*day-bohl-BEHR*
■ to send C. O. D.	**mandar contra reembolso**	*mahn-DAHR kohn-trah ray-ehm-BOHL-soh*
shipment	**el envío**	*ehl ehm-BEE-oh*
tax	**el impuesto**	*ehl eem PWEHS-toh*
■ tax-exempt	**libre de impuestos**	*LEE-bray day eem-PWEHS-tohs*
■ sales tax	**el impuesto sobre ventas**	*ehl eem-PWEHS-toh soh-bray BEN-tahs*
■ value added tax	**el impuesto sobre el valor añadido**	*ehl eem-PWEHS-toh soh-bray ehl bah-LOHR ahn-yah-DEE-doh*
trade	**el comercio**	*ehl koh-MEHR-see-oh*
transact business (to)	**hacer negocios**	*ah-SEHR neh-GOH-see-ohs*
transfer (noun)	**la transferencia**	*lah trahns-fehr-EHN-see-ah*
transportation charges	**gastos de transporte**	*GAHS-tohs day trahns-POHR-tay*
via	**por vía**	*pohr BEE-ah*
yield a profit (to)	**rendir una ganancia**	*rehn-DEER oo-nah gah-NAHN-see-ah*

QUICK GRAMMAR GUIDE

Your facility with Spanish will be greatly enhanced if you know a little of its grammar. Here are a few simple rules governing the use of the various parts of speech.

NOUNS

In contrast with English, in which inanimate objects are considered neuter, Spanish nouns are designated either masculine or feminine. In addition, if a noun represents a male being, it is masculine; if it is for a female being, it is feminine.

Examples of some masculine nouns are:

el hombre (the man)
el hermano (the brother)
el padre (the father)

Some feminine nouns are:

la mujer (the woman)
la hermana (the sister)
la madre (the mother)

As a general rule, nouns ending in *o* are masculine while nouns ending in *a* are feminine.

el minuto (the minute)   **la joya** (the jewel)
el médico (the doctor)   **la manzana** (the apple)

But there are some exceptions, such as:

la mano (the hand)   **el día** (the day)
la foto (the photograph)   **el mapa** (the map)

To make singular nouns plural, add *s* to nouns that end in a vowel and *es* to those that end in a consonant.

el muchacho	**los muchachos**
la rosa	**las rosas**
el tren	**los trenes**
la mujer	**las mujeres**

ARTICLES

Articles *(the, a, an)* agree in gender (masculine or feminine) and in number (singular or plural) with the nouns they modify.

el libro (the book)	**los libros** (the books)
la casa (the house)	**las casas** (the houses)
un libro (a book)	**unos libros** (some books)
una casa (a house)	**unas casas** (some houses)

Two contractions are formed when **el** *(the)* combines with either **a** *(to)* or **de** *(of* or *from)*.

a + el = al (to the)	**Voy al cine** (I'm going to the movies)
de + el = del (of or from the)	**Es el principio del año** (It's the beginning of the year)

ADJECTIVES

Adjectives agree in gender with the nouns they modify. Generally, descriptive adjectives follow the noun.

la casa blanca (the white house)
el hombre alto (the tall man)

Adjectives also agree in number with the nouns they modify. The plural of adjectives is formed in the same way as in the plural of nouns. For adjectives ending in a vowel, you add *s;* for adjectives ending in a consonant, add *es.*

el papel azul (the blue paper)	**los papeles azules** (the blue papers)
la casa roja (the red house)	**las casas rojas** (the red houses)

Limiting adjectives agree in number and gender with the nouns they modify, and usually precede the noun.

muchas cosas (many things)

pocos americanos (few Americans)

Demonstrative adjectives *(this, that, these, those)* are placed in front of the nouns they modify. They must agree in number and gender with the nouns, and in a series they are usually repeated before each noun. Use the following table to find the correct form of these demonstrative adjectives, then notice how they are used in context, agreeing with their nouns in gender and number.

SINGULAR (PLURAL)	MASCULINE	FEMININE
this (these)	este (estos)	esta (estas)
that (those)	ese (esos)	esa (esas)
that (those) (meaning far away)	aquel (aquellos)	aquella (aquellas)

Now, in context.

este zapato (this shoe)	**estos zapatos** (these shoes)
esa blusa (that blouse)	**esas blusas** (those blouses)
aquel edificio (that building—in the distance)	**aquellos edificios** (those buildings)

estos hombres y estas mujeres (these men and women)

Possessive adjectives must agree with the nouns they modify. Use the following table to locate the appropriate form to express what you mean.

	SINGULAR	PLURAL
my	mi	mis
your (familiar)	tu	tus
your (polite) his her its	su	sus
our	nuestro(a)	nuestros(as)
your (plural familiar)	vuestro(a)	vuestros(as)
your (plural polite) their	su	sus

Here are some examples of possessive adjectives, as they modify their nouns in number and gender.

mi amigo (my friend)

mis amigos (my friends)

nuestra casa (our house)

nuestro coche (our car)

nuestros libros (our books)

tus zapatos (your shoes)*

*This is the familiar form, used when talking to a friend, a child, or among members of the same family. **Sus zapatos** (your shoes) would be the polite form, always used when talking to strangers.

Since **su** and **sus** have six possible meanings, it is often necessary to use a prepositional phrase **(de usted, de ustedes, de él, de ellos, de ella, de ellas)** to avoid any possible ambiguity.

su casa (could mean your, her, his, its, or their house)

la casa de usted (your house)

la casa de ella (her house)

PRONOUNS

Subject pronouns *(I, you, he, she,* etc.) have both singular and plural forms.

SINGULAR		PLURAL	
I	yo	(we)	nosotros(as)
you	tú	you (familiar)	vosotros (as) (used in Spain)
you	usted	you (polite)	ustedes (used for both familiar and polite forms in Latin America)
he	él	they (m.)	ellos
she	ella	they (f.)	ellas

Direct object pronouns *(me, you, him, it, us, them)* are used as direct objects of verbs. They have both singular and plural forms, as the table below indicates.

SINGULAR		PLURAL	
me	me	us	nos
you	te	you (familiar)	os (used in Spain)
you	le, la	you (polite)	los, las
him	le, lo	them (m.)	los
		them (f.)	las
her	la		
it	lo		

Object pronouns precede the verb unless the sentence is an affirmative command or the verb is an infinitive.

Yo te veo (I see you)
Ella me habla (She talks to me)

But in a command or with an infinitive:

Dígame la verdad (Tell me the truth)
Déme el paquete (Give me the package)
Yo quiero verla (I want to see her)
Usted no puede hacerlo (You can't do it)

Indirect object pronouns are pronouns serving as indirect objects. They take either singular or plural forms, as the table below indicates.

SINGULAR		PLURAL	
to me	me	to us	nos
to you (familiar)	te	to you (familiar)	os (used in Spain)
to you (polite)	le	to you (polite)	les
him	le	to them (m.)	les
her	le	to them (f.)	les
it	le		

VERBS

In this phrase book, we limit the use of verbs to the present tense, since this is the most likely one for you to use as a tourist. All Spanish verbs in the infinitive end in either *ar*, *er*, or *ir*.

pas<u>ar</u> (to pass)
beb<u>er</u> (to drink)
viv<u>ir</u> (to live)

In order to conjugate a verb this infinitive ending must be removed and replaced by the appropriate ending. The following are three typical regular verbs.

VERB WITH *AR* ENDING (HABLAR—TO SPEAK)			
yo	habl<u>o</u>	nosotros (as)	habl<u>amos</u>
tú	habl<u>as</u>	vosotros (as)	habl<u>áis</u> (used in Spain)
usted	habl<u>a</u>	ustedes	
él, ella	habl<u>a</u>	ellos ellas	habl<u>an</u>

VERB WITH *ER* ENDING (COMER—TO EAT)			
yo	com<u>o</u>	nosotros (as)	com<u>emos</u>
tú	com<u>es</u>	vosotros (as)	com<u>éis</u> (used in Spain)
usted	com<u>e</u>	ustedes	
él, ella	com<u>e</u>	ellos ellas	com<u>en</u>

VERB WITH *IR* ENDING (ESCRIBIR—TO WRITE)			
yo	escrib<u>o</u>	nosotros (as)	escrib<u>imos</u>
tú	escrib<u>es</u>	vosotros (as)	escrib<u>ís</u> (used in Spain)
usted	escrib<u>e</u>	ustedes	
él, ella	escrib<u>e</u>	ellos ellas	escrib<u>en</u>

Using the conjugation tables above, we give you some examples of verbs paired with the appropriate verb endings.

vender (to sell)	**Yo vendo** (I sell)
pasar (to pass)	**Ellos pasan** (They pass)
vivir (to live)	**Nosotros vivimos** (We live)

Many Spanish verbs are irregular. The following tables show the conjugations for commonly used irregular verbs.

DAR (TO GIVE)

doy	damos
das	dais
da	dan

DECIR (TO SAY, TO TELL)

digo	decimos
dices	decís
dice	dicen

HACER (TO DO, TO MAKE)

hago	hacemos
haces	hacéis
hace	hacen

IR (TO GO)

voy	vamos
vas	vais
va	van

OÍR (TO HEAR)

oigo	oímos
oyes	oís
oye	oyen

PODER (TO BE ABLE)

puedo	podemos
puedes	podéis
puede	pueden

PONER (TO PUT, TO PLACE)

pongo	ponemos
pones	ponéis
pone	ponen

QUERER (TO WISH, TO WANT)

quiero	queremos
quieres	queréis
quiere	quieren

SABER (TO KNOW)

sé	sabemos
sabes	sabéis
sabe	saben

SALIR (TO LEAVE, GO OUT)

salgo	salimos
sales	salís
sale	salen

TENER (TO HAVE)	
tengo	tenemos
tienes	tenéis
tiene	tienen

TRAER (TO BRING)	
traigo	traemos
traes	traéis
trae	traen

VENIR (TO COME)	
vengo	venímos
vienes	venís
viene	vienen

VER (TO SEE)	
veo	vemos
ves	veis
ve	ven

There are two verbs in Spanish that express the various forms of the verb to be.

SER (TO BE)	
soy	somos
eres	sois
es	son

ESTAR (TO BE)	
estoy	estamos
estás	estáis
está	están

The verb **estar** and its various forms are used in three major instances.

1. To tell about or inquire about location.
   Madrid está en España (Madrid is in Spain.)
   ¿Dónde está el policía? (Where is the policeman?)
2. To tell or ask about health.
   ¿Cómo está usted hoy? (How are you today?)
   Estoy bien, graciais. (I'm fine, thank you.)
3. To describe a temporary or changeable condition.
   La puerta está abierta. (The door is open.)
   El café está caliente. (The coffee is hot.)
   Nosotros estamos contentos. (We are happy.)
   Ella está cansada. (She is tired.)

At all other times, use the forms of ser.

Yo soy norteamericano. (I am American.)
El coche es grande. (The car is big.)
El libro es importante. (The book is important.)
Los anillos son de oro. (The rings are (made) of gold.)

The verb **tener** *(to have)* is used in a number of Spanish idiomatic expressions.

tener frío (to be cold, literally to have cold)
tener calor (to be hot)
tener hambre (to be hungry)
tener sed (to be thirsty)
tener sueño (to be sleepy)
tener prisa (to be in a hurry)
tener miedo (to be afraid)
tener razón (to be right)
no tener razón (to be wrong)
tener ____ años (to be ____ years old)

Tener is also used in some examples.

No tengo calor. Tengo frío. (I'm not hot. I'm cold.)
¿Tiene usted hambre? (Are you hungry?)
No, tengo sed. (No, I am thirsty.)
Tenemos prisa. (We're in a hurry.)
Tengo razón. El tiene veinte años. (I'm right. He's 20 years old.)

PREPOSITIONS

The following is a listing of simple prepositions and their English equivalents.

a (to, at; with time)
con (with)
contra (against)
de (from, of, about)
en (in, on)
entre (between, among)
hacia (toward)
hasta (up to, until)
para (for, in order to, to)
por (for, by, through, because)
según (according to)
sin (without)
sobre (on, about)

And some compound prepositions:

además de (besides, in addition to)
al lado de (beside, at the side of)
antes de (before; references to time)
cerca de (near)
debajo de (under, underneath)
delante de (in front of)
dentro de (inside of, within)
después de (after)
detrás de (behind)
en vez de (instead of)
encima de (on top of)
enfrente de (facing, opposite, in front of)
fuera de (outside of)
lejos de (far from)

Used in some examples, here are some prepositions:

El policía está delante de la tienda. (The policeman is in front of the store.)

Voy con mi familia. (I'm going with my family.)
¿Está cerca de la estación? (It is near the station?)
Tomo el tren a las cinco. (I'm taking the train at 5:00.)

TO FORM QUESTIONS

Some common interrogative words in Spanish are the following.

¿Adónde (Where; to what place?)
¿Cómo? (How?)
¿Cuál? (Which?)
¿Cuándo? (When?)
¿Cuánto? (How much?)
¿Cuántos? (How many?)
¿Dónde? (Where?)
¿Para qué? (What for? Why?)
¿Por qué? (Why?)
¿Qué? (What?)
¿Quién? (Who?—singular)
¿Quiénes? (who?—plural)

Notice that all interrogative words have a written accent.
To form a question in Spanish, place the subject *after* the verb. For example:

¿Habla usted español?   (Do you speak Spanish?)
¿Tiene María el billete?   (Does Maria have the ticket?)
¿Cuándo van ustedes   (When are you going to the
al cine?   movies?)

Note that in an interrogative sentence there is an inverted question mark before the sentence as well as the regular question mark after it.

TO FORM NEGATIVE WORDS

The most common negative word in Spanish is **no**. It always precedes the verb.

Yo no tengo dinero. (I have no money; I don't have any money.)

Other negative words are:

nadie (no one)
nada (nothing)
nunca (never)
ninguno (a) (none)
tampoco (neither)

Used in sentences, these would be:

Nadie viene. (No one is coming.)
No veo nada. (I don't see anything; I see nothing.)
Nunca comemos en casa. (We never eat at home.)
Ninguno me gusta. (I don't like any; I like none.)
Ella no tiene dinero, ni yo tampoco. (She has no money and neither do I.)

Any one of the negative words except **no** may be used either before or after the verb. If one is used after the verb, **no** is also used before the verb, making a double negative.

Nadie habla.   (Nobody is speaking.)
No habla nadie.

Nada veo.   (I don't see anything; I see nothing.)
No veo nada.

VOCABULARY VARIATIONS

Spanish is an international language spoken by over 300 million people in 19 independent countries and the commonwealth of Puerto Rico. Although there are some differences in pronunciation and a number of regional vocabulary variations, the basic language is remarkably free of mutually unintelligible dialects, and is universally understood in its written and spoken forms throughout the Spanish-speaking world.

The following is a list of some common words in English and their various equivalents in Spain and several Latin American countries.

car:
- **el automóvil:** Universal
- **el coche:** Spain, Argentina
- **el carro:** Peru, Colombia, Venezuela, Puerto Rico, Mexico
- **la máquina:** Puerto Rico
- **el auto:** Peru, Chile

bus:
- **el autobús:** Universal
- **el camión:** Mexico
- **la guagua:** Puerto Rico, Cuba, Canary Islands
- **el ómnibus:** Argentina
- **el bus:** Colombia, Chile
- **el colectivo:** Argentina, Uruguay

gas station:
- **la estación de servicio:** Universal
- **la gasolinera:** Mexico

driver's license:
- **la licencia de manejar:** Universal
- **el carnet de conducir:** Spain, Chile
- **el brevete:** Peru, Ecuador

to park:
- **parquear:** Latin America
- **aparcar, estacionar (se):** Spain

swimming pool:
la piscina: Universal
la alberca: Mexico
la pileta: Argentina

sidewalk:
la acera: Universal
la banqueta: Mexico
la vereda: Argentina, Chile

police station:
la estación de policía: Universal
la comisaría: Spain

apartment:
el apartamento: Universal
el departamento: Mexico, Chile
el piso: Spain

eyeglasses:
los anteojos: Latin America
los lentes: Universal
las gafas: Spain

bootblack:
el limpiabotas: Universal
el bolero: Mexico

(drinking) straw:
la paja: Universal
la pajita: Argentina

eggs:
los huevos: Universal
los blanquillos: Mexico

sandwich:
el sándwich: Universal
el emparedado, el bocadillo: Spain
la torta: Mexico

potato:
la patata: Spain
la papa: South America

beef:
la carne de vaca: Universal
la carne de res: Mexico

string (green) beans: **las judías verdes:** Spain
las habichuelas verdes: Universal
las chauchas: Argentina
los ejotes: Mexico

peas: **los guisantes:** Spain
los chícharos: Mexico
los pitipuá: Puerto Rico
los porotos: Argentina

grocery store: **la tienda de comestibles:** Universal
la tienda de abarrotes: Mexico,
Chile, Peru
la tienda de ultramarinos: Spain
la pulpería: South America

room: **la habitación:** Universal
el cuarto: Mexico

bedroom: **el dormitorio:** Universal
la recámara: Mexico
la alcoba: Spain

soft boiled egg: **el huevo pasado por agua:** Universal
el huevo tibio: Mexico
el huevo hervido: Argentina

fried eggs: **huevos fritos:** Universal
huevos estrellados: Mexico

fruit juice **el jugo:** Universal
el zumo: Spain

orange juice: **el jugo de naranja:** Universal
el jugo de china: Puerto Rico

roll: **el panecillo:** Universal
el bolillo: Mexico

lemon:	**el limón:** Universal **la lima:** Mexico
peanut:	**el maní:** Caribbean (Puerto Rico, Cuba, Dominican Republic), Chile, Peru, Argentina **el cacahuate:** Mexico **el cacahuete:** Spain
tomato:	**el tomate:** Universal **el jitomate:** Mexico
jacket:	**el saco:** Universal **la americana, la chaqueta:** Spain **la campera:** Argentina
postage stamp:	**la estampilla:** Latin America **el sello:** Spain **el timbre:** Mexico
ticket:	**el billete, la entrada:** Universal **el boleto:** Mexico
elevator:	**el ascensor:** Universal **el elevador:** Mexico
rest room:	**los baños:** Universal **los servicios:** Spain
shower:	**la ducha:** Universal **la regadera:** Mexico
refrigerator:	**el frigorífico**: Spain **el refrigerador:** Universal **la heladera:** Argentina **la nevera:** Central America
to rent:	**rentar or arrendar:** Universal **alquilar:** Spain

ENGLISH-SPANISH DICTIONARY

A

a, an un *oon*, una (f.) *oo-nah*

able (to be) poder *poh-DEHR*

about alrededor de *ahl-reh-deh-DOHR day*; **about two o'clock** a eso de las dos *ah EH-soh day lahs dohs*

above arriba *ahr-REE-bah*; encima (de) *ehn-SEE-mah (day)*

abscess el absceso *ahbs-SEH-soh*

accelerator el acelerador *ah-seh-leh-rah-DOHR*

accept (v.) aceptar *ah-sehp-TAHR*

accident el accidente *ahk-see-DEHN-teh*

accountant el contador *kohn-ta-DOHR*

ache (head) el dolor de cabeza *doh-LOHR day kah-BEH-sah*; **(stomach)** el dolor de estómago *doh-LOHR day ehs-TOH-mah-goh*; **(tooth)** el dolor de muelas *doh-LOHR day MWEH-lahs*

across a través (de) *ah trah-BEHS (day)*

adapter el adaptador *ah-dahp-tah-DOHR*

address la dirección *dee-rehk-SYOHN*

adhesive tape cinta adhesiva *SEEN-tah ahd-eh-SEE-vah*

adjust (v.) ajustar *ah-hoos-TAHR*, arreglar *ahr-reh-GLAHR*

admittance (no) se prohíbe la entrada *seh proh-EE-beh lah ehn-TRAH-dah*

afraid (to be) tener miedo *teh-NEHR MYEH-doh*

after después (de) *dehs-PWEHS (day)*

afternoon la tarde *TAHR-deh*

afterward después *dehs-PWEHS*, luego *LWEH-goh*

again otra vez *OH-trah behs*, de nuevo *deh NWEH-boh*

against contra *KOHN-trah*

ago hace *AH-seh*

agree (v.) estar de acuerdo *ehs-TAHR deh ah-KWEHR-doh*

ahead adelante *ah-deh-LAHN-teh*

aid la ayuda *ah-YOO-dah*; **first aid** primeros auxilios *pree-mehr-ohs ah-ook-SEEL-yohs*

air aire *AHY-reh*; **air mail** el correo aéreo *kohr-REH-oh ah-EH-reh-oh*

airline la línea aérea *LEE-neh-ah ah-EH-reh-ah*

airplane el avión *ah-BYOHN*

airport el aeropuerto *ah-eh-roh-PWEHR-toh*

alarm clock el despertador *dehs-pehr-tah-DOHR*

all todo *TOH-doh*; **All aboard!** ¡A bordo! *ah BOHR-doh*, ¡Señores viajeros al tren! *sehn-YOH-rehs byah-HEH-rohs ahl TREHN*

allow permitir *pehr-mee-TEER*

almond la almendra *ahl-MEHN-drah*

almost casi *KAH-see*

alone solo *SOH-loh*

already ya *yah*

also también *tahm-BYEHN*

always siempre *SYEHM-preh*

A.M. de (por) la mañana *deh (pohr) lah mahn-YAHN-nah*

am soy *soy*, estoy *ehs-TOY*

American norteamericano *NOHR-teh-ah-meh-ree-KAH-*

noh; **American plan** la pensión completa *pehn-SYOHN kohm-PLEH-tah,* cuarto y comida *KWAHR-toh ee koh-MEE-dah*

among entre *EHN-treh*

and y *ee;* e *eh* [before i or hi]

ankle el tobillo *toh-BEE-yoh*

annoy (v.) molestar *moh-lehs-TAHR*

another otro *OH-troh*

answer (response) la respuesta *rehs-PWEHS-tah,* la contestación *kohn-tehs-tah-SYOHN*

any algún *ahl-GOON*

anybody (anyone) alguien *AHL-gyehn*

anything algo *AHL-goh;* **Anything else?** ¿Algo más? *AHL-goh MAHS*

apartment el piso *PEE-soh,* el apartamento *ah-pahr-tah-MEHN-toh*

aperitif el aperitivo *ah-peh-ree-TEE-boh*

appetizers los entremeses *ehn-treh-MEH-sehs*

apple la manzana *mahn-SAH-nah*

apricot el albaricoque *ahl-bah-ree-KOH-keh*

April abril *ah-BREEL*

Arab árabe *AH-rah-beh*

are son *sohn,* están *ehs-TAHN*

Argentinian argentino *ahr-hehn-TEEN-oh*

arm el brazo *BRAH-soh*

armchair el sillón *see-YOHN*

around alrededor (de) *ahl-reh-deh-DOHR (deh)*

arrival la llegada *yeh-GAH-dah*

article el artículo *ahr-TEE-koo-loh*

as como *KOH-moh*

ashtray el cenicero *seh-nee-SEH-roh*

ask (a question) preguntar *preh-goon-TAHR;* **ask for** pedir *peh-DEER*

asparagus el espárrago *ehs-PAHR-ah-goh*

aspirin la aspirina *ahs-pee-REE-nah*

at en *ehn,* a *ah;* **at her house** en casa de ella *ehn KAH-sah deh EH-yah;* **at once** en seguida *ehn seh-GHEE-dah*

ATM cajero automático *kah-HEHR-oh ow-to-MAH-tee-koh*

attention! ¡atención! *ah-tehn-SYOHN,* ¡cuidado! *kwee-DAH-doh*

August agosto (m.) *ah-GOHS-toh*

aunt la tía *TEE-ah*

Austrian austríaco *ows-TREE-ah-koh*

automobile el automóvil *ow-toh-MOH-beel,* el carro *KAHR-roh,* el coche *KOH-cheh*

autumn el otoño *oh-TOHN-yoh*

avoid (v.) evitar *eh-bee-TAHR*

awful terrible *tehr-REE-bleh*

B

baby el bebé *beh-BEH,* el nene *NEH-neh,* la nena *NEH-nah*

back (body part) la espalda *ehs-PAHL-dah;* **(behind)** detrás (de) *deh-TRAHS (deh);* **(direction, movement)** atrás *ah-TRAHS*

bacon el tocino *toh-SEE-noh*

bad malo *MAH-loh;* **too bad!** ¡es lástima! *ehs LAHS-tee-mah*

badly mal *mahl*

bag, handbag cartera *kahr-TEHR-ah;* **valise** la maleta *mah-LEH-tah*

baggage el equipaje *eh-kee-PAH-heh;* **baggage room** la sala de equipajes *SAH-lah deh eh-kee-PAH-hehs*

baked al horno *ahl OHR-noh*

balcony (theater) la galería *gah-leh-REE-ah*

ball la pelota *peh-LOH-tah*

banana el plátano *PLAH-tah-noh*

bandage (covering) la venda *BEHN-dah*; **to bandage** vendar *behn-DAHR*

bank el banco *BAHN-koh*

barber el peluquero *peh-loo-KEH-roh*, el barbero *bahr-BEHR-roh*

barbershop la peluquería *peh-loo-keh-REE-ah*, la barbería *bahr-behr-EE-ah*

bargain la ganga *GAHN-gah*

basket la cesta *SEHS-tah*, la canasta *kah-NAHS-tah*

bath baño *BAHN-yoh*; **to bathe** bañarse *bahn-YAHR-seh*

bathing cap el gorro de baño *GOHR-roh deh BAHN-yoh*

bathing suit el traje de baño *TRAH-heh deh BAHN-yoh*

bathrobe el albornoz *ahl-bohr-NOHS*

bathroom el cuarto de baño *KWAHR-toh deh BAHN-yoh*

battery (automobile) el acumulador *ah-koo-moo-lah-DOHR*, la batería *bah-teh-REE-ah*

be (v.) ser *sehr*, estar *ehs-TAHR*; **be back** estar de vuelta *ehs-TAHR deh BWEHL-tah*

beach la playa *PLAH-yah*

beautiful bello *BEH-yoh*, hermoso *ehr-MOH-soh*

beauty salon el salón de belleza *sah-LOHN deh beh-YEH-sah*

because porque *POHR-keh*

bed la cama *KAH-mah*

bedroom la alcoba *ahl-KOH-bah*, el dormitorio *dohr-mee-TOR-ryoh*

beef la carne de vaca *KAHR-neh deh BAH-kah*; **roast beef** el rosbif *rohs-BEEF*

beer la cerveza *sehr-BEH-sah*

beet la remolacha *reh-moh-LAH-chah*

before antes de *AHN-tehs deh*

begin comenzar *koh-mehn-SAHR*, empezar *ehm-peh-SAHR*

behind detrás de *deh-TRAHS deh*

Belgian belga *BEHL-gah*

believe (v.) creer *kreh-EHR*

bell (door) el timbre *TEEM-breh*

bellhop el botones *boh-TOH-nehs*

belong pertenecer *pehr-teh-neh-SEHR*

belt el cinturón *seen-too-ROHN*

best el mejor *ehl meh-HOHR*

bet (I'll …) apuesto a que *ah-PWEHS-toh ah keh*

better mejor *meh-HOHR*

between entre *EHN-treh*

bicarbonate of soda el bicarbonato de soda *bee-kahr-boh-NAH-toh deh SOH-dah*

bicycle la bicicleta *bee-see-KLAY-tah*

big grande *GRAHN-deh*

bill (restaurant check) la cuenta *KWEHN-tah*

billion mil millones *meel mee-YOH-nehs*

bird el pájaro *PAH-hah-roh*

bite (get a …) tomar un bocado *toh-MAHR oon boh-KAH-doh*

bitter amargo *ah-MAHR-goh*

black negro *NEH-groh*

blade (razor) la hoja de afeitar *OH-hah deh ah-fey-TAHR*

blank (form) el formulario *fohr-moo-LAHR-ee-oh*

bleach (clothes) el blanqueador *blahn-keh-ah-DOHR*

blender la licuadora *lee-kwah-DOHR-ah*

block (city) la cuadra *KWAH-drah*, la manzana *mahn-SAH-nah*

blood la sangre *SAHN-greh*

blood pressure la presión de sangre *preh-SYOHN day SAHN-greh*

blouse la blusa *BLOO-sah*

blue azul *ah-SOOL*

boardinghouse la casa de huéspedes *KAH-sah deh WEHS-peh-dehs*

boat el barco *BAHR-koh*, el buque *BOO-keh*, el bote *BOH-teh*

body el cuerpo *KWEHR-poh*

boiled hervido *ehr-BEE-doh*

bolt (automobile) el perno *PEHR-noh*

bone el hueso *WEH-soh*

book el libro *LEE-broh*; **guidebook** la guía *GHEE-ah*

bookstore la librería *lee-breh-REE-ah*

booth (phone) la cabina (telefónica) *kah-BEE-nah teh-leh-FOH-nee-kah*

boric acid el ácido bórico *AH-see-doh BOH-ree-koh*

born (to be) nacer *nah-SEHR*

borrow (v.) pedir prestado *peh-DEER prehs-TAH-doh*; **He borrowed $5 from me** Me pidió cinco dólares prestados *meh pee-DYOH SEEN-koh DOH-lah-rehs prehs-TAH-dohs*

bother (v.) molestar *moh-lehs-TAHR*; **Don't bother** no se moleste *noh seh moh-LEHS-teh*

bottle la botella *boh-TEH-yah*

box la caja *KAH-hah*

box office (theater) la taquilla *tah-KEE-yah*

boy el muchacho *moo-CHAH-choh*, el chico *CHEE-koh*

bra, brassiere el sostén *sohs-TEHN*

bracelet la pulsera *pool-SEHR-ah*

brakes (automobile) los frenos *FREH-nohs*

Brazilian brasileño *brah-see-LEH-nyoh*

bread el pan *pahn*

break (v.) romper *rohm-PEHR*

breakdown (auto) la avería *ah-beh-REE-ah*

breakfast el desayuno *deh-sah-YOO-noh*

breathe (v.) respirar *rehs-pee-RAHR*

bridge el puente *PWEHN-teh*

bring traer *trah-EHR*

broiled a la parrilla *ah lah pahr-REE-yah*

broken roto *ROH-toh*, quebrado *keh-BRAH-doh*

brother el hermano *ehr-MAH-noh*

brown pardo *PAHR-doh*, castaño *kas-TAH-nyoh*, moreno *moh-REH-noh*

bruise (injury) la contusión *kohn-too-SYOHN*

brush el cepillo *seh-PEE-yoh*; **shaving brush** la brocha de afeitar *broh-chah deh ah-fey-TAHR*; **to brush** cepillar *seh-pee-YAHR*

building el edificio *eh-dee-FEE-soyh*

bulb (electric) la bombilla *bohm-BEE-yah*

bull el toro *TOH-roh*; **bullring** la plaza de toros *PLAH-sah deh TOH-rohs*

bullfight la corrida de toros *kohr-REE-dah deh TOH-rohs*

bumper (automobile) el parachoques *pah-rah-CHOH-kehs*

burn (injury) la quemadura *keh-mah-DOO-rah*; **to burn** quemar *keh-MAHR*

bus el autobús *ow-toh-BOOS*

busy ocupado *oh-koo-PAH-doh*

but pero *PEH-roh*

butter la mantequilla *mahn-teh-KEE-yah*

button el botón *boh-TOHN*

buy (v.) comprar *kohm-PRAHR*

by de, por *deh, pohr*

C

cab el taxi *TAHK-see*

cabaret el cabaret *kah-bah-REH*

cabbage la col *kohl*

cable (telegram) el cablegrama *kah-bleh-GRAH-mah*

cake la torta *TOHR-tah*

call (telephone) la llamada *yah-MAH-dah*, la comunicación *koh-moo-nee-kah-SYOHN*; **to telephone** llamar por teléfono *yah-MAHR pohr teh-LEH-foh-noh*

camera la cámara *KAH-mah-rah*

can (container) la lata *LAH-tah*; **be able** poder *poh-DEHR*; **can opener** el abrelatas *ah-breh-LAH-tahs*

Canadian canadiense *kah-nah-DYEHN-seh*

cancel (v.) cancelar *kahn-seh-LAHR*

candle la bujía *boo-HEE-ah*, la vela *BEH-lah*

candy los dulces *DOOL-sehs*, los bombones *bohm-BOH-nehs*

cap la gorra *GOHR-rah*

captain el capitán *kah-pee-TAHN*

car (automobile) el automóvil *ow-toh-MOH-beel*, el coche *KOH-cheh*; **railroad car** el vagón *bah-GOHN*, **streetcar** el tranvía *trahn-BEE-ah*

carbon paper el papel carbón *pah-PEHL kahr-BOHN*

carburetor el carburador *kahr-boo-rah-DOHR*

card (playing) la carta *KAHR-tah*, el naipe *NAH-ee-peh*

care (caution) el cuidado *kwee-DAH-doh*

careful (to be) tener cuidado *teh-NEHR kwee-DAH-doh*

carefully con cuidado *kohn kwee-DAH-doh*

carrot la zanahoria *sah-nah-OH-ryah*

carry (v.) llevar *yeh-BAHR*

case (cigarette) la pitillera *pee-tee-YER-rah*; **in any case** en todo caso *ehn TOH-doh KAH-soh*

cash (money) el dinero contante *dee-NEH-roh kohn-TAHN-teh*; **to cash** cobrar *koh-BRAHR*

cashier el cajero *kah-HEH-roh*

castle el castillo *kahs-TEE-yoh*

castor oil el aceite de ricino *ah-SAY-teh deh ree-SEE-noh*

cat el gato *GAH-toh*

catch (v.) agarrar *ah-gahr-RAHR*

cathedral la catedral *kah-teh-DRAHL*

Catholic católico *kah-TOH-lee-koh*

cauliflower la coliflor *koh-lee-FLOHR*

caution la precaución *preh-kow-SYOHN*; **Caution!** !Cuidado! *kwee-DAH-doh*

ceiling el techo *TEH-choh*

celery el apio *AH-pyoh*

center el centro *SEHN-troh*

certainly ciertamente *syehr-tah-MEHN-teh*

certificate el certificado *sehr-tee-fee-KAH-doh*

chain la cadena *kah-DEH-nah*

chair la silla *SEE-lyah*

change (money) el cambio *KAHM-byoh*; **small change** la moneda suelta *moh-NEH-dah SWEHL-tah*, el suelto *SWEHL-toh*; **to change** cambiar *kahm-BYAHR*

charge (cover) el gasto mínimo *GAHS-toh MEE-nee-moh*; **to charge** cobrar *koh-BRAHR*

cheap barato *bah-RAH-toh*

check (baggage) el talón *tah-LOHN*; **traveler's check** el cheque de viajeros *CHEH-keh deh byah-HEH-rohs*; **to**

check (baggage) facturar *fahk-too-RAHR*

checkroom la sala de equipajes *SAH-lah deh eh-kee-PAH-hehs*

cheek la mejilla *meh-HEE-yah*

cheese el queso *KEH-soh*

cherry la cereza *seh-REH-sah*

chest el pecho *PEH-choh*

chestnut la castaña *kahs-TAHN-yah*

chicken el pollo *POH-yoh*

child el niño *NEEN-yoh*, la niña *NEEN-yah*

Chilean chileno *chee-LEH-noh*

chill el escalofrío *ehs-kah-loh-FREE-oh*

chin la barbilla *bahr-BEE-yah*

Chinese chino *CHEE-noh*

chiropodist el pedicuro *peh-dee-KOO-roh*

chocolate el chocolate *choh-koh-LAH-teh*; **chocolate candies** los bombones *bohm-BOH-nehs*

choose (v.) escoger *ehs-koh-HEHR*

chop, cutlet la chuleta *choo-LEH-tah*

Christmas la Navidad *nah-bee-DAHD*; **(Merry Christmas!)** ¡Felices Pascuas! *feh-LEE-sehs PAHS-kwahs*, ¡Feliz Navidad! *feh-LEES nah-bee-DAHD*

church la iglesia *ee-GLEH-syah*

cigar el cigarro *see-GAHR-roh*, el puro *POO-roh*; **cigar store** la tabaquería *tah-bah-keh-REE-ah*, el estanco *ehs-TAHN-koh*

cigarette el cigarrillo *see-gahr-REE-yoh*, el pitillo *pee-TEE-yoh*; **cigarette case** la pitillera *pee-tee-YEH-rah*; **cigarette holder** la boquilla *boh-KEE-yah*

city la ciudad *syoo-DAHD*; **city hall** el ayuntamiento *ah-yoon-tah-MYEHN-toh*

class la clase *KLAH-seh*

clean (spotless) limpio *LEEM-pyoh*; **to clean** limpiar *leem-PYAHR*

cleaner's la tintorería *teen-toh-reh-REE-ah*

clear (transparent) claro *KLAH-roh*

climb (v.) trepar *treh-PAHR*

clipper (barber's) la maquinilla *mah-kee-NEE-yah*

clock el reloj *reh-LOH*

close (near) cerca *SEHR-kah*; **to close** cerrar *sehr-RAHR*; **closed** cerrado *sehr-RAH-doh*

cloth la tela *TEH-lah*, el paño *PAHN-yoh*

clothes, clothing la ropa *ROH-pah*, los vestidos *behs-TEE-dohs*; **evening clothes** el traje de etiqueta *TRAH-heh deh eh-tee-KEH-tah*; **clothes brush** el cepillo de ropa *seh-PEEL-yoh deh ROH-pah*

cloud la nube *NOO-beh*; **cloudy** nublado *noo-BLAH-doh*

club (night) el cabaret *kah-bah-REH*

clutch (automobile) el embrague *ehm-BRAH-gheh*

coach (railroad) el coche *KOH-cheh*, el vagón *bah-GOHN*

coat el saco *SAH-koh*, la americana *ah-meh-ree-KAH-nah*; **coat hanger** el colgador *kohl-gah-DOHR*

cocktail el coctel *kohk-TEHL*

coffee el café *kah-FEH*

coin (money) la moneda *moh-NEH-dah*

cold (temperature) frío *FREE-oh*; **(sickness)** el resfriado *rehs-FRYAH-doh*; **(weather)** hacer frío *ah-SEHR FREE-oh*

cold cuts los fiambres (m. pl.) *FYAHM-brehs*

collar el cuello *KWEHL-yoh*

collect (v.) cobrar *koh-BRAHR*

cologne el agua de colonia *AH-gwah deh koh-LOH-nyah*

color el color *koh-LOHR;* **color film** la película de color *peh-LEE-koo-lah deh koh-LOHR*

comb el peine *PAY-neh*

come (v.) venir *beh-NEER;* **to come in** entrar *ehn-TRAHR;* **Come in!** ¡Pase usted! *PAH-seh oo-STEHD,* ¡Adelante! *Ah-deh-LAHN-teh*

comedy la comedia *koh-MEH-dyah*

comfortable cómodo *KOH-moh-doh*

compact disc el disco *DEES-koh*

company la compañía *kohm-pahn-YEE-ah*

compartment el compartimiento *kohm-pahr-tee-MYEHN-toh*

complaint la queja *KEH-hah*

concert el concierto *kohn-SYEHR-toh*

condoms condones *kohn-DOH-nehs*

conductor (train) el revisor *reh-bee-SOHR*

congratulations las felicitaciones *feh-lee-see-tah-SYOHN-ehs,* la enhorabuena *ehn-oh-rah-BWEH-nah*

connected (to be ___ by telephone) estar en comunicación *ehs-TAHR ehn koh-moo-nee-kah-SYOHN*

consul el cónsul *KOHN-sool*

consulate el consulado *kohn-soo-LAH-doh*

continue (v.) continuar *kohn-tee-NWAHR,* seguir *seh-GHEER*

convent el convento *kohn-BEHN-toh*

cooked cocido *koh-SEE-doh*

cool fresco *FREHS-koh*

corkscrew el sacacorchos *sah-kah-KOHR-chohs*

corn el maíz *mah-EES*

corner la esquina *ehs-KEE-nah*

cost (amount) el precio *PREH-syoh,* el costo *KOHS-toh;* **to cost** costar *kohs-TAHR*

cotton el algodón *ahl-goh-DOHN*

cough (v.) toser *toh-SEHR;* **cough syrup** el jarabe para la tos *hah-RAH-beh pah-rah lah TOHS*

count (v.) contar *kohn-TAHR*

country (nation) el país *pah-EES;* **countryside** el campo *KAHM-poh*

course (in meal) el plato *PLAH-toh*

cover charge el gasto mímimo *GAHS-toh MEE-nee-moh*

crazy loco *LOH-koh*

cream la crema *KREH-mah*

crystal el cristal *krees-TAHL*

Cuban cubano *koo-BAH-noh*

cucumber el pepino *peh-PEE-noh*

cuff links los gemelos *heh-MEH-lohs*

cup la taza *TAH-sah*

curtain la cortina *kohr-TEE-nah,* el telón *teh-LOHN*

curve la curva *KOOR-bah*

customs la aduana *ah-DWAH-nah*

cut (v.) cortar *kohr-TAHR;* **Cut it out!** ¡Basta! *BAHS-tah*

cutlet la chuleta *choo-LEH-tah*

Czech checo *CHEH-koh*

D

daily (by the day) por día *pohr DEE-ah*

damp húmedo *OO-meh-doh*

dance el baile *BAH-ee-lay;* **to dance** bailar *bah-ee-LAHR*

danger el peligro *peh-LEE-groh;* **dangerous** peligroso *peh-lee-GROH-soh*

Danish danés *dah-NEHS*

dark oscuro *ohs-KOO-roh*

Darn it! ¡Caramba! *kah-RAHM-bah*

date (today's) la fecha *FEH-chah*

daughter la hija *EE-hah*

day el día *DEE-ah*

dead muerto *MWEHR-toh*

death la muerte *MWEHR-teh*

December diciembre (m.) *dee-SYEHM-breh*

declaration la declaración *deh-klah-rah-SYOHN*

declare (v.) declarar *deh-klah-RAHR*

deep profundo *proh-FOON-doh*

deliver (v.) entregar *ehn-treh-GAHR*

delivery la entrega *ehn-TREH-gah;* **special delivery** el correo urgente *kohr-REH-oh oor-HEHN-teh*

dental dental *dehn-TAHL*

dentist el dentista *dehn-TEES-tah*

denture la dentadura *dehn-tah-DOO-rah*

deodorant el desodorante *deh-soh-doh-RAHN-teh*

department store el almacén *ahl-mah-SEHN*

desk (information) el despacho de informes (información) *dehs-PAH-choh deh een-FOHR-mehs (een-fohr-mah-SYOHN)*

dessert el postre *POHS-treh*

detour la desviación *dehs-byah-SYOHN*, el desvío *dehs-BEE-oh*

develop (film) (v.) revelar *reh-beh-LAHR*

devil el diablo *DYAH-bloh*, el demonio *deh-MOH-nyoh*

diapers los pañales *pah-NYAH-lehs*

dictionary el diccionario *deek-syoh-NAH-ryoh*

different diferente *dee-feh-REHN-teh*

difficult difícil *dee-FEE-seel*

difficulty la dificultad *dee-fee-kool-TAHD*, el apuro *ah-POO-roh*

dining car el coche comedor *KOH-cheh koh-meh-DOHR*

dining room el comedor *koh-meh-DOHR*

dinner la comida *koh-MEE-dah*

direct (v.) indicar *een-dee-KAHR*, dirigir *dee-ree-HEER*

direction la dirección *dee-rehk-SYOHN*

dirty sucio *soo-SYOH*

discount el descuento *dehs-KWEHN-toh*

dish el plato *PLAH-toh*

district el barrio *BAHR-ryoh*

disturb (v.) molestar *moh-lehs-TAHR*

dizzy (to feel) (v.) estar aturdido *ehs-TAHR ah-toor-DEE-doh*

do (v.) hacer *ah-SEHR*

dock el muelle *MWEH-yeh*

doctor el médico *MEH-dee-koh*, el doctor *dohk-TOHR*

document el documento *doh-koo-MEHN-toh*

dog el perro *PEHR-roh*

dollar el dólar *DOH-lahr*

domestic nacional *nah-syoh-NAHL*, del país *dehl-pah-EES*

door la puerta *PWEHR-tah;* **door handle** el tirador de puerta *tee-rah-DOHR deh PWEHR-tah*

doorman el portero *pohr-TEH-roh*

double room la habitación para dos personas *ah-bee-tah-SYOHN PAH-rah dohs pehr-SOH-nahs*

down abajo *ah-BAH-hoh*

dozen la docena *doh-SEH-nah*

draft (current of air) la corriente de aire *kohr-RYEHN-teh deh AH-ee-ray*

draw (v.) dibujar *dee-boo-HAHR*

drawer el cajón *kah-HOHN*

dress (garment) el vestido *behs-TEE-doh;* **to dress** vestirse *behs-TEER-seh*

dressing gown la bata *BAH-tah*

drink (beverage) la bebida *beh-BEE-dah;* **to drink** beber *beh-BEHR*

drinkable potable *poh-TAH-bleh*

drive (ride) el paseo en coche *pah-SEH-oh ehn KOH-cheh;* **to drive** guiar, conducir *ghee-AHR*, *kohn-doo-SEER* [first p. sing. (present), conduzco *(kohn-DOOS-koh)*]

driver el chófer *CHOH-fehr*

dropper (eye) el cuentagotas *kwehn-tah-GOH-tahs*

drown (v.) ahogarse *ah-oh-GAHR-say*

drugstore la farmacia *fahr-MAH-syah*

drunk borracho *bohr-RAH-choh*

dry seco *SEH-koh;* **dry cleaning** la limpieza en seco *leem-PYEH-sah ehn SEH-koh*

duck el pato *PAH-toh*

Dutch holandés *oh-lahn-DEHS*

dysentery la disentería *dee-sehn-teh-REE-ah*

E

each cada *KAH-dah;* **each one** cada uno *KAH-dah oo-noh*

ear la oreja *oh-REH-hah*

earache el dolor de oído *doh-LOHR deh oh-EE-doh*

early temprano *tehm-PRAH-noh*

earring el arete *ah-REH-teh*, pendiente *pehn-DYEHN-teh*

east el este *EHS-teh*

easy fácil *FAH-seel;* **Take it easy!** ¡No se preocupe! *noh seh preh-oh-KOO-peh,*

¡Tómelo con calma! *TOH-meh-loh kohn KAHL-mah*

eat (v.) comer *koh-MEHR*

egg el huevo *WEH-boh*

eight ocho *OH-choh*

eighteen dieciocho *dyeh-see-OH-choh*

eighth octavo *ohk-TAH-boh*

eighty ochenta *oh-CHEHN-tah*

elbow el codo *KOH-doh*

electric eléctrico *eh-LEHK-tree-koh*

elevator el ascensor *ahs-sehn-SOHR*

eleven once *OHN-seh*

else (nothing else) nada más *NAH-dah mahs;* **What else?** ¿Qué más? *KEH MAHS*

empty vacío *bah-SEE-oh*

end (conclusion) el fin *feen;* **to end** terminar *tehr-mee-NAHR*

endorse endosar *ehn-doh-SAHR*

engine el motor *moh-TOHR*, la máquina *MAH-kee-nah*

English inglés *een-GLEHS*

enlargement la ampliación *ahm-plyah-SYOHN*

enough bastante *bahs-TAHN-teh*

evening la tarde *TAHR-deh;* **evening clothes** el traje de etiqueta *TRAH-heh deh eh-tee-KEH-tah*

every cada *KAH-dah*

everybody, everyone todo el mundo *TOH-doh ehl MOON-doh*, todos *TOH-dohs*

everything todo *TOH-doh*

examine examinar *ehk-sah-mee-NAHR*

exchange (v.) cambiar *kahm-BYAHR;* **exchange office** la oficina de cambio *oh-fee-SEE-nah deh KAHM-byoh*

excursion la excursión *ehs-koor-SYOHN*

excuse (v.) perdonar *pehr-doh-NAHR*, dispensar *dees-pehn-SAHR*

exhaust (automobile) el escape *ehs-KAH-peh*

exit la salida *sah-LEE-dah*

expect (v.) esperar *eha-peh-RAHR*, aguardar *ah-gwahr-DAHR*

expensive caro *KAH-roh*

express (train) el expreso *ehs-PREH-soh*

extra extra *EHS-trah*

extract (v.) sacar *sah-KAHR*

eye el ojo *OH-hoh*

eyebrow la ceja *SEH-hah*

eyeglasses las gafas *GAH-fahs*, los anteojos *ahn-teh-OH-hohs*

eyelash la pestaña *pehs-TAHN-yah*

eyelid el párpado *PAHR-pah-doh*

F

face (body part) la cara *KAH-rah*; **face powder** los polvos para la cara *POHL-bohs PAH-rah lah KAH-rah*

facecloth el paño de lavar *PAHN-yoh deh lah-BAHR*

facial el masaje facial *mah-SAH-heh fah-SYAHL*

fall (autumn) el otoño *oh-TOHN-yoh*; **(injury)** la caída *kah-EE-dah*; **to fall** caer *kah-EHR*

false falso *FAHL-soh*

family la familia *fah-MEEL-yah*; **family name** el apellido *ah-peh-YEE-doh*

fan (car or electric) el ventilador *behn-tee-lah-DOHR*; **(hand)** el abanico *ah-bah-NEE-koh*; **fan belt** la correa de ventilador *kohr-REH-ah deh behn-tee-lah-DOHR*

far lejos *LEH-hohs*, lejano *leh-HAH-noh*

fare (fee) la tarifa *tah-REE-fah*

fast rapido *RAH-pee-doh*, pronto *PROHN-toh*; **The watch is fast** El reloj va adelantado *reh-LOH bah ah-deh-lahn-TAH-doh*

faster más rapido *mahs RAH-pee-doh*

father el padre *PAH-dreh*

faucet el grifo *GREE-foh*

fear (dread) el miedo *MYEH-doh*; **to fear** tener miedo *teh-NEHR MYEH-doh*

February febrero (m.) *feh-BREH-roh*

feel (v.) sentirse *sehn-TEER-seh*; **to feel like** tener ganas de (+ infinitive) *teh-NEHR GAH-nahs deh*

felt (cloth) el fieltro *FYEHL-troh*

fender el guardabarro *gwahr-dah-BAHR-roh*

festival la fiesta *FYEHS-tah*

fever la fiebre *FYEH-breh*

few pocos *POH-kohs*; **a few** unos cuantos *oo-nohs KWAHN-tohs*

fifteen quince *KEEN-seh*

fifth quinto *KEEN-toh*

fifty cincuenta *seen-KWEHN-tah*

fig el higo *EE-goh*

fill, fill out (v.) llenar *yeh-NAHR*; **to fill a tooth** empastar *ehm-pahs-TAHR*; **Fill it up!** ¡llénelo! *YEH-neh-loh*

filling el empaste *ehm-PAHS-teh*

film la película *peh-LEE-koo-lah*

find (v.) hallar *ah-YAHR*, encontrar *ehn-kohn-TRAHR*

fine (good) fino *FEE-noh*, bello *BEH-yo*, bueno *BWEH-noh*

fine (fee) la multa *MOOL-tah*

finger el dedo *DEH-doh*

finish (v.) acabar *ah-kah-BAHR*, terminar *tehr-mee-NAHR*

fire el fuego *FWEH-goh;*
(**destructive**) el incendio
een-SEHN-dyoh
first primero *pree-MEH-roh;*
first aid los primeros
auxilios *pree-MEH-rohs ah-
ook-SEEL-yohs*
fish (in water) el pez *pehs;*
(**when caught**) el pescado
pehs-KAH-doh
fit (v.) calzar *KAHL-sahr,*
vestir *behs-TEER*
fix (v.) componer *kohm-poh-
NEHR,* reparar *reh-pah-
RAHR,* arreglar *ahr-reh-
GLAHR;* **fixed-price meal**
la comida corrida (completa)
*koh-MEE-dah kohr-REE-dah
(kohm-PLEH-tah)*
flashlight la linterna eléctrica
*leen-TEHR-nah eh-LEHK-
tree-kah*
flat (level) llano *YAH-noh;*
flat tire el pinchazo *peen-
CHAH-soh*
flight (plane) el vuelo *BWEH-
loh*
flint el pedernal *peh-dehr-NAHL*
floor el piso *PEE-soh,* el suelo
SWEH-loh
flower la flor *flohr*
fluid (lighter) la bencina
behn-SEE-nah
fog la niebla *NYEH-blah*
follow (v.) seguir *seh-GHEER*
foot el pie *pyeh*
for (purpose, destination)
para *PAH-rah;* (**exchange**)
por *pohr*
forbidden prohibido *proh-ee-
BEE-doh*
forehead la frente *FREHN-teh*
foreign extranjero *ehs-tran-
HEH-roh*
forget (v.) olvidar *ohl-bee-
DAHR*
fork el tenedor *teh-neh-DOHR*
form (document) el formulario
fohr-moo-LAH-ree-oh
forty cuarenta *kwah-REHN-tah*

forward (direction) adelante
ah-deh-LAHN-teh; **to
forward** reexpedir *reh-ex-
peh-DEER*
fountain la fuente *FWEHN-teh;*
fountain pen la pluma
fuente *PLOO-mah FWEHN-teh*
four cuatro *KWAH-troh*
fourteen catorce *kah-TOHR-seh*
fourth cuarto *KWAHR-toh*
fracture (injury) la fractura
frahk-TOO-rah
free (unattached) libre *LEE-
breh;* **free of charge** gratis
GRAH-tees
French francés *frahn-SEHS*
frequent flyer miles bonos de
vuelo *BOH-nohs day BWEH-
loh*
Friday el viernes *BYEHR-nehs*
fried frito *FREE-toh*
friend amigo *ah-MEE-goh,*
amiga *ah-MEE-gah*
from de *deh,* desde *DEHS-deh*
front (position) delantero *deh-
lahn-TEH-roh,* que da a la
calle *keh dah ah lah KAH-yeh*
fruit la fruta *FROO-tah*
fuel pump la bomba de
combustible *BOHM-bah deh
kohm-boos-TEE-bleh*
full (as in bus) lleno *YEH-
noh;* (**complete**) completo
kohm-PLEH-toh
furnished amueblado *ah-
mweh-BLAH-doh*

G

game el juego *HWEH-goh,* la
partida *pahr-TEE-dah*
garage el garage *gah-RAH-heh*
garden el jardín *hahr-DEEN*
garlic el ajo *AH-hoh*
garter la liga *LEE-gah*
gas (fuel), petrol la gasolina
gah-soh-LEE-nah; **gas station**
la estación de gasolina *ehs-tah-
SYOHN deh gah-soh-LEE-nah*

gate (railroad station) la barrera *bahr-REH-rah*

gauze la gasa *GAH-sah*

gear (car) el engranaje *ehn-grah-NAH-heh*

general delivery la lista de correos *LEES-tah deh kohr-REH-ohs*

gentleman el señor *sehn-YOHR*, el caballero *kah-bah-YEH-roh*

German alemán *ah-leh-MAHN*

get (obtain) (v.) conseguir *kohn-seh-GHEER;* **to get back (recover)** recobrar *reh-koh-BRAHR;* **to get dressed** vestirse *behs-TEER-seh;* **to get off** bajarse *bah-HAHR-seh;* **to get out** irse *EER-seh,* salir *sah-LEER;* **to get up** levantarse *leh-bahn-TAHR-seh;* **Get out!** ¡Fuera!, ¡Fuera de aquí! *FWEH-rah deh ah-KEE*

gift el regalo *reh-GAH-loh*

gin la ginebra *hee-NEH-brah*

girdle la faja *FAH-hah*

girl la muchacha *moo-CHAH-chah,* la chica *CHEE-kah*

give (v.) dar *dahr;* **to give back** devolver *deh-bohl-BEHR*

glad contento *kohn-TEHN-toh,* alegre *ah-LEH-greh*

gladly con mucho gusto *kohn MOO-choh GOOS-toh*

glass (drinking) el vaso *BAH-soh;* **(material)** el vidrio *BEE-dryoh*

glasses (eye) las gafas (f. pl.) *GAH-fahs,* los anteojos (m. pl.) *ahn-teh-OH-hohs*

glove el guante *GWAHN-teh*

go (v.) ir *eer;* **to go away** irse *EER-seh,* marcharse *mahr-CHAHR-seh;* **to go shopping** de compras (de tiendas) *eer deh KOHM-prahs (deh TYEHN-dahs);* **to go down** bajar *bah-HAHR;* **to go home** ir a casa *eer ah KAH-*

sah; **to go in** entrar *ehn-TRAHR;* **to go out** salir *sah-LEER;* **to go to bed** acostarse *ah-kohs-TAHR-seh;* **to go up** subir *soo-BEER*

gold el oro *OH-roh*

good bueno *BWEH-noh;* **good-bye** hasta la vista *AHS-tah lah BEES-tah,* adiós *ah-DYOHS*

goose el ganso *GAHN-soh*

grade (on road) la cuesta *KWEHS-tah;* **grade crossing** el paso a nivel *PAH-soh ah nee-BEHL*

gram el gramo *GRAH-moh*

grapefruit la toronja *toh-ROHN-hah,* el pomelo *poh-MEHL-oh*

grapes las uvas *OO-bahs*

grass la hierba *YEHR-bah*

grateful agradecido *ah-grah-deh-SEE-doh*

gravy, sauce la salsa *SAHL-sah*

gray gris *grees*

grease (lubricate) (v.) engrasar *ehn-grah-SAHR*

Greek griego *GRYEH-goh*

green verde *BEHR-deh*

greeting el saludo *sah-LOO-doh*

guide el guia *GHEE-ah;* **guidebook** la guía *GHEE-ah*

gum (chewing) el chicle *CHEE-kleh*

gums las encías *ehn-SEE-ahs*

guy el tipo *TEE-poh*

H

hair el pelo *PEH-loh,* el cabello *kah-BEH-yoh;* **hair bleach** el descolorante *dehs-koh-loh-RAHN-teh;* **hair lotion** la loción para el pelo *loh-SYOHN PAH-rah ehl PEH-loh;* **hair net** la redecilla *rah-deh-SEEL-yah;* **hair tonic** el tónico para el*

pelo *TOH-ne-koh PAH-rah ehl PEH-loh;* **hair wash** el enjuague *ehn-HWAH-gheh*

hairbrush el cepillo del pelo *seh-PEE-yoh dehl PEH-loh*

haircut el corte de pelo *KOHR-teh deh PEH-loh*

hairpin el gancho *GAHN-choh,* la horquilla *ohr-KEE-yah*

half (adj.) medio *MEH-dyoh,* (n.) la mitad *mee-TAHD*

Halt! ¡Alto! *AHL-toh*

ham el jamón *hah-MOHN*

hammer el martillo *mahr-TEE-yoh*

hand la mano *MAH-noh;* **hand lotion** la loción para las manos *loh-SYOHN PAH-rah lahs MAH-nohs*

handbag la bolsa *BOHL-sah*

handicapped inválido *een-BAHL-ee-doh*

handkerchief el pañuelo *pah-NYWEH-loh*

handmade hecho a mano *EH-choh ah MAH-noh*

hanger (coat) el colgador *kohl-gah-DOHR*

happen (v.) pasar *pah-SAHR,* suceder *soo-seh-DEHR,* ocurrir *oh-koor-REER,* resultar *reh-sool-TAHR*

happy feliz *feh-LEES*

Happy New Year! ¡Feliz Año Nuevo! *Feh-LEES AHN-yoh NWEH-boh*

harbor el puerto *PWEHR-toh*

hard (difficult) difícil *dee-FEE-seel;* **(tough)** duro *DOO-roh*

hard-boiled egg el huevo duro *WEH-boh DOO-roh*

hat el sombrero *sohm-BREH-roh;* **hat shop** la sombrerería *sohm-breh-reh-REE-ah*

have (v.) tener *teh-NEHR;* **to have to** deber *deh-BEHR,* tener que *teh-NEHR-keh*

hazelnut la avellana *ah-beh-YAH-nah*

he el *ehl*

head la cabeza *kah-BEH-sah*

headache el dolor de cabeza *doh-LOHR deh kah-BEH-sah*

headlight el farol *fah-ROHL*

headwaiter el jefe de comedor *HEH-feh deh koh-meh-DOHR*

health la salud *sah-LOOD;* **health certificate** el certificado de sanidad *sehr-tee-fee-KAH-doh deh sah-nee-DAHD*

hear (v.) oír *oh-EER;* **to hear from** tener (recibir) noticias de *teh-NEHR (reh-see-BEER) noh-TEE-syahs deh*

heart el corazón *koh-rah-SOHN*

heat el calor *kah-LOHR*

heaven el cielo *SYEH-loh*

heavy pesado *peh-SAH-doh*

heel (of foot) el talón *tah-LOHN;* **(of shoe)** et tacón *tah-KOHN*

hell el infierno *een-FYEHR-noh*

Hello! ¡Hola! *OH-lah,* ¡Qué tal! *KEH TAHL;* **(on phone)** ¡Diga! *DEE-gah*

help (v.) ayudar *ah-yoo-DAHR;* **May I help you?** ¿Qué desea? *KEH deh-SEH-ah,* ¿En qué puedo servirle? *EHN KEH PWEH-doh sehr-BEER-leh;* **Help yourself** Sírvase usted *SEER-bah-seh oo-STEHD;* **Help!** ¡Auxilio! ¡Socorro! *owk-SEEL-yoh, soh-KOHR-oh*

here aquí *ah-KEE*

high alto *AHL-toh;* **high mass** la misa cantada *MEE-sah kahn-TAH-dah*

highway (auto) la carretera *kahr-reh-TEH-rah*

hip la cadera *kah-DEH-rah*

hire (v.) alquilar *ahl-kee-LAHR*

his su *soo*

Hold the wire No cuelgue *noh KWEHL-geh*

holder (cigarette) la boquilla *boh-KEEL-yah*

home la casa *KAH-sah,* el hogar *oh-GAHR;* **to go home**

ir a casa *eer ah KAH-sah;* **to be at home** estar en casa *ehs-TAHR ehn KAH-sah*

hood (car) el capó *kah-POH*

hook el gancho *GAHN-choh*

hope (v.) esperar *ehs-peh-RAHR*

horn (car) la bocina *boh-SEE-nah*

hors d'oeuvre los entremeses *ehn-treh-MEH-sehs*

horse el caballo *kah-BAH-yoh*

hospital el hospital *ohs-pee-TAHL*

hostel (youth) albergue de jóvenes *ahl-BEHR-geh deh HOH-ben-ehs*

hostess (plane) la azafata *ah-sah-FAH-tah*

hot caliente *kah-LYEHN-teh*

hotel el hotel *oh-TEL*

hour la hora *OH-rah;* **by the hour** por hora *pohr OH-rah*

house la casa *KAH-sah*

how cómo *KOH-moh;* **how far?** ¿a qué distancia? *ah KEH dees-TAHN-syah;* **how long?** ¿cuánto tiempo? *KWAHN-toh TYEHM-poh,* ¿desde cuándo? *DEHS-deh KWAHN-doh;* **how many?** ¿cuántos? *KWAHN-tohs;* **how much?** ¿cuánto? *KWAN-toh*

hundred ciento *SYEHN-toh* [*Cien* is used immediately before the noun: $100, cien dólares *(syehn DOH-lah-rehs)*, but: $160, ciento sesenta dólares *(SYEHN-toh seh-SEHN-tah DOH-lah-rehs)*]

Hungarian húngaro *OON-gah-roh*

hungry (to be) tener hambre *teh-NEHR AHM-breh*

hurry (v.) darse prisa *DAHR-seh PREE-sah;* **to be in a hurry** tener prisa *teh-NEHR PREE-sah*

hurt (v.) lastimar *lahs-tee-MAHR,* hacer(se) daño *ah-SEHR-(seh) DAHN-yoh*

husband el marido *mah-REE-doh*

I

I yo *yoh*

ice el hielo *YEH-loh;* **ice cream** el helado *eh-LAH-doh;* **ice water** el agua helada *AH-gwah eh-LAH-dah*

identification la identificación *ee-dehn-tee-fee-kah-SYOHN*

if si *see*

ignition (car) el encendido *ehn-sehn-DEE-doh*

ill enfermo *ehn-FEHR-moh*

illness la enfermedad *ehn-fehr-meh-DAHD*

imported importado *eem-pohr-TAH-doh*

in en *ehn*

included incluido *een-kloo-EE-doh*

indigestion indigestión *een-dee-hes-TYOHN*

indisposed indispuesto *een-dees-PWEHS-toh*

information desk la información *een-fohr-mah-see-OHN;* **information desk** la oficina de información *oh-fee-SEE-nah deh een-fohr-mah-see-OHN*

injection la inyección *en-yehk-SYOHN*

ink la tinta *TEEN-tah*

inner tube la cámara de aire *KAH-mah-rah deh AHY-reh*

inquire preguntar *preh-goon-TAHR,* averiguar *ah-beh-ree-GWAHR*

insect el insecto *een-SEHK-toh*

insecticide el insecticida *een-sehk-tee-SEE-dah*

inside dentro (de) *DEHN-troh (deh)*

instead en vez *ehn BEHS*

insurance el seguro *seh-GOO-roh*

insure (v.) asegurar *ah-seh-goo-RAHR*

interest el interés *een-teh-REHS*

interpreter el intérprete *een-TEHR-preh-teh*

intersection la bocacalle *boh-koh-KAH-yeh*, el cruce *KROO-seh*

into en *ehn*, dentro de *DEHN-troh deh*

introduce (v.) presentar *preh-sehn-TAHR*

iodine el yodo *YOH-doh*

iron (metal) el hierro *YEHR-roh;* **flat iron** la plancha *PLAHN-chah;* **to iron** planchar *plahn-CHAHR*

is es *ehs*, está *ehs-TAH*

Italian italiano *ee-tah-LYAH-noh*

J

jack (for car) el gato *GAH-toh;* **to jack up (car)** alzar (levantar) con el gato *ahl-SAHR (leh-bahn-TAHR) kohn ehl GAH-toh*

jam (fruit) la mermelada *mehr-meh-LAH-dah*

January enero (m.) *eh-NEH-roh*

Japanese japonés *hah-poh-NEHS*

jaw la quijada *kee-HAH-dah*

jeweler el joyero *hoh-YEH-roh*

jewelry las joyas *HOH-yahs*, las alhajas *ahl-AH-has;* **jewelry store** la joyería *hoh-yeh-REE-ah*

Jewish judío *hoo-DEE-oh*

journey (trip) el viaje *BYAH-heh*

juice el jugo *HOO-goh*, el zumo *SOO-moh*

July julio (m.) *HOO-lyoh*

June junio (m.) *HOO-nyoh*

K

keep (v.) guardar *gwahr-DAHR*, quedarse con *keh-DAHR-seh kohn;* **to keep right** seguir la derecha *seh-GHEER lah deh-REH-chah*

key la llave *YAH-beh*

kilogram el kilogramo *kee-loh-GRAH-moh*

kilometer el kilómetro *kee-LOH-meh-troh*

kind (nice) bueno *BWEH-noh*, amable *ah-MAH-bleh;* **(type)** la clase *KLAH-seh*, el género *HEH-neh-roh*

kiss el beso *BEH-soh;* **to kiss** besar *beh-SAHR*

kitchen la cocina *koh-SEE-nah*

knee la rodilla *roh-DEE-yah*

knife el cuchillo *koo-CHEE-yoh*

knock (v.) llamar *yah-MAHR*

know (v.) **(fact, know-how)** saber *sah-BEHR;* **(person or thing)** conocer *koh-noh-SEHR*

L

label la etiqueta *eh-tee-KEH-tah*

lace el encaje *ehn-KAH-heh*

laces (shoe) los cordones para los zapatos (m. pl.) *kohr-DOH-nehs PAH-rah lohs sah-PAH-tohs*

ladies' room el tocador de señoras *toh-kah-DOHR deh sehn-YOH-rahs*

lady la señora *sehn-YOR-rah*

lamb la carne de cordero *KAHR-neh deh kohr-DEH-roh*

lamp la lámpara *LAHM-pah-rah*

land (ground) la tierra *TYEHR-rah;* **to land** desembarcar *deh-sehm-bahr-KAHR*

language el idioma *ee-DYOH-mah*, la lengua *LEHN-gwah*

large grande *GRAHN-deh*

last (final) pasado *pah-SAH-doh*, último *OOL-tee-moh;* **to last** durar *doo-RAHR*

late tarde *TAHR-deh*

latest (at the latest) a más tardar *ah mahs tahr-DAHR*

laugh (v.) reír *reh-EER*, reírse *reh-EER-seh*

laundress la lavandera *lah-bahn-DEH-rah*

laundry la lavandería *lah-bahn-deh-REE-ah*

lavatory el lavabo *lah-BAH-boh*, el retrete *reh-TREH-teh*

laxative el laxante *lahk-SAHN-teh*

leak (drip) el escape *ehs-KAH-peh;* **to leak** escapar *ehs-kah-PAHR*

lean (v.) apoyarse en *ah-poh-YAHR-seh ehn;* **to lean out** asomarse a *ah-soh-MAHR-seh ah*

learn (v.) aprender *ah-prehn-DEHR*

least (at least) al (por lo) (a lo) menos *ahl (pohr loh) (ah loh) MEH-nohs*

leather el cuero *KWEH-roh*

leave (behind) (v.) dejar *deh-HAHR;* **to depart** salir *sah-LEER*

left (opposite of right) izquierdo *ees-KYEHR-doh*

leg la pierna *PYEHR-nah*

lemon el limón *lee-MOHN*

lemonade la limonada *lee-moh-NAH-dah*

lend (v.) prestar *prehs-TAHR*

length el largo *LAHR-goh*

lens el cristal *krees-TAHL*

less menos *MEH-nohs*

let (v.) dejar *deh-HAHR*, permitir *pehr-mee-TEER*

letter la carta *KAHR-tah*

letterbox el buzón *boo-SOHN*

lettuce la lechuga *leh-CHOO-gah*

library la biblioteca *bee-blyoh-TEH-kah*

lie (down) (v.) acostarse *ah-kohs-TAHR-seh*

life la vida *BEE-dah;* **life preserver** el salvavidas *sahl-bah-BEE-dahs*

lifeboat el bote salvavidas *BOH-teh sahl-bah-BEE-dahs*

lift (of shoe) la tapa *TAH-pah;* **to lift** levantar *leh-bahn-TAHR*, alzar *ahl-SAHR*

light (color) claro *KLAH-roh;* **(brightness)** la luz *loos;* **taillight** el farol de cola *fah-ROHL deh KOH-lah;* **(weight)** ligero *lee-HEH-roh;* **Give me a light** Déme usted fuego *DEH-meh oo-STEHD FUEH-goh;* **to light** encender *ehn-sehn-DEHR*

lighter (cigarette) el encendedor *ehn-sehn-deh-DOHR*

lightning el relámpago *reh-LAHM-pah-goh*

like (as) como *KOH-moh;* **to like** gustar *goos-TAHR*

limit (speed) la velocidad máxima *beh-loh-see-DAHD MAHK-see-mah*

line la línea *LEE-neh-ah*

linen el lino *LEE-noh*, la ropa blanca *ROH-pah BLAHN-kah*

lip el labio *LAH-byoh*

lipstick el lápiz de labios *LAH-pees deh LAH-byohs*

liqueur licor *lee-KOHR*

liquor la bebida alcohólica *beh-BEE-dah ahl-koh-OH-lee-kah*

list (wine, food) la lista *LEES-tah*

listen, listen to (v.) escuchar *ehs-koo-CHAHR*

liter el litro *LEE-troh*

little pequeño *peh-KEHN-yoh;* **a little** un poco *oon POH-koh*

live (v.) vivir *bee-BEER*

liver el hígado *EE-gah-doh*

living room la sala *SAH-lah*

lobby el vestíbulo *behs-TEE-boo-loh*, el salón de entrada

sah-LOHN deh ehn-TRAH-dah

lobster la langosta *lahn-GOHS-tah*

local (train) el tren ómnibus trehn *OHM-nee-boos;* **(phone call)** la llamada local *yah-MAH-dah loh-KAHL*

lock (fastening) la cerradura *sehr-rah-DOO-rah*

long largo *LAHR-goh;* **how long?** ¿cuánto tiempo? *KWAHN-toh TYEHM-poh,* desde cuándo *dehs-deh KWAHN-doh;* **long-distance call** la llamada a larga distancia *yah-MAH-dah ah LAHR-gah dees-TAHN-syah,* la conferencia interurbana *kohn-feh-REHN-syah een-tehr-oor-BAH-nah*

look, look at (v.) mirar *mee-RAHR;* **to look for** buscar *boos-KAHR;* **Look out!** ¡Cuidado! *kwee-DAH-doh*

lose (v.) perder *pehr-DEHR*

lost and found la oficina de objetos perdidos *oh-fee-SEE-nah deh ohb-HEH-tohs pehr-DEE-dohs*

lotion la loción *loh-SYOHN*

lots (of), many mucho *MOO-choh,* muchos *MOO-chohs*

lounge el salón *sah-LOHN*

low bajo *BAH-hoh*

lower berth la litera baja *lee-TEH-rah BAH-hah*

luck la suerte *SWEHR-teh*

lunch el almuerzo *ahl-MWEHR-soh;* **to lunch** almorzar *ahl-mohr-SAHR*

lung el pulmón *pool-MOHN*

M

maid (chamber) la camarera *kah-mah-REH-rah*

mail el correo *kohr-REH-oh*

mailbox el buzón *boo-SOHN*

magazine la revista *reh-BEES-tah*

make (v.) hacer *ah-SEHR*

man el hombre *OHM-breh*

manager el director *dee-rehk-TOHR,* el gerente *heh-REHN-teh,* el administrador *ahd-mee-nees-trah-DOHR*

manicure la manicura *mah-nee-KOO-rah*

many muchos *MOO-chohs*

map (road) el mapa de carreteras *MAH-pah deh kahr-reh-TEHR-ahs,* el mapa itinerario *MAH-pah ee-tee-neh-RAH-ryoh*

March marzo (m.) *MAHR-soh*

market el mercado *mehr-KAH-doh*

mashed majado *mah-HAH-doh*

mass la misa *MEE-sah;* **high mass** la misa cantada (mayor) *MEE-sah kahn-TAH-dah (mah-YOHR)*

massage el masaje *mah-SAH-heh*

match el fósforo *FOHS-foh-roh*

matter (It doesn't matter.) No importa *noh eem-POHR-tah;* **What's the matter?** ¿Qué pasa? *keh PAH-sah,* ¿qué hay? *key-AH-ee*

mattress el colchón *kohl-CHOHN*

May mayo (m.) *MAH-yoh*

maybe quizá *kee-SAH,* quizás *kee-SAHS,* tal vez *tahl BEHS,* acaso *ah-KAH-soh*

meal la comida *koh-MEE-dah;* **fixed-price meal** la comida a precio fijo *koh-MEE-dah ah PREH-syoh FEE-hoh,* la comida corrida (completa) *koh-MEE-dah kohr-REE-dah (kohm-PLEH-tah)*

mean (v.) significar *seeg-nee-fee-KAHR,* querer decir *keh-REHR deh-SEER*

measurement la medida *meh-DEE-dah*

meat la carne *KAHR-neh*

mechanic el mecánico *meh-KAH-nee-koh*

medical médico *MEH-dee-koh*

medicine la medicina *meh-dee-SEE-nah*

meet (v.) encontrar *ehn-kohn-TRAHR*; **(socially)** (v.) conocer *koh-noh-SEHR*

melon el melón *meh-LOHN*

mend (v.) remendar *reh-mehn-DAHR*

men's room el lavabo de señores *lah-BAH-boh deh sehn-YOH-rehs*

mention (don't mention it) no hay de qué *noh ah-ee deh keh*

menu el menú *meh-NOO*, la lista de platos *LEES-tah deh PLAH-tohs*

merry alegre *ah-LEH-greh*

Merry Christmas! ¡Felices Pascuas! *feh-LEE-sehs pah-kwahs*, ¡Feliz Navidad! *feh-LEES nah-bee-DAHD*

message el mensaje *mehn-SAH-heh*, el recado *reh-KAH-doh*

meter (length) el metro *MEH-troh*

meter (taxi) el taxímetro *tahk-SEE-meh-troh*

Mexican mexicano, mejicano *meh-hee-KAH-noh*

middle (center) el medio *MEH-dyoh*, el centro *SEHN-troh*

midnight la medianoche *meh-dyah-NOH-cheh*

mild ligero *lee-HEH-roh*, suave *SWAH-beh*

milk la leche *LEH-cheh*

million el millón *mee-YOHN*

mind (understanding) la mente *MEHN-teh*; **Never mind.** No importa. *noh eem-POHR-tah*

mine mío *MEE-oh*, los míos (pl.) *MEE-ohs*

mineral water el agua mineral *AH-gwah mee-neh-RAHL*

minister el ministro *mee-NEES-troh*

minute el minuto *mee-NOO-toh*

mirror el espejo *ehs-PEH-hoh*

Miss (woman) la señorita *sehn-yoh-REE-tah*

miss (a train) (v.) perder *pehr-DEHR*

missing (to be) (v.) faltar *fahl-TAHR*

mistake el error *ehr-ROHR*, la falta *FAHL-tah*

monastery el monasterio *moh-nahs-TEH-ryoh*

Monday el lunes *LOO-nehs*

money el dinero *dee-NEH-roh*; **money order** el giro (postal) *HEE-roh (pohs-TAHL)*

month el mes *mehs*

monument el monumento *moh-noo-MEHN-toh*

moon la luna *LOO-nah*

more más *mahs*

morning la mañana *mahn-YAH-nah*

mosquito el mosquito *mohs-KEE-toh*; **mosquito netting** el mosquitero *mohs-kee-TEH-roh*

mother la madre *MAH-dreh*

motion picture el cine *SEE-neh*

motor (car) el motor *moh-TOHR*

mouth la boca *BOH-kah*; **mouthwash** el enjuague *ehn-HWAH-gheh*

move (v.) mover *moh-BEHR*; **(change residence)** mudarse de casa *moo-DAHR-seh deh KAH-sah*

movie la película *peh-LEE-koo-lah*

Mr. el señor *sehn-YOHR*; **(with first name only)** don *dohn*

Mrs. la señora *sehn-YOHR-rah*; **(with first name only)** doña *DOHN-yah*

much mucho *moo-choh*

museum el museo *moo-SEH-oh*

mushroom   la seta *SEH-tah*, el hongo *OHN-goh*

must   (v.) deber *deh-BEHR*, tener que *teh-NEHR keh*

my   mi *mee*, mis *mees*

N

nail (finger or toe)   la uña *OON-yah;* **nail file**   la lima de uñas *LEE-mah deh OON-yahs;* **nail polish**   el esmalte *ehs-MAHL-teh*

name   el nombre *NOHM-breh;* **family name**   el apellido *ah-peh-YEE-doh*

napkin   la servilleta *sehr-bee-YEH-tah*

narrow   estrecho *ehs-TREH-choh*, angosto *ahn-GOHS-toh*

nationality   la nacionalidad *nah-syoh-nah-lee-DAHD*

nauseated (to be)   (v.) tener náuseas *teh-nehr NOW-seh-ahs*

near   (adj.) cercano *sehr-KAH-noh;* (prep.) cerca de *SEHR-kah deh*

nearly   casi *KAH-see*

necessary   necesario *neh-seh-SAH-ryoh*

neck   el cuello *KWEHL-yoh*

necklace   el collar *koh-YAHR*

necktie   la corbata *kohr-BAH-tah*

need   (v.) necesitar *neh-seh-see-TAHR*

needle   la aguja *ah-GOO-hah*

nerve   el nervio *NEHR-byoh*

net (hair)   la redecilla *reh-deh-SEE-yah;* **mosquito net**   el mosquitero *mohs-kee-TEH-roh*

never   nunca *NOON-kah*

new   nuevo *NWEH-boh*

New Year   el día de año nuevo *ehl DEE-ah deh ahn-yoh NWEH-boh;* **Happy New Year!**   ¡Feliz Año Nuevo!

feh-LEES ahn-yoh NWEH-boh

newspaper   el periódico *peh-RYOH-dee-koh*

newsstand   el quiosco *KYOHS-koh*

next   próximo *PROHK-see-moh*, siguiente *see-GYEHN-teh*

night   la noche *NOH-cheh*

nightclub   el cabaret *kah-bah-REHT*, el club nocturno *ehl KLOOB nohk-TOOR-noh*

nightgown   el camisón *kah-mee-SOHN*

nightlife   la vida nocturna *bee-dah nohk-TOOR-nah*

night rate   la tarifa nocturna *tah-REE-fah nohk-TOOR-nah*

nine   nueve *NWEH-beh*

nineteen   diecinueve *dyeh-see-NWEH-beh*

ninety   noventa *noh-BEHN-tah*

ninth   noveno *noh-BEH-noh*

no   (adj.) ninguno *neen-GOO-noh*, ningún *neen-GOON* [before m. sing. noun]; (adv.) **no**   *noh;* **no one**   nadie *NAH-dyeh*

noise   el ruido *RWEE-doh*

noisy   ruidoso *rwee-DOH-soh*

none   ninguno *neen-GOO-noh*

noon   el mediodía *meh-dyoh-DEE-ah*

north   el norte *NOHR-teh*

Norwegian   noruego *noh-RWEH-goh*

nose   la nariz *nah-REES*

not   no *noh*

nothing   nada *NAH-dah;* **nothing else**   nada más *nah-dah-MAHS*

notice (announcement)   el aviso *ah-BEE-soh*

novel (book)   la novela *noh-BEH-lah*

November   noviembre (m.) *noh-BYEHM-breh*

now   ahora *ah-OHR-ah*

number   el número *NOO-meh-roh*

nurse la enfermera *ehn-fehr-MEH-rah*

nut (walnut) la nuez *nwehs;* **(mechanical)** la tuerca *TWEHR-kah*

O

occupied ocupado *oh-koo-PAH-doh*

October octubre (m.) *ohk-TOO-breh*

oculist el oculista *oh-koo-LEES-tah*

of de *deh;* **of course** naturalmente *nah-too-rahl-MEHN-teh,* desde luego *dehs-deh LWEH-goh,* por supuesto *pohr soo-PWEHS-toh*

office la oficina *oh-fee-SEE-nah;* **box office** la taquilla *tah-KEE-yah;* **exchange office** la oficina de cambio *oh-fee-SEE-nah deh KAHM-byoh;* **post office** el correo *kohr-REH-oh*

often a menudo *ah meh-NOO-doh*

oil el aceite *ah-SEY-teh;* **castor oil** el aceite de ricino *ah-SEY-teh deh ree-SEE-noh;* **olive oil** el aceite de oliva *ah-SEY-teh deh oh-LEE-bah*

okay (It's) Está bien *ehs-tah BYEHN,* Conforme *kohn-FOHR-meh*

old viejo *BYEH-hoh,* anciano *ahn-SYAH-noh;* **How old are you?** ¿Qué edad tiene usted? *keh eh-DAHD TYEH-neh oo-STEHD,* ¿Cuántos años tiene usted? *KWAHN-tohs AHN-yohs TYEH-neh oo-STEHD;* **I am 20 years old.** Tengo veinte años *TEHN-goh BEYN-teh AHN-yohs*

olive la aceituna *ah-sey-TOO-nah*

omelet la tortilla *tohr-TEEL-yah*

on en *ehn,* sobre *SOH-breh*

once una vez *OO-nah behs;* **at once** en seguida *ehn seh-GHEE-dah*

one un *oon,* uno *oo-noh,* una *oo-nah;* **one-way traffic** la dirección única *dee-rehk-SYOHN OO-nee-kah*

onion la cebolla *seh-BOH-yah*

only sólo *SOH-loh,* solamente *soh-lah-MEHN-teh*

open abierto *ah-BYEHR-toh;* **to open** abrir *ah-BREER*

opera la ópera *OH-peh-rah;* **opera glasses** los gemelos de teatro *heh-MEH-los deh teh-AH-troh*

operator (phone) la telefonista *teh-leh-foh-NEES-tah*

optician el óptico *OHP-tee-koh*

or o *oh,* u *oo* [before word beginning with vowel sound *o*]

orange la naranja *nah-RAHN-hah*

orangeade la naranjada *nah-rahn-HAH-dah*

orchestra (band) la orquesta *ohr-KEHS-tah;* **orchestra section** la platea *plah-TEH-ah;* **orchestra seat** la butaca *boo-TAH-kah*

order el encargo *ehn-KAHR-goh;* **to order** encargar *ehn-kahr-GAHR*

other otro *OH-troh*

our, ours nuestro *NWEHS-troh*

out afuera *ah-FWEH-rah*

outlet (electric) el tomacorriente *TOH-mah-kohr-RYEHN-teh,* el enchufe *ehn-CHOO-feh*

outside fuera *FWEH-rah,* afuera *ah-FWEH-rah*

over (above) encima (de) *ehn-SEE-mah (deh);* **(finished)** acabado *ah-kah-BAH-doh*

overcoat el abrigo *ah-BREE-goh,* el sobretodo *soh-breh-TOH-doh,* el gabán *gah-BAHN*

overdone requemado *reh-keh-MAH-doh*
overheat (motor) (v.) recalentar *reh-kah-lehn-TAHR*
overnight por la noche *pohr lah NOH-cheh*
owe (v.) deber *deh-BEHR*
own (v.) poseer *poh-seh-EHR*
oyster la ostra *OHS-trah*

P

pack (luggage) (v.) hacer las maletas *ah-SEHR lahs mah-LEH-tahs*
package el bulto *BOOL-toh*
packet el paquete *pah-KEH-teh*
page (of book) la página *PAH-hee-nah;* **to page** llamar *yah-MAHR*
pain el dolor *doh-LOHR*
paint (wet) recién pintado *reh-SYEHN peen-TAH-doh*
pair el par *pahr*
pajamas el pijama *pee-HAH-mah*
palace el palacio *pah-LAH-syoh*
panties las bragas *BRAH-ghahs*
pants los pantalones *pahn-tah-LOH-nehs*
paper el papel *pah-PEHL;* **toilet paper** el papel higiénico *pah-PEHL ee-HYEH-nee-koh;* **wrapping paper** el papel de envolver *pah-PEHL deh ehn-bohl-BEHR;* **writing paper** el papel de cartas *pah-PEHL deh KAHR-tahs*
parasol el quitasol *kee-tah-SOHL*
parcel el paquete *pah-KEH-teh;* **parcel post** el paquete postal *pah-KEH-teh pohs-TAHL*
pardon (v.) perdonar *pehr-doh-NAHR,* dispensar *dees-pehn-SAHR;* **Pardon me!** ¡Perdón! *pehr-DOHN,*

¡Dispénseme usted! *dees-PEHN-seh-meh oo-STEHD*
park (car) (v.) parquear *pahr-keh-AHR,* estacionar *ehs-tah-syohn-AHR;* **(garden)** el parque *PAHR-keh*
parking (no) prohibido estacionar *proh-ee-BEE-doh ehs-tah-syoh-NAHR*
part (section) la parte *PAHR-teh;* **to part hair** hacer la raya *ah-SEHR lah RAH-yah;* **to separate** separar *seh-pah-RAHR,* dividir *dee-bee-DEER*
parts (spare) las piezas de repuesto (f. pl.) *PYEH-sahs deh reh-PWEHS-toh*
pass (permit) el permiso *pehr-MEE-soh;* **to pass** pasar *pah-SAHR*
passenger el pasajero *pah-sah-HEH-roh*
passport el pasaporte *pah-sah-POHR-teh*
past el pasado *pah-SAH-doh*
pastry los pasteles *lohs pahs-TEH-lehs*
pay (v.) pagar *pah-GAHR*
pea el guisante *ghee-SAHN-teh*
peach el melocotón *meh-loh-koh-TOHN,* el durazno *doo-RAHS-noh*
pear la pera *PEH-rah*
pedestrian el peatón *peh-ah-TOHN*
pen la pluma *PLOO-mah;* **fountain pen** la pluma fuente *ploo-mah FWEHN-teh*
pencil el lápiz *LAH-pees*
people la gente *HEN-teh*
pepper (black) la pimienta *pee-MYEHN-tah*
peppers los pimientos *pee-MYEHN-tohs*
per por *pohr*
performance la función *foon-SYOHN*
perfume el perfume *pehr-FOO-meh;* **perfume shop**

la perfumería *pehr-foo-meh-REE-ah*

perhaps quizá *kee-SAH*, tal vez *tahl BEHS*

permanent (wave) la permanente *pehr-mah-NEHN-teh*

permit (pass) el permiso *pehr-MEE-soh*; **to permit** permitir *pehr-mee-TEER*

Persian persa *PEHR-sah*

personal personal *pehr-soh-NAHL*

phone el teléfono *teh-LEH-foh-noh*; **to phone** telefonear *teh-leh-foh-neh-AHR*

photograph la fotografía *foh-toh-grah-FEE-ah*; **to photograph** fotografiar *foh-toh-grah-fee-AHR*

pickle el encurtido *ehn-koor-TEE-doh*

picnic la jira *HEE-rah*, la comida campestre *koh-MEE-dah kahm-PEHS-treh*

picture (art) el cuadro *KWAH-droh*, la pintura *peen-TOO-rah*; **(motion)** la película *peh-LEE-koo-lah*, el cine *SEE-neh*

pie el pastel *pahs-TEHL*

piece el pedazo *peh-DAH-soh*

pier el muelle *MWEH-yeh*

pill la píldora *PEEL-doh-rah*

pillow la almohada *ahl-moh-AH-dah*

pillowcase la funda *FOON-dah*

pilot el piloto *pee-LOH-toh*

pin el alfiler *ahl-fee-LEHR*; **safety pin** el imperdible *eem-pehr-DEE-bleh*

pineapple la piña *PEEN-yah*

pink rosado *roh-SAH-doh*, color de rosa *koh-LOHR deh ROH-sah*

pipe (smoking) la pipa *PEE-pah*

pitcher el jarro *HAHR-roh*, el cántaro *KAHN-tah-roh*

pity (What a ... !) Qué lástima! *keh LAHS-tee-mah*

place (site) el sitio *SEE-tyoh*, el lugar *loo-GAHR*; **to place** colocar *koh-loh-KAHR*

plane (air) el avión *ah-BYOHN*

plate el plato *PLAH-toh*

platform el andén *ahn-DEHN*, la plataforma *plah-tah-FOHR-mah*

play el drama *DRAH-mah*, la pieza *PYEH-sah*; **to play (game)** jugar *hoo-GAHR*; **to play (instrument)** tocar *toh-KAHR*

playing cards los naipes *NAH-ee-pehs*, las cartas *KAHR-tahs*

pleasant agradable *ah-grah-DAH-bleh*; **(referring to a person)** simpático *seem-PAH-tee-koh*

please por favor *pohr fah-BOHR*, haga el favor (de) (+ infinitive) *AH-gah ehl fah-BOHR (deh)*

pleasure el gusto *GOOS-toh*, el placer *plah-SEHR*

pliers los alicates *ah-lee-KAH-tehs*, las tenazas *teh-NAH-sahs*

plug (spark) la bujía *boo-HEE-ah*

plum la ciruela *see-RWEH-lah*

P.M. de la tarde *deh lah TAHR-deh*, de la noche *deh lah NOH-cheh*

pocket (n.) el bolsillo *bohl-SEE-yoh*; (adj.) de bolsillo *deh bohl-SEE-yoh*

pocketbook la bolsa *BOHL-sah*

point (place) el punto *POON-toh*, el lugar *loo-GAHR*; **(sharp end)** la punta *POON-tah*

poison el veneno *beh-NEH-noh*

police la policía *poh-lee-SEE-ah*; **police station** la comisaría *koh-mee-sah-REE-ah*

policeman el policía *poh-lee-SEE-ah*, el agente de policía *ehl ah-HEHN-teh deh poh-lee-SEE-ah*

Polish polaco *poh-LAH-koh*

polish (nail) el esmalte *ehs-MAHL-teh*; **polish remover** el acetón *ah-seh-TOHN*
polite cortés *kohr-TEHS*
politeness la cortesía *kohr-teh-SEE-ah*
pomade la pomada *poh-MAH-dah*
poor pobre *POH-breh*
pork la carne de cerdo *KAHR-neh deh SEHR-doh*
port (harbor) el puerto *PWEHR-toh*
porter el mozo *MOH-soh*
portion la porción *pohr-SYOHN*, la ración *rah-SYOHN*
Portuguese portugués *pohr-too-GHEHS*
possible posible *poh-SEE-bleh*
postage el porte *POHR-teh*, el franqueo *frahn-KEH-oh*
postcard la tarjeta postal *tahr-HEH-tah pohs-TAHL*; **post office** la casa de correos *KAH-sah deh kohr-REH-ohs*, el correo *kohr-REH-oh*
potato la patata *pah-TAH-tah*, la papa *PAH-pah*
pouch (tobacco) la petaca *peh-TAH-kah*
pour (rain) (v.) llover a cántaros *lyoh-BEHR ah KAHN-tah-rohs*
powder el polvo *POHL-boh*; **face powder** los polvos para la cara *POHL-bohs PAH-rah lah KAH-rah*; **powder puff** la borla *BOHR-lah*; **powder room** el (cuarto) tocador *(KWAHR-toh) toh-kah-DOHR*
prefer (v.) preferir *preh-feh-REER*
prepare (v.) preparar *preh-pah-RAHR*
prescription la receta *reh-SEH-tah*
press (iron) (v.) planchar *plahn-CHAHR*
pretty bonito *boh-NEE-toh*, lindo *LEEN-doh*

price el precio *PREH-syoh*
priest el cura *KOO-rah*
print (photo) la copia *KOH-pyah*
program el programa *proh-GRAH-mah*
promise (v.) prometer *proh-meh-TEHR*
Protestant protestante *proh-tehs-TAHN-teh*
provide (v.) proveer *proh-beh-EHR*
prune la ciruela pasa *see-RWEH-lah PAH-sah*
pudding el budín *boo-DEEN*
pump (fuel) la bomba de combustible *BOHM-bah deh kohm-boos-TEE-bleh*
puncture (tire) el pinchazo *peen-CHAH-soh*
purchase (item) la compra *KOHM-prah*; **to purchase** comprar *kohm-PRAHR*
purple morado *moh-RAH-doh*
purse la bolsa *BOHL-sah*
purser el sobrecargo *soh-breh-KAHR-goh*
push (v.) empujar *ehm-poo-HAHR*
put (v.) poner *poh-NEHR*; **put in** meter en *meh-TEHR ehn*; **put on** ponerse *poh-NEHR-seh*

Q

quarter el cuarto *KWAHR-toh*
quick, quickly pronto *PROHN-toh*
quiet quieto *KYEH-toh*, tranquilo *trahn-KEE-loh*
quinine la quinina *kee-NEE-nah*
quite bastante *bahs-TAHN-teh*

R

rabbi el rabino *rah-BEE-noh*
rack (train) la red, la rejilla *rehd, reh-HEE-yah*

radiator el radiador *rah-dyah-DOHR*

radio la radio *RAH-dyoh*

radish el rábano *RAH-bah-noh*

railroad el ferrocarril *fehr-roh-kahr-REEL*

rain la lluvia *LYOO-byah;* **to rain** llover *lyoh-BEHR*

raincoat el impermeable *eem-pehr-meh-AH-bleh*

rare (meat) poco asado (hecho) *poh-koh ah-SAH-doh (EH-choh)*

rate of exchange el tipo de cambio *TEE-poh deh KAHM-byoh;* **hourly rate of exchange** la tarifa por hora *tah-REE-fah pohr OH-rah*

rather (have) (v.) preferir *preh-feh-REER*

razor la navaja de afeitar *nah-BAH-hah deh ah-fey-TAHR;* **safety razor** la maquinilla de afeitar *mah-kee-NEE-yah deh ah-fey-TAHR;* **razor blade** la hojita de afeitar *oh-HEE-lah deh ah-fey-TAHR*

read (v.) leer *leh-EHR*

ready (to be) estar listo *ehs-TAHR LEES-toh*

real verdadero *behr-dah-DEH-roh*

really de veras, verdaderamente *deh BEH-rahs, behr-dah-DEH-rah-mehn-teh*

reasonable (price) razonable *rah-soh-NAH-bleh*

receipt el recibo *reh-SEE-boh*

receiver (of packages) el destinatario *dehs-tee-nah-TAH-ryoh*

recommend (v.) recomendar *reh-koh-mehn-DAHR*

recover (v.) **(get back)** recobrar *reh-koh-BRAHR;* **(health)** reponerse *reh-poh-NEHR-seh*

red rojo *ROH-hoh*

refund (payment) el reembolso *reh-ehm-BOHL-soh;* **to refund** reembolsar *reh-ehm-bohl-SAHR*

refuse (v.) rehusar *reh-oo-SAHR*, rechazar *reh-chah-SAHR*

regards recuerdos *reh-KWEHR-dohs*, saludos *sah-LOO-dohs*

registered mail certificado *sehr-tee-fee-KAH-doh*

registry window la ventanilla de los certificados *behn-tah-NEE-yah deh lohs sehr-tee-fee-KAH-dohs*

regular (ordinary) ordinario *ohr-dee-NAH-ryoh*

remedy el remedio *reh-MEH-dyoh*

remember (v.) recordar *reh-kohr-DAHR*, acordarse de *ah-kohr-DAHR-seh deh*

rent el alquiler *ahl-kee-LEHR;* **to rent** alquilar *ahl-kee-LAHR;* **for rent** se alquila *seh ahl-KEE-lah*

repair la reparación *reh-pah-rah-SYOHN*, la compostura *kohm-pohs-TOO-rah;* **to repair** reparar *reh-pah-RAHR*, componer *kohm-poh-NEHR*

repeat (v.) repetir *reh-peh-TEER*

reply (v.) responder *rehs-pohn-DEHR*, contestar *kohn-tehs-TAHR*

reservation la reserváicon *reh-sehr-bah-SYOHN*, la reserva *reh-SEHR-bah*

reserve (v.) reservar *reh-sehr-BAHR*

reserved seat el asiento reservado *ah-SYEHN-toh reh-sehr-BAH-doh*

rest (v.) descansar *dehs-kahn-SAHR*

restaurant el restaurante *rehs-tow-RAHN-teh*

rest room el lavabo *lah-BAH-boh*, el retrete *reh-TREH-teh*

retired jubilado(a) *hoo-bee-LAH-doh(dah)*

return (v.) (give back) devolver *deh-bohl-BEHR*; (go back) volver *bohl-BEHR*

rib la costilla *kohs-TEE-yah*

ribbon la cinta *SEEN-tah*

rice el arroz *ahr-ROHS*

rich rico *REE-koh*

ride el paseo *pah-SEH-oh*; **to ride** pasear en *pah-seh-AHR ehn*, ir en *EER ehn*

right (opposite of left) derecho *deh-REH-choh*; **to be right** tener razón *teh-NEHR-reh-SOHN*; **all right** está bien *ehs-TAH byehn*; **right now** ahora mismo *ah-OH-rah MEES-moh*

ring (on finger) el anillo *ah-NEE-yoh*, la sortija *sohr-TEE-hah*; **to ring** (call) llamar *yah-MAHR*

rinse el enjuague *ehn-HWAH-gheh*

river el río *REE-oh*

road el camino *kah-MEE-noh*, la carretera *kahr-reh-TEH-rah*, la vía *BEE-ah*; **road map** el mapa de carretera *MAH-pah deh kahr-reh-TEH-rah*, el mapa itinerario *MAH-pah ee-tee-neh-RAH-ryoh*

roast asado *ah-SAH-doh*; **roast beef** el rosbif *rohs-BEEF*

rob (v.) robar *roh-BAHR*

robe la bata *BAH-tah*

roll (bread) el panecillo *pah-neh-SEE-yoh*, el bollito *boh-YEE-toh*; (film) el rollo *ROH-yoh*, el carrete *kah-REH-teh*

Romanian rumano *roo-MAH-noh*

room el cuarto *KWAHR-toh*, la habitación *ah-bee-tah-SYOHN*

root la raíz *rah-EES*

rope la cuerda *KWEHR-dah*

rouge el colorete *koh-loh-REH-teh*

round redondo *reh-DOHN-doh*; **round trip** el viaje de ida y vuelta *BYAH-heh deh EE-dah ee BWEHL-tah*

royal real *reh-AHL*

row (theater) la fila *FEE-lah*

rubber el caucho *KOW-choh*, la goma *GOH-mah*; **rubber band** el elástico *eh-LAHS-tee-koh*, la liga de goma *LEE-gah deh GOH-mah*; **rubber heels** los tacones de goma *tah-KOH-nehs deh GOH-mah*

rubbers los chanclos *CHAHN-klohs*

rug la alfombra *ahl-FOHM-brah*

run (v.) correr *kohr-REHR*

running water el agua corriente *AH-gwah kohr-RYEHN-teh*

runway (plane) la pista *PEES-tah*

Russian ruso *ROO-soh*

S

safe (strongbox) la caja fuerte *KAH-hah FWEHR-teh*

safety pin el imperdible *eem-pehr-DEE-bleh*; **safety razor** la maquinilla de afeitar *mah-kee-NEE-yah deh ah-fey-TAHR*

sake (For heaven's sake!) ¡Por Dios! *pohr-DYOHS*

salad la ensalada *ehn-sah-LAH-dah*

salami el salchichón *sahl-chee-CHOHN*

sale la venta *BEHN-tah*

salesperson el vendedor *ben-deh-DOHR*

salon (beauty) el salón de belleza *sah-LOHN deh beh-YEH-sah*

saloon la cantina *kahn-TEE-nah*, la taberna *tah-BEHR-nah*

salt la sal *sahl*
salty salado *sah-LAH-doh*
same mismo *MEES-moh*
sand la arena *ah-REH-nah*
sandal la sandalia *sahn-DAH-lyah*
sandwich el emparedado *ehm-pah-reh-DAH-doh*
sardine la sardina *sahr-DEE-nah*
Saturday el sábado *SAH-bah-doh*
sauce la salsa *SAHL-sah*
saucer el platillo *plah-TEE-yoh*
sausage la salchicha *sahl-CHEE-chah*, el chorizo *choh-REE-soh*
say (v.) decir *deh-SEER*
scalp massage el masaje de cabeza *mah-SAH-heh deh kah-BEH-sah*
scarf la bufanda *boo-FAHN-dah*
school la escuela *ehs-KWEH-lah*
scissors las tijeras *tee-HEH-rahs*
Scram! ¡Váyase! *BAH-yah-seh*, ¡Fuera de aquí! *FWEH-rah deh ah-KEE*
screwdriver el destornillador *dehs-tohr-nee-yah-DOHR*
sea el mar *mahr*
seafood los mariscos *mah-REES-kohs*
seasickness el mareo *mah-REH-oh*
season la estación *ehs-tah-SYOHN*
seasoned sazonado *sah-soh-NAH-doh*
seat (in conveyance) el asiento *ah-SYEHN-toh*
second segundo *seh-GOON-doh*
secretary el secretario *seh-kreh-TAH-ryoh*, la secretaria *seh-kreh-TAH-ryah*
see (v.) ver *behr*
seem (v.) parecer *pah-reh-SEHR*; **it seems to me** me parece *meh pah-REH-seh*

select (v.) escoger *ehs-koh-HEHR*
sell (v.) vender *behn-DEHR*
send (v.) mandar, enviar *mahn-DAHR, ehn-BYAHR*; **to send for** enviar por *ehn-BYAHR pohr*
sender (of mail) el remitente *reh-mee-TEHN-teh*
September septiembre, setiembre (m.) *seh-TYEHM-breh*
serve (v.) servir *sehr-BEER*
service el servicio *sehr-BEE-syoh*; **at your service** a sus órdenes *ah soos OHR-deh-nehs*
set (hair) (v.) arreglarse *ahr-reh-GLAHR-seh*
seven siete *SYEH-teh*
seventeen diecisiete *dyeh-see-SYEH-teh*
seventh séptimo *SEHP-tee-moh*
seventy setenta *seh-TEHN-tah*
several varios *BAH-ryohs*
shade (In the shade) A la sombra *ah lah SOHM-brah*; **window shade** persianas *pehr-SYAH-nahs*
shampoo el champú *chahm-POO*
shave (v.) afeitar *ah-fay-TAHR*
shaving brush la brocha de afeitar *BROH-chah deh ah-fey-TAHR*; **shaving cream** la crema de afeitar *KREH-mah deh ah-fey-TAHR*
shawl el chal *chahl*
she ella *EH-yah*
sheet la sábana *SAH-bah-nah*
shine (v.) **(shoes)** lustrar *loos-TRAHR*; **(stars)** brillar *bree-YAHR*
ship el buque *BOO-keh*, el barco *BAHR-koh*, el vapor *bah-POHR*; **to ship** enviar *ehn-BYAHR*

shirt la camisa *kah-MEE-sah*

shoe el zapato *sah-PAH-toh;*
shoe store la zapatería *sah-pah-teh-REE-ah*

shoelaces los cordones de zapato *kohr-DOH-nehs deh sah-PAH-toh*

shop la tienda *TYEHN-dah*

shopping (to go) (v.) ir de compras *eer deh KOHM-prahs,* ir de tiendas *TYEHN-dahs*

short corto *KOHR-toh*

shorts (underwear) los calzoncillos *kahl-sohn-SEE-yohs*

shoulder el hombro *ohm-broh*

show (v.) mostrar *mohs-TRAHR,* enseñar *ehn-sehn-YAHR*

showcase la vitrina *bee-TREE-nah*

shower la ducha *DOO-chah*

shrimp el camarón *kah-mah-ROHN,* la gamba *GAHM-bah*

shrine el santuario *sahn-TWAH-ryoh*

shut (v.) cerrar *sehr-RAHR*

shutter la contraventana *kohn-trah-behn-TAH-nah*

sick enfermo *ehn-FEHR-moh*

sickness la enfermedad *ehn-fehr-meh-DAHD*

side el lado *LAH-doh*

sidewalk la acera *ah-SEH-rah*

sightseeing el turismo *too-REES-moh*

sign (display) el letrero *leh-TREH-roh,* el aviso *ah-BEE-soh;* **to sign (a letter)** (v.) firmar *feer-MAHR*

silk la seda *SEH-dah*

silver la plata *PLAH-tah*

since desde *DEHS-deh*

sing (v.) cantar *kahn-TAHR*

single room la habitación para uno (habitación individual) *ah-bee-tahSYOHN pah-rah OO-noh (ah-bee-tah-SYOHN een-dee-bee-DWAHL)*

sink (basin) el lavabo *lah-BAH-boh*

sir el señor *sehn-YOHR*

sister la hermana *ehr-MAH-nah*

sit (down) (v.) sentarse *sehn-TAHR-seh*

six seis *seys*

sixteen dieciseis *dyeh-see-SEYS*

sixth sexto *SEHS-toh*

sixty sesenta *seh-SEHN-tah*

size el tamaño *tah-MAHN-yoh*

skates patines *pah-TEEN-ehs*

skin la piel *pyehl*

skirt la falda *FAHL-dah*

sky el cielo *SYEH-loh*

sleep (v.) dormir *dohr-MEER*

sleeping car el coche-cama *KOH-cheh KAH-mah*

sleepy (to be) (v.) tener sueño *teh-NEHR SWEHN-yoh*

sleeve la manga *MAHN-gah*

slip (garment) la combinación *kohm-bee-nah-SYOHN*

slippers las zapatillas *sah-pah-TEE-yahs*

slow lento *LEHN-toh;* **the watch is slow** el reloj va atrasado *reh-LOH bah ah-trah-SAH-doh*

slowly despacio *dehs-PAH-syoh,* lentamente *lehn-tah-MEHN-teh*

small pequeño *peh-KEHN-yoh,* chiquito *chee-KEE-toh*

smelling salts las sales aromáticas *SAH-lehs ah-roh-MAH-tee-kahs*

smoke (v.) fumar *foo-MAHR*

smoking car el (coche) fumador *(KOH-cheh) foo-mah-DOHR*

snow la nieve *NYEH-beh;* **to snow** nevar *neh-BAHR*

so así *ah-SEE*

soap el jabón *hah-BOHN;* **soap flakes** los copos de jabón *KOH-pohs deh hah-BOHN*

soccer el fútbol *FOOT-bohl*

socks los calcetines *kahl-seh-TEE-nehs*

soda (bicarbonate) el bicarbonato (de soda) *bee-kahr-boh-NAH-toh (deh-SOH-dah)*

sofa el sofá *soh-FAH*

soft blando *BLAHN-doh,* suave *SWAH-beh;* **soft drink** el refresco *reh-FREHS-koh,* la bebida no alcohólica *beh-BEE-dah noh ahl-koh-OH-lee-kah*

sole (shoe) la suela *SWEH-lah*

some algún *ahl-GOON*

someone alguien *AHL-gyehn*

something algo *AHL-goh*

sometimes a veces *ah BEH-sehs,* algunas veces *ahl-goo-nahs BEH-sehs*

son el hijo *EE-hoh*

song la canción *kahn-SYOHN*

soon pronto *PROHN-toh*

sore throat el dolor de garganta *doh-LOHR deh gahr-GAHN-tah*

sorry (to be) (v.) sentir *sehn-TEER;* **I am sorry** Lo siento. *loh-SYEHN-toh*

soup la sopa *SOH-pah;* **soup dish** el plato sopero *PLAH-toh soh-PEH-roh*

sour agrio *AH-gryoh*

south el sur *soor,* el sud *sood*

souvenir el recuerdo *reh-KWEHR-doh*

Spanish español *ehs-pahn-YOHL*

spare tire el neumático de repuesto *neh-oo-MAH-tee-koh deh reh-PWEHS-toh,* la goma de recambio *GOH-mah deh reh-KAHM-byoh*

spark plug la bujía *boo-HEE-ah*

sparkling wine el vino espumante (espumoso) *BEE-noh ehs-poo-MAHN-teh (ehs-poo-MOH-soh)*

speak (v.) hablar *ah-BLAHR*

special especial *ehs-peh-SYAHL;* **special delivery** el correo urgente *kohr-REH-*

oh oor-HEHN-teh;* **today's special** el plato del día *ehl plah-toh dehl DEE-ah*

speed limit la velocidad máxima *beh-loh-see-DAHD MAHK-see-mah*

spend (v.) **(money)** gastar *gahs-TAHR;* **(time)** pasar *pah-SAHR*

spice la especia *ehs-PEH-see-yah*

spicy picante *pee-KAHN-teh*

spinach la espinaca *ehs-pee-NAH-kah*

spitting forbidden prohibido escupir *proh-ee-BEE-doh ehs-koo-PEER*

spoon la cuchara *koo-CHAH-rah*

sprain la torcedura *tohr-seh-DOO-rah*

spring (mechanical) el muelle *MWEH-yeh,* el resorte *reh-SOHR-teh;* **(season)** la primavera *pree-mah-BEH-rah*

square (adj.) cuadrado *kwah-DRAH-doh;* **plaza** la plaza *PLAH-sah*

stairs la escalera *ehs-kah-LEH-rah*

stop (v.) parar *pah-RAHR*

stamp (postage) el sello *SEH-yoh*

stand (v.) estar de pie *ehs-TAHR deh pyeh;* **stand in line** hacer cola *ah-SEHR KOH-lah*

star la estrella *ehs-TREH-yah,* el astro *AHS-troh*

starch (laundry) el almidón *ahl-mee-DOHN;* **to starch** almidonar *ahl-mee-doh-NAHR*

start (v.) empezar *ehm-peh-SAHR,* comenzar *koh-mehn-SAHR,* principiar *preen-see-PYAHR*

starter (car) el arranque *ahr-RAHN-keh*

stateroom el camarote *kah-mah-ROH-teh*

station (gasoline) la estación de gasolina *ehs-tah-SYOHN deh gah-soh-LEE-nah*, la gasolinera *gah-soh-lee-NEH-rah;* **(railroad)** la estación de ferrocarril *ehs-tah-SYOHN deh fehr-roh-kahr-REEL*

stationery store la papelería *pah-peh-leh-REE-ah*

stationmaster el jefe de estación *heh-feh deh ehs-tah-SYOHN*

stay (a visit) la estancia *ehs-TAHN-syah*, la morada *moh-RAH-dah*, la permanencia *pehr-mah-NEHN-syah;* **to stay** quedar(se) *keh-DAHR-(seh)*

steak el bistec *bees-TEHK*, el biftec *beef-TEHK*

steal (v.) robar *roh-BAHR*

steel el acero *ah-SEH-roh*

steep grade la cuesta *KWEHS-tah*

steering wheel el volante *boh-LAHN-teh*

stew el guisado *ghee-SAH-doh*, el estofado *ehs-toh-FAH-doh*

steward (deck) el camarero (de cubierta) *kah-mah-REH-roh (deh koo-BYEHR-tah)*

stewardess (airplane) la azafata *ah-sah-FAH-tah*

stockings las medias *MEH-dyahs*

stomach el estómago *ehs-TOH-mah-goh;* **stomachache** el dolor de estómago *doh-lohr deh ehs-TOH-mah-goh*

stop (bus) la parada *pah-RAH-dah*

stoplight la luz de parada *loos deh pah-RAH-dah*, el semáforo *seh-MAH-foh-roh*

store la tienda *TYEHN-dah*

straight derecho *deh-REH-choh*, seguido *seh-GHEE-doh*

strap la correa *kohr-REH-ah*

straw la paja *PAH-hah*

strawberry la fresa *FREH-sah*

street la calle *KAH-yeh*

streetcar el tranvía *trahn-BEE-ah*

string la cuerda *KWEHR-dah*

string (green) bean la habichuela verde *ah-bee-CHWEH-lah BEHR-deh*

strong fuerte *FWEHR-teh*

style el estilo *ehs-TEE-loh;* **(fashion)** la moda *MOH-dah*

sudden repentino *reh-pehn-TEE-noh*, súbito *SOO-bee-toh*

suddenly de repente *deh reh-PEHN-teh*

sugar el azúcar *ah-SOO-kahr*

suit el traje *TRAH-heh*

suitcase la maleta *mah-LEH-tah*

summer el verano *beh-RAH-noh*

sun el sol *sohl*

Sunday el domingo *doh-MEEN-goh*

sunglasses las gafas de sol *GAH-fahs deh SOHL*

sunny asoleado *ah-soh-leh-AH-doh*, de sol *deh sohl*

suntan lotion la loción contra quemadura de sol *loh-SYOHN kohn-trah keh-mah-DOO-rah deh SOHL*

supper la cena *SEH-nah*

surgeon el cirujano *see-roo-HAH-noh*

sweater el suéter *SWEH-tehr*

Swedish sueco *SWEH-koh*

sweet dulce *DOOL-seh;* **sweet wine** vino dulce *BEE-noh DOOL-seh*

swell (v.) hinchar *een-CHAHR*

swim (v.) nadar *nah-DAHR*

swimming pool la piscina *pees-SEE-nah*

Swiss suizo *SWEE-soh*

switch (electric) el interruptor *een-tehr-roop-TOHR*, el conmutador *kohn-moo-tah-DOHR*

swollen hinchado *een-CHAH-doh*, inflamado *een-flah-MAH-doh*

synagogue la sinagoga *see-nah-GOH-gah*

syrup (cough) el jarabe para la tos *hah-RAH-beh pah-rah lah tohs*

T

table la mesa *MEH-sah*

tablecloth el mantel *mahn-TEHL*

tablespoon la cuchara *coo-CHAH-rah*

tablespoonful la cucharada *koo-chah-RAH-dah*

tablet la pastilla *pahs-TEE-yah*

taillight (car) el farol de cola *fah-ROHL deh KOH-lah*, el farol trasero *fah-ROHL trah-SEH-roh*

tailor el sastre *SAHS-treh*

take (v.) (carry) llevar *yeh-BAHR;* **(person)** conducir *kohn-doo-SEER*, llevar *yeh-BAHR;* **(thing)** tomar *toh-MAHR;* **will take time** tomará (llevará) tiempo *toh-mah-RAH TYEHM-poh (yeh-bah-RAH) TYEHM-poh*

taken (occupied) ocupado *oh-koo-PAH-doh*

take off (garment) (v.) quitarse *kee-TAHR-seh*

talcum powder el polvo de talco *POHL-boh deh TAHL-koh*

tall alto *AHL-toh*

tan (color) el color de canela *koh-LOHR deh kah-NEH-lah*, café claro *kah-FEH KLAH-roh*

tangerine la mandarina *mahn-dah-REE-nah*

tank (car) el depósito *deh-POH-see-toh*

tap el grifo *GREE-foh*

tape (adhesive, skin) el esparadrapo *ehs-pah-rah-DRAH-poh*

tasty sabroso *sah-BROH-soh*, rico *REE-koh*

tax el impuesto *eem-PWEHS-toh*

taxi el taxi *TAHK-see*

tea el té *teh*

teaspoon la cucharita *koo-chah-REE-tah*, la cucharilla *koo-chah-REE-yah*

teaspoonful la cucharadita *koo-chah-rah-DEE-tah*

telegram el telegrama *teh-leh-GRAH-mah*

telegraph (cable) el telégrafo *teh-LEH-grah-foh;* **to telegraph** telegrafiar *teh-leh-grah-FYAHR*

telephone el teléfono *teh-LEH-foh-noh;* **to telephone** telefonear *teh-leh-foh-neh-AHR*

tell (v.) decir *deh-SEER*

teller (bank) el cajero *kah-HEH-roh*

temporarily temporalmente *tehm-poh-rahl-MEHN-teh*, provisionalmente *proh-bee-syoh-nahl-MEHN-teh*

ten diez *dyes*

tension (high-tension wires) los cables de alta tensión *KAH-blehs deh AHL-tah tehn-SYOHN*

tenth décimo *DEH-see-moh*

terminal (bus, plane) la terminal *tehr-mee-NAHL*

thank (v.) dar las gracias a *dahr lahs GRAH-syahs ah*

Thank you Gracias *GRAH-syahs*

that (conj.) que *keh;* (adj.) aquel *ah-KEHL*, ese *EH-seh*, aquella *ah-KEH-yah*, esa *EH-sah*

the el *ehl*, los *lohs*, la *lah*, las *lahs*

theater el teatro *teh-AH-troh*

their su *soo*

there ahí *ah-EE*, allí *ah-YEE*, allá *ah-YAH;* **there is (are)** hay *AH-ee*

thermometer el termómetro *tehr-MOH-meh-troh*

these estos *EHS-tohs*, estas *EHS-tahs*

they ellos *EH-yohs*, ellas *EH-yahs*

thick espeso *ehs-PEH-soh*, denso *DEHN-soh*, grueso *GRWEH-soh*

thief el ladrón *lah-DROHN*

thigh el muslo *MOOS-loh*

thing la cosa *KOH-sah*

think (v.) pensar *pehn-SAHR*

third tercero *tehr-SEH-roh*

thirsty (to be) tener sed *teh-NEHR sehd*

thirteen trece *TREH-seh*

thirty treinta *TREYN-tah*

this este *EHS-teh*, esta *EHS-tah*

those esos *EH-sohs*, aquellos *ah-KEH-yohs*, esas *EH-sahs*, aquellas *ah-KEH-yahs*

thousand mil *meel*

thread el hilo *EE-loh*

three tres *trehs*; **three times** tres veces *trehs BEH-sehs*

throat la garganta *gahr-GAHN-tah*

through por *pohr*, a través de *a trah-BEHS deh*

thumb el pulgar *pool-GAHR*

thunder el trueno *TRWEH-noh;* **to thunder** tronar *troh-NAHR*

Thursday el jueves *HWEH-behs*

ticket el billete *bee-YEH-teh;* **ticket window** la ventanilla *behn-tah-NEE-yah*

tie (neck) la corbata *kohr-BAH-tah*

tighten (car, brakes) apretar *ah-preh-TAHR*

till hasta (que) *ahs-tah KEH*

time el tiempo *TYEHM-poh*, la hora *OH-rah;* **on time** a tiempo *ah-TYEHM-poh;* **at what time?** ¿a qué hora? *ah-keh-OH-rah*

timetable el horario *oh-RAH-ryoh*

tint (hair) (v.) teñir *tehn-YEER*

tip (gratuity) la propina *proh-PEE-nah*

tire (car) la llanta *YAHN-tah*, el neumático *neh-oo-MAH-tee-koh*

tired (to be) (v.) cansado (estar) *kahn-SAH-doh (ehs-TAHR)*

tissue paper el papel de seda *pah-PEHL deh SEH-dah*

to a *ah*, por *pohr*, para *PAH-rah*

toast (bread) la tostada *tohs-TAH-dah;* **(drink)** el brindis *BREEN-dees*

toaster el tostador *tohs-tah-DOHR*

tobacco el tabaco *tah-BAH-koh*

today hoy *oy*

toe el dedo del pie *DEH-doh dehl pyeh*

together juntos *HOON-tohs*

toilet el retrete *reh-TREH-teh;* **toilet paper** el papel higiénico *pah-PEHL ee-HYEH-nee-koh*

token (bus or phone) la ficha *FEE-chah*

tomato el tomate *toh-MAH-teh*

tomorrow mañana *mahn-YAH-nah*

tongue la lengua *LEHN-gwah*

tonic (hair) el tónico para el pelo *TOH-nee-koh pah-rah ehl PEH-loh*

tonight esta noche *ehs-tah NOH-cheh*

too (also) también *tahm-BYEHN;* **Too bad!** ¡Es lástima! *ehs LAHS-tee-mah;* **Too much.** Demasiado. *deh-mah-SYAH-doh*

tooth el diente *DYEHN-teh*, la muela *MWEH-lah*

toothache el dolor de muelas *doh-LOHR deh MWEH-lahs*

toothbrush el cepillo de dientes *seh-PEE-yoh deh DYEHN-tehs*

toothpaste la pasta dentífrica *PAHS-tah dehn-TEE-free-kah*

top la cima *SEE-mah*

touch (v.) tocar *toh-KAHR*

tough duro *DOO-roh*

tourist el (la) turista *too-REES-tah*

tow (car) (v.) remolcar *reh-mohl-KAHR*

toward hacia *AH-syah*

towel la toalla *toh-AH-yah*

town el pueblo *PWEH-bloh*, la población *poh-blah-SYOHN*

track (R.R.) los rieles *RYEH-lehs*

traffic light la luz de parada *loos deh pah-RAH-dah*, la luz de tráfico *loos deh TRAH-fee-koh*, el semáforo de circulación *seh-MAH-foh-roh deh seer-koo-lah-syohn*

train el tren *trehn*

transfer (ticket) el transbordo *trahns-BOHR-doh;* **to transfer** transbordar *trahns-bohr-DAHR*

translate (v.) traducir *trah-doo-SEER*

travel (v.) viajar *byah-HAHR;* **travel insurance** el seguro de viaje *seh-GOO-roh deh BYAH-heh*

traveler el viajero *byah-HEH-roh;* **traveler's check** el cheque de viajeros *CHEH-keh deh byah-HEH-rohs*

tree el árbol *AHR-bohl*

trip (voyage) el viaje *BYAH-heh*

trolley car el tranvía *trahn-BEE-ah*

trouble (to be in) tener dificultades *teh-NEHR dee-fee-kool-TAH-dehs*, estar en un apuro *ehs-TAHR ehn oon ah-POO-roh*

trousers los pantalones *pahn-tah-LOH-nehs*

truck el camión *kah-MYOHN*

true verdadero *behr-dah-DEH-roh*

trunk (car) el portaequipaje *pohr-tah-eh-kee-PAH-heh*, el baúl *bah-OOL*

try on (v.) probarse *proh-BAHR-seh*

try to (v.) tratar de (+ infinitive) *trah-TAHR deh*

tube (inner) la cámara de aire *KAH-mah-rah deh AH-ee-reh*

Tuesday el martes *MAHR-tehs*

Turkish turco *TOOR-koh*

turn (n.) la vuelta *BWEHL-tah;* **to turn** doblar *doh-BLAHR*, volver *bohl-BEHR*

tuxedo el smoking *SMOH-keeng*

twelve doce *DOH-seh*

twenty veinte *BEYN-teh*

twice dos veces *dohs BEH-sehs*

twin beds las camas gemelas *KAH-mahs heh-MEH-lahs*

two dos *dohs*

U

ugly feo *FEH-oh*

umbrella el paraguas *pah-RAH-gwahs*

uncle el tío *TEE-oh*

uncomfortable incómodo *een-KOH-moh-doh*

under debajo de *deh-BAH-hoh deh*, bajo *BAH-hoh*

undershirt la camiseta *kah-mee-SEH-tah*

understand comprender *kohm-prehn-DEHR*, entender *ehn-tehn-DEHR*

underwear la ropa interior *ROH-pah een-teh-RYOHR*

university la universidad *oo-nee-behr-see-DAHD*

until hasta *AHS-tah*

up arriba *ahr-REE-bah*

upon sobre *SOH-breh*, encima de *ehn-SEE-mah deh*

upper alto *AHL-toh*

upstairs arriba *ahr-REE-bah*

U.S.A. los Estados Unidos de América *ehs-TAH-dohs oo-*

NEE-dohs deh ah-MEH-ree-kah [abbreviate EE.UU.]

use (purpose) el uso *OO-soh*, el empleo *ehm-PLEH-oh*; **to use** usar *oo-SAHR*, emplear *ehm-pleh-AHR*

V

valise la maleta *mah-LEH-tah*

veal la ternera *tehr-NEH-rah*

vegetables las legumbres *leh-GOOM-brehs*; **green vegetables** las verduras *behr-DOO-rahs*

velvet el terciopelo *tehr-syoh-PEH-loh*

very muy *mooy*

vest el chaleco *chah-LEH-koh*

veterinarian el veterinario *beh-teh-ree-NAH-ryoh*

view la vista *BEES-tah*

vinegar el vinagre *bee-NAH-greh*

visit (sojourn) la visita *bee-SEE-tah*; **to visit** visitar *bee-see-TAHR*, hacer una visita *ah-SEHR oo-nah bee-SEE-tah*

visitor el visitante *bee-see-TAHN-teh*

W

waist la cintura *seen-TOO-rah*, el talle *TAH-yeh*

wait (for) (v.) esperar *ehs-peh-RAHR*

waiter el camarero *kah-mah-REH-roh*; **headwaiter** el jefe de comedor *HEH-feh deh koh-meh-DOHR*

waiting room la sala de espera *SAH-lah deh ehs-PEH-rah*

waitress la camarera *kah-mah-REH-rah*

wake up (v.) despertarse *dehs-pehr-TAHR-seh*

walk (take a) (v.) dar un paseo *dahr oon pah-SEH-oh*

wall el muro *MOO-roh*, la pared *pah-REHD*

wallet la cartera (de bolsillo) *kahr-TEH (deh bohl-SEE-yoh)*

want (v.) querer *keh-REHR*

warm caliente *kah-LYEHN-teh*

was era *EH-rah*, estaba *ehs-TAH-bah*

wash (v.) lavarse *lah-BAHR-seh*

washroom el lavabo *lah-BAH-boh*

watch (clock) el reloj *reh-LOH*; **to watch** mirar *mee-RAHR*; **Watch out!** ¡Cuidado! *kwee-DAH-doh*

water el agua (f.) *AH-gwah*

watermelon la sandía *sahn-DEE-ah*

way (path, mode) la vía *BEE-ah*, la manera *mah-NEH-rah*, el modo *MOH-doh*; **by way of** (por) vía (de) (pohr) *BEE-ah (deh)*, pasando por *pah-SAHN-doh pohr*; **one way** dirección única *dee-rehk-SYOHN OO-nee-kah*; **this way** por aquí *pohr ah-KEE*; **which way?** ¿por dónde? *pohr DOHN-deh*; **wrong way** rumbo equivocado *ROOM-boh eh-kee-boh-KAH-dah*

we nosotros *noh-SOH-trohs*

weak débil *DEH-beel*

wear (v.) llevar *yeh-BAHR*

weather el tiempo *TYEHM-poh*

Wednesday el miércoles *MYEHR-koh-lehs*

week la semana *seh-MAH-nah*

weigh (v.) pesar *peh-SAHR*

weight el peso *PEH-soh*

welcome. (You're) De nada. *deh NAH-dah*

well bien *byehn*; **well-done (steak)** bien hecho *byehn EH-choh*

west el oeste *oh-EHS-teh*

wet mojado *moh-HAH-doh*; **wet paint** recién pintado *reh-SYEHN peen-TAH-doh*

what qué *keh*

wheel la rueda *RWEH-dah;*
steering wheel el volante
boh-LAHN-teh

when cuando *KWAHN-doh*

where donde *DOHN-deh*

which cual *kwahl*

whiskey el whiskey *WEES-kee*

white blanco *BLAHN-koh*

who quién *kyehn,* quiénes (pl.)
KYEH-nehs

whom a quién *ah kyehn,* a
quiénes (pl.) *ah KYEHN-ehs*

whose de quién *deh kyehn,* de
quiénes (pl.) *deh KYEHN-ehs*

why por qué *pohr KEH*

wide ancho *AHN-choh*

width la anchura *ahn-CHOO-rah*

wife la señora *sehn-YOH-rah,*
la esposa *ehs-POH-sah*

wind el viento *BYEHN-toh*

window la ventana *behn-TAH-nah;* **display window** el
escaparate *ehs-kah-pah-RAH-teh;* **(train, post office, bank)** la ventanilla *behn-tah-NEE-yah*

windshield el parabrisas *pah-rah-BREE-sahs*

windy ventoso *behn-TOH-soh;*
it is windy hace viento *ah-seh BYEHN-toh*

wine el vino *bee-noh;* **wine list**
la lista de vinos *LEES-tah deh BEE-nohs*

winter el invierno, *een-BYEHR-noh*

wiper (windshield) el
limpiaparabrisas *leem-pyah-pah-rah-BREE-sahs*

wire (high-tension) el cable
de alta tensión *KAH-bleh deh AHL-tah tehn-SYOHN;* **Hold the wire. (telephone)** No
se retire. *noh seh reh-TEE-reh*

wish (v.) querer *keh-REHR,*
desear *deh-seh-AHR*

wishes (best) saludos *sah-LOO-dohs*

with con *kohn*

without sin *seen*

woman la mujer *moo-HEHR*

wood la madera *mah-DEH-rah*

wool la lana *LAH-nah*

word la palabra *pah-LAH-brah*

work el trabajo *trah-BAH-hoh;*
(creative work) la obra
OH-brah; **to work** trabajar
trah-bah-HAHR

worry (v.) preocuparse *preh-oh-koo-PAHR-seh;* **Don't worry.** No se preocupe. *noh seh preh-oh-KOO-peh*

worse peor *peh-OHR*

worst el peor *ehl peh-OHR*

worth (to be) (v.) valer *bah-LEHR*

wound (injury) la herida *eh-REE-dah*

wounded herido *eh-REE-doh*

wrap up (v.) envolver *ehn-bohl-BEHR*

wrapping paper el papel de
envolver *pah-PEHL deh ehn-bohl-BEHR*

wrench (tool) la llave inglesa
(de tuercas) *YAH-beh een-GLEH-sah (deh TWEHR-kahs)*

wrist la muñeca *moon-YEH-kah;* **wristwatch** el reloj de
pulsera *reh-LOH-deh pool-seh-rah*

write (v.) escribir *ehs-kree-BEER*

writing paper el papel de
cartas *pah-PEHL deh KAHR-tahs,* el papel de escribir *deh ehs-kree-BEER*

wrong (to be) equivocarse *eh-kee-boh-KAHR-seh,* no tener
razón *noh teh-NEHR rah-SOHN*

X

x-ray la radiografía *rah-dyoh-grah-FEE-ah,* los rayos X
lohs rah-yohs EH-kees

Y

year el año *AHN-yoh*

yellow amarillo *ah-mah-REE-yoh*

yes sí *see*

yesterday ayer *ah-YEHR*

yet todavía *toh-dah-BEE-ah;*
not yet todavía no *toh-dah-BEE-ah noh*

you usted *oo-STEHD*, ustedes *oo-STEH-dehs*, tú *too*

young joven *HOH-behn*

your su, sus *soo, soos*, de usted *deh oo-STEHD*, de ustedes *deh oo-STEH-dehs*

youth hostel albergue juvenil *ahl-behr-gheh hoo-ben-EEL*

Yugoslav yugoeslavo *yoo-goh-eh-SLAH-boh*

Z

zipper la cremallera *kreh-mah-YEH-rah*, el cierre relámpago *syehr-reh reh-LAHM-pah-goh*

zoo el jardín zoológico *hahr-DEEN soh-oh-LOH-hee-koh*

SPANISH-ENGLISH DICTIONARY

Only masculine forms of adjectives are given here; in most cases, the feminine form requires dropping the "o" at the end and replacing it with "a." Gender is given by "**m.**" or "**f.**"

A

a   to, at, in, on, upon
abajo   down, downstairs
abierto   open
¡Abran paso!   Make way!
abrelatas m.   can opener
abrigo m.   overcoat
abril   April
abrir   to open
acabado   over, finished
acabar   to finish; **acabar de** to have just (done something)
aceite m.   oil; **aceite de oliva** olive oil; **aceite de ricino** castor oil
aceituna f.   olive
acera f.   sidewalk
acero m.   steel
acetona f.   nail-polish remover
aclarar   to clear up (weather)
acordarse   to remember
acostarse   to lie down, to go to bed
acuerdo m.   agreement; **estar de acuerdo** to agree
acumulador m.   battery
adelante   ahead, forward, onward; **¡Adelante!**   Come in!
adiós   good-bye, farewell
aduana f.   customs, customs house
afuera   out, outside
agosto   August
agradable   pleasant
agradecido   grateful
agrio   sour
agua m.   water; **agua corriente** running water;

agua de Colonia   Cologne; **agua mineral** mineral water
aguardar   to expect, to wait for
aguja f.   needle
agujero m.   hole
ahí   there
ahora   now; **ahora mismo** right now
ajo m.   garlic
ajustar   to adjust
albaricoque m.   apricot
albornoz m.   bathrobe
alcachofa f.   artichoke
alcoba f.   bedroom
alegrarse   to be glad, to rejoice
alegre   glad, merry
alemán m.   German
alfiler m.   pin
aflombra f.   rug
algo   something, anything; **¿Algo más?**   Anything else?
algodón m.   cotton
alguien   someone, somebody, anyone, anybody
algún, alguno   some, any; **algunas veces** sometimes
alicates m. pl.   pliers
allá   there, over there
allí   there, right there
almacén m.   department store, warehouse
almendra f.   almond
almidón m.   starch
almidonar   to starch
almohada f.   pillow
almorzar   to lunch
almuerzo m.   lunch
alquilar   to rent

alquiler m. rent (payment)
alrededor de around, about;
  (los) alrededores
  environs, outskirts
alto tall
¡Alto! Halt! Stop!
amargo bitter
amarillo yellow
amigo m. friend
ampliación f. enlargement
amueblado furnished
ancho wide
anchura f. width
andén m. platform
angosto narrow
anillo m. ring
año m. year
anteojos m. pl. eyeglasses
antes de before
antipático unpleasant, not
  likable (person)
apearse to get off
apellido m. family name,
  surname
apio m. celery
aprender to learn
apretar to tighten
apuro m. trouble, difficulty
aquel that
aquí here
árabe Arab
árbol m. tree
arena f. sand
arete m. earring
armario m. closet
arranque m. starter (car)
arreglar to fix, to repair
arriba up, above
arroz m. rice
asado m. roast
asar to roast
ascensor m. elevator
asegurar to insure, to ensure,
  to assure
así so, thus
asiento m. seat (on
  conveyance); **asiento
  reservado** reserved seat
asoleado sunny
asomarse a to lean out

atrás back, backward, behind
aturdido (estar) to feel dizzy
austríaco Austrian
avellana f. hazelnut
avería f. breakdown
avión f. airplane
aviso m. notice, sign, warning
ayer yesterday
ayudar to help
ayuntamiento m. city hall
azafata f. stewardess
azúcar m. sugar
azul blue

B

bailar to dance
baile m. dance
bajada f. downgrade
bajar to go down, to come
  down
bajo low
bañarse to bathe, to take a bath
baraja f. deck of cards
barato cheap
barba f. beard
barco m. boat
barrera f. gate, barrier
barrio m. district
¡Basta! Enough!. Cut it out!;
  bastante enough (plenty)
bata f. robe, dressing gown
baúl m. trunk
beber to drink
bebida f. drink
belga Belgian
bello beautiful
bencina f. gasoline
besar to kiss
beso m. kiss
biblioteca f. library
bien well; **Bien hecho.** Well
  done.
billete m. ticket, bill
  (banknote); **billete de ida y
  vuelta** round-trip ticket
blanco white
blando soft
boca f. mouth

bocacalle f. intersection
bocado m. mouthful, bite; **tomar un bocado** to have or get a bite
bocina f. car horn
bolsa f. purse
bolsillo m. pocket
bollito m. roll
bombilla f. electric bulb
bonito pretty
boquilla f. cigarette holder
bordo: a bordo on board; **¡A bordo!** All aboard!
borla f. powder puff
borracho drunk
bote m. boat; **bote salvavidas m.** lifeboat
botón m. button
botones m. bellboy, bellhop
bragas f. pl. panties
brasileño Brazilian
brazo m. arm
brillar to shine
brindis m. toast (drink)
brocha de afeitar f. shaving brush
bueno good
bufanda f. scarf
bujía f. sparkplug, candle
bulto m. package
buque m. ship, boat
busear to look for, to search
buzón m. letterbox, mailbox

C

caballero m. gentleman
caballo m. horse
cabello m. hair
cabeza f. head
cabina f. phone booth
cables de alta tensión m. pl. high-tension wires
cada each; **cada uno** each one
cadena f. chain
cadera f. hip
caer to fall
café m. coffee, café; **café solo** black coffee

caja f. box, case; **Pague en la caja.** Pay the cashier.
caja fuerte f. safe (strongbox)
cajero m. teller, cashier
cajón m. drawer
caliente warm, hot
calle f. street
calor m. heat, warmth; **Hace calor.** It's warm, hot.
calzoncillos m. pl. shorts (underwear)
cama f. bed
cámara de aire f. inner tube
cámara fotográfica f. camera
camarera f. waitress, maid
camarero m. waiter, valet; **camarero de cubierta m.** deck steward
camarón m. shrimp
camarote m. stateroom
camas gemelas f. pl. twin beds
cambiar to change, to exchange
cambio m. change
camino road; **camino equivocado** wrong way
camión m. truck
camisa f. shirt
camiseta f. undershirt
camisón m. nightgown
campo m. countryside
canción f. song
cansado (estar) to be tired
cantar to sing
cantina f. saloon
capó m. hood (car), bonnet
cara f. face
¡Caramba! Darn it!
caro expensive
carne f. meat, flesh; **carne de cerdo f.** pork; **carne de cordero f.** lamb; **carne de vaca f.** beef
carretera f. highway
carta f. letter, playing card
cartera (de bolsillo) f. pocketbook (wallet)
casa f. house, home; **en casa** at home; **casa de correos f.** post office; **casa de huéspedes f.** boardinghouse

casi almost

caso m. case

castaña f. chestnut

castaño brown

castillo m. castle

catarro m. cold (respiratory)

catorce fourteen

caucho rubber

cebolla onion

ceja f. eyebrow

cena f. supper

cenicero m. ashtray

cepillar to brush

cepillo m. brush; toothbrush; **cepillo de ropa** clothes brush

cerca de near, close

cerdo m. pig, hog; **carne de cerdo** pork

cereza f. cherry

cerilla f. match

cerrado closed

cerradura f. lock

cerrajero m. locksmith

cerrar to close, to shut

certificado registered (mail)

cerveza f. beer

cesta f. basket

chal m. shawl

chaleco m. vest

chanclos m. pl. rubbers

checo Czech

cheque m. check (bank); **cheque de viajero m.** traveler's check

chileno Chilean

chino Chinese

chirrido m. squeak

chorizo m. sausage

chuleta f. chop, cutlet

cielo m. sky, heaven

cien, ciento hundred

cierre relámpago m. zipper

cima f. top

cincuenta fifty

cine m. movie house, movie show

cinta f. ribbon

cinta adhesiva f. adhesive tape, bandage

cintura f. waist

cinturón m. belt

ciruela f. plum; . . . **pasa f.** prune

cirujano m. surgeon

ciudad f. city

claro light (color), clear; **¡Claro!** Of course!

cobrar to collect, to cash

cocido cooked meat-vegetable stew

cocina f. kitchen

cocinar to cook

coche m. coach, auto, R.R. car; **coche-cama m.** sleeping car; **coche-comedor m.** dining car; **coche-fumador m.** smoking car

cochero m. coachman

codo m. elbow

coger to catch, take

cojinete m. bearing (car)

col f. cabbage

colchón m. mattress

colgador m. coat hanger

color de canela tan

colorete rouge

collar m. necklace

combinación f. slip (garment)

comenzar to begin, to start

comer to eat

comida f. meal; **comida a precio fijo, comida corrida** (or **completa**) **f.** fixed-price meal

comisaría f. police station

como as, like

cómo how

cómodo comfortable

compañía f. company

componer to fix

composturas f. pl. repairs

compota f. preserve; stewed fruit

compra f. purchase (item)

comprar to buy, to purchase

comprender to understand

con with; **con mucho gusto** gladly

condones condoms

conducir to drive
conferencia interurbana f. long-distance phone call
conocer to know, to make acquaintance of
conseguir to get, to obtain
contar to count, to tell
contar con to depend on, to count on
contestación f. answer, to reply
contestar to answer, to reply
contra against
contraventana f. shutter
contusión f. bruise
copia f. print (photo)
copos de jabón soap flakes
corazón m. heart
corbata f. necktie
correa f. strap; **correa de ventilador f.** fan belt
correo m. mail, post office; **correo aéreo m.** air mail; **correo urgente m.** special delivery
correr to run
corriente de aire m. draft (current of air)
cortar to cut
corte de pelo m. haircut
cortés polite
cortesía f. politeness, courtesy
corto short
cosa f. thing
costilla f. rib
creer to believe
crema f. cream; **crema de afeitar f.** shaving cream
cremallera f. zipper
cruce m. crossroad
cuadra f. block (city)
cuadrado m. square (shape)
cuadro m. picture
cuál which?, which one?
cualquier, cualquiera any; **en cualquier caso, de cualquier modo** in any case
cuándo when?
cuánto how much?; **¿cuánto tiempo?** how long?
cuántos how many?

cuarenta forty
cuarto room, quarter; **cuarto de baño m.** bathroom; **cuarto tocador m.** powder room
cuatro four
cubierta f. deck (ship)
cuchara f. spoon
cucharada f. spoonful
cucharadita f.L teaspoonful
cucharilla f. teaspoon
cuchillo m. knife
cuello m. neck, collar
cuenta f. bill (restaurant)
cuentagotas m. dropper (eye)
cuerda f. rope, cord, string
cuero m. leather, hide
cuerpo m. body
cuidado m. care; **con cuidado** carefully; **tener cuidado** to be careful; **¡Cuidado!** Be careful! Watch out! Attention!
cura m. priest

D

danés Danish
dar to give; **dar las gracias a** to thank; **dar un paseo** to take a walk
darse prisa to hurry
de of, from
debajo de under, beneath
deber to have to, to owe
débil weak
décimo tenth
decir to say, to tell
dedo m. finger
dejar to let, to permit, to leave behind
demasiado too much
dentadura f. denture
dentro inside, within
depósito m. tank
derecho right (opposite of left); **todo derecho** straight ahead
derechos de aduana m. pl. customs duties
desayunarse to have breakfast

desayuno m. breakfast
descansar to rest
descolorante hair bleach
descuento m. discount
desde since; **Desde luego.** Of course.
desear to wish
desembarcar to land (from ship)
desodorante m. deodorant
despacio slowly
despejarse to clear up (sky)
despertador m. alarm clock
despertarse to wake up
después (de) after, afterward, later
destinatario m. addressee (on packages or letters)
destornillador m. screwdriver
desviación f. detour
detrás de back of, behind
devolver to return, to give back
día m. day; **por . . .** by the day; **buenos días** good morning, good day
diablo m. devil; **¡Qué diablos!** What the devil!
diecinueve nineteen
dieciocho eighteen
dieciséis sixteen
diecisiete seventeen
diente m. tooth
diez ten
difícil difficult, hard
diluviar to pour (rain)
dinero m. money; **dinero contante** m. cash
dirección f. address, direction; **dirección única** f. one-way traffic
dirigir to direct
disco m. compact disc
disparate m. nonsense
dispensar to excuse, to pardon
Dispénseme usted. Pardon (excuse) me.
distancia f. distance; **¿A qué distancia?** How far?
doblar to turn, to fold
doce twelve

docena f. dozen
dolor m. pain, ache; **dolor de cabeza** m. headache; **dolor de estómago** m. stomachache; **dolor de garganta** m. sore throat; **dolor de muelas** m. toothache
domingo m. Sunday
donde where
dormir to sleep
dormitorio m. bedroom
dos two; **dos veces** twice
ducha f. shower
dulce sweet; **dulces** m. pl. candy
durar to last
durazno m. peach
duro hard, tough

E

elástico m. rubber band
ellas f. they
ellos m. they
embrague m. car clutch
emparedado m. sandwich
empastar to fill a tooth
empaste m. filling (tooth)
empezar to begin, to start
emplear to use, to hire
empleo m. use (purpose), job
empujar to push
en on, in, at; **en casa** at home; **en casa de** at the home of; **en seguida** at once, immediately, right away
encaje m. lace
encendedor m. cigarette lighter
encender to light
encendido m. car ignition
encías f. pl. gums
encima (de) above, over, upon
encontrar to find, to meet
encrucijada f. crossroad
encurtidos m. pl. pickles
enchufe m. electric outlet
enero m. January
enfermedad f. illness

enfermera f.   nurse
enfermo   ill
engranaje m.   gears
engrasar   to grease, to lubricate
enhorabuena f.
    congratulations
enjuague m.   mouthwash
ensalada f.   salad
enseñar   to teach, to show
entender   to understand
entrar   to enter, come in
entre   between, among
entrega f.   delivery
entregar   to deliver, to hand
    over
entremés m.   appetizer, hors
    d'oeuvre
enviar   to send
envolver   to wrap
equipaje m.   baggage
equivocarse   to be mistaken
esa, ese, eso   that; **a eso de** at
    about, approximately (a
    certain hour)
esas, esos   those
escalera f.   stairs
escalofrío m.   chill
escaparate m.   display window
escape m.   exhaust (car), leak
escarpado   steep
escoger   to choose, to select
escribir   to write
escuchar   to listen to
escuela f.   school
escupir   to spit; **prohibido
    escupir**   spitting forbidden
esmalte m.   nail polish
espalda f.   back (of body)
español   Spanish
esparadrapo m.   adhesive
    tape, bandage
espejo m.   mirror
esperar   to hope, to expect, to
    wait for
espeso   thick
espinaca f.   spinach
esposa f.   wife
esposo m.   husband
esta, este, esto   this
Está bien.   All right, okay.

estación f.   season; **estación
    de ferrocarril** f.   railroad
    station
estacionar   to park; **se
    prohibe estacionar**   no
    parking
Estados Unidos de América
    m. pl.   U.S.A.
estanco m.   cigar store (Spain)
estar   to be; **estar de pie**   to
    be standing; **estar de vuelta**
    to be back
estas, estos   these
este   east; this
estancia f.   stay
estofado m.   stew
estómago m.   stomach; **dolor
    de estómago** m.
    stomachache
estrecho   narrow, straight
estrella f.   star
esquina f.   street corner
etiqueta f.   label, etiquette;
    traje de etiqueta m.
    evening dress
evitar   to avoid
extranjero m.   foreign,
    foreigner

F

facturar   to check (baggage)
faja f.   girdle
falda f.   skirt
faro m.   headlight
farol m.   street lamp; **farol
    delantero** m.   headlight;
    farol trasero (de cola) m.
    taillight
favor m.   favor; **Por favor.**
    Please.; **Naga el favor.**
    Please.
febrero m.   February
fecha f.   date; **fecha de hoy**
    today's date
¡Felices Pascuas!   Merry
    Christmas!
felicitaciones f. pl.
    congratulations

feliz happy; **¡Feliz Año Nuevo!** Happy New Year!; **¡Feliz Navidad!** Merry Christmas!

feo ugly

ferrocarril m. railroad

fiambre m. cold cuts

ficha f. token (for bus or phone)

fiebre f. fever

fieltro m. felt

fila f. row (theater), line

fin m. end

flor f. flower

fonda para estudiantes f. youth hostel

fósforo m. match

francés French

frenos m. pl. brakes

frente m. front, f. forehead

fresa f. strawberry

fresco fresh, cool

frijol colorado m. kidney bean

frío m. cold; **hacer frío** to be cold (weather); **tener frío** to be cold (person)

frito fried

fuego m. fire

fuente f. fountain

fuera out, outside

fuerte strong

fumador m. smoker, smoking car

fumar to smoke

función f. performance

funda f. pillowcase

furgón m. baggage car

G

gabán m. overcoat

gafas f. pl. eyeglasses

gana f. desire; **tener ganas de** to feel like

ganado m. cattle

gancho m. hook

ganga f. bargain sale

ganso m. goose

garganta f. throat; **dolor de garganta** m. sore throat

gasa f. gauze

gastar to spend

gasto m. expense, expenditure; **gasto mínimo** cover charge

gato m. cat, car jack

gemelos m. pl. twins, cuff links, binoculars

gente f. people

gerente m. manager

ginebra f. gin

giro postal m. money order

goma de recambio f. spare tire

gorra f. cap

gorro de baño m. bathing cap

gracias f. pl. thanks, thank you

grande big, large, great

granizar to hail (weather)

granizo m. hail (weather)

griego Greek

grifo m. tap, faucet

gris gray

grueso thick, stout

guante m. glove

guardar to keep

guardabarros m. fender

guía m., f. guide; guidebook

guiar to drive

guisado m. stew

guisante m. pea

gustar to like, to be pleasing

gusto m. taste, pleasure; **con mucho gusto** gladly

H

habichuela f. string bean

habitación f. room; **habitación para dos personas** f. double room; **habitación individual** f. single room

hablar to speak, to talk

hace ago

hacer to do, to make, to pack (baggage); **hacer cola** to stand in line

hacerse to become

hacia toward

Haga el favor. Please.

hallar to find

hasta until, even; **Hasta mañana.** See you tomorrow.; **Hasta la vista.** Good-bye. Till we meet again.

hay there is, there are

hebreo Hebrew

hecho a mano handmade

helado m. ice cream

herida f. wound

herido wounded

herir to wound, to hurt

hermana f. sister

hermano m. brother

hernoso beautiful

hervido boiled

hielo m. ice

hierro m. iron

hígado m. liver

higo m. fig

hierba f. grass

hilo m. thread, string

hinchado swollen

hinchar to swell

hoja de afeitar f. razor blade

hombre m. man

hombro m. shoulder

hongo m. mushroom

hora f. hour, time; **¿Qué hora es?** What time is it?; **por hora** by the hour

horario m. timetable

horno m. oven; **al horno** baked

horquilla f. hairpin

hoy today

hueso m. bone

huevo m. egg; **huevo duro m.** hard-boiled egg

húngaro Hungarian

I

idioma m. language

iglesia f. church

imperdible safety pin

impermeable raincoat

importar to be important, to import; **No importa.** It doesn't matter.

impuesto m. tax

incómodo uncomfortable

indicar to indicate

infierno m. hell

informes m. pl. information

inglés English

interruptor m. electric switch

invierno m. winter

ir to go; **ir a casa** to go home; **ir de compras (de tiendas)** to go shopping

irse to go away, to leave, to depart, to get out

izquierdo left (opposite of right)

J

jabón m. soap; **copos de jabón m. pl.** soap flakes

jamás never

jamón m. ham

jaqueca f. migraine

jarabe m. syrup; **jarabe para la tos m.** cough syrup

jardín m. garden; **jardín zoológico m.** zoo

jaffo m. pitcher

jefe m. chief, leader, head; **jefe de camareros m.** headwaiter; **jefe de estación m.** stationmaster

jira f. picnic

joven young, young person

joya f. jewel

joyería f. jewelry, jewelry shop

joyero m. jeweler

judío Jewish, Jew

juego m. game

jueves m. Thursday

jugar to play

jugo m. juice

julio m. July

junio m. June

L

labio m. lip; **lápiz de labios m.** lipstick

lado m.   side; **por otro lado** on the other hand

ladrón m.   thief, robber

lámpara f.   lamp

langosta f.   spiny lobster

lápiz m.   pencil; **lápiz de labios** m.   lipstick

largo long; **el largo** m.   length

lástima f.   pity; **¡Es lástima!** Too bad; **¡Qué lástima!** What a pity!

lastimar   to hurt, to injure, to bruise

lata f.   can (noun)

lavabo m.   sink, washroom, lavatory; **lavabo de señoras** m.   ladies' room; **lavabo de caballeros** m.   men's room

lavandera f.   laundress

lavandería f.   laundry

lavar   to wash (something)

lavarse   to wash (oneself)

laxante m.   laxative

leche f.   milk

lechuga f.   lettuce

leer   to read

legumbres f. pl.   vegetables

lejos   far, distant, far away

lengua f.   tongue; language

lentamente   slowly

lento   slow

letra f.   letter, bank draft

letrero m.   sign, poster, placard

levantar   to lift

levantarse   to get up, to stand up, to rise

libre   free

librería f.   bookstore

libro m.   book

liga f.   garter; **liga de goma** f.   rubber band

ligero   light (adj.)

lima de uñas f.   nail file

limpiar   to clean

limpieza a seco f.   dry-cleaning

limpio   clean

lindo   pretty

línea aérea f.   airline

lino m.   linen

linterna eléctrica f.   flashlight

lista   list; **lista de correos** f.   general delivery; **lista de platos** f.   menu; **lista de vinos** f.   wine list

litera f.   berth; **litera alta (litera de arriba)** f.   upper berth; **litera baja** f.   lower berth

llamada f.   telephone call; **llamada local** f.   local phone call; **llamada a larga distancia** long-distance phone call; **llamada conferencia** f.   conference call

llamar   to call, to knock, to ring; **llamar por teléfono** to phone

llamarse   to be named, to be called; **¿Cómo se llama usted?**   What is your name?

llanta f.   car tire

llave f.   key; **llave inglesa (llave de tuerca)** f.   wrench

llegada f.   arrival

llegar   to arrive

llenar   to fill, to fill out; **¡llénelo usted!** Fill her up!

lleno   full

llevar   to carry, to wear, to take a person or thing somewhere

llover   to rain

lluvia f.   rain

loco   crazy

lograr   to obtain, to get to

luego   then, afterward; **Desde luego.** Of course; **Hasta luego.** See you later.

lugar m.   place, spot, site

luna f.   moon

lunes m.   Monday

luz f.   light; **luz de parada** f.   stoplight; **luz de trafico (luz de tránsito)** f.   traffic light

M

madera f.   wood

madre f.   mother

maíz m.   corn

mal bad, badly; **estar mal** to be ill

maleta f. suitcase, valise, bag

mandar to send, to order, to command

mandarina f. tangerine

manga f. sleeve

mano f. hand; **de segunda mano** adj. secondhand

manteca f. lard, fat, butter

mantel m. tablecloth

mantequilla f. butter

manzana f. apple, block (of houses)

mañana f. morning, tomorrow; **por la mañana** in the morning; **Hasta mañana.** So long (until tomorrow).; **pasado mañana** the day after tomorrow

mapa m. map; **mapa de carreteras (de automovilista)** m. road map

maquinilla f. hair clippers; **maquinilla de afeitar** f. safety razor

mar m. sea

mareado seasick

mareo m. seasickness

marido m. husband

mariscos m. pl. seafood

martes m. Tuesday

martillo m. hammer

marzo m. March

más more

masaje m. massage

mayo m. May

medianoche f. midnight

medias f. pl. stockings

médico m., (adj.) doctor; medical

medidas f. pl. measurements, measures

medio half; **medio crudo** medium rare

mediodía m. noon

mejilla f. cheek

mejillón m. mussel

mejor better, best

mejores saludos m. pl. best wishes

melocotón m. peach

menos less, least, fewer; **al (por lo) menos** at least

mente f. mind

menudo small, minute; **a menudo** often

mercado m. market

mes m. month

mesa f. table, plateau

meter to put in, insert

miedo m. fear; **tener miedo** to be afraid, to fear

miércoles m. Wednesday

mil thousand; **mil millones** billion

mirar to look, to look at

misa cantada (mayor) f. high mass

mismo same; **ahora mismo** right now; **hoy mismo** this very day

mitad f. half (n.)

moda f. fashion, style

modo m. way, mode, manner

mojado wet

mojarse to get wet

molestar to bother, to annoy; **No se moleste.** Don't bother.; Don't trouble yourself.

moneda f. coin; **moneda corriente** f. currency; **moneda suelta** f. change

morada f. stay

morado purple

moreno brunette, dark-complexioned

mosquitero m. mosquito netting

mostaza f. mustard

mostrar to show

mozo m. porter, waiter

muchacha f. girl

muchacho m. boy

mucho much, a great deal of, a lot of

muchos many, lots of

muelle m. pier, dock, wharf

muerte f. death

muerto dead
mujer f. woman, wife
multa f. fine (n.)
muñeca f. wrist, doll
muro m. (outside) wall
museo m. museum
muslo m. thigh
muy very

N

nacer to be born
nada nothing; **De nada.** You're welcome.; Don't mention it.; **nada más** nothing else
nadar to swim
nadie no one, nobody
naranja f. orange
nariz m. nose
navaja de afeitar f. razor
Navidad f. Christmas
necesitar to need
neumático de repuesto m. spare tire
nevar to snow
niebla f. fog
nieve f. snow
ninguno none
niño m. child
noche f. night; **Buenas noches.** Good evening. Good night.
nombre m. name
norte m. north
noruego Norwegian
nos us, ourselves
nosotros we, us
novela f. novel
noveno ninth
noventa ninety
nube f. cloud
nublado cloudy
nuestro our, ours
nueve nine
nuevo new; **de nuevo** again, anew
nuez f. walnut
número m. number
nunca never

O

occidente m. western world
ochenta eighty
ocho eight
octavo eighth
ocupado busy, taken
ocurrir to happen
oeste m. west
oficina office; **oficina de cambio** f. exchange office; **oficina de informes** f. information bureau; **oficina de objetos perdidos** f. lost-and-found
oído m. ear (internal); **dolor de oídos** m. earache
oír to hear
ojo m. eye
olvidar, olvidarse de to forget
once eleven
óptico m. optician
oreja f. ear (external)
oro m. gold
ostra f., **ostión** m. oyster
otoño m. autumn, fall
otra vez again
otro other, another

P

padre m. father
pagar to pay, to cash
página f. page
país m. country (nation)
paja f. straw
pájaro m. bird
palabra f. word
pan m. bread
pañales m. pl. diapers
panecillo m. roll
paño m. cloth
pantalones m. pl. trousers, pants
pañuelo m. handkerchief
papa f. potato
papel m. paper; **papel de cartas (de escribir)** m. writing paper; **papel de**

envolver m. wrapping paper; **papel de seda m** tissue paper; **papel higiénico m.** toilet paper
papelería f. stationery store
paquete m. packet, package, parcel; **paquete postal m.** parcel post
par m. pair
para for; **Es para usted.** It's for you.
parabrisas m. windshield
parachoques m. car bumper
parada f. stop; **señal de parada f.** signal stop; **parada intermedia f.** stopover; **parada ordinaria f.** scheduled bus stop
paraguas m. umbrella
parar to stop, to stall (car)
pardo brown
parecer to seem, to appear
pared m. inner wall
párpado m. eyelid
parrilla f. grill; **a la parrilla** broiled
partida f. game
pasado past, last; **el mes pasado** last month
pasajero m. passenger
pasar to pass, to happen, to spend (time)
pasear, pasearse to take a walk, ride; **¡Pase usted!**; Come! Come in!
paseo m. ride, walk; **paseo en coche m.** drive
paso a nivel m. railroad crossing
pastel m. pie
pastilla f. tablet, cake (of soap), candy
pato m. duck
peatón m. pedestrian
pecho m. chest
pedazo m. piece
pedernal m. flint
pedir to ask for; **pedir prestado** to borrow
peinar to comb, to set hair

peine m. comb
película f. film; **película de color f.** color film
peligro m. danger
peligroso dangerous
pelo m. hair
pelota f. (bouncing) ball
peluquería f. barbershop
peluquero m. barber
pendiente m. earring
pensar to think, to intend
pensión completa f. American plan (hotel)
peor worse, worst
pepino m. cucumber
pequeño small, little
pera f. pear
perder to lose, to miss (a train or boat)
¡Perdón! Pardon me!
perdonar to pardon, to excuse
perfumería f. perfume shop
periódico m. newspaper
permiso m. pass, permit
permitir to permit, to allow
perno m. bolt
pero but
perro m. dog
persa Persian
pertenecer to belong
pesado heavy
pesar to weigh
pescado m. fish (when caught)
peso m. weight, monetary unit
pestaña f. eyelash
pez m. fish (in water)
pie m. foot; **a pie** on foot
piel f. skin, fur, leather
pierna f. leg (of body)
pieza f. play (theater)
piezas de respuesto f. spare parts
píldora f. pill
pimienta f. black pepper
pimientos m. pl. peppers
piña f. pineapple
pinacoteca f. art gallery
pinchazo m. puncture
piscina f. swimming pool
piso m. apartment, suite, floor

pista f.   plane runway
pitillera f.   cigarette case
pitillo m.   cigarette
placer m.   pleasure
plancha f.   flat iron
planchar   to iron, to press
planilla f.   form, document
plata f.   silver
plátano m.   plantain, banana
platillo m.   saucer
plato m.   plate, course (meal);
   plato del día m.   today's
   special
playa f.   beach
plaza f.   square (n.); **plaza de
   toros**   bullring
pluma f.   pen; **pluma fuente
   f.**   fountain pen
poblado m.   village
pobre   poor
poco   little; **un poco**   a little;
   poco asado (hecho)   rare
   (steak)
pocos   few, a few
poder   to be able
polvo m.   powder **polvo de
   talco** m.   talcum powder
polvos para la cara m. pl.
   face powder
pollo m.   chicken
poner   to put, to place
ponerse   to put on, to become
por   for (exchange), by; **pagar
   por**   to pay for; **por aquí**
   this way; **por día**   by the day;
   ¿Por dónde?   Which way?
porque   because
¿por qué?   why?
portaequipajes m.   trunk (car)
porte m.   postage
portero m.   doorman, janitor
poseer   to possess, to own
postre m.   dessert
precio m.   price, cost
pregunta f.   question, inquiry
preguntar   to ask, to inquire
preocuparse   to worry; **No se
   preocupe.**   Don't worry.
presentar   to introduce, to
   present

prestar   to lend
primavera f.   spring (season)
primera cura f.   first aid
primero   first
prisa f.   hurry, haste; **darse
   prisa**   to hurry
probarse   to try on
prohibido   prohibited, forbidden
prohibir   to forbid; **se prohibe
   la entrada**   no admittance;
   se prohibe el paso   no
   thoroughfare
prometer   to promise
pronto   quick, quickly, soon
propina f.   tip (gratuity)
provisionalmente   temporarily
próximo   next; **el año
   próximo**   next year
puede ser   perhaps, maybe
puente m.   bridge
puerta f.   door
puerto m.   port, harbor
pulgar m.   thumb
pulsera f.   bracelet; **reloj de
   pulsera**   wristwatch
pulverizar   to spray
puro   pure, cigar

Q

que   that, which, who
qué   what?, how?
quebrado   broken
quedarse   to remain, to stay, to
   be left; **quedarse con**   to
   keep
queja f.   complaint
quejarse   to complain
quemadura f.   burn
quemar   to burn
querer   to wish, to want, to
   desire, to love; **querer decir**
   to mean
queso m.   cheese
quién, quiénes (pl.)   who?,
   which?; **¿quién sabe?**   who
   knows?, perhaps, maybe
quijada f.   jaw
quince   fifteen

quinto   fifth
quitarse   to take off
quitasol m.   parasol
quizá   maybe
quizás   perhaps

R

rábano m.   radish
rabino m.   rabbi
radiografía f.   x-ray
raíz f.   root
raya f.   part (of hair); **hacer la raya**   to part hair
razón f.   reason, right; **tener razón**   to be right; **no tener razón**   to be wrong
real   royal, real
recado m.   message
recalentar   to overheat
receta f.   prescription, recipe
recibir   to receive
recibo m.   receipt
recién pintado   fresh paint, freshly painted
recobrar   to recover, to get back
recomendar   to recommend
reconocer   to recognize
recorder   to remember
recuerdos m. pl.   regards
rechazar   to refuse, to reject
red f.   net, train rack
redecilla f.   hair net
redondo   round
refresco m.   soft drink
regalo m.   gift, present
rehusar   to refuse
reírse   to laugh
rejilla f.   rack (in R.R. coach)
relámpago m.   lightning
reloj m.   watch, clock; **reloj de pulsera m.**   wristwatch
remendar   to mend
remitente m.   sender, shipper (mail)
remolacha f.   beet
remolcar   to tow
repente   sudden; **de repente**   suddenly

repentino   sudden
repetir   to repeat
reponerse   to recover health
requemado   overdone
resfriado   cold (health)
resorte m.   spring (mechanical)
respirar   to breathe
responder   to answer
respuesta f.   answer
resultar   to result, to turn out to be, to prove to be
retrete m.   restroom, washroom, toilet
revelar   to develop (film)
revisor m.   conductor
revista f.   magazine
rico   rich
rieles m. pl.   R.R. tracks
río m.   river
robar   to rob, to steal
rociar   to spray
rodilla f.   knee
rojo   red
rollo m.   roll (of film)
romper   to break
ropa f.   clothes; **ropa blanca f.** linen; **ropa interior f.** underwear
rosado   pink
roto   broken
rueda f.   wheel
ruido m.   noise
ruidoso   noisy
rumano   Romanian
ruso   Russian

S

sábana f.   bedsheet
sábado m.   Saturday
saber   to know a fact, to know how
sabroso   tasty
sacacorchos m.   corkscrew
sacar   to take out, to extract
saco m.   coat
sal f.   salt
sala f.   living room, hall; **sala de equipajes f.**   checkroom,

baggage room; **sala de espera f.** waiting room

salado salty

salchicha f. sausage

salchichón m. salami

sales aromáticas f. pl. smelling salts

salida f. exit

salir to leave, to depart, to go out

salón lounge; **salón de belleza m.** beauty parlor

salsa f. sauce, gravy

salud f. health; **¡A su salud!** To your health!

saludo m. greetings

saludos m. pl. greetings, regards; **muchos saludos** best wishes

salvavidas m. life preserver

sandalia f. sandal

sandía f. watermelon

sangre f. blood

sanidad f. health

santuario m. shrine

sastre m. tailor

sazonado seasoned

se self, himself, herself, itself, themselves

seco dry; **limpieza en seco f.** dry-cleaning

sed f. thirst; **tener sed** to be thirsty

seda f. silk; **papel de seda m.** tissue paper

seguir to follow, continue; **seguir a la derecha (izquierda)** keep right (left)

segundo second

seguro sure, insurance; **seguro de viaje m.** travel insurance

seis six

sellar to seal

sello m. postage stamp, seal

semáforo m. traffic light

semana f. week

sentar to fit; to seat

sentarse to sit down

sentir to be sorry

sentirse to feel (in health)

señor m. Mr., Sir, gentleman

señora f. Mrs., lady, madam

señorita f. Miss, young lady

séptimo seventh

ser to be

servicio m. service

servilleta f. napkin

servir to serve

servirse (+ infinitive) please (do something); **¡Sírvase hablar más despacio!** Please speak more slowly!

servirse to help, serve oneself; **Haga el favor de servirse.** Please help yourself.

sesenta sixty

setenta seventy

sexto sixth

si if

sí yes

siempre always

siete seven

significar to signify, to mean

silla f. chair; **silla de cubierta f.** deck chair

sillón m. armchair

simpático pleasant, likable

sin without

sinagoga f. synagogue

sitio m. place, spot

smoking m. tuxedo

sobre on, upon; **sobre todo** above all, especially

sobrecargo m. purser

sobretodo m. overcoat

sol m. sun

solamente only, solely

solo alone, only, sole: **café solo m.** black coffee

sombra f. shade; **a la sombra** shade

sombrerería f. hat shop

sombrero m. hat

sortija f. ring

sostén m. bra, brassiere

su, sus his, her, its, their, your

suave mild, soft

subir to go up, to climb

suceder to happen

sucio dirty, soiled

sueco Swedish

suela f. sole (shoe)

suelo m. floor, ground, soil

suelto adj. loose; **m.** small change

sueño m. sleep, dream; **tener sueño** to be sleepy

suerte f. luck; **¡Buena suerte!** good luck

suizo Swiss

sujeto a derechos de aduana dutiable

supuesto supposed; **por supuesto** of course, naturally

sur m. south

suyo his, hers, yours, theirs, one's, its

T

taberna f. tavern, saloon

tacones de goma m. pl. rubber heels

talón m. baggage check, heel of foot

tal vez perhaps, maybe

talle m. waist

tamaño m. size

también also, too

tapa f. lift (of shoe)

taquilla f. theater box office, ticket office

tarde late; **la tarde** afternoon; **¡Buenas tardes!** Good afternoon!

tarifa f. fare, rate; **tarifa nocturna f.** night rate; **tarifa por hora f.** hourly rate

tarjeta postal f. postcard

taza f. cup

té m. tea

techo m. roof, ceiling

tela f. cloth

telefonista m., f. telephone operator

temporalmente temporarily

temprano early

tenazas f. pl. pliers

tenedor m. fork

tener to have, to possess; **tener noticias de** to hear from; **tener prisa** to be in a hurry; **tener que** to have to

teñir to tint

tercero third

terciopelo m. velvet

ternera f. veal

tía f. aunt

tiempo m. weather, time

tienda f. store, shop

tierra f. land, earth

tijeras f. pl. scissors

timbre m. bell

tinta f. ink

tintorería f. dry cleaners

tío m. uncle

tirantes m. pl. suspenders

toalla f. towel

tobillo m. ankle

tocar to play an instument

tocino m. bacon

todavía still, yet; **todavía no** not yet

todo all, everything, every, each; **todo el mundo** everybody, everyone

todos everybody, everyone, all

tomacorriente m. electric outlet

tomar to take

tontería f. nonsense

torcedura f. sprain

toro m. bull

toronja f. grapefruit

toros m. pl. bulls, bullfight

torta f. cake

tortilla f. omelet, cornmeal cake

tos f. cough

toser to cough

tostada f. toast

trabajar to work

traducir to translate

traer to bring

traje m. suit (of clothes); **traje de baño m.** bathing suit; **traje de etiqueta m.** evening clothes

transbordar to transfer

transbordo transfer (pass)
tranquilo quiet
tranvía m. trolley, streetcar
trece thirteen
treinta thirty
trepar to climb
tres three, **tres veces** three times
tronar to thunder
trueno m. thunder
tuerca f. nut (mechanical)
turco Turkish
turismo m. tourism

U

un, una a, an, one; **una vez** once
uña f. nail (finger or toe)
uno one, someone, people
usar to use
uso m. use (purpose)
usted (Ud., Vd.) you (sing.)
ustedes (Uds., Vds.) you (pl.)
uvas f. pl. grapes

V

vacío empty
valer to be worth
válido valid, good for
variedades f. pl. vaudeville
varios several
vaso m. drinking glass
¡Váyase! Scram! Go away!
veinte twenty
velocidad máxima f. speed limit
venda f. bandage
vendar to bandage
vender to sell
veneno m. poison
venir to come
venta f. sale
ventana f. window
ventanilla f. train, ticket window; **ventanilla de los certificados f.** registry window

ventilador m. fan
ver to see
verano m. summer
verdad f. truth
verdaderamente really, truly
verdadero true
verde green
verduras f. pl. vegetables
vestido m. dress
vestirse to get dressed
vez f. time (occasion); **una vez** once; **en vez de** instead of, in place of
viajar to travel
viaje m. voyage, trip, journey; **¡Buen viaje!** Bon voyage! Have a pleasant trip!
viajero m. traveler
vida f. life
vidrio m. glass (material)
viejo old
viento m. wind; **Hace (hay) viento.** It's windy.
viernes m. Friday
vino m. wine
vista f. view
vitrina f. showcase
vivir to live
volante m. steering wheel
volver to return, turn
vuelo m. flight
vuelta f. turn

Y

y and
ya already
yo I
yodo m. iodine
yugoslavo Yugoslav

Z

zanahoria f. carrot
zapatería f. shoe shop, store
zapatillas f. pl. slippers
zapato m. shoe
zarpar to sail
zarzuela f. musical comedy
zumo m. juice

INDEX

Other publications from R. Brent and Company

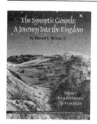
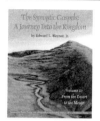

To my family—all of you.

ONE

AIR.

I'm pondering it.

Just random thoughts, like how you're barely aware of it when it's flowing smoothly in and out of your lungs. Or how, if you fall into it, it can't catch you. How it only *seems* weightless. How you can't tie it into knots.

I stole the last one from Buddha, who made me think about air in the first place.

Or I should say Buddhas, because everywhere I look I see his round face. It's on the jewelry, pillows, tapestries, paper umbrellas and paintings in Chiang Mai's crowded night market, where I inch along with my invincible mother. Whenever we accidentally bump someone, we *wai*. That means we put our hands together, fingers pointing up, and bow our heads. Everyone here does it. It's a traditional Thai thing that means "hello," "goodbye," "I'm sorry," "nice to meet you" and probably a lot more.

We are here, in this ancient capital of an ancient empire, to meet our guide. Tomorrow morning he will lead us into the mountains, where we'll trek and live with hill tribes. That means sleeping bags, outhouses and cold showers. Walking uphill for hours. Skidding downhill. Shock-treatment tourism. This trip is for me—to get me out of bed, to get me happy again and, of course, to get me over Amir.

Weird thought. Air is Amir without the *m*.

TWO

I FINALLY WENT TO HIS GRAVE. Mom convinced me to. She wanted me to face my grief. She wanted me to find some closure. And she wanted me to leave my room. Maybe I really wanted to go all along. Maybe I felt I owed her for the pain I'd caused. Or maybe I thought I could knock the very, very heavy thing out of my chest. In any event, I walked the five blocks to the cemetery. I walked slowly. Lying around depressed for a long time can really affect your stamina.

The swinging gates were open, and as I entered them, I had a visceral reaction: sweating palms, pounding heart, swelling lump in my throat. I kept a nervous eye out for Mrs. Ayman, Amir's mother, who, according to Mom, visited his grave every day.

I didn't want to see her. I hadn't seen her since the funeral. I hadn't even gone over to his house to see how they were, and they live just next door. Dad and Mom begged me to, but I couldn't. I'd let him down. Maybe even failed him. And then later, when I wanted to see them, I was too ashamed for not going earlier. I'm sure they hate me by now, and I don't blame them. I hate me too.

It took me forever to find his grave. I wandered endlessly through the rows until I saw his name carved into a shining slab of speckled granite. There was something shocking— air-sucking, in fact—about the headstone, with the stark name and the dates underneath.

Amir Ayman

2000-2016

There were two inscriptions, one in Arabic and one in English:

The heart is the secret inside the secret.

—Rumi

Rumi. The mystical Sufi poet born in thirteenth-century Afghanistan. His full name is Jalāl ad-Dīn Muhammad Rūmī, which I think explains why everyone just calls him Rumi. We studied him in Mr. Singh's class.

I read the inscription out loud. I didn't get it. Why the secret *inside the secret*?

Why did people even write epitaphs? Were they messages for the dead person? Some kind of superstition passed down from the ancient Egyptians? Advice to take to the afterlife? Or were they messages for the devastated people left behind, like me? Something inspirational to ease the pain? If so, this one was a bust.

I didn't cry. I couldn't. I've lost the gift. But the heavy thing inside my chest expanded until I could barely breathe.

My legs buckled, and I sank to my knees in the snow-dappled March grass. I looked like I was praying, but I wasn't. I was railing.

Later, at home, I vowed I would never go back to the place where Amir—beautiful, strong, fast, funny, sweet, warm Amir—lies rotting under a layer of dirt. When I want to remember Amir, I'll lie on the grass and squint at the sun as it glints through the oak trees in my backyard.

Amir loved the sun. He loved all stars. After high school, he wanted to go to the University of Waterloo and study physics and astronomy. He was a geek and a jock, the only hybrid in our grade. He was full of fun facts about football and baseball, especially the Toronto Blue Jays, and the universe, especially stars.

There are ten thousand stars for every grain of sand on earth. Neutron stars are stars that tried to die but couldn't. If you could fold a piece of paper in half fifty times, it would reach the sun. As impossible as this seems, it's true. I've seen the math. We are fifty folds from the sun. Now, every time I fold paper I think about stars. And Amir.

One night last summer we lay on Cherry Beach, looking up at the sky, and Amir asked me if I knew we were made of stars.

"Is this some kind of metaphor?"

"No. It's a hard fact."

"Are there soft facts? Facts you can snuggle with?"

"Are you mocking me? You know English isn't my first language."

"Or are there firm facts? Like pasta? Facts that are *al dente*? Do you know how that translates? 'To the tooth.' So, facts you can bite into. Delicious facts."

He rolled on top of me, not touching, just holding himself up like he was doing a push-up. Then he kissed me. I tasted black licorice. "*Uskut*," he said before he rolled away.

"What?"

"That means shut up."

"That's harsh. Is it less offensive in Arabic?"

"Not really."

"It's a good thing you're a star."

"I'm not a star—I'm *made* of stars. We all are. Every atom in me and every atom in you and every atom in everything on earth, including the earth, is from a star that died."

"So we're all just recycled stars."

"You make it sound a little..." He searched for the word.

"Prosaic?" I asked.

"Huh?"

"The opposite of poetic."

"Exactly."

"Not at all. You know I'm a recycling freak and that no one loves recycling more than I do. The act of recycling," I added, "is a poem."

"What kind of poem?"

He'd called my bluff, and I had to think fast. I am always saying things that I don't really mean, or, at least, I don't know that I mean. He ran his finger down my face, tracing my profile, over my chin, along my neck. He kissed the soft part of my throat, just above my collarbone.

"It's an ode."

He laughed. "To garbage?"

"To the earth. To life."

"I love you, Valentine," he said, nuzzling the skin between my breasts.

That was the first time he ever said it. It's one of those memories that stays sharp, a taste that's always on my tongue—the words, the heat in his skin, the glitter in the sky and the swishing sounds of luminous Lake Ontario against the shore.

THREE

EVEN HERE I can taste that memory. Here in the sprawling Chiang Mai night market, with its canopy of crimson umbrellas and garlands of miniature white lights. I drag my eyes from paper lanterns to golden Buddha statues to hand-painted parasols to shimmering bangles to silk-screen paintings and to cotton sarongs fluttering from hangers. So many colors and shapes, it's like being inside a giant kaleidoscope.

We move with the throng of tourists and the occasional group of monks, bald men in saffron robes. There are other Thais, but they are mostly working behind the booths, selling. All of them seem to be staring at me. Mom says I'm being paranoid until someone actually points. According to *Lonely Planet*, Mom's dog-eared guidebook, pointing is considered extremely rude in Thailand. And Thais hate to be rude. Mom tries to figure out what is so wrong with me that I would force Thais to go against their nature.

"It's your height," she says.

I'm five feet eight—not that tall in Canada.

"Or your hair. It stands out."

I have long dirty-blond hair, the color of wheat. So definitely not Thai-ish.

"Oh no! It's your cleavage. And your shoulders. And your thighs. For God's sake, cover up." She eyes my shorts and tank top and throws her shawl over my shoulders. "We need to dress modestly, remember?"

No. I don't remember anything about that. She could have mentioned it back at the hostel. I swaddle myself in her leopard-print shawl. We stop at a booth displaying silver and jade jewelry. She wants to buy me something and holds up dangling Buddha earrings. Disembodied heads carved from forest-green stone. Instead I choose an elephant pendant in white jade that the merchant—a young woman with an orchid in her hair—fastens around my neck. It feels cool and solid against my skin.

We head to the food market to find our guide. We pause near pails of fresh flowers—orchids, jasmine, lilies. I take a moment to breathe in their sweet perfume. Then we walk past the spice tables, where the combined aroma of nutmeg, cinnamon and cloves reminds me of Christmas. At last we reach the food stalls and inhale the smells of sizzling meat and curry sauces. My mouth starts to water—until we pass by baskets of deep-fried insects.

"Yuck," I say.

Mom wrinkles her nose, then smiles apologetically at the seller.

Our guide is a young guy with a shiny, clean face and shiny, clean hair. He holds a sign with our names— Dana and Valentine Joy—in black felt pen. He wears a golf shirt and shorts that look freshly ironed. I thought he would look more rugged. Disheveled, and maybe a bit dirty. He says to call him Cruise, a nickname he likes for the English-speaking tourists.

"When did you leave Canada?" he asks, offering me a stick of Juicy Fruit gum.

Something about it gives me a homesick pang. Not that I've ever chewed it, but I've seen it in variety stores my whole life. I did not expect to see it here.

"Last night," I say, reaching for the gum. "Or was it two nights ago?"

We left Toronto after dark and stopped in Anchorage to refuel, then changed planes in Hong Kong and Bangkok. We haven't slept or showered. I haven't had a moment to myself in all that time. My head pounds incessantly from being shoved out into the world so suddenly. So rudely.

Mom came up with this crazy trip on, appropriately, April Fools' Day. It had been six months since Amir died and one month since I'd visited his grave.

She sat on my bed, smoothed out my rumpled sheets and laid her hand on my forehead. I was burning up, and her hand was refreshingly cool. Another sleepless night had put my nervous system in a state.

"You've been trying to tie air into knots," she said.

I opened one eye. "Do I know what that means?"

"It means that you've been in search of something, and you've been doing it by hurting yourself. All of it—cutting classes, the drugs, the suici..." Her lips were still moving, but the sound had vanished. A strange effect.

"I didn't try to commit suicide," I said for at least the thousandth time. I was barely a week out of the hospital after an accidental overdose—*accidental* being the keyword. I was just recovering from days of bone-crunching withdrawal, and my voice had no inflection. I didn't even sound convincing to myself, and I *knew* I was telling the truth. Didn't I?

There was a long silence.

"I talked to the school again, and I think it's official," Mom finally said. "You're going to fail eleventh grade." Her voice quivered, but at least she didn't cry. And, of course, neither did I. "If you just write the English exam, they'll give you the credit. Mr. Singh said so himself. He really wants to help."

I'd won the English award for tenth grade, and now I'd be lucky to get a fifty. I thought about how fast everything had fallen away. How meaningless it all was in the first place. If I had known Amir was going to be killed, I would never have studied so hard the previous year. Then I wondered what I would have done instead.

"When Buddha was searching for Nirvana, he did the same thing."

"He failed eleventh grade?"

"Very funny."

Mom recently discovered Buddhism. For the record, it's holy hell living with the newly enlightened.

"He spent six years practicing austerities."

"Which means?"

"Torturing himself, basically," she said.

"How did that work out for him?"

"You don't need to be flippant. He mortified himself by starving. You could see his spine through his stomach. Apparently."

"He seems to have had no trouble gaining the weight back, if the statue in our garden is any indication."

She ignored me. "In the end, he said it was like trying to tie air into knots, and he was no closer to happiness."

"Well, two things. I didn't do anything for six years. It's been more like six months." Six months and nine days, to be precise. I count the days. I don't know why, but I do. "And I think we all agree that I'm not searching for nirvana."

"What are you searching for?"

"Oblivion, I guess." Which actually might be closer to nirvana than I initially realized. And unfortunately it supported the whole suicide theory.

Her nose turned red, and I had only seconds before she cried. I pulled the blanket over my face so I wouldn't see and be reminded of things to cry about, but it didn't help. Amir's face shone there in the dark.

"I wish you wouldn't say things like that." Mom tugged the blanket away from my face. Then she took my hand. We laced our fingers together and stayed like that for a while, quietly holding hands. When I was little, I would jump in her lap, throw my arms around her neck and hug her. That was when I thought she could keep bad things away. That was forever ago.

It was turning into a moment. I had to end it. I was starting to feel things, and that made it hard to hang on. I know it's hard to believe, but you can always go lower.

"April Fools," I said.

"What?"

I nodded at the cat calendar tacked to my wall. It was April first.

"Oh." She stared at the picture of a white kitten peeking out of a paper bag. "I don't get it. Are you tricking me?"

"No. Just avoiding more conversation." I think I fell asleep for a few minutes, but I didn't dream. I need dreams. Without them, I'm never sure I've slept. When I opened my eyes, Mom was tapping her finger on her upper lip, so I knew she was thinking—which scared me a little.

"We're done with the psychiatrist and the group therapy and the whole fucking hospital scene," she said.

I winced. I hate it when she swears. She never used to.

"You're my daughter, and I'm not going to lose you. Do you hear me? *I'm not losing you.* I'm taking you away from here, from this bed and from the school you never go to and from all your memories. We'll go to Thailand, I think. It's full of orchids, elephants and Buddhists. Not to mention mountains to climb."

I stared at her in horror. The only place worse than my bedroom was anywhere else, with the worseness quotient directly related to how far it was from my bed. I couldn't have picked Thailand out on a map, but I knew it was far. Somehow Mom convinced Dad that it was a plan.

FOUR

CRUISE USHERS US to a nearby table and introduces Lish and Pauline, another daughter-mother team, just arrived from England. Lish, the daughter, has a partially shaved head, black eyeliner and multiple eyebrow piercings. She barely looks up from her phone to give me a snarky finger wave.

Her mom, Pauline, lifts her big black sunglasses up to her forehead and holds out a manicured hand with long red nails.

"How old are you, love?"

"Sixteen," I say, sliding my palm into hers. She smiles. "Brilliant! See, Lish? Someone your age."

"She's not my age."

Lish, as it turns out, is fourteen.

"What kind of name is *Valentine*?" she asks.

Mom glares at Lish. Pauline jumps in with a big fake smile and a nervous laugh. "Valentine Joy. That *is* an unusual name. And so pretty. What do people call you?"

"Valentine."

No one calls me Tina or Val or Valli or anything else you can think of. Well, that's not quite true. Mr. Singh, my favorite teacher, used to call me Miss Joy to the World. That was before Amir died. I'm not sure I was ever a joy, and I'm 100 percent sure I'm not one now.

Cruise offers to bring us the Chiang Mai specialty, *khao soi*—flat noodles in curry broth with crispy noodles on top. Mom has the vegetarian option, while I have beef with a side of pickled cabbage and curry paste. It's delicious, and I realize I was starving.

The dinner is awkward. Pauline talks too much, while Mom interjects occasionally. Lish and I concentrate on our food. Cruise mentions an "Australian contingent"—two guys who will be joining our trek.

"Are they brothers?" asks Pauline.

"I don't think so," says Cruise. "They are last-minute add-ons. Why?"

"Because this was advertised as a family trek."

"Well, a family-friendly trek anyway."

Cruise says we'll meet them tomorrow morning. He will pick us up at dawn, and we'll all drive to base camp together. We say goodbye and leave.

"It'll all be great, don't you think?" Mom asks a little desperately as we leave the food court.

I look at her hard for at least ten seconds and bump into a group of monks. I *wai* to say I'm sorry and start to move on. One bars my way, wags his finger in my face and scolds

me in Thai. All of them look angry. I look to Mom for help.
I figure that as a Buddhist she might know what's going on.
She shrugs helplessly and tries to pull me out of their way.

Cruise pushes through the crowd and speaks with them.
He is soft-spoken and respectful. After a lot of *wai*-ing and
backing up, he leads us away.

"What was that about?" I ask.

"You bumped into them, and they are very holy."
Cruise looks embarrassed. "They can't touch a woman."

"Can't touch a woman?"

"No."

"Why not?"

"Because monks are pure." He looks down. "And women
are not."

Mom blanches. Obviously, the Toronto monks aren't such
misogynists.

"Are you serious?" I ask. Hot anger spreads under my
skin. I turn around. The monks are still scowling at me. I *wai*
and smile sarcastically. This time the *wai* means "fuck you."
It really is very versatile.

FIVE

WE BEAT IT OUT OF THERE, leaving the night market and the angry monks behind us.

"Don't be upset," Mom says, putting an arm around me.

"I can't help it. They can't touch a woman! How medieval is that? I don't understand why you're so chill."

"Because I'm trying to be a good Buddhist and follow the tenet of loving-kindness."

"Seriously? That's a tenet? Somebody should tell the monks."

"Never mind them."

"Did you know this was part of Buddhist philosophy? That women are corrupt?"

"It's not, I don't think. Monks struggle to live celibate lives. They don't touch women, because they don't want to be tempted. Not because women are corrupt! Come on. Don't let them spoil our walk. Look how beautiful this city is."

I look around. It is exquisite, with ancient temples, pointed spires and gleaming gold statues. Trees arch over wide boulevards. Purplish mountains silhouette the horizon. Flowers cascade from planters. It's like a fairy-tale city.

"All people are flawed," she adds.

"Some more than others," I grumble.

"Please let it go." Mom's so hopeful that we're going to have a good time. A healing time.

We walk the rest of the way in silence, leaving the old section of the city. The new section isn't nearly as pretty. Or as interesting. We're staying at a hostel instead of a hotel because we need to save money. Truth be told, my parents can't afford this trip, and they'll be paying it off for quite a while. The hostel is a scuzzy place with a hissing neon sign, long dark hallways and bad interior lighting. We get our sleeping bags out of our lockers and lay them over two of the hard cots that line the cavernous room. Most of the cots are empty, because it's not curfew yet.

While Mom showers, I zip myself into my sleeping bag and close my eyes. I'm so homesick, I feel nauseated. I miss Toronto, which is kind of mind-boggling. I never thought I'd miss the city where Neil Carter punched Amir so hard he killed him.

But I miss my home, even though my neighborhood holds so many memories that it feels haunted. I miss the delicate blues and creams of my bedroom. The draping branches of our weeping willow. The futuristic new streetcars that clang down our street. The Italian café next door to the sushi bar next door to the Ethiopian restaurant just around the corner. I miss Dad and his piles of half-marked essays. I miss our lovebirds, Honey and Mooner. And I miss Becca, my best friend, so much I can hardly stand it. Even though I haven't seen her much this year. My fault, not hers.

"What are you thinking about?" Mom asks. She stands over my cot, wrapped in a towel, her hair wet.

"Becca. Dad. The Honeymooners."

"Are you homesick?" She sounds happy. Like the trip has already worked and made me appreciate what I have.

"Only terminally," I say.

"That's not funny, Valentine."

"What's not funny?"

"Joking about dying."

"What? I wasn't joking about dying! I was exaggerating, for God's sake. A rhetorical device called hyperbole, if you're interested."

Mom and Dad are so convinced my overdose was on purpose, so sensitive, so outraged and so hurt, that they get completely irrational whenever they're reminded of it. And almost *everything* reminds them of it. Instead of denying it again or trying to make Mom feel better, I dig my fingernails into both of my palms until I leave deep, purple half moons in the flesh. My temples start to throb, but I don't dare rub them for fear of freaking her right out.

The overdose started with a headache.

The headache started when Becca knocked on my bedroom door. I was in bed, and the door was locked. I hadn't seen her in a month, though she had been texting and calling and messaging me almost every day. I wasn't trying to be mean. I just couldn't bear any kind of human contact. I'd tried for months after Amir died, but at a certain point I gave up. First I quit leaving the house. Then I quit leaving my bedroom. It was the only place I didn't feel raw, like my skin was being scraped with a cheese grater.

I hoped she would go away, not because I didn't love her but because I did, and that made me vulnerable. The lock clicked, and I panicked a bit. She was coming in. My lock could be opened with a small coin, but up to that day, Mom, Dad and Becca had been respecting the concept of a locked door.

She peeked into my room. A dull ache banded my head.

"Hey," she said. She looked nervous. Like she might cry. "You aren't answering your phone."

"That's because I don't want to talk to anyone. Plus it's dead, and I can't find my charger." A metaphor if ever there was one.

"I'm sorry for intruding," she said, sounding really offended. "But I need to talk to you. I miss you." Her voice cracked. I looked at her faded jeans and turquoise sweater. I pondered the colors so I didn't have to feel anything. Blue and turquoise. Egyptian colors. Amir was from Cairo. "I miss you.

And I worry about you. And I get angry—so angry you wouldn't believe it."

"I'm sorry," I whispered.

"I came to tell you about Amir's parents, who, I believe, have at least as much reason to grieve as you do." Her neck and cheeks flared crimson. "Or did you already hear?" she asked.

I didn't answer. I hadn't heard anything and didn't want to. I averted my eyes but managed to resist putting my fingers in my ears.

"They went to school yesterday to meet with the principal. They're sponsoring an annual Fair Play award." Her voice was hard and high and brittle. I thought of glass shattering. I pictured it shattering all over me. "In the name of forgiveness and moving forward."

What can you even say about people who have such big and open hearts? When Amir died, mine shrunk. Now it's as hard and small as a golf ball. It's not like I don't know the difference. I just can't change it. And for the record, a small, hard heart is as heavy as a freaking bowling ball. It's one of those inverse rules of physics—the smaller the heart, the greater the weight.

I turned away from Becca and stared at the ceiling. She climbed into my bed, skooched under the duvet and nestled next to me. We stared at the ceiling together. Blossoming cherry branches painted against a cerulean background. She designed it, and Amir and I painted it with her. She had come up with the idea one day when it was raining and we were stuck inside.

She reached for my hand. "I'm sorry. But I warned you I was angry."

"I don't blame you. I really don't. I'm angry too."

"Are you? You just seem apathetic."

"My therapist says I'm holding my anger in."

"What do you say?"

I shrugged, a tight painful movement.

She sighed, pulled her hair out of its clip and let it fan over the pillow. I reached over and stretched out one of her curly strands. Her hair was as long as mine, which seemed impossible. I let it go, and it sprang up to her shoulder.

I love the dark red of her hair. It's a natural red, not burgundy or cherry. Becca is an artist, but she doesn't seem like one. She's never dyed her hair, tattooed herself or, God forbid, pierced her tongue. She's against all self-mutilation. She thinks ear piercing is barbaric and nearly cried when I did my belly button. Her petite size belies her towering personality. She's only five feet tall and a hundred pounds. When we were younger, people thought I was her babysitter.

I concentrated on the ceiling. The low-hanging sky. I didn't want to remember old times. Or ponder new ones.

"What are you thinking about?" she asked after several minutes.

"'Renascence,'" I answered.

"Renascence" is my favorite poem, written by Edna St. Vincent Millay, a poetic prodigy, when she was nineteen. The poem is about a girl who is in so much despair that she craves death. She lies staring up at the sky, so heavy with the world's pain that the earth gives way. She sinks, inch by inch, until she is six feet under, and her torment eases. Later, though, she frantically wants to live again.

I fell in love with the poem before anything bad had happened in my life. Now I realize it was foreshadowing, something I used to associate only with stories, not real life. I loved it so much, I built my tenth-grade English independent-study unit around it.

I memorized all 214 lines, then recited them to the class. I kept a thirty-day "explore and experience" journal, which just means I jotted down my feelings and thoughts, no matter how random. Finally, I made a five-by-three-foot collage. Becca and Amir helped me carry it to school, and it still hangs in the hallway by the English office. Or it did the last time I was there.

Becca laid her head on my shoulder. "Why?" she asked.

I pointed at the ceiling. "The sky is just above my head."

"So?"

I recited:

The world stands out on either side
No wider than the heart is wide;
Above the world is stretched the sky—
No higher than the soul is high.

I looked into her eyes. "You see the problem?"

She wrinkled her forehead. "You think your soul is flat?"

I nodded. "Well, flattening. Down to six feet or so." Small, hard heart, shrinking soul. It seemed like a crisis.

She wound herself around me, and it felt so comforting that I closed my eyes. Before I knew it, I had fallen asleep. When I started awake from a falling dream, she was gone. I heard once that if you hit the ground in a falling dream, you die. But how, I always wonder, could anyone *know* that?

There was a note on my pillow: *LOVE*. I wasn't exactly sure what she meant, but it made me sad. Like love was an answer to something. And it's not. Love doesn't do anything. All the people that loved Amir couldn't stop him from being killed. And loving him just made his death unbearable. I crumpled up the note and threw it against the wall.

And that's when the dull ache tightened, like an elastic band around my head.

SIX

IT TIGHTENED SO QUICKLY, I got Tylenol from the bathroom. My door creaked on the way back, and Mom bounded halfway up the stairs.

"Valentine! You're up!" She smiled brightly.

"Just went to the washroom."

"I'm making a stir-fry. Talk to me while I set the table."

"I'm not feeling well. Maybe you can just bring it upstairs?" I said, trying to look appreciative.

Her smile dimmed a few watts. "No. You will have to come down. And get dressed."

That was the game we'd been playing. As long as I read a book a week, showered daily and put on some clothes and went downstairs for dinner, the therapist I'd been seeing since Amir died wouldn't send me to CAMH, our local psychiatric hospital. Lately my parents talked about taking me there anyway. Mostly they argued. One day Dad was the one who wanted to take me, but Mom still had faith in the therapist, faith in the future. The next day it was the opposite. Then they'd flip again.

"Okay." I sighed. "Call me when it's ready."

"How was Becca? It was so good to see her!"

"Fine." I wanted to say more, because Mom wanted me to so badly, but I couldn't. "Really fine," I repeated.

I took two extra-strength Tylenols and went back to bed. Half an hour later the ache turned into throbbing. I found a tensor bandage and wrapped my head, covering my eyes. I fastened it as tightly as I could. That felt good for about three minutes, and then it felt awful, and I pulled it off. I smoothed my fingers over my temples but couldn't tell if that felt good or bad. The afternoon light was intense, so I pulled my curtains shut and safety-pinned them together. I took three Trazodones, my antidepressant, even though I'm only supposed to take two before I go to sleep. But they relax me, and I thought they might help my head.

Dad called me down for dinner. When I didn't respond— because I couldn't yell without hurting my head—Mom came up, ready to give me shit. She looked around my dark room, checked herself and sat on the bed. She tried to massage my neck and shoulders, but I couldn't bear to be touched. She brought me a damp washcloth and two Ibuprofens. She didn't ask if I'd taken anything. I didn't tell her I'd already taken some Tylenol, but I knew you could mix Ibuprofen and Tylenol, so I didn't worry.

"I'll make you some soup," she whispered. "And I'll leave the door ajar so I can hear if you call."

That meant I could hear noises from downstairs. Doors opening and closing. Phones ringing. Voices. A timer going off. The TV. And everything was loud—so nerve-shreddingly loud, I was amazed I'd managed to live in such a noisy house for as long as I had. I wrapped the tensor bandage around my head again—under my chin and over the top of my head this time, so it covered my ears. I couldn't sleep, but I half napped— that unrestful state where you don't *think* about worrisome things, you just dream about them.

I opened my eyes to Mom delivering a bowl of vegetable quinoa soup. I didn't want to eat, but she insisted, sitting on the bed and making the mattress move like a choppy lake in a storm. At first the soup tasted good, but my stomach revolted, and I threw up. I missed the bedsheets but hit her, spewing undigested soup all over her Lululemons. She left to clean herself up, then came back with a cup of sweet black tea. She knelt beside my bed.

"You must have the flu," she said. The sound of her breathing rattled my brain. I begged her to leave. She did, but first she brought me a bell to ring if I needed her. It tinkled as she set it down, reverberating in my ears.

Just before she left, I asked for some ice. My head felt hot, even though I was shivering. She brought me an icepack and a heating pad. I tried ice. Then heat. Then ice. Then heat. I held pillows against my ears and tried to sleep. I desperately wanted to sleep. *Desperately.*

That's when I remembered that Mom sometimes took sleeping pills.

I snuck out of my room, holding on to the walls because the floor was tilting, and searched Mom's bathroom cabinet. I found the pills and tried to shake two into my hand. Several spilled out, and funneling them back into the small bottle seemed too challenging. I decided I'd do it when I felt better. I went back to bed, took one and dropped the rest on my night table. They scattered behind a pile of books topped by (most unfortunately, given what happened next) *The Bell Jar* —reading for eleventh-grade English, so not my choice. Anne Michaels's *All We Saw*—a poetry collection that was my book of the week—had slipped onto the floor.

Then, since it seemed like a long time had passed, I took two more Tylenols.

Both my parents came in to say good night. Did I want ginger ale? A popsicle? Did I want one of them to sit beside me until I fell asleep? No. No. No. I said I was feeling better. I wasn't, but I needed to be left alone. I just wanted to go to sleep and escape the blinding pain in my head. I was sure I would. After all, I had taken a sleeping pill. I asked them to close the door on their way out.

I waited at least half an hour, maybe an hour, before I took another sleeping pill. That didn't work either, so I took another. After all, two was the prescribed dose, so I wasn't much over that. I tried to be still, to pretend I was sleeping and fool my body into actually doing it. It didn't work. I started to burn up. I needed another ice pack but didn't want to ring the bell and couldn't call out. I also didn't think I could get out of bed, because I felt so dizzy.

I lay there for what seemed like a long time. I might have fallen asleep for a few moments, because I had a sensation, almost like a dream, that I was an ant on a leaf in a rushing river. I waited another long time, as long as I could—it felt like hours—before I decided to take another sleeping pill. I rationalized it like this: if they weren't even putting me to sleep, they couldn't possibly kill me.

Within minutes I felt sick. And really dizzy. I also had to pee. It was all the water I was drinking with the pills, I guessed. Going to the washroom was a total ordeal. I crawled on my hands and knees down the hall. On the way back I tried to walk, using the wall for support. I fell against my parents' bedroom door, waking them both. Mom called my name. I stumbled through the door, then collapsed onto the bed.

"What's going on?" Mom asked.

"My...headache's...worse." I spoke slowly, enunciating carefully. She moved toward me, then away, then toward me, then away. I had to close my eyes.

"Why can't you stand up?" Dad asked, rubbing his eyes.

"Too...many...pizz. *Pills.*" I kept my words to a minimum because it took such an effort to form them.

"What kind of pills?" Dad sounded angry. I tried to look at him, to see if he *looked* angry too, but I couldn't see past his three noses. And they wouldn't be still, each crisscrossing the others.

"Trazodones, painkillers and some sleeping pills." Actually, that's what I tried to say, but something was happening with my tongue, so it sounded more like "trassdonsom paintkeepers an leaping pills."

"Jesus Christ!" Dad yelled and skyrocketed out of bed.

Mom fumbled with her phone and sent it skittering across the floor. She snatched it up but could hardly dial, she was shaking so bad. She was also very quiet, which isn't like her. It scared me. When she got through to someone, she was unnaturally calm.

"My sixteen-year-old daughter has overdosed."

She gave our address and put the phone on *speaker*. They asked her a lot of questions. What drugs? How many? When? Was I conscious? They told her to hold up her hand and ask me how many fingers I saw.

"Three, I think. Or four," I guessed. "Two?" I couldn't see clearly at all. Dad was hugging me, his arms so tight around me I couldn't breathe. Or I think that's why. My breaths were coming slowly, and they were shallow. I could hear myself wheezing. Mom ran into the bathroom and came back with her bottle of sleeping pills.

"I think she's taken a lot. I don't know though. I don't know." Her voice was shrill. Sharp. Brain-slicing.

"No...No." It was hard to form the words. "I did'n take'em'll. They're bym'bed. B'hind mybooks."

Mom ran into my room. She came back screaming. "There aren't any pills by your bed."

Was that possible? Had they fallen under the bed, or had I taken them all? I couldn't remember. And that's when I got scared. Pretty soon Mom was sobbing, and so was Dad. They held on to me like they thought I was going somewhere far away.

SEVEN

THAT'S HOW THE paramedics found us.

I ended up in an ambulance with Mom, while Dad drove madly behind. One paramedic asked me questions about a bunch of different things—what grade I was in, what my favorite subject was, what I'd had for dinner. He sat really close and stared at me as I answered. He made me answer questions all the way to hospital.

At the hospital they had more questions. I tried to answer but had trouble making sounds. My tongue was too big for my mouth. My head was floppy. My eyes kept closing. Finally I could sleep, but no one would let me. I was quickly wheeled somewhere else.

"How many Trazodones?" another nurse asked.

I knew the answer to that and held up my fingers, but I couldn't tell how many were up. I peered at my hand. By now Dad was there, and he had brought the pill bottles. He was trying to figure out how many Trazodones there should be compared to how many there were. Mom was trying to figure out how many sleeping pills I'd taken. I still couldn't believe I'd taken them all. I told them I was sure they were on or behind *The Bell Jar*.

"Isn't that the book by the poet who committed suicide?" asked the nurse. "Sylvia Plath?"

Mom started to cry. Loud, belching sobs.

I tried to squeeze in a nap, but a nurse shook me awake. Could I stand up? I tried and almost toppled forward. No, I couldn't. More people came. They took my blood pressure. They put a clip on my finger. They asked me if I had tried to kill myself.

I shook my head.

Dad told them about Amir and said I had a therapist at SickKids Hospital.

A doctor ordered several tests.

"What for?" I tried to ask. He understood my slurs.

"Organ damage," he said. That sounded ominous. I began to think I might have really hurt myself, but it was hard to get anything through my fuzzy—and still aching—head. I looked around. The doctor was stern. The nurses seemed angry. Mom's face was the whitest I'd ever seen on anyone, and Dad's eyes were so red it was like they were bleeding.

Suddenly I realized that if I died, I'd be leaving them all alone, drowning in unbearable and never-ending grief.

Then I passed out.

I woke up on a stretcher with an IV stuck in my hand. Mom held my other hand. Dad paced the room. A doctor told me I was a very lucky girl. He said it at least twice.

"I'm sorry," I told Mom and Dad. Then I closed my eyes again.

I woke to a woman shaking my arm.

"But I only just fell asleep," I mumbled.

"No," said Mom, rumpled and bleary-eyed, rising from a cot. "You've slept for eight hours."

The woman turned to Mom. "I'm Dr. Bennet, a psychiatrist, and I'd like to talk to Valentine."

Mom nodded but made no move to leave. She just sidestepped to the end of the bed and held my foot.

"If you don't mind, I'd like to talk to her alone," the doctor said.

Mom looked like she was going to stand her ground, but finally she swiveled and left.

Dr. Bennet leaned in really close. I turned away. My mouth was unbearably dry, and even I could smell my bad breath.

I still felt stoned and also like I was going through withdrawal. At least, I was pretty sure I was going through withdrawal. My headache was worse, my bones ached, my joints throbbed.

"Could I get a painkiller?" I asked Dr. Bennet. She had pale hazel eyes, so pale they were almost colorless.

"No." She didn't say it nicely.

She asked how I was feeling and what I'd been going through. I kept slipping away, but each time, I brought myself back with effort, staring with extra intensity into her pond-water eyes. I tried to look alert and answer her, except when she asked about Amir. She seemed to know a lot about him. She wanted to talk about the day he died and whether I felt guilty. "Not that you had anything to feel guilty about," she added. "But it would explain why you can't move on."

Like that needed explaining.

That was when something happened to my words. I would try to say one word, but another word would come out. And I kept saying "Moroccan" for no reason that I could figure out. I was 100 percent aware of how confused I sounded, a paradox that seemed cruel.

"Did you try to kill yourself?" Dr. Bennet asked more than once.

"I did *not* try to kill Moroccan." I waved my hands at the error. "I mean Moroccan. I mean *myself*. I really didn't," I said. And I really hadn't, but even I wasn't buying it anymore. You can only deny something so many times without it seeming like, well, denial.

Dr. Bennet left and conferred with Mom outside my door.

"You have aphasia," Mom said when she came in. "Word confusion. Dr. Bennet says it's probably temporary, so you don't need to worry."

I didn't mention that *she* looked worried—terrified, in fact. I was too afraid to talk. Afraid I'd say *Moroccan* again.

Dad joined Mom, and they sat on either side of my bed. Time went by excruciatingly slowly, except when I passed out, and then it went by blissfully fast. I lost another day in one blink.

I woke up again and my parents were still there, faces suspended like full moons over my bed. Becca was there too, holding my hand and crying.

"I'm sorry," she said. "I shouldn't have been so angry. I shouldn't have told you about the Aymans."

"I'm sorry too," I said. "But it wasn't your fault. And I didn't try to kill myself. I just had a headache."

And for the record, my headache was now one hundred times worse than it had been when I started taking the pills. I asked several nurses for painkillers, and they either ignored or glared at me.

I was discharged from the hospital before I was steady on my feet.

The next day Dad and Mom had an appointment for me to see our GP, Dr. Pierre, whom we call Manon. I walked shakily into her examining room and again said I hadn't tried to kill myself. I had only wanted to get rid of a headache and go to sleep. A social worker with maroon hair and feather earrings asked questions and took notes. She was very sympathetic and easy to talk to.

After we talked for a few minutes, and with my permission, my parents were invited in. Mom cried so hard, I put my hands over my ears. Dad looked sad and kept wiping his eyes. We talked about Amir. We talked about me. We talked about the future, and I thought about Rilke, the nineteenth-century German poet who said that sadness gets in our blood—

a chilling thought, if you ponder it. He is famous for his mysticism, but he also wrote about the future.

> *The future: time's excuse to make us*
> *fearful; a thought too vast, a morsel*
> *too large for the heart's mouth.*

We'd read his poem on the first day of eleventh grade, and Mr. Singh asked us what we thought it meant. I didn't know, but I liked the last line. I liked the metaphor—that the heart has a mouth and can taste, speak, even sing. We wanted Mr. Singh to explain it, but he said we should think about it.

"For how long?" someone asked.

"As long as it takes," he answered.

"Does that mean you don't know either?" Amir asked.

Mr. Singh only laughed.

But that day in Manon's office, I finally understood the poem. The future isn't a thing to toast on New Year's Eve. It's a frightening place where we lose all of the things we love, either because they disappear or because we do. I didn't say any of this, of course. I didn't want to add any more gloom to the visit. I just nodded vigorously when Manon said the future is an opportunity to heal the past. Everyone agreed, but no one really knew how to make that happen.

EIGHT

MY PARENTS WERE TRAUMATIZED by the overdose. Which is why I am here, now, in Chiang Mai, on a cot with a stranger snoring next to me. Mom has shoved her luminescent watch in my face. It's five thirty in the morning. She kisses me on the forehead and tells me to hurry up. I don't think I've ever been up this early. It feels horrible at first, but I head for the communal showers, where the steaming water soothes me. A naked Swedish woman asks where I'm from and where I'm going.

"You are very young and doing such interesting things," she says in a singsong lilt. "What a lucky girl you are."

Yes, I'm a lucky girl. Everyone seems to agree on that.

We rush through breakfast, slurping hot noodles and gulping tea. Before I know it, we're outside, waiting for Cruise. We're the only people on the sidewalk. Everyone else is on the road, on scooters, bicycles or in the occasional car. The weather forecast is grim. Dark clouds mound threateningly overhead.

I think wistfully of my blue-sky bedroom. Thunder rumbles, sheet lightning brightens the whole street, and the skies open up. It pours. We stand under the hostel's yellow-and-white-striped awning as the rain drums relentlessly on the canvas.

Mom says that spring in Thailand can be wet, something she could have mentioned before. She knows how much I hate rain. She sees my face and says not to worry, that she has rain gear for both of us.

"And the monsoons don't come until summer," she adds.

"Yay," I say dryly.

A van pulls up. Cruise hops out of the passenger seat to greet us, and the driver throws our backpacks in the rear. We crawl in. The two Australians take up the whole of the back seat. Max and Brendan look like hard-core trekkers, with face stubble, wrinkled T-shirts and worn-out boots. In other words, they're way too cool to trek with us. It turns out they've trekked through Africa and are now making their way through Asia. Yes, they trekked *through Africa*— the whole continent, from bottom to top.

"It's how we avoid real life," Max jokes.

"We're committed to that," Brendan adds.

Mom laughs. It's a sound I haven't heard for a very long time. I realize, with a pang, how much I've missed it.

Max has short black hair that sticks up in all directions, and Brendan has a shaved head. They're in their twenties and look like they could wrestle crocodiles. They're related— cousins, they say. They got into Chiang Mai yesterday and booked this trek because it was available. Also, because it goes off the beaten path.

"My company prides itself on that," Cruise says. "It promises that you will never run into another group. Except at base camp, obviously."

Next, we pick up Lish and Pauline from their hotel. They don't look like they're going trekking. Both wear makeup —Lish, eyeliner, and Pauline, bright red lipstick. Lish is in army fatigues, at least. Pauline is in tight stretch jeans with rhinestone-studded cuffs.

"Well," says Pauline, batting her eyelash extensions at Max and Brendan. "You boys look like you should start your own adventure reality series."

Lish looks out the window, either embarrassed by her mother's flirting or just determined not to be friendly. Max and Brendan, totally friendly, laugh with Pauline. They even try to get Lish talking.

"How'd you get sprung from school?" Brendan asks.

"You have to take the opportunities when they come," Pauline says, jumping in to cover Lish's silence. "Traveling is the best education."

When they ask me what grade I'm in, I'm not sure how to answer. I look sideways at Mom. She says I'm in eleventh grade, and I flush, even though it's technically true. She doesn't explain how I got out of school. Now that I think about it, Pauline didn't explain how Lish got out either.

Cruise says we're driving to a base camp near the Thai–Myanmar border. It'll take around five hours. That's a long time in close quarters with total strangers. Lish, who doesn't care if she's rude, puts earbuds in and turns up her music so loud the muted beat thrums through the van.

Brendan teases Cruise about his clean-cut plaid shorts and ironed golf shirt. "Are you sure you've ever been in a jungle?"

Cruise smiles enigmatically and slips on his aviator glasses.

Mom and Pauline turn the conversation back to Africa, plying Max and Brendan with questions. I tune out, laying my head against the van window, my hoodie scrunched into a pillow. Once we are in the foothills, the rain slows to a drizzle, then stops. The sky clears to a brilliant blue. Cruise refers to the landscape alternately as jungle or rainforest, but the rolling hills with lush growth look like regular forest to me. I crack open my window, and the van fills with fresh-earth smell.

NINE

"BASE CAMP," Cruise finally announces, as the driver pulls into a makeshift parking lot on a big patch of flattened grass.

We climb out of the van, and Max smooshes us together for a group selfie. "The adventure begins," he says. He seems truly happy about it.

I'm not sure what I expected, or if I expected anything, but base camp is like the schoolyard before the bell rings—except it's on a grassy hill dotted with wildflowers. Dozens of young hill-tribe guys mill about, smoking and grinning. Trekkers huddle in small groups. Some grungy-looking guys look like they're buying or selling drugs. I note several sketchy transactions. Not surprisingly, Lish is involved in a couple of them, but I think I'm the only one who notices.

There are also vendors—girls and old women selling purses, fabric, fruit, and flower necklaces. Pauline goes on a buying spree, darting from vendor to vendor and holding up her purchases for us to see—a cloth shoulder bag with a puffed-out quilted elephant, oranges, a flower bracelet and a crocheted water-bottle holder that hangs around her neck.

Cruise wanders through the crowd, murmuring surreptitiously to different hill-tribe guys. He looks like he's trying to recruit spies. He finally returns and introduces us to Myo and Myint, who will be our porters. They are from the same village and work as a team. They'll lug our heavier stuff, while we'll carry only small knapsacks with the basics: water, rain gear, bug repellant, sunscreen, toilet paper and hand sanitizer. I add my camping flashlight–knife combo in case I have to crawl through a cave or something. Max and Brandon refuse to let anyone carry their things, but Mom, Pauline, Lish and I hand over our heavy backpacks. Myo and Myint load up with them, even though they are only boys and are wearing flip-flops. By the time they're finished, they are just packages with skinny legs.

We look at each other nervously.

"How old are they?" Pauline asks. "They look so young."

"No labor laws here," Cruise says.

"Let's carry our own sleeping bags," Mom says.

"Don't insult them," Cruise says. He tells them what we've said, and they burst out laughing.

"Are they going to hike in flip-flops?" I ask.

Cruise adjusts his sunglasses and folds a fresh stick of gum into his mouth. "No problem. They do this all the time."

He clears his throat and stands at attention, like he's giving a school presentation. "The hill people we will visit this week have come from all over—China, Vietnam, Laos,

Tibet, Myanmar. Many fled persecution and violence in their own countries and came here for safety."

Brendan and Max exchange a look. Max shakes his head warningly and mutters under his breath, "Don't go there."

Cruise, who appears not to hear, continues his spiel. "The people we will visit tonight—the Karen—are all from southern and southeastern Myanmar. Or Burma, as some still call it."

"That's what I call it," Pauline murmurs. "I hate it when countries change their names."

"The Karen people lived in"—Cruise nods to Pauline—"*Burma* for centuries but originally came from the Gobi Desert. They began fighting for independence, for their own state, just after World War II. The Burmese military has been fighting against them ever since. It is the longest civil war in the world."

"Civil war? You mean a slow, bloody genocide," Brendan says. "Like what's happening with the Rohingya now."

"Rohingya?" asks Mom.

"An ethnic group in Burma," Brendan explains. "They're mostly Muslim, but some are Hindu. The Burmese government doesn't give them any rights, even though they've lived there for over a thousand years. The UN says they are one of the most persecuted minorities in the world."

"Seriously?" Pauline asks. "They're being killed right now?"

Cruise raises his voice. "Back to the Karen. Hundreds of thousands of Karen have died in the conflict, and many were civilians. But one million have escaped to Thailand, where they live in safety and prosperity."

"Maybe not prosperity," Brendan says quietly.

Cruise, annoyed, moves on to our itinerary for the first two days. "Today we'll hike to the village of a Karen hill tribe. Tomorrow we'll hike to a waterfall, where we'll meet our elephants and their *mahouts*. We will ride the elephants up steep hills to a Kayan village—the Kayans are a subgroup of the Karen."

We get ready to trek. Tighten our laces, spray sunscreen and bug repellant, slip on shades and hats. Finally, we check our water. I can't believe I'm going to be doing this for a week.

Lish sidles up to me, stinking of weed. "Elephants. What a joke that is."

"Why?"

She snorts. "It's like a bleeding pony ride at a birthday party. They don't go fast. You can't steer them. You wobble around on top of this chair thing."

I spend several futile moments trying to imagine Lish as the kind of person who ever rode a pony or got invited to a birthday party.

"There was an elephant who murdered her keeper in Florida," I finally say, because the fact just pops into my mind.

"*Murdered*?"

"Yes. It was murder. She planned it. I read about it."

"Seriously?" she asks. "An elephant planned a murder?"

"Yes. So this ride might be more exciting than you think."

Cruise starts walking. I expected a more official beginning, like a gun going off or a flag wave. I go to the end of the line so nobody will notice me stumbling along. Mom gets right behind me, prepared to push me along or catch me if I fall. Even though this trek is designated mild to moderate, and even though I've been hitting the treadmill, I am not fit.

Right, left, right, left. One step at a time under the lemon-yellow sun. I think of the Pablo Neruda poem Mr. Singh gave me four months after Amir died. Neruda is Mr. Singh's favorite poet, a Chilean Marxist who fought for poor people and was murdered by his own fascist government. The poem is about grieving, accepting death—and, appropriately, walking.

If you, beloved, my love,
if you
have died,
all the leaves will fall in my breast,
it will rain on my soul night and day,
the snow will burn my heart,
I shall walk with frost and fire and death and snow,
my feet will want to march to where you are sleeping, but
I shall go on living.

I was confused at first. The poem basically crackles with despair. Falling leaves and rain. Frost, fire, death and snow. There was nothing to console me. But Mr. Singh promised that one day I would see how life-affirming it is. That I would understand it in a profound way. That I would have the "courage and the desire to walk toward life," he said. And that I wouldn't view that as a betrayal of Amir.

Then, because things were getting a little heavy, he joked, "And maybe one day you can walk toward my classroom again. You've missed more classes than you've attended this year."

TEN

WE CROSS ROLLING HILLS, striped gold and green with wild grasses, until the path winds around the edge of a mountain that has been carved into steps.

"Terraced farms," Cruise explains as we stop for a water break and stare at the stunning green staircase sweeping down the entire mountainside. "We do not have a lot of space in Thailand, and though you cannot plant crops on sloping land, you can cut terraces into it, which makes farming possible."

We studied terraced farming in geography, but I never realized how magnificent it would look. Max snaps pictures with his phone until Cruise urges us forward.

After an hour or so, we find ourselves trudging through flat land. A farmer just meters away from us sets fire to his field with a large flaming torch. The acrid smoke gets into my eyes, nose and mouth.

"Slash and burn farming," yells Cruise from ahead. "Don't worry. They do this all the time. It fertilizes the land."

"*Jesus*," says Mom, something she says a lot considering she's a Buddhist. I wonder if anyone ever says *Buddha* in the same way. "At home, we have forest rangers to prevent this kind of thing."

My mouth is already dry, and the smoke just aggravates it. I can't get to my water bottle without stopping, but even though Cruise has told us to call out if we need to stop, I keep quiet. I don't want to be the first one to do that. I want Lish to be first. Or Pauline.

The farms disappear, and we enter a wooded area. Dark clouds gather. Instead of hoping it won't rain, I hope it will. I imagine opening my mouth and rain pouring in. Water is all I think about for at least half an hour. I am about to call out or fall over when we finally stop for lunch, beside a little stream. Completely dehydrated, I rip into my knapsack and down a bottle of water. My legs are like noodles. I have cold sweats and a hot head, and everything is blurry. Mom watches me, alarmed.

"How long were you thirsty?" she asks.

"A while."

"Why didn't you ask to stop?"

I shrug.

Nearby, Pauline moans. Her knitted water-bottle holder has practically guillotined her. She rubs the deep purple groove at the back of her neck.

We each find a patch of ground and spread out. I find a spot far enough away from everyone that I won't have to talk, but close enough that I won't seem antisocial.

Cruise goes farther away and starts a fire in a circle of rocks. Myint and Myo scavenge for branches to keep it going, and the three of them hunker over a pot.

Pauline plops down beside Brendan. "What was all that earlier mumbling and grumbling about?"

This time Brendan ignores Max's warning look.

"Cruise's rosy picture. Yes, the Karen people found sanctuary here, but there are a million hill people in Thailand who are practically treated like criminals and refused citizenship—even the ones born here. Most of them are set up in these tourist villages like animals in a petting zoo."

I watch Mom for her reaction. She doesn't even believe in *animal* zoos. She cranes her neck and listens intently.

Cruise has walked over to call us to lunch, and he hears. He flushes. "The Karen escaped persecution and terrible things to come here. Thailand offers them safety," he says, his voice rising in anger. Myo and Myint leave the fire and come over, their eyes bright with interest.

"No one's saying that's not true, Cruise," Brendan says.

"*You* are saying that! How can you criticize Thailand? Is Australia some kind of refugee heaven?"

Brendan throws back his head and laughs. "Touché. Anyway, I agree. The Karen are far better off here, though I believe they're still getting killed in Mae La. But—"

"That's because Burmese soldiers sneak across the border to set fires and kill them!" Cruise interrupts. "The Thai military tries to protect them. No one else does. Who else here in Thailand is helping refugees?"

"The UN," Brendan mutters. Max pretend-punches him in the arm. But Cruise doesn't hear. He's too wound up.

"And these hill villages are not petting zoos! Yes, tourists like to see them and benefit from their hospitality. It gives the Karen a livelihood. There is nothing wrong with that. It's called tourism."

"Nope. Not a thing wrong with that," says Pauline. "Tourism is a completely legitimate industry. It's why we're all here. What's your opinion, Max?"

He raises his hands as though he's surrendering. "I don't like to judge things I don't know much about."

"Max doesn't have a political conscience," Brendan says. "I've been trying to give him one since seventh grade, when I ran for student council."

"On the pressing issue of our school needing a wrestling team," Max says, laughing.

The tension is punctured, and Cruise relaxes. He beckons us closer to the fire, where he ladles soup into plastic bowls.

Mom and Brendan sit together, close enough for me to overhear them.

"I'm curious," Mom says. "Why did you come here if you find the idea of these hill-tribe villages so offensive?"

"I'm trying to get to Burma, but we couldn't get visas. I thought we'd do this trek, find someone to take us to Mae La and then hop the border."

"What *is* Mae La?"

"A refugee camp."

"And you would sneak into Burma—a police state— without a visa? Aren't you afraid?"

"A bit, maybe. But fear is good. It keeps you safe."

"Why Burma?" Mom asks. "Why not just go to Cambodia or Laos?"

"I want to get inside and see up close what's happening to the Rohingya."

"You said it's a genocide."

"I think it is."

"I haven't heard of the Rohingya."

"You will."

We sit cross-legged in a circle, devouring our chicken-curry soup. I wonder if there really is a genocide happening so close while everyone just goes about their business. It seems unlikely. Even impossible.

When we've finished our soup, Cruise passes around a platter of tuna and cheese sandwiches. I may be trekking in Thailand, but I could be eating at my school cafeteria. After lunch, all of us try to be inconspicuous while finding a tree to pee behind. It's fairly obvious what we're doing, though, because we take hand sanitizer, toilet paper and a plastic bag to put the used toilet paper in. That's to keep the mountains clean.

As Cruise boils water for coffee and tea, I go back to my spot and lie down. My hot and cold sweats have disappeared. I'm hydrated and full. A gentle wind cracks the tree branches, and Max skips stones across the stream. I fall into a semi-sleep with the smell of the sweet burning wood in my nose.

In no time at all, Mom gently nudges me awake and gives me a sip of tea. "We have to go."

I don't waste energy arguing. I finish the tea, get to my feet stiffly and pull on my knapsack. I tell myself that I will make it. I will survive the mountain. Lish, though, has disappeared. We wait for her.

When she comes back a few minutes later—in a cloud of smoke—Cruise sniffs suspiciously. First he looks surprised, then pissed off. He has a serious talk with Pauline about illegal drugs. Pauline looks pissed off and has a talk with Lish. Lish looks pissed off, but that's her regular expression. Mom watches the whole thing closely. I think she is enjoying the fact that, for the first time in several months, I'm not the problem. Truth be told, I'm enjoying it too.

ELEVEN

BY LATE AFTERNOON we reach a grass clearing scattered sparsely with huts. The huts are on stilts, so that monsoon rains and mudslides flow underneath. For now, though, the sun is out, and the raised floors provide shade to lounging pigs, pecking chickens and the occasional goat. One of the dozen huts has burned down, and the charred remains still reek of smoke. My nose twitches as we walk past. So far, smoke has been the dominant theme of the day.

Dark-eyed kids with straight black hair run around playing. They giggle as we pass by. Old people sit or squat and smoke pipes. Some stare, wave or smile, but just as many seem completely indifferent to the fact that we are invading their village. We stop in front of a big hut, and Cruise takes off his boots before he climbs the steps.

A woman throws open the door. She wears a multicolored skirt and some bright fabric wrapped around her head. She welcomes us, smiling broadly.

Cruise turns around. "Come," he says, beckoning us up. We untie our boots and leave them at the bottom of the stairs. Except Pauline, who clumps on up. The woman at the top looks like she might faint in horror. Cruise stops Pauline from stepping onto the top step.

"Take off your shoes, please."

Pauline flushes, and Lish smirks.

Pauline obviously didn't read her *Lonely Planet*. Thais hate shoes. It's because they don't like feet. They really don't. For instance, it's a huge insult if you accidentally point your foot at someone. Worse, I suppose, if you do it on purpose.

Our hut is a big square room made of bamboo slats with a thatched roof. The porters drop off our backpacks and sleeping rolls. We all stake out a spot. Mom and I open our self-inflating air mattresses, then unroll our sleeping bags. We organize the things we'll need for the night: flashlights, towels, shampoo, pajamas, blindfolds, earplugs.

"Are you fluent in Burmese, Cruise?" Brendan asks as he unhooks his iPhone from the solar charger built into his backpack. Mom looks at it enviously. She decided she couldn't afford luxuries like that, and she read that you couldn't really get networks here anyway. She has her phone in her backpack, fully charged and turned off to save juice, in case of an emergency.

"Yes," Cruise says guardedly. There is still friction between them.

"I'm looking for a Burmese guide," Brendan says. "And hopefully one who understands some of the ethnic languages of Burma. You can obviously speak to the Karen."

"A bit, yes. But I have help with the Karen villagers." Cruise thumps Myo on the back. "Myo is Karen, and he speaks perfect Burmese. Also Thai."

"Small English too," Myo says.

A mosquito lands on my arm, and I whack it. Then a pig farts, a loud, long sound like air leaving a balloon. We can see the pigs underneath us through gaps in the floor planks. We all laugh, somewhat ruefully, as the guesthouse suddenly stinks like rotten eggs.

Pauline raises her hand. "If someone doesn't point me in the direction of the loo, I'm going to wet my knickers."

Max and Brendan put on their backpacks, which seems odd, and Cruise walks us to the outhouse. It's not too far, but it is out of sight from the guesthouse. "The shower is right behind the outhouse," Cruise says. Only Mom has thought to bring shampoo and towels.

Lish goes in first, and we arrange ourselves in a line. As we wait, a loud, high-pitched squeal shatters the peace. Three guys pull a pig past us by a rope tied around its neck. They pull it into a nearby pen and, without any warning, hold it down and stick a knife in its neck. Its squeals turn into terrible screams. Its eyes bulge and dart around wildly as the blood gushes out. At first it looks panicked. Then it looks hopeless. Then it looks right at me. The killers are young, and they give me big smiles. Like I'm interested in guys who stick knives in helpless animals.

Lish comes out of the outhouse just in time to see the spurting blood, which stops her in her tracks. Nobody says a word for a long, long moment. Mom rests her hand on my back, like she knows I'm about to collapse, and I rest my head on her shoulder.

"Oh god," I say. "Oh god!"

"I know," she says. "I know. That was awful. Just awful."

Everyone stares at the pig except Pauline, who looks totally chill as she examines her nails. Max looks away first, his face pale.

"Barby for dinner, I guess," says Brendan, grimacing.

"Spareribs, I hope," says Pauline.

I whisper to Mom, "Why are they joking? What kind of freaks are they?"

"I think it's uncomfortable joking," she whispers back.

"Well, it's not funny. It's disgusting."

Pauline hears me. "I grew up on a farm, so this is nothing I haven't seen a hundred times. I guess it's a little shocking if you aren't used to it. Do you eat meat?" She lowers her chin and skewers me with a look.

I nod.

"On the farm, we had a saying: *don't get self-righteous when someone else does your killing for you.* Do you eat pork? Then you should thank those guys. Only vegetarians get to be outraged."

I've never envied my mother so much. As a vegetarian, she's the only one without a guilty conscience.

"If we have pork for dinner, I don't know what I'll do," I say.

"Just try not to think about it," Mom says.

"You know that never works with me. And I'm serious. If anyone eats any of that pig in front of me, I'll do something."

"Only *that* pig?"

"Any pig. I mean it. I will hurt somebody."

She gives me a look that I can't quite read. "Buddha says to practice loving-kindness to get rid of ill will."

"I'm not the one with ill will, for God's sake."

"No?"

Sometimes her Buddhist shit makes me want to pull my hair out. I look away and whisper, "Buddha," like I'm swearing. It makes me feel better.

"What?" she asks.

"Nothing."

Finally, it's my turn. The outhouse stinks, and we aren't allowed to put toilet paper down the hole in the ground. Used paper overflows from a pail. I squat over the hole, my boots sinking two inches into the muck around it. When I'm finished, I burst out gasping, because I've been holding my breath the entire time.

I walk around to the back of the outhouse to find Mom. The "shower" is a pump two feet off the ground, perfect for showering feet and ankles but nothing else. It is also right out in the open, so anyone walking by can see.

"Hmmm," I say.

"Ye-es," Mom says, looking around.

We end up holding towels like curtains to shield each other as we splash ourselves with water. I kneel on the grass to shampoo and rinse my hair. We return to the guesthouse clean and smelling of citrus. It's my most cheerful moment in days.

Several young village women are in our hut, showing off their handmade fabrics and purses. They're part of a program started years ago by the royal family to stop them growing and selling opium, according to Cruise.

Pauline grins. "I'm sure it's *just* as profitable."

Pauline buys some fabric, and I buy a shoulder bag with a geometric black, pink and red design for Becca. It's not my favorite, but I feel sorry for the girl selling it. She's young, maybe my age, with a toddler strapped to her back and a baby on her front. She tells me, through Myo, that she also made the baby carriers—in case I need one. Everyone laughs at my horrified reaction. When she finds out I don't have children, she seems to feel sorry for me.

After the women leave, Max and Brendan take laptops from their backpacks. Max also takes out a serious-looking camera. They unwrap the electronics from waterproof cases and plug them into their solar charges.

"Cool," Pauline says. "And expensive."

"That's why we take them with us everywhere we go, including the outhouse," Brendan says. He opens his laptop and starts to type.

"Are you working or surfing?" asks Pauline.

"Working. There isn't any Wi-Fi."

"What kind of work?"

"It's a travel piece."

"What does that mean?"

"Brendan sells articles to magazines," Max says.

"And Max does the photos," Brendan says.

"Oh! Professional journalists."

"No. Rank amateurs who got lucky with a catchy concept: Cape Town to Cairo on Foot."

"That is catchy," says Pauline. "What are you writing about now? Us?" She fluffs out her hair and laughs.

Brendan smiles enigmatically.

"No," Max says. "Brendan's really only interested in hard news stories—war, politics, corruption."

"And Max is only interested in soft news—animal stories, preferably with gorilla babies," Brendan says.

"Well, have you ever seen one up close?" Max asks us. "Adorable!" He shows us a video he shot in Rwanda. Two baby gorillas swing on vines, annoying their mother, who is trying to relax in the grass. Every time they buzz her head, she swipes at them. Fortunately for the babies, she keeps missing. They are funny and sweet and, for the record, *totally* adorable.

The hostess comes back with her skirt bunched up. She lets it go, and half a dozen small white candles tumble out. She squats, strikes a match and lights the first one, holding it upside down so the wax drips on the floor. When there is a warm puddle of wax, she sticks the upright candle in the wax and leaves it to burn. *On the bamboo floor.* She does the same with each candle.

"Interesting," Max says.

Mom is aghast. "This might explain the burned-out hut we saw coming in."

"At least they save on candleholders," Pauline says.

Just then one of the candles falls over and scorches the floor.

Myo and Myint lug up two big pails with bottles of Coke, water and Singha beer chilling in river water. Max and Brendan invite them to join us while Cruise cooks our dinner. Myint, who can't speak English at all, drinks and smiles while Myo answers all our questions. Lish doesn't ask anything. Her iPod is obviously out of juice, but she puts her earbuds in anyway, just so no one will talk to her.

Myo, who I thought was no more than eighteen, turns out to be twenty-five and married. He has two kids, and his wife is pregnant with their third. We can meet her tomorrow night, he says, because we'll be staying in his village.

Pretty soon everyone learns that Pauline is a nurse from Manchester, Mom runs a yoga studio, Max was a wedding photographer in Sydney who was bored with his job and that Brendan just finished a PhD in political science. His thesis was on Burma. Myo is incredulous that an Australian who has never been to Burma spent several years writing about it.

"Oh, I've been to Burma. I was there over two years ago."

"Vacationing?" Pauline asks.

"No. In the field. Doing research for my PhD. And joining in some student protests in Yangon."

"*You* protested?" asks Myo, his forehead creased with confusion.

"Yes."

"Tell them how it turned out," Max says.

"I got pulled in for questioning. Three days of hell. Then I was escorted to the airport."

Max nods. "And he wonders why I'm not politically active."

"But I learned my lesson," Brendan says.

"What did you learn?" Mom asks him.

"That a mouthy Australian stands out in a crowd." He runs both hands over his bald head and laughs. "And that I was naive. I believed Aung San Suu Kyi had really changed the country and that I would be safe as a foreigner. I went to several protests and never tried to blend into the background. I'll be smarter this time around."

"How did you get interested in Burmese politics?" Mom asks.

"As an undergrad I volunteered at an NGO that helped Karen refugees settle in Australia. I ended up going back and interviewing a lot of them for my thesis."

Cruise brings in dinner, a big pot of curried pork and rice. I bury my face in my hands.

"It's not that pig," says Pauline. "That pig will still be draining. Don't worry about it, darling."

I poke my thigh with my fork to stop from vomiting. I press so hard the skin breaks, and a trickle of blood runs down my leg. I feel better. I move my knapsack beside me to hide any blood that may have soaked through my cotton pants and slip the fork inside it. In case I have to stab myself again.

I go to bed hungry.

TWELVE

A ROOSTER CROWS. Then another. Then another. It's like a crowing competition. Max and Mom both burst out laughing. Pauline swears. Lish groans.

"That is one symphonic alarm clock," Max says.

Brendan yawns. "Morning, everyone."

I run my tongue over my teeth. They feel wooly. Plus, I have morning breath. I drain my water bottle and swish it around my mouth, something I'd rather be doing in the privacy of my own home. But then, I'd rather be doing everything in the privacy of my own home. It was weird going to sleep with strangers, and it's weird waking up with them.

The closest I've ever come to this kind of thing was Katie Chong's sleepover when I was twelve. I only knew one person. We slept on sleeping bags in Katie's cold basement. I didn't really want to go because I got homesick so easily, but she was new to the school and trying hard to make friends.

And Mom made me. *If you're invited to a birthday party, you go.* I spent all night thinking up excuses to leave the party, but in the end I toughed it out, afraid of how Mom would look at me if I returned home early.

Now that I think of it, it's Mom's fault that I'm here too.

I sit shivering in my sleeping bag, looking through the small, glassless window, watching the sky lighten to a pearl gray and trying to get motivated to move. I'm exhausted. I didn't sleep well. A lot of things got in my way—the hard floor, my sore thigh, the snorting pigs and visions of their horrible fate.

Cruise ducks his head in to say breakfast is in twenty minutes and that we should be packed and ready to go then. We'll be at a waterfall later today, so we need to put our bathing suits in our knapsacks. And our flashlights, because the last little bit of the trek might be at dusk.

Mom and I press the air out of our mattresses and roll them tightly around the sleeping bags. Breakfast is toast, bacon and cheese. I don't eat the bacon, and I glare at everyone who does, which is everyone except Mom. The coffee is horrible. I make a face as soon as I take a sip.

"Instant," Max says, laughing at me. "No Starbucks around here. You might want to switch to tea."

Cruise cleans up the breakfast mess and packs the food bin. Myo puts the bin on his head.

"Time to go. Come on, Canada Dry," Cruise says to me.

Myint and Myo laugh. Apparently, it's some kind of tourist joke.

The path is clear and inclines gradually. When it widens, Lish falls in beside me.

"What do you think of trekking?" she asks.

"It's better than I thought."

"So you didn't want to come?"

"No. My mother made me."

"A judge made me."

"*What?*"

"Yeah. I was ordered to come."

"I don't understand."

"Of course you don't. *You've* never been in a courtroom."

She's wrong. I have. The day Neil Carter was arraigned. I watched him say, "Not guilty." He wore a dark gray suit and blue striped tie. I suddenly can't get a breath.

"Do you have asthma?" asks Lish.

"No." I force the face of Neil Carter out of my mind. "So why would a judge make you trek?"

"None of your business," she says, kicking a stone. Her tone isn't as offensive as her words, and for some reason I feel sorry for her.

She pulls a loose cigarette out of her pocket and lights up.

"You smoke in front of your mother?" I ask.

"Yeah. So what?"

I look briefly over my shoulder at mine, trying to imagine what she'd do if I lit up.

"I don't know. You're fourteen. It'll probably kill you. My mother would freak out. It would be genuinely frightening."

"Yeah, well, my mother doesn't believe in parenting."

"Doesn't believe in it?"

"Thinks it's too much trouble. Thinks she has way more important things to do. You know, like look after herself. While leaving me and my dad to fend for ourselves."

"What do you mean?"

Lish doesn't answer. The path narrows, and we return to single file. We start to head downhill, which is surprisingly difficult over loose gravel. Pauline wipes out twice. Going downhill is harder on my leg muscles than going uphill. Or, at least, it's as hard but in a different way. By the time the sun hangs high and hot, we're climbing again, and my skin prickles from the heat.

Finally, I hear water. It's not Niagara Falls, that's for sure, but it has a sound. A trickle and a splash. We emerge from the trees to a refreshing spray of cool water. A slim ribbon of river drops about fifty feet over a ledge. It bubbles into a big basin at our level before it tumbles down again over a rocky hill. The basin is a big, round pool edged by sand and grass.

Cruise starts a fire to heat soup and makes sandwiches. It's the same lunch as yesterday. The only difference is he has two vegetarians now. We have one hour to eat, swim and rest before the elephants come. He tells us that each elephant is coming with its own mahout. Then he uses his official voice to tell us about mahouts.

"Mahouts are elephant keepers and are important to Thai culture. They are very strong, very skilled. The best mahouts are spiritual. They understand and respect elephants. It is a profession passed down from father to child.

"Mahouts are important to Thais because elephants are so important. They are smart and strong and were used in wars. They help with industry, logging when it was legal—"

"Logging isn't legal?" asks Brendan.

"No. Loggers were taking all the trees, and elephants had nothing to eat. Now that logging is illegal, there are more wild elephants.

"Thai elephants came from India a long time ago and are a little different from African elephants. They are smaller, the females usually have no tusks, and they are very agile. They are very, very smart. They even recognize themselves in mirrors, like people and some dolphins. They are also deliberate, unlike African elephants, which are more impulsive."

Brendan and Pauline scoff, but Cruise nods seriously. "Yes, Asian elephants think and plan. They are very smart. And they remember everything."

"The elephant who murdered her keeper must have been from Asia," Lish whispers to me.

"What are the chances we'll see some wild elephants?" Max asks Cruise.

"It's not impossible. I saw five once. Higher up in the mountains. When we go to see the Lahu people tomorrow, that will be our best chance. But wild elephants can be dangerous. Even now, when herds are much smaller than they used to be."

"Why are they smaller?" Max asks.

"Elephants are disappearing."

"We'll have to cross our fingers and hope that we see some," Max says. He raises his camera and snaps photos of birds diving down the length of the falls and skimming over the froth at the bottom.

"They have yellow crests," says Pauline. "How pretty. Like royalty."

"They're yellow-cheeked tits," says Cruise. "Very social. They fly in pairs or families. They love to chat."

I stretch out on a strip of grass, relishing the view—the cascading water, the swooping birds, the white-hazed sky.

Cruise stands over me and nudges my foot with his. "Hey, Canada Dry, time to swim is running out."

"I'm just going to sleep."

"You have a chance to swim under a waterfall, and you'd rather sleep?"

"Yes, I would, actually." But I force myself up, knowing I'll be sorry if I don't swim. I grab my bikini and find a tree to change behind. As I slowly wade into the frigid water, Pauline squeals. I spin around to the sight of six elephants strolling in from the trees. Six massive animals walking as quietly as kittens. They head right toward me.

"Valentine!" Mom calls.

She doesn't have to say another word. I dive into the water and paddle away as fast as I can. I'm not really afraid of elephants. I don't *really* think one is going to murder me. But I did wonder, just for a moment, if one might accidentally step on me. They have tiny little eyes and really big feet.

I stop at a safe distance and tread water. The elephants gather in the shallow side of the basin and fill their trunks with water. They spray themselves and each other, trumpeting with pleasure. They seem to be having a great time. It's undeniably cool to be swimming below a waterfall with elephants bathing nearby.

I float on my back and paddle in circles, luxuriating in the moment. I squint at the sun until I'm half-blind from the bright light. Until the water is a zillion silver sparkles. Until movement at the top of the waterfall gets my attention.

I shade my eyes and bring a person into focus. A half-naked guy with long black hair swishes something in the water, back and forth, back and forth. He wrings it out and stretches it over a large rock. When he straightens, he notices me staring. He laces his hands behind his head and stares back. Finally, I break off our eye contact and do a surface dive. When I come up for air, he's gone.

THIRTEEN

IN THE END, everyone but Pauline swims, and nobody—including the elephants—wants to leave the water. But Cruise orders us out, and the mahouts coax the elephants back onto the grass.

My elephant is incongruously called Tinker Bell. She is gray with brown speckles and very wrinkled skin. Her mahout wears baggy cotton clothes and a straw hat, and he carries a short pole with a hook at one end. Cruise takes pains to reassure us that his company doesn't hire mahouts who use their hooks cruelly. When they do use them, they don't hurt the elephants. I eye the hook and raise an eyebrow.

Tinker Bell's mahout raps Tinker Bell on her legs, and she kneels down, one leg at a time, in a ground-shaking *boom, boom,* the most awkward movement imaginable. He cups his hands for me to step up, and I crawl onto the giant seat, the *howdah,* on her back. It turns out Tinker Bell is the lead elephant. Her daughter, Arial, who looks exactly the same age, follows right behind, with Lish on her back.

"Tinker Bell won't move unless Arial is right behind her," says Cruise. "And vice versa. The mother–daughter bond is very strong in elephants."

Pauline is behind Lish on Elsa, and Mom is behind Pauline on Jasmine. Max and Brendan come up the rear on Aladdin and Prince Charming. Someone is clearly a huge Disney fan. Tinker Bell's mahout tightens the howdah by adjusting the giant strap that encircles her torso. I lean forward and catch his eye.

"Hi. I'm Valentine."

He smiles up at me but doesn't say anything.

"Is her name really Tinker Bell?" I ask. I don't like the irony. It seems mean-spirited, designed to emphasize that she's big and heavy-footed.

He talks to me in his native language, and I, of course, don't have a clue what he's saying. But I smile and nod, because he is smiling and nodding. I imagine he's saying, *I know. Tinker Bell! What kind of stupid-ass name is that?*

Cruise gets the all clear from each mahout, then extends his arm and marches forward.

There are plenty of things I didn't know about elephants. First of all, they are really prickly. They have coarse hair, which you can't even see until you're up close. It actually hurts when the hair pokes through my clothes.

Second, they can balance on very narrow paths. For several minutes only a thin slice of grass separates us from a sheer drop.

We're so close, I can look over the edge and practically see infinity. Every time I do, I'm irrationally afraid I'm going to leap off Tinker Bell and hurl myself into the air—*which can't catch me*. I almost ask Cruise if an elephant has ever fallen down into the chasm but decide that I don't want to know. I have no idea how these hulking animals can walk like ballerinas.

Third, they eat like pigs. In fact, I don't even know why anyone uses that expression. "Eat like an elephant" would make more sense. Tinker Bell sways right and pulls up a plant; it disappears in her mouth. She sways left and pulls up a plant; the plant disappears. She sways right and pulls up a plant. We continue like this until she stops at a tree. She yanks several times, until she pulls up the whole thing. She manages to take a few steps without uprooting anything because she is busy eating the tree. When the entire tree has disappeared, in a matter of a minute or two, she starts all over again. It is really slow going.

Tinker Bell's mahout nags her but has no control. She's like an obstinate pet. She stops to drink at every dirty puddle. He gives her constant shit, but in such a mild voice that she just looks at him and keeps drinking. When he's particularly annoying, she sprays him. The mahout throws up his hands and looks at me as if to say, *What can I do? She's my baby.*

The path finally veers away from the mountainside and into the trees.

"Look at all the banyans," Cruise shouts, pointing at a mass of skeletal trees with gnarled roots that spread above ground.

Tall tree trunks reach for light, their leaves canopying high overhead. "They're fig trees that can grow many trunks. A single tree can appear to be a forest."

Tinker Bell's lumbering rhythm rocks me from side to side and almost puts me to sleep. The farther we go, the narrower the path and the denser the plants. Star-shaped flowers, spiky leaves and trembling ferns envelop us. Cut branches litter the sides of the path. Soon Cruise yells and waves at someone straddling a branch in a tree. The long black hair, now pulled into a ponytail, is familiar. His white T-shirt is impossibly clean. His baggy shorts sit low on his narrow hips. It's the guy who was doing laundry at the top of the waterfall.

Cruise stops. So does Tinker Bell. One by one the whole elephant caravan comes to a halt.

"This is Lin," Cruise says over his shoulder. "He helps the mahouts by clearing the paths."

Flip-flops dangle from Lin's feet, and one falls off. When he looks down after it, he almost loses his balance. I gasp. He catches my eye and smiles. He keeps his eyes on me for a moment as he hacks away at the branch between his legs. When it breaks off from the tree and hurtles to the ground, Lin grabs a vine and swings down, landing in front of Cruise, who slaps him on the back.

"Lin," Cruise says again.

Pointing at each of us down the line, Cruise rhymes off our names. "Valentine, Lish, Pauline, Dana, Max, Brendan."

Lin *wais* to each of us in turn. "Valentine," he repeats, coming back to me and smiling shyly. Then he hugs Tinker Bell's mahout and calls out greetings to the others.

"Lin is one of *them*," Cruise says reverentially, as though mahouts are a special species. "Even though he is only a mahout's helper now, he was raised with elephants."

Lin replaces Cruise at the head of the line, slashing his machete back and forth to clear the way and sometimes climbing trees to hack down branches. I watch, taken with his carefree attitude, his lithe and easy walk, his slender, straight back. He climbs trees easily, pulling himself up and moving around the branches like he belongs in them. There is a scar on his calf, a deep white ridge that runs the entire length, from ankle to knee.

Soon a stream is visible through the trees. Tinker Bell stops and turns toward it. Her mahout scolds her and digs his hook in her hide, near her ear, to pull her along. It looks cruel and makes me feel uncomfortable. Reluctantly, Tinker Bell gets back in line. The stream, however, stays parallel to the path, and the silver sliver of water glistens tantalizingly through gaps in the foliage. Tinker Bell steps off the path. Again she's tugged back, and for a time she walks submissively.

A forked tree blocks our way. Its trunk leans low over the path, and Lin jumps up and straddles it, then starts to hack away. He is focused—cutting, cutting, cutting—biting his lower lip. Suddenly he senses me staring at him. He turns his head and winks. I blush and glance down.

"I sure wish I was sixteen," Pauline calls out.

I turn, my face tingling with embarrassment. Lish puts her finger in her mouth, pretending to gag.

Tinker Bell rumbles, a strange growling sound that sends mild shockwaves through me. Her mahout talks to her, but his voice is drowned out by the rumbles now coming from the other elephants. Lin looks over, his face alert, his eyes wide. He speaks to Tinker Bell in a cooing and melodious voice, so sweet that I'm not surprised when she plods over to him. I think for a moment that she is moving in for a pat, but instead she puts her front foot on the tree trunk.

"Oh, look!" calls out Pauline. "Tinker Bell is helping Lin."

Lin puts his finger to his lips to signal for quiet and studies Tinker Bell's face. She rumbles again. The rumble turns into a roar. I grab the sides of my seat and try to stifle a yelp. The mahout shouts and hooks her just behind the ear again. He pulls with all of his weight until she angrily knocks him across the path with her trunk. He lands in the dirt, mortified, holding his wrist. Two mahouts rush to help him.

Lin talks to Tinker Bell while throwing nervous glances up at me. He sheathes his machete, then holds his hands out, palms down, gesturing to me—I think—to stay calm. Or maybe he is signaling to Tinker Bell, who pushes the trunk right down to the ground and breaks it at the fork.

I shriek as my howdah rocks back and forth. I look over my shoulder at Lish, who for the first time since this trek started doesn't look bored, and at Pauline, who stretches forward to see what's happening. Mom, Max and Brendan are behind us, around a slight bend and out of sight.

Suddenly Tinker Bell trumpets, a resounding blast that rattles the branches and shakes the ground. She swings her trunk around in circles, throwing my seat off kilter. It wobbles violently, and I know I'm going to fall seconds before I do. I reach out frantically for something to hold on to, but there is nothing to grab. I hit the ground with a dull thump, my wrists taking most of the blow. Just as I'm congratulating myself on being okay, Tinker Bell moves sideways, and I'm right underneath her massive belly. I start to panic.

She lifts her giant back foot and moves it over me, letting it hover a foot above my chest. I'm afraid to scream, afraid of angering her. Afraid of being crushed to death. Just afraid. Then she slowly lowers her foot, and before I let out the bloodcurdling scream gathering in my throat, a hand is slapped over my mouth. Lin's.

"Hush. She won't hurt you."

Lish, who doesn't hear Lin, shouts, "Tinker Bell's murdering Valentine!"

"Valentine," yells Mom, a sound almost as powerful and air-shattering as the elephant's trumpet. There's a sickening *thud* and an involuntary shriek. "*Valentine!*"

Lin crouches nearby as Tinker Bell's foot moves gently over my chest and stomach. "You will be okay. Be still. Don't scare her, and don't hold your breath. Let her know you are alive."

Suddenly—as strange as it seems—I no longer feel threatened. Her foot passes over me again, just barely skimming my body, and I'm reminded of a Reiki massage. Then footsteps smack the ground, and Mom tears wildly up the path. Tinker Bell rumbles again, and the other elephants break for the stream, crashing through the bushes and trees as fast and furious as wild horses.

"Hold on to your howdahs!" Cruise shouts.

When the elephants are all gone, Tinker Bell steps daintily over me, sashaying toward the water like she doesn't have a care in the world.

FOURTEEN

A FEW MINUTES LATER we are all at the stream, watching the water slide over mossy boulders. The mahouts have helped everyone off the elephants, who now stand in the shallow water, drinking and spraying. Tinker Bell and her daughter have the tips of their trunks in each other's mouths, ignoring everything and everyone else.

We sit on the grassy bank. Mom twisted her ankle when she jumped off her elephant and is dunking her foot in the cold water to keep the swelling down. Cruise and Lin say she's lucky she didn't break her legs.

"What the bloody hell happened anyway?" asks Brendan, gesturing to the elephants. "I couldn't see. All I heard was shouting, and then we were stampeding toward the stream."

"Nothing happened," says Cruise, the sun reflecting off his aviators. "That was not a stampede, only a short dash. Valentine fell off her elephant, but she is okay. No problem."

I am okay. That's true. Rattled but okay. I dip my scraped hands in the soothing water.

"Valentine fell off," Mom says through gritted teeth, "because Tinker Bell went nuts. What was all that about?"

"She was just naughty," Cruise says, rummaging through his backpack. He pulls out a tensor bandage.

"I'd like to know what Lin says about it," Mom says.

Lin, in the stream with Tinker Bell and her mahout, hears his name. "Yes?"

"What happened back there?" Mom asks. "What was Tinker Bell doing? How much danger was Valentine in?"

"Very simple. Tinker Bell wanted to go to the stream. Maybe she needed to drink, or maybe her howdah strap was too tight. I don't like howdahs. They are bad for elephants. And not needed. But Valentine was not in danger." He opens his knapsack and roots for a ziplock bag full of what looks like joints or hand-rolled cigarettes. I guess cigarettes. He lights up.

"That elephant," says Mom, shaking and pointing at Tinker Bell, "almost stepped on her. On purpose. Lish thought it was murder."

"No. She checked Valentine to see if she was alive. Elephants kill with front feet, but get information with back feet. They hear with their feet. They use their back feet to check if a sick elephant on the ground is still breathing."

"Are you just making that up?" Mom asks, her face softening.

"No. It is true. Is how mothers check their calves."

I relive the moment. That hovering giant foot, seeming to caress as it went back and forth, back and forth. I feel a warm rush of gratitude that she cared enough to check on me. That she saw me.

Tinker Bell still stands with her daughter, their trunks entwined and their foreheads touching. Max wades into the stream to snap pictures of them.

Brendan shakes his head. "He's a sucker for a sappy animal story. But you," he says, elbowing Lish, "you obviously like sensational animal stories. What made you think it was murder?" A smile plays over his mouth.

Lish blushes.

"That was my fault," I say. "I told her about an elephant in Florida who murdered her keeper. It's in a book about a Tampa zoo."

"Ah well. It was nice to see that Lish cared!" Brendan says. He laughs, while she scowls.

"Murdered?" asks Pauline. "You mean she accidentally killed her keeper."

"No. Murdered. She planned it. They had proof."

"It must have been an Asian elephant," Lin says, nodding. "They think and plan."

"Really?" asks Brendan. "You actually believe an elephant planned and carried out a murder?"

"Oh yes. They are very intelligent animals. Sometimes smarter than humans." Lin grins. "Like today."

Cruise, wrapping Mom's ankle, ends the conversation. "Back on the elephants." He waves the mahouts in.

The path is still blocked by the broken tree. Cruise and Lin struggle to move it. Before the others can help, Tinker Bell ambles over, docile and sweet as a lamb. She rolls it up in her trunk and effortlessly tosses it off to the side.

"She's a comedian, that one!" says Brendan, shaking his head.

Mom doesn't want me on Tinker Bell again. She suggests we trade elephants, but I refuse. By now I'm fond of her. We remount and keep going. An hour later, when the afternoon sun dips, Cruise leads us off a path and into a clearing half the size of a school track. There are few trees, and they are almost completely defoliated. The grass is stubble.

"It looks like someone has mowed the lawn," says Pauline. "And the trees."

"Someone has," Cruise says. "Elephants."

The ride is over, and the elephants are going home.

"Where is home?" I ask Lin. I imagine a beautiful refuge, elephants sleeping under arching cherry blossoms.

"Each elephant goes with a mahout. So wherever the mahout lives."

I imagine an elephant squeezed under a hut on stilts.

Lin sheathes his machete in a leather holder that hangs down his back and holds out his arms to me. I swing my legs around to one side and slide into his hands, brushing against his hard body as he lowers me to the ground. I inhale his smell. Cigarette smoke and sweat.

"Valentine," he says.

"Yes."

"What does it mean?"

"Nothing," I say.

"You know that's not true, darling," Pauline says, coming up behind me. "It means 'heart' or 'love,' doesn't it?" She draws the shape of a heart in the air.

"Ahhh," says Lin, staring at me.

"What does Lin mean?" Pauline asks.

Lin just smiles.

"Bright," says Cruise. "Lin means 'bright.'"

We say goodbye to the elephants and the mahouts, since we won't be seeing them again. Except for Lin. He is staying with us. He lives at the Kayan village where we'll sleep tonight. Lin walks Tinker Bell and her mahout partway into the jungle, flip-flops slapping against the hard ground, cigarette dangling between two fingers. He shakes hands with the mahout, they both *wai*, and then he holds his hand out to Tinker Bell. When she strokes his palm with the tip of her trunk, he moves in for a closer caress, rubbing her trunk and laying his face against it.

Cruise tells us to get our flashlights out in case we don't reach the village before dark. I offer to help Mom walk, but she brushes me off in favor of a cane that Myo has cut for her. Pauline walks beside her, and Lin falls in alongside me. I ask him about the elephants' rumbling.

"Elephants talk to each other. Make their plans. *I block the path. You make for water.* Herds in mountains talk to each other. They warn other herds of danger."

"What kinds of danger?"

"Earthquakes, floods, poachers."

"You told my mom there was no danger, but is that really true?"

"Being around wild animals always has danger."

"Aren't they tame?"

"I mean animals who are supposed to be wild."

"How did you know Tinker Bell wasn't going to step on me?"

"I read her signs. Her ears were open but did not flap. Her eyes looked calm. She was not dripping oil down her temples. Her trunk no longer circled in air. Many things."

"Cruise said you were raised with elephants."

"Yes. My father was a mahout. My grandfather was a mahout. My great-grandfather was a mahout, and also my great-great-grandfather.

"A family tradition."

"Yes."

"Those elephants today didn't really have those names, did they?"

"Of course not."

We trade sympathetic glances and hold each other's gaze a fraction too long. The sun, about to disappear, erupts in flames of pink and mauve.

"Does Valentine really mean 'love'?" he asks, fixing his eyes on the path.

"Yes. Kind of."

"Name suits you," he says quietly.

Our bare arms touch, and something shivers over me. I jerk away, stumbling over my feet. I'm acutely aware of Mom and Pauline and everyone else. I feel frantic, and I'm not sure why.

That's a lie. I totally know why. Amir's face has popped up behind my eyes, and I feel like a traitor.

When the sky is purple, Cruise calls Lin to the front of the line, and we walk the final half hour to the village with our flashlights on. Pauline, Max and Brendan have miner flashlights strapped to their heads. I walk all alone, flashlight in hand, eyes on the ground, heart hammering in my ears.

As we enter the village, Mom limps toward me.

"Valentine?"

"Yes."

"Is something wrong?"

"No."

"You suddenly seem upset." She looks uneasily at me. "It's okay if you're having fun."

"Is it?"

"Yes."

"I'm allowed to flirt with a cute guy? Is that what you mean?"

"Yes."

"Tell me this, Mom. If you die, am I allowed to call someone else Mom six months later?"

She recoils.

"I thought not."

FIFTEEN

OUT OF NOWHERE, four huts on stilts appear. "This is the entrance to the village," Cruise says. He sends Myo, Myint and Lin ahead to arrange our guesthouse, then gives his spiel.

"The Kayan, part of the Red Karen, wear neck rings. The girls and women do. They are five when they get their first ring. As they get older and grow, they get another one, then another one, until the neck is long and beautiful." He pauses. "Well, for them it is considered beautiful."

"I don't actually think it extends the neck though, does it?" asks Pauline. "Doesn't it deform the shoulders and compress the rib cage instead?"

Cruise shrugs. He looks irritated, the way Mr. Singh looks when we ask annoying questions.

"Well," Mom says, "I bet they don't wear five-inch stilettos that ruin their feet, knees and spines." Mom hates high heels.

"How true," Pauline says. "Women have always suffered for beauty."

Cruise clears his throat. "Some people call them the long-necks. Twenty years ago they were famous in Mae La. Tourists paid to see them. They became financially self-sufficient."

"What exactly *is* Mae La?" asks Pauline.

"It's a giant refugee camp on the Thai side of the Thai–Myanmar border," says Brendan. "It's where some persecuted Burmese ethnic groups go. The ones who are being system-atically killed by the Burmese military—the Karen, the Shan, the Mon, to name just a few. Some people have been stuck there for a generation."

"No longer such a big camp though," says Cruise, sounding defensive.

I sigh to myself. I wish Brendan would stop commenting on everything. It's not like any of it is Cruise's fault.

"Are you telling me that tourists went to a refugee camp, a place of misery, to gawk at the refugees' necks?" asks Mom.

"Unethical tourism," says Cruise. "My company only does ethical treks. No gawking at refugees."

"But if the Kayan like the neck rings and they are making money, what's the big deal?" Pauline asks.

"Maybe I'll get a neck ring," Lish says.

Everyone ignores her, and we head into the village. The guesthouse is a large hut with a spacious deck. Our backpacks are already piled in a corner. Myo and Myint have disappeared, but Lin has stuck around. He helps Mom up the stairs and asks me if I'm hungry. I don't rebuff him exactly, but I don't give him any encouragement. He *wais* and leaves, stopping on his way out to greet a woman whose hands are full of the little white candles the Karen woman used.

The woman's wide skirt is blue, and her hair is dark. Gold rings spiral up her neck. I examine them surreptitiously when she crouches down and flicks a match into flame. Three teenage girls follow behind her, each with their own children. Babies are strapped to their backs, and shy toddlers hide in the folds of their skirts. They carry bundles of colorful fabric.

"This is Htay, our hostess," Cruise says. "And her daughters. They would like to sell you their handwoven cloth."

Htay smiles briefly as she melts the end of a candle and sticks it on the floor. When she has finished lighting all the candles—when the deck is a blazing fire hazard—she takes two of the little kids with her and leaves. The girls spread their fabric out, and the haggling begins.

"How many kids does Htay have?" Pauline asks after we've each bought a small bolt and the girls have left.

"Five," Cruise says. "Three daughters, two sons. The sons live with their wives' mothers. This is a matriarchal village."

"They must start having kids early. She looks very young to be a grandmother."

"Nothing else to do at night," Cruise says.

"I'm impressed. I can barely deal with one kid," Pauline says. She points at me. "You are awfully quiet."

I nod. "I'm tired."

"Too bad your boy isn't here."

"My boy?"

"Where's Lin, Cruise?" Pauline asks. "Can we invite him for dinner?"

I stand. "I'm actually not feeling well." I slink into the guesthouse.

Mom follows me. "Meditate with me. You'll feel better." She sits cross-legged on her sleeping bag.

"I doubt it."

I lie down and cover my face with my arms.

"Valentine, please. Be kind to yourself."

"I'm fine. I think I just need a nap."

"Dinner is coming. You need to eat."

"I'm not hungry."

"Amir wouldn't want you to put yourself in a living tomb. You know that."

"I don't know it, actually. Strangely enough, we never discussed him dying before he finished high school." I don't mean to sound as sarcastic as I do, and Mom is silent for a minute. Maybe she's already meditating. I peek. She's not. She's staring at me.

"I need to tell you something," she says.

"Okay."

"If I die, I hope and pray that you will...if not *call* someone Mom, *love* someone else and let that person love you. I couldn't bear it if you weren't loved."

Then she hops up and leaves. If I could cry, I would. I wish I hadn't mentioned her possible death. "Touch wood," I say, reaching out to touch the bamboo floor. It is lit with stripes from the moonlight slanting through the shutters. I throw the shutters wide open, and a rush of grass-scented air cools my face.

Air.

Amir without the *m*.

I try to think what the *m* might stand for. Nothing comes to mind except *me*. Air is Amir without me. Or Amir is air *with* me. I search for the profound meaning, but it doesn't make any more sense than the Rumi quote on Amir's tombstone. Less, in fact.

I try to picture Amir as part of the air. It's better than thinking of him as part of the dirt, like at the cemetery. Air is light, and dirt is dark. Air has butterflies, stars, clouds, snowflakes and breath crystals. Dirt has worms. Air fills your lungs. Dirt fills your mouth. Although I suppose that's not such a drawback if you're dead. *For rain it hath a friendly sound / To one who's six feet underground.* More "Renascence." Edna St. Vincent Millay was a glass-half-full kind of poet.

Amir lived in the house next door ever since he moved to Toronto from Egypt, when we were both in first grade. He was a black-haired, black-eyed troublemaker who never saw a tree he couldn't climb, a skateboard he couldn't joyride or a ball he couldn't whip with total, bull's-eye accuracy. He was always laughing—especially if he was getting in trouble. And he was always in trouble.

He came from Cairo. *Cairo*. Even the name is magical. Except for the blue sky and turquoise Nile, everything there is gold—sand, pyramids, camels—or white—Bedouins in flowing robes traversing a sun-hazed desert. Well, that was the Cairo of my dreams. The Cairo of Amir's memory was of buildings. Millions of buildings, some of them with crumbling roofs. He moved to Toronto over Christmas and had never seen snow before. By January he had mastered the snowball slider.

On Amir's first day of school, Jarret McKinney pushed Kamau Stephens into a snowbank. Kamau had a prosthetic leg because he had cancer when he was four. Jarret…well, Jarret was just a total idiot and, sadly, still is. Becca and I were at our usual spot, hidden under the slide, sharing her mother's sugar-free, gluten-free brownies with the squirrels, when Kamau was sent headfirst into the snow. Becca ran at Jarret, calling him names. I trotted behind, a nervous but enthusiastic cheerleader for justice.

Just before Becca reached Jarret, he was totally flattened by a snowball to the face. We looked around, stunned, and there was Amir, grinning and wiping his hands. He didn't have mitts, and his hands were red from the cold. I offered him mine. Then I told everyone that he lived next door to me. At the end of the day, we walked home together. By the time we reached my driveway, we were holding hands.

We got married in second grade. The wedding was in the ravine behind our elementary school. Becca was my maid of honor, and even though we were in French immersion, we invited all the English kids. I divorced him two weeks later when I caught him kissing Michelle Feldman beside the tennis courts. He broke my heart then, but we were friends for years and got back together in the first week of ninth grade, in Mr. Singh's class. Another reason I love Mr. Singh.

Amir used to be at our house so much, Mom and Dad said he was the son they never had.

I'm one of the few people at our school who didn't see Amir die. That's because he died during Friday Night Lights— the only night game of the year, something he was really excited about.

I was on my way there, late, because I had the time wrong. I thought the juniors were playing first. I missed his game because I messed up the time, something I never do. And I think everything could have been different if I hadn't. One little thing can change everything that comes after it. Like the butterfly effect—the idea that a butterfly flapping its wings on one side of the world can cause a tornado on the other.

I've imagined myself at the game at least a hundred times. I'm sitting in the bleachers with Becca, cheering for the home team. I'm enjoying the game, even though my butt is sore and cold, and I'm watching Amir closely, of course, so I notice when he gets in an argument with the big guy, the middle linebacker on the other team. I notice that the linebacker is flattening him almost every time he has the ball, which is a lot, since he's the quarterback. After the game, when the helmets come off and tensions are still high, I'm on alert. I notice when the linebacker goes after him. I yell out, and the coaches run onto the field and stop the linebacker from slamming a fist into Amir's face, so hard it pushes his nose into his skull.

But I *wasn't* there. I wasn't there for the game, or the sucker punch, or the resuscitation attempts on the field. I wasn't in the ambulance with him. I wasn't at the hospital when they pronounced him dead. I wasn't even at the graveyard when they dropped him into the ground. In some ways, I haven't been anywhere since.

SIXTEEN

I DREAM ABOUT AMIR. I'm at his grave, digging to get him out. It's raining, and I'm up to my ankles in muck. The hole I've dug is deep, but I can't reach him. He cries up to me, "Don't leave me here."

I force myself awake and struggle to sit up.

"I'm so sorry," I whisper into the pulsing dark. Because I *have* left him. Here I am, and there he is, and that will never change. Until I'm not here either.

Everyone else is sleeping so peacefully, I want to scream at them. I have to get out before I do. I need to be alone, somewhere private where I can release this awful feeling. I reach for my flip-flops, flashlight and toilet paper. I creak open the door and tiptoe out to the deck, where I slip on the flip-flops and gaze around. I flick on my flashlight. It's so dark. There isn't a streetlight for at least a hundred miles. Maybe a thousand.

I make my way to the outhouse, a five-minute stroll, swinging my flashlight back and forth in a wide arc. Every once in a while, I think I hear something behind me. I spin around quickly, but there's nothing.

I use the outhouse, then find a tree stump and sit down. I stare at the stars. The stars that Amir loved. He wanted me to go to Egypt with him after we graduated from high school, before starting university. He said we'd sail a felucca up the Nile and camp on the banks. He said the best sky in the world could be seen from the Nile, near Luxor, and that when you were there you could imagine that you were living in the days of the pharaohs. I pictured us lying in the felucca, lit from above and below—by the stars in the sky and their shimmery reflections in the river.

Here, the darkness is intense, draping the jungle like velvet. But the sky is spectacular, awash with the Milky Way. I remember the first time Amir pointed it out to me. We were camping with my parents. The Milky Way was a white, gauzy film in the sky. I couldn't understand how we were inside it and yet seemed outside of it, far below. Amir compared it to looking at a cathedral ceiling from the floor.

I can hardly believe that I'm here looking at the same Milky Way. That I've seen it from a mountain in northern Thailand. That I've seen girls with neck rings. That I've seen elephants bathe. Things Amir will never see. In fact, if I were to start listing the things he will never see, I bet I could keep going until I died.

It makes me feel so guilty, I can hardly stand it.

Why me, and not Amir?

This is why I can't get on with my life. Because Amir will never get on with his.

I beam my flashlight into the jungle. The light moves over leaves, vines, trees, flowers, rocks. The indifferent earth orbiting a ball of fire in an indifferent galaxy. The sky was as beautiful the night after Amir died as it was the night before. As though Amir's death was nothing.

What is it all about? Why are we here? I don't believe there is a God or an afterlife, and if I'm right, then this is it. This life is all there is. Amir's life is done. Those sixteen years are all he's ever going to get. I feel my heart shrivel and harden some more.

I haven't cried since the night he died, when I thought I would wash myself away.

I was a block from the school when I saw all the flashing lights, and I ran then, realizing I had been hearing the sirens for about twenty minutes. I arrived to total pandemonium.

There were crowds of kids hanging around outside the front of the school. There were police cruisers and a fire truck. Why was there a fire truck? There was no sign of fire. I ran around back, but I couldn't get near the field. Yellow tape blocked it off. Cops were waving people off the field.

No one was playing football, but there were football players everywhere, talking to cops, sitting on the bleachers, talking to the principal and the vice-principals and the coaches. I looked for Amir but couldn't see him. I looked for his number, actually. The players all looked alike in their uniforms.

I texted him to call me. I saw people I knew, but they all said slightly different things. There'd been a fight between the two teams, there'd been a fight between a couple of players, there'd been a fight when kids who weren't on the team or even from our school ran onto the field. They all agreed on one thing: the field had suddenly erupted into chaos, and the cops, a fire truck and two ambulances arrived in an instant. One of the ambulances left quickly, sirens squealing.

"Who was in the ambulance?"

No one knew.

I tried to talk to three different cops, but no one would tell me anything. I waited for an hour, watching as the crowds thinned to almost nothing, as the players all left the field, as the police drove away.

I phoned Amir, but he didn't answer. I texted him again. **Call me.** I texted him at least twenty more times— **Call me**, with question marks, exclamation marks, **CALL ME**, more question marks. I sat on the curb by the parking lot and felt like something really bad might have happened. Really, really bad.

I called Mom, but she didn't answer. We'd had an early dinner, and she'd said she might pick up Dad from college. He was teaching a night class. I ran to Amir's house and rang the doorbell, but no one was home. Why wasn't anyone home? Someone should have been. I rang the doorbell again. Then again. Twenty times, maybe more. I texted Amir again.

I called friends. No one knew what had happened.

I texted Mom one word: **Help.**

She phoned me, and I told her what was happening. She said she was on the way home with Dad and told me to stay put. She suggested I call the downtown hospitals and see if I could find out which one the ambulance went to. I phoned all of them, but none of them gave me any information. I went next door again. I texted Amir one more time. **I love you.**

Then I sat on my front steps. That way I could see the Aymans when they came home. But by the time Mom and Dad drove up the driveway, I had my head between my knees because I thought I was going to pass out.

They helped me into the house, trying to reassure me and calm me down. Just then the phone rang, and Mom pounced. She listened for a second before turning away from me.

A lot of little things stay in my mind from that moment, the moment I knew my life was going to change. Her head was bent, and she was whispering, but I heard a gasp that she tried to muffle. I noticed how her hair was coming out of its ponytail, how her red sweater was a little pilled. How the slow cooker bubbled over on the counter and how the smell of curry filled the kitchen. Dad walked into the kitchen after hanging up his jacket, and I noticed how his steps slowed down as he took in the scene. How his belt missed two loops. How wary he looked.

He could sense it too.

"Dana?" He said her name, but too quietly for her to hear.

He looked at me. He looked at our lovebirds, Honey and Mooner. They were chirping up a storm, and Honey was flapping her wings. He shushed them, and they stopped chirping, looking at him expectantly with shiny black eyes, cocking their heads to one side as if waiting for an explanation. Dad took off his glasses and rubbed his eyes. He put his arm around me, and I leaned against his laundered shirt. I could feel his heart beating. It was beating as quickly as mine.

All this took only a couple of seconds. Then Mom put the phone down and turned around. She didn't need to say a word. Her face said everything. I shrugged off Dad's arm and stepped back. And back. And back. Because I knew something awful was coming, and I wanted to get out of its way. I stepped back into the hallway.

"Oh, darling," she said, her voice cracking, tears rolling down her face. "Oh, god."

Her arms were out and open, but I kept retreating.

"Valentine, Amir is, oh my god, he is…he's dead, my darling. He was hurt in the football game. He was pronounced dead at the hospital."

Dad made a grinding noise. They both reached out to me, but I tore up to my room. I couldn't bear to be touched or talked to. I locked the door, and I texted Amir again. **Come back. Come back. Come back. Come back.**

Both of my parents cried. I could hear them. I was glad they were crying. It was only right. Amir deserved people crying over him. But I didn't want to join them, didn't want to snuggle in their arms and cry into their shoulders. I didn't want to be comforted. I wanted to be alone. They came to my room. They knocked several times, but I asked them to go away. I sat on my bed and I cried and cried and cried, like I would never stop. I was still crying late at night when Amir's dad came to the door. I heard his voice but not his words, except for Amir's name. I heard that. Then I heard more. "I need to tell you. I want you to hear from me...My son, my son. My boy." I heard more crying.

I looked out the window when the front door closed, and I watched Mom and Dad walk Amir's father home. He walked like he was hurt, holding his side and limping a bit. He looked ten years older than he had the day before. He was between them, but he looked alone.

A lot of people said a lot of things afterward, stupid things like, *It's not the years in the life, it's the life in the years,* and *He's gone to a better place,* and *Thank God, he didn't suffer.* Like they knew whether he had suffered or not. I mean, just think about it. A guy slammed his fist in his face and smashed Amir's nose into his brain, and those people say he didn't suffer? Fuck them and their stupid, stupid words.

Other stupid comments were about his parents. First of all, a lot of people were surprised that the funeral was in a church and not a mosque, as though all Arabs are Muslims. They aren't. Amir was a Coptic Christian. And people said racist things without even knowing they were racist, like *That explains why she doesn't wear a hijab.* Like all

Muslims wear hijabs. They don't. Then everybody, *everybody*, said, *Thank God they have another child, so they have something to live for*.

I thought that was the stupidest thing of all. I was sorry they had Mona, because if they didn't, they could have just killed themselves and ended it all.

And I still can't forget, though I try really hard, his mom holding on to his coffin, half lying on it and wrapping her arms around the sides. She couldn't let it go. And she couldn't stop sobbing. And I'd never felt sorrier for anyone.

But I had stopped crying by then. I'd lost the gift. Mrs. Ayman looked up at that moment. She looked right at me, and I wasn't crying, and I thought she thought I didn't care. And I hated myself. Why wasn't I crying? I was the only one who wasn't.

My therapist says my not crying is a defense mechanism that is actually hurting me. That I would feel better if I had a release.

I take deep breaths, breathing in the jungle's earthy, leafy, tree-bark smell. A scuffling sound sends me jumping to my feet. I hold my breath, listening with my whole body. I flash my light around, spinning in a circle. I don't see anything, but I sense something. I really do. I flick the knife out of my flashlight handle. I back up against a wide tree trunk. Should I scream? Would the sound even reach the guesthouse?

I wait. I shut off the flashlight. Why advertise myself? I look behind the tree. I count to a hundred. I look behind the tree again. Two hundred. Nothing. I decide I've invented the drama. I mean, I'm in a jungle. It's full of living things. Snakes, lizards, monkeys, birds and who knows what else. Maybe even wild elephants.

What I do next isn't planned, but it seems natural.

I pull up my top and put the point of the knife on the fleshy part underneath my left breast, where no one will see it. And I press.

The urge to hurt myself feels like a need, like an itch. A violent itch. It isn't new. I did it last night at dinner when I poked the fork into my thigh.

I gasp. It hurts, but not enough. I press a little harder. Until the knife point breaks the skin. My vision blurs. I have a moment of almost ecstatic calm before the cold sweats start. I close my eyes and roll my head back against the tree. Then the sound of a lighter flicking almost sends me out of my skin.

SEVENTEEN

LISH STANDS IN FRONT OF ME, lighting a joint. It takes everything I have not to scream. I have to hold my hand over my mouth while a storm roars in my ears.

"Cool," she says.

"What are you doing here?" I whisper-screech.

"So you're not Miss Perfect."

"Are you insane? Why are you spying on me? How long have you been there?"

"Long enough. And I wasn't spying. I couldn't sleep, so I followed you out."

"But you stood there watching me! You were there for a while. I *heard* you!"

"Well, yeah. I just wanted to see what you were doing. I wasn't expecting anything as freaky as that." She pulls heavily on the joint. "Cool."

"It's *not cool*, you freakin' dork! What is wrong with you? There is nothing cool about this."

"So why do it?"

"None of your business."

She scuffs the dirt with the toe of her flip-flop as she inhales deeply. "Want a toke?" she asks, offering me the joint and still holding her breath.

I shake my head no.

"Can I see?" she asks.

"See what?"

"The cut."

"I'm seriously worried about you." I move past her and flounce up the path. "That is so messed up."

"Wait," she says. "Can I borrow your toilet paper? I forgot to bring mine."

I grudgingly toss the roll at her.

"Will you wait for me?" she asks.

"You're too much," I say, but I don't move.

"Oh shit. You better take some." She points at my top, to a spreading bloodstain. She rips some squares off for me.

When she comes out of the outhouse, she takes one more toke, pinches the joint out and puts it in her pocket. I hold a wad of toilet paper against the cotton of my pajamas, which are, unfortunately, pale green, a color that won't hide blood. We don't speak, but as weird as it seems, we have moved to a rather comfortable, almost friendly place.

We turn the last bend, and I'm blinded by a flashlight. Someone's on the path. My heart sinks. Mom.

"I woke up and you were gone! I waited at least ten minutes and got worried. You're supposed to wake me up," she says. Then she sniffs like a bloodhound and stares at me questioningly.

"I wasn't smoking dope," I say.

Lish nods. "Yeah, she wasn't."

Mom notices my top and shines her flashlight on it. "Oh my god. What happened?"

"I'll get going," says Lish, running to the guesthouse and flying up the steps.

"Nothing," I tell Mom. I really had no idea how much the cut would bleed. "I just scratched myself on a branch."

"I don't understand. How did you scratch yourself there? Let me see it." Her voice is frighteningly calm.

"You want to look at it here?" I ask, glancing around.

She scans the area. There is no one anywhere. "Here. Now."

I lift my top, then lower it quickly.

She shakes her head. "Let me see it."

I lift my breast. She stares at the wound. "What is that?"

"A cut."

"But what happened?" Her voice is dangerously shrill. "How did you get cut *there*?" She spies my flashlight. The knife is still out. I've forgotten to flick it back in its slot.

Mom grabs it and shines her own flashlight on it. The tip is discolored. "Oh my god, Valentine! What is going on?"

I don't answer. I hear the simple answer forming in my head, and it sounds really bad. Crazy bad.

"Valentine?"

"I cut myself."

Her eyes bug out.

"You mean on purpose?" she whispers.

"Yes."

She tries to speak but just opens and shuts her mouth. She pulls me to the guesthouse and points at the steps. "Sit." The word is like a hiss. "Don't move."

I do what she says.

She emerges from the guesthouse a minute later with a bottle of water, a clean towel and two bottles of hand sanitizer. "Pour water on it—the whole bottle. Then dry it and sanitize. What if you get an infection while we're out here in the middle of nowhere?"

I bite my tongue. Coming here was her idea. I do remind her that she has ointments and antibiotics. She pins me with wild eyes, and I'm sorry I said anything at all.

"Do it now," she orders.

I have to lie back uncomfortably, my spine against the steps, and lift up my top. I check the hut window to make sure no one is looking. It's shuttered. I start the disinfecting. I try not to wince when it stings.

"You have another mark," Mom says. "I noticed it today when you were swimming. A little scab on your thigh. Where did you get that?"

I don't want to answer this either, but I do. "Last night at dinner. When Pauline said the pig was still draining, I was so freaked out I just poked myself with the fork." I start to shake. "I'm sorry."

She sits down beside me and puts her arm around me. She's crying.

"It's not such a big deal," I say. "It's really not."

"And why did you cut your breast? What prompted that?" Her voice is strangled.

"I had a nightmare about Amir. That I left him in the ground."

"Valentine, I loved Amir too. That beautiful boy who ran in and out of our house for years. I loved him. Your dad loved him. We understand how great the loss it. But should we lose you too?" She leans in close, her eyes only inches from mine. "I won't let it happen. Do you hear me? I will drag you all over this fucking earth if I have to before I'll let you just give up."

"It's okay. It's really okay."

"There's nothing okay about this."

That's almost what I said to Lish, which makes me laugh a little. Big mistake.

"You find this funny? It's not funny." Her voice is shrill and loud. I look around nervously.

"Why do you keep hurting yourself? Why?"

"I'm not trying to hurt myself. I'm really not. Everything I do is to try and make me feel better."

Mom buries her head in her hands and sobs. She doesn't even try to muffle the sounds. I look over my shoulder as Max opens the shutters and sticks his head out the window. I try to ignore him and put my arms around Mom. Then I hear a *psst* and look again. Pauline is there too, mouthing something at me. Maybe they're all awake and listening to us. Of course they are. I wave at them to go away. I don't want their help. What could they do anyway?

I sit with Mom until she finally calms down, wipes her face and goes into the hut. Everyone pretends to be sleeping except Lish, who is one sleeping bag over, and who, once my eyes adjust to the dark, gives me a wide-eyed and silent *WTF?*

EIGHTEEN

THE KAYAN PEOPLE have roosters too.

"Does every village have these bleeding birds?" asks Pauline, yawning.

I am unbelievably sore. It takes me longer to sit and then stand up than it does anyone else. Bending over to pack up my things is not even possible. My hamstrings are cement.

Everyone seems awkward about last night. No one speaks. No one looks at anyone. Mom is really, really quiet. She goes to the outhouse alone. I follow as quickly as I can, hoping to catch her, but Lish tags after me.

"So?" she asks. "Who's the freaking dork now?"

"Yeah. It's me."

"Was all that crying about the cut?"

"No."

"Want to talk about it?"

"No."

"I'll tell you something about me if you tell me something about you."

I try not to glare at her. "I think you already owe me something."

"Oh. Yeah. You have a point. Well, let me think. I know. I'm not really fourteen. I'm thirteen."

"Sorry. We're not even. Not even close. But, for the record, why lie about such a stupid thing?"

"To come on the trek. This company doesn't allow anyone under fourteen."

"So why not find a company that allows younger kids?"

"My *mother* doesn't think I have anything in common with kids my own age."

"I can see that. You'd probably scare them to death."

"Thanks."

"That wasn't a compliment."

"I beg to differ."

"Why are you so messed up?" I ask.

"I'm not messed up. My mother's messed up."

We have breakfast on the deck. We sit in a circle, without any conversation, until Pauline can't take it anymore.

"Is anyone going to talk about the elephant in the room?"

Max glances up at Mom and smiles sympathetically. She smiles weakly, but her face goes white.

"Listen. Let me just say this and get it out there," continues Pauline, reaching over and grabbing Mom's hand. "We all heard you cry, but don't worry about it. Sometimes a good cry is better than a bottle of Scotch. Are you feeling better now, love? Because if not, I actually travel with a single-malt."

"Really?" asks Brendan. "I could do with a shot. Hair of the dog and all. Too much beer last night."

Pauline reaches for her bag and pulls out the bottle. Brendan swigs, then offers it to Mom. She refuses and forces a laugh.

"I'm feeling better, thank you," she says. "Sorry I woke you all up." She looks around at everyone and then focuses on her breakfast again. She stirs her tea for a very long time. Then she eats her toast, biting, chewing, swallowing with remarkable concentration.

I feel shitty. I hate to see her so humiliated. I prefer when she's kicking ass. Even if it's mine.

"It was my fault," I say. I stand, get my knapsack on and go down the steps to wait for the trek to start. Mom soon joins me.

"Are you okay?" I ask her.

"I am. How about you?"

"Yes."

"Did you put more sanitizer on the cut this morning?"

"No. I forgot. I'll do it later."

"Please do it now. And cover it with gauze to keep it clean." She hands me a prewrapped packet.

I trudge into a thicket behind the guesthouse for privacy and soak both wounds. The cut is sore, but the fork holes in my thigh are healing nicely. I stick the thick strip of gauze in my bra.

On my way back, I bump smack into Lin, who is carrying two empty pails. I study his face—the high cheekbones and full upper lip. He smells of coconut, and his hair is damp. His expression is serious.

"Valentine," he says.

"Yes?"

"Is everything okay?"

It takes me a minute. Probably because I don't want to acknowledge what he's really asking me.

"Sorry?"

"I worried."

"So you heard? The crying?"

"Yes."

"And you know it was my mom?"

"I peeked out the window."

"Oh god! How embarrassing. I'm sorry. How far does sound travel out here? Did everyone in the village hear?"

He laughs. "No. Most of the village is over there." He nods his head in the other direction.

"Good."

"But is everything okay now?"

"Yes. Fine. Thanks." I duck my head and move away, then feel like I've been rude. "Aren't you coming with us?"

"Yes. First I get water."

"So I'll see you in a bit?"

"Yes."

In front of the guesthouse, everyone is huddled around Cruise. "Today we have a choice," he is saying. "A scenic path or a suicide climb."

"There's a catchy title," says Brendan. "Suicide climb."

"I assure you no one has ever died," Cruise says with a laugh. "It's just a challenge. If you like to test yourself. It's not part of the regular trek, but once in a while I offer it as a special treat."

"Okay," Max says. "Keep talking. I like treats."

"Scenic is a gradual climb around the mountain, with the whole valley below. Suicide is straight over the mountain. The scenic route is very short—maybe four hours—and the suicide climb is long."

"How long?" asks Max.

"Maybe six hours."

"Why? If the scenic is winding around the mountain and the suicide is going straight over?"

"Harder work."

Lish immediately opts for the suicide climb. I shoot her a questioning look, confused by her sudden enthusiasm. And she isn't exactly athletic.

"Like I want to get there early and sit around staring at everyone?"

I roll my eyes.

"I will obviously take the scenic route," says Mom. Her ankle is taped.

"I'm coming with you, girlfriend," says Pauline.

"Me too," says Brendan. We all stare at him, surprised. "Like I said. I'm hungover."

Cruise smiles. "Myo and Myint will go with the moms and Brendan. Lin and I will stay with the girls and Max."

"Do Myo and Myint know the way?" asks Pauline, looking at them skeptically.

Cruise bursts out laughing. "Like they know their own faces. They taught me."

Mom sidles up to me, a deep line between her eyebrows. When she booked this "mild to moderate family" trek—after I'd been lying in bed for a month—nobody mentioned suicide climbs. "I think you should come with me," she whispers, not wanting anyone to hear.

Pauline hears anyway. "Let the girls have some independence," she says. "It would be good for them and good for us."

"Well," Mom says, her face tight, "I don't know."

"She'll be fine, darling. Won't she, Cruise?" Pauline beams at everyone. "Let's just let them go without their mothers."

Pauline's condescending tone makes me wince. For the record, Mom was never like this before my overdose. I mean, she was protective, yes, but not overprotective.

Then Lish surprises everyone by rounding on Pauline. "Well, you're the expert on that—kids without their mothers."

Pauline's face turns a blotchy sort of red, and she's lost for words. The awkwardness just grows and grows, and no one knows where to look. I settle on my feet.

"Valentine?" Mom says really, really quietly. I can barely hear her, though her lips are practically on my ear. "Why don't you come with us?"

"Because I want to do the climb." I'm not even sure this is true, but I'm mortified at being treated like a child.

"She'll be fine," says Cruise, digging around in his backpack. "I have rope and a halter in case a trekker can't make it. I've never used it, but if I need to, we will pull her up."

I stare at the ground and swear to myself that Cruise will not put that halter on me unless I'm dead and he's hauling my lifeless body up the mountain. Mom appears appeased or at least resigned.

Before we split up, Cruise gives us the day's itinerary. "Today we aim for the high altitudes of the Black Lahu people. They're from China. Animal worshippers, ancestor worshippers and slash-and-burn farmers well known for their temples. They're also famous for their weaving skills."

"More shopping," Pauline says, her enthusiasm a little forced. She smiles at everyone except Lish, whom she pointedly ignores.

"Two weeks ago in this area, we came upon a big troop of macaques. Monkeys. They stole people's hats, water bottles, cameras and a phone. And all of our sandwiches. Also, one trekker got bitten." Cruise looks at Mom and me. "A *Canadian*." He sounds so accusatory, we all start laughing.

"No," he says. "It was not funny. We had to leave the trek so he could get a rabies shot."

"You pesky Canadians!" Brendan laughs.

Cruise doesn't really get why we're laughing and becomes more irritated. "If you see monkeys, here are the rules. One, don't look them in the eyes. They take it as a challenge. Two, hide your phone and camera deep in your bags. And three, don't feed them. Unless they insist. If they do, throw the food far away from you.

"Today is also your best chance to see wild elephants. Don't get your hopes up too high, because they can hear us coming from a long way away, and although very big, they're good at hiding. If we do see them, be very careful you don't get between a mother and her calf. Okay now. Scenic trekkers, go left. We suicide climbers go right."

"Wait!" Mom calls. "Take my phone. It's still charged from the airplane."

"Mama Bear!" Cruise says, laughing. "Stop worrying. I have a phone."

NINETEEN

WE SCRAMBLE OVER rocky terrain at a breakneck speed just to reach the start of the suicide climb. By the time we face the vertical section of mountain, my shoulders are already sunburned, my pants are ripped, and my knee is bleeding.

"Ready to take your life in your hands?" Cruise asks, pointing to the wall of dirt, rocks and patches of weeds.

No one speaks.

A vulture circles, which seems like a dire portent.

"It's not as steep as it seems," Max says hopefully.

Lin goes first and tells me to follow. He looks like Spider-Man climbing up a skyscraper.

I get on Max's shoulders to get a solid start. Then I copy Lin's movements, stepping where he's stepped and grabbing where he's grabbed. He waits for me when I'm slow. By the halfway point, my heart pounds so hard I can barely hear him calling out encouraging things. My head is on fire, my hands are blistered, and my lungs are bursting. When I get to the top, or near the top, I'm delirious. I can't quite get my whole body over the ledge, so Lin pulls me over. I roll away so he can't see me gasping for air. I have a moment where I wonder if an out-of-shape sixteen-year-old girl can actually die of a heart attack.

Finally, the pain eases from my chest. When it stops aching, I roll onto my back. Lin crouches beside me, looking worried and holding out a bottle of water. I pour some down my throat. Then over my head. Then down my throat again until the bottle is empty.

"Okay, Valentine?" he asks.

I nod, but I can't talk.

He hands me another bottle. I lift my head and chug, then pour some over my face.

"Hey, take it easy with that water," says Cruise. "You'll need it for drinking."

"Not if my head blasts right off."

"It is okay," says Lin. "You drink. River is not far for fresh water."

My head finally cools down. The air moves smoothly in and out of my lungs. Lish has dropped down beside me, face down, arms spread out. I crawl over to the edge and peer down. Max is halfway up. He catches my eye and grins. I lie back in the grass and wildflowers, gazing at the bold blue sky, making out shapes in the passing clouds.

I made it.

A spritz of rain gets us stirring again.

Cruise hands out energy drinks, and we're as excited as if he's given us iced coffee with whipped cream.

We trek in the warm, mild rain until we come to a dead stop, struck dumb by a mind-blowing view. A valley, magical with floating mist and sparkling blue lakes, encircled by emerald-green mountains. Mountain after mountain after mountain into forever. A rainbow arcs over it all. Even Lish is awestruck.

Cruise gives us just enough time to breathe it in—and for Max to snap some pictures—before he rushes us along a path wide enough for two. We fall into pairs. Lin moves toward me, but Lish scoops his place.

I listen to our feet thudding. At first the sounds are discordant—mine heavier and Lish's lighter—but soon we sync up. There is something pleasing about the synchronicity. I don't talk. I'm too tired. I don't even point out the bunch of butterflies fluttering around a little puddle, dipping to drink the fresh rainwater. Their wings are translucent jade, outlined in black. At first I mistook them for trembling leaves.

I try to remember the collective noun for butterflies, because *bunch* doesn't do them justice. Mr. Singh was a collective-noun fanatic. Every day he'd put one on the board. I had so many favorites—charm of hummingbirds, leap of leopards, ostentation of peacocks.

"A flutter," I whisper, my voice startling Lish.

"What?"

"A flutter of butterflies. The collective noun." I nod toward the butterflies.

Lish glances down without interest. "The what?"

"The collective noun. Or the group noun. You know. Swarm of bees, colony of ants, herd of elephants. But there are others not as common and very creative. They're fun."

She stares at me. "You think nouns are fun?"

"Well, group nouns, yeah."

"I can't believe *you* called *me* a dork."

"I was being nice. I wanted to call you something much worse, but I didn't want to hurt your feelings."

"Hmmph."

I pick up my pace. Lish keeps step, and we move closer to Max and Lin, close enough to hear them.

"Do you ever guide groups yourself, Lin?" Max is asking.

"No. Not yet. I want to. I have been working on my English. I ask for English tours. I talk to people. Some give me books."

"Your English is great. Listen, Brendan has a crazy idea about going into Myanmar—or Burma. Whatever you call it. What do you think about that? We don't have visas, but we know there is an awful lot of cross-border traffic without visas."

"Illegal, you mean?"

"Yes. I guess I do."

"Best to get visa."

"Yes, but we can't. Brendan was kicked out of Burma less than three years ago."

"Why?"

"He was protesting against the government."

"Against *Tatmadaw*?" Lin sounds aghast.

"Tatmadaw?"

"The army. The government."

"Yes."

"He should not go back! Ever."

"So you won't help?"

"No."

"Okay. Frankly, I don't care. I don't want to go. I'd rather be looking for wild elephants. I'd like to be working on something like the hippo piece I shot in Uganda. Hippos in campgrounds. They're bloody dangerous, you know? Snap you in two with one bite. Tourists don't know. They've seen too many cartoon hippos as kids. But Brendan wants to go, and he wanted me to ask you."

"Why me?"

"You can handle the jungle. And you're Burmese."

"What do you mean, *I am Burmese*?"

"Aren't you? Cruise said you are."

"Cruise said I'm Burmese?"

"Yeah," Max says. "What's wrong with that?"

Lin stares at Max. It's the first time I've seen him upset. "Nothing is wrong. It is just not true."

"Okay. Sorry, mate."

"You should not go anyway. Just because Aung San Suu Kyi is elected does not mean she has power. Everyone thinks the soul of the country is saved now. That Mama of country—the beautiful woman with the soft voice, flowers in her hair and British sons—will save Burma. It is pile of elephant shit. Tatmadaw still runs country. And Tatmadaw does not change."

Max whistles. "I guess you don't think she deserved the Nobel Peace Prize."

"Maybe she does because she suffered for Burma. She was in house arrest for fifteen years, not even seeing her sons. She stood up for right. I love Amay Suu—Mother Suu —like everybody, but I know Tatmadaw."

"How?"

"What?"

"How do you know the Tatmadaw?"

I realize Brendan isn't the only one with journalistic instincts. I wait, fascinated, for Lin's answer.

"I hear things," he says after a long pause. "Like everybody."

They walk in silence for a while. I think about Aung San Suu Kyi. Frankly, I didn't have a clue who she was until last month when Mom and Dad made me watch a movie about her, called *The Lady*, as part of getting ready for this trip. She won an election in Burma, and the military got so mad, they arrested her and kept her a prisoner in her house for fifteen years. Dad says she is like Ghandi, a peaceful agitator who brought down the military in the end.

But if Lin is right, Dad is wrong.

"So I guess the Karen don't consider themselves Burmese," Max says.

"What do you mean?"

"Well, you are Karen—or Kayan—but you say you aren't Burmese."

"I am Karen?" Lin starts walking fast, like he's trying to get away from Max. But he doesn't have a chance. Max's legs are really long. I walk faster too, so I can hear, but Lin doesn't speak again.

Max throws Lin several sideways glances but doesn't press.

I check out Lish. She seems oblivious or just uninterested. I'm full of questions though. Isn't Lin Karen? If not, why does he live in a Karen village? Why is he so weird about Max thinking he's Burmese? Aren't all Karen from Burma? He is obviously not Thai. So what is he then? And why did he lie about how he knows the Tatmadaw? Because I am convinced he did.

It occurs to me that Lin isn't as happy and carefree as he seems. In fact, it seems he has secrets that make him miserable. Like I do. His secrets seem serious, like they could get him into trouble. Mine are just things I never talk about.

I imagine myself turning to Lish and telling her everything. *I'm flunking out of school. I was in a hospital for an overdose. I was in bed for a month.* I imagine her eyes sparkling because she's so impressed. I have to tell her it isn't impressive. *My boyfriend was killed after a football game. Punched in the face by a boy, who is out on bail, charged with manslaughter. Neil Carter. Neil Carter. Neil fucking Carter.*

I imagine telling her all of this, but I don't. I'm afraid she won't care.

TWENTY

WE COME TO A RIVER. The bridge across is a fallen tree trunk. Cruise goes first to show us how. He makes it look easy, sure-footing it over the water in less than two minutes. I go next. I put my foot on the trunk, and it rolls slightly. It definitely isn't steady. Underneath, white water bubbles. I hold my arms out for balance and take a few careful steps. I would never do this at home. It would be too dangerous. Stupid.

I remember walking on curbs as a child. The secret is to not try too hard. I take a "cleansing breath"—a meditation technique Mom is always recommending—look straight ahead and move quickly. It works. I'm over the river in no time. Everyone on the other side claps. Max follows fairly easily, with only a few wobbles. Lish doesn't even try to walk. She crawls across, hugging the log like a bear. Next, it's Lin's turn. He makes it look ridiculously easy, like he could cross with his eyes closed.

Lin works harder and harder in the humidity, cutting away brush and vines. He takes his T-shirt off, and I'm relieved Pauline isn't around to comment on his six-pack. The path just gets more and more overgrown. In places it doesn't actually seem like a path. Cruise stops and confers privately with Lin. Then he takes something out of his pocket, and they stare at it.

"I hope that's not a compass," Max says under his breath.

Cruise turns on his heel, facing different directions, looking down into his palm.

"It *is* a compass," Max says.

"Okay," Cruise finally says, turning around. "We will clear this path and go."

"Are we lost?" Max asks, not budging. "Because if we are, I suggest we go back to the fork where we split from the others and take the scenic route. Better late than lost. That's Brendan's motto, and I tell you, it saved our sorry butts in Africa."

Cruise looks at him like he's crazy. "Go all the way back there? No, no. We know where we're going." He asks Lish and me if we want to sit down and wait while he and Max help Lin.

We sink gratefully to the ground, groaning and grunting all the way down. Muscles I didn't know I have hurt. Lin hacks at the overgrown branches, and Cruise and Max start to clear the debris.

"You know what this means?" Lish says with a little grin.

"No."

"It means we aren't going to get to the village on time."
She laughs. "They're going to be all freaked out, waiting for us."

"And that is funny because...?"

"Serves my *mother* right."

"Why do you always emphasize *mother* like that? And why does it serve her right? I don't get it. You imply that she abandoned you, yet she apparently went to court to get you to come on a holiday with her. Unless, of course, the judge ordered her to come too, which doesn't make any sense. What exactly is with you two?"

"Nothing's with us. Absolutely nothing. We're like strangers. She likes to pretend that she's a good mother when people who don't know her are around. But look, you saw how she couldn't wait to dump me today. Not like your mother."

"It didn't seem to bother you."

"No, it didn't. I prefer it. I hate her. I hate her fucking guts."

"Why do you say awful things like that?"

"She *did* abandon me. Left me like a piece of garbage with my dad—who's sick—to go off and have her own life. So good riddance."

"Really?"

"Yes. She just moved out and left us. And my dad needs looking after, so I have to do it."

I think of Zosha, a girl in my grade whose mother left her dad when he got a brain tumor that took away his sight. Everyone thought the mother was the biggest bitch that ever lived. Including Zosha. She lives with her dad now and refuses to see her mother.

"I'm so sorry. What's wrong with your dad?"

"He drinks."

"*Drinks?*"

"Yes. Don't say *drinks* like that! All judgmental. It's a disease."

"Oh. Okay."

"Yes. And my mom thought I'd go with her, that I'd just desert my dad like she did. But I couldn't. He needs so much help."

"O-kay."

"Stop saying *o-kay* like that."

"What kind of help does he need?"

"He needs constant help. He's pissed every night."

"But to be fair, your mom didn't abandon you. She tried to take you with her. To get both of you away from—"

"From what?" she practically spits. "Just say it!"

"Well, from…an alcoholic father."

"Alcoholism's a *disease*."

"Well. Ye-es. But…"

A huge *bang* like a cannon going off blasts us to our feet. A thousand birds erupt from the trees, squawking and beating their wings. A second *bang* has us all shrieking and turning in circles.

An elephant trumpets. Then another. The sound is earth-quaking, tree-shaking. The air seems to shriek, or maybe that's more birds.

BANG, BANG, BANG, BANG. I can't count the blasts, they come so fast. Then more elephant roaring, followed by wailing—human or animal, I can't tell. Lish clings to me in a death grip. There is screaming, high-pitched screeches— some coming, I discover when Cruise motions frantically for us to shut up, from Lish and me.

"Too late," says Lin.

Too late. The words are ominous. Too late for what? I can't ask. I'm too afraid of the answer. I take a deep and shaky breath. A sharp metallic and smoky taste fills my throat.

The yelling and blasts have stopped, and I picture *them*— whoever and wherever they are—standing still, cocking their heads, listening to *us*. The sudden silence is as threatening as all the noise. Maybe more so.

"He's right, Cruise," Max says, his voice hushed. "They've heard us. Whoever they are." He looks at Lin. "Elephant poachers?"

Lin and Cruise slowly nod their heads. Then Lin starts to yell. "Make noise! Much noise!" he tells us.

Cruise also yells, motioning at us like he's conducting an orchestra to bring the volume up. Max hollers too and nods at Lish and me to join them.

It feels like everyone has gone crazy, until I recall that this is how you scare off mountain lions in the Canadian Rockies. Make a lot of noise so they'll think you're part of a big crowd. It's like making yourself big for a bear. Not that we're dealing with lions or bears, but this must be what we're doing, making those suddenly silent men with guns think we're a bigger and scarier group than we actually are. Lish and I join in, our eyes darting wildly as we shout as though we expect men to charge out of the trees and shoot at us. Which, in fact, is exactly what I expect.

When nothing happens, we just naturally wind down. We huddle near Lin, who at least has a machete. He and Cruise speak quickly. When they pause, the silence becomes overwhelming, as if the entire jungle is holding its breath. I picture birds lining branches, wings stilled, beaks clamped, eyes wary.

"What's going on?" I ask Max.

"We don't want them coming this way."

"What would they do? Kill us?"

"I doubt it. They don't want to kill tourists. They might if they think they have to or if we surprise them, but they probably don't want to. The military police would never stop looking for them. This country depends on tourism."

I don't know if this is true—that they don't *want* to kill us—but I try to make myself believe it. "What do we do?" I ask. My voice trembles. We all look at Cruise, our fearless leader—so far.

He lowers his face into his hands like he's going to cry. Lin, at least, looks totally composed. We wait a minute, and then Cruise looks up.

"We keep going. We've scared them away. Max is right: they prefer not to kill tourists. So we go. We have no choice. We have to meet up with the others. Just keep talking. Loudly."

"Has this ever happened before?" Lish asks.

We look hopefully at Cruise. We want him to say, *Oh yeah, all the time.*

Instead he shakes his head. "No."

"The dangers of going off the beaten path," Max says ruefully. He looks almost blasé, but he has trekked all through Africa—even through South Sudan, which Mom and Pauline found shocking. He must be one of those people who craves danger. I am, it turns out, not one of those people. Right now I crave my bed, with Mom in the kitchen and a pot of vegetable soup simmering on the stove, the smell of garlic filling the house. It's hard to believe it's only been a week since I was actually in my own bed.

Lin sharpens his machete on a stone. Cruise takes a Swiss Army knife out of his backpack, as does Max.

"What about yours?" Lish asks, still clinging to me.

I rummage in my knapsack, finding both my flashlight and the fork I stabbed myself with. I hand Lish the fork.

"Thanks," she says, without a trace of irony.

"Go for their eyes," I say. I flick the knife out of my flashlight. Not that I think it's going to do anything. They have guns. Big guns, if the sound was any indication. Maybe I can slit my wrists before they kill me.

It seems like we're heading right toward them, but maybe we're not. The sound bounced around a lot. I tell myself that anyway.

"Lin goes first, then me, then Lish, then Valentine. Then Max. No gaps. Go!" Cruise orders.

Lin has to work hard to get the path cleared, and it's impossible to go fast. But we walk close together, practically kicking each other's ankles, ears pricked like coyotes', listening, because we are afraid someone is watching, maybe even tracking, us.

It's like the feeling you get when you're little and you're suddenly afraid someone is under your bed, or when you're young and you're home alone and the phone rings and the caller hangs up and you're afraid the person who called you is in the house, the basement maybe. Only it's worse, because you know people *are* there, and you know they have guns.

TWENTY-ONE

AFTER JUST A FEW MINUTES of slashing through the jungle, we come to a messy clearing. Lin halts. We crowd around him.

Big boulders and piles of red leaves litter the area, piled in groups. Lin moves forward slowly, holding up his hand to stop us, but we follow anyway. He has the machete, after all.

As I get closer, the boulders arrange themselves into shapes: legs, torsos, heads. Three dead elephants, their heads covered with leaves. I blink. No. The red piles aren't leaves. The elephants' faces have been shot to red pulpy masses. The air reeks of blood. Iron. Rust. I throw up all over my boots.

It's a massacre.

I really, really wish Mom were here.

A lot of things happen, and they all seem to happen slowly except for the last one, which happens really fast. Lish sits down. Just plunks down like she's pushed. Her mouth opens in an O. Max groans, then swings his backpack off and roots around for his camera. Cruise swears, takes his phone off the solar charger on his knapsack and, when he doesn't get a network, throws it to the ground. It bounces but, thankfully, stays in one piece. Lin drops to his knees, lowers his head, upturns his palms and moves his lips, silently praying, I assume.

Then I'm knocked right off my feet.

I fly through the air and land against a dead elephant. I look up in shock. A frantic baby elephant runs in circles around the clearing, making noises I can only describe as screaming. Lin lifts me to my feet, slips my knapsack off my shoulders and brushes me down. Then he squats down, whispering and cooing to the little elephant.

"You okay, Canada Dry?" asks Cruise.

"Well…" I gesture toward the dead elephants. "No! Who did this? And why?"

Cruise just looks at me, then drops his head.

Max ventures in close, snapping photos. "They didn't have tusks, or we'd see big holes where they were hacked out. These elephants were shot in the face. This poaching was for the tourist trade. Right, Cruise?"

Cruise slumps his shoulders. "It's illegal and punished very harshly. It mostly happens in Burma, but…" He shrugs hopelessly.

"What does he mean *for tourists*?" I ask Cruise.

"They steal baby elephants. They have to kill the mama and aunts. It's always a bloodbath, but it doesn't happen much in Thailand now. There are big punishments. It happens more in Burma. Kill the ladies, steal the babies, and torture them until they are tame. For tourists."

"For tourists?" My voice is shrill. Eardrum-piercing shrill.

Lish is as upset as I am. "Tourists want baby elephants to be tortured? Are you insane?"

"No. But tourists like to see baby elephants, and tourists like to ride elephants."

"Those elephants we rode were stolen and tortured?" I ask. The ground seems to give way. The sky darkens. Rain clouds and crows converge. A murder of crows. Max snaps away.

"*Jesus!*" he says as he slips in a puddle of blood and ends up sprawled in it. "Jesus H. Christ!"

Buddha! I think. "Were they?" I stare at Cruise, who slowly answers.

"We use reputable mahouts. Thai mahouts, not Burmese. The Burmese are very bad to elephants."

"Not Burmese," Lin says, furious. "Burmese people love elephants. Just like Thais."

"But where did they come from?" I ask. "Where did Tinker Bell come from? Where?" I'm hysterical. Screeching like a banshee. The baby elephant screams too. Lin hushes me. I clamp my lips together.

"She was born in captivity, like all our elephants," Cruise says. "Don't worry."

"Do you know that, Cruise?" asks Max, walking gingerly around the elephants, trying to avoid the baby. "And if they were born in captivity, weren't their mothers captured then? Or their grandmothers?"

"Tourists like elephants," Cruise yells suddenly, his face red. "Where do you think they come from? Do you think they apply for these jobs?"

"Oh my god!" I say. "I didn't think. Was I supposed to think about that? Why didn't my mom think about that? She's the one who thinks about these kinds of things."

Max clicks away. Lish lights a cigarette with shaking hands. Cruise gives her shit and tells her not to start a fire, which is totally irrational because the recent rain has dampened everything. Lin tries to calm the baby. He crouches down and calls to it, making little clicking sounds like he's calling a dog. The calf rushes him but stops suddenly, before they crash.

"Looks like Lin is an elephant whisperer," Max says.

I try not to look at the elephants, but it's impossible. First, they take up so much space. Like the oak trees that occasionally fall in my neighborhood, they seem so much bigger when they're lying on the ground. The dead elephants are massive—bigger than any I've ever seen. I can't look at the gaping, bleeding messes that were once their heads, so I look at their feet. Their big, gentle, Reiki-massaging feet. Gray with huge whitish toes and markings on their soles that look like the henna designs Indian girls at my school paint on their hands for weddings.

The baby stops running in circles and prods one of the elephants with his little trunk.

"What's he doing?" Lish whimpers.

"Trying to wake his mother up, I think," says Max. "Why didn't they take the baby, Cruise?"

"We interrupted them," says Cruise, looking around nervously.

"But they had plenty of time, no?"

"No. It's not so easy. They don't want to hurt him. *You* try to move a wild elephant, even a baby, and you'll see. They have to catch it, then put a harness on it and pull. Maybe they had a truck nearby." He looks around doubtfully and shakes his head.

The baby gently moves the tip of its trunk over the red pulp of his mother's face. He wails. He mourns. I cannot express how sorrowful it makes me.

Cruise starts yapping at Lin, but Lin waves him away. Finally, Cruise turns to us.

"We go. Now."

Nobody moves.

"The poachers might come back for the calf," Cruise says. "We have to go, get away from here. Let's go to the village and meet the others. We can report this there."

"But what do we do about the baby?" I ask.

"It's a calf, not a baby. A wild animal, not human. We leave it here."

"No."

"No arguing. I am in charge."

"You expect us just to leave it. Don't we have a responsibility?"

"You don't understand. It will die anyway. It is too young. Crazy poachers, stealing such young calves!" We look at him, horrified. He amends his words. "I don't mean it's good to steal a baby elephant, just that this baby will die for sure. It's too young to be without a mother. These idiot poachers don't even know what they're doing."

"Maybe this little calf had an older brother or sister that they already took," Max suggests. "And now they are off and won't be coming back."

Cruise nods noncommittally. "I don't know. I have to assume they might come back. My job is to keep you safe."

"Well, what about an elephant orphanage?" I ask. "They would know what to do, how to keep it alive. Mom and I are going to one when we leave here. Near Chiang Mai."

"For the orphanage to take it, they need to see that the mother is dead. They are really strict with this. If we leave it here, they can come and see the mother, and take care of it. But it will probably die anyway."

"How far to the village, Cruise?" Max asks.

"Maybe one hour. Maybe two. Depending on the path."

"Can we take it to the village?"

"No village wants another elephant. They eat too much. Even if it could survive, which it can't."

"But this is just until we can get hold of an orphanage, right?"

"It is impossible. You see this calf? How do we pull it with us? We can't carry it. It isn't even safe to have the calf with us. My job is to keep you—"

"Safe. Yeah, we know," Max says. "Nevertheless, here we are."

Cruise flares his nostrils and chomps his gum.

"The calf's going to die if we don't take it," Max says. "I have pictures of the dead mother. Won't that work?"

"*We have to go*," says Cruise. "Now. Before the poachers come back for it."

"Him, not it," Lin says. "It is a boy."

Cruise ignores him. "What if they are watching us right now?"

"I don't think so," says Lin, looking around. He looks at the baby. "He would hear them and be even more scared. Great ears on elephants. Maybe the poachers are gone."

"There must be somewhere we can take a baby elephant, for God's sake!" says Max. "Come on, Lin. You must know of a place. This is ridiculous."

Lin crouches down, gently comforting the elephant, waving away the flies swarming the corpses. Lin coaxes the baby's mouth toward a teat showing just inside the mother's front leg. The baby latches on and sucks.

Lish makes a weird sound.

"What?" Lin asks. "The milk is still good. If it comes. If not, sucking alone is soothing."

Cruise yells at him.

"What are you yelling for?" I ask.

"We have to go. He just prolongs the calf's death this way. It is going to die."

"Well, sure," says Max. "If we don't fucking do anything." He kicks a fist-sized rock so hard it soars into the trees.

I kneel beside Lin. "Cruise is making us leave him here," I say.

At the sound of my voice, the calf turns and puts his trunk tentatively on my face. It feels familiar, like soft fingers. I put my arm around his neck, and he nuzzles me. He is trembling.

"He likes your voice," Lin says.

The calf wraps his trunk around my neck, and we hold each other. Something happens to me. My face tingles, and I don't want to let go. I hold him tighter, resting my chin on top of his head, in a stripe of red down. I run my palm over it. It feels like steel wool and looks like a Mohawk.

"I'm naming him Mohawk."

"Mohawk," Lin repeats. "Better than Tinker Bell."

Lin and Cruise talk, if you can call what they do talking. It becomes a screaming match.

"Okay," says Cruise, his words clipped. "Lin also doesn't want to leave the calf here. He will take him to a small sanctuary near the border, run by monks."

"It is not sanctuary," Lin says. "I will take him to monks, who live and pray in the jungle. They look after all living things. They will take him to a sanctuary. I believe so."

"Really?" I ask Lin. "You'll do that?"

He nods.

"That is so wonderful of you."

His face brightens.

"Good," Cruise says sarcastically. "So you are happy."

"Of course we're happy, Cruise," Max says. "Why wouldn't we be?"

"It's too near the border. Thai military police are everywhere. Burmese patrols slip into Thailand. There's a lot of trouble there. It's near a refugee camp. It's dangerous for Lin. And not good for us. Now I'm on my own to get you to safety. So let's go. We have to make up time. Your mamas will be very worried." He tightens the backpack strap around his waist.

I stroke the baby's head one more time. I can't believe how tender he makes me feel. "Goodbye, Mohawk. I'm so sorry."

"Don't worry. I will save Mohawk," Lin says.

I turn to him. "This is such a good thing you are doing. Thank you."

"Don't thank me. This is for karma."

I lean forward quickly to hug him and kiss his cheek. He holds me for an extra few seconds, and he is so warm and comforting that I don't want to let go.

TWENTY-TWO

I RUN AFTER CRUISE and the others, who are already leaving the clearing. We stay close together. Max calls back to me that he will take the rear as soon as he is finished clearing branches. I nod thankfully, because, as it is, I keep looking nervously over my shoulder.

Lish looks over hers at me. "Do you think the poachers are watching us?

"No," I say with bravado. "You heard Lin. Mohawk would have known."

"Mohawk?"

"The baby elephant."

"You think? I feel like they're watching us."

My sense that they're nearby amps up. I feel electrified. I swivel my head right, left, right, left. I spin around and walk backward for a few steps. I wonder when Max will come to the back of the line. I move so close to Lish that I'm breathing on her shoulder.

"Do you think they're going to kill Lin?" Lish asks.

"What? *What*? Why would you say that?"

"Well, even if they aren't watching us—which I think is bullshit—Cruise says they'll be coming back for the baby."

"He said they *might* come back. Lin said they were gone, and Max thinks they took an older elephant. Even Cruise said they don't take babies this young. And Lin knows his way around the jungle better than Cruise does."

"Well, good. Because those poachers are psychos. I mean, you saw those elephants."

Yes. I did. I close my eyes, trying to stop the images filling my head. But I can't. I still see them—the gray flesh and red mush where their faces were. The frenzy of flies. The impatient birds.

"Yeah, I saw them. For that matter, I may always see them."

"Psychos."

"Lin didn't seem worried," I continue.

"Why did Cruise say it was dangerous for him by the border?"

Why *did* Cruise say that? Why is Lish suddenly more aware than I am? "I don't know, but anyway, he wouldn't do it if he thought it was dangerous."

"Sure he would. He's in love."

"With Mohawk?"

"No, you moron. With you!"

"With me?"

"Duh. Don't say you haven't noticed. Why do you think he's doing it? Because you were so upset."

"That's ridiculous. We were all upset. Lin wouldn't risk his life for me. That's the stupidest thing I've ever heard. He is taking Mohawk for his own reasons."

"What reasons?"

"Karma."

"*Karma?*"

"That's what he said."

"Yeah right." Lish laughs.

"That is what he said!"

"Okay. What are you freaking out about then?"

"Because I would never want him to put his life in danger because of me! Obviously."

"Okay."

"Stop saying *okay*."

"Okay. Anyway, I thought you were really worried about Mohawk."

"I was. I am. But now I'm also worried about Lin."

Actually, I'm freaking out about Lin. Did I put his life in danger? Cruise said the border wasn't safe for him. Why didn't that register with me?

Because I wanted so badly for him to take Mohawk. The lump in my throat grows so big I can't swallow. It actually feels like I'm going to suffocate on my own saliva. I trudge along for another minute in total agony, and then I poke Lish in the back and whisper in her ear. "Lish, I have to go back. I'm not telling Cruise, because he would never let me go. Don't tell him. He'll just freak out. But slow down, so Lin and I can catch up later. Please."

Lish spins around, her expression inscrutable. "Really?"

"Yes." I turn around and run.

"Hurry!" she whisper-calls.

The path is narrow, and the tree roots cover it like veins. I keep my eyes on them as I run. I try not to think about poachers. I also try not to think about what I'll do if I can't find Lin. It's just been a few minutes, not even five. He'll still be at the clearing. He can't have cajoled Mohawk away from his mother so quickly.

I follow the litter of branches that Max and Cruise tore away. The jungle feels very different now that I'm alone. A breathing, fluttering, crackling, chirping, buzzing, green thing that eats people, like it did those poachers. They were there, close by, and then they vanished. I push overhanging branches away with my hand. One snaps back, slashing my face. I cry out, then clap my hands over my mouth. I am alone now, and I feel afraid. I'm starting to really panic when I see an opening in the trees.

My heart leaps. It's the entry to the clearing. My heart leaps again when I see Lin and Mohawk. I stop to get my breath. Mohawk looks at me, but he doesn't move. Lin's back is to me. He is tearing branches from a tree. At first I don't understand what he's doing. What *they're* doing. When I do, my skin prickles.

Lin gives a branch to Mohawk and helps him wrap his trunk around it, and then he leads him to the bodies, where other branches are laid like blankets. They are burying the elephants. My heart swells at the respect Lin shows.

I rush toward them, feeling more self-conscious by the second. I softly call Lin's name. He turns and gapes at me. I'm not sure what to say.

"Lin," I start—and then stop. "Don't you need to hurry? What if the poachers come back?"

"I will not leave bodies. Never again. And Mohawk *has* to do this, or he will never be okay. But why are you here?"

"I don't want you to die."

"Also I don't want." He laughs ruefully.

"Don't take Mohawk if it's dangerous. That's what I came back to tell you. Don't do it."

"You want me to leave him?" he asks.

We both look at Mohawk, standing over his mother.

"I don't *want* it," I say. "But it's dangerous. Come with us. Come with me. You are more important than Mohawk."

"Why?" He touches my face where the branch snapped against it. It stings, but I'm surprised to see blood on his fingers.

I shake my head impatiently. "Why what?"

"Why am I more important?"

"Because you're human."

"Are humans more important?"

"I...I don't actually know."

He looks behind me. "Where is everyone?"

"I left them to come and get you."

"No! You go back." His eyes widen. "*Go back now*. Fast. I will take Mohawk."

"Why, though? Why are you taking him?"

"I need to. This is...what is the word? Atone. This is a chance. A chance from the universe. You go! Please."

It's a little humiliating to discover I had nothing to do with his decision and that he would rather I just leave.

"Well, okay then," I say, backing away. "Goodbye. Good luck."

Mohawk raises his trunk and trots toward us. Lin's face changes. He looks around and puts a finger to his lips. Mohawk's trunk points into the jungle. His ears are open wide. He stares, transfixed, at the trees. Lin and I both follow his gaze.

At first there is only the hum of insects and the flap of birds' wings. Then there is crackling, like a strong wind is moving through the trees. By the time I hear voices, Lin is pulling me and Mohawk back into the shade of the jungle. Mohawk shakes visibly, which makes me think he recognizes the voices. Lin keeps putting his finger in front of his lips, and I really freaking hope that Mohawk gets the gesture.

TWENTY-THREE

THE MEN ARE NOISY. Angry. Their yelling gives us sound camouflage so we can keep moving despite breaking branches and snapping twigs. If they kept quiet and listened, they would find us in seconds. For the first minute—maybe two—we walk backward, as though we'll be safe if we keep watching the entry point.

A staccato burst of gunfire rips the sky. Cawing birds explode from the trees. I desperately hope their sounds cloak my involuntary shriek and Mohawk's quick trumpet.

Lin hugs Mohawk close. He strokes his trunk and head and gently shushes him. Mohawk responds with silence. I swear he understands everything that is going on.

What were they shooting? I mouth to Lin.

"Nothing," Lin whispers in my ear, his lips brushing my neck. "They shoot into the air because they are mad." The big blade of the machete, gripped in his fist, glints reassuringly.

I feel the sharp point of my knife, still open in my sweaty hand. It isn't much—not compared to assault rifles—but it's something. I think, with a sick stomach, of the phone Mom tried to hand me before we split up. Even with the patchy coverage here, it would have given me some hope.

Lin takes my free hand in his and squeezes. Mohawk reaches across with his short trunk and holds our hands. Then he strokes my face with the tip of his trunk, feeling each contour. Exploring. Like he's trying to understand who and what I am. Like me, he can't quite believe what is happening.

Lin becomes all business. First, he gets us turned around—slowly. It isn't as easy for Mohawk as it is for us. We have two smallish feet. Mohawk has four big feet. He takes up a lot of room. And there is no room. No path. No clearing. Just jungle.

Finally facing forward, we walk quickly. I get a kink in my neck, though, from looking back. Within a couple of minutes we're in even denser foliage. It's as though dusk has dropped: the sun doesn't penetrate the thick canopy of leafy branches. We squeeze between trees and push through shrubs. We duck under low-hanging branches.

I mostly keep my head down, looking out for roots, vines, rocks and holes so I don't trip or turn my ankle. A sudden movement across my foot almost makes me gasp. A small striped snake flicks its tail and disappears. Gnats prick through my clothes and feast at the back of my neck.

It's damp. It's green. Green is virtually the only color, in fact, except for brief patches of dark dirt. I feel so hidden, almost safe. How could anyone find us in here?

In the distance, the men suddenly yell out. I freeze. Lin turns back and listens, head cocked, eyes narrowed. Then they snap open.

"They come after us. They track us."

I wrestle some air into my lungs and dry my sweaty palms on my pants. The knife won't do me any good if I can't keep it in my grip. Not that it's likely to do me any good anyway, but I refuse to go down without a fight.

Lin makes us wait. My chest nearly explodes with fear as he scales a tall, slender tree. At the top he scans the entire area, and then he shimmies down.

He leads us through feathery fronds, plants so fragile we trample them flat, leaving a clear trail for anyone to follow. I remind myself of what Max said—that they won't want to shoot a tourist. But what if he was wrong?

It is possible, entirely likely even, that very soon I will be dead. Shot to pulp. Mom and Dad won't have a daughter—any child at all. They won't be parents anymore. I feel worse for them than I do for me. It's much worse to be left behind. As I well know.

I have a long moment, while Lin helps Mohawk over a log and then under a branch, to wonder if it is too late to hand Mohawk over to the men. If we could just have a peaceful handoff, and then they could let Lin and me go. It would spare Mom and Dad. They wouldn't have to put me in a coffin and watch me go into the dirt. If they even got a body to bury.

I look at Mohawk. At his wrinkled gray baby skin. His scalloped ears. His silly little pin-the-tail-on-the-donkey tail. Why should I prioritize him over Mom and Dad? They should be my priority. And they are. Of course they are. They're my parents, and I love them. If I can save my life by turning Mohawk in, I should just do it. I would expect them to sacrifice him to help me. That's a no-brainer. So why don't I? Why don't I at least suggest it to Lin?

Maybe I'm afraid of what he will think of me. Maybe I'm afraid of what I will think of myself. All I know is that when I look at Mohawk—his trusting eyes, his affectionate trunk and his scared-stiff ears—I can't betray him. I just *can't*.

The men are on the move, crashing through the same trees and plants we tried to negotiate so quietly. Lin pushes us under a slant of drooping tree branches, and we find ourselves on the muddy bank of a twisting stream. The water runs rapidly, frothing and glinting under a blade of sun. The sudden change of scenery is a surprise. If my heart hadn't been crashing like cymbals, I would have heard the water babbling.

Lin points frantically. I zip my knife into my hoodie pocket and slide down the muddy bank, gasping as I wade into the cold water. I stand shivering in the stream, near the bank, where the water is only up to my knees. It rushes quickly. I'm afraid of getting swept away if I go in too far. Lin cuts a vine from a tree and wraps it around Mohawk's neck. He knots the end and tosses the knotted end at me, gesturing for me to pull. As I tug, Lin gets behind Mohawk and pushes.

Mohawk slides down to the water's edge and puts a toe in the water. He quickly takes it out and tries with the other foot.

I pull hard on the vine. He backs up, stretching out his front legs in resistance. Lin strokes his ears, his trunk. He whispers in his ear. Then suddenly he cuts the vine leash with his machete, and, miraculously, the two walk into the water together.

"Swim," Lin says, going with the current.

Mohawk swims easily but looks awkward, like a cartoon elephant, as he bicycles his big stumpy legs. I didn't even know elephants could swim. I thought they just stood in shallow water to bathe. Lin does the front crawl, and I do a breaststroke, keeping my head mostly above water so I can see what's going on. When the water deepens, Mohawk's head dips beneath the surface, giving me my umpteenth heart attack of the day. Then I notice his trunk's tip above the water. He's snorkeling! Maybe that's where humans got the idea for it. I'm thinking random things like this while I swim for my life.

The stream is reedy at the bottom but clear near the top. I swim alongside Mohawk, catching his eye whenever I submerge my head. I blow water from my nose, making bubbles—just like I was taught at my community swimming pool with its diving boards and a gallery for parents to watch. Now here I am in a jungle halfway around the world, swimming with an elephant.

We make it around the first bend. The stream is now a widening river. Lin and I stop and tread water, catching our breath and taking stock of where we are and what we should do. Mohawk can't tread water, so he swims in circles around us. The current moves us all along. To our left, on the side of the river that we came from, the bank has become grassy. Up ahead on the right side there's a little cove, a catchall area littered with fallen trees, floating logs and tall grasses. An upturned rowboat lies stuck in the mud.

We hear nothing. Either we've outswam the men, or they are still coming after us, quietly, a scenario that makes my skin crawl. Lin chews his cheek and looks around. We are very exposed. If the poachers round the bend now, they will see us.

Lin nods toward the cove. "Quick," he whispers.

It is hard to break away from the current. I am nearly swept away, but Lin grabs my wrist and pulls me with him. In the cove, we stand ankle-deep in mud and thigh-deep in coffee-colored water. Lin turns the boat on its side and sweeps out clumps of slimy leaves that stink of rot. There is just enough room for me and Mohawk to duck behind it, plus there's a hole in the hull that I can look through.

I crouch, and Lin coaxes Mohawk to his knees.

"What about you?" I ask.

Lin looks around.

"I will disappear. Watch." He hyperventilates, filling his lungs to capacity and then emptying them. He does this several times while keeping an eye on the other bank. Then he slips quickly under the water.

The men move out of the jungle, as silent and silky as smoke. Five of them. They wear army fatigues and vests. Three have assault rifles slung casually over their shoulders. One, the leader, has his pointed, ready for firing. It appears to be pointed right at me. One man swings a big ax. I reach underwater for Lin's hand and start counting silently.

Twenty *Mississippis* while they scan the area. Up to forty while they confer quietly. Lin watches me from just under the surface of the water. Waiting desperately for my all clear.

Finally the men run along the grass path, following the river until they disappear. One hundred *Mississippis*. Almost two minutes. I pull frantically on Lin's arm, and he shoots up out of the water, coughing and raggedly sucking in air. He rolls on his back and floats until his breathing is under control.

"Let's go," I whisper, jerking my thumb over my right shoulder.

"No. We go back the way we came. West. To the monks." He paddles out to the middle and looks cautiously down the river.

He waves us over. I touch Mohawk, and he follows me as I swim across, both of us battling the current. We scramble up the bank and dash into the jungle. As soon as we feel safe, Lin and I drop our knapsacks and collapse.

TWENTY-FOUR

My teeth chatter so noisily that Lin takes me in his arms. Mohawk sinks down to his knees, then flops onto his back. He rocks from side to side in the dirt.

"Are you okay, Valentine?" Lin asks.

I laugh, because obviously I'm not okay, and, worse, I imagine the panic I have caused. Because by now Cruise and Max will have noticed I'm not with them. I try to assess how much time has passed. Probably half an hour, though it feels longer. I wonder how much trouble Lish is in. Will she have admitted she knew what I was doing? Will they have backtracked to find me? Are they in the clearing now? Oh my god! I think of the last bit of gunfire. Will they think we're dead?

Then I think of Mom, and remorse hits me like a speeding train. I imagine her learning that I'm not with Cruise, Max and Lish. I imagine her wild fear and uncontrollable grief. And I almost lose my mind.

Lin holds me so tight I can hardly breathe. I'm shaking so hard, it's like I'm having a seizure.

"My mom," I say into Lin's shoulder. "My mom. She will be so scared. She'll think I'm dead."

Lin rocks me gently. "Then it is simple what you must do."

"What?"

"You must not die. Do you hear?" Lin asks. "It will be much worse for your mama if you really die. This can be over soon. But we must move. We will walk until dark, then sleep. Tomorrow we will reach the monks and call Cruise."

"Tomorrow? Not today? I can walk all night."

"No. We will stay alive if we are smart. We will rest ten more minutes, then go." He sits up and pulls me with him, keeping one arm around me as he fishes his ziplock bag of rolled cigarettes out of his knapsack.

He uses his teeth to break the seal on the bag and pull out a cigarette, flicking the lighter with his free hand. The long thin plume of flame comes near my face; the brief sensation of heat only makes me feel colder.

At home I hate being around smokers. Not now. I breathe in the sweet leafy smoke and the mossy smell of the river. I rest my head on Lin's shoulder as he outlines our plan. West toward the border. A day and a half away there is a small refugee camp and, nearby, a monastery where the monks will take Mohawk.

Lin is confident that the monks will help. "They never turn away living things," he says. I hope he is right.

Lin uses my knife to poke holes in the metal cap of his large water bottle. Then he offers it to Mohawk, who sucks it back in half a second. He slurps at the empty bottle. Lin and I exchange a worried look. Mohawk needs a lot more food and drink than we do.

"I will go back to the river for water," Lin says.

"No! What if the men come back? It's too exposed. Please don't. Mohawk and I need you."

"We will all die without water, and Mohawk will go first."

We check our supplies and pool our water bottles. Lin dumps them all in a plastic bag, which he throws over his shoulder as he walks away. I sit huddled next to Mohawk, wondering what we'll do if Lin never comes back

But he does, shortly, sopping wet.

"Did you fall in?" I ask.

"No." He laughs at me, shaking his head. "Water is only good for drinking near the middle, where the river moves fast. Sides are full of bacteria."

It seems crazy to him that I don't know about drinking water. I think of the faucets at home that I just turn on. Right for cold, left for hot. When they don't work, Mom calls a plumber.

"It is good to understand rivers."

"How do you know so much?" I ask. "And how did you stay underwater so long?"

"I breathed in and out quickly first. That helps you hold breath."

"But how did you even know that?"

"I have experience surviving in jungle."

"From tour guiding?"

"No!" His mouth tightens. "Not from tourists."

"From what?"

He answers slowly. "I spent four months in this jungle. Hiding, running."

"From who?"

"Enough talk. We go."

He jumps to his feet, puts out his cigarette on the bottom of his flip-flop and then gives me a hand. After he helps me up, we have a moment, my hand in his for a few seconds too long, his face so close to mine I expect him to kiss me. I lower my eyes and take a step back.

"Ready," I say, feeling both relief and regret. I take off my hoodie and wring it out, then tie it around my waist.

"If we keep moving, we will stay warm," Lin says cheerily.

My sopping hiking boots squish with each step. My wet pants chafe between my thighs. A blister gnaws at my heel. But my legs keep moving, and my mind keeps churning.

"Who were you hiding from?"

Lin throws me a quick glance, his face clouded. He keeps walking, not altering his pace and not answering for so long that I assume he's not going to.

"Tatmadaw," he says finally.

"The Burmese army?"

"Yes."

"*The whole army?*"

"No! Some soldiers."

"Why?"

"They tried to kill me, but I escaped."

"Why did they try to kill you?"

"They like to kill."

Cold fingers creep up my back.

"How did you run into them? What were you doing? Were you in Burma?" I remember Lin telling Max he wasn't Burmese. But why would the Tatmadaw be in Thailand? Then I remember Cruise saying soldiers sneaked over the border to set fires in refugee camps. I also recall Lin's fury when Cruise said the Burmese mistreated elephants. "Were you a refugee?"

"Food," Lin says, stopping suddenly. He scrambles up a skinny tree and reaches a tiered bunch of green bananas. One thwack and they drop, releasing a swarm of the biggest insects I've ever seen. They look like miniature yellow dragons. Their wingspan is the size of my face, and they fly right at me. I scream and wave my hands frantically.

Lin calms me down, stifling a laugh. "Only bats," he says. "Painted bats, you say in English. Harmless, gentle."

"*Only* bats?"

"Yes. They are half-blind. They live in nests in banana trees. Families live together. Mothers, fathers, babies. They squeak to each other. Tonight we might hear them. Very cute. Maybe we will be lucky and see them hunt."

"Hunt? For what?"

"Insects, only. Not girls." He smirks. He peels a banana and offers it to Mohawk, who tries to roll it up in his trunk so he can put it in his mouth. But he can't. It falls out. Lin cleans off the dirt and tries again. It falls out immediately.

"He is so young," Lin says. "He needs his mama to help him eat. He does not know how to use his trunk. Grown elephants can pick up one single flower—or the heaviest log."

I peel another banana and hand it to Lin. Lin puts it directly into Mohawk's mouth this time. Then he helps him chew by manipulating his jutting lower jaw. Once Mohawk gets the hang of it, there aren't enough bananas, so Lin climbs up the tree for more. Lin and I feast on the seedy and chewy fruit too. They're nothing like the squishy bananas at home.

"So were you a refugee?" I ask again.

Lin gives me a searching look, his eyes roaming over my face for so long I start to squirm.

"Yes," he says slowly. "I became one."

I don't understand the distinction between being one or becoming one, but before I can ask, he jumps up to clean up our mess. With his hands and his machete, he digs a hole in a patch of ostrich ferns and buries the banana peels.

Mohawk sucks back another bottle of water. Lin and I only take a few sips. "We have to conserve," says Lin.

I remember how wasteful I was with my water earlier, when I poured two bottles over my head after the climb.

As we walk, I wonder what it was like for Lin to hide in the jungle for months. I wonder if I could ever survive on my own. I wonder if I will survive overnight.

Mohawk stops walking, sinks to his knees and bellows.

"What's he doing?" I ask, glancing around nervously.

"Calling his mama?" Lin suggests.

Lin coaxes him back to his feet and pushes him along the path. But it seems like Mohawk has reached his limit. His trunk sags. His ears droop. He quits looking up at me. He quits talking to me—if his high-pitched whinnies were conversation.

We manage to urge him along until it gets dark, and then Lin finally drops his backpack and machete. "Here we camp."

We're in a small clearing within a tight circle of trees. A stream gurgles nearby. Mohawk sits on a log, but it rolls under him. He jumps up, startled, then settles on the ground beside me. I cuddle him for warmth, but he sits very still and doesn't hug me back. I feed him half of the remaining bananas in Lin's backpack. At least he chomps away at them.

With the dark comes the cold, and it will get worse as the night progresses, Lin warns. Jungle temperature is simple, he says—hot days, cold nights. Mohawk and I watch, half-dazed from the long day, as Lin collects firewood. I jump up when I realize I should be helping. I gather small branches from the ground while he hacks bigger branches into foot-long sticks. I then arrange a ring of rocks.

When the fire is blazing, I get as close as I can to the enticing orange flames, but Mohawk moves away nervously. Lin makes a clothesline out of a vine, takes off his T-shirt and pants and hangs them near the fire to dry. Completely at ease in jockey shorts that seem in danger of sliding down his thin bony hips, he looks at me.

"Don't sleep in wet clothes. Unless you want to be sick."

I'm not sopping wet anymore, but I'm damp, clammy and chilled to the bone. "I think I'm already sick," I say. My hand goes to my throat.

"Sore?" he asks.

I nod. "Like swallowing a knife."

"It's okay. I will make tea. You will feel better." He moves around easily, using his flashlight to search the plants.

Warm, dry clothes would be amazing. I find a tree to change behind and take off my boots and socks. I run my fingers over the bleeding blister on my heel. I strip down to my bra and underwear. It hurts to pull my T-shirt over my head, but I'm too focused on my bra and underwear to think about it. I can't help wishing they were a little prettier, even though it's a ridiculous thing to care about. At least they're black, not white and transparent. They're wet too, but hopefully they'll just dry on their own. I make sure my self-inflicted wound hasn't opened up and bled. It's not bleeding now, so I bury the gauze I'd stuffed in my bra.

I walk gingerly back to the fire, avoiding stones and sharp sticks. I hope I'm not blushing too much when I step into the clearing. Lin doesn't seem to notice that I'm almost naked. He points to my bare feet, alarmed.

"No. You must wear shoes."

"I can't." I show him the blister, and he insists I wear his flip-flops. When I protest, he makes me feel the bottom of his feet. They are hard with callouses. I drape my hoodie, pants, T-shirt and socks over the line, trying not to feel self-conscious. Or, at least, trying to pretend that I'm not.

Lin stares at me, still frowning.

"What's that?" he asks, pointing at my side.

I lift my arm and look down at a bruise that covers my rib cage. "Ah," I say. "That's why it hurt."

"What happened?"

"I don't know."

Lin suddenly nods. "I know. Mohawk did that when he knocked you over. Bad Mohawk," he says softly and strokes Mohawk's trunk. Then he kisses the top of his head.

My fingers go from my bruise to the cut on my face. "I'm a mess," I say.

"No. Beautiful. You are beautiful. *Hla deh.*"

I flush and look away.

"Do you have a boyfriend?"

"No," I say slowly.

"You don't sound sure."

I want to explain but can't find the right words. *I have a boyfriend, but he's dead* would sound bizarre, even to me.

Lin looks puzzled. Then Mohawk bellows, and Lin gets back to work. He wades into the stream to fill the water bottles. When he is back, he pulls an old aluminum pan out of his backpack and drops flat rocks into the fire to make,

I assume, a cooking grate. I give Mohawk water as Lin works on dinner.

Finally, Mohawk's thirst is quenched. He lies down on his side on a grassy patch, and I sit between his legs, leaning against his warm belly. He makes snuffling sounds that I find so soothing, I slouch down, letting my head fall back on his big cushion of a side.

TWENTY-FIVE

LIN CALLS MY NAME, and I force my eyes open. He leans against a smooth tree trunk, a crimson bandanna holding back his long hair. He is dressed now, his T-shirt and shorts dirty but dry. He smokes a cigarette, holding it like a joint as he watches me stand and stretch.

I grab my warm, dry pants and T-shirt from the line and say a mental thank-you to Mom, who insisted I have fast-dry hiking clothes for the trek. I dress behind a tree. I don't know why, but I do. My clothes feel like they're fresh from the dryer. I haven't felt this good in hours. The hoodie is still damp, so I move it closer to the fire.

Lin's pan, our only plate, cools on the grass, and the smell of cooked food makes my mouth water. We use our fingers to eat greens and mushrooms. After we finish eating, Lin boils water and makes tea with a plant he has gathered. It tastes terrible, but it actually eases my raw throat.

We sit around the campfire, warm, dry and full. The moon looks like a silver ball trapped in the tangle of overhead branches. Both Lin and I caress Mohawk. He plays briefly, flipping my hair and hugging my neck. Then he slumps down, despondent again.

"It's time to sleep. He will feel better if he gets rest. Us too." Lin points to a branch, about seven feet off the ground and entwined with a branch from another tree. "A tree bed," he says. "You will sleep there."

"Where will you sleep?"

"Down here with Mohawk. He will be scared alone."

I look up at the "bed" nervously. "And what if I fall out?"

"You won't. I will tie you in. I always slept in trees."

"But won't I be cold?"

"There are bugs and snakes on ground. Many more than in trees."

"But you're sleeping on the ground."

"Because I don't want to leave Mohawk alone."

"I don't want to be alone. I want to be with you and Mohawk."

"Okay." Lin nods seriously. "Okay."

The fire dies down to glowing embers. I pull on my dry, slightly scorched hoodie and snuggle down on the grass nearby. Lin covers Mohawk with branches and big leaves that he first shakes free of bugs.

"What are you doing?" I ask.

"Mama elephants cover their babies when they sleep."

I recall how he covered the dead elephants. "Do they also cover their dead, like you were doing when I came back for you?"

"Yes. That is how they bury them. First, they stand guard for days. Sometimes the whole herd does. If a calf dies, its mama won't let anything near. Will go crazy at birds circling. Elephants have strong feelings, as strong as people's. Maybe even stronger."

"How do you know all this?"

"Mi Mi, my father's elephant, lost a calf. He died only days after born. Mi Mi suffered, and because my father did not know better, he wanted to bury the calf. He thought it would be better for Mi Mi not to see it."

"What happened?"

"Mi Mi almost killed my father. She picked him up and swung him around. We thought she would throw him. But she did not. She only scared him. Then she pushed her calf out of sight. She disappeared. My father did not go after her. In one week she came back, and in two weeks she let my father touch her. Then she went to work again."

"What work? Tourism?"

"Logging."

"And she was okay?"

"Sad, of course, because elephants do not forget. But when they are ready—when they accept death— they bury bodies and move on."

I pause over his words. "When they accept death?"

"Yes. It is important to accept death. Or they stand there forever, roaring at birds."

I take a long, long beat, letting his words sink in. That's been me. Standing over Amir, roaring at birds.

"You're a bit of a poet," I say.

He smiles. "Only a bit?"

I smile too. I have a strange revelation: if I weren't afraid of the poachers and worried sick about Mohawk and Mom, I would be having a good time.

"Tell me more about your father."

"My father was a very gentle man. A good Buddhist."

"Where does he live?"

"In village."

"With you?"

"No. Another village. Far away."

"Do you get to see him very often?"

"No." Lin starts to clean up, wiping the pan clean with leaves.

I stretch out and try to get comfortable on the hard, lumpy ground. Only yesterday I thought a sleeping bag was roughing it.

"Do you think we've lost the men?" I ask.

"Maybe."

"You could understand them?" I try to make sense of the Burmese/Karen knot that Max had tried to untangle earlier today, when he upset Lin.

"Yes."

"They spoke Burmese?"

"Yes."

"Were they soldiers?" I think of their camouflage and vests. And their guns. Then I realize that Lin never really saw them. "They were dressed like soldiers. Oh my god! Could they have been from the Tatmadaw?"

"Could be."

"Is that why Cruise said it's dangerous for you by the border?"

"Cruise would say anything to make me stay with him."

I hope that is the truth, but somehow I think it's not. "But why would soldiers kill elephants?"

"Soldiers take drugs that make them crazy. Makes it easier to do very bad things. Also, they need money. Myanmar—Burma—is a poor country. Once it was rich, but first British, then Japanese, rob the land."

"So could the poachers have been soldiers?"

"Could, yes."

"Why did one man have an ax?"

"To hack tusks out of face if they find male elephants."

"But there was no male there?"

"No. It was a small female herd."

I flash to the carnage again. "Evil bastards." I wonder for the first time how long it took the elephants to die. How many bullets tore away their faces before they fell. "I hate them. I wish they were dead. I wish we could have killed them."

"Don't say that."

"But I mean it. Now they will just keep killing elephants."

"You don't know what you say." Lin smiles bitterly. He reaches over and brushes his knuckles over my heart.

"And it is not good to say. It is bad for your heart." While I am still tingling from his touch, he pulls the bandanna from his head, freeing his long black hair. He lights another cigarette and smokes it, staring into the fire. I lie on my side, watching him. I examine his hands, his long slender fingers, the shiny calluses on the palms.

I imagine them touching me again.

Lin squishes his cigarette into the dirt and stretches out on his side, facing me. He is very close, and once again I think he is going to kiss me. But he doesn't. So I take his face into my hands and kiss him. He kisses me back, tentatively at first. Sweetly, his lips roaming my face. Then hungrily. He rolls on top of me, pressing his body into mine and parting my legs with his hips. Just as suddenly, he pushes me away.

"I need to tell you something."

I expect him to tell me he has a girlfriend. Or maybe even a wife, since everyone here gets married so young.

"Okay."

"I am Bamar."

"What?"

"Or maybe you say Burman. It is the same thing."

"I don't understand."

"Burmese. Of the dominant group. I said I wasn't, but I am."

"I figured."

"My country has been at war with itself my whole life. My father's whole life too. It started in the Second World War when we fought the British. Then the Japanese. Now the Burmans, who run the military, fight all the different people there—the Karen, the Shan, the Chin, the Rohingya and more. The military wants total control. Once upon a time, people from all over came to Burma. It was a beautiful place. More beautiful than you can imagine."

I wasn't expecting a history lesson, but he is so deadly serious, I follow intently.

"But not now. And we are not democracy. In Canada, you vote. Your elections are real. We have elections to make the world happy, but they are—what is word?"

"Shams?"

"Yes. Shams. So the Tatmadaw always win. And if they don't, they arrest the real winner, like Amay Suu."

"A military dictatorship," I say.

"Yes. They came for me when I was fourteen."

"Who?"

"The army."

"Came for you? What do you mean? Is that when you ran?"

"No. I did not run. I could not run. They came for me. They took me."

"They took you where?"

"To fight. To be in the army."

"You were a child soldier? Oh my god." We read about child soldiers in English class, in Ishmael Beah's memoir, A *Long Way Gone*. It all seemed so alien, another world. One day you could be a kid entering a rap contest with your cousins, and the next minute your whole country was at war, and you were a soldier. A world I would never know. Except that—here I am.

"Yes. And I did bad things. Such bad things."

A hole opens in my stomach. "*You?*"

"The army is very bad. They teach…such bad things. They make you do them."

"What bad things?" I ask, but my voice is so quiet I don't think he hears.

"I ran away. I hid in jungle until I came to Htay's village. We could understand each other, because of where I was from, near Irrawaddy River basin. When I was young, there were many Burmans and Karens there. We lived together peacefully. We spoke each other's language. Htay—the lady who owns the guesthouse—took me in. She saved me. Not just my life. My spirit."

"What bad things?" I ask louder.

Lin starts to cry. For a moment it's hard to say who's more shocked—him or me. I take him in my arms, and he cries into my shoulder.

The tears end abruptly, as fast as they started. He pulls away, turning his face briefly to wipe his eyes. "Sorry," he says.

"No. Don't be."

We lie down, facing each other again. He clasps my hands. My face nestles into his. My lips brush against his petal-soft skin. His eyelashes flutter against my cheekbone, and his breath whispers over my mouth. But we don't kiss. We have moved beyond that into a fragile, protective embrace. We close our eyes. Pretend to sleep. Hope to hold on. To what, I'm not sure.

Mohawk makes little agitated noises in his sleep and presses his back into mine.

I wonder what Lin's unit did. I wonder what he did. The wondering is an ache in my heart. I am tired, thankfully. Exhausted. More exhausted than I've ever been in my life. I wait for sleep to take me. Just before it does, little squeaks come from the banana tree. The bats. I picture the mother and father with their babies, and it comforts me. At least that is normal and good. The little bats all together, hidden from view in a nest under the leaves. A snuggle of bats.

TWENTY-SIX

MY EYES OPEN to such opaque darkness that I don't know where I am. The fresh aroma of dirt, the pungent odor of animal musk, the cold, cold air and the two warm bodies sandwiching me are sensations I can't make sense of. I think I must still be dreaming. There is something else too. A new worry—an unfamiliar weight—that I can't identify.

A warm breath on my neck starts a series of recognitions. Lin's hand over mine. Lin spooning me. The wrinkled and leathery hide of Mohawk under my arm. Me spooning Mohawk. The hard ground. The black, starless sky, already shifting into overcast gray. The smudge of a moon. The hooting of owls. The beating of little wings.

I'm besieged with quick flashes of yesterday. Dead elephants. The river. Men with assault rifles. Lin's kiss. Lin's "very bad things."

Mom. Mom, who probably thinks I'm dead. I think of Dad and have a new wave of panic and remorse. Mom will have called him. I didn't think of that yesterday. He is possibly flying to Thailand right now. I look up as if I might see his plane. But maybe she couldn't get a call out. Maybe there was no coverage. I have a fleeting moment of hope. Then it goes. I picture my terrified and terrifying mother. She would have made Cruise get word out somehow. Even if he had to walk to Chiang Mai. No, she would have made him run. I feel sorry for Cruise. And Lish. Oh my god! *Lish.* Mom might actually murder her.

Lin wakes and rolls away from me. Frigid air swoops up my back.

Mohawk stirs too, moving the tip of his trunk over my arm. It tickles. I have a rush of wonder that I am holding an elephant. A rush of wonder at my affection for him. I think of Rumi: *Find the sweetness in your own heart, then you may find the sweetness in every heart.* Maybe it also works the other way.

Mohawk twists his big head around until his trunk touches my face.

"Good morning," I say, tightening my arm around his side, but he withdraws his trunk quickly and lies very still.

I turn to Lin, who is sitting up, his arms around his knees. "Mohawk looked for his mother and found me instead," I say.

His black eyes flicker over both of us sadly. I miss his quick and carefree smile, even if I now know that it covered something dark. I hate the sudden constraint between us.

I try to sit up too, but it's not that easy. My arm is asleep. A sharp pain knits at my side. Every single muscle in my body resists.

Lin piles wood for a fire. I try to catch his eye, but he looks keenly at everything except me. I try to think of something to say that doesn't sound awkward or trite. Nothing comes to mind. I wonder again what he did. How bad it was. I have a brief, panicked moment of wondering if I am safe with him, but I force the thought out of my head. Of course I am. I let myself think of his tears. His remorse. His goodness. He buried the elephants. Mohawk trusts him.

My sleeping arm starts to tingle unbearably. I cradle it until the rush of burning needles subsides. The jungle wakes up too, with warbling from the ground cover, rustling from the leaves, *rat-tat-tat* from woodpeckers. Whistling from Lin while he builds the fire. No friendly rumbling from Mohawk though.

The fire catches, and I move toward it gratefully. The pan sits in the flames, filled with water. Lin hands me a banana. I make sure I touch his hand when I take it.

"Thank you."

He nods gravely, goes to the fire and squats in front of it, all knees and elbows, his hair loose against his dirty T-shirt. As the water starts to simmer, he adds leaves and stirs with a forked stick. His movements are deliberate and focused. He catches me staring, and I smile. He doesn't smile back but holds my eyes for a moment. For a second I feel frustrated. Even angry. I've got my own pressing issues, and *I'm* doing my best.

Then I recall myself lying in bed, shunning Becca, Amir's parents, even his little sister, Mona. Mom, Dad. I was not doing my best then, that is for sure. That was nobody's best. I wish more than anything that I could have a redo.

Random thought on ever getting one: forget it.

When the tea is ready, we sit on either side of Mohawk, greeting him as though he is our child. As we take turns sipping from the pan, we pet him, talk to him, plant kisses on the wide expanse of head between his ears. His eyes open, then close. Other than that, he doesn't acknowledge us. I can't imagine how frightening this must be to him. Until yesterday he had probably never even seen a human.

"We must make him move," says Lin. "He misses his mom. He's sad and doesn't want to face the world."

"God knows I know that feeling."

"Yes?"

"Yes."

"Why?"

I consider for a second. Should I tell him why? Will he even care? Will it sound like I'm only thinking about myself? And how paltry will my own troubles sound to him? Ridiculously paltry. Or will he know I'm trying to share something with him because he shared something with me?

"I've been depressed since September. I was in bed for over a month before I came here. Except for a trip to the emergency department because of a drug overdose."

Lin studies me. "Drug overdose?"

"Yes."

"What kind of drugs?"

"Sleeping pills mostly. Painkillers too. Oh, and Trazodone, an antidepressant."

"Did you try to kill yourself?" he asks, thin eyebrows arching.

"I don't think so. It didn't seem that way, but maybe. I don't know. Maybe I did." My words surprise me. *Was* I trying to kill myself? Is it possible? I was in despair, yes. But if I was really trying to kill myself, why did I take the pills so slowly? And why don't I remember taking them all? I was reckless with my life. Is that the same thing?

"Why?" Lin asks.

"My boyfriend was killed."

"Killed? How?"

"In a game. Another guy." I can't say any more. Neil Carter. Murderer. Still at school because he is out on bail.

Lin looks perplexed. "A game?"

"Football."

"Did they fight?"

"No." I can hardly talk through my clenched teeth. "It wasn't a fight. It was one-sided. But they had fought earlier in the game. I wasn't there to see it."

"Did you love him?"

"Yes."

"I am sorry for you."

"I don't want you to be sorry for me. I want you to be sorry for him. I want you to be angry for him. I know it's unreasonable, since you don't know him, but it's what I want.

I can't help it. It's why I never talk about it—because I know no one will ever be sorry enough." My face heats up.

"I understand, and I *am* sorry for him. But I do not want to be angry. I try, now, to be a good Buddhist."

"Really? I've seen angry Buddhists." I think of the monks in the night market.

"Yes." Lin smiles ruefully. "All Buddhists get angry, except maybe the most holy. We can only *try* to not be angry."

"I'm going to have to tell my mother that. She's a Buddhist, and an angry Buddhist, sometimes."

"Your *mother* is Buddhist?"

"Yes. But she's new, so obviously not very good at it. I drove her to it."

"What?"

"She became a Buddhist because I caused her such worry and distress."

"Then you did something good."

"You think?"

"But I am sorry for your boyfriend. What was he like?"

"He was the most joyous person I ever knew."

Lin waits, expecting more. When I offer nothing, because my throat has completely constricted, he drops his head and stares into the fire. His hair falls forward, shadowing most of his face. He reaches across Mohawk to hold my hand. "I'm sorry."

We finish our tea in silence, then together try to get Mohawk on his feet. We push. We pull. We talk to him, gently coaxing. Eventually he stands, but his legs are wobbly. His head stays down. He looks devastatingly sad. I lift his trunk and upend the bottle into his mouth. I give him all of our water.

Lin tells me to throw dirt on the fire and break up the burning embers while he goes to the river for more water. I am anxious for us to get on our way. I gingerly put on my socks and boots. By afternoon this whole thing will be over. This snake pit of worry in my stomach will end. I rub dirt over Mohawk. I've read that mother elephants spray their babies with dirt to protect their skin from the sun.

"You'll feel better soon," I tell him. "The monks will look after you. And when you're strong, you can go to an orphanage with other elephants. You can make friends."

He doesn't move. Doesn't even lift his head.

"Mohawk, come on! *Come on*." I wrap my arms around his neck and lay my cheek on his head. I impatiently watch the path, waiting for Lin to return. To come back and get us moving. I am watching when Lin appears. Watching when he freezes. Watching when his face changes.

My back prickles with dread. I look over my shoulder. A man stands quietly in our clearing, smiling, his gun casually pointing our way.

TWENTY-SEVEN

MOHAWK IS alert *now*. He shakes and makes gurgling noises. I feel his rumbles before I hear them. He is warning other elephants—wherever they may be—that something is wrong. Or maybe he is warning me. I pat him, telling him I understand, and then I feel for the hard outline of the flashlight–knife in my pocket. Lin edges close to me and calmly tucks the water bottles in his backpack. This is comforting. He still thinks we're going to need them.

He pulls his baggie of rolled cigarettes from a side pocket and offers one to the stranger. As the man moves toward Lin to take the cigarette, he keeps his gun on me. After he has it in his mouth and lit from Lin's Zippo, he lets the gun fall loosely at his side. Several seconds are devoted to smoking.

Lin speaks first. He smiles politely, and his voice is measured. The stranger answers in a similar tone, and for a minute they seem, if not friendly, at least civil. I begin to think everything might be okay. Lin leads the man to a pair of big rocks and gestures for him to sit down. I notice Lin's machete lying beside the rock that he sits on. I quickly look away, afraid the man will follow my gaze.

As the man smokes and talks, he relaxes. He and Lin talk like old friends. The man's front two teeth are missing, giving him a childish, oddly innocent expression. He stabs the air with his cigarette to punctuate his sentences, and once he points it very deliberately at me.

"Valentine," says Lin reluctantly. "This is Bo."

"Hi," I venture.

Bo stands—the cigarette dangling from the side of his mouth, his eyes half-closed against the rising smoke—and cups his free hand behind his ear. He barks something to Lin.

"Bo Shwit," Lin says.

Bo Shwit laughs, stretches out his hand and lurches toward me. When I put my hand in his, he squeezes, then laughs even harder. I wait for him to let go, my smile fixed. My eyes move to Lin, who still looks perfectly composed. So maybe this is normal. I want it to be normal.

Bo finally drops my hand and steps back, lifting his gun until it is pointing at Lin, laughing like everything is a big joke. Lin laughs too, but his free hand, resting casually on the ground, moves almost imperceptibly to his machete. Bo sees and shouts.

Then there's a rush of gray and a startling shriek. Mohawk is trumpeting and running straight at Bo. He knocks him on his back. The gun goes off, whether accidentally or on purpose,

I can't tell, and it shoots up several trees. Pieces of wood and bark splinter, popping like firecrackers. Bullets ricochet all around us, bouncing off rocks. I am too shocked, jumping with each bang, to be really scared. The fear comes after.

Mohawk runs into the jungle. I dash after him, but Bo—amazingly agile—jumps to his feet and, with the gun still in his right hand, grabs my arm with his left. His filthy nails dig into my flesh. He points the gun at Lin.

"No!" I cry out.

Lin talks fast, saying *Canadian* several times. They argue back and forth, Bo screaming, Lin using his splayed hands to try to keep things calm.

Finally, and unexpectedly, Lin steps back and slowly raises his hands in surrender. I stare, unbelieving, as something hard and cold is jammed against my head. The gun barrel. Bile slides up my mouth. The sour taste of terror.

Bo pushes me toward the trees. With each step, I hope Lin will spring up and run Bo down. At the edge of the clearing, I twist my head and catch sight of Lin's face, an unreadable mask, just before I am engulfed by the cold green of foliage and the feathery touch of ferns.

I have to think. These are the only words in my head. Everything else is noise. Feet stumbling. Heart pounding. Bo grunting. *I have to think.* I need a strategy. A plan to stay alive.

I surreptitiously close my hand around the knife in my pocket. I edge the blade out and wait for my opportunity to stab him. Then what would I do? Run back to Lin?

But I don't know the then-whats. I know right now. Right now is all I can deal with—the rocky path, the prickly thistles, the foul-smelling man shoving me forward. The cold circle of steel jammed against my skull.

Bo stops abruptly, turns me around and presses his lips against mine, slobbering into my mouth. His breath is putrid, like he hasn't brushed his teeth—ever. He drops his gun and, using two hands, rips my T-shirt open. He tears my bra half off. When he reaches between my legs, I jab my knife into his side. It gets stuck in bone. In ribs. I should have gone lower. I try again, but I'm too slow. Or Bo's too fast. He bellows, knocks me to the ground and kicks me in the side so hard I can't breathe. It is as though there is concrete in my mouth, cutting off everything. I open my mouth, struggling to get air into my lungs, struggling pointlessly.

There is violence in Bo's narrowed eyes as he stands over me, watching. But I don't care. I only care about breathing. And I can't. There is an agonizing need in my chest that seems to go on forever. Eventually a black shadow at the sides of my eyes moves in like a blindfold, cutting off the pewter sky. All the while, Bo stands over me, watching. Enjoying.

Just before everything goes dark, I suck in a jagged breath. I continue gasping in air, unable to react to Bo, as he undoes his zipper and kneels beside me. There is a small spreading stain of blood on the side of his shirt. He doesn't seem to notice that he's been stabbed, no matter how ineffectually. I think of those drugs Lin told me about. The drugs that make them not feel normal things. That make them crazy.

Lin. How could he just let me go?

Bo yanks down my pants.

Rage displaces my fear.

I decide to fight. As hard as I can until I can't fight anymore. I turn into a flailing, kicking, screaming, punching, biting maniac. And though Bo is strong and I am weak, for a while I fight him off. When he manages to get his hands around my wrists, I bite them. When he kneels on my thighs, I dig my fingers into his eyes. I don't even feel pain. Just fury.

Then I spy Lin above us, his machete glinting in the light. His hand grasps Bo's hair. He lifts Bo's head and holds the machete at his throat. They both scream at each other, Bo on his knees, struggling to stand.

Everything is incredibly vivid. The ever-lightening sky turning to mother-of-pearl. An overhanging branch, its knotty wood, its yellow-green leaves. Lin's enraged black eyes.

Bo sneers. He's not afraid, even though the machete is at his throat and his gun is on the ground. He jerks an elbow into Lin's face.

Lin gasps.

The next vivid thing is the red stain on Bo's throat.

Blood. It's so shiny and red. It spurts in arcs. Bo's mouth opens in disbelief. He makes guttural noises. He slips out of Lin's grasp and slides to the ground, gurgling and gasping. His eyes search wildly. He looks at me. Lin falls on him, pressing his hands hopelessly against the wound, trying to stop the blood. Finally Bo looks straight up into the silvery sky. The panic leaves his face. Something else leaves his eyes.

The stillness is shocking after all the chaos. There is only my wheezing and the whispering of the breeze. The hoot of a single bird.

Lin drops his head in his hands, and I think maybe he cries. I'm not sure, because most of my attention is on Bo. On all the blood. The glistening scarlet blood still trickling from the wound. Splattered over his clothes. Pooled on the dirt.

I watch it soak into the ground.

I marvel at how fast the earth takes us back.

TWENTY-EIGHT

"ARE YOU OKAY?" Lin asks, his voice breaking.

I nod.

"I did not *want* to kill," he says.

I nod again. I'm numb.

I try to sit up but can't. My ribs hurt so much. My pants are down around my thighs. My breasts are exposed. I force myself through the pain, keeping my breaths steady and shallow. I manage to get to my knees.

Lin rushes to help. Crouching down behind my back, he wraps his arms around me and gently helps me stand. I pull up my pants and try to cover my breasts with my torn T-shirt. Lin folds me in his arms. I burrow my face into the curve of his neck.

"You are hurt," he says. He holds me out at arm's length. He runs his eyes, then his fingers, over my ribs. Across my cheek. Around my throbbing left eye.

"Can you walk? We can't stay." He looks around. Grabs my knife from the grass. Untangles a piece of my bra from a thistle and stuffs it into his pocket. "Did you have anything else?"

Did I? I can't think. Can't do anything except stare at Bo. At the gaping wound on his neck. The way his eyes are still open. The awkward angle of his head. I'm glad he's dead— I think. I wanted to kill him myself. I just didn't understand how final, how irreversible, it would be. How real. And I didn't understand how responsible I would feel.

Lin covers Bo with branches, but not gently, not the way he covered the elephants. Quickly. Frantically. Hiding him from view.

He tries to pull me away, but my feet won't move.

"Valentine," he pleads. "We have to go."

I agree. We have to go. I nod. Then I can't stop nodding, as if I'm a bobblehead. I can't move one inch.

"Valentine." Lin takes my hands. His eyes are wet. He is scared. I see that. I do. I *feel* his fear. "We have to move now."

"I don't know if I can. It hurts when I breathe."

"He kicked you. Bruised your ribs. I don't think they are cracked, or you couldn't move." Lin takes off his T-shirt and rips it into strips. "I will wrap them. Bind them. It will help."

"You saw that?"

"Yes. I hid. There." He points to a flowering shrub a few meters back. "Lift your arms, please."

I lift them, wincing. "I didn't see you."

"Of course not. I was hiding."

I register that.

"I'm sorry. Sorry for everything. Sorry he beat you. But I waited for the best moment. I have only one chance with a man like that. Bo is crazy. Crazy strong. He kills with his bare hands. I have seen him. I have seen him fight off three men and kill them all. You did well. You surprised him. You are very brave." He winds the strips firmly around my ribs, over my dangling T-shirt. Then he helps me zip up my hoodie.

"So you know—knew—him well?"

"Yes."

"Was he one of the poachers?"

"Yes."

Lin doesn't say more, and I don't press. "Thank you for saving me. I'm sorry you had to kill him."

"It is okay. The world is better with Bo dead. I am sure."

"But you didn't want to kill him. Why not?"

Lin takes deep breaths and bends over, his hands on his knees. "I did want to. That is what makes me sorry. It is not good to kill, but it happened so suddenly. He moved, and..." He shakes his head. "It is done. It cannot be changed."

An unwanted image of Neil Carter pops up dead center in my mind. I wonder, for a brief moment, how he felt after he killed Amir.

"We have to go," Lin says again.

"Will we just leave him?"

"Yes! What should we do?"

"I don't know. Should we say something? Or write his name in the dirt?"

"Why?"

"To acknowledge him? Acknowledge his life?"

"By his name he will be known. This is for sure." His sarcasm is bitter.

"Why? What does his name mean?"

"*Shwit* is the sound it makes when you do this." He runs his finger across his throat, from ear to ear.

"What?"

"Bo Shwit is not a real name. It is the name for killers in death squads. The name the worst killers like to use. There are many Bo Shwits in Burma." He points to Bo. "He was with Sa Thon Lon, a death squad. This is before I knew him, but he always bragged about how he slit many throats of men. How he cut off many ears and lips of women."

"Oh my god." I stick my fingers in my ears. "Don't tell me anymore. *Don't. Please.*"

"Now we must go. I cannot be caught."

"But you did nothing wrong. He is a monster. And you saved me. I'll tell everyone—"

He grabs my hands, holds them in his. They are ice cold. He stands so close our noses touch. "You cannot tell anyone. *No.*"

"Why not?"

"You cannot tell. I will be killed—or tortured. I will wish I was dead."

"But you were helping me."

"It is not so easy. Just trust me. I tell the truth."

"But I don't understand."

"I know. You can't. You are a rich Canadian tourist. You have money, a mama who loves you. A passport and a country."

I'm taken aback. For a moment I want to say I'm not rich, but of course I see how relative that is. Here I'm rich, just *because* I'm here. Because I've come from so far away.

I follow Lin to the campsite in silence. I don't look back at Bo. I don't need to. I see him anyway.

As Lin helps me put on my knapsack, I'm suddenly seized with panic. "Where's Mohawk?"

"Gone. He went there." Lin points as he gathers our things. He is making sure we leave nothing behind. He even sweeps away our footprints with a leafy branch.

We step down to the stream so Lin can clean himself. He washes his machete, his hands, his face and his T-shirt, swirling it in the water. For a few moments the water is red. He puts his T-shirt on, cradles my face in his hands and kisses my forehead.

"We have to find Mohawk," I say. "Or all this was for nothing. We *have* to find him!"

"I know. We will try."

We walk together, calling Mohawk as loudly as we dare, knowing Bo's friends may be near.

"Did Bo say where his friends went?"

"No."

Thinking of Mohawk alone and afraid and certain to die is as sad as the thought of Mom waiting for me in agony, not knowing if she will ever see me again. I think about mothers and how much they love their children, and what a terrible curse that is. I wonder if Mohawk's mother knew she was dying. I wonder if she had time to wonder what would happen to her calf. I hope not.

I think about Amir's mom, but I regret it immediately. It's too painful. And what about Bo's mother? Is she alive? Does she know what kind of man he is? Does she love him anyway? Is it possible for love to be so unconditional? I picture her crying over his body, remembering him when he was a baby in her arms. Maybe that's how mothers love their monsters: they remember them when they were innocent.

A noise interrupts my tortured thoughts. Elephant yelps! Lin runs toward the sound, and I limp behind. We push through woody shrubs until we come to another part of the stream. Mohawk stands knee-deep in the water, shaking like a leaf.

"Mohawk!" We shower him with greetings and hugs. Lin and I high-five each other, though I can hardly lift my right hand. Lin hugs me softly.

Mohawk seems glad to see us too. At least, he responds to his name and to our attention. He wraps his trunk around my neck and pushes heavily but gently into Lin. He tries to drink again. He sucks the water up his trunk, but before he can spray it into his mouth, the water dribbles out. He can't hold it in. After several tries he drops to his knees and drinks from his mouth directly. I didn't even know elephants could drink like this. He is evidently parched.

As he drinks, I kneel beside him, wrap my arm around his wrinkled neck and whisper, "I love you. I love you. I love you."

Lin is the first to notice that the water swirling around us is tinged pink.

Mohawk is hurt. When he finally stands and wobbles out of the water, we see a bloody hole in his back hip.

"A bullet," says Lin. "We need to sterilize."

I point to my knapsack, and he digs around for my sanitizer. He soaks the scrap of my bra and then gently pushes it into the wound. Mohawk bellows.

"Will clean and also stop flow."

"We have to get him to the monks," I say.

Lin's face shuts down.

"Lin?"

He looks off into the distance, then back at Mohawk. "Yes. Let's go."

"Is something wrong? I mean, apart from—everything."

"They will see the bullet."

"Right?"

"They will ask about it. Ask what happened."

"We can say we don't know. Or that it must have happened yesterday."

"Who will we say beat you up?"

"I'll say I fell out of a tree."

"Lie to the monks?"

"Sure. Why not?"

"It will not bother you to lie to everyone? To monks, to your mama, to police maybe?"

I pause, thinking it through. I don't actually want to lie to Mom or the police, and I still don't understand why we have to lie. I circle back to my original position. "But you were helping me! I don't understand any of this."

"I know you don't. You are Canadian with passport."

He is obsessed with passports. "So?"

"I have no passport. No country."

"But you have a country. You're Burmese. You could go there and get a passport."

"No. I cannot. Never mind. Let's go."

TWENTY-NINE

LIN GETS US BACK on a path. Mohawk and I both limp.

"What exactly happened back there?" I ask Lin. "What were you and Bo talking about?"

"The past."

"The death squads?"

"I was not in death squads."

"What *did* you do?"

"Laid land mines. Forced villagers to give money. Forced them to porter for us. I fought KNLA—Karen who fight for their own state."

"Under Bo?"

"Yes."

"And he was following us all the way? Just stalking us, basically? Why didn't Mohawk hear him?"

"Bo is a match for Mohawk. He is master stalker. He likes games, likes to draw things out. He was angry, he wanted revenge. He probably killed the other men. He told me they were idiots. He *likes* to kill. He asked me to come and join him to kill the Rohingya now. He says we can kill any Rohingya we catch. No one will stop us."

Buddha! I don't dare take Buddha's name in vain in front of Lin, but I get a savage pleasure saying it to myself. *Buddha! Buddha! Buddha!* "So Brendan was right about the Rohingya genocide. I didn't really believe him."

Lin doesn't respond. He just looks sad.

"What was Bo saying when you said *Canadian*?"

"He said we caused him a lot of trouble, that we ruined his chance to take Mohawk when his men were with him. So he asked for you as payment."

"Me?"

"Yes. As payment."

I pause to steady my breath. "And what did he say that made you raise your hands in surrender?"

There is a beat. Then: "I don't remember."

I have to swivel my head to look at him. Because my eye is so swollen, I have no peripheral vision on my left side. He blushes and looks away.

"You don't remember."

"No."

I don't know what to say, so I say nothing.

The path narrows, and Lin moves ahead. I stay next to Mohawk, keeping my hand on him. Sometimes he holds my hand in his trunk. Sometimes he looks up at me, as though to make sure I'm still beside him. He is so human, whatever that means. Or maybe I am so elephant.

Lin and I stop talking. An hour passes. Lin closed down after my last question, and I closed down after his answer. His lie. Why did he lie?

Eventually, Lin points to something in the distance. "There."

I scan the area, using my hand as a visor, but I can't see anything.

"Just there. Behind those trees."

Still nothing. We keep going. Suddenly I see grass roofs, the sun lighting them up like gold. Gratitude wells in my chest.

"We're here," I say to Mohawk. He has reached the end of his endurance. He stumbles over. I barely have time to scramble out of the way as he falls.

"I'll stay with him," I tell Lin. "You go for help."

Lin sprints ahead.

Mohawk closes his eyes. I wrap my arms around his neck and put my face next to his.

"Valentine."

Lin strides toward me, flanked by several figures. I squint up at them, almost blinded by the sun and their bright robes, some saffron, some burgundy. The men stand erect, like birds of paradise, in the cool green of the jungle. My eyes finally focus on the stern faces of eight monks.

Lin helps me to my feet. The monks appraise me from a respectable distance. An old monk in a burgundy robe steps closer, looking long and hard at my face. He asks in broken English if I am okay. I say yes, but that I have to reach my mother.

He nods and says they have already made a phone call. That she knows I am safe and is on her way.

I am light-headed with relief. Light enough to lift my arms and float away. "Thank you so much. When will she get here?"

"Tonight or tomorrow."

I feel an almost irresistible urge to hug him. *Almost.* These monks are not warm and fuzzy, but they are surprisingly tender with Mohawk. They gently slip a slab of wood under him, making sure they don't jar his bad hip. The makeshift stretcher is a door, replete with a tarnished knob. The old monk leans down and runs his long fingers over the bullet wound.

"Will he be all right?" I ask.

No one answers.

Mohawk is heavy. It takes all of them to carry him back to the monastery. Lin helps me stand, and we walk together, close enough that our shoulders touch. He is as pensive as I am hopeful. His face is drawn, his eyes guarded.

"It's going to be okay," I whisper.

The monastery is a simple compound of three bamboo houses on stilts, an intricate and sprawling tree house, a fenced vegetable garden and small yard. A door is missing from the biggest house, the rusted hinges still hanging from the frame. Scattered chickens scrounge for food, bobbing their heads as they move. A goat stands on a fence and stares unblinking at me with strange yellow eyes.

The monks take Mohawk into the shade of a looming and twisted banyan tree. The branches shine with leaves so glossy they look like they've been polished. They slide the door out from under him so he can lie in a soft patch of lush clover. We follow but stand far back, out of earshot.

I ask Lin about Mom. "Did you call her, or did they?"

"Sayadaw did."

"Who?"

"The old monk. *Sayadaw* is a Burmese title of respect. He is Burmese. That is why he wears a burgundy robe."

"And he called Cruise's number?"

"Yes."

"And they got through?"

"Yes. There is coverage here, close to the border."

"Did you hear them actually talk to my mom?"

"No. He only talked to Cruise. But it is okay. Cruise will tell your mama. By now she knows you are okay. Please don't worry."

"Thank you," I say. I lower my voice. "What else did you tell them?"

"Only that we have a baby elephant with a bullet wound and that you are hurt too."

"And did they ask how it happened?"

"Not yet. But they will. They have to worry about trouble too. Everyone has to worry about trouble so close to the border."

"What kind of trouble?"

"The Burmese army sneaks across the border and kills Burmese refugees in camps."

"I don't understand. Why do *Burmese* soldiers kill *Burmese* refugees—regular people who have already left the country?"

"There are no regular people in a civil war. The army thinks refugees are dangerous. That they help insurgents and that they become insurgents."

I think of news clips I've seen of families running from war, trudging down bomb-blasted roads, babies in arms, old people in wheelbarrows. And these are the people the army kills? It is impossible to think of Lin doing anything like this. Absolutely impossible. But still, I glance furtively at him. He *was* a Burmese soldier.

The monks move slowly but efficiently, climbing up and down the ladders to their houses. They bring me a cup of tea, and for Mohawk a giant baby bottle filled with milk. They try to feed him, but he has no interest. They *tsk-tsk*.

"Will he be okay?" I ask Sayadaw when I catch his eye.

He shrugs. "Cannot know."

"Can we sit with him?"

"Wait. Have patience." He shuffles toward us and gestures at a weathered bench.

Lin *wais* before he sits down. I do the same. Sayadaw stands in front of us. He looks hard at me and then at Lin. Then at me again.

"You make *jivita dana*." He points to both of us, looking deadly serious.

I feel like I need to apologize. I turn questioningly to Lin.

"*Jivita dana* is a life-giving deed," he explains.

"Oh." I turn back to Sayadaw. "Thank you."

He frowns. "Don't thank. I only observe. Thanks undoes good, so I will not thank you. You do not thank me."

I nod, a bit confused.

"Tell me," he says, "all that happen to you and to calf."

Lin and I exchange an involuntary glance that doesn't escape Sayadaw's notice.

I tell the story, beginning with how we stumbled on the dead elephants. I tell everything up until we stopped to sleep. I describe the interlacing branches Lin wanted me to sleep in and how he said there were fewer snakes in the trees. Then I look Sayadaw deep in the eyes. I tell him that Lin tied me in the tree, but I was restless and fell out during the night.

Sayadaw frowns. His eyes scare me. They have the same otherworldly look as the goat's. There is a long silence. Then he asks how Mohawk got his bullet wound.

"He was already shot when we found the elephants."

"Why they shoot calf?"

"I don't know."

"Was for tusks? Were faces hacked away?"

"No. They were shot up."

He turns to Lin. They speak for several minutes. Sayadaw fires questions at Lin, and Lin responds calmly.

Then Sayadaw looks at me, and I know he knows I'm lying. I stare defiantly back. When he rejoins the circle of monks surrounding Mohawk, I move closer to Lin.

"What did he say?"

"Just asked me questions. Same as he asked you."

"And?"

"I told him the same thing."

"He didn't believe us, did he?" I lower my voice even further. "How did he know?"

"He is holy man. He sees many things. He knows many things."

"You sound like you know him."

"I do. I was here before, when I was hiding in the jungle."

"Hiding from your unit?"

"From Bo."

"*Bo?*"

"Yes."

"You were hiding from *Bo?*"

"Yes."

"Why won't you tell me what he said? That made you surrender?"

"You don't want to know."

"I *have* to know."

Lin looks past me. "He said if I tried to stop him, he would shoot me, rape you and then burn you alive."

A long time passes before I can choke out a sound. "Oh."

Lin tentatively reaches for my hand. I wrap my fingers around his. "Thank you for saving me."

"Don't thank me."

"Why?"

"You already know. It undoes *dana.*"

The monks motion us over. They have covered Mohawk with a blanket. One hands me the bottle, making sure he doesn't touch my hand. "Feed him. Is goat's milk. Good and sweet."

We sit cross-legged at Mohawk's head, and I try to rouse him.

"Come on, Mohawk!"

At the sound of my voice, he opens his eyes and tries to stand. He flails around for a minute, attempting to get on his knees, then gives up. At last he raises his trunk and latches on to the bottle. I smile at Lin.

"This is a good sign, right? The milk will give him strength."

Lin nods cautiously.

Mohawk finishes the bottle. I lie down beside him. Lin caresses my hair. The sun sparkles between the leaves. A breeze feathers my skin. The clover smells sweet and comforting, reminding me of my yard at home. We made it. We are safe.

My eyes close, the lids like weights. The last thing I hear is Mohawk's breath, which rattles going in and whistles going out. The last thing I think of is my exchange with Sayadaw. How I lied about a man's violent death. How I'm now stuck with the lie.

THIRTY

WHEN I OPEN MY EYES, it's to the muted mauves of dusk. I'm covered in a threadbare blanket, and drool drips down my cheek. It is eerily silent, except for the music of the cicadas. Lin is gone. Mohawk is next to me, but we are no longer touching. I wipe my face, then reach out to touch his trunk. It is hard. Cold.

Stunned, I push myself up and kneel over him. He is still as stone. His blanket has slipped off and is puddled between his stumpy legs.

The long toes and dirty feet of a monk step into my vision. The smell of incense wafts off his robes. I look up into Sayadaw's face.

"Mohawk's dead," I say.

"I know."

"You *know*?" I ask. I'm confused by how accepting he is. How calm. Almost cold. Arrogant.

He offers me chopsticks and a bowl of steaming rice, laying it nearby on the grass so he doesn't touch me. Then he turns and walks away, his sandals flapping, robe swishing.

I eye the rice. Like I could possibly eat next to Mohawk's dead body. The thought sickens me. I sweep the bowl away, and it skitters across the grass.

"Valentine!" Lin sits on the bench. He looks at the spilled rice in surprise.

"Mohawk's dead," I say.

"I know." He momentarily buries his face in his hands. "But it is not good to be angry."

"Aren't you?"

"No."

I don't get it. He has so much to be angry about. We failed in every way. And in the process, he killed a man.

Grief rampages inside me. "Everything we did was for nothing."

"We cannot know if it was for nothing."

"Yes. We can. Mohawk is dead. *Dead.*" I wrap my body around Mohawk's. I stay that way, my ribs aching, arm asleep, head pounding until the sky is black. Until the stars blink. Until Sayadaw and Lin come and pull me up.

"You sleep," Sayadaw says. "Mohawk be gone. You can do nothing more."

"Nothing more? I didn't do anything at all!"

"You tried," Sayadaw says.

We stand over Mohawk's corpse. It looks so vulnerable. So exposed.

"Are we just going to leave him here? Aren't we going to bury him?"

"Tomorrow morning we take him to jungle for hungry birds and beasts. Then we bury bones," Sayadaw says. "You say goodbye now. I come back for you shortly."

I stand helplessly, as though guarding Mohawk's body. Like his mother would do if she were alive. Like Mi Mi did for her son. I can't stand the thought of him in the jungle being eaten. No wonder the grieving elephants shake their trunks at the circling vultures. I also can't stand the thought of him in the ground, rotting—like Amir. I can't stand the thought of anything.

"I can't believe this was all for nothing."

"You cannot know that," Lin says again. "Have hope."

"You sound like a monk."

"I was a novice once. All Burmese boys go to the monastery to learn the way of the monks. I went to a small temple with three other boys from my village. I was at the temple when Tatmadaw came for me."

"You went from a temple to the army?" From praying to killing. I can't process what his life has been like. It's too painful. I take his hands in mine. I don't speak. All the words in my head sound trite.

We kneel beside Mohawk, running our hands over his wide forehead, soft ears and wrinkled trunk. I want to comfort him, but he's not here. He's nowhere.

"How did we fail him?" I ask Lin.

"I don't know."

I cover him with the blanket. Lin smooths out the wrinkles.

Sayadaw returns and leads us to the biggest house. The door is back on its hinges.

"What did we do wrong?" I ask.

"Nothing."

"But why did he die?"

"Does it matter?"

"Do you know?"

"Yes."

"Please tell me."

"He died because he lived. As I will. As you will. As every living thing will." He turns, bunches his robes in one hand and starts up the rungs of the hut's ladder.

Thanks.

We clamber up behind him and step into an airy room with big windows, a polished teak Buddha and an altar. It is sparsely furnished with mats and wooden benches. My room is the first door down a short hall. It is the size of a large closet, with room for only a cot and small table. There is a bowl of water and a towel for washing, a glass of water to drink. My knapsack is already on the floor in the corner.

Lin kisses me—a brush across my cheek—and says good night.

I sit on my cot for a long time, telling myself that Mohawk doesn't matter. He's just an animal. So am I. So was Amir.

Meat for other animals. Minerals for the earth. Random collections of atoms from dead stars.

I try to walk around my little room, but I am too weighted with sorrow.

I think of "Renascence":

> *And so beneath the weight lay I*
> *And suffered death, but could not die.*

Suffered death, but could not die.

All at once the door is flung open, and my mother charges in, sobbing, and sweeps me into her arms. I catch my breath at the pain in my side.

She loosens her grip but doesn't let me go.

"I'm so glad to see you," I say over and over again. "I never meant for this to happen."

She doesn't speak. She just holds me and cries into my hair. Three times, three different monks peek into the room, alarmed. Finally she stops, steps back, holds me by the forearms and looks at me. I look at her too, shocked. Her face is so puffy, and her eyes are so red and swollen, that she is almost unrecognizable. Her ponytail looks like a bird's nest. Her clothes are dirty. She smells as though she hasn't showered since I last saw her. I have been in the water twice, so I'm pretty sure I don't stink as bad. From the look on her face, though, she is just as horrified by me.

She runs her fingers over my swollen eye and cheek.

"Valentine!" she says. "My darling, sweet girl."

"Mohawk died. The baby elephant we tried to save."

"I know. I know. They told me. I'm so sorry."

Someone raps twice, and Mom opens the door. A young monk looks at the floor and gestures for us both to follow him.

The big front room is lit with a dozen little candles, which don't throw much light. I make out Sayadaw, Cruise and Myo, then spy three soldiers by the door. My heart stops. Cruise and Myo greet me enthusiastically. I try to return their smiles.

A soldier steps forward and talks to Cruise. They talk back and forth. It seems to go on forever. When Cruise addresses us, his face is stiff. He talks quietly, which doesn't lessen the impact of his words. The soldiers are part of a Thai border patrol, and they have found a murdered man in the jungle, not far away. They want to question me about it. Mom almost chokes, she's so upset.

"Are you kidding me? Why would she have anything to say about it? What is going on?"

"Let her answer," says Sayadaw.

"This is insane," Mom says.

I shake my head and shrug. "I don't mind answering. But I don't know anything about it." I hope they can't hear my heart thundering.

"I want to know why they are questioning her!" Mom says to Cruise.

"Because Lin is gone."

"What? No he isn't. He's in bed." I look at Sayadaw. "Tell them."

He shakes his head. "Gone now."

We all look at each other, taking it in. Lin has run away. And there is a dead—murdered—man in the jungle. I was with Lin. I am beaten up. Mohawk had a bullet wound.

The soldiers ask me to tell them what happened and how we found Mohawk.

I tell my story again. And again. Cruise translates. They ask me how Mohawk got shot. I say he was shot when we first saw him, that we didn't notice until Lin and I were alone with him. I add this detail because, of course, Cruise was there when we found him. If I can just create enough doubt. *We didn't notice, and neither did they.*

But something twitches in Cruise's eyes, and Mom notices. She interrupts, insisting that I be allowed to sleep. She points to my face and my ribs. She talks about my ordeal, all to save an elephant. She threatens to call the Canadian embassy in Bangkok. She threatens to post everything on Facebook. She threatens to call the Canadian prime minister. She acts as if we know him. We don't.

Neither the monks nor the soldiers are a match for my mother when she's like this. And tourism is a big industry. It's why they allow mother elephants to be murdered and their babies kidnapped. Because it makes the stupid tourists happy. And my mother is *not* happy.

We are allowed to go back to our room. When the door is closed, when we're lying in the narrow cot, she makes me face her and, in a hollow voice laced with dread, orders me to tell her the truth.

I start at the beginning and go all the way to end. I don't leave anything out that happened, but I don't tell her about Lin's past. She doesn't say a word or allow her face to show her trauma. But I know it's there, behind her glassy eyes.

When I'm finished, she holds me, running her hands up and down my back.

"Okay, babe, okay. It's okay. I love you so much, my brave girl. So very, very brave. Let's sleep now. I will figure this out in the morning. You have nothing to worry about. You did nothing wrong. You're okay now. You're safe now. You're safe. Safe."

THIRTY-ONE

MOM TOUCHES MY FACE to see if I am awake. I am. I stretch carefully—aware of all my sore spots—and yawn. Mom is already packed. My knapsack leans against her backpack by the door. She helps me sit up, wraps my ribs with a fresh tensor bandage and ushers me into the front room, where incense and candles burn in front of the Buddha. A monk brings fresh-cut marigolds in a vase to place between the candles. We descend the ladder and look for Sayadaw. There is so much activity, yet no noise. The monks do chores without speaking. They feed the goat, collect eggs, weed the garden, cook rice over an open fire pit and sweep the dirt paths.

Mohawk still lies under his blanket in the clover. Mom starts at the sight. A dead elephant is a terrible thing to see. I need for her to care about him. I tell her Mohawk stories, like how he couldn't chew and how he had to drink with his mouth and how we hid in the water and how he let Lin lead him everywhere. How valiant he was even though he was grieving and scared.

Mom clasps my hands. "You couldn't have done any more."

I stiffen.

"Does that sound like a platitude? Because, darling, it's not. What more could you have done? My god! You tried. You failed. That is true. But you were brave and daring— so daring I am in awe. You risked your life for him. It just wasn't enough."

"Thank you." It wasn't enough. That's all I want acknowledged.

Mom spies Sayadaw milking the goat. She *wais* and thanks him for his hospitality. She says she has to speak to Cruise. A young monk is sent to find him, and Cruise soon arrives, rubbing his eyes, his hair tousled and clothes rumpled.

"We have to go, Cruise. Now. I want to be in Bangkok by nightfall. My husband is joining us."

"He is?" My spirits soar at this.

Cruise looks completely pissed off. "Tonight is not possible. I don't know yet where to go, what to do. And we have to get the others. I am waiting for my company to call."

"Screw the company." Mom is never like this, never rude to people. It shocks me.

Sayadaw interjects. "Soldiers come to speak to daughter."

"Why? She already spoke to them."

"They have more questions."

"She needs medical care, not questions," she says shrilly. "Have you *seen* her?"

Honestly? I don't even know this woman. I scuff the dirt with the toe of my hiking boot. I'm embarrassed too. By all this shit I caused that's making my mother act like this. By how afraid I've made her.

"She has bruised ribs, possibly even a fractured cheekbone. Look at her eye! What if she ends up blind? I am taking her to Bangkok. *Now.* Once she sees a doctor, I'll visit the Canadian embassy, and she can be questioned there, if necessary. You can reach me through Cruise. But not here, not now. We are leaving! Unless you intend to keep us imprisoned against our will."

Mom gets her phone out. Maybe she's going to throw it at someone. Maybe she's going to video everything. Maybe she's actually calling the prime minister. I don't know. The commotion has drawn all the monks. Sayadaw shrugs his rounded shoulders and sweeps his hand toward the jungle. He looks deeply offended.

"Monks do not keep prisoners. Go."

We're on the road in ten minutes. Cruise and Mom argue about what we're doing and where we're going. I interrupt them to ask about Lin. I ask Cruise if he can try to reach him. Cruise shakes his head, and Mom looks really tense. Cruise finally gets a call from his company.

When he hangs up he says everything is settled. We will take a direct route to the nearest village and meet everyone else there. Mom protests. She wants to go to a city, not a little village. She's clearly had it with little villages.

Cruise shakes his head impatiently. Myo needs to go to the village to meet Myint so they can join a new group of trekkers. That's the plan. We will meet the group there. We will spend the night, then pay a villager to drive us to Chiang Mai. The company is booking Mom and me two berths on the sleeper train from there to Bangkok.

Mom hands out energy bars, since we missed breakfast. Cruise moves to the front of the line and Myo to the back. I'm sandwiched in. No one is letting me out of sight.

"What was all that about?" I ask Mom when we are side by side. "Back at the monastery?"

"Getting us out of there."

"Is it okay to talk to a monk like that?"

"No. It's not okay to talk to anyone like that."

"Can you ask Cruise to find out where Lin is?"

"Maybe later," she says. "When he's in a better mood."

"If he's ever in a better mood."

We walk until the sun smolders overhead. Mom doesn't want to stop for lunch, but Cruise insists. Her fear slips under my skin, and awful thoughts fill my head—Bo's head lolling off his body, Lin in front of a firing squad, me in jail.

After a gross lunch of cold tinned soup and crackers, we hit the path again. Mom and I walk side by side, talking in whispers.

"Is Dad really going to be there, or were you just saying that?"

"When we last spoke he had booked his ticket."

"You told him I was missing?"

"Of course!"

"Was he crazed?"

"Of course. He was out of his mind—like I was."

"But you told him I was found?"

"Of course."

"And he's still coming?"

"Yes. We need to be all together, as soon as possible."

"Are you going to tell him what really happened?"

"No. You are. But I will be with you. I'll help. You can't heal from this without the truth. Valentine, my god! What you've been through." Her lips tremble. "And you may—I don't know for sure—but you may have to tell the authorities the truth."

"No. I can't. I won't! I won't get Lin in trouble. He saved me from being raped. Probably from being murdered."

She starts to cry, quietly so Cruise doesn't turn around.

"He was terrified of going to jail or being killed. He said it wouldn't matter what I said. It wouldn't matter that he did it to save me."

"Oh god, Valentine." Mom stumbles over a tree root.

"So I have to help him. And how bad will it look if I change my story? They won't believe the truth now."

"I understand. I do. I really do. But he ran off, leaving you behind."

"That's unfair. You saw the military police! He isn't in Thailand legally. I am. I have you. He has no one. You can't think he should have endangered himself just to be polite and say goodbye."

"No, of course not. I don't know what to think. I'm so sorry."

We stop talking—it's too painful—and concentrate on walking. I stare straight ahead, at Cruise, at his new look. Wrinkled, dirty, rugged. Max and Brendan would be impressed. I think about Lin. I wonder how he left. Did he climb out a window and jump? I wonder if he's okay. I wonder where he is. I wonder if I'll ever see him again.

The sun is on its way down, haloing the tall pines in the distance, when Cruise says we're almost there. He sends Myo ahead to make sure a guesthouse is ready for us. We come out of the trees onto a gravel road with four huts.

"Lin's village!" I say.

Mom bugs her eyes out at Cruise. "It is?"

"Yes."

"Did we have to come *here*?"

"Yes. Believe me, I had no choice. I just do what I'm told."

Pigs laze, chickens strut, kids play. Just like the first day. I look everywhere for Lin, but I only see Htay, waiting for us at the guesthouse, hands on her hips. Mom and I say hello, but she doesn't respond or even smile. She is curt with Cruise, then rushes away.

"What's wrong with Htay, Cruise?" Mom asks.

"Nothing."

"What did she say?"

"Only that there is no water in the rain barrel," Cruise says. "You can bathe in the creek though." He points to a thicket. "Through there. No one will bother you. Don't worry. Nothing is wrong. This is a matriarchal village. All the women are bossy."

"She wasn't bossy. She was upset, and I'd like to know why. Has the patrol been here looking for us?"

"No! You are paranoid. Please trust me. I am getting you to Bangkok."

"Sorry," Mom says, grabbing towels and shampoo.

Cruise starts to roll out his sleeping bag.

"Why don't you ask Htay if she knows where Lin is?" I ask him. "Doesn't he live in her house?"

Cruise almost chokes on his gum. "Don't ask her anything. Don't mention his name."

"Do you know something that I don't?"

He turns away and busies himself with his inflatable pillow.

"Cruise?"

Mom and I both look at his back, then at each other.

"What's going on?" I say as we head down the steps to bathe.

"I wish I knew."

The creek turns out to be a blessing. It is cold and refreshing and deep enough to swim. We dunk and shampoo until we're squeaky clean. We float under arching branches, rippling the water with our feet and hands. We're relieved to be alone. To be together. I think of Tinker Bell and her daughter standing forehead to forehead, so lovingly, so quietly, in the stream.

Mom and I are hushed too. We're too emotionally drained to talk. The silence—the peace—feels healing. We stay until twilight drops, burnishing the leaves purple.

On the short walk back to the guesthouse, Mom warns me that the others, when they arrive, are going to ply me with questions. That they were all traumatized by my sudden disappearance. I ask her what happened when Cruise showed up without me. But she can't talk about it without choking up. She shushes me gently and squeezes my hand.

Cruise is alone on the deck, dishing up rice and zucchini curry, courtesy of Htay. After dinner we dawdle over our tea, waiting for the other trekkers, until Cruise and Mom can't keep their eyes open. I volunteer to stay up and greet them. I need to be alone anyway. Mom and Cruise go inside and blow out the candles before they crawl into their sleeping bags. Mom leaves the door open. I imagine she doesn't want to let me out of her sight.

THIRTY-TWO

CLOUDS SAIL PAST the moon at a rapid clip. I watch them from the top step as I sort through my feelings—my relief at being with Mom, my excitement to see Dad, my anguish over Mohawk, my anxiety over Lin. I think about Bo briefly. I feel nothing. I'm glad he's dead. I push him from my thoughts. He doesn't deserve any of my time.

A whiff of cigarette smoke twitches my nostrils. Seconds later I am shocked into near paralysis by the sight of Lin ambling up the path, a cigarette dangling from his lips.

Startled, he catches sight of me and halts uncertainly at the foot of the stairs. He is not shocked though. Just sheepish.

"Valentine."

"Surprise," I say wryly. "Or maybe not. Not for you."

He puts his finger to his lips and looks past me to Htay's house, where candles flicker on the windowsill and the deck rail, stuck to the bamboo with melted wax. He grabs my hand, pulling me behind the guesthouse, through the thicket of bushes and to the bank of the creek.

"Valentine. I am sorry."

"Oh?" I can't keep the arctic chill out of my voice. "What for?"

"For not coming to see you."

"So you knew I was here."

"Yes."

"And were trying to hide from me."

"Yes. "

"Well. Again, *surprise*."

"You are angry?"

"You think? After all we went through, you just left. You didn't say goodbye. It didn't bother me because I knew—or I *thought*—you were in trouble. Running scared. But here you are. Why not come and at least let me know you're okay?"

"I know. I understand you are upset."

"Do you? I'm in trouble too, you know. The soldiers haven't finished with me! My mother dragged me out of there, but I may have to be questioned in Bangkok. The truth is, I think we should have told the truth. This is much worse. We look really guilty! You left me to deal with the soldiers myself. You *made* us look guilty." Mom's words get under my skin. *He ran off, leaving you behind.* "You just forgot about me."

"Shhh. Htay will hear you."

"So?"

He pauses. "And I did not forget you. Believe me. I will never forget you. I only wish."

"You left me."

"And you will leave me too. No? Your mama will take you back to your nice Canadian life. *You* will forget *me*."

"No. I will never forget you. How could I? After all we've been through? Never."

We are standing so close, we can't resist each other's gravity. Lin's arms go around me, and his hair falls on my face. I feel the heat of his lips even before I feel their pressure. I taste beer and something salty. I explore the contours in his face with my nose and lips. I slip my hands under his T-shirt and run my hands up his back, feeling each vertebra and the spaces in between. His fingers move through my hair.

"Valentine, it is a gift to see you again, and I want to say something. I am sorry for running off. I was sure you would be safe, that nobody would suspect you. If they did—and I would know from Myint or Myo—I planned to confess. To tell everyone I killed Bo. I told Htay I would not let you take the blame."

"So Htay knows you killed him?"

"Yes."

"Does she know why?"

"She is happy I killed him. She does not think I need a reason. She thinks the opposite—that I need a reason to let him live. Htay would not let me back if I did not kill him."

"Why?"

"You will understand, but first I need to tell you more about me. And Bo."

My heart clenches with fear. The bad things Lin did. As if he senses my resistance, he clasps his hands together and entreats me with his eyes.

"Please, let me tell you."

I nod slowly, and he begins.

"We crossed the border, looking for KNLA, who hide in refugee camps. That is—I already told you—Karen fighters. The military wants to kill them all and any Karen who hides them. In truth, some want to kill all Karen."

"Another genocide. Brendan was right about that too."

"But many escaped to Thailand."

"A million of them."

"Yes." He pauses again.

I brace myself. I know something unbearable is coming. It's the same blank dread I felt the day Amir died.

"Bo took us to a small compound at the edge of Mae La, away from the main part where UN soldiers watch. He ordered me—only me, because he said I had not proven loyalty yet—to shoot up the shack. He said KNLA was inside. So I did." Pain contorts his face.

"And?"

"It wasn't KNLA."

I push away from him. "Oh my god."

"It was a family. Mother, father, grandma, aunts and children. A baby too. She was still alive."

I push him farther away.

"You do not understand," he pleads. "You live in Canada. What do you know about war?"

My horror is all over my face. I can tell by his frantic eyes. By his fingers gripping the flesh on my upper arms.

"I did not know. You have to believe me. I know many soldiers kill refugees on purpose. Burn them alive, do terrible things. But I *did not know*. And I tried to help the girl— the baby—when I saw she still lived. Bullets tore off her lower arm. But maybe she could have been saved. Doctors were in Mae La. I wanted to take her. I said I would take her myself and say I alone did the shooting. I would take all the blame. Bo said no. He said she was better off dead, because she had no parents. Then he laughed."

I can't believe such unthinkable words are tumbling out of his mouth.

"I picked her up, and Bo shot my leg. He took my gun. Left me there. Set fire to everything. I asked him to shoot us first so we would not burn, but he said no. Said he would not waste his bullets. I hated him so much, it gave me strength. I refused to die like that. I refused for the baby to die like that. Once Bo and the other men ran off, I crawled out with her. She died in my arms."

I have two such opposite feelings. Revulsion and pity. I step back. I step forward. I don't want to hurt him, but I'm so sickened. I step back. I see his torment, his grief. I fight with myself. Finally, I step in close enough to lay my head on his shoulder. His hands slide up my arms.

"But you didn't want to kill him," I whisper. "I don't understand."

"I promised that night I would never kill again. Anyone. Anything. I would not even kill Bo if the chance ever came. Even to save my own life. But that day it was *your* life. I had to rescue you. I thought I would only hurt him and leave him there. I would tie him up and get away. But I killed him. How? I only remember the blood. Did I just slice his throat? I don't know. I know I wanted to kill him, and that is my shame."

"I know. Please believe me. I saw. Every detail. It was because he moved. He jerked his elbow into your face. It was a reflex. It wasn't your fault." I don't know if this is completely true, but I don't care. I want to spare him *something*.

He bows his head. "Thank you."

"And then what did you do? With the baby?"

"I buried her. Stayed in jungle. Cut out the bullet in my calf. I healed slowly. I was afraid to go back to the compound, but every day I thought about the bodies I left behind. Burned. Maybe just bones. Every night I dreamed of them. I wanted to go back and bury them. But I didn't. I was too afraid."

I suddenly remember what he said when I found him burying Mohawk's mother. *I will not leave bodies. Never again.* And with a stab of pain, I realize that he has. He left Bo's. Now he has that grief. I hate Bo even more, if that's possible.

"I hid, finding food—berries, mushrooms, greens, bananas. At night I slept in trees. After many weeks I came face to face with Sayadaw. He was picking berries. He took me home. The monks took me in. They made me strong again. They asked if I wanted to stay with them, to become one of them, but I did not. I was not clean enough. Pure enough. So I went out to the world again. I am very strong. I can work. I can make good from bad. I asked at many villages, but no one wanted me because I am Burman. Everyone asked the same question: *Were you in the army?* And I did not lie. Finally I came here. Htay felt sorry for me, and she liked that I did not lie. She took me in."

"That was kind of her," I say. "I'm glad she did." My words feel strained and understated. We are talking about his life—his very survival—and I'm saying "kind" and "glad" like an idiot.

"I am not a bad person. Please believe me."

"I do."

"But now I need to go," he says. "I cannot see you again."

"*What?*"

"I need to go forward. To make changes. I hope you understand. I want you to be happy for me. That is what I want to say. Please be happy for me."

"Yes, of course." I'm confused by the word *happy*. It feels like a big reach. Far, far away. Fifty folds away.

Lin steps back, his spine very straight. Before he squeezes between two slender trees and disappears, he whispers something—*I love you.*

The thicket feels extraordinarily empty. *I* feel extraordinarily empty. I try to breathe him in, as though he has left a remnant of himself here. But there's nothing. People never leave anything behind. I know that from Amir.

I slip between the houses. Htay's candles are still burning, though her porch is empty. I half consider blowing them out but don't want her to see me creeping up the steps to her porch. I tiptoe up the steps to our guesthouse, so as not to wake Mom and Cruise. I'm on the top step when a voice spins me around.

"Crikey! Valentine! It is good to see you!" After I adjust to the light shining in my face, I make out Max slogging up the path, his miner's flashlight strapped to his forehead.

Myint, Brendan, Pauline and Lish follow right behind him. I greet them, and they rush me, cheering, with open arms. They start, though, when they notice how awful I look. It feels good to think that everyone cares this much. Max, Brendan and Pauline kick off their shoes, tromp up the steps and cram into the guesthouse, sighing with relief that they are here—that we are all together again. Myint gives me a high five, then heads to his own place. Lish remains on the ground. She lights a cigarette and asks me to stay behind. She doesn't look at me directly.

"I should have stopped you or immediately told Cruise what you were doing," she mumbles. "And I shouldn't have said Lin was saving Mohawk because he loved you. I didn't mean for anything like this to happen."

"I know."

"Not everything, you don't."

"What do you mean?"

"I think I was still pissed."

"Sorry?"

"Because you were so rude about my dad."

"Oh!" *Right.* Her dad, the alcoholic. I stare at her.

"I don't think I started out trying to make you upset, but when I saw how guilty you felt, well, I kept needling you. I wanted revenge."

I'm blindsided by her confession. And distressed. Would I have run back if she hadn't goaded me? And if I hadn't, would Mohawk be alive? Maybe Lin would have been faster without me. Maybe Bo couldn't have tracked him. Maybe right now Lin and Mohawk would be resting happily with the monks.

"So that's why you didn't try to stop me."

"Yes. I guess. But I really thought you'd come right back. When you didn't—I only waited five minutes—I told Cruise. He flipped a shit, and we went charging back for you. Then we heard more guns." She swallows several times. "We all thought you were dead. And I thought it was my fault."

I want to be angry, to blame Lish for everything, but I can't. I'd just be scapegoating her. She gave rise to doubts I already had. Cruise had said that the border was dangerous for Lin, and I just ignored that, because I wanted so badly for Lin to save Mohawk. And who knows? Maybe Lin is alive because I was there. Maybe Bo would have killed him right off if he'd been alone. As Lin says, I cannot know.

"It wasn't your fault, *really*," I say, hugging her. "I made my own choices."

"Do you forgive me?" Her voice is tremulous.

"Yes."

"Thank you."

We turn to go up the stairs. We both stop in our tracks. Pauline is standing on the top step. I wonder how much she heard. From the stricken look on her face, I'd say she heard everything.

"Alisha Rose Robinson!"

It takes me a second to realize she means Lish.

She takes the steps slowly, her hands on her hips. "Put that bloody cigarette out."

Lish drops her cigarette, and I make a speedy exit, scrambling up the stairs and scooting into the guesthouse. I bang the door shut.

Inside, Cruise, awake but groggy, lights candles. Mom sits wrapped in her sleeping bag, stifling a yawn. Max and Brendan unpack their necessities, and Max takes out his camera.

"Where are Pauline and Lish?" Cruise asks.

"Outside," I say. "Talking."

Max calls me over. He is scrolling through his camera. "I'll send you this," he says softly, stopping at a picture of Lin and me crouched by Mohawk.

"Thank you." My voice wobbles.

"And this one I'm sending out with some copy. For media to pick up." The photo shows the dead elephants and Mohawk and me. I'm screaming, and so is Mohawk. "If you're okay with it. It might do some good."

"If you think so," I say. "Sure."

Everyone crowds around to look at Max's pictures. He didn't want to share them earlier, he says—not while I was still missing. It would have been too upsetting. He wanted to wait until we were all together again.

"Great work, man," says Brendan, pretend-punching him in the arm.

The door is thrown open, and Pauline flounces in, followed by Lish. The only sign of their confrontation is Lish's subdued expression. Pauline gathers Mom in her arms and holds her for at least a minute. I'm a little surprised by the intensity of their hug. It seems that a lot happened while I was gone. With everybody here, we sit in a circle, and the questions start. Max and Brendan ask most of them, and I tell an abbreviated version of the past three days, leaving out Bo and ending with Mohawk's death.

Pauline pulls out her Scotch and offers everyone a drink. The bottle goes around the room, and everyone except Lish and me takes a swig. Pauline takes the biggest gulps. I can't help but think about Nathaniel, a friend of mine whose father left his mother because she was an alcoholic and then became one too. Nathaniel had to go live with an aunt while both of his parents went to rehab.

Max asks about Lin. "Where is he? This is his village, isn't it?"

I look around awkwardly, as though I might spy him in a corner.

"Yes," Pauline says. "He should be here tonight. He's part of the trek."

"Lin is not here," Cruise says, his tone curt.

"Is something wrong?" Max asks.

Cruise ignores him. Mom rearranges her sleeping bag around her shoulders. I chew on a hangnail.

"Cruise?" Brendan asks. "What aren't you saying?"

"He is in trouble. Just leave it."

Brendan and Max badger Cruise until he tells them more.

"The military police want to question him. They think he might have killed a Burmese soldier."

First there is shock. There is my shock at hearing the words spoken so casually. There is Mom's shock that Cruise has brought Bo up. There is the shocked disbelief of everyone else. "What?" they ask in unison. Then the guesthouse devolves into chaos as everyone hounds Cruise for answers.

"I don't know any more about it," Cruise says. "Just that there was a dead Burmese soldier not far from Lin's and Valentine's campsite."

Mom grips her sleeping bag, her knuckles white.

"Did you see him, Valentine?" Brendan asks.

"No."

"Did Lin ever leave you alone?"

"No."

"So he didn't do it."

"No! Of course he didn't," I say, rolling my eyes as though it's the craziest thing I've heard in my whole life.

"Where is he?" asks Brendan.

"Not here," Cruise says.

"I see that. But this is his village, isn't it? Where does he live? Let's go talk to him—see if he needs some help."

"No. Don't. Just leave him alone. What can *you* do for him? You are a tourist, passing through," Cruise says.

"Well," says Brendan, ignoring Cruise's barb, "maybe he needs to get his story out. I can help with that."

"No! That is the last thing he needs. This village is his hiding place. He has been hiding here for years."

"*What?*" Max asks.

"I think you need to explain that, Cruise," Mom says, her eyes daggers. "Since you brought him here among us."

I exhale slowly. I've told Mom nothing about Lin's past, something I now regret.

"Yeah. What's he done and who's he hiding from?" Pauline echoes.

"Six years ago he wandered into this village. He was half-starved and filthy. He asked if he could have food. Htay fed him. He asked her if he could live and work here."

"Six years ago? He looks like a kid. How old is he?" Pauline asks.

"Twenty-five, twenty-six—something like that."

Everyone is a little surprised. I'm surprised too but try to hide it.

Cruise continues. "No one wanted him because he had run away from the army. But Htay wanted to give him a chance. The village elder supported her, and he asked the village to also give him a chance. She took him in."

"Ran away from what army?" Pauline asks.

"Burmese."

Brendan whistles. "A Karen woman took in a runaway Burmese soldier!"

"Yes."

"Why is that such a big deal?" Pauline asks.

"No one knows what he did."

"How do they know he did anything?" Mom asks.

"He was a Burmese soldier."

"And are all Burmese soldiers guilty of bad things, Cruise?" Pauline lights a cigarette, as though she is settling in for a long story. No one mentions that she should smoke outside. Not even Mom.

"It's late, and we've talked enough," Cruise says, so Pauline turns to Brendan.

"Will *you* answer that?"

"Well, probably," Brendan says. "Yeah. The army goes after civilians. It's their modus operandi."

"Can you explain why?"

"Sure! If you have an hour."

Cruise groans. "We need to sleep."

"Give us the elevator version," Max says.

"Okay. After World War II, colonial powers—Brits and Japanese—had thoroughly buggered up the country, as colonial powers always do, by playing different ethnic groups off each other. There was a national movement that got rid of the colonial powers. They wanted Burmese ruled by Burmese and were very popular. But the Karen didn't agree. They wanted their own state. The ruling Burmese party refused, and an armed conflict began. Both sides carried out atrocities. It started seventy years ago. Today they are still fighting. Because the military couldn't crush the Karen insurgents, they started a relentless campaign against Karen civilians, driving them right out of the country. The world has done almost nothing, though many observers have called it a genocide."

"And you agree with that assessment?" Mom asks.

"Totally. I still have nightmares from interviewing Karen refugees."

"That's all," Cruise says, jumping in. "The army targets the Karen. Or they used to. Today it's the Rohingya. Valentine needs to rest. And so do I. It has been a really long day."

Cruise blows out the candles and snaps the shutters in place.

THIRTY-THREE

A DOG INSINUATES himself into my dream, barking wildly. Hysterically. Someone is murdering the dog. Typical, I think. Murdered animals everywhere. Elephants, pigs, dogs. The dog keeps barking even though he is dead, his throat slit from a machete. "*You* are next," a man says. "You are a liar." And then I see that the man is Lin, and I don't understand why he's so angry. I lied because he *asked* me to. But he turns into Bo, who has come back to life, good as new except for a black gash across his throat. He sharpens Lin's machete on his lower teeth.

I sit bolt upright, breathing hard, heart pounding in my ears. Everyone around me is stirring—because the barking is real.

"What's going on?" asks Lish.

Mom gropes for me. "Valentine?"

"Right here."

"Will someone murder that dog, please?" says Brendan.

I try to shake off the dread of my dream. I snuggle close to Mom. "I thought the barking was part of my dream," I whisper in her ear, "about Lin and Bo." She puts a cold hand on my forehead. Then she holds my hands in hers, trying to stop their shaking.

"I thought he had come back to life."

Shhh, she mouths, resting a finger against my lips.

But I can't stop talking. "I was scared but also a bit relieved that he'd come back to life. Why was I relieved?" I recall Lin's words. *The world is better without him.* "He was so evil. He did such terrible things."

Mom widens her eyes at me, then quickly checks over her shoulder to see if anyone has heard. She forces my head on her shoulder, squishing my face against her cotton pajamas. For a moment I think she's comforting me. Then I realize she is shutting me up.

Right. *Uskut.* I need to shut up.

"Do you smell that?" Pauline asks.

I sniff.

"Smoke," she says. "Something's burning."

"Maybe someone's cooking," Lish says.

"Now?"

Cruise lights a candle.

"Fire?" Mom asks, springing up.

Suddenly we are all on our feet, sniffing.

Cruise swears and moves the candle in a slow circle. "There!"

Smoke curls into the room through the slats in the shutters. Cruise throws them open. The window overlooks Htay's porch. A line of flame runs along her rail, reaching up and over the six inches to our guesthouse. A plume of dancing orange light.

"Fire!" Mom yells. "Fire!"

"Get your things," says Cruise. "And run!"

"Those bleeding candles!" Pauline cries.

We throw things in our backpacks, leave our sleeping bags and rush outside. Pauline trips down the steps, sprawling face first in the dirt. Lish helps her up.

Htay's house empties too. So many people spill out, it is almost ridiculous. Htay, her mother, her mother's mother, her three daughters, their five kids—and Lin.

"Lin!" Mom gasps.

He hears and looks embarrassed. He *wais* to us. But there is no time for questions or accusations.

Htay shouts orders, and very quickly all kinds of things happen. The pigs and chickens are chased away. Someone bangs a gong. People come running and form a line to the creek. Women find buckets and start passing them down the line. Men appear with shovels, brooms and sticks. Lin stays on the porch and whacks at the burning rail with his machete, the flames leaping around his hands.

I watch, afraid for him.

"They've done this before," Max says. "I think they're going to let the guesthouse go but save Htay's place."

"Oh my god!" says Pauline. "The roof! It's about to catch."

The flames lick at the thatched roof of the guesthouse. It takes several little forays before the grass catches, but once it does, the whole roof makes a sucking sound and goes up in a giant fireball.

"Lin!" I scream, just as the rail falls away. He jumps off the porch, rolling when he hits the ground. When he stands, our eyes lock for a long moment.

Cruise pushes us down the road, out of danger. As the fire spreads, it growls like a ferocious animal. The guesthouse cracks and snaps, creaks and crashes, as it collapses into itself.

Max and Brendan join Myo and Myint and the men shoveling dirt on the collapsing house. Lin gets on Htay's roof and swats away burning bits of grass and bamboo. Mom, Pauline, and Lish help with the water line, which runs to Htay's house. They're soaking it so it won't catch. I can't lift the heavy buckets because my ribs hurt too much, but I run around stomping on fallen bits of burning grass.

By dawn the fire is out, and the volunteers go home. Pauline, Lish, Mom and I collapse on the ground, joined shortly by Max, Brendan and Myo. They have clearly bonded over putting out the fire. Cruise and Myint are nowhere to be seen.

The remnants of the fire—floating, falling embers that for the most part burn out on their own—look like swarms of fireflies. In the east the sky flickers coral behind the dark clouds that have gathered over the mountain. The guesthouse is charred stumps. The smoke has penetrated our hair, nostrils and clothes, and the soot has blackened our skin. Ash coats the ground in a luminescent film.

Htay arrives with a pail of river water stacked with Coke, water and Singha beer. She *wais* to us all several times, then smiles as she glides away. We dive into the bucket for cold drinks to soothe our raw throats.

"She's in a remarkably good mood, given that her guesthouse just burned down," Pauline says.

"Well, her own house was saved, and no one was hurt," Mom says.

"True," says Pauline. "But she's lost her source of income. What will happen to her, Myo?"

"Only good things," he says, his eyes lighting up mischievously.

"What does that mean? Does she have insurance?"

"Insurance!" Brendan snorts. "No one here has insurance."

"What then?" Mom asks.

Myo smiles and shrugs.

Pauline looks peeved. "Maybe Cruise will tell us when he gets back."

"Where is he?" Mom asks.

Brendan and Max huddle with Myo, deep in dialogue. Just then a booming sound makes us sit up.

"What's that? Thunder?" Max asks.

Another boom, this one right over our heads. Then a crash. The sky sparkles with golden veins of lightning. In seconds the rain starts—sheets and sheets of it.

"It's raining *now*?" Max asks.

"Of *course* it is," Brendan says.

We sit in the pouring rain, with nowhere to go for shelter. It has come down so suddenly and with such force, there's no point in digging through our backpacks for our rain ponchos. The water sluices over us, washing the smoke out of our hair and clothes. As it begins to ease, a battered pickup truck bounces down a muddy lane, heading right toward us. Myint drives. Cruise is in the passenger side, sitting on the floor where a seat used to be. We can see him because the door is gone too.

"Ah," Mom says. "They were getting the truck. We might actually be leaving."

"Get in," Cruise calls, hopping out. "Myint is driving us to Chiang Mai. We will be there by afternoon. In a hotel with a pool and restaurant!"

"I thought he was meeting a trek," I say.

Cruise points to the guesthouse. "The trek is canceled. Since the guesthouse burned down. Plus, the village has an unexpected wedding tonight. There is much work to do, and no one else can take trekkers." He slaps his hands together, excited that everything is finally working out. That he's getting rid of us. He looks almost as assured as he did way back in the Chiang Mai night market.

Max and Brendan throw our backpacks in the passenger side and strap them in with a frayed rope. They hitch their own backpacks on their shoulders.

"What are you doing?" asks Cruise.

"Myo's taking us to the border. We're going to sneak into Burma to check out the Rohingya situation. Go to the villages, see if the army is killing civilians—directly or indirectly—by cutting off food and medicine. Document it and show the world."

"Are you crazy?" Cruise asks Myo.

"Yeah," Pauline says. "Isn't your wife due to give birth?"

"My wife says she needs me to make baby, not have."

"These Kayan women are tough!" Pauline says. "So she approves of this crazy plan?"

"Approves? She insists," Myo says. "She hates Tatmadaw. So do I."

Cruise turns to Max and Brendan. "You think *you* can stop the killing? Two foreigners? You might be killed too."

"I don't think so," Brendan says. "No one wants to kill tourists. Or journalists. Well, maybe they want to," he amends. "But they probably won't. The most that will happen is that we'll get thrown in jail. And I've been there, done that. It'll be fine."

"Do *you* want to go?" Mom asks Max.

"Yes."

"I thought you were only interested in animal stories. This is so dangerous."

"That was before," Max says.

"Before what?"

Brendan slaps Max on the back. "Before the dead elephants. Seeing them was the best thing that ever happened to him. He's finally mad. *Mad Max.*"

Pauline shakes her head. "I can't believe you're really sneaking into Burma."

"Well, we are," Brendan says. "Somewhere over there is a story waiting to be written."

"You're doing a profoundly good thing," says Mom.

"*Jivita dana*," I say, though it feels a bit futile—Max and Brendan against the malice of the Burmese military.

We all hug goodbye, and then Mom, Pauline, Lish, Cruise and I crawl into the open back of the truck. Max, Brendan and Myo wave to us as we bump down the gravel road.

"Do you really believe they can change anything?" asks Pauline.

"Photos have power," Mom answers. "As do words."

"*Somewhere a man is repairing the night, one word at a time*," I say.

Mom cocks her head to one side and smiles.

"What's that?" asks Pauline.

"It's a line from a poem by Anne Michaels," I say. "A Toronto poet."

"Well, I like it. I should get into poetry."

Lin doesn't show up to say goodbye. We said goodbye last night, but I still watch for him, for one last glimpse. I watch so intently that my eyes burn with strain. With hope. Finally, with resignation.

"What will happen to Lin?" I ask Cruise quietly, but everyone hears. We all wait expectantly for an answer.

"Lin will be fine. Better than fine, in fact."

"What do you mean?"

"The last-minute wedding tonight is Lin's."

I stare, uncomprehending. "*Lin's?*"

"*Lin's?*" echoes Mom.

"He was flirting with Valentine while he was engaged?" Lish asks.

"He wasn't flirting with me," I lie.

No one looks at me, which gives me time to collect myself. To deal with the sudden ringing in my ears. The fire in my skin. I don't see why they act like he's my boyfriend. He's not. But he could have mentioned his upcoming marriage. Like, oh, I don't know, when he was sticking his tongue in my mouth.

"He is marrying Htay," Cruise says. "It is very good for him."

"Htay?" I say, practically choking.

"The old lady?" Lish asks.

"She is not so old," Cruise says. "Thirty-five, thirty-six, something like that."

"Still!" Mom darts her eyes at me.

"Hold on," Lish says. "Are you actually telling me that Lin is going to shag that old hag?"

"She's not so old," Pauline says.

"And she's certainly not a hag," Mom adds.

"She's a granny!"

"A granny who could still have kids, if she wanted to," Pauline says. "That woman's spunk is off the chart."

"I don't understand anything about this," Mom says. "Not that it's any of my business. But were they a couple? Lin certainly didn't act like he was in a relationship."

"Lin is in trouble." Cruise turns and faces me directly. "Over the soldier. And even if he didn't do it, the authorities know he is here now, in the hills. If they send him back to Burma, he will be shot for desertion. Or worse."

"No wonder Htay didn't want us here tonight," Mom says. "She *was* afraid the patrol would follow after us, maybe to question Valentine or to find Lin."

"Yes," Cruise says. "Htay likes Lin and is very protective of him. He likes her. She is lonely since her husband died. Lin needs help. They both like hard work. Now he will have status in the Karen community. They can build something together. The marriage gives her more power to protect him."

"I still think it's gross," Lish says, sticking her finger down her throat.

There seems to be nothing more to say, and anyway, the rain is pelting down, rattling so loudly on the metal of the truck that we can barely hear each other. We huddle together, miserable, cold and wet. I wonder if Lin had any choice in his future. I doubt it. But then, Lin probably hasn't had any choice since the Burmese army came for him.

Or maybe I don't want to think he had any choice, because I feel so betrayed. Why didn't he tell me? He told me everything else.

The rain slows to a drizzle, the clouds lighten from black to gray, and I realize something. He did tell me—or he tried to—when he uttered that ludicrous word *happy*.

The sun plays peek-a-boo, then gives up.

THIRTY-FOUR

WE REACH CHIANG MAI after lunch. Cruise asks the hotel to call for an English-speaking doctor to see me. Mom and I take long, steaming showers and dress in dry clothes. I shiver, though room service has brought me a pot of steaming peppermint tea and a hot-water bottle.

The doctor is a shy man who seems uncomfortable assessing me in the hotel bed. Mom sits on the other side, explaining that I was lost in the jungle, trying to save an elephant. The doctor shoots her a look of disbelief but says little. He purses his lips as he feels my ribs and listens to my lungs. He shines a light in my eyes and runs his fingers gently around my sockets. In the end he says I have bruised ribs, a swollen eye and some cuts and scrapes, but that everything will heal. That I am "a very lucky girl."

"I've heard that before," I say.

When he leaves, Mom and I go out to the pool, where Pauline and Lish are in their bathing suits, arguing under a striped umbrella. They don't notice us right away.

"I had to stay," Lish is saying.

"No. You didn't have to. I didn't want you to. It never occurred to me that you would."

"Who else was going to care for him?"

"No one. He's a grown man. He doesn't have to drink himself into the gutter. But I have been sick about you. Sick and—"

Pauline abruptly stops talking when she sees us standing uncertainly a few steps away. We are all uncomfortable. Mom lies down on a chaise lounge, and I stand beside the water, my toes curling over the edge.

The sparkling pool nestles amid planters of golden marigolds and trailing morning glories. It is lovely and normal. The normalcy feels absolutely strange. Pauline and Lish in their bikinis under an umbrella. Mom smearing sunscreen on her exposed skin.

I dive deep and rise slowly. I think of Lin staying underwater for almost two minutes. I think of Mohawk swimming, his thick stumpy legs going in circles, his trunk tip above water. I think of him lying still, cold and stiff under the banyan tree. I swim lengths of the pool, ignoring the pain in my side, slicing through the water. I push myself, hoping to clear my head of anything but the effort to swim. I keep my head underwater as long as I can, because I like the feeling of being submerged, the water all around me, the chlorine stinging my eyes. I like the profound silence.

When I climb out, dripping and breathless, I flop onto a chaise lounge. Mom, Pauline and Lish sit at the next table, playing Scrabble. They ask me to join.

"No, thanks. You go ahead."

Pauline wins the draw to go first. She reaches into the bag for her tiles.

"You won't believe this. I have a seven-letter word, Alisha Rose!"

The name takes getting used to.

The tiles click slightly as Pauline places them on the board. "And it's very apropos. R-E-G-R-E-T-S. Regrets."

"Seriously?" asks Lish. "Regrets?"

"Yes. I have regrets," says Pauline.

I wait for Lish to stick her finger in her mouth. She doesn't. Under the table, Pauline reaches for Lish's hand. Lish doesn't slap it away.

We eat an early dinner in the almost empty dining room. Pauline orders champagne. "Not the real stuff," she says. "Just some good sparkly." She pours a glass for everyone. My face feels tight. All of me feels tight. I don't see much reason to celebrate, but I try not to ruin it for everyone else.

Pauline toasts the trek. She toasts Mohawk, never riding elephants again, ethical tourism, putting out fires, Brendan, Max, Cruise, Myint and Myo. She toasts me. And Lin. And Thailand. There is a constant clinking of glasses. Mom's smile, as brittle as mine feels, looks like it might shatter. I don't need to ask her what's wrong. She's thinking about me and Lin and Bo. She's worrying about getting me out of this country.

Pauline looks wistful and says she wouldn't mind taking another trek somewhere. Lish stuns all of us by saying that wouldn't be such a terrible idea. Then she goes to the washroom. Pauline wipes away some tears, and Mom reaches out to pat her hand.

Mom and I have to leave as soon as dinner is over to catch our sleeper train. Pauline and Lish walk us out to the sidewalk.

"What an adventure," says Pauline.

The cab comes, and we all hug goodbye.

"*An adventure?*" I say as the cab merges into traffic. "Really?"

"Don't be so hard on her," Mom says. "She had a rough trip too."

"When did you two become such good friends?"

"When you were lost. Pauline kept me vertical."

"She probably just felt guilty for pushing you to let me do the suicide climb."

Mom looks at me from under lowered lashes and waits a moment before she speaks. Her voice is measured. "She felt guilty, yes, but she also felt empathy. She didn't leave my side, and I was really hard to be around. I was crazy with fear and grief."

"I know," I say, ashamed. "I'm glad she was with you. Did she talk to you about Lish?"

"We talked a lot about Lish, and Lish's dad—until Cruise showed up with the news about you." She shakes her head, and her eyes well up at the memory. "Did Lish talk to you about Pauline?"

"Yes. It was pretty ugly."

"Well, their wounds seem to be healing."

Mom is wistful. That's what she wanted for me.

The train is already at the station. I take the upper berth and make up my bed, then lie down, wary of bumping my head on the ceiling just inches over my head. My face aches from the fake smile I plastered on all day. It takes several minutes of rubbing my jaw to make it feel normal.

The sound of the wheels on the track, the rocking motion of the train and the night sky through the window are soothing. I sleep on and off. Every time I wake, I am overwhelmed with all that's happened. We chug into Bangkok just after breakfast.

The cab drive from the Bangkok train station to our hotel is insanely long, partly because of the overwhelming traffic jams and partly because it is a long way.

"How many people live here?" I ask.

"Eight million or so, and that doesn't include the suburbs," Mom says, riffling through *Lonely Planet*.

"Do they all drive?" I look around at the streets jammed with cars, motorcycles and things that look like golf carts on three wheels, called *tuk tuks*. "Death on three wheels," the cabbie calls them. There are traffic cops in white gloves and masks, flower vendors with elaborate orchid necklaces, occasional gold Buddhas plunked on the sidewalk, and kids in school uniforms. The street our hotel is on is lined with hairdressers, hair salon after hair salon after hair salon.

At the hotel, Mom calls the Canadian embassy and tells them my "story." In other words, she lies. It gives me anxiety to hear her. I picture her being dragged off to jail. But she hangs up completely calm.

"They haven't heard anything. They'll look into it and get back to me."

Then she drags me out, reciting the full itinerary she mapped out on the train: royal palace, lunch, walking tour, dinner theater with traditional Thai dance. She is almost acting like nothing happened, like we just went trekking and had a fine time and now here we are, trying to fill our last hours. Almost. The crazed look in her eyes and the way she grips my hand, as though I'm a toddler who might run off, suggest otherwise. She is, in fact, barely keeping it together. She wants to keep busy. Too busy. Too busy to think or talk while we wait for Dad to arrive. He is in Anchorage, waiting for a connecting plane. Waiting to swoop in and gather his family together. To be with us as we fly home. To make sure we get home. That's if they let me go.

First, we cab it to the royal palace, a massive compound of pointy, glittery buildings. There are endless lines of tourists and enormous piles of shoes at the entrances. Mostly we stand in lines, lines to get into each fairy-tale building and lines to get into each room of each fairy-tale building. Mom's plan to prevent thinking is a huge fail here. The lineups give us endless time.

After three hours at the palace, we find a crowded cafeteria-style restaurant for curried vegetables, then take a short walking tour by ourselves, following a *Lonely Planet* foldout map.

I don't know where we go wrong. But we do. Soon we are looking at very different scenery. Canals with wrecked-up barges. Shacks with tin roofs. Old people rocking in chairs, smoking opium pipes. Gangs of guys in undershirts, whose one activity seems to be chewing toothpicks. They look at us like they've never seen tourists before. One guy wags his tongue at me. We're in a labyrinth we can't find our way out of.

We have been through a lot, however, and Mom is tougher than most yoga-practicing, ponytail-bouncing types. When we pass the tongue-wagging guy for the third time, she appeals to him for help—a bold move that, surprisingly, works like a charm, though he doesn't speak any English. She shows him the map, and he escorts us to a bus stop, where he waits with us, like a guardian angel, for the bus to come and take us away.

"Well played," I say.

"You just have to appeal to people's better natures."

"If they *have* better natures."

We take three buses back to our street and walk the half mile down to the end, where our hotel sits. This morning the hair salons were all closed, but now they're open, and their neon signs are flashing. Behind their big front windows sit the hairdressers—on display.

"What's with all the hairdressers?" I ask.

"Hairdressers?"

"Yeah. Why so many on the same street? And why are they all sitting behind the windows?"

"They're not hairdressers."

"What do you mean?"

"They're prostitutes."

"*What*?"

"Yes."

"That's awful! Are you sure?"

"Yes."

"Do you see how young they are?"

"I know."

"How can you be so calm about it? So accepting?"

"There is good and bad everywhere."

"This country pretends to be so spiritual—with monks and temples and Buddhas everywhere—but it's not."

"That's not fair or true. The tourists—people like us—are complicit. They fund the sex trade. They ignore the animal abuses because they like to ride elephants. Jesus. They go to *refugee camps* to see neck rings."

That really got to Mom.

"Those aren't people like us. Except for the ones riding elephants—and we didn't know better."

"That's right. There is good and bad everywhere. And ignorance. Unintended consequences."

"Brendan says there's a slow genocide happening with the Rohingya. Lin thinks so too. Brendan says the same thing happened with the Karen."

"That's the Burmese military! It isn't everyone."

"And here in Thailand, all those hill people are second-class citizens!"

"It looks like you've finally gotten in touch with your anger. That's supposed to be a good thing." She rubs her eyes. She looks old. "But it shouldn't all be directed at Thailand. Canada has its own shames and—"

"And I almost got raped and murdered in the jungle. Why did you even bring me here?"

She looks like I've kicked her in the stomach. She just shakes her head and doesn't speak for one full block.

"I don't know," she finally whispers. "I really don't." I regret my words. R-E-G-R-E-T. I think of Pauline. But I can't take them back. Nobody can ever take anything back— there are no redos. We walk the last few blocks in total silence. We reach the hotel and join the throng waiting for the elevator. We stare at our feet, mouths clamped. The doors slide open with a *ping*, and we jostle past the people exiting. The elevator is packed. Our room is on the twenty-eighth floor, and we stop at almost every floor on the way up. Once in our room Mom puts on her pajamas and gets into bed with her phone.

"What are you doing?" I ask. My voice sounds odd after such a long silence.

"Nothing," she says, her thumbs moving lethargically over the screen.

"Mom, I'm sorry," I say.

"That's all right," she says in a flat voice.

I sit on my bed and watch her. I walk around the room. I look out the window. I sit back on the bed.

"I really am sorry."

"I know."

I shower and pull my one dress out of the backpack. It's wrinkled and a little damp, but I put it on. Too much skin shows, so I wrap a shawl around my shoulders. I keep glancing at Mom, hoping she will take the hint and get dressed. Hoping we can go out and eat. Hoping we can do something other than sit here in this awful silence.

She doesn't seem to even notice me. I clear my throat and speak again.

"So, dinner? Should we leave soon?"

"I'll order room service." She reaches for the hotel information binder on the night table and examines the menu. She hands it to me.

Mom has given up.

"I don't want to eat here. Let's go out."

"No."

"No, really. Let's go out. What's wrong with you?"

"Me?" she asks.

"Yes, you."

"I don't know."

"Where's your determination? Your aggravating high spirits? Your kick-ass attitude?" Seriously. What happened to it all? I can't believe how much I miss it. "Let's go to that dinner theater and watch some Thai dance. Like you wanted to," I say.

"I didn't want to."

"You were talking about it this morning!"

"I was talking about it," she says. "But I didn't want to."

Honestly? I'm starting to hyperventilate. Mom has become me. And it is *awful. The worst.*

"Please, Mom. *Please*."

She slumps to the washroom and turns on the shower. It runs for fifteen minutes. When she emerges, she is tying the sash of her wrap jean dress. She puts on earrings and lipstick. Her smile, when she turns to face me, is no more than a grimace, but it's better than nothing.

She buries herself in her *Lonely Planet* and then calls the front desk. They recommend a dinner theater near the hotel. We grab our purses and go. Our silence seems exacerbated in the elevator and lasts all the way down. I steal furtive looks at her, and every time I see how dead her eyes look, my stomach plummets.

THIRTY-FIVE

THE CONCIERGE HELPS US into a cab and gives the driver the address. The driver doesn't speak any English, but he smiles a lot—at first. Forty-five minutes later his smile has completely disappeared, and his forehead is furrowed. It's quite obvious that something is very wrong.

"This is an insanely long cab ride," I say.

"Every cab ride in Bangkok is insanely long," Mom says.

"But you said it was close to the hotel."

She leans her head back and closes her eyes. I take her hand and whisper in her ear. "What if we're being kidnapped?"

"Don't joke about such things."

I am actually not joking. "Well, it's a good thing the restaurant is close to the hotel, because it boggles the mind how long we'd be driving if it weren't."

I'm talkative and flippant because she is *so quiet*. Funereal quiet. It's unbearable. If this is what it was like being with me, it's a miracle she didn't lose her mind ages ago. I may not last the night.

We finally drive down a dark, narrow laneway. I elbow Mom in the ribs, but she has already woken up and realized something isn't right. Her eyes dart from side to side, and she fumbles in her purse for her phone. The driver brakes in front of a high gate. He has to coax us out because we don't want to leave the cab. He unlatches the gate, and it swings open onto an elegant outdoor dining room.

I can't believe my eyes. "Holy shit! It's a restaurant."

Mom looks over my shoulder. "It is!"

"It's a *restaurant!*"

We hug.

"But I don't see any dancers. I don't even see a stage. It's not the restaurant we wanted," I say.

"No. But it looks nice." She turns to the driver. He looks warily hopeful.

"Thank you." She *wais.* "Can you come back in two hours?" She points at her watch and holds up two fingers. He nods so energetically, I am afraid he'll dislocate his neck. He *wais.* Mom and I *wai.* He *wais* again. He is as happy as if he got us to the right place. And so are we.

Palm trees dot the patio, and ribbons of tiny pink lights crisscross their fronds. Lots of families are dining under the diffuse light. Families are a good sign. We are the only tourists. A hostess guides us to a linen-draped table.

Mom lays her hand over mine. "Candleholders!"

Every table has a white pillar candle in a blue china bowl.

"Jackpot," I say. Nobody speaks English, and the menu is totally in Thai. It takes twenty minutes just to get drinks. First the server brings us glasses of water. We want bottled water. I shake my head and mime the shape of a bottle. Then I mime drinking from a bottle. The server smiles sweetly and comes back with Coke. Mom tries again. The server brings beer, then wine. We give up on the water. Mom takes the wine, and I settle for the Coke. Figuring out how to order a vegetarian meal takes some strategizing. I prowl around unobtrusively, looking at people's plates, as I breathe in the enchanting smells of coconut and curry. I have to get quite close because it is so dark. The Thais are so polite, they pretend I'm not furtively eyeing their food. When the server comes to take our order, I lead her to a table and order two of a vegetarian (I hope!) dish.

When I return, Mom has downed one glass of wine and is pouring herself another. As we wait for our food, Mom slides back into total apathy. The excitement over finding a restaurant and ordering a meal can only take you so far.

Plus, we have nothing to talk about because everything we could talk about would make us even sadder. I look everywhere but at her, examining every square inch of the restaurant. Finally I settle for looking over her shoulder, so I don't have to see her expression or watch her drink wine like water.

Just then a wave of fog rolls slowly in.

Weather is a safe topic. "It's really foggy," I say.

"It's the pollution," she says.

"And it's dark. It's almost as dark as in the mountains. Why is it so dark?"

"I think it's the pollution."

The fog moves toward us. I blink my eyes and stare incredulously as it takes the shape of an elephant.

An elephant.

A real elephant. Unless I'm hallucinating. It has tusks, so I assume it's a male. A mahout holds on to a rope around his neck. I blink a few times, but every time I open my eyes, the elephant and his mahout are still there, maneuvering the spaces between the tables.

No one else even seems to give a shit.

"Mom, there's an elephant in the restaurant."

"I know, darling. But now is not the time to deal with it."

"What?"

She blots her eyes with a napkin. "Let's just get home before we try to process this trip."

I roll my eyes and turn back to the elephant. He is coming right up to our table—a sad-looking elephant with a broken tusk and an infected eye. The mahout's robes are patched and dirty. Both the elephant and the mahout look worn out, beaten down. Like they have no expectations. Like they've accepted how shitty life is. Maybe this is the lack of desire Buddhists talk about. The ideal state. Accept how awful everything is and never expect anything better.

The mahout holds a bucket over one arm and a corn cob in his hand. He holds the corn out to everyone he passes.

"Mom. I mean a *real* elephant. It's right behind you."

The elephant lays his trunk on her shoulder. She jumps and screeches, scaring both the elephant and the mahout. The elephant's ears flap. The other diners chuckle politely behind their hands. I really don't know how Canadians got their "polite" reputation—we can't hold a candle to Thais.

"There's an elephant in the restaurant!" Mom says.

"Really?" I can't help the sarcasm. The mahout *wais* and offers Mom an ear of corn. She takes it and no sooner gets it in her hand than the elephant snorts it up. The mahout holds out his hand for money.

"Oh. I get it," I say. "This is how he looks after him. It's so sad. A city doesn't seem like a good place for an elephant."

"A bit of an understatement," says Mom, reaching into her wallet.

"Where do you think he keeps him?"

"Some kind of garage?"

"That's horrible. He belongs in the mountains."

"At least he's being looked after." Mom gives the mahout two hundred *bahts*, about ten dollars. He *wais*, bowing deeply, and passes her the whole bucket of corn.

"Do you really call this looking after him? Look at his tusk! Maybe the mahout sawed a piece off to pawn."

"Here," Mom says, handing me the bucket. "You feed him."

The elephant, unable to resist the bucket being passed under his trunk, grabs a cob directly from it. The mahout laughs. I feed the elephant a cob. Then another. I can't keep up with how quickly he puts them in his mouth.

"I don't think he's chewing. He's just snorting them down," I say. I recall the effort Mohawk put into eating. How he struggled to roll up his trunk and how we had to help him work his jaws. Thinking of Mohawk hurts my heart. My eyes blink, and my mouth twitches. I press my lips together and look at my hands. I can't look at the elephant.

"You feed him," I say. "I don't want to."

"It's okay," Mom says gently. "You can't save every elephant, Valentine, but you can feed this one here, tonight."

She's right. I hold up another cob. The whole bucket is gone in a minute, and the elephant waits for more. I look in the empty pail. I show him how empty it is. He feels around with his trunk to make sure. He lowers his head so he can look at me, eye to eye. I can't stand the pus running from his. I wipe at it with my napkin. I expect him to jerk away, but he doesn't.

"It looks like he's crying," I say. I know he's not, but it seems like he is.

The mahout takes the rope and the pail and shuffles away. The elephant shuffles too. I look up at Mom.

"I wish we could take him home."

"I know."

"I mean, at least we have a yard and a park across the street."

"I know."

"It sucks. *It just sucks.*"

I know I'm going to cry about one second before I do. The first sob comes out like a bark. I lower my head, bury my face in the napkin and cry like a little kid, hiccuping and heaving. It seems like I'll never stop. Mom pulls her chair next to mine, puts her arms around me and says that she loves me. When I finally slow down and take a deep breath, she leaves some cash on the table, and we try to leave gracefully. There is a hush over the whole restaurant. No one looks at us, though, as they try to pretend that we haven't made a scene.

Thankfully, the cab driver is there—smoking and sitting on the hood of the car. As he slides off and opens the door for us, the server runs into the alley with our dinner in cartons.

"That is so thoughtful," Mom says. "Thank you."

It's dark and warm in the cab. I curl up against Mom, trying to control the mild tremors running through me like aftershocks.

"I just want you to stop hurting, Valentine. Please stop hurting."

"I need to ask you something."

"Okay."

"Why did you have me?"

"*What?*"

"You must have known what the world is like. That terrible things happen, and everyone dies. So why did you have me?"

I'm not trying to be mean. I want to know. I need to know. Maybe there's something I don't get. Mom doesn't answer. She chokes back a sob. But it bursts out, and then we both cry in each other's arms. The poor cabbie keeps checking his rearview mirror to see how we're doing.

"You don't really mean that, do you?" Mom asks. "That you wish you'd never been born?" There is so much pain in her voice, I can't stand it.

"No. No, I don't. I just feel really bad right now." And then I realize that something else has been weighing on me, suffocating me, in fact. "There's something I didn't tell you that I should have. I need to."

She tries to process this. "Something else? What else could there possibly be?" She presses both hands against her chest, like she's trying to hold her heart in.

I tell her what Lin told me last night. Mom's silence is profound. When I finish, I look at her and swallow hard. "Do you believe Lin?" I ask. "That he didn't know the family was in there?"

She takes a frighteningly long time to answer. She looks out the window. She squeezes my hand. She taps her lip. She takes cleansing breaths. By the time she speaks, my stomach is twisted in knots.

"Yes. I do. But you need to forgive him whether he did or not."

"No! You want me to forgive him if he shot that baby, those people, on purpose? I can't believe what I'm hearing. You can't really mean that!"

"I do. He was a child soldier. You will never—I will never—understand the horror of that. And he is remorseful. He is trying to be a better person. It is remarkable that he even had enough humanity left to be the young man he is. A man who cares about animals. Who saved you. Who liked you.

Maybe even loved you. It is important, really important, that you forgive him."

"Why? He'll never know."

"I am thinking about you."

"What?"

"It is important for *you* to forgive him."

THIRTY-SIX

THE SUN EDGES over the horizon and reflects off the mountain range of glass and mirrored skyscrapers. I lean on the windowsill, watching the bling, holding a damp cloth to my forehead. I have a crying hangover. It's not nearly as bad as an overdose hangover, but my head pounds, my eyes sting, and my chest aches unbearably. All along I've thought that crying would move the bowling ball out of my chest. But no, it's still there.

My sleep hasn't helped. I dreamed about Bo, who continues to resurrect himself in my nightmares. I resent the time my unconscious spends on him. The world is better off without him. That is the truth. Even in death he made misery: now Lin will spend the rest of his life grieving because he killed again. I think about Lin's goodness. I wonder how it survived. I think about justice. Injustice. Amir, who lived like a blazing star. Amir, as dead as Bo, who lived like a black hole.

Mom calls out in her sleep. I sit on the bed and hold her hand until she calms down. I wonder what her nightmares are. Her face is puffy, her breath heavy. She looks a mess, nothing like the person who left Toronto only ten days ago. I lean against the window, waiting for her to awaken, waiting for Dad to get here, waiting to go home. That's the good news. The embassy attaché called last night, and I'm free to go.

I decide to go out for one last walk in Thailand. I leave a note and take Mom's phone, so she can reach me using the room phone. I pull on my jeans, run a brush through my hair and slip quietly out the door. The elevator is empty when I get in but full by the time it reaches the lobby. It doesn't matter how early you get out the door. The eight million people are apparently all early risers. The street is buzzing. The cars, the cops and the people are in full-out hyperspeed.

Only the "hairdressers" are asleep.

I turn down a street and stop outside a little temple, arrested by the gold Buddha on the sidewalk. I wish I understood what people see in this gaudy round guy. I stick my head in the temple's first room for a quick scan. Dark and empty. I kick off my shoes and walk in. The room is bare. There is a second room at the back. It is dark, but I spy an altar with fresh flowers and a basket of candles. I walk in and kneel in front of it.

As soon as I bow my head, I start to cry. Again. It's like once I've started, I can't stop. A voice in my ear almost gives me a heart attack. I shriek and fall back. A monk is crouching down beside me. Even when I see him, I can't stop shrieking.

My voice is a few seconds behind my brain. I notice a little cot and blanket in a shadowy alcove. He was sleeping there. I just didn't notice him.

"Oh! You scared me."

He looks really pissed, and I assume I woke him up. My heart thumps.

"What are you do?" he asks, his brows coming together.

"Nothing."

"Are you cry?"

"Yes." *Obviously.*

"What wrong?"

"You scared me! My heart." It's still pounding. I pat my chest.

"For your heart?"

"What?"

"Your broke heart. You cry for your heart?"

He's not wrong.

"So?" He is impatient, like he wants this settled so he can get back to bed.

"Yes," I say. "I'm crying for my broken heart."

"Only for you?" He looks even madder than before.

"What?"

"You are cry only for your heart?"

I didn't see this coming.

"Only for you?" he asks, his eyebrows meeting in a sharp inverted V. "All the broke hearts"—he flings his arm toward the street—"and you cry only for *you*?"

He's so pissed, I'm afraid to speak.

"Are you understand me?"

I stare at him. He is skin and bones, from his gnarled feet to his shaved head.

"Are you understand me?"

I want to tell him that I'm not only crying for myself. I'm crying for Amir. For Mohawk. For the family that Lin killed. For Lin. For everyone in the world who suffers. And, yes, for myself too.

Suddenly the anger from yesterday comes whooshing back.

"Yes. I understand you. And that's the problem. That's exactly it! Everyone has a broken heart because life is just fucking unbearable. There is misery everywhere."

"And you?"

"What?"

"What misery do you make?"

I don't know how many seconds pass. Minutes even. My face is frozen. My breath stilled. I look deep into his eyes. They're as dark and shiny as black diamonds.

"Hmm?" he asks.

I nod imperceptibly. Then I nod again to make sure he sees it. Sees that I get it. Because I do. I *have* made misery. As recently as last night. And I want to stop. I have no control over anything else. But I can stop causing misery right now.

I have to, because I don't want to be one of the people who does. That's not how I want to be.

I stop thinking about the things other people have done, and I think about what I've done. It's overwhelming. I think of Becca and how I've hurt her. I think of Mom and Dad, and my cheeks burn in shame at the hell I've put them through. And I love them so much. I think of Amir's parents and how I've never gone to see them since he died, because I was thinking about myself. *It was too hard for me.*

I think about Lin. How I judged him, even when I saw how much pain he was in. I relive his last words to me. *I love you.* I relive my silence. I didn't tell him I loved him too. Partly because I was so freaked out about his confession. Partly because I didn't want to betray Amir. But I know now I can love them both. Mom, Mr. Singh and Pablo Neruda were right. Living is not a betrayal. It's pushing back against the darkness. Carrying forward the love.

Finally, I think about Neil Carter, and I admit something I've known all along. He didn't mean to kill Amir. It was a moment of rage—a terrible accident. I remember him in court, how he sat so ruined at that table, with his head down, crying into his hands.

I feel so sorry for him, I almost throw up.

The bowling ball finally rolls out of my chest.

I reach into the basket of candles. I light one for Neil. I hope he can move on. I light one for Lin and Htay. I hope they will be happy. I light one for Mohawk. I loved him and will always grieve for him. I light one for Amir. *Amir.* I wish so much he were here. It's hard to go on without him. I will always feel the pain of his absence. But I won't spread it around. At least, I'll try not to. I light one final candle, for the monk still waiting quietly beside me.

I put some *bahts* into the basket, and then I *wai* to the monk. I clear my throat.

"You speak?" he asks.

"Yes."

"What you say?"

What do I say? I think for a moment. I think about how many layers he had to peel through for me to understand. "The heart really is the secret inside the secret."

He frowns, confused. I want to hug him, or at least reach out and put my hand over his, but I can't. He would be upset. I'm no longer angry that he doesn't want to touch a woman. I smile instead and touch my heart. His face softens.

Outside, the sky is cotton-candy pink and blue. Soon Mom will wake. Dad will arrive, bundle us in a cab and shepherd us home. I walk slowly to savor my last minutes in this percolating city. A memory pops into my head.

A day with Amir. We're in the Rogers Centre, watching baseball. The roof is open. We're eating hot dogs and Häagen-Daz bars. The Jays are up to bat. Amir catches a line drive. He gives the ball to a boy in front of us. The boy looks at Amir like he is a shining hero.

People do leave things behind. Memories. Those memories used to feel like undertow, pulling me down into their dark depths. But maybe that can change. Maybe one day they will feel like air. The air I breathe. The air that infuses my blood with oxygen.

I halt suddenly and almost lose my balance.

Amir is air with an *m*. *Memories*.

I stop at a kiosk and buy stamps and three postcards with images that call to me—an elephant, Buddha and the night sky in Chiang Mai. I duck into a twenty-four-hour Starbucks and order a café au lait. As I sip, I address and write out the cards.

To Mr. Singh, I send the Buddha. *See you next week, possibly before you get this card.*

To Becca, I send the elephant. *You were right. It's all about LOVE.*

To the Aymans, I send the stars. *Thinking of Amir and wishing he were here. Wishing he were anywhere.*

I reread it. It's not enough, of course, but nothing is.

Back on the street I pop them in a mailbox. Just that act, that small effort to make amends, buoys me with hope. I keep pace with the growing crowds, feeling lighter and lighter. The big, bold, brave word *happy*—the word Lin had the audacity to utter—glimmers in my peripheral vision.

I stop at a street stall overflowing with flowers and marvel at the intricacy of the flower necklaces. The vendor hands me one fashioned with purple orchids. It is so exquisite I'm almost afraid to touch it.

"I have to get it for my mom," I tell her. "What do you call it?"

"*Malai.*"

I repeat it, and she smiles. I buy two others—yellow roses for Dad, jasmine for me.

"Did you make them?" I ask the woman.

"Yes."

She drapes them around my neck. The silky petals brush my skin, and the sweet scent fills my head.

As I turn down the busy street to the hotel, I break into a jog, weaving effortlessly through the throng, seized with a need to see Mom, to tell her it's all going to be okay. To thank her for bringing me here. The need is like rocket fuel, shooting me out of my orbit and into the universe. Skimming the pavement, I skirt street vendors, motor scooters and sidewalk Buddhas. Arms pumping, heart racing, *malais* bouncing, I run, faster and faster.

Quick as wind and light as air.

AUTHOR'S NOTE

The world is full of broken-hearted beings, and this novel is about some of them. It's also about hope. While inspired by true events, the characters are all fictitious, and any resemblance to real persons is coincidental. I have had help all along the way, but any missteps or mistakes are mine alone.

ACKNOWLEDGMENTS

HEARTFELT GRATITUDE...

To my agent and muse, Sam Hiyate, for his friendship and unwavering faith—and also his Sunday workshop. I am thankful we traveled this road together. To the entire Rights Factory team, especially kick-ass kidlit agents Ali McDonald and Stacey Kondla.

To my publisher, Ruth Linka at Orca Book Publishers, who saw the potential in my story and guided its metamorphosis from manuscript to book. To Andrew Wooldridge, Jen Cameron, Leslie Bootle, Olivia Gutjahr, Margaret Bryant, Rachel Page, Maria Nguyen—artist extraordinaire—and the whole Orca pod. To editor Sara Cassidy for her profound insights and acute eyes.

To Lee Gowan, director of the creative writing program at the University of Toronto's School of Continuing Studies Creative Writing Program—and my novel's first champion. To Kathy Kacer, Barbara Berson and Dr. Pauline Pariser for early feedback. To Lynn Bennett for her belief.

To Beatrix Montanile for her story about a monk that I held in my heart until I put it in my book. To Alexandra Risen, who pushed and pulled me through stark creative times. To Anne Laurel Carter, Stacey Kondla and Rachelle Saruya for editorial input. To my writing group—Meghan Davidson Ladly, Margaret DeRosia, Linda Rui Feng, Franca Pellacia and Keith Rombough—for honesty and good times. To Barbara Radecki and Joanne Vannicola for inspiring chats over coffee. To Trilby Kent at the Humber School for Writers for mentoring me through a comprehensive rewrite.

To Teresa and Tony at L'Espresso Bar Mercurio, where much of this book was written.

To Janine Manatis, who taught me everything I know about creativity.

To the many people—friends and strangers—who supported this story with expertise, advice, introductions, cheerleading and lunches. To my very earliest readers, including the late and lovely Leanne Coppen, who left us far too young.

To my daughter, Alexandra, who traveled the width and length of beautiful Thailand with me and read several incarnations of this novel.

To my grandparents, who had Shakespeare on their bookshelves and movies on the television. To my mother and father, who bought me books, took me to libraries and listened to endless retellings of my favorite childhood novels. To my long-suffering brother and sister, who wearied of watching me read—especially on cross-country road trips.

To all the writers who have nurtured, enchanted, educated and transformed me. To the poets who inspired Valentine: Rumi, Edna St. Vincent Millay, Rainer Maria Rilke (translated by Anne Marie Kanert), Pablo Neruda (translated by Donald D. Walsh) and Anne Michaels.

To my nieces—Ellie, Carlie, Sira and Sabrina—and to Ross, Allison, Ewa, Nicolas and Chantal for their loving encouragement.

To my husband, Sal, and children, Alexandra, Nathan and Julian, who light up my sky so I can see all the joy in the world.

HOW FAR
WE GO
AND HOW
FAST

NORA DECTER

SIXTEEN-YEAR-OLD JOLENE is from a long line of musical lowlifes. She and her big brother, Matt, are true musicians, but when Matt leaves in the middle of the night, Jo loses her only friend, her support system and the one person who made her even remotely cool.

"A tender story about the
love found in an imperfect,
working-class family."

—*Kirkus Reviews*

Jon is banished from his polygamous community when he is caught kissing a girl. Although he finds support in the friendship of other "Lost Boys," he is utterly unprepared for life outside Unity. He spirals into a life of drinking and drugs, ending up homeless. Then someone from his past appears and helps him find his way.

"The story propels readers
and gives them insight into
the appeal of lives where
decisions are made for you."

—*Booklist*

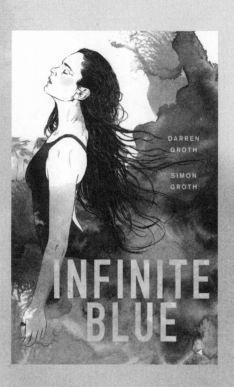

INFINITE
BLUE

DARREN
GROTH

SIMON
GROTH

ASHLEY DRUMMOND is an elite swimmer. Clayton Sandalford is a talented artist. From the moment of their first meeting, they were destined to be together. But a life-altering event demands that both of them let go in ways they never imagined.

"This is a book about
passion, whether it involves
the heat of young love or
the cool of infinite water."

–*Quill & Quire*

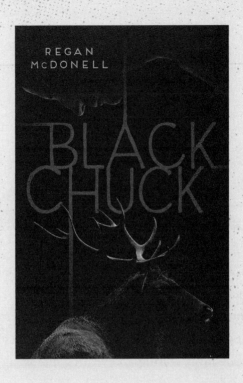

WHEN THE MANGLED BODY of his best friend, Shaun, turns up in a field just east of town, tough-as-hell Réal blames himself. But except for the nightmares, all Réal remembers is beating the living crap out of Shaun the night of his death. As Réal looks to Shaun's girlfriend for atonement, everything goes sideways. Fast.

"Poetic and haunting, tender and gritty—this is a remarkable novel."

– Andrew Smith, Michael L. Printz Honor and Boston Globe-Horn Book Award-winning author

DIANE TERRANA has worked as an actress, a belly dancer and a high-school English and drama teacher. Currently she is the executive editor at The Rights Factory. Born in Alberta, she lives just outside Toronto with her husband and three children. She loves editing and writing almost as much as she loves reading.